Strategic Management

Strategic Management

Colin White

First published 2004 by
PALGRAVE MACMILLAN
Houndmills, Basingstoke, Hampshire RG21 6XS and
175 Fifth Avenue, New York, N.Y. 10010
Companies and representatives throughout the world

PALGRAVE MACMILLAN is the global academic imprint of the Palgrave Macmillan division of St. Martin's Press, LLC and of Palgrave Macmillan Ltd. Macmillan® is a registered trademark in the United States, United Kingdom and other countries. Palgrave is a registered trademark in the European Union and other countries.

ISBN 1–4039–0400–6

This book is printed on paper suitable for recycling and made from fully managed and sustained forest sources.

A catalogue record for this book is available from the British Library.

Library of Congress Cataloging-in-Publication Data

White, Colin (Colin M.)
    Strategic management / Colin White.
        p. cm.
    Includes bibliographical references and index.
    ISBN 1–4039–0400–6 (pbk.)
    1. Strategic planning. I. Title.

HD30.28.W447 2004
658.4'012—dc22

2003062091

Editing and origination by Aardvark Editorial, Mendham, Suffolk

10 9 8 7 6 5 4 3 2 1
13 12 11 10 09 08 07 06 05 04

Printed in China

Brief contents

Prologue   xxi

Part I   Introducing Strategic Management   1
1   Introducing strategy and strategy making   4
2   Thinking and acting strategically   43
3   Adopting a global perspective   78
4   Reading an uncertain future   113

Part II   Strategic Environments and Competitive Advantage   157
5   Identifying opportunity and risk   160
6   Reading the competitive environment   199
7   Analysing resources, capabilities and core competencies   233
8   Creating and maintaining competitive advantage   266
9   Reducing costs   302
10 Differentiating the product   338

Part III   Strategic Dilemmas   375
11 Determining the size of an enterprise   378
12 Integrating the strategists   416
13 When to compete and when to cooperate   456
14 Managing risk   495
15 Participating in the global economy   530

Part IV   Bringing it all Together   565
16 Formulating strategy   568
17 Implementing strategy   614
18 Monitoring strategic performance   651

Part V   Strategic Analysis and Audit   699
Long case studies   702

Epilogue   798

Glossary   802
Bibliography   812
Index   823

Full contents

List of figures		xiii
List of tables		xv
Acknowledgements		xvii
Prologue		xxi
	Who this book is for	xxii
	How to use the book	xxiii
	The case studies	xxix
	Companion website	xxxii
	Introductory reading	xxxiii

Part I **Introducing Strategic Management** 1

1 Introducing strategy and strategy making 4
    What is strategy? 5
    A brief history of the concept 8
    A multiplicity of meanings 13
    Assumptions and metatheories 20
    Strategists and stakeholders 26
    The social web and the 'political' process of strategy making 33

2 Thinking and acting strategically 43
    Case Study Scenario *The IKEA way* 44
    *The distinction between strategic thinking, strategic management
    and strategic planning* 45
    STRATEGY IN ACTION *Quick strategic thinking in unfavourable circumstances* 45
    STRATEGY IN ACTION *Sony – the disruptive innovator* 50
    Principles for the successful use of strategy 61
    *Finding the right strategic mix of entrepreneurial creativity and
    administrative expertise* 65
    Case Study *The IKEA way* 69

3 Adopting a global perspective 78
    Case Study Scenario *The airlines and the integration of global markets* 79
    The meaning of globalization 80
    The five main elements of globalization 83
    Home country bias 90
    A convergent world 93
    Global players 95
    The impact of globalization on strategy 101
    Case Study *Bad strategy and bad fortune – Swissair and Qantas* 103

4   Reading an uncertain future   113
     Case Study Scenario *Airbus Industrie and the next generation*
        of civil airliners   114
     Limited information   115
     Information, knowledge and strategy   119
     Reading the general environment   120
     Coping with the future   124
     Different kinds of risk   132
     Scenario building   136
     Case Study *Airbus Industrie and the next generation of civil airliners*   147

Part II   **Strategic Environments and Competitive Advantage**   157

5   Identifying opportunity and risk   160
     Case Study Scenario *A clean vehicle – the hybrid electric vehicle (HEV)* 161
     General and competitive environments   162
     The nature of the general environment   164
     Change and strategy   167
     Environment segments   169
     STRATEGY IN ACTION *Riding the Internet wave – Amazon.com*   173
     STRATEGY IN ACTION *The Celtic tiger*   178
     STRATEGY IN ACTION *Argentina, a case of recurrent crises*   179
     STRATEGY IN ACTION *The development state – the port of Tanjung*
        Pelepas (PTP)   182
     The main features of global change   185
     Case Study *A clean vehicle – the hybrid electric vehicle (HEV)*   193

6   Reading the competitive environment   199
     Case Study Scenario *Video game wars*   200
     Strategic players   201
     The forces of competition   204
     STRATEGY IN ACTION *Competitive forces for Starbucks*   205
     Risk and market structures   213
     Indeterminateness of outcomes   216
     STRATEGY IN ACTION *Banking in Europe, Germany and market structure*   216
     Country risk   219
     STRATEGY IN ACTION *Business crisis, country risk and the case*
        of Indonesia   219
     Strategic risk   221
     STRATEGY IN ACTION *The Deutsche Bank and investment banking*   222
     Case Study *Video game wars*   224

7   Analysing resources, capabilities and core competencies   233
     Case Study Scenario *Branding a sports team – Manchester United*   234
     Enterprise identity   235
     The nature of resources: tangible and intangible   237
     Resources and capabilities   239
     STRATEGY IN ACTION *Charles Schwab and online broking*   240

The core competencies of an enterprise   243

STRATEGY IN ACTION *Haier: developing a new core competency and pioneering the Chinese export brand*   243

STRATEGY IN ACTION *Business models in broking*   249

STRATEGY IN ACTION *John Doerr and Kleiner Perkins Caulfield & Byers, the leading venture capital firm in Silicon Valley*   256

Case Study *Branding a sports team – Manchester United*   258

8   Creating and maintaining competitive advantage   266

Case Study Scenario *Hutchison and the introduction of third generation wireless communication*   267

The concept of competitive advantage   269

STRATEGY IN ACTION *Inventing a new product – cosmetic contact lenses*   272

STRATEGY IN ACTION *The virtual university and the MBA*   273

Strategies for acquiring competitive advantage   275

STRATEGY IN ACTION *The Mt Buller winter resort and global warming*   280

Focusing   281

STRATEGY IN ACTION *Samsung Electronics: a dramatic turnaround – creating the brand*   281

Remaking the environment by innovation   284

STRATEGY IN ACTION *Samsung Electronics: a dramatic turnaround – investing in new technology*   284

STRATEGY IN ACTION *Vivendi Universal – divesting to survive*   286

Competitive advantage and market structures   289

E-commerce and services   291

STRATEGY IN ACTION *Dell and direct sales*   293

Case Study *Hutchison and the introduction of third generation wireless communication*   296

9   Reducing costs   302

Case Study Scenario *Infosys and the Indian comparative advantage*   303

Cost leadership   304

Cost drivers   305

STRATEGY IN ACTION *The rise of Haier*   309

Pricing strategy   311

STRATEGY IN ACTION *Southwest Airline – the no-frills airline*   315

Focused cost minimization   317

STRATEGY IN ACTION *Packaging a cheap holiday – Club Med*   321

The nature of a technology   322

STRATEGY IN ACTION *Wal-Mart: the origins of a cost-reducing machine*   323

The limits of cost leadership   325

STRATEGY IN ACTION *Caterpillar vs. Komatsu*   325

STRATEGY IN ACTION *Wal-Mart: IT as a source of cost leadership*   330

Case Study *Infosys and the Indian comparative advantage*   332

10   Differentiating the product   338

     Case Study Scenario   *Turning a stone into a jewel – De Beers*   339

     Needs and wants   340

     STRATEGY IN ACTION   *The democratization of luxury*   343

     STRATEGY IN ACTION   *Creating and maintaining demand for luxury and aspirational automobiles*   345

     Marketing as a source of competitive advantage   346

     STRATEGY IN ACTION   *Formula One*   346

     STRATEGY IN ACTION   *Promoting a good image*   352

     Product differentiation   353

     STRATEGY IN ACTION   *Exploiting a brand name – Harley-Davidson*   353

     Intangible qualities   357

     Branding   359

     STRATEGY IN ACTION   *Sir Richard Branson and many wise virgins*   359

     A product differentiation strategy   363

     Case Study   *Turning a stone into a jewel – De Beers*   369

Part III   **Strategic Dilemmas**   375

11   Determining the size of an enterprise   378

     Case Study Scenario   *A merger and a demerger*   379

     The optimum size of an enterprise   380

     STRATEGY IN ACTION   *Communication, information and entertainment – the forces making for fusion*   385

     The strategic gains from vertical and horizontal integration   387

     STRATEGY IN ACTION   *Integration in communications/information/ entertainment*   394

     Acquisitions and mergers   395

     STRATEGY IN ACTION   *The Hewlett-Packard/Compaq merger*   400

     Focusing, strategic alliances and networks as devices for reducing the disadvantages of size   402

     Outsourcing and downscoping   404

     Case Study   *A merger and a demerger*   408

12   Integrating the strategists   416

     Case Study Scenario   *The house of Gucci*   417

     Integrating structures   418

     The influence of the principal/agent relationship on strategy   420

     STRATEGY IN ACTION   *Microsoft, a giant comes of age*   421

     The behaviour of principals and agents   424

     STRATEGY IN ACTION   *Semco and Ricardo Semler – democracy as a management strategy*   425

     STRATEGY IN ACTION   *Finding a new structure and new strategy for Microsoft*   428

     STRATEGY IN ACTION   *Reliance and the death of the founder*   429

     Strategy and organizational design   431

     STRATEGY IN ACTION   *Asea Brown Boveri (ABB)*   437

Monitoring, incentives and corporate culture   441
Outside control   448
Case Study *The house of Gucci*   450

13   When to compete and when to cooperate   456
      Case Study Scenario *The wine industry in Australia*   457
      Dealing with other strategic players   458
      STRATEGY IN ACTION *Benetton: cooperation as strategy*   461
      STRATEGY IN ACTION *The strategic alliance between Renault and Nissan* 462
      The commons and free riding   464
      STRATEGY IN ACTION *Benetton and changing networks*   465
      Game theory and the prisoner's dilemma   467
      The universality of the prisoner's dilemma   471
      How to cooperate   477
      Strategic alliances   481
      STRATEGY IN ACTION *When does a strategic alliance become a merger?* 481
      Case Study *The wine industry in Australia*   487

14   Managing risk   495
      Case Study Scenario *Africa – AIDS and civil wars*   496
      The universality of risk management   497
      Strategic responses to risk   503
      STRATEGY IN ACTION *Enron and the Dabhol project*   504
      STRATEGY IN ACTION *Lloyd's of London and 'long-tailed' risk*   507
      STRATEGY IN ACTION *Responses to the Asian economic crisis*   511
      STRATEGY IN ACTION *Disney and the redistribution of risk*   513
      Risk and diversification   516
      Strategic risk, scenario building and strategy making   517
      STRATEGY IN ACTION *Three different reform scenarios in China*   518
      Case Study *Africa – AIDS and civil wars*   522

15   Participating in the global economy   530
      Case Study Scenario *Entry into the Chinese automobile industry* 531
      Participation strategies   532
      STRATEGY IN ACTION *Wal-Mart and the internationalization of retailing* 535
      STRATEGY IN ACTION *News Corporation and expansion in the USA*   537
      Participation strategies and competitive advantage   539
      STRATEGY IN ACTION *The Japanese entry into the USA automobile market* 541
      Country-specific assets and enterprise-specific assets   542
      STRATEGY IN ACTION *1. Disney and a tale of three cultures*   545
      STRATEGY IN ACTION *2. The trials of Euro Disney*   546
      Internalization   547
      The nature of a world (global) enterprise   549
      STRATEGY IN ACTION *SingTel and its Asia Pacific role*   549
      STRATEGY IN ACTION *Nestlé – a global enterprise?*   554
      Case Study *Entry into the Chinese automobile industry*   555

Part IV   Bringing it all Together   565

16   Formulating strategy   568
       Case Study Scenario *The supreme strategist – General Electric*   569
       Case Study Scenario *Nokia – where did it come from?*   569
       How to learn good strategy making, the 'core' core competency   570
       STRATEGY IN ACTION *Honda and the revival of a stagnant market*   570
       Steps in strategy making   574
       Two alternative models   576
       Strategic thinking – making room for creativity   580
       The nature of strategic management   589
       STRATEGY IN ACTION *IKEA and innovative combination*   594
       Strategic planning   596
       Case Study 1: *The supreme strategist – General Electric*   599
       Case Study 2 *Nokia – where did it come from?*   606

17   Implementing strategy   614
       Case Study Scenario 1 *South African Breweries – a different
          global strategy*   615
       Case Study Scenario 2 *Toyota – still a Japanese company?*   615
       Common weaknesses in strategy implementation   616
       The five Cs and strategy implementation   618
       STRATEGY IN ACTION *Starbucks and being a good citizen*   621
       The interactive or iterative nature of strategy making   626
       Boundaries   627
       Staging   629
       STRATEGY IN ACTION *Lessons from the online broking experience – how
          to stage?*   630
       Leadership and the role of the centre: a specialized strategy division 634
       Case Study 1 *South African Breweries – a different global strategy*   637
       Case Study 2 *Toyota – still a Japanese company?*   640

18   Monitoring strategic performance   651
       Case Study Scenario 1 *Sony – the disruptive innovator*   652
       Case Study Scenario 2 *A blockbuster drug – Imclone and insider trading* 652
       Monitoring   653
       Measuring   657
       The role of financial controls   663
       STRATEGY IN ACTION *Andersen, accounting and the problems
          of monitoring*   668
       Satisfying all the stakeholders   669
       STRATEGY IN ACTION *General Motors and its value added*   670
       STRATEGY IN ACTION *The Enron collapse and others*   679
       Choosing the nature of strategy   679
       Case Study 1 *The disruptive innovator, Sony*   683
       Case Study 2 *A blockbuster drug – ImClone and insider trading*   688

Part V   Strategic Analysis and Audit   699

          Riding the Internet wave: Amazon.com   702

          Finance, a venue for perfect competition: the Deutsche Bank   708

          Haier: pioneering the Chinese export brand   716

          The Hewlett-Packard/Compaq merger   722

          Lloyd's of London and 'long-tailed' risk   729

          The Mt Buller winter resort and global warming   735

          Euro Disney and a tale of three cultures   743

          The strategic alliance between Renault and Nissan   748

          Samsung Electronics: a dramatic turnaround   754

          Going global: Singapore Telecommunications (SingTel)   760

          Starbucks: the third place   766

          Sir Richard Branson and many wise virgins   773

          Vivendi Universal: divesting to survive   778

          Wal-Mart: the cost-reducing machine   783

          Forecasting the price of oil   790

      Epilogue: reviewing the nature of strategy   798

      Glossary   802

      Bibliography   812

      Name index   823

      Organization index   827

      Subject index   833

List of figures

0.1   Andrews' design model xxiii
0.2   An iterative model of strategy making xxiv
0.3   Learning paths xxix

1.1   The four main elements of strategy 5
1.2   Two approaches to strategic thinking 6
1.3   The design school model 10
1.4   Dominant perspectives in strategy making 14
1.5   Stakeholders in the pharmaceutical industry (US style) 27
1.6   The stakeholders (external and internal) 28
1.7   A map of economic stakeholders 31
1.8   A map of political stakeholders 32

2.1   The attributes of strategic thinking 47
2.2   The variations of enterprise circumstance 64
2.3   Value added by customers 74

4.1   The classical model of rational decision making 117
4.2   The different time perspectives 128
4.3   The risk matrix 134
4.4   The demand curve 146
4.5   Movement in demand and supply over time 146
4.6   Price determination under different conditions 147

5.1   The nature of cultural differences 171
5.2   The existing structure of the industry 174
5.3   The causes of economic growth 177
5.4   Representative sources of opportunity and threat in different segments 184

6.1   Porter's five forces of competition 207
6.2   The six forces 211
6.3   Dynamizing the forces 212
6.4   Networking computers 213
6.5   The evolution of markets 215
6.6   The banking value chain 217

7.1   An audit list of resources 239
7.2   Core competencies 245
7.3   The five determinants of a core competency 247

7.4   Primary and support activities 252
7.5   Specialization by activity 254
7.6   Banking activities 256

8.1   Companies with the biggest investment in 3G 267
8.2   The timetable of the global Hutchison 3 strategy 268
8.3   New core competencies and new product markets 271
8.4   Value creation 276
8.5   Strategies for increasing value added (V–C) 277
8.6   Possible 3G technical standards 298

9.1   Pricing stance 312
9.2   The value chain and an automobile manufacturer 319
9.3   Transaction cycle 327

10.1 The range of luxury products and services 357
10.2 Uniqueness drivers 367

11.1 The information industry (2001) 387
11.2 The growth share matrix 393

12.1 The product design structure of the Shougang Company 433
12.2 Regional design structure of Cadbury Schweppes 434
12.3 Functional design structure of British Airways 435
12.4 Customer group design structure of Eastman Kodak 436
12.5 A typical matrix structure 437
12.6 The Galbraith star 441

13.1 Reasons for cooperation within different market structures 460
13.2 The punishment matrix 468
13.3 The possible outcomes of excessive competition in a falling market 472
13.4 Decision tree on entry into a new market 474
13.5 Opportunism in recruiting trained workers 475
13.6 Behaviour in a financial crisis 476

13.7 The Californian wine cluster 480
13.8 Partner selection – risks and strategy 485

14.1 Risk control 497
14.2 Strategic responses to an economic
      crisis 511

15.1 The decision tree for mode of entry 532

16.1 Five phases in the evolution of strategy
      making 572
16.2 A matrix of creativity 582
16.3 Burgelman's process model of internal corporate
      venturing (ICV) or intrapreneurship 587
16.4 IKEA's creative combination 594
16.5 GE's multidimensional portfolio assessment 600
16.6 GE's portfolio of businesses 601
16.7 Handset games consoles 611

17.1 Different strategic routes 1 631

17.2 Different strategic routes 2 632
17.3 A typology of organizations 641
17.4 Toyota's network-level knowledge-sharing
      processes 644

18.1 Monitoring strategy 654
18.2 The relationship of strategic activities 655
18.3 The canvas of a hotel 656
18.4 Performance improvement chain 659
18.5 The virtuous behaviour matrix 676

C.1 The existing structure of the industry 704
C.2 The banking value chain 711
C.3 The demand curve 791
C.4 Movement in demand and supply over time 792
C.5 Price determination under different
     conditions 792

List of tables

2.1 IKEA's expansion 44
2.2 The geographical location of IKEA stores 45

3.1 The world's largest corporations (2001) 100
3.2 Composition of the large multinationals by national origin (%) 100

5.1 Transparency International's bribe payers index (BPI) for 2002 172
5.2 Profit margin for a 'typical book' 174
5.3 Key economic indicators of OECD total and selected small countries 179
5.4 Characteristics of existing HEVs 194
5.5 Relative performance of different technologies 196

6.1 The console cycle 225
6.2 Characteristics of the competing consoles (in 2002) 226

7.1 The discount broker top ten in USA 251
7.2 The cost of Real Madrid's players 259
7.3 2002 market capitalization of the ten most valuable soccer clubs 260
7.4 2001 results (£m) 261

8.1 Sales in 2001 284
8.2 Products in which Samsung now holds number one spot in the world 284
8.3 Status of principal assets (August 2002) 287

9.1 Costs per available seat-kilometre (ASK) – first half of 2001, in cents 316
9.2 Intra-European market shares 317
9.3 Real sales per employee ($1000s) 331
9.4 Top Indian companies by capitalization, in $billion 332
9.5 World spending on IT services 334
9.6 India's ITES companies 334

10.1 The size of the diamond trade (2002) 339
10.2 Budgetary analysis 2002 347
10.3 World rough-diamond supply 370

11.1 Strategic benefits and costs of vertical integration 390
11.2 The range of activities of the main communication/information/entertainment companies 394
11.3 Integration and the value of IBM and AT&T 404
11.4 BHP's planned projects 409
11.5 BHP's recent performance 411

12.1 'Old' versus 'new' management strategies in Asian family firms 424
12.2 Benefits and weaknesses of the product design principle 433
12.3 Benefits and weaknesses of the regional design principle 434
12.4 Benefits and weaknesses of the functional design principle 436
12.5 Benefits and weaknesses of the customer group design principle 436
12.6 Benefits and weaknesses of the matrix design principle 437

13.1 Wine production (million litres) 457
13.2 Gross revenues and net income of Benetton (€ millions) 461
13.3 Benetton's foreign production poles 466
13.4 How Benetton and its competitors configure their business networks 467
13.5 Three patterns of capitalism 486
13.6 The nine principal industry associations 489
13.7 Australian shipments to the US and UK 491
13.8 The top eight wine companies in the world (2000) 491

14.1 Standard & Poor's risk rating scale 502
14.2 The components of Euromoney's risk ratings 502
14.3 HIV prevalence worldwide 523
14.4 Living with HIV/AIDS in Africa 523
14.5 The cost of AIDS to an employer 525
14.6 The typical time frame for costs 525

15.1 Sales of all vehicles in the main markets of the world 531

15.2 Retailers go global – number of new countries entered 535
15.3 Mexico's retail landscape (2001) 536
15.4 News Corp.'s global footprint 538
15.5 Factors influencing the entry mode decision 540
15.6 Percentage of total vehicle production in the USA which is Japanese 542
15.7 A comparison of Singapore and Asia 550
15.8 Before and after entry into the WTO 556
15.9 Joint ventures 557
15.10 Sales and profits in different activities in the automobile industry (%) 559

16.1 The CEOs of GE 569
16.2 The position of GE's strategic business units after ten years of Jack Welch 601
16.3 GE divisional results 604
16.4 Comparison with Citigroup, April 8, 2002 605
16.5 Shares of different activities in turnover (%) 607
16.6 The winning products 607
16.7 Specifications of the standard handset 610

18.1 Profitability ratios 664
18.2 Liquidity ratios 665

18.3 Debt ratios 666
18.4 Time activity ratios 666
18.5 Shareholder return ratios 667
18.6 A typical strategy towards stakeholder groups 675
18.7 The regulatory path 689
18.8 The race for a cancer treatment 693

C.1   Profit margin for a 'typical book' 704
C.2   Performance of Germany's big publicly traded banks 714
C.3   Sales in 2001 757
C.4   The sales and profit situation in 2002 757
C.5   Products in which Samsung now holds number one spot in the world 758
C.6   Characteristics of the two markets 762
C.7   Status of principal assets (August 2002) 781
C.8   Retailers go global – number of new countries entered 784
C.9   Real sales per employee ($1000s) 787
C.10 Mexico's retail landscape (2001) 788
C.11 Crude oil reserves and production in 2001 793

Acknowledgements

The author and publishers would like to thank the following for permission to use copyright material:

Academy of Management for Focus on Theory, Chapter 3 from *Academy of Management Review* by S. Ronen and O. Shenkar. Copyright 1985 by ACAD OF MGMT. Reproduced with permission of ACAD OF MGMT in the format Textbook via Copyright Clearance Center.

Academy of Management for Figure 16.4 from *Academy of Management Review* by D. C. Hambrick and J. W. Fredrickson. Copyright 2001 by ACAD OF MGMT. Reproduced with permission of ACAD OF MGMT in the format Textbook via Copyright Clearance Center.

Academy of Management for Figure 16.2 from *Academy of Management Review* by K. Unsworth. Copyright 2001 by ACAD OF MGMT. Reproduced with permission of ACAD OF MGMT in the format Textbook via Copyright Clearance Center.

Australian Business for Table 13.6 from I. Marsh and B. Shaw, 'Australia's Wine Industry Collaboration and Learning as Causes of Competitive Success', *Australian Business* (2000).

Australian Wine and Brandy Corporation for Table 13.7 from 'Australian brand leaders in the USA', from www.awbc.com.au.

A. M. Brandenburger and B. J. Nalebuff for Figure 1.7 from 'Coopetition' (1996), reproduced by permission of the authors and HarperCollins, Inc.

Blackwell Publishers for Figures 9.2 and 10.2 from R. M. Grant, *Contemporary Strategy Analysis: Concepts, Techniques, Applications* (1991).

The Boston Consulting Group, Inc. for Figure 11.2.

Business 2.0 for Table 16.6 from Kaihla, 'Nokia's hit factory', *Business 2.0*, August 2002, pp. 66–70.

Business Review Weekly for Focus on Theory, Chapter 14: The Principles of Risk Management from M. Hannen and N. Way, 'Run the Risk', *Business Review Weekly*, July 25–31, 2002, p. 51.

Business Review Weekly for Table 11.4 from J. McCallum, 'BHP Billiton's double act', *Business Review Weekly*, April 20, 2001, p. 56; and N. Way and J. McCallum, 'BHP without steel is a political bomb', *Business Review Weekly*, March 30, 2001, p. 39.

Business Today for Table 9.6 from V. Maharta, 'Glut', *Business Today*, Oct 13, 2002, pp. 52–6.

Centre for International Economic Studies, Adelaide for Table 13.1 from K. Anderson and D. Norman, *Global Wine Production: Consumption and Trade 1961–2001 – A Statistical Compendium* (2002).

CRC Press for Focus on Humour, Chapter 1: A fad or a buzzword from R. Vaghefi and A. B. Huellmantel, *Strategic Management for the 21st Century* (1998), © CRC Press, Boca Raton, Florida.

Elsevier for Focus on Theory, Chapter 2: Strategic Thinking from J. Liedtka, 'Strategic Thinking: Can it be Taught?', reprinted from *Long Range Planning*, Vol. 31, No. 1, pp. 120–9 © 1998.

Financial Times Ltd for Focus on Humour, Chapter 18: Simplicity has a price. Why are so many business books written in a style appropriate for 10 year olds? from *Financial Times*, May 7, 2002, p. 8. © 2002, the Financial Times, Ltd; M. Garrahan for Table 7.4 from 'Big players leave the field: the Premiership', *Financial Times Guide*, August 15, 2002, p. 15. © 2002, the Financial Times, Ltd; and Table 8.3 from P. Larsen and T. Burt, 'A Hollywood Studio, a Music Major, TV Assets, Theme Parks: Messier's legacy is up for grabs', *Financial Times*, Monday June 23, 2003, p. 17. © 2003, the Financial Times, Ltd.

Forbes Global for Table 7.3 from R. Heller, 'Big Kick', *Forbes Global*, July 8 2002, p. 34.

Fortune for Table 3.1 from *Fortune*, July 22, 2002, pp. F1–10.

Gomez Advisors for Table 7.1 from www.gomez.com.

Harvard Business School Publishing Corporation for Tables 14.3, 14.5 and 14.6 from 'AIDS is Your Business' by S. Rosen et al., *Harvard Business Review*, Feb 2003, pp. 83–5, © 2003 by Harvard Business School Publishing Corporation, all rights reserved; Figures 17.1 and 17.2 from 'Time Pacing: Competing in Markets that Won't Stand Still' by K. M. Eisenhardt and S. L. Brown, *Harvard Business Review*, March–April, 1998. © 1998 by Harvard Business School Publishing Corporation, all rights reserved; and Figure 18.5 from *The Virtue Matrix: Calculating the Return on Corporate Responsibility* by R. L. Martin, March, 2002. © 2002 by Harvard Business School Publishing Corporation, all rights reserved.

INFORMS for Figure 16.3 from R. A. Burgelman, 'Corporate Entrepeneurship and Strategic Management Insights from a Process Study', reprinted from *Management Science*, Vol. 29, 1983, © 1983.

Inter IKEA Systems B.V for Tables 2.1 and 2.2 from www.ikea.com.

John Wiley & Sons, Ltd for Focus on Practice, Chapter 7: Examples of core (distinctive) competencies from *Scenarios: the Art of Strategic Conversation*, van der Heijden © 1996 John Wiley & Sons, Ltd; and Figure 17.4 from H. Dyer and K. Noeboken, 'Creating and Managing a High-Performance Knowledge-Sharing Network: the Toyota Case', *Strategic Management Journal*, March, 2000, Vol. 21, No. 3. Reproduced by permission of John Wiley & Sons, Ltd.

John Wiley & Sons, Inc. for Figure 12.6 from *Designing Organizations: an Executive Guide to Strategy, Structure and Process* J. R. Galbraith, 2001 by John Wiley & Sons, Inc.

McGraw-Hill Education, Inc. for Table 3.2 from C. W. L. Hill, 'International Business: Competing in the Global Marketplace' (2000), p. 20; Figure 5.1 from G. Hofstede, 'Cultures and Organizations'; and Table 16.2 from A. A. Thompson and A. J. Strickland, *Strategic Management: Concepts and Cases* 11/e (1999).

McKinsey Quarterly for Table 15.2 from L. Catoni et al., 'Travel Tips for Retailers', *McKinsey Quarterly*, 2002, no. 3, Exhibit 3, p. 129; Table 15.10 from P. Gao, 'A tune-up for China's auto industry', *McKinsey Quarterly*, 2002, no. 1, pp. 149–55; Table 18.7 from Heinz-Peter Elstrodt, Pablo Ordorica Lenero, and Eduardo Urdapilleta, 'Micro lessons for Argentina', *McKinsey Quarterly*, 2002, vol 2; Table 5.5 from L. A. Ealey and G. A. Mercer, 'Tomorrow's Cars, Today's Engines', *McKinsey Quarterly*, 2002, no. 3, p. 47; Table 9.1 from P. R. Costa et al., 'Rethinking the Aviation Industry', *McKinsey Quarterly*, 2002, no. 2, p. 97, Exhibit 5; and Table 9.2 from U. Bingelli and L. Pompeo, 'Hyped hopes for Europe's low-cost airlines', Exhibit 1, p. 88 – 'Sky-high expectations', *McKinsey Quarterly*, 2002, no. 4.

Oxford University Press for Table 13.5 from J. Dunning, 'Governments and Macro-Organisation of Economic Activity: a Historical and Spatial Perspective', in J. H. Dunning (ed.), *Governments, Globalisation and International Business* (1997).

Paul & Co Publishing Consortium for Focus on Theory, Chapter 4: The criteria of rationality, Figures 4.1 and 13.4 from J. Forster and M. Browne, *Principles of Strategic Management*, Chapter 8, pp. 161–2.

Pearson Education for Figures 12.1, 12.2, 12.3, 12.4 and 12.5 from *International Business* by Griffin/Pustay, © 2001. Reprinted by permission of Pearson Education, Inc., Upper Saddle River, NJ.

Southcorp for Table 13.8 from www.southcorp.com.au.

South Western College Publishing for Table 14.1 from J. Madura, 'Financial Markets and Institutions' (2001); and Strategic Project, Chapter 17 from J. Siciliano and C. Gopinath, 'Strategize: Experiential Exercises in Strategic Management' (2001).

The Age for Focus on Humour, Chapter 9: Price Differentiation from J. Chessell, 'Greed', *The Age*, Wednesday April 3rd, 2002.

The Economist for Focus on Practice, Chapter 2: A Solution to the Problem of Drug Rape from *The Economist*, June 1 2002.

The Free Press, a Division of Simon & Schuster Adult Publishing Group for Figures 6.1 and 7.4 from 'Competitive Advantage: Creating and Sustaining Superior Performance' by Michael E. Porter. Copyright © 1985, 1998 by Michael E. Porter. All rights reserved.

The Times Newspapers, Ltd for Table 16.7 from P. Durman, 'Nokia bets in a mobile world', *Sunday Times*, June 22, 2003, Business, p. 11. © 2003, The Times Newspapers, Ltd.

Nazdar for Table 9.5 from D. O'Connell and L. Armistead, 'Business Focus: the Great Indian Takeaway', *Sunday Times*, June 8, 2003, Business Focus 3.5. © Nazdar Company. All rights reserved.

Thomson Learning for Figure 1.4 from R. Whittington, *What is Strategy and Does it Matter?* (1999), Figure 1.1, p. 3.

Transparency International for Table 5.1 from www.transparency.org/pressreleases_archive/2002/2002.05.14.bpi.en.html.

Tribune Media Services for Figure 13.3 from A. Camuffo, P. Romano and A. Vinelli, 'Back to the Future: Benetton transforms its global reach', reproduced from *MIT Sloan Management Review*, vol. 43, issue 1, Fall 2001, pp. 49–50.

Every effort has been made to trace the copyright holders but if any have been inadvertently overlooked the publishers will be pleased to make the necessary arrangement at the first opportunity.

Prologue

Why can't strategy be 'everything a company does or consists of'? Is that not strategy as perspective – in contrast to position? (MINTZBERG AND LAMPEL, 1999: 26)

Strategy formation is judgmental designing, intuitive visioning, and emergent learning; it is about transformation as well as perpetuation; it must involve individual cognition and social interaction, cooperative as well as conflictive; it has to include analysing before and programming after as well as negotiating during: and all this must be in response to what may be a demanding environment. (MINTZBERG AND LAMPEL, 1999: 27)

Power takes that entity called organization and fragments it; culture knits a collection of individuals into an integrated entity called organization. In effect, one focuses primarily on self-interest, the other on common interest. (MINTZBERG ET AL., 1998: 264)

Learning objectives

After reading this chapter you will be able to:

- understand the structure of the book
- use the book intelligently
- make full use of the case studies
- discover and explore preliminary reading

Key strategic challenge

What benefit will I receive from reading this book?

Strategic dangers

That an organization does not realize the significant disadvantages of having no strategy, whether implicit or explicit, or having a strategy which is obviously inadequate – fragmentary, imperfectly understood, poorly articulated or badly designed – for an organization's environments.

Who this book is for

The book is written for two particular groups of readers:

- Students about to complete their first degree in the business area or managers beginning a Doctor of Business Administration, that is, those with a theoretical interest
- Active managers undertaking a Master of Business Administration or those who could profitably do so, that is, those with a practical interest.

The book is constructed to benefit both groups. It should also have a wider appeal to senior, and aspiring senior, managers, not just in commercial enterprises but in any organization since it considers strategy in its broadest context.

The starting point for this book is unambiguous; it is premised on two main propositions:

- All successful organizations and individuals, without exception, follow a 'good' strategy, that is, one which significantly improves the performance of the organization. In a sense this is tautology – good strategy can easily be seen, and therefore defined, as what makes the organization successful. Sometimes the strategy is implicit, even unconsciously pursued, but it is always better to make it explicit, that is, to work out its implications as fully as time and resources allow. The degree of success can vary, and vary a lot
- The process of strategy making and the actual content of a strategy must reflect the nature of the world in which it is formulated and implemented. Trying to realize an unrealistic plan is not a sensible thing to do. It is better to take account of institutional and behavioural realities.

Strategy making is therefore challenging and dangerous; it offers significant benefits, if done well, and significant losses, if done badly.

This textbook is intended to do two things:

- Open access to a vast literature, which the student reader cannot possibly master alone. It introduces the key concepts with a maximum economy of effort, saving the reader from spending as much time and effort as the writer has on mastering the material
- Inspire readers with a sense of the excitement to be derived from discovering possible solutions to important theoretical and practical challenges, and therefore giving an appreciation of the critical significance and ultimate value of strategy as a whole.

The second is more difficult to achieve than the first.

The book argues that the only way to assist managers and future managers is by showing them how to think systematically about their problems – to conceptualize and therefore generalize them. It unashamedly confronts the need for theory. If academics often lack a practical feel, managers often fail to recognize the importance of theory. The book balances the demands of the theoretical and the practical, and builds a solid bridge between the theorist and the practitioner.

The text confronts theoretical issues without losing sight of practical aims. Theoretical contradictions need to be dealt with before moving on to practical issues. Having confronted them, the book gives the treatment of strategy a sound practical bias. It asks directly, what is 'doable' in the working world, rather than speculating on what is ideal in the world of reason and imagination.

This is not a textbook on corporate strategy alone, although a subtext can be discovered within it which confronts all the relevant issues covered in courses on corporate strategy, notably in Part II of the book. Rather it is a textbook on strategy for all types of organization. It makes reference more often to organizations than to enterprises, and analyses the way in which various strategies developed at different levels of an economy impinge on corporate strategy. It is impossible to understand fully corporate strategy making without taking into account the broader context in which various players make their own strategy. The organization or enterprise is the focus of analysis but the boundaries assumed to exist between that organization or enterprise and the rest of the world are removed and the strong interconnections between internal and external environments are examined.

For students already enrolled in a business degree, this text has particular relevance to courses or subjects labelled 'corporate strategy', 'strategic management', 'international business environment' and 'entrepreneurship'. It does not claim to be comprehensive in the latter two areas.

How to use the book

Two approaches

There are two alternative approaches to strategy and strategy making:

1. The traditional approach assumes that it is a rational, linear and sequential process, a process in which strategy is determined at the top by a grand strategist and handed down for implementation by others. Diagrammatically it

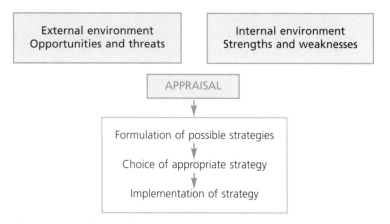

Figure 0.1 Andrews' design model

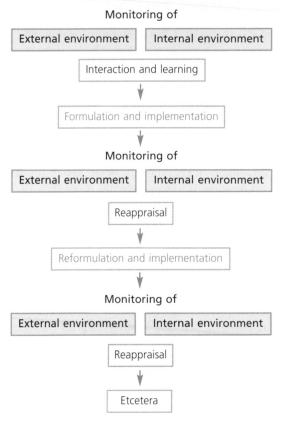

Figure 0.2 **An iterative model of strategy making**

looks something like the original design model developed in the work of Andrews (see for example Learned et al., 1965, in which Andrews wrote the text) and illustrated in Figure 0.1. Strategy is still seen by many managers in this way. It is a simple conception, which explains much of its attractiveness.

2. The second approach is rather different. Strategy is as much intuitive and creative as it is rational; it is also iterative rather than linear, with overlapping rather than discrete steps. Because of the nature of the world, it cannot be sequential. It emerges, unfolds or evolves rather than being created, and comes from below as frequently as from above. It is illustrated in Figure 0.2. If environments were unchanging, each iteration would lead to diminishing adjustments to the strategy. If environments change continuously, as they do, each individual iteration can lead to as much adjustment as any previous iteration.

The position of the author is that the nature of the business world supports the second approach, the iterative model, which determines the structure of this book.

The structure

The text is structured in five sections, as shown in the plan of the book (opposite), which is reproduced in the text at the start of each part:

Task	Parts	Chapters

Starting right

Part I Introducing Strategic Management

WHY?	WHO?	WHAT?	HOW?	WHEN?
Prologue	1 Introducing strategy and strategy making	2 Thinking and acting strategically	3 Adopting a global perspective	4 Reading an uncertain future

Acquiring conceptual tools for the job

Part II Strategic Environments

and Competitive Advantage

General

ENVIRONMENTS Internal

Immediate

GENERIC STRATEGIES

5 Identifying opportunity and risk		7 Analysing resources, capabilities and core competencies
6 Reading the competitive environment		
9 Reducing costs	8 Creating and maintaining competitive advantage	10 Differentiating the product

Resolving particular strategic problems

Part III Strategic Dilemmas

FIVE DILEMMAS

11 Determining the size of an enterprise	12 Integrating the strategists	13 When to compete and when to cooperate	14 Managing risk	15 Participating in the global economy

The strategy emerges

Part IV Bringing it all Together

16 Formulating strategy

17 Implementing strategy	→ **CONTINUOUS ITERATION** ←	18 Monitoring strategic performance

Analysing strategy making

Part V Strategic Analysis and Audit

Case studies

Epilogue

**Part I
Introducing
strategic
management**

A lengthy introduction establishes the topic of strategy and explores the constraints on strategy making, whether they are 'political', social or cognitive. It establishes the practicalities of actual strategy making, placing strategy in a strictly practical context. The four chapters in this section enable readers to answer the following questions:

- What is strategy and what constrains what a strategy can achieve?
- What is the difference between strategic thinking, strategic management and strategic planning?
- What different perspective does a global rather than domestic orientation impart on strategy making?
- How does strategy force us to make predictions and anticipate what might happen in the future?

**Part II
Strategic
environments
and
competitive
advantage**

The core of the book deals with the essential elements of strategy making and concentrates on how the environmental context can be read to identify opportunities which will create and maintain *competitive advantage*. This section develops the main conceptual apparatus of the book and the most important concepts in strategy making and does two main things:

- Analyses, in the first three chapters, the two *external environments* (the *general* and *competitive*) and the *internal organizational environment*. This analysis provides the inputs of knowledge necessary to a good strategy
- Explores, in three further chapters, the meaning of competitive advantage and how it is achieved through the alternative generic strategies of *innovation*, *cost leadership* and *product differentiation*. No enterprise can survive without continuously renewing its competitive advantage. The process of acquiring the knowledge relevant to strategy and the strategies by which it is possible to create and maintain competitive advantage are the central focus of this section.

**Part III
Strategic
dilemmas**

This section moves from the world of the practical and conceptual to an analysis of the kind of recurrent strategic situations in which strategic decisions have to be made. It considers the strategic dilemmas which strategists regularly have to confront and explores the challenges which strategy is intended to solve. In confronting those problems, it weds practice and theory, using the lessons of the practical constraints and conceptual tools discussed in the previous two sections.

This section concentrates attention on five particular strategic dilemmas:

- how big an organization should be
- how to reconcile the interests of different stakeholder groups
- when an organization should cooperate and when it should compete
- how an organization should manage risk
- how an organization should enter a new market, particularly at the global level.

It shows how solving each of these dilemmas is central to good strategy making.

**Part IV
Bringing it
all together**

Here the formulation and implementation of strategy is dealt with directly. This represents the climax of the book, one reached after a steady and deliberate build-up. The systematic development to a discussion of formulation and implementation is deliberate since it echoes the actual process of strategy making which in a real sense emerges rather than being imposed. This section therefore returns to the world of practice.

**Part V
Strategic
analysis
and audit**

The final section offers 15 additional case studies for the purpose of analysis rather than to illustrate concepts or practices. They are carefully chosen to cover a broad area of international businesses and confront the main strategic issues which are covered in the book. The text is deliberately interspersed with questions which promote the process of deeper analysis from the perspective of strategy making and strategic performance.

Key themes

The text incorporates a number of aspects of strategy often neglected or played down by others, including:

- adopting a decisively international or global orientation
- stressing the need in any strategy making to forecast the future
- pointing to the strategic importance of cooperation as much as competition
- drawing out the 'political' processes involved in making strategy.

All these are fundamental to good strategy making and are therefore issues which are fully integrated into the text.

This book also accords a large place to risk management, justified on the basis of the critical role of successfully anticipating threats or shocks, and necessary for the continuing survival of all organizations. However, it accepts that an obsession with the negative factor of risk does not make for good strategy. The starting point for strategy making should be *opportunity*, not *threat*, although every opportunity carries its own threats.

**Learning
aids**

The textual material is complemented by a number of features designed to help student learning. Each chapter includes:

Apt quotation(s) highlighting the significance of the themes contained in the chapter.

Learning objectives each corresponding to a different chapter section, outlining the key areas of knowledge to be gained.

A Key strategic challenge question encouraging readers to consider the main practical issues associated with the chapter topic.

A Strategic danger pointer demonstrating the importance of understanding theory in order to solve real-world problems.

A Case Study Scenario highlighting the main themes of the chapter through the basis of a long case study example.

Strategy in Action mini case study illustrations demonstrating how international organizations apply theory in practice and supporting the key points in the text.

Focus examples highlighting key concepts and contemporary developments within the subject.

A concluding long Case Study illustration containing the resolution of the introductory case scenario which supports the key learning issues within the chapter and demonstrates the application of theory.

Key strategic lessons summarizing the main arguments advanced in the chapter which can be used to check understanding or for revision purposes.

Applying the lessons exercises which have two aims:

• to test knowledge of the concepts and approaches discussed in the text, in particular relating to the achievement of desired learning outcomes
• to develop an ability to make strategy or evaluate another's strategy.

There are suggestions for the use of the Internet as part of these exercises.

A Strategic project which sets a more ambitious piece of work challenging individuals or groups to develop their strategic skills by systematically applying the concepts and methods developed in the chapter.

An Exploring further review providing references which allow further exploration of the issues raised in the chapter, at a level appropriate to the reader's interests and aims.

In addition, the text includes:

Fifteen Long case studies (see below for more details) from Asia, Australasia, Europe, the UK and the USA.

An extensive Glossary containing over 300 entries, to help the reader review and define key terms. For ease of reference, words and phrases that are included in this printed glossary, and on the accompanying website, are highlighted in colour when first encountered in the text.

A comprehensive Bibliography combining all the sources referenced in the text.

Three Indexes – a name, organization and subject listing, to help readers easily search for relevant information or references.

A comprehensive companion Website (see below for details).

Routes through the text

There are two distinct pathways through the book, as shown in Figure 0.3, each designed to suit different reader groups:

• The first is more theoretical, with an emphasis on understanding what strategy making means. The reader's goals are to achieve the learning objectives and complete the first type of exercise. The focus sections, the references and the exploring further sections provide the possibility of a deeper theoretical approach for those students who wish to analyse concepts and problems in greater depth.

Figure 0.3 **Learning paths**

- The other is more practical, with an emphasis on knowing how to construct a good strategy. The reader's goals are addressing the key strategic challenge question, undertaking the second kind of exercise and strategic project and effectively analysing the case studies. The other elements can be dealt with in a cursory manner or even avoided by those whose interest is more practical.

Those with a practical bias should cover the shared ground but should then incline to the activities described as more practical and those with a theoretical bias should cover the shared ground but then incline to the more theoretical activities.

Those who wish to follow a relevant content pathway might divide the book into two distinct parts. Parts I and III have a bias towards the practical, Parts II and IV towards the theoretical. All should read the Prologue and Chapter 1. This is to oversimplify since all chapters have both theoretical and practical content. The better approach is to vary the intensity of reading according to the balance desired, but at least skim read all the text.

Instructors who would like more detail on the structure of the book and how it can be incorporated into teaching programmes, will find more information on the accompanying website.

The case studies

A large proportion of the book is taken up with case studies. The case study organizations, or problems, are selected so that interested readers will be able to improve their understanding of significant strategic issues in the business world. They give a wide coverage of that world, both in a geographical sense and an industry sector perspective, as illustrated in the Case matrix overleaf. Since the strategic position of

CASE MATRIX

Case title	○short ●long	Primary sector	Manufacturing	Air/sea transport	Motor vehicles	Communication/information	Entertainment	Health and education	Retailing	Finance and insurance	Chapters	Region
Three different reform scenarios in China	○	*									○14	Asia
Asea Brown Boveri (ABB)	○		*								○12	Europe
Africa – AIDS and civil wars	●	*	*					*			●14	Africa
Airbus	○●		*								●4	Europe
Aldi	○								*		○9	Europe
Amazon.com	○●					*			*		○5/●Part V	N.America
Andersen	○									*	○18	N.America
Argentina	○									*	○5	S.America
Australian wine industry	●	*	*								●13	Australasia
Benetton	○		*						*		○13	Europe
BHP	●	*									●11	Australasia
BMW	●		*		*						○10	Europe
Boeing	●		*	*							●4	N.America
Brian Epstein	○						*				○2	Europe
Business crisis and the case of Indonesia	○									*	○6	Asia
Business models in broking	○									*	○7	Global
Caterpillar	○		*								○9	N.America
Charles Schwab	○									*	○7	N.America
Club Med	○						*				○9	Europe
Communication/information/entertainment	●					*	*				○11	Global
Compaq	○●		*			*					○11/●Part V	N.America
Cosmetic contact lenses	●		*						*		○8	Global
De Beers	●	*				*					●10	Africa
Dell	●○		*			*					○8	N.America
Deutsche Bank	●									*	○6/●Part V	Europe
Disney	○●					*	*				○14,15/●Part V	Global
Ducati	○				*						○10	Europe
Enron	○●					*	*				○14/18	N.America
Euro Disney	●						*				○14,15/●Part V	Europe
European banking	●									*	○6	Europe
Forecasting the price of oil	●	*									●Part V	Middle East
Formula One	●				*		*				○10	Global
GE	○		*							*	●16	N.America
General Motors	○		*		*						○18	N.America
Gucci	●○		*						*		○12	Europe
Haier	●		*								○7,9/●Part V	Asia
Harley-Davidson	○				*						○10	N.America
Hermes	○								*		○10	Asia
Hybrid electric vehicle (HEV)	●				*						●5	Global

Company	Chapter	Region
Hewlett-Packard	O11/●Part V	N.America
Honda	O16	Asia
Hutchison	●8	Asia
IKEA	O16/●2	Europe
Imclone	●18	N.America
Infosys	●9	Asia
Japanese–English conversation manual	O2	Asia
Komatsu	O9	Asia
Kleiner Perkins Caulfield & Byers	O7	N.America
Lessons from the online broking experience	O17	Global
Lloyd's	O14/●Part V	Europe
Luxury cars	O10	Europe
Manchester United	●7	Europe
McDonald's	O1	N.America
Merlin Biosciences	O7	Europe
Microsoft	O12/●6	N.America
Mt Buller	O8/●Part V	Australasia
Nestlé	O15	Europe
News Corp	O15	Australasia
Nintendo	●6	Asia
Nissan	O13/●Part V	Asia
Nokia	●16	Europe
Qantas	3	Australasia
Reliance	O12	Asia
Renault	O13/●Part V	Europe
Responses to the Asian economic crisis	O14	S.Africa
SAB Miller	●17	S.Africa
Samsung	O8/●Part V	Asia
Semco	O12	S.America
SingTel	O15/●Part V	Asia
Sony	O2/●6, 18	Asia
Southwest Airline	O9	America
Starbucks	O6,17/●Part V	N.America
Swissair	●3	Europe
The Celtic Tiger	O5	Europe
The port of Tanjung Pelepan	O5	Asia
The virtual university and the MBA	O8	N.America/Europe
Toyota	O15/●17	Asia
Virgin	O10/●Part V	Asia
Virgin Atlantic/Virgin Blue	●Part V	Europe/Australasia
Vivendi	O8/●Part V	Europe
Volkswagen	O15	Europe/Asia
Wal-Mart	O9,15/●Part V	N.America

any organization is unique, a large number and variety of case studies are presented, in three different forms:

1. Each chapter is introduced by a Case Study Scenario which prompts the reader to consider the challenges of implementing successful strategy and highlights the main themes of the chapter. The resolution of the case is included at the end of the chapter to demonstrate what happened.
2. Sixty-four Strategy in Action mini case study examples are used throughout the text to illustrate particular issues.
3. The final part of the book includes fifteen Long case studies which are designed to illustrate strategy making in its broadest sense by encouraging students to analyse the situation and performance. They are not directly linked with particular problems or concepts discussed in the text, but the Case matrix summarizes the sectors and issues which each of these support. The best way to approach these case studies is for the individual or student group to conduct a strategic audit of the organization. Additional long case examples are also provided on the companion website.

There are two main uses of the case studies. The first, in the text itself, is illustrative, intended to show a practical manifestation of an idea or concept. The second, in Part V, is analytical, intended to show the way to a full strategic audit.

Case analysis

As a preparation for a class analysis of a freestanding case study, the reader or student might like to carry out the following steps, either individually or in a group:

1. Carry out a first reading of the case study in order to gain an initial perception of the issues raised
2. Carry out a second, more thorough and slower reading of the case study, from the perspective of a strategy audit
3. Do any relevant outside research, in libraries or on the Internet. What is contained in any write-up of a case study is only an introduction which asks questions rather than provides all the answers. Further research is required.
4. Write the first draft of the strategic audit
5. Write the final draft of the strategic audit.

More detail on each of these stages is provided on the accompanying website.

Companion website

This text is accompanied by an extensive companion website hosting resources for both students and lecturers, which can be accessed at www.palgrave.com/business/white.

For students:

- a running case study example, designed to be read alongside each part of the text, ties the different sections together with one coherent illustration

- additional long case studies provide further opportunities for case analysis
- links to further resources help you to navigate the wide range of material available on the Internet
- searchable glossary of strategic terms
- expanded guidance on getting the most out of this book, analysing case studies and further reading.

Instructors have access to all the student resources as well as:

- suggested teaching pathways and objectives
- information on key strategic themes and their use within the book
- suggested case study questions for all the long cases
- comments on the exercises and assignments used in the book
- PowerPoint lecture slides for each chapter which you can edit for your own use.

Introductory reading

The following is a general and introductory guide to reading on strategy. The present text should be supplemented by these other sources. Reading takes three different forms:

1. business newspapers and journals which provide up-to-date information and analysis
2. academic journals, some 'popular' and others scholarly, some devoted to nothing but strategy, others covering management studies in general
3. the body of more extended treatments, some reflective, some primers and some textbooks.

The following indicates those considered most useful and insightful by the author. The focus is on English-language literature.

Newspapers and magazines

The first group includes a number of American newspapers and journals, although in some cases there are versions tailored for and targeted at different parts of the world. For example, the *Wall Street Journal* has an Asian version. *Business Week*, *Fortune* and *Forbes* contain plenty of up-to-date accounts of the strategy of enterprises, mostly the larger multinationals. A European perspective would suggest alternative reading, including *The Economist*, probably the best commentary on current economic events anywhere in the world, although the orientation is consistently pro free market, and pursued with little reservation. The *Financial Times* adds a daily dimension, with more detail and frequently longer and more in-depth articles, perhaps a bit more dispassionate than *The Economist*. *Business 2.0* gives a much more technical perspective on business, with some excellent articles on the strategy of the most dynamic companies. If an Asian perspective is required, *The Far Eastern Economic Review* is worthy of close attention. From India, and largely about India, there are two main journals, *Business Today* and *Business India*.

Each country has its own business press. For example, Australia has *The Financial Review*, a daily, and *The Business Review Weekly*, as the two best sources of business and economic material, mainly but not solely relevant to Australia. Most Asian countries have English-language newspapers, nearly all with good local business coverage, such as the *South China Morning Post* and the *Japan Times*.

Academic journals

The academic literature must start with the *Harvard Business Review*, quite the most accessible journal on strategy, accessible in every sense of the word. It aims to make available new management knowledge to a wide audience. It is a rich quarry of work on strategy, clearly the most quoted journal in textbooks on strategy. The *McKinsey Quarterly* contains a large number of studies of particular industries seen from a strategic perspective; it is probably underrated as a source on strategy. Much more technical and therefore more inaccessible are the articles in either *Long Range Planning* or the *Strategic Management Journal*. Both of these journals contain articles on strategy and little else; they should be major ports of call for those who wish to read at the cutting edge of new research. More rarely found are strategy articles in the broader management journals, such as the *California Management Review*, the *Sloan Management Review*, the *Academy of Management Journal* and the *Academy of Management Executive*. Also worthy of consideration are the journals *Business Horizons* and *Journal of Business Strategy*.

Books

At this stage reference to books is at the 'must read' level for a reader keen to get on top of the strategy area. There are two writers who should be read before all others. Michael Porter is the doyen of all strategy theorists and, because of his enormous influence, should be read, although his work is rather long and not the most exciting of reads. In particular the two main books are *Competitive Advantage: techniques for analysing industries and companies* (Free Press, New York: 1980) and *Competitive Advantage: creating and sustaining superior performance* (Free Press, New York: 1985). Henry Mintzberg is a nice contrast to Porter, very knowledgeable in the area of strategy and a good thinker but sometimes carried away by the exuberance of his own verbosity. The book which is the most analytical treatment of strategy in the whole area is *The Rise and Fall of Strategic Planning* (Prentice Hall International, Hemel Hempstead: 1994). A fascinating romp around the literature on strategy is Mintzberg, H., Ahlstrand, B., and Lampel, J. *Strategy Safari: a guided tour through the wilds of strategic management* (Free Press, New York: 1998).

Rather long, but worth reading to get a sense of historical context and the messiness of any real historical experience, in particular the messiness of business history, are the major works of Chandler, A. D. Jr , *Strategy and Structure: chapters in the history of industrial enterprise* (MIT Press, Cambridge, MA: 1962); *The Visible Hand: the managerial revolution in American business* (Belknap Press, Cambridge, MA: 1977); and *Scale and Scope: the dynamics of industrial capitalism* (Belknap Press, Cambridge, MA: 1990).

There is a rival literature for those who want more rigour in their theory. For very valuable insights into the nature and role of the enterprise, it is worth reading an article which has had an increasing influence over the many years since its publication, Coase, R. 'The nature of the firm', *Economica* 4, 1937: 386–405. Coase has been described as the first institutional economist. The implications of this article are much more fully worked out in Williamson, O. E. *The Economic Institutions of Capitalism: firms, markets, relational contracting* (Free Press, New York: 1985) and in the debate which followed. It has given birth to an enormous literature. Almost as influential as either of these, but in a much quieter way and with a different approach to the topic, is Penrose, E. T. *The Theory of the Growth of the Firm* (Basil Blackwell, Oxford: 1959), probably the most quoted work in this area.

Below are listed the five books on strategy which have given the author most enjoyment and food for thought. They are not traditional textbooks. The influence of these works on the thinking expressed in different parts of the text is obvious to anyone who reads them. All of them offer something but by no means all that is needed for a good text on strategy. For the most part they are not difficult to read, given a commitment to reflect on the issues raised:

Ghemawat, P., *Strategy and the Business Landscape: text and cases* (Addison-Wesley, Reading, MA: 1999).

Forster, J. and Browne, M., *Principles of Strategic Management* (Macmillan, Melbourne: 1996).

Whittington, R., *What is strategy and does it matter?* 2nd edn (Thomson, London: 2001).

Grant, R. M., *Contemporary Strategy Analysis: concepts, techniques, applications* 4th edn (Blackwell, Oxford: 2002).

De Wit, R. and Meyer, R., *Strategy – Process, Content, Context: an international perspective* 2nd edn (International Thomson Business Press, London and Boston: 1998).

Texts on strategy differ enormously in length and the style and depth of analysis. The book by Ghemawat is concise to a fault, at times cryptic. It requires a significant input from the reader. Its approach would probably have greatest appeal to economists. The texts in both Whittington and De Wit and Meyer are also short and highly analytical in tone.

In contrast to the books discussed above, an easy but very much longer read is Viljoen, J. and Dann, S. *Strategic Management; planning and implementing successful corporate strategies* (Longman, Frenchs Forest, NSW: 2000). This is comprehensive and a delight to read. The former works are in the reflective mode, the latter in the primer mode.

Websites

A comprehensive guide to online business magazines around the world is available at http://newsdirectory.com/news/magazine/business/. Links to all the newspapers, magazines and journals cited above are provided below (and are available on the website).

Academy of Management Executive http://www.aom.pace.edu/ame/
Academy of Management Journal http://www.jstor.org/journals/00014273.html
Business 2.0 http://www.business2.com/
Business Horizons http://www.elsevier.com/inca/publications/store/6/2/0/2/1/4/
The Business Review Weekly http://www.brw.com.au/
Business Today http://www.business-today.com
Business Week http://www.businessweek.com/

California Management Review http://www.haas.berkeley.edu/News/cmr/index_.html

The Economist http://www.economist.com/

Far Eastern Economic Review http://www.feer.com/

The Financial Review http://afr.com/

Financial Times http://news.ft.com/

Forbes (Asia, Europe, USA), http://www.forbes.com/home_asia/,
    http://www.forbes. com/home_europe/, http://www.forbes.com/

Fortune http://www.fortune.com/fortune/

Harvard Business Review http://www.hbsp.harvard.edu/products/hbr/index.html

Japan Times http://www.japantimes.co.jp/

Journal of Business Strategy https://www.ecmediagroup.com/Magazines/jbs.cfm

Long Range Planning http://www.lrp.ac/

McKinsey Quarterly http://www.mckinseyquarterly.com/

Sloan Management Review http://mitsloan.mit.edu/smr/main.html

South China Morning Post http://www.scmp.com/

Strategic Management Journal http://www.smsweb.org/about/SMJ/SMJ.html

Wall Street Journal (Asia, Europe, USA) http://online.wsj.com/public/asia,
    http://online.wsj.com/public/europe, http://online.wsj.com/public/us

Part I

Introducing Strategic Management

1   Introducing strategy and strategy making

2   Thinking and acting strategically

3   Adopting a global perspective

4   Reading an uncertain future

Task	Parts	Chapters				
Starting right	**Part I Introducing Strategic Management**	**WHY?** Prologue	**WHO?** 1 Introducing strategy and strategy making	**WHAT?** 2 Thinking and acting strategically	**HOW?** 3 Adopting a global perspective	**WHEN?** 4 Reading an uncertain future

Acquiring conceptual tools for the job — **Part II Strategic Environments and Competitive Advantage**

5 Identifying opportunity and risk — General

6 Reading the competitive environment — Immediate

ENVIRONMENTS Internal

7 Analysing resources, capabilities and core competencies

GENERIC STRATEGIES

9 Reducing costs

8 Creating and maintaining competitive advantage

10 Differentiating the product

Resolving particular strategic problems — **Part III Strategic Dilemmas**

FIVE DILEMMAS

11 Determining the size of an enterprise

12 Integrating the strategists

13 When to compete and when to cooperate

14 Managing risk

15 Participating in the global economy

The strategy emerges — **Part IV Bringing it all Together**

16 Formulating strategy

17 Implementing strategy → **CONTINUOUS ITERATION** ← 18 Monitoring strategic performance

Analysing strategy making — **Part V Strategic Analysis and Audit**

Case studies

Epilogue

All good business performance requires a good strategy; sometimes that strategy is implicit, sometimes explicit; where possible it is always better to make it explicit. The four chapters in Part I are introductory in the sense that they indicate the context in which strategy making is organized and the constraints on content and procedures, constraints which are mainly of a cognitive and organizational nature. There are serious limits on what a strategy can be.

- Chapter 1, Introducing strategy and strategy making, addresses the 'who' of strategy making. It identifies and discusses three particular groups – those who have developed the theory and practice of strategy making, those who at any time are the strategists and those who are stakeholders with a significant interest in strategy.

- Chapter 2, Thinking and acting strategically, addresses the 'what' of strategy making. It

carefully distinguishes between strategic thinking, strategic management and strategic planning. It notes that strategy is a combination of the use of creative imagination and applied reason.

- Chapter 3, Adopting a global perspective, addresses the 'how' of strategy making, although it could be analysed as the 'where'. The key question asked, whether strategy making is different in a global context from a domestic or local context, is answered in the affirmative.

- Chapter 4, Reading an uncertain future, addresses the 'when' of strategy making. By its nature all strategy is concerned with the future and forecasting what that future might look like, allowing for the capacity of the organization itself to remake the future environment.

1

Introducing strategy and strategy making

*Why can't strategy be 'everything a company does or consists of'? Is that not strategy as perspective – in contrast to position? (*MINTZBERG AND LAMPEL, *1999: 26)*

*Strategy formation is judgmental designing, intuitive visioning, and emergent learning; it is about transformation as well as perpetuation; it must involve individual cognition and social interaction, cooperative as well as conflictive; it has to include analysing before and programming after as well as negotiating during: and all this must be in response to what may be a demanding environment. (*MINTZBERG AND LAMPEL, *1999: 27)*

*Power takes that entity called organization and fragments it; culture knits a collection of individuals into an integrated entity called organization. In effect, one focuses primarily on self-interest, the other on common interest. (*MINTZBERG ET AL., *1998: 264)*

Learning objectives

After reading this chapter you will be able to:

- familiarize yourself with strategy as both a theoretical concept and a working tool

- trace the history of the development and use of the strategy concept

- explore the various meanings of the term 'strategy'

- make the link between different meanings and the different academic disciplines behind those meanings

- identify different stakeholder groups and their likely influence on strategy making

- discover the political, social and cognitive constraints on the process of strategy making

Key strategic challenge

Why is strategy important to me as a manager?

Strategic dangers

That strategy is not viewed realistically, with full account of its complexity, but as an oversimplified idea and, as a consequence, the various definitions of strategy are seen as competing and mutually exclusive, rather than representing different aspects of a multifaceted activity.

Strategy is arguably the most important concept in management studies. Strategy making is arguably the most important activity of a practising manager. Yet it is a concept difficult to define, and an activity difficult to pursue with effectiveness.

There are many people involved in the process of strategy making. There are also many different ways of interpreting what strategy is. The main aim of the introductory chapter is to explore the different possible meanings of strategy and to highlight the practical constraints on what strategists and strategy can do. There are clear practical limitations on what is possible which must be understood from the start.

What is strategy?

In its simplest conception strategy is regarded as a unifying idea which links purpose and action. For de Wit and Meyer (1998), in an intelligent treatment of the subject, strategy is any course of action for achieving an organization's purpose(s). In the words of Alfred Chandler, the first modern business strategy theorist, strategy in the area of business is defined as 'the determination of the basic, long-term goals and objectives of an enterprise, and the adoption of courses of action and the allocation of resources necessary for those goals' (Chandler, 1962: 13). Although still tentative and preliminary as a definition, it is possible to advance a little further and say that strategy is 'a coordinated series of actions which involve the deployment of resources to which one has access for the achievement of a given purpose.'

Strategy therefore combines the articulation of human goals and the organization of human activity to achieve those goals. The setting of goals involves the identification of opportunity. Strategy is a process of translating perceived opportunity into successful outcomes, by means of purposive action sustained over a significant period of time. At a minimum there must be a clear intent translatable into specific objectives and some defined and effective means of achieving these objectives by deliberate action involving the use of resources to which one has access (Figure 1.1). Strategy may or may not reflect a fully self-conscious, deliberative and systematic approach to the setting of objectives and their achievement which then require detailed planning. It may be an implicit or unconscious activity.

Figure 1.1 **The four main elements of strategy**

Two types of strategic thinking

Strategy comprises thinking about action in two different ways: vertical (rational) thinking and lateral (intuitive) thinking. It deals with convergent problems, that is, those with one solution, and divergent problems, that is, those with a number of possible solutions. Strategy demands from the strategist(s) both creativity – lateral thinking, often applied to divergent problems, and rationality – vertical thinking, often applied to convergent problems. This means that, in the area of business, strategy combines a vision and managerial effectiveness in realizing that vision, referred to as *operational effectiveness*, and therefore both the harnessing of intuition and the application of reason. In the business world, strategy is about successful entrepreneurship and good management. There is therefore an inherent contradiction in strategic thinking, which makes its full meaning hard to grasp. These two strands of strategic thinking are both essential parts of a strategic orientation and both must be included in any analysis of strategy making (Figure 1.2).

Ways of thinking	Application of creativity, intuition or imagination (lateral thinking)	Application of reason (vertical thinking)
Nature of problem	Divergent: with many solutions	Convergent: with one solution
Area of relevance	Creating the vision: establishing strategic objectives	Realizing the vision: achieving operational effectiveness

Figure 1.2 **Two approaches to strategic thinking**

Different strategic perspectives

The text has introduced the four main elements of strategy and the two main ways of engaging in strategic thinking. A strategic approach also involves a number of distinctive perspectives, which follow from the analysis above. Any strategy lacking the following perspectives is unlikely to be successful:

- Strategy involves looking into the future, not simply focusing on the present or extrapolating what has happened in the past. It involves intent, which both establishes a future direction or destination, and the importance of time because that intent cannot be realized immediately.
- Strategy tries to achieve a balance between flexibility and stability and so avoid either the straitjacket of excessive rigidity or the anarchy of repeated and random changes of direction.
- Strategy emphasizes asking pertinent question(s) as much as providing the answer(s). This means the finding of a problem worthy of serious consideration as much as the resolution of marginal problems thrown up by current operations. Others may be happily unaware that a problem exists or that such a question can even be asked. In this way the strategist moves from known into unknown territory.
- Strategy is complex, dealing in highly intricate systems of cause and effect. It is concerned with what have been called, rather aptly, 'wicked problems of organized complexity' (de Wit and Meyer, 1998: 47).
- Strategy is itself holistic in that it recognizes the many interconnections between superficially different aspects of business activity and different problems. Strategy integrates all the functional business activities – marketing, finance, human resource management, information systems – and gives them coherence.

- Strategy is rooted in particular historical experiences – it is always path-dependent, reflecting the experience through which an organization has reached its present situation.
- Strategy is interactive. The quality of a strategy reflects the degree to which it takes account of the strategies of other players – competitors, governments and cooperators.

Focus on Theory
Strategy

Strategy and a strategic orientation:
- look to the future
- aim for a balance between stability and flexibility
- ask new questions rather than answers old questions
- are holistic and integrative
- are complex
- are path-dependent
- are interactive

Levels of strategy making

Which organizations make strategy and at what levels of an economy? There are inevitably different levels of strategy making, from the functional level within an enterprise to the level of government in a country. Strategy is about the location and significance of boundaries. Such boundaries define an outside and an inside, and thereby potentially a strategy-making unit. These boundaries define the scope of strategy at the different levels, whether the boundaries are between functional departments, strategic business units, corporations, communities or networks, or even countries.

Every boundary can be crossed. Increasingly, corporations actively interact with their outside environment and change it, and through the action of players outside the enterprise, that environment in various ways penetrates the corporation and changes it. This interpenetration is changing its nature over time and is the stuff of strategy making. Simultaneously, there may be a function strategy, a business strategy, a corporate strategy, an industry strategy, a community strategy, even a country strategy, all intertwining with each other.

Does the nature of strategy differ from level to level? Has the internationalization of business, for example, changed strategy making? The content of strategy at the two levels definitely differs. What the local coffee shop does clearly differs from what a large multinational corporation does. Strategy in a global world has begun to change from what it was in a domestic context, if only because of the increasing scale of all the activities. The achievement of competitive advantage and the management of risk at the global level involve different kinds and amounts of functional activity. The global context has begun to have a powerful influence on the strategic dimensions of every enterprise or organization.

Who are the strategists?

Initially, strategy making assumes the existence of at least one strategist, commonly the chief executive officer, who takes responsibility for the successful formulation and implementation of strategy. Few commercial enterprises are run as a democracy, and very few not-for-profit organizations. However, in practice, strategy making is usually done by a large number of people, not just a few. It is often a group activity, involving cooperation.

Not all strategists realize that they are strategists. However, with hindsight, strategy making can always be recognized. Strategy is often conducted in an intuitive way, implicit rather than explicit. Because strategy is universal, embracing a multitude of different activities and circumstances, appropriate definition is difficult. In one sense the whole of this book is part of an attempted definition, one specifically relevant to the area of business, the last chapter providing an informed guide to the making of such a definition.

A brief history of the concept

Today strategy is one of the most commonly used words in management studies, but its use was not, and is not, limited to that area. Thinking and writing about strategy has a history stretching back far earlier than management studies, a history which is interesting in its own right. It has been one of the most debated concepts, both in its definition and significance.

Origins

The history goes back to Greek and Chinese military thinkers, whose insights it has recently become fashionable to quote. In ancient Greek the term *strategos* means an army or its leader. Strategic thinking, in the sense of systematized and institutionalized military thinking, was revived by German military thinkers during the nineteenth century.

In war the overall aim is obvious, the military defeat of the enemy, but the means of achieving that aim need to be carefully articulated. A clear distinction is made between strategy and tactics. For example, Carl von Clausewitz (1984) distinguished tactics from strategy: 'tactics ... [involve] the use of armed forces in the engagement, strategy [is] the use of engagements for the object of war' (quoted in Ghemawat, 1999: 2). Strategy involves both the formulation of the overall aim as specific military objectives and the successful implementation of these objectives. It therefore involves both the marshalling of a wide range of resources to the task and their deployment in a way which maximizes their effectiveness, but also the simultaneous anticipation of what the enemy will do, given its own resources and its likely knowledge of the enemy's resources. The strategy needs to be efficiently implemented, which involves careful preparation, good training and the use of effective tactics. More attention is often concentrated on the effective use of tactics by, for example, Julius Caesar, Alexander the Great or Napoleon than on their ability to get the strategy right, the core of which is the repeated concentration of strength in the right place at the right time.

The military link has continued through to the present day. Many still see a parallel between military strategy and business strategy, drawing a further parallel between tactics and management. The influence of this view clearly underpins the assumptions of the classical approach to strategy discussed below.

While the business enterprise remained small and of low capital intensity and while the invisible hand of Adam Smith appeared to rule economic life, strategy remained dormant as an idea relevant to the business world. When, in the second half of the nineteenth century, the large modern business corporation emerged and, alongside it, the visible hand of deliberate business policy, strategy began its life as a practical application to the business world of a simple principle, shaping one's own fate. As enterprises grew larger, they began to try to control market forces and impose their stamp upon their environment. The first real practitioner in any systematic way was probably Alfred Sloan of General Motors and the first academic commentator was Alfred Chandler (1962), who chronicled, using a number of comparative treatments, the history of the modern business enterprise. Alfred Chandler's main achievement was to explore the implications for strategy of the emergence of the modern corporation. In particular he traced in some detail the interaction between strategy and organizational structure.

Strategy and planning

Strategy is related to planning. Its rise and fall in popularity is linked with the change in attitude to planning. During the twentieth century the techniques of formal and systematic planning became popular in both communist and capitalist economies. It is fitting that the total mobilization of resources for two world wars provided a model of how planning might work. Business planning has quite a long history, both as a practical matter and as a subject of teaching, notably in American business schools such as the Harvard Business School. The case study approach, pioneered by Harvard Business School, highlighted the way in which, in the same industry, different outcomes for enterprises reflected different strategies and different planning models.

The stages of development of strategy

Theory often evolves to cope with a changing world, although the development of such theory tends to lag behind practice. An interesting interpretation of the history of the strategy concept sees it developing over the period from 1945 to the present in four stages, which are defined by the changing problems imposed on enterprises by an evolving socioeconomic environment (see Drejer, 2002: 22–4).

Stage 1

From 1945 to the mid- to late 1960s, the economic context was a relatively stable one, simple to understand, but expansionary. Most economies had been exhausted by war. In 1945, levels of production were well below pre-war levels. During this period overall demand in the world economy tended to be greater than overall supply. There was considerable pent-up demand. There was also a backlog of unexploited technology. The immediate aim of enterprises was the meeting of that demand. Satisfying precise consumer requirements did not matter too much; almost any output was better than none.

The role of strategy in such a context was to mobilize economic resources in an orderly fashion to support a rapid expansion in supply, at first in order to implement recovery from the war and later to use already existing technology to meet the pent-up investment and consumer demand. During this period long-range planning was still accepted as at the heart of any strategy, since economic priorities were clear. Strategy consisted of budgets and programmes put together in one overall plan. The main problem was to plan financially in order to integrate the enterprise internally around the broad aim of profit satisficing within the framework of the plan.

As a separate branch of management studies, strategy was born in 1965 with the publication of two significant books: Learned, Christensen, Andrews and Guth's *Business Policy: text and cases* (1965) (wherein Andrews wrote the text and the other authors wrote the cases) and Ansoff's *Corporate Strategy* (1965). Work in these areas was clearly well developed.

The basic design school model (Figure 1.3), most closely associated with the name of Andrews, is a prescriptive conception. It is intended as a practical guide for dealing with a complex environment in which there are external as well as internal contexts relevant to the enterprise. The approach is best encapsulated in the SWOT model (Strengths, Weaknesses, Opportunities, Threats), probably the most commonly applied method in strategy making. It is often reproduced in flow charts which separate out the key steps in strategy making.

On the other hand, Ansoff prescribed an extremely detailed but potentially overly rigid form of strategic planning, reflecting the nature of long-term planning as it had emerged. He recognized the severe constraints placed on businesses by their existing resources.

During this early period there was a marked reluctance to overgeneralize about strategy and a desire to acknowledge the uniqueness of each experience, as shown by the case study approach. While academics were reluctant to make excessive

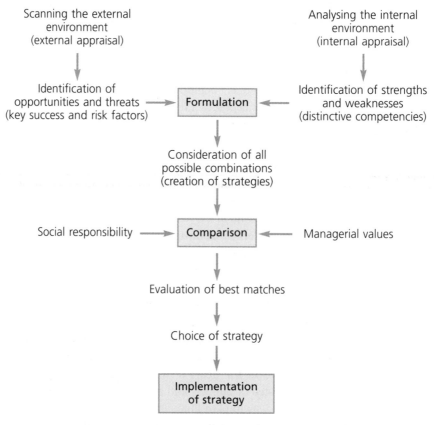

Source: Adapted from Learned et al. 1965.

Figure 1.3 **The design school model**

claims for strategy making of any kind, enterprises themselves were not so constrained. They did not display the same circumspection.

Stage 2

From the late 1960s to the late 1970s, there was more rapid and extensive change, but change of a reasonably predictable kind. Most developed economies were now operating close to the frontier of best-practice technology. Inflationary forces began to emerge, particularly cost inflation involving various commodities and labour, but were still under broad control.

Prioritization became less significant as supply began to catch up with and even run ahead of demand. The consumer became more discriminating. The need to satisfy the consumer in order to make a profit rose in importance. Strategy became more concerned with directing resources into the most promising areas. It began to change its nature, as a changing environment prompted the first efforts to cope with that outside environment, including the choice of desired products and markets. Where an enterprise positioned itself became important.

Further development of strategic thinking resulted from the work of the new consultancies. In the words of the founder of the Boston Consulting Group, BCG was in 'the business of selling powerful oversimplifications' (Ghemawat, 1999: 9), which is true of all consultancies. This work was for the most part based on simplified concepts or partial models which only dealt with parts of a broad strategy, although any recommendations made often involved quite sophisticated modelling. The notion of the experience curve, the growth/share matrix and the profit impact of marketing strategies (PIMS) are well-known examples of the new methods.

Another consultancy, McKinsey's, in conjunction with General Electric, a company which pioneered and developed many different techniques of strategy making (see the case study in Chapter 16), developed the notion of the strategic business unit. Both this and the growth/share matrix marked the entry of portfolio analysis into the area of strategy making. Such techniques were highly relevant to conglomerate and diversified companies in choosing their business units. The practice of some kind of portfolio analysis became common among American enterprises. All these techniques soon came under attack for being overly mechanistic and static in their view of a rapidly changing business world.

Stage 3

Between the mid-1970s and the mid-1980s change became discontinuous. This was the era of the oil price shocks and the later debt crisis in the developing world. Inflation accelerated and growth slowed. The rate of growth temporarily decelerated as the easy gains of the 1950s and 60s were exhausted. In the era of stagflation, inflationary forces temporarily concealed the tendency of supply to run ahead of demand.

The main need of any good strategy was now to allocate resources, including cash flow, in order to develop a competitive advantage, which, in turn, was necessary in order to yield the profits that generated the investment funds required. The focus fell on the portfolio of an enterprise's products and services and the nature of competitive behaviour in the markets. Strategy was increasingly being made at various levels, including business, functional and corporate levels.

In the area of strategy, the 1980s were dominated by Michael Porter, who has done more to develop the theory and application of strategy than any other theorist or practitioner. He published *Competitive Strategy* in 1980 and followed it up with a series of long books, representing a comprehensive approach to the subject. Many of his insights were encapsulated in neat diagrams and summaries which have had a wide and continuing influence, such as the five forces of competition and the competitive diamond, both discussed later in this book.

Porter's originality was to insert the Andrews' approach into the framework of an academic discipline; economics. For the first time an academic was willing to generalize. Porter sought to position the enterprise, and/or its strategic business units, in its strategic environment, principally its competitive environment. It was a matter of selecting appropriate arenas for business activity and a desired mix of products, markets and functional activities. He therefore concentrated his attention on the environmental side of Andrews' analysis. Paradoxically for many readers, this would have the effect of reducing the significance of strategy by assuming away the unique identity of the individual organization.

Stage 4

Finally, during the 1980s, change became not only discontinuous but rather more unpredictable, with new and more complicated dimensions added, as the communications/information revolution began to bite and other demands on business emerged. In the 1990s, growth once more accelerated but in a context in which there were the beginnings of deflationary tendencies. Overcapacity emerged in various sectors of the economy.

It became necessary for strategy to manage and integrate problems in many different areas, including government deregulation, contrasting economic circumstances, rapidly changing technology and new conservationist and environmental demands. Strategy had to expand to embrace these new areas, including a return to a proper consideration of the enterprise's available resources to meet these various requirements.

The 1990s saw the focus of interest shift once again, this time, as might be anticipated, to a greater attention to the other half of the Andrews' concern, the internal resource position of the enterprise. There was an explosion of articles on the so-called 'resource-based view' (RBV) of strategy. The elaboration of this view was not associated with one particular commentator. The debate considered specific capabilities, competencies and even the management of technology as well as resources in general. Various researchers began to explore the context in which the process of strategy making itself occurs, focusing on the social and political constraints on strategy making.

The account above indicates how strategy was cumulative in its build-up of techniques. No strategic method from earlier stages was discarded. Rather they were all improved and used where and when appropriate. As a result, the complexity of strategic management increased enormously. No exact blueprint for strategy making emerged from this history, rather a proliferation of different views about how it should be done.

A careful analysis, as shown in the next section, shows that the difference between strategic methods is much less than often appears, once the changing conditions and fashions of different decades and the changing circumstances for which the different approaches are valid are allowed for. Much has been accomplished in a relatively short history. There is already a good base to build upon in constructing an integrated approach to strategy making.

A multiplicity of meanings

Strategy means something different to every person who uses the concept. There are countless books and articles using different definitions of the term. A powerful concept can have, perhaps should have, a measure of ambiguity in its meaning but it cannot mean all things to all people; it requires some degree of precision in its definition. On the one hand, the multitude of different usages indicates the importance of the concept, the sheer breadth of its scope. On the other, it suggests dangers in the indiscriminate use of such an ambiguous term. Concepts which develop such an elasticity of meaning often lose their significance; their use can become a mere cliché. One aim of this book is to assess:

• the maximum degree of precision possible in defining the term
• the minimum degree required for producing a workable concept.

A starting point – four possible general approaches

An interesting starting point for defining strategy are four general approaches which can be clearly distinguished (see Whittington, 1997; Egan, 1995). Each of these perspectives differs in the way in which it combines two defining elements:

1. Whether the processes of strategy making are deliberate, explicit and handed down from above or emergent and often implicit, coming from different levels of the enterprise, including the bottom, and involving continuous modification of the content of any strategy.
2. Whether the outcomes reflect the single motivation of profit maximization or a more pluralistic motivation, such as satisfying the various stakeholder groups.

Choice of these elements reflects the different emphases obvious in the literature, and indicates a way of separating particular views about what is important in defining strategy making. These are by no means the only elements which could be used to classify different perspectives, but they are undoubtedly significant ones. The combinations of the two elements define four possible perspectives which might dominate (Figure 1.4):

(A) Classical – the traditional view of strategy making. It regards strategy making as comprising deliberate, explicit and rational analysis and emphasizes profit maximization as the only acceptable motivation for any strategy. Classical strategy combines the thinking of the military strategist with some aspects of the economist. Leadership is seen as a key element, since the leader chooses the strategy. The strategy is handed down by the leader, the strategist, to be implemented by the managers. The formulation and implementation of strategy are seen as separate and sequential activities.

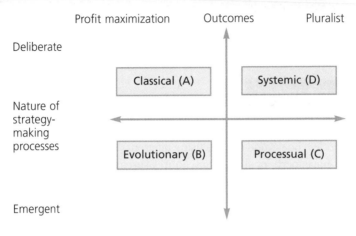

Source: Whittington, 1997: 3.

Figure 1.4 **Dominant perspectives in strategy making**

(B) Evolutionary – the view of the typical economist. It adopts a fatalistic stance, putting the emphasis on the emergence of a strategy as the outcome of the competitive discipline of the market, that is, as the outcome of blind forces weeding out the failures and leaving only the successful. The market operates rather like the process of natural selection in biology, removing those who fail to adjust successfully to a changing environment and leaving only that strategy which is best adapted to the changing economic environment.

Such a perspective stresses an unavoidable profit maximization which is imposed on the enterprise by the dictates of the market environment. In other words, even if managers do not deliberately adopt profit maximization as an objective, they are obliged to do so by the forces of competition. There is in reality little room for strategy in such a situation. This is very much the invisible hand of Adam Smith rather than the visible hand of Alfred Chandler.

According to this view, complex organizations move more slowly than the environments in which they have to operate. Either enterprises adjust sufficiently to the changing environment or they are culled. The most that the leader of an enterprise can do is to recognize the inevitable and encourage mechanisms of successful adaptation when and where they occur.

(C) Processual – the view of the social realist. It moves the observer away from an emphasis on economic rationality and profit maximization, and away from the conception of the market or the organization's leader as infallible. It takes a subtle, more pragmatic view of behaviour and stresses a number of key constraints on the process of strategy making:

- so-called bounded rationality, that is, rationality constrained by the limited knowledge of individuals and their limited capacity to process incoming information
- the messy nature of political bargaining and negotiation
- the prevalence of satisficing in environments which are tolerant of some measure

of underperformance and allow the appearance of significant organizational slack, both typical features of the real world. In such a world, business activity is designed to produce a satisfactory rather than a maximum return.

In this approach strategy is viewed as defined by the nature of the strategy-making process rather than the particular content of any strategy. In this world strategy is usually a matter of incremental change, since nothing more is possible.

(D) Systemic – the view of the social relativist. Strategy reflects the nature of the social system – its attitudes, values and behavioural patterns. Strategy is what different societies make it. Such a view emphasizes a deliberate but relativist approach, one which sees strategy as imposed from above but business behaviour as embedded in a network of particular social and political relations. The motivation of a strategy is itself culturally conditioned, reflecting the society in which the strategy is developed. Both institutional and cultural contexts differ from society to society. For example, in the business world there are enormous differences in the accepted role of government or the family firm.

Each of the major approaches by no means excludes the relevance of the others at the national level; each has its area of relevance, whatever the economic system:

- The *classical* approach is seen as most relevant in mature, stable and relatively predictable environments and for industries where capital-intensive technology predominates and/or some degree of monopoly is the norm. The conditions which favour such an approach are quite rare. In practice the classical approach is more likely to be adopted by start-up companies or those in crisis and attempting a turnaround, if there is the time and the resources to make an explicit strategy. The founder or saviour is often expected to adopt such an approach, at least implicitly.
- The *evolutionary* approach best relates to new industries or those subject to rapid and dramatic change, particularly where a large number of small enterprises exist and compete vigorously with each other. Such competitive conditions are also rare, but apply mostly to what commentators have called the 'new economy', particularly in the period between the action of a first mover in creating a new sector or branch, and the emergence of a mature new sector of the economy. Where technology and tastes are fluid and rapidly changing, the evolutionary approach represents an accurate description of the possibilities for strategy making.
- The *processual* approach is relevant to any 'bureaucratic' system, which means in some way all organizational structures, but it has particular relevance to complex organizational forms. It is most relevant to protected bureaucracies or knowledge-based enterprises where a continuous flow of incremental change coming from the bottom is enough to keep the enterprises competitive.
- The *systemic* approach simply asserts that any strategy must fit its context whatever it is and be dictated by the culture, which varies by time and place. That context determines both what can be done and what is likely to be included in a strategy.

Systemic differences at the global level

The last approach to strategy highlights differences which reflect the social and cultural milieu in which the strategy is made. For example, the first three approaches are preferred in different kinds of society. Many economists in Anglo-Saxon market economies take the evolutionary point of view and see little value in committing significant resources to strategy making. Others in the developed market economies, notably in Japan and Continental Europe, are more closely allied with the classical position. Inevitably in the less developed world the processual approach, with its emphasis on constraints, has much more credibility.

Even views about the nature and role of strategy itself are culturally determined. For example, attitudes on the value of time, the exercise of power or the level of uncertainty differ enormously and colour the whole approach to strategy making:

- Some societies are happy to focus on benefits which are only realized well into the distant future. They are much more ready to take a long-term point of view, while others take a short-term view.
- Some are always looking for the decisive exercise of leadership, others see decision making as requiring a collective consensus. Some accept a significant degree of individual initiative outside the normal processes of collective decision making, while others suppress the exercise of individual initiative in any way.
- Some are prone to be risk-averse, others have a much greater appetite for risk.

There are pronounced national differences in all these areas. Such differences are bound to influence the nature of strategy making in different societies.

In these societies there are relevant institutional differences which involve the roles of market and government and other organizations such as the family. The Anglo-Saxon mode (or American), which is the focus of most textbooks on strategy, is not a good description of what happens in many other economies. It focuses on the business enterprise, and therefore on corporate strategy. It assumes that the family enterprise is not significant and that government adopts, or at least should adopt, a stance of non-intervention in the market. At the beginning of the 1990s, before the persistent problems confronting Japan became evident, an obvious distinction was made between the American and Japanese approaches to strategy. The frequent recurrence in very different societies of various kinds of national planning creates market systems which diverge significantly from the American model. The prevalence of family firms or large conglomerates also affects the nature of strategy making. Others have distinguished a larger number of variants of the capitalist or market economy and therefore of strategy making itself (Hampden and Trompenaars, 1993). For example, there are various European variants, not just one.

Different schools of strategy making

The general approaches described above are very broad. It is helpful to move beyond these to identify the main elements which, according to different authorities, go to constitute strategy making. It is easy to do this by distinguishing as many schools of strategy making as can be found. Mintzberg et al. (1998) distinguished 10 different schools, although as many as 14 are discussed in the literature, each implying a different definition of strategy. The number could be further expanded but the differences then become trivial.

The schools discussed below differ in a substantive way, taking different aspects of strategy and elevating them to the role of defining element. Some of them consider the process of strategy making itself as the starting point, others take the content or context as the initial element. The first three are prescriptive, laying down what strategists should be doing. The others are descriptive, in that they describe what actually happens in strategy making:

1. Strategy as design

A good strategy is designed to fit organizational capability with environmental opportunity. It is best summarized by the SWOT approach and has very close links with the case study approach pioneered by the Harvard Business School.

This school sees strategy as based on the classical approach. It is the rational product of a senior manager, usually the chief executive officer, consciously and deliberately finding a fit between the internal strengths and weaknesses of an enterprise and the external threats and opportunities it faces. A strategy is viewed as an explicit, simple and unique conception. Formulation precedes implementation and is separate from it. There is often a range of options from which the strategy to be implemented is chosen. The one which provides the best fit or best design is chosen. This was the dominant school until the 1970s but still has enormous influence.

2. Strategy as planning

The strategy as plan is a detailed scheme for allocating resources to achieve the objectives specified according to a prescribed timetable. In the view of this school specialist staff planners take over the strategy role. Strategy becomes a highly formalized process, divided into easily decomposable steps, delineated by checklists of necessary actions, and supported by techniques relating to the specification of objectives, the establishment of budgets, the spelling out of programmes and operating plans. This school's view of strategy is again fully consistent with the classical approach. By the mid-1970s this was the predominant school.

3. Strategy as positioning

Strategy is seen by this school as a matter of choosing an appropriate industry or sector to be in, finding the best market segments and focusing on the preferred value-adding activities. This requires detailed analysis of the data relating to the industrial situations in which the enterprise has to operate. Such positioning is consistent with either the classical or the evolutionary approach. By the 1980s this had become the dominant school.

4. Strategy as entrepreneurship

The strategist, seen by this school as the leader, usually the founder and chief executive officer, is concerned with closely controlling the enterprise in order to realize his or her vision. The leader is an innovator who often works by intuition or imagination to create something new. This shifts the definition of a strategy from a precise design, plan or position to an imprecise vision or even a broad perspective which has to be realized. However, the maintenance of an entrepreneurial orientation continues to be important even beyond the period during which the founder is dominant, if the enterprise is to continue to be successful. This school has strong classical elements. This interpretation is not new and has never been absent from strategy making.

5. Strategy as the reflection of an organizational culture or social web

Strategy is viewed as a social process, albeit a complex one. The nature of an organization and its culture constrains what is possible, predisposing the strategic process to certain channels and certain outcomes. Strategy is about integrating disparate elements of the 'social web' and finding common interests among those elements. It is about conserving what the enterprise already has and using its resources to its best ability. It stresses the dangers of dissipating resources which are embedded in the organization itself. This approach is consistent with both the processual and systemic approaches. The debate in the 1960s, which widened the view that economists had of the firm, first introduced such issues. During the 1980s, comparison between the prominent capitalist models and the Japanese variant also promoted this kind of approach among commentators on management.

6. Strategy as a political process

Here the emphasis is on the exercise of power, whether within the enterprise or outside it, specifically as it relates to the making of strategy. The various interests or stakeholder groups, often fragmented and divided, who share power within an enterprise have to persuade and be persuaded, to confront and be confronted. The enterprise itself has to negotiate its way through strategic alliances, joint ventures and other network relationships in order to make a strategy. Strategy results from bargaining, compromise and the exercise of power by the relevant groups. This school is unashamedly processual.

7. Strategy as a learning process

In this conception strategy is seen as a process of exploration and incremental discovery. Strategic knowledge emerges gradually as the result of the interaction of a large number of strategists, possibly all the employees of an organization but certainly key individuals spread throughout that enterprise. There is no difference between strategy formulation and implementation; they occur simultaneously. Strategy emerges from a process of discovery and learning. The views of this school are consistent with the evolutionary and the processual approaches.

8. Strategy as an episodic or transformative process

This school sees strategy as contingent on particular circumstances and moments in the life of an organization. It is a matter of the unfolding in real time of different situations, all heavily contingent on different circumstances, and the temporary emergence of specific configurations. This school emphasizes for different situations the elements highlighted by other schools. It puts the stress on the same enterprise in different circumstances and its ability to handle the relevant transitions. In particular it analyses the quantum leaps from one situation to another, the so-called transformation situation, for example during the start-up of new enterprises or turnarounds of enterprises in trouble. Strategy is a matter of dealing with the demands of these different episodes in an appropriate way. In such an unfolding context, strategy is sometimes classical, sometimes evolutionary and sometimes processual.

9. Strategy as an expression of cognitive psychology

This school concentrates on what goes on in the mind of the strategist, the mental or psychological processes involved in strategy making. It focuses on the cognitive biases of strategists and, even more importantly, on the process of cognition itself, including the way in which information is filtered, knowledge is mapped and conceptualization itself occurs. It emphasizes the subjective element of interpretation rather than the objective reading of reality, but considers both. It takes account of motivation as well as the different ways in which a mind works, using reason, intuition or any other faculty which is relevant. This is present in all types of strategy making.

10. Strategy as consisting in rhetoric or a language game

This school sees strategy as concerned with the way in which strategy is talked about, the kinds of conversations or discussions, both formal and informal, which take place in organizations making a strategy. These are usually aimed at achieving a consensus and encouraging certain kinds of strategic actions. It is about the language required to persuade employees to think strategically or to act to promote a particular strategy. This interpretation of strategy is closely linked with the cognitive interpretation. This occurs in all strategy making.

11. Strategy as a reactive adaptation to environmental circumstances

Strategy is seen by this school as similar to ecological adaptation, leaving little room for the strategic manoeuvre usually associated with a strategy. Strategic action is reactive rather than proactive. This is a variant of the evolutionary approach. Circumstances largely dictate what a strategist should do, although there may be a number of different possible contingencies. Often all the strategist can do is reinforce behaviour which is adaptive to whatever new environment appears. Adaptation is the key to success and strategy is understood as comprising this adaptation. There is an element of this in all strategies.

12. Strategy as an expression of ethics or as moral philosophy

This school sees the strategist as a moral agent, engaging in ethical conduct. The strategy embodies the values of the strategists. Strategy is as much about the nature of the ends and goals of all stakeholders and how they are reconciled. It is also about what strategic action is acceptable. The concern with values might be for good reasons, since a failure to behave ethically can have disastrous results. Strategy is as much about the reputation of the enterprise, particularly in the eyes of its stakeholders, as it is about profit, although in many cases being ethical may not be incompatible with being profitable. The stress is on the content of the strategy.

13. Strategy as the systematic application of rationality

Strategy is applied reason, the application of reason to the leadership and conduct of management within any organization. This school sees an equivalence between strategy and its many elements and an attempt by a strategist to use the differing kinds of rationality. It interprets strategy as only qualifying as strategy if it is an attempt to apply reason to the organization of business activity. The school is concerned with excluding the irrational from strategy making, that is, elements such as whim or intuition. This interpretation of strategy is only consistent with the classical view.

14. Strategy as the use of simple rules

This school interprets strategy in a highly practical way as the application of a limited number of simple rules derived from both general experience and the experience of particular industries. The rules exist because of the degree to which behavior is repeated and particular types of problem recur. Through these rules, strategy enables enterprises to successfully seize opportunities in fast-moving markets and environments of rapid change when there is not enough time for following more elaborate procedures. The rules can apply to a whole range of decision-making areas – notably the 'how to' of business behaviour, setting the boundaries of various types of business activity, fixing priorities for the achievement of objectives and the timing of key decisions, such as when to exit from certain business areas. Such a view is consistent with the processual approach.

There may appear to be a ragbag of other interpretations of strategy which do not have the intellectual standing of those above but nevertheless express important truths (Singer, 1996). For example, formal strategy making may play a number of different roles: acting as ritual, reinforcing a culture of rationality; as glue, bringing together or uniting managers: as a battery, energizing or providing a source of motivation; as a status symbol, for those with access to the secret information: and as pliers, to extract information from subordinates. The use of such graphic metaphors helps us to better understand the multiple roles of strategy making, but do not constitute a sufficient difference of content or process to be the basis for forming different schools.

Each of the different schools illuminates a different aspect of strategy making. The first four indicate what should be done, not what is commonly done. Some are concerned more with process than content. Moreover, they indicate the limits on the process, whether these are cognitive, ethical, social or political. Mintzberg and Lampel (1999) have reduced these in a simplified scheme to the four 'p's – strategy as plan, perspective, position and ploy.

The author likes the term 'strategic thinking without boundaries' (Singer, 1996), which justifies a widening of scope to include the many different elements described above. This book takes all the different schools into account. How a business plan or model or a strategic plan is drawn up is a matter for individual managers to decide, according to the requirements of the particular industry or sector. The main purpose of the book is to clarify the theoretical issues preparatory to actually thinking and managing in a strategic way. The appropriate way of doing this in particular cases should become obvious after the practitioner has analysed the relevant concepts. Analysis of the relevant concepts is not a luxury, it is a necessary preliminary to actual strategy making.

Assumptions and metatheories

Often practitioners find it paradoxical to theorize about a highly practical activity such as business management. Businesspeople are often disparaging of theorists who lack management experience and are therefore dismissive of theory itself. Such an attitude can make its holders vulnerable to an unthought-out addiction to current, or even out-of-date, fashion. All can become prisoners of theorists who unbeknown to them pioneered the fashionable views adopted by many practitioners.

The intellectual influences on a mode of behaviour are often hidden and unconscious. There is a gain in making these influences transparent and deliberate. Otherwise a person may hold contradictory attitudes, some of them at odds with the nature of the world in which he or she operates. Formative years make attitudes but the world changes and, if a person is not careful, he or she does not. Without theory it is impossible to learn since it cannot be known what should be learned. Everyone can gain from occasionally being reflective. Very few people are intuitively right for more than a brief period of time, nor can they know, without systematic thought, when they are right and why they are often wrong.

Differing interpretations of the world lead to different interpretations of what the term strategy means. Each of the above schools has a link with a particular academic discipline, sometimes a strong link. These links sometimes enhance the potential strategy, sometimes they limit what it can be and do. All disciplines have different preconceptions of how the world works. It is necessary to see the link between the preconceptions implanted by the relevant discipline and to have an understanding of what strategy is. This assists in developing an understanding of what strategy making involves.

Whittington (2001: 23) has asserted that strategies 'are a way in which managers try to simplify and order a world which is too complex and chaotic for them to comprehend'. He goes on to point out that for every manager the strategy-making process starts with a fundamental strategic choice: which theoretical picture of human activity and environment fits most closely with his or her own view of the world, his or her personal 'theory of action'. It is impossible to write a book about strategy without taking all sorts of positions, usually implicitly, on such issues as what motivates human beings, or even what constitutes a valid approach to the application of theory to practical activities. Hopefully the assumptions made throughout the book are consistent but it is impossible to justify at length all the positions taken. This would itself constitute another book. It is necessary to make explicit some of the premises on which the book is built.

There must be some treatment of what are called metatheories, that is, the broad cognitive maps which underpin a specific way of thinking. Anyone who reflects even for moment on the nature of the human condition has a veritable atlas of such maps to inspect. These are the implicit models of how the world works and how people behave in that world, models which underpin any text, whatever the discipline, and any mode of thinking. There are economic, political, social, even biological metatheories relevant to management studies. Such metatheories are usually taken for granted or assumed as universally accepted by those working within the discipline in which the text falls. This is seen by the consistency of approach and terminology in most discipline journals.

To take just one example; the body of economic theory known as 'neoclassical economics' is based on a metatheory, a set of assumptions about human behaviour known as 'economic rationalism'. In its extreme form, it claims that all human behaviour conforms to the assumption of economic rationalism; all known human actors are rational economic men. Many management theorists operate within this metatheory. It has been important in the development of thinking on strategy. Part of its power derives from the fact that economic theory is more homogeneous than the theory of other social sciences.

There are three different areas of focus for metatheory which are particularly relevant to any book on management:

1. an underlying view of the nature of the world
2. a position on how it is possible to learn about that world
3. an attitude on what determines human behaviour in that world.

The approach adopted in this book is very much a pragmatic one. It presents an eclectic theory, that is, borrows from different theories. It is both positivist, with significant reservations, and postmodernist, also with significant reservations. It rejects both the total dominance of rationality and the extreme relativist point of view. Human motivation is as much intuitive as rational but the mix is culturally determined.

Uniformity and diversity

Most textbooks on management are written from an American perspective. For this reason these texts use the metatheories which are accepted in the USA. Neoclassical economic theory is certainly part of that perspective. The American perspective includes the assumption that management and the management context is the same the world over, largely because economic theory considers specific cultures largely irrelevant to any economic behaviour. The assumption is that if the world is not like America, it should become so and is, in any event, likely to become so in the very near future. There is some measure of truth in this view but it is far from being the whole truth.

There is one obvious source of difference in understanding both what management is and the activities it involves, that of 'cultural divergence'. There is some literature which explicitly shows the falsity of the assumption of a uniform global culture, and therefore of management practices, but it is not vast. Hofstede (1983, 1991) pioneered this work, showing that Americans have certain characteristics which stand in marked contrast with those of the inhabitants of other countries. Using the terminology of Hofstede, Americans are:

- rational rather than intuitive in their approach
- extremely individualistic
- firmly short term in their orientation
- quite masculine in attitude
- weak in uncertainty avoidance and power distance.

These attitudes are well suited to a reliance on the market in economic life. They also define the nature of management studies in the US. There is a self-reinforcing cycle at work. The market reinforces such attitudes and such attitudes predispose society in favour of the market as the basic mechanism for the allocation of resources and the distribution of incomes. They are also important in defining what is meant by strategy in different societies.

Trompenaars (1983, 1998) has confirmed the different nature of capitalism, and therefore the different role of markets, in different parts of the world. Such different contexts influence the role of strategy. Because of these differences, strategy can mean different things in different countries. Strategic management in the USA is not the same thing as strategic management in Germany or Japan, let alone Kenya or Indonesia. Pascale (1982) reports that the Japanese do not even have a phrase for 'corporate strategy'. The American concept rests, developed in the relatively prosperous and stable world of the 1950s and 60s, on an assumption of 'cultural voluntarism', the exercise of free will, rather than determinism. Global strategic management is itself a problematic concept. Throughout this book there is reference to the fact that operating at the global level requires a sensitivity to these differences. Almost every chapter includes reference to the various ways in which particular strategic questions are answered in different countries.

Academic disciplines see strategy in very different ways. Some disciplines are closely associated with particular schools of thought on strategy. For example, the positioning school has a rather obvious base in economic theory. It is not accidental that economic theory has had the most influence on thinking about strategy. In many ways it is the most rigorously developed discipline in the social sciences. The economic discipline is the one which aspires to be closest to the scientific reliance on a body of logical, internally coherent theory. There are some excellent books on strategy which receive their coherence from the systematic application of such economic theory (Ghemawat, 1999). It is paradoxical, therefore, that strictly speaking economic theory implies either no role, or a minor role, for strategy. Indeed many economists, notably those most wedded to the core neoclassical approach, are disdainful of management studies, except insofar as it is a reflection of the body of microeconomics used by them.

Other disciplines are used to provide an organizing framework in management studies. Psychology, political theory and anthropology link up in rather obvious ways with the cognitive, power and cultural schools which have grown in importance recently and have cast a new light on the relevant aspects of strategy. Management studies is gloriously eclectic in its borrowing from different disciplines. Each of these schools has a very different view of the world. This is not surprising since the solutions to the problems confronted require an interdisciplinary approach.

Language itself is the filter through which it is possible to see and understand the world. It is significant that American English is increasingly the language of business, but even this form of universality has its limitations. The same word has by no means the same meaning for different people. The number of languages in the world may be in the process of significant reduction but there are still enough to guarantee serious disagreement on the meaning of apparently simple concepts.

The opposite position, which stresses a uniformity of approach, is also untenable. Extreme relativism is unacceptable. All players are not islands of comprehension far distant from each other, since it is possible to share understandings. There is also a real world out there and a sequence of events which occurs independently of the observer and is the object of study, a world against which generalizations can be tested. Any strategy must be subjected to a reality check, even if inevitably it is imperfect. All theorizing is improved by such regular reality checks. It is possible to share understandings about those events.

Asking questions

One way of approaching these issues is to keep asking relevant questions since such questions lay out the agenda:

> What are the sources of order? How do we create organizational coherence, where activities correspond to purpose? How do we create structures that move with change, that are flexible and adaptive, even boundaryless, that enable rather than constrain? How do we simplify things without losing both control and differentiation? How do we resolve personal needs for freedom and autonomy with organizational needs for prediction and control? (Wheatley, 2000: 8).

Any serious theorist of management must remember to ask these questions, or a similar group of questions. The reader should add his or her own questions. Such questions lead straight to a confrontation with the metatheories talked about above.

A textbook on strategy is inevitably prescriptive. It advocates a position which should be taken up, in this case with regard to the kind of strategy which is desirable. Prescription must be based on both accurate description, that is, an empirical approach to the world as it is, and careful analysis of that world, expressed in an interpretation or theory of how the world functions, and finally on the way in which the two are brought together. The relative emphasis on each of these aspects, theory and practice, varies throughout the book, but the other is never far way.

Avoiding the fashionable

Some commentaries on strategy reveal a marked lack of historical perspective, a tendency to accept assertions which gain their main strength from constant repetition rather than what is happening in the world of business. There are three myths which illustrate this:

1. The world is one in which it is necessary to take account of continuous change and profit from technical innovation. It is often asserted that the current world is one of unprecedented technical change, with the emphasis on unprecedented. Does this mean that the underlying rate of productivity has increased and, as a consequence, economic growth has accelerated, and if so, by how much? The issue is more complex than often assumed; it is by no means certain that it is true.

   The world is in the middle of one of the great waves of technical change, one which can be called the 'communications/information revolution'. This does not mean that the core of any strategy must be to develop an e-commerce capability, regardless of the other big issues of strategy. In some cases this is appropriate, in others not. Some textbooks give the impression that a failure to apply e-commerce immediately is a sure prescription for disaster. The emergence of the new economy does not suspend all the persistent and surprisingly robust relationships which have always characterized economies. What is happening now is not in substance any different from previous technical revolutions.

2. Another fad is globalization. What is meant by the repetition of the refrain that 'the world is a global one', when on analysis nearly all economic activities continue to have a home country bias? Have the ratios of internationally traded output or internationally financed gross domestic capital formation really risen? If so, over what period of time and by how much? What makes our world more 'global' than any previous world? Surely a robust home country bias is some-

thing which every strategist should take into account? It also needs explanation since the explanation will better inform any 'global' strategy.

3. The alleged 'turbulence' of our times has now entered, in textbooks, into the headings of chapters on strategy. Why? Was the second half of the twentieth century more turbulent than the first, with its world wars, its revolutions and its Great Depression. It would be hard to argue the case. It is easy to argue more persuasively that turbulence has declined, that the current world is more ordered than previous worlds. It is the very regularity of the modern world which promotes the efficient operation of a capitalist economy. The patterns of behaviour are more predictable and less risky than in non-capitalist economies.

None of the usual assertions about technical change, globalization or turbulence should be taken for granted. It is necessary to ask questions concerning each of these issues, ones not very often confronted, let alone answered. In tackling these questions it is necessary to stand back and view, with a degree of justified scepticism, the twist put on current events by many commentators. A sensitive historical perspective is needed, as well as a holistic one, not limited in any way by discipline, fad or personal interest. It is necessary to stand back and to look at empirical data with a dispassionate eye, a historical eye, noting the obsessions of different generations and putting them in a proper perspective. The strategic perspective recommended in this book is meant to be good for all seasons, not just one particular historical conjuncture. Good strategy is born of a sceptical mind. A good strategist reads books on history and novels, even the Bible or Koran and sometimes learns more from them than from management texts. It is better to read both kinds of texts, and even more important to read with an open mind.

Equally to be avoided are excessive claims made for the ability of certain actions to solve major problems. One tendency which mars many commentaries on management is the obsession with the concerns of the immediate present which often turn out to be fickle fashions or fads which come and go at a rapid rate. Management studies are particularly subject to such fads. Its practitioners churn out the appropriate 'buzzword', such as total quality management, re-engineering, downsizing or even downscoping, to name but a few, like a magical incantation. Each of these has some validity, but none has the universal ability to solve all managerial problems.

Focus on Humour
A fad or buzzword

In order to test how authentic a buzzword is, we can apply five tests:

1. It must come from what purports to be an *authoritative* source.
2. It must provide an *instant cure* to your real or imagined problem.
3. It must cause the hearts of managers to go *pitty-pat* with anticipation.
4. It must of necessity *obscure the obvious* and at the same time make the uninitiated feel painfully inadequate for not recognizing the brilliant truth encapsulated in the buzzword.
5. Finally, it must inspire *pseudo-activity*; that is, it must make people think something important is happening while everything remains safely in place.

Source: Vaghefi and Huellmantel, 1999: 24.

Strategists and stakeholders

There is one sense in which all members of an organization are strategists, since all would benefit from thinking strategically, and another sense in which there is but one strategist, the person who leads strategically, usually the chief executive officer. These are extreme positions, but each has some validity.

One key issue is how the strategic thinking of any individual employee fits in with the strategic thinking of the enterprise as a whole. Since the interests of all employees differ, their objectives also differ. This is part of a much broader problem, the existence of various groups of stakeholders with markedly different interests in the organization. There are different aims and objectives envisaged for the enterprise, each reflecting the nature of the different stakeholder groups. One of the first goals of strategy is to reconcile the different strategic interests of these stakeholder groups. The reconciling of these different points of view is a prerequisite for the articulation of the strategic intent of any organization, that is, for a clear indication of what the strategy is trying to achieve.

Before considering the nature of the strategic intent, it is necessary to define what exactly is meant by a stakeholder and classify the stakeholder groups, in the process indicating which stakeholder groups are likely to be important in the making of strategy. There are two elements relevant to defining a stakeholder:

1. An interest in the operation of the enterprise and the nature of that specific interest. The interest may arise because the stakeholder group makes an input vital to the operation of the organization, or it might be an interest which arises because the outcome of any strategy influences the wellbeing of the stakeholder in a significant way, although the stakeholder may be a purely passive recipient of any impact.

A stakeholder has either an explicit claim on the enterprise – service payments on a debt, wage and salary rewards – or the potential to benefit from successful performance, for example lower prices or higher dividend payments. The stakeholder can also suffer from the enterprise's poor performance, for example the receipt of lower taxes or vulnerability to the effects of environmental damage.

Each stakeholder is capable of contributing value to the products or services in return for a reward, which comes in various forms. How much reward is extracted depends on the bargaining strength of the stakeholder.

2. The impact of action by the interest group on the performance of the organization. This action can have a powerful influence on the realization of the strategic intent. The ability of the stakeholder to take action which impinges on the activities, strategic or otherwise, of the enterprise, often as a response to the first element, is a significant factor in the performance of the organization.

Is the stakeholder group in a position to promote the aims of the organization or obstruct the implementation of that strategy? There are many such responses which can harm – a readiness to sell ownership shares, industrial action by workers, political action by community groups or, most importantly, the withdrawal of custom. Such actions constitute potential threats for the enterprise.

A stakeholder is anyone with a significant interest in the performance of an organization and/or an influence on that performance.

The stakeholders

The way in which various stakeholder groups are organized and operate differs from society to society. This is particularly true of the medical industry, where in different countries stakeholder groups have varying influences on the decision making of a pharmaceutical company. These influences reflect, on the one hand, the attitudes, norms and behavioural patterns of the different societies, in short the national culture and, on the other, the attitudes, norms and behavioural patterns of the enterprise, the corporate culture and the way in which these two cultures interact. For example, those societies with a strong civil society have a proliferation of organized groups, outside those which are purely government or commercial, groups which often represent the different stakeholder groups. They have a habit of interacting positively to resolve contradictory interests. This is easily extended to business operations relevant to strategy making.

Focus on Theory
Stakeholders in pharmaceutical companies

There are a number of important players in the pharmaceutical industry, alongside the pharmaceutical companies themselves – patients (the ultimate customers), governments, doctors, pharmacists, insurance companies, health managers of various kinds and biotech research companies. Figure 1.5 indicates the nature of the interactions between these groups.

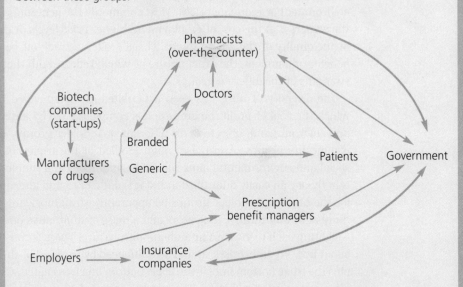

Figure 1.5 **Stakeholders in the pharmaceutical industry (US style)**

Attention is concentrated on the enterprise, but the analysis can easily be extended to any organization, including non-profit-making organizations. Usually the stakeholders are divided into three groups, two external and one internal to that enterprise (Figure 1.6).

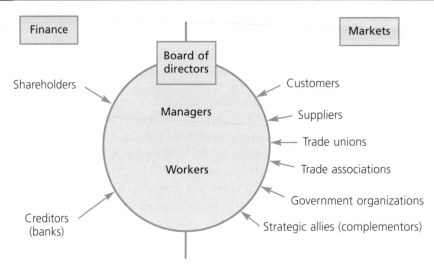

Figure 1.6 **The stakeholders (external and internal)**

Diverse aims

The broad aims and expectations of the different stakeholder groups are disparate and often out of alignment with each other. The aim can be seen as either increasing the benefits or minimizing the damage received by the particular group. For different groups this can take the form of increasing profit, creating more employment, enhancing individual or group power or status, raising tax revenue, protecting the environment or reducing prices. Most commonly the generation of greater profit for the owners is at the cost of employment, higher price levels or even to the detriment of the quality of the environment. There is often a trade-off between the respective benefits or damages, the exact nature of which reflects both the political and market strengths of the different groups.

The diversity of aims has been articulated in the so-called triple bottom line in which the goal of profit maximization is complemented by aims which reflect social and environmental objectives for different stakeholder groups, notably workers and community groups. A criticism often levelled at the triple bottom line is that the social and environmental aims cannot be quantified in a simple way. Whereas profit is in theory an easily quantified index, it is difficult to find alternative success criteria for the other stakeholder groups as apparently straighforward. At best there are a number of quantitative indicators and a mass of qualitative ones, with a problem of weighting each to yield an unambiguous measure. There is considerable controversy about how far enterprises should be influenced by the kind of thinking which underpins the triple bottom line. If the triple bottom line is accepted, why should a quadruple or a quintuple bottom line not be accepted in order to take account of all stakeholder groups, not just three or four?

The most discussed stakeholder groups are still the owners and the managers. The division between ownership and control has always been the focus of considerable attention since the appearance of the public company. The issue needs to be discussed at length, particularly in the context of governance, how a board of directors representing the owners oversees the management of a company.

Profit maximization

The aims of different stakeholder groups are the logical starting point for determining any strategic intent. The simplest model considers only one stakeholder group, the owners, and therefore only one aim, profit maximization. There is a need to specify the relevant time period, profit maximization over the short or long term. The time horizon makes a significant difference. There are many actions which can increase short-term profit at the expense of long-term profit; there are rather obvious trade-offs, often ignored. This simple prescription of profit maximization ignores the interests of the managers who formulate and implement any strategy, an interest which might be very different from the owners. For example, their status and power may be enhanced by simply making the company larger. For the moment it is helpful to assume that long-term profit maximization is an appropriate aim, but that it requires sensitivity to the interests of all stakeholder groups since all are in a position to undermine the ability of the enterprise to make profit.

Social responsibility and profit maximization

The easiest way to alienate various stakeholder groups is to behave unethically, stressing short-term profit at any price. Profits can be increased by cheating customers, exploiting workers, damaging the environment or tax avoidance or evasion. Such behaviour may be unsustainable for a number of reasons – a major loss of customers, the departure of key workers or managers, a seriously negative feedback from environmental damage or the ill will and retaliation of government, at minimum a loss of influence over government policy. By undermining the reputation of the enterprise through these reactions, short-term profit seeking may threaten the level of long-term profit. The aim of managers is usually to perpetuate the existence of the enterprise, not to end it by allowing some members to pillage its sources of capital. One of the functions of stakeholder groups, not always successfully carried out, is to put a check on such pillaging.

Most interests are served by an increase in profit. Such an increase allows action to benefit all stakeholder groups. Increased profit usually means increased dividends and higher share prices and may also mean higher investment and more rapid growth, with increased promotion and employment prospects. Investment may also increase the chance of lower product prices and improved quality in the future. Greater profit may also mean increased scope for supporting community projects. On the other hand, an enterprise which does not make a profit is at serious risk of failure, when all stakeholder groups are likely to suffer.

The twin issues of ethics and sustainability arise in this context. Unethical behaviour threatens the long-term profit of the enterprise by threatening its reputation. Equally, damage done to the environment by practices which are not sustainable over the long term also threatens the good name of the enterprise. In both areas there may be a trade-off between short-term profit and long-term reputation.

Stakeholder groups' organization

The voices of the stakeholder groups might be heard informally or there may be formal channels of communication. This may be a matter of the composition of the board of directors or it may involve a much broader range of communication. Stakeholders have different degrees of organization.

Stakeholders are sometimes aggregated into groups which can express and promote their interests. The power of these groupings varies, both with respect to the enterprise and society at large. Some groups are well organized in certain societies, such as workers in their unions or conservationists in political parties, others are much more diffusely distributed, such as consumers or suppliers. Even these are sometimes organized into consumer or trade associations. There are various ways of institutionalizing the paths of influence from these interest groups to the organization. For example, in Germany, under a system of industrial democracy, workers are represented on supervisory management boards.

There are a number of specific questions which must be addressed in more detail:

- What degrees of aggregation of strategic intent exist? There may be a tacit understanding that different groups will be listened to, an assumption that all groups will be accommodated.
- How is any conflict between the groups resolved and how is a common strategic intent articulated? General aims have to be translated within a strategic perspective into specific objectives. It is at this stage that conflict usually arises.
- Is it critical to have just one general intent, or can intent itself be broken down into separate components which provide the detailed inputs? In this situation the process of iteration, described later in the book, comes into play, as the objectives are defined and refined in the process of transmission from group to company and back.

The government: stakeholder and lawmaker

The government, as maker of the rules of business behaviour and the defender of public interest, is a very important stakeholder. The profitability of a company can be enhanced by its efforts to change the rules of the game or prevent what is perceived as an unfavourable change in those rules. Large multinational enterprises have considerable ability to influence the strategy of government.

The effort of the automobile industry in the USA to shield itself against both Japanese competition and pressure from the environmental lobby is a good example. The exercise of this influence through lobbying, political donations and even corruption is itself part of a company's strategy. All these actions, particularly if they receive significant publicity, will almost inevitably elicit a negative response from other stakeholder groups.

Focus on Practice The political economy of the automobile industry

From the 1970s onwards, the US automobile industry, so long dominant in its ability to outcompete the automobile industries of other countries, came under threat from two directions – firstly from Japanese vehicle imports flooding into the USA, and secondly from a growing safety and conservation movement which saw the automobile as a major source of environmental damage and a threat to individual life and health. What was the reaction of the big three producers, General Motors, Ford and Chrysler, to these threats?

The chief strategy was to seek to influence the government to change the rules and/or retain those rules which already favoured US industry. The big three used their immense resources and significant role in the economy to lobby the government. They repeatedly emphasized the threat to employment in the USA from both foreign competition and stricter environmental rules. They sought and achieved informal

▶

Focus on Practice
cont'd

quotas which shut out the full tide of imports, largely on the grounds of the threat of a significant potential loss of jobs. They also looked to limit the regulatory restrictions on the design of cars, which were intended to improve safety, reduce damaging emissions of pollutants and improve fuel efficiency, all of which they argued would impose an enormous cost on the industry, and which, in the view of the automobile manufacturers, were in some cases impossible to achieve. When bankruptcy threatened Chrysler, another strategy was actively to solicit the financial support of government.

Another strategic response by the automobile manufacturers was to imitate the more efficient methods of the Japanese which made them competitive in the first place, and develop a mentality of innovation, meeting more readily the changing tastes of consumers. In the long term, this strategy was likely to be more effective, since it would satisfy a broader range of stakeholder groups. However, it was more difficult to achieve.

The nature of any political economy, that is, any system of business decision making, draws attention to any inputs which influence market outcomes through their impact on the rules of the game. It is blindness to ignore this aspect of strategy, which is inevitably important for large companies. The larger the company, the more likely that this aspect of strategy becomes important.

Sources: Ingrassia and White, 1994; Luger, 2000.

Mapping stakeholder groups

There is a simple way of presenting the role of external stakeholder groups. This is to map the stakeholder groups and their role in the making of strategy. There are various possible contexts. For example, it is possible to distinguish the market context from the political context. Depending on the problem being discussed, it may be possible to distinguish other contexts. There is a common template, based on the *value net*, which can be used as a basis for mapping the particular situations. This template can be modified to suit different contexts.

In its market activity, the aim of any company is to create a maximum value added. The market context is depicted in Figure 1.7.

Complementors comprise all the groups that can benefit the company in some way. Other producers can act as either competitors or complementors, that is, they can either hinder or help the creation of value by the company. Increasingly they may

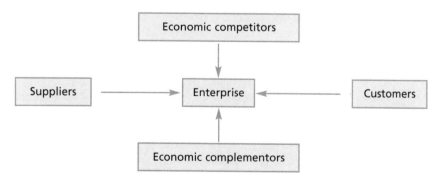

Source: Brandenburger and Nalebuff, 1996: 17.

Figure 1.7 **A map of economic stakeholders**

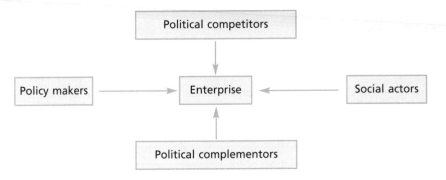

Figure 1.8 A map of political stakeholders

help, both deliberately in partnerships or strategic alliances and without any such organized cooperation. In the economic value-adding process, all these groups are relevant. The way in which they are relevant to strategy making will be developed at some length in this book.

The political context would be similar, but with different players (Figure 1.8). The political aim of the company is to create the kind of *political value*, which can be translated into greater profit or the preservation of existing profit. Political value comes from two sources:

1. the political advantage to be won by instituting a change in government policy or regulation, or even by retaining existing advantageous rules
2. the gaining of social legitimacy by managing important social issues in such a way as to win support for the company and enhance its reputation.

Focus on Theory
Complementing

A complementary product or service is one whose use promotes the demand for another product or service. Very often the successful production or consumption of a product or service does not depend solely on the operations of one company. There are complementors, that is, other company players from whom customers buy products or services complementary to the relevant one, or to which suppliers sell complementary components or resources. In the first case, the complementory consumption enhances the satisfaction received in consuming the main product or service. In the latter case, the supplier has synergies in the supply to different customers which reduce its costs of supply. Complementors, as Figure 1.7 suggests, are therefore the mirror image of competitors. They are players who take action which either increases the buyers' willingness to buy products or the suppliers' willingness to provide inputs. They add value to the product or service.

There are players from whom customers buy or consume resources complementary to the product or service of the enterprise, and in so doing increase the value to the customers of consuming that product or service and consequently the prices that they are willing to pay. Consumption often requires the existence of complementary products, for example the products are consumed together. In the absence of one the other either cannot be enjoyed at all or only in a seriously diminished way:

Focus on Theory
cont'd

- An improvement in the network of roads makes the ownership and use of an automobile more valuable. Some of the complementary goods may therefore be public goods, or goods supplied by a quasi-government organization. An infrastructure capable of reliably supplying petrol and at a reasonable price is also essential. If the hydrogen cell is ever to become the source of energy for the motorcar, there needs to be an infrastructure supplying hydrogen.
- In the pharmaceutical industry, doctors might be regarded as playing the role of complementor, since they are not customers but facilitate the purchase of drugs which complement any treatment recommended.
- The same relationship would apply to that between Intel with its Pentium microprocessor and Microsoft with its Windows operating system; they are complementory. One assists the sale of the other.
- Electricity is used with almost any consumer durable or books with any educational programme. They are both complementary goods.

On the production side, suppliers often need complementary inputs to enhance the quality of their own input or reduce its price:

- This might involve the existence of a training or educational system which improves the quality of human inputs, even making possible the use of some technologies.
- Alternatively the suppliers can take advantage of complementary outputs which reduce the costs of developing or supplying a product. A specific example might be a project mapping the human genome, knowledge which is of definite assistance to a biotechnology company in developing a new drug.
- Wine bottles can be used to contain other beverages. If there are significant economies of scale this might have a dramatic impact on cost. A breakthrough in the technology of glass making may affect all consumers of bottles.
- An explosion of tourist outlets, including restaurants, in or close to a winery will increase the demand for wine by drawing potential customers into the area.
- The makers of films, television programmes or music, in order to sell their product, seek out those who control communication outlets. For the makers of the creative product the communication controllers are complementary, for the communication controllers the makers are complementary.

The social web and the 'political' process of strategy making

The context of strategy making

The context in which strategy making occurs constrains what can be done and therefore determines how the process of strategy making is structured. That limiting context consists of four main parts:

1. a cognitive or intellectual part, which constrains how an individual thinks about strategy
2. an ethical part, which tells the strategist what is socially responsible and what is not
3. a political part which shows what bargaining or negotiation can achieve in support of a particular strategy
4. a social part which consists of the web of rich human interactions in which strategy making is embedded.

A preliminary exploration of the ethical issues is made in the final section of this chapter. The next chapter, in its analysis of strategic thinking, considers some of the cognitive limits. This section deals with the other two limiting parts – the social and the political. Both are important and are dealt with in turn. Here the emphasis is on the internal context of the organization. They are further touched on in the next section as they relate to the external context of the organization.

The human interactions which occur within enterprises involve all the rich characteristics of social life – for example the emotional reactions to people and events and the ever-changing moods of human actors, the continuing likes and dislikes of colleagues, the enjoyment of communication for its own sake and the broad pursuit of personal interests and personal advantage, however defined. Much of the interaction is unstructured and outside formal rules, or becomes structured only slowly. This social web is highly relevant to strategy since strategy making necessarily occurs within the framework of, and partly results from, such an interaction. For example, ideas tend to be thrown about by groups whose members enjoy interacting. Good strategy must take account of the realities of informal organizational behaviour; in such a world, the informal are as important as the formal structures. For example, personal and institutional authority, and therefore influence on decision making, frequently do not reside in the same people.

Corporate culture and strategic stances

Together the formal and informal aspects of enterprise activity mould a corporate culture, a set of attitudes, values and behavioural patterns particular to an organization. Such culture differs from one enterprise to another. It is impossible deliberately to create a corporate culture overnight, or even change an existing one; key aspects of it are often accidental in origin. Something as simple as corporate culture can evolve in unexpected directions without deliberate action. How far culture can be used as a tool in creating good strategy depends on the nature of the organization. Corporate culture is partly the result of the example given by leaders who play an important role in its evolution. They seek to shape the culture and move it in a certain direction, sometimes in order to realize a particular strategy.

Before starting to analyse the kind of corporate culture which an enterprise might need in order to realize its strategy, an observer needs to understand its strategic situation and why an enterprise might adopt a particular stance. There are three possible *strategic stances*:

1. The enterprise might be deliberately seeking to shape, or reshape, its environment. In Gary Hamel's (1996) terminology, it might play the revolutionary and seek to break or remake the rules of the game. This requires a culture which stresses the acceptance and promotion of change.
2. It might try to adapt incrementally to changes in its environment simply to remain viable. This does not threaten the existing culture, provided the changes are small and the adjustment marginal.
3. It might reserve the right to postpone strategic action until it reads the changing environment better, and therefore adopts a stance of inaction, at least temporarily. This is the most conservative of the stances, the one least likely to upset the existing culture.

Many commentators have noted that revolutionary change is unusual, limited to start-up or turnaround situations. There is an obvious temptation for any organization to adopt the last position, unless forced to do otherwise. The best description of the normal pace of change is logical incrementalism, that is, incremental or marginal change which logically grows out of the existing situation; this broadly corresponds to the second stance.

The paradigm

Logical incrementalism is the normal stance, because an enterprise has an existing paradigm, which is difficult to change. The paradigm can be defined as 'the core set of beliefs and assumptions which fashion an organisation's view of itself and its environment' (Johnson and Scholes, 1993). The ideology at the core of the enterprise encapsulates the identity of that enterprise, how it wishes others to see it. The paradigm is closely related to the corporate culture.

The paradigm may involve a ruthless pursuit of profit. It may reflect an obsession with being first, always innovating. The values, and therefore the paradigm, of any organization often go well beyond a desire to maximize profit and involve behaviour towards a whole series of different stakeholders, not just the owners. The values may involve behaving in a way which is honest and transparent, one which returns significant benefit to the community as well as to workers or customers. It may place an emphasis on a good reputation for ethical behaviour, respect for the environment and therefore sustainability. It may place corporate social responsibility at the heart of the enterprise's value system.

Every organization has a web of behavioural modes which are heavily influenced by the values and attitudes and therefore are consistent with and reinforce the paradigm. Broadly these patterns of behaviour can be considered as belonging to six overlapping areas:

1. The repeated patterns of behaviour:
   - The *routines* which govern everyday activity. Most activities are structured into repeated patterns of behaviour which reflect the demands of work but also the shaping of any activity by habit.
   - The *rituals* which mark special occasions. Rituals relate to the way that less usual events are organized, particularly in such areas as training, promotion, new appointments or retirements.

2. The *control systems* which seek to regulate behaviour and guide it into paths acceptable to the organization. These may include:
   - Any measuring systems which are used to benchmark and monitor performance.
   - Any reward systems which link up with these measures to reward the desired behaviour, and provide the incentives to guide behaviour in the desired direction.

   Clearly these control systems link up and interact with routines and rituals, both influencing them and being influenced by them. On occasions there may be some tension between them but usually an accommodation is reached in which the two do not contradict each other too seriously.

3. *Organizational systems*, both formal and informal, are the ways in which an organisation is both integrated and divided into specialized units. The divisions are both horizontal and vertical:

- The horizontal comprises the division of the organization into separate functional units
- The vertical includes the separation of different layers of hierarchy, each level with its ability to integrate those below. Many organizational systems are highly detailed, particularly at the bottom level of the hierarchy.

4. The *power structures*, again some formal and others informal. A formal authority structure defines the span of control of individual office holders. The exercise of power is discussed in more detail in the next section.

5. Many *symbolic expressions of its identity* and the authority held within them. The logos, trademarks and slogans are outward, and often vivid, marks of the identity of the organization. Others are easily understood expressions of identity, and therefore power, within the organization, such as the size and location of offices, the brand of company car for a particular job level or the distribution of parking spaces.

6. The *stories or legends*, sometimes amounting to myths, which encapsulate the meaning and history of an enterprise, usually stories of great success or great failure. The founders are often referred to in these stories. These exist to give expression to the values and beliefs which are part of the paradigm and act as a measuring rod against which current employees assess themselves.

All these areas interact within the central paradigm to create a cognitive, and even emotive, structure through which individuals interpret the world of the organization for which they work. They also ensure that strategy is viewed in a way that is understood by all staff. Both the intellectual and emotional support of the individual employee is harnessed by the use of such mechanisms.

At times such a structure becomes a conservative force which inhibits change. Built for one purpose, it is difficult to divert to another. All the problems thrown up by the external environment, whatever their impact, are interpreted in the light of the paradigm, with the result that the amount of change accepted is nearly always limited and often resisted. As a consequence, in most organizations there is a tendency to strategic inertia, which can be interpreted as an inability to change strategy in anything other than a marginal manner and a tendency to defend the status quo. This is a good explanation of the prevalence of logical incrementalism.

Strategic drift, turnaround and paradigm shift

The most difficult problem is how to achieve a paradigm shift, that is, a significant change in the existing paradigm. Such a shift usually requires and is associated with simultaneous change in all the above areas, and is difficult to achieve. In practice, most change arises as a result of the emergence of new enterprises or organizations. This also explains why there is a continuous churn of enterprises, some rising rapidly, others falling almost as fast. The situation of McDonald's indicates the results of such drift and the need for a turnaround.

The typical picture is one in which an enterprise is subject to strategic drift as it adapts incrementally to environmental change. Strategic drift is the result of a process of gradual adaptation in a context of change which requires more than just adaptation. As a result the organization's strategy imperceptibly moves away from

A turnaround situation arises when an enterprise's performance deteriorates to the point that it needs a radical change of direction in strategy, and possibly in structure and culture as well. The example used is the fast-food chain McDonald's, which, after many years of success and continuous growth, has entered a potential turnaround situation.

Causes

The loss of competitive advantage underlying the need for a turnaround may be due to a number of possible factors:

- Poor management at any level, but particularly the top
- The enterprise overexpanding to exhaust the market and in the process reducing the quality of the product
- Inadequate financial controls and the resulting high costs
- New competition, sometimes arising from innovation
- A significant change in tastes which is unforeseen
- Organizational inertia or complacency: the success breeds failure syndrome

For McDonald's, the particular causes are:

- An extremely rapid rate of expansion throughout the world
- A change in attitude to fast food, now perceived by many as unhealthy food
- An enormous growth in competition, for example Wendy's and Panera Bread in the USA
- Some organizational inertia and management failure

Characteristics

- Slowing in the rate of profit growth, culminating in reduced profit and actual loss making
- Slowing in the growth of sales, culminating in an actual fall of sales
- Loss of market share in key markets
- Loss of share value

For McDonald's:

- First ever quarterly loss
- Fall in sales
- Significant fall in share price

Consequences

- Consolidation and divestment
- Change in business model
- Change of key personnel
- Change in strategy
- Change in structure
- Change in culture

Within the old model, McDonald's is trying to:

- Improve the current business model by reducing prices and speeding up service
- Initiate an ambitious advertising campaign (US$20 million)
- Provide a facelift for the stores (US$300–400 million)
- Change the CEO with the return of former successful CEO, James Cantalupo replacing Jack Greenberg

Focus on Theory
cont'd

- Push through the closure of a large number of loss-making stores (175 with 700 employees)
- Retreat from three countries
- Try an experiment with new foods and an extended range of products.

There is as yet no real change in strategy, structure or culture.

what would fit it best to meet the new environmental forces at work. The organization experiences an increasing gap between where it actually is and where it should be, which creates a steadily increasing tension within the organization and eventually a crisis when key performance indicators deteriorate, sometimes with an apparent suddenness. This is the moment when the strategic situation may change to a revolutionary one, in which there is a conscious and deliberate attempt by individuals within the organization, or by a key stakeholder group, to reshape the organization and its environment, although the latter is difficult to achieve at this stage. This is the moment for a turnaround, that is, a dramatic change of strategic direction.

Very often the success of a business is associated with the name of a particular person, frequently the founder, and its renewal with the person responsible for a turnaround. One role of a new leader might be to snap the enterprise out of its strategic drift. Such persons become the focus for the making of the strategies which are responsible for the success of the business. The founder or the new leader can be an inspiration to the enterprise and also a powerful source of leadership. There is a tendency for one person to provide the direction or coherence, or simply to become the focus for the strategic thinking which both initiates success and continues that success in a different context. This is particularly true during the infancy of an enterprise or a period of crisis. At the stage of maturity, or during long periods of stability, leadership can become routine, but this itself can lead to a loss of competitive edge, if the enterprise is not suitably organized. Leadership often provides that appropriate edge.

Leadership and strategy

Once organizations go beyond a certain size, strategy inevitably becomes a matter of teamwork. No one person can control everything. All teams need to be motivated and guided; this is one of the functions of leadership. The key issue is to select able lieutenants. It is paradoxical that a leader can even consider imposing a democratic style, in a strange mixture of autocracy and democracy. This would be a style which encourages others to speak up and makes transparent the process of strategy making. Styles of leadership differ greatly. The degree of consultation and transparency differs from organization to organization. Moreover, under any regime, whatever its nature, the succession and legitimacy of a new leadership is always a problem. Does the predecessor anoint the new leader or does the process involve a wider group?

There are three different kinds of *leadership*:

- *Traditional* leadership in which roles are ascribed because of divine validation or as a consequence of birth or age, or a combination of all three. Divine appointment or even age are no longer as important as they used to be, particularly in the business world. However, there are economies where family enterprises are still the norm. In such enterprises, birth is still important in determining who leads. Even in these economies nobody can take leadership for granted because of birth. A poor performer is likely to be ousted, whoever is his or her father.

- *Charismatic* leadership is a reflection of the special characteristics of the individual, particularly the ability to inspire others to do what is wanted. A charismatic leader often has a unique strategy, one appropriate to the place and the time. There is a marked tendency to try to turn all leaders into charismatic leaders, even if they initially lack any charisma. Here the main problem is finding a mechanism to identify potentially charismatic leaders and put them in the right position. The succession becomes a particular problem.

- *Institutional* or *bureaucratic* leadership, where authority resides in particular positions because of the nature of the position. Such positions are filled as a result of the carrying out of proper procedures. The incumbents of the positions must have particular qualifications, skills or experience. They might know the organization well, or be well qualified to deal with a new situation. Such leadership is the norm in most organizations.

There is no doubt that successful business leaders are often of the charismatic type, but they often need the backing of bureaucratic leaders imbued with appropriate skills and knowledge. The frequent emphasis in the literature on the 'heroic' leader who determines everything assumes the omnipotence of that leader. There is no such a thing as the omnipotent leader, able or even willing to override the opposition of key strategic players within the enterprise. A *leadership team* might combine the different kinds of leadership in an appropriate mix which suits the times and circumstances.

Strategy is not determined solely on the basis of an ideal fit with a hypothetical set of organizational objectives determined by a grand strategist, the leader. There is often an overemphasis on the development of formal structures and procedures, just as there is on the leader. There are various ways of building flexibility into the enterprise but one is to ensure that there is not an overemphasis on the exercise of formal authority.

In any organization there is likely to be competition for position and the adoption of positions on strategy which reflect the nature of political groupings and the self-interest of players in the promotion of their own careers. Decision making is often the result of negotiation and bargaining, political competition and ultimate compromise. It is the result of the exercise of power by different stakeholder groups, internal or external. Any leader has to take into account the existence and potential power of these groups and win support by persuasion as well as by the naked exercise of authority.

Sources of strategic power

What are the sources of power for stakeholder groups both within and outside an organization? It is possible to map both the sources and indicators of that power. Within any organization, location in the hierarchy is a key element defining power; the higher in the organization an individual is located, the greater is that person's power. However, some staff have an influence which transcends their actual position. A control over strategic resources, such as finance, or an influence over key people helps. Relevant and scarce knowledge or skills, particularly those relevant to the situation of the organization, also increase power. Control over aspects of the external environment through access to markets, customers or sources of capital is another relevant factor. Finally, it must be asked, how much discretion does a person actually have? What is the size of his or her domain of independent decision making? The greater the discretion and the wider the domain, the greater the power.

The power of external groups often reflects the degree of organizational dependence on that group for key resources. The providers of necessary finance are powerful people. Some decisive involvement in the implementation of the strategic plan is another source of power. Again possession of the relevant skills or knowledge needed by the organization is important. Finally, connections with key persons within the organization are a further source of power. Networks of influence exist all over the world. Personal alliances can give access to considerable influence over decision making, and therefore constitute another source of power.

Both internally and externally, the formal status of a person is often an indicator of power. Investment with the symbols of power is usually closely correlated with that status. Regardless of formal position, any claim on resources on which the enterprise depends is also a source of power. Power is also indicated by representation on key committees or the nature of the negotiating arrangements involved in bargaining with outsiders.

Key strategic lessons

- A preliminary working definition of strategy is 'a coordinated series of activities which involve the deployment of accessible resources for the achievement of a given purpose or purposes'. Emerging challenges in the changing environment affect the development of strategic ideas and approaches.

- There are four broad approaches to strategy making – classical, evolutionary, processual and systematic – distinguished by two criteria: the adoption of a single motivation of profit maximization or a pluralistic one, and the nature of strategy making as a top-down process or a bottom-up one.

- It is possible to identify 14 different schools of strategy. Some of these schools are concerned with the limits on strategy making – notably the cognitive, ethical, political and social schools. There are links between these different schools and metatheories borrowed from different disciplines, such as economics, sociology, anthropology, biology and political theory.

- Stakeholder groups include owners, managers,

workers, bankers, suppliers, customers, the local community, government and complementors, that is, groups of enterprises whose activities are closely associated in a positive way with the organization. Each of these groups has a different set of interests which must be taken into account and all have a role in the development of strategy and can be considered potential strategists.

- Motivation is pluralistic, but to a varying degree. To act against the interests of many of these groups is socially irresponsible. Inevitably the current ethics of any society constrain exactly what can be done.

- The set of values, attitudes and behavioural patterns specific to an organization have a significant influence on the making of strategy. Change tends to be slow because of the strength of the paradigm and strategic inertia is the norm.

- It is important to see strategy making as a political process, in which there is bargaining and negotiation reflecting the power held by different stakeholders.

Applying the lessons

1 Define the following terms: vertical thinking, lateral thinking, a convergent problem, a divergent problem, bounded rationality, satisficing, a meta-theory, an eclectic theory, a stakeholder, complementing, the cultural web, the paradigm, strategic drift and a paradigm shift.

2 Under what specific circumstances do you think that each of the four main strategic approaches has validity in describing the nature of the strategy-making process? List the approaches and describe in detail the relevant circumstances which make each of these approaches an accurate description of strategy making.

Consider the circumstances of your own enterprise. What approach best describes the strategy making which is appropriate in those circumstances?

3 Using the IKEA case study in Chapter 2, indicate which aspect in that case, if any, fits the interpretation of each of the various schools defined in the text above.

                                             Relevant aspect

Design
Planning
Positioning
Entrepreneurship
Organizational culture
Political process
Learning
Transformation (revolution)

or configuration
Cognitive process
Rhetoric
Adaptation
Ethical stance
Rationality
Simple rules

4 Use the relevant websites to find the following mission or vision statements. How far do they suggest that the strategic intent of the organization is to satisfy the customer stakeholder group?

Qantas
Swissair
Lloyd's
Royal Dutch Shell
BRL Hardy
Southcorp
Beringer Blass
Nissan
Renault

5 What stakeholder groups does the board of directors represent? Consider the composition of the board of any company and indicate from the information available to you the likely role of each director and the criteria upon which board membership is based.

6 Using the case studies in Chapters 2 and 3, indicate the important stakeholder groups and how stakeholder interests and power appear to influence the strategy adopted.

Strategic project

1 Choose any case study included in this book.

2 Consider the different schools of strategy with their defining characteristics.

3 Select elements which could be seen as comprised within the area of strategy relevant to that school.

4 How far are all the schools compatible in that they simply describe different aspects of strategy making?

Mintzberg has written more about the different views of strategy than any other writer. A short version of his views is to be found in Mintzberg, 1996: 5–11. A whole series of Mintzberg's papers addressing the main issues relevant to strategy making is to be found in Mintzberg and Quinn, 1996. The best and fullest exploration of the different schools is Mintzberg et al., 1998. A synopsis of this book is to be found in an article by Mintzberg and Lampel, 1999: 21–30. A discussion of the criteria for evaluating whether a strategy is a good one or not is to be found in Rumelt, 1996.

A brief history of the development of the concept of strategy is to be found in Chapter 1 of Drejer, 2002.

Perhaps the most interesting of all attempts to classify the different approaches to strategy is that of Whittington, 2001, whose book makes the very important distinction between the classical, evolutionary, processual and systemic approaches. This distinction is further developed by Egan, 1995.

The classical approach is best exemplified by the design and planning texts recommended below. The evolutionary approach is that adopted by most neoclassical economists. The work of Herbert Simon is still the best introduction to the processual approach. See below for the relevant references, including other commentators on the social web and the political process.

The best articulations of cultural differences have been made by Hampden and Trompenaars, 1993 and, later, Trompenaars, 1998 and Hofstede, 1991, a shorter version of which can be found in Trompenaars, 1983 particularly pp. 54–5. A particular comparison is Hitt et al., 1996: 159–67.

Source texts which indicate clearly the nature of the different schools are:

Design: Learned et al., 1965. Planning: Ansoff, 1965. Positioning: Porter, 1980, 1985. Entrepreneurial: Baumol, 1968: 64–71; Mintzberg, 1973: 44, 53; Schumpeter, 1947: 149–59. Learning: Quinn, 1993. Cultural: Johnson and Scholes, 1993. Power: Macmillan and Jones, 1986. Cognitive: There is no one good reference. It is best approached by reading Chapter 6 of Mintzberg et al., 1998. Environmental: There is no good reference. It is best approached by reading Chapter 10 of Mintzberg et al., 1998. Configuration: Hamel, 1996: 69–82. Rationality: Singer, 1996. Ethics: Humble et al., 1994: 28–42. Simple rules: Eisenhardt and Sull, 2001: 107–16.

It is interesting to trace the development of a number of new concepts by consulting firms. The experience curve is dealt with at length in Chapter 9. Variants of the growth/share matrix are discussed in Chapter 16. The role of the Boston Consulting Group and in particular its founder, Bruce Henderson, in developing both concepts is discussed in Henderson, 1979 and 1984. The writings of Sidney Schoeffler, the founder of the Profit Impact of Marketing Strategies (PIMS), are also of interest. See Schoeffler, 1980; Schoeffler et al., 1974: 137–45; and Buzzell et al., 1975: 97–111. The roles of McKinsey and General Electric are discussed in the case study in Chapter 16. There is a lengthy discussion of the strategic innovations made as a result of this partnership in Vaghefi and Huellmantel, 1999.

The resource-based view (RBV) is discussed at length in Chapter 7 and a full bibliography given. However, a good introduction summarizing the then state of play is Drejer, 2002.

Much of the literature on the nature of the business enterprise is relevant to the sections on both stakeholders and the political and social restraints on strategy making. For example, the classic work by March and Simon, 1958 provides an excellent introduction. This is reinforced by Hill and Jones, 1992: 131–54. Brandenburger and Nalebuff, 1996 have introduced the notion of complementors which focuses attention on the importance of cooperation and helps to place the relevance of various stakeholder groups to the enterprise.

A more extended treatment of the political dimension can be found in Macmillan and Jones, 1986. The social web is best discussed by Gerry Johnson, particularly in his text, Johnson and Scholes, 1993. The best source on the economic or political value nets is Ghemawat, 1999.

2 Thinking and acting strategically

Strategic thinking involves the integration of several types of mental skills and techniques, as well as certain habits and attitudes, in the context of defining the problem to be solved from an initially ambiguous sea of unconnected data, and then solving it. There is an element of risk in strategic problem solving because complexity causes uncertainty. (LOEHLE, *1996: 1*)

Great strategies, like great works of art or great scientific discoveries, call for technical mastery in the working out but originate in insights that are beyond the reach of conscious analysis. (OHMAE *cited in de Wit and Meyer, 1998: 94*)

Creativity cannot be taught, but it can be learned. (OHMAE *cited in de Wit and Meyer, 1998: 100*)

Learning objectives

After reading this chapter you will be able to:

- understand and explain the difference between strategic thinking, strategic management and strategic planning
- define strategic thinking, strategic management and strategic planning
- choose which strategic activity is appropriate under different circumstances
- understand the difference between entrepreneurship and management and recognize different mixes of the two in strategy making

Key strategic challenge

What do I gain by becoming a strategic thinker, a strategic manager, a strategic planner, or all three?

Strategic dangers

That an organization neglects either the creative activity associated with strategic thinking or the administrative activity associated with strategic management; it therefore gets the mix badly wrong, either having no vision or making no realistic attempt to realize that vision, or in some cases both.

Case Study Scenario　The IKEA way

Keep making furniture less expensive,
without making it cheap.　　　*IKEA's battle plan*

The furniture and furnishings industry is a mature one,
not one which, superficially at least, lends itself to creative
strategic thinking, to global activity, or even to innovation.
It is an industry with relatively stable, slowly growing
markets, and is very much part of the old economy.

Ingvar Kamprad founded IKEA in Sweden in 1943 as
a mail-order company. The name IKEA is an acronym
for Ingvar Kamprad Elmtaryd (the name of his family
farm) Agannaryd (the name of his home village). Its
Swedish origins are unmistakable even today, although
it has moved its management centre to the Netherlands
and is Dutch-owned.

Kamprad is a man with a clear vision and a support-
ing philosophy, which was expressed in the book,
Leading by Design: The IKEA Story (Kamprad and
Torrekull, 2000):

- He wished to promote the 'democratization of consumption' by offering good value furniture and furnishings at a price that all could afford.
- He believed that everyone deserved to have an aesthetic sensitivity enhanced rather than diminished
  by the immediate environment.
- He believed in a non-hierarchical world and was distinctly anti-bureaucratic in his attitudes.
- He wished to empower his staff.
- He wanted to set a good example of frugal living,
  travelling economy class and sharing hotel rooms
  with his sons on business trips when they worked for
  IKEA. His most striking act was to give IKEA 100% to
  a Dutch-based charitable trust in order to avoid conflict between his three sons and the possible break-up
  of the company.

- The first, starting in 1963, was restricted to the Scandinavian region.
- The second, from 1973, saw an extension to Western
  Europe, which was to become its major market
  centre, with Germany at its heart. This move into an
  area with a similar culture and a similar market was
  comparatively smooth.
- The next move, in 1974, beginning very quickly after
  the second, was into North America, first into
  Canada but then gradually into the USA. The initial
  strategy came under pressure during this stage, but
  the difficulties were overcome.
- The final stage, as difficult as the move into North
  America, was first into Eastern Europe and next into
  Asia, both undertaken during the 1990s. Both moves
  have benefited from the previous move into the USA.
  This expansion is still in process.

IKEA has plans to accelerate its rate of expansion and
to extend its reach. Currently IKEA is moving into Japan,
opening two stores in the Tokyo region and a further
new store every six months. It is a sign of its confidence
that it is venturing into such a different and, for outsiders, difficult market. However, the current crisis in
Japan has created favourable conditions for such an
entry, for example a desire for low-cost furniture and furnishings. IKEA, having learnt from its American experience, produces a range of products suitable for the small
spaces characteristic of Japanese homes.

At the same time IKEA is consolidating its position
in existing markets. Up to now IKEA has opened one
or two stores in North America each year. In 2003
IKEA became more aggressively competitive in that
market, planning to open as many as five stores a year
for a ten-year period. To serve the new stores in the

IKEA opened its first showroom
ten years after its foundation. Initially the growth of IKEA was
steady and gradual. Only internal funding was used to support
the growth, and therefore significant debt avoided. The norm was
to reinvest the equivalent of at
least 15% of revenue each year.

From a global perspective,
there have been four distinct
stages in the growth of IKEA
(Table 2.1):

Table 2.1　**IKEA's expansion**

	No. of outlets	Countries	Co-workers (000s)	Catalogue circulation	Turnover in millions of euros
1954	1	1	15	285,000	1
1964	2	2	250	1,000,000	25
1974	10	5	1,500	13,000,000	169
1984	66	17	8,300	45,000,000	1,216
1988	75	19	13,400	50,535,000	
2001	172	32	70,000	110,000,000	11,300
2003	190		85,000	131,500,000	12,370

Source: www.ikea.com.

Table 2.2 **The geographical location of IKEA stores**

Scandinavia	22	(Sweden 13, Denmark 4, Norway 5)
West Europe	91	(Germany 27, France 12, UK 11, Netherlands 8)
North America	29	(USA 19, Canada 11)
East Europe	16	(Poland 8)
Asia	17	(Hong Kong and China 7)
Others	5	(Australia 5)
Total	172	

Source: www.ikea.com.

USA, IKEA opened two new distribution centres in 2003, one on the east coast and one on the west. It has been seeking an advertising agency to help promote this campaign.

The wide coverage is a considerable achievement, given how culturally sensitive the demand usually is for furniture and home furnishings (Table 2.2). The aim has always been, in the words of IKEA's website, 'to bring the IKEA concept to as many people as possible'.

In 2003 it was estimated that around 347 million people visited IKEA stores worldwide. IKEA has become the world's largest home furniture and furnishings retail chain.

How has IKEA managed to achieve this successful growth? What combination of strategic thinking, strategic management and strategic planning has this achievement required?

In order to clarify the nature of strategy, this chapter concentrates on the distinction between different strategic activities, notably between strategic thinking, strategic management and strategic planning. By linking this distinction with the terminology usually employed in business studies and economics, it is possible to put in place a useful framework for developing a discussion on the nature of strategy.

The distinction between strategic thinking, strategic management and strategic planning

What is strategic thinking?

Some strategic ideas are so simple and so obviously relevant to meeting a particular need that it seems with hindsight that anyone could have conceived them. Ogawa Kikimatsu's idea, described below, illustrates this.

Strategy in Action Quick strategic thinking in unfavourable circumstances

After total defeat in World War II, there were those in Japan who had the foresight to identify strategies for making money, other than black-marketeering and prostitution. Ogawa Kikimatsu, a publishing editor, was one such person.

Ogawa was on a business trip when he heard the emperor's surrender broadcast. He returned to the capital, immediately considering how to get rich in the changed situation. In the words of John Dower (1999), 'By the time the train pulled into Tokyo, he had hit upon his great idea: and, like so many enlightenment experiences, it was the essence of simplicity. As soon as the country was occupied, people would be clamouring for an easy guide to everyday English conversation. He would provide it.' This was the vision: the vision then had to be realized.

First Ogawa sold the idea to a publisher. He had no particular competence in English and used two conversation books as models, a Japanese–Chinese manual ironically used during the occupation of China, and a Japanese–Thai manual. It took only one to three days to complete, the exact time varying according to different authorities. *Nichi-Bei Kaiwa Techo* (Japanese–English Conversation Manual) was only 32 pages long and appeared in print one month to the day after the initial idea had been conceived.

The initial printing of 300,000 disappeared almost immediately. By the end of 1945, 3.5 million copies had been sold. The book remained the country's all-time bestselling publication right up to 1981.

Ogawa may not even have realized that he was engaged in strategic thinking.

Implicit and explicit strategic thinking

Although strategic thinking has its early origins in military activities, the notion of strategy has been applied to a wide range of activities including scientific discovery and even artistic expression. In a sense strategy is everywhere, but is not always recognized as such. It is helpful at this stage to distinguish between *explicit* and *implicit* strategic thinking. Not all strategy is deliberate or self-conscious, and therefore made explicit. Some people engage in strategic thinking without realizing what they are doing. As Kenichi Ohmae (1991) has put it, many outstanding performers 'have an intuitive grasp of the basic elements of strategy'. Strategic thinking is often an unconscious process. There is a breed of instinctive strategists operating in most areas of human activity. In this sense strategic thinking is all around us.

An example to illustrate the use of implicit strategy can be taken from an activity superficially distant from the area of business, one basic to human survival and immensely important to human enjoyment, but one in which there has been radical change – eating, both private and public.

Elizabeth David was an English cook and food writer who changed the eating habits of the English. She recreated the world around her, by publicizing a cuisine very different from the one she found in England, writing a series of highly influential books which were pioneers in promoting what could broadly be called the Mediterranean style. She wrote these books for three reasons:

1. She wanted to convey her deep enjoyment of good food and good cuisine to others; she was an enthusiast as good strategists often are
2. She saw an opportunity, even a need, to raise the quality of what was eaten in England
3. She needed to secure a living.

She had motivation, both intrinsic and extrinsic or pecuniary. She also had the skills to become one of the major strategy makers of the food world and a progenitor of all those 'foodies' who grace our television screens and the pages of journals, magazines and newspapers. Her name became synonymous with good eating in England.

Focus on Theory
Strategic thinking

Liedtka has selected five major attributes of strategic thinking. There are specific techniques which, by promoting the attributes, deliberately encourage this kind of thinking.

▶

Focus on Theory
cont'd

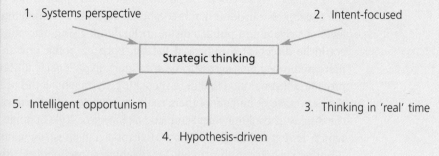

1. Systems perspective   2. Intent-focused

Strategic thinking

5. Intelligent opportunism   3. Thinking in 'real' time

4. Hypothesis-driven

Figure 2.1 **The attributes of strategic thinking**

1. Strategic thinking takes a holistic or systems view

Strategic thinking requires an orientation to the whole, rather than a focus on just part of the whole.

The possible techniques which deliberately foster this attribute are: various kinds of stakeholder mapping, any value system analysis, and conferences which focus on building the future, whatever the exact method adopted.

2. Strategic thinking focuses on intent

Strategic thinking involves purpose – it is not aimless, but has a definite direction. It also unfolds in a process of discovery or learning which takes time to complete, if it is ever complete. It inevitably involves some delay in the achievement of objectives, as the journey unfolds.

The main technique used can be broadly described as story writing.

3. Strategic thinking encourages thinking in real time

'Strategic thinkers link past, present, and future' (Liedtka, 1998a: 31). Strategic thinking is a dynamic process of reading from one's knowledge of past behavior what is likely to happen in the future.

The most important techniques which can be employed are: scenario building, gap analysis, and the systematic use of analogies, as in case studies.

4. Strategic thinking is hypothesis-driven

This attribute links strategic thinking to scientific method. It is necessary to generate new hypotheses and to test them, an iterative process which has no end. Strategic thinking is therefore both creative, in conjuring up the hypotheses, and critical or analytical, in subjecting the hypotheses to testing.

The techniques involved are those common in developing a system of analytical thought: Asking the questions, What if … or, If then … ; and distinguishing what are knowns, what are unknowns and what are assumptions; and finally asking Alexander's question – what new knowledge will change a specific presumption?

5. Strategic thinking is intelligently opportunistic

There must be room for the exercise of 'local' intelligence by anyone anywhere in the organization. This requires room for the adaptation of existing strategies or the emergence of new strategies to accommodate such new insights.

The relevant techniques are: the process of share and compare, and any simulation techniques.

Source: Liedtka, 1998a: 30–5, 1998b: 120–9.

Unconsciously Elizabeth David stumbled on an opportunity which was implicit in the environment around her. It combined a number of enabling factors – a very low level of private and public cuisine in England; rising discretionary incomes which could be directed to improved eating, both at home and in restaurants; vastly increased travel and access to new culinary experiences; a high level of migration, providing those skilled in different cooking styles who could accelerate the spread of the new cuisines and adapt them to the host society; the birth of a medium made for the display of cooking, television, and a change of style in publishing and journalism which lent itself to the display of 'exotic' cuisines, for example the paperback (another strategic innovation of far-reaching consequences). She was present in the right place at the right time or, putting it another way, she read the times right. The indirect result of her pioneering is visible in the variety of restaurants offering different cuisines throughout British cities, a result copied, or rather occurring simultaneously, throughout the world.

Elizabeth David both read the environment right, exploiting opportunities contained within that environment, and changed or remade the environment for those who came after her. This is the core of any strategic thinking, in this case a clear example of implicit strategic thinking.

By contrast it is possible to look at a more deliberate, or even explicit, strategy. A revolution simultaneous with the culinary revolution was the birth of the popular music industry, which reflected some of the same factors – the rise in discretionary income, particularly but not only among the young; the advent of new media, such as radio and television; and the appearance of the gramophone and vinyl records, as a mechanism for disseminating popular music. Much of this revolution occurred in the USA, partly because pop music there was an offshoot of native jazz and partly because the USA pioneered in mass entertainment generally. However, perhaps the most successful popular group ever was the Beatles, a British group, which was at the centre of the process which fully internationalized and made respectable popular music. The Beatles were therefore not the pioneers, but they were the product of an explicit strategy. Others, such as Bill Haley and Elvis Presley, played the pioneer role.

Brian Epstein, the Beatles' manager, was an explicit and very successful strategist, planning every aspect of the group's success, including a very careful creation of an attractive and acceptable image, both for the group itself and its music. This could be described as 'domesticated wildness' or 'domesticated rebellion', terms which encapsulate the essential features of the new group. Epstein took the raw energy of generational conflict and made it acceptable. He created the first pop group to have international star status, one on which all later groups tried to model themselves. He orchestrated in every detail the move of the group from obscurity to fame. He taught them how to dress, what kind of music to write and record and the right combination of live and recorded performance, all with the aim of creating the most powerful brand name in this industry. For this purpose he used all the media most effectively. He internationalized the group in a way which was not true of other British performers who have had a similar longevity in the popularity of their music, such as Cliff Richard.

Brian Epstein had almost an ideal background for the role of manager of the Beatles. He was the son of a Liverpool businessman, in some ways an outsider, being both Jewish and a homosexual. Before becoming a successful manager he had run a successful record shop as part of his father's business, in which he displayed a remarkable talent for spotting future hit recordings and ordering the right number of records, despite the fact that he had a strong personal preference for classical music over popular music or even jazz. He had also spent one year at the Royal Academy of Dramatic Art, aspiring to be an actor at this stage in his career. He had an acute theatrical sense. He was in the right place, Liverpool, at the right time, the 1950s and 1960s, but he was partly responsible for the explosion of the Mersey sound onto the world scene. Without him the Beatles might never have had their London opening and other groups would not have followed them.

Epstein was not a great businessman, although he was charming enough to effect the necessary openings for the group and a stickler for detail. He was the first manager to look after every detail of a group's activities when they were on tour. He was most of all a visionary who could see the golden future for the group and make it happen. He created the imagery of the boy group which became as important as their music. He smartened them up, converting their leathers into mohair suits and giving them the distinctive haircuts. He taught them stage discipline. On stage they were not to swear, not to joke with the girls, and to stop smoking or drinking coke. He made them acceptable to the vast middle class which yearned for an exciting wildness but one somehow under control or tamed. His own homosexuality and neurosis made him identify with the group and made him able to win their respect and even inspire them. In the words of one associate Nat Weiss, 'Brian was the fuse that created the explosion or set it off – not only set it off but controlled it and made it work'. Weiss goes on to add that there was no precedent and a strong measure of pure instinct in what Epstein did. He was a creative pioneer, not of the music itself but of the way the music was presented.

Source: Geller, 2000.

The two examples above illustrate on the one hand an implicit strategy – pioneering a new way, which others benefited from as they developed it with their own explicit strategies – and on the other an explicit strategy which built on the previous implicit strategies of others. The two business areas are firmly positioned in the service sector, which is fitting as this has been, since the middle of the twentieth century, the area of most dramatic expansion and therefore of new opportunity.

The many contexts of strategic thinking

Strategic thinking has many contexts, including here the business context, although in the real world the business context can overlap many others, such as the scientific, the technical, the social, even the aesthetic. A major construction project, for example the renewal of an old docklands area, will have relevance in areas which are aesthetic (the urban landscape), scientific (engineering), political, social, managerial and economic. Strategic thinking is therefore not limited to the area of business, appearing, as it does, in a much wider range of human activities. The scope for strategic thinking extends well beyond commercial activities. Artistic activities offer the justification of an aesthetic experience of some kind. Scientific discovery is prompted by intellectual curiosity. Sport concentrates a blend of competitive instinct and tribal loyalty, the desire to identify with a group to which one belongs. The motivation for strategic thinking in all these areas is always an intrinsic one. The activity is in its own right a pleasurable one.

Strategic thinking is much more than simply having a new idea; that idea must have a context, one in which the idea has a meaning defined by the specific aims of the activity, whether it comprises scientific discovery, artistic expression, making war, winning an important sporting championship or simply the business of making a profit. It therefore involves both systematically developing an idea together with its implications and testing the empirical validity and usefulness of that idea against the real world. This requires the conducting of a reality check – does the idea work in a way which enhances the wellbeing of those for whom it is intended?

It is a matter of identifying both a problem, and therefore an opportunity, and a solution in a highly complex world in which so-called 'wicked' rather than tame problems abound. Strategic thinking comprises a creative but ordered sequence of intellectual activities including the generation of completely new ideas, followed by the application of rational thinking to the development of those ideas. It comes down to the never-ending asking of questions, which have the potential to lead to a significant reinterpretation of the complex world around us, showing how that world can yield a new way of meeting basic human needs. This involves the providing of answers to the questions, often using concepts, approaches and procedures which are themselves innovative but most importantly reveal how a beneficial outcome might be realized. An enterprise which almost epitomized this process was the Japanese company, Sony.

Strategy in Action Sony – the disruptive innovator

Sony was the joint foundation of Masuru Ibuka, a passionate inventor and humanist, in short a dreamer, and Akio Morita, a highly competent administrator and a man of great charisma, a realist. Both had a background in electronics. The Japan Precision Instrument Company, Ibuka's company, had produced vacuum tube volt meters and other instruments during World War II. After the war he sought to continue to employ his workforce. In May 1946 the company was formally incorporated as the Tokyo Telecommunications Engineering Company (TTK). TTK later became Sony. Sony's first location was a burnt-out store in Tokyo's Ginza district. TTK tried a whole host of possible products. Ibuka set very high standards of design and quality, with the result that the company was given the responsibility for converting the equipment of Japan's broadcasting network to modern standards.

Sony became the first company in the world to make the entire range of products involved in tape recording – tapes, circuits, recording heads, feed systems, amplifiers and testing instruments – using skills involving nearly a dozen basic technologies. It did this from knowledge of an existing American tape recorder, for which at the time there was no word in the Japanese language. Sony was forced by postwar shortages to use as tape a specially calendered paper with a slick surface. This compelled it to compensate for the low quality tape by designing extra quality into every other aspect of the recorders. The first tape recorder made was the G-type in 1949, which weighed over 100 lb and sold for $400. It then worked very hard to reduce both price and weight, in a way which was repeated on later products. The first market turned out to be the Japanese broadcasting network's English-language programmes for use in schools.

A visit to the USA acquainted Ibuka with the transistor, which he became convinced would revolutionize electronics. In 1954 the company acquired access to the relevant technology. Ibuka's goal was to produce a pocket-sized radio but with Japanese technology. This seemed a hopelessly overambitious goal. Yet by 1957 Sony had achieved success with the Type 63 radio, which fitted into a shirt pocket. The product was both small and cheap. The company soon sold one million. At this stage Sony had a two- to three-year technological lead over its competitors which it used to provide the world's first transistorized short-wave and FM receivers.

Sony turned to transistorized television and in particular to the mini-TV, first selling the product in the early 1960s. In 1967 the company pioneered a new technology for colour television, the Trinitron system, very different from the existing shadow mask technology, and won the first Emmy ever given for a product innovation. The stress was again on a mini version, which was wildly successful.

Sony moved on to video tape recorders, producing the first commercial model in 1963, a model one-twentieth of the size of the American pioneer, the Ampex, and one-fourth of its price. The first home VCR, the CV-2000, was produced in 1965. Sony chose the Betamax system rather than the VHS system, although it was responsible for much of the research work for the latter. The general view of technical experts is that Sony was right, since Beta offers superior quality, but the market decided otherwise.

Sony then introduced the Walkman, a compact cassette player with small earphones for portable listening, and the Mavica, an all-electric still camera. It pioneered the compact disc audio record player, a small video camera (camcorder), a digital audiotape system of very high sound quality, and a HDTV system with outstanding picture quality.

The general approach adopted to innovation gives an interesting insight into the development and use of creativity. Ibuka's goal was 'to have fixed production and budgetary requirements but within these limits to give Sony employees the freedom to do what they want ... This is the way we draw on their deepest creative potential' (cited in Quinn, 1993: 286). The key unit was the cell, in which a small number of workers were free to determine their own work methods and how to evaluate their performance, in the process developing team spirit. There were net-works of such interacting teams. The job of managers was to set the overarching goals, to assist where requested, particularly to help to solve any problems arising and, even more important, to praise superior performance. The approach of the cell teams was to try as many options as possible, developing two or three alternatives for every subsystem needed, something which became a common practice in the best Japanese companies (see the case study on Toyota in Chapter 17). Staff were appointed on the basis of talent and then given a free hand. Staff were moved around, potential executives exposed to the production line and/or marketing. The decisions to innovate were freed from the constraints which in established companies often lead to the rejection of innovations outside the core activities. Throughout its history Sony carefully avoided involvement with either government or banks.

Christensen et al. (2002: 30) have argued that Sony is the only company in history to have successfully launched such a long series of 'disruptive' innovations, each of which initiated new business. Between 1950 and 1980 there were as many as 12 such disruptions. The last of the successful disruptions was the Walkman, launched in 1979.

By contrast, more recently Sony has been engaged in sustaining innovations, innovations which build on the platform of existing technology and markets. Sony's PlayStation and the Vaio computer notebook are successful products, but they are targeted at well-established markets rather than new ones and use technology which is not revolutionary.

How did sustaining innovations squeeze out disruptive ones? The answer lies mainly in the passing of the old guard and the maturing of the company. In the early 1980s, Morita withdrew from an active role in Sony. The role of Morita and his small group of immediate associates had been critical. They made every product launch decision themselves. They did this largely on the basis of an intuition grounded in well-practised procedures for shaping and launching such innovations. With Morita's departure, a change of balance occurred and the ability to generate disruptive innovation was steadily lost. There appeared to be a loss of creativity. During the early period, there was no market research done since there was no existing market for the new products. The transition was accompanied by a beefing up of the marketing side of the company, with the result that only sustaining innovations tended to pass muster.

Focus on Humour
*An example
of strategic
thinking*

The Australian farmer is well known for his ingenuity and ability to improvise and I think that this tale proves this point.

I own a small electronics business where we specialise in design and service of various types of electronic equipment. A few months ago I was approached by a local farmer to design a monitoring system to detect when the feed pipes in his high-pressure seeder were blocked.

The seeds are carried down the pipes by high-pressure air and delivered to the soil. However, if one or more pipes block the farmer has no way of knowing and a whole day's work can be wasted.

I duly went to the farmer's paddock, inspected the equipment and told him I would be back in touch when I had designed a prototype. The electronics and sensors required turned out to be quite complex. When I mentioned that it would be a month or so before I had some results for him, the farmer surprised me by saying there was no hurry because he had temporarily fixed the problem.

After consultation with his neighbour, they had come up with a novel solution. I think De Bono would be proud of their lateral thinking.

Realising that a lack of air pressure denoted a blockage, a hole was drilled in each of the six feed pipes and a small nozzle fitted. Then a condom was tied to each nozzle (I assume they picked a colour that could be easily seen). This solution apparently worked very well. When the air pressure was present six condoms stood erect on the top of the seeder. A drop in air pressure in any pipe caused the relevant condom to sag. So much for my sophisticated design.

Apparently the only problem is a high wastage rate, because the condoms tend to last only a few days. After I controlled my mirth at the vision of a seeder rumbling over the paddock with six erect condoms waving in the breeze, a thought occurred. I wondered where the farmer bought his replacement condoms and, given his usage of a dozen or so a week, what effect this had on local gossip.

Source: B. Johnson, letter published in the *Age* newspaper on December 27, 2000.

Strategic thinking sometimes consists of using a single new idea or a novel combination of old ideas to solve a major problem. The nature of the combination is itself often the strategic innovation, as the case study on IKEA in this chapter illustrates.

Focus on Practice
*A solution to
the problem of
drug rape*

An increasing number of women are becoming the victims of 'drug rape'. Their drinks are spiked by male companions who slip a drug into their drink, which reduces them to a helpless state, unable to protect themselves. The prime suspect is flunitrazepam, which is a drug ten times as strong as valium. How can this problem be approached and a solution found which prevents the rape? There are many possible ways of thinking about the problem.

A very simple solution has emerged. A small biotechnology firm in England, SSD of Derby, has discovered an immunoassay test in which the antibodies on the surface of

Focus on Practice

cont'd

an agent react with the molecule being tested for, activating a dye, one colour for positive and one for negative. The creativity comes with the way in which this is to be done. The reactive agent is to be placed on a beer mat. All the suspicious woman needs to do is to dip her finger in the drink and touch the test area on the mat. A number of tests can be carried out on the same mat.

The firm teamed up with large beer-mat makers in June of 2002. Sponsors were not hard to find and advertising helps to reduce the cost. This help is needed since the simplest of tests costs more than double the normal price of a beer mat (2p or 3c).

Source: The Economist, June 1, 2002: 97.

This solution puts together two elements in a new combination – the immunoassay test and the use of a beer mat as the location of the test. The solutions to other problems can be a combination of a much greater number of ideas or different elements. The example above reveals a highly successful implementation of a complex combination.

A complex and dynamic world

There is a complexity about the real world which defies the simple classifications of academic disciplines. It is full of wicked problems. Indeed, as de Wit and Meyer assert (1998: 156), strategic problems are inherently wicked, that is, they share some striking characteristics: they are essentially unique, highly complex, linked to other problems, they can be defined and interpreted in many ways, have no correct answer, nor a delimited set of possible solutions. They cannot be reduced to simple, or even complicated, problems of optimization, which have one correct solution. There is usually a number of possible solutions.

In general terms, strategic thinking is devising creative new ways of thinking about a complex world, the consequent application of systematic logic to the working out and development of these ideas and their translation into operational proposals with practical outcomes. This may involve deliberate remaking of the problem's context. Strategic thinking creates as well as recognizes future scenarios. A strategic thinker seeks to understand the world but also to change that world, even if in a limited way. IKEA is a good example of this at work.

Strategic thinking is proactive rather than reactive; it is innovative rather than imitative; and forward thinking both in the sense that it deals with the future and in the sense that it is ahead of its time. All strategic thinking occurs in the context of the achievement of clearly defined objectives, even if those objectives manifest themselves only at a late stage or gradually. Such thinking is inevitably set in a dynamic rather than a static context. It has a potential for significant development and extended application. It often sparks off a continuing stream of fresh ideas. There is an envisioned end result, or series of end results, increasingly indistinct as they stretch into the future.

A strategic thinker breaks out of normal routine thinking, very often moving beyond the accustomed ways and outside the explicit or implicit models through which the world is normally conceptualized, the so-called 'cognitive maps' which already exist in highly developed forms in our minds. He or she finds connections unperceived by others. For that reason strategic thinking involves breaking free of the constraints of traditional thinking and at the same time requires the gathering of new information. In the mind of a strategist, relevant information can become valuable knowledge. The strategist thereby creates a new but valuable knowledge base relating to an uncertain future. Strategic thinking comprises devising a plan for the continuing acquisition and use of such knowledge. It may involve the exploitation of knowledge created by another but in a way not previously envisaged.

The relevant thinking must be driven by the nature of existing and emerging opportunities and problems, not by the concerns of existing academic disciplines or theory alone. Yet the problems cry out for the insights provided by new conceptualizations. Strategic thinking is directed thinking, linked to an application to real-world opportunities and threats and the need to address real-world problems. It is not restricted solely to the cognitive area, it is thinking applied to practice. Neither a narrow scholasticism, nor a narrow empiricism is enough.

Strategic thinking is therefore an approach which combines a number of characteristics: a creative cognitive process; flexibility in reading and responding to changing circumstances in a changing world, particularly those marked discontinuities which are much more common than often thought; and a ruthlessly self-critical evaluation of the validity of that thinking, both from a deductive and an inductive perspective.

Strategic objectives

For an enterprise, strategic thinking is the process of continuously redefining its objectives, undertaken in the context of the intended creation and maintenance by the enterprise of increased value for its customers and competitive advantage over its competitors, both actual and potential, and the management of risk to levels regarded as acceptable by the enterprise's main stakeholders. It anticipates wants before they are perceived and problems before they manifest themselves. It is an inherently creative process.

Changes in the nature of the modern economy have raised the significance of strategic thinking. The perceived universality of change itself has made this increasingly a prerequisite of business success. Particular changes reinforce this perspective: the progressive replacement of labour by capital; the automation of most manufacturing processes; the increasing importance of human capital; and the emphasis on the provision of services.

Strategy requires a serious consideration of how the enterprise will achieve the continuously redefined objectives, particularly in a competitive environment. The ultimate test of strategic thinking is the long-term success of the enterprise, expressed most strongly in the bottom line, the ability of an enterprise, through a new idea, or set of ideas, or the recombination of old ideas, to generate above-normal returns at an acceptable risk level. Success is due not to luck or chance but to strategic intent, systematically pursued. This involves an appropriate blend of creativity and systematic and logical reasoning. Luck is largely opportunity recognized, risk managed, but strategy is required to turn this luck into good performance.

A good starting point for strategy making is to encourage all employees to think strategically, notably by providing some relevant training to enable them to do so. All the employees of an enterprise can, and perhaps should, think strategically. Indeed it is highly, and increasingly, desirable that they do so. Part of the empowerment of such employees is to be able to define a domain in which they can think and act strategically, their own personal strategic domain. All staff in any organization are potentially strategists – what differs for individuals is the size of their domain.

Vision and mission

All strategists, whether engaged in implicit or explicit strategic thinking, have a vision. In the business world, strategic thinking has its most visible manifestation in the vision of the enterprise, written or unwritten. The vision of an enterprise defines what that enterprise is. It is at the core of the enterprise's identity, representing the reason why the enterprise exists. It is closely linked with what the enterprise can do, reflecting its resources, capabilities and competencies. The vision is an expression of the dynamic of the enterprise, where it has come from and where it is going to – in that sense it can remain implicit, unsaid; it exists whether it is made explicit or not. However, it is better made explicit, if only to motivate those who flesh out and realize the strategy.

The vision precedes but overlaps strategy. It is very much the creative or imaginative part of strategy. The existence of a clear vision is a precondition for the formulation of a good strategy. For a new enterprise, it is the very raison d'être of its creation. For an existing enterprise, the vision comprises both the unchanging core and the variable strategic aims and objectives, the strategic intent. For a new enterprise, this distinction is not meaningful: the core identity, even the corporate culture, has to be created in the course of the realization of the new project. For an existing enterprise, one important preliminary question to ask is what constitutes the core, the essence of the existing enterprise, and thus what is a given and what is temporary and changeable and needs to be changed. The latter indicates what should be the focus of strategy.

There are two parts to the vision:

1. The paradigm, discussed in Chapter 1.
2. An explicit core purpose or strategic intent. It can never be fully realized since it puts the emphasis on aspiration. It is intended to guide and inspire. It is not intended to differentiate the enterprise from others. Indeed, other enterprises may have the same purpose, for example to be the best in some specific area, that is, to be the market leader, the most innovative, or to provide the best service.

Vision also incorporates the strategic thinking particular to the enterprise. It includes an envisioned future, which also has two parts:

1. Long-term, challenging goals for the next 10–30 years.
2. A vivid description of what it will be like to achieve those goals, necessary to enthuse the implementers. These have been described as BHAGs – big, hairy, audacious goals. Usually they should have a 50–70% chance of success. They might take a number of different forms:

   • specific quantitative targets
   • a common enemy to be defeated or outcompeted
   • a role model to be emulated in some important respect
   • some internal transformation to be achieved.

They must be clearly articulated.

The vision may be expressed in writing, or left unwritten and expressed only verbally at relevant times. Even if the vision is left unwritten it is not left unsaid. It is internalized. This may occur through meetings and face-to-face contact. Some leaders are superb at expressing a vision verbally, without any resort to the written word.

A written mission statement may articulate the enterprise's vision. Not all enterprises have mission statements. There are other ways in which the vision may be articulated in writing including corporate profiles. Probably the majority of enterprises, if they have a mission statement, have it for internal consumption. In a large number of cases it may be there as a form of tokenism, without real meaning. Sometimes the statement is so bland as to have no specific meaning. A minority of enterprises have it for external consumption by key stakeholder groups outside the enterprise, although in many ways it is an ideal mechanism for such a role. It is intended to alert the stakeholders as to what is being done in their interests and persuade them to acquiesce in enterprise policies. The mission can be constructed to appeal to the broadest stakeholder constituency.

Even fewer companies include the mission statement in their annual report, which is the commonest method of communicating with these groups. In the USA, for example, the stakeholders at whom the mission statement is most often targeted tend to be the customers. What is most frequently communicated includes the benefits for each stakeholder group, most of all the customers. Value statements and expressions of self-image are uncommon. There may be an indication of the focus of the enterprise, that is, what is produced, how it is produced and where it is sold.

A definition of strategic management

As an initial working definition, strategic management is any management action taken to realize a strategy, in particular to realize the vision which results from creative strategic thinking; it is action taken within the framework of the strategy. Successful strategists in the business area are not only engaged in strategic thinking, they also move on to the next step of strategic management. They do not limit themselves to thinking about strategy, they act to carry out their vision. Strategic management therefore translates strategic intent into strategic action. All such actions are organized around the realization of that intent, or should be. Intent defines the direction in which action should be taking the organization. This can be done loosely, or it can involve much more detailed preparation and articulation.

This represents a change in emphasis from the individual to the organization, which consists of teams of individuals working to realize the strategy. Whereas it is conceivable that one individual could formulate a strategy, it is inconceivable that one individual could implement it. Strategic management is carried out by specialist units or teams within an organization who translate the objectives into functional programmes which can achieve those objectives. The relevant functional units engage independently in strategic management. Both within the teams and between them there needs to be significant coordination, which in itself will necessitate strategic action.

Mintzberg and Quinn (1996) have labelled something very similar as *strategic programming*, which represents the process of converting strategic thinking into strategic action. From the opposite perspective, the operational one, it means interpreting the role of particular actions in the context of strategic intentions, but sometimes only recognized and articulated after the event. Sometimes strategy making gives shape to and legitimates what has already been done. Mintzberg identifies three separate steps in such programming – codification, elaboration and conversion, which are each part of the process of strategic management. Strategic management or programming is therefore focused on various strategic activities which can be grouped under the three headings:

1. the identification by the enterprise of specific strategic intentions, identified as a result of strategic thinking (codification)
2. their formulation as proposed actions which will facilitate the achievement of those intentions (elaboration)
3. the efficient and timely implementation of these actions (conversion).

Often one of these activities is much more developed than others. Good strategy making requires all three to be carried out imaginatively and efficiently.

Any effective strategic management is premised on the previous articulation of the strategic intent, often expressed and communicated in general terms through the vision or mission statement. Codification means the translation of a general intent into specific objectives, the spelling out of specific objectives, such as the rate of growth of sales of key products or profit levels in particular units. Sometimes the objectives are only relevant to one part of an organization, for example financial or marketing targets.

In strategic management, elaboration and conversion are not always comprehensive; they are often piecemeal, involving only small parts of the whole organization and certain functional areas. A particular business unit may lend itself to systematic elaboration and conversion, while others may not (see the difference between electronic hardware and entertainment software in the case study on video game wars in Chapter 6 and in the Sony case study in Chapter 18). Some functional areas, such as finance or marketing, are more common venues for systematic strategic management.

The role of the business plan and financial controls

It is often assumed that the central element in any strategy is the business plan, or more specifically the financial mirror of that plan. For most enterprises the most important parts of the business plan are seen as the financial targets, broken down into specific streams of revenue and expenditure. This is because financial control is seen as vital to business success, as expressed in the level of profit, and is found at the heart of any business plan. The most common form of elaboration in strategic management is therefore the production of an annual business plan, sometimes called a corporate plan, the core of which is a set of financial targets (see Chapter 18 for a list of possible targets).

Focus on Theory
Above-normal profit

The broad aim of strategy is often seen as the making of 'above-normal' profit. What exactly is above-normal profit?

For economists normal profit has a specific meaning; it is the return which characterizes an equilibrium situation in a perfectly competitive market. An equilibrium price is reached when competition has fully worked itself out. A normal profit is

▶

earned in a market in which there is a homogeneous product traded by many buyers and many sellers, and in which there is complete freedom of entry or exit. All players have access to the same technology and the same inputs. Competition would ensure that any above-normal profit was eroded by a new entry or expanded sales from an incumbent. In such a market profit will be driven down by competition to a level at which a normal profit is made on the assets employed.

In a riskless world, this normal rate is equal to the opportunity cost of the capital employed – what could be earned on the funds invested in the enterprise if they were invested elsewhere. Putting it another way, it is equivalent to the going rate of interest on an alternative commitment of the same investment funds to the purchase of financial assets with the same risk profile – in a riskless world, the return on a government treasury bill. In such a riskless world, it is assumed that the normal rate of profit is the same in all industries throughout the economy. In such a world all earn the same return.

The normal rate of profit is not the average rate for the economy as a whole nor is it the average for individual industries.

Any profit above the normal level can be described as a monopoly profit. It emerges because there are a limited number of sellers; there is not freedom of entry into the industry; the product is not homogeneous; or one enterprise has a cost advantage over the others. In other words, there is a market imperfection which prevents the operation of perfect competition.

In the real world, as against the theoretical world of the economist, there is no such thing as perfect competition. What motivates an entrepreneur is the possibility of above-normal profit. No self-respecting businessperson would be content with earning only a normal profit.

It is worthwhile to explore for the moment the place of the financial side in strategic management. There is a tendency to see both the elaboration and conversion elements of strategic management as revolving around financial targets and financial controls. It is certainly true that any decision, whether it involves an investment or not, can in theory be reduced to a present value of cash streams which result from that decision. It could be put as a stronger argument, that any plan must be so reduced to ensure successful elaboration and conversion. There are two streams, revenues and costs:

- *Revenues:* these are streams generated by particular sales occurring at different times. In some cases there are delays in the initiation of such a stream or a gradual build-up of the level.
- *Costs:* these are expenditures on a variety of particular inputs occurring at different times. The expenditures may be made as one-off fixed costs, such as the cost of equipment or a promotional campaign, some now, some at an indefinite time in the future, or as operating expenditures which change or vary according to the level of sales, so-called variable costs.

It is often difficult to disentangle the revenues or costs which result from any specific decision. There may be an overlap in both revenue and cost between the business or accounting units. In some cases a project or business unit is independent and stands apart, although there may still be costs shared with other projects or units. In other cases the decision is part of a much larger set of decisions, for example a decision to introduce a particular marketing campaign, raising the general profile of the enterprise which affects all units. The standing of particular budgetary controls may not be closely linked with a clear understanding of where specific revenues and costs are located.

The business plan and its contents provide the financial controls which are used in strategy elaboration and conversion. However, the process of strategy making requires a careful consideration of the assumptions, and therefore the limitations, of any financial analysis. There are a number of powerful assumptions which underpin the stress on financial analysis itself and the interpretation of strategic management as mainly consisting in the implementation of a business plan. It is clear that the financial streams, just as the business plan, are the results of rather complex strategic decisions which reflect different scenarios and can yield different outcomes. There is so much uncertainty that any such estimate has a rather dubious value unless the assumptions on which it is based are made explicit.

All such estimates usually have a spurious degree of exactness. They mask the qualitative judgements which support them. They tend to put the cart before the horse, in the sense that the indication of financial streams should come at the very end of the process of strategy making when their meaning is clear, not at the beginning, after which they are used to justify strategic decisions made later. A successfully implemented marketing strategy will boost the revenue stream. A well-thought-out and implemented operations strategy will keep costs down. A properly focused research and development strategy can yield a series of planned innovations which both reduce costs and add quality to the product. All these functional strategies, and others, are the base on which a business plan, with its streams of income and costs, rests.

The financial part of strategic management is necessary, even vital, but only a part and certainly not the most important part. At best the narrowly financial approach is an oversimplification of the issues at stake. At worst it often drives the whole process of strategy making. A good financial strategy comes at the end of the strategy management process. Focused strategic management should occur in every functional and business unit. Strategic management shows the implications for these units of the overall strategy and what is needed to make an efficient conversion. The degree of elaboration might vary from functional unit to functional unit, from an elaborate marketing plan to one in which there is little in the way of what can be described as planning, as in the uncoordinated use of information systems or a poorly developed human resource strategy. Strategic management can be variable in its effective application. The degree of coordination between such strategic actions might also vary.

| A definition of strategic planning |

The definition of planning is as problematic as the definition of strategy itself. Sometimes it is assumed that strategy and planning are the same thing, at other times that strategy sets the objectives or targets and planning shows how to achieve them. The clearest way to distinguish them is to talk of strategy, not just as a plan but as a whole range of manifestations – as pattern, perspective, position and ploy.

Planning always assumes the pre-existence of a strategy. It is impossible to plan without an explicit strategy; the aim of any plan is to realize that strategy. Strategy does not necessarily imply planning, or planning as it is normally understood, but provides the framework within which planning can be successfully implemented. Nor does strategy necessarily require the development of a formal planning process with a structured planning department.

An organization blessed with good strategists does not necessarily have to produce, in a deliberate way, comprehensive and detailed strategic plans; it may produce strategic plans with a strictly limited functional scope. Planning is analytical, in that it reduces everything to the formal and systematic. Such planning requires a careful consideration of how all resources are to be used in order to achieve the strategic objectives, which themselves have to be spelt out in detail. It requires the collection of detailed data relevant to the achievement of such strategic targets. This data is processed in order to produce a plan. Planning is about:

- *departmentalization*, the setting out of separate functional plans
- *disaggregation*, the breakdown of a plan to suit the lower levels of an organization where this is necessary
- *planning horizons*, the time period over which targets should be achieved. Most plans are broken down into short-term plans, quarterly or annual plans.

Strategic planning is understood here as involving the use of formal planning methods, including the development of explicit plans with a full range of objectives, and its application to all business units and functional areas within the organization, and at all levels. The emphasis is on comprehensiveness. All parts of the enterprise have a carefully defined role to play in the realization of such a plan.

What is the main aim of planning? This aim has a profound influence on the nature of strategy. Planning can have two orientations:

- conservative – premised on the constraints of resources currently available within an enterprise, that is, what can be done with the present resources. Each unit must have the resources required to carry out its part of the plan
- radical – directed chiefly at the creation of new resources in an attempt to break out of current constraints.

Planning is partly about targets, restructuring the company and reshaping its environment, and partly about using as effectively as possible what it already has. It is better to find a balance, that planning involves something of both orientations, respect for existing constraints and the desire to break free of those constraints.

The definition of strategic planning used in this book includes:

- The systematic formulation of fully coherent and comprehensive written plans, setting out all the relevant strategic management actions for the achievement of the enterprise's strategic intent, as expressed in the objectives of its long-term vision.

- The translation of such long-term plans into short-term operational and administrative plans. It involves organization of the actions which are needed to implement in the short term the long-term plans.
- The specification of the exact resources which are needed to carry out those actions and how they can be accessed.
- A fully developed planning process, with the communication and implementation of those plans and the monitoring of their implementation, with any related adjustment of the plan during the period of its currency.

A summary of three different strategic activities

The three strategic activities can be interpreted as three separate steps in the incorporation of strategy making in a systematic process:

1. *Strategic thinking* describes well the establishment of the vision, which includes the process of defining and achieving objectives in a complex world in which there is considerable uncertainty about the future. It is about rethinking that future, sometimes in a small way. In some industries this may be as far as any strategist wishes to go, providing the cognitive framework, which explains how all current operations are to be organized.
2. *Strategic management* is strategic thinking applied to action, allowing an organization to subordinate all its functional activities to the achievement of clear objectives and to integrate them, insofar as this is possible. It is about the remaking of some part of the future. In a world of change this remaking is a precondition for the long-term success of an enterprise. The first step is pointless without at least some move into this second one.
3. *Strategic planning* assumes a further step in the moulding of the future in which strategic management, often fragmentary and inchoate, is translated into highly formal and coherent written plans and action to realize those plans. Any plan imposes the human will upon an environment which is full of unpredicted change.

For most enterprises, strategic planning is simply too hard and too risky. It is better to concentrate on the operational problems within a long-term strategic framework and marshal those elements of strategic management made necessary by those problems. Most of what is usually described as strategic planning does not correspond to what is described above under that label. This issue is discussed at greater length later in the book.

Principles for the successful use of strategy

A key issue is how far an enterprise needs to go in developing strategy making, where on the spectrum from strategic thinking to strategic planning it should locate itself. The definitions above provide us with a checklist of key factors which influence the exact role of each of the possible strategic activities – thinking, management and planning – and their relationship to each other.

The argument has been put that all staff should be strategic thinkers, at least with reference to their own domain, however small. That domain tends to get larger as a staff member rises in the hierarchy of an organization. Within that domain there is, or at least should be, strategic empowerment of the individual, that is, the giving of as much discretion for strategic decision making within the scope of the domain as is consistent with the overall strategy. This discretion must be exercised within the framework of strategic decisions made by higher levels of the hierarchy.

On the other hand, strategic planning is likely to be much less common than usually thought. Certain conditions make strategic planning inappropriate. It is obvious that rapid change in technology and market conditions discourages the introduction of detailed plans. Any risk reinforces this reluctance. An overly detailed plan can act as a straitjacket, removing the flexibility needed to maintain competitive advantage and survive in a rapidly changing environment. Any plan would have to be adjusted so quickly and comprehensively that it would cease to be helpful.

How to classify an industry or market

It is appropriate to consider how to classify different markets or industries by their degree of instability. There are three classifications which can be used:

1. *Level of competition in the market*

   In a certain sense there is an incompatibility between the operation of planning and the market. The key issue is the number of sellers. Monopsony is possible, that is, when there is only one buyer in the market, but rare; usually there are more buyers than sellers. At the extremes the possibilities range from monopoly to perfect competition, from one seller to many sellers. The more typical case falls between the extremes; it is either oligopoly, a few sellers, or monopolistic competition, a limited number of sellers, more than a few but less than many.

   How does the number of sellers influence the nature of the market?

   - The main characteristic of any monopoly is that the player has some control over price and therefore the level of profit that can be earned. The more sellers there are, the less likely it is for such control to exist.
   - A second feature, often assumed rather than discussed, is that the more sellers there are, the more likely it is that the market will be stable, and not subject to price fluctuations; the fewer sellers there are, the more unstable the market and the more likely price fluctuations. This is not always true. There is not necessarily a close relationship between the number of sellers and the level of instability, as will be seen.

2. *Age and degree of development of the particular market, industry or segment of either*

   - The market may be young and small but with enormous potential. At this stage it is the subject of significant entrepreneurial activity. Even rapid growth has little effect, since it is from a low base, but growth may be far from rapid in the early stages of industry life.
   - Later it may be in its adolescence or adulthood during which there is increased competition, more rapid growth but more standardization of product and price. Growth may initially be very rapid but may decline towards the end of this period.
   - It may be at the mature stage, entering middle age when growth is very slow or non-existent.
   - The market may be old when the search for any new markets, often abroad, becomes critical. Growth may become actual contraction.

These stages trace out the conventional S-shape of a life-cycle curve, which is often assumed to have universal validity.

In such an approach it is possible to easily define a new product which remains the same throughout its history, and therefore a new market or industry. In reality there may be modifications of the product which continuously renew it, sometimes quite dramatically. It is as if the industry re-enters childhood.

3. *Speed at which competitive advantage is won or lost*
   - In a slow-cycle market, for various reasons, including natural monopoly or the existence of considerable barriers to entry, there is little threat to the existing competitive advantage held.
   - In a fast-cycle market, competitive advantage can only be sustained for a short period. Competitors quickly imitate the first mover or even take the initiative, leapfrogging the early leader by introducing fresh innovations. There are a multitude of new processes, new organizational methods and new ways of differentiating the product which are introduced one after the other in rapid succession.
   - A standard cycle market is between the two extremes. Here, competitive advantage can be retained for longer than the short term, but still a finite period of time.

It is possible to simplify the classification of circumstance. It is likely that fast-cycle industries are those which are new whereas slow-cycle industries are those which are old. The two can be combined while recognizing that some industries by their nature are fast and some slow cycle. By also aggregating monopolistic competition with oligopoly and infancy with adolescence, it is possible to reduce the classes to three. Figure 2.2 helps to indicate what circumstances are appropriate for different strategic activities. The variants which are in bold are the most common, those italicized are the least common.

Variants:
A. This is the typical situation of an industry in extreme infancy. Such a situation is unlikely to last for long. It is possible to plan in such a situation, indeed highly desirable, but there may be resource constraints on engaging in such planning. Given the speed at which the situation is likely to change, it is unlikely that any planning will occur.
B. As other sellers enter the industry, it becomes harder to retain competitive advantage and therefore it becomes desirable to employ strategic management but impossible to plan in any realistic manner.
C. With many sellers in a young industry, it is only possible to apply strategic thinking and impossible to go beyond this. Enterprises are jostling each other with their competitive innovations.
D. A monopolist can always attempt to plan. However, there are few industries with a natural monopoly. This variant, just as A, is rare.
E. This is a common situation, possibly the most common of all. It lends itself to considerable strategic management. Enterprises might or might not try to speed up the introduction of innovations, that is, to accelerate the standard cycle. If the oligopoly involves stability of market share and price, this is unlikely. There is a

Number of sellers

	One	Few	Many
Young (fast)	A	B	C
Mature (standard)	D	E	F
Old (slow)	G	H	I

Enterprise age (speed of cycle)

Figure 2.2 **The variations of enterprise circumstance**

danger in too much planning which might make an enterprise vulnerable to any change in circumstances.

F. Such an industry is likely to be highly competitive and possibly unstable. In such an industry it is difficult to apply too much strategic management, but there is likely to be some.

G. This is the most likely situation in which there is strategic planning. Competitive advantage is not an issue and unlikely to become one.

H. Such an industry may oscillate between stability and instability. There may well be very significant amounts of strategic management in this variant. They are used to gain some marginal competitive advantage.

I. This is a very unusual situation.

Under what conditions is it likely that an enterprise should go the whole way from strategic thinking to strategic planning? Such conditions do not occur frequently, both A and D being very unusual. Only G is likely to occur and this is also exceptional. Clearly a fiercely competitive fast-cycle market which is in the growth stage is unlikely to be right for strategic planning. The younger the industry, the faster the cycle; the greater the number of competitors, the more unlikely the step to planning. An industry sharing any of these attributes may be ripe for the frequent exercise of creative strategic thinking. How much strategic management is possible depends on the stability of the industry.

When strategic planning is appropriate

As seen above a monopoly in a mature slow-cycle market is much more likely to be ideal for strategic planning. Under what conditions is strategic planning an appropriate strategic activity? There are three situations in which it might be desirable, although there are good reasons why, even in these situations, strategic planning may be unusual:

1. The situation of *predictable change*, at least as predictable as change can be. Both innovation and competition are sources of unpredictability. The absence of one,

or both, makes for a predictable context. This may be true of a mature industry in which technology and tastes are not changing very rapidly, or changing in a wholly anticipated manner, and in which the number of competitors is stable. An enterprise which is faced by an environment which changes little, and then only in a manageable way, can engage in strategic planning without fear that it will impose a straitjacket on the enterprise, which will prevent the exploitation of opportunities inherent in a changing environment and also inhibit the successful management of risk.

2. The *crisis situations* which confront all enterprises at some point in their life, often described as *turnaround* situations. These situations, which threaten the very existence of the organization, typically happen when strategic drift creates a wide gap between where an enterprise should be and its actual situation. This is when the priorities of the enterprise become so obvious that the strategic position is clarified for all. All have the same interest, the survival of the organization. Any planning requires absolutely clear-cut priorities which help to spell out the objectives. Planning enables a strategist to concentrate resources on the achievement of such priorities. Witness the assistance planning provides in conditions of war, at least modern warfare which demands a total mobilization of resources at every level of an economy.

   However, the speed of the necessary response may make it difficult to plan in the way described. Since the turnaround is forced on the enterprise, there may be no time to plan.

3. The *launch of any new venture*, which is best undertaken with a detailed understanding of the resources available and the strategic actions needed to achieve enterprise objectives. There should be an indication of what should be done in various contingencies. In other words, a new venture needs to be planned in a detailed manner. This is situation A above. The frequent lack of any such planning, indeed even of significant strategic management, helps to explain the extraordinarily high attrition rate for small businesses in all types of economy. The critical problem is that a small business may not have the resources to engage in planning.

These remarks provide only a general set of principles and need to be applied to the particular conditions of different industries. Since the world is complex, there are no simple solutions and no simple choices. Rather there are an endless series of unique events which combine to constitute environments which are not only different for every enterprise but never remain the same from period to period. The capacity to generalize about such situations is limited. It is necessary to learn how to read this complexity and create some order. Such uncertainty and complexity influence the whole nature of strategy making.

Finding the right strategic mix of entrepreneurial creativity and administrative expertise

Any successful enterprise needs both the vision and its realization by efficient management. Can the same individual manager or the same organization be good at both? This amounts to asking the question, what does a manager do or rather what should he or she do? Or, putting it differently, should all managers be entrepreneurial?

Entrepreneur and manager

It is helpful to ask these questions in the context of making a distinction between entrepreneurship and management. There is considerable misunderstanding concerning the nature and role of the entrepreneur, in particular a failure to distinguish between the entrepreneur and the manager. These are different roles. The distinction may be solely conceptual, in that it is possible for the same person to be both entrepreneur and manager, or at one time to be entrepreneurial and at another managerial. It may be highly desirable that this is so.

The key conceptual distinction is between innovation and imitation. Broadly speaking, the entrepreneur innovates and the manager imitates. The entrepreneur is the pioneer, the manager the applier of existing best practice. The entrepreneur engages in strategic activity, the manager focuses on tactical or operational activity. The entrepreneur formulates a strategy, the manager implements that strategy. Conceptually the distinction is clear.

The situation from the perspective of strategy is also clear. The strategist must allow for both entrepreneurial and managerial inputs:

- Strategists must sometimes play the role of entrepreneur; they must be entrepreneurial in their attitudes, confronting the need to innovate as part of strategy making. There is a considerable overlap between the role of strategist and entrepreneur. Both entrepreneurs and good strategists must display creativity, sometimes of a very high order. Both must manage change. Entrepreneurs are often implicit rather than explicit strategists, not having the time or the inclination to make the strategy explicit.
- The strategist must also put in place an efficient management team skilled in all the relevant functional areas. This is necessary in order to realize the vision of the entrepreneur.

Business success depends on the continuing renewal and application of the entrepreneurial spirit. This is difficult to achieve since it is in short supply. Business success depends on the application of efficient management. Few enterprises last very long. The attrition rate of new businesses is notoriously high. In the US, the bastion of the entrepreneurial spirit, almost 50,000 new enterprises fail each year. Even large enterprises seldom last more than one or two generations. In a long-term historical perspective, business success is ephemeral. Only a handful of the 100 largest companies existing in any country at the beginning of the twentieth century exist today, typically less than 10%. Even those enterprises are likely to be unrecognizable as the original creations.

Intrapreneur-ship

It is not only new enterprises which are the vehicle for innovation. Existing enterprises can innovate. The term 'entrepreneurship' has been modified to coin a new concept intrapreneurship, which captures the way in which in some companies the upper echelons of management, or the main strategists, manage to structure the enterprise to encourage innovation at middle and low levels. The enterprising individuals at these levels are given scope to discover new processes and products, develop new and more efficient organizational methods and identify new market segments. The upper managers promote the new strategic initiatives and put the intrapreneurs into a position to oversee the new ventures. Sony, in its early history, was a good example of successful intrapreneurship. Intrapreneurship is the key to innovating for a competitive advantage. Most enterprises at some stage lose the ability to generate and/or support intrapreneurship and intrapreneurs. The most successful Japanese companies, such as Sony, had strategies which at least implicitly aimed at doing just this.

There is a very real sense in which success itself is often the cause of failure. It does this by persuading the successful that they know all the answers, despite the fact that the environment has changed and therefore the answers have changed. The success of one enterprise, maybe a brash newcomer, may well be the cause of the failure of another. Schumpeter's famous phrase 'creative destruction' (1934, 1950) summarizes the role of the entrepreneur in both creating and destroying. The entrepreneur's job is to convert new ideas into profitable innovations. By so doing they subvert the viability of existing companies still using old technology or producing old products.

The mix

The obverse of creativity is the humdrum routine of administration. Creativity is not enough for business success. Routine management functions must be carried out efficiently. The relevant functions can be broadly referred to as 'administration', but the functions are rather wider than the term usually suggests. The manager is hired to apply best-practice managerial techniques, invariably well-tried techniques, that is, to carry out the basic operations of the enterprise in as efficient a manner as possible. The realization of entrepreneurial goals requires, for its success, adequate, even high-quality management inputs. Many of these management inputs involve specialist knowledge of functional areas.

The proportion of entrepreneurs and managers required within an enterprise, or indeed the desirable blend of these characteristics within the same individuals, can vary markedly. Some periods are periods of rapid change, others see greater stability. Equally, some sectors are characterized by unchanging technology and stagnant markets. This is the basis of the usual distinction made between the new and old economies. Old established industries often offer little scope for the entrepreneur but much for the manager, whereas new industries offer the reverse.

The number of genuine entrepreneurs available is limited: entrepreneurship requires a particular combination of qualities which is not common. Not least are the characteristics of creativity, imagination and originality, including the ability to think strategically. Further, there are the linked characteristics of persistence and realism, which allow the original ideas to be translated into operational innovations and recognize the importance of implementation through the processes of strategic management and strategic planning.

Entrepreneurs can be found as chief executive officers of large multinational enterprises or creating and running their own small enterprises, converting them into the successful companies of the future. Potential entrepreneurs achieve their greatest success by being in the right place at the right time, usually more by design than luck. Often entrepreneurs mould their own future.

It is also the case that each person, given the opportunity, is able to exercise some degree of entrepreneurship, that is, to reshape and innovate in the relevant functional areas, just as each can also act as a strategist in the relevant domain. Empowerment develops some entrepreneurship in all and gives scope for its exercise. The domain in which this is done may be very restricted. The impact of many small manifestations of this activity can add up to an enterprise which continues to be competitive. The ability of individuals to engage in innovation is the result of an appropriate strategic context, reflecting the input of appropriate strategic leadership and strategic decisions on structure, culture and procedures. Moreover, such entrepreneurial activity helps to make possible the realization of a strategy.

In seeking out and taking opportunities, the entrepreneur is seen as an unusual person; he or she deliberately takes risks, that is, is a risk taker instead of being risk-averse. Often the entrepreneur is seen as glorying in an exposure to risk. One of the main features of an entrepreneur may be the willingness to accept a challenge, therefore to be less risk-averse than the average person, to have a greater appetite for risk. However, successful entrepreneurial activity requires significant risk control. This is an important facet of any successful entrepreneurial activity. Successful entrepreneurs are often good at devising new ways of managing their external environment, controlling everything from suppliers, to competitors, customers, access to finance and technical expertise. Certainly they are good at making full use of any new methods of risk control.

The goal of the entrepreneur is to make above-normal or monopoly profits, at risk levels no higher than the norm for the industry. The monopoly arises from the ability of an enterprise to create a significant imperfection in the market, to erect a barrier to the entry of rival enterprises into the industry or sector, often simply by getting to know something which others do not know and using that knowledge to create value for customers. The ability of an enterprise to generate monopoly profit often depends on the ability of the entrepreneur to pioneer, to be 'first mover' in developing a new product, process or form of organization. On occasion it reflects the ability to quickly follow up after others have suffered the initial development problems which sometimes attach to being first mover.

It is a matter for strategy to determine the appropriate mix of creative entrepreneurship and good management. There is a time and a place for an emphasis on entrepreneurial activity and a time and place for an emphasis on managerial activity. For example, in fast-cycle markets there is both an opportunity and a need for continuous entrepreneurial activity, whereas in slow-cycle markets there is no such opportunity and no such need. The enterprise requires both structure and personnel suited to its circumstances.

It is possible to have too much entrepreneurship or too much administration:

• An organization which is excessively entrepreneurial can dissipate its energies in generating a stream of promising new ideas but never bringing any of them to fruition. It pays all enterprises to encourage a continuous display of creativity and to have a pool of ready-to-utilize ideas available. However, there should also be effective procedures for processing these ideas and selecting those which are worth taking beyond the ideas stage. Successful entrepreneurial activity consists in both generating the ideas and evaluating them effectively, in the context of both the general environment and the conditions of a particular industry.

- On the other hand, an organization which is obsessed with attaining the ideal structure, procedures and job descriptions and with the efficiency of its administration, and nothing else, will steadily lose its competitive advantage, even if it is a slow-cycle market. It will be obsessed with observing proper procedures and rules. It is likely to suffer continuing strategic drift. It will never generate those ideas which can be converted into continuing competitive advantage. At some stage the enterprise's products will become old and tired, its markets established and undynamic and its cost structures increasingly uncompetitive. It is what the typical enterprise often becomes and why the life of most enterprises is so short.

A successful organization needs both an ever-renewed vision for the future and an efficient routine management and administration, the balance between them changing with changing circumstances. Nor should the functional specialists be always limited in their perspective by their specialization. While an entrepreneur must have a strong feeling for the feasible, what is doable, administrators must have an eye for improvements, whatever their scale and impact. All managers need some entrepreneurial perspective, all entrepreneurs some managerial perspective.

The primary aim of any strategist is to maintain the long-term economic viability of the enterprise. The key to realizing this aim is to create and maintain competitive advantage over the long term. This is achieved by securing, on a continuing basis, an acceptable or satisfactory rate of return at an acceptable or satisfactory level of risk. The return ensures that the owners of an enterprise receive a reward which ensures their continuing participation in the enterprise. The managed risk guarantees that there will be no moments of illiquidity, however temporary, which might threaten the continued operation of the enterprise.

To achieve all this the strategist must behave on occasions like an entrepreneur and on others like a manager. The strategist must be an entrepreneur, at least some, if not all, of the time, notably by sponsoring the kind of change which provides value to the customers and keeps the enterprise ahead of its competitors. The key issue for the enterprise is to put together a team of strategists who combine the roles of entrepreneur and manager in the right combination. For an individual it is achieving the right blend of activity at the right time. In an increasing number of industries characterized by fast-cycle markets, there should be maximum scope for the expression of the entrepreneurial spirit: this is a strategic necessity. The industries which are characterized by slow-cycle markets need good management. Strategy is about achieving the right balance and the right timing. The entrepreneur/management mix and the strategic thinking /strategic management mix are therefore closely linked.

Case Study The IKEA way

IKEA's aim is to provide customers with 'affordable solutions for better living'. The better living comes from a range of furniture and household furnishings offered at prices which appeal to those just starting up their own homes and expanding their families, offered in a style and a context which satisfies the desire for beauty and modernity. Nearly all the products on offer by IKEA are sold in IKEA stores throughout the world. IKEA has achieved the impossible, to create a range of products attractive to consumers everywhere, in countries with very different cultures, and to apply a formula for presentation and sale of those products which reinforces the attractiveness.

IKEA has put together a number of creative ideas in a combination which explains its success. It is not a matter of just one creative idea. IKEA is at the same time the McDonald's and Harley-Davidson of the world of home furnishings. It has combined the cost-reducing benefits of mass consumption and production with the attention to style required to persuade consumers to buy items which will be on display and in the eye of the purchaser for many years, unlike the humble hamburger or cup of coffee which are consumed quickly and as quickly forgotten. In short, like Harley-Davidson, it has created a global brand. It has managed to innovate continuously and respond to changes in the world, continuing to convey a sense of excitement and modernity.

It is the originality of the overall IKEA concept which explains its success, a concept which comprises a number of different elements. The key aspect of creativity is how the IKEA package is put together as a coherent whole. It has features unique to IKEA but the uniqueness derives principally from the way in which these different features are combined.

The first, and in many ways most important, of these elements is the role of the customer. The 'IKEA way' elevates the customer above what is the norm. Customers choose, transport and assemble the furniture themselves, in a way untrue of the customers of other furniture and home furnishings retailers, although others are now imitating the IKEA model.

IKEA offers its products in a natural setting which encourages creative thought by the customer about how an individual item might enhance the look of the ensemble in different parts of the home. There is little fear of sameness since consumers can place the products in different combinations with other products, according to personal taste. IKEA encourages a holistic way of thinking about the home and its furnishings but also an attention to the details of design and functionality. It recognizes that there is an aesthetic component to furnishing a home, even if there is a limit on how much can be spent. It also recognizes that there are environmental implications to what is produced and sold, which must be taken into account.

Given this starting point, the concept can be summarized in the following way.

Target market

There is a clearly defined market. It may sound corny but the self-proclaimed focus of IKEA is 'young people of all ages'. In reality the market is primarily young people, who are well educated, liberal in cultural values, white collar, but with limited means because of their stage of career and family cycle, and in the process of setting up or expanding their homes because they are having children.

Canada is typical in its customer profile and can be used to represent the global customer. In Canada the target customer household has an income of $35,000 – 40,000 (middle level), owns a condominium (apartment) or a townhouse, has members with a university degree, has both husband and wife with white-collar jobs, who are in the primary age group 35–44, or the secondary group 25–34, has two children, and is prone to move residence relatively frequently.

Product

The IKEA products on offer exceed 12,000 items in number, an enormous range, in the words of Czinkota et al. (2000: 357), 'from plants to pots, sofas to soup spoons, and wine glasses to wallpaper'. The product is homogeneous worldwide, that is, it does not tend to differ from country to country. There is a complementarity between the large and small items on offer which creates the ensemble effect in IKEA stores. The design is light and modern. There is also a stress on pastel colours and the use of textiles. The emphasis is on individual design which still has a Scandinavian feel. The heart of the company's design capability was, and to some degree continues to be, a 50-person Swedish workshop. Considerable time and effort goes into the design of each product. The products are redesigned at regular intervals in order to retain the modern feel.

IKEA designs but does not manufacture. The products are purchased from a wide range of different sources, both in terms of the network of contracted manufacturers, which runs into the thousands, at present more than 1,800 suppliers, and in terms of countries, 55. Because of initial resistance from existing furniture retailers and their attempt to prevent suppliers cooperating with IKEA, from the beginning IKEA had to go to small cheap suppliers outside Sweden, notably Poland in the early years. This meant that IKEA had to play a prominent role in assisting the suppliers. Buying or trading offices, of which there are 43 in 33 countries, and production engineers perform the job of vetting candidates; their decision is then referred to and ratified by headquarters. The policy is to avoid the pitfalls of vertical integration while avoiding the suppliers' excessive reliance on IKEA.

There is an increasing emphasis on cheap manufacturing sources such as China, now the largest single source, and increasingly Poland, as well as Sweden, and suppliers in the main European markets. A precondition is that these sources maintain the quality of design. Today there are more than 500 suppliers in Eastern Europe alone.

IKEA is an example of what is called a strategic centre enterprise, that is, a company which works at the centre of an alliance network, in this case a global alliance network of thousands of manufacturers who supply IKEA with its products. IKEA can afford to outsource activities in which it does not think it has a core competency, notably manufacturing, concentrating on those activities in which it has, such as design, marketing, logistics and distribution/retailing.

Some of these alliances have been in existence for many years. As Margonelli (2002: 109) has said, 'Yet even as IKEA fosters competition among suppliers, it also treats them as long-term business partners'. It is difficult to become an IKEA supplier, but becoming one gives the supplier access to an enormous global market. The trick in maintaining low costs is high volume production. IKEA, through IKEA Engineering, which employs a dozen technicians, is ready to give suppliers technical assistance to reduce costs and improve quality. IKEA does everything, from leasing equipment to suppliers to offering frequent advice, in order to bring production up to world standards and keep down costs.

The typical product usually comes in kits which have to be assembled by the customer. The components of the kits, once manufactured, are sent to large warehouses, at present 18 distribution centres worldwide, and from there on to the retail stores which themselves act as mini-warehouses. The cash registers of the retail stores are directly connected to the distribution centres, providing immediate information on changes in demand patterns. The warehouses are at one and the same time storage facilities, logistical control points, consolidation centres and transport nodes. They are the key to reducing inventory to the minimum while ensuring immediate access to stock by the customer.

Price

There is a lot of emphasis on a competitive pricing strategy. IKEA prices are as much as 30–50%, certainly at least 20–30%, below those of fully assembled competing products. The exact level of undercutting varies from country to country and from period to period. There are also BTIs, 'breathtaking items', which have a very low price.

IKEA does everything to keep the price down. There is a ruthless drive to reduce costs. For example, the Poang chair has been reduced in price from US$149 in 2000,

to US$99 in 2001 and US$79 in 2002. This follows the establishment from the beginning of a competitive price. As shown below fixing the level of price comes first. This cost and price leadership is achieved by a combination of strategies – large-quantity purchasing, the push to discover ever-cheaper suppliers in ever-cheaper markets (sourcing in developing economies has risen from 32% to 48%), low-cost logistics, store location in relatively cheap suburban areas, and a do-it-yourself approach to marketing and distribution. Low costs are translated into low prices as IKEA pursues a deliberate price leadership strategy. For example, IKEA does not deliver, although it will organize delivery at the purchaser's cost, if it is needed. At a cost it will even organize assembly for the customer.

Distribution

IKEA has constructed its own global distribution and retailing network, with 18 distribution centres in 2003, most near container ports and major truck and rail routes and 4 more under construction – 70% of the total product line is handled by the centres, the other 30% going direct from supplier to store.

Its stores are usually located well outside city centres but with plenty of free parking space. The stores themselves are large and take some time to walk around. IKEA owns the larger scale outlets, but is prepared to franchise in markets which are smaller or carry a bigger risk because of initial unfamiliarity with or hostility to the IKEA concept. They are decidedly family friendly, with supervised crèches and playgrounds or video rooms for older children, both available in order to free the parents from outside distraction in their shopping. There are also free buggies, reasonably priced restaurants and cafes. Such facilities allow for a lengthy visit.

The stores have been described as a kind of 'theme park masquerading as a furniture outlet' (Margonelli, 2002: 112). In the easy accessibility of the products, the experience of shopping is rather like a supermarket experience, but in the encouragement of family participation, it is more like an outing. The normal rules and expectations of a furniture store do not apply to IKEA. The combination of these superficially contradictory features is one aspect of the achievement of IKEA. It is also true that each store is a meticulously constructed 'virtual' Sweden.

In some regions, where the cost is not prohibitive, IKEA has used a mail-order system.

Promotion

One of the best-known features of IKEA is its *catalogue*. It is itself well designed, almost a collector's item. This catalogue has become something of a design icon, rather like the London underground map or the Coca-Cola bottle. It is the main mechanism of advertising. Promotion is centred on this catalogue. The aim of the company is to use the catalogues to promote innovative approaches, which are then talked about and publicity generated by word of mouth initiated by those who have seen the catalogue. The catalogue also helps the consumer to find the relevant product before entry into the store. The catalogue is uniform in layout throughout the world, with very minor regional differences – 110 million copies of the 2002 catalogue were printed in 34 different languages. It is much imitated.

The catalogue is reinforced by the existence of a *customer magazine*. IKEA doubled the print run of its customer magazine to 400,000 copies in 2002, again making it the largest circulation of any publication within the area of home furnishings. The recorded circulation in 2001 was 171,620. Half the copies are mailed to cardholders' homes, the rest are sold in-store and on news-stands. Each issue has a specific theme and tackles concerns relating to everyday life in a manner which makes the ideas easily accessible to the readers, rather than concentrating the focus on an aspirational lifestyle, which was formerly the case.

A second feature of promotion is the colourful and attractive nature of the *retail outlets*, where the furnishings are set out as they would be in actual homes. The usual approach to selling furniture is to have multiple versions of the same product in the same room, such as beds, lounge suites, or tables. Such an unnatural setting creates problems of choice for the customer. Such a situation often requires the shop assistant's assistance in enabling the purchaser to imagine the item in a natural setting. In IKEA by contrast there is not very much direct service; the stores have the do-it-yourself style of the supermarket. Customers are provided with tape measures, pens and note pads to assist them in making a choice. Information on the availability of items in different colours, including where they should be picked up, is clearly provided. The number of shop assistants is kept to a minimum in order to keep down costs. The attractive presentation offsets any notion that IKEA is a low-cost, low-quality supplier.

IKEA's strategy has been described as a focused cost leadership strategy, focused because it is targeted at a particular market niche, those who want style at low cost (Hitt et al., 2001: 169). However, this oversimplifies the approach adopted and underplays the complexity of the product, with its packaging of different services. If it were true that the strategy was no more than a form of focused cost leadership, it would be difficult to understand why IKEA has been so successful. Rather it is the

combination of low price and high quality which attracts the consumer, which is not an unusual situation.

The attributes of the product offered by IKEA differ markedly from those of other retailers. Instant accessibility, customer participation in value-adding, the combination of low cost and high quality – all mark the product out as unique and therefore as carrying a competitive advantage, one which is continuously renewed as products are improved and renovated. IKEA is always ready to innovate. Two examples illustrate this; the introduction of the Children's IKEA in 1997, which meant both the addition of about 600 new products, from egg-shaped cribs to multiethnic fabric dolls, and the revamping of store layout; and, more recently, the distribution of a model kit for designing one's own kitchen.

A typical IKEA product – the Bang mug

The object of this section is to show briefly, with one of the humblest of products, the Bang mug, the IKEA method of developing and renovating a product, noting the sequence of steps in the development of a product. This is one of the most popular, although also one of the cheapest, of the IKEA products. IKEA will probably sell as many as 25 million worldwide in 2003. Its history is typical of many products. The product originated from the idea of a co-worker.

Typically the first step is to set the price, which is suggested by the location of the product in a matrix of price range and product style created by the strategists. The second step is to choose a manufacturer. Only at the third stage does the company design the product. When the process of design began for the Bang in 1996, the starting point for Pia Eldin Lindsten, the product developer, was the price, set at a very low level of five Swedish krona. This was regarded as a powerful knock-out punch, hence the name, Bang. The concern with cost was comprehensive. This price had to be taken into account in choosing materials, colours and design. For example, the mug is made in green, blue, yellow and white, as these pigments cost less than other shades, such as red.

However, price, while the starting point, was not everything. In addition to price there were also requirements of functionality, modern design, environmental sensitivity and production under acceptable working conditions. Some of these were at odds with the cost constraint but all were regarded as important. The team of specialist designers, product developers and purchasers had to satisfy all the requirements.

Often the existing suppliers are able to make suggestions for change. One producer of Bang, a factory in Rumania, has been a supplier for 15 years. This is not unusual. Such a long-term relationship helps in developing an awareness of the expectations of both IKEA and its customers. There is often a mutual exchange of suggestions which assists in the continuous improvement of the product. This was certainly the case with the Bang mug.

There have been three occasions on which the Bang has been designed and redesigned. In the case of the Bang it is possible to interpret the design aim as maximizing the number of mugs which can be stored on a pallet. Originally 864 mugs would fit, after the redesign with a rim, 1280 and after another redesign 2024. This allowed the shipping costs to be reduced by 60%. The launch of a new Bang in 2001 was an opportunity for further improvement and further cost saving. The new mug became shorter and the handle has been redesigned so that it stacks more efficiently. This helps to reduce costs since it saves space for all concerned, from the manufacturer to the customer. It assists the manufacturer since it makes better use of space in the kiln. The new design also helps in transport, warehousing and store display. Probably most importantly of all it assists the customer in saving cupboard space.

The final step is to sell it. The mug is presented in a natural context in the room in which it is likely to be used.

IKEA's competition

Throughout the world the initial competition for IKEA consisted of much smaller companies, often family concerns. Such concerns have neither the negotiating strength to keep costs down nor the opportunity to reap the economies of scale in manufacture or distribution that IKEA has created. They are also accustomed to deliver sometimes weeks, or even months, after the receipt of a specific order.

IKEA has been prepared not only to undercut the price of competitors, but to take on the purchasing risk which those who sell and manufacture to order do not. Calculating the product requirements of each store accurately and in a timely way is critical to ensuring that the products are always available in the warehouse and that the suppliers are producing the right number to maintain this availability. Easy communication of sales information helps. This allows IKEA to supply the consumer with what he or she wants with little or no delay, another product attribute which is very attractive to customers. Inventories are kept down to a minimum. The concentration and coordination made possible by the global coverage of IKEA enables a degree of long-term planning which is unusual for this industry. Planning is absolutely critical in balancing the supply of and demand for individual items of IKEA furniture and furnishings.

The existence of IKEA has raised the game of its competitors and stimulated imitation. As time has passed it has become more difficult for IKEA to maintain a competitive advantage. While the strategy for going global and entering different countries has been a carefully prepared and implemented one, some problems have emerged for the strategy.

This is best illustrated by the experience of IKEA in entering the North American market. Before entering the largest world market, the USA, IKEA went into the much smaller Canadian market. Entry into the Canadian market was gradual, partly by design, partly because IKEA could not do otherwise. This allowed a significant learning process. In 1976 the first store was opened. By 1986 there were still only nine stores, hardly a Starbucks or McDonald's pace of store opening. The range of products on offer was about half the total range available in Europe, a range selected on the basis of what the consumer wanted and what IKEA could sell at a competitive price. A central warehouse was set up in Montreal. Demand tended to exceed supply, which was partly countered by the establishment of a network of Canadian suppliers, 30 by 1984. Rather reluctantly the company ran a mail-order business, less profitable than its normal business.

IKEA took its time in building a platform for rapid growth in what could be its largest potential market, the USA. The American market represented a real challenge to the earlier strategy since it had already been the graveyard of many a European retailer. Bjorn Bayley, who headed the successful Canadian management team, moved on in 1985 to organize its entry into the USA. However, the entry was probably IKEA's most difficult one to date. This is shown by the fact that between 1985 and 1996 IKEA opened only six stores in North America.

The stores were much slower to become profitable than the European stores. Previously in Europe entry into a new market was typically followed by two or three years of loss making but profits began with the third or fourth store after this brief learning and adjustment period. In the USA four years after entry the stores were still losing money. They broke even for the first time in 1993. One problem was an adverse movement in the exchange rate, with the Swedish krona increasing in value, from $1 equal to 8.6 krona in 1985 to $1 equal to 5.8 in 1990. This had the unfortunate effect of removing the price competitiveness of IKEA's products.

A worse problem was the reluctance of the consumers to buy. They entered the stores but did not buy. American consumers did not find the dimensions of IKEA's products to their liking. For example, the beds were too narrow and were not sold with matching bedroom suites. Sheets and curtains were of European sizes, not American. Drawers in bedroom cupboards were not deep enough, and glasses too small to accommodate the American liking for ice.

The previously successful strategy had to be modified. By 1991 IKEA had decided that it needed to customize its products to American tastes and source many more of its products from American suppliers. By 1997 about 45% of supplies came from American sources, compared with only 15% in 1990. By 2000 about one-third of the products were also customized. The results were positive. By 1993 the American operations were profitable. By the end of the 1990s the gross profit was well over one billion dollars and growing rapidly, although not yet as profitable in its profit margins as the European operations.

There are further ambitious plans for expansion. In 2002, beyond the period for which figures were quoted above, there were 24 stores in North America. A further 9 were planned for 2003. The target is to have 50 by 2013. Growth is now rapid. In 2001 sales growth was 25.5% compared with the industry average of 1.9%. IKEA is still only the seventh largest furniture seller in the USA, so it has much room for expansion.

Wisely the same gradual approach has been adopted in Asia and Eastern Europe.

What about the nature of the competitors in different countries? It is possible to make some generalizations. Figure 2.3 does this by choosing two attributes of such players which are particularly important to IKEA.

Most of IKEA's competition comes from businesses with local roots. There are four kinds of competitor:

1. Enterprises not dissimilar to IKEA, that are aiming to give the customer the opportunity to add value, particularly by self-assembly, usually without the level of global activity of an IKEA. These include enterprises set up on the same principles as IKEA or existing enterprises which have adjusted to absorb some of the IKEA ways. The former include Freedom in Australia, IDOMO in Canada and Sauder Woodworking in the USA, although the latter supplies to and sells through department stores such as Wal-Mart, Office Depot or Staples – it does not retail itself. An example of the latter is Sears, with their so-called 'Elements' programme.

2. Specialist chains of furniture stores, so-called specialty chains, such as The Brick in Canada or Andersons in Australia. Both these and the next competitor group do source furniture and furnishings from abroad but most of the product sold is locally produced, whatever country is considered.

3. Large department stores which sell furniture as one of very many different product lines, such as Wal-Mart in the USA and Meyers in Australia.

4. The independents. Typically they account for most sales but have been losing market share, not just to IKEA-type enterprises, but to specialty chains and department stores. These are retail outlets, sometimes closely linked with a particular manufacturer or manufacturers, which sell to order. Some of these are specialists, such as the Sofa Workshop in Australia. The resulting product differs according to customer requirements.

The future

IKEA has an excellent platform for future growth since it has succeeded in branding itself, which helps it to enter new markets. It has an unchallenged reputation for producing stylish home furnishings at a low cost and continuous innovation. In 1999 it ranked as high as 43rd in the aggregate world ranking by brand value. No other home furnishings company was ranked in the top 60. This is a good indication of its competitive success and the special identity that IKEA has established for itself.

One key issue is to manage the brand well. This require a pace of expansion such that there is no loss of quality or efficiency and that sufficient homogeneity is retained to generate the economies of supply which have been so important in the past. Some adjustment of the business model is inevitable, but the main features of the old model will continue. The IKEA model has a lot more mileage in it. The interaction between the

		Value added		
		None	Medium	Maximum
Scope of sourcing	Global			IKEA
	Mixed		Large department stores, Meyers, David Jones Furniture chains, Andersons, The Brick	
	Local	Made-to-order stores		Freedom, Sauder, IDOMO

Figure 2.3 **Value added by customers**

core company competencies and the tastes of its customers will be extended to further parts of the globe as the company expands.

In 1996, when IKEA became Dutch-owned, it was split into three parts – an organization comprising the retailing operations, one holding the franchise and trademarks of IKEA, and a finance and banking organization. The first two are controlled at arm's length by the Dutch charitable foundation. The intention is to try and avoid either the break-up of the organization or its takeover by a predator.

IKEA diverged from the usual way of doing things in a number of ways.

• In its international activities it continued to stress its Swedish roots, notably in the design of its many products but even in its international advertising, ostentatiously displaying the blue and gold of Sweden.
• It also applied the same formula throughout the world, putting on offer the same range of goods. It conducted almost nothing by way of market research into patterns of potential demand and local tastes. It engaged in very little market analysis and initially almost no customization to take account of local market differences.
• It did not ease itself into foreign markets through acquisition of an existing business, a joint venture with a successful local enterprise or franchising: it moved in boots and all, establishing operations on its own. Its growth was organic, that is, internally generated.

IKEA defined clearly what it wanted to do – produce and sell furniture and furnishings to the largest possible market in a new and creative manner, but it also met the requirements of logistics and management in a way which pared its costs to the lowest possible level. Selling the same products throughout the world allowed suppliers to reap economies of scale.

In the words of Normean and Ramirez (1993: 66), IKEA has 'systematically redefined the roles, relationships and organizational practices of the furniture business'. They go on to point out that 'IKEA did *not* position itself to add value at any one point in a predetermined sequence of activities (that is, the conventional value chain). Rather, IKEA set out systematically to reinvent value and the business system that delivers it for an entire cast of economic actors' (p. 68). These actors included suppliers, customers and the various groups of staff within IKEA itself. In the view of Normean and Ramirez, the case of IKEA shows that the focus of strategic analysis should not be the company or the industry, but 'the value-creating system, within which different economic actors – suppliers, business partners, allies, customers – work together to *co-produce* value' (p. 66). IKEA is 'the central star in a constellation of services, goods, design management, support, and even entertainment' (p. 68). It put together a strategy and a business model which was new and highly successful and, most dramatically, contributed significantly to a redefinition of the industry.

Case Study Questions

1. How has IKEA succeeded in expanding across the world using a standard range of products and a standard strategy in the home furniture and furnishings industry, in which divergent cultural influences are likely to be at their strongest?
2. Is there a limit to this expansion? Does IKEA's history illustrate the nature of such a limit?
3. How has IKEA managed to creatively combine the benefits of mass consumption and mass production with the desire for style and modernity of product?
4. Has IKEA chosen a strategy of cost/price leadership or one of product differentiation?
5. How far do you think that IKEA can look into the future in framing its strategic management?

Reading

Beamish, P. W. and Killing, P. 'IKEA (Canada) Ltd', in Grigsby, D. W. and Stah, M. J. *Cases in Strategic Management*, Blackwell Business, Cambridge, MA: 1997: 239–48.

Flynn, J. and Bongiorno, L. 'IKEA's new game plan', *Business Week*, October 6, 1997: 45–7.

Economist, The 'Furnishing the world', November 19, 1994: 83–4.

Hill, C. W. 'Management Focus on IKEA', in Hill, C.W. *International Business: competing in the global marketplace*, McGraw Hill, Boston, MA: 2003: 424–5.

Hitt, M. A., Ireland, R. D. and Hoskisson, R. E. *Strategic Management: Competitiveness and Globalization*, South-Western, Cincinnati, 2001.

Czinkota, Rivoli, P. and Ronkainen, I. A., *International Business*, Dryden Press, New York: 2000.

Johnson, G. and Scholes, K. 'IKEA case study', in *Exploring Corporate Strategy: text and cases*, Prentice Hall, London: 1997: 6–7.

Margonellli, l. 'How Ikea designs it sexy price tags', *Business 2.0*, October 2002: 106–12.

Normean, R. and Ramirez, R. 'From value chain to value constellation: designing interactive strategy' *Harvard Business Review*, 71(4) July–August 1993: 65–77.

Relevant website

www.ikea.com

This case study is also relevant to Chapters 9, 10 and 13.

Key strategic lessons

• There is a significant distinction between three types of strategic activity – strategic thinking, strategic management and strategic planning – which are employed according to the degree of competition, the age of the organization and the speed of turnover of competitive advantage.

• Strategic thinking uses the power of creative imagination to generate innovative ideas which enhance the ability to create and maintain competitive advantage. It can be focused on one new idea or combine a number of different concepts and is often expressed in the vision or mission statement of the organization.

• Strategic management applies known methods in a range of functional areas to the realization of these innovative ideas. It involves codification,

setting specific objectives and targets; elaboration, clarifying the implications of the objectives; and conversion, the implementation by strategic action.

• Strategic planning formally develops detailed plans, which are comprehensive horizontally, covering all specialized functional units, and vertically, covering all levels in the hierarchy of an organization.

• Strategic thinking is always desirable; strategic management is employed to a varying degree; and strategic planning is only rarely possible.

• Entrepreneurship is linked to strategy, in particular to strategic thinking. Entrepreneurial activity differs from management activity since it involves innovation rather than imitation.

Applying the lessons

1 Give definitions of the following terms: strategic thinking, strategic management, strategic planning, entrepreneurship, intrapreneurship, vision, mission statement, strategic intent, strategic activities or action, strategic orientation and strategic domain.

2 Give ten examples of implicit strategic thinking which have radically reshaped the world of business in the recent past. Divide the examples into those which involve the application of a single idea and those in which the creative originality results from the combination of several ideas put together in a complex pattern.

3 Take any example of strategic thinking discussed in this chapter. How far does it share Liedtka's attributes of strategic thinking?

4 Answer the following question on planning. What do you understand by the term planning? What are the problems associated with planning of any kind? What are the usual arguments put in favour and those put against the use of planning?

How and why does a large multinational organization find itself unable to avoid planning? In what sense does it plan? What implications does the growing internalization of transactions within a large organization have for planning?

5 Answer the following questions:
   i What should be the relationship between a business plan or business model and a strategic plan?
   ii Why does the former exist in much larger numbers than the latter?

6 Classify the following industries, breaking the industry into parts if necessary, in the three ways described in the chapter and then evaluate their suitability for the exercise of strategic planning on the basis of these classifications.

	Degree of competition	Stage in life cycle	Market cycle
1 Pharmaceuticals			
2 Electricity generation			
3 Sports footwear			
4 Watches			
5 Wineries			
6 Airlines			
7 Automobiles			
8 Aircraft manufacture			
9 Electronic equipment			
10 Furniture retail			

Strategic project

1 Consider an organization which you know well. The scope for individual decision making has implications for strategy making. How might this organization empower its staff members within their individual strategic domains?

2 What meaning does the notion of the domain of an individual staff member have in the context of the formulation and implementation of a strategy? What role might staff at different levels of the organization play in that strategy making? What might empowerment mean for the making of a strategy?

3 How far might such empowerment encourage the ability to innovate? What might it mean for the promotion of intrapreneurship?

Exploring further

There are an enormous number of works relevant to the creative process and therefore to strategic thinking in general, many relevant to areas much broader than business. The classic work on creativity in general, although one which puts a particular point of view very persuasively, is Koestler, 1989. Also relevant to a wide range of different activities is Loehle, 1996. The best-known writer on creativity in the area of management studies is Edward de Bono who has been extremely prolific. His most helpful works are de Bono, 1970, 1971, 1992 and 1999.

Two articles which establish the link between strategic thinking and strategy are Liedtka, 1998a: 30–5 and 1998b: 120–9. One of the virtues of the work of de Bono is that he answers Liedtka's question in the affirmative and tries to show how it should be done.

The military parallel with business studies is extremely popular. In studies on business strategy there is much reference to and quotation from the work of Sun-Tzu, 1971, and to von Clausewitz, 1984.

The various kinds of planning have been much debated. Still the best on Soviet centralized planning is Ellman, 1989. Very interesting on the transitional state in reform from a planned economy to a market economy is Nolan, 1995. On guidance planning the most balanced treatment is World Bank, 1993.

The best source on different speeds of market cycle is Williams, 1992: 29–51, 1999a or 1999b. To balance the views of one person it is useful to read Bower and Hout, 1988: 110–18.

The classic theorist of entrepreneurship and creator of the term 'creative destruction' is Schumpeter, 1934 and 1950. A much more recent work which looks within the enterprise at the continuing sources of innovation is Pinchot, 1985. A comprehensive treatment of a subject which is rarely dealt with very well is Legge and Hindle, 1997.

3 Adopting a global perspective

Globalization 'is not a single, unified phenomenon, but a syndrome of processes and activities.' (MITTELMAN, 2000: 4)

Rather than being a world within our control it seems to be an erratic, dislocated world. If you like a runaway world. (GIDDENS, 1999: 2)

The dilemma that we face as we enter the 21st century is that markets are striving to become global while the institutions needed to support them remain by and large national. (RODRIK, 2001: 19)

Learning objectives

After reading this chapter you will be able to:

- understand the term 'globalization'
- recognize the degree to which the world is not global and has continued to have a home country bias
- recognize the degree of uniformity attained in the world
- distinguish the main players in the global economy
- understand the ways in which globalization influences strategy making

Key strategic challenge

How will 'going global' change the strategy of my enterprise?

Strategic dangers

That the process of globalization offers opportunities and poses threats that are ignored at the cost of the future viability and profitability of the enterprise; that failing to go global causes a loss of competitive advantage which may threaten the very existence of the enterprise.

Case Study Scenario   The airlines and the integration of global markets

'Air transport has always been a global industry, but one served by national firms. Some airlines now want to become global firms, but to do so they may in the end have to lose their nationalities.'   *Hanlon, 1999: 2*

Since most airlines are involved in moving people and freight internationally, they are a critical part of globalization. There are forces encouraging increased globalization in the airline industry:

- *The deregulation of the airline industry by governments, involving:*
  - the replacement of bilateral agreements by regional or multilateral agreements on traffic rights, even by 'open skies' agreements
  - privatization of state airlines
  - relaxation of foreign ownership rules
  - privatization of airports
  - free entry of airlines into any country or any route
  - free entry of airlines into any airport through open access to gates and the associated terminus
  - self-regulation of safety
  - removal of government subsidies and intervention in the industry

- *The use of new technology, mainly communications technology for air traffic control and booking systems*

- *Increased competition*

- *Increased demand for international air travel*

There are constraints:

- *Vulnerability to external shocks, including recession, accidents, terrorist attacks and hijackings*
  These shocks reduce the number of travellers and raise costs by pushing up insurance rates, creating a need for increased security measures and disrupting normal travel.

- *A tendency to reregulate*
  Any event which reduces profit and pushes the airlines into loss making encourages increased government intervention. Governments intervene to save national airlines, such as Swissair or Air New Zealand. Nearly all American airlines have been heavily subsidized since September 11, 2001. The existence of subsidies corrupts competition by allowing subsidized lines to reduce prices on competitive routes, forcing others to imitate. Different bankruptcy arrangements may favour certain countries, such as the Chapter 11 mechanism in the USA, which allows

an airline to continue trading even if insolvent and reduce costs in a summary fashion, for example by tearing up employment agreements.

- *A tendency to oligopoly*

- *Persistent home country bias*
  All airlines remain tied to their countries of origin, for which many are flag carriers. Government policy still determines who flies what routes. The airlines have been heavily regulated in the interests of retaining domestic markets for domestic airlines and of international routes radiating from the relevant country for national flag carriers. The main mechanism is the control of traffic rights negotiated by bilateral air service agreements, usually encapsulating a reciprocal granting of rights by two governments. Countries with considerable traffic and large airlines are in a stronger position in such negotiations. There have also been severe restrictions on foreign ownership. Governments and customers prefer their own, especially at a time of crisis. A pronounced increase in home country bias results from crises such as terrorist attacks or hijackings.

  Government policy now favours a competition policy which outlaws discrimination in favour of domestic lines. There has been an attempt to deregulate the industry and open it to competition. The transition is occurring at different rates in different countries, more slowly in Europe, but fastest in the USA. The American market is largely deregulated, although foreigners are restricted by the limitation on foreign ownership and voting rights to 25% and travel on foreign airlines by public officials. Some large players, such as Pan Am or TWA, have disappeared.

Increased competition with surplus airline capacity leads to either:

- the absorption of some airlines by others, constrained by ownership restrictions (49% in the EU) and the persistence of bilateral agreements, since specific traffic rights are vulnerable if an airline is taken over by a foreign airline, or
- the substitution of worldwide networks for such consolidations. Airlines have used franchising, code sharing and bloc spacing together with worldwide alliances to gain the effects of increased concentration without actually concentrating.

There are two relevant features of the industry:

1. Between 1945 and 1960, the average annual rate of growth, in passenger kilometres, was 12%, but dropping thereafter to 9% a year. In the 1990s, the rate of growth slowed further, to between 5 and 7%, slower if the recession years are factored in.

The airline industry has an S-shaped demand curve – slow growth during infancy, fast growth during adolescence and slow growth again at maturity. Some countries, such as African countries, are still in slow-growth infancy. Others such as the East Asian and most European nations, are in the adolescent, rapid-growth stage. The United States is in the mature, slow-growth stage. The overall movement of the industry reflects a balance of countries at different stages.

2. The industry is low profit, the return on capital typically less than half the general average. Profitability is highly vulnerable to a downturn in the economy since the income elasticity of demand for airline services is high. The participants in the industry are increasingly vulnerable to serious loss making during recessions.

The industry is vulnerable to any shock. Accidents can destroy the reputation for safety of individual airlines. A major terrorist attack involving hijacking and a threat to lives, or a major outbreak of disease, can destroy general confidence. In 1991, as a consequence of the combined effect of recession and the threat of hijacking arising from the Gulf War, passenger traffic dropped by 3%.

On September 11, 2001 four planes were hijacked and flown into prominent targets in the USA. This shock hit an industry already in recession, causing a jolt to confidence which reduced the number of passengers dramatically and raised costs significantly. Some routes were more badly affected than others, such as transatlantic routes and routes within the USA. In most markets passenger numbers fell by at least a quarter. While there was a steady recovery from the bottom, in the middle of 2002 demand again declined. The ability of airlines to ride the shocks differs greatly, as the experiences of Swissair and Qantas, discussed in the case study at the end of the chapter, show.

There are two questions which define the subject matter of this chapter:

1. Why should an enterprise engage in global transactions, or, why should it have a strategy which deliberately moves it from the domestic to the international?
2. Do global transactions differ sufficiently from domestic transactions to require a different kind of strategy?

The meaning of globalization

Globalization can be simply defined as a process of movement towards a 'global world'. In this book there is no speculation about how long it will take to reach a global world, if it is ever reached. It is the process which is the focus of interest and whose nature needs to be explored.

The term globalization encapsulates for many the perceived uniqueness of the

Focus on Theory **A global world**	Characteristics of a global world:	
	A world government	No national boundaries
	World law and order	Multilateral economic institutions to oversee
	A common language	implementation of the business rules
	A common culture	Fully integrated markets
	A common currency	No barriers to trade and investment
	No transport or	
	communications costs	

present. The current world is a global world, the current era a global era. Every generation thinks that there is something exceptional about the nature of the world in which it lives and the particular environments it faces. The commentators from any generation like to choose a label which highlights the exceptional features of their world and describes that world. 'Global' is currently that label. Depending upon one's view of the world and the changes occurring in it, the term can be used as a compendium of either positive or negative features, or, alternatively and more realistically, a combination of both such qualities. This means that the reaction to the label, as to the process, is as much emotional as it is rational, and as much concerned with values as with knowledge. It is certainly not neutral.

Unfortunately, while it may not be all things to all people, the term 'global' is certainly many things to many people. Its exact meaning is unclear. Consequently it seldom fails to elicit an emotional response, both positive and negative. It brings together a variety of changes, experienced differently by every person, some attractive, some unpleasant. The term is therefore by its nature an ambiguous one, bringing to mind a myriad of different outcomes.

Focus on Theory
The benefits and losses from globalization

There are many outcomes imputed to globalization, both positive and negative. The following lists illustrate the point, but are not claimed as exhaustive. Others might wish to switch an item from the positive list to the negative or vice versa. What are advantages to one are disadvantages to another.

Benefits
- A positive stimulus given to technical change
- Gains from increased competition, in lower costs and raised productivity
- A more efficient allocation of world resources as the result of a reduction in home country bias
- Faster growth, creating more jobs
- A higher standard of living in most countries
- A reduction in poverty in some parts of the world
- A broader access to consumer products at lower prices
- Widespread dissemination of information and knowledge
- Undermining of traditional social hierarchies in many parts of the world
- 'Democratization' – both more choice and more informed choice, in a whole series of different areas

Losses
- A loss of sovereignty by the nation state
- More uneven income distribution in most countries
- Damage to the environment
- Erosion of health and safety standards
- Erosion of regional, national and local cultures
- Local unemployment
- More cultural imperialism
- Loss of independent decision making
- Increased power of large companies
- Increased power of international organizations

Different viewpoints on globalization

There are four different ways of viewing globalization as a process:

1. A significant expanding of mental horizons and viewpoints, stimulated by a stronger consciousness of the global world towards which globalization is taking everyone. It is possible to characterize the process as an increasing tendency for key actors to look beyond the nation state at the wider world. In this sense globalization is a *change of mental perspective*, one that could be seen either as deliberately chosen or imposed upon the relevant actors. Modern communications allow all, even compel them, to view instantaneously what is happening on the other side of the globe. In such a global world a single event such as the act of terrorism of September 11 has an immediate and powerful global impact.

2. A change of perspective, but one focused on the changing nature of individual behaviour. The changing viewpoints are translated into *changing behaviour*, including such activities as international travel, international trading or investment activity and employment abroad. Such behaviour changes its orientation, from the domestic to the global level.

3. Increasingly institutionalized patterns of global interaction, sometimes amounting to a *real integration* at the international level – whether political, economic or cultural – and sometimes simply an increased interaction between existing national units. The world becomes one space. By most accounts, the advent of a global world has changed the perspective of strategy making for all enterprises and organizations.

4. A new *discipline*, which dictates that in a global world you behave in a particular way in order to survive or remain competitive. Open economies have exposed domestic enterprises and organizations to the forces of global competition. In the words of Bryan and Rafferty (1999: 12):

   Globalization is about businesspeople having to consider international investment and international borrowing, whether they end up engaging in it or not. It is also about consumers having to consider imported products and satellite television whether they purchase them or not, about domestic wages being constrained by what companies may have to pay equivalent workers in other countries, whether they are migrant workers or not.

   The competition need not be actual, it is enough that it is potential. The potential threat of competition exerts the discipline; it is summarized in the use of the term hyper-competition, the notion than a much more intensive and heightened level of competition characterizes a global world. The disciplined have no choice but to behave in a certain way. This viewpoint can be summarized in the simple assertion that a global world is a much more competitive world.

For most commentators globalization is rather more than simply a change in mental perspective or an imposition of increased discipline, comprising at the very least a marked change in behaviour and institutional structures.

The five main elements of globalization

This following section selects five main elements which qualify as parts of any definition of globalization and discusses each of them in turn.

**1
The
integration
of world
markets and
the world
economy**

On one understanding, probably the most popular one, globalization is the integration of the world economy and its markets. Integration in this context means the creation of a genuinely global economy, one which is no longer tied to the nation state. It involves the appearance of global enterprises, global products and global markets which have no specific location. In this conception markets are no longer tied to a particular place or time, which become irrelevant.

How far down this road the world has gone is contentious. There is less integration than often claimed, although the tendency is for more rather than less. The market, which once played an important role in integrating national economies, is now actively integrating the global economy. The most significant movement has been made in the market for finance capital in which there is some evidence of a genuine integration.

Globalization, when it occurs, usually involves interaction between national units and not the full integration of those units, although there may be some element of the latter. The *supranational* is only one view of the globalization process. There is an alternative view that it is a process of increasing interaction between existing national units, with all their differing political, economic and cultural characteristics. Integration in the sense of increased interaction between different national units is what is usually meant when integration is discussed. A fully integrated world is better described as a supranational world in order to distinguish it from what is commonly meant by global in current commentary. The former does not really exist, because of the persistence of national boundaries and the differences associated with the existence of national units, whereas the latter clearly does. The interpretation based on integration exaggerates the extent to which full integration has been achieved and ignores the host of differences from one region to another, differences which are both substantial and persistent and which prevent a full integration, putting a break on the process of globalization understood in this way.

There are two kinds of globalization, what can be called supranationalization (literally beyond the national), something which may exist in the future and towards which the world may be headed, and internationalization which already has a long history. There is a need to identify clearly what it is that is different about an allegedly global world from what has gone before. Many of the elements which constitute globalization are not new; the present global world is not so different from previous worlds, nor is the process often referred to as globalization different from the process of internationalization. There are three possibilities:

1. Globalization is not new: it originated many centuries ago and will continue into the future
2. Globalization is a phenomenon specific to the present era, and no other
3. Globalization is new but will continue into an indefinite future.

There are arguments which could be put in favour of each of these three positions. The position argued here is closest to the first.

Mittelman (2000: 19) talks in terms of a period of *incipient globalization*, which began with the origins of civilization, 5,000 years ago; a period of *bridging globalization*, which stretched over the last four centuries when capitalism and the market took root; and finally *accelerated globalization* since the 1970s. In this chronology the term internationalization could be substituted for globalization. What is currently understood as globalization is then what Mittelman calls accelerated globalization. Many of the tendencies which are significant today were important in previous periods. The extension of commodity markets beyond political boundaries and the growth of international trade have happened over many centuries. International investment across international boundaries is not new. Both grew greatly during the nineteenth century. In this sense most global markets have become much more integrated, over a long period of time but with many temporary reversals.

The ratio of exports to GDP or foreign investment to total world investment are little higher today than before 1914. There is less migration today than before 1914. Global integration does not apply to labour markets although there is considerably more short-term international travel by businesspeople and tourists than in the past. One further simple statistic summarizes the situation; almost 90% of the American economy produces goods and services for the domestic market rather than for export markets, a situation which is typical of large economies. Smaller economies do trade more but not usually more than half their GDP. There is much empirical evidence of a marked reluctance to engage in international transactions, which is true of all areas of economic life.

The process of internationalization is reversible, as past history has shown. There have been many significant periods of reversal, the last as recently as the Great Depression in the 1930s, and there is no guarantee that this will not happen again. There was a significant reduction in the level of economic integration as a result of two world wars, when trade and investment ratios declined dramatically. The recovery was a result of:

- continuing technical and organizational change, catching up on an enormous backlog of innovations which had not been implemented in the period of reversal, and the resulting increased incomes
- relative political stability in the second half of the twentieth century, which made possible the removal of significant barriers to the free international movement of products and factors of production.

Recovery may carry the world well beyond the levels of internationalization achieved before 1914 – it has not yet done so. On the other hand, political instability could return and the pace of technical change slow, particularly when the full implications of the communications revolution have worked themselves out.

**2
The
accelerated
diffusion
of new
technology**

The communications revolution is said to have compressed time and place, so much so that space has completely replaced place; in cyberspace location has allegedly lost its meaning. At the level of simple communication the impact is both obvious and dramatic; the price of a three-minute telephone call from New York to London has fallen from $244.65 in 1930 to $31.58 in 1970 and to $3.32 in 1990. In the future the cost will approach zero.

There are two specific influences of the communications revolution, one relating to the nature of contemporary technical change and the other to the impact of technical change on the rate of diffusion of new technical knowledge. The first involves the impact of the new technologies at the core of the communications revolution in directly encouraging other global tendencies – integration of markets, loss of national sovereignty, homogenization of culture and democratization of key activities. This draws out one strong characteristic of globalization, that each of the elements is interconnected with and reinforces the others. The second comprises the role of the communications systems in accelerating the rate at which any new techniques are diffused throughout the world economy. Again the process is encouraged and accelerated by the extension and deregulation of the market.

Innovation in communications is not new; the telegraph previously had the same kind of effect. There has been a steady acceleration over the last 250 years in the speed at which information has moved. At the birth of Australia a message would take more than a year to make the round trip from Britain to the colony of New South Wales. The advent of the clipper reduced the time to less than a year. The telegraph reduced this dramatically to several days. The communications revolution is part of globalization seen as a continuing process of internationalization, even an acceleration in internationalization. The communications revolution has carried the acceleration to a higher level, so that communication is now virtually instantaneous. Improved technology has also enabled a simultaneous transfer of vast amounts of information.

The revolution has gone further by making possible the storage and processing of information on a massive scale. In doing this it has had an enormous impact on the rate of technical change, both by enabling the processing of large amounts of information and encouraging the widespread diffusion of technical knowledge, particularly that concerning new technology. It has allowed some inventions and innovations to occur, since they require an ability to process enormous amounts of information, such as in mapping the human and other genomes, called bioinformatics. The computer has eased one of the constraints inherent in bounded rationality, the limited ability of the human mind to process large amounts of information. It has done this by linking networks of researchers located across the world.

The revolution has vastly improved the accessibility of information. The mechanisms for the international diffusion of new information have been immensely strengthened. This has created an a priori case for the more rapid take-up of new ideas, provided information can be converted into knowledge that is recognized as relevant to the strategy making of an enterprise. Whether this potential becomes reality depends on the nature of the incentives to exploit the relevant information.

In the modern world, history is largely made by the interactions of the governments of nation states. During difficult times, such as war or economic depression, the interaction between these national strategies dominates all other interactions. This also applies when there are global shocks which have to be dealt with at an international level. The general environment in which all international business activity occurs is one in which the governments of countries pursue separate political, economic and military strategies, which are themselves continually being translated into specific policies of a great variety. The particular groupings of nation states which are relevant to any particular problem may change but the general interaction continues. Strategic alliances are not new, nor limited to the business world.

A subsidiary theme, one growing in significance recently, has been the interaction between large multinational enterprises and between those enterprises and governments. In peaceful and more stable times this subsidiary theme rises in importance. The interconnections created appear very brittle when bad times return. It was once argued that war was impossible when international business connections were strong. That was on the eve of World War I, possibly the most damaging war of all time. The argument is being repeated today.

Probably the most common definition of globalization refers to a reduction in the sovereignty of the nation state, both actual and potential. At the core of this reduction is the rise of a global economy, defined in its transnational sense. It involves the alleged reduction in the significance of location-specific factors in influencing business decisions, in particular the factors which are specific to national sovereignties and national territories. It also involves the disciplining or controlling of government policies in order to make them fit the requirements of a global polity or economy, in the currently fashionable terminology of the economist, to fit the requirements of an international competition policy. Thomas Friedman (1999) has referred to this as the 'golden straitjacket' because it simultaneously promotes an improvement in prosperity and limits significantly the scope of government policy.

National boundaries continue to create imperfections in global markets, some arising spontaneously as a result of such factors as the uneven distribution of natural resources, cultural differences, transport and communication frictions. Others are government-induced, either consciously or unconsciously, as governments pursue their own strategies and frame distinctive policies. In practice there has been little overall reduction in such imperfections.

In some areas of policy there has been a clear reduction. The dominant economic power has always had an interest in promoting free trade and the extension of integrated free markets. This usually means the removal of tariffs. Britain aimed to do this in the nineteenth century and the USA tries today; others, the followers, have a compensating interest in resisting such policies. This applies in particular to the commodity and capital markets. It applies both to tariffs and non-tariff barriers. Curiously labour markets have become more, rather than less, regulated. Immigration laws are strictly applied by governments, arguably with less effect as the number of illegal migrants snowballs.

Achieving common action at the international level is very difficult, whether the action relates to economic affairs or other areas. Multinational institutions are still weak, reflecting the interests of the most powerful nation states in their policies. They have supported the push to adopt certain rules of the game. The so-called 'Washington Consensus' is an example. The 'Washington Consensus' represents a set of policies imposed on states in economic crisis – fiscal rectitude, monetary restraint, an open economy, market deregulation and a diminished public sector. Competition policy is the clearest expression of this point of view. The present war against terrorism is another. However, persuading several hundred countries to move quickly in a common direction is impossible. The new Doha round of trade negotiations is likely to take anything up to a decade to complete.

The bilateral approach to international relations is still far more significant than the multilateral. A compromise is to adopt a regional approach, which has become increasingly popular, under the influence of the success of the European Union. In the step-by-step movement towards economic and political unification there is an imperative to harmonize a series of policies, notably commercial, fiscal and monetary policies, and to withdraw from certain types of government intervention in the economy, such as industry or income policies. Ultimately even defence and foreign policy are harmonized but this is a long way down the track in most parts of the world.

Some areas of government policy are very slow to see significant harmonization, including environmental and health and safety rules. Local planning and control of crime are other areas of difference. More important, from an economic perspective, are policies on education, health and social services, including superannuation. There is still an enormous area of discretion for government policy. A genuinely transnational world would be one in which policy differences disappear in preparation for the dissolution of nation states and their governments and their replacement by a world government.

The number of nation states has risen inexorably, although many of the newer ones are small. The dissolution of multinational states, particularly within Europe, such as the USSR and Yugoslavia, has been the main story of the twentieth century. All the colonial European empires have now disappeared, although many of their multinational creations survive, some showing distinct signs of wear and tear, such as Indonesia, but most surprisingly resilient, such as India or Brazil. In many cases, the political boundaries created have been resistant to change, maybe a lasting legacy of the effectiveness with which the colonial empires broke up the existing political structures.

The resilience of the nation state is displayed in the significance of country risk (see Chapter 14). Governments remain as important economic actors, often actively encouraging the process of globalization, but also, through the linked existence of multiple currencies and multiple sovereignties, creating country risk. Country risk stands in the way of an increased interaction between nation states, but such an increased interaction does not necessarily subvert those states.

4 The homogenization of culture

Some believe that the important divisions in the world today relate to culture, not to ideology or nationality as defined by political boundaries (Huntingdon, 1996). Some cultural links extend beyond the nation state, for example the use of a common language in the English- or Spanish-speaking worlds or the sharing of a religion such as Islam or Christianity. Commonalities of language and religion have a particular strength and create loyalties which are supranational. Commonly the world is divided into at least ten main cultural clusters, with some areas of distinct independence.

Focus on Theory
Cultural clusters
in the world

The Anglo	Outliers
Latin American	Brazil
Germanic	Israel
Nordic	Japan
Latin European	India
Near Eastern	
The Arab	
Far Eastern	

Source: Ronen and Shenkar, 1985.

This particular division is based on divergences in attitudes, values and behavioural patterns. The classification is controversial. Huntingdon has placed more emphasis on religious difference, reducing the clusters to seven by making a single division of Europe between the West and East, the dividing line being the boundary between Catholic Europe and Orthodox Europe, and by adding another cluster, sub-Saharan Africa. It is also possible to add Polynesia.

There may also be subcultures within national cultures, some regional, some socioeconomic and some belonging to those who reject the prevailing culture, such as criminal fraternities. Often significant minorities live within a dominant culture and have loyalties beyond that culture, such as the Parsi community in India, Jewish communities in the USA and Australia, parts of the Chinese and Indian diaspora throughout the world.

The norm is for culture to reinforce national difference. There is a continuing interchange between political, social and economic systems within particular countries which reinforces difference. Patterns of behaviour, even economic or business behaviour, have roots which are deeper and broader than the narrowly economic. They have persisted over long period of time.

One element in the supranationalism of globalization is the 'alleged' breakdown of these cultural divisions, the sharing of a common culture which transcends all boundaries, both political and cultural. The communications revolution has assisted in promoting this, through the medium of radio, gramophone and their more sophisticated antecedents, television and film. As a counterweight to cultural difference there is without doubt in certain areas a growing homogeneity of culture, resisted bitterly in some cases but one which imposes itself on all groups, often unconsciously. Increasingly, for example, the world plays the same sports.

However, homogenization affects most strongly the young. English is rapidly becoming the only international language of business, its spread aided by its use in the media. English is simultaneously the language of international business and international popular culture. Consequently English is almost everyone's preferred second language and is taught as such throughout the world from an early age.

British economic dominance until 1914, followed by American dominance up to the present, first established the dominance of English. Through the medium of fast food, film and popular music, American culture is sweeping the world. The way the world eats, the way the world sings, the way the world entertains itself has largely been determined by American pioneers. Interestingly the way it plays has stronger roots in Britain. There is also a growing but still limited number of internationally branded commodities, mainly American such as McDonald's, Coca-Cola, Nike and Disney. It is hard to resist the encroachment of these products. They are very visible manifestations of a tendency to homogeneity, but not necessarily of the dominance of one culture. Perhaps the market is becoming more standardized but this remains to be proved.

**5
The democrat-ization of key activities**

Paradoxically, some have argued that another aspect of globalization is the increased scope for individuals to be involved in the process of decision making at all levels. Put more broadly it refers to a greater scope for choice. There is, it is true, a massive potentiality for decentralized decision making which goes largely unrecognized. The cult of choice and the identification of choice with freedom encourage this emphasis. There has been a steady increase in the ability of individuals, or individual house-holds, to make informed decisions and exercise choice in a growing number of differ-ent areas. This has several aspects – ease and low cost of access to information, and an increasing capacity to exercise a decision-making capacity. Such choice applies both to consumption and economic activity, and to more basic life choices.

This extended choice is partly a result of higher incomes. It is also a result of changing technology, particularly increased flexibility in energy sources and trans-port. The innovations of electricity and the motorcar were critical in making possible an early decentralization of decision making. The individual can in theory choose to work where he or she wishes, at home or abroad, provided of course he or she has saleable skills. The Internet also opens choice as a global phenomenon; for the indiv-idual it gives an unrivalled access to information and entertainment, commodities and capital in a way never previously experienced. In 1990 only one million people were connected, by 1995 50 million and by 2001 490 million. Individual households therefore have easy access to cheap energy, cheap transport, and now cheap capital and cheap information.

Choice increasingly extends to all, to women as well as men, to those living in undeveloped economies as well as developed. Already the emancipation of women and the availability of items of consumption competing for discretionary income have led to a fall in fertility rates, as women have exercised their option to reduce the number of children in a family and promote their own careers at the same time as they enjoy the fruits of increased consumption.

Perhaps this democratization still remains only a possibility for most, an actuality for few. The problem is that not all individuals are capable of exercising this choice, since they lack the means. There are also those who make the wrong choice and finish as losers in the market game.

The global tendencies described above bring to individuals, enterprises and countries both benefits and losses. Some see globalization as an opportunity, others as a threat, depending on the exact perspective adopted and the exact position in the global world of the individuals concerned. There may well be a conflict between two power-ful tendencies, the one constraining the scope for choice by the individual, the other expanding that range of choice:

- For neoliberals, the term globalization involves *the empowerment of the individual*, as indicated below. Clearly globalization is seen by many as reflecting the growing dominance of global markets and the corresponding decline of state power; it is beloved by neoliberals who advocate the further extension of market power.
- For others, the reverse is true and globalization is associated with *the increasing helplessness of the individual* before the increasing power of global institutions, notably the multinational enterprises, which fill the global void in the absence of genuine transnational institutions, and the multilateral financial institutions. Worse, it places more power and more wealth in the hands of the few.

Globalization is clearly not a concept free of preconceptions about the desired nature of the world, and arguments about where the world is actually headed. The term is inevitably and unavoidably value-laden. The balance of opportunity and threat and the formation of interests groups for and against globalization on the basis of the outcomes of the process ensure that governments will continue to retain a considerable discretion in decision making and make policy which has a significant effect on business decisions. The impact of globalization on the mix of decision making by governments, enterprises and individuals is unclear and therefore controversial. What is clear is that the nation state remains the most powerful decision maker in the world, as the case studies in this chapter clearly show. The business world has some features of a global world, but they are limited.

Home country bias

From a business perspective, the most persuasive argument for the continuing importance of international borders, and the need to take proper account of them in making strategy, is the continuation of a significant and universal home country bias. There is a general aversion on the part of most decision makers to economic transactions which cross international boundaries. Consumers consume the products of their own domestic producers; managers and workers prefer to work in their own countries; investors build plant and equipment at home rather than abroad; and savers prefer to hold the financial assets of their own countries. Government policy often validates and reinforces these preferences.

Home country bias is a general tendency at the international level, illustrated by the analysis of the airline industry in the case study. Bryan and Rafferty (1999: 3–33) point out that in the mid-1990s OECD production devoted to exports made up less than 10% of total production; foreign direct investment made up only 5% of world investment (20% if all sources of investment finance used to finance multinational enterprises, including domestic sources, are considered); multinational enterprises contributed just 6% of world production; around 2.3% of the world population had 'migrated'; and another 1.5% of the world's workforce worked outside their country of citizenship. None of this speaks of a high level of globalization, and it says nothing about the direction or the rate of change, or the movement of these key magnitudes. The position varies somewhat from country to country but not by very much. Smaller countries are forced to be more international.

The bias is most dramatically manifested with respect to equity investment, despite the alleged integration of world financial markets. In theory capital can be moved without any transport cost. However, savings pools are still separated by national frontiers. Savings do not flow freely to where there is investment demand and the return is highest, or at least higher than in the domestic economy. Perhaps the most powerful argument for this is the strong relationship between the level of national savings and that of national investment in each economy throughout the world. This suggests, but does not prove conclusively, that domestic investment is almost invariably financed by domestic savings. Furthermore, when there is an increase in savings, it tends to raise domestic investment directly. There are therefore pronounced constraints on the integration of international capital markets. Finance and asset markets have retained a distinctly national flavour, despite the tendency to focus on so-called international markets.

This is easily illustrated. Americans hold only 8% of their financial portfolios in foreign equities, despite the fact that such foreign equities – for this purpose equities which are not American – represent well over half the world's total equities. It is not only America and large economies which are characterized by this home country bias. Small countries share the bias. Australian citizens own 2% of the world's corporate shares. In a world of perfectly mobile capital, two things should follow. The 2% would be evenly spread across the world and foreigners would own 98% of Australian shares. Neither is true. Australian shareholding is heavily concentrated on certain economies with which Australia has a close connection. Foreigners own only 31% of Australian shares.

The reasons for a home country bias

'Irrational' preferences for one's own affect most business decisions, whether they take the form of the decision where to work and live, where to place one's savings or from whom to purchase both goods and services. But are these preferences so irrational?

In the past the costs of international participation were high and a major deterrent to international business activity, whatever the form of transaction considered. These included transport and communication costs, and even more the costs of dealing with the inhabitants of a foreign country. These costs are very much lower today and much less of a barrier to entry.

Often the argument put today rests on the volatility of exchange rates in a world of floating rates, as opposed to the stability of a world of fixed exchange rates. This is said to discourage foreign investment because nobody can be certain of what will be the return in the domestic currency. Moreover, hedging can only cover some of the transfer risk, rather more in trading than in investment. Such investment is typically over the long term, rather than the short term covered by hedging.

Ignorance is still a significant factor. It is expensive both to gain and process the required information in order to dissipate this ignorance, and there exist major constraints on the capacity to process such information. Everyone still knows much more about their own world than that of the other. This is called asymmetrical information, and applies to political, economic and social systems.

Home country bias also reflects the overwhelming importance of separate political sovereignties. Within these sovereignties, policies affecting business can change in unexpected ways. Foreign governments are difficult to read right. They can unexpectedly change their membership and their strategies. They are answerable to a different constituency which it is difficult to identify and understand. A sense of lost control is implicit in *political risk* unless the country concerned has political, economic, cultural and social systems similar to those of the country of origin. Otherwise there is a pronounced nervousness about international business connections which is fully justified, for example if the legal system does not protect intellectual property rights or foreign governments favour their own, as is often the case.

Cultural difference itself presents a serious barrier, particularly where there is a need to cooperate, even negotiate, with foreign partners. The risk of something going wrong increases across international boundaries. Thus the bias often has cultural roots, reflecting the socialization of individuals into particular cultures.

Globalization is seen by many as both undermining political sovereignties and moderating cultural difference. It has not yet done so to any significant extent. Much of the apparent change is superficial. It is possible for different cultures to absorb and adapt foreign entrants without changing the basic culture, and in a way which misleads outside observers.

The concept of country risk embraces those factors which deter foreign involvement and encourage a home country bias. From a business perspective, a global strategy requires a change of approach, the deliberate overcoming of home country bias. This applies both to the initial decision makers and those who have to implement the decisions.

The removal of the bias

There are two possible mechanisms for the removal of the bias:

1. The voluntary ceding of sovereignty to international institutions which fix the rules of the game in a way which is easily understood by all. There is some movement in the direction of a uniform set of informal rules but it is unlikely that the formal rules will change dramatically in this way. At present the rules of the game differ from country to country and from culture to culture.
2. The development of multinational enterprises which have outgrown their country origins. The multinational enterprise can be the agent of globalization. However, most enterprises, and indeed most individual managers, remain with roots firmly planted in particular national soils. It is difficult to sever completely these roots (see the point made in the Strategy in Action on Nestlé in Chapter 15). The breaking of the home country bond would create what are genuinely global, or transnational, enterprises. Such enterprises do not currently exist.

The global environment in which enterprises operate is a complex one. It is impossible to ignore the intermeshing of the political and the economic. Most recent history has tended to confirm that the political dominates the economic. Governments set their own objectives and to achieve them frequently intervene in markets and work upon local prejudices. Sudden shocks or risk-creating events can have the effect of reinforcing such a home country bias or suddenly undoing, or threatening to undo, any movement in the opposite direction (see the case study on the airlines, particularly the section on Swissair at the end of the chapter).

This book makes a clear distinction between a global world and a transnational world:

- A global world involves a significantly heightened level of transactions between national units. These transactions are of various kinds but may also comprise some genuinely transnational elements, which are growing in importance. The growth of such transactions is not inconsistent with a strong and persisting home country bias.
- A transnational world involves forms of organization and strategy that have no national focus. This would mean the ending of home country bias.

A convergent world

Convergence can occur in any area of human activity – in political or economic systems or in culture. In *The End of History* (1992), Francis Fukuyama saw a convergence of the world on a common political and economic system, one centred on representative democracy and the market. The world can converge or become homogeneous in two principal ways, by a process of individual or even group choice or one which is in some sense 'forced'.

The citizens of the world can choose to become more like each other by adopting common patterns of behaviour, whether these are political, economic or simply social. They can engage in consumption of goods and services which are genuinely global, available everywhere and consumed in the same form everywhere. This tendency might result from exposure at an early age to common influences or stimuli, such as the global media and a dominant culture, often seen as the American one. The communications revolution has reputedly democratized choice by giving everyone the same information and exposing them to the same influences. As a result, the world could adopt a common culture which removes differences of taste, even attitudes, values and behavioural patterns. If this were to happen, there would be just one market for consumer goods and one market for managers or workers.

This is inevitably a gradual process, likely to take a long period of time. There is also at present considerable resistance to such voluntary homogenization, particularly on the basis of a dominant culture. The evidence of existing markets is that there is a tendency for increased differentiation of product and service. Cultural difference persists, which is why there are so few genuinely global brands and so few standard products at the global level.

Alternatively the world might be forced to become homogeneous by the operation of political or market forces. There may be a ruthless process of weeding out what is different. In the economic sphere cost differences and the actions of large multinational enterprises could be the instrument for doing this. How far is the market likely to play such role?

A homogeneous world is an integrated world, and one in which national units have ceased to have importance. If the world is not integrated, it is extremely unlikely that it will become homogeneous. It has been argued already that world markets are not as integrated as often thought. An integrated world is a notional world in which the integration of markets produces a set of predictable outcomes. The existence of these outcomes would indicate that integration was really occurring. There are severe limitations on how far this process has gone.

The first outcome is what economists call 'factor price equalization', in particular a world in which interest rates or the rates of return on investment are equalized everywhere – there is one uniform price for capital. There is some tendency for this to happen in short-term financial flows as a result of the normal process of arbitrage, or the operation of what is known as the law of one price. There is evidence that covered interest rate parity, an expression of the law of one price for the price of capital, holds in certain restricted financial markets. There is no evidence that rates of return have been equalized throughout the world for major long-term investments. There is a very good reason for this – the differing risk premiums required from investment in different countries. Some of the differences are very marked; they also fluctuate significantly over time

The second outcome would be for an international convergence of national business cycles. This is a highly dubious proposition which has been asserted as true since the Industrial Revolution. Only in extreme circumstances does the whole world economy move together. On the contrary, it is unusual for the three main centres of the world economy to be at the same stage of the cycle, except in exceptional circumstances. This is fortunate for the relative stability of the world economy.

The third outcome is for certain structural changes to occur in economies on the basis of specialization at the global level. This reflects the particular circumstances of the specific economies. For example, a high wage economy with small markets might find it very difficult to compete in selling labour-intensive manufactured goods. Creating more integrated and open markets might push such an economy in the direction of a reduced manufacturing share, but this might happen in any event, since it is part of the transformation which occurs with a rise in income levels and the associated rise in wage costs. Disentangling those structural changes which are part of the process of market integration and those which result from rising GDP is difficult.

The world may be moving in the direction of integration and homogeneity but it is a long way from this ultimate destination, and there are powerful forces slowing the movement. The dramatic reduction in costs of and acceleration in transport and communications have shrunk the world, creating new opportunities but also generating new threats. It is impossible and undesirable to isolate a country, let alone an enterprise, from global markets. There will be more interaction. The multinational enterprise will be at the vanguard of this movement but it has to make the movement with the greatest care.

Global players

There are three main ways of 'playing' globally:

- multilateral relations through global organizations
- regional relations within such units as the European Union
- bilateral relations, which can comprise both direct country to country interactions and interactions between governments and multinational enterprises, including interactions among the latter.

Multilateral organizations

The main candidates are the World Trade Organization, the World Bank and the International Monetary Fund. Given the emphasis on globalism, it is perhaps surprising to note the continuing weakness of all multilateral institutions, including the ones above, but not all surprising in view of the continuing strength of the nation state. Multilateral institutions which straddle different regions can take many different forms.

Focus on Practice
Multilateral organizations

- The UN and its agencies
    - United Nations Conference on Trade and Development
- World Bank and its agencies
    - International Development Association
    - International Finance Corporation
    - Multilateral Investment Guarantee Agency
    - The International Centre for Settlement of Investment Disputes
- World Trade Organization (WTO)
- International Monetary Fund (IMF)
- Bank of International Settlements (BIS)

- Greenpeace
- Red Cross
- Amnesty
- Oxfam

Some multilateral institutions, which were important in the past and aspired to a reach beyond the nation state, have lost their influence, such as the various churches. Some weak echo of past influence survives as a cultural legacy, that is all. Islam has more influence than Catholicism and does still influence particular nation states, including their political and legal systems, such as Iran or previously Afghanistan. However, most countries with a Muslim majority are still secular states. Moreover, there are as many differences of doctrine and attitude within the Muslim world as there are in the Christian.

Recently, there have been no real secular replacements for the churches which had a sustained existence for many centuries. Communism, which had universalist pretensions, never realized its potential, certainly not in the operation of important international institutions. Communism has been in retreat for more than 20 years, and the communist experiment appears to have failed, both politically and economically. Only a few communist states survive ideologically, and in most their economic systems are tending towards market economies.

There are a few non-governmental organizations (NGOs) which operate internationally and are powerful enough to have an influence on key decision making, such as Greenpeace or Oxfam.

The lack of multilateral institutions translates into a series of particular absences:

- no world government, and therefore no real forum for resolving global problems; witness the series of ad hoc meetings on carbon emissions. With so many nation states in the world these are difficult to organize
- no such thing as international law in any enforceable sense
- no international currency, and no central bank serving as lender of last resort for the world as a whole.

The increasing number of problems which extend beyond the jurisdiction of the nation state can only be resolved by ad hoc action, organized by groups of nation states. The multilateral organizations simply act as facilitators of international interactions and agreements.

Into the political vacuum at the global level step the most powerful of the nation states. Occasionally in the modern history of the world one state has had imperial pretensions and has sought to impose its will through military strength. In other words, it has sought to substitute for the weak multilateral institutions at the global level. These attempts have failed. In peaceful times such a state has been able to help impose solutions to global problems. The forced alliance of others invariably defeats attempts to realize ambitious military pretensions. In practice a powerful state can only use its influence to persuade others to support its policies. A failure to win such support can lead to disaster. For example, the Great Depression of the 1930s had as its backdrop the willingness but inability of Britain to play its traditional role of leadership, and the ability but unwillingness of the USA to play such a role. After World War II the USA played such a role with a much greater degree of success (see Kindleberger, 1987), initially within one part of the world which was 'democratic' and market-based. The ending of the Cold War has left the USA with a clear military superiority, and an economic advantage which, despite recent events, is being steadily eroded. Nevertheless global problems can only be resolved with the support of the USA.

The main multilateral institutions, such as the UN and its linked organizations – the IMF, the World Bank, the BIS and the WTO – have limited powers and limited resources. In the past they have been a vehicle for the transmission of American policy, although this is less true today than it used to be. As a result institutions have also become a focus for opposition to those global tendencies which are disliked and a focus for anti-Americanism.

Regional organizations

In every part of the world there has been an immense amount of activity of a regional kind because it is difficult for a large number of nation states to reach a consensus on any issue. Some of the tendency to regionalism results from informal alliances, some from more formal organization.

Focus on Practice

Regional organizations

- Regional Development Banks
    - African Development Bank
    - Asian Development Bank
    - Inter-American Development Bank
    - European Bank for Reconstruction and Development

- The European Union (EU) and its agencies
    - Council of the European Union
    - European Central Bank
    - European Commission
    - European Court of Justice
    - European Parliament

- Free Trade Areas
    - Andean Community
    - Association of South-East Asian Nations (ASEAN)
    - Australian and New Zealand Closer Economic Relations Trade Agreement (ANZCER)
    - Caribbean Community (CARICOM)
    - Central American Common Market (CACM)
    - Economic Community of Central African States (ECCAS)
    - Economic Community of West African States (ECOWAS)
    - European Free Trade Association (EFTA)
    - Gulf Cooperation Council (GCC)
    - Mercosur
    - North American Free Trade Agreement (NAFTA)
    - Southern African Development Community (SADC)

- Others
    - Asia-Pacific Economic Cooperation (APEC)
    - North Atlantic Treaty Organization (NATO)
    - Organization of Petroleum Exporting Countries (OPEC)

There are also broad umbrella organizations which allow Muslim countries or countries from the Americas or Africa to meet. These tend to be talking shops without any practical effect on global decision making. A clear precondition for success in establishing any formal organization which has real decision-making power has been both a similar political system and a similar level of economic development. It also helps if the countries concerned share a common culture.

There is therefore a limited number of regional organizations which have had a real effect. The EU is the most successful case. The main catalyst for such regional activity has been the terrible consequences of the naked pursuit of national self-interest in two world wars. A major motive has been to stress cooperation rather than competition and to prevent such competition becoming military, as it has with catastrophic results in the recent past.

The progressive integration of Europe, both extensively in a wider membership and intensively in the harmonization of an increasing number of policy areas, has been one of the most important events of the last 40–50 years, beginning with the establishment of the European Coal and Steel Community (ECSC) in 1952 and the Treaty of Rome in 1957. This treaty created the European Economic Community in 1958 which merged with the European Coal and Steel Community and Euratom to form the European Union in 1967. It is a process which is continuing and intensifying, most recently in 2002 with the introduction of a common currency, the euro, in 2004, with 10 more, mainly East European, countries joining the present 15 EU members.

There is a pronounced tendency for increased intervention by European institutions into business activities. The European Commission for Transportation, for example, is intervening more frequently and more forcibly to restrict government action in rescuing bankrupt airlines or bankrupt telecommunication companies.

Some areas of regionalism elsewhere in the world have been a response to the success of the European experiment. This is true of NAFTA and also the recent attempts to create stronger Asian groupings, although these remain very weak, largely because they satisfy none of the prerequisites of successful integration indicated above. Most of these organizations have either never gained any momentum for working together or have lost their initial momentum.

One other highly influential regional organization is OPEC, whose unifying factor is the enormous reserves of oil located in the Middle East and Persian Gulf area (see the discussion in Chapter 4). The non-membership of major oil-producing countries outside these areas, such as Russia, Norway and Mexico, has weakened its influence.

Regionalism has two faces:

- A movement in the direction of an integrated global world with strong multilateral organizations.
- A mechanism of self-defence against such a movement, and therefore an obstacle to such movement. Regionalism is sometimes encouraged by the threat of protectionism as states place themselves in fall-back positions adopted in case the global situation deteriorates.

The regional players can either promote the development of integrated markets or they can stand in the way of such integration. Such regional groupings look, Janus-like, in two directions.

Bilateral organizations

Because of the importance of the nation state and its government, bilateral relations and bilateral organizations are still significant, but some more than others, notably those between members of the triad. The world is very uneven in its level of economic development. Most world production, investment and trade is concentrated on what has been called the triad, a tripolar structure of economic activity linking the main economic and political centres of the world – North America, Western and Central Europe (largely the EU) and Japan. These tripolar centres account for as much as 60–70% of world GDP, the exact level depending upon the nature of the measures used. Because of innovative activity, the degree of concentration of economic activity on the triad has increased. However, recently within the triad, there has been a tendency to a more even distribution of economic activity.

The triad does most of the world's trade, receives and dispatches most of its investment, constitutes the largest part of the world market and generates most of its tech-

Focus on Practice
The triad

There are 20–25 developed economies in the world, the number depending on the exact threshold level selected, comprising about 20% of the world's population. These countries are grouped in three main areas – North America (the USA and Canada), Western and Central Europe (the 15 EU countries plus Norway and Switzerland) and Eastern Asia (principally Japan but some smaller economies such as South Korea, Singapore, Taiwan and Hong Kong). In each region, for various reasons including size and location, there is a core economy which acts as its centre, respectively the USA, Germany and Japan.

nical progress. However, it represents a declining share of world population, a trend which has enormous significance for the future. This process of decline is offset to some degree by the fact that the triad is the main magnet for immigration.

A number of countries are in the process of developing, mostly a limited number of economies in South America, Eastern Europe and Eastern Asia – Chile, Poland and coastal China are the best examples. Some of these countries have a potentially large political influence because of their size, in both territorial area and population. China, India, Russia and Brazil stand out.

Most countries are still undeveloped. Whole areas of the world remain at extremely low levels of development with little sign of change, including most of Africa, Central America and broad areas of Asia. These countries have little influence over political decision making at the global level. Unless they have a valuable resource like oil they are ignored. This is the fate of most of Africa.

Indeed broad swathes of the world are not sharing in globalization, however it is defined. Most countries in the world are either too small in population or territory or too poor to have any influence on decision making in the global economy. The informal rules of the game, whether it is political or economic, are set by the powerful, for example in the General Agreement on Tariffs and Trade (GATT) and the seven successive rounds of trade negotiations, which were replaced in 1995 by the WTO.

Multinational enterprises and organizations

A growing number of business enterprises are international in the nature of their activity. Some enterprises, in the size of the gross income they generate, exceed the GDP of smaller countries. However, this is not an appropriate comparison since GDP is really a measure of value added and gross income is not. For example, Microsoft, at one time the largest company in the world in the US, at the end of the 1990s boom had a gross income which exceeded the GDP of the USA's main trading partner, Canada. In value added it is more like the size of Uruguay.

No multinational enterprise has the sovereign power of a nation state. They are subject to the jurisdiction of such states. However, because of their size and economic strength, some multinationals are capable of exerting more influence than many governments, although the source of their power is very different. They can negotiate in certain areas with many governments, sometimes as superiors or sometimes as equals.

In Table 3.1 the size of enterprises is judged by gross revenues but it could have been the value of assets or the number of employees.

The original multinational enterprises were American but now there are many European and Japanese multinationals, and even a few from developing countries (see Table 3.2).

Although the source country has declined in importance, most multinationals are still strongly rooted in particular national soils, and mostly in the countries of the triad.

Table 3.1 **The world's largest corporations (2001)**

		Revenues		Profits	
		$m%	change from 2000	$m%	change from 2000
Wal-Mart	US	219,512	13.7	6,671	6,0
Exxon Mobil	US	191,581	(8.9)	15,320	(13.5)
GM	US	177,260	(4.0)	601	(86.5)
BP	Britain	174,218	17.7	8,010	(32.5)
Ford	US	162,412	(10.1)	(5,453)	(257.3)
Enron	US	138,718	37.6	N.A.	
DaimlerChrysler	Germany	136,897	(8.8)	(592.8)	(108.1)
Royal Dutch Shell	Neth/Britain	132,211	(9.3)	10,852	(14.7)
GE	US	125,913	(3.0)	13,684	7.5
Toyota	Japan	120,814	(0.5)	4.925	15.5
Citigroup	US	112,022	0.2	14,126	4.5
Mitsubishi	Japan	105,813	(16.4)	481	(42.2)
Mitsui	Japan	101,205	(14.2)	442	(5.1)
Chevron Texaco	US	99,699	107.4	3.288	(36.0)
Total Finn Elf	France	94,311	(10.9)	6,857	7.5
Nippon Telegraph and Telephone	Japan	93,424	(9.5)	6.495	(254.8)
Itochu	Japan	91,176	(16.9)	241	(62.1)
Allianz	Germany	85,929	21.0	1,453	(54.5)
IBM	US	85,866	(92.9)	7,723	(4.6)
ING Group	Netherlands	82,999	16.6	4,098	(63.0)

Brackets indicate a contraction.
Source: Fortune, July 22 2002: F1–10.

Table 3.2 **Composition of the large multinationals by national origin (%)**

	1973	1990	1997	2000
USA	48.5	31.5	32.4	26
Japan	3.5	12	15.7	17
UK	18.8	16.8	6.6	8
France	7.3	10.4	9.8	13
Germany	8.1	8.9	12.7	12

The first column is a proportion of the largest 260 multinationals and the last three of the top 100.
Source: Hill, 2003: 20.

Focus on Practice
cont'd

They are still therefore very much associated with particular countries. The largest multinationals are also concentrated in certain industries – notably automobiles, oil, insurance, banking and the communications area. This partly reflects the importance of the sector and partly the degree of concentration in that sector.

There may be other kinds of players, equally as important as those already discussed. Sub- or micro-regions within countries, for example the state of California, and 'global' cities, such as Shanghai Municipality, can play important roles.

The impact of globalization on strategy

There is no a priori reason to think that, in a fully integrated and competitive world, the nature of strategic thinking at the global level would differ from that at the domestic level. In a global world national boundaries no longer have an economic significance, particularly since national governments cease to have discretionary policy-making power and transport and communication costs have been greatly reduced. In a world without national governments, zero transport costs and instantaneous communication, strategy is easily transferred from the domestic to the global level, with no change of substance, style or approach. Globalization simply requires an extension of the domestic perspective to the global venue; global becomes local.

Paradoxically the obstacle to such a simple transfer is the continuing existence of national governments and major obstacles to the integration of markets. A realistic approach in any definition of globalization 'is to view the world as a single unit while recognizing the uniqueness of each operating context' (Mische, 2001: 54). Globalization therefore involves increased interaction between different countries, different cultures and different political or economic systems.

The current situation requires emphasis on two possible perspectives in a global strategic approach:

1. To take a genuinely global or transnational approach. Viewing the world as a single unit, sometimes described as adopting the perspective of equidistance (Ohmae, 1991: Chapter 2), is better regarded as a transnational approach. It means viewing customers and markets on a geographically indiscriminate and culturally inclusive basis, 'in a manner that best leverages the organization's capabilities, optimizes its worldwide identity, and de-emphasizes geographical uniqueness and national identity or origin' (Mische, 2001: 54). Few enterprises have reached the stage at which this broad perspective dominates their strategy, although many may aspire to eventually achieve this. IKEA, which has sought to take a global approach to product tastes, ran into some difficulty, even in selling to developed economies.

2. To recognize the uniqueness of all operating contexts. Part of that uniqueness is the particularity of the nation state. A global orientation, as against a transnational orientation, requires the recognition of the existence of the many different nation states in the world and a growing level of interaction between them. Any

global transaction must involve activity which occurs outside the home country but which is located within the jurisdiction of one or more of these other states. Primarily for that reason the global environment is different from the domestic environment.

The second approach is the one most frequently adopted.

Globalization drivers

There are four main *globalization drivers*, that is, drivers which compel an enterprise to become global in at least one of our two senses:

1. the lure of interconnected or integrated markets, often called global markets
2. the prospect of and pressure for reduced costs, even within domestic markets
3. the persistence of some government policies favouring globalization, although these are not unchallenged
4. the forces making for increased competition.

Global opportunities and risks

A global orientation in strategy making requires recognition of the greater opportunity yielded by the drivers but also the higher associated risk.

The nature of opportunity at the global level differs from that at the domestic level. A global enterprise must have the capabilities which allow it to exploit such opportunity. This involves the ability to sell in different markets, source components and materials from different nations or regions and access knowledge available at the global level. It involves the recruitment of managers and workers capable of operating in an international environment. It is possible to develop these capabilities through megamergers or strategic alliances at the global level. A global enterprise must take account of the strategies of a different mix of players, particularly other global players, such as governments and competitors.

A global strategy would exploit all opportunities for revenue enhancement and cost reduction offered by a much larger market, whose component parts are all growing at different speeds. The markets open for entry are diverse. A so-called multidomestic strategy recognizes the differences in these markets. The opportunities for profit are difficult to exploit since they involve entering markets for which standardized products are often inappropriate. The relevant methods of production are themselves diverse and subject to adaptation in interesting ways in order to suit local conditions.

The nature of risk at the global level is different from that at the domestic level, largely because globalization has developed alongside the nation state and is promoted or hindered by the nation state. The return demanded differs according to the risk premium which is deemed appropriate to a particular country in which an investment is made. In some cases the risk premium is so high that no international transaction involving that country is possible.

Global enterprises tend to be larger than domestic enterprises, although it is not easy to see the reasons why this is necessarily the case. Many small and medium-sized enterprises engage in international business. In order to operate at the international level one alternative to getting bigger is to develop a network of independent enterprises through strategic alliances. Large multinational enterprises are much more likely both to produce a range of different products and operate in a range of different markets, and for these reasons to be much more difficult to organize. The intra-enterprise international connections must be planned more carefully than domestic connections. An international logistical system is likely to have a complexity which a purely domestic enterprise does not exhibit. The logistical networks within the enterprise make demands which do not exist at the domestic level, except perhaps in markets as large as the American or perhaps in the future, the European. There are very pronounced differences in corporate philosophy, ranging from the ethnocentric – focused strongly on the domestic scene, through the polycentric – which recognizes the existence of many domestic scenes, to the geocentric, where there is one scene, the global. Only the last is really suitable for a genuinely transnational enterprise.

Global enterprises contain within them a much greater diversity than domestic enterprises – of cultures, structures, personnel, markets and resources. They must devise a corporate culture which makes it possible for them to use all these resources while operating at the global level, but a culture which is at times likely to be in conflict with the culture of at least some of the countries in which the enterprise has a presence. This interaction between national and corporate culture is itself a distinguishing feature of global enterprises. It must be allowed for by those who make strategy.

All of this – the complexity, the opportunity, the conflict and the risk – requires a different kind of leadership, a global leadership. One of the core competencies of a global enterprise is the ability to manage diversity and develop strategies which embrace a global approach, what could be termed a genuinely multicountry and multicultural approach.

Case Study   Bad strategy and bad fortune – Swissair and Qantas

It is interesting to compare the recent experiences of Swissair and Qantas in the airline industry. Relevant to a comparison are the following points:

- Both Australia and Switzerland have a small population
- Both have flag carriers which aspire to be major world players, although probably not quite in the top tier, more at the top of the second tier
- Australia is large in territory relative to Switzerland and therefore offers a far larger domestic market. The share of revenues generated by the domestic sector is much larger for Qantas than for Swissair
- Qantas' location, far from the main centres of population, even in Asia, and from potential competitors in the world, has also influenced its route configuration and the degree of competition on those routes
- The two airlines have had a contrasting experience in the recent past.

Swissair is the national carrier of Switzerland, in key respects typical of national carriers in Europe. Many of the European countries, like Switzerland, are small. As a result the average flight haul of Swissair, while well over 1,000 kilometres, was by international standards short. The impact of any deregulatory transition is likely to be more far-reaching in Europe than in the USA and Australia, because numerous countries of the former are much smaller than even the larger American and Australian states. European airlines are smaller than American airlines and have much higher unit costs. As a consequence many European airlines have been chronic loss makers, such as Olympic in Greece, Alitalia in Italy, Iberia in Spain and TAP Air Portugal.

Swissair was a national icon, its senior managers arguing that the role of Switzerland as a major financial centre was linked strongly with the success of its prestigious airline which carried its managers and customers at a level unusual for other airlines. Switzerland and

Swissair were strongly 'branded' as reliable, prosperous and efficient. One problem for the airline is that in 1992 the Swiss rejected membership of the EU, thereby denying the country the benefits of being a member of a much larger organization.

Qantas was for many years the flag carrier for Australia on international routes, while being excluded from domestic routes. Even when it was allowed to come into competition with the other major Australian airline, Ansett, on the internal routes, there was an almost exact duplication of service and price, so that the monopoly position was modified, not removed. Australia stood at one extreme of the regulation spectrum; routes, schedules and prices being controlled, both internationally and domestically. The regulation was intended to guarantee a profit and the government stood ready in bad times to bear any losses. The initial limitation to international flights, combined with the geographical factors associated with Australia's location, partly explains the still long, average flight haul of well over 4,000 kilometres for Qantas, which in turn explains its low average cost per passenger kilometre.

All this was done with a particular regard for both safety and technical best practice. Qantas has maintained an excellent record for safety, often expressed in its claim to be the only airline in the world which has never had a fatality (a feature referred to in the film *Rain Man*, with a very beneficial effect on the reputation of the airline).

Swissair and bad fortune

During the 1990s Swissair adopted an ambitious twofold strategy: to enlarge its non-airline business and acquire minority holdings in other airlines, mainly European. It had significant aspirations to be a major international player. By the middle of 1998, Swissair was the eleventh largest airline in the world. Its routes radiated from Switzerland and were at their most dense within Europe but extended to all parts of the globe. Zurich, its main centre, had become one of the European hubs.

As elsewhere in Switzerland, the industry was highly regulated. As late as 1998 the airline was more than 20% government-owned. For a long period it was, like other national airlines, a recipient of subsidies from the Swiss government. Other European carriers were in a worse situation. Sabena, the Belgian airline in which Swissair invested, made a profit only twice in its 75 years of existence. It made the highest annual loss of all European airlines during the 1990s, almost US$1 million in 1991, an amount not far short of its total sales revenue in that year.

In the new competitive environment the European airline industry has suffered and still suffers from overcapacity. It is highly fragmented. There are two ways of reacting to this situation:

1. to consolidate existing lines by purchase
2. to join an existing, or form a new, network to rival the Star Alliance or Oneworld.

Some airlines like Swissair have sought to expand in both ways. One proposal, strongly promoted by Swissair, has been to consolidate the small European airlines around Swissair.

Swissair expanded its capacity, buying into other national airlines. It bought 49.5% stakes in Belgium's national airline Sabena and France's Air Lib, which combined Air Liberte and AOM. Swissair also owned 49.9% of German charter operator LTU, 49.7% of Italy's Volare, 37.6% of LOT Polish Airlines, as well as 20% of South African Airways. It also owned small parts of Delta (3%), Austrian (10%) and even Singapore Airline (0.6%). It code shared with 20 other airlines and had bloc space agreements with 12.

Swissair was also at the centre of the Qualifying Alliance, which included Sabena, Austrian (for only a short period), THY Turkey and TAP Air Portugal. With the inclusion of Delta this constituted the Atlantic Excellence Alliance. However, American Airlines quickly replaced Delta as Swissair's American partner. This represented a fourth potential world alliance, one which was more fluid and much smaller than the others.

Transition problems

2000 – a bad year

In 2000 Swissair had moved from a small profit in 1999 to a significant loss, largely as a consequence of the rising oil price and an appreciating currency. For the SAir Group as a whole these losses were compounded by the losses on investment in other airlines. The slide into loss making came at a difficult time for Swissair.

An overambitious growth strategy

Swissair had tried to bring together a group of small European airlines to compete with the large airline alliances. Many of these airlines were in poor condition. Unfortunately Swissair did not have the financial resources to sustain such a policy, as British Airways, Air France or Lufthansa might have. The success of the various non-core businesses – maintenance, catering, booking, shopping, cargo transport and airport handling – could not compensate for the problems of the core business. By 2000 it was obvious that the growth strategy had failed.

Partner weaknesses

SF3.3 billion was invested in other airlines. The airlines which were acquired, notably Sabena, Air Liberte and LTU, while small, were relatively weak financially. The business risk was initially hidden by the complexity of the structure of cross-holdings. Because of financial weakness these partner airlines imposed demands upon Swissair which weakened its position. It was difficult to sell such unprofitable airlines and escape from the burden. These demands on Swissair further increased with the crisis of September 11, 2001.

Debt problems

Swissair had considerable debt, which, by the end of December 2000, had reached SF9.4 billion, rising to over 10 billion by the end of June 2001. The restructuring plan envisaged a reduction of debt of 2 billion by the end of 2002 and a further one billion by the end of 2003. This was not to happen. This situation caused Swissair's bankers Credit Suisse and Union de Banques Suisses considerable disquiet. The debt to equity ratio rose dramatically, from just over one in 1999 to as high as 4.68 in 2000, largely as a result of the ambitious growth policy and the increasing weakness of the partners from which Swissair could not disentangle itself.

Greater competition

Deregulation has meant that new 'no-frills' competitors have appeared within Europe, such as Virgin, EasyJet and Ryanair, and insofar as routes and airports have been genuinely deregulated, new competitors also from outside Europe. The level of competition has increased enormously. This creates particular difficulty for a high-cost airline.

New strategies

From January 1, 2001, there was to be a change of direction, described as the 'new strategic course'. This strategy had at its centre the reversal of the previous policy of acquiring equity in other airlines and extending beyond the core business of air travel. Such a shedding would take time, particularly where loss-making airlines were involved. Swissair did not have the time. Its aim of reducing debt was not to be achieved. Almost as soon as the new strategy came into existence, it was superseded by a new strategy forced on Swissair by world events, notably the terrorist attack of September 11, 2001.

The shock and its results

A fall in passenger numbers

Passenger numbers, already falling because of the slowing of the world economy, fell dramatically after September 11, 2001, by as much as 30% on some important routes. It was unclear how long this fall would last. However, recovery was aborted by further shocks in 2003, the Iraq War and SARS.

Increased costs

An increase in oil prices had already increased costs for the airlines. September 11 increased the cost of insurance by a large amount and imposed much heavier security demands on the airlines. The price of oil oscillated significantly, rising again in 2003 and including a significant war premium.

Loss making

Airlines already making a loss before September 11 found themselves with enormous unsustainable losses which could only be covered by government subsidy.

Partner problems

The potential or actual bankruptcy of partners, such as Sabena and Air Lib, made the situation worse. Swissair was unable to meet its commitments to provide these airlines with development funds, which hastened its slide into a crisis.

There were two main results of the shock:

1. Swissair was rescued and recapitalized, just as Air New Zealand was to be. Other airlines in trouble, such as Ansett and Sabena, have been allowed to fail; Swissair was not. The Swiss government rescued the airline and bailed it out of its immediate financial difficulties. It also received an injection of US$1.7 billion from a number of Swiss investors including Nestlé and Swisscom who regarded the airline as an important feature of the Swiss economy and potentially redeemable, with a change of strategy. In operation phoenix US$3 billion new capital was raised, and the resurrected airline, called Swiss International Airlines (SIA), was more than 30% owned by the Swiss government and more than 60% owned by Swiss corporations.
2. The airline had to change its strategy yet again. It was forced to accept a much diminished international role which amounted to closing many of its longer international routes and concentrating on the domestic routes of its 70% owned subsidiary Crossair. It has a fleet of 128 planes, most of which are short-haul planes inherited from Crossair, 102 in all. Overall capacity was down about one-third on Swissair's previous level.

Initially the new airline seemed to do well. In two months, SIA achieved a 69% load factor, good for the post-September 11 world, but reflecting a significant withdrawal into largely European routes. The new Chairperson Pieter Bouw, formerly head of the well-performed KLM, and André Dosé, the new CEO, started the process of reducing costs. Plane leases were renegotiated with the banks and leasing companies, with discounts as high as 30–40%, and pilots' salaries reduced by about 35%. However, in 2003 conditions deteriorated further.

There were renewed difficulties of survival for SIA. In June 2003, the airline was once more threatened with insolvency and bankruptcy. There were a series of problems:

- Costs were still not low enough, for example labour costs were 30% higher than Lufthansa's. The airline had trouble negotiating a reduction in pilots' salaries and the freedom to lay off whichever pilots it wished.
- The image of the new airline was poor.
- The new airline was clinging to high-prestige, low-profit routes. Most of the routes to Latin America and to Asia were losing money. Increasingly, the shorter routes were also becoming unprofitable. Of the 40 overseas destinations, only 15 were profitable. A comparison with Finnair and Austrian with similar home markets is illuminating. They have 6 and 19 destinations respectively and both airlines were profitable.
- Swiss was not a member of any alliance and unlikely to gain entry.
- Most of the regional flights don't make a profit. They had a seat occupancy almost 10% below the European average.

The airline was already engaged in a major cost-cutting exercise, with a 10% reduction in the workforce, 22 short-haul aircraft out of service and a delay in new purchases, when it was forced to rewrite its strategy once more. It had established Swiss Express with costs 20% below its current levels in order to take on the 'no-frills' airlines. There was an urgent need to cut medium-length routes in Europe where losses were significant and cut some long-distance routes. The new plan was to reduce capacity and its labour force by about one-third and raise significant amounts of fresh capital. It was necessary to renegotiate labour contracts in order to make the new business plan acceptable and justify the purchase of new aircraft. Breaking even was postponed until 2004 and was to be achieved at a much lower level of gross revenue.

The position of the new Swiss International Airlines was unsustainable. The combination of a tiny domestic market, only seven million people in a small territory, and many competitors, something like 130 in the European region, was always likely to force the new airline to give up many of its medium- and long-haul routes.

There was still a need to articulate a clear, long-term strategic plan which is realistic.

The general dilemma

The industry is very fragmented, especially in Europe. American Airlines, the largest airline, accounts for only 7% of the market (compared with General Motors' 25%). There are in all 267 international carriers, 500 plus domestic and 23 flag carriers in Europe, and high barriers to exit. It is difficult to stop governments propping up their national carriers.

One result of the series of shocks beginning with September 11 might be to accelerate change, provided that governments are not allowed to simply bail out their troubled carriers. The European Commission of Transportation is seeking to avoid the latter outcome. It has secured the right to negotiate on behalf of all European airlines, possibly to create an Open Aviation Area which would combine the two largest regional markets of Europe and the USA, 60% of the world market. If the market were allowed to operated unimpeded, one forecast is that only a handful of European airlines with real international aspirations, those with a large domestic base, will be left – notably British Airways, Air France and Lufthansa. There will also be a number of small regional or domestic players, such as Crossair, and some 'no-frills' airlines, such as Ryanair and EasyJet. In this context the strategy of Crossair would cease to embrace the international aims of Swissair.

Qantas and good fortune

Qantas was for most of its life state-owned. The government, using the usual mechanism of bilateral agreements, carved out a niche for Qantas by guaranteeing limited competition on routes in and out of Australia. The industry was retained for Australian airlines with foreign competition excluded as much as possible, except where there were reciprocal rights which were considered beneficial to Qantas. Access to airports, themselves state-owned, was also controlled. The airports were run as a single government-owned unit, without competition between them. Gates and terminal facilities were allocated according to the regulated airline policy. It was impossible for other new airlines to get such access without strong government backing.

As elsewhere the industry has been undergoing a radical change of government policy. The change of policy came at the end of the 1980s and began to take effect at the beginning of the 1990s; this new policy was aimed at increasing competition, mainly domestically but also internationally. The means of achieving this was to be deregulation and privatization.

Qantas has been combined with the state-owned domestic carrier, AA (previously TAA), and floated as a public company. It is now fully privately owned and operates both domestically and internationally. There has been a deregulation of routes and prices, at least internally. The amount of deregulation internationally has been more limited. A degree of foreign ownership has been allowed, in the case of Qantas 25% by British Airways (now down to 19%), and in the case of the other main domestic carrier, Ansett, 49% by Air New Zealand. There is still a limit on foreign ownership which is 49% on all ownership and 25% on any single owner. Recently the Australian government refused a request from Qantas to ease this policy. Qantas wanted the rules eased because it believed that it could raise more money, more cheaply in a less regulated environment, which it believed it needed to do in order to remain competitive.

Qantas has joined the Oneworld network, where it joins American Airways, British Airways, Cathay Pacific, Aer Lingus, Iberia, Finnair and LanChile.

Other airlines have been allowed to enter the Australian market. There were two attempts to establish a third airline to compete internally with Qantas and Ansett, on both occasions with an airline called Compass. Both attempts quickly failed. More recently a third airline, Impulse, was established, but aggressive pricing policy on the part of the other two airlines quickly led to the voluntary absorption of Impulse by Qantas. The entry of an outside airline has been more successful. Virgin Blue operates a 'no-frills' service within Australia on the main routes. It is steadily increasing its share of domestic traffic, currently at 20%, with a target of 30%. There is no competition for the business traveller. It is unclear how many airlines the domestic market can accommodate. There is a deliberate policy by government and the Australian Competition and Consumer Commission (ACCC) to maintain competition on the domestic market and prevent what is called 'predatory pricing', that is, the deliberate undercutting of new airlines on routes they begin to operate by existing and much stronger airlines.

On the other hand, there are major restrictions on competition. There are all sorts of restriction ensuring that Qantas remains Australian, including the 49% limit on foreign ownership and an even more restrictive limit of Qantas' ownership of other airlines. At the time of writing Qantas is bidding to own 22.5% of Air New Zealand. The government is negotiating an 'open skies' agreement with Singapore. The Australian government still acts to manage all traffic rights on a bilateral basis.

Positive features

Low costs

The long average haul on Qantas' routes has helped to keep its costs per passenger kilometre at a low level. It has also managed to sustain a high load factor which has steadily increased in recent years, to 75%, compared to about 70% for Swissair. It has also kept its debt to equity ratio close to one, although because of fleet expansion and deposits this ratio has tended to rise but only marginally compared to the dramatic and simultaneous rise for Swissair.

Little competition

Qantas has managed to keep a very strong competitive position on its domestic market. Even on its international routes, competition has been limited, even more limited with the diminishing activity of United Airlines on Pacific routes.

Strong partners

Qantas' main partner has been British Airways which has a route structure complementary rather than competitive with that of Qantas. British Airways is one of the largest airlines in the world and has been financially strong for a long period, although the terrorist attacks have diminished traffic on its main routes. Membership of Oneworld has offered Qantas major advantages, giving strong connections with routes in most parts of the world.

A relatively good 2000

For most airlines the year 2000 was a bad year. Sharply increased fuel costs, up by at least 50%, the beginnings of recession and much more intense competition turned most airlines into low-profit or loss-making enterprises. Qantas was affected, particularly on its domestic routes but not as badly as others. However, earnings before tax and interest on domestic flights fell by more than 50%. This was offset by an increase in international business of more than 20%, which partly reflected the favourable impact of the Olympic Games held in Sydney in that year.

The shock

Simultaneously with the events of September 11, Qantas' main domestic competitor Ansett went into bankruptcy. It had been outcompeted by Qantas, and poorly managed in an uncertain ownership environment. It ceased for a short period to provide any air services and even when it resumed it only provided a very limited service on the main routes. Attempts to refloat failed and the airline later went out of business for good.

The demise of Ansett opened a major gap in the servicing of the domestic market which the new entrant Virgin Blue could not fill immediately. As a result, Qantas came to provide as much as 90% of the domestic services, declining to 80% within six months and probably headed down to 70% at some time in the near future. The situation has greatly increased the profitability of Virgin Blue and its ability to expand. Both airlines have committed major resources to filling the gap in the domestic market. There is still a possibility that Singapore Airlines, or another third carrier such as Cathay Pacific, will enter the Australian domestic market, but not in the near future.

The gap in the domestic market provided an opportunity for Qantas not only to switch planes from international routes hit by the September 11 crisis but also to update its fleet by purchasing new planes. Since it was a minor player on the main routes hit by the crisis, the Atlantic route between North America and Europe and to the Middle East, Qantas found it relatively easy to switch planes from these international to domestic routes and still to keep its capacity utilization levels high, both internationally and domestically. It even found itself having to acquire extra planes to meet the increased demand. This helped to keep its fleet modern and its costs low. It has deliberately taken the decision to purchase from Airbus, where previously it had a fleet which consisted solely of Boeings. This is in preparation for the later acquisition of the A380 (see the case study on Boeing and Airbus in Chapter 4), for which Qantas put in an early order.

The contrast in the situation of Qantas with that of Swissair is illuminating. There were three main areas of advantage for Qantas.

1. Although both operate in high wage, and therefore high-cost, countries, the Swiss franc is a hard currency which has tended to appreciate, whereas the Australian dollar is a soft currency which has depreciated significantly. For most international airlines costs are mainly incurred at home either in the home currency or in American dollars, whereas revenue is generated abroad. Where costs are raised by the decline in the Australian dollar, Qantas is willing to hedge, as it does with its fuel costs. The net impact has tended to reduce Swissair's net revenue stream, accentuating any rise in cost, and increase Qantas' net revenue in both their home currencies.
2. The difference in the size of their respective domestic markets has been reinforced by the bankruptcy

of Qantas' main domestic competitor, Ansett. This has left Qantas to take over most of the other half of the domestic market, compensating for any loss elsewhere, and at a time when the assistance was most welcome.

3. The fall in the share price of Swissair had badly damaged its capacity to raise cheap capital, whereas the rise in the share price of Qantas has made it much easier to raise such capital. In October 2001 Qantas was able to raise A$450 million by an equity placement, up on the A$300 million originally announced because of oversubscription. This has enabled Qantas to continue to expand and modernize its fleet of aircraft. By contrast Swissair's shares plunged from SF500 in 1998 to SF262 in January 2001 and SF1.25 in September 2001, before its bankruptcy. Qantas' price has continued rising, marking it out as the airline with probably one of the highest capitalizations on the market. One possible weakness is that Qantas owns its planes and therefore bears the risk of any decline in value. This is not a problem while demand keeps the fleet fully utilized.

The future

It is interesting to speculate on Qantas' strategy for the future. How will it shape up in the new world?

The new world is one which has not been kind to the industry. There is a view that the huge losses of the industry in both 2001 and 2002 will force a process of consolidation on the industry. The continuing spread of no-frills air travel is increasing the competition. The success of Virgin Blue shows this. Qantas, under the label of Australian Airlines, has already initiated a mainly 'no-thrills' service from Cairns in northern Queensland to a number of Asian cities, including the main Japanese cities and Shanghai and Singapore. It intends to expand the service in the future so that it will serve other Australian cities. This has created an interesting and novel blend of two strategies which superficially do not appear to go together well.

Qantas has announced its intention to purchase 22.5% of Air New Zealand which nearly disappeared in 2001 but was rescued by the New Zealand government, which now owns 82% of the airline. This will give the combined entity 100% control of the trans-Tasman route and also the domestic New Zealand market, if the regulatory authorities and governments in the two countries approve it in its present form, which does not seem very likely. In this case the demands of competition theory present an obstacle to further consolidation. There is also talk of the sale of some part of British

Airways remaining 19% stake in Qantas, with purchase possibly by Singapore Airlines which, despite its losses on Air New Zealand and Virgin Atlantic, is still one of the strongest airlines.

Such partnerships create an even bigger problem in the structure of alliances since Qantas is a member of Oneworld and the other two airlines members of the Star Alliance. There is likely to be a major rethinking of these alliances.

The opportunities for Qantas are:

- it consolidates its already strong hold on the Australian domestic market, probably with a target of 70%
- it extends its dominance to routes from Australia to other parts of the region, including New Zealand, Singapore and across the Pacific to the American west coast.

The threats for Qantas are:

- the Australian government or the ACCC, in the case of the purchase of part of Air New Zealand, the New Zealand government, intervenes to limit Qantas' market power on the grounds that it is anti-competitive
- a no-frills competitor such as Virgin Blue builds up as a major competitor with much lower costs, because it has only one class, leases its planes and is linked to a strong partner, an integrated freight transport company, Patrick
- a third airline, Singapore Airlines, Cathay Pacific or even Emirates, either in alliance with Virgin Blue or on its own, enters the domestic market
- the terrorist attack in the Australian region, in Bali on October 12, 2002, and further shocks such as SARS, reduces the movement in the region of both tourists and businesspeople
- consolidations of international carriers and restructuring of other players, such as United, creates much stronger competition on international routes and Qantas has to compete with much larger transnational airlines with low costs
- Qantas has trouble controlling its costs, notably its labour and airport costs
- Qantas has trouble renovating its out-of-date airline fleet because it cannot raise the enormous amount of finance required.

The airlines are at a critical stage in the move to a global market. The shocks have encouraged a return to old practices, although the extent of loss making in the industry prevents a full return. Qantas is one of the stronger players, but has its own problems. It has withstood the shocks of the last few years much better than Swissair but it needs both a good strategy and good luck to build on its current strength. At the time of writing, there is a rumour that Lufthansa is willing to acquire Swiss International, provided the current cost-saving measures are fully implemented.

Case Study Questions

1. How have Swissair and Qantas participated in the transition from a regulated to a deregulated industry?
2. Identify the three different strategies adopted by, or imposed upon, Swissair during the last decade.
3. Why did Qantas deal with the shock of September 11, 2001 much better than Swissair?
4. What should be the strategy adopted by Swiss International Airlines? What assumptions concerning the future are relevant to the formulation of such a strategy?
5. What strategies should Qantas adopt domestically and internationally? Should it adopt a strategy of significant growth?

Reading

Done, K. and Dombey, D., 'EU set to give Commission mandate to negotiate aviation treaty with US', *Financial Times*, June 5, 2003.

Hall, W., 'Setback for Swiss low cost service', *Financial Times*, June 20, 2003: 31.

Hall, W., 'Swiss Air Line set to cut workforce and fleet', *Financial Times*, June 24, 2003: 30.

Hall, W., 'Swiss to make huge cuts in capacity', *Financial Times*, June 25, 2003: 28.

Hanlon, P., *Global Airlines: competition in a transnational industry*, Butterworth Heinemann, Oxford, 2nd edn, 1999.

Hargreaves, D., 'Airline industry sets course for consolidation', *Financial Times*, June14/15: M21.

Sparaco, P. and Flottau, J., 'Bailouts of Swissair, Sabena may allow both to survive', *Aviation Week and Space Technology*, October 8, 2001.

Tierney, C., 'A smooth takeoff for Swiss International', *Business Week*, June 17, 2002: 28.

Relevant websites

www.swissair.com
www.qantas.com.au

This case study is also relevant to Chapters 8 and 13.

Key strategic lessons

- Globalization is the movement towards a global world which features a uniform polity, economy and society where national boundaries cease to have meaning.

- This movement involves the integration of the world economy and its markets, the introduction of communications technology, the loss of national sovereignty, the increasing homogenization of culture and a democratization of choice for the individual in a series of different areas.

- The core of globalization is an increased interaction between national economies but there is still a pronounced home country bias due to ignorance, cultural difference, significant transport costs, multiple currencies and multiple sovereignties.

- A convergence on representative democracy and the market system has not led to equalization of factor prices or similar political regimes. Cultural differences are still strong and necessitate customization by country. There is resistance to such increased conformity whether through market or demonstration effects.

- There are many players who can influence an organization's strategy including multilateral financial institutions, regional organizations, key nation states and multinational enterprises.

- Global strategy differs from domestic strategy for many reasons, including the existence of national boundaries creating a significant degree of risk. The type of leader needed to operate at the global level must be able to manage the logistics of a complex organization and put together a team of managers able to take opportunities and manage risk.

Applying the lessons

1 If a global world is defined by the final state to which globalization is headed, what might be the nature of that final state?

2 Using the Focus on Theory – benefits and losses of globalization – list the following elements of globalization: causes, characteristics, consequences.

3 Define the following terms: multilateralism, regionalism, bilateralism, multidomestic strategy, global enterprise, transnational strategy, ethnocentric philosophy, polycentric philosophy, geocentric philosophy.

4 One of the major constraints on global involvement by an enterprise is home country bias.

i Consider the different aspects of such a constraint. In turn, consider what the constraints are on different kinds of international transactions which involve entering an international environment: exporting; foreign investment, either portfolio or direct; and working abroad.

ii How is it possible to counter each of these different elements and break down home country bias?

iii One way of counteracting home country bias is to establish strategic alliances at the global level. Consider how such alliances might be constructed in order to deal with the constraints.

5 The world does not have a fully homogeneous culture. Differences of culture have a strong influence on the pattern of tastes in different countries and the nature of products and services consumed in different countries. Such differences therefore influence the nature of international marketing. What is the nature of this influence?

One interpretation distinguishes between a multidomestic, an international and a global strategy. List which products would lend themselves to these different strategies.

6 E-commerce is one important element of the globalization revolution which is occurring. However, so far e-commerce is more effective 'business-to-business' than 'business-to-customer'. Why is this? Compare www.ford.com, www.gm.com and www.vw.com with www.amazon.com, www.federated-fds.com, www.7dream.com and www.tesco.com.

Strategic project

1 Choose an enterprise in a specific industry or sector of the economy. What is needed, in terms of strategic inputs, to make that enterprise a successful global, indeed transnational, player?

2 An airline might be considered as a potential transnational player. What kind of strategy would be necessary to turn an existing airline into such a transnational player? Choose an example of an airline which has successfully pursued the appropriate strategy.

Exploring further

There has probably been more written recently about globalization than any other single topic covered in this book. The newspapers and journals are full of discussion concerning its implications. There is also an increasing number of academic treatments. However, there has also been considerable confusion among the debators about what exactly is being discussed and committed positions are held by the participants on all the issues.

There are three basic approaches to discussion of the topic:

1. What we might call the approach of global political economy. It is about who has the power in the world economy and therefore makes the decisions. It sees globalization as embracing every facet of life – economic, political, social and environmental. Some of this literature is popular in its orientation, much of it very polemical and 'ideological', on either side, for or against.
2. A highly technical approach, that of the economist trying to consider in a theoretical manner those economic tendencies which affect the world economy. For example, it assesses the degree to which factors of production are mobile across international frontiers and how far world markets are really integrated.
3. One that considers whether and how far globalization affects both the process and the content of strategy making for enterprises which engage in international business. It is concerned with how managers should react to the main elements of change in the international environment.

It is appropriate to start with the approach of global political economy. An excellent general introduction to globalization are the Reith Lectures given by Anthony Giddens, now updated as Runaway World: The Reith Lectures revisited (1999), to be found at www.globalisationguide.org. Probably the best detailed introduction is Held et al., 1999.

The argument that what is called globalization represents nothing new is well put in Hirst and Thompson, 2001. This makes an explicit comparison between the present and the period 1870–1914. It also argues that most economic activity in the world today is concentrated on the triad. It interprets what is happening at the global level in terms of the harmonization of the policies of the major powers. There is a review which evaluates these arguments, accepting that it is a necessary corrective to the most extreme views, Perraton, 2001: 669–84.

There are many other globalization sceptics. There is a good book on the resistance to globalization and its reasons: Mittelman, 2000. A supplement of *The Economist*, 'A Survey of Globalization' (2001) has set out the arguments rebutting the sceptics. This article is particularly good on the argument that globalization is reducing national sovereignty.

On the other side are the hyperglobalizers, like *The Economist*. Probably most typical of this group is Kenichi Ohmae. His most interesting and relevant work includes the 1991 and 1995a books and, more briefly an article of 1995b: 269–85.

Exploring
further
cont'd

For a review of the development of the international economy over almost two hundred years, see Kenwood and Lougheed, 1999. There is a lucid discussion of the general concept as it relates to a particular economy in Bryan and Rafferty, 1999.

The domination of the world by the triad was first explored in a chapter under that heading by Ohmae, 1991 and developed by Thurow, 1992. Sachs, 2000 is an interesting article emphasizing the concentration of innovative activity on the triad.

Cultural difference is explored in Ronen and Shenkar, 1985: 449–55. This interpretation can be supplemented by Huntingdon, 1996, probably better considered in the shorter version in *Foreign Affairs*, 1993.

The potential for democratization implicit in globalization is put most strongly in Friedman, 1999.

Economists take a much more limited approach. Although it is a much more general concept, home country bias is often focused in economists' work on foreign investment and placed in the context of portfolio choice and risk management, see Levi, 1996, particularly Chapter 18. The article which raised the problem and started the search for an explanation is Feldstein and Horioka, 1980: 314–29. A much more recent reconsideration of the issue is Coakley et al., 1996: 620–7.

The classic article raising the relevant issues is Levitt, 1983: 92–102. The relevance of globalization to management starts with management and continues with the definition of a global enterprise. The relevant definitions of global enterprises are to be found in Ghoshal, 2000: 51–80, or at greater length in Bartlett and Ghoshal, 1992. Other useful discussions are Hirschhorn and Gilmore, 1992, or 'The stateless corporation', *Business Week*, 1991: 98–104. *Fortune* updates annually, in July, its ranking of the 500 largest multinationals.

More general books are Bartlett and Ghoshal, 1989 and Prahalad and Doz, 1987. There is an excellent introduction which relates globalization to strategy – Nelson, 1999. There are many general texts which are good introductions to internationalization. The author has often used Mahoney et al., 2001. There is a good chapter on competing in a transnational world in Mische, 2001.

4 Reading an uncertain future

The most fundamental aspect of introducing uncertainty in the strategic equation is that it turns planning for the future from a once-off episodic activity into an ongoing learning proposition. (VAN DER HEIJDEN, 1996: 7)

Long-range forecasting (two years or longer) is notoriously inaccurate. (HOGARTH AND MAKRIDAKIS, 1981: 122)

Buy Futures. (AIRBUS advertisement for the A380)

Learning objectives

After reading this chapter you will be able to:

- assess the limitations of the information available for strategy making

- recognize what kind of information is relevant to strategy making

- learn how to read the general environment

- understand what is involved in forecasting the future

- identify the different kinds of risks to which the enterprise is exposed

- build different scenarios of the future

Key strategic challenge

What do strategists need to know?

Strategic dangers

That there is an absence of any systematic attempt to predict what will happen in the future and as a result a significant failure both to take advantage of important new opportunities and manage the risk arising from unanticipated threats.

Case Study Scenario   Airbus Industrie and the next generation of civil airliners

The production of civil airliners is an industry in which there should be strategic planning, mainly because of the need to look a long way into the future and commit enormous resources to projects which only produce a return with a significant time delay.

This applies to the demand side, where it reflects the need of the purchasers of civil airliners, the airlines, to plan in a coherent way the development of their fleets well into the future, despite considerable short-run volatility of demand from potential travellers, and remain competitive in both the price and quality of the service they offer.

It also applies to the supply side where there is a need for planning because of the enormous commitment of resources required to develop a new generation of airliners. Initially, this usually means a pioneer model and later the associated family of related planes of differing range and size. The existence of such a full suite of planes is critical to eventual success, since it allows the enjoyment of significant economies of scale for various components, both at the production and maintenance stages, and also in the training of crew to operate the new planes.

No manufacturer can afford to make a mistake over such a large commitment of resources. Avoiding a mistake means reading the future correctly.

Airbus Industrie began in 1970, significantly the same year that saw the first commercial flight of the jumbo jet, the Boeing 747. It began as a consortium of European companies from different countries, notably Spain, Germany, the UK and France, which was established to compete with American civil airliner producers of that time. The competition for Airbus has always been American. When Airbus started there were three significant manufacturers in the USA – Lochheed, McDonnell-Douglas and Boeing. The first two merged and the resulting company was then taken over by Boeing in 1997, leaving Boeing the sole American producer. The industry is now a duopoly.

Airbus sought to integrate the different European industries. British Aerospace only became a full consortium member in 1979. Two of the consortium members, DAS (a DaimlerChrysler company) and Aerospatiale, merged in 1999, to become the European Aeronautical Defence and Space Company. On July 11, 2001 Airbus became a single integrated company, a French simplified joint stock company or SAS (Société par Action Simplifiée), with it headquarters at Toulouse in France. There are two main shareholders: EADS owns 80% of the company and BAE Systems 20%.

Airbus claims to be the first genuinely European company. There was considerable government involvement in its inception and development. The partners received generous subsidies from their governments to finance Airbus projects and ensure the consortium's long-term survival. For the development and manufacture of its first three models, government assistance to Airbus amounted to as much as $10 billion. A further $4–5 billion was needed at the start of the A330/340 project.

Such assistance threatened to generate a trade war, with the American manufacturers arguing that Airbus was in breach of GATT rules. They claimed that Airbus had an unfair competitive advantage because of the subsidies received. Allegedly, the subsidies allowed Airbus to set unrealistically low prices, offer concessions and attractive financing terms to airlines which bought its products, and write off development costs without detriment. It was also alleged that Airbus had a captive market, in that it could use state-owned airlines to obtain orders. In response, Airbus argued that the American government had indirectly subsidized Boeing by financing military development and the associated contracts. The 707 was originally a military project.

A bilateral agreement between Airbus and Boeing was finally reached in 1992 which represented a recognition that any subsidy war was a 'beggar my neighbour' policy from which neither Boeing nor Airbus could benefit. The agreement limited government subsidies to Airbus to 33% of total development costs, while at the same time restricting indirect R&D funds to 3% of the total revenue received by the American manufacturers. Although European governments have continued to support Airbus, they have kept within the terms of the bilateral agreement. For example, the main four participant governments have made US$4 billion available in development loans for the A380 project, the main focus of this case study, a sum to be repaid from sales revenue. Nor has the American industry resurrected the issue since 1992, despite efforts by both individual politicians and government members to do so.

However, a second critical confrontation arose when the proposal for Boeing to merge with McDonnell-Douglas was made in 1996. Airbus objected on the grounds that the merger violated the rules of fair competition.

Without government involvement, the Airbus consortium would never have counteracted the first-mover advantages of the American industry. The barriers to entry into the industry were such as to make that assistance critical. After 25 years of losses Airbus finally made a profit in 1995. Although the respective European governments are still important for its development, it now acts as a fully private and competitive company. To survive as such it is essential that Airbus reads the future correctly. With the commitment to the A380 project, Airbus has read the future demand for airliners very differently from Boeing. Each manufacturer has its own model of the future, forecasting the demand for airliners 20 years ahead. For Airbus it is critical that the project has been initiated on an accurate forecast of future demand.

Chapter 2 considered significant constraints on strategy making, in particular the cognitive or intellectual, social and political contexts which influence the strategy-making process in any organization, constraining what can and cannot be done. This chapter expands on the first constraint, the cognitive, exploring the imperfect information available to strategists and the limited ability of any one individual to process the mass of available information. Any organization has a limited information-processing capacity. This chapter considers what a strategist needs to know in order to make good strategy. It stresses the nature of strategy making as a learning process and an organization as a learning institution. The major area of ignorance is what will happen in the future. Since most of the life of any organization lies in the future, this is important. There is no way of avoiding the problem of uncertainty about the future. How does a strategist deal with this uncertainty? One response is to try to remove as much of it as possible.

Limited information

Strategy makers operate with imperfect information. To a limited degree, they can choose the degree of imperfection with which they operate; that choice is itself a strategic issue. However, whatever they do, they cannot possible know with certainty what is going to happen in the future, nor can they know the exact degree of their own ignorance. Are they right even on those things about which they are confident? Strategists cannot possibly attain what is called 'perfect information'. The challenge for them is to know enough about the future to give any strategy adopted a good chance of success. They must be able to make a strategy flexible enough to accommodate the unexpected events which lead to failure, in particular those which come as a surprise.

In a world of apparent information abundance, the message of the first paragraph seems rather paradoxical. The problem for any strategy is rather more than just the limitations on available information. There is a sense in which there is far too much information. The strategy maker is faced with a limited capacity to process the information which is available; there is far too much of it. Probably only a small proportion of all the information available is relevant to the enterprise or organization.

Bounded rationality

Together, these two limitations, imperfect information and a limited capacity to process the information which does exist, constitute *bounded rationality*. The successful application of reason depends on the availability of relevant information; it is bounded by the existence of imperfect information and an imperfect capacity to process what does exist in order to discover what is relevant.

Rationality involves two types of reason, the pure and the practical:

- Pure reason involves the application of a particular style of reasoning and argument to problem solving, one which uses the normal criteria of logic. It involves the deduction of true inferences from a given set of axioms or propositions.
- Practical reason involves the application of reason to the problems of action. Such problems involve achieving clearly set out objectives in a logical manner, effectively using the resources available, given the circumstances or environment in which the appropriate action must be taken.

Decision making in strategy making is a form of practical reason.

Simon has distinguished substantive rationality from procedural rationality:

- Behaviour is substantively rational 'when it is appropriate to the achievement of given goals within the limits imposed by given conditions and constraints ... Given these goals, the rational behaviour is determined entirely by the constraints of the environment in which it takes place' (Simon, 1976 quoted in Forster and Browne, 1996: 159).
- Behaviour is procedurally rational 'when it is the outcome of appropriate deliberation. Its procedural rationality depends on the process that generated it' (p. 160).

Focus on Theory
The criteria of rationality

- Rational decisions are conscious, explicit and deliberate.
- Rational decisions must be free from errors of logic, that is, they must be internally consistent and logical.
- Rational decisions are fully informed, taking comprehensive account of relevant information, particularly about the context in which action is proposed to be taken.
- Rational decisions are goal-oriented, that is, they are purposeful, aimed at the achievement of a preferred end.
- Means and ends are analytically independent, that is, the choice of ends is independent of the means for achieving them.
- Rational decisions involve choice between alternative ends as well as between alternative means for achieving them. The choice of means will be determined by the evaluation of alternatives in terms of the ability to achieve to a maximum degree the chosen ends. Rational choice therefore implies maximization.
- Means and ends are causally related, that is, rational decisions depend on the action taken being reliably expected to result in the achievement of the stated objective.

Source: Forster and Browne, 1996: 160.

Optimization

One variant of the rational approach assumes that all problems can be reduced to problems of optimization. Optimization is one way of achieving defined goals within the constraints of the existing supply of available resources. It assumes that there is a clear maximand or minimand, something to be maximized like output or profit or something to be minimized like costs or inputs. It assumes that there are a number of possible solutions but that there is just one optimal solution to any problem. It is

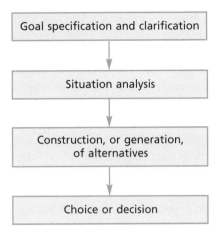

Source: Forster and Browne, 1996: 161.

Figure 4.1 **The classical model of rational decision making**

simply a matter of discovering the optimum solution. There are various techniques for doing so, which are not very helpful in strategy making because the nature of the problem means that is does not satisfy the assumptions above.

In all sorts of areas of human activity there are problems which are solved by rational thinking; for example it is at the core of science and its advances (Figure 4.1). Some see strategy making as nothing more than an application of reason (Singer, 1996). Is the application of reason at all feasible, or even desirable, given the difficulties of defining with precision both objectives and resources in the world of strategy?

One position is to accept that decision making should aspire to be rational but that the application of reason has its limitations. Rationality only takes the strategist so far. Beyond this point strategy making enters the world of creativity, with all that involves. This dichotomy has already been discussed under the heading of strategic thinking in Chapter 2. All the activities in which reason is important have an element which is beyond reason, one which is genuinely creative. The element of creativity necessary in both determining objectives and creating the resources necessary to achieve these objectives moves the analysis beyond routine applications of rationality and embraces a much wider area of human motivation and behaviour.

At best rationality is subject to serious constraints, at worst it is impossible. These cognitive constraints need to be added to the social and political ones already discussed in Chapter 3. There appear to be severe limitations on what can be achieved in following such a narrow approach. These limitations arise from constraints distorting the process of decision making itself.

Rational economic man (or woman)

Many economic models of human behaviour assume not only that perfect information is available to all market actors, whether they are consumers or investors, but also that all actors behave rationally. Such actors are assumed never to be inconsistent, to act on a whim, a momentary sensation, intuition or what we might call a gut feeling. It is not simply that they know fully their own preference map (their ranking of consumer goods) and the price of all products, but that they apply a set of easily deducible criteria to decision making, one which includes consistency.

A typical approach which illustrates the weakness of an overreliance on rationality is the notion of an efficient price. Indeed this notion is one which assumes that the actual price existing in any market reflects all the relevant information on both demand and supply conditions available at that time. It is efficient in that sense. It is often argued that individuals cannot do better than the market in anticipating future price movements because they cannot possibly have more information than the market. Prices change as soon as the market receives new information. It is conceivable that the amount of information available, and therefore the price, can change dramatically and quickly.

This view of an efficient price defies common sense. Such an assumption undermines the very nature of management studies. Its acceptance would reduce severely the discretionary element in business decision making. It also runs contrary to the reason why strategy is valuable to an enterprise. Anyone concerned with real business decisions and the associated managerial behaviour must have a different starting point.

An alternative starting point

There are four elements of an *alternative starting point* which need to be emphasized:

1. Rationality is not the only ground for making a decision, and is often mixed with other grounds. The previous discussion on creativity neatly illustrates this. Because information is necessarily imperfect, there may be very good grounds for not limiting oneself to rational arguments. This applies to all players who make their own strategy.
2. No strategic player has immediate access to anything like perfect information; but access can be improved in a number of ways. It is possible to have access to different amounts of information or deliberately increase the amount of information to which you have access. Therefore access to information is itself a variable. Making an effective strategy depends on having better information than competitors or processing and therefore using it better.
3. Even if these actors had access to perfect information, their capacity to process that information is limited. Again there is a variable amount of processing which can be applied to that information. Effective processing may give the strategist the advantage he or she seeks.
4. Prices may be efficient in the limited sense indicated above, but the inadequacies of that information render this a meaningless definition. There is an inherent uncertainty about market behaviour, and in particular enterprise behaviour, which itself creates an uncertainty about price. Price fixing is a strategic matter which can and should be analysed in advance.

All these are issues which must be taken into account in any realistic approach to strategy making. Strategy concentrates attention on the future, or at least on information concerning the future. Imperfect information about the future generates uncertainty and risk. There is a common distinction made between risk and uncertainty. Risk occurs in a world in which different outcomes have calculable probabilities, whereas uncertainty occurs when you have no idea of probabilities – you simply do not know whether an event will occur or not. Risk allows rational decision making, uncertainty does not. In this sense the world of the strategist is more an uncertain world than a risky world. This accords rather better with a common-sense view of the world.

Levels of uncertainty

What can be said about uncertainty? The key starting point is that the level of uncertainty is never binary, that is, there is never a simple either/or situation – there is neither zero uncertainty (complete certainty), nor total uncertainty (complete ignorance) (Courtney et al., 1997). Such a binary position itself oversimplifies the world. Instead there are in practice four different levels of uncertainty about the future:

1. the vision of an almost definite future
2. the recognition of a number of discrete, alternative futures which are possible
3. the awareness of a broad range of possible futures, with clear boundaries which demarcate what is at the limits but a continuity of possibilities within the limits
4. an ambiguous future fraught with unknowns, a state of near complete ignorance.

By one's own actions it is possible and obviously desirable to move from one state of knowledge about the future to another, in so doing reducing the level of uncertainty. This requires an information strategy which takes the observer as close as possible to the first of the four states. Usually the aim is to move from an ambiguous future to a defined range of possibilities, or from a defined range to a limited number of possibilities. What is possible may differ markedly from one part of the economy to another. The observer should try, through, for example, the process of scenario building discussed below, to have a clear view about the future.

Information, knowledge and strategy

Today there is access to much more information than in the past. Certainly the mechanisms of access have expanded enormously to include electronic media as well as a vastly increased face-to-face contact. Today all potentially suffer from information overload. There appears to be no limit to the amount of information available through the different media. The bulk of the available information is overwhelming. This constitutes both a source of opportunity and uncertainty.

Theoretically, everyone is much better able to understand what is happening now. There is much less of a monopoly over access to information, that is, a democratization of information access. However, the greater volume of information, by creating an enormous amount of background 'noise', makes it more difficult to hear a significant message loud and clear, even if you are aware in the first place that there is such a message. The noise obscures the message. It is critical who hears the message because the expertise of the hearer will determine whether the message is recognized for what it is and correctly interpreted. There are a host of messages, some of which go forever unheard.

This means that the notion of perfect information is hypothetical; it never exists and never will. The common condition is a general state of imperfect information, which has a profound influence on behaviour and strategy making. To dispel even a small part of such ignorance requires a significant investment of time and resources – itself a strategic decision as to how many resources to devote to the process of converting information into knowledge. The returns from such activity can never be known before the event, only after. Since each conversion is unique, it is only possible to learn about the potential in a general way.

Raw information is not knowledge, it only becomes knowledge when it is put into a theoretical framework, or rather placed within a strategic dimension. It is the strategic framework which yields the criteria for selection. It is a chicken and egg situation, in that strategy is impossible without the relevant information and its conversion into knowledge, but the relevant information only becomes knowledge within the context of the strategy itself.

The cost of most information is very low – in many cases it is costless. The communications revolution has massively speeded up and reduced the cost of the storage, transmission and retrieval of information. While in its raw form, information is apparently costless, in practice its conversion into knowledge bears a significant cost. Since it must be processed, the real cost is the time devoted to the process of reading and interpreting that information. It is necessary to analyse the process of reading this information which makes possible the conversion; this is an important strategic activity.

Reading the general environment

The aim of reading the general environment is to identify, at least in general terms, opportunities and threats specific to the organization which might emerge in the future. It is impossible to keep abreast of all future developments, nor are all developments relevant to a particular enterprise. Reading is therefore a selective process, one which is a matter of judgement and experience. It is a critical one since circumstances can change quickly, for example as the result of a risk-generating event such as terrorist attacks, and the early identification of a change in trend, or even mood or atmosphere, may be the difference between success and failure. A good reader of the general environment is in a position to take advantage of opportunities and avoid the threats, thereby minimizing risk.

The reading of the general environment can be done by those employed specifically for the task or by others performing different duties. There is a massive task of selection which demands considerable expertise and enormous effort. The opportunity cost is the time, effort and resources devoted to processing the information, time which could be used for other purposes. This is just one element of what are often called search costs, the costs which are incurred in seeking the relevant information on potential transaction partners and the nature of possible transactions. Making such searches and incurring the relevant search costs are preliminaries to strategy making and the organization of the business transactions which realize any strategy.

Readers and the difficulties of reading

Particular kinds of information are relevant to strategy making. There is a need to recognize opportunities and threats and then strategic actions either exploit the opportunity or counteract the threat. Recognizing a potential threat or opportunity is not easy. Reading the general environment for that recognition is a skilled task. There are three main stages in this recognition – selection, transmission and incorporation into strategy making:

1. The reader has to gain access to the relevant information. Initially the information may be in places normally inaccessible to the organization and its readers. It may also take the form of fragmented and superficially unrelated scraps of information which need to be put together from disparate sources. It is vital to be able to recognize the relationship between these fragments.
2. This information must be conveyed at critical times to the strategist and be seen as representing something of relevance to the organization. This conveying of information may be a regular or irregular process, structured into the process of strategy making or merely incidental.
3. The person must persuade the decision makers that the information merits a strategic response of some kind, for example its embodiment within a strategy.

All three stages involve 'political' relationships, not simply a transfer of useful information in a neutral manner. At each stage the motivation for what is happening may not be a simple desire to make an effective strategy. A particular reader may be selected in order to suppress information of a certain type and this may be well known to the reader; or the reader may be expected to confirm a particular view about future strategy. It is necessary to understand the expectations and interests of those involved in the identification, selection and transmission of such information.

One of the problems is that there may be considerable delay in the movement of information through the various stages of strategy making. This delay reflects a number of causes:

• Sometimes the reason is simple ignorance, a failure to understand what is happening, or even stupidity, either on the part of the reader or the strategy makers themselves.
• Sometimes there is dishonesty or corruption. There may be a motive for concealment. Acknowledgement of knowledge may require a recognition of previous mistakes, the admission that a senior person or persons was wrong. Some individuals may be profiting from the status quo in such a way as to make any acknowledgement of the information contrary to their interests.
• There may be general knowledge of a threat, but for a number of reasons nobody is prepared to respond. The culture of the organization may discourage rocking the boat. Previous success or the commitment of key figures to an opposite point of view may be the problem.
• In large impersonal organizations, the reader or the messenger may not have the standing to be believed. Shooting the messenger is frequent enough to deter indiv-

Focus on Theory
An information strategy

Such a strategy would consist of decisions on:

- What maximum level of uncertainty to aim for, or what level of uncertainty to be comfortable with
- What resources to commit to removing uncertainty by generating new information
- How to identify relevant information from the general environment
- What resources to commit and mechanisms to develop for processing the information which is available
- Selecting the readers
- Establishing channels for the transmission of relevant information from the readers to the strategists
- How to link information gathering and processing to strategy making

iduals from becoming the messenger. Nobody may want to be the messenger, particularly if the messenger appears to be the bringer of bad news.

- The reader who wishes to remain the reader may also be apt to communicate what he or she believes is expected and/or what is acceptable, but not what might jeopardize a continuing and remunerative relationship with the enterprise.

All this shows that if information is almost costless, knowledge is expensive to acquire and therefore valuable to possess. It is expensive because it is generated by a process of reading the environment which requires both time and expertise.

Knowledge is valuable because it is specific and only a few have access to such specific knowledge. The value may diminish rapidly as others read the same message. If it were freely and immediately available to all, it would be without value. Strategy defines what that knowledge is and is based on the possession of such knowledge. Knowledge is the raw material from which strategy is made.

It is possible to break reading into four separate activities – scanning, monitoring, forecasting and assessing. This is rather an artificial distinction but it allows the isolation of the key features of the reading process. Each stage is important. In the end all the reading must be targeted in order to be useful. It can be assumed that all employees are capable of doing it, in appropriate circumstances. It might be a consulting firm, a public research organization, a specialist department in the enterprise or the key decision makers within the enterprise working together and providing an input relevant to their own domain, however narrow that might be. In the last case there must still be someone who puts together all the separate pieces of information.

Scanning

Scanning is the process of acquiring, selecting and processing information which is relevant to the particular enterprise. Information does not stand out in an obvious manner, thrusting itself before the reader and offering itself for conversion into knowledge. It has to be analysed for what is relevant. Because of the amount of information, scanning has to be done quickly – a rapid and cursory review of incoming information rather than a deep analysis, but it must be an insightful review.

Any reader has preconceptions about the nature of the world. The world has been likened to an *iceberg*: a submerged foundation of structures which change only slowly; a higher level of trends or patterns which manifest the interaction of underlying structures; and above the surface, events which are the individual elements of such trends or patterns, although difficult to recognize as such. It is possible to have a good notion of the nature of the submerged parts but also be aware that sometimes those submerged parts change. The only hint of the change is to be found in the visible events (see the attempt in Chapter 5 to identify such trends or patterns).

The reader also has to select those bits of information which help to reveal significant new patterns. Of particular interest are those which are relevant to the part of the economy in which the organization operates. The information can come from a host of different sources, such as the Internet, newspapers, journals and magazines, or word of mouth.

Scanning involves covering of an enormous amount of ground and a sensitivity to any news item which hints at relevance. It must involve the use of 'off-centre' information which is likely to indicate unforeseen or previously unrecognized changes, information which is far more important than may appear at first glance. Much of what is read has already been processed and simply rehashes the known in various guises. It is necessary to consider what does not represent the conventional wisdom. Knowing what everyone already knows is not enough. The successful strategist knows already what nobody else knows – that in itself is a source of potential competitive or strategic advantage. However, it is critical to know more. This is not to advocate that everyone becomes a contrarian, although it recognizes the rationale of such an approach.

Monitoring

Monitoring requires the targeting of particular types of information as relevant. Interpretation of this information may lead to the identification of a new development as important enough to constitute a potential threat or opportunity. It may not be either yet but it has the potential to become so. The change may constitute a modification of the macroenvironment, that is, large enough to have a significant impact in the industry with which the monitor is concerned. For example, IBM should have been monitoring the development of the PC in its infancy, and Microsoft the development of the Internet at its birth. The development of the PC and its enormous potential to change the way communication occurs, or the way in which information is stored and processed, was clearly something a good reader should have spotted as early as the 1960s and 70s. Any information relating to such a development requires careful analysis to see how the issue is developing, whether it will in practice manifest itself as a specific threat or opportunity.

Monitoring often involves the application of theory to data, a shrewd reading of cause and effect. This requires a knowledge of the theory which enables an observer to trace a sequence of causal events. Some of this knowledge may be scientific, involving a deep knowledge of the potential of new discoveries, or it might be economic. It does not require a genius to link the ageing of the population of developed countries with an increased demand for medical and nursing care and pensions. Anticipating the direction of future change sometimes requires the application of such theory, whether simple or more subtle. The process is one of homing in on a particular sequence of developments and anticipating the future unfolding of those developments. For example, demographic change drives many of the political, economic and social tendencies which remake the environments in which relevant players operate. Demographic relationships are not difficult to read and are more robust than often thought.

Forecasting The next stage is the attempt to *forecast*. This is so important that it is discussed at some length in the next section. Forecasting is difficult, even for a short period of one or two years. Stability of key relationships may allow the extrapolation of past trends – the relevant systems may remain dominated by predetermined elements. However, unstable times make forecasting very difficult as critical uncertainties emerge, for example the complex unknown of environmental factors. For longer periods it is almost impossible to forecast, except in very general terms.

Forecasting involves looking at the future in a systematic manner, notably at likely macro-change. It may involve generating the kind of scenarios indicated below, and then considering how such change is relevant to a specific enterprise. The scenarios may identify various change elements as driving forces – new political groupings, new fashions in policy, new technologies, extensions of and changes in the market or dramatically new patterns of consumer demand reflecting a new demographic picture. All these may constitute elements which drive the process of change. It is not difficult to recognize the driving forces which are at work in different parts of the economic system.

For example, it is easy to recognize the relationship between the nature of the economic reform process in China and its rate of economic growth, and in turn the relationship between this growth and China's strategic role in both Asia and the world at large. It is also easy to recognize a general process by which growth slows as an economy nears the frontier of best practice, whether in technology or organizations. Japan's current problems will likely apply to China 20–30 years into the future.

Assessing The final stage, after forecasting is complete, is to *assess* the direct relevance of the predicted changes to the competitive advantage held by the enterprise, or the risk environment in which the enterprise has to operate. A key issue is the interaction between the macro and the micro, the broad aggregative scenario and the specific scenario relevant to a particular industry. What do the macro-changes mean in terms of micro-change relevant to an enterprise? Such an ability to look ahead is vital to the ability to develop effective strategies. What opportunities will help in creating new competitive advantage or maintaining an old advantage? What threats are likely to undermine the viability of the enterprise or any of its activities?

Coping with the future

Focus on Practice
IBM, Fishkill and Fab (chip fabrication plant)

Currently a new best-practice plant to manufacture silicon chips, the basis for computing, communications and all consumer electronic equipment, can produce at a level which adds as much as 5% to total world productive capacity. The plant is large and costs US$3 billion or more to build, an enormous commitment of resources. From 300mm silicon wafers, such a plant produces something like three times as many chips as an older plant using 200mm wafers, with costs 40% lower. There are therefore very significant economies of scale which make it impossible for the much smaller, older plant to compete in a contracting or slowly growing market. IBM's new Fishkill plant is best practice and capable of producing US$8 billion worth of chips a

Focus on Practice
cont'd

year. It requires considerable technical expertise to build and bring on stream; this is an expertise which is lost if a company outsources to a specialist 'foundry'.

Given the supply situation for new plants, there is a need for an enterprise to identify adequate demand to dispose of the chips. Construction of a plant of the size indicated above is only justified if the output can be sold. It is necessary to look ahead to see whether future demand will validate any decision to build a new plant. The record in forecasting demand for chips is terrible. At the end of 2000, the Semiconductor Industry Association, the leading trade group, predicted for 2001 global demand at US$240 billion (a 17% growth). In the event the level of demand was US$140 billion (down by one-third). The errors in other years are less dramatic, but still significant. They show the difficulties of making such forecasts.

Given the desired size of a new plant, what should the main player do in preparing for the future? The risk level is high, given the exposure and the volatility of demand, which will tend to deter investment in new plant. Japanese producers such as Toshiba, NEC and Hitachi fell behind during the 1990s by failing to invest. For the main players such as Intel, Samsung and Infineon, there are three options open to them – to work with a partner, withdraw completely from manufacture or take a risk and commit to building a new best-practice plant. In order to do the last there has to be confidence that there is sufficient demand to keep the plants at a high level of capacity utilization. This requires a forecast of future demand which is reasonably accurate.

The success of most human activity is based upon some measure of accuracy in 'predicting' future outcomes. As individuals in their everyday lives and as employees in business activity, all people do this as a regular part of their lives, but unconsciously. However, the future is by its nature uncertain; exact and successful prediction is impossible, but it must be attempted in order to attain business success. A sure failure will follow from assuming that nothing will change or failing to adjust to a general change in trends or the particular behaviour of a key player.

Ways of thinking about the future

There are three distinct ways of thinking about the future:

1. To reject the possibility of, or need for, accurate forecasting. This is done on two opposed grounds:

   • It is impossible to forecast, particularly as change is rapid in most sectors of the economy. This contradicts common sense and would leave no room for an effective strategy.
   • The aim of the strategist is to create the future, or rather to recreate the present, not to take the future as a given.

This second argument embraces a particular notion of *strategy as revolution*. In this situation what the strategist needs to do is to think ahead of action. In the words of Hamel and Prahalad (1994: 82): 'To create the future the company must first be capable of imagining it' and 'Companies fail to create the future not because they fail to predict it but because they fail to imagine it' (p. 120). This view argues that the future is made by many strategists trying to implement their vision. This activity can be called foresight, the ability to think of the future as the potential outcome of specific strategy making.

2. To consider a limited number of possible futures, each reflecting a different way in which key variables might evolve over time. This is usually called scenario planning or scenario building, and assumes a finite and limited number of likely potential outcomes, which reduces the level of uncertainty significantly. It is possible to say something meaningful about the future, which helps to anticipate and prepare for that future. This approach is premised on the notion that there is sufficient stability and knowledge of the future to construct different scenarios, different stories of how the future will unfold. The Royal Dutch Shell Group pioneered this way, making explicit a process of scenario building which is often left implicit. There is no doubt that scenario building is implicit in the way most strategists have dealt with the future. Scenario planning can fill the gap in knowledge.

3. To predict exactly. There are areas where prediction can take the form of forecasting, that is, the exact prediction of an outcome or the attaching of exact probabilities to possible outcomes. There are more of these areas than often thought:

   • Demographic behaviour has unchanging elements which make it possible to look quite a long way into the future, forecasting the size and structure of populations with some precision
   • Technical change also has stable elements which make it possible to foresee the general nature of a future economy
   • Organizational structures have considerable continuity.

In other words there are a significant number of macroparameters which constitute unchanging elements. At the microlevel some industries are mature and slowly changing. They display little development in market conditions or technology. There are clear microparameters within which the organization operates.

Many of the successful predictions that individuals make appear banal. They are constantly ruling out a host of possible future events, doing this automatically, assuming that from day to day there is a considerable repetition of behaviour. This allows the development of *routines*. Human beings have a propensity to routinize their activities, partly because this makes life liveable and partly because it is a source of control, security and efficiency. Such routines allow everyone to save the time and effort otherwise spent organizing the minutiae of everyday life. Also they prevent paralysis as the result of the threat of the worst happening. However, such routines can become inappropriate if unexpected events occur.

It is a reasonable assumption that risk-creating events do not usually occur. In many areas the present reproduces the past and will continue to do so well into the future. Stability in any pattern of human behaviour depends on this characteristic. The persistence of any culture or set of institutional arrangements demands a strong measure of such stability. However, cultures, corporations or individuals can threaten their own survival chances by failing to change or adapt to a changing environment.

Often it is easy to predict that a certain event will occur at an indeterminate date some time in the future. Many of the superficially unexpected events of the recent past were not in themselves surprising, but it was difficult to predict their exact timing. Successful prediction requires more than a statement of eventual occurrence, it requires the specification of the exact timing of the event. From a strategic and business perspective, timing is of the essence. It is often easy to make a vague prediction; it is much more difficult to specify the precise timing. Getting the timing right is often the difference between success and failure.

What is often surprising is the speed with which an event unfolds, such as the oil price hikes of 1973 and 1979 or the collapse of the Soviet Union. A political system may be observed as under stress but its collapse may be sudden and unexpected. It is often obvious that an overvalued market will see a correction in the future, but when will it occur?

In the business world, decisions involving investment of any kind necessarily reflect a view about the future, a comparing of future income and cost streams and often an implicit prediction that certain events will not happen. Nearly all decisions made in the business or economic areas involve reading the future in some way.

Focus on Theory
The time horizon

It is necessary to expand on the significance of the time horizon. There are commonly three different time perspectives, into which any specific strategic future can be divided – the short, medium and long term.

- In the *short term*, say the next two to three years, predetermined elements may outweigh uncertainties in importance, allowing successful forecasting and possibly even a significant level of strategic planning.
- In the *medium term*, say three to ten years, the number of predetermined elements diminishes and that of critical uncertainties increases, with the result that forecasting usually becomes impossible and scenario building, as described in the text, becomes appropriate and critical to successful strategy making.
- In the *long term,* there are almost no predetermined elements but many uncertainties so that strategy making often becomes a waste of time. However, an exercise in strategic thinking might find it useful to consider this far ahead, especially if the nature of investments in the industry involve facilities which last this long. The best that can be done is to trace out the unfolding of the main forces for change.

The length of the various terms in years depends upon the nature of the industry and the pace of change in its environment. If change is rapid, as in the communications sector, the short term is very brief. If the industry is a mature one, changing very little, the short term is likely to be relatively long. In that case predetermined elements will be dominant and critical uncertainties few and weak. The goal of a strategist is to lengthen the short term, in order to expand the scope for strategic management, and to bring the long term within the perspectives of the short or medium terms. The means for achieving this is to reduce the level of uncertainty by reading the environment appropriately.

▶

Focus on Theory
cont'd

Features

Periods		Degree of stability	Stage of uncertainty	Appropriate strategic activity
	Short	Predetermined elements predominate	Almost complete certainty	Strategic planning
	Medium	Mixed strength	Discrete options, continuous but limited range	Strategic management
	Long	Critical uncertainties predominate	Total ambiguity	Strategic thinking

Figure 4.2 **The different time perspectives**

Focus on Theory
The planning period

By its nature strategy relates to the future. How far should a strategist look into the future? It is useful to ask a series of rather obvious strategic questions which help to answer the bigger questions:

- How long does it take to design a new product and put it on the market? The time taken depends whether the new product uses the existing competencies of the enterprise. It also depends on the sophistication and complexity of the product. In some cases, where no new competency is involved and in an industry in which the turnover of new products is swift, the time period might be very short. However, in other cases the period is much longer. Ten years is not a long period for an airliner or a motorcar, if the innovation is to introduce a whole new family, much shorter if it is a variant within an existing family. Even a pharmaceutical product takes up to ten years to develop and put on the market.
- How long does it take for an enterprise to completely change direction, that is, to change an underlying generic strategy? This may involve developing competitive advantage in completely new industries and acting strategically in a completely different way. The period may be five or six years if it is a well-developed strategy.
- How long does it take to change a corporate culture, and/or restructure an enterprise? Probably even longer, maybe ten years if it is to be done effectively.
- How long does it take to create a new brand name? Sometimes months, more probably years and on occasion decades.

All the changes which have significant strategic implications take much longer than usually assumed. Often there is a minimum time period of five years, sometimes ten years might be required. Strategic management or planning, rather than strategic thinking, involves much shorter periods of time. Strategic planning may be relevant only in the shortest of periods when the stream of events is predictable.

▶

Focus on Theory
cont'd

Unpredictability necessarily shortens the relevant time period. If competitive advantage changes quickly, this may cause the time perspective for strategy to be shortened. Different decisions require different time perspectives.

Strategic thinking can be relevant to long periods of time, decades during which significant trends work themselves out, offering both opportunity and risk. It may be possible to anticipate in broad terms technical change or changes in demand patterns which will occur over a longish period of time.

The relevant time perspective depends on the nature of the strategist but it also depends upon the nature of the sector in which the strategist is operating. There is a tension between these two time frames. Should the strategist as strategist, and not as a private individual, assume the enterprise has eternal life? Or does he or she discount the future so strongly that he or she ignores events beyond a target date in the near future? The answer to these questions, highly specific to particular sectors of the economy and particular enterprises, helps to determine the relevant time horizon for strategy. Aligning the time horizon of different strategists within the same organization and different strategic partners is one of the major problems in strategy making.

For the enterprise the length of the product cycle is relevant. This reflects the nature of the industry because the rate of change varies from one industry to another, and also because the investment in facilities or products is for different periods of time. Some industries see rapid rates of change which obscure the likely outcomes of strategic decisions:

- Some industries, such as clothing, require new products or new styles every year.
- A personal computer has to be changed every three years because the speed of technical change and the improvement in the underlying technology is so dramatic.
- Others, such as resources sectors or public utilities, demand a much longer perspective. A power station, a harbour facility or an airport might take years to make operational and might last for 20 years, at least in its main configuration.

The answer to the big question is that there is no one planning period. There are a multitude of different time perspectives relevant to different kinds of strategies, decisions and industries. There is no simple answer and no simple formula.

The inevitability of prediction

All successful enterprises surviving for a significant period of time anticipate future events with a degree of accuracy sufficient to avoid the full negative impact of significant risk-creating events. They also anticipate the conditions of opportunity under which they can create a temporary monopoly sufficient to generate a stream of above-normal profits, in whatever area they are operating. In other words, they can make a strategy which both ensures survival and, beyond that, significant enterprise development.

There is, however, a potential for prediction built into any theoretical model of behaviour. Recognizing and identifying causal mechanisms allow an observer to follow a chain of events as they unfold. Practically, and perhaps intuitively, some get it right sufficiently frequently to reap impressive rewards – witness Warren Buffett, for example – but generally the record is poor. There is a paradox in the contrast between the need for implicit prediction in many areas of life, indeed in any area which involves decisions with implications stretching well into the future, and the limited success of explicit attempts to actually predict on a systematic basis. It is important to have a clear understanding of the limitations of prediction.

There is one area where prediction is a precondition for success and a continuous process. The commercial offer of insurance is an area which, for its viability, depends on successful prediction. What is predicted is the typical behaviour of large numbers of people, not specific individual scenarios. Insurance has been on offer for many centuries. Predicting actual outcomes for one particular individual, enterprise or society is one thing, predicting a probabilistic outcome for many is another. Insurance profits from the law of large numbers. Insurance is possible where there is a sufficiently large body of data and low probability of an event occurring to make premiums small enough to be affordable and claims infrequent enough not to create even a temporary financial embarrassment. Successful insurance requires a repetition in broad terms of past behaviour. The future in some sense reproduces the past and can be extrapolated from that past. Nevertheless, the unexpected can create losses even for insurance companies, as can be seen in the Strategy in Action on Lloyd's in Chapter 14.

Focus on Theory
Public or professional liability

Insurance requires a clear view about the probability of certain events happening in the future. Insurance against public or professional liability is an essential risk management strategy (see Chapter 14). It is extremely difficult for any organization, either public or private, or indeed for any vulnerable professionals, such as doctors, travel operators or sportspeople, to operate without a public or professional liability insurance. This also applies to those who organize festivals, carnivals and special events of various kinds.

Such an insurance provides a means of controlling a particular kind of risk and guarding against the negative consequences of the occurrence of certain risk-generating events. The ability of a person suffering harm of some kind, whether a customer or not, to sue the responsible agency for negligence creates the potential for very large losses for that agency, which it is better to guard against. Negligence arises because of a failure to maintain the quality of a facility or service, a failure which might result in injury or damage of some kind. The same principle applies to the conditions of employment and their impact on workers. Or it might apply to the provision of services by various arms of the government. A pedestrian tripping up on an uneven pavement can be a cause for litigation against the local authority responsible for the pavement.

There are three separate problems which contribute to these difficulties and therefore potentially the costs of the organization, all involving an element of uncertainty about the future and therefore ignorance:

- The degree to which individuals, sometimes encouraged by certain law firms, are litigious. How likely are those suffering injury to sue? How far do those held responsible accept responsibility for the consequences of risk taking?
- The frequency of such events. The problem is twofold:
  1. There may be a long period between cause and effect, such that the initial cause is not immediately recognized as such. The effects are long-tailed. They may go unrecognized for a significant period of time. They may threaten a large number of people in a completely unforeseen manner.
  2. Which events should be counted?
- The attitude of courts, since they define the nature of negligence and the penalties imposed. In the nineteenth century the courts in the USA usually found against

Focus on Theory
cont'd

those who were the victims of negligence, particularly in the area of business (Scheiber 1981: 103–11). In this way they minimized the costs to business as the new industrial economy emerged. Today courts are much more likely to make large awards to such victims.

In a litigious society in which courts are victim-friendly, any negative impact can result in a case in which an organization is sued for negligence. The chain of causation may be long and indirect. The damages awarded by a court can be so big and the number of individuals affected so numerous that they threaten the very existence of the organization.

Without insurance, the organization might not be viable. In many cases the enterprise might find that potential customers insist that there is appropriate insurance in place. They will do this in order to ensure that they themselves are protected. The problem may be the size of the premiums. For small or medium-sized enterprises this may be a very real problem.

Successful strategic thinkers must have a view about the future. They should be able to read when human behaviour is stable and can be relatively easily anticipated, including the special case when the law of large numbers allows easy interpretation of probabilities or when theory provides us with sequences of linked cause and effect, confirmed by empirical analysis. In such a case change is described as *endogenous*. They must also be able to read when there is a good chance of a change in trend, or an event indicating such a change, which has the potential to remake a significant part of the environment. Such thinkers also accept the inevitability of the occurrence of some events which can only be described as *exogenous*, those without obvious immediate cause and not part of any obvious pattern of past behaviour. On deeper analysis there are few such events. The vast majority of unforeseen disasters which have afflicted enterprises should have been anticipated by them. The aim of the strategist is to convert all exogenous events into endogenous ones by finding a theory which helps to predict the chain of events. The aim, in the words of Watkins and Bazerman (2003), is to convert unavoidable surprises into predictable surprises.

Reasons for a failure to predict accurately

There are good reasons why prediction often fails, but it is not because it is impossible to predict. In fact, the reasons for failure are easily understood and thus can be addressed. The failures arise in three main areas:

1. *recognition:* not identifying the threat in the first place
2. *prioritization:* not according the threat the significance it deserved, even if you recognize it
3. *mobilization:* not committing the resources needed to cope with such a negative event.

This chapter is concerned with the first two areas. Scenario building, as described below, can deal with them. The reasons for failure are:

- *psychological:* resulting from various cognitive biases, usually the result of a self-serving orientation which means that we see the world as we want it to be, not as it is

- *organizational:* resulting from the fragmentation within any large organization of information and responsibility, a tendency which means that nobody sees the whole picture
- *political:* resulting from flaws in the decision-making process which allow interest groups to push their own barrows.

The implications are obvious. Any prediction process must be structured to avoid them. It should include outsiders to stop the self-serving bias of insiders, and involve cross-functional and cross-departmental teams to stop fragmentation.

Methods of dealing with uncertainty about the future

There are various ways in which a strategist can deal with an uncertain future. In some way the strategist must construct a likely future and then run a strategy against this construction. The strategist has as his or her goal the translation of information about future events into knowledge. This involves a process of selection of the relevant information.

There are three main methods of doing this. The first two involve running different strategic options to test their robustness to changing external events:

1. Contingency testing assumes the prior existence of a strategy and involves testing its robustness, its vulnerability to various contingencies, that is, the occurrence of various events. In this the strategist evaluates the effect of a given contingency on the strategy, that is, any event or set of events which may cause serious difficulty in the achievement of the objectives of the strategy.
2. Sensitivity analysis in which the values of different key independent variables are varied to test which ones are critical to strategic performance. One such variable might be the level of demand for the product(s) or the cost of a vital input. Some variables can change by a large amount but do not have a serious impact on strategic outcomes. Others require only small changes to have such an impact. Again this assumes the previous formulation of a strategy which is then tested for its robustness.
3. Scenario building which is more ambitious in its scope than the previous two but is ultimately the only approach which directly confronts the uncertainty of the future. Scenario building does not assume the previous existence of a strategy. Scenario building has an important strategic role to play. It can be used to encourage staff to become keen readers of the environment.

Different kinds of risk

Uncertainty about the future creates an environment of risk for the enterprise. In this context, risk is interpreted to mean the possibility of some unforeseen event imparting a significantly negative effect on a key performance indicator, such as profit.

Risk-generating events are common and constitute part of the environment of every organization. Risk exists at all levels of society. There are risks which could be regarded as specifically global and those which are national, industrial, organizational or even individual.

Global risk

There is some evidence that global threats are appearing with increasing frequency and having a more significant impact than in the past. *Global risk* takes a number of different forms:

- epidemic disease, whether human, animal or even plant, which does not respect national boundaries. These have been around for millennia. There are numerous examples: for humans, AIDS, SARS and new virulent strains of malaria; for animals, mad cow disease and foot-and-mouth disease; and for plants, rusts and smuts and, specifically for vines, phylloxera.
- general economic depression, the last major case being the Great Depression of 1929 and after. Some financial crises, such as the Asian economic crisis of 1997, only affect particular regions of the world.
- world war, such as the two wars of the twentieth century in 1914–18 and 1939–45 or a war which expands beyond a single country either in locational impact or the level of involvement of other countries – the Gulf War of 1991 certainly qualifies, the Iraq War of 2003 probably.
- acts of international terrorism.
- the impact of global warming and other environmental damage, such as acid rain and the depletion of the ozone layer.
- a virulent computer virus.

Such risks consist of threats which extend beyond international frontiers, and cannot be dealt with solely on a national level, but require global control. However, because of the weakness of international organizations and international law, they usually have to be dealt with at the national level and by ad hoc international cooperation between the affected nation states. The rising importance of such threats may encourage the process by which enterprises become truly global. It may also encourage the strengthening of global institutions. It throws more importance onto the global institutions which do exist, such as multinational enterprises.

The risk matrix

As we saw in Chapter 3, country risk arises mainly because of the existence of multiple sovereignties and multiple currencies. The existence of national boundaries is central to the notion of country risk. It is the risk which arises because of the increasing interaction between nation states. Any global activity must take account of country risk. Chapter 6 explores fully the meaning and significance of this concept.

Industry risk arises because of the different characteristics of different industries. These characteristics involve different competitive conditions, technologies and ways of satisfying consumer demand. The rate of change of these environmental conditions within different industries also determines the incidence of risk.

Focus on Theory
The risk matrix

Any enterprise operating on the global scene in specific industries must consider a combination of country and industry risk. It is probably best to picture the risk environment of an enterprise as a risk matrix in which country risk is on one axis and industrial risk on the other. All enterprises are faced with this matrix of risk, shown in Figure 4.3.

Focus on Theory

cont'd

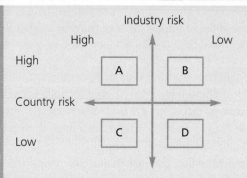

Figure 4.3 **The risk matrix**

- Investing in 3G technology in the telecommunications industry in Indonesia might be an example of A
- Investing in the gas extraction in the Persian Gulf might be an example of B
- A commitment of resources to the steel industry in the USA might fall within C
- Investing in computer software in Ireland might be an example of D.

Enterprise risk

The enterprise has no choice but to take account of the higher level types of risk not specific to it which are filtered down and have an impact on its performance. Enterprise risk, however, exists over and above the matrix of risk referred to above. It comprises the issues specific to a particular enterprise, notably its *creditworthiness*, which in its turn reflects both its economic viability as a profit-making organization over the medium to long term and its ability to remain liquid and crisis-free in the short term. This risk can be further broken down into its different components. A common classification for any enterprise would include the following but this is far from being the only possible classification (Saunders, 2000):

- *Price, specifically interest rate, risk*
This is the risk of an unexpected change in price, particularly of the price of capital. The latter has a particular importance since it can affect the value of all assets since it changes the basis for capitalization.

Some price change is anticipated but price risk refers to the non-anticipated change. Price change can be systematic, that is, affect all markets in the same way. On the whole businesses prefer a moderate degree of price inflation, say 2–3%, to any level of deflation or a more significant level of inflation. This is because a moderate rate also inflates nominal profits without disrupting the economic system and diverting investment into particular kinds of inflation-proof assets.

Risk also arises from individual price movements, again when they are unexpected. It is sometimes possible to anticipate the effect of a change in market conditions, as demand runs ahead of supply or vice versa (see the scenario-building exercise on the price of oil later in this chapter).

- *Differing maturities risk*
This is the risk which arises because of the different maturities of assets and liabilities held by an organization and combines with unexpected interest rate changes to

create a vulnerability for enterprises. This is particularly true of financial institutions but it applies to any enterprise which has assets and liabilities whose maturity date differs and therefore can only be liquidated at different times.

- *Off-balance sheet risk*

Not all obligations show up on the balance sheet. Loan guarantees do not, but they create a vulnerability to risk. Enterprises often deliberately create entities which are off-balance sheet to which they shift costs or liabilities from the balance sheet in order to make their profits appear higher and raise their share price. A special case of an off-balance sheet entity is the captive insurance company set up to insure a risk specific to an enterprise. Such an entity is not a genuine controller of risk.

- *Operational risk*

Breakdowns occur on the operational side, which halt production or threaten the economic viability of the enterprise. There are a variety of sources – labour troubles such as strikes or working to rule, resource scarcities or power cuts. These may arise as a consequence of events completely beyond the control of an enterprise. The cause may also be a fault in engineering systems or a problem of quality control. It is critical to spot such a change quickly.

- *Technical risk*

The introduction of new technology always brings unforeseen teething problems. It is often much more difficult to bring a new technology on stream than usually thought or planned (see the case study on 3G wireless technology in Chapter 8). In any event, the disruption resulting from the introduction of new systems is a source of risk. The new technology may not initially deliver what is expected.

- *Liquidity risk*

An enterprise sometimes does not have the cash to meet its immediate obligations, which may have increased above the norm, although in every other sense it is a viable concern. There may be a bunching of demands which cannot be met from working capital or cash reserves available at the time.

- *Insolvency risk*

The basic cause of insolvency is the inability to make a profit over a significant period of time. It is illegal in most countries for directors of an enterprise to allow it to continue operating if it is insolvent. Enterprises can continue to operate if they can command financial resources. Amazon.com continued to trade without making a profit, and continues to make only a small and uncertain profit. It never became insolvent because it continued to command the necessary financial resources to operate. If an enterprise ceases to be creditworthy and cannot raise new resources, it is in danger of becoming insolvent.

- *Political risk*

Politics intrudes into the life of an enterprise through policies which impinge directly on almost every feature of its economic life. These policies range from tax changes to changes in the regulatory environment, and from foreign policies to social welfare policies. A change of policy can have a profound effect on an enterprise. Policy can change for various reasons. The critical issue is anticipating such a change of policy, which is usually easier to achieve at the domestic rather than international level.

• *Transfer risk*

Exchange rates change with direct and indirect effects on the revenue and cost streams of an enterprise. There is a *translation problem*, dealing with the accounting implications of the change in values. There is also a *transfer problem*, moving funds between countries at exchange rates which are unexpected. There is also an *economic problem*, which arises from the combined impact of price changes and exchange rate changes. Exchange rate changes are linked, in the medium term, with relative price changes in a complex chain of cause and effect. Both kinds of change need to be considered simultaneously.

Other kinds of risks are referred to in the literature but they are not strictly comparable since they apply at different levels and in different ways. They also overlap in both characteristics and outcomes. They all involve the unexpected happening and a failure to forecast accurately.

Risk-generating events which have an impact at all the levels discussed above can and do occur. There are decision makers of varying importance at all these levels trying to cope with or manage the different kinds of risks. General risk management has to be built at these different levels into each and every strategy adopted by organizations. While there is a trade-off between risk and return, it is clearly in the interest of all decision makers to minimize risk at any given level of return.

Scenario building

Scenario building is a technique developed in the nineteenth century by the military for the conduct of war games. The pioneer work in extending the technique to the business world was done during the 1960s and early 1970s by Peter Schwartz at Royal Dutch Shell, with some significant success. As a result it is sometimes called the 'Shell method'. It has since moved beyond this limited sphere as individual practitioners have moved on from Shell.

Underpinning any reading of the general environment is the aim of generating scenarios which represent different views of the future. This can be done explicitly or implicitly. Most of us do it implicitly all the time. It is better done explicitly so that the strength of assumptions made can be spelt out and tested. The problem is finding the necessary time and resources to do a proper job. It is also often necessary that the full implications of different scenarios are explored.

Any major decision assumes a twin scenario for reading the future:

1. a *goal scenario* expressing the aims and objectives of the individual or enterprise and how they might be realized
2. a *general environment scenario*, specifying the changing nature of the context in which the individual or enterprise seeks to fulfil these goals.

There are therefore both microlevel and macrolevel predictions, those made by individuals in the course of their everyday lives or organizations in the course of their business activities, and those made at higher levels, concerning the unfolding of events at the global or national levels which reflect an expectation of how a host of micro-actions made by others will unfold and interact.

This dichotomy is matched by two very different purposes in scenario building:

1. To assist in making a particular decision. The nature of the decision helps to give scenario building a focus. The process of scenario building has a finite life, corresponding with that of the analysis which precedes the project.
2. As a perception device, one which alerts all the participants in strategy making to future opportunities and threats. This assumes that the process of strategy making should involve as many as possible of an organization's managers. It encourages all to engage in strategic thinking. This second kind of scenario building is an ongoing process.

How many scenarios?

Scenario building is best done when an uncertain future presents several discrete and identifiable alternatives. 'Scenarios are a set of reasonably plausible, but structurally different futures' (van der Heijden, 1996: 29). It is more difficult if there is a continuous range of possibilities, or if there is complete ambiguity concerning the future, which may be the case if an organization looks too far ahead. In the medium term, complete ambiguity is extremely unlikely. In any event such ambiguity can be removed by the preparatory work done on scenario building. Even a continuous range can be reduced to a finite number of possibilities, with some having markedly higher probabilities than others. The chosen scenarios are initially seen as equally likely to occur. The key issue is the underlying structure of cause and effect which defines the separate outcomes.

Usually it is enough to generate a minimum of two, three or four scenarios from which to select the most likely outcomes, but which also allow decision makers to accommodate other possible scenarios, should they be realized. The number of scenarios will reflect the nature of changes which might occur. There may also be sub-scenarios which are variants of the main scenarios.

The problem with using three scenarios is that two of them will tend to be classified as at the extremes, an optimistic and a pessimistic view of outcomes, and the third, in the middle, seen as the most realistic. The last will inevitably be taken as the scenario most likely to eventuate. It is preferable that the different scenarios represent real differences in the way events might unfold, not some average of possible outcomes, which itself is not really a possible outcome. It is not sensible to exclude extreme outcomes by simply averaging all possibilities. Weighting possible outcomes by their probability produces a similar kind of result, that is, a single forecast, but not a result which is helpful for strategy making. Scenario building is usually set up to avoid an oversimplistic approach to forecasting and take full account of the uncertainty which exists.

<table>
<tr><td>

The components of scenario building

</td><td>

There are three main components of a scenario which must be identified and distinguished. The illustrations are from an imaginary scenario-building exercise to forecast the price of oil:

1. *The driving forces:* those factors which ensure that any system changes and then mould the nature of the new system and the way in which it changes. For the determination of oil prices they might be:
    - Environmental concerns requiring the reduction in the consumption of carbon fuels and encouraging energy efficiency and the development of alternative sources of energy
    - Muslim fundamentalism and the nature of international conflict in a post-Cold War world, particularly as it relates to issues relevant to countries in the area of the Persian Gulf, including Israel, and members of OPEC (Organization of Petroleum Exporting Countries)
    - The energy position of both developed and rapidly growing economies, for example the rising dependence of some major oil consumers – USA, Japan, China and India – on imports from the Middle East.

2. *The predetermined elements:* those factors from the past which continue as before, providing stability to any system:
    - The size of existing oil reserves, and the level and rate of growth of potential production in the near future
    - The relationship of energy consumption to economic development as determined by the nature of known technology
    - National and cultural divisions in the world.

3. *The critical uncertainties:* the areas where there are markedly different possibilities but whose influence will determine the nature of the new world (see Schwartz, 1996):
    - The possibility of an 'oil shock' of various kinds. This might take the form of a war which closes significant facilities or the overthrow of moderate political regimes in oil-producing countries
    - The exact rate of growth of the world economy over the medium to long term, with the implied level of world activity in ten years time
    - The strength of environmental pressure to reduce carbon fuel use and the level of investment in new technology determining the economics of alternative energy sources
    - The external political environment of OPEC countries
    - The nature of political regimes in OPEC countries such as Saudi Arabia and Iraq
    - The state of the Israeli/Palestinian conflict
    - The productive potential and attitude of non-OPEC oil-producing countries.

</td></tr>
<tr><td>

The steps in scenario building

</td><td>

There are a number of steps in building a scenario (Schoemaker, 1993; Schwartz, 1996). The following exaggerates the number of steps, but does so in the interests of spelling out exactly what needs to be done. In practice the process can be simplified. It also indicates how this might be done if the aim were to forecast the price of oil.

</td></tr>
</table>

Step 1
This involves defining the scope of the exercise, which can vary according to the nature of the problem under analysis. It is helpful to start with a specific problem, or decision to be made, which provides focus and concentrates attention on a limited area of interest. This could take the form of a specific question: should the enterprise make a particular investment? Should it enter a particular market? Should it, as part of a policy of diversification, acquire an enterprise in a quest to enter a new industry? The problem to resolve might be whether to open a new oil or gas field and undertake the enormous investment required.

It is possible to examine the scope. Is it a big problem with macro-implications? Or is it a micro-problem with restricted links to the macro-scene? In the former case there are broad questions to be asked. They may not be simply economic. In the latter it may be that the problem is more circumscribed and limited to economic or business issues. For example, for the price of oil, the interest might be:

- A broad one, that of a government considering the implications of oil import dependence at different price levels, particularly if it concerns an unstable region.
- A narrow one, that of an oil company wishing to open up a new oilfield, asking the question whether it should do so. The decision might hinge upon the level of the price of oil. Or an automobile producer planning a new car, where the type of car, with its power source, its planned size and engine capacity, might depend on the price of oil (see the case study on the HEV in Chapter 5).

Focus on Theory
Macroeconomic stability

Macroeconomic stability is usually understood in the context of the movement of aggregate prices. Those who have grown up in the postwar world have lived all their lives in a scenario of persistently rising prices or inflation. This has not always been the normal condition. Throughout history there have been significant interludes of falling prices, not just brief adjustments after wars or other events (for the regularity of such cycles see Fischer, 1996). From 1873 to 1896 the general price level fell consistently, and it did so again in the 1930s. Today prices are falling in a number of significant Asian economies, notably in Japan and China. There is some concern that the world is about to enter a new interlude of falling prices.

Falling prices create a much more difficult scenario for most decision makers than rising prices, particularly if there is a high level of debt in an economy. The real value of debt rises in a situation of fixed nominal debt value and falling price and income levels. However, if the fall in incomes lags behind the fall in prices, consumers benefit. There are two factors which might cause deflation:

1. A tendency of potential output to run ahead of actual output and create an output gap. Excess capacity is really a symptom of the problem since it is in theory possible to lift demand to the appropriate level. The 1870s' deflation was associated with the massive surge in agricultural and commodity output which resulted from the opening up of new areas of settlement in the world. The primary sector led the way. Today the excess output is much more likely to be in manufactured goods, automobiles for example. If output grows at less than its potential rate of 3–3.5%, surplus capacity will appear and grow, especially if the disparity persists for a number of years. The growth of the Japanese economy has limped behind its potential to produce manufactured goods, as a result of a

stagnant domestic market – export markets cannot take all the surplus. Attempts to sell the surplus on world markets tend to push down prices on these markets.

2. A failure of combined fiscal and monetary policy. In theory it is not difficult for governments to prevent an economy moving into the deflation zone. If the government allows the economy to move into the deflationary zone, it is difficult to reverse the movement since it becomes self-reinforcing as consumers postpone purchases to take advantage of lower prices later and react to a declining wealth effect. As Keynes rightly pointed out many years ago, there is a liquidity trap since it is impossible to shift interest rates below a minimum threshold level, which might be zero or something close to it. Deflation keeps the real rate of interest above zero even if institutions literally give away the money at zero interest. It is not always possible for government deficits financed by printing money to solve the problem, since a decline in confidence can lead to an accelerating decline in private consumption and investment levels which more than offsets government increases.

It is an important task to anticipate price movements, particularly during the transitional periods when the direction of movement is reversed. Scenario building can be used to explore the paths which might lead to varying rates of change – rapid price inflation, significant deflation or relative stability.

Step 2

This involves identifying the key players and driving forces in the environment immediate to the problem. This requires knowing who the main stakeholders are since they will define what is meant by success and eventually indicate whether success has been achieved. What exactly would indicate success for them? Very often profit is the key performance indicator. What factors influence whether success is achieved for players other than the owners? Who is likely to be affected by the success indicators?

The interests and actions of the main stakeholders are a vital part of the exercise since their responses to ongoing events will help to determine the actual outcomes. Some players may not be stakeholders in the narrow sense of the word. Their actions may be unconnected with the problem area. The forces which affect all groups may differ widely, including everything from changes in government policy to immediate environmental concerns.

In the case of oil, the main stakeholders are the governments, the owners of the enterprises which produce and use oil or produce and sell products complementary to oil or oil-using products, and those who manage or work in such enterprises:

• For the governments of oil-producing countries, revenue from excise taxes or directly from oil sales is the main success indicator. It depends upon both price and quantity sold.
• For the government of an oil-importing country, it might be to keep the cost of such imports at a manageable level.
• For an oil company or an automobile producer, profit is the main performance indicator. In the first case, the price has a direct impact on profitability, in the second an indirect impact, since the demand for automobiles and their use when purchased will reflect to some degree the running costs of cars, including the cost of the petrol consumed.

Step 3

This involves identifying in a general way the three factors which influence outcomes: the driving forces which underpin the motivation and actions of the key local players; the predetermined elements which provide stability; and the critical uncertainties whose unfolding underpins the existence of markedly different scenarios. The predetermined elements will be the same for all the scenarios. What distinguishes one scenario from another are the critical uncertainties.

This step requires identifying the basic trends which are relevant to the area under analysis, specifically the macro-driving forces operating in and on that industry. It is breaks in trends, or large unexpected events, with which it is most difficult to deal. Are there technical changes which are revolutionizing the methods and costs of production or the use of the product or service? Are there demographic changes which are changing the nature of demand? There is a need to link these in a theoretical way to performance indicators which are important to the enterprise.

Probably the chief driving force in the oil industry is the behaviour of OPEC. The conditions of supply and demand remain stable over time. Most oil production in any period comes from existing fields. Reserves are well known. Equally, in the short term, demand is relatively fixed, except that the level of activity in the world economy determines the overall level of demand, which fluctuates with the business cycle. The overall supply and demand conditions create the environment in which OPEC seeks to set the price. In normal circumstances OPEC seeks to fix the price at between $18 and $24 per barrel. There are four critical uncertainties:

1. the general political environment
2. how far OPEC remains united and reacts in a concerted way to changes in that environment
3. how non-OPEC countries behave in response to OPEC initiatives
4. how much of world production OPEC controls.

Step 4

The fourth step is to focus on the identity of the key uncertainties and investigate the levels of uncertainty associated with them. This involves identifying the areas of critical importance which have a significant impact on outcomes, but where it is uncertain what might happen. Is government policy a critical variable, or is technical change more important?

For example, in the oil industry it needs to be asked whether OPEC will limit production in the interests of higher prices. Or will production in countries outside OPEC increase in a way which undermines OPEC's ability to control prices? Or is it the overall increase in the level of demand for oil, which reflects the rate of growth of the global economy, that dominates, rather than supply factors?

What determines the behaviour of OPEC? What are the influences beyond the narrowly economic? The political situation in the world, in particular in the Middle East is a major factor in this, as the price hikes of the 1970s showed. The state of the Israeli/Palestinian confrontation, the role of Iraq and its stance vis-à-vis the outside world, Islamic fundamentalism and its popularity, the nature of the regimes in Iran and other oil-producing countries are all key issues.

How homogeneous is OPEC? Equally, how far can OPEC persuade non-OPEC countries to go along with it? Specifically, what are the policies of countries such as Russia, the former Soviet republics, Norway and Mexico which are possibly important sources of new reserves of oil and significant reserves of gas that are competitive with oil?

Step 5

This involves a first drafting of possible scenarios since the main themes, or *scenario drivers*, have been identified. There should emerge a clear logic for each scenario, a sequence of causes and effects. If, for example, there are two key variables, these could be presented as a matrix which offers four possible scenarios. The price of oil which determines whether a new field is economic to develop may reflect the price and production policy of OPEC and the supply of oil outside OPEC. At this stage the scenarios take a crude form but the main variables are all put into place.

The scenarios involve the choice of a *plot* or *narrative story*, of which there are a number of different kinds. It might be one in which there are winners and losers – a zero-sum game – or it may involve a particular challenge and response or simply be part of a process of evolution of an industry or market. The scenario may reflect the nature of that narrative story.

A preliminary outline of the oil scenarios might develop three possible outcomes from the unfolding of the element(s) of critical uncertainty:

1. At one extreme, it might assume a resolution of the Israel/Palestine problem and the prevalence of moderate Arab governments in charge of the oil-exporting countries, with a decline in the influence of extreme views. It would also assume a resolution of the problems in Iraq.
2. At the other extreme, there is the continuation of major conflict, and the domination of fundamentalist governments prepared to use their oil muscle to reduce output and push up the price of oil as a political weapon.
3. In between these two extremes, there is the continuation of the present uncertainty, with unresolved conflicts and a mixture of moderate and fundamentalist regimes. This regime may be an uneasy one, punctuated by intermittent crises. In this case there are occasional events which threaten to destabilize the situation.

These possibilities give us the basis for three scenarios, which represent three feasible futures:

1. A relatively low oil price of $10 per barrel
2. A price at the high end of $30
3. A medium price of $20 which is close to the level before the Iraq War of 2003.

Step 6

The sixth step is to check the scenarios for consistency and plausibility. At this stage this is not a full reality check, more a check of the internal logic or coherence of the narrative story, and a cursory evaluation of the persuasiveness of the scenario constructs. Do they look and feel right?

At the same time it is possible to develop them into what can be called *learning scenarios*, in other words, to try to give expressive titles to the relevant scenarios, titles which encapsulate the essence of these scenarios, identifying their nature. These titles should sum up the possible outcomes and highlight the essential features of these different scenarios.

Focus on Practice **Naming the** **scenarios**	Ericsson, the large Swedish multinational, conducts a major review of the telecommunications industry every two years, using scenario building. At the last review Ericsson identified three main scenarios, distinguished by which sector of the industry would attract customers first, and therefore was likely to be in a strong position to fashion the tastes of the consumer in the future. The scenarios were called: 1. *Grand traditionalonie:* the major carriers will continue to dominate the industry 2. *Service mania:* companies providing the Internet and information services will dominate the market, with customers taking whatever carriers and devices these companies provide with the deal 3. *Up and away:* the hardware manufacturers dominate and customers simply accept whatever services and software come with the PC which they buy. Peter Rule, director of strategic development at Ericsson, indicated that Ericsson had tended to opt for scenario 3 as an accurate description of the unfolding situation.

It is possible to label the oil price scenarios to give them some focus. The first could be called *peace reigns*, the second, *clash of cultures* and the third, *continuing instability*.

The peace reigns scenario means that political intervention in the market determination of price is mild and the price simply fluctuates within the desired range according to market conditions. If there is significant growth in the developed economies, the price may be relatively high, at around $24; if these economies are in recession, the price may be at the lower end, at about $18. Even in this scenario, if OPEC loses its control over price as new producers enter the market, or as members become free riders maximizing their own advantage by increasing production and hoping that price stays up, prices could drop to $10 per barrel, particularly if the world economy is in recession.

The clash of cultures scenario means that production will be badly and significantly affected by damage to wells, deliberate curtailment of production or embargoes and sanctions from outside. Depending on who was affected and by how much, and how far producers outside the area could compensate for lost production, the price may rise to $30 and above, in some cases well above, even to a level of $50.

The continuing instability scenario is the most difficult to interpret. Within this scenario, there might be a whole range of possible prices, from $10 to $30, possibly all these prices at different times. It depends on the exact mix of economic conditions, the strength of OPEC, the share of oil production accounted for by OPEC and the nature of the political environment at the time.

Step 7   This comprises fleshing out the scenarios, including the gathering of detailed information which can be fed into the analysis as the basis for the different scenarios, broadly through the process of scanning and monitoring described earlier. On the basis of the previous analysis, research needs can be identified and action taken to find the information, if it is not readily available.

This step might include the application of quantitative techniques, including modelling where appropriate. The key issue is to use quantitative techniques as a servant, not to allow them to become the master, and avoid giving the analysis a spurious degree of accuracy. In most cases this will result in the construction of a number of possible narratives, showing how the economy moves from point A to point B, point C or point D.

This stage involves developing a narrative of how, in each oil price scenario, the political situation will develop and how OPEC will respond to this situation. This needs to be done at different levels, both at the global political and economic level and at the level of the oil producers themselves. This is a major task. For example, it requires an analysis of the stability of key regimes such as Saudi Arabia and Iraq.

Step 8

This involves the drawing out of the implications of the scenarios. How do they look in terms of the decision being made? Does the identity of a realistic scenario make a difference to a project decision? Under how many and which scenarios should the decision be made? Part of the analysis is to assess the impact of these scenarios on the performance indicators of the enterprise. If only one scenario indicates success and this is an unlikely outcome, then the decision is obviously a risky one. If one or more scenarios give a result which is not as positive as might be desired, then it might be worthwhile to see how the result could be improved under the relevant scenarios. Such work enables more robust results to be derived. This allows the analysis to evolve towards clear recommendations on making particular decisions.

The number of realistic scenarios may differ according to the nature of the balance between the different elements. Different probabilities could be attached to these scenarios but it is better to assume equal probability. It is important not to exclude consideration of all scenarios but the most probable. The key issues are the causal mechanisms which explain the unfolding of the different scenarios, not some artificial estimate of probabilities.

At this stage it is necessary to start to draw out the implications of the scenarios for the decisions. Are the outcomes sufficiently different to make a difference to any decisions to be made, whether by governments or private enterprises? Are there ways of making a strategic decision more compatible with all scenarios?

Step 9

The final step is to identify some leading indicators which are easy to monitor and can tell us which scenario is being realized. These are sometimes called *signposts*. The greater the logical coherence built into the scenarios, the easier it is to draw out such leading indicators or signposts and check whether what actually happens conforms to the expectations built into the different scenarios. Where is the world actually headed?

Oil prices move continuously from day to day but may not be the best means of tracing the unfolding of the actual scenario (Figures 4.4, 4.5 and 4.6 show the effect of different behavioural assumptions on the price of oil). Political events in combination with economic trends may be more helpful. There may be a combination of signposts, such as the rate of growth of world output, the proportion of world reserves within OPEC countries compared to the proportion of output accounted for by OPEC and the level of income per head in the oil-producing countries.

Scenario building as a part of strategy making

Scenario building is not something to be engaged in as a brief supplement to other activities or as one of a number of ways of confirming what has already been decided. It is a significant aid to decision making and an essential part of strategy making. It can even be elevated as part of the strategic culture of an organization, as with Royal Dutch Shell.

The construction of relevant scenarios requires careful preparation and considerable research; it inevitably absorbs significant resources and is not to be undertaken lightly.

When should scenario building be used? Generally the level of uncertainty increases the further an organization looks into the future. This uncertainty usually diminishes as the time perspective shortens and approaches the short term. In the medium term, scenario building is very useful. However, since the degree of uncertainty varies from industry to industry, or from sector to sector, the exact length of the medium-term scenario differs.

Reasons for using scenario building

There are a number of situations when the use of scenario building becomes valuable, even critical to an enterprise:

- The general or industrial environments are ones in which there is a high level of uncertainty
- There have already been a number of costly surprises in the industry which have caught out the enterprise and had a significantly negative impact on its performance
- The industry is a new one and/or one which is subject to major change.

Therefore, for various reasons, past experience already suggests turbulence and the future offers the likelihood of more. It is sometimes argued that scenario building is a defensive rather than an offensive exercise, that is, it is more threat- than opportunity-focused. This need not, and should not, be the case. Other more positive reasons for pursuing scenario building are:

- Competitors are already using the technique, and using it effectively
- The enterprise is bad at recognizing opportunities and has failed to exploit opportunities which other enterprises have used to create competitive advantage. The failure may result from group thinking, a conservative view which restricts the diversity of ideas, acting as a straitjacket on creative thinking and/or excessive fragmentation, with each individual doing their own thing and no consensus existing.

The key is to achieve an appropriate balance between integration and differentiation, so that there is enough creativity to identify opportunities and enough harmony to draw out the implications of these opportunities. Scenario building may be the means of achieving this. The failure by the organization to use scenario building may reflect an inability to engage in strategic thinking at any level of the enterprise. By providing a common language and framework to look at the future, the use of scenario building will help in adopting a strategic perspective. Scenario building will help to highlight and resolve existing differences of opinion concerning the future which, in a sector undergoing major change, may be significant. For that reason it is a precondition for good strategy making.

This is a construct of the economist. A demand curve is drawn for a given moment in time. It represents the level of demand for a particular product at different price levels, assuming that it is known. A comparison of different points on the curve does not represent change over time. Change over time is shown by comparison with a new curve. A demand curve can be drawn for a whole market or an individual; the former is an aggregation of the demand curves for the latter.

A well-behaved demand curve is one which shows consistently higher levels of demand at lower and lower prices; it is consistently downward sloping. The relationship between a change in price and a change in quantity demanded is referred to as the price elasticity of demand (% change in quantity demanded divided by the % change in price). Demand is said to be elastic if the ratio is greater than one, inelastic if less than one. Elasticity is sometimes represented as the slope of the demand curve – the steeper the slope, the more inelastic the demand.

Price determination
The price of a product is determined by the intersection of a demand and a supply curve for that product. These curves trace out the quantity of the product demanded or supplied at different price levels. It is assumed that well-behaved curves fall in the case of the demand curve and rise in the case of the supply curve, so that there is always an equilibrium price which equates demand and supply. The stability of the equilibrium price, that is, the ability of the market to return to that level, depends on the exact slope of the curves.

Change over time would be represented by shifts in the curves. For example, the situation for oil might be as follows. As world demand increases with world output, the demand curve shifts upwards. The rate of shift is likely to reflect the rate of substitution of other sources of energy for oil. As new sources of supply are found, this tends to push outwards the supply curve, but it can be countered by using up existing reserves.

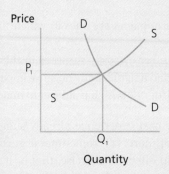

Figure 4.4 **The demand curve**

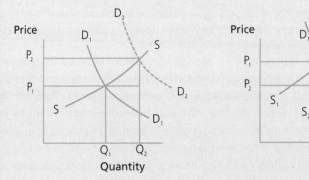

Figure 4.5 **Movement in demand and supply over time**

Focus on Theory
cont'd

In an extreme case, the demand curve may move upwards and outwards and the supply curve downwards, increasing the equilibrium price of oil. If OPEC totally dominated supply, then it could either fix the price and supply as much oil as is demanded at that price or it could fix the quantity and allow demand to fix the price. In the first case, the supply curve is horizontal at the given price, that is, infinitely elastic with respect to price. In the second case, the supply curve is vertical at the given quantity, that is, has zero elasticity with respect to price. The former better represents the behaviour of OPEC. If the non-OPEC producers are willing to sell at a lower price than OPEC, the supply curve will be well-behaved up to the point at which the OPEC price cuts in. It is possible that OPEC policy may change from one position to the other in an unpredictable way.

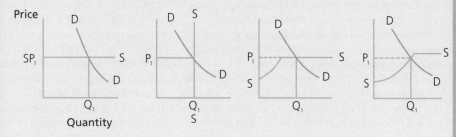

Figure 4.6 **Price determination under different conditions**

Case Study   Airbus Industrie and the next generation of civil airliners

Nature of the industry

The industry which builds airliners has a number of special features which are relevant to the case study:

1. Fixed costs are a large part of the total costs for the production of any airliner. The R&D costs of a new airplane are high, reaching billions of dollars. In order to cover these costs, a manufacturer has to sell a large number of planes, internationally as well as domestically. A generation of airliners must have a long life in order to allow production to cover fixed costs. The present generation is 20–30 years old. To break even on a new airplane requires sales of 400–500 planes, at a rate of about 50 a year over a 10-year period.

   Because of the complexity of aircraft production, there is also a very significant process of learning how to produce new aircraft efficiently. An experience curve typically shows a reduction in costs of 20% for every doubling of production.

2. These two characteristics – economies of scale in the spread of development costs and significant economies of learning – partly explain why the

industry is currently a duopoly, one which could easily become a monopoly if one of the players makes a serious mistake, although it seems likely that the relevant governments would step in to rescue the company in trouble. It also explains why government intervention has been important in this industry.

3. An airliner is an expensive and highly complex product – its manufacture involves thousands of different components. Major employment opportunities and income streams are generated in the region in which production is located. The manufacturer is faced with a proliferation of make-or-buy decisions.

   The industry resembles a pyramid, in that there are a few mainframe integrators at the top, dozens of primary subcontractors in the middle and thousands of secondary subcontractors at the base. Subcontracting, which accounted for less than 10% of operations in the 1930s, rose to 30–40% in the 1950s and to 60–70% by the 1970s. Only those processes which are critical to the core competencies basic to the manufacture of an aircraft have been retained. Others which are not critical are outsourced to those with the relevant core competency. This is partly in order to reduce cost and create flexibility, and partly to raise the quality of components. It is also a method of risk sharing. The component producers share the cost of failure. Sometimes there is a desire to share design and production work with firms located in the countries of purchase of the airliners, so as to be better able to sell the airliners to the local airlines.

4. Because of this complexity and the associated costs, new aircraft are not stand-alone products, but members of extended families of related planes which will share many components and procedures for use in their operation.

5. The demand for new airliners reflects market conditions in the airline industry. These can be quite volatile in the short run and have become increasingly so over the last 20 years, so that demand can fluctuate dramatically from year to year.

In a downturn airlines have surplus planes. In the recession at the beginning of the 1990s, this reached just below 10% of all planes in operation, in the present recession it is as high as 15%. As a consequence airlines slow the rate of new orders and try to delay the delivery of planes already ordered. Even those planes which are ordered and delivered often have to be financed with the help of the manufacturing company which becomes a banker to the airline. The revenue impact of such events on airliner manufacturers is to restrict the money available for new projects.

The past

Initially Airbus aimed for market niches which were free of major competition. It started with just one model of a plane which it designed and built over a seven-year period beginning in 1967. In 1970 the A300 made its maiden flight. The standard A300 carried 226 passengers in two classes. It was built for the short- to medium-range European market. It was the first twin-aisle, twin-engine airliner. It first saw airline service in 1974. By the end of 1975 Airbus had captured 10% of the market segment. Eastern Airlines was the first American airline to use the A300, leasing four aircraft and then confirming an order in 1979. This purchase represented a decisive coming of age for Airbus.

The Airbus strategy was very similar to that of Boeing – to innovate technically, continuously cut costs and develop a whole family of related aircraft. If anything it attached even more importance to its own profits and the operating costs of customer airlines. From the initial one model, Airbus developed a family of 15 different airliners, from short- to ultra-long-haul planes. It now produces a plane for every market segment.

The key events in the history of the A300 series were: the introduction of the A320 in 1988, the first fly-by-wire system (fully electronic control of rudder, flaps and all key mechanisms), a system then extended to the whole family of planes; the introduction of the A340 in 1993, the first new four-engine, long-haul airliner in the world for 20 years; and the announcement of the launching of the A380 programme in December 2000, planned to make its maiden flight towards the end of 2004. The A380 is the focus for this case study.

Airbus has grown into a fully mature company, a manufacturer of civil airliners for the global market. In 2000, its total turnover was US$17.2 billion. By the end of June 2001, it had 4,300 orders outstanding. It was turning out a new plane every working day. As of 2002, 2,500 Airbus aircraft were in service, with 186 different operators in all regions of the world.

From the beginning there was a clear demarcation of responsibility for different functions in building the airliners, although competition for orders was encouraged. The different national parts of the consortium specialized in different areas. In Toulouse, there are 3,000 people from 25 countries working together. Transnational working patterns are very important to Airbus, indeed critical to its success.

The future

The launch by Airbus of the A380 represents a bold coming of age. The standard new plane, it is planned, will seat 555 passengers and is being designed with stretched versions in mind. The A380-200 is planned to have 656 seats. A fully stretched version could carry as many as 800 people.

The range of the A380 is designed to be 10–15% longer and its operating costs 15–20% less than current planes. These are significant gains and likely to be the source of a pronounced competitive advantage for the airlines who operate the plane, if they can be achieved and if no competitor betters them in the meantime. The plane is also intended to be very environmentally friendly, with low fuel burn, less noise and a smaller injection of pollutants into the atmosphere.

The project represents a major challenge to Airbus, both technically and managerially. It requires the application of state-of-the-art technology, using new materials, such as carbon composite for the 'wing box' which joins the wings to the fuselage. As much as 45% of the plane will be constructed from such materials. Fortunately Airbus has been a leading pioneer in the use of carbon fibre over the last 20 years. The managerial challenge is as great, since it is the first project undertaken by the new integrated company. Airbus will need to become leaner and more commercial in its working practices in order to keep the price down and keep to the timetable proposed.

The aircraft has already proved to be popular with the airlines, with orders at a high level. The first planes are due to be delivered in 2006. Airbus's record of achievement leads most airlines to take at face value the timetable which Airbus has proposed for the new project, although some specialists expect a stretching by one year of that timetable. If it comes into existence, no significant airline operating the long-haul routes can afford to be without the new mega-liner. Many are hedging their bets and establishing their place in the queue by ordering now.

Competition

This is an industry in which there are major barriers to entry. It is unlikely that in the near future there will be a new entrant into the industry. This could only occur in the distant future with major government backing combined with the support of a captive market. The main barrier is the sheer size of the cost of developing a new airliner and the long period of time taken to develop a full suite of planes which can compete in every market niche. It has taken Airbus 30 years to become competitive with Boeing. Both the cost and time needed are increasing. The development of the A380 is likely to cost as much as US$12 billion.

Airbus has been assisted in its rise by a considerable degree of complacency on the part of Boeing, resulting from its previous success, a self-satisfaction which constitutes the greatest threat to a continuing competitive advantage for any enterprise. The culture of Boeing was one traditionally dominated by engineers, which did not encourage mention of profit. When Harry Stonecipher took over the day-to-day running of Boeing, after its merger with McDonnell-Douglas, he is reported as being horrified by the state in which he found the civil airliner business. Boeing, clearly losing the competitive battle with Airbus, had entered into a self-destructive price war in order to try to block the rise of the new manufacturer. Production planning was so disorganized that the production lines had to be stopped in the autumn of 1997 in order to allow the suppliers of components to catch up with the level of existing demand.

Airbus and Boeing compete head on for every airline purchase. This is a comparatively recent phenomenon. Of the aircraft currently in the air, Boeing has provided 65% and Airbus 33%. Other players are bit players. More recently, Airbus has been winning the competition, so the proportions in the air are changing. In 1999 Airbus won 470 compared with Boeing's 391 new orders, that is, 55% of the market. For the first half of 2003, Airbus was winning orders at a rate more than five times that of Boeing. It is outcompeting Boeing in every aircraft type. Already Airbus has orders from 10 airlines for 124 of the A380 passenger jets, the largest being for 45 from Emirates. Qantas put in a significant order. Boeing is yet to solicit orders for a new plane; it is at a much less advanced stage in the development of a comparable project.

However, Boeing is less dependent on this industry than Airbus, and is in the process of becoming even less dependent. It always has the option of exit and is taking action which could facilitate such an exit. Boeing has considerable military and space interests. It is one of the largest players in this area, a market much more stable and consistently profitable than that for civil airliners, largely because of government involvement. Boeing has begun to develop an interest in aircraft services – air traffic management through satellites (potentially a greater revenue raiser than civil jets), broadband communications and financing through Boeing Capital, a route which General Electric took when Stonecipher headed its engine division.

Focus on Theory
First-mover advantage

In certain circumstances there is an enormous advantage to being the first mover. It is useful to construct a numerical example for the A380 to show the potency of the cost factor for a first mover. The total development cost of the new aircraft is $12 billion which has to be recouped by sales of the aircraft. If the sales are 100 then the fixed costs per aircraft are $120 million for each plane. If the variable costs are $100 million per plane when 100 built, probably conservative for such a pioneering aircraft, then the total cost of a plane will be $220 million. If the sales are 200, then the fixed costs fall to $60 million and the total cost to $160 million. If the sales rise to 300 then the fixed costs fall to $40 million and the total costs are $140 million. In the unlikely event that production rises as high as 400, fixed costs per plane fall as low as $30 million and total costs $130 million.

▶

Focus on Theory
cont'd

There is no allowance made in this estimate for the effect of experience, or learning by doing, on variable costs. A doubling of production would reduce the variable costs by 20%, which means that costs come down to $80 million for production of 200 and just over $60 million for production of 400. The total costs then decline from $220 million per plane, at a production run of 100, to $140 million at a production run of 200 and to just over $90 million for a production run of 400.

The other important issue is how much an airline is prepared to pay for the aircraft. It is not unrealistic to assume a list price of $150 million per plane. Planes are typically sold on a considerable discount on list price, particularly in a recession. This means a loss of $70 million per plane at a run of 100, a profit of just $10 million per plane at 200 and a significant profit of $60 million per plane at 400. This ignores the timing of costs, mostly incurred early, very early for fixed costs, and revenue, mostly flowing late in the project, as much as five, ten or even twenty years after completion of development. On any reasonable calculation of present value (at a discount rate of 5%) this would mean that at 200 aircraft produced there is still a significant loss. Allowance for a reasonable risk premium in the discount rate ups the ante. The breakeven point may be as high as 250 planes, more realistically 300. Beyond this point the manufacturer begins to make real profits.

Also of relevance is the size of the market. This may vary according to the price, but it is possible to assume away the problem of the price elasticity of demand. If the market were 1,500 as Airbus anticipates, on the most optimistic assumptions this would allow as many as six producers to break even. If the market were only 500, as Boeing anticipates, on the same assumptions, there is room for only two manufacturers. However, no self-respecting manufacturer could be happy with sales below 300. This means either five possible manufacturer slots on the Airbus forecast or just one on the Boeing. Competition really hots up with the latter situation. It will pay to get in first and sell as many aircraft as possible.

Since all the estimates are rather conservative, the situation is even more stark than it appears. There are very real first-mover advantages.

Strategic issues

Strategic risk

In a duopoly any strategy must be formulated with the strategy of the other duopolist in mind. Each is seeking to gain a clear competitive advantage, trying to deter the other from a strategy which would give that player a competitive advantage. In such circumstances there is always the possibility of cooperation but also the possibility of opportunism and deception. This is very much a prisoner's dilemma situation (see Chapter 13).

The decision by Airbus to develop a new super jumbo aircraft which will hold more than 500 passengers is bound to have an impact on Boeing. Boeing, which would have preferred to stay with its existing 747-400, which carried up to 414 passengers, was forced to respond. Initially it responded with a plan for an extended 747, the 747X. Boeing pioneered the habit of

stretching basic planes. In this case the 747 would be stretched to 550 seats, with improved wing aerodynamics and fly-by-wire technology. Such a project, if implemented, would cost it only one-quarter to one-third the cost of the A380 project. However, it soon realized that this was not enough. Boeing had become excessively cautious, whereas before it had kept ahead of the field by being the pioneer. It tried to leapfrog ahead of Airbus by making public a much more advanced project. It responded with the sonic cruiser, in essence a revival of an old supersonic project. However, this project never really took off, and the focus is now on the Dreamliner, a more efficient mid-sized aircraft.

History has shown the problem of launching similar planes simultaneously in a limited market. Lochheed and McDonnell-Douglas launched the L-1011 and the DC10 into a market which could only accommodate one such plane and also failed to compete with the existing

Boeing 747. The DC10 exited in 1980 and L1011 in 1981. Both failed to cover the development costs. The result was mutual suicide and the extinction of both manufacturers as separate entities.

Airbus has become the leader and Boeing the follower. For a short period, during 1993–5, there was a temporary cooperation between the two on the very large commercial transport project. The Airbus managers believed that this might have been a ploy to try to extend Boeing's dominance which was under threat throughout the 1990s.

The managers of Airbus rightly thought that the sonic cruiser was a bluff, but have admitted that they have a trans-sonic project code-named E2 under analysis. For example, one of the artist impressions of a sonic cruiser for a period adorned a billboard just outside the Qantas Jet Base at Sydney Airport. It read, 'Let the Future Begin', and was pitched at eyeball height, not for motorists, but for the Qantas team working in nearby buildings on the introduction of the Airbus A380, for which Qantas had made a very significant order. It was removed when it became obvious that the project was a non-starter with very little airline interest.

The sonic cruiser was intended to fly at just below the speed of sound, about Mach 0.98, slower than Concorde but faster than Boeing's existing jets, thereby reducing significantly air time on long routes, for example by two hours on the Sydney–Los Angeles flight. Future members of the family would fly even faster, at Mach 1.08. In a positioning statement, Walt Gillette, the vice-president of the sonic cruiser programme, said that it would be a family of jets, the first carrying 250 passengers between 10,000 and 16,000 kilometres non-stop. One problem for Boeing was that the first plane would not be likely to be in service until 2008, two years after the A380. Even this was doubtful since the technology was new, with at least 60% of the plane made of composite material, and completely new engines required. There is also on the Boeing drawing board an even more revolutionary plane, a 'blended-wing-body' aircraft which is ten years into the future.

The Boeing approach may be bluff, but it is consistent with the history of the company. The company originally designed the 747 as a military aircraft but it lost the tender. It therefore conceived the aircraft as a freighter which explains its blunt front. For Boeing the jumbo was simply a stopgap to fill a transitional period until supersonic flight became the norm for mainstream long-haul flying, already pioneered over the last 20 or more years by the Europeans with Concorde. The jumbo was a stopgap which surprised the world, saturating it, with 1,300 so far sold, at a total sales value of US$200 billion. There are still about three jumbos rolling off the

production line each month. Whatever happens at the top end of airliner competition there will still be a mighty struggle at the lower end and in the middle ground between the Boeing 737 and the Airbus A320, and between the Boeing 777 and the Airbus A330 and A340.

Anticipating the future

Airbus and Boeing have adopted different strategies which can be summarized briefly as scale versus speed. The two companies have read the future market differently. Boeing thinks that most future passenger growth will come from frequent point-to-point flights, rather than longer flights between the hubs, or major airports. Airbus thinks the opposite.

Accurate forecasting is an essential precondition for the successful launch of a new airliner. Both Boeing and Airbus have their own econometric models of the future demand for airlines, models which they improve and update each year. These models are a critical part of the justification for any project. An ability to anticipate the future accurately is critical to the development of strategies which work (see Chapter 5). The further into the future goes the prediction, the more room there is for disagreement. The forecasters in Toulouse and Seattle differ significantly in their vision of the market 20 years into the future.

The two manufacturers agree on two issues. They agree that growth for the services of airliners, both for passengers and freight, will grow at about 5% per annum over the next 20 years. This will be translated into a threefold increase in the number of planes over the next 20 years. They also agree that there will be a market for some mega-liners, jets which will carry more passengers than any previous airliner, 500 passengers and above.

Where they differ is on how many large airliners are needed. Boeing anticipates a demand for more than 18,000 new planes, of which one-third will be twin-aisled, that is, large. Airbus sees the demand as 20% less, a little more than 14,500, but with almost half twin-aisled. This translates into a significant divergence of view. Airbus believes that there will be a market of 1,500, 1,200 mega-liners and 300 freighters. Boeing thinks the market will be as small as 500, 330 passenger liners and 170 freighters. This is a large difference and has a powerful influence on the strategy adopted by the two manufacturers. The former prediction is much more friendly to a project for developing a mega-airliner.

There are other assumptions which feed into this divergence of forecast. Boeing believes that there will be more deregulation of the skies than Airbus does. Airbus thinks that the influence of this on patterns of passenger flow will be countered by the capacity constraints at airports which will require the arrival of fewer, and therefore larger, planes.

Future strategy

Given the different views of the future held by each, what strategy will these players choose to pursue? The strategy depends on three main factors:

1. The exact size of the future market or, more accurately, the view of the size of market taken by the manufacturer, in particular whether the market is big enough for two players or just one, or optimistically more than two.
2. The confidence with which the manufacturer might embark on a project which will make significant new demands. That confidence reflects a combination of factors, including:
   - present market share and the ability to translate that into orders for a new airliner
   - technical expertise and the capability of mastering all the problems involved in creating a new generation of airliners
   - access to the financial resources needed to make the project a success.
3. The abilities of the leaders of the airline to formulate and implement an appropriate strategy. Any self-doubts will probably yield a strategy which tries to avoid commitment to a new project, or a significant delay in its inception. A high risk level might also lead to a strategy of diversification away from reliance on civil airlines, an option which is ignored for the moment.

Airbus has already won more than 100 orders for the A380, enough to keep the production line going from 2006 to 2009. There is every prospect of Airbus reaching the putative breakeven point of 230 planes in the relatively near future. At this stage it appears unlikely that Airbus will withdraw, although the project could be delayed.

There are a number of possible strategies to be adopted by the two players. Assume that the demand for planes is only sufficient to support one project, not both. The aim of each would be to become the only supplier:

- Both try to bluff each other out of the game. A possible outcome is that one goes ahead, after succeeding in bluffing the other whose bluff fails.

   One airline could decide not to go ahead with the project, even if it has already been publicly announced. It is faced with the problem of dissuading the other player from going ahead. If the other does continue with a rival project, it could establish a competitive advantage in the operational effectiveness of the new plane which could take years to emulate; it would have considerable first-mover advantage. This may mean each player trying to give the other the impression that its new project is still going ahead, come what may, in other words bluffing. The two might then compete in the ambitiousness of the projects announced in the hope of intimidating the other.

- Both agree to delay the development of the new generation because demand is inadequate and the manufacturers lack the resources to complete the projects.

   One resolution of the situation described above is that the two airlines get together and agree not to introduce a new generation of planes, or at least to delay the inception until they could be certain of a large enough market to accommodate both. The present uncertainty of demand for air travel resulting from the danger of terrorist attack, 'the constant shock syndrome', encourages such an approach. It may be obvious that, should both go ahead, the sonic cruiser might cream off enough business traffic to make the A380 unprofitable while not justifying its existence.

- Both go ahead in conditions of healthy demand but they target different market niches.

   If there is enough demand to justify the completion of both projects, the scenario above might still be repeated since profits would be significantly higher for a sole player who completes the project. On the other hand, the game may be played openly and possibly evenly, if both projects have their counterbalancing strengths and weaknesses, which make the relevant planes appropriate to different market segments.

What of other key players, including stakeholder groups? The two manufacturers are not the only players.

Customers

A key question, particularly apt in the difficult environment of post-September 11, is how many airlines can afford to buy the new aircraft. The airline customers are very important. Without their orders no project can go ahead. Has September 11 permanently changed the nature of the market or reinforced changes which were already underway? This is unlikely.

Suppliers

Suppliers of components, such as the engines, are also important. They have to be involved from an early date in the development of a new airliner. They will help determine its price. Contracts for supplies are often used to help win orders from the local airlines. For example,

Airbus has awarded contracts worth US$3 billion over 20 years to 15 different Japanese suppliers, including Bridgestone for the tyres, in an effort to persuade the Japanese airlines to place orders for the A380.

Government

Also important is the government or rather the governments which fix the regulations which determine the structure of supply in the airline industry over the next few decades. It does matter to the manufacturers whether in 10 years there are many small airlines or simply a few consolidated and very much larger airlines. The latter would be likely to have the resources to buy mega-liners whereas the former might not.

Boeing seems keen to adopt a strategy in which it avoids direct confrontation with Airbus by putting the emphasis on a strategy which diversifies its interests. This may suggest to Airbus that Boeing is not serious about its proposals for the next generation of airliners. It is dangerously overreliant on the 737 and to a lesser extent on the 777, with the 757, 767, 717 and 747 having very few orders. Purchase of McDonnell-Douglas raised Boeing's profile in military and space, assumed to be a more stable source of revenues, one less subject to the cycles of the airliner business. In 2003 for the first time defence overtook commercial aviation as a source of revenue. Boeing is seeking to become the 'systems integrator' for high-profile defence contracts. One example is the US$16 billion contract to lease 100 new 767 air-fuelling tankers to the US Air Force. Boeing's leaders have also noted the success of IBM in turning from manufacturing to supplying services. Maintenance is an obvious service which is profitable, but one which reflects the number of planes already sold. Success in providing an air traffic control system based on its satellite system would establish a significant alternative source of revenue. The financing of aircraft purchase by Boeing Capital is another area ripe for expansion, but again might be strongly linked with aircraft sales. Insofar as Boeing ceases to be dependent on aircraft sales for most of its revenue and profit, the nature of the strategic context for its rival also changes.

The element of strategic risk for both companies is high. Once a decision is made to initiate a new project, and Airbus seems to be fully committed to the A380 project, then every move has to be closely planned, whether it relates to production, finance or marketing. Airbus must ensure that:

- enough finance is available to see it through the deficit period and at a reasonable price
- all the technical problems are fully under control
- all costs fall within the planned range

- all suppliers are properly prepared
- every sale is won and sustained, even in recessions.

The main features of the timetable of the project have little flexibility once a commitment is made.

Case Study Questions

1. Why has the industry manufacturing civil aircraft become a duopoly?
2. What would be the influence on both the manufacture and the operation of civil airliners if one manufacturer was to cease production and the industry was to become a monopoly in the near future?
3. What are the factors likely to determine the demand for mega-liners in 10 or 20 years time?
4. How are the following industries related to each other – tourism, the airline business, airliner manufacture, jet engine production? Does the growth of one of them drive the growth of the others, or is there a third factor which drives the growth of all?
5. Why should strategic planning be a must in this industry? What would be the particular aims of such planning?

Reading

Daniel, C., 'Condit focuses on domestic problems', *Financial Times*, June 19, 2003: 29.

Daniel, C., 'Boeing vow to stay in commercial aviation', *Financial Times*, June 19, 2003: 23.

Done, K., 'Emirates Airbus deal is a blow to Boeing', *Financial Times*, June 17, 2003: 25.

Done, K., 'Airbus set for Asian deal', *Financial Times*, June 18, 2003: 30.

Economist, The, Special Report: 'Boeing v. Airbus: towards the wide blue yonder', April 27, 2002: 71–3.

Hill, C. W., 'Boeing versus Airbus; trade disputes', in *International Business*, 2003, McGraw-Hill Irwin: Boston, pp. 295–9.

Sanchanta, M., 'Bridgestone wins Airbus tyre contract', *Financial Times*, June 4, 2003: 31.

Sandilands, B., 'Boeing's jet has everyone guessing', *The Australian Financial Review*, April 9, 2002: 68.

Wine, E. and Simensen, I., 'EADS shares surge as Airbus outsells Boeing at Paris', *The Financial Review*, June 21/22, 2003: M20.

Relevant websites

www.boeing.com
www.airbus.com

This case study is also relevant to Chapters 6, 9 and 14.

Key strategic lessons

- It is necessary to understand the influence of 'bounded rationality' on the strategist, that is, the constraints on the application of reason to strategy making. These constraints arise because of the limitations of the information available and the strategist's ability to process what information does exist.

- The further the strategist looks into the future, the greater is the uncertainty. It is impossible to avoid all uncertainty but the level can be reduced.

- It is possible to distinguish four levels of uncertainty with respect to any future event or series of events: absolute or near absolute uncertainty; a range of possibilities with known limits; a finite number of discrete options; and complete, or near complete, certainty. The aim is to move as far as possible in the direction of complete certainty.

- The strategist converts information into valuable knowledge by selecting what is relevant to strategy making and placing it in the context of a strategy which can be realized. This requires considerable resources including the expertise of a number of 'readers' of the external environment.

- Reading the general environment for information about potential opportunities and threats is critical to successful strategy making. This requires scanning, monitoring, forecasting and assessing.

- The future can be dealt with by rejecting the possibility of forecasting, reducing future possibilities to a finite number of discrete options or believing in the possibility of exact prediction.

- Ignorance and uncertainty involves risk at the country, industry and enterprise levels. Risk can take a variety of forms at the enterprise level, all of which need to be anticipated in advance and managed.

- One effective way of forecasting is through scenario building which allows prediction relevant to a particular project and a sensitivity to future possibilities. The key is to distinguish between forces of change, predetermined elements and critical uncertainties.

Applying the lessons

1 Define the following terms – reading the environment, scanning, monitoring, prediction, foresight, forecasting, assessing, uncertainty, risk, scenario building and scenario planning.

2 In what ways does ignorance or, more specifically, the lack of certain knowledge of the future influence the process of strategy making and the content of any strategy?

3 Indicate how you might set about establishing an information strategy. What factors will determine the level of commitment of resources by an organization in converting information into knowledge relevant to strategy making? Who might do the relevant reading of the environment? Should they be full-time readers? What should their relationship be to the strategists?

4 In an industry of rapid change and intense competition, it may not be possible to predict outcomes with any precision. Choose one such industry and indicate how it is possible to develop a strategy without the availability of accurate forecasts.

5 Consider the industry in which you work or have had experience. What are the risks to which you would be exposed if and when you create a new enterprise or business unit in that industry? How might you classify these risks?

6 Imagine that you are either the lead underwriter of a Lloyd's syndicate or a name backing that syndicate. How might scenario building have assisted you in anticipating the problems of the late 1980s and the early 1990s (see the Strategy in Action in Chapter 14)?

Strategic project

1 It is possible to set up scenario-building exercises in many different areas of interest. There are several examples given throughout the book. The object of this project is familiarize the reader with the procedures for implementing scenario building.

2 Set up a scenario-building exercise on the general movement of prices in future world markets, not just local markets such as Japan. Under what conditions would a deflationary outcome be likely to occur? This requires a careful analysis of relevant forces for change, predetermined elements and critical uncertainties.

3 Take a particular industry and a project in that industry and refine the scenario building to take account of the specifics of the project and the industry in order to evaluate the consequences of deflation.

Exploring further

The main authority on bounded rationality is Simon, 1955: 99–111 and 1976.

Quinn, 1993, is the person most associated with the notion of the enterprise as a learning organization. This book should be read with Senge, 1990.

There is a relatively sparse literature on reading the environment. On scanning there is Elenkov, 1997: 287–302. See also Yasai-Ardekani and Nystrom, 1996: 187–204. More generally there is Hilmetz and Bridge, 1999: 4–11, Goll and Rasheed, 1997: 583–91 and Aggrawala, 1999: 83–104.

A good introduction to the problems of dealing with the future is Ackoff, 1983: 59–69. A more weighty treatment, exploring the notion of foresight, or remaking the future, is Hamel and Prahalad, 1994, or in a shorter version, 1989.

The problem of uncertainty and how to classify its level is analysed in Courtney et al., 1997: 66–79. A general introduction to the various kinds of risks is Saunders, 2000.

There is a rich literature on scenario building which originates with the attempts by Royal Dutch Shell to undertake such work. Many of the leading thinkers in this area worked at one time for Royal Dutch Shell. However, their influence has spread widely. The pioneer was Wack, 1985a: 73–90, 1985b: 131–42 and 1989: 60–3. Another early pioneer was de Geus, 1988: 70–4. Another early work is Mack, 1986: 125–33.

Closely following the pioneers was Peter Schwartz, 1996, who has written perhaps the most popular and accessible book on the subject. However, for those with an inclination to a more theoretical approach see van der Heijden, 1996. Outside the Shell school there is a book which has very much the feel of a primer for practising managers, Ringland, 1997. A useful but shorter treatment is Schoemaker, 1993: 193–213.

For a negative view of the attempt to forecast see Hogarth and Makridakis, 1981: 115–38, or at greater length Makridakis, 1990. Mintzberg has generally supported this position in his work. The reasons why many enterprises read the future very badly are discussed in an interesting paper and a powerful argument put that this is avoidable: Watkins and Bazerman, 2003: 72–85.

Part II

Strategic Environments and Competitive Advantage

5   Identifying opportunity and risk

6   Reading the competitive environment

7   Analysing resources, capabilities and core competencies

8   Creating and maintaining competitive advantage

9   Reducing cost

10   Differentiating the product

Part II puts together the conceptual ideas needed to think about strategy in preparation for making strategy. It deals with the conditions (or environments) in which an organization operates and pursues its strategy and also with the core element in any strategy, the creation and maintenance of competitive advantage.

The total context in which strategy is made by the enterprise comprises two parts, an external context and an internal context, divided by the boundary between the inside and the outside of the enterprise which is assumed to be a well-demarcated and watertight boundary. There are therefore two main environments, one external to the organization, and the other internal to the organization.

The external environment also comprises two parts, the general environment, sometimes called the contextual environment, and the industrial or competitive environment, sometimes called the transactional environment. The first, despite its breadth, is important for an organization but the organization has a very limited influence on it. The second is much more specific and one in which the organization influences outcomes as much as it is influenced itself.

All these environments are complex, dynamic and subject to rapid change over time. At a given moment in time, it is impossible to describe them in all their detail. It is necessary to select aspects relevant to the strategic intent and objectives of the enterprise which then become subject to investigation and candidates as inputs of knowledge vital to the process of strategy making. The process of selection of relevant aspects and the associated information is a critical part of strategy preparation.

Task	Parts	Chapters				
Starting right	**Part I** Introducing Strategic Management	**WHY?** Prologue	**WHO?** 1 Introducing strategy and strategy making	**WHAT?** 2 Thinking and acting strategically	**HOW?** 3 Adopting a global perspective	**WHEN?** 4 Reading an uncertain future
Acquiring conceptual tools for the job	**Part II** Strategic Environments and Competitive Advantage	5 Identifying opportunity and risk	General ENVIRONMENTS Internal	6 Reading the competitive environment Immediate	GENERIC STRATEGIES	7 Analysing resources, capabilities and core competencies
		9 Reducing costs		8 Creating and maintaining competitive advantage		10 Differentiating the product
Resolving particular strategic problems	**Part III** Strategic Dilemmas	**FIVE DILEMMAS** 11 Determining the size of an enterprise	12 Integrating the strategists	13 When to compete and when to cooperate	14 Managing risk	15 Participating in the global economy
The strategy emerges	**Part IV** Bringing it all Together	17 Implementing strategy		16 Formulating strategy CONTINUOUS ITERATION		18 Monitoring strategic performance
Analysing strategy making	**Part V** Strategic Analysis and Audit		Case studies		Epilogue	

The creation and maintenance of competitive advantage represents the core of the strategic approach. The main aim of any strategy is to promote the continued viability of the enterprise. Few wish to terminate the life of an organization because it has achieved all that was hoped for and all that was possible. In order to survive, the organization must create value for the customer in a way that others cannot and therefore create and maintain a competitive advantage. This core section therefore focuses on the nature of competitive advantage and the challenges of ensuring that the enterprise retains such advantage. The justification for the existence of an enterprise, and the explanation of the associated above-normal profits necessary to do this, is the holding of some competitive advantage over competitors. In order to maintain a continuing advantage, enterprises have to innovate. At any given time there are two main ways of achieving competitive advantage – minimizing costs and differentiating the product. These are discussed in turn.

Part II can therefore be described as dealing with the dynamic interaction between the enterprise and the environment of opportunity which confronts the enterprise. It is structured in the following way:

- Chapter 5 considers the general environment and its different segments. It shows how this environment can be 'read'.

- Chapter 6 turns to the industrial and competitive environments, analysing the nature of strategic risk, notably in the context of the different forces of competition.

- Chapter 7 considers the internal environment, appraising the significance of the resource position. This chapter describes how resources are integrated into capabilities and how capabilities become core competencies within a specific strategic context.

- Chapter 8 discusses how competitive advantage is created. The second section of the chapter analyses the problems of maintaining that competitive advantage by innovating in an environment of rapid change.

- Chapter 9 considers cost leadership or minimization, and the related price leadership, as one way of achieving competitive advantage.

- Chapter 10 discusses product differentiation as an alternative strategy for creating competitive advantage.

5 Identifying opportunity and risk

Learning objectives

After reading this chapter you will be able to:

- understand the difference between the general environment and the competitive or industrial environment

- identify those features of the external environment relevant to strategy making, notably opportunities and threats

- know how to manage change

- explore the different segments of the general environment – STEP – social or cultural, technical, economic or financial and political or legal

- recognize the main trends or tendencies which are part of global change over a strategic time period

Key strategic challenge

What is the nature of the external environment in which the organization must position itself?

Strategic dangers

That the various segments of the general environment change in a way which is unanticipated and has a significant influence on the business context, but that the strategist fails to read the implications of the change, notably the appearance of new opportunities and new threats.

Case Study Scenario   A clean vehicle – the hybrid electric vehicle (HEV)

'I've heard it said that hybrid technology is a bridging technology to eventually arrive at fuel cell vehicles, but that idea is completely mistaken. Hybrid technology is itself a core technology because it stores energy and enables its efficient use. For many years to come, various types of hybrid cars that combine an internal combustion engine and secondary battery or a fuel cell and secondary battery (like the Toyota FCHV) will coexist and compete against each other.'

Watanabe (Toyota website)

One of the most important and influential movements of current times is the environmental movement which expresses the desire to conserve the natural world and avoid the extreme effects on that world of modern economic development. The movement has implications for all sectors of the economy. For business these implications open new opportunities and create threats. There is, for example, enormous pressure on the automobile industry to innovate in a way which will at the same time remove damaging emissions and reduce its use of energy. The important aim of any innovation is to tap into relatively clean energy sources.

The role of government in financing research and promoting innovation is important. For example, in the USA the state of California has introduced zero emission rules. To a large degree government regulation drives the pace of change. There are a number of possibilities for achieving the aims of the environmental movement and also satisfying government regulation.

This case study considers three of the possibilities and compares them with the existing technology, given its potential for improvement. The alternatives are the all-electric vehicle using batteries, a hybrid vehicle using both electric battery(ies) and an internal combustion engine, and a vehicle using the hydrogen cell. The control situation is what can be achieved in fuel savings and emission reduction with existing technology, that is, a continuing use of the internal combustion engine.

The alternatives of electric battery or hydrogen cell, whether used in combination or not, not only require mastering a new technology at cost levels which are acceptable but establishing a new infrastructure of electricity and/or hydrogen supply. The investment required is enormous. A whole series of related technical problems await resolution. The changes involved have extensive ramifications.

The realistic alternatives, given likely government regulation, are really two, either a hybrid use of fuel and electric or the use of the hydrogen fuel cell, which might also be used in a hybrid form with an electric battery. The all-electric car is a non-starter for all but a few niche uses. Although General Motors (GM) has spent over one billion dollars on the project, it has now discontinued its EV1 battery electric car on the grounds that the economics of such a technology are unacceptable. The technology which can be envisaged for the next 10 years would involve batteries which were too big and heavy to be viable. The range of any vehicle would be poor and the batteries would need regular recharging. Heavy investment is going into the other two alternatives and improvement of the current technolology. The money is being bet on these technologies.

The HEV is a motor vehicle with two power sources, a comparatively small conventional combustion engine and an electric motor. The two power sources can be used individually or together. The combustion engine is designed to perform best when the vehicle is at cruising speed. At other times, when the vehicle is either starting up or changing speed significantly, the electric motor can be called into use. A computer determines when the two power sources are used and in what combination. It does this in order to maintain power in the battery system, so that the need for regular and periodic recharging is eliminated. The combustion engine combines with a generator to supply electricity for both the electric motor and the battery pack.

The HEV represents a compromise and a real option, one which is already with us. There are two such Japanese vehicles on the market, the Honda Insight and the Toyota Prius. In late 1997 Toyota was first to put an HEV on the market. Honda released its model in late 1999. In the next few years a number of American HEVs are likely to follow. For example, GM has three types of HEVs which it plans to sell in the next five years. These cars incorporate new technology and are a competitive threat to all existing vehicles. In December 2002, the two Japanese companies began releasing fuel cell cars to the Japanese government, which unfortunately still cost over ¥100 million to manufacture.

As seen in Chapter 4, an important activity which makes possible the continued success of any organization is an accurate reading of what the business landscape looks like today and in the future. It is a matter of reading a dynamic process of change. Any change will throw up new opportunities and new risks. A strategist needs to anticipate any significant future change. It is the complexity of the changing environment which makes it difficult to make an accurate reading. It is critical to the continuing success, and potentially even the viability of an organization, to read these changes and their relevance to the enterprise.

General and competitive environments

In the next two chapters it is assumed that there are no constraints on the ability of the organization to position itself as it wishes, primarily by selecting an appropriate business and an appropriate market in which to operate. The key aim is to position the organization so that it can exploit any profitable opportunities and avoid any unnecessary risk. This positioning requires an accurate reading of the environment and changes in that environment. At least in theory an enterprise can enter any industry or sector of the global economy it chooses. During the 1980s many enterprises behaved as if this were true. The focus is on what the organization *should* do, given the opportunities and risks which a reading of the general environment reveals, rather than what it can actually do.

The external environment of the enterprise can itself be divided into two parts, the general environment and the competitive (industrial) environment. The latter is dealt with more fully in Chapter 6. It is appropriate to limit the present discussion of the industrial context to some preliminary remarks which are necessary to place the discussion in a proper perspective.

The competitive environment is made up of the immediate competitors of an enterprise. Industries overlap national boundaries. The general environment, viewed from an economic perspective, consists of a whole series of different industrial environments. A different way of dividing the general environment is by segment – political and economic, social and technical, demographic and legal. These segments overlap, but they are a useful mapping device. Both are useful ways of thinking about and mapping the world.

This chapter focuses on the global aspects of the general context but links these with those aspects which are specific to local contexts. Returns, even in the same industries, differ from country to country. Enterprises must position themselves appropriately in the external environment in order to make an above-normal rate of return, one which gives a guarantee of their continued existence. Positioning involves location as to both industry and country and comprises identification of an appropriate industry and an appropriate country in which to have business dealings. Such positioning only relates to the general location, and not to a particular location. Reading the general environment only results in general positioning.

Positioning

Some interpretations of strategy see positioning as the essential feature of strategy design. The work of Michael Porter is closely associated with this point of view. Positioning involves a range of different strategic decisions – the choice of product or service, market or even market segment, location of various facilities concerned with production and selling and, not least, the choice of a specific technology. In this sense reading the external environment could be said to determine the nature of the strategy. On these accounts the external environment is at the very least the starting point for the articulation of any particular strategy.

One very graphic image used to describe this environment is as a three-dimensional landscape (in theory it should be multidimensional to take account of all the influencing factors, but this is impossible to visualize). In such a landscape, the height above sea level can indicate performance, usually measured by rate of return. Location and proximity represent the difficulty of access. The simplest conception of the strategic task is that it identifies the highest peak and then positions the enterprise to climb it.

Focus on Theory
The use of metaphor

The use of metaphor is very common in management studies, much more common than in other disciplines. The systematic and sustained use of a metaphor is called 'allegory'. Some works in management theory amount to the use of allegory. Analogy is a related technique. It is used deliberately in case studies which are selected to give insights into comparable experiences.

Metaphor is built into any language and is often used unconsciously. The use of a vivid metaphor is a helpful heuristic device, one which through the suggestion of a striking image sensitizes the reader to an important concept or idea. Talking about the entry into modern economic development, the 'take-off' conjures an image of an aircraft on the runway, an image which has had a lasting influence on the literature on the acceleration of economic growth in the modern period.

The more systematic use of metaphor often reflects assumptions about the nature of human behaviour and the links between management studies and other disciplines. For example, the aspiration to make economics or management studies like science, and therefore academically respectable, leads to the regular employment of mechanical metaphors, or analogies borrowed from engineering systems. Human behaviour is then sometimes squeezed into the straitjacket of inanimate systems. Feedbacks of various kinds are often discussed, sometimes in a way which infuses a whole book, such as Senge's interesting exploration of learning processes. More recently there has been a tendency to pursue the biological analogy in talk of organic growth. For example, the metaphor of natural selection leads to the application of notions such as punctuated equilibrium to management studies.

A number of examples of metaphor used graphically in the area of strategy spring to mind. The danger is that the metaphor takes over and imposes a meaning on the analysis. The metaphor of war is probably the oldest one used. Much of the vocabulary of strategy is borrowed from this source. Business anecdotes are often referred to as 'war stories'.

Ghemawat's 1999 book systematically uses the metaphor of a physical landscape. This has various meanings: the existence of mountains or hills of different height, the scaling of such heights and the use of a map to find such peaks.

▶

Focus on Theory

cont'd

Another very popular metaphor is that of a game. The whole of game theory is based on a likening of decision making to playing a game. Hambrick and Frederickson (2001) talk of arenas as if strategists were performing in some way. Mintzberg et al. (1998), in a popular text, talk of strategy making as a safari and liken strategy to an elephant, or rather each of the different schools of strategy to different animals encountered on a big game safari.

Metaphors should be recognized as such and not taken too seriously.

It is important to be able to read the environment in such a way as to identify elements of opportunity and elements of threat in that environment, that is, to identify the mountain ranges and valleys in the business landscape. Enterprises will tend to move into areas of opportunity, the mountain chains, and avoid areas of threat, any landscape of steep gradient. This begs the question of how and by what route the move to the peak is pursued. Sometimes threat is a necessary companion of opportunity, so that it is impossible to completely avoid the threats. There are chasms and precipices in the mountain ranges. Such a reading of the landscape guides the enterprise into areas of activity which are profitable and suggests ways in which the associated risk can be managed to sustain a consistent minimum profitability. Strategy sets the goals – the peaks to be ascended – and also sets the path to be followed in order to reach the peaks. Reading the general environment is like reading the map of such a business landscape.

This is to oversimplify the overall picture. The problem is that this landscape is not stable and given for all time; it is highly unstable. Powerful forces are causing it to change dramatically and rapidly. Geological forces are causing new mountain ranges to appear. Old ranges are descending. The whole topography is changing in a way which it is difficult, but not impossible, to predict. Strategy is therefore not only concerned with geography but with geology, not only choosing the peaks to ascend but with identifying the location of future peaks. It must see that the organization is in the right place at the right time, close to these new peaks, but not necessarily pioneering overly dangerous routes which expose it to possibly dangerous falls or dangerous earth tremors. It might be sensible to allow others to pioneer the dangerous routes and locations.

In order to locate the mountain peaks, it is also necessary to learn to read the different maps rather than to wander aimlessly using only eyesight to look for them. The nature of such maps differ, one may show height contours, another transport routes, yet another areas of different tectonic instability. For the strategist the two main notional maps which are relevant are those relating to the general environment and the industrial environment. These are the maps the reader needs to learn to read.

The nature of the general environment

The general environment is complex, uncertain and characterized by rapid change. It is extremely difficult to read.

Complexity

The complexity arises from the multiple interactions between different segments of the general environment. It is common to see change as resulting from segments of the environment which are already an immediate focus of interest. For example, a strategist may be tempted to read the environment simply as an economic environment and other segments as irrelevant. This is a mistake. The nature of the interaction which produces the flow of global events and trends is difficult to read clearly. It involves many different elements and complicated interactions between different segments.

There are numerous ways in which the general environment influences the profitability of an enterprise, or the profitability of future ventures likely to be undertaken by the enterprise. Many of these influences are indirect, not immediately obvious to the observer. The pathway of causation may be very circuitous. The general environment is amazingly complex, particularly, but not only, at the global level.

Uncertainty

There is significant ambiguity and uncertainty. The nature or strength of the pressures building beneath the business landscape is far from obvious. The sources of these pressures can be anything from a change in the birth rate to major technical breakthroughs. Sometimes the economy is overwhelmed by catastrophic events, such as war or a general depression, which may have causes which are complex and not simply a reflection of economic change. Understanding change is not simply a matter of observing the symptoms of that change and detecting patterns in it. It is much more a matter of recognizing in a series of apparently unrelated events relevant chains of cause and effect.

Rapid change

The general context is a dynamic one. It offers both threat and opportunity. Change is imposed upon the enterprise by the instability of the environment in which the enterprise has to survive. The enterprise has no choice but to change with its environment or cease to exist. The trick is to ride the wave of change, exploiting the opportunities which arrive with the change and controlling the threats.

It is essential that any enterprise anticipates all the threats which loom on the horizon and rapidly change the relevant context:

- extreme political events such as revolution or war
- the appearance of a new product or technology, or rather a family of products or processes
- a fundamental market change, say a shift from inflation to deflation
- difficulties in factor markets
- a worsening shortage of labour
- a change in the level of government regulation
- the appearance of a new competitor or competitors, sometimes from abroad.

On occasions the unanticipated changes are political, sometimes demographic, sometimes simply economic, sometimes all of these rolled into one. The relevant parts of the general environment are broad indeed. These interactions have little stability; they change their nature from moment to moment, so that the environment never returns to what it was before. Each momentary context is unique. Each period of time has its own characteristic pace of change, its own mix of stability and volatility. It is often unclear what will be the source of the next change and what impact it will have on the business landscape. It is hard to make an accurate prediction if there is no understanding of the causes of the instability.

Very often a threat is associated with an opportunity, the chance of moving into a new area of profit. This is not uncommon. The difference between opportunity and threat is not very great. Failing to anticipate significant events is not just a matter of missing a chance for enhanced profit, it is often a sure prescription for disaster.

The tools of understanding

How can anyone learn how to read this environment? The social sciences have sought to provide the relevant concepts necessary to read the environment and provide the kinds of theories which allow a significant degree of successful prediction. Because every situation is unique it is hard to elaborate valid generalizations. Helpful ones are few and far between. Economists have made more claims in this area than the other social scientists. Historians have woven much more elaborate explanations which pay proper attention to the uniqueness of every experience. There is considerable causal ambiguity in explaining any historical event.

Any identification of opportunity or risk requires both an organizing conceptual framework and a proper regard for the specifics of individual situations. Strategists need to develop rules of thumb which allow them to read the environment in order to provide the knowledge vital to effective strategy formulation. Such rules of thumb allow the rapid processing of a mass of information and selection of what is relevant.

For example, it is very difficult to read political change and anticipate the historical moments when that change becomes overwhelming. At one extreme is revolutionary change, the kind which overturned existing political regimes in Iran in 1979, in the Soviet Union in 1991 and in Indonesia in 1998. It is clear that revolution is not caused by poverty and ignorance, but more likely by the denial of rising expectations, often in the context of an improvement in both wellbeing and education, which is suddenly truncated by extreme events, war, disease or a deterioration in economic performance after a period of improvement. It is also obvious that governments, faced with mounting difficulties, often tend to scapegoat, turning their attention to the role of outsiders. These are simple empirical patterns which combined with a persuasive theory help the strategist to anticipate threats.

The environment is full of shocks, unexpected and unpredictable events which have a potentially negative impact on business enterprises. Are these events really unpredictable? Particular events are often difficult for anyone to foresee, but the trends are rather easier to trace but often at first slow to be recognized. Some changes represent a change of trend, others are simply short-term changes which are quickly reversed but still represent a threat or an opportunity, or indeed both. For this reason any generalization may have only a short shelf life. However, there are some changes which are very robust, for example the relationship between higher income and lower fertility, or the rising income elasticity of demand for services, as compared with either primary (agricultural) or secondary (manufacturing) sector products.

Reading the environment as economic

Naturally most attention is concentrated by the managers of an enterprise on what are regarded as conventional economic factors. Often those running an enterprise see little need to go beyond these. Economic factors relate to the cost and availability of necessary inputs such as labour, capital or even resources, and the nature of the technology which links such inputs to outputs. The process of technical change is continuous and expresses itself in the economic world in a never-ending stream of innovations. Economic factors also take the shape of market elements such as changes in the nature of products or services, the level and distribution of income, the level of unemployment, foreign competition and even the mode of transportation to the market. It is unsurprising if strategists limit their attention to these.

It is possible to read the environment solely in terms of such economic changes but this would be to make more difficult the interpretation of what is happening in that environment and delay the recognition of potentially important changes. What is causing the economic change? It is obviously sensible to identify the general changes as soon as possible. It is true that most changes in the general environment at some stage translate into economic changes which directly affect the enterprise. Reading the change in these other segments is an important element of successful strategy making. This is not to assume that there is a prime mover, one segment which moves the others, but rather that there may be early signs of an impending change which can be seen elsewhere than in the economic system. It is useful to become expert in recognizing these connections.

Change and strategy

Managing change is seen as one of the chief managerial challenges of the present time. The first issue is the rate of change which has to be managed. There is much disagreement on this issue, despite the temptation to simply assume a faster rate of change in the contemporary world.

Patterns of change

Broadly it is possible to distinguish four possible patterns of change, although it might be that, at the same point in time, different patterns characterize the situation in different parts of the world. The present era is characterized by stability, alternating periods of stability and change, continuous change and discontinuous change.

1. *Stability:* the forces of inertia seem to prevail and no significant change appears to be occurring. It might be assumed that the 80% of the world which is not developed would be inert. This pattern is more unusual than might be thought. In all societies there is change, even if the main source is external, resulting from competition and external demonstration effects. Such stability can only occur when the population size is steady and economic growth is close to zero. This is very unusual. Countries which show no economic growth are often characterized by rapid population growth, an unstable mix. Countries which are demographically stable tend to grow economically, at least in output per capita.

2. *Alternation* of periods of stability and change: there are some regions in the world which display this oscillation in growth, with brief periods of rapid growth inter-

rupted by crises and periods of contraction. Latin American countries have long conformed to such a pattern, with periodic financial crises often associated with political instability.

3. *Continuous change:* the rate of change is relatively steady and at a manageable rate. Manageable in this context means at a speed that allows the political and social systems to accommodate the tensions which economic development inevitably brings. This is the norm in some parts of the developed world. It is certainly the main characteristic of the developed world in its relatively prosperous periods, such as the 1950s, 60s and 90s.

4. *Discontinuous change:* can be uneven and rather violent, with a dramatic rate of change in a whole series of different sectors. The change can be in either direction, up or down. Enormous political and social tensions accompany the growth. China today is experiencing rapid economic change, an experience through which many of the currently developed economies once passed, with great stress imposed on their political and social systems. Even some unlikely developed economies can go through such an experience, as the USA in the 1930s or late 1990s.

The proponents of change see the second pattern as at times valid, at other times the fourth. The third is desirable as a context in which to run a business. Whatever the situation change has become the norm. One aspect of globalization is that if one pattern of change characterizes significant parts of the world, other parts are confronted by the same pattern. Change intrudes from outside into societies which are not generating their own impulses to change.

The temporary nature of success

The dangers of trying to freeze out change and achieve stability at any cost have been revealed by the failure of central planning systems. These systems collapsed because of their inability to innovate, even their inability to translate the broader trends into specific opportunities or threats. In a market system a failure to absorb the unpredictable changes in technology and taste means a loss of competitive advantage. This leads to a financial deterioration and the eventual collapse of enterprises. These changes provide not just threats to existing enterprises, they offer opportunities which will be taken up by other players. Many of the changes are the result of actions by successful enterprises. Successful enterprises create the new environment.

Business success is by its nature ephemeral. Successful enterprises quickly lose their dynamism because they fail to anticipate change. Their previous success breeds failure. They become less efficient at reading the changes which occur and adjusting to those changes, and less responsive in acting on such knowledge. They are consequently in danger of being taken over or they steadily diminish in size and importance. The average lifetime of an enterprise is short, a matter of decades rather than generations, years rather than decades. Few survive more than one generation. New enterprises appear all the time, and most disappear within a short period of time. Even within periods of stability or a stable rate of change, the process of appearance and disappearance continues. Beneath a superficially stable exterior, there is often considerable change occurring.

A properly developed strategy addresses the issue of continuous change, reading carefully the nature of that change. Such a reading helps the older enterprises to diversify and survive and the newer enterprises to move beyond their infancy. Good strategy formulation and implementation, sensitive to the nature of the changing context in which the enterprise operates, is a vital underpinning of business success. It helps to extend the lifetime of the enterprise. In a world in which there was no change, least of all unanticipated change, there would be no need for strategy. There would be nothing beyond the making of simple operational decisions.

Environment segments

The general environment, one half of the external environment, can usefully be broken down into environment segments. In the analysis sometimes called PEST, but more accurately STEP, the four main segments are identified – social, technical, economic and political. As any such classification, this is an oversimplification, since it is easy to add other segments which can also stand independently, such as the religious, the demographic or the financial. It is possible to break down the whole into increasingly smaller segments. To do so is to lose a useful conceptual framework. To ensure the manageability of the discussion, the present treatment keeps to the four main headings, while noting that some degree of flexibility of treatment is highly desirable. The smaller segments are subsumed under the more general headings.

The main problem with the acronym PEST is that the word has negative connotations, which STEP does not. In practice the environment has both positive and negative features. In reading that environment the strategist should be looking for opportunities, although also noting threats. The emphasis should be on the process of reading, a positive series of sequential steps by which the knowledge of the general environment is built up.

The danger of segmenting the general environment is that it removes the element of dynamic change in the system as a whole, freeing the analysis of the interconnections which actually move the process of historical change and underpin the chains of cause and effect which operate across segment boundaries. The original sources of change may lie in one particular segment but, if they are significant, they affect all other segments. There are numerous subtle feedback effects.

In reading the environment there is no real substitute for a good sense of history. There are patterns in history which help us to understand the present and where an organization or economy is headed. For example, it should not have been difficult for a perceptive observer to have predicted the economic success of Ireland during the 1990s or the apparently sudden failure of Argentina at the end of that decade. A good historian is often better than a good economist in anticipating the changes which are likely to be important in the future. Economists persuade themselves that economic reform alone can change the direction of an economy. Historians do not compartmentalize change in the same way, considering simultaneously political, social and economic change. The discussion below shows the importance of recognizing these patterns in history. Because all experiences are path-dependent, the springs of change are to be found in previous history.

The aim is to provide some framework for identifying the factors which influence the nature of opportunity and risk for the individual enterprise. The treatment considers each of the segments in turn. Later in the chapter specific trends which are important today are examined, noting in which segment they have their origin.

The social (or cultural)

Huntingdon (1996) has argued that the significant conflicts of the future will be between different cultures, not between different nation states or ideologies. The Huntingdon argument is probably exaggerated but it does suggest the potential significance of social factors in influencing the nature of business activity. This view asserts the primacy of the cultural, at least in one important area. What truth does such an assertion of primacy have? The topic is very broad and the present treatment inevitably selective.

Culture embraces the underlying patterns of behaviour which characterize different societies as well as their attitudes, values and assumptions. Culture also includes for many the typical creations of those societies – their works of art, their enduring institutional innovations and engineering constructions. Culture is therefore both the institutionalized pattern of thoughts and behaviour which characterizes a society, embracing every aspect of human behaviour from family life and recreational activity to sexual mores and business activity, and the artefacts of that society. Culture is by definition all-embracing and therefore, unless the focus of interest is narrowed, it is self-evident that a cultural explanation will embrace all that is happening.

Cultural patterns are integrated, each part internally consistent with the others, although there may be subcultures within a given society or nation state. Cultures differ markedly one from another. Sometimes the interaction between such cultures is a positive one and sometimes a negative one, which often deteriorates into violence. As indicated in Chapter 3, some see as few as six, seven or eight major cultural clusters in the world, while others have identified a much larger number, including variants of the major groups. These clusters share similar main cultural features.

The basis for cultural difference may be religion or the general mode of social organization, including the structure of families and households. The two are connected. The rise of Islamic fundamentalism has reinforced the apparent importance of the social or cultural segment. It would be a great mistake to underestimate the importance of religion in any part of the world.

The role of socialization and language as a mechanism for the transmission of culture to children and therefore its perpetuation is critical. The roles of family, schooling and peer groups are critical in this. However, children are exposed to the influence of global culture, as expressed in popular music and film, an influence sometimes described as *cultural imperialism*. The origin of today's most potent influences is the USA. This affects everything from clothing and food to the language used and sexual habits.

There is often, but not always, considerable resistance to threats to a specific culture perceived as coming from other cultures. Measures taken to protect a culture can lead to either opportunities for enterprises operating within that culture or threats to enterprises from outside the culture. There are even those who manufacture *ersatz cultural differences* which become the basis for a commercial tourist trade. After all, who wants to travel to societies which all look the same? The differences have to be acceptable or saleable differences.

No culture is completely uniform. There may be a dominant culture, but there are also subcultures. Even within nation states there are ethnic, social and regional differences of various kinds. In most societies there may even be a youth or a criminal counterculture which contradicts all the main values and norms which prevail in the overall society.

Focus on Theory
Cultural differences

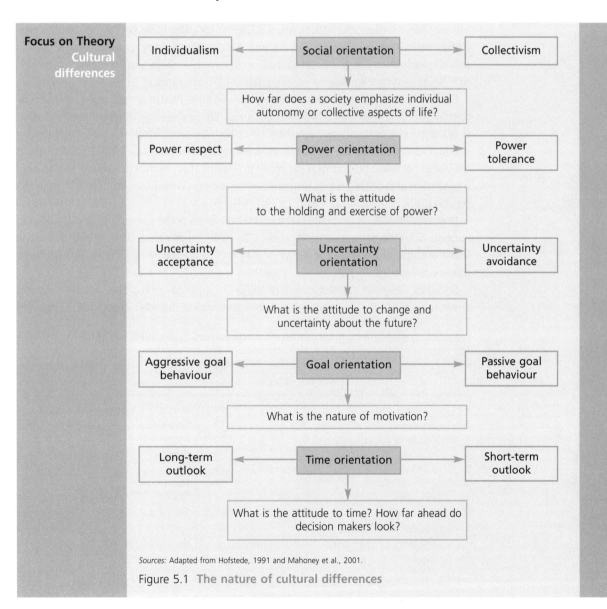

Sources: Adapted from Hofstede, 1991 and Mahoney et al., 2001.

Figure 5.1 **The nature of cultural differences**

The most underestimated social element is demography and demographic change. As discussed later, demographic change is, in the short term, possibly the most predictable element in all segments. In theory it is possible to predict population years or even decades ahead. For example, it should not be difficult to forecast the need for schools and teachers, or hospitals and doctors. In practice it is difficult for other reasons, mainly because of the volatile nature of political decision making. Demographic change is most far-reaching in its social effects. It is closely linked with the nature of the family and the location of both consumption and production within different economic systems.

There is no doubt that technologies are embedded in cultures in such a way as to make some societies more amenable to technical change than others, and also to lead to those technologies actually differing from society to society. Some societies are technically dynamic, others are not. Some societies have very rigid social structures, which oppose innovation of any kind. Others have considerable levels of mobility, whether social, occupational or geographic. Some embrace risk, others do not. Some embrace authority, others encourage its flouting.

Equally, consumer tastes vary from culture to culture, implying a product differentiation which is systematic between cultures. There are even different ways of consuming products, such as toiletries or entertainment. Methods of advertising a product also differ markedly from culture to culture. Genuinely global advertising is unusual. National branding is far more prevalent than global branding. Methods of negotiation also differ greatly from society to society. Misunderstandings between the representatives of different cultures can easily occur.

One area of significance to international business is the nature and extent of corruption in different economic systems. The differences are striking (Table 5.1). The index is constructed from the views of 835 business experts in 15 leading 'emergent market' countries.

Societies differ on the definition of what constitutes corrupt behaviour, or what constitutes a bribe. It is noteworthy that the emerging market countries themselves

Table 5.1 **Transparency International's bribe payers index (BPI) for 2002**

Rank	Country	Score (10 = no propensity to bribe)	Rank	Country	Score (10 = no propensity to bribe)
1	Australia	8.5	13	USA	5.3
2	Sweden	8.4	14	Japan	5.3
3	Switzerland	8.4	15	Malaysia	4.3
4	Austria	8.2	16	Hong Kong	4.3
5	Canada	8.1	17	Italy	4.1
6	The Netherlands	7.8	18	South Korea	3.9
7	Belgium	7.8	19	Taiwan	3.8
8	UK	6.9	20	P.R.China	3.5
9	Singapore	6.3	21	Russia	3.2
10	Germany	6.3		Domestic companies	
11	Spain	5.8		in the emerging market	
12	France	5.5		countries	1.9

Source: www.transparency.org/pressreleases_archive/2002/2002.05.14.bpi.en.html.

have the worst reputation for taking bribes. Should an enterprise decide to offer a bribe, the act of corruption imposes a cost on the business. Such activity can open up avenues of business in highly regulated economies, which are otherwise closed. Corruption often simulates the operation of a market. The higher the value of bypassing the obstacle presented by a government regulation, and by implication the higher the value a free market would place on this right or privilege, the greater the value of the expected bribe. On the other hand, there may be a long-term cost in gaining a reputation for corruption, whether it be a country or an enterprise. A good strategy may require avoidance of countries where corruption is prevalent.

For these reasons, economic activity is set in a social context which cannot be disregarded, again a changing as well as varying context. This is true at both the enterprise level and the society level. Often the most persuasive reason for a strategy of entry into international business based on joint ventures is to allow an outsider to tap into an alien culture, which is not understood. It is not difficult to understand this or to understand the impact of shocks such as the terrorist attacks of September 11, 2001 in encouraging a home country bias.

The technical

Strategy in Action   Riding the Internet wave – Amazon.com

'everything, everywhere'

Amazon.com slogan

There has been a lot of talk about the potential for e-commerce at the retail level and its capacity to revolutionize the nature of business. There has also been a rapid uptake of the Internet. E-commerce at the wholesale or business-to-business (B2B) level is catching on fast. Many of the preconditions for e-commerce at the retail level also exist, yet there has been little success, outside a few areas, such as pornography, gambling, share broking and travel.

Amazon.com has revolutionized the selling of books, but without making a profit. In December 2001 for the first time Amazon reported an 'honest-to-GAAP' (generally accepted accounting principles) quarterly profit of US$5 million, but one which reflected favourable exchange rate movements. There have been three quarters of small operating profits, and two quarters of positive cash flow. Perhaps Amazon has really turned the corner. Before 2002 the losses were prodigious, US$1.4 billion in 2000 alone.

In most respects Amazon.com is a great success. It had a total revenue of US$3.1 billion in 2001. The total number of active customers has risen steadily – 14.1 million in 1999, 19.8 in 2000, 24.7 in 2001 and 27.3 million in 2002.

Jeff Bezos, a computer science and electrical engineering graduate who became the youngest vice-president in the history of D. E. Shaw, a Wall Street-based investment bank, saw the rise of the Internet and read its implications. After careful research on 20 possible products for sale on the Internet, he chose books as the best candidate, largely on two grounds:

- the largest physical bookstore in the world held only 175,000 books, as compared with the 1.5 million English-language books in print and 3 million books in all languages worldwide
- there was no dominant player or players in the industry. The two largest booksellers in the USA, Barnes & Noble and Borders accounted for only 12% of total sales. There were also 4,200 publishers in the USA alone.

Bezos launched his new venture in July 1995 in Seattle, a carefully thought-out venue. Within a year sales were at a level comparable to a large Barnes &

Noble superstore. The rapid rise in sales meant that the company had to move warehouse several times in the first year.

Publishers sell books on a consignment basis, bearing all the risk. They tend to print far more copies than they can sell, so that about 25% of all books distributed to wholesalers are returned. The profit comes from about 10% of the book titles. Some 90% of publishers are barely making money. There is some consolidation in the industry, with the 20 largest publishers accounting for 60% of retail sales.

Effective wholesaling depends on the range and speed of turnover of stocks – the latter helped by electronic ordering. Profit margins are about 1.5%. The wholesale side is more concentrated, with one company, Ingram Book, accounting for as much as 50% of sales in the USA. Only about 30% of book sales go through wholesalers.

In 1994, 35–40% of book sales were accounted for by bookstore chains, independents and general retailers, but during the 1990s the relative proportions within these groups changed dramatically. The superstores expanded and the independents closed. Librarians and institutions provide a stable and important share of demand, particularly for books with a limited market. Textbooks for schools and universities offer the highest profit margins of all sales. Sales by mail order are declining but book club sales are increasing.

The superstores are already bypassing wholesalers. Virtual bookstores offer the possibility of the retail layer disappearing altogether. Electronic book publishing and online distribution by computer-literate authors threatens even the publishers and the virtual bookstores.

Amazon.com provides four desired attributes of book buying – low price, convenience of purchase, a wide selection and rapid and reliable service, although service may be significantly slower than for a normal retail outlet. Its website provides fun and a wealth of relevant information. What it lacks is the feel of the book and the opportunity to browse and skim a book.

Marketing costs are down from 12.5% in 1999 to 4% of gross

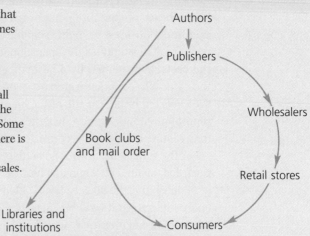

Figure 5.2 **The existing structure of the industry**

revenue today. Amazon.com has a potential cost advantage in that it turns over the inventory much faster than a normal bookstore, every 19 days. It has also managed to reduce its capital expenditures to 1 cent in the dollar, from 10 cents in 1999, although it found that it had to build warehouses to meet its delivery targets. Amazon needs to spread the fixed costs incurred in the technology of setting up its online systems, organizing its customer service operations and customer base, building its warehouses and marketing. How can it do this?

- By selling as many products as possible
- By expanding its customer base
- By selling in as many countries as possible
- By finding as many partners as possible who can sell through Amazon.com, paying a commission to do so.

Table 5.2 **Profit margin for a 'typical book'**

Book list price	US$19.95	
Revenue to publisher (paid by wholesaler or bookstore)	10.37	48% discount off suggested price
Manufacturing price	2.0	Printing, binding, jacket design, composition, type setting, paper, ink
Publisher overhead	3.0	Marketing, fulfillment
Returns and allowances	3.0	
Author's royalties	2.0	
Total publishing costs	**10.0**	
Publisher's operating profit	0.37	A margin of 3.7%

Bezos has developed the website and created an interactivity which has changed the selling of books for good. He has used the brand name well, extending sales to videos, CDs, toys, electrical goods, tools and kitchen utensils. However, today in the USA only 7% of book sales are accounted for by online sales.

Technical change comes in waves, concentrated in particular time periods and affecting most dramatically particular sectors of the economy. The whole economic growth process, wherever located, is always variable, despite the common tendency to present it as if it were an even and stable process. The cyclical waves of technical change drive the growth, so the process is an uneven one.

Since the inception of modern economic growth, there have been three major waves of technical change. These can be described as:

1. the initial Industrial Revolution centred on Britain and Western Europe
2. the beginning of mass consumption, overwhelmingly concentrated in the US, but to a lesser degree Germany
3. the communications revolution, again American-based.

The first wave occurred in the late eighteenth and early nineteenth centuries. The second began in the late nineteenth century but, because of the delaying effect of three major shocks – two world wars and a depression – stretched well into the middle of the twentieth century and took time to spread from its epicentre. The present, third wave will continue for several decades yet. What might constitute a fourth wave is unclear – it might be a biotechnology revolution or the hydrogen fuel cell.

Usually these waves are associated with major technical change in certain limited areas, in particular the areas of transportation, communication or energy supply. This is because these sectors provide basic inputs for all parts of the economy and require enormous investments in infrastructure which are large enough to determine the level of activity throughout the affected economies.

Each wave comprises a small number of macro-inventions, which are set in a multitude of micro-inventions. The latter help to realize the macro-inventions and allow the adventurous to profit from the opportunities opened up by these inventions. The application of steam power, the introduction of the internal combustion engine and electricity, the combined development of new communication systems and the PC are the macro-inventions characterizing the big waves. In their turn, they required the use of large central power sources, the laying of railway or road networks, the establishment of electricity grids and satellite and cable networks. These take time to put in place and have far-reaching effects on the organization of economic life. The macro-inventions create pressure for a multitude of micro-inventions, which provide enormous opportunity for profit making. During these waves, there are many opportunities to develop micro-inventions.

Growth rates and rates of productivity accelerate during the peak of the waves, although much less than often assumed. There is a tendency to overdramatize these waves. The positive effects take a long time to work through the economy. While they create an environment of opportunity, they also undermine the viability of existing enterprises. In a significant restructuring of the economy, existing physical and human capital is threatened and devalued.

The economic

The economic is the best documented segment of the general environment. This is true whether the focus is on the theory of economic behaviour or the nature of economic institutions. Economists assume that what moves the world is a desire to improve income or profit. In an age of economism everything is given an economic interpretation, including the motivation of most decision makers, from criminals to family members. The market is the favoured institutional device for allocating resources and distributing income. It is cogently argued that it is the most efficient mechanism for such an allocation.

There are two areas of economic theory of particular interest in any reading of the environment, the theory of economic growth and the theory of the firm. It is an advantage to be able to anticipate the different economic growth performances of a broad range of countries. For example, it is useful to be able to identify recent high flyers – the Asian tigers since the 1960s, the Chinese turnaround since 1978 or the excellent performance of some smaller economies such as Ireland, the Netherlands, Finland or Australia during the 1990s – to recognize the difficulties which maturity can bring to some economies, such as Britain particularly in the 1960s and 70s or more recently Japan and Germany, and anticipate the fall from a brief grace of economies such as the Russian, with its associated republics, the Indonesian or Argentinian. This is hard to do but not impossible.

Focus on Theory
Economic growth

There is no good theory explaining the sources of economic growth, because the uniqueness of each experience limits the validity of the kind of generalization demanded in a theory. This is true at the enterprise and national level. There are some general principles which help us identify potential high flyers and laggards:

1. It is usual to divide the world into three groups of countries according to their level of development, usually expressed in GDP per head of population – the developed, the developing and the undeveloped.
2. Most countries stay in one group, but it is an interesting exercise to try to identify those who are changing group. In the past 20–30 years, these have been Asian countries, earning them the label the 'Asian miracle'.
3. There may be a tendency to convergence in the level of income or output per head among the developed, but little or none between the different groups.
4. There is a limit on the maximum annual rate of growth among the developed economies which is about 4%.
5. The conventional neoclassical approach is an exercise in comparative statics which does not help understanding of the dynamics of economic growth. It puts the emphasis on the production function which expresses the relationship between the inputs of the factors of production and the output of the product. Some growth is due to an increase in such inputs.
6. Any residual growth is the result of the change in the nature of the relationship between inputs and outputs, which is seen as comprising the impact of technical and organizational change. The residual is often referred to as total factor productivity

▶

Focus on Theory
cont'd

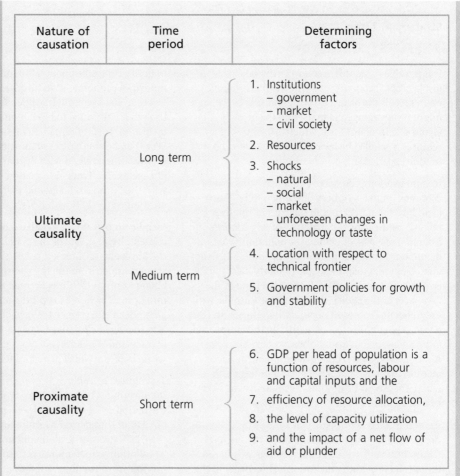

Nature of causation	Time period	Determining factors

Ultimate causality	Long term	1. Institutions
		    – government
		    – market
		    – civil society
		
		2. Resources
		
		3. Shocks
		    – natural
		    – social
		    – market
		    – unforeseen changes in
		      technology or taste

	Medium term	4. Location with respect to technical frontier 5. Government policies for growth and stability
Proximate causality	Short term	6. GDP per head of population is a function of resources, labour and capital inputs and the 7. efficiency of resource allocation, 8. the level of capacity utilization 9. and the impact of a net flow of aid or plunder

Source: Adapted from White, 1992: 47–50.

Figure 5.3 **The causes of economic growth**

7. The key factors in economic growth are therefore:
   • An increase in relevant inputs, including demographic change, exploitation of natural resources and capital accumulation
   • Technical change
   • Organizational change
   • Infrastructural improvement.
8. There are factors which influence growth in the short term and those with long-term influence.

The complexity of the problem of predicting growth rates is shown by the number of determining factors. They all interact in a way which is difficult to analyse without a detailed study of a specific experience. Figure 5.3 sets out the main framework and illustrates the complexity of the theory. It identifies nine different sources of causation. The author's inclination is to play down the short-term effects and play up the longer term ones, especially the institutional ones which are in their turn influenced by the resource and risk environments.

Strategy in Action The Celtic tiger

Is it possible to identify a country which is likely to display rapid economic growth? Such an identification reveals the fastest growing markets to which it might be advantageous to sell and the most favourable locations for productive facilities. It requires a detailed historical knowledge of each unique experience.

Ireland was long considered a relatively backward economy on the periphery of a much richer European heartland, whether in the level of relative income per head or the structure of its economy. Ireland had a past of colonial domination by its neighbour Britain, and significant population settlement from that neighbour, particularly in its northern part, the Six Counties. Ireland was one of the first parts of the British Empire. It was Catholic with a significant Protestant population in the north and a thin veneer of Protestant gentry in the countryside and in government and the professions. The colonization of Ireland stimulated economic development in the north but it hindered it in the south, where the Anglo-Protestant ascendancy was seen as a foreign intrusion.

Ireland has a recent history of serious overpopulation. Rapid population expansion in the late eighteenth and early nineteenth centuries was based on the spread of potato cultivation. At its peak, at the beginning of the nineteenth century, the population of Ireland represented about one-third of the total population of the British Isles. However, the potato famine of the 1840s killed thousands and sparked off a dramatic emigration which saw almost 3 million depart, especially to the USA.

This contraction created a vicious circle. Ireland's best people seemed intent on enriching the cultural life of areas of new settlements outside Europe and Britain.

Ireland was poor, held back culturally by an ultra conservative Catholic Church which dominated the attitudes of its population to economic development, and by the continuing loss of its most adventurous and most able. Ireland, after a long period of mounting unrest and internal strife, managed to assert its political independence in 1922. Unhappily independence led to the separation of the North, with its majority Protestant population and its relatively industrial economic structure and higher income levels. Ireland separated politically from Britain, even though it continued to be economically dominated by Britain. Ireland remained neutral during World War II and chose to remain outside the British Commonwealth. It joined with Britain in setting up the European Free Trade Association in 1960 in rivalry with the European Economic Community (EEC) and only joined the EEC with Britain in 1973.

Membership of the EU created a new economic context. Ireland, one of the poorest and most rural of the European economies, received significant financial assistance from the EU – subsidies totalling €30 billion as of 2002. It has become a platform for entry into Europe by non-European companies, a particularly cheap entry, since the cost of labour in Ireland is markedly low relative to its quality, with the level of literacy and education always high, witness the six winners of the Nobel prize for literature.

The figures in Table 5.3 reveal the extent of the turnaround. The beginnings of such growth lay in the period 1979–90, mainly the late 1980s. Growth of GDP in that period was already slightly ahead of the OECD average. Ireland did not escape from the 'stagflation' which characterized developed economies at the time, high unemployment and a high rate of price increases. Ireland exhibited the symptoms worse than most. In the 1990s the situation changed dramatically, as growth accelerated above the average.

This economic growth generated an impressive rate of job creation. Inflation came down to a manageable level. There were dramatic turnarounds in the current account and the fiscal position of the government. Ireland had no difficulty in satisfying the conditions required to enter the European Monetary Union in 2000. On any indicator the economic performance improved, with incomes rising.

The government, committed to transforming the Irish economy, played an important role in accelerating economic development. The helping hand has been gentle and indirect. Some of the stimuli used are traditional. A low corporate tax rate has helped, initially zero for the profits generated by foreign

▶

Table 5.3 **Key economic indicators of OECD total and selected small countries**

	Total OECD	Ireland	Australia	The Netherlands
Real GDP growth				
1979–90	2.7	3.5	3.1	2.1
1990–98	2.1	5.7	2.9	2.4
1993–98	2.4	7.4	3.7	2.8
Inflation				
1979–90	5.4	8.2	8.0	2.7
1990–98	2.5	2.2	2.4	2.3
1993–98	2.0	2.1	2.3	1.9
Employment growth				
1979–90	1.2	0.0	2.3	0.9
1990–98	0.8	2.1	1.2	1.6
1993–98	1.0	3.0	2.4	1.6
Current account balance (% of GDP)				
1979–90	–0.6	–5.6	–4.4	2.6
1990–98	–0.5	1.7	–4.2	3.6
1993–98	–0.4	–2.4	–4.3	4.2
Current government financial balances (% of GDP)				
1979–90	–2.9	–9.0	–1.3	–5.0
1990–98	–3.1	–1.9	–2.1	–3.3
1993–98	–3.2	–1.7	–2.1	–3.0

investment, but generally at the 16% level, compared with an EU average of 30%. The government has provided a helpful infrastructure, including education.

The focus has been on computer software. Entry into the EU led to a dramatic increase in foreign direct investment, with almost every large company in the new economy building facilities there. The weight of so many foreign companies has sustained the most rapid economic growth rate, not only in Irish history but also within the EU. The government has established a network of linked institutions which have encouraged research and development in this area.

When Ireland entered the EEC it had an income per head about 60% of the EEC's average. Today it has an income per head about 120% of the average. The net outflow of the Irish has been reversed. Property prices have risen dramatically. Ireland has become a focus for tourism, and Dublin the trendy European city to visit.

Strategy in Action Argentina, a case of recurrent crises

The financial collapse in Argentina in 2001/02 has taken the economy down further than the Great Depression of the 1930s. Was it unexpected? Such an economic crisis is not an isolated event. There is a tradition in Argentina of financial crises and political coups d'états, characteristics of Latin American countries. Not only have none of these countries succeeded in becoming developed economies, but nearly all have been the venue for abrupt changes of political regime, often associated with financial crises. Both economic and political life are afflicted with a winner-takes-all philosophy. Argentina belongs to the group of Latin American countries

which have always teetered on the edge of sustained modern economic development. Parts of its economy have been able to generate high incomes, but this has not sustained a high average level of GDP per head.

There is seldom a decade in which a Latin American country does not experience a financial crisis. The cause is often ascribed to an appetite for excessive debt, mistaking a characteristic for a cause. Argentina's experience is not unusual, Mexico and Brazil having similar problems in the 1990s. Such crises are also contagious.

▶

The causes of the Argentinian crisis lie in an overvalued exchange rate combined with an excessive amount of foreign debt. At the end of the 1980s Argentina was suffering from hyperinflation, which at the beginning of the 1990s was 200% per month. Between 1991 and 2001 the value of the peso was pegged at parity with the American dollar. In order to control inflation, in 1991 the government introduced the currency board system, a return to the system prevailing throughout the 1950s and 60s.

The government pegged the value of the currency by guaranteeing that it could convert pesos into dollars at the going exchange rate. The key issues were the level of the exchange rate and the monetary reserves held by the financial system. Provided the rate was right, the government could deal with any wish to convert pesos. The government had enough reserves to back the currency in circulation, but not enough to cope with a desire to convert all the bank accounts in existence. The government could react to any conversion by reducing the money supply, partly in order to free up the necessary reserves. The effect would be to increase interest rates and encourage a return of the lost savings to the peso accounts.

A loss of confidence in a currency, almost inevitable in the Argentine context at some stage, makes impossible the retention of a fixed rate. The government should have assumed a future move to a floating rate system, but in advantageous circumstances. Initially the system seemed to remove a dangerous inflation from the economy. Together with other policy measures, this stimulated an improvement in economic performance. Between 1991 and 1994 the rate of growth of GDP accelerated to over 7% in a short, sharp boom.

There were three critical issues:

1. Was the exchange rate at an appropriate level, one which avoided a significant and persistent current account deficit?
2. If a problem emerged on the current account, would the government be prepared to push interest rates to a high enough level to cause the adjustments required, even if this meant a much higher level of unemployment and social unrest?
3. Was the economy flexible enough to adjust to the higher interest rates, so that relative price reductions would play the role which a devaluation played elsewhere?

The currency was overvalued. In a young democratic system the government was never willing to jeopardize its position by taking unpopular measures. Nor was the economy flexible enough, partly because of strong unions and 'rigid' labour laws.

The result was a vicious circle, compounded by:

• the rise in the value of the American dollar
• the fall in the price of Argentina's exports
• the devaluation of other Latin American currencies, notably the sharp fall of the Brazilian real in 1999.

Argentina's economy became uncompetitive, with a rising current account deficit and mounting debt levels. There was a rise in interest rates and unemployment of 15%.

Why did the government not head off the crisis? There was a fear of inflation and bankruptcies resulting from any devaluation, given the build-up of dollar-denominated debt. By late 2001 the ratio of debt, mostly central and provincial government debt, had reached 50% of GDP. The main events of the crisis were the default on the $155 billion central and provincial debt in December 2001, the largest sovereign debt default ever, and the devaluation of the peso in January 2002, by as much as 70% of its recent value.

The currency board system of opening the economy, deregulating markets and privatizing public organizations had encouraged the entry of foreign banks in significant numbers after 1991. The size of bank deposits rose dramatically from 4% of GDP in 1989 to 37% ten years later. Foreign banks accounted for 75% of these deposits.

The crisis had catastrophic effects – US$20 billion was lost by the forced conversion of dollar loans and deposits into pesos. The drain in lost deposits reached a rate of US$100 million per day. Some foreign banks have written off their entire investment. The government tried to head off the crisis by issuing bonds to compensate the banks, but they were in no position to honour such debt. Nor are the banks keen to acquire such paper. The IMF withheld a US$20 billion rescue package, until it got assurances on the policies to be adopted, which were slow in coming. The banking system ceased to function; there were no new loans and no new deposits.

One ultimate cause of such crises is the political context of policy making. The alternation in power, between the Peronista party, representing workers and pubic servants, and the other parties which represent opposed and more traditional rural and business interests, is an example of winner-takes-all politics, the modern manifestation of a situation which stretches back into the early history of independent Argentina. In the past, changes in government were much more violent.

At the microlevel where economic development originates with the efforts of the business enterprise, there is a considerable and growing literature on the theory of the firm. The approaches range from a straightforward neoclassical approach to a broader study of institutions such as the typical enterprise, in particular explaining why they exist in the first place and why some are more dynamic than others. Much of this literature is relevant to strategy making by enterprises. Increasingly enterprises have become the focus of studies which consider what influences the organization of any economic activity. The many business histories written concerning nearly every kind of major economic enterprise are of considerable interest in a study of business behaviour. Analysis at this microlevel supplements the macro-analysis relating to national units. Putting the two together to explain economic success is an illuminating exercise which has not been done systematically.

At the global level, the patterns of international trade and investment are given an economic interpretation. Recently country-based theories of trade have given way to enterprise-based theories, just as demand-driven theories have replaced supply-driven theories. There are also quite elaborate theories of the determination of foreign direct investment. The economic basis for the existence of economic opportunity as an explanatory factor for patterns of world trade and investment has been fully studied. None of the theories are completely persuasive, probably because they do not exhaust a complex list of determinants.

The interaction of the political and the economic leads to a treatment of global political economy. At the country level, it is appropriate to look at international relations from three perspectives – the multilateral, regional and bilateral. Multilateral institutions such as the WTO, the IMF and World Bank are the focus of much discussion, particularly because of the economic policies they are seen as supporting. All regional groupings involve government institutions of various kinds. However, most international business policy is conducted on a bilateral basis between national states. The institutional structures at each of these levels influence powerfully the market patterns and the pattern of distribution of resources at the global level.

On the other hand, the evolution of the financial sector as one which is designed to control risk is strongly emphasized in most of the literature. This sector certainly has a strong market base, probably the strongest of all sectors. A whole list of so-called 'derivatives' of increasing sophistication has developed to cope with the risk thrown up by change. The financial market is at the cusp of economic change. Paradoxically it is the mechanism for moving resources from the old to the new economy. The financial sector is the focus of new opportunity in its role of intermediation and new risk in its role of risk control.

In the end the intermeshing web of markets throughout the world is the context in which all business decision making occurs. It is change in these markets which is an important bearer of change.

Strategy in Action The development state – the port of Tanjung Pelepas (PTP)

In all economies the government has played an important role in promoting modern economic development, in some being an extremely active participant. The strategy of government is an important part of the strategic context for other players. Often, where the starting point of the country's economy is a relatively low level of GDP per head, the role of the government is likely to be an interventionist one, actively guiding the private sector through the provision of necessary infrastructure, including transportation, the pooling of information with key decision-making groups and the use of credit and price signals. The development effort is a competitive one, in which the country is competing for markets and foreign capital with neighbours or other developing countries.

Malaysia is a 'third tier' Asian economy which began the process of modern economic development in the late 1980s and 90s. It shares some characteristics of the previous two tiers of countries, notably rapid economic development with a model which stresses the development state but which has been described as crony capitalism. Often prominent entrepreneurial figures work with the government to provide the infrastructure of energy, transport of various kinds, telecommunications and education.

This intervention is described as guidance planning. Most important enterprises have had a strong element of government control, including significant levels of ownership. Asian governments have had pronounced views about the structure of the economy and which industries to promote. In Malaysia this has been complicated by the desire to increase the economic role of the native Malay population, called the *bumiputras*, against the local Chinese and Indians who have traditionally dominated the economy. Various measures have been taken which give priority to this group, not wholly successfully. Malaysia was initially badly affected by the Asian economic crisis of 1997. Alone it tried to impose restrictions on the inward flow of speculative capital, restrictions which were unpopular but later vindicated.

Until 1966 Malaysia and Singapore were part of the Federation of Malaya, established in the process of decolonization. Frictions quickly developed, partly as a result of a different ethnic composition – Singapore is mainly Chinese, whereas 60% of the inhabitants of Malaysia are Malay and Muslim – and partly as a result of different economic interests.

On separation, Singapore saw a rapid rate of growth which has taken its GDP per head into the range of the developed economies. Now one of the four Asian tigers, the government of Singapore has played an active role in stimulating this growth, picking winners, actively seeking to bring a desired economic structure into existence.

Malaysia is already the 17th largest trading nation in the world, with US$80 billion of exports and imports; 90% of this trade moved by sea, mostly through Singapore, the second busiest port in Asia after Hong Kong. For 40 years Malaysia has depended on the neighbouring port of Singapore for the export of its goods. On one estimate the possible loss in freight and insurance payments is as high as US$2.1 billion over the last decade (Cheng, 2002).

The country's premier port is Klang-West Port in Pulau Indah, only 40 kilometres from the capital Kuala Lumpur. Almost half a billion dollars has already been invested in improving the facilities of this port. This investment has not stopped the flow of exports through Singapore, since Klang is not a realistic competitor.

In 1999, the US$1 billion state-of-the-art container port of Tanjung Pelepas was opened. More money has been poured into the new port than the old one of Klang, almost three-quarters of a billion dollars by 2003. The government has been active in encouraging this development.

The new port is located on the southern tip of Johor province, which borders Singapore and is directly competitive with Singapore. Like Singapore, PTP is at the confluence of the world's busiest shipping lanes. Its location is ideal for capturing some of Singapore's traffic. It is a realistic potential competitor. As a result PTP has become one of the world's fastest growing ports.

Already the port has a number of advantages over Singapore. It has abundant land and a 2.16 kilometre linear wharf with a 15 metre deep-water clearance. Tankers can use the wharf with ease. Shipping companies can acquire dedicated space which allows quick access, rather than, as at Singapore, having to wait in offshore anchorages for a berth to become free. The port facilities and the infrastructure are modern. Because of the pool of much cheaper available labour, operational costs in the port are 30–40% lower than at Singapore. The port has duty-free commercial zones, distribution parks and banking services. There is a plan to build a petrochemical plant and refuelling facilities close to the port.

Singapore is not in any position to win a price war, if it should develop. It can still claim technological excellence. At Singapore's new Pasir Panjung facility, a single stevedore manipulating a computer-controlled crane can unload and load a 3,000-container ship overnight. It is unclear whether the Malaysian port will be able to equal this rate. Higher productivity can compensate for lower costs.

While the number of container units handled at Singapore between 1999 and 2001 has fallen from 15.9 to 15.2 million, over the same period PTP has gone from nothing to 2 million units, a long way behind but closing the gap. It has already won some significant customers away from Singapore such as Maersk.

The port is 70% owned by Seaport Terminal Sdn Phd, a company controlled by Syed Mokthat Al-Bukhary, a shipping tycoon close to the Prime Minister Mohammed Mahathir. This is not untypical of the way in which the government promotes the kind of developments it wants, working with favoured individuals. Such a pattern has much criticized and to some degree played down, but it persists. The other 30% is owned by the Danish shipping company, Maersk-Sealand, which has been lured into this partnership, away from its former location at Singapore. This is an interesting and potentially very positive partnership.

As seen in Chapter 3 the nation state is still the basic political unit in the world. The strategy of governments and the policies that realize those strategies are key elements of any general business context which cannot be ignored by business enterprises. The world is divided into a growing number of separate political jurisdictions in which legal systems and the systems of political organization differ. The mechanisms through which policy is developed differ markedly from country to country. Some are representative democracies, other have more authoritarian governments. There are patterns of alliances which are relevant to the political scene.

The nature of the political system affects the probability of policy change. Some degree of political stability is a precondition for successful business activity. It is difficult to conduct successful business either with a hostile government or in conditions of unpredictable political change. Policy may change because:

- the government is under pressure from groups with the ability to make their voice heard
- the government itself changes, either in an orderly manner through a democratic election or through a coup of some kind
- the government has a change of heart, itself reacting to changing circumstances in the general environment or social unrest. One important issue is the way in which a government gains its political legitimacy.

All governments have to adapt policy to the changing environment. The degree of policy stability differs markedly from region to region and country to country. It largely depends upon whether there is a broad social consensus. In developed liberal democracies, the rival parties' sensitivity to the social consensus ensures that radical policy change is a rarity. In developing countries with authoritarian governments, the situation varies enormously. It is much easier to share a large and growing cake than a small and fixed one. Successful economic development is used to legitimize authoritarian regimes. Winner-takes-all politics is much more likely in the latter case. This may involve frequent and dramatic changes of policy. Ratings of country risk reflect these differences in policy stability.

A second major issue is the ability of any government to make its policies work. An apt distinction in this context is between infrastructural power and despotic power. How far a government can carry out policies which achieve its aims in the fields of transportation, communication, education and health depends on its ability to penetrate the society and consistently implement its own policies. On the other hand, some governments can satisfy the whims of the governors but not realize major policies.

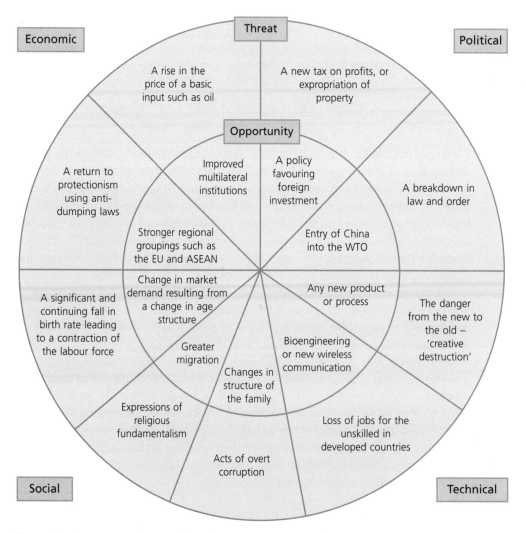

Figure 5.4 **Representative sources of opportunity and threat in different segments**

Through a range of policies, governments have a profound influence on the way in which a business operates. This is true even though governments may appear to be moving away from industry policy or incomes policy, that is, away from direct intervention in markets. The current fashion is for deregulation of markets, for government to withdraw and contract in size. There is enormous pressure on governments from key international players to conform to this view.

Some of the influences of government on enterprise are direct, in that the policies impinge directly on revenues or costs. Fiscal, monetary or commercial policies do this. Other policies, such as social policies or foreign policy, have a more indirect influence.

The effects are by no means always negative. Policy can promote business activity. Multinational enterprises actively encourage this process. Their degree of influence on the governments of the country of origin and the host country may vary, but cannot be ignored. In a world which is moving, if slowly, towards integration, there is a powerful sense in which the governments of different countries are in competition with each other to locate desirable economic activity within their own boundaries. They compete to be the location of foreign investment. This makes them amenable to pressure from the multinationals who make this investment. An obvious way in which they assist business is through promotive policies, including the provision of a suitable infrastructure, but there are numerous other ways. The government may seek to provide cheap loans or tax holidays. It may encourage the establishment of all sorts of institutional mechanisms helpful to business, encouraging the exchange of information or the undertaking of research. This is a very important part of the context in this environmental segment.

Figure 5.4 indicates a few important opportunities and threats which might arise within each segment of the general environment, some are general, others more specific.

The main features of global change

The opportunities and threats created by the rise of the global economy reflect various significant tendencies occurring in the world, many of them global tendencies.

The choice of tendencies made here is by intention subjective, illustrative of the kind of analysis which is often implicit in the thinking of strategists but which ought to be made explicit. It represents the context in which scenario building for any particular industry must be undertaken and a background to such scenario building. There is an attempt to indicate the nature of the threat or opportunity created by these trends, limiting the number of trends to the ten most important and including only those which have had a major impact throughout the world.

The trends in the next 20 years often represent a continuation of what has already occurred over the previous 25 years. However, there are some major changes of trend which should be noted, especially the first one, which is going to have a profound effect on every aspect of business life. The trends are not placed in any order, but clearly some are more important than others. The length of the treatment is some indication of the extent and depth of impact.

Falling birth rate

The falling birth rate, occurring in an increasing number of middle-income countries but predominantly in the developed world, is now well below the net reproduction rate in about 60 countries.

This is a robust and powerful social phenomenon. While fertility rates fluctuate in the short term, they have a long-term tendency to decline. There is an almost universal law that as incomes rise birth rates fall, a law which is demonstrated by long-term studies of particular countries and cross-sectional studies of a particular country in a given year. Sometimes this trend is obscured by short-term term fluctuations but it always reasserts itself. This decline is also associated with lower mortality rates and a tendency for increased longevity and improved health at what used to be considered advanced ages. Life expectancy has been rising at an average rate of about 2.5 years each decade for the last century.

Maintenance of the existing population level in any region or country requires either a gross net reproduction rate of 2.0 or net immigration which offsets any shortfall below 2.0. In reality because of deaths before child-bearing age, the rate has to be somewhat higher than 2, more like 2.1 or 2.2. Typically, as of 2002, the rate has fallen in developed countries below 2.0, in the most extreme cases as low as 1.3 or 1.4. Even in countries with significant immigration and therefore a younger population like Australia, the ratio is well below 2.0. The fall has affected both developed and developing countries; it first affects the higher income groups and then works through to lower income groups.

The fall in birth rate is part of a long-term trend, resulting from two powerful factors:

- The treatment of children as another consumption good, a good which is increasingly expensive, particularly compared with other desired goods, both in terms of the cost of supporting the child to an ever greater age and in the opportunity cost of lost income while the child is in secondary and tertiary education.
- The growing equality of women. Women now desire a career and an equal opportunity with men. It is difficult, with the current organization of child rearing, to have both career and children.

There are significant implications which follow from the anticipated demographic behaviour:

- There is no population problem in the world, only a development problem in those parts of the world where incomes are not rising. The poor will continue to have lots of children.
- World population will reach a peak some time in the second half of this century, at a lower level than most people have expected and still expect, and the population of certain countries, some with large populations, such as Russia or Japan, will peak at a much earlier date.
- Population growth in the developed world is only sustained by immigration. Over the next 20 years, the conflict between the labour needs of countries with contracting populations and labour forces and the conservatism which seeks to preserve existing cultural integrity will become a focus of intense conflict in various

parts of the world. There is a significant and growing net movement of people from the undeveloped world to the developed world, some legal and some illegal. Migration-friendly countries, such as the USA, Canada, Australia and New Zealand, will do best economically by selectively topping up their population in key areas where there are skill needs. The development problem of the poor countries will be compounded by a loss of the skilled, educated and most adventurous.

- There is a major stimulus to migration, legal and illegal, short and long term, and as a result an increasingly 'forced' multiculturalism, embraced by some, resisted by others. There will be more diversity within countries but less in the world as a whole, that is, between countries (the trends in biodiversity mirror those in population composition). The key major constraint on migration is not the economic capacity of countries to absorb the newcomers, although this is a factor, but rather the cultural conservatism of existing social groups in the receiving countries who resist significant immigration.

- There is a changing distribution of world population, notably less in Europe and Japan, and more in undeveloped countries, worsening their development and environmental problems.

- There is a significant ageing of the population of developed economies, with a growing problem of financing retirement and health. Although the health of the old is improving, dependency ratios are rising. As a result, compulsory retirement ages are being progressively removed. There will be an additional incentive to work beyond the normal retirement age.

- High participation rates among women in the developed countries allow little further increase in the employment of women, another factor compounding the slower likely rate of growth of the labour force in the future and making faster any contraction. The rate at which women occupy senior positions in any organization will accelerate.

- Labour markets in the world are being systematically deregulated. An integrated world market for labour, particularly skilled labour, is making its appearance. The developed countries will reduce and transfer elsewhere economic activities which rely on cheap and abundant labour and where possible substitute capital for labour by automating processes and extending the use of robots.

- There will be significant changes in the nature of consumer demand, with less emphasis on youth and the products consumed by the young. The 60+ age group will grow in importance as a market segment. A pattern of demand which emphasizes health, recreation and entertainment will emerge and become much more important. Ageism and grey power will be new movements of some significance.

Uneven economic development

There will no automatic spread of economic development from country to country. It will continue to be difficult, but not impossible, to make the breakthrough to a high level of income per head. So far there have been two major breakthroughs, the European/US one, mainly in Western and Central Europe and North America, and the Eastern Asian one. The breakthrough will spread to areas adjacent to the existing centres, such as Eastern Europe or Southern Asia, but not as quickly as might be hoped. There is no automatic process of spread, or guarantees attaching to the success of particular policies. There can be significant reversals.

The implications of this failure are significant:

- There will be increasing disparities in rates of economic growth between different regions and countries, associated with disparities in the rate of population increase. Growth rates in the developed world will continue at close to their long-term maximum level of 3–4%.
- Unemployment will be much less of a problem in developed countries but a growing one in the undeveloped world. The level of unemployment will steadily fall in developed countries.
- There will be an increasing unevenness of world income distribution which will encourage the movement of people described above.
- Cases of new economic success will remain few, mostly economies adjacent to the triad, that is, parts of Eastern Asia and Eastern Europe, perhaps even Latin America. The one major exception may be the Indian subcontinent which is likely to emerge as the next miracle economy.
- There will be continued marginalization of some areas of the world, for example Africa.
- The increasing disparity in incomes will result in continued North–South tensions.
- There will be a re-emergence of a debate about desirable economic strategy, particularly the role of governments and markets in the process of economic development.
- One aspect of this reappraisal will be a rethinking of excessive reliance on the market but in practice it will continue to be difficult to isolate an economy from the global economy without serious short-term difficulties. Countries will continue to quietly pursue non-tariff protection of their economies.

Continuing communications revolution

This technical revolution has by no means fully realized its enormous potential to change the world. There are a number of implications:

- The world will recover from the bursting of the dot.com bubble, in 2000–02, and the overextension of new broadband communications networks. Demand will eventually catch up with supply. There will be a continuation of the third wave of technical change, with a tendency to keep the global economy prosperous – high investment, productivity acceleration, increased business opportunities.
- This will result in a restructuring of employment. The decline in the share of employment in the primary and secondary sectors will continue. There will be a reduction in employment in some core service areas, such as finance, insurance and government, but matched by an enormous increase in others, tourism and entertainment, medicine, research and consulting. This will create structural difficulties in the skills composition of the labour force of the affected countries.
- There will be an enormous reduction in transaction costs generally and an improvement in the efficiency of market operation. The process of global market integration will continue.
- There will be an increased tendency to periodic outbreaks of extreme market volatility and threatened meltdowns in capital markets. The capital markets will show less growth than in the 1990s, as price/earnings ratios are restored to normal levels.

- There will be an increasingly homogeneous global culture but with local resistance to the process of homogenization based on subnational regional identities.
- There will be opportunities for small enterprises which are quick on their feet and an emphasis on flexibility of organizational design to accommodate the needs of the IT revolution.

| **Increasing focus on Asia** | Asia will continue its rise, eventually becoming the dominant economic region in the world. There are dramatic implications: |

- This period will see the emergence of a number of Asian economic giants, their interaction creating the dominant economic region in the world: a recovery of Japan with a redefinition of its role, the continuing rise of China and India emerging as the next centre of rapid economic development. Indonesia will make a slow recovery.
- There will be a significant slowing of the rate of population increase in most of Asia as birth rates fall, but in a context of already very large populations, which in aggregate will continue to dominate the world distribution of population and ultimately world demand.
- There will be the same tendency to increased migration, as in North America and Western and Central Europe, both across national boundaries and within countries, particularly from areas of low income and poor employment prospects to areas of higher income and better employment prospects.
- There will be a much greater awareness of cultural difference between the different areas of Asia and a resulting increase in cultural tensions within Asia itself.
- Within Asia there will be a reproduction of the 'uneven' world economic scene: some advanced areas with high income levels, some intermediate but rapidly changing areas and some backward areas, with low income levels and low growth rates.
- The Asian consumer market will emerge as a significant global factor. There will be great competition to open up these markets and a reluctance on the part of the governments in Asia to allow free entry for imports.
- Intra-Asian political frictions will become common and the achievement of economic cooperation will be difficult; as a consequence economic and political union within Asia will make slow progress.
- Asia will see the spread of various single interest movements – conservation, feminism, minority rights – with these movements strongest in the most developed of the countries, such as Japan and South Korea.

| **Reinforcement of tripolar world** | The triad will continue to dominate economically but the relative weight of the different parts will change, becoming more equal. The implications are: |

- There will be an increasing concentration of world output, investment, trade and the generation of intellectual property in the triad, although the triad will marginally extend its boundaries.
- Economic development will take the form of an extension of the triad to areas adjacent to the main centres.

- There will be a slow and steady erosion of American primacy: military withdrawal from Asia, the contribution of a declining proportion of world output, investment and trade. But the USA will remain the main source of intellectual capital, the world's cultural capital and its political and military leader.
- There will be further consolidation of Europe; an increase in the number of member countries of the EU and a slow movement towards further economic and political integration.
- There will be a slow revival of Eastern Europe as part of Europe, still very limited in the areas in the extreme east, furthest from the EU.
- The Asian tripolar centre will broaden beyond Japan, South Korea and Taiwan in Northern and Northeastern Asia to include some smaller economies and an increasing part of China.
- There will be difficulty in the assertion of international leadership by any one country; the existence of rival political centres, the increasing power of multinational enterprises and the continuing weakness of international organizations are the main reasons for this. This could make for increased instability in the world. There may be serious terrorist attacks, directed at targets in the developed world or related targets elsewhere, which are costly in their short-term consequences but do not change the world in a significant way.

Increasing importance of multinational companies

Multinational enterprises (MNEs) will continue to grow in number and size, with a continuing influence on the nature of the global economy. The implications are many:

- There will be an increase in the number, and economic and political power, of such enterprises, which will extend their influence to all sectors of the global economy. There will be an increasing number of such multinationals within and outside the triad.
- Acquisitions and mergers at the global level will grow in importance. Many industries will become oligopolistic, dominated by a few giants at the global level.
- MNEs will become one of the main engines of world economic development, with an increased emphasis on the internalization within these enterprises of global investment and commodity flows.
- There will emerge a genuine international market for management and labour, especially skilled labour.
- The attempt to reinforce branding and product differentiation at a global level will become more pronounced, but there will be few genuinely global brands.
- There will be increasing level of both foreign direct investment and foreign portfolio investment, both in absolute terms and as a proportion of gross domestic product and total capital formation.
- There will be increased attempts to control MNEs by international organizations and governments setting the rules of international business.

Rising environmental concerns

The environment has become an important focus of concern. This concern will increase but will change its nature. There are several developments which are relevant:

- The rate of world population growth will slow more quickly than envisaged and move towards an earlier stabilization, with an obvious effect in relieving the pressure on the environment.

- Improvised solutions to the problems requiring increased need for global controls will predominate: particularly in the areas of global warming, acid rain, nuclear waste, the threat to biodiversity and forest depletion.
- MNEs will become increasingly sensitive to the issue of sustainability and actively seek a reputation as environmentally sensitive.
- Developed countries will further improve their environment and develop a virtuous circle of improvement as income levels rise and more resources are devoted to this area. There will be much less pressure on the natural environment. The developed countries will continue to develop renewable energy sources.
- Undeveloped and some developing countries will see further deterioration of the environment and develop a vicious circle because of a failure to raise income levels significantly. There will be a redirection of polluting activities to the undeveloped world.
- The environment will be increasingly recognized as a development rather than a population problem. As incomes rise the demand for conservation rises too.

Internationalization of services

The economic importance of the service sector will rise to the point at which it accounts for nearly all employment and nearly all of any rise in production. The number of people employed in manufacturing and agriculture will continue to decline. This has the following implications:

- Services will be traded on an increasing scale and account for an increasing proportion of exports. There will be an increasingly important connection between the consumption of goods and the consumption of services, as part of the general process of customization of all production.
- Growth in international trade of some services, including tourism, specialized medicine and education, will be very fast. Consultancies will operate more and more on a global level. Much of this will be conducted on the Internet.
- As services continue as the main source of employment in the developed world, manufacturing, particularly of a labour-intensive kind, will be more and more limited to developing countries.
- There will be an enormous increase in e-commerce, with e-commerce developing faster for businesses than for consumers.
- Value chains will become increasingly complex, involving international links of great intricacy.
- There will be an enormous increase in foreign travel. Special events will go increasingly global, on the model of the Olympics or the World Cup.

Bioengineering and clean car revolution

The bioengineering revolution has only just started. This period will see the beginning of a new wave of technical change but one rather different in nature from previous waves. It is mainly based on the enormous growth of knowledge of the biochemical basis of life, including the mapping of the human and other genomes. This is a knowledge-based revolution but the growth of knowledge has also emphasized the complexity of the genome. The revolution will be much slower coming than originally thought. Depending on the degree of encouragement from governments, the hydrogen cell will be introduced on a significant scale in the next 20 years. There are changes which are already happening:

- There will be less investment in infrastructure in the early stages of the bioengineering revolution, but large investment in a network of hydrogen supply to replace the network of petrol supply. The demand for oil will not decrease since it will be used in the petrochemical industry. There will be a rise in the level of competitive research as countries position themselves to take advantage of both revolutions. The development of bioengineering products and the new automobiles is expensive. Such research and development expenditures will raise the level of demand.
- The initial impact of the bioengineering revolution will be on medicine, agriculture and pharmaceuticals. This is already becoming significant. The potential in terms of raising productivity levels in agriculture and stabilizing output is large. There are already genetically modified crops being planted, especially in the USA.
- One immediate impact of the revolution is to massively increase the cost of pharmaceuticals and medical treatment in general. In the near future it will be possible to tailor drugs to personal needs. These will be designed specifically, on the basis of personal DNA, to accommodate an individual's reaction to an ailment. For diabetes such a drug is only two to three years away. This process will accentuate the improvement in both longevity and health. These changes will precede the revolution in personal transport, but be more gradual in their build-up.
- The revolution will eventually spread to materials, energy sources and even to communications, but much later than usually anticipated, probably beyond the next 20–25 years.
- There will be much conflict over the ethics of genetic engineering. The issue of genetically modified food, much debated, illustrates the nature of the likely debates which will take place. On the other hand, conservationist needs will accelerate the introduction of the hydrogen cell.

Changing nature of households

One of the most distinctive features of family structure in the developed world is the nuclear, as compared with the extended, family. The nuclear family will become even more flexible, both in its structure and ability to encourage mobility of various kinds, involving larger numbers of temporary partnerships and single member households. There will be even more mobility geographically, socially and occupationally, particularly internationally. This will be aided by the decrease in the average size of household unit, which will become a global phenomenon:

- In the developing world, the extended family will weaken and gradually be replaced by the nuclear family.
- Most women in the developed world, and an increasing number in the developing world, will be in paid employment. Household roles will gradually become more homogeneous, particularly in developed countries.
- Much of the employment in the new world will be casual. It may also involve work

at home. In the developed world the household will again become an increasing focus for work, as well as for consumption, but working at home will only be for the minority.

- There will be a growing importance of lifetime education, with periodic retraining and re-education. This will be associated with a more frequent change of job and occupation.

It is possible to draw out in detail the full implications of each of these tendencies. Scenario building is premised on such a view of the world.

Case Study   A clean vehicle – the hybrid electric vehicle (HEV)

The first question is why should anyone buy and use an HEV? This is a question of the advantages which such a vehicle offers.

Advantages

These are mainly environmental, but are achieved at some damage to those attributes of the vehicle which are highly valued by users:

1. There is a significant reduction in the emission of air pollutants, as much as one-third to one-half, compared with vehicles with internal combustion engines only. This is because the combustion engine is never used for idling, short trips or when the engine is cold.
2. There is a massive improvement in fuel economy. HEVs can achieve as much as twice the kilometres per litre or gallon that a conventional vehicle can achieve. HEVs are also more energy efficient, since they convert forward momentum during deceleration into energy used to recharge the battery system.
3. For personal and light commercial use in urban areas, HEVs have the flexibility of normal combustion motors. They can even be used for some commercial hauls over longer distances.
4. HEVs address the main deficiency of electric cars – their limited range of about 80–140 kilometres and the significant downtime required for the recharging of batteries.

Disadvantages

1. There is an additional weight of several hundred kilos because of two power sources, including generator, electric motor and batteries. This is already taken account of in the estimate of fuel efficiency, but there is a consequent reduction in the availability of space.
2. The maximum horsepower of the combustion engine is only used about 1% of the time, during acceleration.

3. There are currently additional costs reflected in the high price of HEVs which reflect particularly the high level of R&D expenditures and the low volume of sales.

Probably the most significant technical development in this area is the cooperative project developed between the Department of Energy in the USA and the main automobile producers, GM, Ford and Daimler-Chrysler, called the Partnership for a New Generation of Vehicles (PNGV). This was established in 1993 as a five-year, shared-cost programme. The brief of the partnership is to pursue any technology which will improve fuel consumption by motor vehicles. It has a specific objective of tripling fuel efficiency to 80 mpg or 3 litres/100 km for the standard motor car from the norm of 27.5 mpg or 9.5 litres/100 km at present. It sees the HEV as an instrument for achieving this target. The project has received US$319.6 million in funds for research and development.

The work of the Partnership is supplemented by other initiatives. The Department of Energy has, through the Cooperative Automotive Research for Advanced Technology (CARAT), dispensed more than US$3.7 million in grants to small companies, universities and institutes of technology to develop low-cost, advanced automotive components and subsystems. The USA's National Renewable Energy Laboratory (NREEL) also assists the Partnership with technical support. In January 2003, President Bush announced that his government would spend $1.2 billion so that 'America can lead the world in developing clean, hydrogen-powered automobiles'.

Competition

What has already been achieved? Table 5.4 shows the features of the two HEVs on the market in mid-2002.

The Honda has been selling poorly, for the reasons indicated above, whereas the Toyota has accumulated 70,000 sales internationally since 1997. At 2003 petrol prices, neither vehicle is likely to repay the additional cost of purchase, nor are they the ultimate environmental answer since both still need unleaded petrol. They are very much pioneers, showing what will be the norm in five to ten years.

These two vehicles will soon face major competition. There are two types of competition for the existing HEVs: competition from HEVs produced by rival automobile producers; and competition from vehicles using alternative technologies, including improved versions of the existing technology.

The American HEV programme is about to bear fruit. General Motors has at least three versions of HEV vehicles in the pipeline, including passenger and light commercial vehicles. Ford has two models, the Escape and the Prodigy. DaimlerChrysler has two passenger and one light commercial vehicle under construction. Other automobile manufacturers that are not far from launching their own HEVs include Fiat, Daihatsu, Mitsubishi and Renault-Nissan.

The use of compressed natural gas (CNG) is another source of competition, particularly for light commercial vehicles including taxis. In the USA there are already well over 100,000 vehicles using CNG and the number is growing rapidly. CNG has a similar environmental impact to the HEV and is currently much cheaper.

Present technology

From the mid-1950s to the early 1980s a complacent industry dominated by the large American producers made little effort to improve the technology of the internal combustion engine. During this period there was no increase in the horsepower per litre of car. Three things happened to change this situation. The oil price hike made energy efficiency important. The amended US Clean Air Act of 1990 began the effort to reduce emissions from cars. The flood of Japanese automobiles pressured the Americans to lift their game.

From 1980 to 2002 there was a doubling in the net horsepower per litre. The annual rate of gain was as high as 1.5%. The cost of running a car and the emissions fell. All emissions, apart from carbon dioxide – the Achilles heel of the internal combustion engine – have fallen 90% since 1968, prompting Ealey and Mercer (2002: 51) to say: 'by 2000, late-model cars emitted less pollution while running than 1970s-era cars did while turned off.' This was because the older models leaked large amounts of fuel vapour.

Table 5.4 **Characteristics of existing HEVs**

	Honda Insight	Toyota Prius
Price	A$48,900 (equivalent to over US$20,000)	A$39,990
Features	56kW 1.0-litre three-cylinder engine 10kW electric motor Trip computer Other usual features – dual airbags – anti-lock brakes – air-conditioning – CD player – power windows – remote central locking – power steering	53kW 1.5-litre four-cylinder engine 33kW electric motor the same the same
Pluses	Impressive fuel consumption – 3.0 litres/100 km/(47–8 mpg) – digital dashboard includes a computerized fuel consumption readout Decent luggage space	5.9 litres/100 km/ (54 mpg)
Minuses	For urban areas only Feels gutless Terrible ride quality and handling Poor styling (aims for least aerodynamic drag) Seating for only one passenger High purchase price (three times the basic small cars)	Handles much better but surges Looks better Seating for four passengers (five doors) Still relatively high price
Assessment	Impressive technology but impractical Positive from green perspective	Same kind of technology but much more practical Somewhat less environmentally friendly Price more acceptable

Patents for the internal combustion vehicle have risen by 25% in the past five years. There are still significant new gains to be had:

1. The use of 36- and 42- rather than 12-volt alternator systems
2. Continuously variable transmission
3. Infinitely variable valve lift and timing
4. Direct fuel injection (diesel, and gasoline (US))
5. Plasma ignition system (gasoline)
6. Turbo-charging and after-cooling
7. Cylinder disconnecting with variable camshaft timing.

There is also the opportunity, pioneered by Airbus for airliners, to introduce what is called drive-by-wire, a system which replaces an automobile's hydraulic and mechanical system, such as the braking, throttle or steering systems, with fully electrical systems. This requires a high voltage system, such as the fuel cell, which is scalable by the introduction of additional plates, or the use of 36- or 42-volt alternators. Drive-by-wire is therefore compatible with either system, the internal combustion engine or the fuel cell. The best-known example of drive-by-wire is GM's Hy-Wire.

Fuel cell technology

In this system the hydrogen cell is the source of power. In the hydrogen cell the proton-exchange membrane (PEM) stack electrochemically converts hydrogen and air into electricity and water. The catalyst in the conversion is usually platinum or another rare metal, which explains the current high cost of such vehicles.

Advantages

1. It is clean, with no emissions, at least from the car. There may be emission if the hydrogen is extracted from carbon fuels elsewhere.
2. There are few resources needed to make the system work.
3. There is an instant on torque response.
4. The vehicles are less noisy than the internal combustion vehicles.
5. Maintenance is cheaper.
6. There is greater energy efficiency.

Disadvantages

1. It is an expensive producer of energy. The cost per kilowatt produced is $500–2,500 compared with $30–35, although ten years ago the former was $500,000, so the cost is coming down rapidly.
2. Under driving conditions the reliability and durability of the system are both suspect. For example, the stack currently does not generate power at low temperature.

3. The fuel cell has been, and still is, a very significant absorber of R&D funds, both government and private.
4. There is almost no infrastructure for the upkeep and maintenance of fuel cell vehicles or the supply of hydrogen, or enough work done on how the latter might be achieved. A reliable infrastructure might cost as much as $100 billion to install. It will require government action.
5. There are problems in extracting hydrogen from relevant compounds.
6. There are serious safety hazards.
7. Hydrogen tanks are heavy.

The future

It would be simple to construct a future scenario exercise on the possible options.

There is a question mark about whether there is a genuine market for the HEV. In 2001 Honda sold only 3,788 hybrids in the USA and Toyota 15,556, a good proportion of which probably went to local municipalities and corporate fleets. Honda itself thinks that its 2003 Civic SULEV will match the emission status of the Civic Hybrid and will at the same time achieve better fuel efficiency.

There is preference in the American market for large cars, in particular pickups and SUVs. There is a claim that the saving on petrol from the operation of an HEV is only about 12% and that this saving could easily be achieved using existing power sources. If the saving is as little as this, then the high initial capital cost means that the extra cost would not be recouped for many years. Table 5.5 shows the relative performance of different technologies.

GM has claimed that it will start to put fuel cell vehicles on the market as early as 2010. Other producers think that it will be five to ten years later. The Japanese government has an ambitious goal of having about five million fuel cell vehicles on Japanese roads by 2020. The biggest problem is the lack of an infrastructure similar to that currently supplying petrol. The general expectation is that as late as 2015 as many as 90% of new vehicles sold in developed countries are still likely to use the internal combustion engine. For a decade after that they are likely to remain dominant.

There is one critical uncertainty which could produce a different outcome, government regulation. If governments were to opt for zero emissions, as the state of California has already, then only the fuel cell could achieve this. Government could push the manufacturers who are already spending very large sums on new technology to accelerate the process of introducing the new generation of vehicles. Otherwise, whatever the

Table 5.5 **Relative performance of different technologies**

Fuelling hope	Miles per gallon, 2001 or fuel cell equivalent	Carbon dioxide emissions, 2001 grams per kilometre
Conventional internal combustion engine	28	72
Advanced ICE		
Gasoline	49	42
Diesel	56	37
Hybrid ICE		
Gas	71	30
Diesel	83	27
Fuel cell engine		
Compressed hydrogen	94	34
Onboard refiner	42	49

Source: Ealey and Mercer, 2002: 46.

R&D funds expended on the fuel cell, and these will be large, both in the public and private sector, and whatever the tax credits given to car purchasers in order to persuade them to choose the fuel cell, in the immediate future the situation is unlikely to change more than marginally.

Case Study Questions

1. What are the main features of the external environment influencing the strategy of automobile manufacturers in designing new vehicles?
2. How will these features have an impact on the choice of vehicle made by consumers?
3. Using the steps of the analysis described in Chapter 4, carry out a scenario-building exercise on the future of the motorcar.
4. What implications do the different possible futures have for the strategy to be pursued by the automobile manufacturers?

5. What is the relevance of government strategy to the choices made by automobile manufacturers?

Reading

Armstrong, L., 'A mean green machine', *Business Week*, April 22, 2002: 63.
Ealey, L. A. and Mercer, G. A., 'Tomorrow's cars, today's engines', *McKinsey Quarterly*, 2002(3): 40–53.
Flint, J., 'Don't count on hybrids', *Forbes*, 06.03.02.
Nakamura, A., 'Fuel-cell cars now have a place to fill up', *The Japan Times*, March 13, 2003: 9.
O'Dell, J., 'GM hydrogen-fuel car looks lean, mean', *The Japan Times*, March 4, 2003: 9.
Rifkin, J., 'The forever fuel', *The Australian Financial Review*, November 1, 2002: 1–2.
Watanabe, H., 'Toyota FCHV – the first step toward the hydrogen society of tomorrow', Special Report on Toyota's website.

Key strategic lessons

• There are differences between the general environment and the industrial or competitive environment and different ways in which the general environment can be divided.

• Strategists should consider the rate at which the general environment changes and quickly recognize the implications in terms of opportunities and threats and complexity.

• A prerequisite for business success is to anticipate the different patterns of change and manage the implications of change. The transitoriness of business success indicates the failure to achieve this.

• It is useful to divide the environment into four segments: the social, technical, economic and political.

• There are ten main tendencies which may be

important in influencing the business environment over the next quarter century: falling birth rate; uneven economic development; continuing communications revolution; increasing focus on Asia; reinforce- ment of tripolar world; increasing importance of multinational companies; rising environmental concerns; internationalization of services; bioengineering revolution; and changing nature of households.

Applying the lessons

1   Define the following terms: the general environment, and its segments, political, economic, technical, social and technical, the competitive environment, the business landscape, a cultural cluster, a macro-invention, a micro-invention.

2   List all the different sources of information which you can use in developing your view of the general environment in which you operate as an individual.

• What are the most useful of these sources?

• What are the most accurate in indicating future trends?

• How has the communications/information revolution influenced the flow of relevant information?

3   'Knowledge is power.' Choose an important issue such as hormone replacement therapy or genetically modified crops and answer the following questions. In what sense is the statement true? What implications does it have for the business world if it is true? What are the ethical issues involved in the deliberate withholding of information? Select a particular issue and show how transparency is relevant to this issue.

4   Imagine you are modelling the business landscape of a specific part of the world in which you are interested. This world consists of different industries and different countries. How would this landscape look? Note the frequency of mountain chains and peaks, the frequency of plains and valleys and the gradient between them. Justify your modelling by reference to what you know about the business world.

5   Write down the most important but most unexpected events which have had the most influence on your personal life. How far could these events have been predicted?

6   Choose three countries belonging to different cultural clusters. Comment on their differences in their attitude to the following:

• risk or uncertainty

• time

• authority or power

• age

• goal achievement

• the individual or community.

Strategic project

1   Divide the class into small groups of 5 or 6.

2   Choose a particular sector of the economy.

3   Consider what you think to be the most important changes in the external environment, which occurred in the 1990s and have had an impact on that business sector.

4   Select the ten most important changes in refashioning the business environment. List the opportunities and threats which these changes have created.

5   Reassemble as a class and consider how many of these you have in common.

Exploring further

Any textbook on the international business environment will have a section on the different segments of the general environment, on STEP or as it is sometimes called PEST. The one used by the writer is Mahoney et al., 2001. This text divides the economic into international and national sections but has individual chapters on both the political and social segments. An alternative is Hill, 2003, particularly Chapters 2 and 3. Each text of this kind has its strength on different segments. Hill recognizes the close connection between the economic and the political. The difficulty is presenting enough theory to make it possible to read the environment through chains of cause and effect. This requires quite an in-depth knowledge of a discipline.

Two general pieces on how to read the general environment are Zahra and O'Neill, 1998: 36–42 and Thomas et al., 1999: 70–82.

There are still major gaps in the literature which on this topic is neither broad nor deep. Both the above texts lack a chapter on the technical segment. For this there is an excellent introductory book, Mokyr, 1990, which provides the conceptualization for interpreting technical change.

The literature on culture is often superficial. For further reading it is worth reading Huntingdon's 1996 work which is rather controversial but thought-provoking. More prosaic but just as illuminating is the work of Hofstede, 1991 and Trompenaars, 1983, 1998 which stress cultural difference; there has been little work building upon this base. The original source on cultural clusters is Ronen and Shenkar, 1985: 449–55.

6 Reading the competitive environment

I know more about them than they know about themselves. (ALAIN PERRIN, *President of Cartier, talking about his competitors*)

Case Study Scenario   Video game wars

The video game industry is a product of the information and communications revolution and a new way of satisfying the desire for entertainment. During the 1990s the industry developed quickly and was profitable for the successful players.

There are two elements in the delivery of video games, the hardware and the software. The hardware consists of the machines, platforms or consoles needed to deliver the games. The software consists of the games themselves. It is possible to specialize in one or the other, or try to do both well. Success in one may encourage success in the other.

Not all players have been consistently successful, the successful players having changed over time. During most of the 1990s Nintendo and Sega were the leading players, outcompeting the American and European players such as Atari, 3DO or Philips Electronics. In the mid-1990s, Sony entered the industry as a major player and in 2001–02 came Microsoft's decisive move into the industry. The competitive position in the industry has changed rapidly and will be subject to further changes in the future. For example, in 2001 Sega ceased to produce games consoles and became solely a producer of the games.

It is possible to configure the hardware so that it will accept only certain software, namely those games which are produced by or for the company which sells the platform. There are therefore strong network effects which protect the incumbent console providers who already have a good list of games. This reduces the competitiveness of any new entrant to the industry. However, it is not difficult for skilled hackers to succeed in breaking this link, and in at least one country such activity has been deemed legal.

This is one of the most competitive industries in the world economy, whether the console or the video game itself is considered. There is competition on both the hardware and software sides, competition which has been, and still is, very fierce. The industry is currently going through a period of particularly intense competition as a new generation of consoles have been introduced.

How difficult is entry into the industry? The ease of entry differs between the hardware and software sides, with different barriers for the two areas. The hardware is subject to rapid technical change which affects the nature of the platform and the mechanism for delivery. New platforms are expensive to develop, requiring a major investment of resources, and are introduced only

intermittently. There are only three hardware players. It is difficult to develop a pool of attractive games to go with a completely new console. New consoles are at a disadvantage in lacking such a pool of existing games, since consoles are sometimes configured to allow the playing of the games made for previous generations. For example, games made for PlayStation 1 can be played on PlayStation 2.

On the other hand, the software requires creative and imaginative ability which is always in scarce supply. However, there are a large number of games makers, both attached to the console makers and independent. It is much easier to build upon an existing foundation, upgrading already popular games and redeploying existing characters, than it is to create games from nothing. Alliances with creative individuals or companies is critical to success. These have to be created from nothing by newcomers.

Demand for either console or games is price elastic. Price does matter to consumers, especially price relative to that of competitors' products. A price premium can be charged for superior technology or a strong games link, but serious price competition is not infrequent.

Why would an enterprise, such as Sony or Microsoft, wish to enter such an industry? The obvious answer is that for the most part the industry has been immensely profitable, with some exceptional periods, such as 1994/5 or 2001 when demand fell precipitously. Sony's PlayStation currently generates about 60% of the company's profits, and at times this share has exceeded 100%.

The industry is surprisingly large. In 2002 games sales reached US$17.5 million and console sales US$8.7 million. The games industry is now generating almost as much revenue as the box-office receipts from films and rapidly catching up with the value of sales of music CDs. Only the sales of DVDs and videos are growing as fast. In 2002 as many as 45 million consoles were sold. The market grew on average at a rate of 10% per annum in 2001. During the rest of the current cycle, the growth rate is expected to be as high as 15–25%. In North America nearly two-thirds of children aged 6–14 now play video games. This proportion would be repeated in other parts of the world if the children had access to consoles or the purchasing power to give them that access. The rewards for a successful competitor are large.

Even where the coverage amongst children is already high, there is great potential for the development of the market, particularly the segments accounted for by adults and women. The demographic profile of the typical games player in the USA is changing. More than 60% of players are now adult, and more than 40% female. The average age is already 28, which explains why the mature-rated game Grand Theft Auto: Vice City,

launched in October 2002, turned out to be the fastest-selling game ever, with 1.4 million copies sold in the USA alone during its first three days on the market. An ability to anticipate the changing nature of demand is a significant competitive advantage.

The external environment of an enterprise has an element, the competitive or industrial environment, which has a much more obvious and direct influence on strategy making than the general environment. That environment is made up of various players – existing competitors, potential competitors, complementors and both government and multilateral institutions who set the rules of competition and also have a strong influence on the distribution of any rewards. No maker of strategy can ignore the responses of other players to any attempt to implement a strategy. There is inevitably a continuing process of action and reaction.

Strategic players

No strategy can be made without account being taken of the intentions and possible strategies of other important strategic players. It takes little imagination to realize that within the external environment of any organization there is a multitude of strategic players, all pursuing their own interests and contributing to the continuous change which is occurring in that environment. Some are potential allies, others serious competitors. Some set the rules by which this strategic game is played, others try to influence those who set the rules. There are numerous strategic players whose actions influence, directly and indirectly, the success or lack of it of any enterprise and its strategy.

Often strategy making is discussed as if it is formulated in isolation and in an environment in which all is given and unchanging. This is not the real world of strategy making, which is constantly being remade by the strategy of others. By making its own strategy, an enterprise in its turn contributes to that remaking for others.

Some of the strategic players operate in the general environment, others within the immediate competitive environment, which is the focus of interest in this chapter. The first problem is to identify the playing field. On the industrial playing field, there are those whose actions have a direct influence on the enterprise – competitors, complementors and lawmakers. By contrast those in the general environment develop their strategy completely independently of the enterprise and have only an indirect influence.

Players at both global and national levels mould the general environment, usually without considering specific feedback effects, as individual enterprises react to their action, since most of the latter are small and indirect. This is not true for the players in the industrial environment. Since most markets are dominated by a few players, the actions of one enterprise inevitably influence directly the actions of others, with a feedback effect from the ensuing response on the first player. For example, the fixing of a price level by one significant player has an impact on the price level set by all competitors. Their reaction then influences the initial price maker. Few enterprises are pure price takers, that is, completely unable to influence the level of price within a market. It is impossible to frame strategy without taking account of the universality of such feedbacks effects.

<table>
<tr><td>

Who are the players?

</td><td>

Players are not stakeholders, although there may be an overlap between the two groups. It is a different role, although the two roles can played by the same organization. The most important players are:

</td></tr>
</table>

- Competitor enterprises (including potential competitors, that is, those who could easily enter the industry and might do so in the future, and those who produce substitute products whose output could be expanded), both domestic and foreign
- Complementor enterprises (including those who are potential complementors but might currently be competitor enterprises)
- Large suppliers
- Large customers
- Various lawmakers and implementers, including different levels of domestic government
- Foreign governments with jurisdiction over large international players, for example the USA. This includes all foreign governments with economic relevance, for example venues of investment or destinations for exports
- International economic institutions influencing the rules of the game
- Industrial associations
- Large non-governmental organizations.

The most important players, defined in terms of the strength of their likely impact on the successful outcome of strategy and therefore on strategy making in the first place, fall into three categories – competitors, complementors and government organizations. In this section of the book, the focus is on competitors, with some reference to complementors, and on governments who might sometimes act as complementors.

Circumstances vary from industry to industry and the circumstances specific to an industry must be taken into account. For example, as the consumers of their products, airlines are of critical importance to the manufacturers of civil airliners, determining what and when they produce. In some industries, such as the wine industry, industrial associations, which bind together the players, are very important. In others the lawmakers are critical. The Food and Drugs Administration (FDA) in the USA and its counterparts elsewhere are important players in the pharmaceutical industry. The circumstances of a particular industry define exactly who is a significant player.

Even players in the general environment can have an impact on an enterprise through their own strategic actions, both direct and indirect. For example, the actions of governments, both domestic and foreign, can directly affect many economic factors relevant to the enterprise, through the level of taxes or the cost of capital, trade policy or a policy on foreign investment. Sometimes the effect is indirect, for example a change in world trade rules by an international institution such as the WTO or the introduction of a new technology by a potential competitor abroad.

The nature of an industry

The situation becomes more immediate as the focus shifts to players closer to the enterprise, since the potential impact increases and the feedback effects become more significant. Usually the enterprises which are in close competition with each other are regarded as constituting an industry or sector of industry. What is an industry? How is it defined? There is a standard classification of industrial sectors, but the boundaries move with technical change and changes in the nature of the product. They are not fixed. In some industries the boundaries are very flexible – communications, financial services and medical services are current examples.

An industry can be defined in terms of supply-side factors, the common attributes of a product or the nature of the process of production, or demand-side factors, that is, the degree to which the consumer views the products as satisfying the same utilities and therefore alike. In the jargon of the economist, an industry is defined by the level of the elasticity of substitution in the demand between the products of different enterprises, that is, how significantly demand shifts to another product in response to an increase in the price of one product. An infinite elasticity would mean that any movement of the price of one product above that of the other would cause the other to be wholly substituted in consumption; they are perfect substitutes. Clearly the enterprises producing them are part of the same industry.

The problems are twofold:

1. there is some degree of substitutability between most products, not just those within a given industry
2. there is no obvious threshold of substitutability above which the product can be regarded as part of an industry group and below which it is not.

The greater the degree of substitutability between two products, the greater the impact of the strategy pursued by one player on the other, and not just its pricing strategy.

Sequences of action and reaction

Strategy cannot be formulated and implemented independently of the expected reactions of other competitive players, particularly the larger players, to any strategic action taken. Clearly this response will determine the outcome of the original strategy. In some cases the impact of the response may dwarf that of the original action. Somehow an accurate anticipation of that response must be achieved, or an allowance made for a range of possible responses.

The aim becomes something more than reading the environment. It entails understanding the types of situation which can develop and the likely behaviour of players in these recurrent situations. Part of strategy is to read the strategic intent of other players, and read their ability to successfully formulate and implement that intent, and also to weigh the consequences of different courses of action.

Strategy is a dynamic process of action, response and further reaction. Relevant players come and go. The interaction can be limited to a brief moment or it can be one which stretches over a lengthy period of time. Once the response stretches over a significant period of time, it is possible for players to note the predominance of certain responses by players to particular types of action. The market ceases to be impersonal, since the reputation of known players becomes important. It becomes possible to read the behaviour of other players, since players tend to behave with some consistency.

Sometimes players have an interest in suppressing information about their possible reaction, even in deceiving others as to the likely nature of that response (see the case study on Airbus Industrie in Chapter 4). In this situation it may be appropriate to try to guess what the competitor is doing, or intends to do. The intention may be highly specific, such as the decision to begin a new generation of airliners. It may also be appropriate to build a considerable degree of flexibility into a strategy to allow for different strategic responses from other players, and allow for the inevitable ploys which are intended to bluff or deceive.

The role of the complementor

There are players who assist an organization to achieve its strategic objectives through strategic alliances of various kinds. Other organizations do this without any kind of formal alliance. These are complementors, who are the mirror image of competitors. Complementors are not necessarily strategic allies but they act like allies and may become allies.

Complementors are everywhere, but are most important for new industries and those where the standards achieved by the product are not yet fixed. The increased availability of complementary products or services with an associated reduced price will have a beneficial impact on an enterprise. Often the enterprises grow together, sometimes in clusters or networks.

A focus on complementarity redirects our attention away from competition to cooperation. There is still competition of a kind, in that the value added by an enterprise and its complementors must be divided up amongst them. For example, in the distribution of the overall value added, video game console manufacturers are less threatened by small games developers than by large ones, who can exert more pressure to increase their share of the gross income generated. The size of the switching costs incurred in moving from one complementor to another is also relevant in the proportions of this sharing. Complementary goods can also be unbundled in the same way as any product to reduce them to the attributes which are really necessary as complements.

It is possible, but unfashionable, for government to act as either competitor, producing and selling itself, or as complementor. The latter is much more likely than the former. Government is an important player in any market, in that it sets the rules for the interactions which occur and then arranges for their implementation. In this sense it is a very important complementor. First it decides on the nature of the regulations. Then various regulatory agencies apply them. Government here is a broad label covering a range of different levels of decision making – some supranational, most national, regional or local. There may be various layers of regulation. Government is not the only organization which helps to determine the rules but it is the most important since it has the authority to make those rules stick.

The forces of competition

The forces of competition are key elements in defining the recurrent competitive situations which are the focus of interest in this chapter. According to Michael

Porter (1980), there are five competitive forces, which are the main determinants of the level of competition in any one industry:

1. the nature and level of the barriers to entry into a particular industry
2. the availability of possible substitutes for the product or service
3. the bargaining strength of the suppliers to enterprises within that industry
4. the bargaining strength of the customers of those enterprises
5. the degree of intensity of competition within the industry.

One of the great competitive success stories of recent times is the growth of Starbucks in an industry which appears to be dominated by competition from a large number of small players. It is interesting to note how the forces of competition have affected Starbucks.

Strategy in Action Competitive forces for Starbucks

BARRIERS TO ENTRY

There are few barriers to entry into this industry. There is nothing in the technology of coffee production which creates a significant obstacle to entering the industry, for example no significant economies of scale or scope. A small player can easily set up a coffee shop.

The major entry problem is location. There are a limited number of locations in the centre of any town, easily accessible to potential customers, such as shoppers or businesspeople during the day and those attending entertainment venues during the evening. With the advent of the expresso cart, the importance of location is retained but access to suitable locations made much easier.

The saturation of good locations by Starbucks is a deterrent, the company being prepared to cannibalize existing stores, with an initial loss of as much as 30% of sales, on the assumption that the additional stores will expand total demand to compensate. Starbucks has a reputation for predatory rental behaviour, paying over the odds in rent for a good location. It might even rent or lease and keep a venue empty.

Although Starbucks spends as little as $30 million on advertising, or 1% of its revenues, its brand name is an increasing factor in deterring entry, established by word of mouth and repeated visits.

EXISTENCE OF SUBSTITUTES

In its broadest sense, a substitute is anything offering the same experience. The sale of specialty coffee in grocery stores and its consumption at home is a substitute. In its narrow sense tea, juice, soft drinks, alcohol and other flavoured coffee and non-coffee-related drinks are possible substitutes. Starbucks provides some of these.

The Starbucks coffee experience is a package of attributes. The overall experience comprises the ambience of the venue, including decor and musical background, the acceptability of the clientele, predictability of the product, convenience and ease of payment and even the availability of Internet facilities. Starbucks innovates to cut transaction costs and speed up service, introducing automatic expresso machines in some stores and prepaid Starbucks cards. In its 60 Denver stores it is possible to prepay on the phone or the Starbucks Express website and have the coffee waiting on arrival at the store.

Starbucks claims the largest Wi-Fi network in the world, a high-speed wireless Internet service to about 1,200 stores in North America and Europe, developed together with Mobile International and Hewlett-Packard. The coffee house works as an office where you can check your emails and download multimedia presentations. Starbucks provides an initial 24 hours of free wireless broadband, backed up by a variety of monthly subscription plans. The aim is to fill the stores in the period between the breakfast and lunch rushes, and win the support of the generation just entering the workforce.

▶

BARGAINING POWER OF SUPPLIERS

Because Starbucks purchases high-quality coffee, suppliers give priority to Starbucks and work closely with the company to ensure prompt delivery and good quality.

During the last 13 years the price of coffee has plummeted, peaking at US$3.15 per pound, but now at an average price as low as US$45 cents. The grower receives far less, since the intermediaries take their cut. The first International Coffee Agreement was negotiated in 1962, a complicated set of quotas for more than 60 coffee-growing countries, designed to keep prices reasonably stable. This it managed to do for 25 years, despite endless renegotiation. In 1989 the USA withdrew its support; the agreement was suspended and the price began to fall. Before 1989 the price had hovered around the US$1.20 mark. Supply ran ahead of demand, with new producing areas such as Vietnam becoming significant. During the 1990s world production rose by 21%, demand by 10%.

The typical coffee producer is small, although the purchase by cooperatives or middlemen, including exporters, increases somewhat the market power of suppliers. The cooperatives do not have the market clout of Starbucks, which could easily apply considerable pressure on producers, hardly necessary, given the level of coffee prices in world markets. To access a wide variety of coffees and hedge the risks to local supply, Starbucks buys 50% of its beans from Latin America, 35% from the Pacific rim and 15% from East Africa. Increasingly Starbucks blends the coffees. With a global reach and access to modern procurement techniques, Starbucks makes purchases to minimize cost.

BARGAINING POWER OF PURCHASERS

The typical customer purchases a cup of coffee at one of Starbucks' retail outlets and has little bargaining power. Starbucks has agreements with retailers, wholesalers, restaurants and other service providers to carry Starbucks coffee. Starbucks sought out leaders in the various fields, including the airline United Airlines, supermarket chains Nordstrom and PriceCostco, using a special brand name Meridian, bookstore Barnes & Noble and a supplier of business services ARAMARK. Starbucks has worked to develop new products: with PepsiCo to develop the frappuccino, a milk-based cold coffee beverage in a bottle; with Red Hook Breweries to supply an ingredient for a stout; and with Dreyers' Ice Cream to develop its own ice cream which it distributes through Dreyers' grocery channels. These companies have many more resources than the usual Starbucks customer and can negotiate from a stronger position.

INTENSITY OF COMPETITION

In developed economies there is a 'retailing war' between coffee chains, and between the local retail outlets of such chains and individual coffee shops. Starbucks is the largest player. In the USA there is no nationwide competitor. McDonald's McCafe outlets are expanding rapidly, but they have a downmarket image. The strategy of McDonald's has changed, from simply capturing the passing trade through low price, to making the outlet a 'destination'. In 1997 in North America when Starbucks was beginning to take off, there were 3,485 competitors, mostly one-store establishments with no plans to expand. Starbucks' main competitor in the specialty coffee area was Second Cup, a Canadian company, a franchiser, traditionally mall-based but increasingly using stand-alone locations like Starbucks.

The forces of competition are strong in this industry, so it is remarkable that Starbucks has established itself as such a dominant player. The notion of an aspirational product largely explains this (see the Strategy in Action on the democratization of luxury in Chapter 10).

A sixth competitive force, neglected by Porter, should be added, the availability of complementors and their own bargaining power.

The present analysis seeks to extend this classification to the international level, applying it to global markets. The forces of global competition are increasing as barriers to international competition disappear, whether these are significant transport and communication costs or simply government policies seeking to protect home enterprises.

The analysis proceeds in three stages: it outlines Porter's five forces, adds a sixth feature, the role of complementors and makes the analysis dynamic rather than static.

Figure 6.1 **Porter's five forces of competition**

Barriers to entry

The greater the barriers to entry into a particular market or industry, the higher tends to be the above-normal profit which can be earned in that market and, of course, the greater the incentive to get in. If there were no barriers, any above-normal profit would be quickly competed away by new entrants into the industry. How quickly this might happen depends on how long it takes to set up in the industry. Clearly no entry can take place instantly.

It is much quicker for a new entrant to enter an industry by acquiring an existing player. Most foreign direct investment entails such mergers and acquisitions. Entry into many parts of the global market is through this mechanism. In this case, entry is instant but does not increase the number of players, although it might lead to an expansion of productive capacity, depending on the intentions of the newcomer concerning that productive capacity.

What prevents this occurring frequently, especially where above-normal profits are being earned? At the international level, a government may put limits on the ability of a multinational enterprise to acquire an enterprise within its jurisdiction. Barriers can also be erected by existing players, on the demand and supply side. Clearly it is in the interest of enterprises deliberately to erect such barriers but it is much easier in some industries than in others. Some industries lend themselves to the existence of such barriers, while others do not. The nature of the production technology and related organizational structure and the way in which the demand for the product or service is satisfied determine the level of existing barriers.

The differentiation of a product, whether real or perceived, constitutes one such barrier, since it implies an attachment by the consumer to a particular product or brand. For the consumer there may be switching costs which attach to a change in the brand purchased, and these are often considerable. Such costs are sometimes financial and sometimes psychological. The preference for a particular brand can seem irrational to many non-consumers. In the extreme case branding ensures that the attachment is difficult to break. Advertising and general marketing of the product encourages such differentiation. There are still few genuine international brands, that is, brands which have currency in all countries. Most brands are national but they are many and have real value.

Existing players may also have all sorts of cost advantages over new entrants. In most industries there is a learning process which gives a decided advantage to those already established in an industry. This process of learning by doing allows movement down the experience curve.

Fixed costs associated with marketing, distribution, R&D and design are growing in importance. The existence of such large fixed costs rewards those with already large sales. They can spread these fixed costs more widely and thereby reduce unit costs. Often it appears that there is a race to grow large in order to reap benefits of scale. Any other economies of scale attached to the manufacturing process encourage this process. The nature of the technology may dictate a size of plant which is large. There may also be economies of scope, which arise from producing a range of related products or services. There may be significant synergies in such production which allow costs to be shared among the products.

The entry of any new player will change the competitive context of existing players in a way which has an important impact on the latter. Newcomers must take account of the impact of their own production and sales on existing markets, even if there is no response from the existing players. The bigger the desired output of the entrant, the greater the impact on existing players. The potential entrant is unlikely to ignore the impact of entry. Entry may be deterred simply by the expected impact on price and profit levels of the output of the new entrant, especially if it is large.

Powerful players already in the industry can also be expected to retaliate, making the life of new entrants difficult and unprofitable, through price wars or major marketing campaigns. Any player wishing to enter a new market must take account of the likely strategic response of existing players. Sometimes existing players may use bluff to suggest action they do not intend to take; sometimes the bluff is translated into action.

Existing players may also use their influence with government to create barriers. They may exploit existing rules to maximum effect in order to prevent entry, in fact they may already have influenced the nature of the rules. Previous success may reflect their ability to use such contacts effectively. Pharmaceutical companies are notorious for their ability to delay the end of patent protection, preventing the introduction of generic alternatives to existing drugs.

Existing players may also exploit control over important inputs, such as sources of vital raw materials through vertical integration or long-term contracts, over supply networks through a carefully crafted set of close relationships with the suppliers, or over skilled labour or managerial assets through attractive contracts. Existing players may have a particular expertise in working all the networks in order to keep out newcomers.

The barriers may also be in a market imperfection, for example the legal barrier of patents or restricted access to necessary inputs. The imperfection may be introduced by the government deliberately to keep out foreign competition. There are a multitude of interventions, such as quotas, often informal, tariffs, or quality controls of various kinds, reinforced by elaborate and time-consuming inspection.

One obvious barrier to entry at the global level is ignorance, notably of the nature of a market, or ignorance concerning the way in which economic activity is organized. The influence of cultural difference, where it exists and is significant, at the very least imposes a cost on entry into another market, the cost of learning about the nature of the different market and how to do business there.

Traditionally another important barrier at the international level has been distance, which has always imposed significant transportation and communication costs on the players. Such costs, while much lower than used to be the case, are still weighty, more significant than often assumed. How significant they are depends on the nature of the product, its bulk to value ratio or its perishability.

In the end the biggest barrier is the specificity of the resources held by an enterprise, particularly as those resources are translated into the core competencies which give that enterprise a competitive advantage. It is impossible to 'codify' such resources. They are often tacit, that is, their exact nature is unclear. It is impossible to explain from what source the relevant competitive advantage is derived. Often the resources or competencies cannot be easily or quickly imitated (this is discussed at length in Chapter 7).

Given the wide range of such barriers, there can be few industries without at least one or two significant barriers to entry. In a number of markets the barriers are very high. The height of such barriers changes over time, sometimes in a non-trivial manner.

There are also barriers to exit which may cause below-normal profit to be earned for longer than the short term. Enterprises making such a profit are unable to leave the industry. The nature and strength of the barriers to exit also determine how long below-normal profit may be earned. Contractual or regulatory arrangements may prevent immediate exit.

The existence of substitutes

The second factor is the existence of possible substitutes outside the industry concerned. As already noted the definition of industries is a matter of convention; strictly speaking the elasticity of substitution would define clusters of closely related products or services produced in a particular industry. There are also broader groupings of products which are substitutes. The industry might be considered as broad, such as energy in general, or it could be one of the various components of energy – oil, gas or electricity. Gas is clearly a substitute for electricity, just as train or bus travel is for car travel. Computer games can be played on PCs as well as consoles. Going to a film or a football match is an alternative form of entertainment to playing a video game. Drinking coffee at home is an alternative to drinking it at a coffee shop. Of course a thirsty person might go to a bar. Most products have a range of such substitutes, some close substitutes, others not so close.

The closeness of any other product in terms of its physical characteristics and attributes or its ability to satisfy the same need determines the extent to which prices tend to move together. Higher petrol prices push consumers onto public transport. An increase in cinema prices increases the use of videos at home. Clearly the existence of such substitutes restrains the level of profit which can be made, since potential customers move to a substitute if the price rises too high. Changing technology is continually providing new substitutes, making inappropriate the existing classification of an industry and changing the structure of prices of possible substitutes.

The bargaining strength of suppliers and customers

The bargaining strength of suppliers and customers determines the price paid and received by the enterprise. This is not solely a matter of the negotiating ability of the player. The level of competition between suppliers or purchasers may determine bargaining strength; usually the larger the number of suppliers or customers, the greater the competition and the lower the bargaining strength. The smaller the number of suppliers or customers and the larger they are, the more powerful is a particular player likely to be in any negotiation. A single supplier or customer is in a potentially very powerful position.

A powerful supplier can exert pressure to increase the price of necessary inputs. A powerful customer can drive down the price at which the end product is purchased. Either can also change the quality of the product in a desired direction, which is equivalent to a price change. If the supplier or customer has a diversified range of other products or services, it may be even more powerful in any negotiations over price or quality, since it is not dependent on a successful conclusion to negotiations on that one product.

The nature of the relationship with a partner is also critical. There may be asymmetrical investment and *asymmetrical information*. The existence of such asymmetry affects the mutual bargaining strength:

- An enterprise which has invested heavily in a particular relationship, whether in terms of staff or investment in facilities or organization, is at a disadvantage, particularly if there is a strong asymmetry in the relationship, the partner having made no such investment. Such an investment creates something akin to a hostage held by the partner.
- One of the negotiators may know much better the true position on the costs of production or sale. Again there may be significant switching costs for either partner.
- It may not be easy for one partner to switch to another partner, since it requires both time and the commitment of major resources to develop a new partnership. It may be much easier for the other.

It is a matter of strategy to limit such vulnerabilities, to avoid both dependence on one partner and any asymmetry of investment or information.

The intensity of competition

Within any sector the intensity of competition depends on a whole range of different factors, including those already discussed relating to the barriers to entry and the existence of possible substitutes. Such factors, and the previous history of the industry, largely determine the number of producers. The number and size of the players are critical. Globally the number of producers in different countries is a key factor, since they can move relatively easily into foreign markets. Even the level of diversification by existing producers is relevant since it determines how far they can go in meeting increased competition or how far they are dependent on the revenue from a single product.

Intense competition reflects the strategy adopted by different players in the industry. It can take a number of different forms, including vigorous marketing campaigns, aggressive pricing policies and the threat of intermittent takeover bids. The relative size of the various enterprises is a key issue. Another one is the homogeneity of the product. How far are competitors serving different market segments and therefore not really competing at all?

The existence of complementors

It is useful to add a sixth force, the existence and bargaining strength of complementors (Figure 6.2). Complementors assist particular players to compete better and make a higher profit. The greater the significance of complementarity in a particular industry and the greater the number of complementors linked to the enterprise, the greater the potential help given to that enterprise in competing effectively. Efficient complementarity is a major benefit. There is always a price at which such help is given, and the price may be too high. Complementors can compete for the extra profit, exerting their bargaining strength. The issues which arise concerning the bargaining strength of suppliers and customers are therefore relevant to the bargaining strength of complementors. This issue is fully explored in Chapter 13.

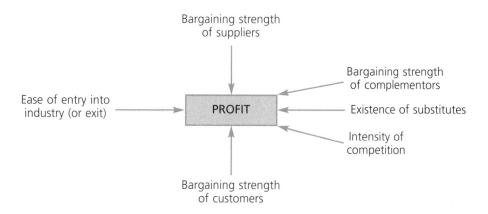

Figure 6.2 **The six forces**

Dynamic forces

Finally, the picture must be made dynamic, as in Figure 6.3, rather than static, as in Figure 6.2. Uncertainty about the future requires the addition of another dependent variable, risk. There is obviously a varying degree of uncertainty about possible outcomes. Both the level of anticipated profit and the degree of risk are influenced by factors which change over time, in particular:

1. the growth of market demand – clearly the higher the better
2. the capacity of innovation to increase or decrease profit, usually through price
3. the level of market instability.

• A growing market invites more competition. It makes entry easier since new customers are cheaper to win than those already linked with another producer, but

Figure 6.3 **Dynamizing the forces**

eases the intensity of competition since there is more room for the newcomers. A rapidly growing market allows profit to remain above the normal level longer than would usually be the case.

- Innovation can benefit those innovating and can create a new barrier to entry for those who cannot quickly imitate. It might make possible an increase in price for a differentiated product or service, or an increase in profit if costs are reduced. A rapid rate of innovation increases the level of risk for all players, since they all need to catch up.
- Market instability raises the risk level by causing profit rates to fluctuate in an unpredictable way.

These are relevant to the competitive situation in an industry and are discussed at greater length in Chapter 8.

Focus on Theory
Network economics

Network economics apply when the demand for a particular product or service increases with the size of the existing network of complementary products. For example, the value of, and therefore the demand for, a telephone or email connection increases with the size of the existing network of connected subscribers. There is a positive feedback loop, in that every new entrant increases that value for existing users. The same would apply to the incentive of an enterprise to supply information or commercial services on the Internet. The bigger the network, the greater the incentive, with two obvious results.

- Demand grows rapidly since it is cumulative.
- There is often a concentration on one producer, or a limited number of producers, in the supply of complementary products or services, since the standardization of systems imposes significant switching costs on those who have existing attachments. For example, Windows became the standard operating system for PCs and Intel the standard microprocessor, largely because IBM installed Windows in its PCs and software was written for those PCs which had both these systems installed and was specific to these systems.

Focus on Theory
cont'd

Through the positive feedback loop, a small initial lead can lead to a massive advantage even when superior systems or components become available. These are 'winner-takes-all' markets. As a result, Microsoft and Intel have acquired enormous bargaining power and earned large profits.

The strategic trick in this instance is to position the complementary product or service so that its installed base grows quickly as a result of positive feedback loop effects and significant switching costs prevent the substitution of an alternative.

The positive feedback loop in the computer industry is shown in Figure 6.4.

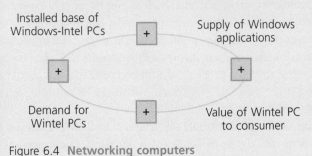

Figure 6.4 **Networking computers**

Risk and market structures

The forces of competition described above help to determine the market structure. Some markets are highly competitive and have a large number of players, such as coffee shops of the Starbucks type. Others may have a small number of players but still be intensely competitive, such as video game console production or airliner manufacturing. However, the intensity of the competition tends to change with the number of competitive players.

The four types of market structure

As shown in Chapter 2, there are four basic types of market structure: monopoly, monopolistic (imperfect) competition, oligopoly and perfect competition. The number of players varies according to the market structure.

In theory the level of profit in an industry is determined by the nature of the market structure. A monopolist is a price maker. The key feature of perfect competition is that any single enterprise cannot influence price, since it produces such a small part of output; in that sense it is a price taker. The more players there are, the smaller the influence of any one player on the level of price, since its output is likely to account for only a small proportion of the total output in the industry. The more competitive the market, the lower tends to be the rate of profit. Under perfect competition, only normal profit can be achieved.

In practice, there is no such thing as a pure monopoly or perfect competition, and therefore no such thing as a pure price maker or price taker. These are ideal types, theoretically definable but impossible to find in the real world. A pure monopoly would assume that there is no possible substitute for a product and that the demand curve demand is always inelastic. This would mean that the supplier could take all the income from customers by simply raising the price. This might be possible for water in the middle of a desert but for nothing else. In practice there are always substitutes, however remote. There are always stretches of the demand curve where demand is elastic; consequently, a rise in price begins to reduce demand more than proportionate to the increase in price. In a rational world, price would not be raised above this point on the curve.

On the other hand, the conditions of perfect competition are so demanding that they cannot exist, for example the assumptions include a fully homogeneous product, no economies of scale, perfect knowledge on the part of both producer and consumer, no barriers to entry into the industry, independent tastes (no aspirational products), no transport or communication costs and so on. The implications of these assumptions are dramatic and not always fully understood. Perfect competition would greatly simplify the strategic problem of an enterprise, since it would remove any space for varying the strategic approach. Strategy is simply imposed by the forces of competition.

Under perfect competition all producers also have access to and use the same technology and the same factors of production. Consumers all perceive the product in the same way and derive a pleasure from consumption which is unaffected by the consumption of others. There are no advantages in either being the first mover or the largest producer. There is a known optimum size of plant, well below the overall size of the market, the level of output of which becomes the norm since competition will force all enterprises to this point. These features bear no relationship to the real world.

The iron law of oligopoly

The real world typically consists of monopolistic or oligopolistic markets. Monopolistic markets can be competitive but the market is in practice a series of niche markets, or separate market segments, separated by the differentiation of the product. Some products lend themselves to such differentiation – cosmetics or toiletries for example. The degree of differentiation determines the degree to which the price can be raised above a notional competitive price. Profit margins are raised by successful differentiation, often well above what they would be with a homogeneous product.

Because of significant factors on the cost side, such as economies of scale or scope and learning effects which drive enterprise to become large, there is a tendency for all markets eventually to become oligopolistic. It is easy to observe this but not so easy to give a definitive explanation of why it happens. It is not just because of economies of scale but also because the big and powerful have an enormous advantage, if not in competing as such, but rather in controlling competition or competitors.

Figure 6.5 shows a temporary starting point which eventually becomes one of three outcomes. Perfect competition is very unusual. Strategists prefer to attain the third option and usually achieve this, if only when a market or industry has matured. There are many markets of the second kind, which is a temporary resting point in some industries but the normal final outcome in others. Where an industry finishes depends on the nature of the industry, its history and the current strategies being pursued.

Governments seek to slow, and even to reverse, any process of consolidation which

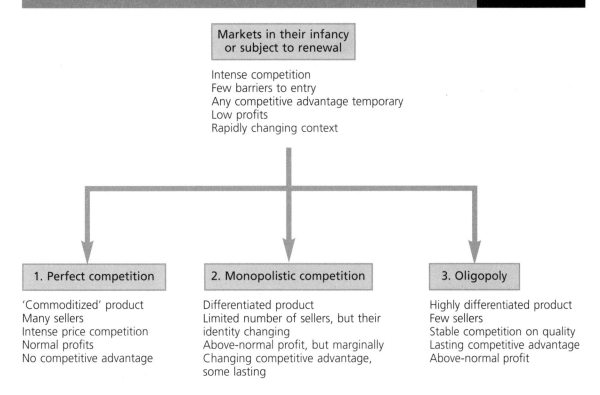

Figure 6.5 **The evolution of markets**

results in the third outcome. They have a particular interest in certain sectors, where the tendency is so strong that it results in something close to monopoly. They try to curb the process of consolidation through anti-monopoly legislation. Today this is more often called *competition policy*. There may be restrictions on foreign investment which prevent the takeover of domestic companies. Major international acquisitions may require government approval.

In the extreme case the large enterprise can absorb the quick-moving small ones and often does. This is a way of compensating for the tendency of the large to find it difficult to generate and put into practice their own innovations. Most industries which begin as competitive ones at some stage enter a period of ferment during which acquisitions and mergers abound. The large enterprises have enormous political clout, an ability to influence or pressure other players and keep key stake-holder groups happy. They can even influence governments. The large have an incentive to manage the rate of change within an industry in order to prevent the undermining of the value of their existing assets, even inadvertently by them-selves. This may mean acquiring control over relevant technical knowledge and sitting on it for a period of time. Managing the nature of the market is part of man-aging change and therefore also a valid part of strategy. Large enterprises have a much better capacity to ride the bad times, whereas smaller enterprises do well in the good times.

Indeterminateness of outcomes

Strategy in Action   Banking in Europe, Germany and market structure

In recent years the banking industry has seen more change than most other sectors of the economy. The information/communications revolution has had a dramatic impact on the finance sector. By improving access to information, the revolution made all the various markets for financial services potentially more efficient. The efficient operation of a market depends partly on the speed at which information is communicated. Financial markets are closest to the perfect market beloved by the economist.

The term 'the democratization of finance' summarizes well aspects of a revolution opening financial transactions to most people in developed economies. The generalization to a majority of the population of share ownership and trading, the management by financial institutions of investment portfolios, and the extension of loans by a wide range of international institutions – these are elements of the revolution. Most visible has been online financial activity of various kinds, including retail banking and the broking of shares and bonds. Even efficient markets suffer from two problems, those of volatility and malpractice.

Every market is based on confidence, the level of which can change rapidly. Attitudes are subject to cumulative change. As market participants rush to join in, rising asset values can create bubbles which accentuate and prolong an expansion. The greater the rise, the further the subsequent fall. Success reinforces the overshooting, in both directions. During the 1990s the finance sector was part of a protracted boom in the new economy, which overshot badly. Acquisitions and initial public offers generated enormous investment banking business for institutions. The Deutsche Bank built its strategy around this feature of the boom. Often volatility and corruption go together. Expansion removes the usual restraints on behaviour; prudential checks are not properly made and margin borrowing re-emerges. The risk appetite sharpens. Conflicts of interest proliferate. All upturns are accompanied by some corruption.

In 1989 the reunification of Germany highlighted problems which now confront that economy. Since that date the rate of economic growth in Germany has averaged barely 1% per annum. Unemployment has rarely dipped below 10%. Reunification of Germany proved a much bigger problem than expected. At the parity exchange rate adopted on reunification, most of the industry of East Germany was bankrupted and unemployment spiralled. Massive transfer payments to the East have kept public spending at more than half of gross national product. Labour costs in the West are high and employment regimes overly rigid, both tending to undermine German competitiveness.

Germany has led the way in integrating Europe, willingly giving up its strong currency, the mark, in favour of the euro, and subordinating the conservative Bundesbank to a European Central Bank. It is willing to accept a modelling of Europe on its own federal structure. The expansion of the EU eastwards, by the Treaty of Nice (2001), to a tier of eight new countries in Eastern Europe becoming members of the EU in 2004, will shift the centre of economic gravity of the EU towards Germany, providing Germany with great opportunities to restore its trading and investment pre-eminence in Central and Eastern Europe.

Germany's model of economic development in which the investment bank had an important role has developed its own difficulties. Like Japan, Germany has to shake off the political legacy of the successful recovery model of the 1950s and 60s. This is another example of success breeding failure, of circumstances changing but the strategy remaining the same.

The European banking industry is still fragmented, with the five largest banks accounting for a tiny 16% of the overall market. There are as many as 15,000 separate institutions within the European industry and in Germany more than 2,500 banks distributing banking products. Since 1996, within national economies there has been a considerable quickening in the pace of consolidation, with as many as 60 mergers and acquisitions, each worth more than US$1 billion. In Germany this process is constrained by the existence of savings banks owned and operated by regional governments, not

▶

currently on offer for privatization. There is little room for further domestic consolidation.

With the integration of the EU, the time is ripe for international consolidation. It is impossible for governments to prevent consolidation. There are many less barriers as a consequence of differing currencies and practices. Both the drive for profits and the scope for economies of scale encourage this process. The potential synergies from domestic mergers are typically much larger than those from international mergers. However, once one merger occurs, it significantly encourages others. The harmonization of government regulations, notably on the Basel standards, assists concentration, as does the perfection of the automated clearing house.

Currently many European banks conduct almost every kind of banking business; they are universal banks. There are four alternative models for the

banks of the new era:

1. *Regional retail distributors*
Banks offering the ordinary commercial banking services required by the typical retail customers, but offering them in a concentrated way in limited regions.

2. *Pan-European product specialists*
Banks specializing in the provision of particular services, such as insurance, leasing, asset management or the provision of consumer credit.

3. *European and global wholesale banks*
Banks which assist in the finance of investment in production facilities at the European level and beyond.

4. *Pan-European service providers*
Banks which help to provide the necessary infrastructure for payments, settlement or exchange to Europe as a whole.

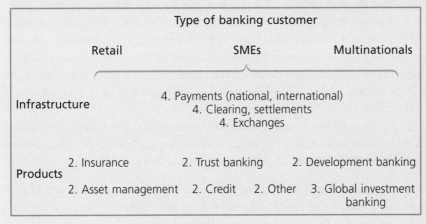

Figure 6.6 **The banking value chain**

Figure 6.6 shows the range of activities in a simplified banking value chain.

Technological change and the expansion of the EU encourage competition, but the degree of competition differs from banking service to banking service. German banks have to use the new technology to compete at a higher level.

According to economic theory there are clear economic rules which determine the level of key variables such as price or productive capacity. The attractiveness of monopoly or perfect competition for economists is that in theory there is a clear equilibrium output and equilibrium price in any industry, which, given the availability of the appropriate information relating to the levels of demand or costs, could be easily determined. In these circumstances there would be little difficulty in selecting a strategy on the desirable level of output or price.

Path dependency

In practice this is never the case. Indeterminateness of such levels and therefore of strategies is a feature of all the market structures between monopoly and perfect competition, the structures which occur in the real world. The existing levels of both price and profit are themselves the result of past strategies and their evolution; both are determined by the particular histories of individual enterprises and the industry as a whole. The structure of an industry reflects its previous strategic history. In an indeterminate world the unique historical experience determines where the industry is at today. This is called *path dependency* or *hysteresis*. Even minor differences in the early strategy of a player can have far-reaching effects in influencing later outcomes. At any given time there are many such paths which could be taken, but the nature of the strategy adopted at any given time closes off some future outcomes and opens others. Such indeterminateness means that it is not possible to know the future level of output or price which will prevail at any given time without knowing the strategies of the main players and how they are likely to evolve. This indeterminateness also means that it is impossible to know the performance outcome for any single enterprise.

Indeterminateness is compounded by the universality of change. There is no such thing as equilibrium in a world in which a market is always moving towards equilibrium but never quite arriving, because conditions have changed, defining a new equilibrium before the old one is attained. So many things are changing, such as elements of technology or taste, the number of competitors, the reputation of individual players and even government policy.

Each enterprise has to devise its own strategy to take account of this indeterminateness. Price strategy is part of a much wider strategy relating to entry into a market and positioning in that market. The many possible sequences of initial action, response and counteraction, which are inherent parts of strategy making, increase the degree of indeterminateness. A strategy must be formulated in the knowledge that it will induce a response from others, which it is not possible to know exactly. This creates what might be described as 'strategic risk', a concept developed later in the chapter.

In principle it is not difficult to articulate the main features of any strategic situation, even to explore the various ways in which a situation might develop. This is done in much greater depth in Chapter 13, where it is analysed in the context of game theory.

The importance of infancy

There are moments in the life cycle of a product which are more important than others. In particular the strategies adopted during the infancy of the industry are a critical determinant of the later structure of that industry:

- A move by an early player(s) to exploit short-term monopoly advantage arising from the development of a new product, for example, by raising the price to the highest possible level, a move which invites new entrants. There may be many new entrants and the resulting price competition may eventually ensure a relatively low price.
- A decision to keep price down during this key period may discourage such new entrants. In the longer term this may paradoxically result in fewer players and higher prices.

The pattern of action and response determines the specific structure of the industry. This depends on the various strategies adopted which, in their turn, partly reflect the culture of the enterprise and the personality of the key players. There are always alternative possibilities. In that sense the typical situation is indeterminate.

Country risk

The existence of a global market for any product or service is constrained in a number of significant ways by the existence of national boundaries. There are no parts of the world beyond the reach of sovereign governments and no body of international law and legal institutions which can supercede national jurisdictions, except in a minor way as with the development of regional law in the EU. This means that governments are important players, not so much as suppliers of products and services, more as the lawmakers, if only to set the structure of rules by which the market operates and the competitive and cooperative game is played. The problem of country risk is illustrated neatly by the case of Indonesia.

Strategy in Action Business crisis, country risk and the case of Indonesia

In Indonesia in 1998, partly as a consequence of the economic pressure of the Asian economic crisis of 1997, there was an abrupt transition from what was perceived by many as a 'benign' authoritarian regime under Suharto to a democracy. It was a regime in which the army played a much less benign role. The transition ended a period of relative political stability and rapid economic growth. The economic crisis was accompanied by a political and social crisis, which prevented a proper recovery from the economic crisis of 1997 and added its own ingredients.

The continued existence of the new democratic system has been somewhat precarious, with rapid changes of leadership, from Habibie to Wahid and Wahid to Sukarnoputri. Any democratic leader was faced with the need to meld together disparate interests groups and control the army and police whose role in a democratic system was much reduced and changed from what it had been before.

The events which provided the context for the downfall of the Suharto regime created a deep unease in the Chinese community which has traditionally dominated Indonesia's business life. As often before in periods of unrest and street violence, the wealthy minority of Chinese who run the business life were under immediate threat of murder, rape and destruction of their property. This led to a movement of many of this community abroad.

Another task of the new regime was to rid the economic system of endemic corruption and cronyism which had surrounded the president. Indonesia is a graphic expression of crony capitalism in action. It is by no means clear that cronyism has ceased, since companies under government control seem destined to return to many of the same people who controlled them under Suharto. There is evidence that the judiciary were open to bribery to act in the interests of particular business interests, and sometimes against the interests of foreign companies.

The transition to a democratic system was accompanied by a series of frictions within what is a multiethnic empire, the attainment of independence by East Timor representing only the most dramatic of these. Unrest generated by independence movements in Irian Jaya and Aceh in northern Sumatra, and intercommunal violence between Muslims and Christians in the Moluccas, have further destabilized the political system. Such events have changed the level of political risk, not just in the areas concerned but also at the centre, thereby massively increasing the level of country risk.

Because of unease with various aspects of country risk in 2001 and 2002, there has been a net outflow of foreign direct investment (FDI). FDI approved in 1997 totalled a very respectable US$34 billion, but this had fallen to US$9 billion by 2001. Typical of the decline is the decision of Sony to close its audio equipment factory in western Java, with 1,000 jobs lost. The facility has moved to Malaysia. The explanations offered to explain this include labour troubles, high taxes and rampant smuggling, with perhaps as many as half the electronic goods sold in Indonesia smuggled in to avoid the 50% tax rate. Japanese investment has fallen to an insignificant amount, about 7% of the 1997 level.

The situation has worsened markedly with the terrorist attack of October 12, 2002 in Bali. The Balinese economy, dependent on tourism, has been devastated by the attack. Although Bali is a small part of the Indonesian economy, the ripple effects from the Bali attack are affecting all the country.

Recent bombings in Indonesia:

August 1, 2000: 2 killed in bombing of the Philippines ambassador's residence

September 13, 2000: Car bomb explodes at Jakarta Stock Exchange, killing 10

December 24, 2000: 30 bombs explode in churches across the country, killing 19

August 1, 2001: Bomb explodes at Atrium shopping centre in Jakarta, injuring 6

September 23, 2002: Grenade explodes outside the home of US aid worker in Jakarta

October 12, 2002: Huge car bomb explodes outside Sari nightclub in Bali, killing at least 192 people. Another bomb explodes outside the US consulate in Bali

December 5, 2002: 3 killed by bomb at a McDonald's restaurant and a Toyota showroom in Makassar, Sulawesi

August 5, 2003: 12 killed in the bombing of the Marriott Hotel

The Bali attack and its repercussions have heightened the frictions both within and outside Indonesia. There are obvious tensions between the Indonesian government and its moderate Muslim supporters and the fundamentalist groups which favour terrorist acts in support of a greater Muslim state stretching across southern Thailand, Malaysia, Singapore, southern Philippines, Brunei and Indonesia. Outside governments have perceived the Indonesian government to be weak in dealing with extremists. Internally many resent what they see as intervention in their own affairs by Western countries, notably Australia. The cultural divisions are exacerbated by the danger of further terrorist attacks. Travel directives by Western governments not to go to Indonesia makes the conduct of business by foreign companies even more difficult. Temporarily a potentially large economy appears to be out of bounds for foreign businesspeople. Only the very bold are prepared to venture in at this time.

The level of country risk in Indonesia has become, at least temporarily, prohibitively high. The danger of the collapse of the present government is seen as a real threat. At best it is seen as maintaining law and order internally with difficulty and having trouble in creating the predictable environment required by business in order to operate effectively. This is a situation which can change very quickly.

Risk at the supranational level is different from risk at the domestic level. There are the obvious and severe limitations on the globalization of markets which result from a home country bias, which is not simply a matter of additional cost. To some degree the bias reflects ignorance. It is impossible to know about all the products available or all the factors which influence the viability of production in a foreign country. It reflects systematic and significant asymmetries of information, since it is impossible to know as much about other countries as about your own. It results from cultural differences, the different ways of perceiving products or services or the different ways of organizing business operations. For example, for many products it is difficult to use the same advertising campaign in different countries. Even negotiation for international transactions is made more difficult by such cultural differences. This problem has already been considered in the last chapter in discussing the need to read carefully the cultural segment of the general environment.

The bias is also induced by country risk, the reluctance of enterprises to enter particular markets because of the risks of revenues or costs varying in a way which threatens the profitability of their ventures, but varying as a result of the existence of national boundaries. The factors which explain home country bias are components of country risk.

Country risk arises from two main sources, so-called political risk and transfer or economic risk, defined below. The former follows from the policies of governments, or rather from the danger that such policies may change in an unexpected way. For that reason, governments are key strategic players, intruding directly into the competitive or industrial environments of the enterprises.

Political risk

Governments may at any time, but most often during a crisis, introduce a whole swathe of policies which encourage exports or the inflow of FDI, or discourage imports or the outflow of FDI. Attitudes to trade tend to be neomercantilist, even today. Attitudes to investment vary enormously across countries and across time. More to the point these policies may change, because the government has a change of heart or the government itself changes, democratically by election or more dramatically by coup d'état, or even because the government is under threat during a crisis. Political risk is ever-present for enterprises operating outside the jurisdiction of the government of their country of origin. The context within which they operate may change significantly and unexpectedly. The ability of the home country government to defend them varies.

Transfer risk

Transfer risk follows from the fluctuations in the relative value of different currencies. Currencies usually move within national boundaries unless the currency is a reserve currency – few can play that role. In a world of floating exchange rates, the relative value of these currencies fluctuates all the time. It is a simple matter of supply and demand, both of which change from day to day. For that reason there is often a *dirty float* in which the government authority intervenes in the market to even out short-term fluctuations.

In such a world any revenue received in a foreign currency or any cost incurred in such a currency can rapidly change its value in the home currency. This is a kind of risk which is much more easily dealt with than political risk, increasingly by all sorts of hedging or risk management techniques. However, hedging is a short-term phenomenon. In the longer term the movement of exchange rates and relative prices reflects the performance of a particular economy, and once again this is related to the policies of the government. In this context, it is perhaps better to refer to this kind of risk as *economic risk* since it reflects the broader performance of the economy. It is better, for all sorts of reasons, not to have invested in a country whose economy is performing badly. The poor economic performance may become a source of political risk, if the performance is bad enough.

Strategic risk

Strategic risk can be defined as the risk which arises as a result of the impossibility of knowing what strategy other players will adopt in any given situation. Such risk is inherent in any competitive market in which there are a limited number of players. Risk is inherent in situations in which, even if you have perfect knowledge of the whole range of possible strategies of players and the possible outcomes – which you do not, you cannot know with certainty which of these strategies will be adopted by any one player.

The situation is even more risky. It is impossible to know all the possible strategies of other players or the possible outcomes. Risk is closely connected with uncertainty, which in it turn reflects a lack of information, particularly, but not only, concerning the future behaviour of other players. In many cases, whatever the investment of time and effort, the ignorance cannot be fully dissipated.

Opportunism

Since no strategy is written on tablets of stone, there can never be certainty of others' intentions, which may change. There is always a significant degree of uncertainty concerning the possibility of opportunistic behaviour by another player, represented by a sudden shift of strategy. A strategy can be dropped or modified and often in a very short period of time. Reading the situation correctly now does not guarantee that it is read right in the future.

If there is a major return to be made, opportunistic behaviour can be very tempting. This is an option available even to governments, which can change their policies to exploit foreign players. It is much more open to competitors to pursue similar opportunistic behaviour. The threat of such opportunistic behaviour guarantees the existence of some strategic risk.

Strategic issues arising from strategic risk

There are three issues:

1. What strategy to adopt, given the likely strategy of a competitor, assuming that strategy is well known
2. What action to take in order to ensure that the strategy is well known, if it is not
3. What chance there is that the other player will change strategy to exploit a developing situation.

The strategy of the competitor is often unknown, so all three elements are significant.

The situation of Deutsche Bank neatly illustrates the nature of strategic risk in an industry dominated by a few large players.

Strategy in Action The Deutsche Bank and investment banking

In Germany there has been a tradition of investment or wholesale banking, once more accurately referred to as 'development banking'. This means holding for a significant period a sizeable share ownership, helping to see companies through the start-up period and any bad times. It involved having representatives on the board of directors of the company, joint directors who made a significant and positive entrepreneurial input.

As the investment bank model changed, the advisory and underwriting functions rose in importance, which proved immensely profitable, particularly when the stock market was booming. On the basis of this strategy and economic recovery, the German banks became masters of European banking. Led by the Deutsche Bank the banks tried to extend the model abroad. They attempted to carve out global empires.

The high spot of the old strategy came in March 2000 when Deutsche Bank, the largest, announced that it would merge with the Dresdner Bank, the third largest, with the goal of creating a European investment and asset management institution which was large enough to be competitive with the 'bulge-bracket' of Wall Street – Citigroup, Goldman Sachs and Merrill Lynch. Neither investment bank had the weight to compete on its own, but such a fusion would create a global investment bank.

Because profit margins on the wholesale business were much higher than on the retail business, the former was regarded as a better strategic focus for banking activity. The acquisition of Bankers Trust and the old Morgan Grenfell showed Deutsche's ambitions. The aim was to integrate Dresdner's

▶

investment arm Kleinwort Benson with the investment arm of Deutsche.

An important part of the strategy was the absorption of all the retail operations into Deutsche's retail banking division, Bank 24, and the spin-off of that division as an independent entity in which the merged bank would have less than a 10% ownership stake. The existing retail branch networks were fragmented and unprofitable, needing rationalization. The Dresdner deal was intended to yield at least €3 billion from savings made in fusing the two retail networks. The new bank would shed its retailing operations and act as a global wholesale bank. Out of the two large universal banks would emerge two institutions specialized in retail and wholesale banking.

The merger failed because of the inability to win the support of their own specialist staffs for the merger. By April 5 2000 the merger was dead. Within six months Deutsche's strategy had completely changed. Previously the investment bank tail wagged the whole. The high-tech crash and the recession of the early 2000s provided a good reason for rethinking such a strategy. Investment banking looked a different proposition.

Bank 24 became the heart of a new strategy, in which Deutsche built a pan-European retail channel. It decided to reintegrate under one management all the services offered, including the retail operations, and rebrand Deutsche Bank 24, and other divisions, as a unified Deutsche Bank. Deutsche has identified a rich market segment of some 60 million well-educated and prosperous 30–40-year-olds within the EU, who are switching their money from deposit accounts to equities and investment funds as part of a savings management strategy and in preparation for retirement. Retail banking would link these savers with the wholesale banking business. Such affluent private clients and prominent business clients would provide a profitable core business, in Germany and in both the southern part of the EU and Germany's neighbours, where Deutsche has most of its foreign branches. Access to such savers would be helped by the introduction of the euro.

The aim is to offer the full range of banking services, through a single bank account and through branch offices, the telephone and particularly the Internet. Despite the high level of expenditure required, after initially trying to find a partner for its retail oper-

ations, the bank has opted to go it alone. Deutsche intends to close more than one-third of its 1,240 outlets in Germany. To offset these closures, Deutsche will set up 300 self-service banking terminals and 120 mobile consulting units. Most of the branches outside Germany will be retained.

Less than ten years ago, in terms of market capitalization, the Frankfurt-based Deutsche bank was, outside Japan, the biggest bank in the world. Given the setbacks received by the Japanese banks during the 1990s it might expect to be the leader now, but it is not even in the top 20. The value of its assets is still second only to Citigroup, but they have been poorly managed. For a period, it was a bank vulnerable to acquisition, rather than one looking for acquisitions. Citigroup showed interest in buying Deutsche.

All the German banks are confronted by sky-high costs and mounting bad debt – the consequences of reckless lending practices and ill-conceived forays outside core areas. In European banks costs are typically 60% of income, but as high as 80% in Germany, with scarcely any profit being made.

There are a number of reasons for the banking malaise:

- The bank receives unfair competition from the state-controlled banks, which offer guarantees on deposits and have close links to municipal and state governments. This special status is to be phased out by 2005.

- The recession has affected badly the German economy, with a rising tide of bankruptcies and consequent bad debts.

- Germany is being opened up to competition from outside banks.

- Deutsche Bank has an exposure to the collapses in the USA. Its aim in accepting such exposure was to win more lucrative advisory and underwriting business.

The year 2002 was a critical year. Deutsche announced a buy-back of 10% of the bank by September 2003. The aim of the buy-back is to improve investor returns and boost the market value of its shares, thereby avoiding becoming prey to a takeover. The buy-back will be funded by the sale of holdings in the bank's large industrial portfolio and a cost-cutting campaign, including job cuts of 10% of the workforce.

The principal players here are competitors and governments. Earlier sections of this chapter dealt with the industrial or competitive context in which the forces of competition determine the number of players and produce an indeterminateness of market outcomes. It went on to deal with the general context in which governments operate, as they create and maintain their policies, and the associated notion of country risk.

There are therefore two main components of strategic risk, competition risk and country risk.

1. Competition risk is determined by the forces of competition in any industry and the resulting structure of the market. Tracing the appropriate sequences of initial action, response and further reaction is difficult and unlikely to yield a certain outcome. In a typical oligopolistic market, this kind of risk becomes significant.

2. Country risk reflects the role of government policy. There are many countries where there is no consistent history of policy in the key areas which impinge on business activity. Policy changes with fashion, the membership of governments and the pressures exerted on governments by various interest groups. The rules of the game change. Winner-takes-all politics in which there is often a complete reversal of policy is a sure prescription for policy instability. Such a situation is not uncommon.

Managing such risk often involves getting to know the other players and their likely strategies, and establishing with them cooperation of some kind. This cooperation may be conscious and deliberate, or it may be tacit. The desire to manage risk is often the main motivation for such cooperation. The problems involved in converting competition into cooperation are discussed in Chapter 13. On the other hand, players may make a decision to compete head-on. For any individual player this may be a chosen path of behaviour or it may be imposed by the behaviour of other players who are unwilling to agree to cooperation.

Case Study   Video game wars

The nature of the industry and the driving forces

The main driving forces in the industry are:

Technical change
There is enormous potential for the kind of technical change which will revolutionize the industry. Video games are part of a much broader revolution (see the case study on Sony in Chapter 18). In the near future consoles may disappear, and be replaced as a delivery platform by the PC or mobile phone. There is a continuing convergence of all digital devices including games platforms. The PC-based hardware segment of the market is ripe for growth. Future opportunities are linked to the development of the information superhighway, or in the words more common today, broadband. There is strong interest in interactive multimedia forms of entertainment. Does this mean that independent games developers will in the future link themselves with the PC side of the industry? The nature of the present generation of consoles, which are inclining towards convergence, does suggest that this might be the case.

• Digitalization and convergence
• Improvement in the quality of graphics and sound

Increasing demand and the changing nature of the market
The industry is like the airline industry, in that there are countries where the market is mature and growth slowing, countries in a rapid expansion phase and countries where nothing significant has yet happened. The overall rate of growth of the industry worldwide reflects the relative importance of these different groups. At present the main markets are in the triad.

- Geographical extension of the market
- Demographic extension

The nature and number of the main players
Any of the large information-entertainment (infotainment) conglomerates are possible players.

- The creativity of games makers.

The main features of the industry relevant to competition are:

- This is an industry in which it is possible to adopt a cost leadership strategy, each player, or at least some, seeking to undercut rivals by offering a lower price. It is possible for the seller of a console to make a loss on console sales provided this is offset by a profit on the sale of games. This is not an unusual strategy. The producers of consoles incur increasingly large R&D costs which they must eventually recoup. If the console acts as a loss leader, the period of recoupment may be quite long.
- It is possible to use a product differentiation strategy, based on use of the most updated technology, so that the quality of the picture and the graphics is of potential concern to consumers. With video games the quality of the game is the key success factor (KSF). The strength of a console is judged in terms of the games which can be played on that console. It is impossible to predict with precision the taste of consumers for games, which tends to change in unexpected and abrupt ways.
- The industry requires significant cooperation. For example, like IKEA, Nintendo is a strategic centre firm, at the centre of an alliance network. The other console providers are in a similar situation. The network is made up of independent games creators as well as component producers. These networks are bound together by commercial links but also by bonds of loyalty and respect for the quality of partners' work.
- Those who create the games have high skill levels in graphics, and are creative people who need the kind of treatment given to successful entertainers. The game developers pay a charge for the production of a game disk and then a royalty for each sold. There is intense competition to secure the most able game developers as partners.
- At present video games have a well-defined market consisting of young males below the age of 30, usually in their preteens and teens. It is interesting to ask what will happen as this group grows older. Will they turn to different games or give up game playing? As a new generation emerges, computer-literate and familiar with game playing, will the market change its nature?
- One of the key issues raised in the making of games is the level of violence or sexual activity depicted which is regarded as acceptable. Clearly these features are seen as helpful in selling the games. What standards should the industry adopt or should it be left to self-regulation? Should the standards be imposed by government? How effective will any regulation be in the future when access to games is by broadband Internet? This is a particularly sensitive issue, as the main consumers of games are young and assumed to be impressionable.

The contending hardware

There has been a dramatic improvement in the nature of the hardware in the video game industry. In the late 1980s and early 1990s, the consoles of video machines were 8-bit or 16-bit. By 2003 the consoles were 128-bit, which massively increased what a game can do. Complex 3-D graphics are now possible. In the 1990s a game title took several months and several hundred thousand dollars to develop; in the 2000s it takes two years and usually between $2 million and $5 million, but anything up to $10 million. This is a far greater commitment and obstructs the ease of entry into the industry.

There is a console cycle of about six years (Table 6.1) which seems to be independent of the business cycle, since console sales seem to be unaffected by the latter, although by contrast games sales are. During these cycles, the software cycle is usually two years behind the hardware cycle.

Table 6.1 **The console cycle**

Technology and products	Period	Peak
Atari cycle	1980–85	1982–83
8-bit (NES, Master System)	1983–96	1989–90
16-bit (Megadrive/Genesis SNES, 3DO)	1990–94	1992–93
32/64-bit (PlayStation 1, N64 Saturn)	1994–2006(?)	1997–98
128-bit (PlayStation 2, XBOX GAMECUBE, Dreamcast)	1999–2007(?)	2002–04

At the moment there is a bitter competition between the providers of new hardware. There are three main competitors, shown in Table 6.2.

PlayStation 2 was the first of the new generation of consoles to be introduced, in Japan as early as March 2000 and in Europe, America and Australia in the autumn of that year, with immediate and dramatic success. PlayStation 2 led the way in that it was viewed by Sony officials 'as a sort of Trojan horse that will enter the house as a videogame player and then become a secret weapon to access the Internet, play movies and download music, rivalling the PC as the hub of entertainment in the home' (Guth, 2000).

Where Sony led Microsoft followed, with full embellishments and power. The XBOX is basically a PC, built around a Pentium 111 processor and an 8GB hard drive. The hard drive allows XBOX to do much more than is normal in a console and to improve games performance. For example, it allows the copying of an entire music disk and its play as background to a game. It allows the XBOX to avoid the annoying frozen delays that afflict most game machines as they swap CD data in and out of memory, with the hard disk acting as a high-speed buffer. GAMECUBE is much less technically ambitious.

In 2001 Sega was forced to withdraw its Dreamcast console because sales lagged so far behind those of its competitors that developers of games began to desert the company. This is the danger for any competitor which fails to maintain its sales.

Because by the end of 2001 only 1.5 million units of XBOX and GAMECUBE had been made available for sale, demand tended to exceed supply. By the end of the same period, 8 million units of PlayStation 2 had already been shipped. Sony had managed to gain a lead on the others by bringing out PlayStation 2 ahead of its competitors. The competition to get the console onto retail shelves was intense. In its timing PlayStation 2 had established a clear advantage. In 2003, PlayStation 2 dominated what is a US$2 billion console games market. However, as soon as XBOX and GAMECUBE began to appear in significant numbers on retail shelves, an intense price competition exploded.

Sony pre-empted the entry of Microsoft into the market by cutting the price of PlayStation three times after the

Table 6.2 **Characteristics of the competing consoles (in 2002)**

Main competitors	Microsoft: The XBOX	Nintendo: The GAMECUBE	Sony: PlayStation 2
Price (in A$)	Initially $699 reduced to $399	$329	$499.99
Specifications:			
1. Processor	32-bit custom Intel Pentium CPU 733MHz 23MHz graphics chip	64-bit custom IBM Power PC 'Gekko' CPU 485MHz 162MHz graphics chip	128-bit emotion Engine CPU 294MHz
2. Memory	64 MB	40MB	32MB
3. Extras	DVD player, also plays audio CDs (optional remote control $50) An MP3 player An Internet terminal Dolby Digital 5.1 surround sound Ethernet point	Peripherals needed	DVD player, also plays PS2 CD, PS1 CD, audio CDs
4. Size	310 270 100mm 3.8kg	301 178 78mm. 2.1kg	150 161 110mm. 1.2kg
Advantages	Computer powerhouse (as much power as a PC) – less time loading games – designer platform for more intense graphics – good audio – suited to online gaming	Cheaper than rivals Has legendary game developer, Shigeru Miyamoto (the Walt Disney of video games) Pokemon Relatively compact	Builds on success of PS1 (34 million sold) More than 144 games titles (1,000 plus forward compatible from PS1)
Disadvantages	Only 12 games Relatively bulky	Only 20 games but 50 by end of year	Only two controller points (compared with four for the others) Least power

release of the XBOX. Microsoft has had to respond by cutting the price of the XBOX which now, according to some authorities, is selling as much as US$375 below cost. It is estimated that Microsoft will lose as much as US$2 billion before XBOX starts to break even as late as 2005. XBOX appears unlikely to reach its target sales figures, especially in Europe and Japan. Although Microsoft has a deep purse, this could turn out to be a very expensive foray into a new industry. Competition showed itself in an advertising and price war.

It is likely that there is room for only two hardware producers. Sega gave up when it become number three. Microsoft's entry has again created a situation in which there is one more player than can be accommodated within the market.

Software

For the moment software must take centre stage since the consoles on the market are only as good as the games which can be used on them. The creative side of the industry, the software producers, whether they are the console producers themselves or independent games makers, is in the process of producing an unusually large collection of new games. According to the companies involved, new games for the leading consoles were expected to number between 350 and 400 in 2002 alone. These games included both those produced in-house and those produced by outside developers. The number represented a record output and indicated the growing intensity of competition.

Traditionally the games companies have been disorganized and fragmented. However, there is some tendency for the sector to consolidate. The largest publishers, such as Electronic Arts and Activision, now have revenues of about one billion dollars. They are the darlings of the stock market. There is a tendency to diversify beyond one game and even beyond one console.

In many respects the games are more important than the consoles. For example, the dollar value of games sales exceeds that of console sales. The sale of a console is a preliminary to the sale of various games. About US$10 is passed from the games publisher to the console maker for each game sold, at an average price of US$50. Both sales of consoles and games are rising rapidly. One forecast was that games sales would rise by 18% in 2002 and console sales by 16%.

In this area the console contenders have different strengths and weaknesses. Microsoft has as many as 900 software writers employed to develop games for the XBOX. It lacks well-known legacy titles on which to build. It is starting from scratch. Sony has most of the current bestsellers, including the number one, Grand Theft Auto 3, but these have been produced by outside developers, who could move elsewhere, if either Sony falters or others provide the right inducement. Nintendo has a very strong pool of legacies, such as Mario, the acrobatic Italian plumber. However, it developed these to suit a young market which has aged and demands different kinds of games, largely those which include a great deal of action.

The strategies adopted to win this battle are threefold:

1. Develop new games
2. Win away either games or their creative developers from rivals. This is likely to be particularly important for newcomers to the industry like Microsoft
3. Spend a lot of money in promoting existing and particularly new games.

Producing a new game today is rather like producing a Hollywood spectacular. The total cost has ballooned well beyond the level of ten years ago. The new Tomb Raider, which is a multimillion dollar project, is being musically scored by the London Symphony Orchestra. Staff of 40 or more are required to develop them. It is common to upgrade an old, already popular, title rather than to come up with a completely new title. However, the return is enormous since a successful title can bring in $200–300 million, as much as a blockbuster film. Some return $100 million in the first few days of sales.

The year 2002 was regarded by the long-established player Nintendo as a make or break year. In an unprecedented move Nintendo aimed in 2002 to update two of its well-known games, the Mario and Zelda games, and hoped that sales of each would eventually top one million. These projects are headed by its best creative mind and probably the most famous games maker of all, Shigeru Miyamoto. As important is a new game which Nintendo is working on, 'Eternal Darkness: Sanity's Requiem'. This project has been four years in the making. It is a psychological thriller, which includes mild violence and adult language. It is pitched, as other new games being developed by Nintendo, at a more mature market, the older-teen and adult market, to take account of the ageing of Nintendo's customer base.

Microsoft announced the planned autumn release of an XBOX version of Crimson Skies, a PC version of which has been available since September 2000. Microsoft has feature film ambitions for this game. It will include several film-like scenes spliced into the game action to enhance that part of the story. The story concerns a flying ace who duels with sky bandits in dirigibles in a 1930s America that has been split into separate nations. For the film version there is the essential love interest.

Sony had announced that a new version of their bestseller game, Tomb Raider, would be out by Christmas

2002; usually such announcements are kept for the industry's big trade fair in May. The game is produced by Eidos, a London-based company. However, it was only released, after delays, in June 2003. As an example of the second strategy, Microsoft officials flew to London to try to persuade Eidos to make a version of this hit game for the XBOX, in other words to lure Eidos away from Sony, but without success. Tomb Raider has outsold all other games, with 17 million copies sold since its initial release in 1996. In an attempt to beef up the number of games which are tailored to the XBOX, Microsoft has also tried to become a major shareholder in Rare, a British games maker known for its high-quality games, which is already 49% owned by Nintendo.

The third strategy involves promotion of the games already available. Microsoft has indicated it will spend as much as US$500 million from the time of the launch of XBOX until the end of 2003 just to promote its games. Despite the level of expenditure, success is not assured. One illustration shows the quirkiness of tastes. Minoru Arakawa of Nintendo America had a vision, one not shared by his staff or observers of the market. This was the enthusiasm of American children for the Japanese video game, Pokemon, a game with 150 collectible monsters. He ignored resistance from all those who were experts and should have known about these things and scored a huge hit by bringing Pokemon to the USA over the objections of co-workers and the negative market research. In a short period it became the game to have. Between 1998 and 2000 Pokemon's sales in the USA exceeded $1 billion. *Business Week* included Arakawa in their top 25 managers of 1999.

The crunch comes

A danger moment comes when games developers begin to lose confidence in a console. At the time of writing this is happening to Microsoft, and for good reasons. PlayStation 2 has been outselling XBOX by more than two to one in the USA, and almost two to one in Japan, largely because of the much larger choice of games titles on offer. By January 2003, 50 million PlayStation 2 consoles had already been sold worldwide. Overall Microsoft has had to downgrade its global sales expectations, from 4.5–6 million to 3.5–4 million.

In Japan, as elsewhere, Microsoft is relying on the quality of a game to rescue it, one which can be played only on XBOX. The game Halo has already had one million sales in the USA. It is a shooting game which can be played simultaneously by four users on a split screen. The players try to fight aliens after crash-landing on an unknown planet. It may be that the games are

the key to success, but it is also true that the games may go elsewhere if the console cannot establish a strong position in the market, notably as number one or number two. The games competition will help to determine who will be left in such a duopoly.

The games developer THQ, which make the game WWF Raw for XBOX, has already called on Microsoft to cut the price of its console earlier rather than later, a sign that a strategic ally is becoming worried by the lack of sales. Microsoft has responded by slashing the price by 40%. There is a major price war which has brought the respective prices of consoles well below their cost levels. The reduction in price appears to be working, but it is unclear whether or not the increase in sales is a temporary spike.

The future

A completely new long-term strategy is 'network gaming'. This requires the use of plug-in adaptors to link the boxes with networks over the Internet. Both PlayStation 2 and XBOX are designed to do just this. In the first week of launch in November 2002, Microsoft had sold 150,000 starter kits for 'XBOX Live', by March 2003 this had risen to 350,000. Sony claims 175,000 subscribers for the rival online service launched in August 2002. Both were launched in Europe in 2003. The model for this strategy is the popularity of online gambling.

This is just a start. The main constraint on the spread is access to broadband. The introduction of such network gaming is slowed by the surprisingly slow speed at which the high-speed broadband Internet connection has been accepted. That connection is critical since the quality of graphics is very poor without broadband. Its time will probably come in the next console cycle.

Microsoft has already accepted the challenge, taking an aggressive approach, planning to spend $2 billion over the next five years building a dedicated network, XBOX Live, to support online gaming for XBOX owners. The subscription fees will go to Microsoft which will run the network. This will clearly upset the games makers. The other players have taken a more passive approach, waiting for others to set up and make the infrastructure work before they commit themselves. It is unclear which strategy offers the better outcomes for the players.

The way of the future is being made by John Smedly, 33, chief operating office of Sony Online Entertainment, master of EverQuest, which is an online role-playing game, modelled on The Sims, that now has 433,000 paying customers, each paying $13 per month, already generating $5 million a month and a 40% gross profit margin. Profit margins could be even higher in the future as companies learn how to develop the games. Alternatively competition could cut these margins.

Sony has worked with the company Electronic Arts (EA) to bring online the computer game, The Sims, which is the biggest selling game so far, with sales of 9 million since its debut in 2000 and 8 million expansion packs, a separately sold add-on software. The game is like a doll's house simulation of real life, which allows players to choose jobs, buy houses, furnish them, date, marry and have kids. Most games players are young males, but half of the players of The Sims online are 10–30-year-old girls and women.

Other companies such as Microsoft, Vivendi Universal and Disney are involved in the same general project, to build online theme worlds, virtual worlds, which can be based on all sorts of sources, such as books – the Harry Potter series, films – *The Matrix*, or television programmes. One of Smedly's ex-partners McQuaid is now working for Microsoft. The next project for Sony is to develop, together with Lucas Arts entertainment, the first online colony, based on *Star Wars*. The Star Wars Galaxies game came online in December 2002 and is anticipated to have 500,000 players within three months. All such games have console versions. In the future Hollywood films may well act just as trailers to publicize online games. The key competitive issue is the quality of the graphics for the medium, whether it is online or through a console.

The story of EverQuest is an interesting one. When Smedly and his team first developed EverQuest, Sony nearly pulled the plug on this project because its costs soared to $5 million. Smedly and the others formed their own company to continue the project, Verant Interactive, in which another Sony division took a 20% share. When EverQuest was launched in 1999, 12,000 signed up in the first few days and 75,000 within the first week, at a fee of $10 a month. Within six months, there were 150,000 subscribed players. The project was not planned to break even for two years, but was soon very profitable. In 2000 Sony, observing this success, bought the rest of EverQuest for $32 million. The company now has 480 employees at stations in San Diego, Austin and St Louis.

Another country which is pioneering online games is South Korea. Nearly half the population of South Korea has a broadband, or fast Internet, connection, compared with only 12% of Americans. As a consequence, South Korea is the largest online game market in the world. As much as 6% of the population already plays games online. The main game is Lineage, which has 330,000 players. It is run by NCSoft with its dynamic CEO Kim Taek Jin. The monthly subscription is $21 per month, which helped to generate a revenue of $100 million in 2001. The game really took off after 1997 when unemployed managers, created by the crisis of that year, set up something like 20,000 Internet cafes.

The loyalty of game players to a particular game is very strong. According to studies in the USA a typical player spends as much as 20 hours a week playing. Already there are 42 versions of EverQuest and 12,000 new players are signing on each month. There is also an illicit market for items from the games which are in high demand, a real market with real prices. Although Sony is nervous about this, it may be that such a market will be built into future games.

Usually the games makers pay other companies for the right to use their logos in the games. The popularity of the games, which has made the overall market larger than the market for Hollywood films, has reversed this. Intel and McDonald's have entered into multimillion dollar deals with EA in which they pay EA to use their logos in the games. This followed the precedent of a deal with Reebok which was on a much smaller scale. Online games, just as films, are becoming a favourable platform for product placements or the promotion of consumer products.

The alternative to online gaming is mobile gaming. Mobile phones are already sold with one or two simple games built in. Mobiles now have much better graphics, with colour screens and the ability to download software remotely. The cost of downloading a game is much cheaper than buying one for console use. Nokia is pioneering in this area, planning to gradually launch a handset aimed at specific use with games, the N-Gage, a competitor for Nintendo's Game Boy Advance. The advantage of mobiles is their already wide coverage.

Currently PlayStation 2 is clearly number one, outselling the other two consoles by a handsome margin. However, Microsoft may win out in online gaming and Nokia in mobile gaming. They represent real competitors in a rapidly changing competitive environment.

Case Study Questions

1. How competitive is the video games industry and how does that competitiveness show itself?
2. What are the main factors which determine whether a games platform is competitive or not?
3. How do the strategies of the main players in this industry differ from each other?
4. Analyse the nature of the video games industry, both hardware and software, in terms of the role of the main actors – suppliers and customers, competitors and complementors, and various stakeholders.
5. What is likely to be a successful strategy in the video games industry in five years time?

Reading

Chang, G., 'Game over for Nintendo if rivals buy stake', *The Age*, September 13, 2002, Business 5.

Economist, The, 'Strong plays', December 14, 2002: 62.

Guth, R. A., 'Inside Sony's Trojan horse', *Wall Street Journal*, February 25, 2000: B1, B4.

Moon, P., 'Microsoft makes its box of tricks a serious player', *The Australian Financial Review*, May 7, 2002: 34.

Nicholas, K., 'Xbox scores a hit with price cut', *The Australian Financial Review*, May 6, 2002: 16.

Pereira, J., 'Games war: it's survival of the hippest', *The Australian Financial Review*, April 23, 2002: 40.

Taylor, C., 'Game wars', *Time*, March 20, 2000: 44–5.

Relevant websites

www.gamecube.com
www.xbox.com
www.playstation.com

This case study is also relevant to Chapters 8 and 13.

Key strategic lessons

• The main players in the competitive environment are competitors, including potential competitors; complementors, who have a positive role rather than a negative one; and lawmakers, mostly various arms of government.

• Within the competitive environment, the impact of any strategic action takes the form of a sequence which is repeated many times – initial action, response and further reaction.

• Porter defined five forces of competition: ease of entry into an industry (or exit); the existence of substitutes for the product or service; the bargaining power of both suppliers and customers; and the intensity of competition. A sixth force, the bargaining power of complementors, can be added to these and dynamic factors, such as the role and impact of market growth, instability and innovation, should be considered.

• Under perfect competition and monopoly, there is no scope for the independent making of strategy but perfect competition and monopoly do not occur in a pure form in the real world. The typical situation is one of imperfect competition, either oligopolistic or monopolistic, and there is scope for the independent making of strategy.

• Under conditions of imperfect competition any strategy maker can influence the level of price or output in that market. Consequently the implementation of a strategy has a direct impact on other players who respond to that strategy.

• The exact nature of response and further reaction cannot be determined in advance, even if an enterprise has accurate information on demand and supply conditions. There is a strong measure of path dependency, the shaping of the current situation by the exact sequence of past decisions.

• Government and its various arms act as independent strategy makers, and are subject to the same temptation to opportunistic behaviour and influence from various stakeholder groups.

• Strategic risk comprises the competitive risk arising from other players competing in the same market and the country risk arising from the role of the government as lawmaker and strategy maker.

Applying the lessons

1 Define the following terms: competitive or industrial environment, strategic risk, market structure, perfect competition, monopolistic competition, oligopoly, monopoly, competition risk, country risk, transfer risk and political risk.

2 Focusing on the enterprise for which you currently work, or one for which you have worked in the past, list all the main players who occupy the competitive environment, directly relevant to your enterprise, as both competitors and complementors.

Applying the lessons cont'd

3 Are there ethical considerations which influence the choice of how an enterprise might compete? In what ways might these ethical considerations affect the long-term health of the enterprise?

4 Consider the following rating scale, based on the key success factors (KSFs) considered appropriate in the video games industry:

Innovative /creative games	0.25
Reputation/image	0.15
Technological innovation	0.25
Marketing skills	0.15
Relative cost position	0.10
Financial strength	0.10
	1.00

Using this scale, assess the competitive strengths for the main players in the current video game war: Nintendo, Microsoft and Sony.

5 What rating system would you adopt for the following industries – pharmaceuticals, airlines and fashion houses?

6 Take an imaginary situation relating to pricing or investment policy in a selected industry in which there are few sellers and show how the adoption of different strategies by a leading player defines different possible paths. Use a decision tree to illustrate these different possible paths.

Strategic project

1 Choose a particular industry such as the automobile or pharmaceutical industry. Consider the possibility of a new player entering that industry. This might be either an existing player in another industry or a start-up company.

2 Consider in detail the forces of competition which face that enterprise. Are these forces changing over time?

3 Evaluate the impact of the change in forces of competition on the timing of entry.

Exploring further

The starting point for discussion, the five forces of competition, originates with Porter, 1980, and is discussed in just about every text on strategy. It is quite a useful way of discussing the influences on competition. It requires development. It can be supplemented by the inclusion of complementors, see Brandenburger and Nalebuff, 1996, an insertion discussed at length by Ghemawat, 1999. It has been dynamized by a recent article reviewing the area, Slater and Olson, 2002: 15–22. Porter himself sought to dynamize his own analysis, 1991: 95–118.

There is some interesting literature on whether positioning in distinct industries makes a difference in terms of the return likely to be made, that is, whether there are markedly different returns in different industries. It began with Schmalensee, 1985: 341–51. An influential article was that of Rumelt, 1991: 167–86. Replying to the general negative inferences was McGahan and Porter, 1987:15–30. See also Mauri and Michaels, 1998: 211–19 and Schmalensee, 1989. This shows how a theory should be tested against the empirical data of the real world. The conclusion is that there are significant, but not large, differences and that they are not as significant as differences in returns between enterprises within the same industry.

There are a number of treatments of competition and its influence on strategy making. Most tend to exaggerate the degree to which competition prevents the appearance of oligopoly. Certainly globalization has encouraged the process of competition. One of the best treatments is D'Aveni, 1994. An alternative treatment is Smith et al., 1992.

One school which is associated with the perspective that innovation is the source of competition is the so-called Austrian school which goes back to the work of Schumpeter. See Jacobson, 1992: 782–807, or Hill and Deeds, 1996: 429–51.

An interesting discussion of political risk, the key component of country risk, is to be found in Robock, 1971: 6–20. Regular assessments of country risk appear every year in *Euromoney* and *Institutional Investor*. Both indicate the complex formulae used to estimate the level of country risk. They also show the high level of variability in the level of country risk for most countries.

7

Analysing resources, capabilities and core competencies

Learning objectives

After reading this chapter you will be able to:

- recognize what gives an organization a particular identity and see how, over time, it accumulates different resources
- distinguish between tangible and intangible resources
- understand how capabilities are created by the combination of different resources
- identify the core or distinctive competencies of an organization which make a strategy achievable

Key strategic challenge

What is my enterprise capable of doing?

Strategic dangers

That the enterprise is either unaware of its own resources, notably those which are intangible, or, more significantly, ignorant of the way in which those resources can be combined to support the creation and maintenance of competitive advantage.

The resource position of an enterprise largely defines its identity by determining what it can do, rather than what it should. Most organizations have a core activity or activities, which it is inconceivable that they change and which require the possession of specific resources. The activity helps to define the identity. An organization may add other activities not necessarily directly connected with the core activity, sometimes in order to package better the main activity and make it even more attractive to consumers, or at other times to diversify away from the core activity. In order to do either the organization needs resources, or rather the capabilities made possible by those resources. Not all organizations recognize their own capabilities, only discovering the full range of their resources by exploring strategic possibilities.

Case Study Scenario   Branding a sports team – Manchester United

'The world's most popular sport.'
'Arguably the most valuable sports team
brand in the world.'   *Heller, 2002: 32*

Today sport is big business. Sports such as golf, tennis, Formula One motor racing and soccer are much bigger income generators than sports with only a minority following. Certain sports, such as darts or bowls, can have their popularity raised by attractive television coverage, sometimes only briefly.

Major sporting events, such as the Olympics or the World Cup, require considerable preparation and are in any terms big events. That is why these particular events occur once every four years. They are important in raising the profile and increasing the popularity of a sport, and also in generating enormous flows of money, not least through the sale of broadcasting rights and the media coverage of the sports themselves. There is the money spent by those attending the events and by later visitors following the promotion of the venue as a place to visit. For this reason there is enormous competition to stage such events, despite their enormous cost.

Major events create an enormous potential for the sports to generate future revenue by creating stars – individuals or teams who can be sponsored and used in marketing a range of different products. In the process they become brands, often global brands. David Beckham, the former captain of Manchester United and captain of England, is one such star. Branding is so strong for successful sportspeople or sports teams that enterprises, often with no direct connection with the sport, wish to identify themselves with the sport and benefit from that branding. They are happy to sponsor an event, a team and even an individual.

The process of commercializing sport began during the 1950s and 60s, initially in the USA, as in entertainment generally, and first with golf and tennis at the international level. An illustration of this is the history of Mark McCormack and the International Management Group (IMG), which developed initially by representing sportspeople in all their legal, financial and marketing activities. From a beginning acting as an agent for the golfer Arnold Palmer and using his name to generate income in sponsorship and endorsements, McCormack has developed his enterprise to the point at which in 2001 it received not far short of £1 billion in income.

In 2000 IMG had no interest in soccer. With a stated aim to be the 'House of Football', by 2002 it was one of the top management groups in the sport, representing 250 (mostly European) players, 35 national teams, including those of Turkey, Norway, Scotland and the USA and nearly 100 professional clubs, including Manchester United and Liverpool. IMG, together with other consortium members, manages the rights of eight premier league teams outside the UK. In a short period IMG has become a big player in the promotion of soccer, its teams and players.

During the 1980s and 90s, one major development was a realization of the value of sports television rights. In 1988 the aggregate amount paid for the TV rights to broadcast soccer in the UK was over £3 million; in 2002 it was closer to half a billion pounds. Some organizations, such as ITV Digital (a joint venture of Granada and Carlton Communications) or in Germany Kerch Media, paid too much for these rights and paid the ultimate price of business failure.

The bread and butter of sport comes, not from the big events, but the weekly fixtures which are part of regular annual competitions. A good example is the premier league of English football. The World Cup undoubtedly has spread the gospel of soccer to traditionally non-playing regions such as Africa and Asia. However, it may inadvertently divert attention away from more humble levels of competition.

European soccer clubs began their existence as not-for-profit organizations. After World War I they evolved into closely held enterprises, usually owned by a local businessman, just as today Juventus is owned by the Agnelli family which owns Fiat. These businessmen were enthusiasts, investing because of a love of the game or a wish to be prominent in a local community. Recently the motivation in running a football club has become much more commercial, not with the most desirable of outcomes.

Soccer, as it is called to distinguish it from other football codes, is popular throughout the world, although that popularity is at its greatest in Latin America, Europe and increasingly Africa, less so in North America and Asia. The sport's growth in Asia has been promoted by the success of South Korea in reaching the semi-final of the 2002 World Cup, Japan in reaching the quarter-final and China in getting to the finals. The successful staging of the event by Japan and South Korea helped in selling the game in the region.

The sport is simple to play. Boys begin playing in the playground at school or in the back garden at home. Most began watching the sport at a very humble level. The writer began watching Aldershot, which once played in the fourth division of the English league. There were scarcely any seats and the stands were barely functional. The spectators stood for the whole match and endured the elements. Most fans developed a strong identification with such a local team.

Soccer is both a mass participatory sport – its appeal now extending to women, as the film *Bend it like Beckham* and the popularity of the women's world championship shows – and a mass spectator sport. FIFA claims that 33.4 billion people watched some part of the 1998 World Cup, obviously including repeat viewers. On one estimate, the football industry is worth £135 billion worldwide.

If soccer is the most popular sport in the world, Manchester United is the best-known team. It is not just a soccer team, but a commercial organization with a brand name recognized the world over.

Enterprise identity

What gives an organization its identity?

Success in its core activity is one source of identity, but not the only one. It is assumed here that the organization has clear, well-defined boundaries which divide what is within the organization from what is outside, just as the analysis of an industry assumes the same clear boundaries. For the moment the analysis assumes that the resources available to an enterprise do not include access to resources outside that boundary, with the obvious exception of access to finance. It assumes away, for the time being, the accessibility given by strategic alliances. In this case identity reflects elements contained within the boundary of the organization.

Core defining resources

The nature of the services or products provided by the organization helps to define its identity, particularly if the organization is good at providing them. What it produces reflects what it has in the way of resources. Continuity in the provision of products or services helps since it allows a reliable evaluation and widespread acceptance of the quality of the service provided by the organization. It allows learning which further extends the range of resources available to it. The organization may have a strong identification with a particular industrial area. However much an enterprise may diversify, it is usually associated with the particular activity, or activities, which have placed it in a clearly demarcated field of human activity and given it a name. It is unusual for the field of primary activity of any organization to change dramatically. Man Utd is unlikely to stop playing soccer.

What is sold or supplied can differ enormously. The organization may or may not be a for-profit organization. A university lecturer teaches and does research, the Red

Cross is concerned with organizing to solve medical problems and a football team plays football. It is unlikely that there will be much movement outside these defining areas.

Very often the core defining resources are those which obviously go with the relevant activity, often human resources. For most enterprises it is clear what 'core' resources they need in order to support the core activity. A football team needs good footballers and a coach to integrate them. A fashion house needs good designers and attractive models to display the designs. A hospital needs good doctors and nurses, but also the equipment needed for effective medical treatment and easy access to medications.

But all organizations need more than just the core resources in order to have continuity of existence and be effective as enterprises. The more successful they are at their core activity or activities, the more they need a range of well-run supporting activities and a range of supporting resources. Such organizations become a repository for a highly specific set of resources which support the core activity, both directly and indirectly.

The accumulation of core resources

Organizations derive their identity from the specific resources that they have developed over their history, often the core resources. These resources define what the enterprise can do now and what, with some adjustment, it might be able to do in the future. Often these resources are accumulated as a result of a long and difficult process. Each enterprise has its own specific history and its own set of specific resources built up over that history. No two enterprises have the same history of accumulation or the same set of resources. The nature of these resources ensures that for most organizations there is considerable continuity in what they do.

These resources also mark out the enterprise as different from other enterprises. The resources consist in a wide variety of assets which are shown in Figure 7.1. They include human and physical assets, tangible and intangible assets.

A precondition for the continuity of any enterprise is economic viability, the ability to make a satisfactory profit; for a not-for-profit organization it is a continuing demand for services and access in some way to the resources needed to meet this demand. In the end the resources which constitute the organization are identified by their ability to support the creation of value for the customer. A resource is only a resource if it has the potential ability to help in creating such value. In this book a resource is taken as anything which has the potential ability to help generate a revenue flow by encouraging purchase by a potential consumer. This ability naturally reflects both the nature of technology and consumer tastes.

Transformation

A change in that environment can undermine that ability to create value by removing a demand for the product or service. In all periods some past resources cease to be current resources. Renewal may require the combination of new with old resources or the recombination of both. Clearly enterprises have to renew themselves if they are to survive. This may involve diversifying activities into new areas as well as changing the mix of resources.

The renewal may be the result of a continuous, but incremental, process or it may require a quantum leap made necessary by some major change of external context. Because resources are specific to the enterprise, the enterprise itself cannot be transformed, at the wave of a wand, into an entirely different enterprise. Some transformations are simply impossible, others are managed only with great difficulty and at enormous cost.

This is not to deny the possibility of some transformation but to emphasize the difficulties. There may be no choice in attempting a transformation if the organization is to survive in a changed environment. To make such a transformation requires a set of resources appropriate to the new situation; it may be difficult to put together these resources. There is a major risk of failure in so doing.

A resource-based approach

For these reasons, it is impossible to identify an advantageous position for an enterprise and locate the enterprise accordingly, without comparing its existing resources with those needed for the relevant positioning. An alternative to the positioning approach is first to define the resources available to the enterprise and then consider what these resources allow the enterprise to do – this is known as the resource-based model. Resources offer both opportunity and constraint.

The starting point for strategy making becomes the resource position, defined in this broad way, rather than the identification of a desirable position in the general or industrial environment in which to place the enterprise, a process described in the last two chapters. All resources have some measure of flexibility. Some allowance can be made for the acquisition of new resources. However, there are limits on the degree to which resources can be changed in the short term. A strategic orientation stressing the resources is a much more realistic one to adopt, and is also a better description of the usual setting in which strategy is made than one which assumes potential malleability of resources.

The nature of resources: tangible and intangible

There is a tendency to focus on resources as natural resources only, such as a benign climate, good soils or rich raw material deposits found in a particular location. However, the concept of a resource is much wider. Many resources are created by human action rather than occurring naturally. Over time the proportion of created assets to natural assets has increased, as has the proportion of assets which are mobile.

For any organization the concept of a resource is a wide one, including any inputs which aid the production and selling processes of an enterprise. Such inputs take a wide range of different forms. They include an enormous range of assets – any piece of equipment, the skills of a group of engineers, a patent, the ability to borrow from a bank or raise money on the stock market, a branded product, the capacity to innovate. The list could easily be further lengthened. On its own each cannot produce a competitive advantage in the market, but in the right combination, they can.

A resource audit

In theory it is possible at a given moment of time to take a snapshot of the enterprise and list its assets. It is a good starting point for strategy making to have access to such a listing of resources. It is rare for organizations to conduct such a resource audit. Because enterprises are not encouraged to conduct a full resource audit, it is impossible to draw up a full and completely accurate inventory of an enterprise's resources. It is also hard to define the full complement of such resources, indicated below. For various reasons the traditional balance sheet gives a distorted and incomplete view of the true resource position of an enterprise.

The most important distinction is that between a *tangible* and an *intangible* asset. Most assets are considered to be tangible but this is far from being the case. The assets which most differentiate an organization and create its separate identity are those which are intangible.

In theory a tangible resource is easily defined as that which can be seen, touched or felt. However, this is not an adequate touchstone. Perhaps it is better to describe a tangible asset as one which can be measured in some way. This does not help us very much if the units of measurement differ from asset to asset. A building or a piece of equipment is a tangible asset but how can it be measured or quantified? It is possible to count the number of workers or the number of PCs, but this tells nothing about what the worker can do or how the PC is used. How is it possible to quantify, and with what precision? The distinction between the tangible and the intangible is not anything like as clear-cut as might seem at first glance.

If market value is what defines a resource, it can also act as a measuring rod. Perhaps the most relevant distinguishing feature between the tangible and the intangible is the possibility of sound and stable valuation for the former, and not for the latter. There may be a good market for such an asset which gives it a relatively easily determined value. The distinction is therefore not based solely on a physical manifestation or its absence.

What about a resource such as technical know-how, which clearly cannot be seen or touched? A patent is an asset with a value, which might be estimated. On the other hand, the capacity to innovate is a much more nebulous characteristic, obviously an intangible resource. The capacity to innovate, or the related knowledge underpinning this capacity, may be tacit, difficult even to codify, let alone value.

It is possible to talk about assets as being tangible if they have a transparent and stable value. Any such value may be ephemeral. There may also be value which is difficult to impute to a particular asset. A brand name has a lasting value, although it often comprises tangible and intangible attributes or characteristics. There are methods of trying to value each attribute. Even the capacity to borrow has a specific value. Figure 7.1 illustrates an audit of resources.

There is no doubt that the value of any enterprise reflects both kinds of resource or asset. Many of the assets on which the overall valuation of the enterprise is based are intangible assets.

It is the intangible assets which give the organization its specific identity. Intangible assets often appear as a result of continuing patterns of positive interaction both within enterprises or between members inside the enterprise and those outside it. Such interactions are embedded in the nature and structure of the organization. Together they embody what is called the tacit know-how of the organization and constitute its underlying identity. The patterns of interaction reflect and reinforce the network of common beliefs, values and shared commitments. Many of these interactions are fashioned to deal with the typical or recurrent problems which emerge, such as the need to reconcile conflicts of interest, reduce the danger of asymmetrical

Tangible resources

Physical resources:

- These include production facilities, comprising buildings, plant, equipment and the land on which they are located. The size, location, technical sophistication or vintage of plant and equipment are all relevant.
- All this productive capacity has a value outside its current use. Alternative uses for land and buildings should be considered. Access to raw materials and other inputs obviously affects value.

Technological or intellectual resources:

- These include intellectual property rights, such as patents, trademarks, copyrights and trade secrets, as well as the capacity of an R&D department, with its laboratories and research staff.

Financial resources:

- The enterprise's ability to: borrow from financial institutions; generate or find

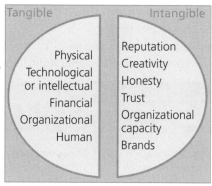

Tangible	Intangible
Physical Technological or intellectual Financial Organizational Human	Reputation Creativity Honesty Trust Organizational capacity Brands

funds internally; raise money on the stock market.

Organizational and human resources:

- These include the formal structures for control, command, communication and coordination, and for the reporting of financial information, together with the human capital of its managers and employees.

Intangible resources

Reputation of the enterprise:

- but with whom?
  - Competitors
  - Customers
  - Suppliers
  - Employees
  - Government
  - The community at large

Human qualities of individual staff:

- Creativity
- Honesty
- Trust

Organizational qualities:

- Capacity to provide leadership
- Capacity to innovate
- Capacity to think strategically

Intangible attributes of products or services:

- Brands

Figure 7.1 **An audit list of resources**

investment, cope with the universality of uncertainty and risk or manage the relentlessness of change. On the other hand, what is codifiable is easy to imitate and easily shared by others.

Resources and capabilities

Resources can be put to together in a wide variety of different ways, each constituting a different capability. Such capabilities result from the combination of tangible and intangible resources. Very often it is the intangible resources which help to translate a physical resource or resources into a capability. The capabilities may be specific to a particular industry or sector, a particular functional area or a particular part of the value-adding chain, even a particular situation, or they may be much more general.

Whatever the scope of the capability it is usually highly specific to a particular organization. Many of a firm's employees have a particular functional expertise which is usually related to that enterprise's organizational requirements and its position in the market. That functional expertise, initially general, quickly becomes specific to the organization. It might involve financial skills or an ability to apply new ways of processing electronic knowledge, but it relates to specific financial control and specific information systems. The enterprise will deliberately seek to develop that expertise and make it more concrete. Part of the capability is learning to apply an expertise to the changing circumstances of the organization. The resulting capabilities are the foundation on which the enterprise will build the competitive advantage which is at the core of any strategy.

The stockbroking industry is one in which such capabilities were important, but their nature has changed with the communications revolution.

Strategy in Action   Charles Schwab and online broking

Traditionally broking was an expensive activity, accessed by the rich few. Brokers were well rewarded, developing a close relationship of trust with their clients. The one-to-one relationship explains the high cost. As incomes have risen and the number of transactions has increased, there has been a greater demand for broking. The proportion of shareholders in the population has risen steadily, accelerated by privatization. When the Internet appeared, there was much discussion of its potential for supporting the retailing of products or services (B2C); online broking is a pioneer in the development of e-commerce.

Online broking involves:

- the provision of information
- the facilitation of online trading in financial assets
- the provision of a means of payment, including credit where desired.

The broking is the main service provided.

Whatever the opportunities, someone has to pioneer the use of the new technology. The pioneer in stockbroking was Charles Schwab, whose aim was to offer the cheapest service, and to offer value, particularly to the small investor. It did this by innovating, typically spending a high 13% of its revenues on new technology.

In 1973, Schwab set up a brokerage firm to exploit the end of fixed-rate broking which became law in the USA in March 1975. It was the first brokerage firm to discount its commissions, thus triggering the appearance of discount brokerage. By the mid-1980s Schwab had pioneered the use of independent financial planners as complementors to the brokers.

The discount brokers could cut their prices because they reduced costs in a number of significant ways:

- they reduced the time devoted to each client
- they did not engage in major research into the behaviour of investments in the way full-service brokers did

- they operated mainly on the telephone, rather than from branch offices.

At their peak they accounted for about a quarter of retail brokerage. Charles Schwab never engaged in discounting for its own sake, having a sufficiently good reputation and a wide enough range of products and services to charge a price premium. Schwab has 400 branches nationwide.

Charles Schwab set up a one-source and no-fee mutual fund supermarket. It launched its innovative OneSource and Mutual Fund Marketplace programmes which, by 1988, provided customers with the ability to purchase 1,400 mutual funds through their Schwab account without having to open an account directly with a mutual fund provider. This made it possible to switch easily into and out of funds. It had particular appeal to those who had retired.

In 1998, following E*Trade, Charles Schwab initiated online trading through the Internet. The firm aspired to be the leader in electronic brokerage. Provided a certain minimum account was held and a certain minimum trading undertaken, the customer had free access to his or her own webpages in which the information was customized. 'In the late 1970s about 95% of Schwab's business was done through branch walk-ins or telephone calls to branch office personnel; in 1998, only 5% of the firm's business was done in branch offices' (Thompson and Strickland, 1999: C-235). The company occupied a 'mid-market' position. It charged $29.95 for an online trade, whereas E*Trade charged $14.95 and other online brokers as little as $8.

Market leaders adopted a wait-and-see attitude, expecting those who had gone over to the new electronic broking to return to a full professional service. Online traders were rapidly rising in importance and were expected eventually to reach 75% of all trades. Growth in online brokerage was so explosive during the years 1997, 1998 and 1999 that all were eventually forced to imitate. Information providers were

▶

forming alliances with the online brokers and it was possible for investors to get an enormous volume of information. Online brokers were continually improving their websites. By mid-1997 a major advertising campaign was in full swing everywhere. Online broking seemed to encourage much more trading. By 1998 the retail brokerage industry was a $12 billion-plus business, with well over 200 competitors. There were three kinds of broking firms:

1. traditional full-service brokers like Merrill Lynch
2. limited-service discount brokers like the original Charles Schwab
3. Internet brokers like Schwab Online, E*Trade and Waterhouse Securities.

There were significant differences in the price charged for providing broking services, with the first kind of firm more expensive and the third cheaper than the other two. Brokers made their money in four ways:

1. commission income from executing customer trades – increasingly a flat fee per trade
2. interest earned on loans to customers engaged in margin trading
3. interest earned on the balances held in customer accounts
4. payments for orders received from the market makers in each NASDAQ-listed stock.

Online brokers made their income increasingly from the last three.

Recombining resources as new capabilities

Capabilities have only a short life span. Tangible and intangible resources are endlessly coming together to form new capabilities. It demands a certain degree of creativity to put resources together in new ways and fit them into a changing context.

Many capabilities are incorporated into the human capital of the enterprise, including the more general ability to put together such capabilities, that is, they reflect the growing knowledge of those who work for the enterprise. The capabilities are very much knowledge-based. If a staff member departs, a particular capability might be lost. To lose staff is always to lose part of the enterprise. However, the capabilities of the organization are more than the sum of the individual capabilities of its staff members. Such capabilities reside in a team rather than in individuals. The break-up of such teams is often more damaging than the loss of a valued individual.

Learning what an enterprise can do

Given that, in the development of any capability, whether it is tacit and organizational or codifiable and individual, there is a learning process, completely unforeseen and unplanned but difficult to replicate, the human capital needs to be carefully protected and nurtured. The process of learning needs to be given direction but the organization must be sensitive to the unexpected turns of the learning process. In some areas repetition and practice are important elements of this learning process. Many enterprises have appointed chief learning officers to oversee the deliberate development of knowledge within the enterprise.

There is a paradox for any organization. The more general a capability, the easier it is to adjust it to a changing environment. The more specific a capability, the more difficult it is to imitate and the more likely it is to be a source of competitive advantage. There is an obvious trade-off between maintaining flexibility and reinforcing an existing competitive advantage which might prove to be transitory.

Leveraging existing resources

It is much easier and less expensive to use the resources and capabilities which already exist within an organization than to look for new ones outside. The enterprise must leverage creatively those resources which it already has. It can achieve this leverage in a number of different ways:

1. By concentrating resources, linked together as appropriate capabilities, on the achievement of clear and specific strategic objectives. These objectives are given the highest priority and are consistently and persistently pursued. This may require significant focusing which itself reflects the identification of particular competitive advantages which the enterprise desires to create and maintain. Resources must not be wasted on low priority objectives.

2. By efficiently accumulating any other resources needed. This involves developing the ability to recognize and identify resources, or *extract* them from the resources the enterprise already has, minimizing the need to go outside the organization. It includes the ability to recognize and borrow resources which exist outside the enterprise but which can be tapped into relatively cheaply and easily, for example through a timely strategic alliance.

   The foundation of such a process of accumulation is learning. It is necessary to be fully aware of the resources implicit in the vast experience of existing staff members or readily available because of the existing network of contacts of the organization. Such resources can be easily and flexibly released for use.

3. By putting together potentially complementary resources. This involves a process of simultaneous blending and balancing, that is, putting the resources and capabilities together in a mix within a desired strategy. *Blending* comprises three possibilities; enterprises can aim for just one kind of blend or all three. These are:
   • a new technological integration, which is more the capacity to develop a new technical area than knowledge of actual processes
   • a new functional integration
   • an imagined new product.

Balance requires the achievement of high standards in all the areas relevant to this blending.

4. By conserving the resources it already has. This is made possible by recycling resources away from activities which no longer deliver competitive advantage to new ones which do. This includes:
   • the redirection of a resource into a different part of an enterprise in order to: boost a technical capability; help to produce another product; or assist another functional area
   • the cooption of partners into actions which both reinforce existing resources and shield them from damage. Again strategic action can highlight the value of resources already held.

5. By recovering or recycling in the shortest possible time resources already invested in a particular project, in so doing taking advantage of any success to spin off resources for new projects. In other words, the aim is to release financial or human resources for other purposes. For example, the enterprise might find it useful to speed up its cycle of product launch and development.

By leveraging resources in an effective way the organization is creating new core or distinctive competencies. These are now considered.

The core competencies of an enterprise

Simply having a resource or a capability is not enough. An enterprise must make good use of its resources or capabilities. The process of strategy making provides the opportunity to discover the specific use and identify the aspirations or intentions to which that use is linked.

A core competency is a strategic capability, that is, a capability which has strategic value. The possession of certain capabilities influences the nature of the strategy adopted but it is the strategy which turns a capability into a competency. The strategy shows which activities the enterprise should develop and which functional areas or activities on the value chain are of greatest importance to the organization. It indicates the core competencies which are relevant to that strategy.

The term 'core' refers to the role of the competency in strategy and indicates that the competency is central to that strategy. Without the competency, or competencies, the strategy could not be implemented. The strategy allows all the existing capabilities to be prioritized and then harnessed to the achievement of particular strategic goals. This is the sense in which they are core or central.

Strategy in Action **Haier: developing a new core competency and pioneering the Chinese export brand**

'We work in a mixed economy. You have to have three eyes: one for the market, one on the workers, and one on policy.' *Zhang Riumin, CEO of Haier*

'We have a broad product line with a wide price range. We need lower price models for price-only stores that sell commodity goods. We need higher price models for stores that will display our products and have salespeople on the floor.'

'We promote Haier as a global brand – not Chinese or American, but global.'

'I saw opportunity in the Haier brand. The appliance market is old and has a lot of hang ups like product recalls. Here was a new brand of good products with no baggage and the chance to develop its own Image. I believed in the Haier Brand.'
Mike Jemal, president of Haier America

China appears the natural focus for a cost leadership strategy. The potential for exporting from China is enormous, as the rapid growth of exports since 1978 has shown. This potential is largely based on the vast supply of cheap but often skilled labour in China. It is argued that China can become the manufacturing base for the rest of the world. At the moment this requires the participation of foreign companies which invest directly in China.

One reason for the activity of foreign companies in China is that there are few Chinese companies which have an international profile for their products. Most have no international exposure. If they do, it is usually to export and sell under a variety of brands either relatively unknown or belonging to some other company. Within China there is growth in the profile of Legend, China Keijian and TCL, but as yet these names mean little outside China. There are good reasons why most Chinese enterprises lack such an international orientation. Even today the economy is only half-open. Before the initiation of reform in 1978, it was a fully closed economy. The size of the domestic market means that companies can still grow to a reasonable size without having to export.

It is revealing that *Fortune*'s first China 100 list contains no privately owned company. There is still a strong legacy from the period of centralized physical planning. Most enterprises are either state-owned or in collective ownership of some kind. There may be governance problems which make operation within a market economy difficult.

In order to succeed internationally, Chinese enterprises need to develop two competencies, firstly the

▶

ability to create and manage a brand name and secondly an ability to operate in a competitive market environment with its sudden changes in demand, particularly at the international level. Haier is something of an exception, in being the world's number two refrigerator maker, after Whirlpool. It has quite deliberately cultivated its own brand name and targeted the most competitive markets. Its CEO Zhang Riumin has global ambitions, aspiring to place the company in the Fortune 500. Haier already sells its products in 138 countries. It is the market leader for small refrigerators in the USA. Its total worldwide sales are $7.5 billion, not dramatic by the standards of most large multinational companies, but impressive by the standards of a country just entering the global economy. While Haier is in collective ownership and rated only 57th in the China 100, it has a high international profile. This is an unusual combination.

Haier produces not just refrigerators, but a wide range of white goods – air-conditioners, freezers, washing machines, colour televisions, water heaters and microwave ovens, even computers and mobile phones. It has also ventured into the area of financial services. White goods are fairly standard products produced by the same methods throughout the world, for which there is a stable market. This market is not growing quickly in developed economies, where the demand is largely a replacement demand. As the rate of population increase has declined, the growth of the market has decelerated. An Electrolux planning review several years ago found that the growth of the market was unlikely to exceed 2–3% in the near future. Today the expectation might be even lower. On the other hand, Electrolux saw demand growing at a rate of

20% per annum in developing areas within Asia, Eastern Europe and Latin America. There is a rapidly growing demand in the fast developing economies of Asia, including China.

China offers an excellent base for a producer of white goods. Any domestic producer which reached a significant size might start to consider foreign markets. Up to now it has been a market difficult, but not impossible, for foreign producers to enter, as Electrolux has showed. Through joint ventures, Electrolux developed a manufacturing facility in China which it then used to export white goods to other Asian countries. Both Siemens and Samsung have also entered the market, as have a plethora of local producers. All this competition has cut profit margins significantly. However, Samsung has shown a sensitivity to the constraint on profit margins on standard products and has sought to move upmarket.

In the developed world, white goods are products which have been largely commoditized. The technology is well known and not subject to rapid change; the product is a standard product with standard technical specifications. There are significant economies of scale which tend to lead to a concentration of production within mature markets, but worldwide there is plenty of competition for markets. In order to differentiate the product, there are only relatively small features which can be adopted. It is a real challenge to discover a differentiating feature which allows an enterprise to brand its products. A name for quality and reliability is one, while a key issue for the purchaser is value for money. The challenge for Haier is to develop a core competence to brand its product.

The distinctive competency

Core competency is the term used in most texts on the internal environment. Some texts use the term *distinctive competency* for the same concept. 'Distinctive' focuses attention on the ability of the competency to define the organization. It is seen as unique to that enterprise and difficult to emulate, even beyond the short term. There are two main sources of distinctiveness; knowledge and competencies.

The knowledge which supports the competency is specific to the organization. Much institutional knowledge, particularly that which underpins the competency, is uncodified, that is, not spelt out in sufficient detail to allow the transfer of the competency to another enterprise and, probably in most cases, uncodifiable or unspecifiable, that is, impossible to specify in such detail.

Uncodified and uncodifiable knowledge refers to knowledge which is *tacit* rather than *explicit*, that is, cannot be described or articulated exactly. Such knowledge cannot be possessed by the individual alone but in some sense only by the institution or a team within the institution, that is, it cannot be fully appropriated by the individual. In other words, it can only be defined with reference to 'networked' people and 'embedded' processes. Without the networks specific to the enterprise and the processes which give meaning to these networks, there would be no competency. Neither networks nor processes can be disentangled from the enterprise itself. They help to identify the enterprise.

The competencies are the result of sunk costs, that is, past investments or commitments which are irreversible and cannot be retrieved. They usually have to be repeated by others if they wish to imitate or recreate the competency. A first mover, or an incumbent, has the advantage of having already sunk the relevant resources in such a commitment or investment. A follower may find a faster route to developing the same capability, but the process is never instantaneous.

However, sunk investments refer to commitments whose opportunity cost is lower for incumbents than for new entrants since the latter have to repeat in some form the investments undertaken in making the commitment. This would include the many investments in the establishment of a good reputation, securing full legal protection for intellectual property rights or developing the specialized techniques or methods associated with operating well within a particular sector of the economy.

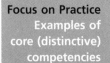

Focus on Practice
Examples of core (distinctive) competencies

Institutional knowledge
- Institutional R&D capability
- Company know-how
- Exceptional technological capability
- Rapid transformation of technology into new products and processes
- Functional knowledge pools

Engineering
- Development of sophisticated engineered elevator control systems
- Digital technology
- Deep knowledge of silver-halide materials
- Miniaturization of components and products

Design
- Production of technologically sophisticated automobile engines

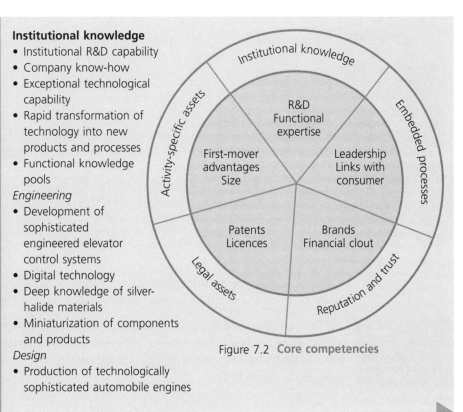

Figure 7.2 **Core competencies**

- Design of advanced running shoes
- Knowledge of customer value systems
- Shared assumptions and values

Embedded processes
- Leadership style and commitment
- Links into (institutional understanding for) the world of the consumer
- Effective and efficient control of inventories through point of purchase data collection methods
- Access to distribution channels
- Effective use of logistics management techniques
- Institutional relationship with government
- Internal communications, systems/culture
- Staff identification and commitment
- Motivating, empowering and retaining employees
- Staff training and development

Reputation and trust
- Brand
- Effective promotion of brand name products
- Dominant size and presence
- Installed base
- Financial clout

Legal protection
- Concession or licence agreements
- Patents
- Ownership of prime sites

Activity-specific assets
- Investments in dominant size, market share and image
- Sunk investment in sites, exploration, experimentation, specialized equipment
- Investment in economies of scale, such as in distribution (low unit stock levels, low unit delivery cost)
- First-mover investments in production capacity

Source: van der Heijden, 1996: 64–5.

The information above illustrates the great variety of competencies which can exist. There are two ways of testing whether a competency is genuinely a competency.

Testing the basic characteristics

The first test requires a five-point check of whether a given strategic asset or capability possesses the basic characteristics to qualify as a competency. The translation from capability to competency depends on the satisfaction of each of the five criteria indicated in Figure 7.3.

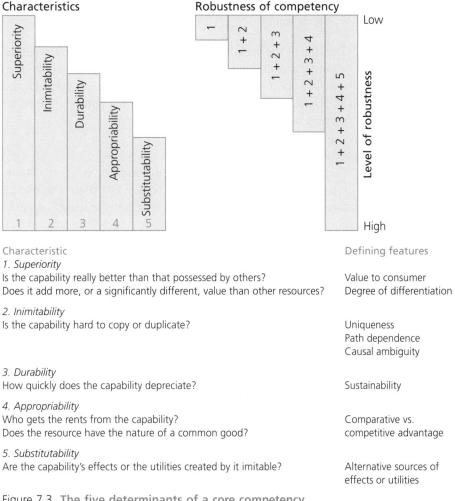

Characteristic	Defining features
1. Superiority	
Is the capability really better than that possessed by others?	Value to consumer
Does it add more, or a significantly different, value than other resources?	Degree of differentiation
2. Inimitability	
Is the capability hard to copy or duplicate?	Uniqueness
	Path dependence
	Causal ambiguity
3. Durability	
How quickly does the capability depreciate?	Sustainability
4. Appropriability	
Who gets the rents from the capability?	Comparative vs.
Does the resource have the nature of a common good?	competitive advantage
5. Substitutability	
Are the capability's effects or the utilities created by it imitable?	Alternative sources of
	effects or utilities

Figure 7.3 **The five determinants of a core competency**

Superiority

Firstly, the resource, or more exactly the capability, must contribute value to the organization by contributing value to the consumer of the product or service, yielding the latter a utility of some kind. The value derives from its ability to help the enterprise to exploit opportunities or neutralize threats in the external environment of that enterprise. It derives from the ability of the organization to meet a customer's wants, and to meet those wants in a way superior to that of other enterprises. If a capability has value, but not the other characteristics, then the enterprise has competitive parity in the relevant area, but not competitive advantage. It can only aspire to earn a normal profit.

It must also be unusual in its capacity to do this, at best unique. Uniqueness rarely attaches to one resource alone, but to a combination of resources put together as a capability:

- A particular mine is almost invariably unique in that no two minerals are ever exactly the same

- 11 footballers play as a team, with a unique style of play and mix of skills, not as individuals.

The sum of the parts is more than the individual parts and once more unique.

For a capability to be rare, few enterprises should possess the same capability and, from the point of view of the enterprise possessing that capability, preferably none. Rarity allows the creation of at least a temporary competitive advantage and the earning of a temporary above-normal return.

Inimitability

Even if it is not unique, a competency must be costly to imitate, or it must require a significant commitment of time to achieve such a duplication. There are three factors which might make it costly to imitate, in some cases extremely costly:

1. The competency is the product of a unique historical experience, which may be long and difficult to trace out in all its detail. An enterprise imitating the experience might somehow have to repeat this history. In the most extreme case the enterprise was in the right place and at the right time to develop the competency, a conjuncture unlikely to be repeated since the context is forever changing, in which case the experience cannot be repeated.
2. The competency has an ambiguous cause. Often it is unclear what it is that constitutes the core competency. Something with undefined characteristics is difficult to explain in terms of cause and effect. It is impossible to explain why the enterprise has it. Competitors have difficulty working out what the competency comprises, and therefore how to recreate it.
3. The competency has its origins in socially complex interactions. Again the issue is the dense system of networks in which individuals interact closely with each other, combining individual skills and experience in ways which cannot be fully described, let alone explained or imitated. There is a collective embodiment of the competency.

Durability

The competency may be of transitory uniqueness, in which case the competitive advantage is only short-lived and of little value. Because machine tools may last for a long time – as long as 50 years – they are heavily patented, whereas computers are not, because both the product cycle and the technology cycle associated with them are so short. The presence of durability makes advantage sustainable and above-normal profit a real possibility.

Appropriability

Can the enterprise take full advantage of the value created by the competency, or do others also benefit? Does the competency have any characteristics of a public good so that it is a 'common' good, which others can share? Even if it is not a common good, can other stakeholder groups capture some part of the benefit? If the asset could be acquired in the market, would the operation of a competitive market compete away any rent and the seller rather than the buyer gain from the value created?

If there is a genuine core competency, the answer to all these questions is no. There is no common good aspect and the market is imperfect. Who is able to earn the rent from a particular asset or competency? The assumption is that all the gains are made by the enterprise.

Substitutability

The competency must not be capable of substitution. Substitution should be understood in its broadest sense, as the utility derived from, or the effect of consuming, the product or service, not the nature of the product or service with its particular attributes. For example, an alternative to a new oilfield might be a better method of extraction from an existing field or a better method of refining the raw material. The lack of substitutability means that no competitor, through its own action or strategy, could find an alternative for the asset, capability or competency.

Making a checklist of these characteristics and answering the key questions in Figure 7.3 enables a strategist to prioritize the development and exploitation of different competencies. It allows the enterprise to select those activities for which it genuinely has a competitive advantage.

But what are the activities which add most value to an enterprise's products or service, or, in which activities do the core competencies find their obvious home?

The following Strategy in Action shows how capabilities are developed into competencies.

Strategy in Action   Business models in broking

'For years consumers have been paying exorbitantly high prices to get information that is selectively controlled by their brokers. What we've done is to totally eliminate the back office process, automate it and provide institution-quality information by putting it at their fingertips.'

Christos Cotsakos, CEO of E*Trade

'Our mission is to empower the investor. All our information is for free.'

CEO of an electronic broker

The adjectives used to describe online trading are expressive of the difference in service provided – simple, convenient, user-friendly, private, safe, informative, pleasant and cheap. As of 1996 the full broking service cost was as high as $150 per trade and the price nearer $200. Discount broking was much cheaper, at a cost just under $50 and a price just over $50. Online broking costs and prices were between $15 and $20. Since then the price per trade has fallen as low as $10 per trade, and finally to nothing for two brokers.

The advent of online broking has made it much more competitive. There are four main groups of business model employed. Between them they manage to realize customization by large market segments:

Click-and-brick models (just over half)

1.   Inquiry model (about 25% of all brokers)
The brokers provide the clients with the traditional full-service offerings. There may be detailed account information provided online, but no trading occurs online. Brokers include A. G. Edwards, D. A. Davidson and Dain Rauscher. The level of personal face-to-face advice is high and consequently the level of commissions charged is also high.

2.   The layered model (about 15%)
These brokers could be described as providing a flexible full service, both a traditional full service and online trading, in other words a bundle of rather complex services. It is up to the customer to choose which to use. This may cause some channel confu-

sion. The minimum account balance required may be high, for example Morgan Stanley asks for $50,000. The costs of such brokers are likely to be high. This group includes a lot of the big names – Morgan Stanley, Goldman Sachs, Merrill Lynch, Paine Webster and Prudential Securities.

3. The discount model (slightly more than 15%)
This group deliberately set out to undercut the traditional brokers by charging low commissions. Technically this group was always innovative. It includes Fidelity, Schwab, CSFB Durel and TD Waterhouse.

Click-only models (just under half)
4. E-broker model
This service is designed for active traders. E-brokers compete on price rather than quality. Free Trade.com and Brokerage America charge no fee. They derive their income from banner advertising sales and kickbacks on order placements from market makers as payment for maintaining an order flow. Others do charge a fee, including Ameritrade, Dutek and E*Trade. There is therefore fierce price competition between members of this group.

What is likely to happen in the future? Group 1 is likely to merge with group 2 as more brokers and their customers become confident about using e-broking. The discount group, group 3, is likely to disappear in the future, moving in two directions, one part moving to group 2 and the other part moving into the specialist broker group, group 4. The end result may therefore be two groups, 2 and 4.

There are a number of ratings systems that rank the various e-brokers, which illustrate the core competencies of such enterprises. The best and most comprehensive of these systems is that of Gomez Advisers; others include Barron's and Smart Money. Ignoring the heading of commissions and charges, that is, the price charged by the broker, there are four main competencies contained within the Gomez categories:

1. Creating a website which is easy to use
The main elements facilitating ease of use include functionality and the simplicity of account opening and the process of making a transaction. The degree of integration of different features and the consistency of design and navigation through the website are important.

It is best to address the issue by asking the following questions. How easily can a consumer get access to the information he or she wants? Is access customized according to the nature of the particular customer segment, whatever the nature of the customer, whether he or she is a life goal planner, a hyperactive trader, a serious investor or a one-stop shopper? Are tutorials available explaining how to use the site? If the answer to these questions is yes, then the site is easy to use.

2. Instilling confidence in the client
This is largely a matter of reputation, which would reflect the financial strength of the organization, including the size of its capital, degree of independence and technical capacity. Can the information from the broker be regarded as objective and unaffected by any other relationships which the broker might have? Clearly the running form of the broker considered over as long a period as possible, particularly times of crisis, is significant in making such an appraisal.

Will the firm be there if there is a crisis for the client? The phone response times and the ability to deal quickly and effectively with simple technical questions are relevant, as are the backup between phone, email and branches in reinforcing the provision of the customer services required. The transparency of operation and easy availability of information concerning these operations is important. Is it clear what the firm is promising and does it deliver on its promises?

3. Providing on-site resources
Again there is a long list but the heart of this competency is the ability to do the appropriate research and disseminate the results of that research, or a means to enable the client to do the necessary research and understand the results. The resources comprise information organized in an easily usable way, including real-time quotes, charts, new updates, editorial comment and screening tools for stocks and mutual funds. The customer should be able to know the availability of specific products, his or her ability to transact in each product line and his or her ability to seek and have met service requests online.

4. Establishing a strong relationship with the client
This depends on the ability to understand the client and provide exactly what the customer wants, for example in online help, tutorials, a glossary or the

answer to frequently asked questions. It should be possible to customize a site and use specific customer data to facilitate future transactions. It should be possible to meet a wide range of personal needs in a fully secure environment. This includes the personalization of all data, including the real-time updating of stock holdings and account balances. It should include a facility to update the client on anything important which might happen to a specific asset held in the customer's portfolio.

Most of the leaders, as might be expected, have improved their performance, but one or two of the top ten have lost ground and need to renew their strategy, such as TD Waterhouse and Datek (see Table 7.1).

Table 7.1 **The discount broker top ten in USA**

	Overall score (2002)	Score and position 1998	
Charles Schwab	7.27	6.68	7th
Fidelity Investments	7.21	5.97	17th
E*Trade	7.01	6.50	9th
Harrisdirect	6.57		
Ameritrade	6.30	5.71	20th
TD Waterhouse	6.13	7.21	2nd
Datek	5.98	6.32	11th
Merrill Lynch	5.95		
Cititrade	5.94		
WellsTrade	5.93		

Source: www.gomez.com.

Analysis of the value-creating chain

It is possible to generalize about the nature of the activities engaged in by any enterprise, whatever the sector. A fully integrated company producing a simple product like steel engages in a range of different activities. These activities comprise both *upstream activities*, such as procuring the raw materials of coal, iron ore and limestone, and their transport to blast furnace or smelter, and *downstream activities*, such as selling the finished steel to companies using that steel, like automobile manufacturers or construction firms. It also comprises production and, where appropriate, assembly, in this case making the steel in furnaces and then rolling it into appropriate shapes.

Primary and support activities

Porter has introduced a rather different distinction, that between primary activities and support activities, as shown in Figure 7.4.

Primary activities are those which are most important in adding value to the product or those involved in either producing or selling the product, that is, the core productive processes, the sale and distribution of the product and its later maintenance or service. The primary activities include operations, inbound and outbound logistics, marketing and sales, and service:

- *Operations.* These are often considered as the activities which define the nature of the enterprise. They are the activities which help convert the inputs provided by inbound logistics into the finished products distributed by outbound logistics. They include such activities as machining, assembly, testing/quality control, packaging and equipment maintenance.
- *Inbound logistics.* This includes activities, such as materials handling, input or component warehousing and inventory control, used to receive, store and distribute to the appropriate place the inputs necessary in producing the final good. These activities require a broad range of physical, financial and human resources.

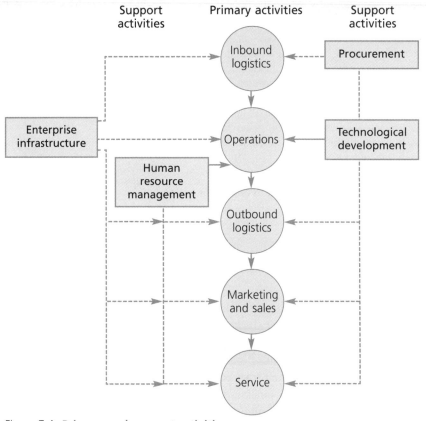

Figure 7.4 **Primary and support activities**

- *Outbound logistics.* This includes activities, such as finished goods warehousing, materials handling and order processing, which involve collecting, storing and physically distributing the final product, either to the distribution channels or directly to the final customers.
- *Marketing and sales.* These include the activities in which the enterprise develops advertising or promotional strategies, selects appropriate distribution channels, and selects, develops and supports its sales force in order better to identify potential customers and persuade them to buy the product. It includes purchase order processing, customer account management and the transfer of data on sales to headquarters or suppliers.
- *Service.* This comprises activities designed to enhance and maintain a product's value, such as installation, repair, training in use and product adjustment to suit particular needs. It also includes the giving of guarantees and warranties.

Support activities are those which provide support for the primary activities, helping to bind them together, including servicing the enterprise's infrastructure, such as its control systems, human resource management (staff development), technological development (R&D) and procurement or purchasing.

- *Procurement.* These are the activities involved in purchasing any of the inputs required for production. Some are consumed in production, such as raw materials, others continue in existence over a period of time much longer than the production cycle, such as intermediate goods of various kinds, equipment, plant and buildings.

- *Technological development.* These are the activities involved in improving the product or developing a new product. They include R&D and product design or engineering.
- *Human resource management.* These include all those activities which are intended to develop and improve staff – recruiting, hiring, training, appraising, devising reward systems and motivating staff – in order to ensure that the enterprise has staff with the right skills, experience and motivation.
- *Enterprise infrastructure.* This includes a number of systems which facilitate the operation and development of the enterprise. The systems infrastructure includes the whole apparatus of strategy making itself, as well as more general operational supports, such as accounting or financial controls, management information systems, legal services and public and government relations.

Not all sectors of the economy can be analysed in terms of a value chain. It is most apt where manufacture is involved, less relevant where services are involved.

The value chain can be analysed from different perspectives, which link up with the generic strategies analysed in Chapters 8, 9 and 10:

- the location or concentration of core competencies and resources in general, particularly in the context of maintaining a competitive advantage through innovation
- cost minimization
- product differentiation.

Each of these is dealt with in turn in this and the next three chapters.

A fully vertically integrated enterprise would include all these activities. However, it need not do so since different firms will have competencies which are relevant to different areas of activity. The stress on different competencies can lead to a focusing on certain activities as the source of competitive advantage, sometimes without the other activities being relinquished, at others with significant outsourcing. It is easy to envisage specialization in what an enterprise is good at.

Specialization
This might involve, for example, a three-way split of an integrated enterprise. One company might concentrate on inbound logistics, one on the production process and the other on marketing and sales. The picture might then look like Figure 7.5.

In steel production the first company might be the mining company which produces the iron ore, the second the steel company and the third the company that trades in steel. It is also possible to break up the company even further, separating almost all the activities into independent enterprises.

Non-linear value creation
The picture created by Porter is a generic one, one which is supposed to encompass all enterprises. The value creation envisaged by Porter, in which activities occur in a

Primary activities   Support activities

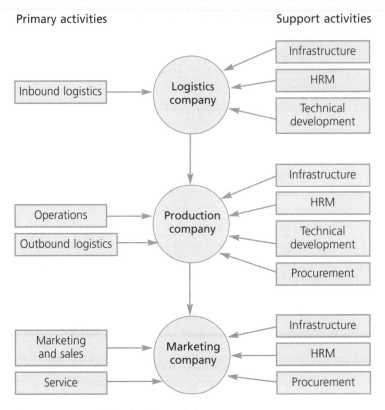

Figure 7.5 **Specialization by activity**

linear sequence, may not be a good description of the modern service enterprise, or even the modern manufacturing enterprise in which a package of services surrounds the product or products. Not infrequently, the modern enterprise is a complex, non-linear value creator in which different customers put together their own products by picking and choosing the combinations of value activities which most satisfy their needs. The supplying enterprise should not organize itself in a series of sequential activities.

Focus on Practice
Merlin
Biosciences

Merlin is the brainchild of Sir Christopher Evans (nicknamed Dr Strangebug), a representative of the new breed of scientist entrepreneurs. It is a $375 million venture capital company specializing in the funding of projects in the area of cancer, heart disease and other areas of medicine, founded in 1996, and part of the rather late wave of biotechnology start-ups which has been occurring in Europe over the last five years. Sir Christopher epitomizes the changing role of universities in the English-speaking world. He has an early academic background in bioscience and then a history of participation in biotechnology companies in both the USA, between 1983 and 1987, and after 1987 in England. He currently holds six professorships at English universities. The company is located near Cambridge University and therefore near to the Wellcome Trust Sanger Institute, which is part of the human genome project, or at

Focus on Practice
cont'd

least its public university stream. Cambridge has become an example of what Evans calls the biovalleys, clusters of companies around major research facilities.

Evans has himself founded 20 companies and through Merlin funded another 75. So far there has been no investment failure. This is because out of the 1,000 or so projects vetted each year, only 15–20 are chosen for funding. The team making the selection and overseeing it have considerable expertise and experience in the areas of bioscience. Merlin partners sit on the boards of all the companies in the Merlin portfolio, keeping a close eye on the development of the relevant projects. The focus is very much on the progress of research and the successful application for a patent.

Source: Adapted from Orr, 2002: 19.

It is much more difficult to map such an enterprise, what has been called a *'value constellation' enterprise*, an organization which appears to be becoming more common. Merlin Biosciences is such a company.

Focus on Practice
The modern bank

A contemporary bank can be used to illustrate a value constellation enterprise (see for comparison the Strategy in Action on Deutsche Bank (Chapter 6) and Charles Schwab earlier in this chapter) .

There are three possibilities:

1. The activities could be provided by just one company, a universal bank.
2. The core competencies could define three separate companies:
   - a computer service company which could handle the ATMs and the phone banking
   - a core bank doing traditional retail banking work
   - a financial advice and management company.

In other words the structure could be driven by market segmentation rather than by competencies in particular activities. There may be a number of distinct market segments:

- One group of customers may require only savings accounts
- Other customers want only ATM services and cheque account access
- Others want the full deposit services
- A further group wants the full retail services including both savings accounts and cheque accounts, and mortgage or home finance
- A fifth group is looking for portfolio management services and access to phone banking.

3. In theory the activities could be unbundled, so that there might be as many as five firms providing the different services:
   - a core bank providing cheques, mortgages, savings and deposit taking
   - an investment house providing superannuation and financial management activities
   - a clearing house to do the clearing services for the core bank
   - a trading house which handles the financial market transactions of the investment house
   - a computer services company which services the above companies.

Focus on Practice
cont'd

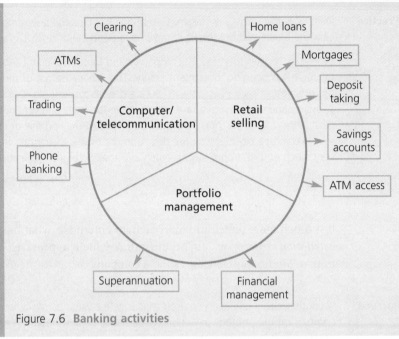

Figure 7.6 **Banking activities**

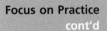

Strategy in Action John Doerr and Kleiner Perkins Caulfield & Byers, the leading venture capital firm in Silicon Valley

'We are participating in the largest legal creation of new wealth in the history of the planet.' *John Doerr*

The main role of a venture capital (VC) firm is linking those with funds with those who need funds. Venture capital firms provide capital to small companies which are capital-poor but ideas-rich and risk-high. They specialize in such areas as computing and biotechnology, in which the partners have an expertise, developed by participation in previous start-ups and floats. Their ability to persuade those with funds to invest depends on their reputation and growing expertise for making good investments. The main role is to provide capital, taking a share in that company proportionate to the contribution, but lesser roles are to contribute inputs necessary to success. This is a matter of a timely initial public offering (IPO), and assistance of a more general kind – placing personnel on the board of directors and providing advice and contacts. The role of the venture capital firm should end when the target is able to operate independently.

John Doerr, an electrical engineer with an MBA from Harvard Business School, worked for Intel between 1974 and 1980 as one of the firm's top-ranked sales

executives. He familiarized himself with communications and information and in 1980 joined the venture capital firm Kleiner Perkins. His timing was perfect. By 1983 the computer revolution was in full swing, with IPOs becoming popular. In that year venture capitalists invested US$2.9 billion in start-up companies, something like five times the amount three years earlier. Annual investment hovered around $2.2–3.9 billion over the next decade.

John Doerr has been called 'the avatar of the Web', the first person to recognize the potential of the Internet. A main feature of his strategy was to create a network of Kleiner Perkins' companies assisting each other. Intuit's Quicken software would incorporate the Netscape Navigator; Netscape and Macromedia were early adopters of Sun Microsystem's Java software. Through regular meetings of senior managers, these companies built up strong relationships and helped each other.

Doerr's early successes in raising money for high-tech companies included Compaq, Sun and Lotus. In 1993 *Forbes* described him as the finest venture capitalist of this generation, and in 1998 *Fortune* called him the 'industry's only celebrity venture capitalist'. In 1995 the total venture capital investment suddenly jumped to US$7.1 billion and peaked in 2000 at US$104.9 billion invested in 7,656 deals. By that stage the demand for attractive start-ups exceeded the supply.

The presence of John Doerr on the board of a private company was enough to guarantee the success of a float. The firm and its client investors, early to invest in the new dot-coms, saw the value of their holdings soar by as much as 300% a year. During this period Kleiner Perkins assisted Amazon.com, Juniper Networks, FreeMarkets, @Home Network and Handspring as well as Netscape Communications. It also financed Cerent, maker of optical equipment, which was sold to Cisco in 1999 for $7.2 billion.

Usually Kleiner Perkins waited two and a half years between putting together a new fund. The funds put together in 1994 and 1996 were very successful, the funds of 1999 and 2000 much less likely to succeed. The latter two were originally intended to raise a combined $1 billion. Investors included such prestigious organizations as Harvard University, the Ford Foundation and Stanford University as well as wealthy individuals such as Michael Dell and Steve Case. The 2000 fund was scaled back from US$600 million to US$475 million.

Kleiner Perkins makes its money by collecting an annual fee of 2% of the fund's committed capital and taking 30% of the fund's net profits after payment to its limited partners of all their invested capital, 5–10% higher than the industry standard. Profits are booked on the basis of the price of the shares at the time they are distributed to Kleiner investors.

The example of Kleiner Perkins identifies three main competencies:

1. The ability to identify a start-up with the potential to become a winner. This depended on reading the market for new products well and judging the ability of the new enterprise to exploit that opportunity.

2. The ability to manage a portfolio of specific assets, the investment in the start-up firms, in such a way as to make the capital available at an opportune time.

3. The ability to make a broader contribution to the start-up firm when required. The role of the venture capital firm was to help fill any entrepreneurial gaps and present the firm to the investors in a favourable light.

Between 1995 and 2001, 439 dot-coms went public, raising US$33.5 billion. Many were to fail when the market went into reverse in 2000–1. Companies were floated which had little prospect of making a profit. Some were not genuinely high-tech. Kleiner Perkins departed from its usual role by investing in companies before public sale.

A typical investment was Amazon.com. By 1996 Amazon.com, needing finance to allow the company to expand, sought a venture capital firm, with the obvious candidate being Kleiner Perkins. A number of venture capital firms were interested, notably General Atlantic, which valued the new company at US$50 million, raising this to US$60–70 million, with some conditions, when Bezos claimed a value of US$100 million. Amazon.com opted for Kleiner Perkins as a partner and it provided US$8 million in cash based on a US$60 million valuation. Doerr came onto the Amazon.com board and persuaded Scott Cook, the chairman of Intuit, to join him. When the company went public in 1997, a process supervised by Kleiner Perkins, Kleiner Perkins still held about 11% of the company. The preferred stock was converted to more than three million common shares in the IPO, by the end of 1997 worth $156 million, an increase in value of about twenty times the original investment achieved over a period of about a year. Those shares were later distributed to the funds' limited partners, which included the chiefs or founders of Intel, Sun Microsystems, America Online, Lotus and @Home.

Banks illustrate well the departure from a linear sequence of activities, which is common among service companies, but such companies are still characterized by their core competencies. Obviously the market segments define the relevant core competencies required. A banking institution will be inclined to specialize where it already has a distinct competency. The market segments chosen as the focus of activity, or the associated core competencies which support them, together define the core business of the enterprise.

'Core' core
competencies
and core
activities

Some competencies are so obvious they can be regarded as 'core' core competencies. Any bank, retail or wholesale, must have the ability to carry out the prudential checks which identify good credit risks, that is, by its nature it must be in the business of risk management. The image or good reputation of the bank is also important and follows largely from this ability to carry out the proper prudential checks.

There are many examples of 'core' core competencies. A football club must have players who can play football well, and play well together as a team. A fashion company must have designers who have flair and creativity. A biotech company must have researchers who are good at research.

In the end, however, the 'core' core competencies are not enough. The enterprise must be able to sell a product to the customer that the customer actually wants and it must deliver the product at a cost and with an efficiency which enables the enterprise to be viable. This involves a number of core competencies which are specific to the product area. One core competence is never enough – there must be a minimum of at least two.

How many?

If there is a minimum number of core competencies for a viable business, is there a maximum? There appears to be a limit on the number of core competencies which any enterprise can have at a given time. This follows from the nature of a core or distinct competence. An attempt to expand the number of competencies beyond a limited number is likely to result in a weakening of all the existing competencies. Keeping the core competencies in good condition requires a significant effort. That effort must be rationed. For example, trying to be a universal bank might mean trying to retain too many core competencies and doing nothing well.

Just how many a maximum might be is difficult to say. The absolute maximum is said to be five, but it is more usual to think in terms of three or four.

Case Study   Branding a sports team – Manchester United

The lifeblood of soccer lies not at the international level but in club competition. The really big money is concentrated on the elite European football clubs. Ever since the European Commission ruled that it was in breach of fair trade to deny a footballer the right to earn his living wherever he chose to, the best footballers in the world have made a beeline for Europe, or at least those parts of Europe which have teams capable of paying them handsomely. The best go to the elite leagues – the English premier league, Italy, Spain and Germany.

Real Madrid, the European champions league winner of last year, has a habit of purchasing the player of the year. In 2003 it was David Beckham. In 2002, at £33 million, it was Ronaldo, the match winner for Brazil in the World Cup and the 1997 European Footballer of the Year. In 2001 it was Zidane for £47 million (European Footballer of the Year in 1998 when he helped France

win the World Cup), and in 2000 Figo for £40 million (European Footballer of the Year in 2000). At the time of writing, the whole team looks like Table 7.2 in terms of its prodigious cost.

Even within the lesser leagues, there are elite teams such as Rangers, Celtic or Feyenoord which can afford to employ at least one or two of the highest paid. Those with lesser ability or unrealized potential can find other European leagues and other teams. This is very much a cosmopolitan industry. The 2002 World Cup was kicked off by two teams, France, whose members largely play in Britain, and Senegal, whose members largely play in France, a contrast which very much captured the essence of the times.

The most famous of all the clubs is Manchester United. It has a very rich tradition. The Munich air crash in 1956, in which most of the famous Busby Babes were killed, is

Table 7.2 **The cost of Real Madrid's players**

	(£m)
Zinedine Zidane	47
Raul	40
Luis Figo	40
Ronaldo	33
David Beckham	25
Roberto Carlos	18
Ivan Helguera	12
Claude Makelele	12
Iker Casillas	8
Michel Sagado	5
Esteban Cambiasso	5
Fernando Hierro	3
Total	248

part of that tradition. Busby, the coach, and Bobby Charlton, probably England's most famous player, survived that crash, the latter to become famous helping England to win the World Cup in 1966 and Manchester United the European Cup in 1968. Other clubs, such as Real Madrid and Bayern Munich, are as well known but are not quite in the same 'branding' league, and with nothing like the value of Manchester United, the Red Devils. Indeed Real Madrid has enormous debt problems which it staves off by property manipulations allowed by a supportive local government.

Worldwide, Manchester United is said to have 50 million fans, 30 million of whom are in Asia, and 200 fan clubs – 151 in the UK, 25 in Ireland and 24 in the rest of the world, including one in the USA. Four of the 23 main England squad at the 2002 World Cup were Manchester United players, but it also had players playing for England's great rival Argentina, South Africa, France (2) and Ireland, whose controversial captain Roy Keane was probably the most famous absentee from the World Cup. It included for many years one of the great names in world soccer, David Beckham, who has increased his fame by marrying Posh Spice. By American sporting standards, Beckham is paid a modest amount, £7.5 million a year over the term of his new four-year contract. He has the ability to make many times this in sponsorships and endorsements. His team gains greatly from his presence, both in skill and spectator support.

The problems of football clubs as business enterprises

It is possible that, by the end of 2003, Manchester United will be the only premier league club to make a profit. In

2001 only seven of the twenty clubs made a profit and three of those only just broke even. Arsenal, which achieved the double, made the highest but not much more than Man United. Three clubs lost more than £20 million. Lesser teams have even bigger problems.

Many clubs rely on broadcasting fees. The most famous clubs would prefer to see most of the fees come to them, rather than spread amongst all the members of the leagues. Getting the right to broadcast live games in the major leagues and competitions is costly but generates enormous advertising revenue because of the mass audience. The success of BSkyB, one of the only pay-television networks to make a profit, is due to its securing the rights to televise live the English premier league, probably the most popular league in the world. The pay-television companies understand this very well.

The difficulties of pay television have spread to the clubs who should receive revenues from the networks. Many of the lesser English clubs are bankrupt as a result of the collapse of the ITV Digital network, which had bought the rights to televise live their matches. Instead of receiving £69 million from ITV Digital, the clubs are to receive only £20 million from BSkyB. Very often it is only the largesse of a private sponsor which has saved the teams from disappearing.

One of the strengths of Manchester United is the diversity of its sources of income. It receives its income in three roughly equal parts: gate receipts (its ground Old Trafford holds 67,500 people and is usually full); the sale of broadcasting rights; and an assortment of other sources, including the sale of merchandise by the club, sponsorship (Vodafone and Nike are the main sponsors) and the renting out of facilities for conferences. This healthy balance of sources is unusual for a soccer club. Man United has the least local support base of all the premier league teams, with almost half the fans being born more than 20 miles from Old Trafford. In 2001 Man United had a turnover well above any other premier club, including Arsenal, at over £130 million ($190 million). Its expected revenue in 2003 is nearly £150 million. As a consequence of such a good and relatively stable income stream, its capitalization on the stock market at one time reached £1 billion.

Man United was listed on London's stock exchange in 1991. Thirty-seven other clubs in Europe are now listed (Table 7.3). Only the British government prevented Rupert Murdoch purchasing Manchester United. In 1998 Murdoch's company BSkyB bid over £600 million for the club but was thwarted by the regulators who prevented the takeover. Currently the club is worth less than £325 million.

The recent fall in market capitalization partly reflects

Table 7.3 **2002 market capitalization of the ten most valuable soccer clubs**

	US$mill	£ mill
Man United (England)	466	300
Juventus (Italy)	241	155
Rangers (Scotland)	139	90
Arsenal (England)	135	87
Lazio (Italy)	111	72
Roma (Italy)	96	62
Ajax (the Netherlands)	73	47
Borussia Dortmund (Germany)	58	37
Newcastle United (England)	50	32
Parken (Denmark)	49	31

Source: Heller, 2002: 34.

the general fall in the market but also the particular problems of soccer clubs and the industry in general. On Forbes' simple formula of value (value being four times revenue), Man United should be worth something closer to more than £650 million, or approximately what Murdoch was willing to pay for the club. The most valuable sporting clubs in the USA, the Washington Redskins and the New York Yankees, are worth a little less.

The biggest problem for most clubs is not so much on the income side, although many are dangerously dependent on the revenue from the sale of TV rights, as on the cost side. The greatest difficulty arises first from the need to pay their players. Transfer fees have reached dizzying heights, as the figures for Real Madrid, given in Table 7.2, show. Weekly salary bills are also huge and growing. In the last five years the total wage bill of Manchester United has moved from 27% to 39% of its total revenue, 33% being down to the players alone. Other clubs have a much higher proportion. There are other demands for financial resources. Players have to be kept fit and well. There are teams of staff to do this. Training facilities must be up to date. Clubs also have to keep their stadium modern and attractive to the fans. They also have to use the most up-to-date communications and information technology.

The 2002/2003 season

The scramble by institutional investors during the early 1990s to cash in on a lucrative future for soccer has come to an end. While attendance at matches is increasing and the income generated by the spectators is on the rise, some sources of income are contracting and costs are still rising dramatically. The situation for the premier league teams and the promoted teams, in order of league position, in 2001 is shown in Table 7.4.

In 2001 the 20 English premiership clubs spent as much as £234 million on the transfer of players. In 2002 the figure was very much less, at £146 million. 20% of that, £30 million, was spent by Manchester United on one player, Rio Ferdinand, the English international star of the 2002 World Cup, partly as a response to Man United's failure to win a trophy in 2001. In response to tightening financial constraints, there have been many loan deals in which a player is lent to another club, thus removing him from its wage bill but not adding through transfer fees to the costs of the other club.

The fall in the share prices of soccer clubs has reflected low returns, poor corporate governance and rising wage bills. Market capitalizations have been falling below the value of the player squads. This fall has made it difficult for clubs to raise equity capital to pay for stadium improvements and player transfers. As a substitute source of finance, a number of teams, notably those with a large and loyal spectator base, have negotiated deals in which they securitize future ticket receipts, that is, they issue securities to raise a form of debt finance. These securities are attractive for pension funds to hold. This method of raising finance is popular in Britain with famous clubs such as Leeds and Newcastle and is rising in popularity in other European countries. Such debt has its dangers if the numbers of spectators dwindle for a team facing short-term difficulties.

The pressure on club income and the significance for club survival of declining income from television rights is shown by the postponement by two weeks of the start of the Serie A Italian soccer league in 2002. This resulted from a dispute over television rights. Two pay-television networks were involved, the Telepiu network of Vivendi Universal, which was in the process of being bought by Murdoch, and the Stream network, already controlled by Murdoch, which have been in competition to secure the rights for individual teams, a competitive element which will disappear with the merger of the two networks. Lucrative contracts were signed by the high flyers such as Juventus and AC Milan, at respectively €54 million and €49 million, to televise live the home matches of the clubs. Lesser clubs without contracts expected €10 million but were offered only four. RAI, the state broadcaster, offered to pay only half of what it paid in 2001 to show highlights of games on free television, €44 million instead of €88 million. In the season 2001/2002 Serie A teams made a combined loss of about €700 million, with the famous club Fiorentina going bankrupt.

In England the threat came from the European Commission who, to provide an opening for BBC and ITV, ended BSkyB's exclusive contract. However, BSkyB won the relevant tenders.

Table 7.4 **2001 results (£m)**

	Pre-tax profits and losses	Turnover	Main shareholders
Arsenal	29.4	62.94	Star Alliance (D Fiszman) Lady Nina Bracewell-Smith David Dean Granada
Liverpool	0.41	82.37	David Moores Granada Stephen Morgan
Manchester United	21.78	130.64	BSkyB The Cubic Expression Company Moutbarrow
Newcastle United	−8.85	54.92	Douglas Hall
Leeds United	−7.59	86.25	Schroders
Chelsea	−10.45	67.26	Ken Bates
West Ham United	−4.74	38.07	Terence Brown
Aston Villa	0.14	39.42	Ellis Family
Tottenham Hotspur	−3.47	48.40	Enic
Blackburn Rovers	−31.06	17.50	BRFC Investments
Southhampton	−0.20	24.38	Invesco
Middlesborough	−21.91	29.96	Gibson O'Neil
Fulham	−23.25	9.91	Fulham Leisure Holdings (Mohamed Al Fayed)
Charlton Athletic	0.32	28.32	Richard Murray
Everton	−3.65	32.85	True Blue Holdings (Bill Kenwright Consortium)
Bolton Wanderers	−8.9	14.49	Eddie Davies
Sunderland	3.01	46.02	Robert Murray
Manchester City	−0.62	32.36	Trust interests of D. M. Makin and J. C. Wardle
West Bromwich Albion	1.69	8.51	Paul Thomson
Birmingham City	−2.63	13.29	Sport Newspapers

Source: Garrahan, 2002b.

Even if the number of games televised is increased, the net impact is likely to reduce the revenue below one billion pounds.

An appropriate strategy – seeking both silver and gold

The appropriate strategy depends on who is considered. What is good for the club is not necessarily good for the league, the national team or the global state of the sport. It is useful to concentrate attention on the club, specifically on the strategy adopted by Man United itself.

Man United's self-proclaimed twin-track business strategy is expressed on their website in their own words:

Manchester United's ambition to be the most successful team in football will be achieved by developing a successful and sus-

tainable business. To this end, the football and the commercial operations of Manchester United work hand-in-hand. There really is 'only one United'.

Success as a football team depends very much on whether the team is winning and whether it wins national or European championships. In 1999 Manchester United managed to win the English premier league, the English Cup and the European Champions Cup, a trio of victories which reinforced the already high profile of the team. In 2002 it won none of these, in 2003 just one, the English premier league. How much a lack of success damages the brand name is unclear, nor is it obvious how long you can continue without a major win and without significant damage.

Success also depends on whether the team has players who draw in large crowds, stars like George Best, Pele or Zidane. David Beckham was the star of Manchester United, known all over the world, as well as captain of England. It is unclear how far he benefited from the Manchester United brand and how far it benefited from the Beckham brand. At the time of writing, Beckham at the age of 28 has moved to Real Madrid. The price was sufficient to allow Man United to add players who might enhance its chance of winning the European championship. The advantage to Real is both a price which is lower than has been the norm in recent years and a commercial potential which is enormous. Real has obtained a 50% entitlement to the proceeds from any exploitation of Beckham's image. The club scarcely needs another attacking player, but rather a defensive one – the motive for acquisition is commercial. In the year after Zidane arrived at the club, Real sold almost half a million jerseys in the first year, worth about £14 million. This shows the commercial potential of some stars.

The strategy to be adopted in football depends on the rules, not of the game itself but of the way in which the league is conducted and teams recruited and paid. European soccer has a particular set of rules which encourage self-perpetuating success. It is based on the deregulated market model. In other words, there is nothing to stop a club in difficulty seeking to buy success by buying good players. The rich can rescue themselves from failure by buying the best, whether coaches or team members. Of course they need someone capable of recognizing the best and putting together a team rather than a set of brilliant but ineffective individuals.

Elsewhere, for basketball or football in the USA or for the local football championships in Australia, the rules are set very differently from those in Europe. This is done deliberately to try to prevent the self-reinforcing cycle of success which seems to be the norm in Europe and which tends to focus attention on a small group of elite teams. The rules are much more egalitarian in their effects. Whether they are successful in achieving their aim is another matter:

- There is a salary cap for each club which prevents the richest clubs competing for all the best players and using their financial muscle to buy a successful team, unless of course they find a way of quietly breaking the rules without too much penalty. The cap often forces team to part with expensive players against their own wishes.
- There is also a draft which gives preference in recruiting new players to the teams which are at the bottom of the league, young players with lots of potential who might otherwise go to the most glamorous teams. Sometimes it is possible to trade draft spots if a team wants a particular player.
- Since there is no relegation in either the American or the Australian championships, a downward spiral has a limit and can be halted. In England in a downward spiral, a team without success and therefore without support and finance can get into a vicious circle in which it is relegated, loses crowd support and has to sell good players to make ends meet. The team is faced with declining levels of player ability and ever-dwindling crowds as it descends the ladder, in theory all the way from the premier league to the bottom league, the fourth one. Some teams in the rust belt of northern England have done just that.
- It is true that the money from broadcasting rights might be more fairly distributed in the USA and Australia, although the league negotiates in both areas rather than the individual teams. Teams still lose money and incur debt.

Within these parameters, Man United can achieve a footballing success, which follows from a policy of using its financial resources to secure such success, that is, by buying good players like Rio Ferdinand. What about its commercial position?

Manchester United is more than a soccer team; it is a growing commercial organization. Its stadium complex includes, in addition to the ground, a museum, conference rooms, executive dining rooms, a restaurant and a mega-store. The holding company Manchester United plc includes three companies, one of which is the football club, the other a TV channel and the third a finance company.

Since 1998 Man United has had its own TV channel, MUTV, which is available on cable, satellite or broadband digital, owned equally by Man United, Granada and BSkyB. It has a four-year agreement with Terra Lycos, a web portal, for its website, manutd.com. Man United has a joint venture with the New York Yankees, which shows Man United's matches on Yankee Entertainment Sports, a subscription sports channel. It has a deal with Ladbroke's which allows betting on the Man United website. It also has the company MU Finance making joint ventures with the Bank of Scotland and Zurich Financial Services to provide financial services for its fans.

Almost certainly it can do far more to exploit its brand name. The name rivals Coca-Cola or McDonald's for recognition, yet the business of Manchester United is small beer compared with these enterprises. With 50 million fans and an annual revenue of about £150 million, the club is on average only tapping each fan for less than £3 a year. It could easily double this and therefore double the income. Already the club has mega-stores in Singapore and Kuala Lumpur, and another soon to open in Bangkok. There is a firm plan for a chain of Reds (United's nickname) Cafes. There is also a branded family restaurant, an idea which could be extended.

All over Asia Man United is seen as a model to be emulated. It often plays preseason friendly games in the area, games very well attended. Even its training sessions are attended by thousands of fans. In China a United match may be watched by more people than live in the whole of Britain.

Annual revenue has been rising dramatically, up almost 50% over the last five years. Net profit is as high 12% of the gross revenue, at the last count. From a commercial perspective Man United is in a very healthy state. It has enormous potential to improve that state. At least two core competencies are critical to this – the ability to play football well and manage well its brand name. The former is a matter for its coach Sir Alex Ferguson and the team, the latter for its CEO the 47-year-old Peter Kenyon, who before he moved to Man United worked in marketing for the producer of sports clothing Umbro.

A failure to maintain the first core competence and its link with success in the second is shown by the following anecdote. The threat of poor performance to a sponsor is illustrated by the early season loss (2002/2003 season) by Manchester United to Hungarian champions Zalaegerszeg in the European Champions League. United's chief sponsor Vodafone has been struggling to increase its market share in Hungary, which has barely reached 10%. Seizing the opportunity, Vodafone managed to get tickets for 12,000 of the 27,000 seats available, handing out 10,000 free to its subscribers. This did not prove a popular move among the Man United fans who queued unsuccessfully for tickets. For the return leg, Vodafone ran a competition for 400 places at the match, open this time to anyone. A failure by Man United would have denied Vodafone further opportunity to take advantage of its sponsorship role. Fortunately this was not to be. Man United went through to the quarter-final when they were defeated in an exciting encounter with Real Madrid.

Case Study Questions

1. What in detail are the core competencies of Manchester United football club?
2. What threats exist to the retention of those competencies?
3. Identify a strategy for a football club wishing to succeed 50 years ago and one wishing to succeed now. What are the changes of environment which have made necessary or desirable a change of strategy?
4. What might be the environment in 10, 20 or even 50 years? How might the strategy of a top-flight football club evolve over the next few years?
5. How can a football club with a brand name as well known as Manchester United make use of that brand name? How can it best manage that brand name?

Reading

Betts, P., 'Italian fans mourn soccer season delay', *Financial Times*, August 21, 2002: 5.

Bond, D., 'Fans get result in pay table', *Sunday Times*, June 22, 2003: 2–6.

Christy, J. H., 'The alchemy of relationships', *Forbes Global*, July 8, 2002: 24–9.

Financial Times 'Quizzical' Observer, August 21, 2002: 13.

Garrahan, M., 'Big players leave the field', *The Premiership Financial Times Guide*, August 15, 2002a: 15.

Garrahan, M., 'Just the ticket for financing football', Companies and Finance, *Financial Times*, August 19, 2002b: 23.

Garrahan, M., 'FA faces cash crunch as TV bids fall short', *Financial Times*, June 4, 2003: 7.

Garrahan, M., 'Beckham is the clear winner if he is sold', *Financial Times*, June 9, 2003: 25.

Garrahan, M., 'Man Utd would incur few penalties in Beckham sale', *Financial Times*, June14/15, 2003: 20.

Garrahan, M. and Guerrera, F., 'BSkyB risks losing grip on live football', *Financial Times*, June 20, 2003: 1.

Hawkey, I., 'New gold dream', *Sunday Times*, September 1, 2002: 2.8.

Heller, R., 'Big kick', *Forbes Global*, July 8, 2002: 32–5.

Steinberger, M., 'Baffled by Beckham's fallen star', *Financial Times*, June 17, 2003: 18.

Wheatcroft, G., 'Real will want more than the shirt off Beck's back', *Financial Times*, June 20, 2003: 16.

Relevant website

www.manutd.com

Key strategic lessons

• An enterprise must know what resources it has and continuously consider how to recombine them to develop new capabilities or core competencies which create and maintain competitive advantage. This is part of a process of learning.

• A resource is any potential input into the process of production or sale which adds value for the final consumer, or anything which could, on a continuing basis, assist in providing such value. The specific resources held by an organization help to define the identity of that organization, particularly the intangible resources.

• Most organizations have a 'core' core competency which creates the identity of the organization and determines which resources are critical to its performance.

• The resource position is a good starting point for strategy making because it defines what an organization can, rather than should, do.

• Tangible resources include all resources which have a physical manifestation, such as a piece of equipment or a building, and resources which can be 'codified' or described in detail, those that can be

Key strategic lessons cont'd

recreated easily with little delay and which can be valued exactly.

* Intangible resources include all resources which do not have a physical manifestation, such as the ability to innovate or an organizational skill and those that cannot be 'codified', recreated easily or valued exactly.

* An organization can use different resources in combination to develop capabilities which give it the potential to provide goods or services which are wanted by consumers. Over time these combinations must change to tailor the output to the external environment of the organization.

* Capabilities become competencies when they are given a strategic dimension. A competency is therefore a strategic capability. There are core or distinct competencies which are critical to the successful implementation of a strategy and are important in establishing the identity of the organization. The number of core competencies must lie between two and three to five.

Applying the lessons

1 Define the following terms: corporate identity, a boundary, tangible resources, intangible resources, capabilities, core competencies and path dependency.
2 What is meant by the identity of an organization? Consider ten well-known organizations and briefly describe what determines their identity. How far is this identity determined by the organization's interactions with the rest of the world? How far is such an identity linked to the existence of specific resources, notably a brand name, or specific competencies?
3 How far is it possible to use the brand name of a product or an organization outside the areas in which it was developed? Give at least two examples of a brand name being used in this flexible way.
4 What are the ethical issues which arise in the course of the exploitation of a brand name? Which stakeholder groups are affected by these issues? How do such stakeholders stand to gain or lose?
5 Is it useful to distinguish between a 'core' core competency and a core competency? What is the

basis for such a distinction? How far is it possible for an enterprise to change its identity by using the core competencies which it has which are not 'core' core competencies?
6 Choose any company with a wide range of diversified activities, such as Johnson & Johnson or General Electric. Consider its history over the last two or three decades. Fill in the following:

Product or service	Market segment	Core competency

When you have completed the diagram, evaluate the present company in terms of the fit between its core competencies and the market segments which it is currently targeting.

Strategic project

The project is designed to show how many core competencies a typical company is likely to have.

1 Choose an enterprise in an industry which is likely to be characterized by a large number of core competen-

cies, preferably the highest. As a contrast choose an enterprise in an industry which is likely to be characterized by a few, preferably the lowest.

2 Consider both the theoretical and practical arguments for the possession of these competencies. In what sense can there be too many or too few competencies?

3 Give the arguments for and against developing a different number of core competencies as they have emerged from this project.

Exploring further

Two general articles which are helpful in understanding what it is that an enterprise is doing are Meyer, 1991: 821–33 and Seth and Thomas, 1994: 165–91.

Generally, on resources, Chapter 4 in Grant, 1991 offers the best introduction. Their role in creating and maintaining competitive advantage is tackled by Aaker, 1998: 91–100, or Stalk et al., 1992: 57–69.

During the 1990s a group of theorists focused close attention on the role of the resources, capabilities and competencies of an enterprise in the making of its strategy, that is, on the nature and role of its internal environment, which became known as the resource-based view of the firm (RBV). This body of theory is the 1990s' main contribution to strategic theory. For a student it is an interesting example of the way in which theory is constructed piece by piece, partly to cope with the deficiencies of existing theory and partly under influences from outside the area. For those interested in the way in which theory develops this is an interesting literature. RBV has a coherence which justifies and rewards further attention.

Probably the most influential article in kicking off the debate is Prahalad and Hamel, 1990: 79–93. There is an informative review on the usefulness of the resource-based view of strategy making in the *Academy of Management Review*, **26**(1), 2001: 22–66. The outcome of the exchange is in the view of the author very much in line with the arguments expressed in the first three sections of Chapter 16. See Priem and Butler, 2001a and 2001b and Barney, 2001.

The original view was set out in Wernerfelt, 1984: 171–80, and further developed by Barney, 1991: 99–120, Barney et al., 2001: 625–41, and Peteraf, 1993: 179–91. It was reviewed by Wernerfelt, 1995: 171–4, and Barney, 1995: 49–61. A more dynamic treatment can be found in Collis and Montgomery, 1995: 118–28.

A good example of the application of the view is Miller and Shamsie, 1996: 519–43.

The start of value chain analysis can be found in Chapters 2 and 3 of Porter, 1985. There is an excellent application of such analysis in Grant, 1991, which is applied to both the cost and quality sides.

8 Creating and maintaining competitive advantage

Key strategic challenge

How do I achieve and maintain competitive advantage in an ever-changing world?

Strategic dangers

That the enterprise pursues an inappropriate generic strategy which puts too much emphasis on either cost leadership or product differentiation and too little emphasis on innovation and as a consequence fails to maintain its old competitive advantage and create a new advantage.

Case Study Scenario   Hutchison and the introduction of third generation wireless communication

'A new entrant with zero customers, zero cash flow and zero revenue to protect has a fundamentally different approach to the market from incumbents with customers and revenues and in a position where growth opportunities are limited. They try to protect and generate as much revenue as they can and spend as little as they can. There is not great upside for a Telstra, an Optus or a Vodafone here. There is great upside for us.

If you go to every single global market, you will find the incumbents following similar strategies. Holding onto as many customers as they can, spending as little capital expenditure as they can and spinning as much noise negatively as they can about 3G.' (Kevin Russell, CEO of Hutchison Australia, cited in Hewett and Kruger, 2003)

One of the most explosive technical and consumer developments of the 1990s was the spread of wireless communication. The mobile phone quickly established a market segment which increased enormously in size throughout the 1990s. Together with the Internet this was the new product of the decade. The technology of wireless communication moved forward rapidly, a technology which it is conventional to classify by different generations (see the end of the chapter). Currently most equipment in the sector is working in the second generation, although many players have committed themselves to paying vast sums for licences for the use of the third generation (3G) spectrum, with an as yet untried

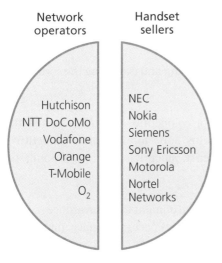

Network operators	Handset sellers
Hutchison	NEC
NTT DoCoMo	Nokia
Vodafone	Siemens
Orange	Sony Ericsson
T-Mobile	Motorola
O_2	Nortel Networks

Figure 8.1 **Companies with the biggest investment in 3G**

technology. One of the factors influencing the current choice of technology is the need to use the full 3G spectrum in the 2GHz band and therefore for such new licences. For 3G, an unproven technology, there is no accepted standard. It is easy to anticipate major teething problems.

The first 3G service in the world was FOMA (NTT DoCoMo) in Japan, launched in October 2001. This was slow to get started, with 140,000 subscribers one year after its introduction. In 2003 the number of subscribers started to grow at a much faster rate, 140,000 signing up in March 2003 alone. One prediction sees as many as 1.5 million by March 2004. The key to better performance was probably much extended battery life, a lighter, longer-lasting and much cheaper handset and a 90% plus potential network coverage of Japan's population. South Korea's KTF also offers 3G services.

Initially neither consumers nor commentators found a 'must-have' application to justify subscribing in large numbers. The main potential applications are:

1. video conferencing
2. media on demand, such as news and sport
3. shoot and send – photos or video
4. mapping services – global positioning satellite
5. games
6. mobile Internet browsing and email.

Because there were confident expectations that the technology would be quickly applied, companies were willing to pay handsomely for licences to use the technology. The bill for 3G licences in Europe amounted to US$150 billion, much of which has since been written off. Unfortunately those applications which are currently most exciting can be provided with 2G technology.

The high-tech crash and the telecommunication over-expansion brought to a virtual halt the application of the technology.

Hutchison Whampoa, led by Li Ka-Shing, is going it alone, hoping to gain major first-mover advantages. The commitment is large, US$17.5 billion to set up nine 3G operators across the globe, in seven of which Hutchison will compete, as a newcomer, against entrenched players. This is a major move to try to develop a significant lead in the use of new technology. With minor partners Hutchison planned and started operations in Britain and Italy before Christmas 2002 and Australia and Sweden at the beginning of 2003.

Mobilkom, Telekom Austria's mobile arm, has also started offering a 3G service in Austria. In Britain

	Europe		Asia	
2002	Britain Launch: Nov–Dec Owned: 65% Licence: $6.8 billion	Italy Nov–Dec 88.2% $3.2 billion		
2003	Sweden Q1 60% $107,000	Austria Q2 100% $135 million	Australia Q1 46% $108 million	Hong Kong Q1 75% $68 million
2004 (possibly)	Ireland 100% $49.4 million		Israel 42.8% $46 million	

Figure 8.2 **The timetable of the global Hutchison 3 strategy**

Hutchison must persuade potential customers not to renew their contracts with five major players – Vodafone, Orange, O$_2$, T-Mobile and Virgin Mobile. Only in Hong Kong and Austria, relatively small markets, does it already have active subsidiaries.

Is Hutchison trying to do too much too fast? Are there genuine first-mover advantages in using the third generation technology? Are those who are waiting adopting a better strategy?

Without a significant competitive advantage there is no hope that an enterprise can earn above-normal profit. Initially the problem is to create such an advantage, later it is to maintain it in a rapidly changing world. The creation of advantage is the result of two activities:

1. Discovering what you *should* do. This means positioning the enterprise to take the opportunities and avoid the threats offered by the market, that is, by successfully anticipating the potential demand of consumers and/or ensuring the absence of competitors able to deny you such an advantage.
2. Discovering what you *can* do. This means identifying and exploiting the core competencies already possessed by the enterprise.

There is a danger of regarding the creation of competitive advantage as a static accomplishment which, once achieved, remains done for all time. Competitive advantage must be maintained. This is not easy, since it requires two kinds of approach by the enterprise:

1. adopting a proactive stance in remaking the environment to its advantage
2. developing a flexible response in managing changes occurring independently in the external environment.

In other words the enterprise needs to innovate.

The concept of competitive advantage

What is meant by competitive advantage and why is it important? Hutchison is seeking to gain such an advantage by introducing 3G technology in wireless communication. This is an example of an attempt to create competitive advantage by winning first-mover advantage through technical innovation.

Causes, characteristics and consequences

As with any concept it is appropriate to start by distinguishing causes, characteristics and consequences. The main concern in any definition is with characteristics. However, the difference between cause, characteristic and consequence is a critical issue. There is a tendency in most definitions to look first at consequences since these determine the significance of the concept.

The main *consequence* of having a competitive advantage is clear. Such an advantage translates into the positive outcome of a profit earned by the enterprise above the average for the industry, or alternatively a loss less than that earned by others. It does not necessarily mean an above-normal profit since this depends on the nature of the industry. It is easy to recognize when competitive advantage exists, when an enterprise, competing with another enterprise or enterprises, for the same customers in the same market, is able to earn either a realized, or potential, profit which is higher than that of competitors, or a loss which is smaller. Provided the accounting is accurate, it is not difficult to identify the enterprise with a competitive advantage.

The consequence of better financial performance is made possible by the key *characteristic* of any competitive advantage, the greater utility or value given to the customer by an enterprise. Customers buy the product or service either in greater numbers or at a higher price because of this greater utility. Competitive advantage is then the ability to better satisfy customers than competitors can.

The *causes* of the existence of such an advantage reflect the combined ability to recognize opportunity and therefore position the enterprise accordingly, and produce what is wanted at a cost and therefore a price which is acceptable. Both these abilities are the result of the appropriate application of the core competencies possessed by an enterprise.

Focus on Theory
Competitive advantage

Cause:	an appropriate application of the core competencies possessed by the enterprise and an appropriate positioning of the enterprise in the relevant industries or market segments
Characteristic:	the ability to provide utility to, or to satisfy, customers better than competitors can
Consequence:	the ability to win market share or make a higher profit than competitors

The use of the term 'potential' as well as actual profit indicates that the enterprise could choose to sacrifice profit in order to:

• win market share
• provide some additional benefit to one of the stakeholder groups other than the shareholders.

In either case the profit would not be actually realized. Either action might well mean that the enterprise is looking to maintain competitive advantage beyond the present, well into the future, as will be seen in the next section. In other words, there may be a deliberate policy of taking a lower profit, or even incurring a loss in the short term, in order to maximize the market share of the company and earn the enterprise a greater profit over a longer period of time.

The impact of poor positioning

Competitive advantage is a necessary, but not a sufficient, condition for continued participation in a market since the enterprise at some point of time needs not just the ability to do better than its competitors, but the ability to earn an above-normal profit in order to justify such participation. How far the profit earned in one industry differs from that earned in others depends on the nature of the industry, particularly on the degree of intensity of competition and the point in its life cycle that the industry has reached. It is possible that no enterprise operating in that particular market can earn as much as the normal rate of profit. Some industries do persistently offer a below-normal profit over a significant period of time, that is, one which is longer than the short term. The airline industry is a good example of such a situation.

If the enterprise is badly positioned, that is, in an industry, or pursuing an activity, which is not characterized by good returns, then competitive advantage is not sufficient to support a continued operation in that industry. The enterprise may be faced with a declining number of customers due to external factors beyond its control. The industry may be past its maturity and in decline. In that situation the strategic aim of the enterprise might be to seek another industry in which it could generate a different competitive advantage.

An enterprise may have a competitive advantage but be badly positioned. Or it may be well positioned but lack a competitive advantage because it cannot attain the relevant core competencies. The achievement of competitive advantage involves the leveraging of an enterprise's resources, developed by strategy into capabilities and core competencies, to take advantage of opportunities which a reading of the external environment has revealed. Positioning is part of this, but the development of competitive advantage reflects both positioning and an effective use of any resources the enterprise has or can gain access to.

Outcompeting competitors

Competitive advantage is, therefore, the greater attractiveness of any product or service produced by a particular enterprise to a significant group of consumers within a given market. That attractiveness arises from either the lower price of the product or a preferred range of attributes as perceived by the purchaser of the product, or some combination of the two. It is a relative rather than an absolute concept. The enterprise is better able to satisfy the wants of the consumers than others active in the same industry, or is at least perceived by the consumers to be better able.

To sustain any advantage beyond the short term requires both the further development of existing capabilities and the recombining of relevant resources into different capabilities and competencies. This must be done in the light of a careful reading of changes in the environment. It involves a combination of a better reading and a better harnessing of resources than other enterprises operating in the same market can manage. The enterprise needs to keep ahead of the competitors in reading any change in that environment.

Without a potential competitive advantage there is no point in developing a strategy. Identification and development of a competitive advantage is central to strategy making. Any strategy has at its core the creation and maintenance of such competitive advantage.

A dynamic context

The overall situation of an enterprise at any given moment for both old and new core competencies and for old and new products can be represented as in Figure 8.3.

What are the possibilities?

- Option C is the starting point for any analysis since it represents the status quo. Competitive position and product life stage determine how far improvement is possible. A stable external environment would favour such a strategy.
- By contrast the strategy involved in option B is an unusual one involving high risk. It requires not only entering new markets but developing the core competencies to do this, which are themselves new. It represents a complete change of strategic direction for the enterprise. Such a turnaround might be attempted in a crisis situation, but rarely otherwise. Only extremely dynamic organizations could attempt such a strategy. The risk of failure is very high.
- Clearly any realistic diversification of product or service should involve option D, putting together existing resources and capabilities in a novel and effective manner to enter new markets and produce new products.
- Option A implies staying in the same markets but developing new core competencies to allow this to happen. It assumes that within the industry consumer tastes and technology are changing and require the modification of competencies to suit such a changing context.

The Strategy in Action below is an interesting illustration of the way in which there can be a recombination of existing core competencies held by an enterprise with a new one and the identification of a new market segment to whom to sell. It represents a partial movement by the enterprises into the B quadrant.

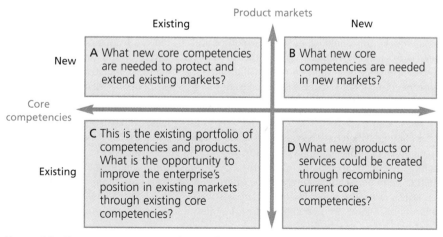

Figure 8.3 **New core competencies and new product markets**

Traditionally contact lenses have been supplied under medical prescription to deal with some defect of the eye of a patient. The lenses have been seen as performing the same function as glasses. This has also affected the mode of distribution, since it is usually illegal for the lenses to be sold over the counter in a supermarket or even a chemist shop. Glasses or contact lenses have been supplied by optometrists or opticians. This has traditionally given the optometrist some element of a monopoly, although optometrists could compete with each other.

The preference for contact lenses over glasses is a cosmetic one, in the sense that it is thought by the wearers that glasses mar the natural appearance in a way that contact lenses do not. Contact lenses can be worn unobtrusively. Statistical evidence on Australia shows that something like 65% of wearers are women. Studies have also shown 80% of women are willing to wear cosmetic lenses.

It is also the case that the traditional method of manufacture implied high costs. Soft lenses were lathe cut, an extremely labour-intensive process requiring a highly skilled input, which produced a high price. The frequency of replacement, and therefore the level of demand, is influenced by price. Replacement normally occurs at 3, 6 or 12 monthly intervals.

The new method, very much cheaper than the old, is to cast mould the lenses. The original cost of the moulding plant is high but there are considerable economies of scale, which can bring down the price of a lens by a significant amount. This makes possible frequent replacement, so that the lenses become disposable. This method of manufacture has also opened possibilities for the moulding and use of coloured and tinted lenses to meet wants which are other than medical. The price is now low enough to allow purchase for cosmetic rather than strictly medical reasons. Not only can a woman become a blonde overnight, she can become a blue-eyed blonde.

Other changes which have been occurring relate to a broadening of the distribution system and an opening up of optical products to advertising, whether on radio, in print or even on the Internet. This is part of a more general easing of the restrictions on professional promotion by doctors, lawyers

and others. The product is now open to the normal commercial process of branding.

The traditional approach to the prescription of lenses reflected the ability of the optometrist to prescribe properly. This was based on the relevant training at university level. The traditional certificate on the wall was a symbol of this competency. There were serious constraints on the freedom to advertise, which limited the degree of competition, although chains of specialist optometrists did appear, often well represented in shopping malls. The approach also reflected the ability of the skilled craftsman supplying the end product to produce exactly what was being prescribed. In turn, he or she had to receive the appropriate training.

The competencies required by the new product are rather different from the traditional ones. The medical competency becomes marginal if the lenses are solely used for cosmetic reasons. The new technology also means that there is nothing difficult about production – the old skills are much less important.

The key issues of generic strategy are finding the right cost level for an optometrist to be competitive, and differentiating the product for the consumer in terms of different consumer utilities and different intangible product attributes. The utility of health is replaced by one of attractive appearance. The two aspects of generic strategy – cost and differentiation – are connected, since getting a greater market share by deliberately differentiating the product enables a reduction in costs through economies of scale. Since this is a new market segment, innovating ahead of the competitors or getting in first are critical. There may be pronounced first-mover advantages. It is also critical how the product is advertised and distributed. The ability to promote a different product in a different way, through a different distribution system, becomes relevant.

Some players already produce coloured or tinted lenses, or are in an advanced planning stage before doing so. The most likely entrants, and the ones with least barriers to entry, are those who already produce contact lenses, particularly those that can benefit from scale production and sale. Those already with a well-known brand name, such as Johnson & Johnson, have an added advantage. In some cases they clearly have

▶

considerable marketing strength relevant to the distribution of toiletries and cosmetics. In terms of Figure 8.3, such companies start off in quadrant C, a much more favourable starting point than quadrant B. However, such companies may be slow to move, being distracted by a broad range of other interests. Smaller players may have more flexibility. It may be an advantage to outsource manufacture to the lowest cost location and concentrate on promotion and distribution.

A whole series of relevant strategic questions are raised:

- Who should provide the new product? Existing producers or newcomers?
- Should the product be sold through distribution channels different from the existing ones, such as supermarkets or chemists over the counter?
- Should the same manufacturers produce both the medical and the cosmetic product?
- How will a company time its entry into the market? There may be first-mover advantages.
- What kind of pricing policy will be adopted – an aggressive one or one which seeks to reap some monopoly profit when the market is a new one?
- How will the product be promoted and distributed – stressing what attributes?
- What are the exact differences in the core competencies required in the production and selling of these two different products?

A balanced portfolio of products

Where an enterprise provides different products or services, it may have to weigh the potential competitive advantage in various industries against each other. It is no good having a decided advantage in one industry if it is a contracting or stagnant industry. One of the arguments in favour of a diversified portfolio of products is that the products will be at different points in their life cycle and in industries which are characterized by different rates of growth and levels of profit.

One aim of strategy is to choose a balanced portfolio of products. Different products may have sources of competitive advantage which require different underlying core competencies. The limit on the number of core competencies limits the degree of diversity which is appropriate. This is the argument for doing what you know best. The exact meaning of balance will be discussed later in the book. The present chapter assumes that the choice of portfolio has been made and that the concern is with particular products or services and the strategy to be adopted for the creation and maintenance of competitive advantage in particular business units. In the Strategy in Action above, there is an opportunity for companies to add to their portfolio of eye care products a product which has a high potential growth rate and which uses core competencies similar to those already in use. There is a significant overlap in the competencies needed.

The tertiary education sector is one which has moved from being supply-driven to being demand-driven and therefore needs to take action to provide a balanced portfolio of products which meet the wants of a changing market, themselves reflecting a changing labour market.

Strategy in Action   The virtual university and the MBA

Education combines a role as an investment, made either by individuals or organizations, and a role as a consumption good, to be enjoyed at the time of delivery. Education is allegedly critical to the efficient operation of the modern economy, more so than used to be the case because of the rising importance of innovation. There are very considerable externalities not captured by the individual being educated, rather by the society in which the individual works and plays. This explains the important public role in education. The tendency is to progressively raise the age to which compulsory education is pursued. In most societies education is compulsory until about the age of 14,15 or 16; the more developed the economy, the higher the level. The need for lifetime education has become the norm since knowledge is becoming rapidly outdated. Frequent and multiple career changes make the re-education or retraining of individuals highly desirable. At the tertiary level, many societies, particularly English-speaking societies, distinguish between education and training, the former a training of the mind, the latter vocational. There is usually a binary system of institutions specializing in providing one or the other.

The MBA is an American innovation, which has spread to all countries. There was a time, as recently as the 1960s, when the MBA was only taught by a small number of institutions. It was a qualification which, partly because of its rarity, had real value in promoting the career of the holder. At that time, full-time 'on campus' study was the accepted mode of delivery. For this reason few people had the opportunity to participate in the programme. The general recognition by the business world of the usefulness of the degree led to a rapid expansion in the number of programmes taught throughout the world. The MBA has become the universal tool of management training. There is hardly a university today which does not offer an MBA. There has also been an increase in the flexibility with which the MBA is taught. Part-time programmes have been introduced. Choice has been extended in that there are also specialist streams within the MBA itself. The MBA is often the focus of distance learning. For example, the largest number of MBA students taught by one institution in the UK is by the Open University. In the terminology of the textbooks the MBA is now practically a commodity. Management studies itself is a newcomer to many universities, both at postgraduate and undergraduate levels, often regarded as lacking the rigour of other disciplines, more training than education.

In traditional teaching the emphasis is on face-to-face contact and teaching informed by research. There are two mechanisms of such face-to-face contact – the delivery to a large number of students of lectures by a staff member, usually of some seniority, supplemented by the organization of appropriate activities, such as laboratory experimen-

tation under supervision, and the conduct of regular tutorials with much smaller numbers attending, often under the guidance of a more junior member of staff. The student is expected to undertake about four or five hours of private study for every hour of face-to-face contact. The staff are employed to carry out research, administrative and professional activities as well as teaching.

The teaching of an MBA has always involved a significant degree of innovation. It is much more hands-on. Entry into such courses in some countries reflects managerial experience as much as intellectual achievement. Activity learning has been an important component. The case study approach has also placed a significant emphasis on such a practical orientation.

The university has ceased to be supply-driven and become demand-driven. In the traditional university research tended to dictate what was taught. For a number of reasons universities now have to attract students by offering courses which the students see as interesting/relevant. The universities increasingly compete for students by offering what students see as relevant which is likely to be related to possible careers.

In most countries there are still tight restrictions on who can teach a degree course. The government very often sets the standard below which the universities cannot go – it accredits their courses. The level of government participation, in the sense of government funding, also differs markedly from country to country. The period of free tertiary education has come to an end. In all countries the students contribute to the cost. In many the proportion of costs borne by the student has tended to rise. In many areas there are quotas on the maximum number of students who can undertake a course. The tendency of the government to withdraw has meant that the universities must seek new sources of income. One such source is the fee-paying student, such as the MBA student. Universities have begun to compete for such students. Those countries which have a good reputation for their educational level have an advantage in such competition.

The other great change is technical, a massive improvement in the means of delivering a degree from a distance. Initially the post was the means of delivery, later radio and television were mobilized to assist, today teleconferencing and the Internet are used. Cheaper and faster air travel has also con-

▶

tracted the world, making possible the entry of teachers from outside, sometimes for short periods of time for the purposes of block teaching.

There have always been degrees awarded through correspondence systems. The assessment through examinations may be the same as in a traditional system, but the student conducts nearly all the study required privately with a minimum of guidance. That guidance may be limited to suggestions on reading and the written word.

The Open University model, developed in the UK in the 1970s, was originally designed for mature adults who had missed out on a tertiary education at the usual earlier age. It provided limited exposure through face-to-face lectures and seminars, both on a monthly basis and through a week's summer school. Most of the time the lectures were provided through the medium of radio and television, supplemented by course material which was organized in a textbook format. The courses were assessed on the basis of assignments written and completed at various stages during the course. The course material was highly innovative, both in content and mode of exposure. Once the pool of those who had missed out on an earlier education had been used up, the model was opened to more extended use.

What does the future hold? The Internet opens up the whole world as the prospective market. Courses could be provided anywhere at any time, provided the student has access to a personal computer or the equivalent. Courses can be updated continuously. The place, method and pace of study can be regulated by the student, as can the assessment system. The speed of movement through a course is determined by students according to their circumstances. Contact through email with a tutor can be maintained continuously, although the cost situation is likely to restrict the amount of access. There may be no face-to-face contact at all. There is certainly no limit on numbers. The virtual university has the advantage of flexibility and low cost. It is ideally suited to training, perhaps not so much to education. Traditional universities might see such a mechanism as simply enhancing face-to-face contact.

There are two possible strategies – cost leadership and product differentiation:

- The new technology could be used to provide standard courses to large numbers at a very low price. For those for whom cost is important, the virtual university offers obvious advantages.
- Alternatively the new technology could be used simply to enhance face-to-face contact. Courses could be customized to meet the needs of the student, even including in an MBA exposure to the business environment of different countries. Quality could be built into such an education.

Strategies for acquiring competitive advantage

The underlying aim of the strategies for developing competitive advantage is to maximize the economic value added, not just by the enterprise but in the whole chain of value-adding activities from raw materials to final consumption. For the moment it is possible to assume a situation comprising three separate and 'unintegrated' players – the suppliers of various inputs, the enterprise and the customers for the final product. Figure 8.4 represents the situation in a simple diagram.

The total value added for the product is the difference between V and C. The higher is V and the lower is C, the greater is the value added.

The enterprise will seek to minimize V–P, but is usually unable to charge a price equivalent to V since it cannot differentiate price by individual customer. In some sectors, such as travel or accommodation, it is possible to differentiate to some degree but in a typical case there is no price differentiation at all. Most consumers therefore enjoy a positive consumer surplus which represents what they would be willing to pay above the going price in order to enjoy consumption of the product. Competition from other suppliers also limits the degree to which P can be raised towards V.

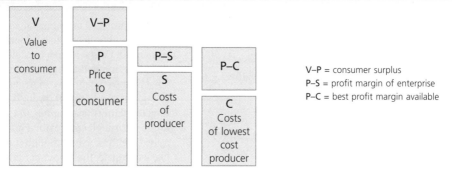

Figure 8.4 **Value creation**

The enterprise will also seek to raise V, but this may depend on joint action by the industry, for example in the generic advertising of Australian wine in foreign markets.

The enterprise will seek to minimize S–C, but again individual suppliers who can produce at a lower cost, closer to C, can enjoy a producer surplus. Bargaining and strategy will determine the size of the gap between S and C. Other things being equal, the company will seek to maximize the profit margin by minimizing the gap. An enterprise can also seek to lower C by innovating in the areas of technology and organization.

For any specific transaction at a given moment, the value added is a simple concept; it is the difference between the total opportunity cost of the inputs necessary to produce the unit of output – the raw materials, intermediate goods, capital equipment and labour and the final price of the product or service:

- The opportunity cost is the smallest amount that any supplier would be prepared to accept to deliver the specific inputs
- The end price is the largest amount that the customer is prepared to pay for the product.

The actual cost could be higher and the actual price lower than defined, which is a matter of strategy and relative bargaining strength if different enterprises are involved in the value-adding chain which produces the final product. In other words, either the supplier or the customer could capture more of the value, with or without the acquiescence of the enterprise. The distribution of the total value between the three players is therefore something to be determined by negotiation or bargaining. In conditions of unrestricted bargaining, the sum of the shares cannot exceed the total value.

Any strategy of an enterprise is therefore a twofold one:

- maximizing the economic value added for the transaction
- ensuring that the enterprise captures an acceptable share of that value.

There are competitors in the industry who are in a different situation in terms of both costs and consumer value, adopting strategies which involve the application of bargaining strength which is itself different, and which aim at a differing share of value added.

It is clear from such a definition that the overall value added for the transaction can be increased either by improving the willingness of the customer to pay, in other words in some way adding value to the product, or alternatively by reducing the opportunity costs of the various suppliers. This may involve cooperative action between the enterprise and its suppliers or even between the enterprise and its customers.

Strategic options

The strategic options on how to add value and acquire competitive advantage can be illustrated with the help of Figure 8.5. This is a static point of view, the competitive situation as envisaged at a given moment of time, which assumes that all the competitors are vertically integrated enterprises.

On the horizontal axis is the level of price, which we can take as a proxy for costs (therefore for C above). There are three possibilities: a price lower than the standard price, in other words a low-cost situation; a standard price; or a price higher than the standard price, in other words a high-cost situation.

On the vertical axis is the value added to the product or service by the enterprise, as perceived by the consumer, a measure of the willingness of the customer to pay (V above); it is the degree to which the product or service is seen as differentiated. Once more there are three possibilities: a lower than standard value added or product differentiation; a standard value or product differentiation; and a higher than standard value or product differentiation.

There are eight possible combinations. However, strategies 6, 7 and 8 would be destined for ultimate failure, since they involve either a high price or costs with standard or less than standard value (an undifferentiated product), or a standard price or costs with low value. In other words, they are strategies which cannot yield a competitive advantage and are therefore uncompetitive, unless for some reason there is a monopoly in the market. If adopted they would lead to a steadily declining market share.

This leaves five generic strategies for developing competitive advantage which are feasible and can be clearly distinguished.

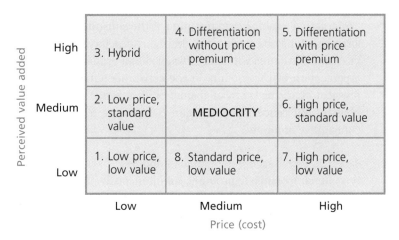

Source: Adapted from Bowman and Faulkner, 1996.

Figure 8.5 **Strategies for increasing value added (V–C)**

1. Cost leadership (1 and 2)

General cost leadership refers to the need to get all costs lower whatever their nature, whether they are fixed or variable costs, whether they relate to labour, capital or resource inputs, and whether they relate to design or distribution. For an existing enterprise capital costs will be sunk costs and irrelevant to current operating strategy.

Cost leadership is not the same as price leadership, but is often a prerequisite for the latter. It is possible to lead on costs but not on price and enjoy the higher profits. An enterprise with lower costs has much more scope in developing a strategy, particularly in developing a pricing policy. Lower costs mean a wider range of possible prices without the outcome of making a loss.

Lower costs mean the possibility of higher profit and a higher share price, thereby lowering the potential price of additional capital. There is a virtuous circle in which lower present costs make possible lower costs in the future.

2. Focused cost leadership (1 and 2)

Since the enterprise may produce a wide variety of products, the desire to minimize cost may fall on a particular product or products at critical stages in their life cycle. The effort to minimize cost is concentrated on this product. A critical issue relates to the choice of product on which to focus. It may focus on a product for which there is intense competition.

The same might apply to the possibility of focusing on different activities in the value-adding chain. Focusing on particular activities, particularly those which account for a large proportion of costs, may produce better performance outcomes.

3. Product differentiation (4 and 5)

Most industries produce products which are not homogeneous. There are tangible and intangible differences which are important to consumers. The quality of the product, or rather the perception of quality by the consumer, is a key variable. The better a product satisfies the perceived wants of the consumer, the more attractive is the product to the consumer. This is partly an issue of production technique and design, partly an issue of promotion and marketing.

Marketing establishes in the mind of the consumer the existence of intangible differences. It may be a matter of desired characteristics or the whole package of services and attributes which are attached to a product. Branding involves implanting a perception of the product in the consumer's mind which may have no basis in physical characteristics, or it may build a range of intangible benefits upon real physical differences. The key aim is to create a perceived advantage over other competitive products.

4. Focused product differentiation (4 and 5)

It is often impossible to promote, simultaneously and with the same intensity, all the products of the enterprise. Marketing campaigns focus on particular products or particular market segments, usually those which warrant the charging of a price premium. Of course such campaigns may have an influence on the other products of the enterprise insofar as the name of the enterprise itself, as a result of such a strategy, becomes the brand name.

5. *A combination of cost leadership and product differentiation* (3)

This may turn out to be the only sensible strategy, and the one which best describes the strategy adopted by successful enterprises. The two main strategies of cost leadership and product differentiation are often described as if they were mutually exclusive – you can either pursue one or the other, but not both. You can either minimize cost or you can aim for the highest quality of product and customize according to the requirements of the market niches. To some degree this is true.

Some products are by their nature homogeneous. However hard you try, it is impossible to differentiate the product in the mind of the consumer. This tends to put all the emphasis on cost and therefore on price. There is no point in the consumer paying extra for the same product.

Other products are by their nature heterogeneous, notably any service or product which has significant service components. An increasing number of products have intangible attributes and service components which are critically important in persuading customers to buy, for example the drinking of premium coffee in an attractive place surrounded by congenial people.

Generic strategies as hybrids

The comments above refer to the extremes. Very few products fall at these extremes. Between the extremes there are many products which share aspects of both homogeneity and heterogeneity. The separation of strategies presented above may, therefore, be an illusion.

In practice no enterprise can minimize costs, completely ignoring the perception by consumers of the quality of the product. One mechanism for reducing costs is obviously to reduce the quality of the product and to fail to customize that product according to individual customer needs.

Nor can any enterprise develop a perception of high quality regardless of the cost of developing that perception. Product differentiation necessarily involves the expenditure of resources in design or marketing and the general promotion of the product or service, which pushes up the overall costs of production and distribution in the enterprise.

There is another cost associated with product differentiation. With a homogeneous product it is possible to reap economies of scale. Where the product is customized in some way, the production line must be adapted to meet the particular requirements of the market. The production line is adjusted to meet the varied needs of the different customers. This involves a cost, the loss of economies of scale. However, there are always ways of retaining economies of scale for component producers.

There is a strong link between the strategies; the two go together. In practice there may be no real choice between generic strategies. All enterprises have to adopt a combined strategy. Typically an enterprise which is performing exceptionally well does both: it is at the same time a cost leader and a product differentiator. IKEA not only organizes a very cost-efficient system of production, logistics and sales, but also differentiates its products by style and continuous improvement and updating.

This analysis has been conducted on the assumption that the strategist is making a once and for all choice at a given moment in time, or repeating the choice at a series of different moments. In practice the choice is a dynamic one. In order to create and maintain competitive advantage the enterprise must continuously innovate. Successful innovation can ensure the simultaneous achievement of both lower costs and higher quality. Since competitors do not cease to innovate there is no choice; the enterprise must keep ahead of the pack. In any event the enterprise must respond to a changing environment.

The Strategy in Action below explores the way in which a changing environment may require a change of strategy.

Strategy in Action The Mt Buller winter resort and global warming

Mt Buller is the premier winter resort in Victoria, Australia, one of six such resorts. It competes for customers with these other resorts as well as with winter resorts elsewhere. It is only a three-hour drive from the city of Melbourne which has a population well over 3.5 million. The Buller resort raises the linked issues of seasonality and global warming. Global warming could reduce the skiing season below its present four months. In the absence of other activities attracting visitors, this could have disastrous consequences for the resort.

Winter resorts require considerable infrastructure for normal everyday life: transport systems with the outside world and within the resort; utilities – energy, water, communications, rubbish disposal; police; sometimes educational and medical services; plus the usual retail outlets selling food and other daily necessities; even hotels and motels; and for the recreational activity, ski lifts.

Most facilities demand a minimum size of permanent population, or a regular flow of visitors all year. There is a threshold level of demand below which any facility is not viable, even supermarkets, restaurants or cinemas.

It is difficult to build up a significant permanent population which justifies keeping facilities open out of season. There is a vicious circle – poor facilities, few permanent residents. The closing of such facilities out of season compounds the problem of increasing the permanent population. The domination of a resort by temporary visitors, particularly day visitors, and by part-time workers, or workers who live somewhere else, influences the nature of the resort.

The unit costs of supplying services may be relatively high in a resort. If the resort is remote, transport costs are a significant element of the final price of

goods and services. The resort may not be large enough to reap significant economies of scale for basic services. There may be a lack of competition in the provision of goods and services. Wage costs may be higher because it is necessary to attract staff to a remote place, or because living costs are higher, including accommodation, or simply because most staff are employed on a part-time basis. Skiing is already an expensive sport in terms of equipment and clothing.

Most resorts involve networks of cooperating enterprises. Such enterprises may be involved in providing inputs of various kinds, others may be directly operating part of the resort, a few may even be involved in assisting in the marketing of the resort or providing its services. Some of the cooperating organizations may be government organizations. The strategy maker must operate the resort in a way which keeps these stakeholders happy.

It is important that all the cooperating enterprises have a clear idea about the likely future development of the resort. Plans for investment must be consistent. There must not be any serious bottlenecks arising from the lack of a critical service or input. Where the resort has one owner, the enterprise concerned has the coordinating role. Where there are many different enterprises, such strategic coordination may be provided by a leading enterprise, an industry association or a government body. Since the resort has a very significant impact on the local region, generating both jobs and income, there may be a strong government interest in stimulating resort development, for example by providing infrastructure or services at a low price.

The arrival of visitors is uneven, because resorts are seasonal. A short winter season leaves the infrastructure of a resort underutilized for the rest of the year.

▶

The short season is a major deterrent to the provision of the full range of facilities required by a permanent alpine village. A lack of out of season activities worsens the problem. During the off-season facilities are underutilized. This creates a problem for the employment of staff who must be part time. The problem can be solved by the availability of a range of different seasonal activities which maintain year-round employment.

There is a definite interest in evening out the patterns of visitation to a resort. The kinds of activities that might be pursued include walking, climbing, mountain bike riding, horse trekking and other sporting activities, even golf. The existence of good sporting facilities allows the provision of training facilities for sporting teams. Educational pursuits might be appropriate. Where there are good hotel and restaurant facilities and good lecture and seminar rooms, conferences can be attracted to the resort.

Attending a resort may involve a main experience, such as skiing, and a range of other experiences ranging from good eating and drinking to sporting activities. The range is extended if it is a family affair.

The skiing season is defined by the presence of adequate snow. The fall of snow at the beginning of the season, and its publicising, is particularly important in setting the tone for the season. Snow making itself, while of increasing importance, can only occur if the temperature is low enough. Artificial snow is used to supplement natural snow. Where the snow season is short and dependent on advantageous weather conditions, there may be bad years when there is little possibility of skiing. Fluctuations in the length of the season affect the level of revenues and costs in any particular year, not only for resort management but for all businesses in a resort. It is hard to break even with bad conditions and even harder to finance investment in improvements.

With global warming the frequency of bad seasons may increase for marginal resorts such as Mt Buller. Any strategic plan needs to take account of the incidence of bad seasons and any change over the years in such incidence. Reading the environment includes tracking the degree and effects of global warming. The problem is larger for resorts which are marginal in the sense that their seasons are already short and variable, generally because they are at a relatively low altitude. Anticipation of global warming may encourage a diversification of resort activities.

Focusing

Focusing is the mechanism by which an enterprise concentrates on certain parts of its operations and not others, for example on certain products, services or market segments for which it has a strong competitive advantage. In the Strategy in Action below, Samsung is concentrating on creating a brand name in the important American market. Focusing may also involve the choice of an activity, or functional area, in the value chain to concentrate on, which is critical to the achievement of such a competitive advantage.

Strategy in Action   Samsung Electronics: a dramatic turnaround – creating the brand

'Samsung Electronics has become a global company living in accord with global standards.'
Jeffrey D. Jones, president of the American Chamber of Commerce in Korea

The economic structure of South Korea is similar to that of Japan. Between 1910 and 1945 South Korea was a colony of Japan. Japanese influence was, and still is, strong, despite the legacy of hostility from World War II. The keiretsu organization of the Japanese economy was closely paralleled by the chaebol system of Korea. Samsung was one of the leading chaebols, an enormous group, comprising

▶

25 different companies and producing a wide range of products, catering mainly for the domestic market. In the pre-1997 world Samsung Electronics was by reputation a 'low-end' maker of refrigerators and VCRs. It was an imitator rather than an initiator.

The South Korean economy was badly affected by the Asian economic crisis of 1997. However, recovery was speedy and dramatic. Samsung responded to that crisis extremely well, much better than the other two large *chaebols*. It developed a turnaround strategy which has left it much better placed in the world economy than previously, although it still carries a legacy of the old Korea Inc., notably in its top-down hierarchy.

Samsung has reinvented itself as a breathtakingly innovative competitor seeking to 'snatch Sony's crown' (Larkin, 2001: 36). It has set out to establish a reputation for quality and innovative ability. It has focused on certain key markets, principally the largest and most demanding of all, the American market, and also on the fastest growing, the Chinese market. It has emerged as a top three player in a host of product areas and a top five receiver of patents on a worldwide basis.

In the depths of the 1997 crisis, Samsung was losing millions of dollars every month. Yet by the next year the *chaebol* was once more profitable. In 2000 the position improved further, with a net income of over US$5 billion. Since then it has flourished. How was this turnaround achieved?

Until 1997 Samsung was hierarchical in structure and deferential in its corporate culture. In 1997 Yun Jong Yong became the CEO. He spoke fluent Japanese and had a Japanese background. He turned the group into what amounted to South Korea's first great global company. There was a pronounced change of leadership and leadership style. The turnaround required a profound shift of attitude, in particular a stress on performance, creativity and open-mindedness. Initially Yun Jong Yong dispensed the traditional medicine, a 30% cut in costs over five months. Overall the company shed 30,000 of its 70,000 workforce and a number of non-core units.

The group began to hire American-educated staff or those with significant experience in the USA. Three non-Koreans become members of the board of directors. Two of the three possible heirs to Yun Jong Yong could speak English. Sixty per cent of the shares of the group were owned by foreigners, including significant ownership by such companies as Apple. The company now generates 70% of its revenues outside South Korea. It manufactures in 14 different countries, including China and Mexico.

There was a deliberate attempt to upgrade the image of Samsung, particularly in the USA. In the words of Idei, Sony's CEO, Samsung 'found Sony a model or a benchmark of their brand image'. In 1999, Eric Kim, a marketing director with considerable experience in the USA, was attracted to the company and set out his strategy immediately: 'Samsung is going to be the first Korean company to create a truly global brand' (Solomon, 2002: A1). The first step in the rebranding of Samsung Electronics was to reduce the 55 advertising agencies working for Samsung to just one. Samsung signed a US$400 million contract with a Maddison Avenue firm, Foote, Cone & Belding Worldwide, whose task was to create a global brand image for Samsung Electronics. An expensive marketing campaign was undertaken, the cost of which in 2002 was $450 million. The aim was to rebrand Samsung as a maker of stylish best-practice products.

At the same time there was a move to effect a partnership with the main purveyors of American technology. At the beginning of 1997 Samsung had almost no presence in mobile phones outside South Korea, but later that year it had won an order for 1.8 million handsets worth $600 million from Sprint, an order which most might have expected to go to Nokia or Ericsson. Not only did Samsung complete the order but it did it in 18 months, half the contracted time. As a consequence the partnership with Sprint has grown, involving the new 3G Sprint wireless system. Samsung now has a reputation for high-end mobile handsets.

Three years ago Samsung had no retail presence in the USA. It has changed that by forging new partnerships, like those with Best Buy, Radio Shack and Circuit City. In these stores there are often lavish displays highlighting Samsung's products. The best sellers are its DVD/VCR players and the mobile phone, which also serves as a PDA (personal digital assistant).

It has succeeded in upgrading the brand name of Samsung. Samsung became a regular and reliable supplier to the main computer companies in the USA,

▶

suppling digital components to Dell and forming a US$16 billion R&D partnership with that company, supplying set-top boxes to AOL Time Warner, digital products to Microsoft and components to the giants, IBM, Compaq and Hewlett-Packard.

Since 1996, but accelerated by the crisis of 1997, it has aimed to differentiate its products on the basis of design. It sought to rank alongside Sony and Motorola as brands, not to outcompete them by undercutting them through price. Over the past few years only Apple has won as many design awards as Samsung. Even with the TVs and DVDs it has deliberately moved upmarket. There are 300 talented designers in Seoul and four design bureaus in the USA, Europe and Japan.

Focusing can occur for three reasons:

- As an unconscious strategy, a spontaneous reaction to the changing circumstances of the market, resulting from adjustments of strategy or operation, which reflect an acute sensitivity on the part of enterprise staff to changes in that market. Any enterprise which automatically takes account of changes in technology or tastes may find itself unconsciously focusing on the areas of greatest opportunity or risk. A product may be subtly differentiated to suit a particular market segment which is newly emerging. At some stage directing attention at a particular market segment creates a new product. Where an enterprise has a portfolio of different products or services, focusing allows the adoption of a strategy which automatically commits resources appropriate to the location in the life cycle of these different products or services.
- As a reaction to the time limitations for senior managers and their staff and the limitations on the resources available to the enterprise. Within any organization it is only possible to concentrate on a few priority areas simultaneously. It is impossible to attach equal importance to all products and activities and to all parts of the enterprise. There is a need, even an inevitable tendency, to prioritize.
- As the obvious benefit of expanding areas of relatively high return and contracting areas where the return is either negative or low. The latter may simply be a matter of benign neglect. Focusing is an aspect of explicit portfolio choice. The enterprise will concentrate on business units which offer the highest return or the best possibility of a high return. It will also concentrate on market segments which offer the best prospect of successful sales.

In other words, whatever the wishes of the managers of an enterprise, events and circumstances inevitably lead to focusing. However, implicit focusing may not be adequate. Given that for various reasons focusing tends to occur everywhere, it is logical to take the next step and make it an explicit strategy. Focusing becomes a deliberate strategy.

The recent history of Samsung illustrates both the advantages and limitations of focusing. Samsung has focused on R&D and the US market but has persisted in producing most of its own inputs for the final products.

Remaking the environment by innovation

Strategy in Action Samsung Electronics: a dramatic turnaround – investing in new technology

Samsung Electronics is the most dynamic part of Samsung. While it generates only a quarter of total revenue, it accounts for three-quarters of net income. The capitalization of Samsung has now overtaken that of Sony. Samsung is behaving like a Korean Sony. It is investing heavily in expanding its electronic capacity, by research and putting in best-practice plants.

In the restructuring of the late 1990s, three strategic business units were created within Samsung Electronics – digital media, telecommunications and semiconductors (memory chips). Samsung is aiming for world leadership in all these areas. The biggest advance was in the first business unit, which now accounts for the largest share of sales (Table 8.1).

The home market of South Korea gives Samsung an advantage in a number of the product areas in which they operate. Fifty-six per cent of South Koreans have mobile phones, which they typically upgrade every eight or so months. This creates a market for the most up-to-date products. More than 50% are already broadband subscribers, way above comparable figures in developed countries. Samsung has made an enormous investment in research in order to place it at the cutting edge of best practice in the three areas above. They adopted what has been called a 'digital-convergence strategy', similar to Sony's strategy.

Today Samsung is the world's largest producer of memory chips and flat-panel monitors (Table 8.2), number two in DVD players, number three in mobile phones, well behind Nokia but catching up on Sony Ericsson. It is most definitely by reputation a 'high-

Table 8.1 Sales in 2001

	%
Telecommunications (mainly mobile phones)	27.9
Digital media (mainly TVs and PCs)	29.1
Semiconductors	27.4
Home appliances (refrigerators, microwave ovens etc)	9.6
Other	6.0
Total US$26.64 billion	

Table 8.2 Products in which Samsung now holds number one spot in the world

	Market share (%)
DRAM (dynamic RAM)	27
SRAM (static RAM)	27
TFT-LCDs (thin film transistor/liquid crystal display)	22
CDMA mobile handsets	26
Computer monitors	22
VCRs	17
Microwave ovens	23

end' maker of mobile phone handsets, DVD and MP3 players, and digital TVs. It has emerged as a leader in the linking of wireless technologies with gadgets ranging from PDAs to refrigerators.

Samsung is investing significantly in order to develop its markets for handsets, in which it is gaining ground rapidly, and memory chips. The biggest commitment is in flat screens. Samsung is investing US$17 billion in the manufacture of sleek flat-screen devices for home and office, TV and PC, on the assumption that demand is expanding rapidly for the flat screens to replace existing thick screens as prices drop significantly. One forecast is that the price of a 40-inch television will fall from $7,500 to $3,500 by 2005, and that sales will double in the next four to five years. The goal for Samsung is to be a first mover in this rapidly expanding market, building production lines at Asan in South Korea which yield a scale of production which make it competitive with any other manufacturers. Already the South Korean producer LG Philips has made a similar commitment, soon to be followed by investments by the threatened Japanese and Taiwanese manufacturers, so that the boom is likely to result very quickly in a significant expansion of capacity and the danger of overcapacity. Other producers, such as Sharpe, are targeting niche markets such as those for large plasma display panel TV screens and yet others small screens for digital cameras and wireless handsets.

In the course of renewing competitive advantage, the really successful companies remake their own environment. In doing so they ignore the normal constraints on size or rate of growth, whether the constraint is the organization's resource endowment or the existing market size. In remaking their environment, most enterprises grow bigger, sometimes very quickly. Growth is generated in two ways:

- internal action as a result of innovation initiated and organized by the enterprise and occurring within the enterprise, referred to as organic growth
- the absorption of other enterprises by acquisition or merger.

The role of innovation

The two mechanisms of growth may be linked since the latter may be a vehicle for helping to realize the innovation which is a result of the former. The enterprise may target new market segments as output grows. Or it might be that the acquisition is targeted to obtain the new technology or new organizational expertise itself.

Innovation takes two forms: a change in technology or a change in organization. Again the two may be closely linked. Often a new business area is organized as a separate strategic business unit within an enterprise, which allows the unit to be structured appropriately. Since the implications of strategy making for already established business activities and new ones are very different, this is probably sensible.

How is it possible to manage change which is both rapid and radical? It is not simply a matter of adjusting to the minimum necessary degree to the change that is going on around the enterprise. Nor is it a matter of marginal or incremental change occurring within the existing business models, that is, change which is simply helping to sustain existing mainstream activities. It is an issue of what has been described as discovery-driven planning, the kind of change which is necessary for an enterprise to suddenly become a major player in a new industry or an already established enterprise to dramatically renew its impetus to growth by innovating in its old business areas.

The emphasis is on both innovation and 'planning' for that innovation. The enterprise is generating the change and deliberately so, not allowing it to happen accidentally. How can it manage or plan that change in a way which ensures the enterprise is not only in control of its own destiny but gets the most out of the opportunities thrown up by the innovation?

Managing disruptive innovations and turnarounds

An enterprise has to develop a viable strategy for generating and successfully managing so-called disruptive innovations, that is, innovations which change radically the nature of an enterprise but also the nature of the industry in which it is operating. This is partly a matter of taking positive measures such as encouraging intrapreneurship or absorbing small companies which are already highly entrepreneurial and partly a matter of avoiding certain obvious mistakes. For an enterprise which has been successful in the past there is a danger that nothing will be done, that success will be allowed to implant its own immunity to further change. In good times there is no need to innovate and no motivation to do so and in bad times the resources are not available to support innovation.

It is in the good times of positive growth that an established enterprise is best able to create the conditions for future growth. It is critical to do so. The enterprise needs to turn an initial ability to create a single new disruptive business into an engine capable of repeating the success.

Other sources of failure Another frequent cause of failure is trying to grow too fast too quickly (see the Strategy in Action on Vivendi). Time is often what is most needed – time to massage markets into life and define a new business model to fit that market. Success is not simply a matter of throwing resources at a project and moving as quickly as possible. Success must be planned and enough time allowed to prepare the ground for success.

Success also requires a business unit to be unprofitable for only a limited period, if at all. However strong the wish to stimulate creativity, there needs to be proper governance and proper financial controls. The discipline of a limited resource availability and an emphasis on the need to cover costs within a relatively short period, if not immediately, is good for any project and concentrates attention on the effective formulation and implementation of an appropriate strategy.

Strategy in Action Vivendi Universal – divesting to survive

Vivendi, an 149-year-old French water and sewerage utility, was converted through takeovers, which amounted to US$77 billion, by its CEO Jean-Marie Messier, a 45-year-old former investment banker, into a communication/entertainment giant to rival in size and spread of assets even the new AOL Time Warner. Messier's strategy was an ambitious one. In 2000 he bought Seagram, the owner of the Universal Music Group, one of the big five music companies, and Universal Studios, a major Hollywood studio; Canal Plus, Europe's biggest pay-TV business; US publisher Houghton Mifflin; and the broadcasting interests of Barry Diller's USA Interactive. Vivendi rode the stock market boom to put together the giant conglomerate in a remarkably short period of time.

At its peak the value of the company reached €154 billion, but, when Messier resigned under pressure on July 1, 2002, the decline in the share price, which had followed Moody's cut in the company's credit-worthiness rating to below investment level, had reduced its value to one-tenth of that high, about €15 billion.

The company had reached a crisis point because:

- it lost the confidence of the capital market
- its strategy of delivering movies and music via mobile devices did not work; it is unlikely to be successful for a number of years
- the build-up of the company left it with €17 billion worth of debt which has to be serviced.

The liquidity position of Vivendi became critical, with €5.6 billion of debt to be refinanced by March 2003.

The refusal of the main bankers to grant a new standby credit line at the end of June 2002 and the final loss of confidence by the French directors, who joined the Americans in seeking a replacement of the CEO, spelled the end for Messier.

The company is likely to be unbundled at an even faster rate than it was constructed. Fortunately many of the businesses are performing well in operational terms.

As a distressed seller, the company needed to divest about US$20 billion of assets. A fire sale threatened and still threatens at the time of writing. The implications of this weak position are clear. News Corp was originally prepared to pay €1.5 billion for Telepiu, but because of Vivendi's parlous position it has managed to drop the price to only €1 billion. A French publishing unit and a Norwegian pay-TV unit have been sold off, at rock bottom prices.

The new CEO, Jean-Rene Fourtou, has to deal with the immediate crisis. In order to do this he has to devise a new strategy. This may involve both a short-term and a long-term strategy. In the short term, there is limited scope for choice of strategy. It involves selling off non-core assets in order to allow Vivendi to service and roll over its debts. This raises the question, what is a non-core asset? How is such

▶

an asset to be defined? Non-core assets may not be the assets for which there is any kind of a market in a recession. This may make inevitable a sale of assets which might be regarded as core assets. A successful short-term strategy would provide more scope for a long-term strategy. A longer term strategy might even involve the sale or demerging of Vivendi Universal Entertainment and Universal Music Group.

It is difficult to read the strategic intentions of Fourtou. Table 8.3 is just one reading of the situation.

What is for sale reflects partly what can be sold, what there is a market for. Prices reflect both the current state of the market and the urgency of sale. A turnaround strategy involves some difficult decisions. What should Vivendi sell?

Table 8.3 **Status of principal assets (August 2002)**

Assets	Comment	Estimated value €billions
For sale		
Houghton Mifflin	US publisher	1.5–2.0
Canal Plus International	Non-French pay-TV (includes Telepiu)	2.0
Canal Plus (after proposed purchase and IPO)	51% of French pay-TV operator	2.0
Canal Plus Technologies	Decoder manufacturer	0.25–0.35
Express-Expansion	French press	?
Vizzavi	50% of internal portal	up to 0.15
Paris St Germain	Football club	0
Undecided		
DuPont	16.4 million shares	0.7
Maroc Telecom	35% stake	1.3–1.5
Universal Pictures	Hollywood studio	2.2–4.0
USA Networks/SciFi Channel	Cable channels	4.0–5.0
Universal Music	Global music group	6.3–8.5
Recreation	Theme parks	1.8–2.5
Echostar	10% stake	1.2
Not for sale		
Cegetel	44% of telecoms subsidiary	5.0–6.5
Vivendi Environnement	40.6% stake in water utility	3.5
Canal Plus	49% of French pay-TV operator	2.0
Vivendi Universal Publishing	Rump European business	3.0

Source: Johnson and Burt, 2002: 20.

<table>
<tr><td>**Encouraging innovation**</td></tr>
</table>

How can innovation be encouraged? There are two main strategies for creating the disruptive innovations which will generate change and growth, in the process remaking the environment. Both require identifying what product offers the best chance of success.

The first sees the enterprise as competing, not with real competitors, but with the consumer's preference to save and not consume at all. This is frequently the case in Asian economies where savings rates are very high and consumer debt levels low. Several questions need to be asked:

• Why is it that a particular product in which the enterprise is interested is currently not being consumed?
• Does the product not fit neatly and easily into the underlying structure of potential consumer needs? If it does, the consumer must be made aware of this in a simple way.
• Has the market not been exploited for one of the following reasons?
  – The potential consumer lacks the relevant information needed to understand the availability and usefulness of the product
  – He or she does not have the money to purchase it

        – He or she lacks the skills to use it
        – Some combination of all these.
- Can such deficiencies be easily rectified?

The second is to tackle competitors head-on. This means taking some part of their market. This is best done by introducing a new 'disruptive' business model which significantly changes the consumer perspective on a particular product. Such an approach does not necessarily demand a disruptive technical change. This may mean asking whether existing products overperform. A simple check on whether this is true or not is to ask whether consumers, faced with the removal of a specific attribute or attributes, are prepared to pay a premium to retain it (them). Are these attributes part of the standard expectation or are they superfluous or redundant? If they are clearly superfluous for the consumer, a low-end strategy may work well, one which separates out a market segment for the product without these attributes.

The no-frills model does exactly this. It removes a number of surplus features from air travel – such as food, free drinks and early booking. By so doing it reduces costs significantly, and makes possible a reduced price. There must be significantly lower costs associated with such a strategy in order to allow the newcomer to make a normal profit. In the airline case the profits arise from the use of secondary airports with lower charges and less delay, a single type of plane with lower training and maintenance costs, and minimal terminal and booking facilities.

Such a strategy works best if the competitors are prepared to give away this part of the market. The strategy most likely not to invite retaliation is one which removes only a small part of the market, small relative to the whole. In this case the incumbent may be reluctant to compete on price with the newcomers, since it will hurt existing profits. For the incumbent or incumbents it is not worth the effort of taking action to prevent loss of this market segment.

Evaluating innovation

How can an enterprise evaluate such a strategy? Preparation for the adoption of such a strategy can take a number of different forms. One suggestion is to start with a reverse income statement, which runs from the bottom line up. In other words, the enterprise starts with a target profit level and works from there to test the viability of the particular project. The target level for the new price and the target number of consumers are known. The income statement is based on many assumptions which need to be articulated and questioned. Projects come unstuck because they accept without query assumptions based on past success. It is appropriate to list the range of activities or operations which must be undertaken in order to ensure the operation of the business, and the costs of these. If all this is done and the project is viable, there must be a timetable, a chart of what needs to be done and when.

Implications of remaking the environment

There are positive features of riding the unpredictable, answering a challenge and making a large return for a small outlay. There are also negative features, risks which can undo the unwary.

Managing risk often involves trying to control the environment in a quite deliberate manner, taming the forces of change to yield opportunity at the minimum risk. This requires ironing out all technical problems, preferably by and at the expense of others; marshalling all the necessary resources – organizational, financial, political; eliminating competitors, if possible; and massaging all the appropriate markets.

Enterprises can remake their internal environment by developing new capabilities and competencies, renewing and reintegrating existing resources, acquiring new resources in the market or gaining access to new resources by selective strategic alliances. It is much harder to remake quickly the structure or culture of the enterprise, but even such a remake can be achieved as the result of deliberate action taken at the appropriate time over a long period.

The relevant strategies often involve trying to avoid a competitive backlash. This may not always be possible. Enterprises can remake their competitive environment by aggressive strategic behaviour which leads to acquiring other enterprises or outperforming and outgrowing them in various ways, or by persuading others to act passively, usually with the implicit backup of a threat of even more aggressive behaviour. Such behaviour is not sensible unless the enterprise knows that it can succeed.

Much strategic analysis makes it appear that the external environment is a given. In reality strategy is usually concerned with remaking the environment in some way, for some that is the main aim. Operational decisions tend to perpetuate the past, strategic decisions to remake the present as a more desirable future. The further ahead the strategy looks, the more parameters become variable and the greater the possibility that the enterprise can have a hand in making that future.

Such a remake may involve the introduction of a new product or process or an attempt to influence tastes directly, that is, open up a new market or expand an old one. Change is the consequence of countless individual decisions of this kind, many of them by their nature radical and strategic. All the main players are engaged in this exercise.

Change is an interactive process in which each enterprise, by remaking itself, is remaking the external environment of others. Since any enterprise is part of the environment of other enterprises, a change in the structure, culture or resources of that enterprise represents at least a partial remaking of both the general and the competitive environments of all other enterprises.

Competitive advantage and market structures

Another method of acquiring competitive advantage is to remove those who can outcompete the enterprise or, if removal is impossible, in some way neutralize the advantage held by these enterprises. The actions taken to achieve this may not be limited to the two strategies of cost leadership and product differentiation. There are various methods of achieving the removal or neutralization of competitors. Most of these methods have a lasting effect on the degree of competition in the market.

Alternative strategies for gaining competitive advantage

There are four such strategies:

1. *Acquire, or merge with, a competing enterprise*, particularly if it has gained, or threatens to gain, some distinct advantage. There are three constraints on this kind of action:
   • Limited access to the financial resources required to do this. It may be a very expensive strategy.

- The unwillingness of the other enterprise to be acquired. There may be resistance not only from senior managers but also from key stakeholder groups, if the target is a public company.
- Barriers erected by government. The diminution of competition may be unacceptable to the key lawmaker, the government, or one of its regulatory agencies which administers the policy. The legal rules of anti-monopoly policy may constrain this process.

2. *Drive another enterprise out of business*. This requires that the enterprise has sufficient resources to do this, or has an underlying cost advantage. This may also require substantial financial resources, usually resources in excess of those held by the competitors. The strategy might be to reduce price to a low level and hold it there for sufficiently long to threaten the viability of the competitor or competitors. A price war can be expensive for all concerned. Predatory pricing also upsets governments and their regulatory agencies. There are other means; the strategy may be to get control of a key input and deny this to the competitor.

3. *Persuade consumers that you are offering a vastly superior product*. It helps if there is some reason to believe this. There is a clear overlap between this strategy and a product differentiation strategy. This strategy may involve a major marketing campaign and expenditure of resources. An advertising war can be as expensive as a price war. It is likely to take much longer to achieve a clear victory. Such a strategy may encourage competitors to engage in defensive marketing and ratchet up costs generally in the industry.

4. *Persuade government to change the rules in favour of the enterprise*. This can take an infinite number of forms including: extension of the period of validity of a patent (as in the pharmaceutical industry); restriction of foreign imports through informal quotas (as in the automobile industry); and restriction on the number of players in a market segment (as in the airline industry). Almost every industry has its restrictive rules, and these rules are not immutable. The main aim of an enterprise is to limit in some way the degree of competition and the number of players.

Competition and competitive advantage

In considering these strategies, the analysis above has assumed implicitly a market structure which is oligopolistic. In a perfectly competitive market, as defined by economists, there is no strategy which could possibly achieve competitive advantage in the way described above. The more competitive a market, the less the strategies described above are available to any enterprise. All enterprises become reactive rather than proactive, unable to impose their will on the market. They cannot control price, they cannot differentiate their product. Competition denies them the resources to acquire other enterprises. In reality cost positions differ, often significantly, and products are perceived to be different, sometimes so different that some are branded. This generates both the scope and resources needed for acquisitions, aggressive price behaviour or a major marketing campaign. Moreover, acquisitions and the other policies described above push the industry towards oligopoly.

Market imperfections

All strategies share one common characteristic. Any competitive advantage is created by market imperfections, in particular by the introduction of elements of monopoly, whatever their nature. These imperfections involve creating and maintaining barriers to entry of various kinds, barriers which are not insignificant. They might involve a monopoly control over knowledge of a process or product, the ownership of a brand or the putting into place of rules which limit the number of players. Other players can also be removed by aggressive action of various kinds, including purchase. All enterprises are on a ceaseless quest to create these elements of monopoly.

E-commerce and services

> There is no such thing as e-business; there is just business and some of it is electronic.
> (Coltman et al., 2002: 72)

The business world is in the middle of the so-called information/communications revolution. The present revolution has only just begun to reveal its full nature. Such revolutions create threats to existing capital, both physical and human, but they create opportunities for new investment and new enterprises and organizations.

Most visionary predictions made concerning e-business and the notion of an info/communications revolution are unlikely to be realized immediately, and in some cases not at all. The revolution is alleged to have the following outcomes:

- the influence of brand names will dissipate
- the role of middlemen of all sorts will disappear, sales to the consumer will become much more direct, as in the Dell model
- the scale of production or delivery is now irrelevant to the level of the unit costs of production or sale
- the price of affected products will become significantly lower.

If a technological change is genuinely revolutionary, it should be accompanied by some of these anticipated changes, but, judging by previous revolutions, the outcome is likely to be incremental, unfolding over a long period of time, at least in its eventual impact.

The objections to the notion of a revolution are therefore partly semantic, hinging on what, in terms of speed or extent, constitutes a true revolution and partly empirical, hinging on the outcomes of the revolution and their significance.

Some commentators have rejected the notion of a revolution on the grounds that:

- the term 'revolution' should only be applied to radical change, either in the way the vast majority of people shop or consume their purchases or in how most business is conducted on a day-to-day basis.
- the degree of productivity change which has been caused by the so-called revolution has been exaggerated. All figures on the acceleration in productivity increase which has occurred in the key economies are controversial, particularly where they relate to the productivity of services.

- many B2C (business-to-consumer) and B2B (business-to-business) strategies have often failed to deliver what was promised.

Opportunities created by the revolution

Since communications are inputs into every part of the economy, every aspect of the activity of an enterprise and every sector of the economy will eventually be affected by the communications revolution. The revolution creates pressure for the application of a mass of micro-inventions to help exploit the opportunities created by the macro-inventions at the core of the revolution – the new means of communication represented by the Internet. In order to maintain competitive advantage, every organization has to absorb the lessons of this revolution.

The revolution creates opportunities for new enterprises and allows old enterprises to diversify. It creates opportunities for:

- reducing costs dramatically through B2B e-commerce
- differentiating the product through new marketing schemes based on company websites, which are becoming more elaborate and sophisticated
- selling directly to the final consumer, that is, engaging in B2C e-commerce.

The most important current result of the Internet is the better branding of an enterprise through its website. There are other gains; for example new information systems allow better financial control systems and more sensitive booking systems. For example, systems such as Sabre or Fidelio are revolutionizing the airline business by linking up booking systems.

The way in which the new systems are relevant to different industries varies enormously. Any organization faced with competitors taking advantage of the new technology has no choice but to imitate, or even better to innovate ahead of the others.

The revolution has a twofold impact, establishing two opposed tendencies:

1. It encourages centralization, by making possible better control in larger and larger organizations.
2. It makes possible a greater decentralization of decision making. It can have a similar effect to the introduction of electricity or the motorcar in democratizing communications, as energy supply and transportation have been democratized. It encourages the activity of many small enterprises, often working from a home base. It increases enormously the ability of such enterprises to move quickly and operate without expensive infrastructure.

Constraints on the development of e-commerce

The most dramatic manifestation in the future is likely to be the development of e-commerce. E-commerce has not as yet realized the great expectations placed on it. It is still at a formative stage. Many of the dot.coms, set up to sell a wide range of products, extending to such oddities as pet foods, have failed, in whatever country they were founded. Few companies have been successful, and only in specialized categories of goods and services, for example discount brokers, Amazon or eBay. One group of experts has predicted a maximum online penetration for books of as little as 15% which shows the severe constraints on e-commerce, even in an area where it has a distinct advantage. There is a general tendency to use the Internet, not so much for online selling, but for creating websites as marketing and information tools.

One example illustrates the distinction nicely. In Australia, as elsewhere, there have been a series of failures of dot-com companies, for example companies trying to sell wine online – Winepros, Wine Planet, Bottleshop.com.au and possibly Wine Online have all tried and failed. The reason is simple; 95% of wine bought in Australia is consumed within 24 hours of purchase. Online selling requires purchase in lots of a dozen bottles and delivery with a delay of at least several days. Purchase of high premium bottles might be organized through the Internet since it is not for immediate consumption and, because of the high price, might be worth transacting singly. On the other hand, in Australia there are as many as 22,100 websites providing information on the wine industry and seeking to promote the branding of a particular product. Naturally all the wineries have such sites.

There are many specific reasons for not buying online, which usually relate to the nature of the product, its purchase or consumption. There are some difficulties which affect all potential buyers, including:

- problems of security – initially there were serious security problems which have limited development at the retail level. There is a general perception that the system is insecure, in that credit card details become available to those who will misuse them
- a possible invasion of privacy – information acquired by a customer's use of the Internet can be misused
- heightened uncertainty – there are more unknowns than for normal purchase, for example doubts about quality or delivery time
- issues of consumer protection – many of these issues lie in areas of uncertainty from a legal perspective
- continuing low bandwidth for most potential consumers
- limited access by the consumer to the relevant network.

E-commerce depended for its expansion on the spread of the PC. One of the great success stories in developing a business model which yielded significant competitive advantage is Dell.

Strategy in Action Dell and direct sales

'Michael Dell looms over the PC landscape like a giant, casting a shadow over all his unfortunate competitors.'   *Serwer, 2002: 55*

In the sale of computers to businesses, one supplier has becoming increasingly dominant. Dell revolutionized the PC industry though its direct sales model. It adopted a strategy which has proved very

successful. That model made use of both the Internet and a highly customized approach which tailored the attributes of a product to the particular needs of the customer. It provided a personal service which was highly regarded by its customers. It divided the business market from the ordinary retail market, carving out a separate market segment. Dell made its machines to order and delivered them direct to the customer. It customized according to the requirements of individual enterprises and individuals within those enterprises. There were to be no middlemen, which reduced costs significantly. Direct sale gave Dell a tremendous advantage in the speed of delivery and the cost of the computer to the final customer. It meant that the product was differentiated to meet particular customer wants.

Dell has been likened to Wal-Mart, in that it extracts more and more from its component suppliers. Its rapid growth and high market share has given it considerable bargaining power. It has been able to push its costs down in this way to supplement the impact of direct sales. It is able to compete through cost leadership.

From 1995 to 2001, Dell has grown at a compound rate of 42% per annum, well above the rate of growth of even Wal-Mart. The share of the business market accounted for by Dell reached just under 25% in 2001 and on industry expectations is headed for as high as 40%. By contrast, the next two suppliers, Compaq and Hewlett-Packard (HP), accounted for only 13.3% and 9.7% respectively. Less than ten years ago, in 1994, Compaq was at 13.6% and HP 2.4%, but Dell at only 4.2%. HP has been losing ground, Compaq just maintaining its position. By contrast, in dominating this particular market, Dell was rapidly translating itself into the equivalent of Microsoft or Intel. In order to do so, it has used the new technology of e-commerce and has provided not only low costs but a highly differentiated product.

Can Dell continue to use its existing strategy and business model in the way which has made it very successful? There are problems:

- *A maturing industry.* Even before the recession it was obvious that the market for computers was becoming a mature one, the product becoming a commoditized one. Moreover, the product, its components and the services associated with it had been separated and commoditized. There were clear industry standards. Specialist suppliers provided the products, components and services. A sign of the times was that IBM had largely withdrawn from producing computers to concentrate on computer services. Others such as Hewlett-Packard and Compaq are trying to follow suit. Computers are likely to be a slow-growth business with increasingly tight profit margins.
- *Increased competition.* Many computer manufacturers competed to produce what had become a fairly standard product. There is already a tendency to seek out lower cost sources for component production and assembly. The industry is subject to competition from a host of new devices, with attributes superior to the humble PC. The industry was, and still is, ripe for consolidation.
- *Recession.* The recession of 2000–02 knocked the bottom out of a market which was already growing at a slowing rate and which had become fiercely competitive. Demand fell dramatically, partly because the market in developed economies was saturated and partly because users could easily postpone replacement in the absence of any major change in technology which added significant new attributes to a computer. In 2001, for the first time since the product was launched, PC sales actually fell. The era of rapid growth had come to an end. The industry has come of age.
- *Imitation of the business model.* Other manufacturers have sought to imitate the model. With the fall in demand, the computer manufacturers have been under immense pressure to cut their costs. One way of achieving this is adoption of the successful Dell model.

Dell is itself seeking to apply its business model to a wider area:

- the sale of printers and servers
- the sale of computers to individual home consumers.

It is unclear whether the business model is relevant to these areas.

Areas of e-expansion

There are some areas where the problems of security and so on have not limited growth – the purchase of books and airline tickets, private auctions, stockbroking and the sale of pornography or gambling. A homogeneous or standard product, the ease with which partners to a transaction are brought together, the desire for anonymity of purchase or consumption and the parallel use of a normal bank account for payment explain the greater success in these areas.

However, at the B2B level there has been a much more significant increase in the use of e-commerce, particularly for the procurement of components. It has proved much easier for a small number of companies to get together to exploit the benefits of e-commerce. The motorcar industry is one of the best examples of what is happening. Large companies generally are better equipped to communicate electronically. They are much more cost conscious. There are particularly strong network effects in any scheme as membership grows. All have an interest in extending the networks in order to reap network externalities. These network effects explain why over time the impact of e-commerce will grow dramatically.

In the usual manner of market systems, there is a tendency to overshoot and exaggerate the consequences of the revolution. The rise and fall of the new economy is not a new phenomenon, rather the result of the natural fluctuations of a market economy faced with any technological revolution. The crash of numerous dot-coms offering information services and the massive oversupply of telecommunications capacity are part of this overshooting. The activity of such dot-coms will eventually become standard, at least in areas where they either reduce costs significantly or allow a better package of services to be associated with purchase. Demand for the services of the telecoms will eventually overtake the capacity.

Such revolutions change the way of doing things but they do not remove the strategic constraints which always exist. The principles of business success have not changed. At some stage all enterprises have to make a profit. The price–earnings ratio may reflect the expectation of future profit streams but cannot move far away from the norm. Every enterprise must remain liquid, able to meet any sudden cash requirement. It cannot continue making a loss indefinitely. The only way to survive a revolution is to remain cool and appraise the full implications in a calm and collected manner. There will be many casualties of this revolution. As with every revolution it is consuming, and will continue to consume its own children. All such technological revolutions are examples of 'creative destruction'.

The present revolution contains within itself the seeds of the next revolution, the bioengineering revolution, since the complexity of the genome and its unravelling depends upon the computing power of modern communications technology. The level of biochemical complexity is much greater than often assumed and this revolution will be rather longer coming than is usually assumed. Its influence will eventually spread well beyond the pharmaceutical industry and medical sector. Assisted by government regulation, the hydrogen cell is more likely to indicate the next technical boom.

The services transition

There are a number of important changes occurring, which have been referred to earlier, which are dramatically changing the general environment of all enterprises. The rise of the manufacturing sector relative to the agricultural sector merited the graphic description of 'Industrial Revolution'. There is no such name for the rise of the tertiary sector or services relative to the secondary sector, a far more sweeping change. The arrival of postindustrial or postmodern society is equally as dramatic and significant for business life.

The rise in the importance of services is almost as important as the communications revolution to which it is linked, but it is far less obvious. One characteristic of the revolution relates to the rising proportion of GDP and employment accounted for by services. The vast majority of the labour force in developed economies is employed in services, largely because a rising proportion of income in these countries is spent on the products of this sector. An increasing proportion of services are being traded, and traded at the global level. The share of exports consisting of services such as education, health, tourism, entertainment, travel, financial services and consulting is rising all the time.

The services package

Another aspect relates to the rising importance of services as part of the products produced, packaged and sold from manufacturing or agriculture. Service inputs are a vital part of product differentiation. For example, less than 10% of the price of most food products is accounted for by on-farm production costs. The other 90% consists mostly of the services needed to get the product to the consumer in a form which is desired. Services are linked to the physical products in ways which enhance their attractiveness. They are critical to the whole process of product differentiation. Since they are so important, the improved delivery of service inputs is also a vital part of cost reduction for all sectors of the economy.

The communications revolution has allowed an enormous increase in productivity and reduction in costs to occur in the service sector and the influence of that reduction to spread to all industries. There is now an ongoing process of cost reduction which is sweeping through every part of the services sector, including banking, insurance, health, education and all government services. Some of these industries are shedding labour at a rapid rate or expanding significantly without adding to their labour force. The revolution is having a profound effect on the organization of production and selling. It cannot be ignored.

Case Study   Hutchison and the introduction of third generation wireless communication

Hutchison has pushed through a movement to the new generation of wireless communication. In order to understand the implications of this, it is necessary to review the development of the technology.

The technology

1G (first generation)

This was the beginning of wireless communication. The first truly mobile phone system came into being between the late 1970s and early 1990s. In Australia, for example, the analogue mobile phone system was first introduced in 1987. At first the mobile or cellphone was known as the cellular mobile radio telephone (see the case study on Nokia in Chapter 16 for comments on its early history). The voice signalling system was entirely analogue, that is, it sought to reproduce the frequency of the voice with all its modulations.

2G (second generation)

The second generation began in the early 1990s. This is the period of sustained takeoff in wireless communication. The introduction of digital voice encoding began. For the first time the networks allowed data services – in Australia in 1991. Much of the technology in use today is second generation technology. There is a 2.5 generation, a stretched version of the second generation.

3G (third generation)

The main distinguishing feature of the different generations is speed of data transmission. This determines what can be transmitted. The International Telecommunications Union defines 3G by two speed requirements – data transmission speeds of at least 144 kilobits (thousand bits) per second in wide area mobile environments, and 2 megabits (million bits) per second inside buildings. Only W-CDMA and CDMA2000 1EV-DO satisfy these requirements.

This generation has barely begun. Technology has become fully digitalized and makes full use of available bandwidth, significantly broader than in earlier generations. The technology can be used in personal and business communication. It is available in all popular modes, such as mobile phone, email, paging, fax, video conferencing and Web browsing. There is a facility for enhanced multimedia communication.

During the second and third generations, the technology applied was initially CDMA (code-division multiple access), the protocol most popular in the Americas, South Korea and Japan. The protocol allows numerous signals to occupy a simple transmission channel, optimising the use of available bandwidth. An alternative is global system for mobile communications (GSM), which has an estimated 825 million users worldwide, the most popular system, one used by most operators in Europe and Asia.

W-CDMA (wideband CDMA) is currently the core technology of the third generation. It offers much higher data speeds to wireless devices than previously or commonly provided for. It greatly increases the potential range of possible applications. A substitute which does not generally fully satisfy the requirements of 3G is CDMA2000. General packet radio service (GPRS) is an upgrade of GSM. A further upgrade is EDGE (enhanced data rates for GSM evolution).

For 2G GSM had speeds of 9.6 Kbps, and CDMA 14 Kbps. For 2.5G the GPRS upgrade of GSM has speeds of about 40 Kbps although in theory it could extend up to 170 Kbps. EDGE offers up to 437 Kbps in theory, but in practice closer to 100–120 Kbps. The CDMA2000 1XRTT sometimes operates at about 70 Kbps, with usual speeds of 144 Kbps, although in theory it could reach 307 Kbps. For data alone CDMA2000 1XEV-DO offers 2.4 Mbps, and a further version, not yet operating, CDMA2000 1XEV-DV, offers both voice and data.

In view of the high licence fees for the use of third generation wireless it is not surprising that one of the licence holders has decided to go ahead with the development of the technology, seeking first-mover advantage. It was a matter of which player would take the lead in doing this. Given the circumstances of the market, it is unlikely that other players will quickly imitate.

First-mover advantage

Hutchison is taking a significant risk in introducing the third generation wireless technology, committing a high level of resources to this project. It is likely that in the short run its competitors will simply observe how Hutchison is doing. Whether this investment is justified depends on working out the relative advantages and disadvantages of being a first mover, and the speed with which others can respond if it proves a success.

The advantages of being the first mover are that the first mover:

- establishes an important, if not the, brand name in the new area. In an extreme case the particular product becomes synonymous with the technology. Hutchison's use of 3 as its brand name emphasizes the generational leap. However, this primacy can backfire if the teething problems of a new product undermine the good name of the pioneer seller. There are many possible teething problems, as shown below. Hutchison needs to establish itself not only as an innovative pioneer, but as one which is a reliable and relatively cheap provider of a new consumer product
- develops considerable expertise both in the new technology and in the bundling of consumer services and product attributes in a process of learning by doing
- plays an important role in setting the commonly accepted standards for the new technology.

There are offsetting disadvantages, which are that the first mover:

- has to take a wager on which new standard will emerge as victor
- bears the costs of technical development as well as the investment required in setting up a new network. It is estimated that, including the cost of the licence, it costs 50% more to build a 3G network than a traditional one. This requires a market share of at least 25–30% in order to break even, a difficult ask of any new product
- has to turn new technology into consumer products which are in demand; in other words it has to establish a new market segment, with product attributes which satisfy consumer needs. As already indicated, it is unclear at this stage what these will be
- has to win that market segment by drawing customers from existing players, customers who may be well content with the existing products.

The market is already a fiercely competitive one. One problem is that the costs of the hardware and the software of the new technology are likely to be high, which, if reflected in the price, will reduce the competitiveness of the new product. The new handsets, since they will include a digital still camera, a video camera, an MP3 player and an Internet-connected computer, are likely to be expensive, probably twice as expensive as existing handsets, at least if price reflects the real cost level. This will limit the size of market. It is likely that the monthly charge, covering the fees for each service, needed to break even is going to be high. It is open to the first mover to charge at below cost, but this requires both ample resources and a confidence that future returns will justify such a strategy.

The 3G handsets, at least initially, are also likely to be big, heavy, short on battery life as well as expensive, since the technology is immature. This was certainly the case initially with DoCoMo. This reduces their attractiveness to potential purchasers. It does appear to have been true of the first handsets sold in Europe and Australia.

What does Hutchison stand to gain or lose? Success will establish it as a major player in the industry. Failure will lose the company a lot of money. One of the reasons why Hutchison has a good appetite for risk is that it is a conglomerate, with very significant interests in ports, infrastructure, retail and property, and only 13% of its revenue coming from the telecommunication sector in 2001. It is in a strong position to undertake a difficult and expensive project. Failure would not necessarily destroy the company. Fortunately all the other players, including its partners, want Hutchison to succeed since this will help them to recoup their own commitment of resources.

Alternative technical standards

Recently the Chinese government surprised all the main players with announcement that it was backing the standard TD-SCDMA (time division-synchronous code-division multiple access). This is important since China is the largest mobile phone market in the world, with 190 million subscribers. The government in China has allocated a substantial portion of the scarce 3G radio-frequency spectrum for networks using the home-grown standard, two blocks representing 55 MHz as against just one block of 60 for the other two. It has also established a TD-SCDMA industrial alliance between the German firm Siemens and the state-owned local company Datang to develop the new technology. There is some disagreement on when the technology might be commercialized, with Siemens claiming a starting date as early as 2003, and Datang indicating late 2004.

Nokia/Texas Instruments and Luck Goldstar have entered an Rmb230 million venture to develop the handsets and other equipment for TD-SCDMA. Qualcomm has leapt in with a charge that this alliance is violating its patents for the technology. This is a matter which has been fought out in the courts, resulting in various settlements and will continue to be so.

The American standard is much cheaper to establish since it needs less base stations and very often no new licence. The EDGE technology improves performance but can be applied with the existing base station network. The network cost is as little as one tenth of the cost with the W-CDMA standard. However the W-CDMA standard is technically superior, carries much more traffic and has the greatest potential in the future. The choice by China will have large implications since it is by far the largest potential market. Whichever is chosen, experience shows that it will take years before the technology is stable, as introduction of the previous generations has already shown.

Some of the companies are hedging their bets by being involved in the development of more than one standard. It is no means clear which is going to predominate in the future. There are short-term advantages in not going for the technically superior technology. Path dependence shows that choices now will determine the future course of development of the industry. Financial demands may incline operators to a second-best technology, or there may be a compromise in which the superior technology is limited at first to densely trafficked urban areas.

The early outcomes

There is a conviction among observers and in the market that Hutchison is making a mistake and this is affecting its ability to raise money. Hutchison is suffering, in that its shares almost halved in value over 2002, largely as a result of fears about 3G. The company had to cancel a bond issue of US$1.45 billion. Even a company with Hutchison's resources is not immune from damage caused by the failure of such a large project.

This view has discouraged others from entering the play. Even minor players who have entered a partnership with Hutchison have showed an inclination to withdraw. The reaction of most other players has been to stretch the capacity of the second generation technology to provide as many of the third generation services as possible. The more popular of these – picture messaging, access-

	W-CDMA	CDMA2000	TD-SCDMA
Backers	EU countries	Qualcomm (USA)	China
Supply companies	Nokia, Sony Ericsson	Lucent, Samsung	Siemens, Datang
Key markets	Europe, Japan	USA, Japan, South Korea, China	China

Figure 8.6 **Possible 3G technical standards**

ing corporate email, online ticket booking – are already available using second generation technology, supplied by Nokia and Samsung. In some cases, the services are not far short of those provided by Hutchison. This may act as a stopgap until it becomes clear how the market is responding to the Hutchison initiative. It is possible that an unexpected service such as global positioning will turn out to be the prime seller.

For its competitors the entrance of Hutchison 3 represents, and will continue to represent, a competitive challenge. The British market is a good example. The launch of the new system was not impressive. The bad press for clunky handsets with low battery life and poor network coverage and connections inevitably led to a poor subscription rate running well short of target levels. There was a rumour of a significant number of handset returns because of poor quality. As a consequence the strategy of Hutchison was quickly changed from an emphasis on product differentiation, with the next generation services of video and high-speed data transfer, to one based on price. The price was reduced to a level only one-third of the average level, supported by low handset prices. The response in the market has been positive, with sales rising by five times. The other players may be forced to follow suit with the result of a price war. How long Hutchison can sustain such a price war is unclear.

The difficulties of Hutchison were compounded by two events soon after the launch of 3 in Britain, firstly, a downgrading of its credit rating by Standard & Poor's and secondly, difficulty with a minority shareholder partner in the British venture. Hutchison has a 65% share while the minority partners are the Japanese pioneer DoCoMo (20%) and the Dutch carrier KPN Mobile (15%). Hutchison 3 made a £1 billion cash call to assist in securing loan extensions from its banks to finance the new project. KPN refused to meet its obligation of £150 million, on the grounds that it was a breach of its shareholder contract. It demanded that the Hong Kong group buy it out at '140% of fair price'. Hutchison sued for damages, having had to fill the gap by raising capital, thus creating further exposure to the project.

Case Study Questions

1. What are the main problems which might arise when an enterprise is seeking to gain competitive advantage by being at the cutting edge of technological innovation?
2. What is the nature of the relationship between a new technology and a new product?
3. Why is Hutchison adopting such a risky strategy in being the first mover on 3G?
4. If Hutchison is successful, what will be the impact on the industry and the other players in that industry?
5. Indicate first-mover advantages and disadvantages in at least one other industry compared with mobile communications.

Reading

Bolande, H. A., 'Hire wireless act', *Far Eastern Review*, October 31, 2002: 36–40.

Bolande, H. A. and Drucker, J., 'China's schism on cell-phones rocks industry', *Wall Street Journal* (Eastern edn), November 1, 2002: B1.

Budden, R., 'New entrant Hutchison sees big surge in 3G phone sales', *Financial Times*, June 21/2 2003, Money and Business: 1.

Financial Times IT Review, June 18, 2003.

Hewett, J. and Kruger, C., 'Hutchison readies for space-age mobile attack', *The Age*, April 14, 2003.

Kruger, C., '3G, opening on a screen near you', *The Age*, April 11, 2003.

Kunii, I., 'DoCoMo gets a clearer sign', *Business Week*, April 21, 2003: 22.

Kynge, J. ,'China backs home-grown 3G technology', *Financial Times*, November 1, 2002: 17.

Leahy, J., 'Hutchison Whampoa downgraded', *Financial Times*, June 13, 2003: 31.

Leahy, J. and Bickerton, I., 'Hutchison threatens to sue as KPN finds 3 a crowd', *Financial Times*, June 12, 2003, Companies and Markets: 23.

Leahy, J. and Nuttall, C.,'Li Ka-shing's 3G plan hits a snag', *Financial Times*, June 13, 2003: 31.

Nutall, C., 'Hutchison mobile price cuts represent a tough call for rivals', *Financial Times*, June 6/7, 2003 Money and Business M3.

Key strategic lessons

• Competitive advantage is a relative notion, referring to the ability of one enterprise to satisfy customers better than other enterprises.

• All generic strategies have the aim of maximizing the value added in transactions. This involves maximizing the difference between the value of the output for the consumer and the cost of inputs for the suppliers. The division of the value added between the players – customers, producers and suppliers – is a significant strategic issue.

• There are five possible generic strategies: cost leadership, product differentiation, focused cost

Key strategic lessons cont'd

leadership, focused product differentiation and a combination of cost leadership and product differentiation.

• Focusing, or concentrating on certain products or services rather than others, is a separate strategy. Often an implicit response to external change or resource constraints, focusing should be made explicit.

• Every generic strategy involves some remaking of the external and internal environments. Sometimes the remaking is radical and implies a significant disregard for market or resource constraints. This 'disruptive innovation' includes changes to process, product or organization.

• The remaking can involve the creation of new markets, by encouraging customers to buy new products, or the segmentation of old markets by stripping attributes from existing products.

• Deliberate removal or neutralization of competitors can be achieved by acquisition of (or merger with) a dangerous competitor, the use of price or promotional wars, or by persuading governments to change the rules of the game.

• E-commerce in the form of B2B and B2C is a significant issue, but it can be exaggerated, as the slow rate of change, low rate of productivity acceleration and necessary commitment of large resources show.

• The e-commerce revolution can either encourage centralization, since the efficiency of information control systems is enhanced, or promote decentralization, since individuals have much better access to information and the means of communication.

• E-commerce is part of a much broader revolution, which is the rising importance of services.

Applying the lessons

1 Define the following: a cost leadership strategy, a focused cost leadership strategy, a price leadership strategy, a product differentiation strategy, economic added value, disruptive innovation and focusing.

2 What is the time period over which competitive advantage can be retained without any action on the part of the enterprise? How far does this period differ from industry to industry? What factors influence the length of the relevant period?

3 Give any examples of the pursuit of a pure cost leadership strategy or a pure product differentiation strategy that you might be aware of. If there are no or few such examples, explain why this might be.

4 The rate of innovation differs from one sector of the economy to another. How might it be possible to measure the rate of innovation in these different

sectors? What are the factors which determine the rate of innovation?

5 How has the communications revolution affected the creation and maintenance of competitive advantage in the following industries?

> Automobiles
>
> Entertainment
>
> Electronic hardware
>
> Airlines
>
> Pharmaceuticals

6 In what sense have services become the main focus of the economic system of any developed country and the new economy, and therefore critical to the creation and maintenance of competitive advantage in that economy?

Strategic project

1 Comparative advantage in the pharmaceutical industry depends on the development of an appropriate portfolio of drugs. There are a number of alternative ways of gaining access to such a portfolio.

2 What are the strategies adopted by the following

pharmaceutical companies in maintaining a balanced portfolio of drugs?

> America Home Product Corporation; Merck; Pfizer; Novartis; GlaxoSmithKline.

Exploring further

Porter is the originator of the distinction made in generic strategies between cost leadership and product differentiation, and introduced focusing as part of the distinction. Once more this approach has its limitations.

Much of the reading relevant to the previous chapter is also relevant to this one. It provides the building blocks for competitive advantage. There is usually a distinction made between creating competitive advantage and maintaining it. In Ghemawat's 1996 book, in which competitive advantage and value creation are central ideas, Chapter 3 is devoted to the former and both Chapter 4 and Chapter 5 to the latter. This is appropriate since innovation is a key to maintaining competitive advantage.

An excellent introduction to the requirements on an enterprise to maintain competitive advantage in a context of change can be found in Tushman and O'Reilly, 1996: 8–30.

There is quite a literature on the role of innovation in achieving competitive advantage. There is an argument that disruptive innovation rather than sustaining innovation is what is required. A short introduction to the argument can be found in Christensen and Bower, 1996: 197–218. The issues are discussed at much greater length in Christensen, 1997. See also Hill et al., 1993: 79–95. An interesting and original approach is Kim and Mauborgne, 1997: 102–15.

First-mover advantages are discussed in Liberman and Montgomery, 1988: 41–58.

There is quite a literature on turnarounds. The first extended treatment looks at the reason why they are needed: Argenti, 1976. There is another longer piece which deals with the turnaround itself: Siafter, 1984. Shorter pieces are Hoffman, 1984: 46–66 and Schendel et al., 1976: 1–22.

The role of the Internet is discussed in Hamel, 1999: 70–84 and in Porter, 2001: 63–78. Quinn, 1993, is particularly good on the role of services.

9 Reducing costs

Key strategic challenge

How do I keep my costs as low as possible?

Strategic dangers

That the enterprise fails to pay sufficient attention to all aspects of its cost position, particularly those elements which account for the largest part of costs, with the result that the enterprise is easily outcompeted in price by other enterprises and experiences a deteriorating profit performance.

Case Study Scenario   Infosys and the Indian comparative advantage

'Global standards at Indian costs.'   *Company slogan*

India may be the next economic miracle waiting to happen, following the miracles in Japan, the four little tigers and China. For most of the 1980s and 90s, India sustained unprecedented growth rates of GDP, around 5–6%. In 1991 the Indian government of Rao and Singh began the process of switching from a planned economy to a market economy, repeating China's gradual reform. It began to open up the economy, deregulate markets and withdraw the government from direct economic activity, quietly reforming the 'licence raj' of the planning era. In a democratic context, the Indian central government promoted the reform process, but with difficulty against opposing groups with a vested interest in the status quo.

The rate of population growth is higher in India, ensuring that within a short period India will overtake China as the most populous nation on earth. Because of its population of over one billion, India has the same capacity as China to change the global picture through its rapid growth, notably relative market size, and in terms of national economic and political strength. Between them, India and China account for almost 40% of the world's population. India has the potential to do what China has been doing for the last 25 years, generate rapid economic growth, enter global markets as a major player and attract a high level of foreign direct investment. At present India is much less involved in international trade than China and receives much less foreign investment, but both activities are rising rapidly in importance.

On the basis of GDP calculated on a purchasing power parity exchange rate, China and India are respectively the second and fourth largest economies in the world and powerful magnets for an inflow of imports and investment. They have become sources of highly competitive exports. In their cheap but skilled labour, India and China are potential rivals.

India has certain advantages over China:

- A democratic political system since independence in 1947. One of its major achievements has been to preserve that democracy, despite the immense stresses and strains caused by the multiethnic and multireligious composition of its population and the resulting conflict in areas such as Kashmir
- A developed legal system
- A well-educated middle class whose usual language is English, the international business language

- A highly respected educational system, particularly in the areas of technology and management
- A major Indian diaspora throughout the world, similar to that of China. As with China this provides a pool of highly skilled and experienced labour which India can draw upon
- Contact networks throughout the world. The role of Indians in setting up small software companies in Silicon Valley and elsewhere is well known. The flow of remittances from Indians working abroad and the willingness of Indians abroad to hold rupee accounts assist the balance of payments.

One of the tasks for India is to establish large competitive multinational companies as exporters. There are two areas in which Indian success has been most marked:

- Computer software, the focus of interest in this chapter
- Back-office services; increasingly India is playing the role of the world's back office.

Both industries are ITES (IT-enabled services). In the financial year 2001–02, ITES grew by a prodigious 71% (Maharta, 2002: 52). Without the Internet these services could not exist. Another link is the pool of educated, but relatively cheap labour which can be drawn on to support these two industries. It is a paradox that the Indian government did not exploit a natural comparative advantage in labour-intensive consumer goods. Indian enterprises could easily have developed a competitive advantage in such areas.

Back-office work requires an intelligent English-speaking workforce which India certainly has. One estimate has 50 million English speakers in India who might be employed in this sector and could each reasonably expect to earn US$20,000 a year for doing so. This would translate into an aggregate income of $1 trillion, or twice the size of India's current GDP. The potential for stimulating economic growth is therefore enormous, and the future impact on the Indian economy likely to be dramatic.

GE Capital Services opened India's first international call centre in the mid-1990s. It now employs more than 5,000 people. British Airways and American Express have followed the GE example. The range of activities undertaken as back-office services include data entry and conversion (for example medical transcription), rate processing, problem solving, direct customer interaction (call centres) and the provision of expert 'knowledge services'. Some services are provided by the arms of foreign companies set up in India, that is, the services are said to be 'captured' ones, others are provided by independent contractors.

The success of this activity is indicated by the role of GE in India. GE now employs more people in India than in the USA. As a symbol of its participation in India and India's potential role, GE has established the John F. Welch Technology Centre which is intended in three years to act as GE's research and development centre.

Can Infosys continue to exploit India's cost advantages and even move on to innovate in order to retain the competitive advantage?

Other things being equal, lower cost is a significant competitive advantage. One of the basic variables in achieving competitive advantage is price, which in its turn rests on costs. There are various ways of both reducing costs and employing price in a strategic manner to achieve competitive advantage. It is time to consider a pure strategy of cost leadership. This chapter is concerned with analysing the relevant issues.

A common view of the typical consumer is that cost is his or her primary consideration and that the consumer is engaged in an unceasing quest for the cheapest source of any product or service. A naive view of the typical producer is that the search for cost reduction is a ruthless one which dominates all other considerations; it is almost the *raison d'être* of the enterprise.

Cost leadership

The lower its costs, the better able is an enterprise to charge a lower price. The more successful an enterprise is at achieving this, the more likely it is to outcompete other enterprises who cannot charge the same price without squeezing their profit or even starting to make a loss.

For the moment the supply and demand sides in any product market are assumed to be completely independent of each other. There are two main situations when this is certainly not the case:

1. Where the incurring of a cost allows the enterprise to set the price at a compensatingly higher level, most typically when the increase in costs finances a successful marketing promotion or any activity which changes the perception of the product in a positive way. The demand for the product is then positively correlated with the level of expenditure. In this case, by shifting the supply curve upwards to accommodate the higher costs, the enterprise can also shift its demand curve upwards. The key issue for the enterprise is then, which moves further?
2. Where a reduction in costs leads to a reduction in the quality of the product or service offered. This might include a reduction in the quality of inputs in the production process or a reduction in design activity. In this case, short-term cost reduction is at the expense of one of the key stakeholder groups, the customers of the enterprise. A negative reaction by this stakeholder group might reduce demand in the medium or longer term.

These exceptions are discussed in the next chapter. Independence of the two curves is an unrealistic assumption, since it means that it is not possible to increase demand by incurring costs in promoting, marketing or distributing the product, or even in improving the design or quality of that product. The independence is therefore invalid but the simplification is necessary to focus the analysis on the cost side. This chapter therefore concentrates attention on the cost side, and the next considers the demand side, only at the end of the analysis relaxing the assumption of independence to give a more realistic view of the world.

Other things being equal, it is in the interests of all enterprises to keep costs as low as possible, specifically to try to keep them lower than those of competitors. This involves three issues:

1. The enterprise needs to know the costs of a typical competitor and, as far as possible, how that competitor has achieved that cost level. If both can be achieved, the lowest cost producers can be imitated. However, both are difficult to achieve:

   • Enterprises are notoriously secretive about their own cost position, so it may not be easy to discover the true position. In some cases the means for discovering that cost level is quite elaborate, for example reverse engineering
   • There is 'causal ambiguity' – in other words, in some notable cases nobody really understands how low costs are achieved. Toyota is an excellent example of such ambiguity.

2. There is a choice of the technique, or technology, which is to be used; this determines the broad parameters fixing cost levels. Such a choice is made only infrequently. Significant leaps in technology do not often occur and have to be carefully prepared. If a competitor does move to a new and superior technology, others may have no choice but to follow. Such a move has significant initial costs in the investment in new plant and equipment and training staff to operate the new technology.

3. There is a need to take advantage of the detailed knowledge of individuals in their own 'domain' area and therefore to give them the motivation to reduce costs to a minimum level. Such cost reduction occurs in an incremental way rather than in the manner of discrete technological shifts. A multitude of such improvements made together over a period of time add up to a significant advance. Such reduction is the result of a learning process which occurs continuously, with both new and old technologies. This can apply to any functional area. It might be the core production process or something peripheral such as distribution or maintenance. Both primary and support activities are the target for such cost reductions.

Cost drivers

Costs can be classified in a number of different ways, the most common is between fixed and variable costs:

• *Fixed costs* are those which are incurred independently of the level of output
• *Variable costs* are dependent on the level of output.

What constitutes a fixed and what a variable cost may depend on different practices in various industries. For example, labour costs of various kinds may be a fixed costs if there is lifetime employment. Often salaried staff cannot be sacked without considerable trauma.

Other fixed costs are more obvious. They include the costs of buildings, plant and equipment; marketing and distribution; R&D; and administration of various kinds.

Variable costs include labour costs insofar as workers can be hired and fired as the level of output changes, that is, laid off if output falls; the cost of various inputs, including raw materials; component costs; the cost of energy inputs; and the costs associated with the operation of any plant, including maintenance.

The actual mix of costs differs from industry to industry and changes over time. It is likely that the share of fixed costs has tended to increase in recent years, particularly those associated with R&D and with marketing and distribution.

Another way to classify costs is by the nature of the activity in the value chain. Some of the core and support activities require only fixed costs, others variable costs. It is difficult to fully separate all the relevant costs.

There are a broad range of particular ways in which an enterprise can drive down costs. It is possible to identify seven significant sources of cost reduction, which can be distinguished as cost drivers. Together they account for the marked differences in cost levels between enterprises. Some involve the reduction of fixed costs, others of variable costs. Some are more likely to happen in certain activities than in others.

The first four are associated with reductions in cost resulting from greater experience, or learning, usually linked with greater output. In other words, cost reductions result from any increased output, although not always automatically as some commentators seem to imply. The seven cost drivers are outlined below.

1. Economies of scale or scope

There is some controversy over the importance of this cost driver. Economies of scale and scope reflect the existence of some fixed and some shared costs. Economies of scale are when the reduction in average unit costs reflects the spreading of costs over the larger output of a particular product, and economies of scope the spreading of fixed costs between different products in a multibusiness enterprise.

Economies of scale arise from three different causes:

- Technical input–output relationships specific to technologies with differing optimum capacities. Plant is built to have minimum costs at a particular level of output. Usually this means that over a large range of output levels, lower costs are built into the technical parameters of plant and equipment as output increases. Up to a certain level of output, there is an inverse relationship between size and unit costs.
- Major indivisibilities, that is, only certain sizes of plant are possible. It may be impossible to build plant of a continuously variable capacity, only possible to build at certain sizes. For example, a hydroelectric power station reflects the potential of the water flows. In some industries, it is possible to increase output incrementally without major cost disadvantage, but this is rare.

- The specialization of skills and experience which arises from the division of labour, as described in Adam Smith's famous pin factory. As the size of output rises, it becomes possible to develop a sophisticated division of labour, which allows the development of skills specific to particular tasks. A simple example is the emergence of functional specialization as an enterprise moves beyond its infancy. Once important, this specialization is less important as a source of cost reductions in the modern world.

In theory, there is an optimum size of plant or equipment which yields the minimum level of costs per unit of output, beyond which costs start to rise. This optimum size of plant differs from industry to industry. For example, it is clearly highly desirable to build power stations which produce at a very high level of output.

There may be room for only one or two plants to meet the total demand of the market. In other cases the optimum output may be small relative to the total level of output in a particular industry, in others it may be large. The greater the economies of scale, the greater the likelihood that one or two large producers will dominate an industry.

Since investment has to be made in discrete blocks, if demand rises above a certain level, output can only be expanded by building a new plant with a fixed minimum production level. Output cannot be expanded in marginal amounts. Where there is one plant meeting current demand, for example an airliner on a certain route, this may mean that both plants, or planes, are operated at below optimum capacity. This may mean that there is the danger of either overcapacity or undercapacity, both of which will imply higher than necessary costs, or a particular industry lurching between the two situations.

2. Economies of learning
Learning by doing is very important in almost all industries. Economies of learning arise mainly from two sources:

- *Increased dexterity.* This has diminished in importance as production in most industries has been increasingly automated. It is the story of Adam Smith's famous pin factory again, a factory lacking in mechanization, although the breakdown of production into different tasks and their careful definition allowed the development of machinery able to perform the task.
- *Incremental improvement in organization.* In the contemporary world this is increasingly important. It is a continuing process which often does not require any additional investment.

3. Improved production techniques
This improvement is manifested in three particular ways:

- *Mechanization and automation.* There is a substitution of capital for labour, which reduces the necessary labour input. Over the last few centuries labour has tended to rise in price, relative to the price of capital and other inputs. An expectation of a continuing change in the relative price of labour will encourage further substitution of capital for labour, through mechanization and automation, for example the use of robots.

• *Improved efficiency in the use of raw materials.* For example, the requirements for energy or iron ore inputs to produce a ton of steel have dropped to less than one-tenth what they were 100 years ago. This is a universal phenomenon which explains the tendency for the demand for raw materials to run behind supply and for raw material prices to continue to decline in real terms.

• *Improved quality control.* This involves greater precision in the specifications of the component inputs and fewer defects in both inputs and outputs.

4. Improved product design

Improved product design may assist in either production or use. It can encourage other cost drivers, for example aiding the mechanization or automation of production and helping an enterprise to economize on the costs of material input. The number of necessary component inputs may be vastly reduced, or the number of separate stages in production may be reduced. Often, improved quality is associated with this reduction in the number of component inputs or stages of production, both of which enable a further reduction in costs.

5. Reduced input costs

There are a number of possible sources of reduced input costs, whether of raw materials or intermediate inputs (components). There may be technical improvement in the extraction or production of these necessary inputs, which the user can encourage in various ways. There may be a tendency for supply to run ahead of demand, pushing price down as suppliers compete with each other to capture customers.

Some of the decrease in costs may be under the control of the enterprise. There are four sources:

• *Location.* An enterprise can locate itself close to low-cost sources of necessary inputs, for example close to sources of raw materials or energy, or close to enterprises producing low-cost components.

• *Ownership.* An enterprise can take ownership of the sources of low-cost inputs, thus ensuring supply at a reasonable cost and preventing others from monopolizing the exploitation of the supply.

• *Bargaining strength.* The enterprise can develop and use its own bargaining power to drive down costs, if it is large enough and in a position to do so. It can also work closely with the supplier to improve the costs of supply.

• *Cooperation.* The enterprise can enter into cooperative agreements with other purchasers to lower the costs of particular inputs.

6. Increased capacity utilization

Especially where the ratio of fixed to variable costs is high, it is important to keep capacity utilization high in order to realize the economies of scale which are built into the planned size of plant and the costs already envisaged.

It may be necessary to match the degree of flexibility in varying output levels with fluctuations in demand. What is the cost of either installing new capacity in order to expand output or removing surplus capacity in order to reduce it? It might be advantageous to increase the flexibility of plant in varying output levels to match demand, but without incurring significant extra costs.

When demand expands beyond the optimum capacity of the existing plant, it may be desirable to build a new plant rather than be faced with rapidly rising costs. However, a new plant might be utilized only at a low level, at least temporarily, which may sharply increase costs. Alternatively, if demand falls, it is necessary to ask, is it possible to close down plant in order to limit variable costs?

7. Increasing residual operational efficiency or reducing slack

No enterprise can operate at full intensity for long periods of time. Briefly it may be able to lift the intensity of its operational effectiveness in order to meet a temporary need. Normally every organization operates with a considerable amount of organizational slack which has all sorts of advantages during the life of that organization, while appearing to raise costs. The existence of slack is inherent in the way that all organizations are structured, the existing amount of slack differing from enterprise to enterprise.

There are good reasons for operating in this way. In an ideal world any department head prefers to have resources which could be regarded as surplus to requirements, but which give the department flexibility and the ability to cope with any unforeseen crisis. Under certain conditions the slack might be removed and costs lowered, but it usually re-emerges when the pressure for urgent cost reduction is removed. Certain enterprises somehow manage to operate most of the time with a level of efficiency greater than all their competitors, that is, with less slack.

The case of Haier illustrates the importance of cost leadership in selling on a global market, but it also shows the restraints on the pursuit of a pure cost leadership strategy.

Strategy in Action The rise of Haier

The legend which defines how Haier is different from other Chinese enterprises relates to an action of its CEO Zhang Riumin in 1985, shortly after he took over the enterprise. Having observed a disgruntled customer return a shoddy refrigerator and then inspect a large number of other fridges before he selected one which satisfied him, Riumin did the same, inspecting 400 and finding 76 in a condition which prevented their sale. He gathered his management team and in public view reduced the refrigerators to mangled wrecks with the aid of a sledgehammer. The sledgehammer now hangs on the wall to remind all of the need for quality.

When Riumin took over the enterprise in 1984, it was in a poor state, making large losses and incurring significant debt. The workforce was unmotivated and demoralized. Although Riumin had worked his way up through the municipal administration in Qingdao, he had familiarized himself with Western management literature and was open to outside influences. This showed itself in two ways:

1. He purchased German technology from Liebherr-Haushallsgerte, a firm which not only gave Haier its technical base but its name, since Haier is the Chinese phonetic approximation of Liebherr.

▶

From 1994 Haier became a supplier of new technology rather than a receiver.

2. Riumin took the 5-S self-check system from Masaaki Imai, the guru of Japanese quality control. The five S's comprised discarding the unnecessary, arranging tools in order of use, a clean work site, personal cleanliness and the observing of workshop discipline. Riumin added a sixth, safety. In the Haier Enterprise Culture Centre, Su Fangwen, who joined Haier in 1988, taught discipline and quality control to the staff.

By 1986 Riumin had turned the enterprise round so that it was making a profit. He was given three other white good enterprises which together formed the Qingdao Haier Group in 1991.

Already Haier meets a considerable proportion of the local demand for refrigerators, freezers and washing machines as well as air-conditioners. Its rapid rate of growth has been fuelled mainly by the growth of the domestic market. It is becoming harder to sustain growth and profitability in the Chinese market because of intense competition. Haier currently holds 29% of the Chinese market for refrigerators and 26% for washing machines. In capturing this market share, it emphasized product quality, reflected the results of a study of customer needs, demonstrated the ability to respond quickly by selling products which met those needs, and finally exerted a relentless pressure to promote its brand name.

The first international forays were to open factories in Indonesia and the Philippines. The most interesting initiative is the entry into the American market. At first the mode of entry was by export. In this Haier had surprising success, capturing 50% of the American market for compact refrigerators, suitable for a student room, office or hotel room. The market for family refrigerators is harder to crack, since there were four manufacturers holding 98% of the market, between which there is already fierce competition. Haier has been making steady inroads even into this market and now claims 25%. It has been innovative in pioneering the sale of new products, such as electric wine cellars, in which it claims a 50% market share. Market shares for chest freezers, at 40%, and room window air-conditioners, at 18%, are lower but growing. By 2001 overall sales in the USA had reached $200 million, not a startling level, but a good initial base. However, the company claimed to be making a profit and had clearly begun the difficult process of establishing its brand name.

The aim is to increase sales in the USA to $1 billion by 2005. To help achieve this, in 2000 Haier became the first Chinese company to open a major manufacturing facility in the USA – in Camden, South Carolina. While this represented a small investment, $40 million initially, it proclaims Haier's intention to penetrate the family refrigerator market, with an annual output target from the facility of 200,000 family-sized refrigerators. The rationale for establishing this facility is to be close to the market. Haier has a design centre in Los Angeles and a trade centre in New York.

Haier seeks to fit the product to the market niche. The compact refrigerators for the student market have locks. The Haier mini-fridges, with folding computer desks, have been selling well. Door shelves in fridges for the American market are designed to hold gallon jugs. There are see-through vegetable crispers. Haier's chest freezer has an innovative cooling section in addition to the freezing compartment. Most components for Haier's products are locally sourced, although compressors are imported from Brazil. Haier has committed itself to a major advertising campaign to help promote its brand name. It has placed its product prominently in well-known department chains such as Wal-Mart, Macy's, Office Depot, Target and Sears.

Haier faces fierce competition internationally. Three of the most potent competitors are Whirlpool, GE and Electrolux, important players in the American market, who have adopted a global role. These companies have enormous resources and a ruthlessness in keeping costs down to the level of their competitors. With the opening of China, this competition will penetrate the domestic economy. Entry into the WTO means that foreign manufacturers can enter the Chinese market, either by exports or foreign direct investment.

Haier may be overstretching its product range and its geographical spread, although it is trying to earn higher profit margins than those for white goods. Computers, TVs and mobile phones offer a temporary increase in profit margins, whereas financial services, including insurance and securities, offer a continuing profitability. It has bought into both local and foreign securities and banking companies, at considerable expense.

A focused cost leadership strategy might be appropriate, in other words, a concentration on white goods. Not only has the company come under criticism but also under pressure on its profits, for example a 45% reduction in net profits in the first half results for 2002, largely because of reduced returns on sales of air-conditioners. This is a sector with thin and decreasing profit margins. There is concern that the situation on profit levels and debt is rather opaque, and there is frequent reference to a culture of secrecy. The share price of Haier has fallen. The main criticisms have been directed at Haier's investment in air-conditioners and mobile phones, its purchase of a refrigerator factory in Modena, Italy, seen as high cost and less than best practice, and the sheer audaciousness of its overseas ambitions. The response from Haier was not encouraging; it resorted to issuing a lawsuit against a critic, rather than adjusting its strategy.

Pricing strategy

Cost leadership, or cost minimization, reveals nothing about pricing strategy. Low costs do not necessarily mean low prices; there is no necessary relationship between the two. The nature of the relationship depends partly on the nature of the industry and the degree of competition in that industry, and partly on the price strategy adopted by the enterprise.

It is surprising that more attention is devoted to a cost leadership strategy than to a pricing strategy, for two reasons:

1. The impact on profits of a similar percentage increase in price or decrease in particular costs can be very different, in the first case the impact often being a multiple of the proportional price change.
2. In theory it is much easier to change price than to change costs.

Aggressive and tame pricing

There are two relevant distinctions – aggressive versus tame pricing, and active versus passive pricing:

1. In an aggressive policy, an enterprise can use price to try to drive out competitors. Alternatively, price can be left at a level which allows a high margin of short-term profit, encouraging others to enter the industry. In an extreme case, the enterprise can aim for short-term profit maximization, or be forced by competition or the threat of takeover to aim at short-term profit maximization. This would mean an avoidance of aggressive competition.
2. Pricing strategy can be active or passive. Price can be changed often or it can remain stable for long periods of time. It can change in a regular cycle – weekly, seasonally or even annually. The enterprise can be a price leader or a price follower. This partly reflects the size of the enterprise's resources. Price behaviour depends partly on the way in which price changes in the industry, which reflects the competitive nature of that industry – how many players there are and how large they are relative to each other, indeed how aggressive others are.

The various pricing stances (Figure 9.1) are:

A. An enterprise moves price often and deliberately uses price to try to gain a competitive advantage

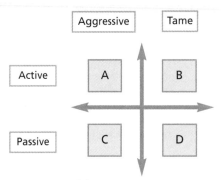

Figure 9.1 **Pricing stance**

B. An enterprise moves price often but simply follows others who initiate the price moves
C. An enterprise rarely change prices but, when it does, it uses price in an aggressive way to enhance its competitiveness
D. An enterprise rarely changes its prices and even then only follows the lead of others.

A large enterprise can be both active and aggressive or passive and tame. It can live and let live, or it can change price often and use price as a strategic device for undermining competitors. It can play the role of price leader to stabilize a market or it can use this role to extend its market share.

The aims and uses of a pricing strategy

Pricing strategy is a key strategic area which must be considered in some detail. Price is a vitally important part of overall strategy. There are a number of possible objectives of a price strategy:

- The enterprise may be trying to maximize profit, either in the short or longer term. The time horizon considered relevant is important.
- The enterprise may be trying to defend its own turf, trying to maximize its market share, deliberately sacrificing short-term profit to do so. Clearly a large enterprise which already accounts for a significant proportion of the market has more options open to it than a small enterprise accounting for an insignificant part of that market.

Given the existence of an experience curve which shows a significant future reduction of cost as dependent on the level of output, pricing may be based on achieving that higher output and premised on the future rather than the existing cost level. An enterprise pursuing a strategy based on current costs may find itself at a severe disadvantage in competing with the more future-oriented strategy. At the international level, it may accuse the other enterprise of exploiting cheap labour or dumping, that is, selling below cost, whereas the strategy is a reasonable one which takes account of cost levels over the near future, not just the present.

Pricing policy must be consistent with other policies, notably marketing policy. For example, if the objective is to sell on the basis of quality, then a policy of minimizing price may be a mistaken strategy. It may give very misleading signals to the potential consumer. The Strategy in Action on Club Med later in the chapter neatly illustrates this. Low price may been seen as indicating low quality. Depending on the nature of the product, price may be viewed as an indicator of quality. This must be taken into account in devising any price strategy.

An appropriate pricing strategy can differ according to the stage in the life cycle of the product being considered. The critical stage for any product is the infant or adolescent stage when price policy determines how many players there are likely to be in the industry at later stages in that life cycle. Price policy during this phase also has a powerful influence on what happens to price in the future. Current prices in any industry usually reflect the previous price history in that industry. There is a strong measure of path dependence in this area. This issue is explored in greater depth in Chapter 13.

A differential pricing strategy

It is possible to take a closer look at the notion of differential pricing. Each potential consumer could be regarded as having an individual demand curve. All sellers, if they could, would like to identify the shape of these individual demand curves and select a range on the curve at which demand becomes inelastic, that is, to move price upwards until the revenue effects of the fall in demand exceed those of the increase in price. Price discrimination of this kind maximizes revenues.

However, there is an offsetting effect, in that such discrimination may well antagonize some customers when they discover that they are paying different prices from other consumers for the same product and purchasers may be upset if they become exposed to a perpetually varying price.

Since no seller knows the nature of all individual demand curves, they have to infer them by trying different price levels. In practice the haggling over price in the open market environment of many Asian countries represents a partial realization of such differential pricing. The initial price is often set at many times the expected final price. The price is negotiated down by the prospective purchaser. To some degree the agreed price reflects the relative bargaining skills but even more the intensity of the desire on the part of the potential purchaser for the product. You pay according to the strength of your desire. Since this process is more transparent and also provides pleasure to those who like to think they have a bargain, it is far more acceptable than other forms of price discrimination.

In some industries there is a more systematic attempt to practise such differential pricing. Priceline.com was set up to do just that. It applied the practice of name-your-own price to the purchase of airline tickets. This worked reasonably well, partly because this is not a practice new to that industry. The company sought to extend the principle to the sale of groceries and fuel through the Priceline Webhouse Club. They failed. The prerequisite for success was that the company could buy in bulk at a discount. The producing companies did not want to give away the premiums which they believed their branded products warranted and earned.

It was no accident that the practice of differential pricing worked for airline tickets. Airlines do pursue differential pricing under the guise of a revenue management policy. Customers sitting next to each other often have paid very different fares for the same service, not always a good thing to do for your reputation, as the tale below shows. There are one or two other industries which pursue a similar policy, such as the hotel industry.

Focus on Humour
Price differentiation

Imagine that you are buying paint from Qantas, which practices revenue management. First you spend days trying to reach them by phone to ask if they have paint. Nobody answers. So you drive to a Qantas store.

Customer: Hi. How much is your paint?

Shop assistant: Well, sir, that all depends on quite a lot of things.

C: Can you give me a guess? Is there an average price?

SA: Our lowest price is $12 a litre, and we have 60 different prices up to $200 a litre.

C: What is the difference in the paint?

SA: Oh, there isn't any difference; it's all the same paint.

C: Well, then I'd like some of that $12 paint.

SA: When do you intend to use the paint?

C: I want to paint tomorrow. It's my day off.

SA: Sir, the paint for tomorrow is the $200 paint.

C: When would I have to paint to get the $12 paint?

SA: You have to start very late at night in about three weeks. But you will have to agree to start painting before Friday of that week and continue painting until at least Sunday.

C: You've got to be kidding!

SA: I'll check and see if we have any paint available.

C: You have shelves FULL of paint! I can see it.

SA: But it doesn't mean that we have paint available. We sell only a certain number of litres on any given weekend. Oh, and by the way, the price just went to $16. We don't have any more $12 paint.

C: The price went up as we were speaking?

SA: Yes, sir. We change the prices and rules hundreds of times a day, and since you haven't actually walked out of the store with your paint yet, we just decided to change. I suggest you purchase your paint as soon as possible. How many litres do you want?

C: Well, maybe five litres. Make that six, so I'll have enough.

SA: Oh no, sir, you can't do that. If you buy paint and don't use it, there are penalties and possible confiscation of the paint you already have.

C: WHAT?

SA: We can sell enough paint to do your kitchen, bathroom, hall and north bedroom, but if you stop painting before you do the bedroom, you will lose your remaining litres of paint.

C: What does it matter whether I use all the paint? I already paid you for it!

SA: We make plans based upon the idea that all our paint is used, every drop. If you don't, it causes us all sorts of problems.

C: This is crazy! I suppose something terrible happens if I don't keep painting until Saturday night!

SA: Oh yes! Every litre you bought automatically becomes the $200 paint.

C: But what are all these 'Paint on sale from $10 a litre' signs.

Focus on Humour
cont'd

SA: Well, that is for our budget paint. It only comes in half-litres. One $5 half-litre will do half a room. The second half-litre to complete the room is $20. None of the cans have labels, some are empty and there are no refunds, even on the empty cans.

C: To hell with this! I'll buy what I need somewhere else!

SA: I don't think so, sir. You may be able to buy paint for your bathroom and bedrooms, and your kitchen and dining room, from someone else, but you won't be able to buy paint for your connecting hall and stairway from anyone but us. And I should point out, sir, that if you paint in only one direction, it will be $300 a litre.

C: I thought your most expensive paint was $200!

SA: That's if you paint around the room to the point at which you started. A hallway is different.

C: And if I buy $200 paint for the hall, but only paint in one direction, you'll confiscate the remaining paint.

SA: No, we'll charge you an extra-use fee plus the difference on your next litre of paint. But I believe you're getting it now, sir.

C: You're insane!

SA: But we are now THIS COUNTRY'S only full-service paint supplier! And don't go looking for bargains! Thanks for painting with Qantas.

Source: Chessell, 2002.

Price is therefore very important and price determination an important aspect of a strategy to differentiate a product. It is not simply a matter of the cost level. The demand curve is not independent of the supply curve. This whole issue is discussed at greater length in Chapter 10.

There is another way in which both cost and price can be reduced. This can be done by peeling away various attributes of the product or service which require expenditures to sustain but which are over and above those required by the customer, the no-frills approach.

Strategy in Action Southwest Airline – the no-frills airline

In recent years Southwest has been by far the most successful American airline, probably the most successful international airline. In 2002 it was almost the only profitable airline in the USA. Its capitalization is as great as the three major American airlines combined. It has come through the crisis of recession and the terrorist attacks of September 11, 2001, avoiding the serious fall into deficit which has afflicted the other airlines. It has achieved its strong position by a strategy of cost minimization and, following from low costs, price leadership.

Southwest has done much more than cost minimization. It has identified a significant market segment which was being supplied with a product which had attributes for which customers did not wish to pay. It has provided for this market segment in a way which has made it impossible for the national and international carriers to compete.

Southwest divided airline customers into business passengers and holiday or tourist travellers, and identified their different needs – convenience and comfort in the first case, economy in the second. It deliberately sought to win the latter from the conventional airlines. In the process it has drawn attention to the heavy cost to enterprises of business travel. Some business travellers are becoming more like tourists in the attributes they seek.

Southwest has a model for others to emulate. In its purest form, the model is only suitable for high-density, short-haul routes and regions where there are many such routes. A favourable deregulated environment helps in supporting the model, particularly the privatization and deregulation of airports. The ideal contexts are the dense air networks of North America and Europe. Elsewhere the density of demand for air travel is too low, the routes too long or the industry too regulated.

The following are some of the features of the model:

- Avoid the existing and often congested hubs of other airlines, thereby reducing both airport charges and delays. Use airports which are less busy and therefore cheaper to use, but which are located favourably for concentrations of potential passengers. Rent or lease terminal facilities and pay according to use. Use your bargaining strength to reduce the charge. Try to persuade the local authorities to offer major pecuniary incentive to use airports in their area. Michael O'Leary of Ryanair, a Southwest imitator, has even suggested that fares could be reduced to zero, since the authorities should be prepared to pay for customers to come to local resorts and shopping malls.
- Avoid international routes which are long and require a significant number of the services indicated below. Fly routes which are less busy and less well served by other airlines. Ignore possible connecting flights and don't operate schedules to link up with other flights – this creates delays and increases the downtime for planes.
- Accept, even encourage, online and 'at the gate' bookings. If possible accept only such bookings. Seat the passengers as they come, without designating seats. Limit the passengers to one class and configure the aircraft for just one such class.
- Turn the planes around as fast as possible. Allow for minimum passenger baggage, carried by the passenger. Use aircraft much more intensively than usual, on average about 50% more intensively than the aircraft of conventional carriers.
- Do not serve meals or provide other services unless the passenger pays. Do not provide

lounges or club facilities. Do not run a frequent flyer or loyalty scheme.
- Use a single type of plane to minimize training and maintenance costs – in the case of Southwest, the Boeing 737. Lease your aircraft.
- Multiskill the staff. This reduces cleaning time and cuts other expenses. Reduce crew size. Keep labour costs low but maintain high morale, empowering staff to recognize potential cost savings. Treat the customers as well as you can.

Individual items can be discarded and a hybrid adopted. In many cases there is no choice but to compromise. The impact on costs is striking.

Lower revenue per seat-kilometre is more than offset by significantly lower costs (Table 9.1). The biggest savings come from lower airport charges and ground handling fees. Competition for cities and towns to be the venue for flights has driven airport fees down. Other major gains come in lower distribution and seat delivery costs. There are possible savings in many other areas including passenger services, crew costs and overheads.

The most successful of the imitators is Ryanair based in Ireland which has done in Europe what Southwest has done in the USA. In a short period of time, its capitalization reached a level twice that of British Airways, Air France or Lufthansa. The aim is to get the price as low as possible, in order to create a new market segment. Its costs are rock-bottom. It actively pursues every feature described above.

EasyJet is the second no-frills airline based in Europe, but one which is a hybrid. It adopts some of the features above, competing with the national airlines for the budget-conscious business travellers, a much more difficult task (Table 9.2).

In the USA the share of airline revenues accounted for by businesspeople was already declining before

Table 9.1 **Costs per available seat-kilometre (ASK) – first half of 2001, in cents**

	Revenue	Cost	Profit	Profit margin per ASK (%)
Southwest	5.7	4.8	0.9	15.8
Jet Blue	5.2	4.5	0.7	13.5
Average of USA majors	6.7	7.0	–0.3	–4.5

Source: Costa et al., 2002: 97.

Table 9.2 **Intra-European market shares**

Year	Total passengers flown (m)	Low cost (%)	International (%)	Domestic (%)	Regional (%)	Charter (%)
1997	365	2	33	25	17	23
2001	435	7	32	23	17	21
2007 (projected)	600	14	30	21	16	19
2001–7 annual growth		20	4.5	4.0	4.0	3.3

Source: Bingelli and Pompeo, 2002.

the terrorist attacks of September 11, 2001. The trend has been accelerated by September 11. There is plenty of room for the expansion of no-frills flights. They still represent below 15% of the revenue-passenger-kilometres in the USA, less elsewhere.

Focused cost minimization

Focusing takes a number of different forms. Depending on the degree of competition and the stage of development in a particular market, it may be appropriate to focus on a particular strategic business unit in minimizing costs, one which appears to offer a much greater potential for cost reduction and a greater impact on the overall cost position if it is achieved. The products involved may be new or in areas in which there is major technical change.

Alternatively the focus may be on a particular market segment. It might be that there is the possibility of targeting a market niche large enough to justify the strategy by removing certain attributes of the product or service, in the process reducing the costs and by implication the price of the product or service.

There is another type of focusing, which can be applied whatever the product. Where costs are relatively stable, the focus may be on certain parts of the value chain which account for a large proportion of total costs. The pressure may be greater in a particular area, especially one where the costs are high, relative to the costs of competitors.

The use of the value chain for cost leadership

One strategy on cost drivers is to go through the whole value chain in a systematic way in order to make sure that costs are at a minimum. As has been seen in locating core competencies, the value chain shows how a product moves all the way from the raw material stage to the final customer. In practice, where an enterprise produces a whole range of different products, there will be multiple value chains. The problem starts when there is significant overlap between the different value chains. This inevitably means sharing costs and the existence of significant synergies.

For the moment, the analysis assumes a single product and therefore a single value chain. As the reader has already seen the value chain is commonly divided into the two parts, primary and support activities. It is unusual for all these activities to be vertically integrated within the one enterprise. Which should be integrated depends partly on the importance of the activity for the core competencies of the enterprise and the differentiation of the product. Activities may also be major cost generators or areas in which the enterprise does or does not have such a cost advantage. Reducing cost may require that other enterprises carry out the activity for the enterprise. For all activities there is a 'make or buy' decision. This is one of the important strategic choices which emerge from analysis of the value chain.

The value chain is a means by which an enterprise can carry out a systematic study of costs. There are separate steps in the use of value chain analysis to achieve a minimization of costs:

- Identify the core activities of the enterprise, a step which gives the basic framework of the value chain
- Allocate, in an approximate manner, total costs between these activities in order to pinpoint where there is the greatest scope for a reduction of costs. Attention can be concentrated in these areas
- Link cost drivers to the different activities. This is done by taking the seven cost drivers outlined above and analysing how each is relevant to specific activities. This can be done as if each activity is independent
- Analyse the connections between different activities. This is done by identifying linkages between different activities, where a reduction in cost in one area may increase costs elsewhere, or vice versa
- Decide on the specific strategy of how to minimize cost and make recommendations which realize this strategy.

One of the most interesting situations in which a clear price advantage emerged at the industry level unfolded in the late 1970s and 80s, when Japanese car producers began to enter the American and European markets in strength. Initially it was thought that the price advantage was the result of producing a smaller product, a compact automobile, and, even more, using cheap labour and even dumping at artificially low prices. However, the price advantage persisted. These producers possessed a clear cost advantage over the previously dominant producers. Some of this advantage had a clear source, some was of an ambiguous provenance. Clearly the Japanese producers had introduced methods which had the result of significantly reducing costs. They relied much more on outside suppliers than the American manufacturers and had an entirely different kind of relationship with them (see the case study on Toyota in Chapter 17). Some of these methods have now been taken up by competitors.

A case study   Figure 9.2 takes the automobile industry as an example of cost minimization through the value chain, illustrating the cost drivers for each activity and highlighting the way in which the cost position is relevant to the competitive position of rival automobile producers.

There are a number of key linkages between activities which the Japanese producers focused on in their efforts to reduce costs. The linkages were critical to understanding the nature of possible cost reductions:

- The relationship of inventories to the size of component orders. The larger the orders and therefore the longer the time period between orders, the greater the inventories which have to be held. The more frequent the component orders, the smaller the orders. The aim of large orders may be to reduce the price of components, which are produced and delivered in a large batch, but this may be at the

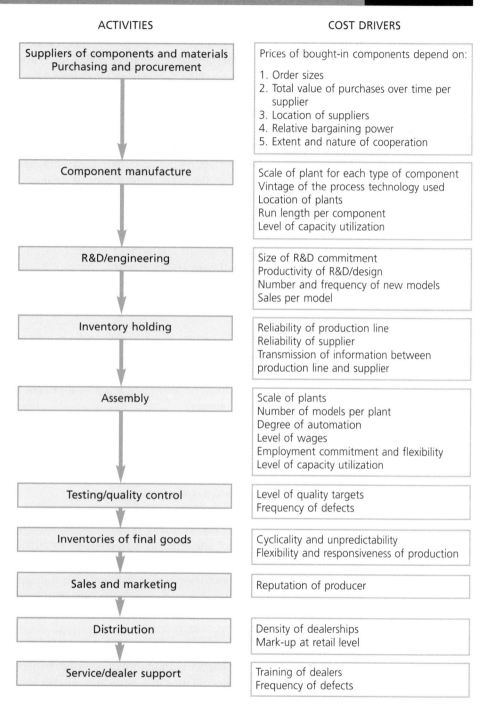

Figure 9.2 **The value chain and an automobile manufacturer**

cost of carrying larger inventory. 'Just-in-time' delivery of components was made possible by better communication systems and had a dramatic effect in reducing costs. It implied a close cooperative relationship with suppliers and a continuous flow rather than a bunching of such deliveries.

- Concentrating component orders on one supplier. This may reduce costs for that supplier by offering economies of scale and therefore reduce the price to the enterprise, but this may be at the cost of a greater risk of interruption to the continued flow of purchases, if something goes wrong for that supplier. Reducing costs over the medium to long term may mean retaining more than one supplier. There may be competition between suppliers and a greater likelihood of one making a breakthrough in costs.
- The relationship between component quality and cost levels in other activities. Higher quality and therefore higher cost components may reduce the cost of later activities, including assembly and quality control. It may be false economy to skimp on components.
- Wiser use of major components. Design of car models with common components, particularly major components, such as platforms or engines, makes possible greater economies of scale in component production and in developing new models which may use the same component.
- Quality control and its effects. Fewer defects in manufacturing reduce warranty costs incurred in the service and dealer support.

The key to using these linkages to keep down costs is information transfer. Good communication between those responsible for different activities is a vital part of cost cutting.

On the basis of the Japanese performance, it is possible to put forward some recommendations on cost improvement.

One key strategic decision which has been identified already is whether to buy in or make an input (or provide a service oneself), in other words whether to outsource. As seen earlier this depends on whether the enterprise has a core competency and a competitive advantage in this area. Often this core competency or competitive advantage is translated into a cost advantage.

It is often a help that others have the relevant core competencies, that is, can produce at a lower cost or higher quality, allowing cost reductions further down the chain. The relationship of the enterprise to component suppliers is an important one, one which recurs throughout the case studies in this book. Vertical integration is not a strategy which should be pursued automatically and without regard to costs.

The nature of the relationship with suppliers is critical. It is good risk management not to put all your eggs in one basket. More than one supplier is desirable. However, it is better to assume that the relationship is a long-term cooperative one, in which both partners will make a significant investment. The enterprise should try to ensure that the investment it makes is less than that of any one supplier, so that the supplier is more closely tied to the relationship than the enterprise is to the supplier. A measure of competition between alternative sources should be kept in the background in order to exert discipline on the supplier and allow a switch of supply if some unforeseen interruption occurs.

Club Med illustrates the importance of cost leadership in a sector in which the value chain is not so clear-cut as in manufacturing, but, like the Haier case, shows the dangers of pursuing a pure cost leadership strategy.

Strategy in Action   Packaging a cheap holiday – Club Med

Cost is a key factor influencing whether a package holiday is taken and which one is taken. Although a holiday packaged on a one-off basis is likely to be attractive, it is also likely to be expensive, particularly if it has to be carefully planned in advance. It is time-consuming for anyone to put together a holiday in its every detail. Most holiday-makers take advantage of the services of a travel agent to choose a package holiday. An individual has less bargaining power than an organization acting on behalf of a large number of like-minded individuals, so these packages are also cost effective. An organization which builds a resort itself can offer an even better price.

A number of factors have expanded the range of package holidays, including a general rise in income levels and the spread to most of the workforce of the right to significant annual holiday leave. There are many alternatives competing for this holiday time and many providers of holidays with varying combinations of attributes packaged together. Holiday packages are complex, but usually concentrate on one or two attributes known to be popular and rely on the scale of sales to make the price competitive. There is a high price elasticity of demand for any holiday package, simply because there is significant competition for a variable discretionary income.

The original package holidays offered basic accommodation and entertainment, the latter often involving significant guest participation. These holiday camps were staffed mainly by young, part-time and cheap workers. The aim was to make the holiday affordable to the maximum number of holiday-makers. Today the package holiday is much more likely to be abroad, reflecting the lower cost and reduced time of air travel. It includes fares, other travel, basic accommodation and sometimes meals and a range of rather exotic recreational entertainments.

Club Med was established by the Trigano family to cater to the demand for package holidays. Although it was by origin a French company, Club Med came to consist of an international collection of resorts located in attractive, even exotic, places throughout the world. The location of the resort was one of the main attractions. These included beach and winter resorts in Europe, North America and Asia, offering a range of activities.

Club Med carried the package to its ultimate. The resort was like a mini-township. In most Club Med resorts there was no need to leave the resort at all during the stay. There was no need to spend money, except on a few optional luxuries such as cocktails in the nightclub. Even then tokens were used rather than real money. A choice of food was offered, which might include a French restaurant with waiter service, an Italian pasta or pizza restaurant and a self-serve smorgasbord. Food was accompanied by free beer and wine or soft drinks, according to taste. The range of activities included archery, sailing, snorkelling, windsurfing, swimming and fitness exercises, or activities specific to the locality, again free. The young organizers also arranged entertainment which followed the Butlin's tradition of visitor participation.

Club Med has experienced a two-phase crisis. The first arose because international competition became so intense that there was a frenzy of price cutting. It engaged in an active policy of cost and price leadership, with dramatic but negative effects on its profit levels and consequently on its share price. As a result the Trigano family lost control of the company. The shareholders brought in, as CEO, Philippe Bourguignon, who had previous experience in rescuing Euro Disney, to revive its fortunes.

Bourguignon tried to spruce up the resorts which were beginning to look a little worn – US$350 million was spent on 70 of the 120 resorts. He also tried to differentiate the clubs more than in the past, in some catering for the young by introducing activities such as rock climbing and in others trying to attract a more demanding clientele. Both holiday-makers and investors liked the new policy. As a result there was a 51% boost to net income in the year ending October 31, 2000, to US$52 million, on a gross revenue of US$1.6 billion. The share price, which had reached its lowest point in 1996 at US$36, climbed to US$159 in July 2000.

Bourguignon intended to turn Club Med into an 'umbrella leisure brand', beginning with a chain of fitness clubs. It moved into running nightclubs, creating Club Med World, starting with two clubs in Paris and Montreal. It also put its name on some fragrances. The brand name had potential for exploitation. However, whereas 92% of the US population knew about Club Med, only 12% wanted to go to a Club Med resort. Club Med had acquired a reputation for cheapness in both senses of the word and perhaps an unjustified reputation for regimentation and lack of variety. The view of analysts, investors and even the French press was that it should get its core business right before it embarked on diversification. Although the Paris nightclub had 400,000 visitors, Club Med World still lost US$5 million in 2001. Old habits die hard. A new resort Oyyo in Bekalta, Tunisia, intended as a no-frills party club turned out to be a failure, perhaps because it reinforced the old stereotype of the cheap Club Med.

Unfortunately the timing of the new initiatives in 2001 proved to be disastrous. There was a growing recession in the USA which affected all parts of the world. Asia was still suffering from the consequences of the Asian economic crisis of 1997. The terrorist attacks of September 11, 2001 hit the tourist industry harder than any other sector of the economy. In the three months ending January 31, 2002, guest numbers at Club Med's resorts were down 20% and gross revenue 14.6%. In the financial year to October 31, 2001, it lost US$63 million on gross revenue of US$1.8 billion. The share price returned to a low $45. Bourguignon was replaced by Giscard d'Estaing as CEO and strategy returned to an emphasis on the core business, but with an attempt to take Club Med upmarket.

The nature of a technology

A technology is a set of productive techniques which characterize a particular industry or group of related industries. The nature of technologies differs greatly across industries. The core of these technologies rarely changes. Such change involves the introduction of macro-inventions. However, techniques are subject to continuous change.

At the core of any particular technique is a process by which specific inputs are converted into specific outputs. Techniques are often viewed simply as sets of technical blueprints, each of which defines the methods of production in terms of specific inputs and outputs, and therefore the parameters of conversion. As such, they are seen as the same wherever in the world they are adopted. It is assumed that a given plant and its equipment can be installed anywhere in the world and will reproduce the relevant parameters.

Choice of technique

Alternative techniques may exist within a given technology. Economic theory assumes that there are a number of known techniques for each process in an industry. In practice new techniques are discovered in adapting an early technique to specific circumstances. There is an important learning process.

What are the criteria for making a choice? If there is a choice of technique, it is assumed that the choice is made according to the relative costs of the different inputs, usually classified as resources, labour and capital. Where labour is abundant and cheap, more labour-intensive techniques will be chosen, and vice versa, if capital is the relatively cheap input. Where natural resources are abundant, techniques which use these resources in what might be regarded as a wasteful manner are chosen. If, in the future, certain costs are likely to rise faster than others, then this may affect the choice today and certainly the direction of future development. A tendency for the price of labour to rise faster than the price of capital encourages a capital-intensive bias, not only in technical choice but in the direction in which future technology is developed. The same will apply if a resource is likely to rise in price.

The question to ask is when the differences in technique are significant enough to constitute a difference of technology, and when choice of one technique locks an economy into a particular technology. The argument of path dependency is based on the notion that such choice cannot be undone except at enormous cost. This is neatly illustrated by the VHS/Beta choice, or the quasi-monopoly possessed by Windows in computer software.

In this conventional view, the nature of both technologies and techniques are simplified. They are not seen as sophisticated interactions between equipment and the people working the equipment, and therefore as much a reflection of the way in which people use the equipment as of the nature of the equipment. The importance of organization in the application of a technology is usually underestimated. Some assume that the organization simply reflects the nature of the technology. In reality there are countless ways in which a given piece of equipment might be used, either in relationship to other equipment or the people involved in the production process. There may be many auxiliary processes, involving the preparation of components or inputs and the transportation of these within the factory, which can be organized in different ways. The many different ways in which a given piece of equipment is used often reflect cultural differences as much as they reflect differences in factor costs. What suits one society does not suit another.

The potential for cost reduction lies in the improvement in physical equipment and organization. After an initial investment, the latter can continue to be a source of cost reduction for many years without any further investment. The process of organizational change defines a possible trajectory for costs which is not knowable in detail at the inception of the new technology but may be obvious in its general outline. Choice may be influenced by the differing nature of these trajectories for different techniques. Different technologies have different potentials for cost reduction. Much of the actual reduction in costs of production is therefore achieved by improvements in organization. Choice is often made because the technology offers a much greater potential for organizational improvement in the future. The process of learning by doing is critical in this cost reduction.

Strategy in Action Wal-Mart: the origins of a cost-reducing machine

'For a lot of years, we avoided mistakes by studying those larger than we were – Sears, Penney, Kmart. Today we don't have anyone to study ... When we were smaller, we were the underdog, the challenger. When you're number one, you are a target. You are no longer the hero.'

Glass, former CEO of Wal-Mart

By 1995, when Wal-Mart finally won its five-year battle with local leaders to open its first store in Vermont, it had a store in every state of the union. This store was in fact Wal-Mart's 2,158th store. By the end of 1997, it had two more stores in Vermont. The typical Wal-Mart store occupies an area of 200,000 sq. ft and is built close to a major highway. In Vermont Wal-Mart showed itself ready to compromise with only a 50,000 sq. ft area located downtown.

The history of Wal-Mart is rather briefer than often thought. Sam Walton opened his first Ben Franklin franchise in Newport, Arkansas in 1945 but failed to persuade Franklin's to go into discounting. The first discount department store was opened by Wal-Mart in November 1962. The Ben Franklin stores were gradually phased out, finally disappearing in 1976. The company was incorporated in 1969 and went public in 1972, with only 18 Wal-Mart and 15 Ben Franklin stores. The $3.3 million raised in the public float went to help meet the cost of a warehouse, which at the time cost more than $5 million.

After that, geographic growth, which began in the south and mid-west, began to accelerate. The pattern of advance never jumped ahead, it was systematic. Steadily it covered the whole country.

The initial store format was the traditional Wal-Mart store that sells a wide range of basic consumer merchandise, from household products to clothes and electronics. When Wal-Mart established its first supermarket in 1962, it was not a new concept. Discount retailing was already known. However, most discounters eventually failed. Wal-Mart did not. Wal-Mart's success did not come from discounting as such, but rather the way in which it was pursued.

Two new concepts were introduced in 1987, which brought in groceries as an addition to the basic merchandising mix:

- The *hypermarket*, the 200,000 sq. ft-plus store which sells everything, including food, and the *super-centre*, a scaled-down version of the hypermarket, combining supermarket and discount store. The super-centre usually covered about 120–130,000 sq. ft. The hypermarket was borrowed from France. It covered an enormous area, carried as many as 20–30,000 items and, when well run, has gross margins as high as 13–14%. After giving it a try, Wal-Mart opted for the super-centre. Today the latter is the fastest growing part of Wal-Mart, mostly replacing existing Wal-Mart stores. In 1995 there were 68 super-centres, by 2000 over 800. The super-centre became the main engine of Wal-Mart's growth.
- The *no-frills warehouse business* which mainly served other businesses. This is real discounting. These warehouses were called Sam's Club. These are deep discount stores that carry a limited range of low-priced merchandise and food.

The Wal-Mart system had a number of unique features which allowed it to achieve unprecedentedly low levels of cost.

Wal-Mart built the leanest supply chain in the industry:

- Wal-Mart pioneered the development of the hub-and-spoke distribution system, in which a central distribution warehouse served a cluster of stores (IKEA has used this system). The speed at which Wal-Mart could replenish stock in its stores was accelerated. Inventories could be smaller, thereby reducing costs, and sales per square foot of store space much greater. This system was introduced for the conventional stores but applied to all the new stores as they were introduced. To supply the super-centres with food, Wal-Mart acquired the McLane chain of warehouses and further developed these. Wal-Mart expanded the number of warehouses rapidly.
- Wal-Mart combined its network of warehouses with an early use of computer-based information systems which tracked in-store sales and transmitted the information to suppliers. This assisted in determining pricing policy and the better management of inventories. Suppliers were encouraged in various ways to keep down their own costs, which became easier to achieve the bigger Wal-Mart became and the more important as a buyer.

Simultaneously, Wal-Mart reconfigured its stores, with the following aims:

- To strip away all inessentials from the store. The physical amenities of the typical department store, such as carpeting or chandeliers, were discarded.
- To rearrange the store in such a way that it could handle the flow of large numbers of shoppers. This applied to the whole store, from parking lots, shopping aisles to checkout points.
- To put fewer salespeople on the floor and rely on customers to serve themselves.

These strategies had obvious cost advantages. Wal-Mart did this in just the same way as Kmart has done, but it went much further putting its individual stamp on the supermarket. The strategy was unique. It combined cost minimization with a strategy which was much more subtle. There were three parts to the strategy which marked Wal-Mart out as different:

1. *Location*. In the words of Walton himself, the key strategy of Wal-Mart 'was to put good-sized stores into little one-horse towns which everybody else was ignoring'. The targeted towns had populations of 5,000–25,000 like Rogers, Arkansas, where the first supermarket was located. Much of America lived in such areas.

Walton believed that, given the opportunity, people would shop locally, provided there was no significant price disadvantage in so doing. In the major cities, competition was intense. By putting in a supermarket of some size into a relatively small place, Wal-Mart pre-empted entry by competitors. In the mid-1980s, about one-third of Wal-Mart stores were located where there was no competition. Entry into such a market would be suicidal for the new entrant as well as the existing player, since it would lead to a fight for customers and probably a price war. Expansion moved Wal-Mart into areas where there was competition, but it was still true that Wal-Mart had an advantage. In 1993, 55% of Wal-Mart stores faced direct competition from Kmart, and 23% from Target, whereas 82% of Kmart stores faced competition from Wal-Mart and 85% from Target stores. The strategy gave Wal-Mart a continuing advantage.

2. *Quality*. Wal-Mart took account of the customer's concern with quality. From the start it promised national brands at everyday low prices, rather than the usual private label goods, second-tier brands or price promotions. Its prices were consistently lower than those of its competitors. It unashamedly copied the good ideas of its competitors, for example taking the concept of Sam's Club from the Price Club of Sol Price.

3. *Branding*. Rather as Richard Branson did later, Wal-Mart used the charismatic personality of Sam Walton to sell itself. Sam Walton was ruthless in his single-mindedness, obsessed with keeping costs down but zany in his behaviour and the way he promoted the stores. He sought to empower his associates but keep an eye on them, use every element of technological superiority he could and build loyalty among associates and staff, customers and suppliers. As a result, the culture of Wal-Mart was dynamic and egalitarian. Staff were empowered to take responsibility, provided they were committed to excellence of performance and motivated to perform by stock incentive schemes. This raised productivity and kept down costs.

The limits of cost leadership

There are many cost factors which can change quickly and unexpectedly. These changes are accentuated at the global level. Changes in exchange rates are one cause of such transitoriness, as the Strategy in Action on Caterpillar and Komatsu shows. It is possible for small changes in exchange rates to deprive an enterprise of a cost advantage, increasing the degree of competition from abroad almost overnight. This can happen either as a consequence of a decline in the value of a foreign currency, making enterprises based in the relevant country much more competitive, or a rise in the value of the home country's currency. It can be the consequence of both kinds of change. When currencies move in opposite directions, these relative cost movements can be very dramatic. They may be totally unconnected with the performance of a particular industry or company.

Strategy in Action Caterpillar vs. Komatsu

The market for heavy earth-moving equipment is a semi-duopoly in which the American firm Caterpillar has had a decisive advantage over its main rival, a relative newcomer, the Japanese firm Komatsu. Between them they typically meet about two-thirds of world demand. In 1980 Caterpillar's share was

▶

about 60%, well down on an earlier 70%, but still well ahead of Komatsu's 15%. All seemed to be well with Caterpillar – it was one of the USA's leading exporters and making a good profit. However, the situation was changing and changing rapidly. Caterpillar entered a period of crisis between 1981 and 1985.

Komatsu had steadily increased its share from a low 9% in 1974 to 15% in 1980, mainly as a consequence of higher labour productivity and lower costs which allowed it to sell its machines at 10–15% below Caterpillar's prices. This gradual encroachment was in spite of its lack of a worldwide dealer network and efficient after-sales support and service functions, which seemed to justify for many potential customers the higher Caterpillar prices.

The gradual encroachment was greatly accelerated by a significant change of price which resulted from currency movements. Between 1980 and 1985 the American dollar rose by 87% against a basket of currencies from 10 other industrialized countries. As a result, the dollar price of Komatsu products fell dramatically, reaching as much as 40% below the Caterpillar price by 1985. Customers began to desert Caterpillar for Komatsu. This happened at a time when the Third World

debt crisis had greatly reduced the demand for construction equipment.

Caterpillar responded to this situation in two ways. It began a cost-cutting campaign which reduced costs by as much as 20% between 1982 and 1985 and it joined with other exporters in pressuring the Reagan administration to do something about the problem of the high value of the dollar. The result was the Plaza Accord in 1985 which reduced the value of the dollar significantly. This allowed Caterpillar to regain some lost ground, in 1989 getting back to about 47% of the market, compared with Komatsu's 20%.

A currency value which has moved dramatically down, between 1985 and 1994 from 240 to 99 yen to the dollar, after a climb in the relative value during the early 1980s, and thereafter has fluctuated at various points in between, is bound to have a powerful influence on the relative prices and competitiveness of American and Japanese products. The movement of the relative exchange rate of the dollar and the yen is not unusual in a world of floating exchange rates. A massive fall in the value of any currency relative to others is likely to affect many competitors in other countries, whatever the nature of the product.

A commodity is an unbranded or undifferentiated product. It is a product which has homogeneous physical attributes or is perceived by the consumer as having homogeneous attributes. One product is identical with another, whoever is the producer. The term 'commodity' is frequently used to describe the products of the primary sector of the economy, that is, agricultural products such as wheat or mining products such as copper. The term has now been extended to include manufactured products which are standard in nature and produced in a competitive market in which buyers perceive little or no difference between the competing products. There may be many sellers, and something approaching perfect competition. Profit margins are normal. However, any economies of scale or learning by doing will favour those who win market share and will eventually reduce the number of producers. Profits may still be low if entry is not too difficult.

Commoditization is the process of becoming a commodity wherein cost factors change their significance in a regular cycle.

Particularly at the global level, cost or price leadership is a tenuous achievement which can disappear quickly. In practice there are cycles in which cost leadership and product differentiation may alternate in importance for the strategy maker, as indicated in the following Focus on Practice on the transaction cycle.

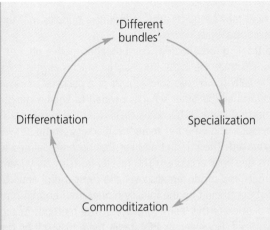

Figure 9.3 **Transaction cycle**

Most products or product groups go through a similar cycle during their lifetime. In some cases this cycle may be repeated a number of times, with intermittent upgrading of the product as the nature of demand changes. Or it might be that there are intermittent remakings of a product as technology itself changes (as in the case of the mobile phone).

This cycle does not necessarily describe what happens in particular cases but does indicate the way in which cost leadership and product differentiation strategies are likely to be pursued at different points in the cycle. The emphasis in strategy shifts from one to the other and back again.

There are four distinct stages in the transaction cycle:

1. When a product is first introduced, it is new to the consumer who is unclear exactly what to expect from the product. This is scarcely surprising since the product may be on offer in different forms. It may rapidly change its attributes over time. This can apply to any major move in adding an attribute to an existing product when it is first made, or removing redundant attributes, a much more likely outcome. At this stage the first mover has a clear advantage. It may not matter exactly what attributes the product has since innovation creates a clear, if temporary, competitive advantage.

    At this stage there is a distinct unevenness of appearance and performance. The product may have many attributes that consumers, or significant groups of consumers, do not need. It may vary in attributes from producer to producer, having all sorts of redundant functions. Suppliers may be producing and putting on the market products which are highly differentiated, difficult for the consumer to understand, compare or evaluate. Because the consumer does not know what he or she wants of the product, he or she may have to devote some time to learning how to use the product. There may be alternative technical systems, certainly no standard industry specification. An example is the major division between Beta and VHS in the early years of video recorders. As a consequence, during the early days there may be serious switching costs in moving from one product to another, as from a Macintosh computer to an IBM.

    The method of production itself may not be settled. There may be alternative products competing in the same niches and alternative ways of producing the same product. At this stage there has been little opportunity for learning by either supplier or consumer. There has been little movement down the experience curve, a movement which eventually settles the issue of system beyond doubt. There is great scope for either the consumer or the producer, or both, moving down the experience curve. It is highly likely that the product will become much more user-friendly over time.

    The consumption or operation of the product may require all sorts of services which are still supplied with the product, often by the same supplier. The bundle of such services may be quite large. Alternative bundles may exist, just as alternative technical systems exist.

Many electronic goods, such as computers or mobile phones, on their first introduction, illustrate the cycle. The way in which petrol is sold serves as another illustration. Initially petrol was sold as part of a package of services including maintenance and all the other services needed to keep a car on the road.

2. During the second stage, it becomes clear what the consumer wants and expects from this product, and whether there are markets segments which can be separately supplied. The product and services become defined and the normal specifications generally accepted. This results from an early learning process as both consumers and producers discover the most useful application of the product. More suppliers, attracted by the initially higher than normal profits, enter the market and accelerate this learning process. The methods of production become more standardized. However, at this stage, there may still be one or two variants of the basic product in competition with each other and even one or two production techniques, such as different generation mobile phones.

3. As the market matures, one variant of the product or process becomes dominant. All the products and services become standard, and visibly so. Consumption becomes easy, the use of the product being user-friendly. Switching costs consequently decline to close to zero. In the jargon, the product becomes 'commoditized'. The nature of the product or service and the production methods used are widely known.

The next move is for the product and services to be unbundled from each other and for specialist suppliers to emerge. Component production becomes specialized. There is much more competition in supplying the products and services and any components. Profit margins come down, in some cases significantly. The emphasis shifts to cost leadership and a race to establish market share. Prices tend to fall.

This is where it might stay unless someone makes a move in adding to the product an attribute which is valued by the customer and not expected by the other suppliers, or even doing the opposite, removing an attribute or attributes.

This is the stage at which self-service petrol stations became the norm (removal of an attribute, assistance in filling the petrol tank) and points systems based on the level of consumption the norm (the addition of an attribute, a loyalty programme which tries to tie a consumer to one supplier). Garages became separate from dealers selling cars and petrol stations and specialized in maintaining and repairing certain vehicle types. Spare parts could be bought in discount department stores.

4. Price competition induces a twofold process at the next stage. Some suppliers react by seeking new ways to differentiate the product. There is an attempt to decommoditize the product by packaging it differently. New attributes are added. This often involves a different system of retailing. There is a stronger attempt to segment the market, to discover and sell to customer groups who want bundles of attributes different from the norm.

In a simultaneous process, others try to dominate the market, making up for poor profit margins with higher sales, racing for market share. There is room for few such sellers. Some are bound to win and some to lose in such a scramble.

The length of each stage in the cycle, and thus the cycle itself, can differ greatly from product to product. The commoditization cycle can be repeated time and

Focus on Practice
cont'd

time again for the same product, sometimes with a complete cycle of weeks or months rather than years (see the different generations of video games consoles as described in the case study in Chapter 6).

The repackaging of petrol saw the addition of retail outlets, often open 24 hours, or close to 24 hours, selling a whole range of non-automobile products from newspapers and magazines to foodstuffs. In some cases, the oil company which is associated with particular outlets has developed a strategic alliance with a bank to establish fully fledged ATMs to pay bills, check credit balances and withdraw cash, even to purchase tickets for entry into resorts. It has even been asked how long it might be before the petrol station becomes a drive-through supermarket.

In a world of floating exchange rates, there is a deterrent to international transactions arising solely from the volatility of exchange rates and the effect of this on future returns. After all, hedging is only possible in the short term. In the long term changes in exchange rates feed through into costs, either directly because of international inputs or indirectly because others use foreign inputs.

There might also be differences in the rate of price inflation between different economies which are not linked with exchange rate variations. These might reflect changes in the cost of particular inputs or tax rates.

There might even be the movement of a new player, a large multinational, into a new market or even a new industry. The entry of a major new player from abroad can have the same effect as changes in the exchange rates, even with stable exchange rates. Important markets become the venue for large global players in competition with each other. Provided the market is sufficiently important, entry may be pre-emptive, directed to preventing others gaining an advantage. New entry may also be the result of a change in relative factor prices which cause global players to seek out cheaper venues, for example to reduce wages levels or the cost of capital.

Domestic players can also take the lead in changing their strategy quickly using price competition as a deliberate strategic device for winning market share. Large players can suddenly shift into a new industry, particularly if the industry is highly profitable. Other unexpected changes can occur, reflecting technical breakthroughs or unexpected reductions in the cost of important inputs such as labour or oil.

For all these reasons a cost or price advantage is likely to be transitory. It is not easy for an enterprise to sustain a process of continued cost reduction and a continued cost advantage.

Keeping a cost advantage is one thing, retaining price leadership is another. Using price advantage in an aggressive manner is not something to be done lightly. Using price to try to drive out competitors is a dangerous strategy which can only be employed if the enterprise has a decided cost advantage and/or if it has the resources to finance the deliberate incurring of losses. It must be confident of success, and usually a quick success. In most cases, it can only be employed for a brief period. The enterprise must be able to manage a sustained and continuing reduction in costs if it wishes to pursue such a strategy over a longer period of time.

Even Wal-Mart is not a pure cost leader, which is best shown by a comparison with an enterprise such as Aldi which is much closer to being such a cost leader.

Strategy in Action Wal-Mart: IT as a source of cost leadership

'Wal-Mart's secret was to focus its IT investments on applications that directly enhanced its core value proposition of low prices.'

Johnson, 2002: 42

The rate of growth of retail productivity in the USA, as measured by value added per hour, jumped from 2% between 1987 and 1995 to 6.3% between 1995 and 1999, which explains as much as one-quarter of the economy-wide acceleration in productivity which occurred at that time and attracted so much attention, often accounted for by the communications and information revolution. Although general merchandising accounts for only 15% of retail sales in the USA, the sector is heavily concentrated in five enterprises – Wal-Mart, Kmart, Target, Costco and Sears – accounting for 60% of the total sales. There is some suspicion about these statistics on productivity acceleration and their implications. It has been argued that the tendency of consumers to favour higher quality items has automatically pushed up productivity, without any real increase.

More than half of the productivity acceleration in retailing of general merchandise is explained by what has happened to Wal-Mart alone. Certainly Wal-Mart has been the market leader. In 1987 it had 9% of the market share, in 1995 27%. At the earlier date, in terms of real sales per employee, Wal-Mart was 40% more productive than its competitors, at the latter date 48%.

The following innovations undertaken by Wal-Mart underpinned this surge in productivity improvement:

- The large-scale, 'big-box' format of the super-centre stores, with the detailed attention to layout and throughput, raised the efficiency with which each customer was served and increased sales per square foot above what any other store could achieve
- The concept of 'everyday low prices' for brand name products allowed a consistent underselling of competitors
- The location of an expanded number of stores around the central distribution centres.

Probably most famously, Wal-Mart pioneered the application of IT to retailing. It was:

- among the first retailers to use computers to track inventory (1969)
- one of the first to adopt bar coding (1980), starting regular use of electronic scanning of uniform product codes at the point of sale in 1983 and installing the system in all its stores by 1988, two years ahead of Kmart
- among the first to introduce electronic data interchange (EDI) (1985), which enables most vendors, including the large ones like Proctor & Gamble, General Electric and Wrangler, to receive orders and interact directly with Wal-Mart electronically, allowing Wal-Mart itself to reduce inventory; and also to put in wireless scanning guns (the late 1980s).

Wal-Mart has a well-deserved reputation for its use of IT. It has the largest private satellite system to control distribution. The first installation of the satellite system was made in 1983. The use of this system allows a much better link between the stores, distribution centres and the head office at Bentonville, Arkansas. It makes possible the daily collection and analysis of sales data. Managers could tell immediately how fast stock was moving and thus avoid, on the one hand, overstocking and the need for deep discounting, and on the other empty shelves and disappointed customers. Between 1987 and 1993, Wal-Mart spent over $700 million on its satellite communications network, computers and related equipment. Each year it spends in excess of $500 million on IT. Today it employs over 1,200 staff in this area alone.

However, at least half of Wal-Mart's productivity edge came from traditional areas of improvement, such as in-bound logistics, cross-training of employees, better training of cashiers and monitoring of the level of utilization in its stores. Distribution is usually through the distribution centres, rather than direct from suppliers. However, a 'cross-docking' scheme allows merchandise to move straight through the distribution centres.

Over the period 1995–99, Wal-Mart's competitors began to catch up. From 1994 they began to copy the Wal-Mart innovations. Wal-Mart's productivity rose by 22%, that of its competitors at a faster rate of 28%.

Table 9.3 Real sales per employee ($1000s)

	1995	1999
Wal-Mart	148	181
Kmart	109	133
Sears	87	118

However, Wal-Mart has outcompeted and outlasted Kmart which has filed for bankruptcy. This is not surprising since Wal-Mart, with about the same number of stores, sells about three times the value of products. Per square foot of area, Wal-Mart sales are about twice those of Kmart. Wal-Mart has been investing about four times the capital each year in expansion and innovation. There is clearly a virtuous circle in which Wal-Mart spends more and therefore makes more, makes more and therefore can spend more.

It is interesting and significant to note that Wal-Mart has the largest and most complex commercial database of all enterprises. It has recently doubled the size of its central data warehouse, so that it now can hold 200 terabytes of information (a terabyte equals 1,000 gigabytes or one million megabytes). As

recently as 1996, the capacity was raised from 3.5 to 7 terabytes. One forecast is that Wal-Mart will be the first commercial enterprise to have a petabyte capacity (one petabyte equals 1,000 terabytes).

The new warehouse could store all the books and research data in the Library of Congress twenty-five times. The attainment of this storage capacity has been made possible by the dramatic reduction of costs. It now costs just 15 cents for the hardware and software to store one megabyte of information. A decade ago it cost $15. Within five years, the cost will be down to one cent.

This facility is a real strategic asset. It enables Wal-Mart to analyse the large quantities of data available to it, in the process interpreting and predicting consumer buying patterns and the demand for particular consumer products on a day-to-day basis. This helps Wal-Mart to meet demand with the minimum of stocks. The main information going into this database relates to transactions within the Wal-Mart stores. Every point-of-sale transaction is reported, stored and analysed. Through the retail link system, this information is made available to Wal-Mart's suppliers. Some information going in may be personal and is likely to be the subject of debate on grounds of privacy.

Focus on Practice
An alternative cost leadership model

The Aldi model is an alternative to the Wal-Mart model. Aldi (short for Albrecht Discount, the name of the founding brothers) is a genuine discounter which Wal-Mart is not. The Aldi group has a chain of 6,324 discount grocery stores spread across Europe and North America. The group has its origins in Germany. It is immensely successful but still has its main base in Germany, where it generates 65% of its sales and operates 3,723 stores. The formula adopted is low prices, limited selection and perpetual cost cutting. In 2001 it managed to generate an unprecedented average of US$8,000 revenue per square metre of floor space, almost twice its main competitors. In recent years a number of competitors have appeared – Lidl, Netto and Penny Market, for example, carrying the discount model to Southern and Eastern Europe.

Aldi has a very different structure from Wal-Mart. It is a private company controlled by a trust. To avoid disclosing the financial accounts and also the usual intrusion in Germany of a workers' council, considered by the Aldis bound to push up labour cost, the organization is divided into north and south parts and 60 legally separated operating units.

Apart from the form of its organizational structure, Aldi differs from Wal-Mart in two key respects:

1. Aldi operates more like Sam's Club than the Wal-Mart super-centres. It offers only 700 separate items for sale, compared with Wal-Mart's 80,000.

▶

Focus on Practice
cont'd

2. The items offered are often store-brand versions of food products, that is, generic or cut-price products, not the national brands which Wal-Mart sells. Aldi's brands are typically 30% cheaper to buy wholesale. Aldi uses its buying clout to purchase cheaply from small producers.

This comparison shows that even Wal-Mart does not pursue a pure cost leadership strategy.

Source: O'Brien, 2002a: 72–3, 2002b: 8.

Case Study   Infosys and the Indian comparative advantage

'One bad customer experience is all it will take to erode brand equity that the country has built over the years.'
Maharta, 2002: 56

The leading sector in Indian economic growth is the computer software industry. Clearly in the world at large this is part of the new economy, linked to computing, telecommunications and entertainment, which has shown such rapid growth. Once the hardware is in place, and there has been a tendency to build telecommunication networks ahead of demand, notably broadband, the most powerful growth area is in software applications. There are a myriad of possible innovative applications.

India has developed a strong information industry, centred on the cities of Bangalore and Hyderabad. This industry has grown from almost nothing at the beginning of the 1990s, when the credibility in the outside world of such an industry in India was low. Since 1991 the industry has had an annual growth rate of over 50%. Total sales in 2000 were $8.3 billion, employment was about 400,000 and the industry accounted for 15% of India's exports. The main trade association,

NASSCOM, has predicted $50 billion worth of exports by 2008 and an employment of 1.1 million people. The research company IDC believes that India has already captured 80% of the market for 'outsourced offshore' software development.

A number of software companies have taken the lead, replacing the rather tired family conglomerates which used to dominate the Indian economy. Reliance Industries is a notable exception to this. There are now three software companies in the top ten, whereas there were none as late as 1992 (Table 9.4).

Can this success be maintained?

The history of Infosys

The Bangalore-based Infosys was founded in 1981 by Naraya Murthy and five others. To do so they had to borrow US$2,000. Murthy, its chairman and managing director, has been the moving spirit for the company. Growth has been very rapid. The company was launched on the stock market at a capitalization of $60 million dollars in 1993. By 1997 the capitalization was up ten times. At this stage, the company already had a strong international orientation, being 30% foreign-owned, and with 80% of the sales of its products and services abroad, mostly in the USA. Total sales in 1996 were still only $40 million, but profits were $9.4 million. It was a bit player but in an industry which was on the rise. In 1997 software exports were $2 billion, up 66% on the previous year.

By February 2002 the market capitalization was almost US$8 billion. Murthy alone had accrued a personal fortune in excess of US$550 million. This is not large by American or triad standards but by Indian or non-Japanese Asian standards it is very large indeed. In the year to March 2002 the

Table 9.4 **Top Indian companies by capitalization, in $billion**

	1992		2001
Tisco	2.21	Hindustan Lever	10.30
ITC	1.20	Reliance Industries	8.84
Telco	1.14	*Wipro*	6.65
Century Textiles	1.13	*Infosys Technologies*	5.79
Hindustan Lever	0.89	Reliance Petroleum	4.65
Reliance Industries	0.77	ITC	4.29
Grasim	0.74	Oil and Natural Gas	4.05
GSFC	0.71	Indian Oil	2.73
ACC	0.67	State Bank of India	2.26
Colgate	0.57	*HCL Technologies*	2.22

annual revenues of Infosys reached well over US$500 million, small beer compared with IBM Global Services which sells US$9 billion of technology services a year, but again impressive in the Indian context.

The compound annual growth rate of Infosys revenues over the last five years has been 70%, although this eased off to a still impressive 30% in the crisis year of March 2001–02. In that year the net income was still well in the black, at US$155 million. Infosys has become the model for success in the newly liberalized environment of India. It has shown how an Indian company can compete with the best abroad.

The nature of the company

The Infosys business model has transformed the global IT industry, so much so that Murthy was named by *Time* magazine and CNN as one of the 25 most influential global executives for 2001.

What is that model? Infosys was founded on principles of deliberate globalization, or internationalization. According to Murthy, the aim is: 'Source capital from where it is cheapest; produce where it is most cost-effective; and sell where it is most profitable. All without worrying about national boundaries.' Because of the limitations of the home market, Murthy believed that the company had to go global from the beginning and attack the established players on their own turf. That meant that the company had to be at the cutting edge of best practice. It had to be reliable, quick and efficient. In order to foster initiative and ownership, each Infosys project was run as an independent mini-company, rather as Sony had run its own projects. Infosys has its own in-house management development programme, the Infosys Leadership Institute, which prepares the managers for this competitive environment.

The company was the first in India to use a stock option plan, with 60% of the 1,900 employees holding stock options. Job satisfaction has been so high that staff turnover was as low as 10–15%. When the company went public in 1993, this immediately created 400 'paper' US-dollar millionaires. It also has an Infosys Foundation which puts back profits into the Indian economy.

There have been three main problems:

1. The attitude of the Indian government. It clearly believed that a home industry could be developed by closing the frontiers to outside competition and outside influence, that is, by continuing the import substitution strategy which underpinned the industrialization which had been achieved in the five-year plans. In the late 1970s it expelled the American computer giants such as IBM. There were severe import restrictions which slowed the early development of the company. It held up the first telephone line for Infosys for nine months and the import of computers on which the company could write its software for three years.

2. An overdependence on the American market. The company's first overseas outpost was set up in the USA in 1987. The first successes were in persuading large multinationals like Reebok and Nordstrom to go to Infosys for their cheap, back-office processing, again with an American bias. In 2001 something like 74% of sales were generated in the USA. The company is now looking to increase the share of Europe (currently about 20%), Japan, Australia and even South America.

3. Competition from other home-grown companies such as Wipro and HCL as well as multinationals such as IBM, setting up in India to take advantage of the cheap labour. The Indian companies are seeking to reinforce their position by strategic acquisitions abroad and a continuing attention to quality, including transparency and disclosure.

The nature of the competitive advantage

The advantage of India in the area of computer software can be summarized as, 'global standards at Indian costs'. Infosys develops made-to-order computer systems for a fraction of the cost of a typical US- or European-based integrator. The Internet allows this to be done, even at a significant distance, with minimum delay. If necessary, teams of specialists can be flown to wherever in the world they are needed. The low cost of Indian software developers enables Infosys to employ larger teams which allow them to complete a job in a fraction of the time needed in the developed world. Infosys employs a veritable army of 10,000 programmers.

There are many cases where this competitive advantage has been revealed by the winning of loyal customers. For example, the Belgian mobile operator Belgacom Mobile wanted to develop a customer loyalty programme which could handle data stored in different languages and provide flexibility for customers. The company wanted a quality programme at a low price and wanted it delivered quickly. Infosys delivered in eight months to a highly satisfied client. The Belgian company has gone back to Infosys for other systems development work.

A reputation for quality was essential to the company. Foreign companies were nervous about going abroad for their software work. One way of counteracting this was simply to continue to exceed customer expectations. Other deliberate action was taken. The company undertook a series of quality assurance initiatives to bench-

Table 9.5 **World spending on IT services**

	IT services spending US$bn	Exports to India US$m	India's market share %	Share of India's exports %
North America	171.1	6,685	3.92	67.6
Western Europe	109.6	2,103	1.92	21.3
Japan	34.9	193	0.55	2.0
Asia Pacific	16.0	311	1.94	3.2
L America and rest of world	17.5	583	3.33	5.9
Total world market	349.1	9,875	2.82	100.0

Source: O'Connell and Armitstead, 2003.

mark itself against the best in the world. The most striking and significant of these was the Capability Maturity Model for Software (SW-CMM). Run by the Software Engineering Institute at Carnegie-Mellon University in the USA, the SW-CMM is a model for judging the quality of an organization's software processes. Infosys achieved the top accolade of the model, a level five certification.

The strategy

At the end of the 1990s, the software industry, including its Indian component, was faced for the first time by a recession. The high-tech crash and rapidly diminishing demand for IT translated worldwide into falling demand and a severe pressure on price levels. Paradoxically, this has favoured India since the desire to cut costs and to outsource business processes favours the low-cost and high-productivity producers. Although there are no new major stimulants to demand such as the threat of Y2K or a boom in e-commerce to offset this fall in demand and carry the supplier companies through the bad times, Indian software exports had grown by 20% in the year to March 2002 and are forecast to grow to 30% in 2003. They will exceed US$7 billion and already India's share of the global market is more than 2% (Table 9.5). Despite intense competition India continues to take advantage of the combination of low costs and skilled labour. The return on capital invested in India's IT companies is almost 50%.

For Infosys an increasing proportion of the company's turnover comes from what could be called 'infotech consulting' (often called 'IT for business transformation'). Much of the IT of major companies is now being outsourced rather than carried out in-house. This is not a completely new departure for Infosys, although it is given a new urgency by the recession. In 1999 the company created a consulting arm, called Infosys Business Consulting Service, the Domain Consultancy Group and a technology-heavy unit, the Software Engineering Technologies Lab. The aim was to be able to seek out the burgeoning consulting business and tailor highly sophisticated IT solutions to the problems of client companies.

In order to promote this shift of emphasis, one strategy of Infosys has been to acquire small boutique consultants. For example, an alliance with the Concours Group, a small consulting firm that specializes in the area of change management, has expanded Infosys' capabilities.

In this volatile and competitive environment, the Indian software companies have to try to enhance their long-term competitiveness and switch their emphasis temporarily at least, but probably permanently, away from software services to more general services. If they are to survive as major global players, they have to make a successful transition from $350–500 million players to the billion dollar club, not an easy thing to do when they are faced with competition from players such as the big five (now big four) accounting firms which have all spun off consulting divisions, and other majors such as IBM, CSC and EDS.

Table 9.6 indicates the intensity of the competition faced. In order to achieve sustained competitiveness,

Table 9.6 **India's ITES companies**

	Examples	Number	Employees
Back-office giants	GE, American Express HSBC, Citigroup	30+	30,000+
Software converts	Progeon (Infosys) E. Serve (HCL) Spectramind (Wipro) Msource (Mphasis – BFL)	30+	6,000+
True third party cos	Daksh, EXL, Transwonder Customerasset.com	100+	45,000+
Global ITES cos	Convergys, ACS Sitel, Teletech	10+	6,000+
Consulting leaders	Accenture CSC	2+	500+

Source: Maharta, 2002: 55.

companies such as Infosys, or rather its consulting arm Progeon, have to do three things:

1. ensure that what they deliver is of the highest quality and delivered at the lowest price
2. extend their expertise to a wider circle of industries, engaging in cross-selling, that is, using the expertise they have developed in one area in others
3. establish long-term links with a significant number of Fortune 500 or Global 1000 companies. They have to have something of value to offer such companies, new strategic initiatives which will assist the clients to raise productivity, increase their return and better satisfy customers.

In this area companies must be proactive, taking the initiative and approaching the prospective client. This is hard to do since many already have close relationships with the major players which means that particular software projects are seldom put out to tender. The aim of Infosys and the other Indian companies will be to win an increasing amount of IT consulting and systems integration work with high margins.

Although in the financial year 2001–02 consulting generated no more than 4% of the company's revenues, the intention is to increase this quickly and dramatically. The general aim is to be among the top ten consulting firms in the world by 2010, an ambitious goal. As Table 9.6 shows, the reference model is Accenture, the former consulting arm of Andersen. Other significant competitors already in this market are IBM, Wipro, Cap Gemini Ernst &Young and EDS, all with significant presences in India. This partly removes an advantage which is that Infosys can afford to charge between $40 and $90 per hour whereas the big four charge as much as $250 an hour.

In order to keep with the competitors, Infosys must sell itself and its reputation, raising its marketing expenditure from about 5% of total income to about 10%. This is a much harder task than anything it has accomplished up to now. To some degree it is reliant on the action of others. It depends on the brand name of India. India, alongside Ireland, offers a broad-based, competitive presence in the ITES area. In India the costs of telecommunication services have fallen 85% since 1994, whereas in Ireland they have been constant. Moreover, India is five times larger than any competitor (Maharta, 2002: 54). Already ITES employs more than one million people and generates almost US$1.5 billion worth of business. There are something like 200 to 300 companies.

What Infosys has to counteract in order to maintain a competitive advantage is:

- undercutting on price by small players in India
- a possibly bad experience by a major customer of an Indian company
- overcapacity in the sector, which incidentally discourages entry by some strong international players
- continuing problems of regulation and poor infrastructure.

Case Study Questions

1. From what sources is Infosys' competitive advantage derived?
2. What elements of Infosys' competitive advantage derive from its location? Which other countries offer comparable advantages?
3. How has Infosys achieved the success which it has? What has been its strategy in doing this?
4. What strategy should an enterprise with its main activities in the new economy adopt when the new economy goes into recession?
5. What has accounted for the rise in significance of consulting services? Can Infosys create a competitive advantage in this area?

Reading

Economist, The, 'Outsourcing to India,' May 5, 2001: 61–3.

Maharta, V., 'Glut!', *Business Today*, October 13, 2002: 52–6.

Merchant, K., Alden, E. and Foremski, T., 'India fears impact of bid to curb jobs exports', *Financial Times*, June 4, 2003: 12.

O'Connell, D. and Armitstead, L., 'The great Indian takeaway', *Sunday Times*, June 8, 2003, Business focus: 3.5.

Sibillin, A., 'The best of both worlds', *Eurobusiness*, April 2002: 41–2.

Sukumar, R. and Shulda, S., 'Infosys Ver 2.0', *Business Today*, September 1, 2002: 64–8.

Unger, B., 'A survey of India's economy', *The Economist*, June 2, 2001: 3–22.

Utland, T., 'India's software sector progress', *Far Eastern Economic Review*, December 12, 2002: 54.

Key strategic lessons

● The main element of a cost or price leadership strategy is an attempt to keep costs as low as possible and use prices to maximize the gains of this competitive advantage.

● Whether this is the strategy to be adopted depends on the nature of the industry, the nature of competition and the culture of the enterprise.

● There are seven principal drivers of cost reduction: economies of scale, learning by experience, design improvement, technical change, a reduction in the cost of inputs, increased capacity utilization and reduced organizational slack.

● The pricing strategy adopted is not necessarily linked to the need to keep costs down, but the lower the costs, the more flexibility the enterprise will have in its pricing strategy.

● Focusing in cost leadership might be on a particular market segment or business unit. The simplest manner of focusing is to consider each of the activities in the value chain and their importance within the total cost position.

● Technical management is part of the more general cost leadership strategy. It is an ongoing and changing set of arrangements reflecting a mass of small technical and organizational changes which define and redefine the technology.

● Short-term cost fluctuations influence price behaviour and make the use of a pure cost and price strategy dangerous. Any price leadership is ephemeral since exchange rates, technology, the rate of inflation and the intensity of competition can all change quickly.

Applying the lessons

1 Define the following concepts: cost driver, cost leadership, price leadership, economies of scale, economies of scope, learning by experience, a technique and a technology.

2 Choose one industry with which you are familiar. What are the factors which influence the level of costs in that particular industry and the speed at which these costs can be, and are, reduced? Assess the relative importance of the different cost drivers in that industry.

From your own experience, give an example of an enterprise which operates closest to a pure cost leadership strategy. Explain why the enterprise behaves in this way. What is the nature of the product? Is this an appropriate strategy to pursue?

3 It is possible to distinguish between cost minimization pursued in the context of current operations and cost minimization pursued in the context of innovation, that is, in the context of the introduction of new products or new processes. Take one industry and give an example of each type of cost reduction. Which predominates in this industry?

4 'Price leadership is not cost leadership.' Give an example of an enterprise which pursues a price leadership strategy without being a cost leader, and one which pursues a cost leadership strategy without being a price leader. In what specific ways can you distinguish the two strategies?

5 Choose an enterprise with a high level of vertical integration and show how internalization can be used to assist in the minimization of costs. How does the nature of the supply chain influence strategy on costs?

6 It is clear that the exchange of information, particularly information relating to elements relevant to market demand, has helped to make enterprises more responsive to consumer wants and reduce costs. The reduction in inventory (just-in-time) depends on the rapid transfer of such information. However, there are problems of privacy which arise in the storage, use and transfer of such information. Consider a large enterprise such as Wal-Mart, or even a bank or an airline, and analyse the privacy issues which can arise with respect to the information systems which they use.

Strategic project

1 Choose an industry with which you are familiar and an enterprise typical of that industry. Imagine you are a consultant asked to advise how the enterprise can reduce its costs in order to achieve cost leadership.

2 Divide the value chain into its constituent activities.

3 Estimate the relative importance of each activity in total costs.

4 List the cost drivers which are relevant to each activity, noting in particular those relevant to the high-cost activities.

5 Evaluate how a significant decrease in costs can be achieved and make recommendations on the basis of this evaluation.

Exploring further

An article which is strongly in favour of separating the cost leadership strategy from the product differentiation strategy in the way which Porter suggests is Hambrick, 1983: 687–707.

There is no shortage of published work on costs. A thorough treatment is Shank and Govindarajan, 1993, especially Chapters 2–6 and 10. A shorter version is 1992: 39–51. The issue is particularly well dealt with in Grant, 2002. A rather shorter piece is Cooper and Kaplan, 1988: 96–103. For the accounting perspective see Hegert and Morris, 1989: 175–88.

The learning or experience curve is discussed in the work of Henderson, 1979 and 1984. The strengths and weaknesses of the curve are assessed in Abernathy and Wayne, 1974: 109–19. The significance of the curve for strategy is analysed in Ghemawat, 1985: 143–9. The loss of interest in the curve is discussed in Kiechel, 1981.

The supply chain and its importance for costs is discussed in Kulkani, 1996: 17–20, and Fisher, 1997: 139–47. The importance of operations, particularly manufacturing and materials procurement, on costs is argued by Miller, 1986: 21–231.

10 Differentiating the product

After reading this chapter you will be able to:

- recognize the difference between needs and wants

- understand that marketing is a broader notion than just selling or advertising

- understand the nature of product differentiation

- identify the various attributes of a product and the utilities required by the purchaser of such a product

- see branding as an extreme form of product differentiation

- establish a generic strategy based on product differentiation

Key strategic challenge

How do I persuade consumers that I have a superior product?

Strategic dangers

That the enterprise misses the opportunity to develop a market segment in which the price of its product permits a relatively high operating profit margin, and that this failure results from an inability to identify an appropriate product and develop a strategy to differentiate, even brand, that product.

Case Study Scenario   Turning a stone into a jewel – De Beers

'In reality, diamonds are not scarce and the main role of the Central Selling Organisation (CSO) has been to regulate supply and demand to bring stability to the diamond markets.'   *Lewis et al., 1999: 440*

The trade in diamonds is rare but lucrative (Table 10.1).

Table 10.1 **The size of the diamond trade (2002)**

	US$ billion
Annual value of rough diamonds	7.9
Cutters' product	9.6 in rough stones
	12.8 in polished gems
Wholesale diamond jewellery market	27
Retail market	57.5 (USA share 45%)

Prices at the retail level make this a valuable industry. Yet a diamond is only a sparkling stone with an unusual hardness and a stone in surprisingly plentiful supply. It is possible to create demand by attaching attributes to the product which link with a consumer utility such as luxury.

This case study tells the story of how a stone for which there was little demand, beyond an industrial one, was converted into a highly valued and therefore valuable product, most commonly found in diamond rings worn by women in the developed world. It discusses how the marketing of small and coloured diamonds revolutionized the industry. The case study shows how branding was achieved for diamonds.

Previous studies of the diamond trade have concentrated on the supply side, the way in which De Beers has maintained a monopoly position. For most of the twentieth century De Beers dominated the diamond industry as a monopoly seller. In this period 80–90% of the rough diamonds marketed in the world were normally sold through the Central Selling Organisation (CSO). What is often forgotten, even by De Beers in the years of its dominance, is the importance of final consumer demand.

The demand for diamonds has tended to fluctuate with the business cycle. In bad times the demand is low. Even before the 1930s, there had been periods when the market had been flooded with diamonds and prices severely depressed. As might be expected, the Great Depression of the 1930s created an unprecedented surplus of diamonds. As a reaction to the low demand, in 1934 Sir Ernest Oppenheimer put together the CSO and its trading arms in order to control the supply of diamonds onto the market. He established a system in which all producers channelled their diamonds through the CSO, a system which continued to operate well into the 1990s, and still exists today, if as a pale reflection of its former self. Even today De Beers still controls about two-thirds of the global trade in cut diamonds and wields enormous power in this market.

Until the 1950s Africa was the main source of supply of diamonds. There always was a problem of diamonds being stolen and smuggled out of Africa. After the 1950s new sources of diamonds appeared in the Soviet Union and Australia, and there were intermittent attempts by producing countries to operate independently of the CSO, for example in Israel in the 1970s and in Botswana/Zaire in the 1980s. These attempts were rebuffed. The biggest crisis came during the 1990s, when, during the early 1990s, the Soviet Union, later Russia, put enormous pressure on the system and then, in the second half of the 1990s, Australia emerged as an important source of supply. As a result, the share of the CSO fell as low as 63% in 1995. Today the pressure is coming from new sources of supply in Canada. Canada is already the fifth biggest diamond producer after Botswana, Russia, Namibia and South Africa. Significant exploration is still continuing throughout the world. During the 1990s, the key date in a dramatic change of strategy on the part of the main players was 1996, when the Australian producer Argyle broke free from the De Beers cartel and began to sell its diamonds independently.

Until recently De Beers sought to retain a monopoly of supply and persuade others to support this monopoly. In such a monopoly, limiting supply was critical to the setting of a premium price. The control over supply was matched by an attempt to stimulate and maintain demand. A higher demand was a prerequisite for the maintenance of a premium price. If De Beers was surprisingly successful for so long at controlling supply, it began its dominance by excelling at marketing. De Beers managed to create a demand where little had existed before, to put in place a whole new market segment.

What is the demand for diamonds? Individual diamonds differ markedly in their quality. Diamonds can be divided into three groups – those of gem quality, those of near gem quality and industrial diamonds. The category to which the diamond belongs depends on the four Cs; carat, colour, clarity and cutability, meaning shape. The first group is worth per carat about ten times the second, the second about ten times the third. There is a very sophisticated system of grading developed by the CSO.

The demand for gem-quality diamonds is for jewellery, although there may be a fluctuating level of investment demand. The only other demand is an industrial one for diamonds as a cutting tool, which is unreliable since it has been reduced by the substitution of cheaper synthetic diamonds, whose price had been falling steadily as the technology of production has improved. Since there are few barriers to entry into this industry, the existence of such substitutes keeps down the price of industrial-quality diamonds. This segment of the market has become highly competitive, and increasingly so.

The demand created by De Beers rested on a different attribute of the diamond, its attractive appearance and sparkle when polished, rather than its physical characteristics of hardness.

Today it is unusual to find products which are homogeneous and unusual to see the competitiveness of a producer based solely on price. Most products differ in some respect, if only in the perception of the consumer. Consumers can perceive even homogeneous products as different.

There are three elements of the product differentiation triangle:

1. the product itself, together with its attributes
2. the customers – their wants and needs or, more explicitly, the various market segments defined by a common evaluation of the usefulness of the attributes of a product or service to the customer
3. the capabilities and therefore core competencies of the enterprise, which define what the enterprise can do and where the enterprise is able to position itself.

A policy of strategic market segmentation, or product differentiation, must include each of the three elements – product and attributes, consumer and needs, and supplier resources and competencies. A strategy of product differentiation can be described variously as 'segmentation', 'targeting' or 'market positioning'.

Needs and wants

It is appropriate to ask what is likely to motivate a consumer to purchase a particular product. This desire is the basis for differentiating that product and representing it as more attractive to the consumer than other competitive products. One simple answer is that it allegedly satisfies some human need. On most accounts such human needs are quite stable. The enterprise selling the product must therefore identify and understand these needs, and be able to translate them into wants or specific utilities which a particular product or service satisfies for the consumer.

Maslow's hierarchy of needs

The number of human needs is finite but how they might be the classified is infinite and therefore uncertain. In his well-known analysis, Maslow (1954) hypothesized a hierarchy of five human needs. He argued that, as each need is satisfied, the next need becomes dominant. This is useful for gaining an intuitive understanding of needs and helping to classify those needs, while at the same time making clear the distinction between needs and wants. The five levels, in ascending order, are categorized as:

- physiological
- safety
- social
- esteem
- and self-actualization needs.

The first two focus very much on the individual in isolation and his or her needs, although the specific ways in which these needs are satisfied are often determined by society. Maslow describes these two levels as lower order needs, which need to be satisfied before any social activity can be sustained. The next three levels are higher order needs. More explicitly, the five levels are:

- *physiological needs*, which are generally instinctive, those necessary for survival. The list might include food and drink, shelter, clothing and sex
- *safety needs*, which comprise the desire for security and protection from physical and emotional harm
- *social needs*, which are a result of a person being part of a community or social group – the need to belong, that is, to be accepted in a membership group, as well as the basic need for friendship itself, for fellowship and affection. There is a need to be entertained by others, in a variety of different ways
- *esteem needs*, which are met by the interaction with others. They include feelings which arise within the individual, such as pride, self-respect and a sense of autonomy or achievement, and external factors contributed by others such as power, status, a recognition of achievement and the attention of peers or colleagues
- *self-actualization needs*, which centre on a person's drive to turn potential abilities into actual achievements. The individual can realize any inherent promise and become what he or she is capable of becoming.

Focus on Humour
The club of one

'Exclusively for everyone', Marks & Spencer advertisement seen by the writer on the side of a bus in Norwich, England, in August 2002.

'Modern man has a need to let the world know that he has succeeded. To do this, he needs to be able to buy symbols of social prestige. True luxury objects produced by the great jewellers cannot give him the recognition he yearns for, since they are exclusively one-of-a-kind.' Robert Hocq, owner of Cartier.

The advertising slogan of Marks & Spencer quoted above highlights the issue, how can a product or service be exclusively for everyone? There is an obvious contradiction in simultaneously trying to be exclusive, that is, to appeal to a limited group of potential customers, in the extreme case just one, and trying to appeal to all, or at least as many as possible. The quotation displays clearly the tension between the desire to sell a differentiated product to a limited market segment at a price yielding a high profit margin and the desire to sell as many items of the product as possible, which is better achieved with a lower profit margin and a lower price. The quotation does capture the desire and the increasing tendency to 'democratize luxury'.

▶

Focus on Humour
cont'd

The second quotation leads to a distinction between luxury goods, those which can only be afforded by the very rich, and aspirational goods, those which are available to a wider group and help to realize an aspiration to feel successful. The contrast is nicely captured by the following:

'Gary wanted to enjoy being a man of wealth and leisure but the country was making it none too easy. All around him, millions of newly minted American millionaires were engaged in the identical pursuit of feeling extraordinary.'

As he goes on to lament the wave of pseudo-sophistication that has lifted even the hog farmers and cleaning ladies of middle America, he continued to muse: 'Gary wished … all mid-westerners (could be) encouraged to revert to eating pasty food and wearing dowdy clothes and playing board games, in order that a strategic national reserve of cluelessness might be maintained, a wilderness of taste which would enable people of privilege, like himself, to feel extremely civilised in perpetuity.'

Source: Franzen, 2001 quoted by Cornell, 2002: 47.

Wants as social constructs

The present work makes an important distinction between needs and wants. Needs are translated by social processes into specific wants which a society can satisfy in a variety of particular ways. Human beings need food but can satisfy that need with a wide variety of food prepared differently and served in different contexts. The variety of this one need is infinite and continuously being added to. Society is continually creating a variety of new ways to satisfy such lower level needs.

Much of this process of creation of wants is unconscious, the result of attempts to meet everyday problems but increasingly the role of marketing is to deliberately create new wants, or rejig old ways of satisfying needs as new wants. The multitude of wants is one result of the creativity of human beings. They are socially created, the result of the normal social interactions which are part of living in communities. Each community devises its own ways of satisfying the full range of needs and passes knowledge of these onto new generations in a process of socialization. Often a younger generation rebels by creating its own ways of satisfying needs.

The higher the level of income in a particular society, the greater tends to be the number of ways in which particular needs are satisfied, and the more indirect and complex tends to be the methods of satisfying these needs. The marked increase in discretionary income earned by those in developed countries allows this to happen. It is an open invitation to suppliers to discover new ways of satisfying the basic needs.

In the process of satisfying wants, the lower order needs become invested with elements which assist in satisfying higher order needs. Different needs are satisfied simultaneously in complex ways, or the satisfaction of one need is linked to the satisfaction of another. Products and services are invested with a range of attributes which satisfy different needs. Needs are jointly and simultaneously satisfied. The hierarchy of needs breaks down. Pleasure is derived from particular ways of satisfying these wants. The medium very much becomes the message.

Luxury stores are not new; they have always existed. Cartier is a good example of a store with a long history and considerable reputation. Today none can surpass Hermes in the cachet its stores give to the products it sells. It is a notable example of aspirational selling.

When in early 2002 Hermes opened its brand new, 11-storey, glass headquarters, designed by Renzo Piano, in the Ginza district of Tokyo, where property is the most expensive in the world, respectable middle-class people queued for days waiting for the opening. Some were waiting to buy handbags which cost anything up to $40,000.

The Kelly and Birkin bags of Hermes are deliberately kept in scarce supply. A Kelly (named after Grace Kelly) would cost over half a million yen. There was a range of bags, none of which could be described as cheap. Most of them were handmade, which increased the feeling that the product was differentiated from the ordinary standard product.

Such stores exist all over the world. There are a surprising and increasing number of them, ten in Tokyo alone. In the whole world the number is in triple figures, not quite at Starbucks dimensions, but well beyond the exclusiveness of, say, Harrods. Most of the Hermes stores are concentrated in the places where large numbers of people with middle-class incomes live, shop, spend their holidays or simply regularly travel through, in the last case airports in the main centres such as New York and Paris. As might be expected, the heaviest concentrations are in the USA, rich European countries like France, Germany, Italy and the UK, and Asian countries where there are significant numbers of rich people, such as Japan. Affluent small cities like Kuwait, Singapore, Monaco and Hong Kong are also venues for Hermes stores. The stores often occupy, as with the Ginza, the most prestigious and expensive streets in the best-known cities in the world. In London there are stores in Sloane Square, Harrods in Knightsbridge, New Bond Street and at the Royal Exchange. The location is part of the attractiveness of the product. It lends the store the image of exclusiveness which attaches to the area.

In a strange combination of the democratic and the exclusive, you can buy Hermes products on the Internet – fragrances, ties and scarves in an infinite variety of colours, sensuously displayed on the screen. A silk tie is over US$100, a silk scarf US$250 and a man's eau de toilette US$400. They are not cheap, but nevertheless within the reach of many today and easily purchased.

Hermes stresses that a strong component of the luxury which resides in its products is the absence of machines in its production process. Most of the products are handmade, particularly the leather products, which are made from the most expensive leather, those in the top 3% by value. The resulting price partly reflects the time taken by craftsmen to make them but also the cost of the raw materials. The limited number of skilled craftsmen and their finite working period helps to limit the supply and maintain a significant waiting list.

Hermes is like an haute couture fashion house – there is no 'off-the-rack' label. Hermes rejects anything which is redolent of the machine – a word they reserve for what is unacceptable, that is, it rejects not just machine manufacture but also the practice of marketing, seen as indicative of a machine mentality. The managers of Hermes see no need to market, except by the appearance of their products and the physical presence of the store. Bags carried by the rich and famous market themselves. Hermes abstains from all the usual marketing methods, but takes great pains to control fully the whole manufacturing process for all its products.

Hermes illustrates the nature of aspirational demand which reflects the desire for status, prestige and luxury. One problem for the sellers is that traditionally the range of genuinely luxury goods has been limited. The democratization of luxury is accompanied by its opposite, the conversion of the mundane or ordinary into luxury. There is a tendency, encouraged by the deliberate action of sellers, to extend the range of aspirational goods so that it becomes almost unlimited. At the opposite extreme to an expensive luxury good is the humble loaf of bread. There is an interesting example of a product which is an everyday one converted into an aspirational one, the Poilane loaf. In the words of Durack (2002: 35): 'Pain Poilane is not just a loaf of bread. It is a work of art; a global celebrity; a Gallic icon; a symbol of artisanal purity; a natural medicine; a crusty, salty, sour piece of proof that there are still some things the French can do better than anyone else in the world.' Whereas an ordinary loaf commonly sells in an English supermarket for about 70p, the Poilane (sourdough) loaf, also made from just flour, salt and water, sells in the British supermarket chain Waitrose for £9.62 (Fitzmaurice, 2002: 1). Of course, it is twice the size of an ordinary loaf and baked in an oak-burning oven for six hours, characteristics which add to its cost. The Poilane loaf is an extreme example of a more general phenomenon, the designer bread boom.

In many sectors of the consumer market there has been an attempt to tap into this aspirational demand. All products and services are affected by this phenomenon. Aspirational goods or services are substitutes for each other since they provide the same utility to the consumer – status, prestige or luxury. In the case of many commoditized products there has been an attempt to create an upmarket brand or brands. This often means giving a new cachet to an old product.

There are plenty of examples. The introduction of premium beers, such as Hahn and Cascade in Australia, but similar products all over the world, fits the bill. It is the only rapidly growing market segment in the selling of beer in developed countries. Even more striking has been the successful pushing of coffee into the area of aspirational consumption by purveyors such as Starbucks, again stressing quality. Allegedly you can tell whether a residential area is on the rise by whether or not it is possible to get good coffee in the area. The cachet has always attached to wine, the drinking of which has always elicited what some call the mystique of casual consumption of the very expensive, others just plain snobbery.

Sometimes the differentiation is a deliberate attempt to give the product a style which it previously did not have, such as Apple's iMac. Samsung is pursuing the same goal of elegance. This is not so much luxury as style, although with some products such as the electrical goods of Bang & Olufsen it merges into luxury. Often the aim is to prevent commoditization of the product which tends to send prices and profit margins tumbling. Commoditization is the reverse process by which a product is democratized but in the process loses its prestige.

The aim for the consumer is the creation of the perception of luxury in goods which are hardly luxurious. Such a potential always exists. The obvious outcome for the successful supplier and seller is to increase or protect the profit margins which can be earned.

Alternatively companies which once produced only luxury goods for the very rich have been tempted to go downmarket, exploiting their brand name to sell a much greater quantity of goods, in the way BMW is attempting and Gucci has tried in the past with resulting difficulties. Prestigious companies such as Royal Doulton, Waterford or Wedgwood now produce everyday items or sets. This practice has been common among the producers of expensive clothing or accessories such as Yves St Laurent.

There are degrees of aspiration. There is a fairly large group of consumers who are not concerned with finding a bargain or discovering the lowest possible price. They do not queue up for the sales, nor do they queue to enter a new Hermes store. They are interested in good personal service, knowing about the product and quality and status. They want to buy ahead of the crowd, before a product takes off and rises in price. This group typically accounts for something like a quarter of the buying public but accounts for half of all consumer expenditure. It is rising in importance, which shows itself particularly during the upturn of an economy. It is not a group to which Wal-Mart seeks to sell. The husbands drive BMWs and the wives carry Gucci bags. The children already play online games.

Focus on Humour
'Icon' bags

Handbags are bought for purposes which are not purely utilitarian, although they do have ordinary functions. 'Must-have' handbags are the best example of an aspirational good. They are so important that they still account for 40% of the profits of the rapidly expanding luxury company Louis Vuitton-Möet Hennessy (LVMH). With their lead products – the Fendi baguettes (Fendi is part of LVMH), the Gucci Jacky bag (named after Jackie Onassis), the Prada metallic or bowling bags, the Louis Vuitton graffitis to the Hermes Kelly and Birkin bags, and finally to the current leader, the

▶

Focus on Humour
cont'd

Yves St. Laurent Mombasa bag (YSL is now owned by Gucci), the main players have vied for a dominant market position, and still do so. The rate of turnover of the latest fashionable bag is very high. The time at the top is brief.

The icon bag has symbolized the aspirational ethos of the 1990s. The bag which was 'in' at any particular time changed with a dizzying speed. Keeping up with the fashion could be an expensive business when a bag had a average price of $AU3,000, perhaps a minimum of $AU1,000 to even qualify as an 'in' bag of any kind. Somewhat ironically the Beggar's bag from LVMH retails at between $AU1,000 and $AU5,000 depending on its size and the materials used in its manufacture.

There were short-cuts for the aspirant; one was to buy a 'genuine imitation'. Fakes abounded everywhere. Just how accurate and therefore valuable an imitation might be is shown by the case of the Hermes bag. The Hermes Company took a counterfeiter to court in the USA and won the case. The fake bags were apparently so good that the counterfeiter could charge half the normal Hermes price, which meant significantly more than $AU3,000. At this price the counterfeit bags were more expensive than the bags of nearly all other designers!

Source: King, 2002: 4.

Strategy in Action Creating and maintaining demand for luxury and aspirational automobiles

How does a car manufacturer sell a AU$1 million car, the Mercedes Maybach, or a AU$2 million car, the Enzo Ferrari? This is pure luxury. In Australia you devise a AU$100,000 direct marketing campaign for the Maybach, selecting 160 prospective buyers from the *Business Review Weekly* Rich 200 list, and hand-delivering a AU$50 coffee-table book detailing the car's history and specifications, presented in a handcrafted, high-gloss, timber box worth about AU$300 and personalized with the potential customer's name in brass on the lid. Purchasers can use a AU$30,000 software program to configure the car to their personal taste.

At the Ferrari factory in Maranello near Bologna, there are two production lines – one for the V8 models, including the 360, and one for the more expensive V12s, including the 456 GT and 575 M. A third is prepared for the Enzo, named after the brand's founder, Enzo Ferrari, who died in 1988. At present only 16 or 17 Ferraris are produced each day, 4,289 in 2001. The Formula One Ferrari team, whose racing success lends status to the brand, is based at Maranello.

The attention to detail means the production lines move very slowly. At each of the 32 stations on the production line, the car has up to 45 minutes of Italian craftsmanship devoted to it. It takes three days to complete a 360, closer to two months for a 456 or 575. At the heart of a Ferrari is the engine. Each day 20 engines are produced but some are rejected after three hours of rigorous testing. More obviously expressive of the luxury is the separate room for leather crafting, in which 35 people hand stitch everything from seats and dashboards to steering wheels and roll cages. The Exclusivity programme gives a choice of 13 standard leather colours, along with a range of stitching types, sizes and hues. There are also 14 standard exterior colours. The Ferrari red and the stand-out yellow have a fixed shade. Most cars go for sale in the USA but some go all over the world. Workers are generally paid less than at rival companies, but work for the prestige and the enhancement of their career prospects.

To draw out the nature of democratization, it is possible to compare the motorcar producers Lamborghini and Ferrari, genuine producers of luxury, with BMW and Porsche, producers of aspirational products. Porsche is a brand with luxury written all over it but with greater sales than Ferrari. It is the car which the

▶

newly rich businessman or woman aspires to drive, as a badge of success. In its 54-year history Porsche has manufactured only sports cars, currently two – the 91 and the Boxster convertible. Despite a level of production which is miniscule by the standards of the big companies, about 50,000 vehicles a year, Porsche has moved from near bankruptcy in the early 1990s to being the most profitable carmaker in the world. It is a niche player which has managed to keep down its level of fixed cost and developed the flexibility and the ability to outsource effectively.

Porsche is using its brand name to sell a new vehicle, a fashionable sports utility vehicle (SUV), the Cayenne, which, at €60,000 for the standard model, is very much cheaper than its other products. Porsche will build the new car in partnership with Volkswagen; Volkswagen will produce the chassis and other major components, whereas Porsche will produce about 5–10% of the car. Will Porsche's customers purchase a car that carries its brand name but is largely produced by another company? Performance and technology will determine its competitiveness with rival vehicles. The danger is to undermine the value of the brand name. The level of production is planned to double to about 100,000 by 2005; scarcity will help to retain the kudos of the name.

BMW is very much a producer of aspirational vehicles – alongside others such as Mercedes or Alpha Romeo. The average BMW purchaser is younger than the purchaser of a Mercedes or a Lexus, which will assist future demand. Premium or aspirational cars are, in price and size of market, somewhere between luxury and standard vehicles. This is a market segment growing at twice the rate of the demand for the standard car. The market segment targeted consists of the older and more affluent.

Among producers of premium or luxury cars, only Porsche has higher profit margins than BMW. Porsche makes only 50,000 cars each year, whereas in 2002 BMW made one million, and the number is growing fast. This has prompted Holloway (2002) to comment: 'BMW is facing a difficult balance: how to extend its market but maintain the illusion of exclusivity.' Helmut Panke, CEO of BMW, has reinforced this view: 'For us, the experience of driving a BMW has to be aspirational, special. The research and development is designed to take that ultimate driving experience one step further. There will never be a boring BMW.'

BMW is consolidating its position as the biggest manufacturer of premium cars. In 2001 BMW brought out a revamped mini, a new, top-of-the-line 7-series, in 2002 the Roadster, in 2003 a new Rolls-Royce and a smaller SUV and in 2004 a compact car, the 1-series. By 2005 BMW expects to be selling 1.2 million vehicles, 50% up on 2000.

The BMW brand outperforms fashion brands such as Chanel, Gucci and Louis Vuitton, or Mercedes, Jaguar and Audi. Can this reputation withstand the increase in sales? BMW has defended its brand by the patient consistency of its claim that BMW produces dynamic sporty cars. BMW must pay attention to costs, by having common power sources or other components, outsourcing 65% of its 7-series, and having flexible production facilities which can tailor specifications to customer needs.

Marketing as a source of competitive advantage

Strategy in Action Formula One

Formula One racing is the most glamorous of sports. The initial championship goes back to 1950. Today there are both drivers and team championships. Formula One began with limited exposure and a limited number of venues. Today the carefully selected grand prix venues for the 17 races are located all over the world. Formula One returned to the USA in 2000 and there are plans to establish a race in Russia. Countries and cities vie with each other to be venues for these events. In Australia fierce rivalry saw the grand prix move from Adelaide to Melbourne.

The races are attended by hundreds of thousands of fans. Practice events are supported by vast crowds and generate major revenues. They are widely televised and reported. Television coverage generates

▶

enormous income. Consequently Formula One is big business as well as a popular sport. There is fierce competition to succeed, both at the individual and the team levels.

By its nature Formula One must attract sponsorship. In 2002 it attracted over US$2 billion in external sponsorship. Why should any company choose to sponsor or own a racing team?

The motivation for sponsorship varies greatly. The automobile producers have an obvious interest in associating themselves with the sport, particularly with success in the sport. The races are a vehicle for the automobile companies displaying best practice in technology. The same applies to those who have a manufacturing connection, such as an oil or tyre company. Traditionally, because other outlets have been steadily closed to them, cigarette companies have used Formula One to promote their product. Their role is already less important than it was and this will end in 2006, since the sport is unwilling to continue being tainted by such an association.

BUDGETARY SUPPORT

The costs of running a racing team are high and mounting rapidly (Table 10.2). The Arrows team collapsed in 2003, the Minardi and the Jordan teams struggle to raise enough money to survive. Together with Sauber they are the only teams not supported by a manufacturer. In 2003 the manufacturers' teams have agreed to bail out Minardi and Jordan by providing each with $8 million to offset the higher engine cost they face without the backing of a big motor manufacturer. Seven of the sponsors own or have equity in the teams which they support. Most are automobile companies which derive a range of benefits from the involvement and as a matter of strategy use the teams to promote their global image. They wish to control what is happening to their team since they are in fierce competition with each other.

The largest owner is Renault, also the second largest sponsor, chiefly because it does not want its own role to be diluted by that of others or its image to be tarnished by the nature of other sponsors. Renault

retained an unofficial involvement even when it temporarily withdrew from the sport at the end of the 1997 season. It is once again seriously committed and keen to succeed.

Toyota has recently become a major player and is likely to be the biggest player in the future. It is highly likely that Toyota will be the biggest spender, if marketing support and capital investment are taken into account. Toyota intends to invest over $1 billion during its first three years of involvement.

DaimlerChrysler has a rich pedigree in Formula One since its very beginning, having had five world championship winning years. The company invests both in McLaren and in the engine-builder Ilmor. The presence of DaimlerChrysler as an owner has attracted a whole raft of other German investors, such as Siemens and Warsteiner.

Ford entered Formula One as long ago as 1967 and has been fully involved ever since. In 1999 Ford decided to run its own team and invest it with the Jaguar name. It may or may not choose to continue to own. Recently it instituted a full review.

BMW has proved itself the best engine-builder in Formula One, despite the fact that it has only been in the sport three years. Its engines have a clear power advantage over the others. BMW is said to have invested about $150 million in a state-of-the-art engine design and build facility four years ago. Every season it builds about 200 new engines. There has been some conflict between the Williams team and BMW over who controls the design of the car. The

Table 10.2 **Budgetary analysis 2002**

Rank	Team	Direct cash ($m)	Trade support ($m)	Other income ($m)	Total ($m)
1	Ferrari	224.85	34.55	43	302.4
2	McLaren Mercedes	144.30	124.50	19	287.8
3	Renault	139.50	101.30	15	255.8
4	Toyota	163.20	53.20	22	238.4
5	BAR Honda	98.25	123.15	14	235.4
6	BMW Williams	110.50	101.50	18	230.0
7	Jaguar Racing	101.25	95.53	15	211.775
8	Jordan Honda	64	112	14	190
9	Sauber Petronas	55.15	32.20	17	104.35
10	KL Minardi Asiatech	24.55	42.90	16	83.45
11	Orange Arrows	31.15	4.40	14	49.55

performance of the team determines the level of such conflict.

The most lucrative element in Formula One is the broadcasting rights. The promotive impact of broadcasting is very strong. Until 2008 these rights are held by the company SLEC, a Swiss company established by impresario Bernie Ecclestone, the man who more or less controls the sport, and named after his wife, Slavica. Each year this company takes something like US$1 billion from the sale of the media and commercial rights to Formula One. It is estimated that worldwide there are about 350 million television viewers for each race.

Currently there is a crisis concerning the ownership of SLEC which has raised a number of significant issues. In 2001 Leo Kirch, German media owner, took US$1.5 billion in bank loans in order to acquire a 75% stake in SLEC. He overpaid for the stake, fell into financial trouble and became bankrupt. Under bank pressure he has had to sell this stake.

The car manufacturers, the main sponsors of Formula One, have resisted attempts by Kirch to put the races on pay TV, a plan designed to generate revenue for him. Currently they receive wide coverage on free-to-air television. The pay-TV coverage would be much more restricted. The car manufacturers are willing to purchase SLEC but value it at only half what Kirch has paid. They are in the best position in making such a purchase since there is a plan to set up a rival racing series when the present contracts expire in 2008. At the moment the racing teams receive only 47% of SLEC's revenues and believe this is too small. They wish to increase this significantly, some think to a sum as high as 85%.

Marketing as the creation of new wants

All strategy must be made with the broad aim of satisfying the consumer. In that sense all strategy is market-driven. The process in which strategy confronts the consumer is a dynamic one. Like all other strategic action it involves some measure of remaking the environment in which the enterprise operates. There is a sense in which marketing often creates a new want, previously unperceived, or hives off a new market segment from an existing market. It is always devising new ways of satisfying old wants. In this sense the enterprise is as much a creator of new wants as simply a flexible responder. The enterprise briefly reduces the competition to which it is normally exposed. It can exercise its market power to make an above-normal profit.

The marketing concept is a much broader concept than just advertising or even selling. In the view of some commentators marketing includes every aspect of enterprise behaviour and is closely associated with the whole process of strategy formulation and implementation. For some, strategy is simply one aspect of marketing.

Marketing as everything the enterprise does

Marketing today involves literally everything the enterprise does, everything which could make an impression on the consumer, and not just the consumer, since the other stakeholder groups are important in promoting the good name of the enterprise. Any enterprise should be, and usually is, concerned with the ultimate objective of branding itself. Success in this endeavour means that it can sell its products on the basis of the name of the producer alone. In such a situation a new product would require little in the way of new marketing. In order to establish such a reputation the company must pay attention to the multifaceted way it does business and the way it relates to the customer, whatever the activity involved. Exactly how it gains a reputation for quality depends upon the nature of the market segment.

Branding not only establishes a reputation for quality, and in particular for responsiveness to consumer needs, it makes the enterprise attractive as a good corporate citizen, as a desirable strategic partner or as a caring and worthwhile employer. All sorts of different variables might be relevant to the reputation or image of the organization:

- innovativeness and the ability to renew itself
- the functional expertise of management
- its ability to communicate an exciting vision
- employee talents
- the quality of the enterprise's products or services
- the long-term investment value and behaviour of share prices
- financial soundness
- social sensitivity and responsibility
- the effective use of corporate assets.

Such a reputation encourages the repetitive buying which underpins the value of any brand. Every producer creates a brand by attracting such repetitive buying.

Branding

Branding is a matter of degree. Some achieve what could be called super-brand status. There are two main routes to super-brand status:

- to offer good and functional value or utility to the stakeholders, whether they are customers, employees or any other group. Literally this means being good at whatever activity creates the utility for the group. It means being able to sell a good product at a good price, pay good wages or yield a high level of taxes.
- to offer good psychological value to stakeholder groups, that is, to tap into their emotions, motivating them in an appropriate way to actively support the organization.

Or you could do both. If you succeed, the result elevates a super-brand into an icon-brand, such as Disney or Coca-Cola.

The consumer society

The general context in which this happens is always important. In particular it is necessary to consider the relationship between overall supply and demand. In the decades which followed World War II, overall supply tended to lag behind demand. It was easy to sell whatever was produced. Since the 1970s the situation has been reversed; supply has tended to run ahead of demand. Today there are numerous sectors of the economy with overcapacity. In recent times the emphasis has therefore changed from the necessity of selling whatever is produced by the enterprise to accommodating production to the needs of the customer, producing only what the customer wants, or rather what he or she thinks she wants. This change in emphasis became obvious about 1970 when the postwar situation of product shortage changed to one of potential surplus and when the incomes of a large number of people had risen to a level which made consumers more demanding. Another way of describing the situation is that an increasing number of products, which were new, were 'commoditized'. This is a characteristic of the age of high mass consumption.

The four Ps of marketing

Marketing has often been discussed in terms of *the four Ps* of product, place, price and promotion, but this is to oversimplify marketing. On this account marketing is a straightforward matter, although an all-embracing one, of putting the right product in the right place at the right price, presented and promoted in the right way. It sounds simple but it is not.

Product

What is it that the consumer wants to consume? There is always discretion for the producer and seller on exactly what attributes to attach to the product. Defining the product is not always a simple task. It is recognized that what is consumed includes all the services which go with the product, including both tangible and intangible qualities possessed by the product. Putting it more exactly, individual consumers desire different attributes of that product. They seek to satisfy different combinations of utilities. Certainly everyone has a slightly different perception of a product and what the product is. They consume the product in a different way.

Place

Place is a matter both of the venue of consumption – consumption may be in some sense a public act – and the venue at which the product is assessed by the potential purchaser and where the negotiation on purchase occurs. Convenient access to the information and the product is one important element for all products and services. The nature of the interaction with staff of the enterprise is vitally important. The growing importance of e-commerce has already changed the venue of purchase and the venue at which information is received.

Price

Price is a significant marketing tool, discussed in general terms as part of overall strategy in the last chapter. It is possible to take a closer look at this notion. All sellers, if they could, would like to identify the shape of individual demand curves and select a range on the curve at which demand became inelastic, that is, a further increase in price would cause the revenue effects of the fall in demand to exceed those of the increase in price. Prices would be raised to this point. Price discrimination of this kind would maximize revenues.

Generally it is assumed that the demand curve is always well behaved, that is, that demand increases with a reduction in price and decreases with an increase in price. However, the phenomenon of the backward-sloping demand curve is not uncommon, that is, the association of a higher price with greater demand. On first consideration this appears paradoxical, but is not so, for the following reasons:

- it stresses the desire for exclusivity in consumption – at best the club of one, me and me alone
- it emphasizes that many products are not worth consuming if they are consumed by all or by people who belong to negative reference groups
- it ignores a general identification of quality with price, an uneasy feeling that a low price is achieved at a cost, usually, of lower quality. The greater the likelihood of successful product differentiation, the more likely is this to be the case.

Price policy must reflect the nature of the product. Price is very important and price determination an important aspect of a strategy to differentiate a product.

Promotion

Promotion can take many different forms, but it includes any action which helps to put the product in the hands of the consumer in a favourable context, that is, a context which makes the consumer positively disposed to buy and consume the product. It might include sponsorship by the company of a popular event or a consistently friendly disposition of company workers to outsiders.

Aspirational demand

One strategy of gaining a competitive advantage and putting a price premium on a product or service is to persuade consumers that the product is like a luxury or prestige good which they wish to consume. It is possible for shrewd marketers to deliberately exploit the desire of consumers for luxury as part of a strategy of product differentiation. 'Aspirational' consumers read the product market intuitively and attribute to various goods a status value, and they do this to an ever-increasing degree, as income levels rise and more consumers join the upper-middle income group. The level of price in itself is important in this process. It has to be relatively high since much of the satisfaction from having or consuming the product comes from the high price itself, beyond what your neighbours, friends or even relatives can afford, and the way in which the high price excludes others from the act of consumption.

The Boston Consulting Group (quoted in Christensen, 2003) defines democratization of luxury as middle-market consumers trading up to higher levels of quality, taste and aspiration. As incomes rise, more consumers are capable of doing this and there is more opportunity for sellers to take advantage of the situation. A greater number of products begin to qualify as aspirational goods. The economist expresses this in the rather prosaic definition of a luxury good as one which has an income elasticity of demand greater than one, that is, a good on which the expenditure takes up an increasing share of income as that income rises. Indeed it may be a product for which the income elasticity of demand goes on rising as income rises.

The aspirational phenomenon is quite different from the desire of the genuinely rich to be part of a club of one, but it could not exist without that desire and the existence of the rich as the ultimate reference group. The upper-middle income group wishes to be like the rich, to associate itself with that group by the act of consuming expensive goods which they imagine that the rich themselves consume.

Because retailing is usually so intensely competitive (see the case study on Wal-Mart in Chapter 9), profit margins are normally very low, often in single figures. In some cases the profit margins are barely above zero, but the sheer volume of sales still ensures large profits for the retailer, whether it is Wal-Mart, Aldi or a specialist retailer such as Starbucks. Revenue comes from the quantity of sales, not from the profit margin on individual items.

Creating a sense of luxury in a good or service can easily double or triple the usual margins earned on goods in the same category without the differentiation. It pays to aim at this aspirational market. It is difficult to generalize about how this is done. Luxury involves a strong human element, whether in the producing – the use of expensive raw materials and an emphasis on the handmade helps, or the selling – the direct, even individual, marketing approach, or even in the consuming, done in exclusive company but ostentatiously displayed in front of those excluded. It almost invariably involves a limited supply, preferably a persistent tendency for demand to exceed supply. It involves a recognition of value by those who are not directly involved in any of the activities – producing, selling or consuming.

There is always a temptation on the part of the supplier to spoil it all by undermining exclusivity by allowing the product to go downmarket as more are sold, in the process stressing quantity rather than quality (see the case study on Gucci in Chapter 12).

Strategy in Action Promoting a good image

The effort to use Formula One to promote an image can backfire badly, as the two excerpts from newspaper articles show.

THE FRAGILITY OF REPUTATION
Not everything always runs smoothly.

Defending formula one world champion Michael Schumacher of Germany faces charges of betting fraud in Italy and Austria following his controversial victory in Sunday's Austrian Grand Prix.

Schumacher owed his win to team-mate Rubens Barrichello, who led the race until just before the end when he pulled over to let the German by, under orders from the Ferrari team.

'We are not going to let Ferrari make fools of us,' said Austrian businessman Wolfgang Poetl, who also intends to take Barrichello and the Ferrari team to court in a class action.

In Italy two consumer protection organizations have contacted the state prosecutor with a view to legal action.

Ferrari defended the team order in the wake of heavy criticism after the race, arguing motor racing was a team sport and other formula one stables had done the same in the past.

Nevertheless Ferrari, Barrichello and Schumacher, who was announced as the Laureus Sportsman of the Year, have been summoned before the sport's governing body, the FIA, on June 26 to explain their conduct.

Critics say the team's actions have damaged the image of formula one.'

Reuters, 2002: 5

'If the wheels can come off an empire, they came off Bernie Ecclestone's formula one empire in Austria on Sunday, when Rubens Barrichello, under team orders from Ferrari, slowed down to let Michael Schumacher take the win.

A zillion petrol-heads all over the world were thus given an unmistakable television signal that they might as well have been reading the business section of their local newspaper. The fix was in.

The bottom line and the finishing line had revealed themselves as being identical. The chequered flag was a chequebook.'

James, 2002: 8

A different problem has confronted the sport. The repeated and easy success of Ferrari and Michael Schumacher during the 2002 season has removed much of the interest in viewing the races which have had on almost every occasion an all too predictable result, so much so that the numbers attending the races and watching on television have diminished significantly, threatening both the flow of income and the promotive capacity of the sport.

This is a new phenomenon. It has led to a variety of proposals for change, some of which have been radical. For example, it has been suggested that weight be added to any racing car which reaches a certain level of points in the competition, or that the cars be rotated between drivers for each grand prix race. There has been a change in the rules to try to add interest but it is a relatively benign change.

Product differentiation

'Other motorcycles are wimpy.'
   L. Dennis Kozlowski (55 years of age, ex-CEO of Tyco International, who has three different types of Harley-Davidson – the Softail, the Fat Boy and the Road King)

'Harley-Davidson. It's the master at creating a whole world of activities around what it sells.'
   David Gross, director of strategic planning and product development at Ducati Motor

After it fell under the control of the AMF corporation in 1969, Harley-Davidson appeared headed for oblivion. In 1981 it was bought out by 13 of its management employees, including one Willie Davidson, a grandson of one of the founders. In 1985 it nearly went bankrupt, having to shed half its labour force.

The company was given, by a significant increase in import tariffs by the Reagan administration, breathing space to get its house in order. This required improving manufacturing efficiency and product quality. Its managers and engineers took advantage by literally riding their own company bikes and going directly to the customers. They noted preferences for seat heights, control positioning and features of general comfort, but most of all the tendency of owners to customize their bikes, by using parts from a burgeoning after-sales industry. This was deliberately brought in-house by producing a range of 'custom production models' and significantly extending the accessories' catalogue.

By the end of the 1980s the company was once again in control of its own destiny. Since then the performance of Harley-Davidson has been remarkable:

- It established control of its distribution system
- It set up a renting facility, Harley-Davidson Authorized Rentals, which now rents half as many bikes as it sells
- In 2001 it sold 234,461 bikes
- It set up Hog, the Harley Owners Group, in 1983, which has 600,000 members. Its 1,200 international chapters are coordinated through Harley-Davidson dealers. An important mechanism for encouraging loyalty to the brand is the annual Sturgis Rally, started some 60 years ago, by a group of bikers in the town of Sturgis. It is now deliberately promoted by Harley-Davidson. The 2001 rally attracted more than half a million enthusiasts.

An initial public float of Harley-Davidson shares was made in 1986. Since then the share price has increased by a prodigious 15,000%. This can be compared with other high flyers, such as Intel, up 7,200%, and GE, up 1,056%. Earnings have grown at an average annul rate of 37%, continuing to grow even through recessions.

During a significant recession and in a year in which many companies either lost money or saw their profits seriously reduced, Harley-Davidson turned in a gold-plated set of figures. Its estimated sales in 2001 increased by 15% to $3.3 billion, its earnings by 20% to $435 million and its share price leapt 40% (compared with an S&P fall of 15%). In the first quarter of 2002 Harley-Davidson's revenue was a record US$927.8 million, a 19.4% increase on the year before. Harley-Davidson sells 243,000 bikes a year, which is 26% of the American market.

The traditional Sportster which sells for $8,000 accounts for 20% of this total. Accounting for 50% of sales is the Softail, a heavy bike which sells for $15,000. Even more expensive, at $22,000, is the touring bike which has plush seats, fibreglass saddle bags, cruise control and a six-CD player, and accounts for the other 30% of sales. All in all, it has 26 models in five families: Sportster, Softail, Dyna, Tourer and V-Rod.

This success has prompted the remark, 'All this from a company founded a century ago that is making a product that hasn't fundamentally changed since then: an internal combustion engine bolted between two rubber wheels' (Fahey, 2002: 30). Harley-Davidson has succeeded by leveraging that history, presenting the choice of motorbike as a lifestyle choice. Performance is not the reason, since a thoroughbred Ducati two-cylinder engine has three times the power of a typical hog (the nickname for a Harley-Davidson bike).

In the past Harley-Davidson chose to focus on the heavyweight motorcycle. This laid it open to competition by enterprises which wished to focus on an even

▶

more narrowly defined market segment and 'outfocus' the focuser. This outfocusing could reflect an attempt to create a new brand name. For example, Honda chose small motorcycles for its entry into the industry, initially not deliberately but more as a result of a chance discovery of a market niche which it did not know existed. BMW has sought to project class into the touring part of the market. It could also be a deliberate attempt to outdo Harley-Davidson in the very attributes which unpinned its brand image. Big Dog has deliberately focused on the heavy end of the market.

Harley-Davidson is unusual in exploiting a first-mover advantage for so long. It has a group of consumers intensely loyal to the brand. The brand name can be extended to a whole range of other products. The stronger the brand name, the greater the leverage which the enterprise can use in exploiting the market. The motive for doing this is the much larger profit margins on accessories and apparel, as high as 45%, more usually 20% or so, and on spare parts, even higher at 70%, than those on the bikes themselves.

Harley-Davidson Motorclothes, exploiting the appeal of the hog lifestyle, generates more than $100 million in revenue each year. However, the Harley-Davidson logo adorns not just black leather jeans, but fashions for young children and French-style lingerie for women. The brand name even adorns a limited-edition Barbie doll. The range of use includes a popular restaurant in New York and a line of L'Oreal cologne.

There are problems:

- The average age of buyers is increasing, from 37 in 1990, to 46 in 2002
- Harley-Davidson is slowly losing market share to both Japanese motorcycles and look-alikes
- Many features of the strategy adopted can be easily imitated.

In order to appeal to younger buyers and meet the competitors head-on, Harley-Davidson has introduced a radical new motorcycle, the V-Rod, the first of a new family of high-performance bikes, a 270-kilo bike, priced at $17,000. It has 110 hp, twice the power of a typical hog, a more efficient water-cooled engine, which allows greater acceleration, and can do 225 miles per hour. It is designed for young, hip Americans and Europeans.

Focus on Practice
Ducati

Ducati is a company founded in 1926, which has gone through a history similar to Harley-Davidson. A loss-making period led to a leveraged buyout by the Texas Pacific Group. It was listed on the New York Stock Exchange in 1999. Ducati has paid Harley-Davidson the ultimate compliment of copying its strategy of brand development. Fortunately Ducati is not in the same market segment as Harley-Davidson, producing sports rather than cruising bicycles. Its bikes win the World Superbike Championship.

The key is marketing, although the product was already there, winning world championships, just as the Harley was already there. Ducati has sought to turn itself into an icon or star brand in the same way as Harley-Davidson. It has brought its distribution under the control of its own subsidiaries; introduced a new international standard 'Ducati Store' design; cultivated a worldwide Desmo Owners Club (named after the marque's distinctive engine valve-train system); and in 1998 held the first World Ducati Weekend.

The World Ducati Week, held biennially, is loss making and modelled on the Sturgis Rally. The third Week was held at the Santa Monica motor racing circuit in Misano in June 2002 and attended by some 20,000 Ducati owners with their distinctive bikes. The Week coincided with a round of the World Super-bike Championship, won by Troy Bayliss on a Ducati. Tickets were over €100 for a full week, half for the weekend, most purchased in advance on the Ducati website. The Week included stunt shows, racetrack sessions and organized motorcycle tours through the mountains of Emilia-Romagno.

Ducati is still small, producing only 40,000 units, a level of production similar to Harley-Davidson in the early 1980s. This represents only 7% of the sports bike market,

Focus on Practice
cont'd
which is dominated by the Japanese, who take 90%, but significantly up on the 4% which was the situation when the new management took over. The target is 10%. Ducati have also imitated Harley in bringing accessories and spare parts in-house. The spare parts now account for just under 10% of total revenue, and the accessories and apparel over 5%. Ducati has recognized the attractiveness of the Harley strategy.

What is differentiation?

The object of a deliberate and conscious product differentiation is to persuade potential purchasers that the product is unique, different from all other products, that it has qualities which justify the charging of a higher price. Economists describe this as making demand more inelastic; a rise in price will not shed so many customers that it will result in lower revenue. In particular the objective is to persuade the market that there is a distinct gap between this product and others competing with it in the market. It is also preferable to do this in such a way that the competitors cannot replicate the differentiation, or can only do so at a significant cost or with a long delay.

This gap may have its origins in real or physical differences of the product, particularly when seen in isolation from, and therefore uninfluenced by, its context of purchase or consumption. There is a difference which can be confirmed by some objective test. Alternatively it may simply be a perception of difference created by the supplier. This perception may be related to the context in which information about the product is discovered, or it may relate to the circumstances of purchase and consumption.

The sources of differentiation

It is difficult to differentiate certain kinds of product, however hard you try, although the list is shrinking all the time. The product may be a technically simple consumer good, such as a brick or a pair of socks. However, even a pair of socks can be differentiated by material, colour or the design placed on the sock, and a brick by its material, colour or texture. It makes a great deal of difference whether the product is visible or not, and to whom and in what circumstances. Is the active promotion of lingerie intended to satisfy the wearer's wishes or those of someone likely to see it? If it is seen, it is easy to differentiate in a meaningful way. If it is not seen, then it would be a pointless exercise to differentiate it.

Alternatively the product may be a standardized industrial product, such as an aluminium ingot or a random-access memory chip. It is much more likely that such primary inputs are undifferentiated and therefore become 'commoditized', with the homogeneous qualities of commodities. The further down the value-adding chain a product is located and the closer to the final consumer, the more likely it is to be differentiated. Compare wheat with bakery products, sugar and cocoa with confectionary, or gold with jewellery. There is a much lower potential for differentiation of textile materials such as wool and cotton than there is of a shirt made of cotton or a dress designed by a fashion company.

Some goods satisfy the need to carry out uncomplicated functions, such as a corkscrew or a nail, or they have to meet highly specific technical standards which dominate their design and appearance, such as a spark plug or a thermometer. These functions or design standards determine their nature and even their look, making differentiation difficult.

It is much easier to differentiate a product which is complex by design such as an airplane or an automobile, which consists of hundreds of thousands of different components which can be put together in an infinite variety of ways. The same applies to products which satisfy complex wants, such as a holiday, a time share or a serviced apartment. Any transport vehicle may move a person between locations A and B but at varying speeds and with a varying degree of safety or comfort. A vacation can provide an infinite variety of different experiences for the holiday-maker.

If a product does not have to conform to rigorous standards, it can also be differentiated easily, particularly if there is no commonly accepted standard of quality. Wine or toys would fall into this bracket, since the ability of either to satisfy wants is entirely subjective. There may still be some limitations, such as safety requirements for toys and the use of generic regional names for wines.

There are physical characteristics which mark out products as different. The features which can be used to differentiate a product include:

- size
- shape
- colour
- weight
- design
- material
- technology embodied.

These are visible and verifiable by all, often the result of deliberate design and marketing. The physical differences may be 'packaged' to accentuate the contrast with other competing products and packaged so that they emphasize particular intangible characteristics which are considered desirable and can be linked with the physical characteristics.

On the other hand, the performance of the product or service may be the key difference. This would include reliability, consistency, taste, speed, durability and safety. These are not so obvious to the potential purchaser and difficult, but not impossible, to verify. For example, the product may be robust and easy to repair, because of the use of interchangeable parts. Product design becomes even more important, particularly when you want to emphasize, through the look of a product, the ability of the product to perform. A fast car needs to look fast. A comfortable piece of furniture needs to look comfortable.

Alternatively, there may be other products and services complementing the product in question. There may be an attractive form of pre- or after-sales service which appeals to the customer. There may be accessories which can be acquired, either immediately or later. The availability and speed of delivery may be an issue. Credit may be necessary to allow purchase. The method of financing the purchase may also be innovative; the more expensive the product, the more important this is. How easily can the product be upgraded in the future? Is maintenance a problem? Leasing rather than outright purchase may be desirable. All products come invested in a package of services of this kind. They are often the key to effecting a sale.

Yet again, the difference may simply be a reflection of a sales pitch or marketing ploy which makes it seem different when it is not. The association of the product with non-tangible utilities such as youth, a healthy lifestyle or a fashionable elegance may differentiate it as effectively as a tangible characteristic. Perception is as important as actuality. Or it may simply be that the product both is and appears innovative, reflecting cutting-edge modern technology. Keeping up to date is an obsession of some. The product may also in some way impart a sense of luxury, or prestige or status to the owner or consumer. All these are utilities which attributes of the product can satisfy. Certain attributes of the product may trigger in the potential consumer the hope of the satisfaction of a utility.

Intangible qualities

Most products competing in the market are able to satisfy at a minimum level the utilities expected. They have the required physical attributes to achieve this. A car can get the driver and passengers from point A to point B within a reasonable time. A pair of shoes are comfortable and protective. A food item is nutritious in the necessary way and edible. However, selling any of these products against great competition depends on doing more than simply telling consumers that they achieve the minimum requirements. It involves the association of a product with attractive intangible qualities which give the product that 'something extra' which invests it with uniqueness. These intangible qualities must be appropriate both to the product and the market segment for which the product is intended. Some products, such as cosmetics or toiletries, lend themselves well to this approach.

Consumer utilities

The differentiation of the product is achieved by linking certain attributes of the product or service itself with certain utilities sought by the consumer. There may be many attributes in a complex product, but the main attributes are defined by the nature of the industry in which the product or service is produced. Some utilities may have much wider scope; they may not be linked to particular industries, but to a range of industries. For example, the desire for luxury or prestige, described in the De Beers case study, can be satisfied by a wide range of products (Figure 10.1).

As luxury goods, all these products are substitutes for each other. They are different ways of satisfying the same utility. It is possible to identify many other utilities such as healthiness. They too comprise products which overlap different industrial sectors.

Figure 10.1 The range of luxury products and services

The basis for attaching the intangible attributes varies from product to product, and market segment to market segment:

- It may be targeted demographically or socially, that is, plays on the attitudes and values of particular age or social groups or those often regarded as reference groups by these groups
- It may have an emotional orientation, that is, it deliberately provokes an emotional response(s), based on known stimuli which are often culture-related
- It may be psychological, designed to play to the known fears, hopes or aspirations of the consumer
- It may be aesthetic, designed to trigger a reaction which is favourable to what in a particular culture or generation is considered beautiful or stylish.

Underlying what is being done is the association of the product with a stable set of attributes linked to particular needs and the utilities which satisfying these needs gives to purchasers. The trick is to emphasize attributes which highlight the need which can be satisfied. This may involve, for example, a desire for security or status. For consumers, utilities are linked to these underlying needs.

Intangible qualities are linked closely with human psychology and deep underlying human desires, such as those involved in being young, innovative, attractive or simply living a long healthy life. Whereas fashions quickly pass, these human desires never disappear. Most marketing is designed to exploit these desires, to invest a product with the ability to give the consumer the desired utility in a way which enhances the appeal of the product.

On the other hand, some market areas are particularly prone to changes of taste. The whole area of popular culture is subject to rapid and dramatic shifts. In this area there are clear opinion leaders, the pop personalities admired and envied by the consumers of such culture. The packaging of a whole range of products is influenced by these fashions. Intangible qualities are sometimes linked closely with fashions or fads which have an unpredictable life and are very much culture-linked. Linking a product in some way with what is in vogue is a clever marketing ploy but it may only achieve a short-term gain. Creating a new fashion or fad, and therefore being ahead of the market, is even cleverer.

Some opinion leaders manage to set the fashion and keep ahead of the market by continuously innovating. The sales pitch of an enterprise may be directed at those known to be opinion leaders or the target groups from whom a desire for the product will spread, for example film or sports stars, or what today are called celebrities.

The importance of marketing is shown in a number of sectors by the tendency to outsource areas unconnected directly with the nature of the product. In the process of outsourcing many other activities in the value chain, the enterprise often retains those critical to marketing. Sports footwear is a classic case. The manufacturing of the shoes is often outsourced to low-cost labour enterprises or regions. However, those activities connected with product design are not. R&D and design are as important as marketing in creating products which have the characteristics required by potential purchasers.

In some areas of apparel, new designs are produced every year. Again manufacture is not as important as design. It may be that in the future the same process will occur with the automobile, with assembly outsourced, but design, R&D and promotion retained by the 'branded' company.

Branding

Strategy in Action   Sir Richard Branson and many wise virgins

Successful leadership, particularly when based on charisma, can lead to the favourable branding of the person. The name then sells the product. While there is obviously a relationship between the reputation of the leader and business success, in some cases the relationship seems a tenuous one. The degree of success does not seem to justify the branding. The company may never quite achieve the success it promises. The reputation of some leaders survives repeated failure; they display an uncanny ability to bounce back.

Sir Richard Branson, the founder of the Virgin brand, has created, over 35 years, a stable of companies with a gross turnover of over £4 billion. Sir Richard (1986) describes his business as a 'branded venture capital' organization. Virgin looks at business sectors around the world which are 'fat, lazy or oligopolistic and do not serve the customers well' and inserts the Virgin brand.

The companies operate in competitive industries, often outside the new economy and with a questionable management competency; many of the enterprises are scarcely profitable. What is it about Richard Branson which attracts attention and wins respect?

- He has obvious good looks and charm
- He behaves with a flamboyance attractive to the media
- He is seen as a counterculture figure, prepared to cock a snook at the stuffy gentility of old Britain and represent the entrepreneurship and glamour of new Britain. His behaviour is most unBritish but much admired. His appeal transcends class despite his upper-class background
- He sees no division between public and private life, involving in his business dealings all those who come into contact with him. Often he has

operated his businesses from home rather than an office
- He immerses himself in a new project before passing it over to good management and financial people who are given a stake in the enterprise and room to make it succeed
- He puts his staff first, followed by the customers, and only then by the shareholders
- He looks much more to long-term than to short-term profit
- He prefers organic growth to acquisitions which have been rare
- He accepts the challenge of entering markets where there are long-established incumbents who have become conservative, enjoys confronting them, as he did famously with British Airways and Coca-Cola
- He is popular for his emphasis on fair play.

The Virgin family is a sprawling alliance of about 270 companies held together by the trade name and Branson's role as shareholder, chairman and public relations supremo. The Virgin group has been likened to a Japanese *keiretsu* or a franchising operation. The companies are nominally independent of each other but linked by the small group of executives and advisers who guide strategy, plan new business development and exercise overall financial control. There is no real headquarters and almost no middle management, the aim being to empower the managers to act in an entrepreneurial way. Close personal ties and a strong culture substitute for a formal structure.

Two characteristics mark out the Virgin companies as different. The first is that all the enterprises are private companies. In 1986 Branson briefly flirted with the notion of a public company, floating his music and entertainment empire. The timing was

▶

very unfortunate because the stock market crashed in 1987 and the economy went into recession, leaving Virgin shares at almost half their initial offer price. In 1988, at a cost of about £100 million, Branson reprivatized the company, buying back the shares at their float price.

There are trusts acting as holding companies for the enterprises. Because they are private companies, Branson argues that they are not driven by short-term profit and avoid the short-term obsessions of the stock market. He maintains that they are much more concerned with cash flows and capital value. The downside is that nobody knows just what is the profit position of the various companies. Branson has shown a marked reluctance to close down or dispose of any company he has created, whatever its profitability.

Second, Branson almost always operates with a partner, often excellent partners who supply much needed managerial expertise and credibility in the relevant areas. Singapore Airlines owns 49% of Virgin Atlantic. Patrick has recently acquired half of Virgin Blue in Australia. Stagecoach holds 49% of Virgin Rail, T-Mobile 50% of Virgin Mobile (UK), and AMP half of Virgin Money.

The Virgin brand name is the most valuable asset which the Virgin group of enterprises possesses, one closely associated with the name of Richard Branson, reflecting his sense of fun, humour, style and irreverence. The extension of the brand carries its own dangers, having been applied to a wide range of products and services, including airlines, railroads, cosmetics, financial services, music, mobile phones, retailing and soft drinks. How far the brand name can be used in an international context is unclear since Branson is so quintessentially British. It does seem to work in North America and Australia, but not so well elsewhere.

A brand is a unique bundle of tangible and/or intangible attributes, which in the mind of a significant number of consumers, or potential consumers, gives the product a quality superior to that of competitors and persuades the customer to repeat the purchase. For various reasons the bundle is difficult to imitate. There may or may not be an underpinning of strong physical characteristics supporting the reputation of the product. It is likely that physical characteristics can be relatively easily imitated. The key to effective branding is the way in which the product or service is perceived. For a branded product there is a perception of quality in the mind of consumers which creates a strong preference for this product over others. A new consumer is likely to try the known product before any other, simply by virtue of the brand name.

The broader the portfolio of business units within the Virgin stable, the greater the potential need for financial resources to cover losses and meet the needs of future expansion. A diverse portfolio can hide a multitude of sins. In recent years, Branson has regularly raised money to finance expansion. In 1999 he sold 49% of Virgin Atlantic Airways to Singapore Airlines for £600 million, either a shrewd choice of partner for future development, or a recognition of a need for cash. Since then he has raised a further £700 million by selling stakes in a number of companies including Virgin Blue, Virgin Radio, Virgin Cinema and Virgin Active, a chain of health clubs. The partners were all well chosen. There is a further plan to float as many as eight of the companies, beginning with Virgin Blue in 2003, but stretching over a period of eight years. This will raise at least £2 billion, supplementing the £1.3 billion already raised over the last three years.

Focus on Theory

What's in a name?

The simple answer is, sometimes not much and sometimes a lot as the name conjures up whole layers of meaning. It is desirable to use effectively a name which is already known and therefore has value. It pays not to overuse it, but to use it in such a way as to preserve the kudos attached to that name. On the other hand, it is good strategy to change a name which has developed a negative connotation. Recently Philip Morris, one of the world's largest companies, received permission to change its name to the Altria Group Inc. Since Philip Morris has been diversifying its interests, for example purchasing the food processing firm Kraft and creating a conglomerate with disparate products and services in which cigarettes are a minor part, it is logical to break the link with its one-time 'hero product'. However, the main objective in doing this is to play down the link with what is now a 'villain product', the cigarette.

▶

Another example of a conglomerate changing its name to better reflect what it was doing was the creation of Diageo, following the merger of Guinness and Grand Metropolitan. Also British Petroleum prefers to be called BP, in order to remove the emphasis on its British origins. Its rebadging as Beyond Petroleum rather than British Petroleum did not last long.

There are examples of the reverse, a conglomerate seeking to exploit the brand name of one of its products. Consolidated Foods became the Sara Lee Corporation, Elders became Foster's. In these cases the conglomerate wanted to use the strength of the brand name to promote itself.

Increasingly corporate names are made up. The insurance giant CGU has become AVIVA, after months of research. Sometimes the name change works, sometimes it does not. Sometimes the company is lucky. In 2001 Andersen Consulting, looking for a new identity after the split from its parent, changed its name to Accenture, which was fortunate given the poor reputation now associated with the Andersen name (best known for the paper-shredding scandal). Without the name change, the company might have disappeared with its parent.

In Britain, the Post Office changed its corporate name to Consignia in March 2001, but a year later announced a loss of more than £1 billion, and promptly decided to change its name back to Royal Mail.

Some changes are logical, BHP to BHP Billiton after the merger of the two companies, or Pacific Dunlop to Ansell, its most successful brand, after a decade of share market underperformance. Others are made to escape from association with a losing cause, such as the high-tech and dot.com collapse. WorldSchool has become Tribeca, Davnet is now DVT Holdings, and ehyou.com is now Destra.

Clearly a name change on its own is not likely to have a beneficial outcome. However, if introduced as part of a new strategy and/or new structure, it can reinforce a change of direction and assist in implementing that change.

It is difficult and potentially expensive to create a new brand. It is a long and costly process. In the end branding reflects repeated consumption and the resulting general reputation for quality of a product. Advertising can initiate and reinforce the process, but the retention of a positive brand name comes from the interaction of the advertising and a positive experience in consuming the product. There are cases where because of so much repetition the brand becomes the name of the product – in the UK a Mackintosh, Wellington boots, or Sellotape, but every country has its examples.

Even the amount spent and the spread of the advertising can help in the process of brand making. Every enterprise aspires to create or own known brands, hopefully a whole portfolio of brands, and brands which have not just national but international standing. Success for one brand rubs off on others. There are few brands which have genuine global standing, few with the cachet of, say, Coca-Cola.

The pervasiveness of branding

Everything is branded today. Most branding is deliberate but some is the unconscious result of events. Countries can be branded as national stereotypes emerge. Sports stars or public persons can be branded as a reflection of their achievements or successes. Places are branded. Often the brand name of an enterprise is promoted by association with brand names of this type, some free to use, others costly. Much advertising plays on the use of existing brands, on faces which are easily recognized, and reputations for quality. The advertising exploits existing brands. An enterprise can leverage a branded product to brand itself and extend the influence of the brand to other products.

Sometimes a brand is like a common good which can be shared. In other words in branding a product, existing reputation can be exploited, whether that reputation attaches to a country, region or enterprise. Free riding can dissipate and even destroy the brand reputation. 'Brand capital' can be used up.

Brand names and trademarks have a value which can be quantified. They are an important part of the basket of intellectual property rights which have become so important. Many franchises are based on the use of brand names and derive their value from the brand. However, there is still a problem of maintaining the brand quality which can easily be destroyed.

Focus on Practice
Reflections on and of an entrepreneur – Sir Richard Branson

'The Virgin name was inspired by the nubile young women who passed through Sir Richard's west London squat in the 1960s, by the entrepreneur's lack of business experience, and by a religious experience he had at a funeral, depending on which story he feels like telling.' *The Economist* (2002: 22)

Branson has used words to publicize himself and the Virgin companies. He has also become a favourite target for the comments of others.

'The biggest risk any of us can take is to invest money in a business that we don't know. Very few of the businesses that Virgin has set up have been in completely new fields.'

'Branson does not expand Virgin Blue to Hobart (as he did recently). Rather, he 'allows grandmums and granddads to come and see their grandkids on the mainland'. He does not push Virgin Mobile into the US (as he did recently), he 'helps ordinary Americans get a better deal on phones, and make it fun along the way'.

'I have not depended on others to do surveys or market research, or to develop grand strategies. I have taken the view that the risk to the company is best reduced by my own involvement in the nitty-gritty of the new business.'

'Greed is fun' – that's true says Branson

'I think he sees his business as having a definite social value, rather than just as a way to make money.' Brown, M., *Richard Branson: the inside story*

'Reduce the scale of … risk through joint ventures … (and) have a way out of a high risk venture.'

Branson's headmaster: 'You will either go to prison or become a millionaire.'

'As businesses grow, watch out for management losing touch with the basics – normally the customer.'

Rowan Gormley, CEO of Virgin Wines: 'A big part of why he's successful is because he's instinctive. Rather than analysing things backwards and forwards, he simply asks, "Would I like it as a customer." '

▶

Focus on Practice
cont'd

'My goal is to set enormous, some say unachievable, challenges and rise above them.'

Brown: 'You can go to any Virgin event or get on any Virgin plane, and everybody seems to feel that they know him personally.'

'(Our) 'keep it small' rule enables ... more than usual numbers of managers the challenge and excitement of running their own businesses.'

'He *is* the little guy'

'Pursue a 'buy, don't make' strategy.'

Source: Adapted from Mintzberg et al., 1998: 130, with the help of Elder, 2002.

A product differentiation strategy

The initial discussion in this section is on the general nature of a differentiation strategy, which is then compared and linked with a cost leadership strategy. Are the two mutually exclusive or can they be combined in some way?

There are two sides to any differentiation strategy:

1. the potential for differentiation which exists on the *demand side*, the receptiveness of a potential market to such differentiation, reflecting a market segment which needs to be identified and then activated
2. the potential which exists on the *supply side*, the ability of the enterprise to achieve a differentiation of the product. In a sense this ability might be one of its core competencies. The ability to differentiate may consist of a number of capabilities put together to create one key core competence.

Each of these sides is dealt with in turn.

Focus on Theory
Segmenting
the market

The analysis in the text assumes that it is always desirable to add attributes to any product and that an enterprise will go on doing this until the value of the additional attribute added is less than the price increase necessary to cover the cost of adding that attribute.

The segmentation of a market can be carried to the point at which each individual demand for an attribute is taken into account. One example might be the computer industry in which there are home users, or normal retail customers, group A, and business users, group B. Business customers could be approached directly to discover their exact needs, customizing the product to suit individual requirements. Dell has done just this. Such an approach might lose some economies of scale but enable the enterprise to save on delivery costs of various kinds, including the use of middlemen, the need for general marketing and the accumulation of inventory at the retail level. More importantly, it allows the enterprise to differentiate its product.

Another example might be the postal industry, in which most consumers are not overly fussed by the exact delivery time, whereas there is a particular consumer group which places a high value on overnight delivery. In the USA Federal Express defined an important market segment which wanted this rapid delivery, but it also showed that by concentrating on overnight package delivery it could reduce overall costs since it could decrease the handling, sorting and ground transport costs more than it increased the air freight costs. In this case not only had the added attribute a value but it could be provided at a negative cost. Even a positive cost would have been acceptable, provided it was less than the additional value.

The real value of an added attribute is not always positive. It may be the case that redundant attributes are already sold with products or services and that overall costs can be reduced, not just by focusing on a given market segment but also by removing those attributes from the product or service.

Suppose an existing enterprise is supplying what appears to be a 'generic' market. It treats the market it faces as if were one homogeneous market with no differences in the evaluation of the products' attributes by the different consumers. It charges a common price to all consumers. Suppose in reality that the market is not homogeneous but consists of two groups of customers, groups A and B, who look for different combinations of attributes. A, the dominant group, wants all the existing attributes but B, a group large enough to warrant attention, is not interested in some of these attributes. Will it pay a new enterprise to try to meet the needs of group B with a separate product or service? Let us suppose that there are no significant economies of scale, that is, they are not sufficiently large to produce cost reductions which exceed the difference in attribute valuation by the two groups. If this were the case, it would not be worthwhile to separate out the two market segments.

This might be the airline industry, in which there are business passengers, group A, and holiday travellers, group B, who take a very different attitude to the frills, regarding them respectively as of significant value and almost no value. A new entrant might come into the industry but deliberately target the B group. It will price the product lower than the existing enterprise according to the value of the attributes desired and/or the costs saved. The existing enterprise might have overall costs which are lower because of learning or some economies of scale, but nevertheless finds it is losing market share because this second market segment is happier with the lower price and the reduced attributes of the product sold to it. As shown in Chapter 9, Southwest Airline has done just this.

On the demand side, there is a critical interaction between the product and the customers:

- The technical nature of the product, its physical characteristics, defines how it might satisfy customer requirements. Initially it is necessary to identify the principal product attributes, whatever they are. Such attributes are not always as obvious as often thought. Any product may be perceived differently in terms of its attributes by its consumer. It is possible to ask what are the particular needs or wants of the consumer that any given attribute satisfies.
- On the other hand, customers have certain criteria by which they choose a product, principally its ability to satisfy certain utilities. It is possible to identify the pattern of customer preferences by the degree to which individual attributes and their combination satisfy these utilities.

What are the attributes? This is initially tackled by a broad approach. Most products have a number of attributes. Some have only one or two, some many. This is illustrated with the help of the motorcar. A motorcar has a capacity to move an individual from point A to point B in a certain period of time determined by its speed. In so doing, it has other attributes, provides other services and satisfies other utilities:

- a degree of *comfort* – space, ease of position, freedom from outside noise, availability of audio entertainment, a comfortable and stable temperature
- a level of *safety*, strictly relevant only in certain contingencies – this includes fixtures over and above what the law requires – airbags, ABS brakes, a strengthened frame
- some aspects of an *exclusive good* – it conveys status by its very cost and rarity
- other attributes, such as the *ability to go very fast*, or incorporate best-practice technology
- *environmental friendliness*, at a level not simply able to satisfy existing regulations on exhaust emissions or energy efficiency but to be ahead of the norm
- *an economy of cost* in terms of petrol consumption or maintenance and repairs.

Each of these six main attributes can be seen as independent, or they can be joined in different combinations.

The value of attributes

It is also possible to identify, and even estimate, the price premia which the customer is prepared to pay for particular attributes. How much are they prepared to pay for comfort, speed, safety, exclusiveness, high technology or low running costs? What value do they attach to each of these attributes or to any combination of different attributes? There are ways of estimating this. The value of each attribute may change over time according to external circumstances.

It is appropriate to consider how consumers are motivated or influenced to behave in consuming any product. This requires analysis of the demographic, socioeconomic, and psychographic factors which correlate with customer behaviour. Can separate groups with well-defined utilities be identified? Are there distinct patterns in the ways in which the potential customers within the different groups regard the attributes?

Customers can be divided into different groups of varying sizes according to their evaluation of the different attributes. There are two possible approaches:

1. The first starts with a generic product and then disaggregates by key attributes. The weakness of this approach is that it takes the existing market as given and as the starting point.
2. The other assumes that the extreme in segmentation is a segment of one consumer. It aggregates from this starting point. This has the advantage of focusing on what the individual consumer wants. From the point of view of market segment targeting, it helps that there are distinctive clusters of homogeneous customers who evaluate the attributes in a similar way. Such groups need to be large enough to justify targeting them. It is hard to customize a product on the basis that each group consists of just one individual.

In this way it is possible to identify an opportunity in the market. Is the enterprise in a position to exploit this opportunity?

The supply side of differentiation

On the supply side the key issue is whether the enterprise can actually implement the strategy:

- Does it have the capacity or core competencies to do so? Can it produce a product with the relevant attributes?
- If the answer is yes, the next question is, can it do so at a cost which is within the price premia which it can charge? Can it produce the product at a cost which allows a profit to be made?

It may be that the potential supplier is unable to manage this. The attributes of the product referred to above may be varied. They may involve the whole package of attributes which go with the product, including various physical and intangible features.

The steps in a product differentiation strategy

There are four steps in the formulation of a product differentiation segmentation strategy:

1. Select the target customer group, one which occupies a particular market segment with its specific utilities, or in some cases constitutes the whole market
2. Choose the specific product attributes desired and their levels, thereby selecting a product position, sometimes called a product bundle
3. Ensure compatibility between product bundles of attributes, and the utilities or preferences of the target customer group or groups
4. Evaluate the potential returns from differentiation, relative to the costs of differentiation.

Uniqueness drivers

The next step is to identify the uniqueness drivers and offset these alongside the cost drivers talked about in the previous chapter. The cost drivers, notably economies of scale, may overwhelm the uniqueness drivers.

The creation of uniqueness is not simply a matter of choosing an appropriate product and then marketing it intensely, using certain intangible features to sell it. It may also involve every aspect of the enterprise and its activities:

- its design capacity and technology
- from whom it purchases inputs
- what quality control mechanisms it has in place
- the experience and skills of its labour force.

The approach to identification of uniqueness drivers through the value chain is the same as for cost drivers. The potential for differentiation on the supply side can be identified with the help of a diagram (see Figure 10.2) setting out the value chain and the uniqueness drivers associated with each activity.

ACTIVITIES	UNIQUENESS DRIVERS

SUPPORT

Infrastructural activities	1. Build corporate reputation 2. Management information systems supporting innovation and responsiveness to customer needs through close internal coordination

Research, development, design	1. Unique product features 2. Fast new product development 3. Design for reliability/serviceability

Human resource development	1. Training which supports the goals of quality and responsiveness 2. Incentives which are consistent with differentiation goals 3. Developing commitment to customer service

PRIMARY

Purchasing, inventory holding, materials handling	1. Quality and reliability of components and materials

Production	1. Fast manufacturing 2. Defect-free manufacturing 3. Ability to produce to customer specifications

Warehousing and distribution	1. Fast delivery 2. Efficient order processing 3. Sufficient inventories to meet unexpected orders

Sales and marketing	1. Advertising which enhances brand reputation 2. Effective sales force 3. Quality sales literature

Dealer support and customer service	1. Training for customers 2. Fast, reliable repairs 3. Availability of spare parts 4. Financial support for dealers 5. Training for dealers 6. Customer credit

Figure 10.2 **Uniqueness drivers**

This provides the template for a specific analysis of an enterprise. It is useful to show how a particular case can be used to illustrate the method. There are four stages in the evaluation of potential:

1. Construct a value chain for the enterprise and its customers
2. Identify the specific uniqueness drivers
3. Select the key variables, that is, the drivers which are likely to make a significant difference
4. Identify the linkage between uniqueness drivers, and between such drivers and cost drivers.

The costs of developing uniqueness

The costs of imparting such uniqueness may be various but significant:

- *Direct costs.* Promotion or advertising can be costed in an unambiguous way
- *Indirect costs.* These are more difficult to identify and estimate. They include the carrying of larger inventories in order to customize and satisfy consumer needs quickly; the loss of economies of scale; and the beneficial effects of moving down the experience curve.

To some degree these costs can be minimized by following certain principles:

- to design in a way which allows component producers to reap economies of scale
- to differentiate as late as possible in the value chain
- to use new technology to reduce the changeover time on a production line.

The basic rule is – incur additional costs of differentiation up to the point at which they are equal to the additional returns resulting from the price premia and the additional market share won by the strategy.

Advantages of a differentiation strategy

There are two distinct advantages of a differentiation strategy over a cost leadership strategy:

1. It is much less likely to be overturned by turbulence in the external environment than a cost advantage. Consumer taste and the structure of particular market segments are usually more stable than many of the variables which affect the immediate costs of production and the sale price of a product, including relative exchange rates. This is not always the case since there are products where fashions change quickly, but it is usually so.
2. A cost leadership strategy can be pursued with greater ease and its main elements more easily imitated by others. It is much more difficult to remove the uniqueness of a product.

A false distinction in practice

In practice the distinction made between the two strategies is rather artificial, although making the distinction helps us to understand the full implications of different generic strategies. This can be easily argued. One method of cost leadership in the short term would be to reduce marketing costs to zero, clearly a prescription for self-destruction. Such costs are incurred for a purpose. In the end the value created for the consumer may greatly exceed any additional cost incurred.

There is a critical exercise to be carried out which assesses how much it costs to impart various degrees of differentiation, which then result in the charging of different price premia. An assessment of how far to go may involve a high level of analysis, or it may simply reflect a great faith in the powers of intuition.

If both cost and differentiation strategies are sensibly constructed, the two can be combined or pursued simultaneously. The enterprise may aim for good value for the customer, that is, a product which combines good quality and a reasonable price, although not perhaps the best in either area.

A focus on the future and innovation will remove any residual incompatibility between the two strategies. Both quality and price can be sought together. Often the effort to minimize costs leads to a situation in which it also becomes clear how quality can be improved. There is not an inevitable incompatibility. Very often those who are cost leaders are the leaders in product differentiation. Unnecessary costs can be removed but costs which raise the quality of the product sufficiently can also be accepted.

If there is a focus on the value chain and the dictates of core competencies in deciding what to outsource, it is possible that the emphasis in strategy may differ according to which activity is the focus of attention. It is possible to pursue different strategies for different activities. Focused cost leadership and focused product differentiation are sensible approaches.

Particular activities are the key to product differentiation. Clearly marketing and distribution are key activities, but design and R&D are increasingly important to such differentiation. For running shoes, cost minimization is the name of the game for manufacturing, but not for marketing or design where the emphasis is on product differentiation. The same applies in the motorcar industry or even the aircraft industry, where an increasing proportion of component production is outsourced and it is likely that contract assembly will emerge in the future, but where branding through marketing and design still involves a strong degree of product differentiation.

Case Study   Turning a stone into a jewel – De Beers

The first major marketing campaign by De Beers came as early as 1939, in order to try to reduce its excessive level of stock. The full impact of the campaign was felt in the postwar era when incomes were rising and there was a general air of prosperity.

J. Walter Thompson, De Beer's advertising agency adroitly promoted the notion of the diamond engagement ring, where possible building on existing customs and linking the gift of a ring with occasions already celebrated for different reasons in different countries. It succeeded in establishing the near-universal tradition of diamond engagement rings and popularized the slogan 'a diamond is for ever'. At the peak of the custom, 80%

of American males bought a diamond ring for their partner. The scope of the practice was even more dramatically extended in Japan where it was linked to *yunio*, the exchange of gifts between bride and groom. J. Walter Thompson used this to lift coverage from a low 5% in 1966, when it was an unusual Western custom, to 60% by 1979. In Germany, where there was the tradition of the gift of two gold bands, promotion of diamonds was supported by the insertion into the custom of the gift of a third gold ring studded with diamonds.

Further creative promotion established markets for eternity rings, diamond-studded cuff links and tie pins featuring diamonds. Considerable resources were committed to promotional campaigns. In 1995 US$168 million was spent on the 'Shadows' campaign, with the theme that diamonds were addictive.

In such a way a stone of little usefulness was converted into one of great value by continuing promotion which created a market where there was almost none before. De Beers was careful not to encourage the appearance of an investment market for the stones because such a market would have been outside its control. In any event the grading of diamonds is inexact, an art rather than a science.

Argyle's diamonds

In 1996 the Australian producer Argyle broke free from the De Beers cartel and began to sell its diamonds independently. The development of Rio Tinto's Argyle diamond mine in Western Australia (formerly belonging to CRA and Ashton) revolutionized the world diamond market. The main processing plant at Argyle was commissioned as late as 1985. The mine is the world's single biggest producer, with 40 million carats annually compared with De Beer's aggregate of 31 million. As early as the 1990s, Argyle was producing 40% of the world's diamonds in terms of volume, but nothing like this in terms of value, since many of the diamonds were small and of lower-than-average quality. Only about 25% of these diamonds were of gem quality and 40% of these were coloured, the price of which could be as much as 30% below that of clear gems. This did not apply to the pink, green or blue 'fancies' which commanded a rather higher price.

A five-year agreement with the CSO in 1986 allowed Argyle from the beginning to dispose of 25% of its own production. The agreement was renewed in 1991 but with the pink diamonds excluded, retained for distribution by Argyle. This was a very unusual agreement for the CSO, since it allowed Argyle to sell a significant proportion of its output while disposing of most of it through the CSO for a 10% marketing surcharge. The industry was never to be the same again. Argyle opened offices internationally, in Antwerp and Bombay, and domestically, in Perth, through which it could distribute its share of the diamonds. In the mid-1990s, Argyle became increasingly unhappy with the role of the CSO and in particular its inability to sell the low-grade material coming from Argyle and its tendency to defer purchase of its diamonds. It found unacceptable its reduction of the price of low-quality gems; valuations were being fudged. The agreed arrangement was breaking down and in 1996 the sales contract was cancelled.

Marketing of diamonds from the new source had begun already, but became more important. Argyle Diamonds built upon the existing success in product differentiation. It had cleverly turned a weakness into a strength. It started to use the terms 'champagne' and 'cognac' to describe the pink and brown colours of some of the gems. A Champagne Diamond Exhibition was held to promote the diamonds. On display was a 200-piece jewellery collection designed by Stuart Devlin, jeweller to the Queen, which included 10,000 Argyle gems. The centrepiece of the exhibition was a Fabergé-style egg, worth US$2.9 million. This was encrusted with 400 champagne and cognac gems on the outside and inside there were diamond-studded golden horses on a revolving carousel. The collection was sold in 1990. Fired by the success of the first exhibition, Argyle later staged a second, much larger exhibition, this time with 20,000 gems. A Kutchinsky egg was created which had a diamond-studded library and miniature portrait gallery inside. The pink diamonds created a special interest, encouraged by their sale through auctions and tender.

The end of the monopoly

Over the past decade, De Beers has been in crisis, faced with a number of significant problems. The supply of diamonds has been running well ahead of demand, with a flood of diamonds coming onto the market, initially from Russia and Australia but later from northern Canada – the Ekati mine, majority-owned by BHP Billiton, and the Diavik mine, owned by Rio Tinto. The Ekati mine now produces about 6% of the world's total output by value. The Diavik mine began production in 2003.

Table 10.3 **World rough-diamond supply**

	Value (US$ billion)	Market share (%)
De Beers (SA)	3.4	43
Alrosa (Russia)	1.6	19
Rio Tinto (Aus/Can)	0.6	8
BHP Billiton (Can)	0.4	6
Others	1.9	24
Total	7.9	100

The supply situation was made complicated by a worldwide campaign against so-called 'conflict' or 'blood' diamonds, those mined and sold by combatants in war-torn countries such as Sierra Leone and Angola. There was an active search for sources of supply outside Africa.

This situation does not prevent the CSO controlling something like two-thirds of the world's cut-diamond trade. The CSO still wields enormous, although not any longer dominant, influence in the industry.

On the other hand, there is a decline in the demand for diamonds compared with other luxury goods. The demand for luxury goods (this would include what have been called aspirational goods in this book) is said to be growing at a rate of 10% per year, whereas the retail demand for diamonds has contracted, especially in Japan. The price has not fallen, partly because there is a residual investment demand arising from the fact that a diamond is more than 300 times the value of gold on a weight-for-weight basis, and partly because the CSO is still acting as a buffer purchaser. As a result of falling retail demand, the value of the stockpile held by De Beers during the 1990s doubled, from US$2.5 billion to US$5.0 billion.

One problem which is looming large for De Beers is its anti-competitive practices. Anti-monopoly legislation in the USA is reputed to prevent senior officials of the CSO even stepping on American soil for fear of arrest and gaol. The Europeans are beefing up their own anti-monopoly legislation. De Beers is aware of the problem. It knows that the old monopoly is a thing of the past and that it must turn its attention to better marketing and increased demand.

De Beers' leaders have been impressed by the success of Argyle in marketing what appeared to be unattractive stones. They have begun a major shift in strategy, which is really a return to fundamentals. De Beers is trying to shift from an emphasis on stocking and warehousing diamonds to one of selling them. It realizes that such a consumer-oriented policy cannot happen overnight, but might require five years of careful work. During this period profits will be low and therefore the market valuation of a public company poor. Consequently in 2001 De Beers was privatized, with the Oppenheim family retaining 45%, the large mining company Anglo American holding the same proportion and the remaining 10% owned by a joint venture of De Beers and the Botswana government. The price was still US$18.7 billion, despite the various factors dragging down the share price.

De Beer's new emphasis on marketing has taken a number of different forms:

- There has been a rethink about the sightholders, the distributors, cutters and traders, to whom De Beers sells at prices determined by the CSO. Firstly, it has reduced the numbers from 125 to about 85. Secondly, it has changed the criteria for selecting sightholders. In choosing the sightholders to whom the diamonds have been allocated, it has traditionally only considered a capability to process the diamonds and the strength of financial backing. Now it is looking for the ability to stimulate demand in the retail trade. It intends to shake up its client list every two years.

- De Beers itself is opening its first retail outlet, in London on the corner of Old Bond Street and Picadilly, a joint venture, to be called De Beers LV, as the name suggests one between De Beers and the well-known purveyor of luxuries Louis Vuitton-Möet Hennessy (LVMH). This is the start of a US$400 million programme to open as many as 100 stores worldwide. The joint venture now owns the De Beers name. A new range of jewellery carrying the name was launched in the London store in October 2002.

- The Diamond Trading Company of De Beers is to start a global marketing plan, important since De Beers still controls the marketing of at least 60% of the world's diamonds.

- De Beers is changing from a single-channel to a multichannel business, in which, although it hopes to be the 'supplier of choice', it recognizes that there will be many retailers whose job is to undertake most of the marketing. De Beers now believes that the total market will be expanded by a kind of 'brand warfare', as producers and retailers develop their own brands in competition with each other. All will gain, some more than others.

  This will require new products and specific diamond brands, such as Chris Evert's tennis bracelet, inadvertently publicized some years ago. Roland Lorie, joint chief of the International Gemological Institute in Antwerp, one of whose tasks is to evaluate diamonds for retailers, is quoted as saying: 'the weak point of diamonds has been that it's one of the few things that you cannot put a name on, not like a Rolex or a Swatch' (Simon, 2002: 8).

- Currently the industry only spends about 1% of its sales revenues on marketing, about US$200 million. De Beers hopes that the industry will at least double this and eventually push the proportion up to 4%.

The impact of Argyle has been widespread. It did an excellent job persuading Indian cutters to cut the new diamonds and major American retail chains to sell brown (cognac) diamonds at prices between US$99 and US$199. Its B2B programme left De Beers for dead. It understood very well the 'aspirational' nature of the demand for diamonds and exploited it to the hilt.

The whole structure of the industry is in the process of change. Until recently, the world diamond distribution system and processing activities were controlled by a small group of Hassidic Jews, with the main centres in Clerkenwell, London, Antwerp and Israel, just as the Jewish Oppenheimer family owned and controlled De Beers and the CSO. This group specialized in cutting and polishing large diamonds. The flood of small gem-quality diamonds from Argyle rapidly subverted this system and made possible the substitution of a different dominant group on the supply side and a different mode of sale on the demand side.

It is not only Argyle which has broken the monopoly. BHP Billiton has set up Aurias, a new direct-to-consumer retail business, which was launched in October 2000, selling diamonds from the Ekati mine. Even BHP Billiton has engaged in direct marketing of the Canadian stones under the brand name Aurias, widely promoting it on TV, in print media advertising and on the Internet, but bypassing the CSO. The name Aurias itself, based on the aurora borealis, or northern lights, emphasizes both the rapidly shifting and sparkling light patterns seen as diamonds are moved and the northern hemisphere origins of the diamonds. The diamonds are only available in their cut form, not as jewellery. BHP recognizes its lack of expertise in this area. The diamonds can be viewed in a gallery at the BHP headquarters in Melbourne. BHP's aim is to try to establish a brand name. Only 1% of the Ekati diamonds are being distributed in this way, and, of the rest, 65% went to the wholesale trade through the BHP sales office in Belgium and the other 34% through the CSO.

Another sign of the times is the way in which Ben Bridge, a Seattle-based chain of jewellers with 68 stores in 11 states, has recently begun to sell diamonds from the Ekati mine under the brand name Ikuma. Both Ikuma and Aurias stones are etched with a tiny maple leaf. Typical of the new marketing regime is the recent creation of Diamond Stratagem, a Perth-based independent diamond marketing consultancy set up by ex-Argyle executives. This process is likely to gather momentum, since the New York-based retailer Tiffany has an indirect stake in the new Diavik mine and the rights to buy at least US$50 million in stones from Diavik each year for ten years.

What happens in the American market is critical since in 2001 the USA accounted for 49% of the world retail demand for diamonds compared with Europe's 14% and Japan's 12%. The Middle East and the rest of Asia Pacific each accounted for 10%.

The bypassing of the traditional network by most of the Australian diamonds is linked with the move of the main diamond-cutting centre in the world to India. About 80% of India's diamond processing is concentrated in the northern state of Gujerat and more than half in and around the city of Surat. Ahmedabad is another important location. The work is done in thousands of small family-controlled workshops. Labour costs are so low that a single diamond can be processed for as little as one dollar. The Indian system made possible the sale of the Australian diamonds and has democratized demand for diamond jewellery through low costs and the polishing of very small diamonds of only 0.01–0.06 carats. Many more purchasers could afford to buy such low-priced diamonds; the aspirational market was vastly expanded in this way. Thus the changes on the supply side have both promoted changes on the demand side and been promoted by changes in demand.

The industry, notably its lower end, is once more controlled by a small group, the Jains. It has taken this group about three decades to displace the previous dominant group. The dominance of a small group is not surprising, given that the international trade requires security since it is based upon the handling of small but valuable consignments. Secrecy, trust and strong cross-border connections are obligatory for successful trading. Jain companies are run by families, linked together in all the main centres in networks of brothers and cousins. Jainism is a subsect of Hinduism. There are about 3.5 million Jains, a non-violent group of vegetarians who live mainly in Rajasthan, Gujerat and Mumbai. Certain family names recur, such as Mehta. There are now Jain dealers in all the main diamond centres, including Tel Aviv, Antwerp, London and New York. Jain firms such as the Gembel Group and B. Vijaykumar and Company dominate the trade, even in Tel Aviv. Most of the Australian diamonds pass through this network to Mumbai and the processing workshops in Gujerat and back through Mumbai to the main gem markets in the world.

Case Study Questions

1. What are the intangible attributes which the CSO managed to associate with diamonds and use to brand a product which previously had a limited value and limited market?
2. Which was more important in the De Beers strategy, the control of supply or the control of demand? Did the relative emphasis in the strategy change over time – if so, why?
3. How will the changes in the structure of the industry, both on the demand and supply side, affect the perception by the consumer of these attributes?
4. How does the Argyle strategy differ from the De Beers' strategy and how does the new De Beers' strategy differ from the old?
5. What will the industry look like in the future?

Reading

Backman, M., 'Argyle cuts in on diamond monopoly and Jains polish off the competition', *Business Age*, May 16, 2002: 5.

Case Study 1, Argyle Diamonds, in Lewis, Morkel, Hubbard, Davenport and Stockport, *Australian and New Zealand Strategic Management Concepts, Context and Cases* (Prentice Hall, Erskineville, New South Wales: 1999: 435–51).

Hannen, M., 'BHP plays shop with diamonds', *Business Review Weekly*, February 2, 2001: 30–32.

Lamont, J., 'De Beers to reduce its client list', *Financial Times*, June 9: 27.

Simon, B., 'Girls' best friends will soon be branded with names', *Business Age*, July 5, 2002: 8.

Treadgold, T., 'Diamonds are for everyone', *Business Review Weekly*, June 6–12, 2002: 66–70.

Key strategic lessons

• Product differentiation results from the interaction of the consumer, the product bundle itself and the enterprise.

• Consumer needs are stable, but wants, because they are socially constructed, change. The satisfaction of different needs can be combined. As incomes rise, the means of satisfying wants tend to become more complex.

• The origin of any differentiation is not solely the consumer. The reputation of the enterprise, or its brand name, is a key to product differentiation.

• The aim of differentiation is to make the product or service unique so that it can better satisfy the unique wants of every consumer. This is the basis of customization on an individual basis.

• Product differentiation involves not only physical attributes, which satisfy basic utilities, but intangible attributes which promote a perception of quality. The perception is as important as the reality.

• Intangible attributes are becoming increasingly important and must satisfy basic utilities such as luxury, status, prestige or even health. These attributes must be tailored to suit particular market segments.

• Everything can be branded, including a country, region, person, company and product. The main characteristic of a brand is purchase on the basis of name alone and repeated purchase expressing an attachment to one product or enterprise. A brand allows a price premium.

• The current fashion for outsourcing various functional activities usually omits marketing and other related functions such as R&D and design.

• A generic differentiation strategy requires the linking of products and their attributes with the consumer group and its utilities. The enterprise needs to produce the product with the desired attributes at a cost which is less than the price premium made possible by differentiation.

• There are also uniqueness drivers such as design, quality of inputs, quality control mechanisms and the experience and skills of the labour force.

• Tastes are more stable than costs, and differentiated products less easy to imitate, both of which favour a product differentiation over a cost leadership strategy.

Applying the lessons

1 Define the following terms: wants, needs, attribute, utility, market segment, commoditization, uniqueness driver and an aspirational good.

2 Can you indicate utilities other than 'luxury' which can be satisfied by a broad range of products and services? Which products are likely to satisfy these utilities?

3 Choose a range of different products, at least six. These might include agricultural or mining products,

luxury goods and complex products such as an MBA or a packaged holiday. Which ones can be described as a commodity? Compare the products in terms of the list of attributes attaching to the different products. Is it the case that the greater the number of attributes, the greater the product differentiation?

4 Choose five different brand names which are well known to you. Are they local, national or global

Applying the lessons cont'd

brands? How was the branding achieved? How might the value of the branding be lost?

5 Show how the differentiation of products relates to the transaction cycle described in Chapter 9.

6 Consider the support and core activities which are important in the value chain of any enterprise in which you work or have worked. List the uniqueness drivers and evaluate the potential for differentiation of that enterprise and its products.

Strategic project

1 Devise an imaginary new product which satisfies a utility which is important to consumers. Answer the following questions.

2 What attributes, both tangible and intangible, will that product possess?

3 What is the nature of the consumers in that market segment?

4 How will the enterprise promote that product?

5 What changes in the external environment are likely to undermine competitive advantage?

Exploring further

A good starting point for product differentiation is a concern with quality, see Garvin, 1984: 25–44. A more focused introduction to the same topic is de Souza, 1989: 21–5. An article explicitly relating quality to strategy is Raynor, 1992: 3–9.

Product differentiation is at the heart of marketing. One of the first treatments in the context of strategy, apart from Porter (1980), is Hall, 1980: 78–81. Two marketing texts which develop the issues well are Kotler, 1996 and McColl-Kennedy and Kiel, 2000. Customization is closely linked to product differentiation. See Pine 1993. Branding, the ultimate in differentiation, is best approached through the work of David Aaker. See Aaker and Joachimsthaler, 2000 or Aaker, 1996. Aaker is probably most interesting when branding is placed in the context of a business strategy as in Aaker, 2001.

Pricing strategy is dealt with at length in Nagle, 1987. A shorter treatment is Cravens, 1997, particularly Chapter 11, and Jeannet and Hennessey, 1998, particularly Chapter 13.

There is a growing literature on whether it is possible to have both low cost and high quality, in other words an implicit critique of the Porter point of view. In favour is Sanchez, 1995: 105–40. Putting the position that trying to do both may leave an enterprise stuck in the middle is Miller and Dess, 1993: 553–85.

Part III

Strategic Dilemmas

11 Determining the size of an enterprise

12 Integrating the strategists

13 When to compete and when to cooperate

14 Managing risk

15 Participating in the global economy

The previous section equipped the reader with the basic concepts necessary to understand the process of strategy making and interpret the likely context in which a strategy must emerge. These concepts included the general environment, the competitive environment, the internal environment (including resources, capabilities and core competencies and their role in establishing competitive advantage) and the generic strategies such as cost leadership, product differentiation and focusing. The identification and exploration of these separate environments and the different generic strategies for exploiting opportunities open to the enterprise enables the reader to understand the recurrent strategic dilemmas which are continuously unfolding and requiring a resolution.

One main conclusion of the previous section was that it is impossible to sustain fully all these separations; environment merges into environment, and generic strategy into generic strategy. Boundaries are sometimes present, at other times not, and even when present turn out to be porous. There cannot be a pure cost leadership strategy or a pure product differentiation strategy. There is a significant overlap between these concepts.

Managers make a host of particular decisions, some strategic, some operational. The strategic decisions usually involve some kind of investment, a commitment of resources now for benefits in the future. Such managers build new plant and decide to enter new markets, in the process fixing the prices of products, hiring and firing employees, purchasing supplies and confirming a multitude of routine day-to-day decisions. All this is performed with the goal of developing the enterprise in line with

Task	Parts	Chapters				
Starting right	**Part I** **Introducing Strategic Management**	WHY?	WHO?	WHAT?	HOW?	WHEN?
		Prologue	1 Introducing strategy and strategy making	2 Thinking and acting strategically	3 Adopting a global perspective	4 Reading an uncertain future

Acquiring conceptual tools for the job

Part II Strategic Environments

5 Identifying opportunity and risk

General

ENVIRONMENTS Internal

7 Analysing resources, capabilities and core competencies

6 Reading the competitive environment

Immediate

and Competitive Advantage

GENERIC STRATEGIES

9 Reducing costs

8 Creating and maintaining competitive advantage

10 Differentiating the product

Resolving particular strategic problems

Part III Strategic Dilemmas

FIVE DILEMMAS

11 Determining the size of an enterprise

12 Integrating the strategists

13 When to compete and when to cooperate

14 Managing risk

15 Participating in the global economy

The strategy emerges

Part IV Bringing it all Together

16 Formulating strategy

17 Implementing strategy → **CONTINUOUS ITERATION** ← 18 Monitoring strategic performance

Analysing strategy making

Part V Strategic Analysis and Audit

Case studies

Epilogue

strategic objectives and exploiting the competitive advantage which is held.

Presenting concepts and describing the decisions to be made is only the beginning of learning how to make strategy. The concepts have to be used creatively in order to explore a number of strategic decision-making situations. Certain situations are recurrent and give rise to common challenges. The aim, therefore, is to identify the nature of these strategic situations and explore how to make appropriate decisions to resolve the recurrent dilemmas.

In theory such decisions could be reduced to a *choice* between alternative programmes which offer different present values or different internal rates of return. The criterion of choice is to maximize whatever financial target is selected as appropriate. Provided all the future streams of revenue and costs are known, this choice would be a simple matter. This view of the decision-making process is a gross oversimplification of the nature of strategic decision making.

For the moment, discussion of this way of posing a problem is postponed, since the concern is with the nature of the recurrent situations. These decision situations are characterized by certain fixed parameters; situations in which key elements sometimes threaten the achievement of the strategic objectives, while others promote such an achievement. It is unclear exactly how many such situations there are; they sometimes overlap for different decisions. Senge talks of 'systems archetypes'; this book refers to them as 'dilemmas'. In this section a number of such archetypal situations or dilemmas are discussed.

The chapters in this section select five principal strategic dilemmas which recur in repeated strategic situations:

• Chapter 11 analyses what is an appropriate size of the enterprise.

• Chapter 12 focuses on how it is possible to integrate the interests and roles of different strategists and different stakeholder groups.

• Chapter 13 considers when to compete and when to cooperate.

• Chapter 14 asks how it is possible to manage the risk which confronts enterprises.

• Chapter 15 considers the choice of participation strategy, what mode of entry into international business transactions to adopt.

These dilemmas focus attention on two broad interactions; that between strategy and the external environment in which the organization operates and that between strategy and the structure of the enterprise. In discussing how to deal with these dilemmas. this section assists the process of making valid generalizations about strategy making and prepares the ground for discussing strategy making as a distinct process.

11 Determining the size of an enterprise

After reading this chapter you will be able to:

- understand the reasons why an organization should be a particular size

- identify the benefits which come from either vertical or horizontal integration

- trace the influence of acquisitions and mergers on the creation and maintenance of competitive advantage

- evaluate membership of a network and focusing as devices to counter the negative impact of excessive size

- understand when outsourcing or downscoping are appropriate

Key strategic challenge

How large should my enterprise be?

Strategic dangers

That the enterprise is either too large or too small to be able to create and maintain competitive advantage, and that managers are unable to exploit fully the advantages associated with optimum size or counter the negative effects of failing to be at the optimum.

Case Study Scenario   A merger and a demerger

'Smaller, traditionally structured resource groups that see cash flow and earnings ebb and flow with the economic cycle and commodity prices are "a gamble" ... We're an investment.'

Chip Goodyear, CEO of BHP Billiton
(quoted in Maiden, 2003)

'BHP Billiton is giving its steel business to its shareholders.'

Rennie, 2002: 38

Broken Hill Proprietary (BHP), the 'Big Australian', is the largest company in Australia and one of the largest resource companies in the world. It originated as a non-ferrous metals miner, from the 1880s onwards exploiting the rich metallic ores of Broken Hill in the dry centre of Australia. It became Australia's main steel producer at the time of World War I and has continued to be so right through to the present. In recent decades it has added further strings to its bow with the acquisition of major gold mining and oil and gas interests.

Many of the successes of BHP have arisen from its ability to diversify into the right areas at the right time. Until recently it had not divested any of the activities acquired. BHP is a genuine conglomerate; in this it has been rather unusual for a mining company. It is a large conglomerate with activities which differ markedly, one from the other. Its divisions have been run separately and independently, even to the extent that the different headquarters have been located in different countries. There has been a tendency for BHP to do everything itself; it has preferred to make rather than buy.

When any company generates significant profit and cash streams, as BHP has – being the first Australian company to generate net revenue of over A\$1 billion, it has to decide what to do with the revenue.

It can seek out projects within the areas in which it is already active, further developing the interests it has. This may involve some degree of horizontal or vertical integration. The sectors in which it is operating may be mature industries offering little further opportunity for expansion, with low profit margins and low rates of return.

It can reward the shareholders, either by distributing the net profits as dividends or buying back its own shares, thus increasing the net earnings per share for the remaining shareowners. At a time when the issue of share options has become common, it is often seen as desirable to reduce the dilution of stock by buying back shares in this way.

A final option is to look for new areas for diversification, to consider moving outside the existing core areas, preferably into areas offering rapid expansion and high profits.

In recent times BHP has had a rather 'up-and-down' history, with significant debate and differences of view on strategy. These came to a head in 1995 and again in the early 2000s. Its main businesses, at different stages in their life cycle, have had a mixed history. Some have done well, notably minerals and at times oil and gas. These businesses, especially the commodity businesses, are cyclical in performance and suffer from a slow general decline in price, which reflects a tendency of supply to run ahead of demand, fortunately offset in their impact on profitability by an increase in productivity and reduction in costs. The price cycle is by no means the same for the different minerals. The steel industry has been a mature industry with low profits, which tend to fluctuate markedly with the business cycle; at the global level there is significant overcapacity.

The main focus of analysis in this chapter are the various advantages and disadvantages of size, considered from the perspective of the maintenance of competitive advantage. There are strategies which can minimize the disadvantages of being either too big or too small. Choice of size, and the related choice of strategies which minimize any associated disadvantages, is a key strategic dilemma, which is confronted on a regular basis.

So far the discussion has been focused on the enterprise or organization as if it always consisted of a single business unit. The analysis has considered the search for competitive advantage in this narrow context. Yet there are few single-unit enterprises. Those that exist are usually small. Most enterprises have more than just one unit. They are either diversified enterprises in which the separate business units share the use of at least some resources and are characterized by synergies of various kinds, that is, by connections which are mutually cost-saving or revenue-generating, or genuine conglomerates in which the business units are separate from each other and capable of being operated as independent profit centres.

Any enterprise can integrate varying numbers of different activities and functions, including both downstream activities such as distribution and upstream activities such as materials procurement.

The optimum size of an enterprise

There are various ways of measuring size, either by the value of gross revenue or sales, or by a measure of a key factor input such as employment or the value of all assets used, or even by the value of the company's market capitalization. While ranking by size yields a different order according to the measure used, a large enterprise is inevitably large by any of these measures. Since the other measures give undue weight to the factor intensity of an industry – its capital or labour intensity – total sales is considered to yield the most relevant measure for the purposes of this book.

While the choice of size is clearly a strategic question, it is unfortunately a matter of fashion and fashions change dramatically. Not so long ago it was part of prudent risk management to diversify the activities of an enterprise, with a clear implication that as enterprises acquired new business units, they grew in size. Corporations learned to put together under their control very disparate groups of business units. The essence of all good risk management was the creation of a sufficiently large portfolio of diverse assets whose performance was independent of each other. As a consequence enterprises came to consist of a range of different business units, in some cases involving very different products or services, often well outside the core area of interest and therefore often lacking synergies. In some countries this is still the norm. The task of central headquarters or the treasury department was then to manage these different business units by distributing resources among them according to the relative rates of return earned by the different units and the risk attaching to them. On this account strategy looked like an exercise in good portfolio management.

By contrast today, the fashion has changed, partly as a consequence of the bad experience with diversification. It is now considered desirable to stick to a core activity and where possible to divest an enterprise of all non-core activities, whether selling off unwanted units or outsourcing activities in which others have a competency. The problem is to identify the business units in which there is a strong competitive advantage and the strategy-critical activities which must be retained. In doing this it is possible to identify those which are better outsourced to others. The prescription is to do only what you do best and to allow others to do what they do best, particularly if they can do these things better than you. Size, once seen as an advantage, is now interpreted as a decided disadvantage, if it conceals underperforming units or activities.

In the debate on the influence of the size of an enterprise, there are strong but contradictory views held by protagonists on its impact on the maintenance of competitive advantage.

What are the advantages and disadvantages of size? The wide range of advantages and disadvantages needs to be reviewed.

Advantages

There are those who argue strongly that size gives a series of obvious and weighty advantages:

- The most powerful argument in favour of such a point of view is an empirical one, the domination of the real world by large enterprises, that is, the sustained tendency of organizations in the real world to get bigger and bigger. There seems to be no limit to this process, which reflects an iron law of oligopoly, that is, the tendency of a few to dominate nearly every single market at whatever level in the world economy. The tendency for the size of enterprises to continue to increase and for oligopoly to reassert itself at all levels, global, national or regional, confirms that, whatever the theoretical reservations, there must be some significant advantages encouraging such a trend. It is necessary to consider these advantages since they are obviously relevant to strategy making and must be taken into account.
- The existence of large fixed costs indicates likely economies of scale, at least over a wide range of outputs and sales. Fixed costs have tended recently to increase in importance relative to variable costs and some costs, such as labour costs, have taken on the characteristics of fixed costs, whereas before they were more like variable costs. Economies of scale exist when the total unit costs of production decline as production is increased.

Also it may be that there are significant economies of scope rather than of scale, synergies which attach to the production and sale of different products or services. Economies of scope exist when the sale of more than one product leads to a reduction of total unit costs for that product. Often intangible resources such as technical know-how or organizational skills can be used for a number of different but related products.

It is usually assumed that there must be a maximum level of production or sales at which the tendency to a reduction of costs is exhausted, some point at which an increase in variable costs, that is, in the costs of labour or various inputs, offsets the lower per unit fixed costs. This follows mainly from the organizational problems of size. However, this optimum point may be well above the current level of production.

- As has been discussed, size may not mean simply more of one particular product or service. Rather size may reflect the production and sale of a diverse range of products, including differentiated variants of the same product. This may deny the enterprise the advantages derived from economies of size but, provided there is unsystematic risk, that is, that conditions in the different markets vary, diversity itself may cushion the enterprise against the risk of a downturn in any one market. This promises lower risk, or the possibility of making a higher return at a given risk level.
- A large enterprise is usually in a much stronger position to gain access to resources of various kinds and procure those resources at a lower price. Generally, the larger it is,

the greater its bargaining strength. This is as true of labour as of other inputs. A large enterprise is often more attractive as a potential customer or an employer. Those seeking an exciting career path are much more likely to enter a large organization which offers better prospects of internal promotion. The work is more likely to be challenging, and the experience a more assured qualification for securing a job elsewhere at a later date. Altogether the possible rewards are much larger.

- Political clout is very important when an enterprise seeks to negotiate favourable treatment by governments or other key bodies – again, the bigger, the better. The enterprise may be in a stronger position to influence either the setting of the rules of the game or their implementation. The influence of the organization on any industrial association or strategic alliance is also likely to be greater, therefore indirectly influencing government or regulatory bodies.
- Competitive strength is often linked with size since a large enterprise is likely to have access to financial resources which allow it to initiate strategies which can damage competitors – by using internal funds, borrowing or raising capital in the stock market. It can more easily retaliate if others initiate an aggressive strategy. It is in a much stronger position to take over enterprises, which pose a threat or offer an opportunity, in order to gain access to valuable intangible assets.

Disadvantages

On the other hand, there are those who argue, just as vehemently, that size is a disadvantage, that large organizations are like dinosaurs, destined for eventual extinction:

- Large organizations are seen as lumbering giants unable to match the nimbleness of smaller enterprises. Some commentators stress that the nature and speed of innovation and technical change today encourage the notion that small is beautiful, and if not beautiful, at least effective and efficient. The underlying assumption is that large organizations inevitably become bureaucratic in structure and thinking; bureaucratic used with its commonly understood negative connotations. As they become more bureaucratic, large organizations reveal a slowing response to a changing environment. The eventual loss of entrepreneurial dynamism by all enterprises, however much they may shine for a brief period of time, and the limited life of nearly all enterprises argue strongly for this point of view. There may be a progressive tendency for enterprises to get bigger and bigger, but the enterprises filling the key slots at the top of the size ranking are not the same enterprises: the leaders turn over quickly.
- Diseconomies of scale or scope depend on the optimum size of an enterprise and the degree to which different products or services can share functional facilities. The nature of the product is a key issue. The more a product or service is differentiated, the less is it possible to use techniques which reap economies of scale. In some cases the optimum size of a production run may be very small. An enterprise may be faced with producing a host of different products all differentiated or customized in some way. Intangible resources, like tangible resources, may be highly specific to the production of particular products. The associated costs cannot be shared.

- As an organization becomes larger, it must specialize. It must develop both horizontally with separate specialized functional departments and vertically with different layers of authority. The system can easily become inflexible, often difficult to change. The enterprise develops job descriptions and procedure manuals, articulating the rules of behaviour in some detail. In so doing it faces a multitude of problems of coordination and communication. Control becomes much more difficult. Conflict becomes a threat to unified action.

- In such an organization there are a number of different stakeholder groups and a multitude of principal/agent problems which make it difficult to keep the organization integrated, that is, problems connected with ensuring that the agent does what the principal wants. Different interests mean that the organization must resolve problems in a 'political' way, different parts of the organization often moving in divergent directions.

- The organization may grow over time in unexpected ways, with little rational thought given to restructuring. The structure may severely constrain the strategy which can be formulated and implemented. The whole organization may be a mish-mash of different design principles inherited with the acquisition of different business units or enterprises.

Whether the benefits or the costs of size predominate reflects the condition of the industry or sector.

Optimum size and optimum growth

It is necessary to note that optimum size is a static concept and what is required is a dynamic context. The optimum size may change over time, becoming either larger or smaller. There are therefore corollary questions to be asked:

- What is the optimum rate of growth?
- Is all growth good?
- Do most rewards go to the organization which grows the fastest and captures most of the advantages of size?
- Is it a race to become the biggest?
- Or is it sometimes desirable for an enterprise to contract in size?
- If so, when should this contraction occur?

The single-product enterprise

The picture is simple to understand if initial attention is limited to a one-product enterprise. There is a definite limit on size if the enterprise continues to be a one-product enterprise. There is a common pattern of varying growth throughout the life cycle of a typical product. It takes time to persuade consumers to adopt a new product, in other words to develop the market for such a product. Growth, when it comes, can be at a rapid rate, but only for a finite period of time. The expected pattern is for an initial acceleration to a maximum rate followed by a gradual slowing until the potential for further growth is exhausted. If the enterprise is limited to one product, the implications are clear. This is true at the global level if, when the domestic market is saturated, attention turns to export markets. This is the origin of the well-known *S-shaped growth curve*. For example, the airline industry sees slow growth both in its infancy and when it is fully mature.

It is useful to dwell on a single-product enterprise for a moment. A new product cannot fully satisfy all the wants of the customer. It takes time to develop the product to a point at which the customer has identified exactly what are the utilities or wants which the product satisfies and becomes happy with the nature of the product. For this reason, there is a tendency at this stage for all activities related to its production and development to be integrated, that is, under the control of a single enterprise. When the product has matured, it is possible for this to change, that is, for specific activities to be divested as specialization occurs. The emergence of separate enterprises providing necessary inputs, services or complementary products or services puts a limit on size.

The single-product enterprise can sustain its growth, where this is possible, by developing new variants as substitutes for the original product. These variants may be dramatically cheaper or constitute a different bundle of attributes. Such a development renews the dynamism of that particular market, but there is a limit to how far this is possible. As tastes and technology change, the market for the product can be renewed in this way.

A portfolio of products and services

If the potential market of a specific product is exhausted or further growth is limited, the producing enterprise can grow by taking the further step of introducing new products. They may or may not be related to the product area in which the enterprise started. This process can be repeated a number of times so that an enterprise can develop a pipeline of products. With a balanced portfolio of products at different points in their life cycle, the enterprise can better sustain its growth.

Even so growth may slow. There must be a stage at which the growth slows because the enterprise has a high proportion of largely mature products in its portfolio. Simultaneously it is confronted by the difficulties faced by any large organization. It becomes more and more difficult to design an efficient structure in order to manage all the products in a diverse portfolio, although not impossible.

The advantages and disadvantages of size reflect the path on which an enterprise has grown and is growing, in particular whether it is growing organically or through acquisition, through a stable rate of growth or in fits and starts. The specific history of the organization will determine at different points of time the exact mix of advantages and disadvantages arising from size. This mix reflects the nature of the historical process of growth.

At any time the enterprise could introduce new products and simultaneously contract the number of old. For many enterprises, a contraction, even if it is matched by an expansion, represents a difficult challenge. One strategic option is simply to moderate the rate of expansion without totally suppressing growth. The answer may lie in simultaneously expanding some parts of the enterprise and contracting other parts in a deliberate strategic plan, a difficult thing to achieve successfully. Any contraction tends to become cumulative and difficult to control. It is also difficult to reverse growth and reduce the size of an enterprise without having seriously negative effects, resulting in the loss of some competitive advantage. There is often damage done to the morale of staff.

Ways of reducing the disadvantages of size

Both advantages and disadvantages may be potentially significant. Where the advantages of size clearly predominate, it is beneficial to have large organizations, and where the disadvantages clearly predominate, it is better to outsource and down-scope, in the process systematically reducing size. There are creative ways in which it is possible to avoid the disadvantages and reap the advantages of large organizations without opting for a strategy which emphasizes either large or small size.

• Potential disadvantages can be played down by choice of the appropriate design structure. However, design cannot fully remove all the disadvantages and inappropriate design can reinforce them.
• By forming strategic alliances and creating networks, it is possible to develop a mechanism which benefits from the advantages which hierarchy and large size give and avoids the disadvantages.

The bias in favour of large size

There is no doubt that, whatever the 'objective' balance of advantages and disadvantages which size brings, there is a bias in the attitude and experience of managers which favours growth and larger size. In a successful organization, it is difficult for managers to hand back all, or even most, of its profit to its shareholders and let them make the decision how to distribute the finance to other enterprises. Most of the possible motivations of managers are better satisfied in a larger organization than a smaller one – status, power and position all incline them in favour of growth and size. It is much easier for the enterprise to look around for new investments, and plenty of good rationalizations for entering completely new areas in order to avoid the negative effects of growing maturity. There is a tendency for key staff to weight the arguments heavily on the side of advantage.

Strategy in Action   Communication, information and entertainment – the forces making for fusion

Technical change can alter the classification of different sectors of the economy. The so-called information/communications revolution is doing just that in three sectors:

• the computer industry, including both hardware and software
• the companies who provide the conduits which carry the data or voice communication from device to device, commonly called the telecommunications industry
• those companies which provide what can be sent down the conduits, the providers of entertainment such as films, music or television programmes.

Recently the first two have been subject to radical

change. That change is at the heart of the communications revolution which has dramatically reshaped the economy over the past 15 years and will continue to do so over the next 15. The basis of the revolution is clearly technical. This is best summarized by Moore's law, which says that the capacity of the microchip doubles every 18 months.

There are several technical changes which have had a wide-ranging impact on organizations:

• the advent of the PC and its operating and application systems
• the massively increased capacity of both wireless and broadband communication, including the mobile phone
• the development of satellite communication

▶

- the introduction of fibreoptic networks
- the development of a multitude of software systems
- the development of digital communication to replace the analogue system.

One result has been to reduce the potential cost of everything concerned with communication. The technical changes have emphasized product differentiation, offering the customer much enhanced attributes for electronic devices such as the PC and the mobile phone, and even the humble TV. The supply revolution is driving a revolution in the definition of consumer wants.

The environment is highly competitive, with many enterprises trying to anticipate the nature of the change occurring. Unfortunately it is subject to rather violent fluctuations in the relationship between supply and demand, with a tendency to violent lurches in which supply runs ahead of demand. There have been enormous fluctuations in the valuation of the relevant companies on the stock market.

Traditionally there has been considerable government intervention, with the aim of promoting competition. The new technology has necessitated a change in regulation to allow more competition and therefore less necessity for government intervention to prevent the misuse of monopoly power. There is a process of deregulation going on, highly specific to particular countries, whose nature affects the structure of organizations, particularly the amount of cross-ownership.

The resulting changes are fourfold:

1. An explosion in the number of companies trying to use the technology to increase their selling power. Most of the high-tech start-ups, notably the dot-coms, are in this area. The potential in terms of e-commerce has been perceived to be very large. The importance of both cable networks and wireless communication systems has stimulated significant interest. The revolution has underpinned an asset bubble in which unprofitable companies were valued at surprisingly high stock market prices and it has been easy for initial public offers to occur. New companies have appeared, some growing very rapidly, others disappearing just as rapidly.

2. New ways to satisfy a number of consumer wants:

   - purchasing
   - communicating with others, for example with instant messaging
   - entertaining through video games in virtual worlds
   - gaining access to data and information
   - engaging in efficient administration using spreadsheets and so on.

New products have appeared and quickly reached a high level of coverage of the relevant markets. There is a need for material to be available to the consumer and therefore considerable interest in those companies which have access to films, music, games, the written word or even data. There are all sorts of possibilities of integrating different services.

3. The internationalization of the related sectors. Some companies aspire to have interests in all aspects of the broad communications/information/entertainment sector in all major markets.

4. Redrawing of the boundaries between different sectors of the economy. There has been a convergence in what equipment can do. The PC can do everything that a television, stereo system, video or even games console can do. The mobile phone will soon be able to do exactly the same things. There is also a convergence between office equipment and consumer electronics, partly as a consequence of the enormous reduction in costs. There has been a rapidly changing series of strategic alliances. Those enterprises which can, through appropriate alliances, recognize the implications of future technical change for the nature of effective organization can safeguard their competitive advantage, despite a dynamic context.

In 1991, at Harvard University, John Sculley of Apple forecast how technical change would power fusion within the information industry in 2001, as shown in Figure 11.1.

Figure 11.1 illustrates the fluidity of the boundaries between products and service and between sectors of the economy. Some changes have still not fully worked themselves out.

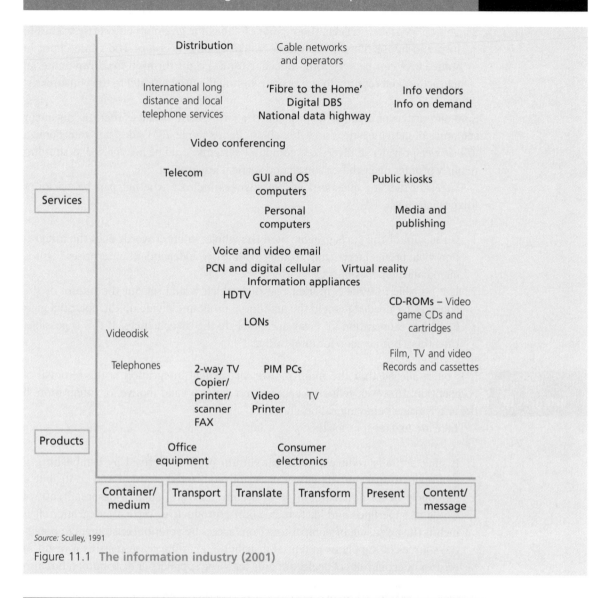

Source: Sculley, 1991

Figure 11.1 **The information industry (2001)**

The strategic gains from vertical and horizontal integration

An enterprise can get larger by merging with other competing enterprises or integrating related but separate activities. There are two dimensions in which an enterprise can integrate, the horizontal and the vertical:

1. Horizontal integration reflects the range of products or services the enterprise chooses to produce or sell, the so-called 'portfolio of business units', and the markets in which it chooses to sell those products or services. However, the existing range may be the result of two factors, a history of long-forgotten decisions to enter new areas and a reluctance to divest any business activity once it is adopted.

2. Vertical inegration reflects those parts of the value chain an enterprise wishes to locate in-house. This is the classic 'make or buy' decision. The value chain in some cases can be very long indeed, running right through from raw material extraction and refining to the act of retailing the final product to the consumer.

Sometimes it is difficult to distinguish the two, partly because there is no linear sequence of activities, no true value chain. For example, IBM's decision to become a full-service provider of diversified computer systems could be interpreted as simultaneously promoting both horizontal and vertical integration.

There are two key questions whose answers indicate whether it is beneficial to integrate or not:

1. Is the sum of the parts greater than the whole: in other words does the integration yield profits larger than would exist for two independent enterprises? This is often called super-additivity.
2. Is it possible to write a market contract which would set out the nature of the cooperation needed to yield the additional profit and divide up the potential gain from that cooperation in a way acceptable to the two partners? If this is possible, then there is no reason for integration.

Vertical integration

It is often alleged that the main motive for vertical integration is the removal of competition. However, reducing competition is not a valid motive for integration, if the enterprise is behaving rationally.

There are two reasons for this:

1. It may actually reduce profits. Maximum profit is derived by establishing a monopoly in just one activity, it does not require the creation and control of a monopoly in all downstream or upstream activities; such widespread control would be superflous and likely to be counterproductive. Vertical integration, if it means the exclusion of competitors from access by potential customers to potential sources of supply or potential distributors, can increase costs as a result of the loss of economies of scale, not only for those suppliers or distributors, but also for the monopolist.

    This principle is well illustrated by the case of Microsoft, which has successfully established a monopoly at a narrow 'choke' point, but has an interest in sustaining competition elsewhere.
2. The attempt may have the opposite effect to that desired. An increased price, even if behind the barrier raised around a vertically integrated enterprise, is likely to encourage entry. If new entrants need to be vertically integrated themselves in order to operate within the industry, the overall commitment of resources on entry is massively increased, which itself might constitute a major barrier to entry. Whichever is the stronger tendency – the lure of high profit or the deterrent of greater commitment – if the outcome is a smaller number of players dominating the industry, there is a greater likelihood of collusion between those players in what has become a completely different kind of strategic game.

There are two sources of additional profit which drive the process of vertical integration, namely, joint production economies and transaction economies.

Joint production economies (JPEs) arise from the use of two types of joint or complementary assets shared in producing the different outputs:

1. Economies of scale, which can apply to any of the primary activities in the value chain, for example core activities such as operations and marketing
2. The sharing of support activities among the most significant core activities. Where there are large and repetitive transactions between different activity areas in the value chain, coordination of these activities by means of some overarching supervision is likely to lead to a reduction in costs of various kinds. Some of the most important examples are:
   • a reduction in the need for paperwork and formal record keeping
   • the removal of a need for the provision of specific quality control checks as products move between activities
   • the avoidance of a long and costly search for suppliers
   • the avoidance of costly transport between facilities
   • a sharing of administrative facilities.

A minor driver may be the desire for tax minimization which arises when tax rates differ between activities, are progressive in their incidence on enterprises, or asymmetrical, in that losses are dealt with differently from profits, for example if, for some reason, losses cannot be offset against profits.

Transaction economies result from the trade in intermediate products (TIPs) taking place within an organization rather than in the market outside. The existence of a TIP mainly reflects the widespread danger of market failure.

Market failure arises because in any market contract it is impossible to fully specify all contingencies. It is impossible because of the long time perspective of such a contract and the impossibility of anticipating all possible contingencies. The kinds of conditions which are needed in such a contract are those which ensure that each party to the contract has an incentive to honour that contract and that each has agreed, in a transparent way, how to share any revenue or costs which arise from the activities covered by the contract.

The likelihood of market failure, combined with these economies, explains the need for vertical integration.

There are many elements which combine to create the likelihood of a significant market failure, but three stand out:

1. Small numbers contracting, in an extreme case, the existence of a bilateral monopoly – there is little or no choice of transaction partner
2. Large-scale asset specificity, which might be a specificity of site, technology or human capital. Assets are extremely limited in their use and have almost no value outside the relevant areas
3. The commitment of significant resources to making the particular relationship work, that is, the assets are developed in a way which is specific to the particular transaction(s).

Table 11.1 **Strategic benefits and costs of vertical integration**

Strategic benefits	Strategic costs
Economies of combined operation	Increased capital investment requirements and financial commitment
Economies of internal control	Higher overall investment barriers and loss of coordination
	Increased operating leverage
Economies of information	
Offsetting of the bargaining power of suppliers/buyers	Differing managerial requirements
	Maintaining required coordination
Establishment of stable relationships	
Enhanced ability to differentiate product	Reduced flexibility to change partners
	Foreclosure of access to supplier or consumer research or technology
	Dulled incentives

Together these three elements create scope for possible opportunism which would subvert the intent of the two parties in making a market contract. At least one partner has a strong interest in breaking the contract. If the investment in specific assets is asymmetrical, that is, it is much larger by one partner than the other, it makes one partner vulnerable to opportunistic behaviour by the other. Strategic risk becomes a real issue when it is unclear how the gains from any exchange will be shared. This issue is discussed at length in Chapter 13. One resolution of the problem is vertical integration, but, as Chapter 12 shows, this creates its own problems.

The kind of market failure discussed above is highlighted when, rather than a product, information is the major intermediate good being passed along the value chain. This will mean that there can be extremely ambiguous definitions of what is being exchanged. Moreover, when information becomes public, it loses its value for the generator. It is much easier in the case of information to conceal the level of commitment on either side or even hide what is being exchanged.

The information revolution has made the transfer of information between separate organizations much easier, with more likelihood of transparency in the exchange. Together with the improvement in organization made possible by such a revolution, it has tended to reduce the significance of joint production economies, but has raised the relative importance of non-marketed trade in intermediate products or services. The latter is rising in relative importance.

Types of vertical integration

Vertical integration does not have to be full equity ownership. It can be what is called taper integration. In such integration the integration is not total. Alternative suppliers or distributors are still used, and the capacity of the integrated enterprise is maintained at below the level of market demand for the services. When demand falls, the alternative suppliers and distributors are the first to lose business. In conditions of frequent market fluctuations, this may be an effective approach to adopt in order to limit any threatened rise in costs and provide flexibility.

The integration might also be a quasi-integration, which includes franchises, minority ownership, joint ventures or other similar limited ownership relationships. Most franchising is focused on two main resources which can be combined effectively – the product and/or process of the franchisor and the local knowledge and familiarity with investment opportunities of the franchisee. In this case the range of choice of organizational design is much extended.

Horizontal integration

When should horizontal integration occur? Horizontal integration is another label for diversification. The question is equivalent to asking, when should such diversification occur? As with vertical integration, diversification is only desirable if the benefits outweigh the costs. There are a number of possible areas of benefit:

- A reduction in risk
- The development of potentially profitable new products or markets which require and benefit from the use of the resources, capabilities or competencies already possessed by the enterprise
- A reinforcement or enhancement of the existing asset base of the enterprise and the creation of future innovations which generate increased profit.

Again this is not enough since a strategic alliance could produce the strategic actions which are profitable. The same comments about market failure are relevant. Horizontal integration requires the need to resolve a market failure or a combination of market failures in the same way as vertical integration does.

The enterprise is much more likely to generate new profit opportunities by integrating only products or markets which are in some significant sense related to their existing products, activities or markets. Profit opportunities arise in two cases:

1. Increased efficiency in the use of the existing asset base in producing the existing products. This increased efficiency results from:
   - the existence of joint production economies in the way already described for vertical integration
   - a complementarity in management skills, particularly those tacit skills which are clearly the least amenable to codification or exact specification
   - the avoidance of customer rigidities or switching costs, often associated with the branding of a particular enterprise and its products and the holding of a significant reputation for quality
2. A build-up of new assets, which increases the potential for successful future products.

Putting such activities, products and marketing projects together produces greater value than can arise from their separate existence.

Choosing the portfolio of business units

The strategic aim in horizontal integration is to build a portfolio of products or markets which meet the requirements implied above. Such a portfolio will promote the present profitability of the enterprise and healthy growth in the future. It is easy to claim such benefits, much harder to prove their existence in any strategy and realize them as part of that strategy. Size partly reflects the number of different products or business units within an enterprise. How many businesses should an enterprise have and how should they be chosen?

The level of diversification differs markedly from enterprise to enterprise. It is possible to distinguish five different levels of diversification:

1. A very low level of diversification, where a single business unit generates more than 95% of the revenue of the enterprise. This is the situation of Amazon.com in its first years
2. A low level of diversification, where the core business remains dominant, generating, say, 70–95% of the revenue of the enterprise
3. A moderately diversified situation, in that less than 70% of revenue comes from the dominant business, but that all businesses continue to have strong product, technical and distribution linkages
4. A high level of diversification, in that less than 70% of revenue comes from the dominant business but businesses are weakly linked
5. A very high level of diversification, with less than 70% of revenue coming from the dominant business and no links between the businesses. General Electric would qualify a such an enterprise.

The use of choice matrices

This book has at different times touched on the issue of putting together a portfolio of businesses without directly confronting the question of how such a portfolio might be chosen. This is a critical part of strategy making. The most common approach to articulating the key issue of choice is to use a matrix. There are a number of matrices which have been used to illustrate the relevant problems. The first and best known is the growth share matrix, developed by the Boston Consulting Group. A variant of this is the competitive strength matrix, developed by McKinsey, which broadens the dimensions on the axes. A third one uses the life-cycle stages as an indicator of market strength, dividing products into the four stages – infancy, adolescence, maturity and old age. There is little difference between these matrices and so only the growth share matrix is discussed.

In the allocation of resources between business units, the relevant factors are the competitive strengths of the enterprise, that is, existing market share, and the potential for market growth or industry attractiveness, that is, where it should position itself, and the sales growth of the product category or the GDP growth.

The dividing line between high and low market share is taken to fall at the lowest of the two or three largest industrial enterprise shares, and for market growth it is some median in terms of market or GDP growth.

It is an oversimplification to fit all cases into the four, but it helps in developing and understanding the criteria for portfolio choice. It is possible to expand the number of squares by introducing a greater degree of gradation of either competitive strength or industry attractiveness, but this only introduces subtlety at the expense of understanding.

A. The *cash cow* exists in a market which is mature or even declining, but in which the enterprise has a large market share. The product or market is generating

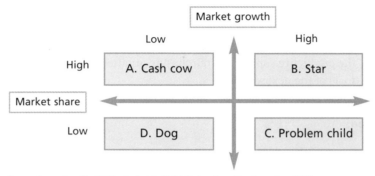

Source: *Perspectives*, No. 66 'The Product Portfolio' (Boston Consulting Group, Inc., 1970)

Figure 11.2 **The growth share matrix**

significant revenues at a low cost. The aim is usually to hold and defend the position, as far as this is possible. Cash cows are a vital part of any portfolio.

B. A *star* is a product or market which is in a rapid growth phase, possibly because it is new, and in which the enterprise has a strong position. It requires significant investment, having high costs as well as high revenues and may or may not be profitable. It certainly promises to be profitable in the future. The aim is to convert a star into a cash cow, protecting its market position as far as possible.

C. A *problem child* is a product or market in a rapid growth phase, again because it might be new, but in which the enterprise is weak, holding a small market share. It requires significant further capital expenditure and is almost certainly making a significant loss. The aim should be to either divest the problem child, or possibly invest at a level which turns it into either a star or a cash cow. Decisive action is required.

D. A *dog* exists in a mature or declining market in which the enterprise has a poor market share. The dog has high costs and low revenues and consequently makes a loss and promises to continue to do so. It should be divested as soon as possible.

However, the world is not divided so simply. There are clearly units which are marginal, and could either be harvested for a short period before divestment or invested in for a period to see whether they are worth developing. The portfolio should be a balanced one, consisting of cash cows, stars and problem children. As far as possible, dogs should be avoided, stars nurtured, problem children rescued and cash cows safe-guarded as the source of finance to look after the stars and problem children.

It is possible to draw a parallel between a pipeline of drugs at various stages of their life and an enterprise which sells products which are at different points in their life cycle. It is not sensible to have products which are all sold in a mature market, nor is it sensible to have a portfolio of only immature products.

The main difference between a conglomerate and a diversified company is that a conglomerate consists of business units which are independent of each other and a diversified enterprise has businesses which are linked in some way. Most enterprises produce a wide range of related products – either on the demand side or the cost side. On both sides there might be shared value-creating activities, such as R&D or promotion. This means that the costs of this activity can be shared.

Where the business units are related, portfolio choice must be made on different principles. In order to put together such a portfolio, the enterprise has to either develop the productive capacity itself, assumed to be a fairly long process, or acquire the productive capacity by purchasing another enterprise. The latter approach is the topic of the next section.

Strategy in Action Integration in communications/information/entertainment

From the late 1980s onwards, a process of fusion has occurred at a frantic pace in this area. There are seven major companies with significant involvement, as shown in Table 11.2. The exact mix of activity varies between the companies. The analysis considers ten activities, excluding the areas of wireless communication through hand-held sets and games consoles. All the main players have TV production and, bar one, film-making and publishing facilities.

Sony led the way, as can be seen in Chapter 18, but is the least represented in the activities, having only TV, film and music production. It does have a games console, PlayStation, and produces the hardware, such as TV sets and so on. It has been joined by another six main players. AOL Time Warner has eight activities and represents the most dramatic fusion of all, only lacking a telecom network and theme parks. Vivendi has eight, lacking broadcast TV and data transfer. Disney and Viacom have seven, both lacking an Internet portal, a telecom provider and a music facility.

From the late 1980s onwards there was a wave of mergers. The motive was simple, the need to ensure that the new communication channels had enough content. The favourite term was 'convergence', which came to have a host of meanings, both technical and organizational. The distribution systems needed film, TV programmes and music to go over the new broadband and wireless networks. The latter needed to spread their huge fixed costs across customers attracted by good content. Potentially the complementarity would result in lower costs.

In a sense technology was driving the whole merger process, technical convergence bringing an organizational convergence. The merger movement created a small number of large consolidated companies which now dominate the sector. The acquisitions were made possible by the enormous rise in share price of companies associated with the new communications revolution and highly regarded by the capital market. The role of the new high-tech economy was exaggerated by commentators and highly regarded by investors. This rise gave companies, such as AOL, the leverage to purchase companies they would otherwise have been unable to purchase, such as Time Warner. A high level of debt also resulted.

Table 11.2 The range of activities of the main communication/information/ entertainment companies

	AOL Time Warner	Viacom	Vivendi Universal	News Corporation	Disney	Bertelsmann	Sony
Internet portal	*		*				
Broadcast TV	*	*		*	*	*	
Cable TV	*	*	*	*	*		
Telecom			*				
Film production	*	*	*	*	*		*
TV production	*	*	*	*	*	*	*
Music	*		*			*	*
Publishing	*	*	*	*	*	*	
Theme parks		*	*		*		
Data transfer	*	*			*	*	

There are two major advantages in linking together content and distribution systems:

1. Economies of both scale and scope which result from vertical integration. Any film or TV series requires a major commitment of resources to produce. The marginal cost of giving the content more exposure falls to almost zero, after a few years of significant initial exposure.
2. Clever management of brand names, as Disney has achieved with *The Lion King* and *Toy Story* or Bertelsmann with *Pop Idol*. All the media can be used to take advantage of these, whether it is film, TV, video, DVD, games or publishing.

There are disadvantages:

1. The exclusive favouritism which often results from fusion can stifle creativity. All managers of media outlets want to tap into the best, whatever the source.
2. The expression of independent editorial opinion, whatever the media, whether press, TV or radio. There may be rather obvious conflicts of interest, which can result in a loss of reputation.
3. Size itself which may be an enemy of creativity. This might be solved by having small independent creative centres within the organization. The alternative for the ambitious large organization is to take over small independent organizations as they emerge.

The whole sector quickly ran into considerable difficulty. Three of these companies clearly overextended: Vivendi having to divest activities; AOL Time Warner having lost an enormous amount of share capital in the merger and having changed its CEO; and Bertels-mann was struggling, having changed both its CEO and its strategy. Michael Eisner at Disney was under pressure to improve performance. News Corporation weathered the storm in its usual way, while Sony lost money. Only Viacom came through comparatively unscathed. News Corp. and Viacom were the only companies further consolidating their empires.

Unfortunately the process of consolidation was premature. The ability of the new technologies to deliver convergence was overestimated. Extensive fibreoptic networks were put in but neither wireless nor wired broadband systems had the customers to justify the investment; 3G licences were bought at vast expense (see the case study in Chapter 8). Loss making became rife and share prices tumbled. The market value of all the companies has fallen dramatically. The communications companies have lost value relative to the traditional media companies. The fall in share prices has tended to reveal a high level of debt which must still be serviced.

Pressure is on some of the giants to divest themselves of purchases in order to reduce their debt ratios and cover losses in key areas. For example, Vivendi Universal has been forced to sell off key assets. There have also been large write-downs of asset values, particularly of goodwill built into purchases, as well as the writing off of investments in underutilized fibreoptic networks. The degree of difficulty varies from player to player. All need to change strategy to survive. The model was not necessarily a bad one; some of the giants will eventually succeed. The timing of fusion was wrong, but waiting gives others an opportunity to be first mover.

Acquisitions and mergers

The simplest and quickest way of getting bigger is to acquire another enterprise. The reasons for getting bigger may be many, including simply the productive use of surplus profit or cash flow. Most companies take growing bigger as a mark of success. It may be a matter of eating or being eaten, a race to avoid being absorbed by another enterprise, a race down the experience curve. An acquisition may be defensive, the need to grow big enough to avoid being taken over by some more adept at getting bigger. It may be a matter of diversifying while it is still possible.

The motive may be that the industry has matured and offers much lower profit margins, so the acquisition is motivated by the need to gain market share. Another motivation may be a change in the external environment which is significant. This might involve sweeping technical change such as the communications revolution, a dramatic change in market segmentation or a significant change in government regulations, such as removal of the restrictions on the cross-ownership of different media or foreign ownership.

The present analysis is not concerned with acquisitions which are motivated simply by the prospect of asset stripping. Asset stripping is engaged in for the financial reward of breaking up and selling all the assets of the acquired enterprise, because the buying price of that enterprise, its market value, is less than the aggregate value of its assets when they are resold, its book value.

The assumption made here is that the primary motive for acquisition is strategic, either to improve the competitive advantage of the acquiring enterprise or better manage the risk to which that enterprise is exposed.

The vast majority of foreign direct investment, particularly during boom times, takes the form of mergers and acquisitions, for example 80% at the height of the boom in 1999. Even domestic acquisitions may have an international orientation. A merger may be intended not so much to remove a domestic competitor as to build up the size of the acquirer so that it becomes internationally competitive. Even if there is an anti-competitive aim at the domestic level, the merger might be approved on the grounds that it improves the ability of the larger unit to compete on the international stage.

From a strategic perspective, the underlying rationale for an acquisition should be to acquire assets complementary to those already held by the acquirer. The identification of such assets assumes that there is a clear strategic purpose in the acquisition, which has been carefully thought out beforehand. One motivation may be that vital assets are not otherwise available to the acquiring enterprise. Such assets might include a whole range of resources, which either build on the existing core competency or add a different core competency, such as:

• technical expertise, sometimes formalized in patents
• branded products
• access to particular markets and their distribution systems
• organizational know-how, often tacit.

The acquisition of complementary assets does not preclude the sale of unwanted parts of the acquired enterprise as part of a linked restructuring. Almost all acquisitions are followed by this restructuring, with a varying time delay. Sometimes the restructuring is half-hearted and does not fully integrate the acquired enterprise. In other cases there may be rapid and radical restructuring.

In many cases the exact motivation of the acquisition is not very sophisticated:

• to pre-empt a competitor getting hold of resources
• to discover a short cut to growth
• to purchase an expanded productive facility
• to expand market share, particularly in regional markets to which the enterprise has not previously had access.

The difficulties of acquisition

If the acquisition extends the range of unrelated products or services in the portfolio of the acquirer, the problem of assimilation may be less. The usual structure of multidivisional enterprises which frequently places strategic business units in different divisions is well suited to acquisitions of new products or services, since the addition of a different product to the portfolio of business assets can be accommodated simply and easily. Within a holding company, such units are managed separately. The sole issue in this case is whether the new business unit offers a good return.

The problems start when the diversification offers synergies which are often advanced as the main justification for mergers. In other words, the products or services acquired overlap in their inputs or in some common activity with existing products or services.

Whether acquisition is a good way of growing depends on a number of key issues:

- the degree of preparation which has gone into the acquisition or merger. In order that the enterprise is confident about what is being acquired, it must carry out due diligence studies and audit the whole range of assets. This should be done with a degree of scepticism about the strength of the data presented. Consequently, coming cold to an enterprise about which you know little because there has previously been little contact is not a good idea. It make the enterprise vulnerable to deception.

- the degree of goodwill and trust between the acquirer and the acquired. Enterprises which have been strategic allies for a significant period of time are in a much better position to understand each other's philosophy, culture and core competencies and consequently can read accurately the financial data. They will understand each other's resource position and core competencies. They are unlikely to be ignorant of each other's strategic intent and also more likely to be less vulnerable to opportunistic behaviour by the partner. In this situation they are better able to detect suspect claims and put a realistic valuation on the enterprise.

- the way in which the new enterprise fits into the acquiring enterprise:
  - Is the corporate philosophy and corporate culture compatible with that of the acquirer?
  - Is the organizational design similar?
  - Do the acquired resources complement those the enterprise already has?
  - Is there a strong possibility that the staff of the acquired enterprise will accept the new situation and not depart?

- the price at which the acquisition occurs and how the payment is made, including the question of the nature of the assets in which that payment is made. However desirable the acquisition might be in terms of reduced costs or increased revenues, there is a price at which it becomes unacceptable. Any negative impact on the acquiring enterprise is compounded if the terms of the acquisition have a significant effect on its debt position. In order to secure a purchase, the price usually has to include a premium over the market price. Relevant to most acquisitions is both the market price of the acquirer and the acquired, since an exchange of shares usually takes place, sometimes accounting for all the payment, and the price which is implicit in such a deal. Sometimes there is no other exchange. For that reason, the shareholders of the acquired company are usually in the best position to benefit from the acquisition, provided they dispose of the shares quickly.

Very often the acquirer offers a price which reflects recent growth and future potential. This is said to justify the premium over the market price which is needed to persuade the owners of shares to sell. The shares of the acquirer may have a price-earnings ratio which is high, well above typical market levels and certainly well above that of the acquired. This is likely to be the case where the enterprise is in a sector of the economy favoured by the market. This gives such enterprises enormous leverage in the capital market and reduces the real cost of any acquisition, whether in raising more equity to make the necessary payment or in directly using equity in the purchase itself. It reduces both the need to incur debt and use up valuable cash reserves.

In estimates of whether an investment is worth making, a comparison is usually made between the likely return on the investment, which might be a purchase of another company or investment in new productive facilities, and the weighted average cost of capital, which includes a component for risk. Such a weighting combines the cost of debt and equity according to the existing ratio of total debt to total equity. This is probably reasonable if the decision, yes or no, is under analysis, but it says nothing about the source of funds to make a purchase, which does influence the level of weighted cost. In practice the situation appears to the company managers and strategists rather differently from the way it appears to the shareholders, for whom it makes no difference whether the company uses cash or new equity to make a purchase – they are either finding new funds from their pockets or being denied an additional dividend payout. The cost therefore depends on whether the company is considered as consisting of the shareholders only or as a coalition of all stakeholder groups. For whom is the strategist acting? This is a question touched on a number of times before being directly addressed in Chapter 18.

- For the company, cash is cheapest, at least if the opportunity cost of safe alternative investments for such money is considered. Such a use causes least immediate risk. However, its use reduces the scope for other strategic action by the enterprise in the future; it may also deplete the liquidity of the enterprise and therefore expose it to higher risk. For a company, cash is a necessary buffer against liquidity problems. For the shareholder, the cash held by the company is simply part of its equity.

- For the shareholder, the cost of debt is the interest paid relative to the size of the debt. For the company, debt can appear more expensive and be the most expensive source of funds since the level of gearing is relevant to the risk level. Debt appears much more expensive if the gearing ratio is 80% rather than 40%. The acceptance of a high level of gearing involves a much higher level of risk of loss making since the level of company income may fluctuate. The ratio of debt to equity does matter. What is an acceptable level of gearing differs from industry to industry.

- For the shareholder, the cost of equity is considered to be the aggregation of three components:

  - a base risk-free return (usually the redemption yield on a two-, five- or ten-year government bonds, depending on the time span)
  - plus an equity risk premium (the excess return on all equity compared with risk-free investment)
  - plus the beta of the company (that is, the tendency of the company's price to deviate from the average in the sector or market).

  To the shareholder, equity appears to be more expensive since by its nature it is riskier. However, the latter two elements are based on past performance, which is of no interest to the strategist, except insofar as it may affect the potential supply and cost of new equity. For the company, equity may appear much cheaper, particularly if this sector is currently flavour of the month, with a high share price. In difficult times future dividends can be reduced or in extreme times not paid at all.

- The nature of the resources which are being acquired. Can the acquirer retain the capabilities or core competencies that may be the initial lure? This usually requires the cooperation of the acquired and is best delivered by a merger or an uncontested takeover. Most acquisitions make the acquirer bigger, in that sense potentially stronger, but they do not necessarily promote the competitive advantage of the acquiring enterprise. There is a large literature pointing out that most acquirers have suffered from the acquisition, as shown by the decline in their share price in the year after acquisition. The expected advantages have not materialized or have materialized so slowly that they can be heavily discounted. In the meantime the acquisition and associated restructuring has diverted attention and resources away from other activities, leading to a deterioration in the effectiveness and efficiency with which the enterprise is run.

The worst scenario is where the acquisition is resisted. A contested takeover is likely to lead to a higher price. It is easy to get swept away by the contest. If the target enterprise is an unwilling party to the acquisition, the acquirer may eventually lose key managers, especially senior mangers in the acquired enterprise, and with them the intangible assets which made the enterprise a desirable target in the first place. The resources of the acquired may disappear into thin air; intangible assets become invisible; the expected synergies do not occur.

Growth by acquisition can hide a multitude of sins; it certainly delays the revelation of the disadvantages of size. Some enterprises become addicted acquirers. Acquisitions are sometimes used to conceal a failure to meet growth targets for earnings or profits. In conditions of rapid growth, the transparency of both advantages and disadvantages may be limited. While the process of repeated acquisition promotes learning, which means that the obvious mistakes can be avoided, it makes necessary regular restructurings which again absorb resources and raise the real cost of any acquisition. Repeated acquisitions compound the problem of how to structure the new entity and put a severe strain on scarce managerial resources.

Despite the problems revealed by the history of acquisitions, they continue, particularly in the good times. The simplest explanation is that the managers of an enterprise have an incentive to expand the enterprise since it gives them a better possibility of satisfying all their aspirations for power, status and position. Secondly, the enterprise itself may gain increased political negotiating strength and competitive force from the growth made possible by such acquisitions. Or, the aim may be much more complex than simply maximizing present value. Successful acquisition places the acquirer in a good light and reinforces an apparent momentum of growth.

The Hewlett-Packard/Compaq merger illustrates many of the difficulties faced in a merger, particularly one in which there is significant opposition.

Strategy in Action The Hewlett-Packard/Compaq merger

A merger which has attracted much attention is that between Hewlett-Packard (HP) and Compaq, two of the large players in the computer industry.

Hewlett-Packard originated as the world's largest manufacturer of test and measurement equipment. During the early 1960s it moved into the area of medical equipment and in the mid-1960s computers and peripherals. It has always remained technically dynamic, often spinning off employees who 'seeded' numerous small start-ups in Silicon Valley.

By the late 1990s the leaders of the company were concerned at the slowing rate of growth and an inability to take advantage of the Internet revolution. An internal review by the CEO Lewis Platt decided that the company was too big and diversified: it lacked corporate focus. The non-computer areas were to be spun off. Platt resigned in favour of Carly Fiorina who previously had run the global services division of Lucent. She was clearly a new broom and the architect of the merger.

In the late 1990s, Compaq rapidly began to lose market share and make losses. Compaq had achieved number one position in overall PC sales in the mid-1990s. An attempt to compete with Dell through direct sales has fallen foul of its distributors. Compaq wished to extend into the area of services and to achieve this bought Digital Equipment Corporation in 1998 for the large sum of US$8.4 billion. It had great difficulty absorbing the company and began to lose customers in the services area. In 1999 the former CEO Eckhard took the blame for the deterioration in performance and was replaced by Michael Capellas who later strongly supported the merger with HP.

Although there was agreement on the merger between the senior management of both companies, one group on the HP board associated with the founding Hewlett family was bitterly opposed and took their opposition into the courts. This took up significant time of the main protagonists and generated considerable animosity. Fiorina had to resist the opposition of the old Hewlett interest and later defeat an effort from an ally, the former CEO and now president of Compaq, Michael Capellas, to accelerate the process.

The process of acquisition and merger absorbs resources. Staff from HP and Compaq allegedly devoted more than one million hours of their time to planning this merger, before it was even approved. In the short run the process pushes up costs before any savings are realized. It is a major problem to fuse two large organizations which operate throughout the world and which may have an entirely different culture, structure and strategic philosophy. The same process has to be repeated in each country in which they operate, and in very different contexts, which might be more hostile to the very concept of a merger. This involves a significant rationalization of products, markets and staff, a process which differs according to the nature of the enterprises in each country.

In scoring a merger there are four main areas to consider:

1. *Financial performance.* Most mergers or acquisitions are judged in the short term by the impact of the merger on share values and the combined capitalization of the two companies. Initially nearly all acquisitions involve the payment of a premium on market value. The acquiring enterprise often sees a fall in price. Market value usually reflects profit levels and growth. After two or three years the impact of the merger on key indicators such as profit or the rate of growth of net revenue is clearer.

2. *Impact of the merger on the range of products or services produced and sold.* Many mergers may be designed to diversify either the output or the markets of the company involved. What each company has may be complementary to what the other has. In this case nothing needs to be given up, or is given up, by either company as a result of the merger. When the merger involves similar companies producing competitive products and services, the issue is how far the product range can be rationalized, or who should give up what? What happens when one gives up a product or service? Are some customers lost?

3. *Potential synergies.* Does the merger allow a cutting of costs, through the reaping of economies of scale or scope, increased buying power or the avoidance of duplication? Fixed costs may be spread much wider, whether the costs relate to R&D, the system of distribution or promotion. There may be possibilities for cost saving in merging the procurement of the two enterprises, the removal of duplication in staff or facilities. Their joint buying power may give them the opportunity to drive down the prices of components.

4. *Significant differences of culture between the two organizations.* Are managerial styles compatible? Will staff who are a valuable resource leave because of this?

The situation with respect to the HP/Compaq merger is:

1. It appears that the new company is being turned around successfully, from loss making to profit, but the resulting growth is unbalanced.

The loss from the enterprise systems group making high-end servers, storage machines and enterprise software has risen to a very significant figure.

The personal systems group (PCs, notebooks, hand-held devices and workstations) also has problems. It has seen a serious loss of revenues and is making significant losses. It is in these areas that there is a serious loss of jobs.

The new HP still depends on printers and other services for its profits. There is an enormous expansion in the number of models sold. In this area there are record revenues and a dramatic increase in profit, almost a doubling, so that the area accounts for most of the profit made by the company. Profit margins in this area are up to 13–15%.

2. In theory the new company has settled on an aggressive adopt-and-grow policy. It has lined up the products of the two companies, adopted the better ones and dropped the worst. The products rejected include most of the HP-branded server computers using processors from Intel, Compaq's Tru64 Unix operating system and HP's business PCs and the Jornada hand-held computer. HP is bound to lose more of its products since it produces 62,000 of the two companies' enormous range of 85,000 products. There is room for much more pruning.

The major problem is in the area of PCs. A decision has been made to retain both ranges of PCs, on the grounds that dropping one would almost certainly lead to a net loss of sales and revenue slippage and, more important, to lose the company add-on sales in printers and digital cameras. Together the two products hold 60% of the retail market. They are different in their market orientation. Compaq's PC is designed for home offices and making a wireless link with the Internet, HP's PC is a home entertainment device and a digital imaging camera for photography enthusiasts. HP is betting on the success of Intel's improved pentium chip in which it is a first mover.

3. It is anticipated that by the year 2004 annual costs will be cut by $3 billion a year, up from the $2.5 billion originally thought. There is an attempt to accelerate the savings. More recently it is claimed that the $3 billion will be saved by the end of 2003. At least $1 billion can be saved by common procurement alone, because of the increased bargaining power of the very much larger company.

The savings from the payroll are targeted at $1.5 billion, which means the shedding of 15,000 jobs, with 10,000 to go by November 2002 and 4,000 on a 50-year plus, early retirement buyout offer. As of December 2002, 17,900 have been laid off, again ahead of schedule. The problem is morale – $55 million has been committed in retention bonuses to try to stop a brain drain of key staff, notably technical staff.

4. There is a different corporate culture in the two companies. HP is rather more laid-back than Compaq. This can affect the nature of the cutbacks and who bears the brunt of them.

The new HP sees its main competitor as IBM rather than Dell. However, it is under threat from both.

Customers view HP as a printer and PC company, not a provider of powerful servers and services. HP needs to win more package deals from its corporate customers. Typical of the current situation is a contract which HP won for 40,000 PCs from Home Depot. IBM took the much more valuable long-term contract for servers and software designed to help Home Depot to analyse all its logistical and sales data. Dell is entering a whole series of HP markets, intending to sell printers and ink cartridges from Lexmark under the Dell label. It is also moving into the area of services and advice. One strength of HP is the raft of technical partnerships it has with good companies. Technically it is still extremely dynamic.

The timing of acquisitions

One interesting issue is the timing of acquisitions or mergers. Acquisitions tend to peak on a rising stock market. Most acquisitions are concentrated in the periods of upturn. The reason for this is simple. High and rising share prices protect against takeover and provide the means to achieve the takeover of others. If the market favours a particular sector, it provides that sector with the potential to undertake such takeovers. The movement of share prices often explains the timing of mergers.

Some mergers may be premature, running ahead of the realization of genuine synergies which are promised by a change in environment. The use of shares as an acquisition currency which is ever-more valuable is one good reason why this timing might be appropriate. As P/E ratios rise, it becomes easier for companies to use their own shares to purchase or their own share value to raise money. The high valuation put on any company in the new economy, particularly in the communications sector, promoted acquisitions by companies in this area. The general acquisition frenzy which reached a peak in 2000 with the expenditure of $1.8 trillion shows the truth of this. This is offset to a significant degree by the increasing prices of the acquired.

The cycle is now in reverse, with an enormous drop in acquisition activity. The process is not symmetrical, in that demergers never completely reverse the previous mergers.

Focusing, strategic alliances and networks as devices for reducing the disadvantages of size

Focusing (discussed in Chapter 8) is one way of avoiding the negative consequences of size. The enterprise focuses on what it does well and relies on others for the provision of necessary services. An enterprise can specialize in a limited number of activities which exploit its core competencies. It is surprising how far this can be taken. The enterprise avoids the disadvantages of an elaborate hierarchy. A network of small enterprises, each concentrating on the provision of specialist services, can behave as if it were one large enterprise. This reliance can become a long-term one if there is continuity in the network of relationships.

Reliance requires a significant degree of trust. It can take many different forms, perhaps being formalized in a joint venture or simply based on a cooperation superficially contractual, in reality based on nothing but the goodwill and trust of the partners, sustained over a long period of time. One enterprise buys from another, trusting it to maintain quality and price at levels acceptable to the purchaser.

This continuing interaction can be a source of risk. One partner may build up a considerable investment in the partnership, an investment which is not reciprocated by the other.

Strategic alliances

Strategic alliances take a multitude of different forms, some stable in that they are likely to continue, others unstable, that is, either self-liquidating, when a problem is resolved, or likely to lead to closer integration (strategic alliances are discussed at greater length in Chapter 13). An alliance can be just a matter of purchasing a particular input or it might mean more than this, a technical collaboration or a joint sales campaign. Sometimes the cooperation is comprehensive, covering all areas, but if this is the case, it is often only a prelude to a merger.

Stable strategic alliances, if sustained, can grow into genuine networks, which involve alliances with more than one enterprise, sometimes with very large numbers of enterprises involved. A whole strategy can be based on the existence of networks in which all are committed to work for the common good. Sometimes there is a strategic centre enterprise which coordinates the network, acting as its leader. Some networks are stable over a long period of time, others exist only briefly.

Networks

Sometimes the enterprise tries to act as if it were a network. A large enterprise tries to avoid the disadvantage of size by deliberately simulating within itself the operation of a network. It structures itself as if it were a network. In this case the initiative might come wholly from above, whereas in many networks the initiative comes from below.

In this way related enterprises can develop different core competencies and the enterprise can plug in to exploit the competencies of others. Since no enterprise can develop more than a limited number of competencies, this seems a sensible strategy to adopt. Networks proliferate in certain industries and certain regions of the world in which their geographical proximity often makes them into clusters. (This is discussed at much greater length in Chapter 13.)

Focusing

The alternative is to continue to produce a range of outputs but to focus on particular areas. Focusing is a mechanism for further moderating the disadvantages of size:

- Select a market segment and develop an integrated set of actions designed to deliver goods or services to that segment. It is possible to describe this as a market niche, a part of a broader market but with particular needs and customers
- Choose a particular activity to concentrate on, taking actions to minimize the costs of production or distribution in this area
- Differentiate particular products or services.

Outsourcing and downscoping

It is possible at any time to decide to reduce the size of an enterprise, or at least certain parts of an enterprise. Focusing can achieve only a reweighting of the different parts. Divestment actually removes non-performing parts. The processes of vertical and horizontal integration can be reversed. The processes are outsourcing and downscoping. Both processes lead to a significant reduction in the size of an enterprise.

The advantages of being smaller

There are powerful arguments which can be advanced why an enterprise should be reduced in size, if sometimes only temporarily. Some of the arguments are empirical, based on an observed pattern of increasing failure of large enterprises to withstand the competition of much smaller and younger enterprises. This can be shown by a simple comparison.

The difficulties of IBM have been much talked about and used as an example of what can happen to a slow-moving giant. A comparison of the impact of deintegration on the market capitalization of AT&T and its divested companies and the market capitalization of IBM has posed the question in an interesting way (Table 11.3).

Table 11.3   Integration and the value of IBM and AT&T

	Market valuation of AT&T plus the Baby Bells (US$ billions)		Market valuation of IBM (US$ billions)	
	January 1982	June 1992	January 1982	June 1992
AT&T	$47.50	55.40	$33.60	$55.70
Pacific Telesis		16.10		
US West		14.70		
Nynex		15.80		
Ameritech		16.80		
Southwestern Bell		18.00		
Bell Atlantic		19.30		
Bell South		23.80		
		$179.90		

The much greater increase in value for AT&T and its offshoots is obvious and prompts us to ask whether a similar increase in capital value would have followed the break-up of IBM.

In most industries, there is a concentration of the increase in stock market value on a small number of enterprises. A slight competitive advantage can lead to a very different performance in the relevant share prices. The winners are often the smaller, more agile competitors. The larger ones struggle. As has already been argued, all enterprises lose their dynamism unless they remake themselves. This is a normal part of the 'creative destruction' taking place in any dynamic economy. Every year in the USA about 30–50 of the companies in the Standard & Poor's 500 fall out. Paradoxically, the more successful an economy is, the more likely there are to be enterprises which fail. Success and failure are the two sides of the same coin.

Outsourcing

Outsourcing involves breaking up the vertical integration of a value-adding chain. It refers to the desirability of purchasing products or services from outside rather than producing them within the enterprise itself, the shedding of activities in the value chain. This may mean that the enterprise needs to go through all its primary and support activities to see in which of them it has a genuine competency. The aim is a reduction in costs, and a reduction which is not just temporary but secured on a continuing basis. Such a reduction will free up resources to further develop the core competency.

In some cases, such as cleaning or accounting, the argument seems well based but it can be carried surprisingly far. For some enterprises, particularly in the clothing and footwear industries, the apparently core activity of manufacturing is outsourced. The goal is to emphasize the core competencies, which might be research, design or marketing rather than manufacturing. It has been said that a university might in theory consist of only three staff – a programme director to select consulting lecturers to deliver the academic programme, an accountant to receive payment from the students, or prepare the necessary accounts and organize the system of making payments to contractors, and a caretaker to prepare and open on time the rented buildings for classes.

It is important not to outsource activities which might be relevant to the retention of a core competency or activities critical to the maintenance of the knowledge base of the enterprise. Outsourcing such activities can have a twofold negative outcome:

1. Undermining the core competency of the enterprise
2. Giving another enterprise the opportunity to replicate the core competency and outcompete it in its area of strength.

Downscoping

Downscoping involves breaking up the horizontal integration of different business units. It refers to the desirability of limiting production to the core product or service and the need to shed other products and services, particularly if they have no connection with the core product. The first process is applicable to one business. This second process relates to the number and mix of businesses. Shedding might simply mean 'spinning off' a business unit or it might mean selling it. This approach recognizes that it is difficult for an enterprise to organize effectively the production of a wide range of products and that the costs of trying to do this exceed the benefits of managing risk in this way. The enterprise should concentrate on what it does best. If it does not, it is likely to lose competitive advantage. At the very least it should apply some simple rules on what businesses or companies it retains, reacting to a target rate of return or a target position in the market. It also recognizes that some businesses reach a maturity, which means that the profit margin or return on assets falls away.

For example, Jack Welch set the target that any GE company should be at least number one or number two in its market or be shed. BHP has more recently adopted the same aim. As a consequence divestiture became a cornerstone of GE's strategy under Jack Welch; it is the policy of BHP, as the case study shows. In all, 117 business units were cast off during Welch's incumbency of the CEO's position, constituting something like 20% of the value of its total assets.

Barriers to exit

Exit from a business is sometimes difficult. Barriers to exit are as important as barriers to entry. Without a planned exit, an organization tends to develop more slack than is good for its performance indicators. Good strategy requires thinking about how to manage contraction. When a company has a significant free cash flow, it is tempting to develop unconscious, implicit contracts with stakeholders which amount to buying their acquiescence in a continuation of old policies. It is tempting to continue previous policies of growth and think that any problem simply requires more of the same.

In this context only a crisis will induce a rewriting of the implicit contracts, a crisis which might take the form of the threat of takeover through the capital market, a serious declining performance in the product market or even the threat of a political or regulatory intervention. Internal control systems are not good at recognizing problems and dealing with them in an incremental manner. They tend to react belatedly, being slow to recognize a relative deterioration in performance. They take far too long to effect a major change. The history of General Motors illustrates this (see Chapter 18). Its performance during the 1980s was poor and the response to this worsening performance slow. Only significant losses which totalled US$6.5 billion in 1990 and 1991 led to the eventual removal of the CEO in 1992.

The asymmetry between acquisition and divestment

The evidence for the USA shows clearly that there is a marked divergence between the pattern of behaviour which promotes the wellbeing of companies and what actually occurs, a pattern likely to be true everywhere. That evidence tends to show that:

- active managers of business portfolios, those who actively acquire or divest, do better in terms of the return on their assets than passive managers
- balanced acquirers/divestors do better than either pure acquirers or pure divestors
- there is a clear preference for acquisition over divestment reflected in actual behaviour
- a vast majority of divestments are reactive rather than proactive; they are a reaction to problems which have already emerged and reached crisis proportions. Many responses are delayed until there has been a significant period of weak performance which has reduced the share price of the company
- incoming CEOs are those most likely to make divestments.

This evidence points to a general tendency for companies to divest too little and too late. This is a major strategic weakness, one which often accounts for a deterioration in performance and ultimate failure. There are a number of reasons for the resulting asymmetry between acquisition and divestment:

- There is a perfectly natural prejudice against the divestment of companies or business units, since this signals at best weakness, at worst a failure on the part of the managers responsible for divestment. There is little incentive for managers to discontinue business models and business activities which have previously brought success.
- It is relatively easy if there is a good free cash flow, generated by the success of other business units, for the existing management to buy support among the key stakeholder groups for existing policies which protect the less efficient business units.

- Internal control systems are often poor and tend to get worse, frequently as a result of complacency.
- A policy of growth and acquisition can hide a multitude of sins, even if the final retribution is only postponed and a final unravelling is far worse than it might have been.

The costs of such behaviour for an enterprise can be significant:

- an excessively stable portfolio, particularly one which includes poor performers, gives the wrong signals to employees, removing the desire to aspire to be the best
- the company can become inflexible and risk-averse, emphasizing the need to protect at all costs what it already has and certainly not to innovate
- the retention of the wrong business units can divert scarce investment funds or entrepreneurial inputs away from new or better performing units, stunting their growth
- the wrong mix of businesses can confuse customers and other stakeholder groups as to the identity of the company and where its strengths lie.

For the business unit, the costs of failing to divest can be significant:

- the unit itself can suffer from a lack of expertise suitable to the stage it has reached in its life cycle
- separation of the unit could have liberated it from 'bureaucratic' control and given it the freedom to grow.

A divestment strategy

In order to make it successful, there should be, as part of good strategy, a proactive divestment programme, which should include the following elements:

1. The employees of the organization should be prepared for such a programme. Its general rationale should be clearly explained as part of that process, just as for scenario building and other important strategic activities.
2. There should also be a forcing mechanism which ensures that the programme is not sidelined and forgotten, for example the stipulation of a periodic and regular review.
3. Suitable candidates for divestment should be identified and the impact on both divestor and divestee analysed. The following issues should be considered:
   - the 'cultural fit' of any business unit with others in the organization
   - market valuations
   - the overall balance of the business portfolio.
   Any other practical issue relating to divestment should be considered.
4. The method of divestment to be pursued must be chosen: should it be spun off to shareholders or sold? The timing adopted in either method is critical.
5. In order to minimize uncertainty, the decision should be communicated to staff as soon as possible.
6. As part of the overall strategy, the divestment should be placed in the context of the creation of new businesses.

Case Study   A merger and a demerger

Recently the strategic ability of BHP's leaders seems to have deserted them. In the late 1980s BHP was almost taken over by Robert Holmes A'Court, with the prospect of being asset stripped, that is, broken up and sold in parts. Later it made investments which resulted in massive losses, such as the A$3.2 billion write-off of the investment in the Magma copper project in the USA, and the investment in a hot briquetted iron (HBI) plant in Western Australia.

Two events occurred in 1995 which were highly sig-nificant for the future strategy of BHP:

1. At the BHP strategy conference in May, the then CEO John Prescott, expressing a widely held view, forecast a poor future later in the 1990s for its main activities, particularly steel. Prescott believed that the six main generators of BHP's profit had peaked, that is, Bass Strait oil, flat-products steel, the North-West Shelf (the only area of likely future growth), coal, iron ore and copper.

Prescott devoted considerable time to thinking about strategy. At that time Prescott flagged the possible demise of BHP, indicating the urgent need for a shrewd diversification. The senior managers at BHP looked at as many as 27 industries or activities, ranging from power, paper, timber to transport, as possible new areas of investment, but mainly at telecommunications.

2. In September Paul Keating, the then Australian prime minister, asked Prescott whether BHP was interested in buying Telstra, the monopoly telecom-munications operator in Australia, at that time still 100% owned by the government. Unknown to the prime minister, Prescott had been working on such a plan for some time, but was opposed by a signifi-cant number of directors of BHP.

Despite the intense review in the second half of 1995, the board made a series of unfortunate decisions, includ-ing the commitment of A$5–6 billion to the two projects indicated above, both located within the range of exist-ing activities. Other decisions included a rejection of the purchase of Telstra and a proposed merging of BHP's steel business with British Steel. At the time senior man-agers even considered and rejected the sale, at peak prices, of its petroleum business. The view of the board was that, in its existing state, BHP was still profitable and that diversification had grave dangers. The disagreement created a situation of strategic disarray, leading to a delay in making the strategic decisions necessary to put BHP in a strong position for the future. The ability to diversify or divest sensibly seemed to desert BHP in the 1990s. In the end Prescott proved more prescient than his board.

The merger

In 2001 BHP decided that it needed to get bigger in order to survive as a resources company. Size would ensure that it was competitive and could attain a stabil-ity untypical of the commodity markets in which it operated. The company embraced the rather unfashion-able view of diversifying in order to manage risk. The aim was to create a company diversified enough for the fluctuation in the earnings of any one business unit to be unable to affect earnings in a significant way. Two decisions were made: to build up the company's resources base and divest its steel manufacturing, a process already started in the previous year. The main driver of this strategy was the new CEO, Paul Anderson.

Billiton, the partner company in the merger, was only formed in 1994 and had seen rapid growth under the guiding hand of Martin Gilbertson, who became CEO of the merged company in 2002. Gilbertson was both chairman and CEO. He controlled the company in a highly centralized manner and was strongly in favour of rapid growth. In the year before the announcement of the merger, Billiton had absorbed Rio Algom, a Cana-dian company, at a cost of US$1.7 billion, increased its stake in the Worsley aluminium oxide refinery, from 30% to 80%, at a cost of US$1.49 billion, and opened the Mozal smelter in Mozambique (85% owned), at a total cost of US$1.2 billion. Billiton was reaching its debt limit. For Billiton the merger offered the ability to remove this constraint and finance further expansion.

The merger with Billiton, a South African resources giant, has created, it is claimed, a A$57 billion resources giant, one of the biggest resources firms in the world. However, because of declining prices on the world's stock markets, the value is only A$39 billion. The company is dual listed on the London and Australian capital markets. The 'Big Australian' is now a world corporation with a listing on the London stock market. Its headquar-ters remains in Australia, one of the conditions on which the government allowed the merger. Rio Tinto is the only other diversified resources company which is in the same league. Anglo American is the third of a trio of large diversified mining companies.

The general view is that the shareholders of Billiton did better out of the merger deal. Theoretically Billiton shareholders own 42% of the merged company. There has been much debate about the price and the relative shares of the two parts of the company. From the time of the announcement of the merger, the share price of the two companies rose, showing strong fund manager and investor approval of the marriage, although the share price of Billiton rose more than that of BHP. The rise in share prices prevented any concerted and effective opposition to the merger from small shareholders and those who wanted, for example, to keep BHP a pure Australian.

At the time of the merger the new company had a transparent five-year plan, consisting of a list of major projects, which was put on the table from the very beginning (Table 11.4).

This comes to a grand total of investment of about US$7–8 billion. Since the initial outline of this particular plan, BHP firstly accelerated its implementation, but then as a result of deteriorating product markets slowed it. Some parts of the plan were and are still more problematic than others. For example, the nickel plans are more uncertain. In the absence of a catastrophe the new company would have enough profit to generate the cash to fund all the ambitions plans, and still look

around for a substantial acquisition, if this is deemed desirable. There has been a major disagreement on the desirability of this.

There are two questions which might be asked.

1. Was it the right strategy to stay in resources?
2. Is Billiton the right partner to give BHP the mass to be successful in the markets?

The rationale announced for the merger was as follows:

- The joint base consisted of a broad range of exceptionally low-cost and long-life operations
- The merger created significant cross-country and cross-commodity diversification
- The merger established a leading world position in a number of different areas – including aluminium, coal, fero-alloys (manganese and chrome), iron ore and titanium minerals
- It established substantial positions in oil, gas, liquefied natural gas, nickel, diamonds and silver
- It increased overall access to capital
- It extended the range of management skills, including marketing and risk management skills, available to both partners
- It offered the prospect of sustained growth through new projects and the expansion of existing ones.

BHP brought to the merger a collection of valuable assets, including the Pilbara iron ore operations, a collection of Queensland coalfields, the Bass Strait oil, North-West Shelf gas, the Ekati diamond field in Canada and the Escondida copper mine in Chile. It has potentially valuable oil leases in the deepwater Gulf of Mexico, leases which are now beginning to bear fruit with a series of successful discoveries.

Billiton has its own range of assets. It is the third largest producer of aluminium in the world. It has a majority interest in the Worsley aluminium oxide plant in Western Australia and aluminium smelters in both South Africa and Mozambique. This will fill an obvious gap in BHP's portfolio of assets. It also owns half of the Richards Bay mineral sands deposit in South Africa, for years a dominant force in the mineral sands industry. Billiton also has significant coal and nickel interests.

One problem which the merger has

Table 11.4 **BHP's planned projects**

Year and project	Value (US$ million)	Location
2001		
Typhoon – oil field (BHP)	250	Gulf of Mexico
South Blackwater – coal (BHP)	139	Queensland
Antamina – copper/zinc mine (Billiton)	1,000	Peru
2002		
Tintaya – copper (BHP)	250	Peru
Escondida Phase 4 – copper (BHP)	600	Chile
San Juan – coal (BHP)	250	New Mexico
2003		
Ohanet – oil and gas (BHP)	450	Algeria
Mining Area C – iron ore (BHP)	200	Western Australia
Mt Arthur North – coal (BHP)	333	NSW
Ravensthorpe/Yabula – nickel (Billiton)	500	Queensland and WA
BBRS/ROD – oil (BHP)	190	Algeria
2004		
CdC – coal mine (Billiton)	150	Colombia
Escondida Norte – (BHP)	600	Chile
North-West Shelf – LNG (BHP)	250	Western Australia
Mozal 2 – expansion (Billiton)	710	Mozambique
2005		
Hillside – expansion (Billiton)	446	South Africa
Spence – copper (Billiton)	809	Chile

Note: A US dollar is worth 50% more than an Australian dollar, and in the past sometimes twice as much.
Source: McCallum, 2001: 56.

created is a greater exposure to areas of the world in which political risk may be a problem. Approximately 23% of the current value of its assets are accounted for by businesses located in Africa and 21% by those in Latin America, very much the result of what Billiton has brought to the merger. It is true that BHP has had its own problems in Papua New Guinea. Generally the market spread for the new company is wide, with 31% of the product selling in East Asia, 28% in Europe, 17% in North America and 12% in Australia.

From the point of view of geography and minerals coverage, there was little overlap between the two companies. Therefore from the perspective of commodities and markets the two companies complement each other. They are natural cooperators rather than competitors. Because of the lack of overlap there are few possibilities for synergies or savings in costs. The rationale for the merger is the classic one of diversification and the management of risk, reinforced by the increase in the size of this major player in the resources area, with all the accompanying gains including the ability to negotiate with governments from a position of strength.

The first year of the merger

The first year of the merger could not have produced a worse environment. The market for resources was at its worst for 20 years. Even the price of oil fell significantly, before it began to rise again under the threat of war and the influence of first the Venezuelan oil strike and later civil unrest in Nigeria. Between them the falls had the potential to reduce BHP Billiton's EBIT (earnings before interest and taxes) by US$1.5 billion. However, the modelling by BHP of the risks of its diverse portfolio of resource assets predicted that in a bad year, even the worst one for 20 years, EBIT would be unlikely to fall by more than US$1 billion. In the words of the current CEO:

'The central tenet of the BHP Billiton business model is that its diversified portfolio of high-quality assets provides more stable cash flows and greater capacity to drive growth than the traditional resource cyclicals.' (Bartolomeusz, 2002: *Business* 3)

In practice EBIT fell only US$440 million to US$4.9 and its operating cash flows actually rose from $3.8 billion to $3.92 billion. This is a remarkably stable result in such a volatile context, one which BHP Billiton does not think will improve dramatically in the short-term. Six quarters in a row BHP generated a cash flow of US$1.2 billion.

This result has allowed BHP Billiton to sustain more than $2.6 billion in capital investment in 2001 and, as planned, US$2.9 in 2002. As we have seen, there is a continuous flow of new projects coming online, particularly and increasingly in the oil and gas area. The company is continuing to pursue an aggressive investment policy. The company even paid down US$500 million of debt, increasing its EBITDA (earnings before interest, taxes, depreciation and amortization) interest coverage from 8.5 to 11 times. Its gearing is at a low 35%. It has an A rating from the two major credit rating agencies.

The anticipated cost savings resulting from the merger are not large. Common purchasing and selling may produce some synergies. In the first year of the merger the figure was US$220 million of savings. However, the figure of A$270 million to be won in 2003 from savings in duplicated overheads and other activities is not large. Over the next three years a saving of US$500 million is anticipated.

One result of the merger has been a clash of cultures. The growth culture of Billiton clashed with the much more conservative policies of BHP with an emphasis on a good rate of return and a desire to improve dividend payouts. Gilberton had plans for acquisition, perhaps Alcoa or Western Mining Company, even Rio Tinto or Anglo American, or a significant player in the oil and gas industry. Gilbertson found himself having to win support from the board in a governance system which gave a much more active role for a separate chairperson and a board with a significant number of independent members. As a result of these differences, Gilbertson resigned in early 2003. The absorption of other managers from Billiton seems to have been achieved much better.

The demerger

BHP, under new leadership, decided to concentrate on its core business of resources, not steel. Steel is also a business which does not quite fit with the range of other activities in which BHP is engaged, which are concentrated on mining and the early processes of metal refining. It is logical to organize a demerger and divest this business.

BHP moved into steel production when it opened its integrated steelworks at Newcastle in 1915, a move which had been planned before World War I, but was accelerated by the onset of war. Other key moves in the history of BHP Steel were the acquisition of the Port Kembla steel works in 1935 and the opening of the Whyalla facility in 1941 and that at Western Port in 1972. Initially steel represented a diversification of activity for BHP, but it became very much a core activity.

The Newcastle works was eventually closed in 1999, after long debate on its continuing viability. By this time such integrated works were having problems competing with the new mini-mills appearing worldwide, including Australia. Such mini-mills use scrap metal. Today there is much more profit in processing steel into the shapes and forms suitable for its main uses, rather than in the basic processes.

The steel industry is a mature industry, slow growing and subject to quite significant cyclical fluctuations. It is not a glamorous industry, one suffering at present from the recession. Substitute materials such as aluminium and plastics have eaten into steel's market. Once an index of the extent of industrialization, steel production today is more an index of a failure to use new materials. Steel still has a significant market in construction, albeit a cyclical one, and automobile manufacture.

There is a worldwide overcapacity in steel production. According to the OECD, this amounts to 12% of annual global capacity, or 850 million surplus tons. Moreover the industry is highly fragmented, with the five biggest producers accounting for just 15% of total world production. In the past there has been a twofold tendency for governments to protect their own steel industries and newly industrializing countries to create their own industry.

Because of the overhang of the surplus and the cyclical nature of demand, prices are volatile. In 2001 profits were low, just about everywhere. In 2002 prices picked up, with demand and the imposition of higher tariffs in the USA. Profits also recovered.

There is much room for consolidation of the industry, even across international boundaries. This has been happening, with the creation of Arcelor, a A$6 billion merger of Arbed of Luxembourg, Usinor of France and Acerdia of Spain, and the A$8.5 billion merger of British Dutch Corus and Brazil's Companhia Siderurgia Nacional, which appears recently to have broken down. There is room for further consolidation, particularly for flat-product manufacture and distribution.

However, BHP Steel is a solid business, generating a good free cash flow. In the 13 months to June 2000 it generated A$658 million (Table 11.5). This represented a return on investment of 10%, which is shy of the BHP target return for all its businesses of 12%. In a good year, it is a solid, but not outstanding performer.

The first step was taken in October 2000, when the A$1.9 billion long steel products business OneSteel was spun off, the smaller part of the steel business, very much focused on processing steel into a form which makes it useable. OneSteel owns the Whyalla steelworks and an electric arc mill at Rooty Hill near Sydney. The spin-off was done on the basis of a one for four share distribution. The start was poorly managed. It has been a disappointing spin-off since the share price has gone down and stayed down.

The plan was to divest the rest of the steel division, a much larger enterprise. The main assets of BHP Steel is the Port Kembla steelworks and the Western Port facility. It owns a steelworks in New Zealand, 50% of an electric arc mill in the USA and factories for coated steel products in Australia and Asia. It is a significant exporter, sending abroad as much as 60% of its output, needing to do this in order to keep the level of capacity utilization high. By international standards it is an efficient unit, in the lowest quartile of costs in the industry. The intention once more was to give ownership of the new company to the shareholders of BHP Billiton, without any cost and without changing the distribution of ownership between the former Billiton and the former BHP.

The spin-off was not accompanied by a capital raising. Each shareholder in BHP Billiton Ltd was to receive one share for every five held. The shareholders in BHP Billiton plc, the other half of the dual listing, did not receive BHP Steel shares but a share allocation. To compensate for the loss of this unit, the shareholders received bonus shares in BHP Billiton, based on the average market price of BHP Steel in the first five days of its listing, an amount which was intended to balance the ownership of the larger company.

The BHP Billiton shareholders received 94% of BHP Steel's shares. The other 6% was offered in a prelisting sales facility to help meet the inevitable institutional requirements for shares. Shareholders could sell their shares into this facility before listing, if they wished. There was an institutional tender and book-bid for stock before listing and the price announced. It was thought likely that foreign institutions would wish to sell, and this was countered as much as possible. Since at a likely price of, say, A$3.59 a share, the capitalization of A$2.8 billion would place the new company in the top 50 of listed Australian companies, funds which tracked the share index would automatically buy them.

As it turned out, the shares were issued at A$2.80, within the predicted price bracket. The price then moved upwards.

Table 11.5 **BHP's recent performance**

	1996/97	1997/98	1998/99	1999/2000 (thirteen months May 30–June 30)
Sales (A$ mill)	5,040	5,232	4,773	5,185
After-tax profit (A$ mill)	214	406	205	320
Total capital (A$ mill)	4,527	4,137	3,753	3,498
Dispatch tonnes (mill)	5,522	5,528	5,586	5,891

Source: Way and McCallum, 2001: 39.

BHP Steel remains closely linked with BHP since it is a major customer, taking 13% of the Pilbara iron ore mined by BHP, and one half of the coal from BHP's Illawara coal operations. There is, however, an advantage for BHP Steel standing on its own, rather than being the poor relation in a family which is reluctant to devote time, effort or resources to this industry.

By mid-2004 BHP Steel must shed its BHP name. At some expense it has to rebrand itself and establish a separate identity. It is highly likely that the industry will see a further process of consolidation, which may even have an international perspective. BHP Steel is open to the possibility of joint ventures, mergers or acquisitions.

There is now a stable and visible steel sector in Australia, in which there are now three pure steel companies: Smorgon floated in February 1999, OneSteel spun off in 2000, and now BHP Steel. Smorgon and OneSteel each have 35% of the steel distribution market, even jointly purchasing, for A$815 million, Email, the third largest steel distributor which they acquired for its metals distribution business. They will divest the Email white goods business at an appropriate time.

The strategy

The strategy adopted by BHP is an interesting one in that it involves the divestment of what was defined as a non-core business, steel, but the simultaneous diversification of its minerals interests, both from the point of view of products and producing locations. It chose to retain its oil and gas interests, an interesting add-on for a resources company, one which helps to safeguard the company from cyclical fluctuations in revenue. There is considerable room for further projects in this area since BHP is far from being one of the larger players in oil and gas.

The new CEO has made great play with the impact of diversity on the cash flow of the company. For the last six quarters since the merger, the cash flow has remained stable at about A$1.2 billion. As some areas have seen decline, others have seen expansion, such as oil. The merger with Billiton was justified by the complementarity of the two companies' resources and by the attainment of a size by the new company which makes the new entity a major player as a resources company, if not the major player at the global level.

The main arm of the strategy of BHP is to concentrate its energies on the resources sector and improve its ability to operate in this area worldwide. It has defined its core competencies as the production and selling of mining products. One core competence has been defined as a knowledge of resources. Billiton complements this competence.

The second arm of the strategy is to hold a diversified portfolio of mining products and sell in a diversified range of markets. The rationale for the merger is the classic one of diversification and the management of risk, reinforced by the increase in the size of this major player in the resources area. The nature of the assets allow the new company to maintain its cash and profit stream in a stable manner, immune to major fluctuations. This is intended to ensure that the company keeps its profits stable, growing at a good rate from year to year. There is still the question of what it should do with its profits. There is room for relatively risk-free expansion.

The strategy which has been developed has the following specific features:

1. It has brought forward two projects – the Mt Arthur North coal project and the expansion of the Mozal aluminium project.
2. It has designated iron ore and nickel as areas of expansion.
3. In the style of Jack Welch, it set the target of making all the businesses number one or number two in the world.
4. It stressed the importance of an orientation to customers. As the charter of the new company, issued on July 2, 2001, said: 'its [BHP Billiton's] purpose is to create value through the discovery, development and conversion of natural resources, and the provision of innovative customer and market-focused solutions.' Some restructuring has moved the company in the direction of a customer–group principle.
5. To assist the fusion of what might be the two different cultures, reflecting the South African and Australian origins of the companies, there was to be a significant intra-company transfer of staff.
6. Small business units which generated little revenue or profit but which absorbed significant managerial resources were to be sold off.

One possible problem which the merger has created is a greater exposure to areas of the world in which political risk may be a problem. The focus on political risk has already pointed out the dangers of exposure to a sudden change of policy on the part of host governments in Africa, including the South African government. Fortunately BHP Billiton's interests in South Africa are already at a mature stage, with expansion having already occurred. There is little immediate threat to the company. It is also aware of the AIDS threat, having tested all its workers. It sees both problems as manageable.

Case Study Questions

1. What should have been the strategy of BHP in the mid-1990s? How did the delay in making a new strategy affect the company?
2. What are the advantages and disadvantages of the merger between BHP and Billiton?
3. How far does the BHP Billiton merger show that one way of effectively managing risk is to diversify? Is this a good strategy?
4. Was it a wise decision for BHP to divest the steel division? What are the benefits and the disadvantages for BHP Billiton and BHP Steel?
5. How should BHP use its huge profits? In what way does their existence influence the strategy of BHP Billiton?

Reading

Bartholomeusz, S., 'BHP Billiton passes stress test of the worst trading year in 20', *The Age*, August 8, 2002, Business 3.

Hitt, M., Ireland, R. and Hoskisson, R., 'BHP Billiton: a resources giant is created', *Strategic Management: Competitiveness and Globalisation*, Pacific Rim Edition, 2002: 259–63.

Maiden, M., 'Now is a Goodyear for BHP', *The Age*, April 12, 2003.

McCallum, J., 'BHP Billiton's double act', *Business Review Weekly*, April 20, 2001: 56–9.

McCallum, J., 'BHP Billiton straight down to business', *Business Review Weekly*, July 20, 2001: 32–5.

McColl, G., 'Steel stocks command new investor strength', *Business Review Weekly*, July 25–31, 2002: 42.

Rennie, P., 'BHP risks floating into indifference', *Business Review Weekly*, vol. 24, no. 18, 2002: 38.

Ries, I., 'Dust settles but the hard yards lie ahead', *Australian Financial Review*, May 19–20, 2001: 13.

Sykes, T., 'A deal short on great synergies', *Australian Financial Review*, March 20, 2001: 14.

Way, N. and McCallum, J., 'BHP without steel is a political bomb', *Business Review Weekly*, March 30, 2001: 38–9.

Key strategic lessons

- The desire for maximum size, and therefore often for rapid growth, should not be taken for granted. The steady increase in the size of enterprises and the rapid turnover in the composition of the largest are associated with significant advantages and serious disadvantages.

- Advantages can include economies of scale, reduction of transaction costs, increased capacity to access outside resources such as capital, gaining political 'clout', reinforcing competitive advantage and developing an ability to negotiate from a position of strength.

- Disadvantages can include diseconomies of scale, inappropriate structure and 'bureaucratization', such as slow responsiveness to change, reluctance to innovate or coordination and communication problems.

- Any act of integration, whether at vertical or horizontal levels, must be justified by significant additional profit from the joining of the two units and by a market failure, preventing the generation and sharing of the same benefits through normal market operation.

- Growth often occurs by an addition to the portfolio of new business units. A successful enterprise needs to build a balanced portfolio of businesses at different points in the life cycle of the industries in which it operates.

- Optimum size can be attained through organic growth or acquisitions and mergers. The latter approach is more rapid.

- Many acquisitions fail to deliver the gains promised because of inadequate preparation, ignorance about the enterprise, too high a price, opposition from incumbent managers, poor restructuring, cultural differences or the acquisition of new businesses outside the core area of activity of the acquirer.

- There is a tendency to retain existing businesses and continue to acquire because success breeds complacency and a neglect of innovation. Divestment is usually viewed as an admission of failure. Acquisition promotes the interests of the senior managers by increasing their status, power and income and makes the massaging of key performance indicators such as profit growth easier.

- An appropriate organizational design (discussed in the next chapter) can reduce the negative impact of size along with the formation of strategic alliances, networking and clustering and explicit focusing.

- There should be a deliberate strategy of divestment, including policies of outsourcing and downscoping, which counter the tendency towards growth for its own sake.

Applying the lessons

1 Define the following terms: outsourcing, downscoping, vertical integration, horizontal integration, network, strategic alliance, merger, demerger, divestment and a portfolio of business units.

2 What are the main indicators of the size of an enterprise? What does each of them tell us about the company? Which is the most informative and why?

Repeat the same exercise using the indicators of growth.

3 Take the following industries, estimate the size of the top three global players in that industry and list the factors which influence the average size of the enterprises within that industry.

Automobile
Pharmaceutical
Wine
Airline
Computer
Telecommunications
Clothing
Furniture manufacture and retailing
Banking
Insurance

4 Take the largest enterprises in the industries above and place them on the following diagram:

Products and markets
(Degree of horizontal integration)

Activities in value chain
(Degree of vertical integration)

5 Choose an example of a major acquisition which has occurred more than two years ago, but less than five. Consider the stated reasons for the acquisition. Review the behaviour of the share prices. Consider what you think are likely to be the most important factors determining whether there has been, and will continue to be, a net advantage or disadvantage.

6 Is it true that divestment is less likely to occur than acquisition? Why might this be the case? Consider the results of question 4 and indicate what it tells you about the reluctance to divest.

Strategic project

The project is intended to explore the way in which a network or cluster makes possible the avoidance of the disadvantages of size while allowing the exploitation of any advantages. There are a number of steps in the project.

1 Choose an industry in which networks or clusters have been important in generating competitive advantage. What are the likely reasons for the emergence of networks in this sector of the economy? Are these networks likely to persist in the future?

2 Select a specific network of related organizations which has been successful and map out in detail the

links between the different members of the network. Is there a typical structure to such networks?

3 Compare the network or cluster with a 'large' enterprise operating in the same industry, preferably where the two are competing directly. Pay particular attention to any significant differences in cost or product quality.

4 Compare the advantages and disadvantages of each competitor at different moments in time. Which tends to win out in the dynamic context? Which has proved more competitive, better able to generate innovative activity?

Exploring further

There is almost no literature on optimum size or optimum growth as such. There is however a wealth of comment on issues such as diversification, horizontal and vertical integration and acquisitions and mergers, all relevant to the issue of desirable size.

The classic 1959 text by Edith Penrose is a good start for exploration of the issue. There is a piece by Tom Peters (1993: 7–29) which raises some of the relevant issues. Of more indirect relevance but providing the rationale for the fashion of outscoping is Biggadike, 1979: 103–11. As a counter to this there is Lauenstein, 1985: 49–55.

Why do enterprises exist in the first place? Why does the economy not consist of a network of individual contractors? This is a question raised by Coase in his 1937 article and followed up much later by Williamson, 1975 and 1985. Since the appearance of the latter, there has been a veritable explosion in publications on the topic, too many to refer to here. However, the relevance to strategy and structure is explored in Jones and Hill, 1988: 159–71 and 1995: 119–31.

An introductory article on vertical integration is Harrigan, 1983: 3–7. This can be followed up with 1984: 638–52 and 1985a: 397–425. If your taste is for an extended treatment see 1985b. Two articles which further develop the arguments for and against vertical integration from another perspective are Stachey and White, 1993: 71–93 and Venkatesan, 1992: 98–107.

There is quite a large literature on mergers and acquisitions, both a theoretical one on how to plan for a successful acquisition and an empirical one considering their impact on performance. On planning acquisitions there is an extended treatment in Haspeslagh and Jemison, 1991, and a rather shorter one in Anslinger and Copeland, 1996: 126–35. The problems of a merger which has gone wrong are confronted in Marks and Mirvis, 1992: 18–33. On the empirical side see Brush, 1996: 1–24.

An introduction to the area of strategic alliances and networking is Henderson, 1990: 7–18. Simulating a network internally is discussed in Hannan, 1969: 55–66.

12 Integrating the strategists

I know of textile units in the UK which source fabrics from India, cut them in the UK, send them to Africa for stitching, source laces from the Middle East, convert them to garments in Latin America and sell in the US and Europe to high end stores and retail chains.
This requires management of a different kind in global sourcing of material and marketing, on-line, real time supply chain systems and virtual manufacturing discipline and organizational commitment to resources and talent. (MUKESH AMBANI *in a speech to the 7th International and 58th All India Textile Conference*)

Learning objectives

After reading this chapter you will be able to:

- understand who are principals and who are agents in the making of strategy and how the interests of the two diverge

- explore the general nature of the mutual interaction between principals and agents

- understand how strategy influences the design of an organization's structure

- see how monitoring, the choice of appropriate incentive structures and the role of corporate or organizational culture are useful mechanisms for making compatible the interests of principals and agents

- evaluate the role of external discipline in solving the problem of integration, notably the threat of takeovers by other players

Key strategic challenge

How can I build a strategic team which is capable of both formulating and implementing a common strategy?

Strategic dangers

That the managers and workers at different levels of an organization, the different stakeholder groups and the various divisions and departments will have divergent interests and different objectives which fragment their contributions to strategy formulation and implementation and create an organization which is fractured rather than integrated.

Case Study Scenario   The house of Gucci

'Gucci is like a Ferrari that we are driving like a Cinquecento.'

Maurizio Gucci (cited in Forden, 2000: 142)

'What if things had turned out differently? If the Gucci family had been more united, would Gucci today be a quiet, predictable family firm happily churning out plastic-coated GG shopping bags with the red and green stripe or brown, bamboo-handled handbags? If Maurizio Gucci had achieved his vision – already radically different from that of his relatives – would Gucci be more like Hermes, a safe, respectable luxury firm with beautiful products and no fireworks?'

Forden, 2000: 330–1

Gucci is one of a number of Italian companies which have developed a name for style and fashion; it could be said to have been the pioneer of this kind of company. Throughout its recent history, it has developed and exploited a powerful brand name. The Gucci name became the company's most obvious and most valuable asset, one which it took some time for those in control to understand and cherish. Although the brand name has been one of the company's main assets, as with other brand names it has fallen on hard times, being for a period overused and cheapened, notably in the early 1990s, when a licence to use the name was granted to all and sundry provided they paid. The overuse led to the attachment of the Gucci name to a widening range of products and the granting of the licence to use the name to a expanding group of other organizations, over which the company had little control. Quality is one victim of such a strategy. In the course of its history, Gucci has taken full advantage of the desire to purchase aspirational goods, referred to in Chapter 10 as the 'democratization of luxury'.

The Gucci company was created in 1921 in Florence by Guccio Gucci as a sole proprietorship, initially selling high-quality leather goods which he bought from Tuscan manufacturers, but later establishing his own workshops which made the goods themselves. The emphasis was on the high quality of work by the fine craftsmen employed by the company and the special nature of the service provided to customers. The firm produced and sold bags of delicate kidskin and genuine chamois, telescope purses with gussets on the sides and suitcases inspired by the Gladstone bags which Guccio had seen when he was employed in his early career at the Savoy in London. Other products were linked to a similar kind of luxury market, exotic items such as car robe carriers, shoe boxes and linen carriers. The market was a relatively high income one, which the Gucci firm excelled at supplying. The company had a flair for pleasing the rich and powerful. The designs for Gucci products came from within the company, from family members and the ideas of workers. The famous bamboo-handled bag and the brindle pigskin originated this way. Aldo, Guccio's eldest son, had a particular talent for marketing. He emphasized quality and in order to enhance the aura surrounding the family enterprise created the family myth of the long line of noble saddle makers. Design played to and emphasized the link with stables and horses and the pursuits of the aristocracy.

The whole family became involved in working for the rapidly expanding enterprise; from the beginning it was very much a family business. The key figure after Guccio was Aldo who expanded the company within Italy beyond Florence, into other European countries and later into the USA. Guccio's youngest son Rodolfo was for a period a well-known actor in silent films, only returning to the family business when his career in the cinema came to an end. Rodolfo's son Maurizio represented the third generation controlling the family business. By that stage contrasting views of how the company should be led had resulted in conflict, often spilling over into courts cases.

Instability of strategic objectives is often the result of a number of key strategists pulling in different directions. This instability is typical of family enterprises like Gucci. It is often the reason why in the end family control is lost. The control of the founding figure disappears and an increasing number of family members all have their view on how the company should be managed. The main focus of interest in this case study is the transition from a family company firmly under the control of the Gucci family to a public company, greatly expanded by acquisition but no longer run or owned by the Gucci family. This movement is typical of many such enterprises and represents a coming of age. In retrospect the movement at each step looks avoidable. In Gucci's case the loss of control followed from a mix of opportunities and threats, some of which resulted from its nature as a family firm:

- divisions within the litigious and quarrelsome Gucci family itself
- the inevitable failure of family skills and talents to match the full range of professional management skills required by a large and growing enterprise
- the obvious interest of outsiders with money to invest in a family company with such a name.

The case study deals with the issue of how to combine creativity, in which the Gucci family excelled, both understanding the potential of aspirational and luxury demand and designing and marketing new products, with the administrative skills necessary to control costs, raise capital and manage the brand name, in which it did not excel and needed help. The blending of creative and managerial talents is a requirement for success in companies like Gucci. Tom Ford and Domenico de Sole managed this with great flair, creating a partnership which stabilized the company and promoted its growth. The experience of Gucci highlights the problems of integration which come with growth.

There is never only one strategist within an enterprise; even the founder entrepreneur needs a supporting team. Nor is an enterprise a monolithic entity with a uniform set of attitudes and interests held by its members; it is not even desirable to have such uniformity. An implicit assumption of much analysis is that cooperation reigns within an enterprise and competition outside. In reality, there is significant competition within the enterprise, between individual members of staff and different units, as this chapter will show, and significant cooperation outside, alliances between different organizations and enterprises, as the next chapter will also show.

Any organization has a formal structure with a number of different levels and a varying number of positions at each level. The bigger the organization, the greater tends to be the number of hierarchical layers. The organization has specialist divisions and units. The team of people who formulate and implement strategy must be organized effectively in order to ensure that these different levels and divisions pull together. The nature of that organization is an important input into strategy making.

Integrating structures

Typically, any economy, including market economies, consists of enterprises of varying size with a hierarchical organization. Some multinational enterprises are very large indeed, others much smaller. Even smaller organizations, once they move beyond the stage at which an owner and one or two linked people run the enterprise, have a hierarchical structure. Within such organizations functional specialization becomes the norm. The organization is departmentalized by such specialist functions. Within the larger organizations there are various levels of authority as well as various specialized functional departments and later even separate business units. There is 'line and staff' as the traditional description has it, neatly summarizing the existence of both hierarchy and specialization.

There are increasing numbers of employees at lower and lower levels of the organization. Sometimes the number of layers of control reaches double figures. The need for different levels follows from the assumption that there are strict limits on the span of control which can be exercised by any one individual manager, on how may subordinates that one person can supervise. This may vary with the nature of the industry and even more importantly with the nature of the communications technology. There is a never-ending attempt to limit the number of such layers.

An increasing number of transactions are not market transactions, but intra-enterprise transactions. The bigger the enterprise, the greater the number of transactions, a good proportion of them often international transactions. This process of internalization is unavoidable and in most cases highly desirable. As the last chapter has shown, the rationale for such a system is that with such an organizational structure transaction costs are lower than they would be under alternative organizational systems. Hierarchy persists because such bureaucratic systems are usually more efficient than any alternative, including, for example, a dense network of contractual relations between individuals.

In theory these organizations could act like large holding companies, comprising a mix of separate business units which are independent profit centres and behave like small, independent organizations. The number of these independent units might be very large indeed. It is possible to treat different functional units in the same way. The transactions occurring between the units within the enterprise could simulate the nature of market transactions.

There is a need for integration of the enterprise, a need which is partly met by action coming from the top levels of management within the enterprise. The role of leadership is partly to help bind together these large organizations.

The principal/ agent relationship

The relationship between the different levels may be a supervisor–subordinate one – a relationship in which authority is clearly defined, but it is also a principal/agent relationship. The latter relationship captures better the essential nature of the organization. The principal/agent relationship is one which is common to all hierarchical organizations, of whatever kind, as well as to a host of other relationships.

Put in its simplest form, the principal hires the agent to carry out a defined job. This is not necessarily a relationship in which one has greater authority than the other, although this might be the case. An agency relationship is one in which one or more people, or some entity such as an enterprise, contracts with another individual, or entity, to act in their interest as their agent Such a contract involves a continuing relationship of significant duration, not a single transaction. It is the continuity of the relationship which distinguishes the relationship from a market relationship, which is assumed to be capable of being renegotiated on a one-off basis. Each transaction is a new one. However, the principal/agent relationship includes market relationships as a special case of this broader relationship.

Although the agent is obliged by contract to act in the interests of the principal, whether he or she actually does so is another matter. The principal might be the board of directors who appoint the senior management of a company or they might be the immediate boss of workers or junior managers. As officers of the enterprise, one level of supervisors or managers can be seen as acting in a principal role relative to the level below, although the contract of both is with the enterprise as a whole. The principal/agent relationship includes not only the superior/subordinate relationships within the enterprise but relationships outside with customers and suppliers, usually but not always market relationships.

The interaction between principal and agent may be mutually beneficial – it is intended to be – but is not necessarily so. It is mutually beneficial if the interests of the two are compatible or if the agent is constrained in some way to mould his or her interests to those of the principal. The interests of the two may differ significantly. They both have a personal interest which may create a situation which amounts to a zero-sum game, or is perceived as such by both. The gain of one is at the cost of the other. Such situations do not exhaust the nature of the relationship because there are aspects which are non-zero sum, that is, both can desire and actually extract some gain from the relationship.

The agent almost inevitably has a much more detailed knowledge relating to the carrying out of his or her role and the conduct of the job. He or she knows much better than the principal the problems and the opportunities which show themselves in his or her own limited domain. There is a pronounced information asymmetry. There may be an asymmetry of commitment. If there is a serious divergence of interest, the asymmetry of information often gives a significant advantage to the agent in hiding what he or she is doing and why. He or she has the ability to pursue his or her own interests rather than those of the principal, and hide the fact that this is what is being done. This may involve shirking, stealing, deliberate sabotage or simply the pursuit of personal advantage over and above the realization of enterprise objectives.

The influence of the principal/agent relationship on strategy

Whatever the enterprise's strategy, its implementation depends on the actions of many agents who act in the way described above. The classic divergence is between the interests of the owner and the manager. The debate over the motivation of managers has pointed out the clash between the desire of owners to make a profit and that of mangers to expand the organization. Whoever the agents are, they need to be motivated to achieve the objectives of the principal. This is often seen as the problem of an appropriate governance system, but in reality it is a much broader problem than that which is commonly understood under the label of proper governance, a problem dealt with later in this chapter.

As regards strategy, it might be postulated that those who formulate strategy are the principals and those who implement that strategy the agents. This is a reasonable first assumption but an oversimplification. The situation is much more complex. The nature of a strategy and the strategy-making process determines exactly who are principals and who are agents. Even if it were argued that all the employees had a hand in the formulation of strategy, it is true that the domain of strategy making for those at the top encompasses all the strategic domains of those below, but the reverse is not true. Since this corresponds with the allocation of tasks and the hierarchical relationships of authority within the organization, it is still reasonable to talk of principals and agents. Strategists actually fill multiple roles, most managers being both principals and agents insofar as they are both supervised and supervisors.

Founder enterprises

Many new enterprises which have grown quickly are associated with a founder who, during the period of success and rapid growth, often combines ownership and control, even for a period after the company is publicly floated. The rapid growth of founder enterprises reflects the adoption of a successful strategy closely associated with one person, or at least a small team of people closely linked to the founder, which carries the enterprise through its early years. The initial team imparts a momentum which can last for a number of years, but not for ever. Every new enterprise eventually reaches what has been called an inflection point, that is, a point at which it needs to rethink its business model and change its strategy.

The strategy of such a company initially exploits a competitive advantage which is new and cannot for a number of reasons be easily or quickly imitated. The competitive advantage reflects the creativity of the founder, his or her ability to read a changing environment and identify an opportunity with enormous potential. The trick is then to go on to defend that competitive advantage, sometimes through the use of the law in an era dominated by a tendency to broaden the protection of intellectual property rights.

During this period of early growth, the enterprise is structured in a way which allows the founder to implement the strategy. There tends to be more central control than is typical of organizations of similar size. Problems are dealt with as they arise by action taken at the centre. Often the strategy being pursued is not fully formulated and exists rather in the mind of the founder. It is formulated at the same time as it is implemented. In this way there is no principal/agent challenge, no divorce of interest between owner and senior manager. The situation looks very much like the classical view of strategy (as described in Chapter 1), something handed down from on high and implemented by those who are appointed to do just that. Its success and robustness depends on the commitment, energy and health of the founder. It also depends on the capacity of the founder to adjust as the company grows larger and the environment surrounding it changes. Two issues arise:

1. how to sustain the growth beyond the period of birth and infancy into the period of adulthood
2. how to organize the company to achieve this.

Strategy in Action   Microsoft, a giant comes of age

'The scale of Microsoft and the scope of his [Gates'] responsibilities had become more than one person could handle. A new division of labor was required.'
Steve Bullmer, the current CEO of Microsoft

Even after the high-tech collapse of 2000–01, Microsoft is one of the largest companies in the world. Within a period of 24 years, Microsoft had grown from a small bit player to its present size. It is a company with extensive global interests, subsidiaries in 74 countries and a product portfolio of 227 products and services. Its annual revenue is still in excess of US$28 billion, with a profit in the financial year 2000–01 of nearly US$9 billion. It employs 50,000 people. It has access to US$39 billion in cash, which can be used for acquisition or internal growth. Few companies have sustained the rate of growth of Microsoft over such a long period, 29% in 1999 alone. The company is by any indicator a giant.

However, more recently the growth rate has declined, coming down to 10% in 2001, and the stock value has halved between 1999 and 2002. The company is in a transition, partly induced by a changing context and partly by its own previous growth. It is a giant which has dominated one era. Can it continue to do so?

For most of this period, Bill Gates has been almost synonymous with Microsoft. He had the creativity and the entrepreneurial ability to see the importance of creating computer software systems and software applications in the new world of the communications/information revolution. The company was not necessarily the inventor, rather more the innovator or exploiter of certain key systems.

Microsoft has been driven largely by a rapidly changing technology and structured to reflect the nature of the new technology. There were originally two divisions in Microsoft. One focused on Windows applications software such as Microsoft Word, Excel and

PowerPoint and associated software products. The other focused on operating systems, ranging from the Windows range, culminating in Windows NT and including the stripped-down Win CE for hand-held consumer devices.

There is a cost to the 'entrepreneurial' pattern of development usually associated with a strong degree of centralized control. Sometimes the founder becomes overwhelmed by the sheer pressure of decision making. The division heads had to go to either Gates or Bullmer before any significant decision of any size was made. This link was bound to become a bottleneck as the company grew in size. Inevitably the system became bureaucratic.

The Windows operating system has given Microsoft a monopoly at a key point in the operation of the PC, especially on the Internet, almost a licence to print money, but it has caused Microsoft immense problems with government authorities who saw this as a misuse of market power. Microsoft sought to use the monopoly to sell other software products to a captive market. Microsoft has had to fight very hard to retain this monopoly. It has used the monopoly during the recession to increase fees for the use of its systems and improve its profitability when that of others has declined badly.

As a result of these difficulties, in 2001 Bill Gates decided to step down as CEO to become the chief software architect with a responsibility to drive forward the technology. Steve Bullmer, a colleague for the whole early period of growth of the company, took over as CEO. There were two motives for this change:

1. the need to maintain creativity in the technological area
2. the need to create a different type of enterprise, one with a more efficient structure.

Because he has been so closely associated with Gates in the development of the company, Bullmer has shared the same culture of centralized control. The break with the past is not as decisive as it might appear at first glance. It is an interesting problem whether Bullmer can break out of the old culture and create a new one.

What are the main difficulties which Bullmer has to confront? There are three internal challenges and one which is associated with the high-tech crash:

1. Managerial control was overcentralized, with a feeling of disempowerment on the part of most managers. This resulted in slower decision making since it became increasingly difficult for senior management to cope with the immense amount of detail; illustrated by the failure of Microsoft in the 1990s to see the rise of the Internet and the Java program. Also, frustrated staff began to leave, often the very people whom the company needed in order to continue successful creativity.
2. The company was not focused on its customers. It acquired a reputation for arrogance, for thinking that it knew better than its customers what they wanted. The company needed to refocus on customer wants.
3. Microsoft ran into a deluge of law suits and bad publicity, which diverted attention from the main game and began to wear down those at the top. The disgruntled included not only the government, but its own employees, its customers and its competitors. Clearly Microsoft had deliberately used its muscle to stop other enterprises using different products or failing to promote Microsoft's. In 1999 the government took action, which could easily have led to the break-up of Microsoft, but in the settlement of 2002 resulted in nothing more than a hard rap over the knuckles.
4. As PC sales contracted, Microsoft's two major products, the Windows operating system and the office suite of applications, saw declining demand. Microsoft needed successful new products to sustain further rapid expansion. It committed significant resources to producing new products such as the games console and research into the new generation of software.

Family firms   In some parts of the world family companies are still important. Even in developed economies, there is a problem of succession when a founder passes a company on to his or her children. The succession problem highlights the inflection point if it occurs more or less simultaneously with a change of structure and strategy. Family firms experience the same problems as all enterprises, but one magnified by the need to identify a successor.

Focus on Practice
The family
business in Asia

In Asia the corporate structure in common use has been largely one which reflects the overseas Chinese model. The typical company has been patriarchal and family-controlled. Depending on the ability of the controlling member, the family enterprise has often been quick to respond to opportunity, even entrepreneurial in its approach. It has seized opportunity wherever it has showed itself, in property, shipping or any other area, which partly explains the conglomerate nature of its activities. It almost looks as though the different businesses have been put together by chance. Some of these family companies have become very large. They are centrally organized with autocratic leadership and little separation between owners and management. Often appointments within these companies are made on the basis of family connections or circles of friends.

There are numerous examples in Asia of large conglomerates which are the result of this kind of process, and which comprise within them a wide range of activities, sometimes banking or financial services, trading and a number of disparate manufacturing or service activities. The family link may become weak, but the structure does not change. The businesses may have more of a logic about them. The *keiretsu* of Japan fit the pattern, as do the *chaebol* of Korea. These are often vast organizations held together by cross-shareholdings, although the level and importance of these have probably been exaggerated. Where they exist, they have insulated the organizations from competition within the domestic market and the effects of general fluctuations in the economy.

From his study, in 1997, Dumaine estimated that the top five business families in an arc of nine countries from India to South Korea controlled 77 companies, with sales of at least $1 billion each, generating anything from 6% to 60% of a nation's GNP. Although the role of family firms has diminished, it is still there and still important.

However, the circumstances of regulated and protected markets which encouraged the development of family conglomerates has been changing, and changing everywhere. For example, the regulatory system in India is known as the 'licence raj', wherein, within a broad planning system, production licences were dispensed to favoured businesses, with a use of patronage which could be regarded as corrupt. Now there is much more competition from outside and much less regulation inside. Existing companies have to adapt to a new deregulated and competitive environment or go out of business.

In the words of Alex Liu, vice-president of AT Kearney: 'The top family companies are trying to create a kind of hybrid organization that combines the best managerial aspects of the East with those of the West' (Dumaine, 1997: 42). There is no desire to drop completely the strengths of the family system, but there is every desire to imitate the best practices of the West and market economies.

The strengths of the Asian model are, at its best, an emphasis on entrepreneurial behaviour, access to strong contact networks and sources of capital, a tendency to shrewd commercial dealing and a corporate culture which stresses a sense of family among employees. The Western strengths would include the use of formal strategy making itself, transparent and consistent accounting, a focus on innovation and an orientation to customer service and product quality. Rather than offering a different model of enterprise structure, Asian companies could be regarded as simply at an

▶

Focus on Practice
cont'd

earlier stage of development compared with their Western counterparts. There are three issues which must be raised:

1. The system of governance, how family members can be held responsible for the consequences of their actions, if they can.
2. The nature of leadership and the rules for the transition from one kind of leader to another, in particular a move from traditional autocratic leadership to institutional or even charismatic leadership. Even the succession to the leadership role could be regarded as a matter of governance.
3. The control of the potential abuse of power and influence, notably in taking measures to protect the company from cronyism.

There are a number of changes which can be observed in many Asian and Indian companies. These occur everywhere but at a different pace and include:

- The use of professional managers rather than family members
- A simplification of ownership
- An emphasis on functional expertise
- The need to take a hard look at the portfolio of businesses and focus on those which use core competencies
- The need to avoid conflicts of interest arising from family position.

These changes reflect the influence of large multinationals on Asian practice. The main differences between old and new management structures are shown in Table 12.1.

It is still the case that 38 of India's top 100 businesses, by market capitalization, are family-owned, as against 51 in 1986. Some clearly cannot adjust. Others can adjust, partly because it is a matter of survival. The family enterprises account for 28% of sales by the top 100 companies. How far is the problem of transition a general one, or one specific to Asia and the family firm?

Table 12.1 'Old' versus 'new' management strategies in Asian family firms

Old	New
Conglomerate	Intense focus on one's core competency
Autocratic and centralized leadership, with family members occupying all or many key positions	More use of professional managers
Informal structures	More formal organizational processes such as training and strategy making
Large networks of personal contacts	Harnessing info-tech to integrate the organization and improve the business
Willingness to secure the deal without detailed study	Willingness to secure a deal only after detailed study

The behaviour of principals and agents

Who are the principals in a corporation? The simple answer is everyone who is not at the bottom level of the organization, that is, anyone who supervises another employee. However, unless you are the CEO, every principal is also an agent; each is supervised by another. Even the CEO is an agent of the board of directors. The effectiveness of an organization depends on the way in which each employee performs both tasks, those of principal and those of agent, how all the principals interact with all the agents. Much of this interaction is of an informal rather than a formal nature, but both types of interaction must be considered. The example of Semco illustrates the informal.

Strategy in Action   Semco and Ricardo Semler – democracy as a management strategy

'The purpose of work is not to make money. The purpose of work is to make the workers, whether working stiffs or top executives, feel good about life.'

'People will perform at their potential only when they know almost everyone around them, which is generally when there are no more than 150 people.'

Ricardo Semler (quoted in Caulkin, 2003)

In 1982, at the age of 24, Richard Semler took over from his father the Brazilian company Semler, later to become known as Semco SA. At that time the company was a typical Latin American enterprise – paternalistic, hierarchical, pyramidal, run by an autocratic leader and having a rule for every contingency. Semler had graduated with an MBA from Harvard Business School at the unusually early age of 20. Despite a difficult business environment in Brazil, he guided the company from a turnover of about US$4 million to one of US$160 million, achieving a growth rate of 30–40% in many years. It is now a conglomerate with a diverse business portfolio, from machinery to information technology, property to professional services, employing 3,000 workers. He managed to do this with an unusual business model which has attracted much attention, partly through Semler's own literary efforts (1993, 2003).

It is what Semco lacks that has drawn so much attention. It lacks a formal organizational structure, even a human resources department and a headquarters. After much trial and error with a matrix organization and autonomous business units, Semler hit on the lattice organization as the answer to the organizational problem of motivating staff. The lattice consisted of self-managed groups of 6–10 manufacturing employees who were placed in charge of all aspects of production. Semler believes that everyone in the right context is capable of excel-

lence. This has led to a form of management or, rather, entrepreneurial democracy, which stresses:

- the maximum employee participation in decision making of every kind
- profit sharing, which has risen as high as 39% of existing profits, but is normally 25%
- the free flow of information, including all financial data as well as salaries.

Where once there were twelve layers of bureaucracy, now there are only three, usually described as 'concentric circles', rather than layers, of management: an inner circle of counsellors, a second circle of 7–10 leaders of Semco divisions, known as partners, and the rest, called associates. Real decision-making power lies as much with the last as with the other two.

The associates can determine everything, should they so choose, including who is employed at all levels, what is produced and the allocation of resources for this purpose. The system breeds conflict, real dissent, argument and diversity. 'Trust' and 'delegation', even empowerment, are made a reality. The corollary of such democracy and empowerment, the only real rules existing at Semco, is peer pressure and self-discipline. Everyone is accountable in terms of the bottom line. A failure to perform can result in a loss of job, and quickly. As far as anything can, peer group pressure and the self-discipline of full accountability ensure good performance.

There is a distinctive corporate culture, where managers become facilitators, providing workers with the tools, mainly information, to make informed decisions. Semco has no mission statement, no rule book and no written policies. Policies are never devised looking more than six months ahead. Innovation and entry into new areas are pioneered by small satellite organizations, the first of which was spun off and called the Nucleus of Technological Innovation (NTI) team. This initial experiment, using a small group of workers brought up in the Semco culture, was such a success that it was expanded. There are now many such teams generating something like two-thirds of the new products and employing about the same proportion of staff. Their aim was to invent and reinvent new products, refine marketing strategies, expose production inefficiencies and dream up new lines of business. The teams were fully account-able, being regularly appraised every six months, and fully responsible, receiving rewards based on performance. Poor performance leads to extinction of the team.

Most functional areas were either outsourced or moved to satellite companies. The centre retained only top management, applications, engineering, some R&D and a few other high-tech, capital-intensive functions considered to be among Semco's core competencies.

Semco's attitude to strategic planning is that it inhibits spontaneity and creativity. The external environment, with its opportunities and threats, makes too much planning a danger. In practice there is a lot of strategy making going on, all the time, at countless meetings, but it is not being made by Semler himself. The staff makes strategy. In the words of Semler: 'you've got to hope that the system itself and people's interest in self-preservation and self-motivation will take you to a place that's approx-imately what you'd like to have. I haven't suggested anything in a long time.' In the words of one observer, 'The company recently held a party to com-memorate the tenth anniversary of the last time he made any decision at all' (Caulkin, 2003: 13). As the system has evolved, it has, perhaps surprisingly, put a great emphasis on profit performance. So far the system has worked well; productivity and profit have risen dramatically and there is a long waiting list of people wishing to work for Semco. How long can it continue to work so well?

Supervision

The easiest method of ensuring the harmonization of interests is through continu-ous direct supervision of staff, that is, of the agent by the principal, supervision which ensures that the staff are always performing their jobs in the expected manner. Continuous supervision is not possible or desirable, since it removes all dis-cretion from the exercise of the agent's functions. Most supervision must be in some sense indirect, not requiring the physical presence of the supervisor.

Any supervision requires a proper job description and a definition of procedures, without which it would not be possible to define the role and supervise in an effective way. Even with the most detailed specification of tasks, no one person can supervise all the staff in an organization, even indirectly and only occasionally directly. Obvi-ously, the more staff one individual supervises, the less comprehensive the control and the less able the supervisor to know exactly what the agent is doing. There is a limit to the number of staff any one staff member can supervise without losing control. The exact number will reflect the degree of control expected and the way in which it is exercised. Where control is direct and detailed, it is impossible to supervise more than a dozen people effectively. Where the control is indirect and general, it is possible to supervise many more but practical problems begin to emerge, particularly where there is a divergence of interests.

Equally, the more levels of authority there are in an organization, the less likely it is that the supervisors at the bottom will understand and share the objectives of the CEO and senior management at the top. The distance between the two levels becomes too great. As in the game of Chinese whispers, the message may look very different when it has passed through many levels. Even direct contact, for example the memos sent to all staff by successive CEOs in Microsoft, bypassing the usual channels of communication, can lead to misunderstanding, if the immediate context of the agents is providing contradictory signals in the interpretation of these memos. It is a clear contradiction to encourage decentralization by sending out memos from the centre.

The degree of supervision varies from supervisor to supervisor, partly reflecting personality. Authority does not follow only from position. A simple diagram of an organization does not show the full activity of all the principals. Very often the most influential people are those with the least formal authority. One of the key issues which arises is the nature of leadership and how it is exercised.

Good leaders persuade others to follow without the backing of formal systems. They lead through the strength of their personality and are usually good communicators. However, leadership does not operate in a vacuum; the leader is leading in a certain direction, although that direction may not be specified early on. The best expression of leadership is to inspire others to follow without the need for detailed instruction. The development of trust in the leader allows supervision to be lightly exercised. Choosing the right people as leaders is critical to success.

The effect of organizational structure on agents

How does the structure, both formal and informal, influence the behaviour of the agent? What kind of behaviour does it encourage? The starting point is a detailed strategy, which specifies target levels of the key performance indicators, although as already seen this is a gross oversimplification. The types of problem likely to arise in achieving strategic targets are now discussed.

Setting any target initially involves a process of negotiation, either explicit or implicit, in which the agent seeks to have a target or targets specified which are well within reach and achievable without the commitment of too much effort. There is also every incentive for the agent within his or her particular domain to hide the full productive potential of a unit and keep in reserve for future use, particularly in a crisis, resources which are not fully used. This is the origin of organizational slack.

Another problem which can arise is 'storming', the last-minute effort at the end of a planning period to reach a target after a previous tendency to lag. This arises particularly in the context of the kind of planning which articulates clear planning periods – one, two or three years. This gives rise to all the problems associated with a campaign mentality, the focus for a short period on the achievement of certain key targets. Since there may be a lag in the reading of the current situation, that is, a tendency to react to yesterday's news, this may result in serious 'overshooting', moving too far in the apparently desired direction.

Since it is not always obvious who is responsible for either success or failure, the responsibility for performance almost always being shared by a number of agents working in a team, there is much scope for passing the blame for failure onto others and claiming the credit for success, even where it is not justified. It might also be possible to shift costs or revenues in a way which helps individuals to achieve targets or make performance look better than it really is.

One way of seeking assistance in achieving the objectives is to look for outside help. The most common way of achieving this within an organization is to tap into the use of free or underpriced resources available elsewhere in the organization. This is discussed at length in Chapter 13 under the heading, The commons and free riding.

Another way of reacting to the possible conflict implicit within the principal/agent relationship, particularly as it relates to its strategic context, is to lower those targets that relate to an individual or a unit. If everyone does this, the outcome is to erode the successful achievement of the strategic intent.

Finally, there are a multitude of short-term fixes which can be adopted by the agents, which make short-term performance look good but threaten long-term performance. For example, there may be serious underinvestment, a failure to commit resources which have no short-term benefit. Outright cheating may also occur, in which the key performance indicators are doctored. Performance is presented in a way which exaggerates achievement. This is all too common. Both these responses are more likely if there is a high staff turnover and they are not likely to be around when the consequences of the responses become obvious.

Motivating agents

Incentive structures within any organization may play on different motivating factors. Organizations may seek to recruit staff with particular motivations. Each agent differs in this motivation and has to be treated in a way which is designed to get the most out of them. One agent may be deeply committed to the enterprise, another may be always on the lookout for opportunities elsewhere but, from the perspective of the company, may have skills and experience which offset the poor motivation. The market system encourages a short-term view and a focus on pecuniary reward. It also encourages a high turnover of staff who are seeking to improve their position.

An effective system of performance appraisal will help to harness any motivation to the goals set. It is through such a system that principals can discover and explore the necessary information concerning the motivation and behaviour of their agents, information which will enable them to guide the agents to act as they wish. They can provide the necessary incentives to reward good behaviour, that is, that which promotes the implementation of the strategy, and the necessary sanctions to discourage poor behaviour, that is, behaviour which obstructs the achievement of the strategic intent.

The Microsoft example is revisited below to show how Steve Bullmer used organizational structure to try to drive a successful strategy, while the Reliance example demonstrates how the family firm can continue without its founder.

Strategy in Action   Finding a new structure and new strategy for Microsoft

Bullmer followed his predecessor in setting out his mission through a memo. In 1995 Gates had sent out a memo to all employees, entitled 'The Internet tidal wave'. The stress was squarely on technology. In 2002 Bullmer sent out his own memo, 'Realizing potential'. His new mission was 'to enable people and businesses throughout the world to realize their full potential'. This is a very broad aim, but one which puts the focus on employees and customers. It contrasts with the previous aim of building software for

any device, anywhere. The new memo talked about sales and quality, the need to decentralize and review all practices. It emphasized the need to move away from ad hocracy and develop a reputation for honesty, integrity and respect.

The company has decided to enter new businesses, such as video game consoles and the linked software, notebook tablets and even accounting software. It is also aiming to develop software to go in the sophisti-

▶

cated mobile phones of the future. These are decisive moves, involving a major commitment of resources.

The reorganization of the company can be divided into two phases whose existence reflects an element of uncertainty about what to do at this point in the history of the company.

PHASE 1: ORGANIZATIONAL STRUCTURE
Here the intention was to create a new organizational structure which divided the company's product development into six different divisions. These divisions were by customer group in order to connect product development with these different users:

- Corporate leaders
- Knowledge workers
- Home PC buyers
- Those who shop for computers and video games at retail outlets
- Software development
- Those surfing and/or shopping on the Web.

Another interesting idea considered was to introduce so-called tracking stock, that is, shares linked to particular company assets, with the hope of decentralizing and focusing the company. This might enable business-level managers to have a clear indication of the performance of their business area and benefit from their own entrepreneurial ideas.

PHASE 2: STRATEGY
Bullmer has fashioned a new strategy for the company. He is trying to soften the image and practice of the company by seeking to:

- settle any outstanding claims against the company
- empower managers to participate in making strategy and introducing new products
- and have a proper sense of their own performance.

He wanted to move away from the mentality of the monopolist and deal with competitors as potential complementors. Above all, he intends to listen much more to the customers.

There is a sense that during the first period as CEO, Bullmer was finding his feet and asserting himself against the control of Gates. He was on a steep learning curve, discovering what he needed to know about the company, before changing its culture in a significant way. The customer structure has its own problems, with the strategies of different groups in conflict.

Under the new organizational order, Gates has been freed to oversee the development of new technology. As Schlender (2002: 41) has written, Bill Gates' greatest gift is 'that uncanny ability to foresee how emerging software technologies can be woven together and parlayed into must-have "industry standard" products, which, in turn, reinforce demand for other software from Microsoft and its allies'. The current project is an ambitious integration project, the attempt to produce a radically new version of Windows, code-named Leghorn, which is to come out sometime after 2005. The idea, starting from scratch by asking what exactly the customer wants, is to put together a simple but unified technological vision.

To achieve this Gates has used transformative scenarios. In the words of Craig Mundie, the chief technical officer for advanced strategies and policy, who reports directly to Gates: 'The scenario is the dream, not something defined in super-gory detail. It's what Bill and I focus on more than the business plan or P&Ls. For a project as big as Leghorn there could have been 100 scenarios, but Bill does this thing with his mind where he distils the list down to a manageable set of functions that we can organize developer groups around' (Schlender, 2002: 43). The ten key scenario categories include people, accommodation, real time, communication, storage, authenticity and security and the new look. Gates is backed up by a 600-person think-tank, Microsoft Research.

Strategy in Action Reliance and the death of the founder

In 2002, Dhirubhai Ambani,the 69-year-old founder of the Indian conglomerate Reliance, died. Ambani was the most admired, in many ways the most feared, businessman in India. He had a strong appeal to the

▶

ordinary Indian. During the licence raj, he had a remarkable ability to make deals with politicians and bureaucrats, building market dominance by exploiting his government contacts. The big family-run conglomerates prospered by exploiting contacts with the politicians and bureaucrats who controlled most commercial activity in India and made most of the decisions, issuing the key licences. Reliance's network of contacts has been second to none, and still is. It grew by adopting a strategy well suited to the licence environment.

Ambani began his career 50 years before at a Shell petrol station in Aden. He returned to India in 1959 and started a yarn-trading company. Ambani's most effective strategy was to backwardly integrate within the textile industry. This meant setting up petrochemical plants to make polyester filament yarns, polyethylene and other raw materials that feed into the spinning and weaving which produces the textile fabrics. Petrochemicals depend on hydrocarbons so Ambani set up a refinery to process the oil and gas he extracted off the coast of Bombay. From a small beginning he built a business empire, which extended from oil exploration, extraction and refining, petrochemicals, to the spinning, weaving, finishing and trading of textiles. Not content with this level of vertical integration, he diversified horizontally into areas of major growth such as telecommunications, electric power, financial services and biotechnology.

In 1986 Ambani had a stroke and went into semi-retirement. He began a gradual withdrawal in favour of his two sons, Mukesh and Anil, who are very much creatures of the new era, but so is the company.

Mukesh, a Stanford MBA, using the basics of good management, masterminded the construction of the core refinery and petrochemical projects, earning a reputation for completing projects ahead of time and within budget. Anil, a Wharton MBA, took charge of promoting the company name, with a high-profile public articulation of business policy and financial strategy, and the conduct of the associated ambassadorial duties. The brothers have very different temperaments.

In the words of one commentator: 'Reliance is a link between two stages of evolution in Indian business' (*The Economist*, 2002: 364: 52). Liberalization of the Indian economy began in 1991 and, although slow, has been proceeding ever since. A new strategy is required and Reliance has shown itself sufficiently successful at developing it to have become arguably

not only the largest Indian company in terms of its capitalization, but the most successful.

Often in such a situation there are quarrels over who controls or owns what (see the case study on Gucci), which means that too much energy is devoted to managing kinship tensions rather than directing company growth. The Ambanis successfully managed to separate the roles of ownership and management. Between 1986 and 2002, the brothers put in professional managers, helping to create a structure which emphasized professionalism.

Reliance was the pioneer in a number of areas:

- It built production facilities which are globally competitive, rather than reliant on a guaranteed market. It showed how to survive in an increasingly competitive environment and exploit the opportunities offered by the opening up of the Indian economy. Any facilities must produce at competitive cost levels. This is epitomized by the Jamnager oil refinery in Gujerat, with a 27 million tonne capacity, the largest in Asia, which came on stream in 2000. Mukesh claims that the operating costs of the plant are such that it is viable even in a downturn.

- Almost single-handedly Reliance popularized the ownership of shares among the Indian middle class. The two holding companies, Reliance Industries and Reliance Petroleum, part of the Reliance Group, together had as many as 3.5 million shareholders. The aim is to sustain the 20% annual growth in profits which characterized the 1990s.

- Reliance has combined entrepreneurship with the employment of professional management methods to create a modern competitive company. Mukesh Ambani is relying on the ability of Reliance to build industries from scratch, in the process raising cheap capital and operating the resulting facilities efficiently. An 'infocom' initiative builds on the strengths of the labour force in India. The level of investment projected is a minimum of US$5 billion. This is an industry with a deregulated market in which there is real competition from other companies offering services and products at fiercely competitive prices. Ironically, Reliance, as other fixed-line service providers, has received preferential treatment from the government, not having to pay high cellular licensing fees. Reliance has previously dealt with only industrial customers, providing inputs to other companies. It hopes to build up revenues from consumer services to a third of group sales within four years.

On March 1, 2002, the amalgamation of Reliance Industries and Reliance Petroleum was announced, following a series of previous amalgamations of Reliance Petrochemicals, Reliance Polyethylene and Reliance Polypropylene. This was clearly intended to give the new company the gearing potential to acquire further companies and finance its most ambitious project to date, a nationwide fibreoptic cable. One goal is to complete the energy chain by moving into petrol retailing, either by building a network itself, or by bidding for the state-owned Bharat Petroleum or Hindustan Petroleum when they come up for sale. Reliance has mostly grown by organic growth. It has already shown itself willing to reverse this policy by building through purchase of the plastics producer IPCL. It has ambitions to build its international position by further purchase.

Mukesh Ambani, the new chairperson, says he wants an 'organizational architecture that is like a centipede – one that walks on a hundred legs and where individuals are irrelevant'. What might he mean by such a comment?

Strategy and organizational design

It is said that strategy should determine structure, but that it does not always do so. This was the message of Alfred Chandler's (1962, 1977, 1990) series of long-term studies of Western enterprises. Unfortunately it is often the case that structure determines strategy.

The argument is that the external environment has been subject to more dramatic change and in order to retain competitive advantage, strategy has to embrace innovation. During the 1990s, there was considerable discussion about the need to flatten hierarchies, in particular to remove the middle layers of management in order to make the enterprise more flexible and responsive to customer needs. The aim was to make the enterprise better able to respond quickly. In the discussion on the need for less hierarchy, there was talk of all sorts of exotic structures, as illustrated by the Focus on Theory.

Focus on Theory
Non-hierarchical structures

- *spider's web* organizations, which are really elaborate networks. They may be the result of the simulation within an organization of the networks which often exist outside an enterprise
- *starburst* organizations which continuously shed new second-generation companies
- *federal* or cluster organizations in which the clusters continuously form, disperse and reform with a different membership
- *inverted* organizations in which the usual pyramid is inverted and the number of contact points with customers is maximized.

However, all this talk often failed to recognize the universality of hierarchy and the fact that what was being discussed were organizing principles for the achievement of greater customer responsiveness or a more rapid rate of innovation, not the overall organizational design principle. Provided some part of the organization satisfied the requirements of these new forms, the rest of the organization could continue to be structured along old lines. The need to restructure along these lines was extremely limited, the ability to do so even more constrained.

In any organizational design there is always a trade-off between the requirements of integration and those of specialization. Once they move beyond a certain size, all enterprises must have specialized units which must remain part of an integrated unit. The more layers of control in any organization, the greater the danger of a failure of integration, in particular what might be called vertical fracturing. This is one of the principal disadvantages of size. In order to make integration easier, there has been a tendency to support the removal of as many middle layers of an organization as possible.

There are five basic design principles, that is, principles on which the construction of such units or departments might be based. The first four are based on product, region, function and customer group. The fifth is what is called the matrix design where two principles are superimposed. There is a sixth type of design, the hybrid, which simply recognizes that all designs are the product of history and for that reason each is unique. It is possible to deal with each of these in turn, dwelling on the advantages and disadvantages of each design.

Product design structure

The product design principle is desirable where the emphasis in achieving competitive advantage is on the supply side, that is, either on a technology and its development or the costs of various inputs. This is often made possible by the existence of a reasonably standard or homogeneous product, one which is not differentiated or customized to any significant degree. However, rapid technical change and the typically short life cycle of the products may also incline the structure towards this principle.

This is the most popular of all designs, well suited to an enterprise which produces a range of different products, with very different technologies. Sometimes the division is simple. Most large enterprises produce hundreds, if not thousands of different products. The key is to be able to group them easily. Often such divisions, or the departments which group the products, are called strategic business units. They bring together businesses which are related in some strategically important way, by sharing markets, technology or key activities in the value chain.

There are two forms of product design, the multidivisional form (M-form) and the holding form (H-form). The M-form is relevant where the products are related; there are self-contained operations but overlapping functional activities. The M-form lends itself to a diversified company in which there are synergies between the different product groups. The H-form contains unrelated businesses which can have complete autonomy. It is the natural organizational design of a pure conglomerate and can be demonstrated by the Shougang company, as illustrated in Figure 12.1.

Shougang illustrates the tendency within Asia, and more recently in China, to put together conglomerates operating in highly disparate product areas. There is little relationship between the different divisions. As used to be true of BHP, a company which is also organized on a product design principle, Shougang's core business is steel. Shougang has moved into unrelated areas but ones with enormous appeal in a rapidly growing economy – the financial services, property and high-tech sectors. The financial services group includes Canadian Eastern Life Assurance and the

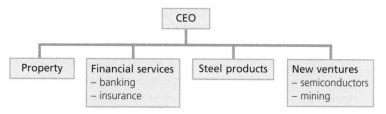

Figure 12.1 **The product design structure of the Shougang Company**

Huaxia Bank. Like many other Chinese enterprises, it has not resisted the temptation to move into property and information technology, and has a semiconductor joint venture with NEC of Japan.

Table 12.2 **Benefits and weaknesses of the product design principle**

Benefits	Weaknesses
• This design concentrates expertise in the relevant product areas, encouraging a technical dynamism which rapidly moves the enterprise down the experience curve	• Any design type has its own specific problems of reconciling integration with differentiation. This might be dealt with by having a corporate services and a strategic section attached to the office of the CEO which acts as the focus for integration
• It lends itself well to global organization, that is, to the logistics of an organization which sources from many facilities in different parts of the world	• The problems of this design structure are usually concentrated in the areas of coordination and communication between the business units
• It allows an enterprise to take from the lowest cost source or develop a flexible system in which the risk of an excessive dependence on one source is avoided	• Getting the different product groups to work together is difficult. Empire building within departments is a universal phenomenon. It does not matter whether the departments are organized by product, region, function or customer group, they will still develop a loyalty to their department and tend to promote the interests of that department over those of others. It is difficult to avoid this tendency
• Where there are economies of scale, this is clearly the preferred organizational design, as it allows their full exploitation	• Horizontal fracturing between units at a similar level, whether they are business or functional units, is common
• It allows the development of a global approach to marketing	• Information is power and the release of that information from one unit to another is often not a main priority but difficult to achieve
	• Within each product division, there may be the same functional departments. Each group has its own functional specialists who are likely to duplicate much of the work done elsewhere

Regional organizational structure

The regional organizational design shifts the emphasis from the supply to the demand side. It is better suited to a market or customer orientation, particularly where markets and customer wants differ significantly in character. In this design structure the departments are demand-oriented.

This may be because of the nature of the product, as with electric power, cement or dairy products, which have strong 'locational' characteristics. Alternatively, it may be because of the importance of keeping the customer happy by providing the kind of food and service required by locals, as with restaurants or discount retailers.

In some cases the product may not be marketable at all in some regions. In other words, the products are not readily transferable across regions. The marketing of the product must be customized by region, according to the nature of the market. This market orientation, reflecting differences in taste, is relevant within and between national markets. Where there is significant product differentiation and major cultural differences characterizing the markets, this is the desirable design type.

There is likely to be a functional structure, both attached to the CEO's office and within the separate regional organizations, supporting the main structure but subordinate to it.

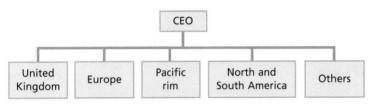

Figure 12.2 **Regional design structure of Cadbury Schweppes**

Food and beverage companies such as Nestlé (discussed in Chapter 15) and Cadbury Schweppes (illustrated in Figure 12.2) are commonly organized in this way. More elaborately, the pharmaceutical company Pfizer, the largest of all pharmaceutical companies, has ten geographic area managers and under each of them country managers. Sometimes the enterprise then splits up according to product type. This is appropriate to the pharmaceutical industry since the nature of the market and distribution system, and the regulatory environment specific to it, differs dramatically from country to country. This principle is also most common for products such as toiletries, confectionary and entertainment of various kinds.

Table 12.3 **Benefits and weaknesses of the regional design principle**

Benefits	Weaknesses
• It is appropriate for industries in which cultural difference is important. At the international level, products which have significant intangible attributes lend themselves to this design since the attributes themselves are often culture-related • It suits industries in which the system of distribution differs • It helps to meet the increasing emphasis on product differentiation and the need for customization	• This design loses the advantages of cost reduction which accrue to the first design principle • It may even act to discourage technical change • It moves the enterprise away from a global organizing principle • It encourages an even more tenacious form of empire building based on regional units. Geographic distance and language barriers tend to reinforce this • Almost certainly the application of this organizing principle adds another layer of management to the organizational structure. The centre may have to make up its mind how much decentralization it will allow • There may be duplication and a loss of coordination between the regions. For these reasons the Ford Motor Company dropped its regional design structure

Functional organizational structure

The functional organizational design is usually the first form of specialized design structure to appear in any organization, certainly where there is only one business unit. The design is appropriate where the enterprise produces a narrow range of similar products or services, perhaps best of all, where there is only a single product or service. Mining enterprises or those producing energy, such as oil, electricity or gas, often but not always (see the BHP Billiton case study in Chapter 11) fit this principle.

The functional divisions that might exist in an enterprise are many, but reflect strategy-critical processes. The departments could be:

- accounting/finance
- human resource management
- public relations

- operations, marketing
- research and development
- law

However, the nature of the product and the business unit determine which functions are important and may break these large generic activities into more specialized process ones. A hotel might have departments based on:

- front-desk operations
- building maintenance
- quality control
- personnel

- housekeeping
- food service
- marketing
- finance/accounting

A discount retailer might have departments for:

- purchasing
- warehousing and distribution
- advertising
- customer service

- store operations
- merchandising and promotion
- corporate administrative services

As has been shown, the previous two organizational designs may comprise a functional specialization within them, at a lower level in the organization.

British Airways (Figure 12.3) sells just one main product, air travel. It is therefore organized on a functional basis, but with a large number of separate departments, some of which are specific to an airline. Security and the environment are critical to air travel, and government relations are also important.

One way of counteracting the weaknesses of a functional structure is to 're-engineer' it into a 'process' structure, which is a variant of this design.

Figure 12.3 **Functional design structure of British Airways**

Table 12.4 **Benefits and weaknesses of the functional design principle**

Benefits	Weaknesses
• It gives enterprises a high degree of centralization which tends to make them potentially closely integrated • It concentrates functional expertise in one area and makes possible easy central control of these functional areas and the quick diagnosis of functional problems. When there is a deterioration in performance, it is difficult to identify the problem without a significant delay. A functional organization allows this to be done more quickly • It also promotes in-depth promotional expertise, an expertise which can become a core competency	• Empire building derived from functional myopia and an overemphasis on function-directed career paths • Strategy-critical activities may be cross-functional, so that the functions may get in the way of making good strategy and building core competencies • In order to achieve cross-departmental cooperation, much work may be thrown onto the CEO, who may deliberately put in place a department responsible for strategy

Customer group structure

The customer group design is appropriate where there are customers with different needs who divide into discrete groups. This structure is appropriate where the needs of the different customer groups differ significantly and/or where different marketing or distribution systems are required. For example, an appropriate division for a bank might be between government, corporate and individual customers, whereas for a tyre producer it might be between motor vehicle manufacturers, retail customers and agricultural users. The structure reflects the nature of the different customer groups.

For Eastman Kodak (Figure 12.4), the market for film differs between ordinary camera users, specialized business, particularly medical, users and professional film makers. The markets are quite separate.

Figure 12.4 **Customer group design structure of Eastman Kodak**

The first group of consumers consists of film studios, the second businesses and the medical community (scanners, copier-printers and high-tech medical film and imaging systems) and the third amateur and professional photographers.

Table 12.5 **Benefits and weaknesses of the customer group design principle**

Benefits	Weaknesses
• It allows a significant degree of customization by market segments • It caters for significant differences in the system of distribution	• There are serious duplication problems • There are major problems of coordination and communication

Matrix design structure

In the matrix design structure type, two of the other principles are combined, so that the enterprise has a dual structure. The most common combination is one which is both product and function-based (Figure 12.5), but this is not the only combination which is possible. For example, a product structure may have a regional structure superimposed on it.

	R&D and engineering	Manufacturing	Marketing	Finance
Business venture 1 (SBU 1)	Engineering/R&D specialists	Production/ operations specialists	Marketing specialists	Finance specialists
SBU 2				
SBU 3				
SBU 4				

Figure 12.5 **A typical matrix structure**

Companies which are using or have at some time used the matrix type of organizational structure include General Electric, Texas Instruments, Citibank, Shell, Bechtel, Boeing, Dow Chemical and ABB, as illustrated in the following Strategy in Action.

For these reasons, often the matrix principle is applied to only part of an organization, not the whole. The structure does allow the operation of separate project teams which are very much part of strategy making.

Table 12.6 **Benefits and weaknesses of the matrix design principle**

Benefits	Weaknesses
• This structure reflects the importance of two organizing principles	• The structure is a complex and probably confusing one
• It is intended to promote integration, by assisting coordination and communication and countering the usual problems which emerge in these areas	• It can lead to conflicting influences slowing communication and creating delays. The whole decision-making process may be slowed unless one line of authority prevails
• From the perspective of strategy, it gives deliberate attention to more than one dimension of strategic priority	• Having two bosses, or two principals, may be an opportunity for agents to make space for the pursuit of their own interests or can even be a source of confusion about what their objectives really should be. There are likely to be many trade-offs and compromises
	• There may be a significant deterrent to entrepreneurial activity and the design may be seen as disempowering middle-level managers

Strategy in Action Asea Brown Boveri (ABB)

ABB is a diversified multinational company of joint Swedish/Swiss origin, with headquarters in Zurich, and core competencies in electric power technolo- gies. It has had a chequered history. It once had a strong matrix organization.

At the top of the corporate organization was an executive committee, consisting of the CEO and 12 members from various parts of the world, which was responsible for the company's corporate strategy and performance. It met every two to three weeks in different parts of the world.

One dimension of the matrix consisted of 50 or so business areas (BAs), each representing a group of related products or services. These BAs were in turn grouped into six 'business segments', each supervised by a different member of the executive committee (the number has varied from year to year).

The other dimension of the matrix consisted of national groups of enterprises, each headed by a president, with boards of directors, financial statements and career structures. Inside the matrix were around 5,000 'local' ABB companies, relatively autonomous and entrepreneurial profit centres, but seen as subsidiaries of the national enterprises. Each company president answered to both the national president, on its global role, and the leader of the BA, on local issues.

The intention of the matrix was to combine global strategy with sensitivity to local needs. ABB saw itself as a federation of national companies with a global coordination centre. Decision making was decentralized, but control and reporting were centralized. The HQ in Zurich had about 100 staff, but received a regular flow of information which enabled it to monitor performance against targets.

This is the theory and for a period it seemed to produce good results. Unfortunately, the matrix did not always work well, with frequent conflicts of interest between the two elements of the matrix. The negative elements began to predominate over the positive and ABB has serious problems of poor performance. Recently the structure has been reorganized so as to dismantle one half of the matrix, the country management, beginning with the regional groupings. This experience shows the possibilities and the dangers of the matrix structure.

Sources: Uhlen and Lubatkin, in Hitt et al. (2000); Thompson and Strickland (1999).

Ideal types and hybrids

The five structures discussed above are ideal types. The actual organizational structure of any company rarely coincides with what is ideal or with any of the structures described. There are a number of reasons why this might be so:

- As the environment changes, it often makes appropriate a different organizational structure. It is difficult to keep adjusting the structure to keep up with the demands of a changing environment.
- Personnel change all the time, notably at the top of the organization. What is good for one leadership team or CEO is not good for another. This may be associated with a change of strategy and therefore a change of structure.
- Any recent acquisitions mean that a company inherits different structures which are tacked onto the existing structure. Even the fastest restructurings cannot rid the actual structure of the influence of its particular history, another example of path dependence.
- Any restructuring disrupts normal operations, requires the investment of significant resources and diverts attention from other important activities.

In an ideal world it might be desirable to use a pure structure. However, an enterprise's structure is very much determined by its history, which might include the acquisition of other enterprises with their own structure, which is inherited by the acquiring enterprise. Most actual structures are hybrids, the result of a process of acquisition and organic growth bringing together substructures which differ in basic principle. This increases the complexity of organizations so that most are hybrid organizations with complex and apparently irrational structures. Many have different parts of the organization which separately use as many as three or four different design principles. The complexity of most large enterprises is quite daunting and one of the significant disadvantages of size. Most organizations become bureaucratic in some sense, sometimes in a wholly negative sense.

Restructuring

To modify complex structures in a significant way is a costly exercise. Restructurings are rare events which need careful preparation. For that reason, structure, having developed a life and history of its own, sometimes determines strategy. The existence of structures ill-suited to the changing environment may mean that severe constraints are exerted on strategy making and, in an extreme case, it is possible that structure determines strategy. The two-way interaction is far more subtle than often thought. Like resources, structure is often a given, part of the internal context which must be taken into account at the beginning of any strategy-making process; it also helps to define the enterprise.

Smaller, younger organizations have more flexibility. As an organization gets bigger, it is difficult to retain this flexibility and reproduce the advantages of a small organization as well as reconcile the demands of functional specialization with those of integration. As the organization develops new departments, the main challenge shifts to the need to coordinate the operation of all these departments. Successful growth increases the need for a deliberate analysis of the advantage and disadvantages of formal organization.

The five Cs

The effective formulation and implementation of strategy depends upon satisfaction of what can be called the five Cs:

- commands issued at the appropriate time
- control, whether formal or informal, direct or indirect
- coordination of the different parts of the organization
- communication flows through proper conduits
- conflict being contained and creatively channelled. In some countries, such as Japan and others in the Confucian world, conflict might be replaced by consensus, with the emphasis on avoiding overt conflict.

Any structure must make possible an effective realization of these elements. They are discussed at greater length in Chapter 17. In this chapter they are considered in the context of the need to integrate the organization. Much of what is said provides insights on the issue of size and how an organization might gain the advantages of both large and small size.

Command

In theory any agent can be compelled to follow commands. A failure to do so leads to punishment. However, this is to oversimplify the situation. The regular use of commands is counterproductive. Centrally planned economies rested on the fallacy that instruction was all that was needed to realize a plan. The problem is that any command or instruction has to be indirect in two senses, firstly, its realization has to be supervised by someone other than the issuer of the instruction and, secondly, it has to be given a specific meaning at the appropriate point in an organization. In other words, commands move down an organization.

Commands can be distorted as they move down, in the way Chinese whispers distort a message or story. Commands have to be disaggregated to fit the various levels below the top one. They can be disaggregated and interpreted in a number of different ways, ways which suit the interests of the interpreter.

It is appropriate to grant some discretion to those below in order to empower them to be entrepreneurial in the way they behave. This is helpful since subordinates may be in a position to innovate in a desirable manner and confront unexpected contingencies. It is better to persuade them to identify with the commanders, as a result anticipating their wishes, and allow them to interpret and adjust the command in accord with the demands of the immediate context.

Control

Control is a broad issue. It cannot, nor should, mean control of every minor detail of activity or behaviour. Rather, it means direction within the broad parameters of the strategy. Control assumes that those parameters have already been fixed. There may be different ways of accomplishing the main objectives of the strategy. Some of these options may be unknown to those in authority. Some may be superior to existing or already envisioned ways, even to those conceived by the top-level strategists. Control is often indirect, rather than direct.

Coordination

All organizations are vulnerable to empire building and the politics engendered by the pursuit of personal ambition. Departments may systematically favour their own. They may fail to keep other departments aware of what they are doing. They may duplicate what is done elsewhere. They may compete for scarce assets, acting as free riders. They may make decisions inconsistent with those of other departments. All of these problems may threaten the implementation of the strategy adopted. Both formal and informal mechanisms of coordination are critical to avoiding such negative effects.

Communication

The communication of information is essential to both good strategy formulation and effective implementation. In the process of communication, information is converted into knowledge. Communications can move down the organization. Equally as important are those communications which move up. Again distortion can occur as communications are aggregated in the upward movement.

In order to further coordination between different departments, horizontal communication is as important as vertical communication. Structures usually ignore the horizontal dimension of communication. There must be efficient conduits for all such communication, whether vertical or horizontal. Cross-functional or cross-regional teams, designated liaison people and informal managerial networks all help.

Conflict/consensus

Conflict can be used in a positive way. It is not always a bad thing, since it does not need to be damaging in its consequences. A healthy organization generates different ideas, different ways of doing things and different ways of resolving problems. This should be encouraged. Diversity inevitably gives rise to conflict. It is the nature of the conflict which is significant.

Informal structures

Textbooks usually consider formal structures at some length but ignore informal structures. Informal structures are often as rich in their variety of forms as formal structures. Communication exists outside the formal conduits. Control is exercised by informal persuasion and influence. Conflicts may be entirely personal. There may be a proliferation of temporary teams or committees created to focus attention on a specific problem, prepare for a particular project or bridge the gaps between departments or divisions, whatever their organizing principle (see the Strategy in Action on Nissan and Renault in Chapter 13).

While informal or temporary structures may have less resilience than formal structures and reflect the temporary membership of the organization, some do survive beyond the short term. Some aspects of the informal structure, such as corporate culture, develop over a long period and cannot be created overnight by deliberate action. No formal structure can work without a working informal structure. The two operate together to make an organization effective. In a healthy organization they interact positively. An organization with a strong formal structure may be weakened by the lack of a healthy informal structure, or one which has a dynamic informal structure may find itself hindered by an inappropriate formal structure.

Monitoring, incentives and corporate culture

It is often argued that any change in strategy must lead to a change in three other areas in addition to structure – processes, culture and the incentive system. The so-called Galbraith star (Galbraith, 1995), as shown in Figure 12.6, illustrates this.

This view places the clear articulation of the objectives of a strategy as a precondition for successful integration. The star suggests that, apart from the structural aspects discussed above, there are three main ways in which all members of an organization can be integrated in the implementation of an agreed strategy: the monitoring of behaviour and performance; an incentive system; and integration of the agents into a corporate culture. Each of these is discussed in turn.

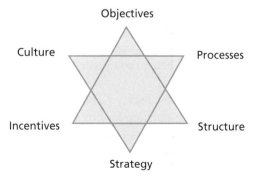

Source: Galbraith, 1995.

Figure 12.6   **The Galbraith star**

Monitoring and sanctions

Monitoring is the systematic supervision of subordinates and the regular appraisal of their performance. It assumes that there is some follow-up action which results from such monitoring.

At its simplest monitoring comes down to observing the behaviour of a staff member. It usually requires a regular reporting system with clear performance indicators. The downside of monitoring is twofold. First, it requires the commitment of scarce managerial or supervisory time and the collection of information, which is time-consuming and expensive. Second, there is a maximum number of staff who can be effectively monitored at any one time by any one supervisor. Expanding the number of supervisees rapidly reduces the effectiveness of such supervision.

An organization needs to be structured to take account of these limitations. The better the information conveyed in the reporting systems available to the enterprise, the larger the number of subordinates who can be monitored. At some point, time becomes a constraint. It is always a problem for the person doing the monitoring to have sufficient information to monitor effectively and enough time to gather and interpret the information.

There is always a distinct asymmetry in the information available to the monitor and the monitored, and it may be in the interest of the subordinate to perpetuate this situation. The latter knows much better the details of all the operations directly relevant to the position than the supervisor.

The most important form of monitoring occurs at the top of an enterprise. The board of directors monitors the performance of the CEO and senior management on behalf of the shareholders. That is the chief *raison d'être* of any board. This monitoring raises a number of issues. First, it raises the issue of information:

- What information does the board have and what does it need?
- Do board members have enough information to do their job effectively?
- What financial control mechanisms exist?
- How effective is the auditing system?

Clearly an ill-informed board is in no position to control senior management, even if it is motivated to try to exert such control.

Second, how far is the board independent of senior management? This reflects the number of senior mangers on the board, notably relative to the number of independents. In many cases the CEO tends to dominate the board. Again an asymmetry of information becomes relevant, since insiders know much better than outsiders what is happening. They are in a much better position to interpret that information which is available.

What sanctions exist if monitoring discloses a failure to pursue the achievement of strategic objectives? The ultimate sanction for any employee is loss of employment. The same should apply to board members. However, the loss of a job can be counterproductive since it may unsettle other employees or other board members

There are many sanctions which fall short of this extreme. Some involve material loss – the denial of bonuses and other social punishments – or marginalization and exclusion from the decision-making process. Since sanctions have a negative effect on both the individual concerned and others, they are better avoided and more positive mechanisms used, if possible.

In any system of monitoring and reward, it is better to encourage staff to admit their mistakes and learn from them, rather than conceal them. Staff with a high morale, who are willing to risk making mistakes, are more productive. After all every success is accompanied by failures. In a typical case, the successes more than compensate for the failures, but not always.

Incentive systems

One way to enforce desired behaviour is to have an incentive system which strongly influences behaviour. This is to emphasize extrinsic motivation, which has its own dangers. An extrinsic incentive system is usually based on a system of bonuses. If employees learn to respond only to extrinsic motivation, that is, to a material or pecuniary reward of some kind, this may have the result of limiting the contribution made to strategy making in its broadest sense. An organization may be training its staff to limit their behaviour to actions which only respond to such signals. Extrinsic motivation may suppress intrinsic motivation, that is, the desire to achieve for its own sake. There is a danger that this may suppress the creative urge.

The degree to which individuals are influenced by different incentive systems varies from individual to individual. It also reflects, as we shall see, the culture of the organization and what kind of behaviour that culture encourages. It reflects the culture of the country in which the organization is located. There is plenty of research work which emphasizes the remarkable differences in the way the capitalist system works in different countries and the different motivations which characterize those countries. What works in one country does not work in another.

For the moment it is useful to assume a clear set of objectives, which can be translated into defined targets and measurable performance indicators, linked explicitly to the achievement of those targets, and articulated in a way appropriate to the different levels of the organization. The situation is simple if short-term profit is taken as the performance indicator but this is only one possible approach. It is possible to widen the approach later, but a concern with long-term performance may incline an organization against a simple extrinsic reward system.

At the top of the management hierarchy, stock option schemes which link the rewards of management to the share price can guide behaviour in the direction of satisfying the shareholders' interests. A good performance which has a beneficial influence on the share price rewards the managers through their stock holdings. However, this may overfocus the managers in their behaviour, in such a way that they actually begin to cheat by doctoring the accounts to produce profit or earnings figures which influence the share price in a way which provides them with the greatest reward. This is a good example of how extrinsic motivation can drive out intrinsic motivation and distort behaviour in such a way as to ultimately prevent the pursuit of strategic objectives.

Bonus schemes of a similar kind can be introduced throughout the enterprise, linked to the performance of a particular department, performance which is measured in a way desired by the principals. It is often better to provide such bonuses to a group since it is often hard to isolate individual performance and such a reward system is less likely to damage intrinsic motivation.

As can be seen, one major issue which clearly informs responses to incentive systems relates to the nature of the general motivation of managers and workers. What are most employees looking for from their work? Clearly they are not motivated solely by short-term profit for the enterprise. Even the desire to maximize their own short-term income is qualified by their sense of self-worth and pride and in challenging themselves to achieve well, in the words of Maslow, to self-actualize. At another level, they must consider their medium- to long-term career possibilities and the danger of a loss of employment. There are major differences of attitude in the world, revealed in different cultures.

One such difference relates to that between the Japanese employment model and the typical Western model. The Japanese model was once a major focus of interest, but is now out of fashion. It is based on three pillars – lifetime employment, promotion by seniority and enterprise unions. The Japanese model of lifetime employment, although never completely universal throughout Japan, focuses on promotion by seniority rather than ability. It focuses on the long-term career chances of the employees. An employee's loyalty to the enterprise is secured by the loyalty of the enterprise to the employee. A manager can expect regular promotion simply on the basis of seniority. A lifetime career path is easily mapped out and security given to the worker. Career advancement is not achieved by moving between enterprises, but by staying within the same enterprise. Equally, the enterprise union works to harness the loyalty of the workers to their enterprise in order to fulfil the objectives of the enterprise. Labour relations are not adversarial, as in the Western model.

In Western enterprises, appointments to higher positions are made from inside and outside the enterprise, but on the basis of ability rather than seniority. Individuals compete for jobs on the basis of their skills, qualifications and experience, and of course their network connections. In the last there is little difference from country to country. Managers often improve their position by moving to another enterprise. They acquire jobs which pay more, provide more power, responsibility and status, or some combination of these, whatever it is they want. There is therefore a continuous accretion of new talent to any given enterprise, entering the organization at all levels, not just the bottom level, as in the Japanese system. There is also a pool of disappointed aspirants for more senior positions who accumulate within an enterprise, a situation which can create problems for performance. The senior management hopes that these potential discontents will leave, but their presence can be a source of low morale. Certainly this employment regime does not encourage loyalty, at most a short-term loyalty on the part of many staff. The underlying rationale for the system is that it is motivated by short-term profit for the enterprise and a pecuniary reward system for the workers and managers.

In this world performance is often judged by short-term results, partly as a consequence of the obsession with the one stakeholder group of shareholders and therefore with share values on the market. Since in this system staff often move on quickly, the more long-term results of their activity are not readily apparent and cannot be easily blamed on them. The danger is that this is likely to produce a kind of short-termism which is destructive of any longer term strategy.

Both systems have their strengths and weaknesses. Some combination of the two may avoid the obvious weaknesses – in the one case failing to encourage an efficient allocation of labour, and in the other encouraging an obsession with short-term results at the cost of long-term performance.

Organizational culture

A corporate or organizational culture consists of a complex set of common values and symbols, shared by all members of the organization, which are capable of influencing the way in which members of the corporation or organization behave. From the perspective of strategy, it can clearly be both another tool assisting in the formulation and implementation of strategy and a constraint on the process and content of strategy making itself.

It is possible to start by considering in a descriptive manner the different general types of culture which might exist, particularly in their structural contexts, asking how far different cultures help to produce an effective fit between, on the one hand, the people, systems and structures within the enterprise and, on the other hand, the tasks to which the enterprise is committed and the environment of the organization in which they have to be undertaken.

According to Handy (1983) there are four general types of corporate or organizational culture which differ significantly; power, role, task and person. They are associated with very different external contexts and often with different structures.

Power culture

The defining feature of power culture is the central power source. The structure is like a spider's web, with circles of power and influence radiating from the centre. Decision making is highly 'political'. Everything depends on the quality of those at the centre and the effectiveness and efficiency with which they operate. There is little bureaucracy in such a culture – few defined rules or procedures. The culture is homogeneous and strong, since only the like-minded continue long in employment positions in such an organization. The organization is capable of being flexible and quick-footed. It is possible to shift its strategic direction very quickly, provided it is not too big. Such a culture is therefore typical of small entrepreneurial enterprises, notably those in their infancy and those dominated by the personality of the founder.

Problems arise with the success of an entrepreneurial organization, as it grows in size and complexity and reaches adolescence or even maturity. It outgrows the ability of the founder, or even of a small team around the founder, to control. Change management becomes difficult and the succession is always a problem. This culture is a favourite topic for journalists, historians and biographers to write about since it revolves around charismatic individuals. The personal interest draws attention. This interest tends to deflect attention from other cultures, so that to many the power culture appears typical of all organizations. The classical approach to strategy is the one which best describes such a situation.

Role culture

Role culture is beloved of management textbooks and sociologists. The defining feature is functional specialization, reflected in the existence of separate functional units, coordinated by a top layer of senior managers. There may be professional standards, professional values and professional codes of behaviour which are important. The structure is sometimes likened to a Greek temple, with its columns and roof resting on those columns. Decision making is structured and rational, occurring within an elaborate bureaucratic structure. The clear definition of roles within the organization makes the position more important than the individual.

Such a culture is appropriate where the organization has grown beyond a certain size. It is relevant where the organization has become large and has some significant influence over its environment, as in markets dominated by a few producers or sellers. Change can be very difficult to manage with such a culture, particularly where the structure is replicated within the functional units of the organization. There may be many layers of responsibility. In such an organization there is a tendency to interpret the future in terms of the past, that is, in terms of what is already known. All mature enterprises eventually reach this structure.

Task culture

The defining feature of task culture is the immediate project and the tasks associated with it. The undertaking of the task requires expertise, and therefore the knowledge that expertise brings. The structure is likened to a net, with the strands representing specializations relevant to the task at hand and the knots the centres of power and influence. Decision making is usually made by teams dealing with a stream of specific projects and tasks. These teams are flexible, with variable membership according to the task at hand.

Such an organization is suitable for turbulent times in which the organization has little control over a rapidly changing environment. The existence of such teams makes it easier to manage that change. Of course the teams can create their own turbulence. However, the teams themselves are difficult to control, since they gather their own momentum as they explore different problems and their solutions. They can go off in a completely arbitrary direction. This culture is an unstable one, in the sense that it unlikely to survive for very long. Generally there is a tendency for such organizations to regress to the role culture, particularly where the organization is failing and resources are limited or becoming so. Such a culture is seen by many as appropriate to the new economy and an environment of rapid change. It is the culture which is desired when creativity becomes significant. It is the mechanism through which innovation is achieved in organizations which can become both bureaucratic and conservative.

Person culture

Person culture occurs when for some reason the individual possesses talents or skills which are critical to success in the industry. The individual is the dominant factor, so that the organization consists of a cluster of individual stars carefully recruited or developed. The success of the organization depends on recruiting and retaining these individuals. This culture is unusual. It is very attractive to those who seek full empowerment, that is, the maximum scope for the free exercise of their talents. There is no control and no hierarchy. Again it is hard to sustain such a culture in existence beyond a brief moment of time. It is rare for the requirements of the organization not to eventually prevail over the aspirations of individuals, except in limited parts of an enterprise. Sociologists are fond of studying the interrelationship between the individual and the organization.

Again an organization might combine aspects of these different cultures in different parts of the organization. The culture might also change over time from one to another. For example, the interaction between a power and a role culture reflects the maturing of the enterprise and the overcoming of a crisis, often confronted when the enterprise gets too big for the founder to control and when the original business model has lost its sparkle.

Cultures are closely linked to structures. Culture has a profound influence on the informal ways of doing things. The classic tension between creativity and its expression and the requirements of an efficient bureaucracy often manifest themselves in the culture of an organization, so that:

- where creativity is important a task or person culture might be cultivated
- where efficiency is important a role culture is necessary.

Culture develops a life of its own which largely reflects the particularity of an organization. Like the structure, culture reflects the specific history of the organization. The transition to both a functional structure and the role culture associated with it is difficult. The nature of the role culture reflects the influence of past strategy.

The leader(s) of an organization cannot wave a magic wand and create a new culture over night. Culture cannot be built deliberately and instantly. An organization builds up its own corporate culture over time. The culture reflects the heroes and legends of its past. It is partly a result of the past actions of strategic leaders. Corporate culture is a manifestation of that leadership. It may reflect the character of the original founder or those who have been important at different times in developing the enterprise, notably in turnaround situations. In that sense the culture in the early years of an organization is an expression of a power culture, deliberately shaped by those strategic leaders, but does not always develop in the way envisaged by those leaders.

Culture is encapsulated in the logos and ethos of the enterprise, or the nature of the services provided. It takes time for any enterprise to develop its own way of doing things and its own set of values. While in theory it is desirable to be able to fashion culture according to the needs of strategy, in practice there are severe limitations on the ability of any leaders to do this. Leaders do not act in a vacuum. Their personality and behaviour sometimes reflect the existing culture as much as they influence that culture.

Corporate culture helps to bind together members of the team as they internalize the values of the particular corporate culture. It helps to regulate and control their behaviour. Individuals entering the enterprise for the first time are initiated into the culture in various ways, sometimes through a deliberate programme of induction, and persuaded to identify with this culture which then influences their behaviour. As a consequence, all will act in the desired way regardless of and in the absence of any sanction or incentive. In an ideal world neither incentive nor sanction are needed. Strictly speaking, neither is necessary in an enterprise with a strong corporate culture.

But what kind of behaviour should the culture encourage? Obviously it is not just a matter of any behaviour. In an ideal world, the culture should encourage:

- strategic thinking at every level of the organization
- employees to be entrepreneurial, not just managerial
- creativity rather than simply carrying out instructions
- a cooperative effort to formulate and implement the strategy.

This kind of behaviour has two major dimensions. First, it should empower the employee, giving him or her considerable discretion or room for decision making, sometimes referred to as 'autonomy'. The concept of self-direction or self-organization captures this element. Any organization can repress or suppress such behaviour but at a terrible long-term cost. An appropriate culture harnesses the self-interest of the employee to the interest of the organization

Second, the employee is encouraged to be receptive to new ideas and look for new ways of doing things, that is, to be personally innovative. Every improvement, however small, helps the enterprise retain its competitive advantage. The weight of many small changes may be the difference between holding a competitive advantage and failing to do so.

Following from these features are other characteristics, such as a propensity for risk taking, adopting a proactive stance in reading market change and being aggressive in a competitive sense. With all these characteristics, there should be a measure of restraint. Risks should not be taken for their own sake. Customers and competitors should not be antagonized unnecessarily.

There is therefore a danger that a culture which discourages non-conformity will undermine the development and maintenance of strategic advantage. An overly rigid conformity to the wishes of those in the principal position may discourage the kind of initiative by agents which improves performance and conserves competitive advantage. Culture should be framed to encourage initiative, or strategic thinking as it has been defined. As will be seen in Chapter 16, an emphasis on strategy as emergent is linked with the giving of significant discretion to all agents, even in the apparent formulation of strategy.

Much of the change referred to above is marginal or incremental, but what if a major change is required? A new strategy may mean a new culture. The appropriate culture may become once more, if temporarily, a power culture. The re-engineering of culture requires the support of a large number of key managers, probably all the senior managers and a sizeable proportion of middle managers. This is only likely to happen in a turnaround situation. The recruitment of key change managers who take the initiative in pushing through the necessary change of culture is a must.

Culture can assist in addressing the principal/agent problem. However, it may be that a full solution is bad for the organization. It may be that a degree of conflict provides the motivation to change and a continuous review of what is currently being done. All the mechanisms for solving the principal/agent problem described above can be employed simultaneously. They are not mutually exclusive. They reinforce each other. A well functioning organization is easy to recognize; it is one in which, while there may be many tensions, all staff are moving in the same direction.

Outside control

Obviously the outside world intrudes on the internal workings of an enterprise, particularly if there is competition in the markets. There has been much discussion of commodity markets and the impact of the forces of competition on the enterprise. In a developed economy the pressure is at its most intense in the capital market. Any loss of performance is usually reflected in a fall in the share price of a company. For that reason the share price of a public company is seen as an indicator of its good, indifferent or bad health. If the share price falls far enough, two results are likely to follow: a sacking of the management team and perhaps the directors and, even more drastic, a takeover of the company. The capital market can be a relentless driver of short-term performance. It exerts a discipline over management which can be severe.

An inappropriate structure, or a situation in which too many agents are allowed to pursue their own interests, can mean an enterprise, which is operating ineffectively, failing to implement its strategy or even formulate an appropriate strategy. It may appear to be moving without direction. This ineffectiveness will be reflected in the price of the company's shares.

Alternatively, an enterprise which has a strategy but is perceived as neglecting the bottom line, or working less effectively than it might to realize that strategy, may represent an opportunity for another enterprise to acquire resources relatively cheaply and quickly improve performance.

Often both these situations are revealed in a tendency for the valuation ratio to fall below one, that is, for the market value of the enterprise on the capital market to fall below the real or book value of its assets. Such an enterprise is clearly not realizing its full potential. If the capital market is 'efficient', this will lead to a takeover of the enterprise and a restructuring of that enterprise. This is the ultimate discipline on any public enterprise. A threat of takeover also threatens the jobs of the senior management team. It constitutes another form of risk.

Fortunately no capital market is perfect. It is obvious that policies such as the dividend payout affect the share price. It is not unusual for valuation ratios to fall below one for lengthy periods of time without a takeover occurring. This might be because a large share of profits is retained for investment in the enterprise. The potential threat of takeover provides the motivation for behaving in a certain way. It may involve structuring the enterprise in a way which is effective for its strategy making while tending to increase the importance of profit as the key indicator in any strategy, and even its distribution as dividends to shareholders. It is impossible to ignore the bottom line. However, provided the enterprise makes a reasonable rate of return, there is usually considerable freedom to make strategy. Many shareholders are just as much satisficers as are the managers. They are long-term holders of shares.

Sometimes a potential threat has the perverse effect of integrating all agents in resisting an undesired takeover. This is unusual since various management groups have different interests.

In the absence of the likelihood of a takeover threat, outside control, or discipline, can come from the commodity market, but it may be a long time coming. The change in the situation of the enterprise may not be sudden or dramatic. Increasing uncompetitiveness or a concentration of resources in mature or poorly performing businesses can lead not just to declining profit margins, but also to a steady loss of market share, a decline in the rate of future growth of either gross or net earnings, and eventually to loss making and a slowly mounting debt. If the industry is one important to government, for example one regarded as a pillar industry, it might lead to government intervention.

Case Study   The house of Gucci

The expansion of the Gucci enterprise was not supported by Guccio Gucci, the founder. Against resistance from his father, Aldo's first step in the company's growth was to open a shop in Rome in 1938, not a very propitious time to take such a step, but the first step in moving beyond the Florentine base. After the major setbacks of the 1930s, such as restrictions on leather imports, and World War II which closed all the normal markets and when attention was turned temporarily to shoe production for the military, the company flourished in the period of postwar recovery when incomes rose and consumers were free to buy luxury goods if and when they were available. Working in the Gucci leatherworks became a much-desired job and many skilled craftsmen started at Gucci, only to create their own enterprises later, often still supplying the Gucci company. The Gucci enterprise became the centre of a network of such craftsmen. Gucci established the foundations of a whole industry.

Particular attention was paid to the location and decor of the sales outlets, which were always located in expensive areas and furnished luxuriously but stylishly. They were set up to attract what are called today celebrities. The rich and powerful were individually feted. Their presence attracted others and gave the stores an ambience which helped sell the products. By the early 1950s possession of a Gucci bag or suitcase established its owner as someone with refined style and taste. Royalty and celebrity displayed their ownership. The press photographed them with Gucci products. Thus public display helped build the name. Gucci products were the first status brands to appear in postwar Europe. At the same time Italian clothing designers began to promote their products at *prêt-à-porter* fashion shows.

The first step in internationalizing the company was expansion into the USA, an obvious move given that Americans in the early postwar world had far more money to spend on aspirational goods. Aldo inaugurated the first New York store as early as 1953, much against the wishes of his father Guccio. The conflict between the different generations became something of a family tradition, unfortunately often reaching the courts. Aldo took a particular interest in the US project, recognizing the importance of the US market at this early stage in recovery from war. Gucci Shops Inc., the first US company, was given the right to use the Gucci trademark in the US market – the only time that the trademark was ever granted outside Italy. Elsewhere Gucci's foreign operating companies were franchise agreements. Gucci America became a flagship for the Gucci group. The first store in London was opened rather later in 1960, and in Paris in 1963. The three stages in the restructuring of this family company are discussed in turn.

Seeking a partner

A major role in the rise of the modern company of Gucci was played by the investment bank Investcorp, little known until it became involved with Gucci. It was created by its founder Nemir Kirdar in 1982 to act as a bridge for wealthy clients in the Middle East to invest their increasing wealth, based mostly on oil, in Europe and North America. There was a large pool of such money. Investcorp was set up as an Anglo-Arab counterpart to Goldman Sachs or J.P. Morgan, with a mission to buy up promising but struggling companies, restructure and improve them and then sell them off at a profit. Investcorp came of age and made a fortune by purchasing the American jeweller Tiffany & Company for US$135 million in 1984, rehabilitating the company and then selling the shares on the New York Stock Exchange. The company played an important role in sorting out the complicated share ownership and resurrecting the brand name. This deal put the company on the map. When approached by Gucci, Investcorp saw it as its means of entry into the closed business community of Europe. It proved to be a difficult and expensive, but finally triumphant entry.

Maurizio Gucci, son of Rodolfo, grandson of Guccio and the rising star of the family, was the next family member who was important. He managed to manoeuvre to take control of the company. In 1987 Maurizio Gucci and Investcorp reached what was called the 'Saddle Agreement'. They would collaborate to relaunch the brand, install professional management and establish a unified shareholder base for the company, in other words buy out the other family members, naturally against the wishes of these family members, including Aldo and his sons, one of whom he was in bitter conflict with. After this was done, they would seek a stock market listing for the family company. Investcorp agreed to acquire up to 50% of the company.

The acquisition took 18 months to complete and was made possible by the already bitter divisions within the Gucci family. It was carried out by Morgan Stanley, with the role of Investcorp as purchaser remaining secret for the whole period of negotiation with the different members of the Gucci family. This was a real turning point for Gucci, since it was the first time an outsider had owned a significant block of shares in the family company.

It was extremely difficult for a family-owned firm such as Gucci to attract and control the new capital and the professional management resources it desperately needed to stay viable. Having a creative idea was not enough. Most other fashion houses have been built on a strong relationship between the creative figure and an efficient business manager. Maurizio had great creative flair. His vision for the company turned out to be correct. It was Maurizio who appointed Tom Ford as the company's chief designer. However, the strategy was very expensive in the resources needed to give it back its name for quality. By 1993 Maurizio faced personal bankruptcy and so did the company. Investcorp was losing patience in financing the company. Between 1987 and 1994 Investcorp had poured hundreds of millions of dollars into Gucci with no return. The house of Gucci was in total disarray, each part having a serious debt problem. Sales had been static for three years and losses were mounting. Morale was low. The only solution was for it to cease to be under the control or ownership of the Gucci family. By the end of 1993, Investcorp had acquired 100% ownership, buying out Maurizio Gucci for US$120 million.

The company returned its headquarters to Florence from where Maurizio had moved it to Rome. It rationalized its activities and labour force. One key turning point was when Tom Ford was given sole charge of design in May, 1994. He single-handedly turned Gucci into a fashion house. Another turning point came with the appointment of Domenico De Sole, for ten years CEO of Gucci America, as chief operating officer in the autumn of 1994 and in July 1995 as CEO. De Sole knew Gucci very well and, more to the point, knew how to motivate the staff and restore morale. At last Gucci had the partnership of creativity and management expertise it required. Maurizio had given it the right strategy. In 1994 profits became positive and sales began to turn upwards.

Investcorp had grown tired of the effort to revive the company. In 1994 it tried to sell Gucci for US$500 million, offering it to either LVMH or the Vendome Luxury Group, owners of Cartier, Alfred Dunhill, Piaget and Baume and Mercier. The offers received were between US$300 and 400 million, an unacceptably low level. However, the company was ready for listing.

The public float

Investcorp used two top merchant banks to lead the listing, Morgan Stanley and Credit Suisse First Boston. Fortunately sales were already on the rise. They were far exceeding the expectations at the time of the offer from LVMH and Vendome, one year before. In August 1995, Vendome, realizing its mistake, came back with a raised offer of US$850 million, twice the previous level. However, Investcorp's advisers valued the company at more than $1 billion so they continued with the initial public offering planned for the autumn of that year. The initial plan was to offer 30% of the company on international stock markets, Investcorp retaining the other 70%. The road show promoting the issue went so well that Investcorp increased the offer share to 48%. The share price was to be $22, at the high end of the previously estimated range. In the event the offer was 14 times oversubscribed. In April 1996 the secondary offering was completed. Between them they raised a grand total of US$2.1 billion, which, after intermediary costs, left Gucci with US$1.7 billion.

This was an amazing turnaround for a company which had seemed to be headed for bankruptcy just two years before. Investcorp was completely vindicated in its commitment. Maurizio's creative strategy was also vindicated. Gucci, as a publicly traded company owned by large and small investors across the US and Europe, was an anomaly in Italy where even such companies were usually controlled by a shareholder syndicate. Most fashion companies remained privately owned.

Gucci created a new sector on the stock market. It was a true pioneer and was imitated by other luxury goods companies. Gucci encouraged the emergence of analysts in the international investment banks who specialized in 'fashion risk', meaning what a poor collection might mean to a company. They began to analyse the business cycles of fashion companies, including sourcing, delivery and sell-through as well as the importance of show reviews, glossy fashion spreads and the style arbiters of Hollywood. They also appreciated the impact of recession on the market and how companies might insulate themselves from its effects.

Meanwhile Tom Ford was integrating the total image of Gucci – the apparel and accessory collections, the new store concept, advertising, office layout and decor, staff dress and even the flower arrangements at Gucci events.

Expansion

The team of the designer Tom Ford and the manager Domenico De Sole completed Maurizio's strategy successfully by rescuing Gucci's tarnished brand and turning the company round. The success of the public float and the ensuing rise in the share value was made possible by this turnaround. What was to be the strategy for further expansion?

The public float made Gucci a possible target for takeover. In June 1998 Prada announced that it had bought a 9.5% stake in Gucci, but Prada was not large enough to constitute a threat to Gucci, at that time a $3 billion company with sales in that year of more than $1 billion. Prada took no further action. In the autumn of 1998 the corporate offices of Gucci were moved to London, reinforcing its international status. This move was taken deliberately to help Gucci to recruit top-level international managers.

In January 1999, LVMH acquired more than 5% of Gucci. LVMH already included in its stable Christian Dior, Givenchy, Louis Vuitton and Christian Lacroix as well as the vintners Veuve Clicquot, Hennessy and Chateau d'Yquem, the perfume house Guerlain and the cosmetics emporium Sephoria – this was a real threat. LVMH was dominant in France, and was likely to look to Italy which was a rising player in the world of fashion and aspirational goods. LVMH even had separate discussions with Georgio Armani which came to nothing. Arnault, the CEO of LVMH, has a style of continuing to build his stake in a 'creeping takeover' until he controlled the company. LVMH bought out Prada's 10% share, and by the end of January 1999 held 34.4% of Gucci. Prada in its turn continued to expand, buying control of Jil Sander and Helmut Lang, and joining with LVMH to buy Fendi, winning out in a bidding war with Gucci.

Threatened in this way, Gucci sought a white knight to help it fend off LVMH. To buy time it initiated an employee stock ownership plan, in so doing diluting LVMH's ownership share. This was combined with the putting in place of a golden parachute for both De Sole and Ford in the event that the company was taken over, a threat of removal of Gucci's main assets. The white knight eventually emerged in the form of François Pinault, controller of the largest non-food retailer in Europe, Pinault-Printemps-Redoute (PPR).

Pinault not only offered to buy enough of Gucci to block the purchase by LVMH, he also offered to buy Yves Saint Laurent, which he later did for $1 billion, and turn it over to Gucci. Pinault invested $3 billion for a 40% share in Gucci, later raised to 42%. This had the effect of reducing Arnault's share to 21%. In reaction Arnault made a bid which valued Gucci at $8 billion which was rejected, even when the price was further raised. However, the agreement in place today is that PPR is obliged to buy out the rest of Gucci if the share price of the company is below US$101.50 in March 2004. PPR is now Europe's biggest distribution company, with annual sales of US$27 billion, but a debt of $6 billion. It is currently at a debt rating just a notch above junk bond status and in no position to buy out the rest of the Gucci company.

In 1999 the Gucci Group bought the Yves Saint Laurent brand for US$1 billion from Pinault, at least its ready-to-wear and beauty businesses. It did not acquire the haute couture part of the company, which was acquired by Pinault himself. Gucci then made YSL the cornerstone of its global multibrand strategy. Gucci had become a profit machine on the basis of $5,000 dresses and $700 purses. It now intended to do the same with YSL: it was a test of its ability to extend and develop the model.

The Yves Saint Laurent story parallels in some respects the story of Gucci, although it is a much more recent one. Yves Saint Laurent began as the chief designer of Christian Dior. He made his name at the early age of 26 when he began his series of collections which changed the nature of modern fashion. He initiated his own label in the same year. He opened his first ready-to-wear Rive Gauche boutique. In all of this he acted as one of the pioneers.

In 1972 Squibb bought the YSL company and started the process of licensing. Quite quickly this ran out of control. There were a myriad of licences sold, without coordination and no desire to prevent the valuable brand name being sullied, for everything from YSL cigarettes to plastic YSL shoes, which could be bought on the Tokyo subway for as little as $125. There were as many as nine different store designs around the world. By the early 1990s, a time when Gucci also reached a similar stage, most upmarket shops had ceased to stock YSL products. YSL was overtaken by Giorgio Armani and Chanel, and later the revived Gucci.

After acquisition, Gucci was faced with the task of restoring the YSL name, a task in which they already had valuable experience. The number of licences was reduced to just 15. Royalties from these licences declined from 65% of revenue in 1999 to 25% in 2001. Most of the manufacturing of shoes, bags and clothes was brought in-house. The number of directly-owned stores with the YSL name was tripled to 43, with a promise of 60 within 18 months.

YSL once more became the fashion trendsetter. Ford put on three critically acclaimed shows, the first at the Rodin Museum in Paris in October 2000. Ford regularly placed his designs on the front pages of fashion magazines. The first outstanding success for the revived YSL came with a $2,500 purple silk peasant blouse in March 2001. There was a heavy commitment of financial resources to advertising. Quite the best advertising came when A-list celebrities began to wear YSL – Nicole Kidman at the Cannes Film Festival in 2001 wore a black silk strapless YSL dress and Gwyneth Paltrow carried a Mombasa bag at a fashion show in January 2002.

The Mombasa bag is typical of the world of luxury and the worlds of Gucci and YSL. It was a soft, oyster-shaped leather shoulder bag with a curved deer-horn handle, which was priced at $700. Such accessories carried a profit margin of over 40%. It sold out as fast as shops could stock it.

YSL was still making a loss but a return to profit was planned for 2003. Sales were growing so fast that an earlier return seemed likely. In 2001 YSL sold only $90 million worth of ready-to-wear items and accessories compared to $462 million of beauty products, and compared with Gucci label sales of $1.5 billion.

The strategy and its implementation

The Gucci history shares many events and circumstances with other similar companies – the identification of appropriate partners, the movement to a public company, the loss of family control, the problem of the professional management of creative people, the development and misuse of a brand name. All these issues pose strategic problems which must be resolved. The twin achievements which make success possible are a positive balancing of creativity against managerial efficiency and the managing of the brand name so as to preserve the aura surrounding the brand but at the same time taking advantage of that aura to make a significant profit. These are problems which have confronted many similar companies.

Gucci always had the creative flair; it did not always have the administrative expertise. It grew alongside the aspirational market which emerged in the postwar world, once recovery was complete. It understood well that aspirational market. The family members, notably Aldo and Maurizio, understood very well the nature of and potential for development of the market which had appeared for the kind of product which the company sold. They did not fully understand the commitment of resources and the level of management needed to translate this vision into a reality.

Gucci set the model which has been imitated by many other companies. Some have remained private companies, other have been floated and taken over. Some have become parts of much larger organizations. To some extent all purveyors of luxury or aspirational goods are competitors with each other. Each chooses to highlight one particular attribute of its goods. As Goldstein (1999: 95–8) has written of another company:

'Prada is not beautiful like Dior, classic like Armani, sexy like Gucci, or tacky like Versace. But at various times it is each of those things. ... Prada is fashion's future.' All have tried to draw out the attributes which the customer prizes.

One particular problem with the sellers of luxury or aspirational goods is how to ride recession. In the second quarter of 2002 Gucci's profits were down 55% and sales down 7%. The problems of the white knight PPR are more of a problem. Riding a boom is easy when rising income and wealth levels fuel demand. In a recession the reverse effect becomes prominent. Luxury or aspirational good are easily struck off the list of purchases when it is necessary for consumers to retrench. This makes it essential to take a number of strategic decisions to ensure survival. Polishing the brand names to give them advantage over others helps, as does the expenditure of US$200 million to open and refurbish 70 stores. Positioning the company is a key strategy.

Case Study Questions

1. How should an enterprise be structured where the core competency of that enterprise involves 'creative' activity?
2. Is it inevitable that a family company goes through a difficult transition in order to come of age?
3. What does the history of Gucci tell us about the successful management of a brand name?
4. Does the history of Gucci show that a company selling luxury or aspirational goods is different from the norm in both structure and strategy?
5. What strategy should be adopted by such a company in a recession?

Reading

Ball, D., 'Makeover after takeover', *The Asian Wall Street Journal*, May 27, 2002: A7–8.

Forden, S. G., *The House of Gucci* (William Morrow, New York: 2000).

Goldstein, L., 'Prada goes shopping', *Fortune*, September 27, 1999: 95–8.

Matlock, C. and Edmundson, G., 'Maybe buying Gucci was too much of a luxury', *Business Week*, October 14, 2002: 30.

Relevant website

www.gucci.com

Key strategic lessons

- The dilemma of how to integrate all stakeholders and managers in the effective formulation and implementation of a strategy is a universal problem, affecting all types of organization.

- A principal engages an agent to carry out a particular task on his or her behalf. This principal/agent relationship is a key issue in strategy making and includes the relationships between shareholders, managers, staff, suppliers and strategic allies.

- This relationship creates challenges in integrating an organization in order to achieve strategic targets because continuous and detailed supervision is impossible and the principal and agent have divergent interests and asymmetrical information.

- Behavioural patterns which affect the way in which strategy is made include excessive concentration on achieving strategic targets at the end of a planning period, scapegoating, seeking less demanding goals or adopting short-term fixes such as underinvestment or misrepresenting performance.

- The formal structure of an organization can be determined by the product, regional, functional or customer group design principles. The matrix principle systematically combines any two of these and the hybrid principle reflects the actual history of growth of an enterprise.

- The informal structure of an organization can be determined by command, control, coordination, communication or conflict factors.

- An organization can solve the principal/agent dilemma through monitoring and/or internalization of the corporate culture. The former involves direct and indirect supervision and incentive structures.

- Corporate culture can be power, role, task or person-centred.

- The main source of outside discipline on the various groups in the enterprise is the operation of various markets, principally the capital market.

Applying the lessons

1 Define the following terms: principal, agent, formal structure, informal structure, matrix design structure, power culture, role culture, task culture, and person culture.

2 Select an organization with which you are familiar and list the kind of principal/agent relationships which exist within that organization and indicate the way in which differing interests influence the behaviour of principal and agent, particularly behaviour with a strategic perspective.

3 What is meant by governance? Consider the use of the term in recent comments on corporate performance. Is it possible to widen the meaning of the term to include relationships between all stakeholder groups? How is governance relevant to strategy making?

4 Give examples of the various ways in which the behaviour of any agent might obstruct the making and implementation of good strategy.

What are the ethical issues which might arise in the attempt to reconcile the interests of principals and agents and prevent obstruction of the strategy-making process? In any divergence of interest, what are the procedures which might be adopted in order to reconcile principal and agent?

5 Often the reorganization accompanying a takeover or the initiation of a major new project requires a structure different from the one characterizing an organization which is stable and mature. How should this problem be dealt with? What are the key challenges? Illustrate from an example of one such reorganization.

6 Select one example of a takeover threat and show how the threat influenced the behaviour of the threatened managers. What influence does such a threat have on strategy making?

Strategic project

Choose a company which is currently in a turnaround situation or a situation likely to result in a turnaround situation. This might be a company which is in the news or a small company with which you are familiar. The important issue is access to information about the problem. The aim of the project is to prepare a report which will suggest how the turnaround might be achieved, following the procedure outlined below.

The project should involve the following steps:

1 Analysis of the nature of the problem which has emerged. Is it the result of a poor or non-existent strategy or a failure to realize the strategy already adopted? The focus of this project is on the latter kind of problem.

2 Diagnosis of the causes of the problem with the help of the concepts introduced in this chapter. What are the causes, characteristics and consequences of the crisis?

3 Comparison with a similar turnaround problem or problems in the past.

4 An indication of what is required to turn the company around.

Example: The recent and current problems of Asea Brown Boveri display the difficulties of using a matrix model of organization.

Exploring further

For a discussion of agency problems see Fama, 1980: 375–90. The literature relevant to various issues in this chapter is overwhelming in its extent.

Going back as far as the early work of Chandler, 1962, there is an immense literature on the subject of structure and its relationship to strategy. The starting point might be Duncan, 1979: 59–80. There are a range of other introductory papers, of which Macmillan and Jones, 1984: 12–16 and Mintzberg, 1981: 103–16 are excellent examples. Mintzberg has written a series of papers considering different kinds of structure in Mintzberg and Quinn, 1996. All textbooks introduce the main organizing principles and provide examples of the application of these principles.

There is a good paper on the problems of the matrix organization – Davis and Lawrence, 1978: 131–42.

The various issues of control and motivation are discussed in an extensive literature. The following provide a good introduction: Simons, 1995: 80–8, Katzenbach and Santamaria, 1999: 107–17, Latham and Slajkovic, 1999: 49–57, Herzberg, 1987: 109–20, Kohn, 1993: 54–63 and Kerr, 1995: 7–14.

Many texts devote significant space to the role of corporate culture in the implementation of strategy, usually something short of a chapter length. Often culture is put alongside leadership. Both topics are well covered in the literature. There are some good introductions to the issue of the interaction between culture and strategy: see Scholz, 1987: 78–87, Bettinger, 1989: 38–41, Clement, 1994: 33–9; O'Reilly, 1989: 9–25; and Schwartz and Davis, 1981: 30–48. A rather longer treatment is to be found in Kotter and Heskett, 1992.

A description of a specific case can be found in Quick, 1992: 45–56.

13 When to compete and when to cooperate

Strategic rivalry, unlike competitive rivalry, is the search for cooperation. (DAVIS AND DEVINNEY, 1997: 286)

Learning objectives

After reading this chapter you will be able to:

- take account of the actions and responses of other strategic players in making a good strategy

- understand what is meant by the commons, or public goods, and free riding

- use game theory to understand the structure of a number of recurrent strategic situations

- describe the different ways in which cooperation can be initiated

- note the proliferation of strategic alliances as an expression of the increasing importance of cooperation

Key strategic challenge

When should my enterprise compete and when should it cooperate?

Strategic dangers

That an enterprise foregoes the strategic advantages of cooperation by regarding all situations as involving competition for a fixed reward and displaying an excessive desire to compete, and that all other players are regarded as adversaries whose sole aim is to deceive in an opportunistic way.

Case Study Scenario   The wine industry in Australia

'It was the wine industry's efforts in strategic collaboration that were the cornerstone of its remarkable business growth and export achievements.'

Marsh and Shaw, nd: 7

There has been a wine industry in Australia almost since the first white settlement. Conditions in many parts of Australia are ideal for grape growing, particularly in those parts with a Mediterranean-type climate. However, as in Europe, the industry was almost completely destroyed by the outbreak of the disease phylloxera at the end of the nineteenth century. As a consequence the industry disappeared as a major part of the economy for well over half a century. The modern industry has been a product of the last 30 years.

The development of the industry has been one of the great economic success stories in Australia, if not *the* major success story. The Australian wine industry has been very successful and has grown rapidly over the last 30 years, establishing an international reputation and presence. It has displayed an impressive record of innovation and an impressive switch into the high premium market (for example, the average price per litre of Australian wine rose from A$2.49 in 1986/7 to A$4.20 in 1996/7 and is still rising). Growth has been sufficiently fast to override any short-term fluctuations in the level of demand and any tendency for supply to run ahead of demand, at least until now. If anything, the rate of advance has accelerated in recent years, with all indicators almost doubling in the five years since 1997 – the number of wineries, the area under vines, the wine grape crush and wine production itself.

The growth is mainly due to exports. For example, as late as the mid-1980s, only 2% of production was exported. A decade later this had risen to 37%, way above what is achieved by Italy and France. In 2002 exports overtook domestic sales. More than one million bottles of wine are exported every day. The target of A$1 billion worth of wine exports by the end of the 1990s was exceeded. A$2 billion is now very close to achievement.

As an exporter, in 1999 Australia accounted for 3.7% of world exports in volume terms, fifth behind Italy, France, Spain and the USA and 5.3% in value terms, fourth, behind France, Italy and Spain. France is the clear leader in value, producing and selling a high proportion of premium wine. The big three European producers between them account for more than 68% of world exports in volume and over 70% in value.

As a world producer, Australia still has a long way to go, but it is climbing the rankings. In 1995 Australia produced less than one-tenth the amount of wine of France or Italy. Over the next five years it rapidly closed the gap to about one-seventh, but it is disadvantaged by the small size of the domestic market, reflecting a small population and a relatively low level of consumption per head. The industry has no choice but to be export-oriented if it is to grow. So far the industry has more than met this challenge; in 2001 BRL Hardy, one of the big four producers, was the Australian exporter of the year.

It is interesting to speculate what the industry has done right in order to achieve this success. The case study focuses on the blend of competition and cooperation which has underpinned that success.

The industry in Europe is an old industry, with enormous prestige attached to particular labels or brands and particular regions such as Burgundy, Bordeaux and Champagne. The traditional producers have prevented these generic labels being used by Australian producers. This is probably a blessing in disguise since it has forced the Australian producers to develop their own branding and has reinforced the development of a strong local identity and a highly differentiated product.

The main wine markets in the world are in the old areas of production or the areas close to them. Consumption per head in European wine-producing countries exceeds by a considerable amount consumption in Australia. In 1999 it exceeded 60 litres per head in France, almost 55 in Italy and a little short of 50 in Portugal. However, this represents a significant decline in consumption from past levels – in the French case from about 100 litres, and therefore a contraction of the domestic market. Australia was 18th, at a little less than 20 litres per head. Some of Australia's main markets, such as the USA,

Table 13.1 Wine production (million litres)

		1995	1997	1999
1	France	5,435	5,356	6,023
2	Italy	5,570	5,089	5,807
3	Spain	2,088	3,322	3,268
4	USA	1,867	2,200	2,069
5	Argentina	1,644	1,350	1,589
6	Germany	851	849	1,229
7	South Africa	845	881	914
8	Australia	503	617	851
9	Portugal	725	612	781
10	Romania	672	669	650

Source: Anderson and Norman, 2003.

Canada and Japan, have by comparison very low levels of per capital consumption and are ripe for opening up with an appropriate marketing campaign.

There is a long tradition of the accumulation of knowledge relevant to the industry and a snobbery about the techniques used. For example, the industry in France is highly fragmented and subject to all sorts of detailed regulation. Producers have been rather con-temptuous of the application of science to viticulture and wine making. There are new wine areas, principally in California, Chile, Argentina, South Africa and Eastern Europe. These areas have similar conditions to Australia and produce similar products. The industry is therefore a competitive one. Success in Australia has partly resulted from a capacity to cooperate in a number of key areas, such as research, training and promotion.

Dealing with other strategic players

One major problem for strategy making is the existence of other players, particularly if they have unknown strategies. Are they fierce competitors, passive competitors or potential cooperators? Some enterprises have a competitive bias, others a cooperative orientation. The bias can change over time; the same enterprise sometimes acts competitively and sometimes cooperatively.

Any player can act aggressively and opportunistically or in a way which invites cooperation. The style of strategic activity reflects the attitude of the players, the influence of the corporate culture of the organization and the nature of the typical situations in which they have to play. Here, the competitive position of the main players, the other players' strategies and the nature of the strategic situation are relevant.

The nature of the market may not allow cooperation to occur – in some cases the market is too competitive. Chapter 6 dealt with the competitive environment and the forces of competition. Sometimes the nature of competition is such that only a few players are rewarded. For many players, competition appears a zero-sum game, that is, a game in which if there is a winner, there must be a loser. This colours their strategic orientation. However, there are many games in which everyone can win. It is clearly preferable to develop a strategy which allows every player to win, although in such a game the maximum winnings are always less than what could be won, with the very best outcome, in the zero-sum competition. The problem is that the best outcome is unlikely to occur.

Every enterprise has objectives which need to be defined, although there may be an inherent ambiguity even in the apparently simplest of objectives. It is necessary to explore what other enterprises know about themselves and their competitors:

• What is this knowledge likely to be?
• Is there an asymmetry in the knowledge held by the enterprises?
• Does one know more than another?

How are other players likely to react to any initial action? It helps if the interaction with the other player is not a one-off event, that there has been previous contact. The track record of a player tells much about the likely responses of the players in different situations. A player may have a good reputation or a bad one: it may engage frequently in opportunistic behaviour or may follow a long-term strategy which earns a good reputation for consistency. It may attach great importance to keeping its word, seeing this as a significant intangible asset.

Reading such unwritten strategies is difficult:

- The strategy may not exist as an explicit statement and may be implicit
- The reading may be an incentive for others to conceal their intentions. Worse, there may be a deliberate intention to mislead
- The behaviour of different representatives of an enterprise may be inconsistent. The principal problem is to read the differing strategic objectives of all the main players
- There is always the problem of strategists changing their mind or adjusting specific objectives to changing circumstances
- The time frame may differ significantly. One player may be looking ten years ahead, another may be concerned only with the immediate future. This may lead to one looking to emphasize short-term profit and the other to building significant market share.

There is a set of parameters which define the nature of such situations. Where it is relatively difficult to interpret the actions of other players, the best approach may be to look at the situation in order to see what decisions might be made. The three main elements of any situation are the set of rules governing how the players behave, the reward structure and the time frame.

There are the *rules* by which the different players are influenced, if not fully bound. Some rules are self-imposed, others are imposed from outside. The self-imposed rules reflect the values and norms of behaviour of the enterprise or the wider community in which the enterprise operates. These values may relate to key individuals, the enterprise as a whole or its stakeholder groups. They may relate to what is contained within the corporate, community or national culture, which are in a sense imposed on the enterprise from outside. There may be some conflict between these different cultures and between different sets of self-imposed rules. There may be significant sanctions resulting from a failure to observe any rules.

The rules imposed from outside might consist of legal rules or rules that are inherent in the situation itself, such as the rules of economic competition. Some players scrupulously follow such rules, others flout the rules whenever it is profitable to do so. Flouting either legal or economic rules is a dangerous strategic decision since it may involve the incurring of serious future costs.

The degree of competition structures a specific situation. If there is intense competition, there may be no choice but to conform to the demands of the market. If there is less than perfect competition, there may be room for discretionary behaviour which does not aim for short-term profit maximization.

The *reward structure* has a powerful influence on behaviour. The rewards may differ in nature – the expansion of profits or the winning of market share, or they may differ in size, some cooperative activities offering much larger rewards than others. Returns have to be balanced against the risks.

What are the risks associated with different kinds of behaviour? Cooperation creates its own risks. The main risk is that it lays the cooperator open to opportunistic behaviour. This may reflect the changing, indeed worsening, circumstances of the

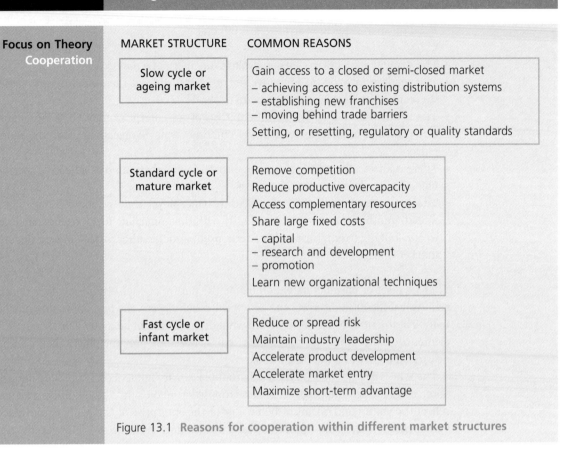

Figure 13.1 **Reasons for cooperation within different market structures**

cooperators or the emergence of an asymmetrical situation in which one of the cooperators has far more invested in the relationship. A desperate player may pressure a partner who has become dependent on the relationship to change the reward structure in a dramatic way.

It is necessary to ask, rewards for whom? The rewards and risks are unevenly distributed among strategists or stakeholders. For key individuals the rewards may be different.

Cooperation tends to produce benefits in the future. It encourages a *time frame* longer than is used in fiercely competitive environments. Opportunistic behaviour is more likely in one-off situations since the victim's opinion is of no relevance since the former partners will not interact again.

The strategic horizon reflects the nature, not only of the decision, but of the industry and changes in its external context. Strong stable cooperative relationships develop over a protracted period of time when circumstances do not change much. Whatever the time frame of the enterprise, or of senior strategists within the enterprise, the interests of any one individual may be to adopt a short-term horizon since the individual may cease to work for the enterprise in the near future or may have an incentive scheme which rewards short-term operational rather than long-term strategic success, a typical situation. The stock market may punish anything other than short-term profit maximization. These sorts of pressure may make it difficult to engage in cooperative behaviour which provides benefits in the distant future.

There are clearly situations in which it is better to compete, and other situations in which it is better to cooperate. It appears from the proliferation of strategic alliances at every level of the economy that the situations promoting cooperation are becoming increasingly common. The following two Strategy in Action modules illustrate the nature of cooperation in two very different industries – clothing and automobile manufacture.

Strategy in Action　Benetton: cooperation as strategy

The clothing industry is a mature industry. Since there is not much scope to change its technology, it remains a labour-intensive industry. Yet it is an industry with a split personality:

- On the one hand, there are the low-cost Asian countries, which produce standard goods of low price and mass sales. Price and the supply side rule.
- On the other hand, there are the high-cost, developed economies, producing high-quality, high fashion clothing for those with significant discretionary income. Product differentiation and the demand side rule.

Italy and Germany are as much exporters of clothing as China and Thailand.

The Benetton Group has about 5,550 shops in 120 countries, 7,000 employees and manufacturing facilities worldwide. The group has greatly extended its range of products since its early days. Benetton became Europe's multinational clothing retailer-producer.

Its revenue comes from three sources:

- casual wear (garments, accessories and footwear), distributed under the United Colours and Sisley brands, in 2000 accounting for about 74% of total revenue
- a comparatively new area, sportswear (the Playlife and Killer Loop brands for clothing, accessories and footwear) and sports equipment (ski boots, skis, in-line skates, skateboards, snowboards, scooters and tennis rackets, marketed under brands such as Nordica, Prince, Killer Loop and Rollerblades), in 2000 accounting for 20% of total revenue

Table 13.2　**Gross revenues and net income of Benetton (€ millions)**

	Revenues	Net income
2001	2098	148
2000	2018	243
1999	1982	166
1998	1980	151
1997	1878	150
1996	1483	127
1995	1518	114
1994	1440	109

- complementary activities (royalties, sales of raw materials, industrial and advertising services), accounting for 6% of total revenue in 2000.

The Benetton Group was founded in 1965 by a brother and sister team. Luciano was a fashion wholesaler and Guiliana a sweater designer. An early success with soft, colourful, wool-blend sweaters attracted two other brothers, Gilberto and Carlo, to join the partnership. The market segment targeted was the young with large discretionary income. The focus was on fashionable, brightly coloured, casual garments made of natural fibres. Since the onset of the influx of cheap imports, nearly half the European textile business has disappeared, but Benetton has survived and thrived. How has it achieved this?

From the beginning Benetton aimed to combine good design and quality at competitive prices with the volume sales which would allow it to reap economies of scale. It based its operations on industrial fashion rather than the handcrafted fashions preferred by

▶

other Italian fashion houses. At the same time it tried to keep close to the customers and be flexible enough to respond quickly to changes in fashion. The approach was to combine centralization where it was beneficial, for example in purchasing, and decentralization where it was beneficial, in manufacturing. Benetton became the single largest consumer of wool. There are more than 400 subcontractors providing the operations needed for manufacture. Only specialist, high-tech operations such as dyeing and cutting are not decentralized.

Benetton pioneered a new relationship with suppliers and distributors. It had a unique system of agents who acted as intermediaries between Benetton and its retail outlets. In the early years, the agents, less than 80 of them, played a vital role in spreading the Benetton brand. They displayed and distributed the Benetton collection, assembled orders for stock and generally supervised the merchandise and pricing at the stores. Agents could easily earn at least US$1 million from the 4% commission on factory sales through their retail outlets, and any profits which came from part ownership of the retail outlets. The agents were responsible for bringing into the partnership small but committed investors. Together they established and stocked the stores exclusively with Benetton products. The store owners or managers acted as if they were franchisees, adhering to a set of understandings which constituted the 'Benetton way of doing things', carrying only Benetton merchandise and following simple rules. The shops offered close market contact and outstanding service. Benetton stores were typically low-capital, high-turnover operations, able to recoup a capital commitment in three or four years.

Benetton saw itself as having core competencies in design and some parts of manufacturing, but not in the distribution of clothing. It took advantage of the skills of others in manufacturing high-quality, fashionable clothing where it could. It sought to outsource the labour-intensive phases of production, such as tailoring, finishing and ironing, to small and medium-size enterprises located mainly in northeastern Italy, especially in Treviso, but some international. Since direct supervision of labour is the key issue in putting together the clothing, Benetton was better off linking with small family-owned workshops, typically with less than 15 workers and every incentive to perform well, than putting together a vast concern with thousands of union-organized workers and no economies of scale or high-tech applications.

For many years Benetton was the archetype of the network organization, like IKEA, a strategic centre firm, linking up with suppliers in the same way. Benetton has developed a number of successful vertical complementary alliances with its subcontractors. Benetton helps the suppliers with production planning and materials procurement, and gives technical assistance when needed. The nature of the relationship assists Benetton to remain flexible and keep its overhead costs low. Benetton retained in-house any strategic activities and operations which required heavy investment (weaving, cutting, dyeing, quality controls at entry and on finished goods, quality control of intermediate phases and packing).

Cooperation lowered costs and increased flexibility over what would have been possible had all the activities been concentrated in one enterprise. At its best, Benetton excelled in responsive merchandising, inventory elimination, customized production and credit management. Worldwide it was able to replace inventory quickly and efficiently. It was famous for its ability to use point-of-sale information to tailor seasonal production to demand. It unashamedly relied on its cooperators to achieve this.

Strategy in Action The strategic alliance between Renault and Nissan

Renault has been one of the smaller global car producers, France's largest, but a relatively efficient one. It has significant government ownership. On the other hand, by the end of the 1990s, Nissan had entered a period of financial distress, having failed to make a profit for the previous eight years and having accumulated over $16 billion of debt. It lagged behind the leading Japanese car producers, Toyota and Honda. Neither was expected to be among the six major world players. However, together they would become the fourth largest producer in the world.

The origin of the strategic alliance was the Renault reaction to a decision by Toyota to build a new small car manufacturing plant in France. Competition was reaching into the core market of Renault. Renault reacted strongly and positively. In early 1998 it announced plans to expand its output by half a million units in the period to 2002, and simultaneously reduce its overall costs of production by a significant amount. One way of achieving this was to form an alliance with Nissan which had significant excess capacity. Nissan could produce annually a million more vehicles than it actually sold. In 1999 this alliance took place. The first task was to turn Nissan round.

The initial core act of the alliance was the transfer of $5.4 billion of the Nissan debt to Renault in return for a 36.6% equity stake in the Japanese company. However, written into the 1999 agreement was the retention of operating autonomy by both partners, despite the equity stake. Clearly Renault saw significant advantage in the alliance for itself, even at this stage.

A proposed link between Renault and Volvo had fallen through, as had a proposal for Daimler-Chrysler to take over Nissan. From the beginning, the companies were genuinely complementary. There were powerful geographical synergies. Nissan was strong in North America whereas Renault was weak. Renault was expert in innovative design, Nissan in engineering. There had been much preliminary discussion, analysis and action. The particular areas of focus in exploiting the synergy were in manufacturing operations, purchasing and marketing.

In an unprecedented move, a Brazil-based high flyer, Carlos Ghosn, later nicknamed 'Le cost killer', was appointed as the new president and CEO of Nissan. He saw his mission as making the necessary changes to make Nissan profitable once more, but to do this while retaining and safeguarding the identity of Nissan.

In its first stage, the aims of the alliance were to:

- formulate a revival plan for Nissan
- update Nissan's products and make them competitive
- introduce systems in Nissan to reward good performance
- cut Nissan's costs to a competitive level so that it could retain profitability
- reduce Nissan's debt
- break down barriers between the different parts of the alliance

- identify and exploit the complementary strengths and synergies of the two partners
- identify a broad strategic direction for the alliance.

One of the main problems of the alliance was that it was between two companies with different cultures and philosophies and, more to the point, different expectations on the part of managers and workers. Ghosn believed that it was imperative to develop trust and be transparent in what was done.

To achieve success required the dropping of some time-honoured Japanese practices. For example, despite the high level of debt, the company held significant non-core assets, financial and property investments, particularly in *keiretsu* partners. This amounted to at least US$4 billion, resources which could be productively used to assist core activities by financing new investments and reducing debt. This investment was disposed of and the resources released for use in the revival plan.

More directly threatening to the gaining of willing cooperation from staff was the need to change the system of employment, in particular to ditch the seniority rule and revamp the compensation system, putting the emphasis on performance. This was done. In the event, it proved possible to introduce stock options.

Ghosn went about this dramatic change by creating two sets of teams:

- a set of cross-functional teams (CFTs) within Nissan itself, important to the formulation and implementation of the revival plan
- a set of cross-company teams (CCTs) between Nissan and Renault, important to continuing successful cooperation between the two companies.

Initially the emphasis was on the first set of teams. The aim of the CFTs was twofold, to encourage managers to think differently from the way they had thought in the past and help to sell the message that change was necessary. There were initially nine such groups, each with ten members from middle management. A vice-president sponsored each team and specialist pilots were there to guide their efforts. Each team could create subteams where it was thought desirable. The areas covered were business development, purchasing, manufacturing and logistics, research and development, sales and marketing, general and administration, finance and costs, phase-out of products and parts complexity, and organization. Each team had three months for the review. About 500 people worked in the CFTs and the subteams, a sizeable part of the management of the enterprise. At the top was a nine-member executive committee responsible for processing the recommendations and producing the revival plan itself. The CFTs remained in existence after the completion of the plan review and have a continuing role. Alongside the CFTs are the CCTs, the cross-company teams responsible for making the alliance work. There were eleven of these. Their role increased in importance as the partnership deepened.

The commons and free riding

The strategic situation of any player is made more complex by the existence of what is called the commons and the tendency of other players to free ride. The term 'commons' is shorthand for common property, that is, a public good, and a resource or simply a property which is accessible to a number of potential users or consumers, sometimes all potential consumers, at a price which does not cover the real cost of its use, in the extreme case at no charge at all. The most frequently cited examples of the commons are fresh air and clean water.

The definition of commons should be broader. Common land might be available to a whole community or public areas within a block of apartments available to all its residents. Both would qualify as 'commons'. The 'commons' exists everywhere, at all levels in a society or an economy. This becomes obvious if the perspective is shifted down to the level of the enterprise. From a strategic perspective, it is this level which is relevant.

Some of the commons is tangible and obvious to all, such as public land, other parts are intangible and often invisible, such as good reputation. Increasingly, the intangible is becoming the more frequent manifestation of the commons. A strong branding for a locality or a country and a good reputation for generic products or services qualify as commons, in that various members or residents can take advantage of this commons. Reputation is an all-pervasive commons. A reputation for hard work or efficiency attaching to a particular group, however large, constitutes a type of commons, since members of the group can take advantage of the general reputation and exploit that commons in an opportunistic way.

Some of the commons is directly relevant to business:

- At the industry level, the supply of trained workers or managers may be part of the commons, that is, freely available to all players within those sectors without the need to incur the cost of training. Anyone can recruit without incurring such a cost
- The results of publicly available research are another example, insofar as the knowledge cannot be patented and is freely available to all.

The existence of commons within the economy at large is generally recognized and has been much discussed, but the existence of commons in the enterprise or at the industry level is often ignored. The larger the enterprise, the larger the problem.

The appearance of commons is constrained by the general application of the principle of *user pays*, that is, a charge which covers the full cost of its use. In theory, the kind of opportunistic behaviour encouraged by the existence of the commons is best prevented by the universal application of the user-pays principle. Where the exclusion principle holds, that is, where the consumption of a product or service by one consumer prevents its consumption by another, the system of payment can be universalized. This principle is far too costly to apply everywhere, and in many cases impossible, where exclusion does not hold.

How is it possible to apply user pays to something which cannot be measured? A service can only be satisfactorily charged for if its attributes can be measured. Because many of the attributes are intangible, they are difficult to measure and difficult to record.

The existence of commons invites opportunistic behaviour. Free riders are those who exploit in some way the existence of the commons, engaging in opportunistic behaviour to take advantage of the low or non-existent price. Such situations are likely to be unstable, in that there is a tendency for such behaviour to become more general once it begins. The process of exploitation can become cumulative. Once self-restraint breaks down, nobody has an interest in *not* exploiting the commons; all become free riders. It becomes a race to take advantage of the commons before it is fully exhausted. The commons is often so overexploited that its very existence is threatened.

The strategic implications of the existence of the commons within any organization are important. Within an enterprise there are all sorts of commons available to staff, since it is impossible, at a reasonable cost, to devise comprehensive systems of charging for their use – an IT or communication system, the expertise of specialists within the organization or the time of senior managers.

Some services are charged for, others are not. There is a degree of budgetary independence of units within an organization, but it is never complete. There are always services provided centrally. The provision of such services can never be organized so that the commons does not exist. Any individual can trade off the resources of others, including their good name and their work efforts. Where it is difficult to measure individual performance because performance is so often a team effort, it is easy for free riders to appear undetected, exploiting the efforts of others who carry the main load. Where a staff member has every intention of seeking, within a short period of time, a better position elsewhere, this might appear to be economically rational behaviour. If allowed to start, such opportunistic behaviour becomes the norm and the efficiency with which any strategy is implemented deteriorates. All try to take out rather than to put in. The danger of such opportunistic behaviour may become a key influence on the making of a strategy.

Strategy in Action Benetton and changing networks

Benetton's attitude to ownership of the stores which distribute its products has changed. Recently Benetton has decided to change the nature of its network. Its motivation is to have first-hand contact with customers, to be able to respond quickly to changes in demand and also ensure that it has direct control over its supply chain. It wishes to benefit from economies of scale in sales and purchases. The

▶

assumption is that demand has become more homogeneous. The forces of globalization and the communications revolution have changed the context in which Benetton must operate. This requires some degree of centralization and a significant measure of vertical integration.

In order to achieve this, Benetton has decided to reduce the customization of its products to particular markets and hopefully in the process to reduce the unappreciated and therefore unnecessary variety. It will reduce the proportion of products customized from 20% to between 5 and 10%. It will also reduce the number of articles offered in its biannual collections by as much as 35–40%, but engage in more in-store testing and increase the number of flash collections in order to keep up with changes in fashion. It has streamlined its family of brands under the two main brand names.

With the increase of sales and production volumes by the mid-1990s, Benetton set up a high-tech production pole at Castrette, not far from its headquarters at Ponzano, near Treviso. This centre has responsibility for all Benetton's production. It is a large and technically advanced centre. Increasingly Benetton has reproduced the Castrette production pole abroad on a smaller scale in subsidiaries which are partly or fully owned and directly managed by Benetton, each at the centre of a group of SMEs often set up and managed by ex-employees or contractors. Castrette allocates the tasks and each pole specializes in a particular product or products, for example T-shirts in Spain or jackets in East Europe. All products come back to Italy before being dispatched to where they are to be sold.

Benetton has moved to consolidate control over its textile and thread suppliers. The main supplier of woven fabric, cotton knit fabric and carded and combed wool is now 85% controlled by Benetton itself. Quality control is made easier and logistics more cost effective. Benetton has retained close control over logistics generally, making a big effort to take advantage of the new communication technologies.

Most of Benetton's competitors are international retailers with no in-house operations. They have large retail outlets and are aggressive in their selling. Benetton has adjusted its retail strategy to deal with this competition:

1. It has, where possible, enlarged its retail outlets, to make possible a wider display of its products
2. Where this is not possible, it focuses on one market segment or product, for example men's products or underwear
3. It has opened large retail outlets, varying in size from 7,535 to 21,528 square feet, on the main shopping streets and in the main shopping areas of big cities.

After an abortive attempt to expand in the USA during the 1970s that led to an overbuilt retail network with some 600–700 licensed stores, many of them underperformers, Benetton now has just 150 outlets there. It intends to open mega-stores in New York and Atlanta. It already has such mega-stores in the most prestigious locations in Milan, Paris, London, Tokyo and Rome.

Under the retail project started in November 1999, 60 mega-stores were opened by the end of 2000 and the plan was to have 100 by the end of 2002. The aim was to establish a network of large to medium-sized stores owned and managed by

Table 13.3 Benetton's foreign production poles

Name	Headquarters	Workshop locations	Benetton's equity share
Benetton Spain	Castellbisbal, Spain	Spain	100%
Benetton	Maia, Portugal	Portugal	100%
Benetton Tunisia	Sahline, Tunisia	Tunisia and Morocco	100%
Benetton Hungary	Nagykallo, Hungary	Hungary, Ukraine, Czech Republic, Poland, Moldavia, Bulgaria, Rumania,	100%
Benetton Croatia	Osijek, Croatia	Croatia, Slovenia Serbia	100%
Benetton Korea	Seoul, South Korea	South Korea	50% (joint venture)
Egyptian Clothing Manufacturers	Alexandria, Egypt	Egypt	50% (joint venture)
DCM Benetton India	New Delhi, India	India	50% (joint venture)

Source: Camuffo et al., 2001: 50.

Benetton, a radical change of policy and one intended to enable Benetton to transmit information on sales and changes in tastes directly to headquarters which could then adjust its design and production.

Benetton illustrates the necessity of adjusting the network of cooperators according to changes in the external environment. So far only about 8% of

Benetton's sales are made direct to the consumer, but this will rise to 20% after 2002 if all goes to plan. There are possible problems with the new strategy – alienation of existing distributors, the need to develop new skills, the uncertainty about how fast the new strategy can be implemented and the level of commitment it requires from the management.

Table 13.4 **How Benetton and its competitors configure their business networks**

Company	Supply and production network	Distribution and retail network
Benetton (Italy)	Strong upstream vertical integration In-house production in 32 production centres (22 in Italy and 10 abroad) Outsourcing of production to a network of small and midsize enterprises directly controlled by the Italian and foreign production poles	Annual revenue of US$1.8 billion Retail outlets managed by third parties, with about 5,500 stores in 120 countries (old pattern); retail outlets managed directly with about 60 worldwide (new pattern) Average size; 1,292 sq ft traditional shops (old pattern); 10,764 sq ft mega-stores (new pattern)
The GAP (USA)	Complete outsourcing of production	Annual revenue of US$13.7 billion Retail outlets managed directly: about 3,700 stores, mainly in North America Average size; 7,535 sq ft
Hennes & Mauritz (Sweden)	Complete outsourcing of production	Annual revenue of US$13.7 billion Retail outlets managed directly: about 700 stores in 14 countries Average size: 13,993 sq ft
Zara (Spain)	Partial upstream vertical integration In-house production in 23 production centres Outsourcing of production to a network of small shops in Spain and Portugal	Annual revenue of US$1.8 billion Retail outlets managed directly; about 450 stores in 29 countries Average size: 8,072 sq ft

Source: Camuffo et al., 2001: 49.

Game theory and the prisoner's dilemma

The existence of the commons and free riders helps to define with more precision the nature of a strategic dilemma which frequently recurs, the problem of whether in a whole range of different circumstances to compete or cooperate.

In some situations competition can produce a non-optimal solution; in other situations cooperation can produce a non-optimal result. What is optimal can be determined from different perspectives – those of the enterprise, the industry or the whole community. There are cases where a solution may be simultaneously non-optimal at all these levels, and some where it is optimal at only one level. It is rare to talk of a solution simultaneously best at all levels. Corporate strategy does not exhaust the full scope of strategy. If the actions and reactions of competitors are likely to produce a significantly non-optimal solution, it may be necessary to frame a strategy at either the industry or community levels, one which guides the players into conforming to a strategy which produces an optimal outcome. At its heart this strategy often involves avoiding the exploitation of 'commons' by free riders.

One way of conceptualizing typical strategic situations is to use game theory. This can be used to aid understanding of what is happening in various strategic situations. The emphasis on the benefits of competition in most economics texts is based on the operation of Adam Smith's 'invisible hand' of market forces, which is alleged to produce a maximization of the common good through the pursuit of self-interest by all. That this is not always the case can be illustrated by the situation usually described as the prisoner's dilemma.

Superficially, the prisoner's dilemma does not appear to have relevance to the business or management world. However, appearances are deceptive and it is worth describing the dilemma at length before applying it to four typical strategic business situations:

> Two suspects are taken into custody and separated. The district attorney is certain that they are guilty of a specific crime, but he does not have adequate evidence to convict them at a trial. He points out to each prisoner that each has two alternatives: to confess to the crime the police are sure they have done, or not to confess. If they both do not confess then the district attorney states that he will book them on some very minor trumped-up charge such a petty larceny and illegal possession of a weapon, and they will both receive minor punishment; if they both confess they will be prosecuted, but he will recommend less than the most severe sentence; but if one confesses and the other does not, then the confessor will receive lenient treatment for turning state's evidence, whereas the latter will get 'the book' slapped at him. (Luce and Raifa, 1957: 95)

A payoff matrix for this situation can be presented in diagrammatic form, with possible punishments structured to make the point, as shown in Figure 13.2. In this game there is a dominant strategy, that is, one in which, given the rules and the structure of information, there is a preferred strategy for each player. Confessing is the best strategy for each prisoner individually since it offers the least punishment. The worst punishment occurs when one prisoner does not confess and the other confesses. If both confess, the eight years punishment received by each is less than the 10 years which would be received if one does not confess, when the other confesses.

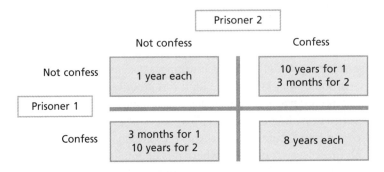

Figure 13.2 **The punishment matrix**

In other words, if both confess or both do not confess, the outcome is better than one confessing and the other not confessing. Both are better off if they cooperate in making their choice. Cooperation has two implications:

1. Each must identify and agree on the best strategy, in this case not to confess.
2. Each must trust the other to keep to this strategy. This agreement exposes both to opportunism; one of them can improve the outcome at the last moment by reversing the strategy, provided the other does not also do so.

There is usually a limit placed on the kind of business game which is discussed in this context. The games are not pure freewheeling games in which there are no constraints on strategy. Rather they are rule-based games, although the nature of the rules is assumed rather than stated, and the consistent observance of the rules is problematic. In practice, business is 'a complex mix of both types of game' (Brandenburger and Nalebuff, 1995: 57).

The game above is a one-off game, in which decision making is simultaneous rather than sequential. Alternatively, the game might involve a real-time sequence of decisions. The game can also be a recurrent one, repeated at a number of different times. This makes an enormous difference since both sequential decision making and repeated games introduce the possibility of learning and gaining a reputation for consistency. Reputation may be based on the tendency of one enterprise to repeat previous behaviour and give reliable signals concerning future behaviour. Can an organization be trusted to do what it has signalled? The outcome of the game can be different in the two circumstances.

Any game requires the assumption of a straightforward objective for each player, something akin to short-term profit maximization, and the articulation of well-defined situations in which profit is being pursued. Game theory focuses attention on the assumptions made concerning objectives and situation:

• What does it assume about the behaviour of other players?
• What are the players trying to maximize?
• What is the game's time perspective?

It should be pointed out that no game is rigid; a good strategist actively shapes the game, changing any of the five elements referred to below in a way which will improve the chance of a good outcome. If possible, a player will change the rules to promote his or her own benefit.

The elements of a game

There are five distinct elements to any game: the identity of the players; the value added by the game; the rules of the game; the players' tactics; and the scope of the game. These are discussed in turn.

The *identity of the players* is not always clear. The players include not only customers and competitors but also substitutors or complementors. The players relevant to any game are defined by the situation of the game, which can change. Most games are set up in a way which simplifies the situation, reducing them to games in which there are just two players.

In a freewheeling game in which players are free to adopt any strategy they wish, no player can take away more than he or she brings to the game, otherwise he or she would be excluded from the game. Typically, the sum of all the *value added* of the individual players exceeds the total value of the game, otherwise there is no point in engaging in the game. At least one player will receive less than he or she contributes. In that sense someone has to lose.

In games with rules a player can take more than its value added, because the rules limit the reaction of other players to certain moves. It is also possible that a player will be paid either to enter or exit a game, or do neither.

The aim is often to turn the game into a win–win game rather than a zero-sum game in which players are competing for a fixed cake. The value added can be defined as a finite amount or it can be seen as a variable.

Game theory assumes simplified *rules* to the game. The rules come from:

- practical requirements, such as the mechanisms for the transmission of information between players
- custom or convention, such as the norms of ethical behaviour or the normal behaviour in a market, including, for example, actions such as refraining from price discrimination
- the law, which outlaws a wide, but varying, range of practices
- any contractual constraints, such as giving the right of last bid to the incumbent in an existing arrangement which is being renegotiated.

Most games assume rigid and unchanging rules. Unfortunately those with market power can often make the rules to suit themselves and may take away more than the value they bring to the game.

The *tactics* adopted in any game reflect a number of factors, such as the perceptions which different players have of the game and the attitudes of other players, the number and nature of other players, and the time horizon of play.

Study of typical games situations show that there are evolutionary stable strategies, which evolve over time and are adopted by all participants. One which is popular is the tit-for-tat strategy, in which a player does to another player today what that player did to it yesterday. This has the virtue of being:

- passively pleasant – not initiating a hostile act, but having the capacity to be provoked, while at the same time implying instant retaliation
- forgiving – whatever the past history, a cooperative act elicits a similar response.

Such a strategy is robust in a broad range of circumstances. Strategies can be mixed rather than pure strategies – they can change. Players can be aggressive or passive, or vary their approach according to circumstances.

The boundaries of a game determine its *scope*. There may be linkages between what appear to be separate games. Players may be simultaneously playing a number of different games, which are linked in some way. Some players may be playing a limited game concerned with price fixing in one product market, while another player may be much more interested in expanding its total market.

The game theory approach helps us to reinforce some important points regarding the nature of strategy making:

- A strategic player can make a new game as well as take the game on offer. The player is a proactive strategist, not just a reactive one.
- Games do not need to be zero-sum games. It is better to create games which have winning situations for all players. Part of the objective of any game is to maximize the value added. Other players may want to compete and force competition on you. Another game is to persuade them to engage in cooperative behaviour.
- In order to be successful, a player does not need to have a unique strategy. There is not one strategy good for all times and all circumstances. Strategies can change. It is possible to imitate the successful strategy of other players.
- A player should attempt to see the whole picture including all its games, not just recognizing the players who can affect the outcome of one particular game, but linking this game with other games with more significant outcomes.
- Allocentric strategies are more effective than egocentric strategies, therefore the respective games should be played the same way. They have to consider the consequences of the actions of other players. The players must take account of the strategies of these other players.

The real world is much more complex than any game, but games are very helpful in drawing out the implications of strategic situations. In the cases discussed below, the game puts a strong emphasis on the potential advantages of cooperation.

The universality of the prisoner's dilemma

The prisoner's dilemma is common in the world of business. In order to illustrate its universality, four strategic business situations are discussed and related to the four possible outcomes of the prisoner's dilemma.

The four situations are:

1. price strategy
2. entry into a new market
3. the commitment of resources to training or other activities closely linked to the core activity of the enterprise
4. and the withdrawal of funds from a threatened financial institution.

Price strategy

The first situation relates to how price levels are fixed in oligopolistic markets. It assumes that under oligopoly, price competition can result in losses for all players and that a price war is to the detriment of all the players. The reduction of excessive price competition benefits all. In such a market there is usually a tacit agreement that each player sells less than they might without constraint and refrains from aggressive price competition.

In anything less than perfect competition, an individual supplier has some influence on the level of price, simply by increasing the quantity of products or services offered on the market. The bigger the player, the greater the potential impact on price of a given proportionate increase in sales. If all expand sales, price falls even more. At a given price, it pays a player to sell as much as possible, provided others do not follow suit. The problem is that such action will push down the price. Opportunism can pay for small players who have little impact on price, but not for large players who by acting this way initiate a breakdown in any agreement.

The example chosen to illustrate this situation is the fixing of the price of oil (Figure 13.3). It has been simplified by assuming a duopoly, but the same basic principles apply to any oligopolistic situation. The conclusions of the simplified example hold for more complicated cases. It is possible to conceptualize this as an agreement between a monolithic OPEC and a group of non-OPEC, oil-producing countries. It is assumed that there is no difference in the costs of producing oil in the two groups of countries, an unrealistic assumption but one which further simplifies the situation.

What is the willingness of suppliers to decrease supply in a falling market or increase it in a rising market? Assume demand for the homogeneous product has already fallen because of recession. How do suppliers react to such a situation?

The figures in brackets in Figure 13.3 represent possible outcomes as proportions of previous revenue and are only meant to be representative. The exact figures in any particular situation depend on the size of the reduction in demand and the slope of the new demand curve. Both could aim to cut back supply by an amount intended to maintain the previous price level. In this case, there would be some loss of revenue because of the decline in sales. This is a possible strategy, but one which would require cooperation.

There might be significant animosity between the two groups which acts as a barrier to cooperation. They are not talking to each other. What then appears to be in their short-term interests? Each supplier in isolation will tend to choose the maintenance of supply as the dominant strategy since this minimizes the loss of revenue. At one extreme, this strategy offers the possibility of maintaining previous revenue, provided the other supplier reduces supply by the amount of the decline in demand. If the other supplier chooses to maintain supply, the player is still better off than in the situation in which it chooses to cut supply and the other player maintains it. If both pursue their short-term interests, the result is that both suffer a major loss of revenue, in this example a fall of 25%.

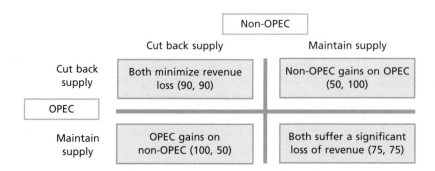

Figure 13.3 **The possible outcomes of excessive competition in a falling market**

Cooperation leads to a different preferred strategy. The players would identify the choice of jointly cutting back supply as the favoured strategy and as producing the better outcome for both, which is a retention of 90% of the previous revenues.

Can each player trust the other to carry out an agreed strategy when the other player will, in the short term at least, gain by opportunism. If the game is repeated, the situation changes. Short-term opportunism produces a decidedly inferior outcome over the longer term. If the size of future revenue streams depends on cooperation, then opportunism would be a misguided policy.

This is not an untypical situation. After the decline in tourism which followed the terrorist attack of September 11, 2001, all hotels were faced with a similar situation. Do they discount the price of a hotel room in order to win a larger share of a declining total demand? A discounting war could easily lead to major loss making.

Entry into a new market

There is an existing monopoly but the possibility of a new entrant. One of the barriers to entry is the possibility of retaliatory action by the incumbent monopolist. There is sequential instead of simultaneous decision making, which makes the second situation more realistic. Each player responds to the previous decision. The key issue is how the incumbent reacts to the initial entry. It is not sensible for the new entrant to expect no reaction. According to the nature of the action and reaction, the payoffs differ dramatically.

An example might be a new airline trying to enter a market in which there is already a monopolist. This is a good description of the Qantas position in the domestic Australian market in late 2001 after the demise of the second carrier, Ansett. Virgin Blue played the role of the new entrant. If Qantas thinks that Virgin Blue wishes to enter a particular route, it can either expand its capacity on that route or maintain its original capacity. In either case, Virgin Blue must make a decision whether to enter.

If the decision is to enter, Qantas must make a decision whether to fight. The action may include a price war with major discounting, a strategy which causes losses on the route for both players. This tactic is sometimes called 'predatory pricing'. It may also involve a major promotional effort and advertising campaign. This example has the advantage of making the situation dynamic.

The decision tree in Figure 13.4 illustrates the situation. The analogy of a tree is used since the diagram has the same shape, broadening out from a narrow tip. In describing the process of action and reaction, it is always useful to construct a decision tree which explores all the possible options (see the decision tree on the mode of entry in Chapter 15).

A threat to expand capacity may be only a threat, which the incumbent, Qantas, has no intention of realizing. The threat alone may deter entry (vi). Qantas may actually realize the threat which can have the desired effect of deterring entry (iii), but Qantas has incurred increased costs which reduce its profit level. If Qantas takes no action at all (v), the new entrant, Virgin Blue, will divert profit to the value of E + S from Qantas. As a consequence, both may be making a loss. If Qantas chooses to fight by lowering the price (iv), there will be a further cost imposed on both – F. If Qantas expands capacity and Virgin Blue still enters, then there will be a transfer of

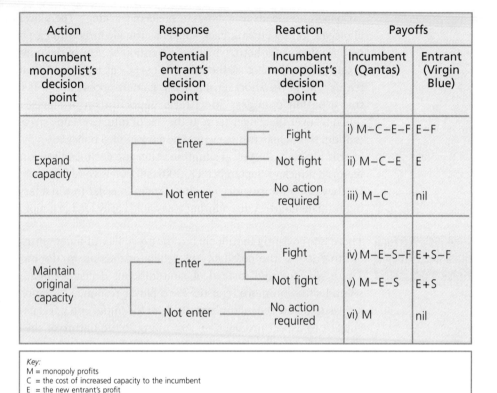

Action	Response	Reaction	Payoffs	
Incumbent monopolist's decision point	Potential entrant's decision point	Incumbent monopolist's decision point	Incumbent (Qantas)	Entrant (Virgin Blue)
Expand capacity	Enter	Fight	i) M−C−E−F	E−F
		Not fight	ii) M−C−E	E
	Not enter	No action required	iii) M−C	nil
Maintain original capacity	Enter	Fight	iv) M−E−S−F	E+S−F
		Not fight	v) M−E−S	E+S
	Not enter	No action required	vi) M	nil

Key:
M = monopoly profits
C = the cost of increased capacity to the incumbent
E = the new entrant's profit
F = fight costs of either the entrant or the incumbent
S = the profit the entrant will take from the incumbent if there is no capacity expansion

Figure 13.4 **Decision tree on entry into a new market**

profit from Qantas to Virgin which may make both players loss making (ii). If Qantas fights, there will be further costs for both (i).

Whether it is worth the new entrant going ahead depends on the short-term profit position and the long-term potential for growth of the market. Assume for the moment that existing capacity can absorb the growth. Suppose that initially there is an above-normal profit which will fall to a normal profit if capacity is expanded. However, fighting in the form of a price or promotional war will convert profit into loss. This is a prisoner's dilemma situation. Both players are better off not fighting. Each could improve their short-term position by establishing a credible threat, either to enter or retaliate, especially if the threat does really deter the other from taking action. Whether this action is likely to deter depends on perceived patterns of past behaviour and a reputation based on that past history, and on the general strategy pursued by each player. The better option is an agreed programme of expanding capacity on the relevant route.

The provision of training

Often training specific to a particular industry is required. This training may involve a significant commitment on the part of both the trainers and the trained. Those trained can derive a benefit from their increased employability which may or may not justify any cost individually incurred. If the trained have read the situation correctly, in the future they can earn a far higher salary.

If the only source of training in an industry is in-house training provided costless to the trainee by the enterprise, one strategy is to train the appropriate number of staff required by the enterprise. In theory, each enterprise in the industry could train the staff it needs.

Training a staff member is no guarantee that he or she will stay with the enterprise. Other enterprises can recruit from the pool of trained staff by offering a higher reward than the enterprise doing the training. Any enterprise could do the same, bidding away the trained from other enterprises. Such recruitment pushes up demand, raising the price of all trained staff. An alternative approach is to train more workers than you currently need on the assumption that you will lose some.

It is useful to analyse the following industrial situation. All enterprises have been doing the appropriate training. There is little competition for trained staff. An enterprise in such an industry realizes that it might gain from a little opportunism. The new strategy adopted by that enterprise is to abstain from training, thus saving its total cost, and then to recruit from enterprises which do train. Again Figure 13.5 simplifies the situation by assuming two enterprises. The figures in brackets are notional costs of training. They ignore two further sources of cost, firstly the salary premium to the trained, necessary to avoid having them enticed away, and secondly the costs which arise from not having properly trained workers, both of which would tend to rise in the future if there were an inadequate labour force.

In the short term it would pay both to abstain from training and recruit from the other; this would reduce costs. This is the classic free-riding strategy. There would be some increase in short-term costs as the two enterprises competed for labour. If only one enterprise trained staff, the cost would be higher than in a situation in which both engaged in training, since even if the training were sufficient for both, competition would push up the salaries of trained staff. In the long term it is better for both to train. This is an example of cooperation constituting a non-zero-sum game, whereas competition is a zero-sum game.

This situation exists wherever there is a commons, that is, an asset available at less than its true cost. This might offer the possibility that others gain from that common

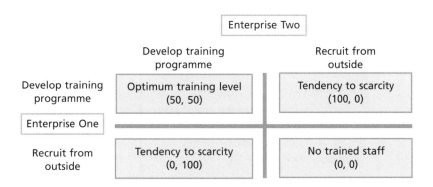

Figure 13.5 Opportunism in recruiting trained workers

asset – improved labour, new technical knowledge or simply innovative organizational expertise – without paying fully for its development. The situation would change if any enterprise which attracts a trained worker or manager, on the user-pays principle, has to compensate the organization for the cost of training or developing the technical knowledge or organizational expertise.

Withdrawing a deposit in a financial crisis

Enterprises which are in danger of liquidation are faced with a number of creditors all concerned with extracting their money. The focus is on such a debtor enterprise, say a bank. The situation is simplified. There are two creditors who have provided short-term finance to the enterprise. In this world there is no lender of last resort, who can rescue the bank in trouble. The short-term liabilities of the enterprise exceed its short-term assets. There is already a crisis in which another similar enterprise has failed. The creditors are concerned:

• What should be the strategy of each depositor?
• Should each seek to take out its money as quickly as possible?

Figure 13.6 captures the essence of the strategic situation in such a financial panic. Neither creditor can take over the whole debt. If both creditors try to withdraw their funds, the enterprise fails. If only one creditor withdraws quickly enough, it loses the opportunity of a return on the funds invested, but it will save its principal. If the other creditor is quicker, the creditor loses everything. An effort to withdraw by both precipitates collapse and they both lose.

If both agree to leave their money invested, they have an excellent chance of losing nothing and making the expected return since the enterprise is fundamentally sound. Communication allows them to recognize the preferred long-term strategy but do they trust each other enough to follow it? Once more this is a prisoner's dilemma.

The generality of the situations described above is striking. A possible fifth situation, easily set up, might relate to the problem of air pollution, in particular the emission of greenhouse gases. Carbon emissions result from the burning of fossil fuels. From a social perspective such emissions are undesirable, but for the individual company there is no incentive not to emit and every incentive to do so since abstaining from engaging in such pollution will impose additional costs on the company if others do

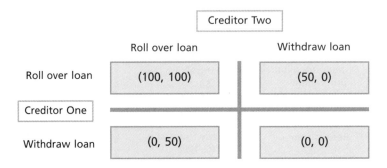

Figure 13.6 **Behaviour in a financial crisis**

not abstain. This of course also applies at the country level, at which individual countries might try to escape from international agreements such as the Kyoto Protocol. Again all such situations could be set up as a prisoner's dilemma. The issue of socially responsible behaviour, such as avoiding pollution, is discussed at greater length in Chapter 18.

How to cooperate

There is a twofold problem for an enterprise: recognizing when to cooperate, and identifying how to organize the situation so that the best outcome is recognized by all the key players and a cooperative outcome achieved.

The situation requires the use of three appropriate cooperative mechanisms: spontaneous self-organization, industry-organized action and government-imposed cooperation.

Spontaneous self-organization

This involves tacit cooperation by the players. Some commentators have a strong belief in the capacity of individuals or enterprises to self-organize. This leaves the initiative to the spontaneous response of individual players faced by the challenges thrown up in the relevant situations. This raises a number of questions:

- Is this realistic?
- Who takes the initiative in promoting cooperation?
- Does a leader emerge spontaneously?

There are both carrots and sticks – inducements to cooperate and threats on what might happen if the players do not cooperate.

The *inducement* to cooperate might be a positive benefit, not just the avoidance of a significant negative outcome. Sometimes cooperation arises spontaneously from the actions of individual players interacting with each other over a protracted period of time. Continued interaction allows a process of learning to occur. The benefit outcomes become clearer. Strategists learn the nature of other players and as a result evolve informal norms of behaviour, or rules of the game, which guide decision makers in the direction of better responses and better decisions. As a result conventions emerge. It is assumed that such rules are voluntarily adhered to. Players learn to trust each other. The inducements are the realized opportunities to increase revenue or reduce costs.

Cooperation may result from one player issuing a credible *threat* of action which will damage the other player(s). Any threat must prompt the necessary cooperative action. Do the other players believe the threat?

Signalling is important for inducements and threats, but more for the latter since the consequences of failure for the latter are worse than for the former. The situation is made less immediately damaging if the 'game' can be broken into smaller steps, which signal an intention to proceed but give time for withdrawal, for example flagging an intention to increase price or mount a new advertising campaign, without actually doing anything. It is a matter of feeling one's way and learning. The credibility of any threat depends on:

- the reputation of the player issuing the threat
- the writing of a specific contract, expressing a commitment to go ahead with the threatened action
- the deliberate burning of one's boats, closing off any alternative paths
- chance – it is out of the control of the issuer of the threat.

The emergence of 'spontaneous cooperation' reflects the effectiveness of signalling by the players. All players must understand the mutual interest in cooperation and be capable of signalling their intentions to cooperate. Misunderstandings are possible. The probability of a cooperative outcome depends on the accuracy with which players can anticipate the expected behaviour of other players. Such accuracy depends on the effectiveness of communication between the players.

The reaction to any signal depends on the objective of the player, which might be more than just cooperation, including a desire to:

- gain more information
- force withdrawal of the original signal, or the intention expressed in that signal
- offer an alternative course of action.

There are two sides to what is called signal effectiveness – accurate interpretation of the signal and appropriate reaction to the signal.

The interpretation of a signal depends on sender characteristics, signal characteristics and receiver characteristics. The commitment to the course of action and the reputation of the sender for having consistently realized an expressed intention are important. Equally as important are the signalling expertise of the receiver and the similarity of situation for both receiver and sender which makes for a greater clarity of interpretation. In order to have most impact, the signal itself should be consistent, clear and unambiguous to both sender and receiver and of maximum aggressiveness.

The signal reaction comprises:

- *magnitude* or size of response: there is a whole range from no response to a dramatic response which signals either total acceptance or total rejection of the proposal
- *domain* or areas of response: is there a behavioural response? What is the nature of the behaviour?
- *speed*: is the response immediate or deliberately delayed?

The coexistence of competition and cooperation

In some activities, cooperation and competition occur at the same time. For example, enterprises, otherwise competing for customers, might agree on a generic advertising campaign to promote the product itself (see the case study on the Australian wine industry). This implies participation in a non-zero-sum game since it means winning customers from other countries or switching customers away from other, different products. Australian wine producers agree to promote Australian wine but continue to compete with each other for the customers who want to buy Australian wine. Competition within a generic market may still be intense despite the existence of obvious cooperation at the industry level.

There may be tacit cooperation which limits the intensity of competition and its possibly damaging effects, for example price leadership by the largest producer. Some competition is potentially very destructive. A classic case is the cycle of petrol pricing, possibly a universal phenomenon, which moves almost by magic in regular weekly cycles, all enterprises tending to move price simultaneously. A price war can affect all the participants, but even some cooperation may also be harmful in slowing the pace of change; it may amount, as Adam Smith suggested many years ago in *The Wealth of Nations*, to a conspiracy against the public interest.

Where cooperation does occur, there is a danger that it may suddenly and comprehensively break down. Circumstances may change and then there is a danger of opportunistic behaviour. An occasional act of opportunism may not matter provided the players are small, but opportunism by a large player is a much bigger problem. The chance of a high, and increasing, return from opportunism or a major deterioration in the situation of one of the players, which forces the player to take drastic and risky action to rectify the situation, may encourage opportunism, dictating that an enterprise abruptly ends the cooperation. Those who choose to cooperate are always vulnerable to opportunism. For this reason, there are some commentators who advocate an extreme wariness towards cooperative initiatives and a disregard for the opportunities inherent in cooperation.

The opposite problem is that cooperation itself encourages a loss of sensitivity to market opportunity and a tendency to rest on what has already been achieved, rather than seeking new opportunities. Cooperation may be extended past the point at which it encourages an improved outcome. The cooperators may become a cosy club resting on the status quo, which may become concerned with suppressing change rather than encouraging it. The club becomes vulnerable to the entry of aggressive new competitors.

If there is ignorance of the beneficial effects of a win–win game or if there is a poor signalling, some other cooperative mechanism is needed.

Industry-organized action

A common, and often more acceptable, alternative occurs when cooperation can be organized within an industry, usually with the leadership of one or several large players, often working within an industry association, sometimes with outside prompting, where it is needed. Some institutional expressions of such behaviour may be potentially illegal, in that they are perceived to be anti-competitive, but there are areas where this is not the case.

Ignorance of the potential benefits from cooperation is less likely in the situation where there is some organizational expression of the common interest. Industrial associations, of various kinds, are not uncommon and they have easy access to information. The danger is that the large players may dominate and that the rules of the game are framed in favour of those large player(s). The association may become an obstacle to change. Of course industry associations can estimate benefits and require contributions from members that reflect the likely size of such benefits, if they are backed up by government.

Focus on Theory
Clusters

'A cluster is a geographically proximate group of interconnected companies and associated institutions in a particular field, linked by commonalities and complementarities' (Porter, 1998a). The potential members may be:

end-product or service companies
suppliers of specialized inputs, such as components, machinery or services
financial institutions
firms in related industries
firms in downstream industries
producers of complementary products
specialized infrastructure providers
government and other institutions providing specialized training, education, information and technical support
trade or industry associations.

An example of a cluster is shown in Figure 13.7.

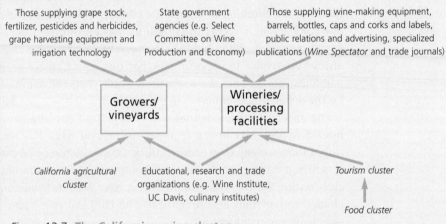

Figure 13.7 **The Californian wine cluster**

Government or industry associations have a number of wide-ranging roles which include:

• Collection and dissemination of economic information • Export promotion
• Regulatory reform • Attraction of foreign direct investment • Science and technology policy • Development of advanced and specialized managers and workers.

Government-imposed cooperation

The third possibility occurs when cooperation is enforced by an outside body, usually by a government or some agency endowed with a statutory authority to force organizations to accept cooperative behaviour. Whether players can be forced to give cooperation in anything but a token way is unlikely, unless the resistance was based solely on ignorance, an ignorance dissipated by the imposition of cooperative behaviour. The success of outside intervention also assumes the possibility of a benevolent and informed regulator with a real interest in implementing the best outcome. Unfortunately there are plenty of examples of malevolence, ineffectiveness and/or ignorance on the part of regulators.

The reaction of the players depends on what the government actually does. The rules of the game are often changed and new rules imposed on all players. Such a solution avoids certain kinds of opportunism, but it may encourage others, and it has its own weaknesses, not least of which is the forced suspension of a willing commitment on the part of the coerced. There are several possible consequences:

- A lack of incentive to reveal the true situation of an individual player or the proposed strategy of that player to the authority imposing the cooperative solution.
- Every incentive to seek ways of cheating. Because there is a tendency for the regulating agency to be kept in the dark, there may be an enhanced chance of secret opportunism.
- Action to avoid the consequences of regulation. This may involve corrupt behaviour or control of the regulators in the interest of particular private players.

If the government wishes to impose a levy to finance important activities, such as marketing or R&D, it must persuade those paying to rate the prospective benefits as greater than the costs.

All three kinds of cooperation can coexist in different sectors of the economy, or even in different functional areas within one industry. The three mechanisms can reinforce each other. Whenever there is the pooling of some significant resources, there is always the danger of opportunism. However, the use of all the different mechanisms makes it more difficult to engage in opportunistic behaviour. Cooperation is not just a theoretically desirable outcome, it is also a commonly observed occurrence.

Strategic alliances

Strategy in Action   When does a strategic alliance become a merger?

An alliance is often the result of a crisis in at least one of the partners. The Nissan revival plan was made public in October 1999. It represented unwelcome medicine. It included cutbacks and closures as well as major new investment commitments. It also included a plan to reduce purchasing costs by 20% and cut the number of suppliers by 50%.

A failure to have achieved a speedy turnaround might have sounded the death knell for Renault. Some analysts predicted that it would take Renault 8–10 years to produce a return on its investment in

Nissan. This was unduly pessimistic, as the revival plan was a rapid success. Not many alliances produce such rapid and striking success. By 2001 Nissan was in the black. Carlos Ghosn became a household name in Japan and a symbol of the way in which a turnaround could be achieved.

The combined automobile sales reached the magical 5 million level in 2001, after being very close in 2000, when the alliance was among the top five world producers. The combined entity is competing to be among the six surviving global players forecast for the industry. The partners were almost equal in size: Nissan sold 2.6 million, and Renault 2.4 million. Together they accounted for 9.2% of the total world market. The regional breakdown is interesting – 2.4 million in the EU, 0.8 million in North America, 0.75 million in Japan – that is almost 4 million, or 80%, in the triad. The increasing importance of other areas is shown by the 1.0 million sales, 20% of the total.

There were a number of different areas of cooperation, areas of synergy in which costs could be significantly cut or sales expanded:

Platforms and power-trains: These are the two most important parts of the car and therefore potential sources of cost saving through economies of scale. Common platforms will account for more than half the two enterprises' production by 2005. There is also an increasing exchange of engines. There is much room for continuing cost reduction.

Joint purchasing organization: In April 2001 the first joint company, equally owned, was created in this area – the Renault-Nissan Purchasing Organization. This will handle 70% of both groups' purchases, a combined invoice amounting to US$50 billion. Combined purchasing increases the bargaining strength of the two companies.

Industrial and commercial cooperation: The aim is for each enterprise to help the other in areas where they are weak: Renault using Nissan to return to the Mexican market and also to get back into Australia, Japan and Indonesia, and Renault assisting Nissan in Brazil and Europe.

Joint distribution in Europe: With a dealership hub strategy, a joint distribution organization is being set up in Europe, again significantly sharing costs.

Joint IS/IT: A common system was set up in September 2001, for which the Renault-Nissan IS/IT Office (RNIO) is responsible.

One example of cooperation and of the first components jointly used is a powerful 3.5-litre, V6 engine which has been developed by Nissan and is being used by Renault in its attempt to break into the lower end of the European premium market, currently dominated by the German companies Mercedes and Audi.

The success of the first stage naturally led to a second stage in cooperation between the two companies. Building on the initial agreement, during stage two of the alliance, there has been a strengthening of cross-shareholdings. Renault has raised its stake in Nissan from 36.65 to 44.4% and Nissan is taking a 15% stake in Renault without voting rights. As a consequence of these cross-holdings, an improvement in the performance of either automatically profits the other.

The alliance has been so effective that the cooperative arrangements are being institutionalized in the second stage. To oversee the making of a common strategy, the plan of October 30, 2001 proposed the creation of a new equally owned management company, Renault-Nissan BV, which will represent a strategic command centre for the alliance, in charge of coordinating all its operations worldwide. The CCTs, the driving force of the alliance since 1999, will now report to Renault-Nissan BV. The new Renault-Nissan Purchasing Organization will also report to R-N BV. These initial steps were completed by mid-2002.

Success in this merger may not be enough. The joint enterprise is still not large enough to compete with the really large players. Renault is still seeking other acquisitions. Logically the alliance should look for another partner in the USA. As the alliance is developing, there is every chance that Renault and Nissan will merge their manufacturing processes and production methods in the near future. In a third stage, a complete merger might take place. This is even more likely if Ghosn moves to become the CEO of Renault.

There is abundant evidence that enterprises are cooperating and cooperating more frequently. Often an enterprise is simultaneously competing and cooperating with the same enterprise, referred to as coopetition. It is not a question of whether to compete or cooperate but rather what combination to engage in and in which functional areas to concentrate on one rather than the other.

There is plenty of evidence of cooperation. One of the most common forms of cooperation is the *strategic alliance*. There are few enterprises today which are not involved in strategic alliances, which number in the thousands or tens of thousands. Over 20,000 strategic alliances were formed in a recent two-year period, more than half of which were between enterprises which were otherwise competitors.

There are various motives for cooperation:

- Reduction of vulnerability to strategic risk. Many such situations can be expressed as examples of the prisoner's dilemma.
- Avoidance of exploitation of a commons and therefore the occurrence of free riding.
- Leverage of existing competencies by accessing and linking with the competencies of other enterprises.
- Increase in the scale of commitment by individual organizations. The growing importance of fixed costs of various kinds forces enterprises to cooperate in order to limit the risk involved in the commitment of so many resources.

Types of strategic alliance

The nature of strategic alliances ranges all the way from equity participation in joint ventures to tacit collusion. The former may be a prelude to merger or acquisition, whereas most non-equity alliances may be only temporary, put together to deal with a temporary problem.

There are three explicit organizational forms of a strategic alliance:

1. A joint venture which combines the assets of two or more enterprises in a new enterprise independent of the partners.
2. An equity strategic alliance which occurs when partners acquire some proportion of the equity of another enterprise. Sometimes there are cross-ownerships, both partners holding a share of the other, with or without voting rights (see the Strategy in Action on Renault and Nissan).
3. Non-equity strategic alliances which occur when a contract between partners indicates a commitment to cooperate in some aspect of the partners' activities.

The motives for strategic alliance differ between the strategic business unit levels and the corporate level. At the business level, there is reference to four common types of alliance, each distinguished by a different motivation:

1. Complementary alliances can be horizontal alliances between potential competitors or vertical alliances linking enterprises which are located at different points in the value chain. In the absence of any significant degree of vertical or horizontal integration, such alliances are inevitable. Enterprises which concentrate on a limited number of core competencies must gain access to the competencies of other enterprises. A complementary strategic alliance is a way of achieving this. This is often the rationale for vertical alliances. For example, the main producers of sports shoes, such as Nike and Reebok, have now concentrated on R&D and marketing, leaving manufacture to partners.

    Complementary alliances are often created with the aim of accessing otherwise unavailable resources. Complementary alliances are more likely to create and maintain competitive advantage than the other kinds of alliance which at best help to manage threats to the status quo.

Several examples of horizontal complementary alliances exist within the airline industry. These alliances open up different parts of the world market, not directly serviced by a particular airline, to individual airlines. The fact that the enterprises are in competition with each other creates tensions in such alliances, which do not exist in vertical alliances.

2. Competition reducing alliances are designed to reduce the intensity of competition within an industry. They are common in industries which are prone to price or promotion wars. Where the aim was to control sales levels or prices, such alliances used to be called cartels. Today these alliances are illegal in many countries and can run foul of anti-monopoly legislation. There is a limit to how far such alliances can be pursued.

3. Competition response alliances are an attempt to cope with increased competition resulting from the entry into an industry of a new player(s). There is a potential for the situation which leads to competition reducing alliances to be created. The aim is to prevent this.

4. Uncertainty reducing alliances are put together to reduce uncertainty or risk, of whatever kind. They become more popular as the commitment of resources to new projects increases. These alliances are discussed in detail in Chapter 14.

Many alliances are related to one particular functional area, such as marketing, distribution or R&D, and are designed to spread the risks or costs in these areas. Or the alliance might be related to the solution of one particular problem, such as software companies looking for a solution to the security or encryption problem or automobile companies trying to solve the problems of the hydrogen cell. Some are comprehensive alliances covering all areas, but these usually result in an eventual merger.

At the corporate level, there are also two main kinds of alliance:

1. A diversifying strategic alliance, which allows an enterprise to begin a move into new product or service areas and helps it to avoid the problems of mergers or acquisitions which do not work; it can reduce uncertainty or risk generally. One variant of this kind of alliance is the contractual arrangements associated with franchising which means a diversification of market rather than product or service.

2. A synergistic alliance, rather like a complementary strategic alliance at the business level, for example the alliance between Nissan's engineering and Renault's design prowess. The broad aim is to discover and exploit economies of scope.

Managing strategic alliances

It is difficult to manage such alliances successfully. They are prone to failure. There is evidence that two-thirds of such alliances have difficulty in the first two years and as many as 70% eventually fail.

The management of any alliance is a difficult and intricate matter. It is often difficult for others to imitate a network which has been developed and themselves develop a competency in the management of such alliances. The ability to cooperate effectively is strategic in that it promotes the attainment of competitive advantage. In some industries it could be described as a core competency.

Focus on Practice
Partner selection

Criteria for partner choice	Partner risks	Risk management strategies
Objectives in requiring cooperation • nature of problem • time perspective • creating customer value	Opportunistic behaviour by partner	Read partner's strategic intent Develop trust Write detailed contracts and monitor enforcement Avoid asymmetrical partnerships, i.e. don't invest markedly more than your partner
Ability of partner to contribute to solution of problem	Inability of partner to contribute in way promised, e.g. in delivery of complementary assets	Withdraw from alliance Don't enter future alliances without basic research
Ability of partners to work together	Failure of mutual understanding due to incompatible corporate cultures	As above

Figure 13.8 **Partner selection – risks and strategy**

Where the cooperative interaction is repeated many times and involves a dense network of separate and independent players who have stable levels of cooperation, it results in a network. Such networks are increasingly common.

When the network involves close proximity of location it is called a cluster. Such clusters congregate in certain regions of the world: northern or central Italy in a number of different industries, ranging from clothing to ceramics; certain parts of Japan around some of the most dynamic large companies; most famously in the computer software industry in Silicon Valley in California; and often in certain industries, such as winery, biotechnology or automobiles. These clusters give a sound institutional and market underpinning to cooperation, as do networks which can link organizations which are not physically close to each other, and sometimes even global in their reach. Geographical proximity may help cooperation but it is not essential to it.

International alliances

Organizations are as likely to engage in cross-border alliances as in domestic alliances. They do this for a number of different reasons:

• Typically, multinational enterprises (MNEs) perform better than domestic ones
• In many industries and many countries the scope for domestic merger or acquisition may have been exhausted

- Other modes of entry or participation in the global scene may be impossible, costly or difficult to achieve
- Such alliances may also help the enterprise to adjust to a rapidly changing environment.

All the issues raised in this chapter become even more pressing at the global level – the need to read other players' intentions, avoid the consequences of opportunistic behaviour and the problem of increased vulnerability to opportunism in undertaking any cooperative arrangement. The criteria for the selection of partners is an even more important issue. Trust is based on knowledge of the potential partner's likely behaviour, a knowledge more difficult to develop at the global level.

The importance of strategic alliances, particular at the international level, has prompted John Dunning (1997b) to go as far as to announce the arrival of a new

Focus on Theory
The nature of capitalism

Table 13.5 Three patterns of capitalism

	Phase 1 Entrepreneurial capitalism	Phase 2 Hierarchical capitalism	Phase 3 Alliance or flexible capitalism
Markets	Small and fragmentary, local and national: mainly competitive	National or international: increasingly oligopolistic	Regional and global: dynamic and more competitive
Specialization	Simple and modest, based mainly on distribution of natural assets	Becoming more complex: both national and international	Extensive and interdependent: the paradox of an increasing global division of labour based on location-specific assets, together with subnational specialized clusters of economic activity
Key resources	Natural assets, e.g. fruits of the land and relatively unskilled labour	Physical and some knowledge capital	Intangible assets, e.g. human competence and knowledge, information, organizational and learning capacity
Mobility of assets	Little except for finance capital, and some emigration	Gradually increasing via MNE operations	Substantial mobility of firm-specific assets. But less mobility of some location-specific assets
Organization	Factory, small firms	Large integrated corporate hierarchies	More inter-firm alliances, single firm hierarchies, corporate networks
Production system	D form, batch	M form, mass or scale	Innovation-driven, flexible
Government role	Limited involvement: active	Growing intervention: growth	More systemic and market-enabling

type of capitalism, alliance capitalism or flexible capitalism. In Dunning's view, the existence and proliferation of strategic alliances defines the nature of capitalism itself. The nature of markets in a global world and the significance of innovation and learning in the modern period make the strategic alliance a critical part of a capitalist or market system.

In a modern economy, since enterprise-specific assets are mobile, enterprises can locate themselves wherever they wish. However, this tendency is offset by the continuing importance of a range of location-specific assets which are immobile; often those assets which are the real rationale for the appearance of clusters. Such 'constructed' assets include the skills of a local labour force, relatively immobile and with no incentive to move; the extra competitive leverage provided by access to complementary and supporting enterprises located in close proximity to each other; political stability, at least at the level of government relevant to the cluster; the availability of sophisticated business services; a transparent legal system; and a government alive to its systemic responsibilities. In this way, global networks can easily become localized clusters. The world is not as footloose as it might seem at first sight.

Case Study   The wine industry in Australia

Defining features of the industry

The wine industry comprises two basic activities – growing grapes and wine making. There are enterprises which specialize in growing grapes and do not make wine and enterprises which make wine but purchase all or most of their grapes. Most of the large enterprises do both. The relationship between grape growers and wine makers is a close one, and where the same enterprise is not doing both, a long-term contractual relationship often exists. The principal interest here is in the wine making.

The industry is highly dependent for growing high-quality grapes on the right climatic and soil conditions. They certainly limit the location, although different kinds of wine can be grown in different areas. These natural assets are location-specific. Micro-conditions vary enormously, even within the best areas. These affect the quality of wine produced. The intensive use of such land has raised the price for the land which is best for grape growing, for which there is great competition.

Conditions in a particular year also affect the vintage – the amount of sun, the damage caused by storms or frost, rain at the wrong time or not at all. There are good and bad years in terms of quality. However, the core of the industry has changed from an essentially commodity-driven industry to a knowledge-based cluster of activities. To some degree the enterprises concerned can control natural conditions, for example through irrigation.

Apart from the appropriate contribution of natural resources, there are three other contributory areas which require creative responses, two on the supply side and one on the demand side.

1. The quality of the *human capital* required in both activities, the intimate knowledge of grape growing in particular localities and the level of training and skill required of both grape growers and the wine makers. There is a vital process of learning which provides the necessary expertise. Education and training are critical elements for a successful industry. The interesting new development is the deliberate use of scientific knowledge by the industry. Grape growers and wine makers need access to this knowledge and the ability and knowledge to apply it, and apply it well. In any winery the wine maker is the key figure.

2. The high *level of investment required in grape growing and wine making*. Irrigation and trellis support for the plants demands a high initial investment per hectare or acre. Between planting and full production there is likely to be a seven-year gap, which pushes up the real cost. The facilities for wine making are also expensive.

Fortunately there are not only large enterprises prepared to put in large sums of money but also many amateurs who are prepared to invest their savings in the industry because they are attracted by the associated way of life. Entry into the industry in the past has been relatively easy, provided the scale of activity is initially low. A larger and more systematic entry requires a commitment of significant resources. Only large enterprise can do this on any scale.

3. The high *level of investment needed to market the wine*, in the process creating valuable brand names, supplemented by the costs of distribution itself and establishing reliable distribution systems. Branding is vital, whether nationally, regionally, by corporation or particular wine type. Product differentiation is central to the wine industry.

The industry is closely linked with one of the most rapidly growing industries, the tourist industry. There are often restaurants and even accommodation and gift shops attached to the larger wineries. It is said that there are as many as 50,000 small businesses serving the industry in various ways. Some contribute obvious inputs like the major producer of bottles, ACI.

The closer these wineries are to major urban centres, the stronger the likely link with tourism. There may be guided tours and large numbers of day visitors. These have the effect of increasing cellar door sales as well as generating other sources of income. Many of the smaller wineries only sell at the door or by mail order. Because of the tourism element, the industry is a godsend to small market towns in the relevant areas.

The market is not a homogeneous one. Product differentiation is probably more important in this industry than any other. Consequently the product differs enormously in price. There is a mass market for wine, highly competitive. There is a premium market, open to those who can persuade consumers that the higher quality justifies the higher price. Sometimes the price is very much higher. A backward sloping demand curve exists in this industry at the top of the premium end.

Tastes change quite rapidly. In recent years there has been a revival in the demand for reds over whites. There has also been a revival of the fortunes of Riesling over Chardonnay.

Because the industry in Australia is so dependent on exports, the exchange rates of the main competing countries are critical. For example, the continuing weakness of the South African rand or the recent more than 50% devaluation of the Argentinian peso can have major consequences at both the premium but particularly the cheap end of the market, creating new competition for Australian wine.

Wine competes in some way with other alcoholic beverages and non-alcoholic drinks. In this sense the whole industry worldwide has an interest in promoting the drinking of wine rather than these other beverages. The industry has to deal with the changing and rather fickle tastes of consumers and the problems of regulation which deter the consumption of wine, such as drink-driving laws. It has also to deal with the marketing campaigns supporting the consumption of other beverages.

Problems in a purely competitive environment

There are a number of disadvantages engendered by a competitive environment. The main problem is the tendency to free riding or the failure to nurture and develop the commons, whether this is technical knowledge or a market reputation:

- Underinvestment in training. This could arise either because of opportunism or because enterprises are too small to afford it.
- Underinvestment in R&D. The same arguments hold as for training.
- Underinvestment in grape growing.
- Excessive price competition. This might happen in conditions of excess supply. It might also happen if there is a stress on cost minimization rather than product differentiation and therefore quality.
- Excessive competitive advertising and promotion at the enterprise level can undermine the reputation of the generic product.
- Linking the grapes grown with consumer tastes fast enough. The taste for red or white wine, or particular grapes, for example Chardonnay or Riesling, can change quickly, much more quickly than the ability to change plantings.

Cooperative solutions

Before the 1990s the industry was fragmented, with no shared interests apparent. Compared with the French or even the American industry, the Australian industry has become highly concentrated. As the industry became more concentrated, the interests of large and small producers diverged more obviously.

All three forms of cooperative guidance were important. Charismatic individuals within the large enterprises took the lead in indicating solutions to difficult problems. Government was happy to play an important role in encouraging appropriate behaviour. Most importantly, various industry associations acted as cooperative mechanisms. The divergence of interests between large and small was offset by the creation of new industry associations and the redefinition of the functions of some old associations. In the wine industry, associations have provided the main context within which collaboration germinated. There are nine main associations, as indicated in Table 13.6.

Table 13.6 **The nine principal industry associations**

	Mission 1997/8	Funding	Sources	Governance	Staff	Outreach
Wine Makers Federation of Australia (WFA)	Represent producers	$1.4m	Members' subs Special levies (graduated scale)	Elected board (11 members)	5	Annual report
Winegrape Growers Council of Australia (WGCA)	Represent growers	$0.2m	Members' subs	Elected board (9 members) Federal organization (3 State Councils)	1	Periodic newsletter
Australian Wine and Brandy Corporation (AWBC)	Statutory authority Quality regulation/ export promotion	$6.4m (1998)	Statutory levy	Mixed nominee/ elected board	26	Annual report Newsletters
Grape and Wine Research & Development Corporation (GWRDC)	Statutory authority	$4.9	Statutory levy	9 members appointed by minister	2.5	Annual report
Australian Society for Wine Education	Facilitate domestic wine education/ promotion	$200,000	Subs and levies ($50,000 WFA)	Subsidiary of WFA	1	
Australian Wine Research Institute	Research & development	$4m	GWRDC Contract research	Nominated board	45 (15Phd)	Annual report Newsletter Technical bulletin
Cooperative Research Centre for Viticulture	Research & development	$6m	GWRDC Contract research	Nominated board	45	Conferences/ training Newsletter Annual report
Wine Industry Education & Training Group	Coordination between industry & educational institutions			Industry reps nominated by associations		1P/T provided by S.A. Wine Corp.
Wine Australia	Stage exposition every two years	$5m	Exhibitor contributions	6 member board (WFA sponsored)	2	

Source: Marsh and Shaw: 44.

There are at least seven areas in which collaboration assists the industry, most of all the largest players. These are trade issues, government relations generally, taxation, education and training, generic marketing, R&D and investor awareness. Statutory levy arrangements avoid the free rider problem and the differential level of the levies recognizes the different stakes that enterprises of different sizes have in collaboration. The size of costs are related to the size of benefits. The pioneer area of collaboration, mainly stimulated by the AWBC, was in exporting, with great success, helped by the significant decline in the value of the Australian dollar. Some in the industry believe that more should be spent on cooperative schemes than has been in the past.

Out of the collaboration there grew a visioning exercise, the preparation in 1996 of Strategy 2025, which identified the opportunities open to the industry in a global setting and a long-term context. The aim was growth of a dramatic kind, growth based necessarily on exports. This strategy was translated into a five-year operational plan released in 1997, with 14 specific strategies covering all the main areas of interest. The WFA initiated the strategy-building exercise.

The Strategy and the plans provided the framework for the marketing and distribution campaigns which focused on important markets such as the USA, the UK, Germany, Scandinavia and Japan. The AWBC, and its subsidiary, the Australian Wine Export Corporation (AWEC), established in 1992, have played the main role in this. AWEC champions national brand awareness.

Marketing was not the only major area of cooperation. Major efforts were made not only to increase the R&D effort but to disseminate its results, with priority areas identified in the Strategy and plans. These concentrated on water management and irrigation, improving the quality of the grapes, pest management and nutrition. This effort was financed by increased levies and the increase in associated government funding. Educational institutions, such as Roseworthy College and Charles Sturt University, were linked with the industry. The links were institutionalized in the Cooperative Research Centre for Viticulture, a joint government and industry venture.

An expanding range of newsletters, journals and pamphlets, published by the industry associations, communicate what is being done. Annual reports of the associations and conferences reinforce this process.

The changing mix of competition and cooperation

There is a comprehensive collaborative structure which is made up of three principal zones which interact strongly.

The *competitive market zone* consists of both domestic and particular international markets. All wineries are operating in a fiercely competitive world in which they must keep down costs and keep up quality. They can only hold their position by gaining a competitive advantage in either or both areas. The market is the domain of the competitive firms, ably supported by the AWEC. All the enterprises operate in a number of different markets or market segments. This is the area of activity which is the traditional focus of attention in the press or by economists.

The *collaborative zone* is made up of the industry associations. They take the lead in identifying common interests, forging from these common purposes and accumulating and disseminating collective knowledge. These activities are translated into the strategic vision for the industry as a whole and medium-term industry priorities expressed in operational plans. Strategy is emergent, in the sense of identifying latent possibilities,

translating them into priorities, recognizing new issues and reconciling the interests of different stakeholder groups. The impact on enterprises is to improve the competitiveness of all enterprises through raising aspirations and identifying new opportunities, national brand development, the deepening of market knowledge, individual brand projection and the stimulation of innovation.

The *negotiation zone* is again dominated by industry associations. The industry associations represent the industry to government and other institutional stakeholders such as the media, the stock market, tertiary training institutions and related and supporting industries. They promote awareness of industry achievements, indicate factor input needs, such as trained workers, and defend the industry from possible negative spillovers in the areas of tax and regulation.

There has been a deliberate cultivation of internationalization, innovation and a shared outlook. It is interesting to ask who are the main change agents in this process – leading enterprises or the visionary managers in some of them, the industry associations or the government? The government is usually seen more as a catalyst facilitator, encouraging the others to play an active role in change. It is difficult to separate and evaluate the role of the other two, both of whom are powerful change agents.

International cooperation

Traditionally the UK has been Australia's largest external market. The USA market is likely to overtake the UK market in the next two or three years. The key to success in the USA is distribution. Because of the importance of each state's rights and a hangover from the days of prohibition, each state has its own laws on sales of alcohol, its advertising and promotion. Both importers and distributors (wholesalers) must be licensed in each state. As a consequence, exporting to the USA is like exporting to 50 different countries. It is critical for Australian companies to form strategic alliances with American companies which can unlock the distribution system. It would be enormously expensive to have to start from scratch in putting together a distribution network.

Casella Wines' Yellow Tail brand is a remarkable story of a successful strategy and also illustrates the importance of finding the right partner in the USA, in this case W. J. Deutsch. Casella only began to sell this label in the USA in June 2001, anticipating, on the advice of W. J. Deutsch, sales of 25,000 cases in the first year. By the end of July the annual sales had topped one million cases, 40 times the target, and are still climbing. This is the most successful launch in the history of the US wine industry. Yellow Tail is already a bestselling Australian

Table 13.7 Australian shipments to the US and UK

	Vol. (litres)	Change (%)	Value (A$ FOB)	Change (%)	Average price/litre (A$)
USA					
1999–2000	49.7m	32.9	315.1	46.2	6.35
2000–2001	67.6m	36.2	417.3	32.5	6.17
2001–2002	94.9m	40.2	584.7	40.1	6.16
UK					
1991–2000	139.1m	35.9	587.7	31.6	4.23
2000–2001	165.1m	18.7	689.9	17.4	4.18
2001–2002	201.0m	21.7	838.1	21.5	4.17

Australian brand leaders in the USA

Brand	Sales by dozen	% change 12 months	Average price – US$/750ml bottle
Lindemans	154,566	55.2	7.48
Rosemount	95,392	34.2	9.39
Jacob's Creek	50,158	10.2	8.47
Yellow Tail	48,404	2561.0	6.81
Alice White	28,067	92.8	6.76
Penfolds	19,345	238.1	10.17
Black Opal	18,694	12.7	9.98
McPherson	14,343	3.7	6.98
Banrock Station	12,160	118.2	6.39
Wyndham Estate	7.495	(12.1)	9.73

Source: Australian Wine and Brandy Corporation website, www.awbc.com.au.

label in the USA, having overtaken Jacob's Creek, Rosemount and Lindemans.

There are all sorts of pluses for the brand: the general popularity of Australian wine in the USA; the purchase of an off-the-shelf brand label with superb graphics; the hire of a general manager, sales and marketing, with the right experience and background in exporting, John Souter; and the targeting of the right price range, one with the most potential, that between US$5 and US$7 in the store. But as important has been the role of W. J. Deutsch. This company has a 44-state network of distributors. It took Casella 18 months to successfully persuade the company to agree to sell an unknown wine and give that wine a prominent place in its stores. Without that help the expansion would have been impossible.

Recent trends in the Australian industry

Until quite recently the industry in Australia was dominated by small enterprises. Over the past 5–10 years the industry has experienced two tendencies. The first is a process of consolidation, with the emergence of four major producers – Beringer Blass (formerly Mildara-Blass and now under Forster's control), Southcorp, which in February 2001 merged with Rosemount Estates with a combined capitalization of A$1.5 billion, BRL Hardy and Orlando-Wyndham (owned by Ricard Pernod). Together these four companies produce about 80% of Australia's wine. By contrast the next 20 in terms of size account for 15%, and about 1,350 wineries make up the last 5%. The big four are large by international standards. Their share in exports is even higher than their share in production.

The second tendency is the establishment of strong international links by the large producers, for example the purchase of the American company Beringer Wine Estates by Foster's wine division Mildara-Blass in October 2000, for A$2.9 billion. There has been particular interest in the US, the third largest wine market in the world, but one in which only 7% of the population accounts for 86% of wine consumption, and therefore one which has an enormous untapped market potential. A number of Australian wine companies have formed joint ventures with American

Table 13.8 The top eight wine companies in the world (2000)

		Sales (US$ millions)	
1	LVMH – France	1,524	(about ¾ of these sales champagne)
2	E&J Gallo – USA	1,428	
3	FBG/Beringer – Australia	1,217	
4	Seagram – USA	800	
5	Castel Freres – France	700	
6	Constellation – USA	614	
7	Diageo – Britain	590	
8	SRP/Rosemount – Australia	538	

Source: www.southcorp.com.au.

companies, notably Southcorp with Robert Mondavi, BRL Hardy with Constellation Brands, the second largest American wine company, and McWilliams with the largest, E&J Gallo.

Australian companies are vulnerable to takeovers by large multinationals unless they can expand by acquisition and gain access to key distribution systems. Some large British players are hovering and the New Zealand company Lion-Nathan is in the process of acquiring two Australian companies, Banksia Wines and Petaluma. The industry in Australia has a number of large producers which are potential world players or potentially part of large global players. There is also a host of smaller producers, boutique wineries, which in any difficult period are likely to be open to purchase. There is also a host of small grape growers, 4,000 in all, some on a continuing contract with the wineries, other selling in a free-market context.

A key transitional period

The industry cannot stand still. It has to adapt to its changing environment or begin to change the global environment by its own actions. It has to accept its previous success as only temporary. Success has two consequences: it encourages imitation and slows the pace of innovation, as the players reinforce what seems to have succeeded in the past. Future success may require a different approach, the ability to adjust in a changing environment.

It seems clear that the Australian industry is moving into a new phase in which continuing growth may be a problem. Initially there seemed to be a potential glut of grapes. World wine consumption is rising only slowly, at a rate of about 2% per annum, whereas the increase in grape production in Australia, given the likely growth of the domestic market for wine, seemed to require a growth of 8% per annum in exports over the next 5–10 years to absorb the supply of grapes. However, in 2003 drought reduced the harvest by 10% and removed this problem. There is even talk of a shortage. This is also a major challenge in marketing within a highly competitive industry. The Australian industry will be threatened by the success of wine industries in new areas of supply and any rise in the value of the Australian dollar.

It is also critical to keep costs as low as possible. The Australian industry is quite highly taxed which makes it more difficult to achieve a significant reduction. There are economies of scale in certain areas, such as marketing and distribution. Such economies encourage consolidation. Diversification internationally also encourages internationalization in order to manage risk.

There is an enormous difference between an industry growing from a very small base and one which is already established as a major player. Further gains then become much harder to make. Expanding market share from an already large base is also difficult. A feature of the industry which is both an advantage and a disadvantage is the small size of the domestic market. Australian enterprises have to export. This makes them vulnerable to changes in their markets but at the same time highly competitive.

Case Study Questions

1. How should a grape grower adjust to the changing environment?
2. How should a small winery adjust to the changing environment?
3. How should a large winery adjust to the changing environment?
4. What changes are likely in the mix of cooperation and competition which has characterized the industry?
5. Do the larger Australian companies need to become international players?

Reading

Anderson, K. and Norman, D., *Global Wine Production Consumption and Trade 1961–2001: a statistical compendium* (Centre for International Economic Studies, Adelaide: 2003).

Halliday, J. A, *History of the Australian Wine Industry* (Corporation/Winetitles, Adelaide: 1994).

Hannan, M., 'Wine companies sparkle in a slow US market', *Business Review Weekly*, January 17–23, 2002: 38–9.

Marsh, I. and Shaw, B., Australia's Wine Industry; collaboration and learning as causes of competitive success (unpublished consultant's report).

Snow, C., 'Australian winery toasts all-American success', *The Age*, September 28, 2002, Business: 3.

Wahlquist, A., 'Volatility on the vine', *The Weekend Australian*, January 19–20, Inquirer: 21.

Relevant websites

www.awbc.com.au
www.beringerblass.com
www.brlhardy.com.au
www.lion-nathan.com au
www.mcwilliams.com.au
www.southcorp.com.au
www.winetitles.com.au/awol

This case study is also relevant to Chapters 10 and 15.

Key strategic lessons

• The danger of one strategic actor making decisions in ignorance of the intentions of other players can result in outcomes which could easily be improved for all players. This applies to all enterprises operating in competition within a given industry, but notably in conditions of oligopoly.

• The impact of strategic risk on the strategic orientation of any player is affected by the competitive position of the main player, the (perceived and actual) strategies of other players and the nature of the strategic situation.

• It is impossible for any player to ignore the strategies of other players and there are many players to take into account, not just competitors.

• Strategic risk can be reduced by a deliberate effort to learn about the strategies of others, and there may be situations in which cooperation achieves a better performance outcome for all.

• The commons is equivalent to public goods which are available at below full cost, sometimes free. Free riding is the systematic exploitation of the commons.

• The commons exists at every level of an economy.

Free riding may be potentially inefficient and the problems arising from this can be resolved by a cooperative strategy.

• The prisoner's dilemma formalizes the result of non-cooperative decision making in a less than optimal outcome. Independent decision making and a lack of trust produces an inferior outcome in one-off games to that which would be produced by cooperation.

• Some common challenges which can be resolved by cooperation include the moderation of price competition, new entry into a market, the provision of a training scheme and the withdrawal of a loan from a financial institution.

• The cooperation which resolves these situations can result from spontaneous action by the players, leadership from one enterprise or trade association or imposition by a government or quasi-government body.

• The proliferation of strategic alliances makes it possible to talk in terms of alliance capitalism. The term 'coopetition' encapsulates the combination of competition and cooperation desirable in most business situations.

Applying the lessons

1 Define the following terms: the commons, free riding, zero-sum game, game theory, the prisoner's dilemma, horizontal alliances, vertical alliances, joint venture, networks and alliance capitalism.

2 Focus on a sector of an organization of which you have good knowledge. Identify as many examples of the 'commons' as you can at the different levels of the economy relevant to this particular sector:
i. Within the organization
ii. Within the industry in which that organization is located
iii. Within the country
iv. At the global level.

3 In what sectors of the economy would you expect cooperation to be given more emphasis than compet-

ition? Use the conceptual framework introduced in this chapter to identify these sectors. Give your reasons for the particular selection made.

4 Construct an illustration of a prisoner's dilemma to illustrate a common strategic situation faced by decision makers in any organization, other than those indicated in the text of the chapter.

5 Under what circumstances might opportunism be a reasonable strategy for an organization to pursue? What are the losses which result from an opportunistic strategy? How might these losses be avoided?

6 Give an example of a network and/or an example of a cluster other than those in the wine industry. Describe the origins, history and main features of the network and/or cluster.

Strategic project

1 Choose an example of a strategic alliance with which you are familiar, which has been in existence long enough to test its effectiveness. In what circumstances did the alliance arise? How extended were the negotiations? How well did the partners know each other before the alliance?

2 How important is the nature of the partner to the effectiveness of the alliance? Give reasons for your assessment. What are the characteristics of a good partner in such a strategic alliance?

3 Give as many examples of the breakdown of such an alliance as you can and the reasons for the breakdown. How far was the nature of the partner responsible for this failure?

Exploring further

Relevant texts differ enormously in the importance given to cooperation. Some have almost nothing on the subject, limiting their attention to competition alone.

Francis Fukuyama's 1995 book is an easily accessible introduction to the significance of trust in economic and business activity. It is a good reminder of the social infrastructure on which enterprises rely in order to keep their transaction costs down. Another work on this theme is Coleman, 1988: 95–120. As a contrast it is worth reading Schelling, 1960.

An early introduction to the notion of the 'commons' is, aptly, Commons, 1934. There is a basic text on free riding, written in a rigorous manner, Alchian and Demsetz, 1972: 177–95, which discusses the case of workers free riding on team effort. The need for government action to counteract free riding is discussed in North, 1981 and 1990.

The classic reference on cooperation interpreted in terms of game theory is Axelrod, 1984. A theoretical treatment of games is Luce and Raifa, 1957. More relevant to the world of business are Ghemawat, 1991 and 1997. There are a number of shorter pieces which are very helpful: Brandenburger and Nalebuff, 1995: 57–71, Dixit and Nalebuff, 1991 and Lyons and Varoukis, 1989.

Defining the recurrent dilemmas is somewhat more difficult. The present text benefited enormously from the treatment of the prisoner's dilemma in the second part, entitled Strategic Situations, of the book by Forster and Browne, 1996. There is also a very interesting interpretation, in terms of the prisoner's dilemma, of the *nemawashi* model of business–government cooperation in Japan, designed to remove excess competition; see Chapter 5 of Reed, 1993.

A good treatment of networks can be found in Coyne and Dye, 1998: 99–109. A more specific application is to be found in Stuart, 1999: 668–98. The principal source on clusters is Porter, 1998a, especially pp. 197–289. Porter also has a shorter piece: 1998b: 77–90.

The best introduction to the subject of strategic alliances in general is Doz and Hamel, 1998. The main source on alliance capitalism is Dunning, 1997a: 31–73 and 1997b.

14 Managing risk

Worst infection-disease catastrophe in recorded history. (ROSEN ET AL., *2003: 81, talking of AIDS)*

Learning objectives

After reading this chapter you will be able to:

- recognize the omnipresence of risk of various kinds
- identify the main strategic responses to the existence of risk
- understand when avoidance is the best form of risk management
- distinguish between the management and mitigation of risk
- understand how diversification is one way of managing risk
- consider how, using scenario building and planning, risk management can be made part of the overall strategic orientation of those making strategy

Key strategic challenge

How do I respond to the existence of risk?

Strategic dangers

That the enterprise will expose itself to risks which can destroy or seriously weaken it. This damage can result from a failure to either assess properly the risk environment or control the enterprise's exposure by appropriate strategies of avoidance, management and mitigation.

Case Study Scenario   Africa – AIDS and civil wars

'Africa has never known anything like this in its history. It is the worst nightmare that we can imagine. It is worse than a nuclear bomb.'

Bunmi Makinwa, head of UNAIDS
in eastern and southern Africa

'We are all engaged in a fight to the death. We are faced with extinction.'

Joy Phumaphi, Botswana's health minister

Each year Africa receives less than one per cent of the world's foreign direct investment (FDI). The only countries in Africa receiving a significant level of FDI are those with obvious opportunities for a return to offset the risk. Usually this means the existence of natural resources of some kind. These would include countries such as Nigeria and the Sudan which have significant oilfields or those with other natural resources such as diamonds, for example Botswana.

The multinationals which invest at an already high level in China and on an ever-increasing level in India do not do so in Africa. Why is this the case?

Economies displaying poor rates of economic growth offer fewer opportunities of a good return for investment than countries which have high rates of growth. Most of sub-Saharan Africa has seen a contraction in its economy over the last 15 years. Growth is negative. Returns for most types of investment in Africa are not good. It is tempting to assert that it is because the risk environment is so bad that no investor is willing to take the risk of conducting business transactions in Africa. The problems are particularly threatening in sub-Saharan Africa, but by no means limited to that region. Only where the prospective returns are very high is it worth investing.

There is a vicious circle in which the high frequency of risk-creating events helps keep income levels down and those same low income levels make the continent vulnerable to risk, unable to respond in a way which effectively mitigates or manages that risk. There is a general perception of Africa as highly risky, which helps to keep out investment. The perception of Africa is such that the news coming out of Africa usually relates to disasters, threats and risk.

Africa has the full range of risk-generating events, from natural events to social sources of risk, from drought and disease to warfare. These include all sorts of human and animal diseases in an environment which, because of its climate, encourages their proliferation, much of it debilitating as well as potentially lethal, including bilharzia and sleeping sickness. AIDS is a new

but potentially extremely destructive problem. Drought is another problem. Much of the pain from the latter is self-inflicted, as with its common consequence famine. There is a progressive desertification of many areas because of the agricultural practices pursued and an inability to raise agricultural productivity. There is a failure to distribute efficiently what is produced.

The negative impact of such risk-generating events results partly from the inability of governments to respond effectively and handle that response in a way which attracts approval. Governments in Africa tend to be unstable, and poorly supported by a public service which is itself often highly politicized and riven with corruption. Again the perception may be worse than the fact and unfair to many governments which are doing their best in difficult circumstances.

Political risk, in the sense of frequent changes of government and policy or general civil commotion, is at a high level. Political stability is hard to find. Tribal divisions often make very difficult the development of national states to which all the population can be loyal. In nearly all cases, decolonization has left a legacy of division between the tribes of different areas. Often the tribal situation is complex but in some cases the divisions are only too obvious. In some cases this has boiled over into genocide, as with the Tutsis and Huttus of Rwanda. In the Sudan there is a continuing civil war between the Christians of the south and the Muslims of the north. Elsewhere divisions have burst out into civil war, as in Biafra in Nigeria back in the 1960s, but now smoulder below the surface. The list of countries suffering from civil war is endless: Nigeria, Ethiopia, Somalia, the Sudan, Angola, Mozambique, Liberia, the Congo, Sierra Leone and the Ivory Coast. Only a handful of countries seem to be exempt – Kenya, Tanzania and Ghana.

The concept of a modern state with an efficient and detached civil service is an alien concept. In both politics and economics there is a winner-takes-all attitude, with the spoils of government enjoyed in lavish and ostentatious but unproductive expenditures and rewards for key groups of supporters, particularly the army or police. A tendency to a winner-takes-all politics, even in stable polities, often translates into corruption at all levels of government from the top downwards. Entering African states and encountering the immigration and customs controls can be the first, but not the last, encounter with corruption.

Decolonization has left an indelible mark on Africa. The colonizing powers redrew the boundaries in Africa according to the fortunes of particular colonizing powers in the competition for colonies. Language and outside links still reflect the influence of the former dominant powers. The creation of independent states came much later to this continent than to the Americas and even Asia, in many cases as late as the 1960s. Settler populations in various parts of Africa have made the problem more, not less, complicated.

The business environment in Africa is seen as very hostile. The usual response to that environment is an avoidance response, which explains both the low level of foreign investment in African countries and the low level of interest in Africa revealed in the business press of the developed world. How should such risk be factored into business decision making?

Whatever kind of business decision is made, and wherever it is made, it is always made in conditions of risk and uncertainty. All strategic situations are characterized by at least some risk, although the exact nature and level of the risk will never be the same in two different situations. As a consequence, whatever decision is made must be made with an eye to the risk exposure created and the likely impact on the risk position for any organization.

The universality of risk management

There is no business decision which does not involve risk management of some kind. Any decision involving future performance comprises some measure of uncertainty and therefore risk. This means that risk management must be a universal phenomenon and an essential part of strategy making.

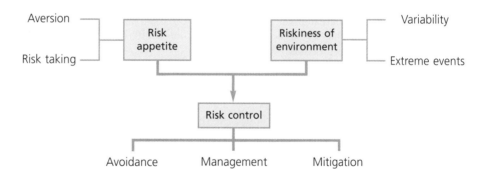

Figure 14.1 **Risk control**

The risk appetite

Effective risk management requires the taking of an explicit attitude to risk and careful consideration of the actual riskiness of possible outcomes.

What should be an appropriate attitude to risk? There are four major elements determining such a risk appetite:

1. The *economic health of the enterprise*, partly its general profitability but notably its immediate liquidity position. Only a cashed-up enterprise, fully used to operating in an environment of high returns, high risk and rapid change, and faced with a project offering fairly certain revenue and cost streams, can afford to totally ignore risk. There are not many enterprises and projects around and not many situations in which these conditions hold.

The more vulnerable the enterprise in which the decisions are made, the greater the reluctance to accept risk. Vulnerability may be a matter of:

- chronically low profits, as with the airlines
- persistent loss making, as with many dot-com companies, such as Amazon.com
- low financial reserves and poor borrowing ability.

An enterprise which has few reserves to tide it over unexpected bad times is bound to be more sensitive to risk than one with ample reserves which can tide it over anything but the most extreme events. There are various such reserves, stretching from cash held to assets which can be easily realized on the market or used as collateral for a loan. Some valuable assets, such as aircraft or a car fleet, can be sold and leased back.

2. The *personality and motivation of the strategists themselves*. The perception of performance outcomes is coloured by the position of the observer and reflects the confidence with which expectations of the future are held by that observer. There is no doubt that some individuals are more risk-averse than others. Risk aversion often reflects the past history of the individual. Recent catastrophic events tend to reduce the appetite for risk and increase risk aversion.

   Confidence is a key issue, particularly the confidence with which views concerning the future are held. A single dominant personality can be the key figure and the critical input in the willing acceptance of risky projects. Without a champion with a belief in a successful outcome, the project would never be undertaken or completed. It is often the role of the leader or entrepreneur to provide such confidence.

   Entrepreneurs by definition have a greater appetite for risk than the average. In reality few strategists can afford to be deliberate risk takers. Even the most adventurous of entrepreneurs seek to manage risk as much as they can. They will make every effort to reduce the risk level or pass the risk on to others. Some are stimulated by the challenge of overcoming risk but they always seek to control the level of risk to which they are exposed. This can be done by proper organization. Teams of staff can massage markets, anticipate technical problems and ensure access to sufficient finance.

3. The *culture of the enterprise*, whether it encourages or discourages risk taking. Corporate culture almost invariably involves an attitude to risk and risk taking. The culture of an enterprise is partly the result of past behaviour and its outcomes – what succeeded in the past and what failed – and partly the result of the attitude and influence of leaders, past and present. A corporate, just as a national, culture can encourage or discourage risk taking. Whatever the views of a single powerful CEO, such a person needs support; an appropriate corporate culture helps.

4. The *'political' interaction between key decision makers*, including the level of conflict within the enterprise. Conflict can prevent decisive action and encourage risk-

averse behaviour. How far do the decision makers pull together? Fear of a mistake can increase in a context of conflict. Different interest groups can clash and prevent decisive action. As a result the whole decision-making process may become much slower. To be successful, risky projects usually require a careful alignment of stakeholder groups and integration of all functional areas.

Reactions to the requirements of a particular situation are therefore based on the interaction between this attitude to risk and the actual riskiness of a particular project, that is, between the appetite for risk and the amount of risk involved in any particular project.

The riskiness of the environment

What about the riskiness of the environment? How is this to be measured?

Outcomes for any particular project are expressed in the movement of chosen performance indicators, such as the level of profit. The measurement of risk depends on the selection of an appropriate key performance indicator which expresses by its possible movements the existence of risk. Often there is an assumption that past behaviour indicates future risk. There are two ways of measuring risk:

1. The variance in a key performance indicator. This approach dwells on the general tendency in some sectors of the economy to variation.
2. The size of possible extreme fluctuations occurring with a defined probability. The approach focuses on the shock of the occasional extreme event.

Risk management entails either reducing the variance or taking action to guard against the extreme event; two different responses. Extreme events can have a dramatic effect on performance indicators such as profit. There is always the chance of an extreme event occurring which would take down even the best prepared organizations. They come with a varying degree of probability, in some cases with a complete uncertainty. Some projects offer the prospect of huge losses, if they fail.

How does the observer compare the possibility of an extreme event, an event which might, for example, reduce net income to a tenth of its anticipated level, with a variance which is 25% of the average value? Which represents more of a threat?

Risk-generating events

Risk can arise from a multitude of particular kinds of threats. Risk-generating events take many different forms. The more turbulent the environment in which such decisions are made, the greater the level of risk. In particular, the waves of 'creative destruction' which define a capitalist economy have always been characterized by high levels of risk. Unforeseen fluctuations of the market economy, such as the Asian economic crisis of 1997 or the Argentinian financial crisis of 2001, are inherent in any market economy. The frequent overshooting and undershooting of demand relative to supply means that prices rise and fall in cumulative movements. This is not surprising, given that within any market system confidence waxes and wanes. Such crises have been happening as long as the market itself has been in existence. Some industries, particularly those in the new economy, are more volatile and more risky than others. They are more subject to violent fluctuations, both upwards and downwards. So-called bubbles are common in these new sectors.

Risk management strategy

Given the risk environment in which there are risk takers with a given appetite for risk and projects offering the opportunity of different and varying returns, there are two strategic decisions which are necessary preliminaries to managing risk – the extent of the risk assessment and who should implement it.

Risk assessment

The first decision is how far decision makers, including strategists, should go in making a risk assessment, that is, what level of resources is it desirable to commit to such an exercise.

Part of risk management is a thorough assessment of the level and nature of risk. Ignorance in the market can never be fully removed, but it is always possible to get access to more information than is currently available. This requires the commitment of more resources, in particular the time and effort of staff members. It is always costly to make a full risk assessment for a particular project, whether country risk or any other kind of risk.

Assessment of risk involves the identification of risk-generating events and the estimation of their incidence. Such an assessment can take a variety of different forms. There are a variety of approaches, including sensitivity analysis and scenario creation, which identify and determine the possibility of a certain sequence of negative events unfolding in the future. Assessment depends on the collection of information about such events and their impact. Any measure can be an exact quantitative measure, sometimes deceptively exact, or it can be a qualitative rating, ordinal rather than cardinal.

In theory, the expenditure on risk assessment should be taken to the point at which the marginal return on the investment made is equal to the marginal cost. Because of ignorance and uncertainty there is no way of knowing in advance what the marginal return will be from making such a commitment of resources. This simple rule is of little operational value. Much cruder and simpler rules must be adopted on the level of commitment. Usually there is a process of trial and error which establishes an acceptable level.

Since the risk situation in a particular country or industry reflects the specifics of the environment in that country or industry, a proper risk assessment requires considerable expertise and knowledge of the country or industry. This includes knowledge of both prior history and current conditions. An in-depth study of country or industry risk, carried out to test the viability of an investment, may take months to complete. It cannot be repeated very often, for example every year, although it might be updated in order to evaluate a rapidly changing risk environment. Any risk assessment is a matter of a careful analysis which must guide action over a significant period of time.

The risk managers

The second strategic decision is whether to do it 'in-house' or use the services of specialists. The outcome of such a decision depends partly on the size of the organization, its capacity to carry out an effective risk assessment and the relative costs of doing it in-house or outsourcing the service.

On the one hand, there are many consulting firms willing to carry out this function for an enterprise. There are many people who set themselves up as experts in risk assessment and sell their expertise as consultants in risk assessment.

On the other hand, many organizations today have their own risk management officers and carry out regular risk audits. In particular, financial institutions have their own risk officers and risk departments.

An enterprise always gains by knowing exactly what the worst is and the consequences if it happens. However, it is not sensible to allow the negative side of a project to completely dominate decision making. A risk assessment is just one among a number of inputs into the decision-making process. The positive side must not be relegated to a secondary place in this decision making.

A sensible approach to any decision making is to consider simultaneously opportunities and threats, to build risk management into the process of evaluation from the very start, rather than apply it as an 'add-on' after a decision is made. It is not a matter of undertaking risk management as an afterthought or a final check on whether a policy is sensible.

All managers must, at least implicitly, manage risk, even if they do not do so explicitly. As with many other aspects of strategy, it is better that it is made explicit.

There may be problems of measurement, whether it is of the actual incidence of the risk-generating events, the degree of the threat, or the strength of its likely impact, but it is advisable to try to assess the approximate level of risk in a systematic manner. This might be a matter of estimating the frequency of events, and evaluating the severity of exposure and impact, that is, how many lives or how much capital is actually at risk. Each decision maker needs to understand exactly what it is which, under the heading of risk, actually threatens him or her.

The first response to the existence of risk is therefore to articulate clearly the nature and level of risk. Only then is it possible to work out what other responses might be necessary. Obviously too little was spent on risk management in the past, with negative results. The debt crisis of the early 1980s led to a significant debate about country risk, mainly by financial institutions which had made large non-performing loans. It was concluded that no significant investment should be made without a proper risk assessment. However, this requires taking a whole series of strategic decisions. This conclusion, reached largely with respect to portfolio investment, applies equally to foreign direct investment (FDI).

An alternative is to consider the country risk rating of *Euromoney* and *Institutional Investor*. These come out once or twice a year. They purport to measure country risk, which typically includes political as well as economic risk. They score each country out of 100, with the highest scores indicating lowest risk. Other assessments, such as those by Moody's or Standard & Poor's, are of creditworthiness.

The first issue is how these ratings are determined. The formula used by *Euromoney* includes ten different elements and is shown in Table 14.2.

As can be seen, there is a strong influence of the factors relevant to creditworthiness in this formula, amounting to 50%. However, both political risk and economic performance play an important role, each 25%.

The ideal may be to see a steady improvement in the risk rating, both for a corporation and a country, but the reality for undeveloped and particularly developing countries or corporations is to see significant fluctuations in the level of sovereign and corporate risk. Sometimes these fluctuations are the result of events elsewhere in the

Focus on Theory
Risk evaluation

There are many different risk rating systems available, some public and others only available on payment. Mostly they apply to financial assets, that is, portfolio investment rather than direct investment in productive facilities, investment in bonds or bills rather than in shares or physical facilities. The most common are ratings of creditworthiness. Moody's, Standard & Poor's and Fitches use letter systems to assess the creditworthiness of both companies and governments. The listing runs typically from the lowest risk AAA rating to the highest risk rating D. The key dividing line is between investment grade and that deemed less than investment grade. The downgrading of a company or country to a non-investment grade not only increases the cost of capital for the recipient, but often has seriously negative effects on share prices.

All countries are assessed for their sovereign credit rating, that is, the likelihood that the government will be able to continue to service its bond or bill issues. All large companies are rated for their corporate risk. Table 14.1 illustrates the method.

Table 14.1 **Standard & Poor's risk rating scale**

Rating	Comments	Numerical equivalent
AAA	Excellent	91-100
AA		81–90
A		71–80
BBB	Satisfactory quality, average risk	61–70
BB		51–60
B		41–50
CCC	Low quality, high risk	31–40
CC		21–30
C		11–20
D	Excessive risk	0–10

Source: Adapted from Madura, 2001: 558.

world, so-called risk-generating events. In other words, broad groups of countries move together in a systematic way.

A good example of this was the Asian economic crisis, which led to the downgrading of the risk rating of many countries in Latin America and Eastern Europe not directly affected by the crisis. Almost all countries in the developing world were affected.

How much importance do decision makers attach to these ratings? For some countries or corporations, a downgrading is accompanied by the reduction in the inflow of FDI or higher borrowing costs.

Table 14.2 **The components of** *Euromoney's* **risk ratings**

	%
Political risk	25
Economic performance	25
Debt indicators	10
Debt in default or rescheduled	10
Credit ratings	10
Access to bank finance	5
Access to short-term finance	5
Access to capital markets	5
Discount on forfeiting	5
(the rate of interest on export finance)	

An interesting case involves Japan. In 2002, Moody's reduced the credit rating of Japan's sovereign debt to A2, which is five ratings below a triple A rating and rates Japan as a higher risk than Botswana. It is not difficult to make fun of such a rating. The revenues from Japan's annual automobile sales alone exceed Botswana's total GDP. In Botswana, despite a good record of growth during the 1990s, 47% of the population live below the poverty line, compared with just 5% in Japan. A major social problem is that Botswana has one of the highest HIV infection rates in the world. As

Powell (2002) noted, Japan's main social problem is to prevent her best baseball players from defecting to the USA. How does this compare with an HIV infection rate of above 38%? Certainly Botswana has some mineral riches, notably diamonds. But why is the comparative rating at the level it is? It is probably because Botswana's banks are solvent and the suspicion is that Japan's are not, but currently there are similar suspicions about the banks in China and Germany but they are not so badly rated.

Strategic responses to risk

There are three main generic strategies which are valid techniques of risk control. They can be summarized under the broad headings of avoidance, management and mitigation.

Risk avoidance

There is no doubt that there are projects too risky to contemplate, markets too volatile to enter and countries where the risk of political instability and detrimental policy change is too great to tolerate. If this is the case, the obvious response is one of risk avoidance. There must be thousands of projects which never get off the ground because they are considered too risky even to contemplate. There are probably many which are never properly analysed; they are dismissed after a cursory examination of their riskiness. What exactly does such avoidance mean?

- Does it mean that you wish to invest in a particular industry but avoid investing in a particular country, investing elsewhere?
- Or does it mean that you wish to invest in a particular country, but avoid investing in this industry rather than that one?
- In other words, does it mean that you reject one project in favour of another? In so doing you make a choice based on relative riskiness and relative return.
- Or does it mean simply that entry into a particular industry or country is far too risky, so that there is no entry at all?

A common-sense approach suggests that there is a potential cost to avoidance, which is the opportunity cost of avoidance or the return which might have been received had the project been undertaken and gone well. An enterprise may refrain from entering a particular market or making a particular investment if the risk level is considered too high, but it has to do this in the context of the return offered. As seen already, there are various ways in which the risk can appear in the figures of any estimate of whether a project is profitable enough.

This mode of proceeding might be modified to take account of the role of the particular project under study in the overall portfolio of business units. The strategy may involve a number of projects of varying risk level. In combination the projects yield an acceptable risk level. Together the portfolio of assets created by these projects does not seem to entail a prohibitively high level of risk, whereas in an extreme case individually they may all seem too risky. This may simply be a consequence of diversification, or it might be a reflection of the way in which various markets or facilities link together or fail to link together.

There may not be a simple one-to-one relationship between risk and avoidance. Many opportunities may be rejected because the expected return is too low – the risk premium demanded is too great for the level of return associated with the project. The higher the level of risk, the greater the likelihood of avoidance. There will be a significant number of projects rejected, not because the return is too low, but because the risk is too high, or rather because the combination of risk and return is unacceptable.

Enron's Dabhol project shows how an enterprise might factor a premium for country risk into the terms of the contract.

Strategy in Action Enron and the Dabhol project

Enron International, before the demise of its parent Enron, had in train an important project to build a power plant at Dabhol in Maharashtra state in India, important in that it would help meet the infrastructural needs of India and prevent intermittent power cuts. This project was associated with a plan for Enron to become a major player in the distribution of liquefied natural gas in India and to be one of the major consumers of that gas. The gas was to come from a project in the Gulf state of Qatar, partially financed by Enron's parent company. The power project was very large, involving a US$2 billion contract with the state government, up to that date the largest single foreign investment in India and the largest independent power project in the world.

Unfortunately, even after careful but long drawn-out and ultimately successful negotiations with the Congress Party, which was in power at the national and state levels, the project became a victim of India's democratic politics, with opposition to the project a major plank in the policies of non-government parties in the provincial election of 1995. The political ploy, based on anti-outsider nationalism, was highly successful in winning the attention and support of the electorate; the opposition won the election and immediately instituted an inquiry into the project by a government committee. The report of

the committee was never published but its findings of deception and cost padding were leaked. In response to the cost padding, Rebecca Mark, who was CEO of Enron International and responsible for the original negotiations, argued: 'In India you are supposed to have a 20 percent import duty on equipment. But when it comes right down to it, very common in a project is that it doesn't end up being 20 percent but whatever the customs inspector wants it to be on the day you get there. So you have to price that risk in' (quoted in Hill, 2003).

In other words there was a risk premium built into Enron's contract with the state of Maharashtra. The risk premium might or might not be associated with additional costs but there was a danger of that turning out to be the case. In many situations, a risk premium might raise the price of the electricity beyond what would justify the project. In this case it did not. Clearly, shifting political circumstances, universal bureaucratic rules and the crosscurrents between national and state governments in a federal system make India a difficult place in which to invest. There is a high level of political risk and therefore country risk, which up to now has kept down the level of FDI. One reason that the project did not fail was that the law courts in India would not have accepted a deliberate breach of such contract. To this degree the risk was limited.

Of course the choice may not be between different investment projects with differing levels of risk. It may be between investing in a project and using those funds to repurchase the shares of the company or pay additional dividends. One argument is that the latter allows the shareholders or ex-shareholders themselves to make investments outside the area strictly relevant to the enterprise. In theory, the shareholder has a much wider range of choice than the enterprise, which is constrained in its target investment by the nature of its own resources and competencies.

Risk management

The second kind of generic strategy or response can be called risk management, defined in a rather narrower sense than that often used. In this sense, management of risk does not affect in any way the overall risk level, which remains the same, but rather consists in attempts to redistribute the incidence of existing risk to others outside the enterprise, thereby reducing its potential impact on the enterprise and its performance indicators. This requires those at risk to persuade others to bear some of the risk. There are three principal ways in which this can be done.

Insurance

Risk management can be part of a commercial arrangement. Those at risk pay for others to take on all or some part of the risk. The enterprise takes out an insurance policy which covers a specific type of risk. It pays a premium to receive this kind of cover. Unfortunately, the cost of insurance behaves in a cyclical fashion, partly reflecting the return which insurance companies themselves earn in the capital market on the investment of their reserves. Since the cost fluctuates, the strategy may be to continuously adjust the amount and nature of its insurance cover.

The insurance may have a minimum threshold, below which level the company self-insures. In an extreme case, this may mean simply placing in a separate account what the company would otherwise have paid an insurance company for this cover.

Conversly, the insurance may have an upper cap, either because the insurance company does not wish to bear this kind of extreme risk or the cost is too high for the company. In the latter case, the company will either have to avoid or mitigate risk, if it is averse to the incidence of such extreme events, however unlikely they are to occur. At least it can limit the exposure to the amount above the cap.

Is it always possible to take out insurance? For many types of risk, possibly an increasing number of different types, it is possible to take out insurance. Lloyd's of London prides itself on the fact that it is willing to insure anything. However, realistically insurance can only be available where the affected population is large enough and the probability of the particular event occurring is low enough to ensure the setting of premiums which are within the means of the insured. Otherwise the premiums to be paid will be prohibitively large. There might also be an excessively high risk for the insurer, which can be covered by either sharing the insurance with other insurers or reinsurance, although reinsurance has itself proved to be very risky for insurance companies.

Insurance can never be the answer where the risk level is too high, partly because of its high cost and partly because of what is called adverse selection. If the cost of insurance is relatively high, only those most at risk will tend to insure. Those for whom the risk is low will consider it better to save the premium costs and even to self-insure, that is, bear the risk themselves, since it involves the occurrence of an unlikely event. This may create an unstable situation, one which might quickly get much worse. High premiums cause those least at risk to withdraw from taking insurance. This raises the probability of claims being made by those with insurance cover and further increases the level of premiums. The cycle is repeated. This can be a highly unstable situation in which the provision of insurance may break down completely.

Focus on Theory

Insurance

One industry in which it is necessary to have an accurate view of future events is the insurance industry. It is possible to insure against the negative consequences of almost any type of future event by taking out an insurance policy and paying the associated premiums on this policy. The degree of risk aversion, as well as the probability of occurrence, determines whether an individual or organization actually takes out cover against damage from a particular class of risk-generating events, for example a road accident or plane crash. The insurer tries to ensure a profit by setting premiums at an appropriate level so they will more than cover the claims made on policies. This requires an accurate forecast of the number of claims.

The viability of the commercial insurance industry, or indeed a particular insurance company, reflects two factors.

The first is the existence of a large number of potential insurees at risk and willing to cover that risk at a feasible price. If the premium is high and the risk for certain groups is low, 'adverse selection' may occur, threatening the viability of insurance. Those least likely to claim do not insure. This may push the premiums up to a non-viable level.

Secondly, that sufficient information, readily converted into knowledge, exists for premiums to be accurately calculated. This information consists of past statistics on the frequency of occurrence of potentially negative events. Traditionally, the probability of such events occurring could be calculated with some accuracy. This applies to marine, fire, motor and life insurance. In principle, the calculations assume that this frequency does not change and also that the cover is for a fixed amount. The insurance company can then fix an appropriate level of premiums and carry reserves adequate to meet a possible bunching of claims. Clearly, since claims will occur at some time in the future, premiums can be invested to yield a return which is added to reserves.

For much of its history, the industry dealt with what it calls 'normal' events but what most of us would call abnormal events, events which cause a determinate amount of damage or a fixed loss of income. These events would include storms, fires, shipwrecks, earthquakes, accidents, illnesses and theft. The law of large numbers meant that the industry had no difficulty with the two factors above. Insurance companies could specialize in different kinds of risks, for example marine, life, medical or automobile insurance.

The same principles were applied to the more costly satellites, oil rigs and airliners of the modern world. With the extension of insurance to a broader class of valuable assets and therefore possible damaging events, the risk is more difficult to calculate, partly because it is difficult to anticipate the frequency of extreme events. The size of the cover and therefore possible losses has become much greater, so that the sharing of insurance, or reinsurance, becomes more important.

The risk of insurance companies can be reduced in two ways. It can be done horizontally, by a number of companies taking a proportion of the total risk. Or it can be done vertically, by one company taking all the initial risk but passing on some of that risk by reinsurance and by further retrocession achieving the same result for the reinsurers. One problem that emerges is that with each layer of reinsurance, knowledge of the underlying risk becomes more uncertain.

Insurance has been extended to many new areas. It can cover an actress's legs, political risk, professional indemnity of various types or exposure to harmful materials

▶

Focus on Theory

cont'd

or polluting agents. Many of these new areas involve 'long-tailed' risks, that is, risks which only manifest themselves long after the policy has been written, for example diseases which have a long gestation period, such as asbestos-related diseases which take 20, 30 or even 40 years to show themselves. In these cases, it is often difficult to assess the real risk. There is a strong possibility of an underestimation of the risk and the appropriate level of premiums.

In the insurance industry there are institutions which specialize in modelling risk, predicting both the frequency and severity of risk-creating events, institutions such as Applied Insurance Research, Eqecut or Risk Management Solutions. This is a highly specialized task. The forecasting has worked quite well for assessing severity which reflects both the possible size of the shock and the value of the capital at risk. Depending on the nature of the event, it is much more difficult to get the frequency right, particularly if it is a rare event. For events such as terrorist attacks, it is very difficult indeed. The insurance cost of the terrorist attacks on September 11, 2002 is something like $35 billion, much of which falls into the lap of Lloyd's.

The problem of assessing frequency and severity is compounded if the law courts, in awarding damages, change their policy, both extending the definitions of negligence and malpractice, and awarding much larger sums than was previously the case. The inclination and practice of law courts may differ from country to country. With the increasingly global reach of insurance companies, the pattern of decision making by courts abroad must be considered. All this has to be allowed for – the amount of knowledge required has become much larger. A core competency of insurance companies is the actuarial expertise to make an accurate estimate of probabilities, which involves having specialist knowledge of a particular area of risk.

Strategy in Action Lloyd's of London and 'long-tailed' risk

Lloyd's is probably the most famous insurance company in the world, claiming to be able to undertake any kind of insurance. It is the reinsurer par excellence. Lloyd's is a market rather than a single corporation. It is like a franchise, in which the managing agencies writing policies are the franchisees. Each syndicate in the market is acting as an independent insurance company, competing for insurance and cooperating in providing reinsurance.

Lloyd's is an unmatched brand name, with an unparalleled reputation. Lloyd's has existed for over three hundred years and boasts that it has never dishonoured an insurance claim, deliberately erring on the side of generosity in meeting such claims. The market needed enough knowledge of the risks to set premiums at appropriate levels and enough capital to deal with any bunching of losses.

Before 1969, the individual providers of capital to the syndicates were all British, who knew each other and knew and were known by the brokers, the underwriters and the agents. The latter had a known expertise and could be trusted. Most syndicates made very healthy and attractive profits.

The role of capital provision was dealt with in an unusual way. Each individual providing capital pledged assets or later put up a letter of credit from a bank, backed by shares or bonds. These assets were backing for the underwriting of insurance risks. The money worked twice, in giving a return from the initial investment and another from the insurance. For any agency, the aggregate of pledges defined the 'stamp capacity', which fixed the maximum permissible level of premiums, and for individuals their share in profits or losses. Those putting up the capital

▶

were individuals, not corporations, and until 1970 a relatively small group of well under 3,000 very rich and carefully elected, as the terminology has it, names (originally they put their names on the back of a policy).

The insuring syndicates were reconstituted at the end of each year, so that individuals could withdraw and be replaced by different individuals. Normally there was immense competition to become a name, so that withdrawals were uncommon. The closing of a syndicate was always done for the year falling three years before to allow most outstanding claims to be settled. This process was called 'reinsurance to close', since a reinsurance premium was paid to cover any outstanding claims. The year was closed if this happened. If it did not, because the outstanding claims were too uncertain, the year remained open. When it became desirable for names to withdraw, few could, because the syndicates remained open.

The underwriters of an agency considered any insurance proposal made by brokers, and put together a syndicate to back a particular policy. Those putting up the money for the syndicates had unlimited liability. Under this system it was impossible for the syndicates to fail to honour a claim unless the individuals putting up the money all became bankrupt simultaneously, an extremely unlikely event. Whereas on the stock market for a typical limited liability company there were potentially unlimited returns but limited risk, here the case was the opposite, unlimited risk and limited returns, albeit very generous, since they reflected the permitted total of the premiums.

A number of critical changes occurred during the 1970s and 80s culminating in a serious crisis at the end of the 1980s. The changes were:

- The range of insured events expanded enormously. Reinsurance rose greatly in importance. At the same time competition in the industry became intense.
- The proportion of insurance abroad increased; the share of the American market rose to 40%.
- To secure an expanded supply of capital, there was a major effort to attract new names and increase the number of syndicates. The number of names expanded to well over 30,000, with the result that entrants were less wealthy. New names were deliberately brought in for fear of

losses. These names were increasingly found in North America. They inevitably had less knowledge of what they were doing. There were over 400 syndicates.

The following were the main inputs into the crisis:

- The new names, blinded by the reputation of Lloyd's, lacked an understanding of their commitment. It was no longer possible for the names to know whether the underwriters had the desired expertise or the managing agents to know whether the names had the necessary wealth to cover claims in an emergency.
- Expansion into new areas meant underwriters were much less expert than they had been. There was a loss of proper risk assessment, certainly the charging of premiums well below what was reasonable, given the real risks. This was complicated by an element of outright fraud and a failure to realize the level of risk.
- In London, the so-called 'spiral' of reinsurance got completely out of control. For some syndicates, a majority of premiums disappeared into a foreign insurance company doing the reinsurance. In some cases the reinsurance involved the same syndicate in reinsuring different tranches of the risk.
- A few syndicates remained conservative, and insiders, aware of the relative riskiness of policies, allegedly kept to these syndicates. By contrast new names often landed up in the highest risk syndicates.
- There was a delayed reaction to the greater riskiness. This was not completely irrational since there were enormous delays in the claims made, the time taken for the court to make a judgement and reclaiming money along the chain of insurers and reinsurers (this alone could take up to ten years). At a time of high returns, premiums could compound to sums way above the initial value. The problem was the persistence of practices out of step with the claims coming in.

In 1991 the first loss was reported, for 1988. The losses quickly escalated to over US$15 billion. Lloyd's was forced to increase contributions to the central fund covering the position of those names who either could not or would not meet their obligations. Names, who found themselves required to find large sums of money to meet losses, began to take legal action against Lloyd's on the grounds that they had not been given adequate information to make informed decisions, and particularly that Lloyd's had not reacted quickly enough to new information on the asbestos claims. For the most part these actions failed.

There has been a major attempt to reform the Lloyd's system. The preference of successive leaders has been to exclude the names completely and attract new capital from corporate investors without limited liability. The names have resisted this, successfully insofar as they have been allowed to survive. While a significant share of Lloyd's capital comes from corporate sources, the old system has not disappeared.

Hedging

An alternative commercial arrangement, similar in some ways to insurance, involves hedging. This requires putting together, in the general market for risk, offsetting risks, whether directly or through a specialist enterprise or specialized financial instrument. It assumes that risk exists for different individuals or enterprises in ways which can be set against each other, that is, in ways which are compensating. For example, the original development of a futures market for pigs was based on the different needs of farmers and butchers. The supply of pigs reflected weather conditions in any given year. The farmers feared a glut and the resulting fall in price which would reduce their income. They wanted to ensure that the price at which they sold in a year's time was not too low. The butchers feared a dearth and the resulting rise in price which would reduce demand for their product and hence their income. They did not want the price to rise.

A futures or forward market allowed them to hedge their risk by entering into a transaction which managed risks for both parties to the transaction. What is risk for one party is opportunity for another; in this case a low price for farmers and a high price for butchers. The key is to find a way of bringing the parties together, either in a market transaction or another type of arrangement. Specialist institutions, because of the high volume of their transactions, can provide the service at a low level of transaction costs. Alternatively the enterprise can put together its own hedges, thereby lowering cost.

The range of derivatives, involving options and swaps as well as futures or operations in the futures market, which make hedging possible, has expanded enormously recently. The principle is exactly as above, the matching of risks. The use of some derivatives is similar to insurance, for example purchasing an option which is not exercised involves covering a risk at a cost which is equivalent to the payment of an insurance premium.

One limitation on hedging is that it usually has a limited time horizon. For example, German car manufacturers have hedged against the decline in the value of the dollar, but to a significantly different degree – at one extreme, Volkswagen for one year and at the other extreme Porsche for above five years. BMW, at above three years, and DaimlerChrysler, at above two years, lie in an intermediate position (Mackintosh, 2003: 23). Hedging can be applied to the near future but usually only two or three years into the future. This is not the case with insurance, although uncertainty about the future shows itself in the flexibility of premiums. The level of premiums may change quite dramatically from year to year to reflect the incidence and size of claims.

The second management mechanism is for risk to be shared with other related enterprises by voluntary agreement. Many strategic alliances are focused on risk management and involve a sharing of the risk associated with particular projects. The greater the commitment of resources, the greater the likelihood of such a strategic alliance. In a global world, the size of projects has increased enormously, leading to a situation where one single failure can destroy a multinational enterprise, say the abortive development of a new generation of civil airliners or the introduction of a new model of motorcar. Where the commitment of resources is such that a failure will threaten the very existence of the enterprise, alliances are highly desirable. They represent a way of redistributing the risk, but the cost is obviously the simultaneous redistribution of some of the return. There has to be an incentive for a partner to enter such an arrangement; the gain must be mutual.

The third way in which risk management can be implemented involves action by the government. The government has the advantage of access, through the tax system and its own borrowing capacity, to much greater resources than any enterprise. The government might be ready to compensate an enterprise for excessive losses arising because of extreme events. This is not uncommon. Whatever the protestation of government, it often finds itself in a position in which it feels compelled to act as the backer of last resort, sometimes to a single enterprise such as Rolls-Royce in the UK, sometimes to a group such as the savings and loans companies in the USA or to farmers just about everywhere in the world.

The government can give a firm commitment to rescue those in difficulty but this is unlikely to be the approach adopted, because of the negative consequences of flagging such an intervention and guaranteeing rescue from the consequences of behaviour freely and voluntarily entered into. It is more likely that the government will indirectly insure businesses against the risk of unexpected events by simply doing so without any prior commitment, if they deem that the situation merits such a response. It is rather similar to its role as lender of last resort. This is often done after rather than before the event, but a continuing pattern of similar interventions may create an expectation of intervention in the future and may be equivalent to the guarantee described above.

The intervention of the government may therefore create another problem, rather curiously described as moral hazard. In the event of a government being willing to intervene whenever an untoward event occurred, there would be no need for enterprises or individuals to take action to manage or mitigate the associated risk. This could encourage a reckless disregard for risk. Intervention would therefore encourage an excessively high level of risk taking, an outcome probably not in anyone's interest. This outcome, potentially very expensive, would eventually restrict the ability of government to use its position as it should to promote the good health of the economy at large.

An enterprise operating in a foreign country can often negotiate with the government of that country to share risk, provided that the enterprise brings to that country something the government wants. Arrangements can be put in place which have the effect of reducing the risk to which the enterprise is exposed.

Sometimes the risk environment in a country changes. For a number of countries, the Asian economic crisis in 1997 illustrates this point.

Strategy in Action   Responses to the Asian economic crisis

How does an enterprise respond in a crisis which is international, involving business activity in a country which is not the country of origin of the affected enterprise? Many foreign companies were already operating within the Asian countries concerned in the crisis of 1997. Others were considering the possibility of entry. It might be assumed that there would be two immediate reactions.

Firstly, the natural reaction to such a crisis is the avoidance response, that is, to try to exit from the economy with as little loss as possible, or refrain from entry in the first place. The inflow of direct investment might suddenly cease. Those already in have a more complex problem since they have considerable sunk costs, which cannot be retrieved. The desire for exit creates the kind of situation described in Chapter 13 on the prisoner's dilemma, the fourth business example which refers to the strategy to be adopted when a financial institution is in trouble, whether to call in a loan or not. The same situation applies to foreign investment in countries.

Secondly, the crisis might change the perspective of the company, inducing a strong degree of short-termism. Such a crisis might be expected to focus attention on operational rather than strategic issues, and short-term rather than long-term matters. These would include the need to get costs down as prices fall in a declining market. Any company could be

forced to react in this way, but it is a mistake, if there really is any choice.

What is clear is that such a crisis creates opportunities as well as threats. Figure 14.2 sets out the broad range of possible responses.

THE LESSONS OF SUCH A CRISIS

As already indicated, the most common reaction was to seek ways of reducing short-term costs, taking advantage of a favourable situation to do so. For example, it is always tempting in such a situation to reduce labour costs, laying off workers and reducing wages. However, this may lay up problems for the future, making the foreign companies very unpopular. Crisis management is an incomplete response to such a crisis, largely because it ignores the strategic dimension. The crisis constituted a major strategic challenge for all involved.

This is not to say that it is not essential for companies to alter, or even question, their basic strategic position during crises. Such strategies should have taken account of the possibility of such a crisis. It is necessary to take a strategic approach, perhaps to adjust or fine-tune the strategy, because the environment has changed. It is certainly better to avoid actions which offer some short-term advantage but at a severe long-term cost, notably to the reputation of the company.

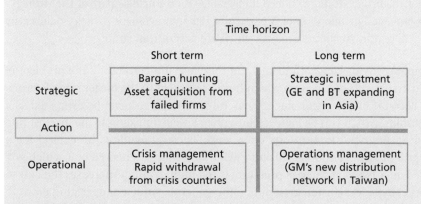

Figure 14.2 **Strategic responses to an economic crisis**

There was no such thing as a common experience in the regional crisis. The general crisis manifested itself in specific ways in the different countries. Each particular crisis emerged from the interaction of as many as eight different subcrises, which interacted in their own special way. These subcrises occurred in the areas of banking, political alignments and realignments, government strategy or policy change, confidence in both government and the economy, currency valuation, demand levels, supply capacity and enterprise viability. Each country experienced these subcrises in a different mix.

The immediate impact of the crisis on the multinationals was to deprive them of markets, as income levels fell and unemployment rose. For example, the sales of many products contracted, including motorcars and computers for which demand fell dramatically. Supplier and buyer chains were disrupted as enterprises within the chain went bankrupt, cutting off the supply of key components or making distribution difficult. Local partners collapsed. Enterprises relying on imports were often faced with significant price rises, caused by the decline in currency value. Cost structures were disrupted. There were increased financial risks, as the cost of capital rose and loans became unavailable.

Initially, there was more political risk since governments changed and changed their policies in unpredictable ways. These changes could have an impact on foreign companies directly or indirectly.

Opportunities exist in every crisis, taking a number of different forms. One involves the availability of bargains for purchase, assets or even companies which are on the market without many prospective purchasers. Potential purchasers must be careful not to seem to be too exploitative.

There are many opportunities for strategic investment. These can take the form of acquisitions of existing enterprises or new alliances, sometimes with enterprises which need support in order to survive, but not always.

It may even be possible to expand or restructure existing operations, for example to take advantage of low exchange rates in order to generate an export boom. The decline in the exchange rate may make many products highly competitive on international markets. It may be much easier to enter new markets on the basis of a cost minimization strategy. Such action must be guided by strategic considerations, that is, it must embrace the whole enterprise, enhance the ability to execute the chosen strategy, be sensitive to competitors and focused on customers and look to the long-term opportunities and threats.

| **Risk mitigation** | The third generic strategy is risk mitigation in which strategic action is taken to reduce the risk level to which the enterprise is exposed. There are various ways of doing this, including building flexibility or diversification into the enterprise's strategy. |

Within each of these general responses there is a range of particular policies which can be pursued. The risk management of an enterprise may consist of a combination of policies which fall within each of these different types. Such policies and their mix are highly specific to industries and enterprises. They can be selected only as part of the broad strategy. Indeed their choice is an intrinsic part of the strategy-making process. The adoption of a particular risk management strategy reflects the level of risk relating to all the projects which are part of that strategy.

| **A risk premium** | The simplest way of conceptualizing and therefore understanding the problem of risk is to assume a risk premium which has to be added to the target rate of return to take account of the particular risk environment. All risk can be expressed as a risk premium, which can be factored into price levels, for example the interest rate charged by financial institutions on a loan. Those providing the capital for a project will in any event build this into what they charge. This is a cost which will be passed on. Clearly, if the risk premium is too high, it either increases the cost to an unacceptable level or makes it difficult to generate sufficient operating profit to justify the project. |

Financial commentators make frequent reference to this premium. In general equity is supposed to offer holders a risk premium of varying size over fixed interest bonds. Risky countries have to offer a risk premium on government paper over the allegedly risk-free New York treasury bills, again one of varying size. The greater the risk level, the higher the risk premium and more unlikely that the project will achieve the target return. There are various ways of building a risk premium into the calculations.

Acquisition of an enterprise in a particular country will reflect the risk level in that country. The higher the risk, the lower the acceptable acquisition price. The greater the risk level, the lower the price the acquirer will be willing to pay, since the rate of discount applied to future net revenue streams will be higher.

The threshold qualifying criterion for a new project is rather different from an existing one. With an existing project, previous investment is a sunk cost, unless of course there is a market and a value for the facility. Even if there is, the price is likely to be much lower than the original cost of creating the facility. Any impact of risk is concentrated on the operating revenue or cost streams. Risk is built into the rate of time discount employed. Only where the application of such a rate leads to a negative net result will there be a withdrawal, or a closure of the enterprise. One issue is the ease of exit. The fact that the investment usually cannot be undone gives a natural advantage to those already operating in a particular market over those who wish to enter. This asymmetry in the bearing of investment costs is itself a barrier to new entry into existing markets.

The possibility of exact quantification does not solve the problem of integrating risk into any decision-making process, since it is often unclear what the choice of risk premium should be. The analysis has simply pointed out their universality, not how they are derived or how their future level is to be predicted. The previous discussion begs this question. The problem is that the use of a risk premium presupposes a level of precision which in reality does not exist. Risk may suggest a precise level of probability attached to different outcomes. The more general situation is one of uncertainty rather than risk, one in which there are no probabilities attached to possible outcomes. Quantification lends the analysis a spurious degree of precision.

It may be tempting to take a conservative approach and choose a high risk premium. However, this is not sensible since it may rule out many projects which offer a potentially high return. The obvious loss resulting from avoidance is the return which could have been made on rejected projects. While it pays to be cautious, a continuing emphasis on negative factors will prevent the enterprise from renewing itself, investing in new products or new markets. The investment funds which are not committed to this project may be invested elsewhere at a lower rate of return.

Strategy in Action Disney and the redistribution of risk

There is sense in the argument that Disney sees its main business as selling videos, movies, television programmes and consumer products, not running theme parks. The theme parks simply highlight these other products. Theme parks are seen as a gateway for accessing new markets for these other products, such as the Japanese, European and Chinese markets. For this reason, Disney wishes to minimize its risk, even if this means reducing the possible return. It stands to make only about US$80–100 million in annual licensing and attendance fees from its new Hong Kong park, compared with overall revenue of US$25.3 billion in 2002. Disney has been adept at managing its risk in opening new theme parks by sharing the risk with others, particularly in its foreign ventures which have taken full advantage of well-negotiated deals with governments, whether French, Chinese or Hong Kong.

The financial arrangements for the Euro Disney project were complex, but amounted to a large amount of debt supported by very little equity. This was highly risky for all concerned in the provision of the debt in the event of the project failing to deliver the target rate of return. Disney had put in place financial arrangements which in theory protected the company from the full effects of failure but rewarded them handsomely for success, if they kept their partners to the letter of the agreements. Euro Disney was a subsidiary in which the Walt Disney Corporation held only a 49% stake. It paid just Fr10 for its shares, whereas the other 51% were sold at Fr72 a share. While the shares did open at Fr165, they quickly fell back to 68, much to the chagrin of the investors.

The parent company also contracted to manage the park for hefty management fees. Royalty payments were also considerable. On the assumption that the planned targets were met, 57% of Euro Disney's operating profit would go to the parent company. In the event of losses, Euro Disney would still have to pay the management fees and royalties, if it could. It could not, so that in the event it proved impossible for Disney to collect such payments.

In Euro Disney they also managed to negotiate partnerships with high-flying allies, such as American Express, Coca-Cola, Esso, IBM, Kodak, Mattel, Nestlé, Philips and Renault, to build or finance many of the attractions and state-of-the-art systems in return for favourable sales and/or promotion opportunities within the resort.

In the end, Disney found itself in a difficult position. Losses from Euro Disney amounted to US$36 million in 1992 and more than US$900 million in 1993. Attendance was down 15% in 1993 compared with 1992. The share price continued to slide throughout 1992 and 1993. Eventually in 1994 a rescue package was put together which raised more money and provided much needed liquidity. It had the goal of halving Euro Disney debt, in practice significantly reducing it but not quite halving it. The creditor banks were persuaded to accept the waiving of a significant interest debt and to postpone repayments of the principal. Disney retained a controlling interest but saw its share of the project decline to 39%, a sign that it did not think that the theme park was going to be a major generator of profits. Euro Disney was renamed Disneyland Paris.

Disney also agreed to waive management fees and royalties for five years and only reintroduce them gently at half the previous level for a further five years. Losses in 1994 still amounted to well over US$300 million. In 1995 there was only a very small profit despite the temporary but significant reduction of costs. The key success indicators, particularly attendance levels, continued to deteriorate.

The arrangements for the Hong Kong project are even more striking. Disney is laying out only US$314 million for a 43% ownership stake. By contrast, the Hong Kong government is putting in as much as US$2.8 billion.

There is a vital distinction between risk management and risk mitigation, based upon certain assumptions about how far an enterprise can control its own environment, including its risk environment.

Risk management assumes that it cannot control the environment, at least in respect to removing risk from that environment; the level of risk is a given. Insofar as it is an unavoidable companion of a high return, its existence is simply a challenge. Provided that the return is high enough to compensate for the higher risk and that the risk not prohibitively high, that is, it falls at what might be regarded as an intermediate level, risk management is the appropriate approach. However, sharing the risk necessarily implies sharing the return. There is a cost to this strategy.

Where risk can be reduced, the approach changes. At the cost of the commitment of significant resources to various methods of risk mitigation, risk can be reduced, preferably to a manageable level as indicated above. Risk mitigation assumes that the enterprise can remove a significant amount of risk, that there are methods of reducing risk which are open to any enterprise. These include:

- Negotiating with government officials or other major players to reduce strategic risk
- Building a level of flexibility into a project to allow for unexpected events and possible setbacks
- Putting together a balanced portfolio of assets or projects.

It is also possible to combine risk management and risk mitigation. Mitigation might reduce the risk to a level at which management becomes possible, or it might reduce it to a level where management is unnecessary. There is no doubt that strategic risk, that is, competitive and country risk, can be both managed and mitigated. It is necessary to look at the different elements of strategic risk and how the enterprise can manage them.

It is also impossible to remove all risk. Removal of even some risk is costly. What are the costs of such risk management or mitigation measures? There are direct costs incurred and revenue foregone, which must be taken into account in assessing the viability of any project. The direct costs can be high. They may be the costs of:

- gaining exact information about the risk to which the enterprise is exposed
- negotiating an alliance or government support
- insurance or hedging techniques.

Indirect costs include revenue sacrificed and revenue shared:

- A loss in revenue may result from sharing risk with a strategic ally
- Flexibility usually has a cost in lost revenue.

One strategy which is not helpful and does not qualify as a valid generic strategy is to hide the risk exposure. There are a number of techniques which are frequently used and have received significant attention when their use has been revealed as distorting the performance of an enterprise. The most common problems of concealment arise with:

- the employment of operating leases for the assets used in key operations
- the securitization of benefit streams, that is, bringing forward future revenue streams
- the use of special-purpose entities to take on obligations, that is, taking liabilities off the balance sheet
- the creation of captives, that is, setting up insurance companies to insure against the risks carried by one company only.

Any enterprise should avoid simply hiding and, by implication, ignoring the risks. The best and most effective policy is to integrate risk management and mitigation into the overall strategy in a completely open and transparent way.

Risk and diversification

There is one risk mitigation device which has been widely applied and recommended – diversification, that is, the deliberate holding of a wide range of different assets, subject to different levels of risk. The recommendation of diversification is based on the so-called portfolio approach.

The portfolio approach to risk

The portfolio approach to risk is borrowed from financial markets where a number of conditions mean that risk can be reduced to a negligible, if not zero, level. The conditions are:

- the existence of something analogous to perfect competition, in which there are a large numbers of buyers and sellers exchanging a wide range of homogeneous products
- the availability of good access to information
- the ease of adjustment of the portfolio composition
- a large data bank, built up from past behaviour, making it possible to calculate the exact level of risk in different asset markets
- independence of price movements and risk from individual assets.

The last condition means that it is possible to divide risk into two types, *systematic*, when the prices of assets move together, and *unsystematic*, when prices do not move together. Price movements vary from asset to asset and may or may not be independent of each other.

The portfolio approach argues that if there is a sufficiently large range of projects or assets in which to invest and if the returns on these assets are independent of each other, that is, risk is unsystematic, then the simplest risk management device is to diversify, that is, to hold a portfolio of assets sufficiently large for the possibilities of gain to offset the possibilities of loss. If one asset falls in value, this is countered by a rise in the price of another. The *law of large numbers* ensures that the risk of the whole portfolio is markedly lower than the risk of individual assets.

In normal times, when markets are stable and change is marginal, the model of risk management used in the financial markets works well. In times of dramatic change, for example when risk becomes systematic, it works much less well. If there is systematic risk of any kind, then the conclusions do not hold. For example, if all markets move together, particularly in a downturn, then this approach does not help to manage risk. If the number of projects is insufficiently large, even if the risk is unsystematic, the mechanism does not fully remove risk.

The argument can be applied to any portfolio of assets. Developing a portfolio is a key strategic aim. In theory it could be applied to domestic investments or FDI. Risk could be reduced by putting together a portfolio of assets spread throughout the world, in countries in which the level of country risk varies greatly. This approach was used as the justification for the acquisition by enterprises of a wide range of non-core businesses and entry into a wide range of foreign markets. On this argument, in theory it is possible to remove all risk by having enough business units and/or entering enough markets. The assumption is that the larger the number, the lower the risk.

There is an additional problem if the focus is on FDI. Most companies do not hold a sufficiently large range of different facilities, different in country or even industry location, for this assumption of unsystematic behaviour to hold. This could be a powerful argument for adopting maximum growth as a strategic aim, if that growth makes possible a significant diversification of the business units and markets. According to the logic of this argument, a typical corporation ought to contain a wide range of separate strategic business units. Even a risk-averse enterprise could choose to produce a wide range of products in unrelated areas and sell those products in a wide range of unconnected markets.

In the 1980s, many enterprises followed a diversification strategy, deliberately acquiring in various ways business units not associated with their core activities. This led to disaster for some enterprises. Many enterprises entered areas in which they had no core competence, perhaps few resources and little market knowledge. For this reason, they found they could not run the disparate range of business units efficiently and at a profit. Since the businesses were usually acquired by purchase, the problem materialized into one of successfully absorbing the new businesses. This often proved too difficult to achieve. Consequently, and not surprisingly, the notion of diversification became unfashionable.

An enterprise which concentrates on its core area may have assets in a variety of countries and markets but they may all be linked in the value-creating chain. They are operated within the framework of an overarching strategic plan. They are not assets whose prices move independently. Poor performance in one area will have an impact on all areas – they are interrelated rather than independent. In this situation, all risk is systematic.

It is not easy to move from one asset to another. There is a pronounced stickiness of investment which prevents a continuous readjustment of the portfolio.

This is not to reject the risk-reducing role of diversification completely. The case study on BHP Billiton in Chapter 11 shows how this strategy is still relevant to large companies, in this case within the limited area of minerals and resources. The basic principle on which diversification is based is sound, but it is necessary to accept the limitations of the approach. There must be a different rationale for acquiring assets which are outside the core area of activity. Risk management is not sufficient justification. In certain conditions it might be quite appropriate to pursue a strategy which involves some measure of diversification, but it should be limited and each step well justified.

Strategic risk, scenario building and strategy making

Stressing the point that risk management is not a science, Michael Chaney, CEO of Wesfarmers, is reputed to have said: 'you have to use your best guess about what's going to happen in the future' (Hannen and Way, 2002: 50). This could not be more true than in the case of China.

Strategy in Action   Three different reform scenarios in China

For some enterprises, a major source of risk is what will happen to China in the future. What is likely to be the speed of economic reform? Will China implement its obligations on entry into the WTO?

Chapter 4 discussed the procedure for scenario building, giving as an example an exercise in forecasting the price of oil. In the case of the future of China, it is necessary to identify the main driving forces, the predetermined elements and the critical uncertainties relevant to Chinese reform.

The main driving force for the Chinese government is to maintain its internal power and extend that power externally by the build-up of economic strength. The latter will give the government the legitimacy which makes the former easier to achieve. Economic success combined with an increasingly influential international role will give the present regime significant legitimacy.

The second driving force is the economic ambition of the ordinary Chinese citizens, already released by rising income levels. There is the growing expectation by the rising managerial middle class and others that they will enjoy the fruits of rising consumption levels. Education stimulates a desire for a change in the standard and style of living. The desired package includes foreign travel and private housing, even automobiles.

For the outside world, the main driving force is globalization, or some aspects of that globalization such as the integration of international markets. The outside world sees China as participating actively in this process.

There are a number of predetermined elements:

*   The present national boundaries and strength of internal integration
*   The existing network of party connections
*   The Chinese diaspora in the outside world, amplified by family connections, both inside and outside China.

The critical uncertainties are:

*   The level of social unrest generated by the workers who become unemployed as a result of the restructuring of the economy. There is a race between the creation of a new economy, largely foreign and private, which absorbs workers, and the destruction of jobs in the old economy.

*   The spread of HIV/AIDS within China and more recently the spread of SARS. However, China has a well-developed medical infrastructure which is being tested but is likely to emerge stronger from present stresses.
*   The role of a significant Muslim minority in China, notably in Sinkiang.
*   The nature of relationships within Asia, particularly those revolving around Taiwan.

Three possible scenarios could be described in the following way.

1.   The conservative backlash
Under this scenario, outside competition and the social unrest resulting from the opening up and associated reform threatens the very existence of the regime and discredits the reform process. The main problem of the economic reforms is the uneven distribution of their benefits and costs. Already there is considerable labour unrest from those who have become unemployed. There are two main groups who are in distress:

*   those in the countryside without means of support who, as the system of attachment to a particular location weakens, often move to the cities to look for work, but do not find it, or find work with a very low reward
*   those who lose their position in the restructuring of state enterprises in the cities.

As many as 200 million people could comprise these two groups, or constitute those most at risk. In these circumstances, the conservatives gain the upper hand on the basis of the fear of losing any control of the situation.

2.   Steady as she goes
This is really a recreation of the experience of the last quarter century. Reform is phased in steadily despite an acceleration in the opening of the economy as a result of entry into the WTO. Under this scenario the economy remains competitive and attractive enough to foreign investment to sustain a growth rate of the overall economy similar to past rates, that is, 7% or above. This is high enough to assist in containing the level of social unrest by keeping the number of unemployed down to an acceptable level. The growth rate needs to be sufficiently high to absorb the new entrants to the labour

force who may number as many as 10–15 million each year. The emergence of the new economy does compensate in general terms for the contraction of the old, but it is a delicate balance. There is a consistent level of unrest but it never spirals out of control; it is manageable without a threat to the regime.

3. Shock therapy
This could occur in two possible situations. Reform is so successful that it might as well be accelerated – an unlikely outcome. The more realistic situation is that the reformers decide to make a desperate pitch to accelerate growth in order to deal with a worsening situation. This might be prompted by a number of different situations:

- A generational change among the leaders of the Communist Party which favours a younger reform group.

- Entry into the WTO might make accelerated reform critical to attaining competitiveness at the international level.
- Pressure from outside may prevent the government from slowing the process of restructuring. Outside powers, including the USA, may pressure the Chinese government into accelerating the process of opening up.
- Conflict in China may lead to the temporary dominance of a group with an interest in accelerated reform, probably the entrepreneurial group.

It is necessary to identify signals through which it is possible to monitor the pace of reform. Those investing in China must know which of these scenarios is likely to prove correct. At present, the second scenario seems the most likely to hold.

Integrating risk control into strategy making

Managing risk is not a strategic process separate from other processes. It must be integrated into the main strategy making. This may require consideration of a notional balance sheet broader than that normally employed, one which includes all economic resources, some of which are difficult to value, and all economic obligations of whatever kind. In the words of Ayres and Logue (2002: 50): 'In short, risk management is simply high-quality management with no readily available, economically relevant information *overlooked*.' Information on threats or different kinds of risks is simply one input into the general process of strategy making.

There are five general principles in an overall risk management policy which help to integrate the control of risk into strategy making in general:

1. The enterprise should concentrate on providing an incentive to strategists and operating managers to undertake any value-adding activities which promise a competitive advantage, particularly for more than the short term. Risk is considered simultaneously with the returns which might be made.
2. The enterprise must not treat the main control functions, relevant to the implementation of a strategy, such as accounting, quality control or even strategy making itself, as profit centres, in which the staff are given an interest in maximizing profit, either by increasing revenues or reducing costs. Clearly defined objectives which require and reflect accurate monitoring are needed but they should not put an emphasis on linking the controllers with the success of the strategy. There needs to be a separation.
3. The enterprise must appoint high-quality external and internal audit committees, independent of the CEO. An accounting audit should be conducted at arm's length from the strategists and operational managers.
4. The enterprise must read the environment carefully, notably for possible threats,

and understand all the implications of that changing environment and those possible threats for the core business activities. Scenario building should be internalized as a way of considering the future.

5. Evaluate all incoming information critically, whatever its source.

Country risk and competitive risk

The way in which global business transactions are organized has to take particular account of differences in the level of country risk and competitive risk, which together constitute strategic risk.

The level of country risk is highly correlated with the level of GDP per head in a country:

- The rich developed countries, which have representative democracies in which the legitimacy of government is confirmed by regular elections, have a low level of country risk, whatever index or rating agency is consulted.
- Undeveloped economies, especially those with governments subject to rapid change or whose legitimacy is doubtful, have high levels of country risk.
- Developing countries have an intermediate level, which also tends to be unstable. For some countries, the level of country risk can change dramatically from period to period (see the Strategy in Action on Argentina in Chapter 5). This may be due to political instability which may be linked to economic instability. The interaction between the two is complex.

The same is true for some industries. The level of competitive risk inherent in the structure of different industrial markets may differ markedly. The level of competition can quickly change.

Strategic risk and scenario planning

Anticipating the onset of instability, of whatever kind, is not easy. Few have anticipated the major changes of government which have occurred in recent years. Few have worked through the implications of significant technical change. Such accurate forecasts may require in-depth qualitative studies of a particular country or a particular industry. Scenario building is the technique which should be used. Most commentators, including the country risk rating agencies, have a poor record in predicting such sudden turns of fortune. Where strategy making is based on scenario building, it is sometimes called scenario planning. Scenario building becomes an integral part of the strategy-making process itself. It is highly desirable to develop both in combination.

However, country risk encapsulates a set of factors which have a powerful influence on patterns of direct investment, acting as a major deterrent where the level of country risk is high. It is a critical aspect of the home country bias discussed in Chapter 3. Once attention is directed to a direct investment in productive facilities which has been made for the medium or long term, the focus also necessarily moves away from strictly economic or financial factors to emphasize political factors.

Focus on Theory
The principles of risk management

The following is a sensible set of principles which can be applied in taking account of risk:

1. Pay attention to all kinds of risk, including both quantifiable and non-quantifiable risk. For example, the risk of pursuing certain practices, notably those which are illegal, is a loss of reputation. This loss can have catastrophic results.
2. Wherever possible, the risk should be quantified. Even if it cannot be quantified, it should be made as precise as possible.
3. Every member of an organization should be made aware of the importance of risk.
4. It should be made clear that every member has a responsibility to control risk.
5. Those who are specifically designated as risk mangers should have the ability to take any necessary action to limit the exposure to risk.
6. Any enterprise should avoid businesses in which they have no real knowledge or the relevant core competencies.
7. Strategists should always accept the universality of uncertainty about the future and engage in scenario-building exercises to explore possible future outcomes.
8. The risk managers must be subject to the same kind of monitoring as any other staff. This might take the form of a regular risk audit.
9. Successful risk management creates value by increasing the chance of a good business performance.
10. It is necessary to understand how willing an enterprise is to take risk, its so-called risk appetite. This is part of its culture.

Source: Hannen and Way, 2002: 51. The principles are loosely based on those developed by PricewaterhouseCoopers.

Focus on Theory
Political risk

On Friday, July 26, 2002, the South African government released the first draft of a new ministerial charter, which can be described as a 'black empowerment policy'. On Wednesday, October 9, a second draft was released, described in a memorable phrase, which captured the uncertainty created by the policy, as 'fog turning into mist'. The first draft had the following main points:

1. In an existing operation, an applicant for a mining licence should have a black economic empowerment partner with at least 30% equity.
2. In a new operation, an applicant for a mining licence should have a black empowerment partner with at least 51% equity.
3. In the event that a suitable parent is not found by the applicant, the South African government, through its associated investment vehicle, the IDC and the Development Bank, will warehouse the relevant equity until a partner is found.

The clear aim seems to be to ensure that within ten years all mining is in the hands of black organizations. The second draft appears to have watered this down somewhat, in that it talks of a 26% black ownership in ten years. It also talks of enormous transfer costs to be borne by the South African mining industry, 40% of all managers to be black within five years and all mine workers literate. The policy imposes significant costs on the mining companies.

This represent a major change of policy which has been interpreted by the resource companies, or rather the shareholders in those companies, as a threat, since the companies are circumspect in their public reaction. The mining company Anglo American,

Focus on Theory
cont'd

which generates about 70% of its operating profits from South Africa, saw its share price fall by 11% over the weekend following the announcement.

Who is vulnerable? The position of BHP Billiton is that it has 6% of its assets in South Africa – notably the Ingwe coal mining operation, its 60% share of Semancor manganese and chrome business and parts of its half-owned Richards Bay mineral sands joint venture with Rio Tinto – but these are mature businesses unlikely to be expanded in the near future. It has 11% of its profits generated there, compared with 5% of Rio Tinto's. BHP Billiton is more vulnerable than Rio Tinto (see the case study on BHP Billiton in Chapter 11).

The resource companies are hoping to get major concessions before the charter becomes law. However, the very threat of such political action is a major source of risk and a major deterrent to foreign direct investment in such countries, even if it is not carried out and even if it is easy to understand the reasons for such an action. The sovereign risk premium demanded for foreign investment in South Africa has risen and is likely to stay high for a significant period of time, whatever happens.

Sources: Fitzgerald, 2002; Hextall, 2002: 58; Oldfield, 2002.

Case Study   Africa – AIDS and civil wars

The present study focuses on Botswana, because this country, while small, has been represented as a model of what might be achieved in Africa. It is a notable exception to the story of negative growth in the southern cone of Africa. Botswana is a land-locked but large country, two-thirds of which is covered by the Kalahari Desert. It became independent from Britain in 1966. It has a well-organized government. It is blessed with a number of natural resources which make it attractive for foreign business. It is using the income generated by these resources to support good and, even more important, free education and health systems.

Since 1966, the growth rate of GDP in Botswana has averaged 7% a year, much the highest rate of any African country. This has already raised per capita income from $80 to $6,600, a major achievement. According to the Cato Institute, a Washington-based think-tank, it is Africa's freest economy, that is, the one least regulated by government. Taxes are low, but budget surpluses the norm. Property rights are respected and so far the government has not nationalized any business. It has the highest per capital foreign exchange reserves in Africa. There is so little poaching in its world-famous game reserves that it has had to cull its elephant herds.

However, there are two major challenges facing Botswana:

• The rising size of government, which has gone from absorbing 21% of GDP in 1971 to about 50% today.

• The catastrophe of HIV/AIDS. Botswana has the highest rate of HIV infection in the world, which has already had a dramatic impact.

Botswana has been proactive in trying to tackle the latter problem, which partly explains the first challenge. If Botswana cannot deal with AIDS, despite its obvious advantages, the problem elsewhere in Africa and beyond looks even more unassailable. Despite the problems, the rate of economic growth in 2002 is likely to remain as high as 5%.

HIV/AIDS

Because of its low level of income per head and the previous success in reducing mortality rates, although, as we shall see, this may be temporary, Africa has seen a rapid rate of population growth. Fortunately, until recently, population densities were low compared with the main population areas of the world, including densely populated parts of Europe and Asia. Fertility rates are still high and have recently offset relatively high and rising mortality rates. Initially, these mortality rates declined with improving medical facilities, but they have been increasing again. As a result of rapid population growth, some African countries, such as Nigeria, have become very populous.

It is almost certainly the case that AIDs had its origins in Africa, where it seems to have leapt the species barrier between monkeys and people about 70 years

Table 14.3 **HIV prevalence worldwide**

North America	950,000	W Europe	550,000	East Europe and Central Asia	1m
Caribbean	430,000	N Africa and Middle East	500,000	S and SE Asia	5.6m
Latin America	1.5m	Sub-Saharan Africa	28.5m	E Asia and Pacific	1m
				Australia and New Zealand	15,000

Source: Rosen et al., 2003: 83.

ago. The first publicity in the West related to the onset of AIDS in the gay community on the west coast of the USA. Table 14.3 gives an indication of the prevalence of HIV worldwide.

Many of these figures are only approximations. Already AIDS has killed more than 20 million people worldwide, with more than 40 million people currently HIV positive. There are many different strains of the AIDS retrovirus active in different parts of the world, including Africa. The developed world has type B, East Africa mostly types A and B. Type C is the most virulent and most resistant to the drugs being used today. It is the type common in the south of the African continent. In any event the AIDS retrovirus mutates very rapidly. Poor and incomplete treatment with the new drugs only encourages and accelerates this process.

Type C is prevalent in Botswana and threatens to sweep India and China. Already as many as 51 different strains of type C have been identified in Botswana alone. In much of Africa, the retrovirus therefore has a different nature, being much more susceptible to heterosexual transmission. In the developed world, the most vulnerable groups are the gay community and the drug users who reuse needles. It has been relatively easy to re-educate these groups to adopt safe practices. In Africa this is not the case. One of the most common methods of transmission there is through contact between highly promiscuous men and the prostitutes they infected, either by not allowing them to use condoms, or a lack of them in the first place. A culture of widespread sexual promiscuity only accelerates the spread of the disease. Unfortunately, education of the population on methods of avoiding transmission is almost non-existent in most places.

AIDS is already a major problem in Africa. It is a potential problem in a number of other regions of the world, notably Asia. The Chinese government has admitted that one million of its people are HIV positive. This is almost certainly a serious underestimate. There are already four million infected in India. The number is growing rapidly. Both Indonesia and Russia have serious problems which are growing dramatically. There are three million dying each year, 15,000 new infections each day and the rate is still increasing. Those infected and dying tend to be in the prime working ages. The impact on the economy of protracted sickness and eventual death is dramatic, particularly as the sick have to be cared for.

Of the 40 million cases of infection in the world, as Table 14.3 shows, sub-Saharan Africa has 28.5 million, including about 2.5 million under the age of 15. In sixteen African countries south of the Sahara, more than one in ten adults aged 15–49 are infected. This is the most important part of the potential labour force of any country. The number of infected is growing rapidly. Last year there were 3.4 million newly infected, of which 700,000 were children under the age of 15. In Africa every minute four people die of AIDS. Last year AIDS killed 2.3 million Africans, including 500,000 children (global deaths from AIDS were 3.0 million).

South Africa has the highest number of people in the world with HIV/AIDS, 4.74 million, or one in nine of the population. Since South Africa is potentially the economic powerhouse of sub-Saharan Africa, this is particularly unfortunate. Nigeria, another African giant in economic and demographic terms with 120 million people, already has 3.5 million people infected.

Botswana, a country with only 1.6 million people, has the highest proportion of its population infected, 38.8%, up from 35.5% in 2001. The disease is spreading rapidly. This has caused the average life expectancy to fall from a peak of 69 to a minimum of 39 today, and it may be moving still lower. Some have anticipated an expectancy as low as 27. Another of the southern cone countries, Zimbabwe, with 2.3 million people, has an infection rate of 33.7%, not far behind Botswana. In some local areas of Africa the proportion of the population infected is much higher than even these figures suggest.

Table 14.4 **Living with HIV/AIDS in Africa**

	% of adult population
Botswana	35.80
Swaziland	25.25
Zimbabwe	25.06
Lesotho	23.57
Zambia	19.95
South Africa	19.94
Namibia	19.54
Malawi	15.96

Fortunately, Botswana has a number of clear advantages over other African countries in the fight with HIV/AIDS. It has the resources to fight the battle and a government structure which helps it to do so. It also has a government leadership which sees this fight as its first priority. Festus Mogae, Botswana's Oxford-educated president, has called for an all-out war on AIDS. He has appealed to the international community to assist.

The international community is beginning to take up the problem. There is a biennial international AIDS conference, which was held in Durban in 2000 and Barcelona in 2002. At Durban the emphasis was very much on prevention, for a number of reasons, some good, including the costs of treatment, some not so good. At Barcelona the emphasis shifted to a combined prevention and cure approach. The focus for the approach to AIDS is UNAIDS and its fund, the Global Fund for AIDS, Tuberculosis and Malaria. In 2002, its first year, the fund already had US$2.1 billion, not enough but a good start. To be really effective it probably needs something like US$7–10 billion. In reality the cost of not doing anything is likely to be horrendous.

Brazil is often held up as the model of how to deal with AIDS. There a well-organized campaign has kept the number infected to about half of what was predicted earlier. The number of people dying is actually declining. The core of the campaign is free treatment and an attempt to cure through highly active anti-retrovirus therapy (HAART). There are now 140 approved variants of HAART. This therapy is expensive to administer, particularly since the virus is mutable. However, the annual cost of treatment has come down from about $12,000 per person in 1998 to $500 in 2002. This is still too high for most people in the world. In Brazil the support for free treatment is allied with an active programme of education in safe behaviour and how to administer systematic drug treatment. The reduction in the number of infected is now generating savings which are greater than the cost of the campaign, at least this became true from 2001 onwards. The cost of treatment has been brought down to about one dollar a day, through the generosity of the pharmaceutical companies and the intelligent use of international agreements such as TRIPS which allows the waiving, in an emergency, of the defence of normal intellectual property rights.

Even one dollar a day is beyond the means of most Africans. In Africa, however, some countries are moving to use the Brazilian model, although at a slow pace. Botswana is a test case for Africa.

For Africa the main response from abroad has been the establishment of the Gates and Merck Foundation, jointly called ACHAP (African Comprehensive HIV-AIDS Partnerships), in the capital of Botswana, Gabarone, into which Bill Gates has pledged to pour US$50 million over a five-year period, matched by another US$50 million from the pharmaceutical company Merck. The Harvard AIDS Institute is providing expert medical treatment, helping to set up the first anti-retroviral clinic at the Princess Marina Hospital in Gabarone, and organizing state-of-the-art research into the type C virus, including the mode of transmission from mother to child and the development of a suitable vaccine. A second clinic is just starting in Francistown, the second largest city, with help from London's Chelsea and Westminster Hospital. The effort is very much dependent on foreign participation.

At the moment HIV/AIDS is, strictly speaking, incurable, but its onset can be postponed and the disease controlled. This needs to be done, while simultaneously the spread of the disease is checked by the adoption of safe behaviour – the use of condoms, abstinence or the reduction of promiscuity. The main problems are gaining access to drugs at a reasonable price and educating the people in safe sex and using the drugs properly. Botswana is the first country to offer free anti-retroviral drugs to everyone who needs them. The danger is that improper use of the drugs will only encourage the development of resistance. The drugs regime is complex and difficult for a relatively unsophisticated population with a rudimentary healthcare system to understand and sustain.

There are a number of cultural problems, which stand in the way of an effective solution to the problem in a society which is largely rural and patriarchal. There is a reluctance of those vulnerable to be tested for the disease. Prevention is a matter of breaking down ingrained attitudes to intergenerational sexual relations and women adopting a much more independent role, such as getting a job. The government favours using the local community and the family to change attitudes and behaviour. The process is labour-intensive in social workers and the medical staff required.

Even in Botswana the problem has only been confronted in a marginal way. It still has only 19,000 patients receiving anti-retroviral treatment, compared with the 110,000 people who should be taking the drugs.

The implications for international business

'Not only is AIDS our business; fighting it also makes good business sense.'

Rosen et al., 2003: 86

'Very simply, AIDS is destroying the twin rationales of globalization strategy: cheap labour and fast-growing markets.'

Rosen et al., 2003: 82

Table 14.5 **The cost of AIDS to an employer**

	Direct costs	Indirect costs
Individual costs (for one employee with HIV/AIDS)	Medical costs Benefit payments Recruitment and training of replacement	Reduced on-the-job productivity Reduced productivity due to employee's absence Supervisor's time in dealing with worker productivity losses Vacancy rate while replacement is hired Reduced productivity while replacement worker learns the job
Organizational costs (for many employees with HIV/AIDS)	Insurance premiums Accidents due to sick workers Cost of litigation over benefits and other issues	Senior management time Production disruption Depressed morale Loss of experienced workers Deterioration of labour relations

Source. Rosen et al., 2003: 84.

It therefore deters foreign investment in countries with high levels of infection. Sub-Saharan Africa is such a region. Clearly AIDS is another serious constraint on the ability of African nations to develop economically, as if there were not enough constraints already. It has imposed a massive cost on the communities and also on the corporations which employ the infected workers.

The capacity of the community to work and reproduce is seriously threatened by the epidemic. AIDS kills primarily the young and middle-aged adults in their most productive years as both employees and customers. For individuals there are many years of impaired productivity, followed by impoverishment of the family after death of the breadwinner and orphanhood for the children if both parents die; for enterprises serious absenteeism, high employee turnover, a pressing need to hire replacement workers and various legal, social and political complications add to their costs. Time horizons for all concerned are shortened by the diminished life expectancy. It is difficult to look ahead. It is difficult for the key decision makers in the societies to even consider, let alone take, those decisions which would accelerate the rate of economic development.

Two of the large resource companies working in the area, the diamond company Debswana, in which De Beers is joined with the Botswana government, and Anglo American have begun to offer free AIDS drug treatment. In Botswana, 80% of the cost of the drugs is born by the government although the pharmaceutical companies are providing the drugs at cost, the pharmaceutical company Merck free of charge. The medical and educational systems have diverted significant resources to meeting the crisis, resources which are badly needed to build an infrastructure to support rapid economic development.

There are strong reasons, apart from the obvious humanitarian ones and the problem of corporate image, why international business should get involved. The epidemic is already imposing a cost on every ounce of gold or platinum produced. Anglo Gold estimates the additional cost to be $6 on a total cost of about $170–180, Anglo American platinum $3. All companies suffer from the costs indicated above. A study of six companies operating in South Africa and Botswana (Rosen et al. 2003), showed annual direct costs ranging from 0.4% to 5.9% of the wage bill, with between 7.9% and 29% of workers infected. Previously the companies simply bore the cost, which might take the form of the employment of two workers where one is needed, on the expectation that one will become sick. Until recently the most that was done was to assist in a programme of education and encouragement to use condoms. Now it is thought that the cost of drugs has fallen sufficiently to justify the expenditure. Not all infected workers take up the offer. Most companies think that the cost of treatment and education is cheaper than the cost of doing nothing, that is, not treating the disease. Even properly discounting the future, the costs of infection prevention and treatment provision are less than the savings which can be made in future costs. This applies to those already operating. For potential newcomers there is an additional cost, higher where the incidence of the disease is higher.

Table 14.6 **The typical time frame for costs**

Year 0	Infection	No costs
Years 0–7	Employee productivity unaffected	No costs
Years 7–9	Sickness begins	Sickness-related costs
Years 9–10	Death or disability	End-of-service costs
Year 10 +	Replacement	Turnover costs

Source: Rosen et al., 2003: 85.

Avoidance of high incidence areas is still an option for potential investors.

The example of Botswana can act as a model for the rest of Africa. As the head of the Gates and Merck Foundation, Dr Donald de Korte, formerly head of Merck in South Africa, has said: 'If you're looking for a self-interested motive, it is that if this model works, it will be repeated throughout Africa and increase the pharmaceuticals' markets.' If it does not work in Botswana, it cannot work elsewhere.

A major debate has taken place in South Africa relating to the cost of the drugs, which was way above what could be afforded either by those suffering from the disease or their governments. The South African government encouraged both parallel importation of cheap drugs and an abuse of patents with generic production of the drugs within South Africa. The drug companies took them to court. The reputation of the pharmaceutical companies became a real issue, which persuaded them to capitulate. Elsewhere in Africa, for the enormous effort required in coping with the disease to be effective, it must combine the commercial with the humanitarian. The model which might work for a small country like Botswana, that is, small in population, will not work in the more populous countries like Nigeria, Kenya or South Africa.

Although there is no formal obligation, there is an increase in the number of companies listed on the South African stock exchange which publicize their anti-AIDS policies, spelling out how AIDS is affecting their business, markets and workers and how they are fighting it. Already about half the largest companies have a formal HIV/AIDS policy, for example Anglo American, Anglo Gold and De Beers give infected workers free anti-retroviral drugs.

The future

It is untrue that Africa has not seen the like of the current AIDS epidemic before. It is easy to liken it, in its potential impact, to the loss of slaves from Africa from the sixteenth to the nineteenth centuries, with the major impact in the seventeenth and eighteenth centuries. In terms of relative numbers there is likely to be a similar impact, certainly in the region of the southern cone, but the impact of AIDS will be packed into a much shorter time period. Like AIDS, slavery took those predominantly in the age group which provided the bulk of the labour force and the ability of the community to reproduce. The Botswana Institute of Development Analysis has estimated that AIDS could reduce growth rates in several African countries by amounts ranging from 0.5% to 2.6%, an impact which is doubly significant since the growth rate for most African countries is already low.

Other comparisons are also apposite. The Black Death in the fourteenth century took about one-quarter to one-third of the population of Europe, with dramatic effects on the nature of the economic system which was left. The influenza epidemic after World War I also took about 20 million people, with less overall impact than the Black Death, but a reinforcement of the negative shock of World War I. It is possible to trace the effects of these events and build possible scenarios of what will happen in Africa. AIDS is by no means the last epidemic disease to strike; the advent of severe acute respiratory syndrome (SARS) has shown that. Epidemic disease has also been a problem for livestock. Fast-mutating fungal and other plant diseases become resistant to treatment and further treatments need to be developed. There are other societies at risk from AIDS. What is happening in Africa is only the tip of an iceberg which might prove to be very large indeed.

Case Study Questions

1. What are the main features of the risk environment in Africa? How important is the political environment for international business?
2. Indicate what future scenarios are likely for Africa given different assumptions about the trajectory of the AIDS epidemic. Indicate carefully what are i. the forces of change, ii. the predetermined elements, and ii. the most important critical uncertainties.
3. What are the implications of the AIDS epidemic for the making of strategy by i. enterprises wishing to invest in Africa, ii. African enterprises, and iii. the governments of African countries?
4. What is the likely future for economic development in Botswana?
5. How should those coming to a foreign country deal with the existence of what are commonly regarded by those outside as corrupt practices? Is there a consistent strategy which should be applied?

Reading

Dyer, G., 'As the pandemic spreads, developed nations must respond to a new challenge from the White House', *Financial Times*, June 2, 2003: 17.

Economist, The, 'Hope for the best. Prepare for the worst.', July 13, 2002: 65–7.

Economist, The, 'The long war', July 13, 2002: 16.

Economist, The, 'Business and AIDS: digging deep', August 10, 2002: 55.

Economist, The, 'Strategic caring', October 5, 2002: 64.

Koppisch, J., 'Lessons from the fastest growing nation: Botswana', *Business Week*, August 26, 2002: 72–3.

Rosen, S., Simon, J., Vincent, J. R., MacLeod, W., Fox, M. and Thea, D. M., 'AIDS is your business', *Harvard Business Review*, February 2003: 80–7.

Focus on Humour

The naked power of the Niger Delta 'mamas'

The 'mamas' are the mothers and grandmothers of the Itsekiri tribe who live in the oil-rich Niger Delta in Nigeria. They have discovered a new weapon to use against the giant oil company, Chevron Texaco, to persuade it to recognize the legitimacy of their demands. This is 'the curse of nakedness'. They have threatened to strip off all their clothes, using their nakedness to shame the oil company into submitting to their demands. Such an act is culturally a potentially very potent one.

The central government in Nigeria is strongly in favour of the oil companies exploiting the oil of the Niger Delta, and is prepared to use the army and police against locals who, up to now, have seen only damage to their local communities from the intrusion. Nigeria is the sixth largest oil exporter in the world, almost all of which comes from the Niger Delta. The whole Nigerian economy has become dependent on the revenue generated by the oil. However, local communities are poor and have seen their local farms and fisheries badly damaged by the environmental impact of the oil drilling.

Most locals do not wish the oil company to go away. Rather they wish for a more equitable distribution of the gains from the oil. In order to achieve this they apply pressure to the company in order to persuade it to pay what amounts to an unofficial local community tax. The wish list consists of a number of possible actions – the creation of jobs for locals, the provision of credit to create local businesses, such as chicken or fish farms, and the establishment of infrastructure, such as improvements in sanitation, the electrification of villages and the building of schools, clinics and town halls.

Local action is not new. Traditional action to try to divert some of the benefits to the local communities has not met with much success. This action has taken the form of local self-determination movements, kidnappings, seizure of cars and helicopters, occupation of facilities and sabotage. Sometimes there is the exaction of overt protection money, sometimes simply compensation for damage to the environment. Such action has failed to achieve very much, only provoking repressive action by the government, worsening the plight of the local communities. The present movement is by contrast a peaceful once, although it means an interruption to oil supply as the women occupy oil pipeline stations.

A historic agreement has been signed which ended the 'mamas' action. Perhaps this is a precedent. The deal will create jobs for 10 people from villages near the flow stations, upgrade 20 contract workers to full-time positions and create 30 new contract positions. Chevron Texaco has also agreed to set up a A$294,000 microcredit scheme to help the women create businesses. All this has been achieved without them having to shed a single garment; the threat was enough.

Source: Branigan and Vidal, 2002: 22; *Financial Times*, 2003.

Key strategic lessons

- Risk is universally present in the business world in the form of strategic risk, comprising competitive and country risk.

- The appetite for risk reflects the liquidity of an enterprise, the personality and attitudes of strategists, the nature of the corporate culture and the 'political' interactions.

Key strategic lessons cont'd

• Risk can be viewed as either the variance in a performance indicator or the possibility of an extreme event occurring.

• A risk management strategy should be an integral and explicit part of strategy making and formulated at the same time as the main strategy. The risk attached to any project should be considered jointly with the return.

• A first step in reducing risk is to reduce ignorance, which requires a decision on the resources to be committed to generating the required information. This is part of an information strategy. A decision must also be made on whether to do the risk assessment in-house or outsource it.

• Generic risk control strategies can include avoidance, mitigation or management strategies. Any strategy based on concealment is to be discouraged.

• Avoidance is a common strategy since many projects are not considered at a preliminary stage. It is a last resort and should be adopted only after careful consideration. Its cost is the return lost from the rejected project.

• Risk management is the sharing of a fixed risk by a commercial arrangement such as insurance or hedging, a strategic alliance with a partner who shares both risk and return, or the backing of a government.

• Risk mitigation reduces the level of risk by methods such as negotiation, building flexibility into any arrangements or diversification.

• Risk avoidance should be adopted where the level of risk is high, risk mitigation where the risk level is intermediate and risk management where risk is low. The strategies can be combined. Each of these strategies involves the incurring of costs, both direct and indirect, such as the loss of revenue.

• Diversification is an acceptable device for reducing risk under certain conditions which hold most strongly in the world of financial portfolio choice.

• Scenario building and planning is part of good strategy making which assists in effective risk management.

Applying the lessons

1 Define the following terms; a risk-generating event, risk avoidance, risk mitigation, risk management, adverse selection and moral hazard.

2 From your own experience, or the experience of an organization with which you are familiar, give examples of business policies which fall under the headings risk avoidance, risk management and risk mitigation. If there are no such specific policies, in what other ways are policies shaped by the need to manage risk?

3 Distinguish risk-generating events which occur at different levels – the global, the national, the industrial and the enterprise levels. In your view which of these levels is characterized by the highest risk? Does the answer to this question differ according to the economic sector under analysis?

4 Imagine that you are considering an investment project in a particular industry in a particular country. You choose both the industry and the country. How would you deal with the issue of country risk? Do you carry out an assessment yourself? If you do, how would you do this?

5 Consider the *Euromoney* formula for assessing country risk. Answer the following questions:
• The use of a formula assumes the usefulness of a synthetic index. What are the advantages and disadvantages of using such an index?
• How might you adapt this formula for FDI rather than portfolio investment?
• What components and subcomponents should be included in such an index? How should different components be weighted?

6 In the process of scenario building, risk arises from

Applying the lessons cont'd

the existence of critical uncertainties. What are the critical uncertainties which are likely to be important in the following industries over the next five years?

Airlines
Wine
Pharmaceutical
Automobile

Computer software
Banking
Share broking
Insurance
Tertiary education
Managing shopping malls

Strategic project

1 You are considering undertaking a new investment project to be implemented in a particular industry and a particular country with which you are familiar. First choose the industry and the country, and the exact nature of the investment.

2 What are the likely returns from this project? What are the likely sources of risk? What sort of events are

likely to generate risk? Analyse the nature and levels of industry and country risk. Evaluate the level of risk attaching to this kind of investment.

3 Consider what kind of risk management strategy should be adopted. What specific measures need to be taken according to this strategy? What is the usual practice in investments of a similar kind?

Exploring further

There is an excellent introductory text on the treatment and management of risk which is an easy read: Bernstein, 1998. For an excellent text on new methods of risk management, but one very difficult to read, see Dow, 1998. A basic but comprehensive text on country risk is Coplin, 1994.

Risk management is often relegated to a minor role in texts on strategy making. There are exceptions, for example Chapter 10 in Daniels et al., 2001. For a specialist article see Aaker and Jacobson, 1990: 137–60.

The early work on risk dates back to the 1980s: see Calverley, 1985 or Krayenbuehl, 1985. An excellent review article which considers not only the nature of country risk but possible responses to that risk is Miller, 1992: 311–31. Another article which stresses the importance of the issue, but also the particular way in which it shows itself, is Reeb et al., 1998: 263–79.

Two evaluations of the type of diversification which is desirable are Lubatkin and Chatterjee, 1994: 109–36 and Goold and Luchs, 1993: 7–25. On the risks in strategic alliances see Das and Bing-Sheng Teng, 1988: 34–41.

For much of the reading on scenario building and its relationship to reducing uncertainty or risk, see the bibliographical review to Chapter 4. These works can be supplemented by Linneman and Klein, 1985: 64–74.

15 Participating in the global economy

Key strategic challenge

How do I enter a new market, particularly a global market?

Strategic dangers

To choose a mode of entry into a particular market that is inappropriate for the time and the situation, which will either lose the enterprise its competitive advantage or waste opportunities for additional profit and/or expose the enterprise to a significant loss of revenue.

Case Study Scenario   Entry into the Chinese automobile industry

'China today is our No 1 geographic priority in terms of market development.'

   Carlos Ghosn, CEO of Nissan (cited in Dwyer, 2002: 1)

China is unusual in attracting an enormous inflow of foreign direct investment, despite the fact that it is still a largely undeveloped, or at best a developing, country. In 2002 the total inflow into China exceeded that into the USA and made China the number one recipient country in the world. Part of that flow has been an investment in the Chinese automobile industry. The size of its population and the rapid rate of growth of income within China has made it an attractive market to enter, whatever the product, although the market is not quite as easy to enter as often thought, or as homogeneous as it appears at first glance. The low cost base has also made China potentially attractive as a platform for vehicle exports to the rest of the world.

The normal mode of entry into the automobile industry, as into many other Chinese industries, has been through joint ventures. The reason for this is government insistence but it corresponds with the belief that the Chinese market is exceptional. In order to gain access to this market, the foreign enterprise typically believes that it is necessary to find a local partner, who understands the local culture and systems. This partner can provide the contacts required to gain the appropriate permissions and effectively use local distribution networks. The foreign enterprise is typically expected to reciprocate by providing technological and organizational know-how and sometimes the capital needed to set up facilities. This pattern is true of all sectors of the economy, not just the automobile industry (see the case studies on SAB Miller and Haier in Part V).

In 2000 sales of motor vehicles of various kinds in China were over 2.1 million, including 620,000 passenger cars. The latter figure rose to 730,000 in 2001, and reached as high as one million in 2002, in a total vehicle figure of almost three million. The growth in sales was 60% in 2002. In January of 2003 the growth on the previous year was as high as 150%. This surge in sales is associated with the rise of the private car buyer in China. The introduction of bank loans for car purchase and an enormous increase in the number of Chinese-made models, from only 8 in 2000 to 65 in 2003, together with the removal of uncertainty associated with entry into the WTO, released a massive pent-up demand. In 2002 for the first time private citizens overtook the government as buyers of motorcars. The most competitive market is that for the compact or subcompact car.

Table 15.1 **Sales of all vehicles in the main markets of the world**

	Units per year in 2002 (in millions)
1. USA	14.2
2. Japan	4.8
3. Germany	2.9
4. China	2.7
5. UK	2.5
6. France	2.2
7. Italy	2.1

In the absence of a major catastrophe, the rate of production will at least double by 2010. Conservative estimates have the market at 2.5 million cars, more optimistic commentators see it as high as 5 million. At present there are in China just 10 passenger cars per 1,000 people, which compares poorly with 250 in Taiwan and over 500 in the USA and Germany. It is easy to calculate the number of cars required to take China to comparable levels. Assuming a car lasts ten years, the level of production required for a population of 1.3 billion to reach an endowment of 500 per 1,000 is 65 million a year. Of course this is an overambitious, even impossible, target in such a short time period. A target of 100 passenger cars per 1,000 would still require production of about 13 million a year. In terms of potential demand in the domestic market, even 5 million a year appears relatively modest. It is likely that the major constraint on demand will be the poor shape of the infrastructure.

The estimates above ignore any export demand. It is not only the size and growth of the domestic market which is acting as a lure to foreign business in China. It is the possibility of using China as a platform for exporting to other parts of the world. This is less clear-cut, but there are persuasive arguments why it might prove to be important. China is positioned in the fastest growing region in the world, one in which the demand for motor vehicles is growing rapidly. It is easy to see a significant part of that demand being met from China. Even more important will be the role of the large global vehicle manufacturers who may use China as an assembly base for a sizeable part of their production. At the moment, component production in China is at a level which makes impossible the achievement of major economies of scale, so that the products are 10–20% dearer than world levels. It is likely to take 3–5 years for this situation to be rectified. Once this occurs, exporting becomes feasible. All the major car companies are positioning themselves in China to take advantage of the opportunities in both domestic and export markets.

How should these companies enter this market? Is the conventional mode through a joint venture the appropriate one, given the likely circumstances of the country and the industry in the future?

In order to enter any market, whether domestic or international, the basic prerequisite is to hold some kind of a competitive advantage. The nature of that competitive advantage is a major influence on the mode of entry. This chapter draws out some important implications of the difficulties of creating and maintaining competitive advantage at the global level. It poses the question, how best can an enterprise exploit this competitive advantage in markets other than its own domestic market? Which participation strategy should it adopt to make the most of the situation?

Participation strategies

There are a number of different modes of entry into a new market, particularly one which is part of the global scene. In order to arrive at the correct mode of entry, a series of decisions have to be made, as illustrated in Figure 15.1. The main choice is between:

- producing the product or service locally and exporting it directly to the market
- setting up a production facility in the country in which the market is located, or organizing the setting up by a local producer.

After a decision is made, there may be a monitoring of the project, which can yield two questions which must be asked on a periodic basis:

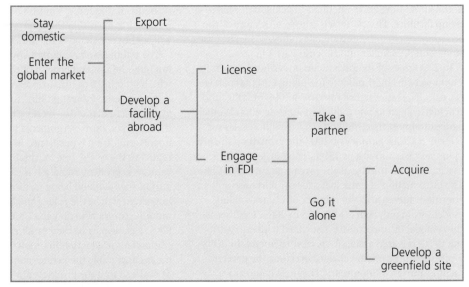

Figure 15.1 **The decision tree for mode of entry**

- Should the company withdraw from the commitment – a different issue from making the initial commitment when significant expenditures have become sunk costs which cannot be retrieved?
- Should the company move to a different mode which represents a bigger commitment, for example from exporting to direct investment?

In the past, the problem of mode of entry was reduced to a simple problem in cost minimization. It paid to produce at the location which was most profitable in terms of sales to the market. This might reflect the costs involved, for example tariffs or wage levels. Often it was interpreted in terms of the relative bulk to value ratio of inputs and outputs which determined whether it was more economic to locate near the sources of raw materials or near the market. In either case the location of the facility might be outside the country of origin of the company. Today, the choice of participation strategy is viewed as a strategic question.

The choice of a mode of entry depends largely on:

- the nature of the competitive advantage held by the enterprise
- the commitment of resources – the greater the commitment of resources, the greater the return and the greater the risk level
- the return to be made – the lure is a higher return
- the level of risk to which the company is exposed – as is generally the case, the higher the prospective return, the higher the level of risk.

The objective in this section is to list the different modes of entry, or participation strategies, which might be adopted. They are listed in order of commitment of resources and organizational effort, and therefore in order of the increasing risk associated with the different modes.

Indirect exporting

An enterprise may sell its product as an input to another domestic enterprise which then exports the assembled product. A component-producing company, such as one producing upholstery for car seats, might sell its product to an automobile manufacturer which exports the assembled car. For products which contain a large number of components, like an airliner or motorcar, this is common. Indirect exporting may involve a significant level of sales, but it does not change the nature of the activities undertaken. Nothing beyond the normal demands of routine domestic activity is required of the enterprise.

Direct exporting

In this activity a company deliberately sells to consumers outside the domestic market. Direct exporting may be:

- reactive, the response to an opportunity arising, perhaps drawn to the attention of staff in the company by others, sometimes unexpectedly, sometimes in the normal course of business
- proactive, the result of a deliberate strategy on the part of the exporter who actively seeks out new markets.

Such trade may take the form of intra-enterprise transfers across international frontiers, one part of a multinational company shipping components to another part in another country, an internal transaction.

The services required in exporting, and there are many – warehousing, transport, insurance, documentation of various kinds – can be organized by the enterprise or specialist organizations, intermediaries such as trade management companies. Distribution in the foreign market can be the responsibility of partner enterprises. It is possible to sell through trading companies which carry out all the necessary functions, so that selling into export markets requires exactly the same activities on the part of the producer as selling into domestic markets. However, this incurs a cost which reduces the size of any profit. The advantage is that it allows specialization by those who know what they are doing.

Management contracts, including turnkey projects

This is an intermediate mode in that it involves both a service export and something equivalent to licensing the use of scarce organizational ability. An enterprise might take on a contract in a foreign country to provide a particular service or packages of services. This might involve hiring out a team of managers or technical specialists, or it might be a specialist enterprise which has competencies in starting up large facilities, such as an airport, port or nuclear power station, known as a turnkey project (also called BOOT – build, own, operate, transfer). The specialist knowledge is what is being bought or hired. This is not unlike licensing in the purchase of specialist knowledge or skills.

Licensing, including franchising

The enterprise can sell the right, either to use a particular process, manufacture a particular product or exploit a particular brand name, to a foreign enterprise in a market into which the enterprise wishes to sell, broadly referred to as licensing. The partner enterprise is then responsible for producing and selling the product. For example, the American company Qualcomm licenses the use of its patents for telecommunications technology to numerous companies in the wireless communication business and generates more revenue doing this than actually manufacturing or selling a product. The licensee may maintain quality or fail to do so. The licensee company may also develop its own variant of what is licensed and drop the licensor as a partner. This is not difficult to achieve particularly if the courts in the country are complaisant.

Franchising is a special case of licensing, involving a more complex and sophisticated movement of assets, beyond the simple transfer of intellectual property rights, including the application of organizational know-how. It involves hiring the good name of the franchiser. Franchising may involve the transfer of management expertise, even amounting to an entrepreneurial input. Maintaining good quality, and therefore a good reputation, is the real issue. The franchisee saves on marketing or promotion costs by using the good name of the franchiser.

Foreign direct investment

In this mode of entry the enterprise both produces and sells in the foreign country. This involves the largest commitment of resources but also carries the highest risk. The commitment can be a small or large one. It might grow over time or it might remain stable. Usually there is a minimum threshold size necessary to make it viable, which is quite substantial.

There are three main ways of engaging in foreign direct investment (FDI) – joint ventures, acquisitions and mergers, and greenfield projects. Each has its own benefits and problems and is designed to deal with different circumstances.

Wal-Mart has used a number of different methods, but has often commenced its foreign involvement with a joint enterprise.

Strategy in Action Wal-Mart and the internationalization of retailing

Wal-Mart recognized that the domestic market in the USA was reaching saturation point, although as late as 2001 it continued to open new stores. To counter the slowing growth of the domestic market, in 1991 Wal-Mart began to internationalize, transferring its successful business model to new markets. By 2001 1,000 of its 4,000 stores were foreign.

The opening up of new markets by deregulation, the saturation of domestic markets and the improvement in the technology of communications and logistics have encouraged the movement of many retailers onto the international stage. As yet this process is in its infancy. In 2000 the market share of the world's 50 largest retailers was only 20%. The 10 largest had on average entered only 10 countries.

Table 15.2 **Retailers go global – number of new countries entered**

	1981–85	1986–90	1991–95	1996–2001
Ahold	1	1	3	20
Carrefour	1	2	5	14
Kingfisher	0	0	3	12
Metro	2	3	1	9
Tesco	1	–1	2	6
Wal-Mart	0	0	4	5
H&M	0	1	2	5

Source: Catoni et al., 2002: 126.

Internationalization is a new phenomenon. No major player can afford not to be in the game. Wal-Mart has been comparatively slow in joining this trend and has concentrated most of its efforts into neighbouring countries such as Mexico and Canada. The other, more recent, area of expansion is in Hong Kong as a possible springboard into China.

The model which underpins this strategy of internationalization differs from retailer to retailer. There are three main models:

1. *Replication.* For some retailers like Benetton and Starbucks, both the focus of case studies in this book, the model is replication. A simple format and business system are reproduced wherever the company goes. This provides significant economies of scale and enormous clout in purchasing from suppliers who themselves are often major international players, such as Unilever, Procter & Gamble and Kellogg's.

   This is very much the model adopted by Wal-Mart. Internationally Wal-Mart sought to reproduce the model which had served it so well domestically.

2. *Performance management.* For Ahold and Kingfisher, the model is one of performance manager. In this model the company acquires a portfolio of existing retail businesses and develops them as almost completely distinct entities with their own brands and product profile. Management is decentralized. The problems with this model are finding cheap acquisitions and managing an enterprise of increasing size and complexity.

3. *Reinvesting.* For Carrefour and Tesco, the model is that of the reinvestor. The company has one or more store concepts such as the hypermarket concept of Carrefour, which are then adapted to suit each local market. There are standard back-end processes and systems which help to achieve economies of scale and economize on costs, at least in these limited areas.

There are threats to such leviathans. There are discounters who undercut even these retailers. Specialist stores are undercutting the department chains at the domestic level. Another threat comes from e-commerce on the model of Amazon.com, discussed elsewhere in the book.

Could the model be exported by Wal-Mart to other countries? Entry into Mexico by Wal-Mart has shown that it can.

Mexico was chosen because of the establishment of the North American Free Trade Area (NAFTA) which removed obstacles to entry. Wal-Mart chose not to establish franchisees because it believed that franchisees could not operate its model, or to establish a greenfield enterprise because it did not know enough about the local culture and business practices to be confident of success. It therefore formed a joint venture with one of the largest Mexican retailers, Cifra, eventually, when it had the necessary experience and confidence, turning its partner into a majority-owned enterprise.

Initially there were serious difficulties which defeated other entrants from the USA, such as Kmart and Sears. Some of these were general to the economy as a whole, such as the peso devaluation of 40% in 1994 and the ensuing recession, and the poor infrastructure, others specific to Wal-Mart. The initial lack of distribution centres represented one such difficulty, as it prevented the recreation of the important logistics system in the USA. It was simply a matter of time and scale before these centres were introduced. It took Wal-Mart a decade to introduce its electronic supply management system into Mexico, partly because of the resistance from suppliers and partly because of confusion in the minds of its own employees, as well as the problem of the local infrastructure. Wal-Mart now has 10 super-efficient distribution centres. The distribution centre in Mexico City became Wal-Mart's most efficient centre anywhere because of the low labour costs in Mexico. Wal-Mart surmounted the teething problems and did so remarkably quickly.

Mexico is now the brightest star in the company's international division, with more than 500 stores generating over $9 billion in sales and $458 in profit. Wal-Mart has half of all Mexican supermarket sales nationwide, just a decade after entering the country. The Mexican companies are losing ground, with their sales and profits falling. Without foreign partners, they find it difficult to achieve the costs to match Wal-Mart's 'everyday low' prices.

Not surprisingly Wal-Mart has a $600 million budget set aside for the establishment of a further 63 stores by mid-2003.

Wal-Mart has entered Germany and Britain through acquisitions, in the latter acquiring Asda, a nationwide discount food chain. The model adopted is very much that of the replicator, but on occasion it can come unstuck, as it did in Indonesia, where local tastes upset the apple cart. In 1996 Wal-Mart established a number of efficient, clean superstores, only to find that the customers preferred Matahari, a chain of shabbier local stores, more akin to the traditional local markets in which the customers loved to haggle and regularly buy fresh produce. In 1998 Wal-Mart left Indonesia. Nevertheless there is much scope for extension of a replicator model since today only 15% of Wal-Mart's total sales are abroad.

Table 15.3 **Mexico's retail landscape (2001)**

	Walmex	Commercial Mexicana	Gigante	Soriana
Net sales ($bill)	9.67	3.61	3.25	3.03
Net profit ($mill)	458.00	82.90	68.70	160.30
No. of stores	579	225	445	115

Joint venture

The first method of FDI involves finding a partner who will share risks and returns. Even the most successful companies like to enter, at least initially, through a partnership. Wal-Mart illustrates this. The existence of a partner can make possible the saving of some investment and it may reduce the risk level in a number of different ways. It also reduces the returns, since any profits have to be shared. Often the partnership involves the establishment of a new enterprise, jointly owned.

Choosing the partner is critical to the success of the joint venture. A good partner should enjoy core competencies different from the main enterprise, competencies which make entry into the market more likely to be successful. The nature of the competencies depends on the level of development of the economy being entered. In countries with a different culture or political system, obvious competencies might be an ability to liaise with local networks or government and access to an already well-developed distribution system. The partner from outside might provide capital or technical know-how.

In developed countries, joint enterprises may involve a different kind mentarity, often specific to a particular functional area.

Acquisition or merger

Foreign direct investment mostly takes the form of acquisition of, or merger with, an existing company in the foreign country. A minimum holding of 10% of shares is generally regarded as necessary to qualify as FDI.

The acquisition of an operating enterprise has the advantage of allowing immediate production and sales in the country but it also means the acquisition of not just productive capacity, but any problems characterizing the acquired enterprise. The technology may be less than best practice. The existing management team may be undynamic or culturally incompatible with the acquiring enterprise. The labour force may be too large but there may be contractual obligations to that labour force. It may turn out to be difficult to change any of these things.

Greenfield projects

To undertake a greenfield project literally means to start with an empty site and build a facility upon it. Even then it is necessary to buy, lease or rent the site. The company has to get all the necessary permissions and permits and oversee construction and the beginning of operations. This approach avoids the problems of acquiring existing facilities. The company can choose best-practice technology and appoint excellent staff. This mode of entry carries different problems. It delays production and sales, sometimes quite dramatically, and presents all sorts of demands in terms of learning how to operate in a foreign country. It is usually very ambitious to undertake such a method of entry.

At a given moment in time, choice may mean moving down the decision tree to an appropriate level where the answer to a question halts the process. It is of course possible that the list of different modes of entry describes not simply a choice at a given moment in time, but a real-time process of increasing involvement in particular markets, a process sometimes stretched over a significant period of time. In other words, it may describe a temporal sequence of stages in the changing nature of participation in the market or economy.

The answer to the questions at different levels of the decision tree may change over time. It is possible for an enterprise to choose to enter or exit at any point in the sequence. There may be powerful reasons for going straight into foreign investment rather than preparing the ground with some intermediate mode of entry.

The next step in the analysis is to consider the conditions under which the particular options are chosen.

News Corporation clearly wishes to enter the pay-TV market in the USA but must decide how to do this. The choice may be influenced by opportunity.

Strategy in Action News Corporation and expansion in the USA

The media giants which have emerged in the last 15 years have very different origins. News Corporation has Australian origins but Rupert Murdoch, its CEO and principal shareholder, changed his nationality in order to allow the extension of News Corporation interests in the USA. News Corporation is a media giant which is still very much in play, in the sense that it is still acquiring other international enterprises, despite a significant fall in its share price and level of profitability.

News Corporation has at different times made unfortunate purchases which have led to a number of recent write-downs, $10 billion in all, notably for Gemstar. At various stages in its history, News Corp. has seemed on the brink of disaster. Fortunately today a number of its investments have begun to generate significant cash flows, especially pay TV. There are clearly significant economies of scale and scope in acquiring the ability to have a pay-TV facility in every major market in the world. Under Rupert Murdoch, the company has always been inclined to expand, using its surplus cash for acquisitions. In so doing it has probably lost its shareholders as much as $15 billion but has also had offsetting successes. Provided the successes outweigh the failures, this is a viable strategy. Not all acquisitions can be successful. Some companies have tended to avoid all acquisitions, for example IKEA.

In a number of advantageous ways, a time of recession is a good time to acquire. The prices of acquired companies are low. Others are not in the market competing for the companies which are for sale. It is possible to put together at a relatively low price combinations of assets with major synergies. There is a good opportunity for rationalization of a sector. All of

this is premised on a company's ability to raise the capital required. A strong cash flow is the best base for such activity.

Table 15.4 provides details on the pattern and level of News Corporation's activities in different parts of the world and different parts of the communications/media/entertainment sector. By exposing the obvious gaps, the picture also helps to indicate those areas which News Corp. might move into in the future:

- The concentration on the USA, Australia and the UK is obvious, as are the gaps in Europe and Asia
- There is a major gap in pay TV in the USA
- Where government regulation prevents activity, it is possible to anticipate lobbying and pressure from News Corp.
- Where News Corp. is a minor player, there is likely to be an effort to lift the level of activity.

News Corporation has tried to acquire pay TV in the USA, but failed to buy the satellite broadcaster DirecTV. It has extended its media interests in Europe, by the acquisition from Vivendi of Telepiu, a pay-TV company in Italy which it got at a bargain price. Merging Telepiu with its own loss-making Stream business into Sky Italia gives it a monopoly in a TV-mad market where there is little in the way of opposition. The refusal in October 2002 by the Federal Communications Commission (FCC) to allow EchoStar to buy DirecTV from Hughes Electrics, a

Table 15.4 **News Corp.'s global footprint**

	Newspapers	TV studio	Content Movies	Cable channels	Books	Distribution FTA TV	Pay TV	Technology Gemstar	NDS
2002 revenue US$ mill	2.411	3,000	1,050	1,869	1,078	4,198	Associate	Associate	368
Australia	***		***	***	*	^	***		**
UK	***		***	***	*		***		**
Continental Europe			***		*		*		*
US	^	***	***	***	*	***		***	**
Latin America				**	*		**		**
Asia		*		***	*	^			**

*** = leading player, ** = major player, * = minor player, ^ = not allowed

Source: Sykes, 2002: 10.

General Motors subsidiary, has put that company in play again, since GM needs the money to help cover its poor pension position. News Corp. lobbied against the purchase by EchoStar and will almost certainly try again to purchase it.

The News Corp. philosophy is that content is king and the form of distribution really does not matter. News Corp. therefore owns, controls and develops content but only owns sufficient stakes in distribution systems to guarantee access to customers for its content and benefit from any advantages which vertical integration may bring.

The sources of income for News Corp. are also revealing. Three-quarters of its revenue and two-thirds of its earnings before interest and tax come from the USA, as might be expected from its level of activity and the relative size of that market. It is very much a USA-focused company. There is perhaps room for diversification and further purchases in Europe and Asia.

For media companies there are four categories of income: advertising, corporate (payment for licences or the use of the pool of existing film and TV), consumer subscriptions and consumer discretionary.

Advertising exists in all the media, but most of all on TV. Unfortunately the level of advertising expenditures fluctuates with the business cycle. There is little a company can do to control those fluctuations. Discretionary expenditure on newspapers, magazines, books, even videos and films also moves with the business cycle. These sources of income are currently reduced.

News Corp.'s income comprises as much as 37% from advertising and 54% from discretionary purchases such as newspapers, magazines and DVDs. These are high figures by industry standards, which tend to make News Corp. more vulnerable to the business cycle than it needs to be. It would be helpful for News Corp. to raise its subscription income. This could be achieved by the purchase of the satellite broadcaster DirecTV which would give it national coverage and a low-cost entry compared with cable. The problem is to get round the barrier created by the regulator, the FCC.

This analysis of the News Corporation portfolio of assets has indicated the areas of the world in which it is interested in entering and the likely mode of entry.

Participation strategies and competitive advantage

Graduated entry

There are good reasons why most enterprises are likely to engage in a form of graduated entry, or what has been called 'creeping incrementalism'. They start with low-risk, low-cost entry modes, such as exporting or licensing, and then, if the experience has been rewarding, they move on to more complex modes, such as investment, which require a greater commitment of resources. This approach is tempting, since in the long term it may save on time and resources and allows a low-cost exit in the early stages if the project fails. It allows for the necessary learning process, usually a prerequisite for success, at whatever pace seems suitable to the circumstances.

Graduated entry has its weaknesses, one of which may be a failure to seize an opportunity which others may be only to happy to take, or a tendency to allow others time to consolidate their position and any first-mover advantage they may already have. It may be inconsistent with an appropriate and decisive strategic approach.

Which mode?

A more systematic approach, one consistent with a strategic approach, is to identify all the feasible modes, perform a comparative analysis on their effectiveness, and then rank the modes, choosing an appropriate one, and then, only after this full analysis, implement the decision. This approach takes time and effort. It may be necessary to simplify the full approach. Table 15.5 assumes a major strategic initiative

Table 15.5 **Factors influencing the entry mode decision**

Factor	
Foreign country	
Sales potential	What is the size of market and nature of demand patterns?
Degree of competition	What is the nature of the market structure and what is the likely presence of competitors?
Marketing infrastructure	What is the efficiency and accessibility of distribution networks?
Production costs	Is it expensive to produce the product in this country?
Import policies	What is the degree of protection against imports?
Investment policies	Is there assistance given to promote investment in the country?
Geographical distance	What is the size of transport costs for goods entering the country?
Dynamism of economy	What is the present and future growth rate likely to be?
Exchange controls	Do they exist? Do they favour particular kinds of activity?
Value of currency	Is the currency in any sense overvalued or undervalued? Is it likely to change in the future? Is there transfer risk?
Cultural distance	Does the country belong to the same cultural cluster as the country of origin?
Political risk	Is this relatively high?
Home country	
Size of market	Are there economies of scale or scope in the country of origin?
Degree of competition	What is the level of competition in the country of origin?
Production costs	What is the relative level of productions costs in the country of origin?
Export promotion	Are there policies promoting exports?

and focuses on the question to ask before a mode is chosen. Each of these entry modes has its own advantages and disadvantages which must be weighed against each other.

Table 15.5 illustrates the complexity of the problem. Many of these factors affect the modes differently. It is possible to simplify the issues, but not by much. The account below highlights some of the most important elements.

Difficulties with profit as the sole criterion

Since profit is usually the main objective, the mode of entry which apparently maximizes the profit earned is likely to be the preferred one, other things being equal. As a starting point, the criterion for choice might be seen as profit maximization over a suitable period of time. However, there are three obvious difficulties:

1. It is necessary to consider carefully the time frame. Some of the costs are incurred immediately as fixed, others are incurred in the process of activity. The initial costs may be high. An enterprise may be willing to incur losses today in order to make profits later. The broader aim may be to build up a position in a new market. When Daimaru, the Japanese department store, came to Melbourne, it said that it was willing to wait 10 years before it made a profit. In the event, it left after 12 years, still making a loss.

2. Higher profit is often linked to higher risk. Each entry mode has a different combination of risk and return. Generally, export and licensing offer much lower returns than direct investment but lower risk. Perhaps the key decision to be

made is a trade-off between risk and return, which obviously reflects the risk appetite of the company. For example, licensing the use of 3G wireless technology is less risky than making a major investment in applying that technology (see the case study on Hutchison in Chapter 8).

3. There may be other non-profit objectives, often strategic objectives, which need to be taken into account. It is the profit of the whole of the value-adding chain, not its constituent parts, which is relevant to the decision makers.

Often the key decisions are made within large multinational enterprises which build up value chains across international boundaries. The creation of these value chains is a strategic issue, in which short-term profit cannot be the determining factor. For example, a company may deliberately create alternative sources of supply for important components in order to build flexibility into the system.

Investment and trade flows are closely linked. Direct investment often follows the build-up of an export market. Direct investment creates the preconditions for a different kind of trade, an intra-enterprise trade which is organized to manage risk of various kinds, in particular to free the enterprise from political risk. It might be undertaken to minimize taxes. The profit might turn up in expected places and at unexpected times.

Strategy in Action The Japanese entry into the USA automobile market

One of the most dramatic entries of a product into a new market was the entry of the Japanese automobile into the American market. The occasion was the oil price hike of the 1970s. This threw a spotlight on the increasing competitiveness of the Japanese car producers, led by Toyota, particularly in the areas of smaller and cheaper vehicles. Initially the Japanese entered the American market through exports to that market.

The surge of demand for compact and subcompact cars as a result of the increase in the price of petrol favoured the imports from Japan. It was not just that the American companies were producing the wrong cars, large gas-guzzlers, but they were being outperformed on almost every performance indicator. By the early 1980s the American industry was in crisis.

American car producers reacted by trying to exclude the competitors. The imposition of informal quotas by the government under pressure from the car companies prevented the continuing expansion of imports. The success of this strategy resulted in the Japanese invasion changing its nature. It moved from product exports to FDI, exporting the Japanese method of production and Japanese plant and facili-

ties rather than the car itself. The Japanese continued to take market share but now from the inside and by allying with domestic producers.

Today some markets are relatively open to imports, or at least more open than they were in the past. As a mode of entry, exporting is still an important mechanism, but probably not the most important. The import share is as high 60% in Australia, 47% in Germany and 34% in the USA. Other countries somehow manage to prevent imports.

Both Americans and Europeans reacted by imitating the methods which had made the Japanese enterprises successful, such as just-in-time inventory control, new long-term cooperative relationships with suppliers, lean production, quality circles and outsourcing. In turn, by the mid-1990s some of the Japanese enterprises, such as Nissan, were in trouble. European producers led the way in the premium markets and used their reputation to extend the branding to other markets.

For political reasons, the Japanese decided that it was much easier to engage in FDI. This had the advantage of creating jobs in the USA, not taking them away, and

▶

had much less impact on the American balance of payments, which was seriously in deficit on its trading account. The substitution of direct investment for exporting is common, and often undertaken in order to get in behind the trade barriers created by governments, which sometimes take the form of tariffs and sometimes quotas, whether formal or informal.

Honda built its first American plant in Marysville, Ohio in 1982. It was closely followed by Nissan and Toyota. Other Japanese manufacturers have at different times had plants in the USA but the big three are by far the largest players. The Japanese players have been successful enough in transferring their methods to steadily win market share. Initially the American companies thought that low prices were a result of dumping or poor wages, but quickly discovered otherwise.

The figures tend to leap during recessions when the well-priced Japanese cars have a particular attraction. Toyota is now poised to replace Chrysler as the number three producer in the American car market. Toyota locally manufactures two-thirds of the vehicles it sells in the USA. The overall market share of the three Japanese players, both exports and locally produced, is about 30%. In order to reach its target of two million vehicles sold by 2004, Toyota needs a fifth plant there. It is already talking about a sixth plant.

The big three Japanese producers make half their

profits in the USA. Their activities are far more profitable than those of the American producers. GM makes only \$330 in profit per vehicle, whereas Toyota and Nissan make \$1,000 and Honda even more at \$1,600. One advantage that the Japanese share is that they have avoided Detroit as a venue and therefore kept clear of the United Auto Workers Union and their constraints on efficient production. The most efficient car factory in the world is Nissan's plant at Smyrna, Tennessee.

The Japanese have a competitive advantage in a number of different factors – durability, economy, good servicing and a reputation for reliability. Even the prices of second-hand Japanese cars hold up better than American cars. Japanese companies have won one-third of the saloon car market and 20% of the light truck market (the pickups and SUVS so popular in the USA), despite a late entry. They are gaining in the luxury market. The American market is the most competitive in the world.

Japanese strategy is more long term in its orientation. The Japanese have deliberately limited fleet sales to car-rental companies. This helps avoid a flood of second-hand vehicles coming onto the market. They have also avoided the financial incentives given to purchasers by their American competitors, such as zero-cost finance.

The change of entry mode by the Japanese companies was timely. For example, Toyota went from exports to a joint venture with General Motors to direct investment. This sequence represented a shrewd strategic response to the opposition within the USA to imports and the need to learn how to use the Toyota model in a new context.

Table 15.6 **Percentage of total vehicle production in the USA which is Japanese**

1983	1985	1987	1989	1991	1993	1995	1997	1999	2001
1	3	5	9	15	15	17	18	17	19

Country-specific assets and enterprise-specific assets

Traditionally the explanation by economists of patterns of foreign trade or investment has been in terms of country-specific assets, that is, assets which are fixed in their location. An alternative approach is to explain the patterns of trade or investment in terms of enterprise-specific assets, which are more mobile than country-specific assets.

Country-specific assets

For trade, the chief theory was based on comparative advantage and differing resource endowments, principally the different factors of production – land or resources, labour and capital; in other words, a supply-based explanation. A country exported those products which it produced relatively more efficiently or cheaply. It was assumed that availability of a factor was simply translated into cost. The relative price of the factor reflected the relative supply. Some countries were resource-rich and labour-poor, others were capital-rich and resource-poor. The former would tend to export resource-intensive products and the latter capital-intensive products.

It was further assumed that most resources were immobile, which, while not fully true, is a close enough description of the situation throughout most of human history, and even today. Certainly natural resources and land are by their nature immobile. In theory people and capital can move. Financial capital is extremely mobile, but when translated into physical capital – buildings, plant and equipment – is largely immobile.

Some labour and an increasing amount of financial capital have always moved across international boundaries but most factors can be assumed to be immobile, even most of the physical capital which has been created over the years. In such a world of relative factor immobility, trade not only reflected the distribution of the factors, it also served to move factor prices more closely together. The export of resource-intensive products raised the price of land or resources in countries above what it would otherwise have been. The export of labour-intensive products would have had the same effect on countries well endowed with labour, raising the price of their labour. In theory, if carried far enough, this would have raised the incomes of those countries to the level of countries with the highest level of incomes. The movement of commodities can substitute for the movement of capital or people.

The traditional picture, which held up to World War II, was that the developed world, the core or metropolis, exported initially labour-intensive and later capital-intensive products, while the developing world, the periphery, exported resource-intensive products. As wages rose in the developed world, labour-intensive products moved their point of origin from the manufacturing centre to the periphery where there was more labour. The core initially exported manufactured goods and imported raw materials and foodstuffs, and the periphery exported raw materials and foodstuffs and imported manufactured goods. Later, some parts of the labour-rich periphery, such as East Asia, began to export labour-intensive products, complicating but not really changing the main pattern of trade.

The driving force behind the expansion of trade since 1945 has moved from the distribution of immobile, country-specific assets, but the pattern explained by the location of these assets still persists. Today there may be an echo of the pattern above in the product cycle in which a given country moves, with a specific pattern of dominant exports and imports according to its changing factor endowment – initially resource abundance, then labour abundance and finally capital abundance. Development frees the country from such constraints, as the export of high-tech products and services becomes important. The different countries of East Asia are at different stages in this cycle. They are moving through such a product cycle, which ceases when the economy reaches the high-tech stage, at which point factor endowment ceases to drive the trade or investment flows.

Enterprise-specific assets

In the pre-1945 world, most foreign investment flows were in some way related to these endowments. Where agricultural conditions or mineral deposits created the possibility of significant exports, foreign investment often helped to provide the facilities to promote the exports, financing the mines or plantations, the transport facilities linking them to the coast and the harbours from which they could be shipped. Investment flowed to the resources, just as labour flowed in the same direction, provided there was not an already dense population, hostile climate or disease environment. Equally, where labour was already abundant, capital would flow in to exploit this abundance.

The situation changed after World War II, but perhaps not as dramatically as the theoretical literature would have the reader believe. Over time, immobile natural resources or assets have declined in relative importance, particularly as determinants of the patterns of both international trade and investment. As technical change has reduced the need for such inputs in production, their importance has declined. A ton of steel requires much less in the way of inputs of iron ore, coal or limestone than was true 100 years ago. Steel itself is much less important as a construction material. The importance of services which do not require such inputs of raw material has risen greatly.

Created assets rather than natural assets now help to determine the patterns of foreign trade and investment. Created assets include the whole range of tangible assets which are mobile such as equipment and skilled people, but also intangible assets such as organizational know-how, technical knowledge and marketing expertise. For an enterprise, its combination of resources, in particular the range of patents, trademarks and brand names it holds, are far more important than access to raw materials.

For that reason, theories of the pattern of trade and investment based on countries and their different endowments have been replaced by theories based on enterprises and their different endowments. The trade of any country was always generated by the trade of many individual enterprises, although often the role of the enterprise was largely ignored. As a consequence of the recent change in perspective and the rising importance of created assets, the emphasis in explaining trade and investment has shifted to the role of the enterprise and the created assets which it holds. Supply-based explanations are giving way to demand-based explanations, that is, explanations based on the need to meet the tastes of consumers with rising discretionary income and the associated product differentiation.

Financial capital has become highly mobile, initially going to the less developed countries but now more often to developed economies. However, FDI is rapidly becoming more important than portfolio investment as a significant generator of economic development. A simple explanation of the location of economic production, in terms of the input of the basic factors of production, is inadequate to explain today's patterns of international trade and investment. For example, trade and investment in Africa can be explained in the old way, but not the trade and investment of the triad or other rapidly developing areas. Any adequate explanation has to refer to the locational explanation and one based on the created assets of enterprises. Technological expertise and organizational know-how have become a major source of advantage.

Location is not irrelevant, as the growing literature on clusters shows. Enterprises wish to capitalize on locational advantages, for example to exploit the advantages of agglomeration in the computer software industry in Ireland, as the Strategy in

Action on the celtic tiger in Chapter 5 shows. They also wish to preserve their created assets. There is a monopoly element in both. Competitive advantage results from a creative blend of location and created assets. The key to success is to be able to spot the creative combinations which offer most in meeting consumer wants, and to use the mode of entry which makes the most of these combinations in sustaining a competitive advantage in the market segments. From a strategic perspective, it is necessary to consider both sets of factors in determining a preferred mode of entry into foreign markets.

Strategy in Action 1. Disney and a tale of three cultures

Everything that Disney undertook seemed to be marked by success. This applied to the theme parks as well as Disney's other areas of commercial interest, developed earlier. Disney had successfully opened up theme parks in the USA, in California and Florida. It had also extended the model to Tokyo in Japan with great success. Could the model be applied throughout the world? The moment had come to enter the European market. Disney was confident of success. The projections of attendance and profits confidently anticipated that the new theme park near Paris would break even within a year and would repeat the success of the other theme parks.

Disneyland, established at Anaheim in Los Angeles in 1955 and Disney's first theme park, was an offshoot of Disney's successful film enterprises. It allowed those who had enjoyed the whole range of Disney characters, from Mickey Mouse to Goofy, to reacquaint themselves with their favourites. This was a successful initiative since the theme parks came to generate a majority of Disney's income. The park was very much in the Disney mould of family entertainment, wholesome but fantastic. It took full advantage of the Disney brand name.

However, Disney made a significant mistake in Disneyland at Anaheim. The company only owned the land on which the theme park and its car parks were located. Consequently it had no control over the sprawl of hotels and motels which were built around it and diminished its image, undermining the wholesomeness and the fantasy element. Nor were the profits made from the attendance fees comparable with those made from the businesses in the vicinity.

As a response to this, when the plans were laid for Disney World in Florida, which eventually opened in 1971, they included the purchase of a huge tract of undeveloped land outside Orlando, 28,000 acres in all, enough to hold a multitude of hotels and amusement parks. Disney attempted to coordinate much better its activities and vertically integrate in order to capture the profit made by others. The aim was to cater for all the needs of visitors, including accommodation, entertainment during the evenings and food.

Disney was successful in its general aim, but not fully. Despite the fact that it built three hotels with over 2,000 rooms, hotel chains, like Hyatt and Hilton, still located themselves just outside the Disney-owned area.

Michael Eisner, who became CEO in 1984, used three strategies to increase the revenue from Disney World:

1. Increase the price. He discovered that the price elasticity of demand was low. The entrance price was raised 45% in just two years, with a resulting 59% growth in revenue, the price increase generating as much as 94% of the total earnings growth.
2. Add attractions and rides to the existing park, and add theme parks. For example, the Disney-MGM Park opened in 1989. The existing infrastructure could serve a much wider set of facilities.
3. Try to capture more of the money spent by visitors on shopping and night-time entertainment by building nightclubs and restaurants on site and by running the food concessions in the park. Disney entered the hotel business, although usually with partners who helped to finance the hotels.

Having successfully established the business model in the USA, the next obvious step was to open a theme park abroad. Disney chose Tokyo as the venue, which turned out to be a very shrewd choice. The Japanese were benefiting from a significant rise in both leisure and income. The park took five years to plan and was opened in 1983. Initially there were some difficulties and the need for some adjustments: the weather made it necessary to put most activities indoors and cover walkways, and there was a need for translators.

However, visitor targets were exceeded and quickly came up to American standards. The park became profitable very quickly. The initial investment of ¥180 billion or US$1.5 billion was recouped in just four years.

By 2002, 25 million people had visited Tokyo Disneyland, about one-fifth of Japan's population. Whereas visitors to Disney theme parks elsewhere in the world have tended to be tourists, in Japan they are locals. Something like 95% are 'repeaters', mainly from the metropolitan Tokyo area. Visitors spent more than had been anticipated, including admission, something like ¥9,600 per person or more than $90.

Overall, the Tokyo park has been a resounding success, more so than other Disney theme parks. This was by no means assured as the rather chequered history of other theme parks in Japan has shown, with some three-quarters of them struggling. More or less the same business model had been applied by Disney with success, although in hindsight it is clear that Disney did not fully anticipate or understand the success factors which were important in Japan. That success bred a confidence about further expansion. The next obvious move was into Europe.

Strategy in Action 2. The trials of Euro Disney

'Euro Disney developed a core strategy and culture of Disney, and then had to work to Europeanise its theme park.'
  CEO Bourguignon (quoted in Hitt et al., 2001: 305).

Two European countries competed for Disney's new theme park, France and Spain. Disney enlisted the support of the French government by stressing the beneficial results in increased tourism and employment but kept as a background threat the Spanish city of Barcelona.

The French government made an offer Disney could not refuse, firstly to purchase 51% of the shares and organize their sale on the market. It dangled very attractive tax breaks and sold Disney 4,800 acres in a prime location only 30 kilometres from Paris, at a price equivalent to 1971 agricultural prices. The French government also contributed necessary infrastructure, extending highways, subways and railway lines to the site in Marne la Vallee, building a station on the high-speed train route opposite the park entrance. The location appealed to Disney. Apart from the proximity of Paris, the main tourist city in Europe, the park was accessible by visitors from a number of Western European countries.

The Disney management appeared to have done everything right in the lead up to the opening of the theme park on April 12, 1992. They succeeded in completing phase 1 of the detailed plan the day before the opening, including the theme park, six hotels with a total of 5,200 rooms, a convention centre, a golf course, and 32 nightclubs, bars and restaurants. The construction, a mammoth organizational effort, had taken five years. By 1992 something approaching $3 billion had been invested, by any standards a major commitment of resources. They also had in mind the start of construction of phase 2, a film studio and a second theme park, by the end of 1993, and at one stage even a third park for the beginning of the new century.

Yet, after an initially good start (in 1993 attendance at one million per month made the resort Europe's most popular paid tourist destination), attendance rates were disappointing, well below expected levels. The park failed to reach its financial targets. By October 1993, the park had lost Fr1.5 million. The reaction was to retrench.

What were the reasons for the difficulties? On the basis of an already successful business model, Disney made a series of wrong assumptions:

- Admission prices at Euro Disney were about 30% higher than at Disney World, food prices as much as twice as high, hotel rates, at $200–300 a night, well above the rates available near the other theme parks. Early strategy in the USA had been to raise an initially low price level. In the early years, satisfied customers 'talked up' the parks. By contrast the price for Euro Disney started high and the park was consequently 'talked down'.

- Disney was ignorant of the vacation habits of Europeans. The typical holiday in Europe is 4–6 weeks as against 1–2 weeks in the USA, but the total expenditure on the holiday was about the same. Disney had anticipated that guests would stay on average four nights at their three hotels. It turned out to be two, partly because of the high costs of hotel accommodation and partly because there were initially only 15 rides in the park, as compared with 45 at the inception of Disney World.
- Eating and drinking habits were different. Disney had planned for all-day grazing at the park, as happened in the USA and Japan. European eating habits were different. Visitors looked for a dinner at noon, putting unsustainable pressure on the eating facilities. They were used to eating bread and cheese and drinking wine, compared with the usual fare of burgers, fries and coke.
- Purchases of merchandise at the souvenir shops was at a lower level than anticipated, not surprising since the money was going on the basics of entrance, accommodation and food. Many fewer high-margin items such as T-shirts or hats were bought.

The result was expenditure per visitor well below the expected level. The times were not auspicious, with recession in Europe. Devaluation of a number of neighbouring countries' exchange rates raised the relative value of the franc to levels which implied prices for foreign visitors well above those anticipated. This reinforced the feeling that prices were excessively high.

A graphic phrase applied to the theme park, a 'cultural Chernobyl', encapsulated a further problem. There was a backlash against the American nature of the park. The press argued that it was a prime example of American cultural imperialism, certainly unlikely to be accepted by the French, and probably not by other Europeans.

Disney recognized the validity of some of these argu-ments since within months of the opening they replaced the American CEO of Euro Disney, Robert Fitzpatrick, by a Disney insider of French origin, Philippe Bourguignon. The replacement was seen as a move from an American style of management to a European style. Fitzgerald had already prefaced the 1992 annual report: 'that looking at the future, Euro Disney had two primary objectives: to achieve profitability as quickly as possible, and to better integrate Euro Disney into its European environment while reinforcing our greatest asset – our Disney heritage'. The view of the new CEO was that Disney should, as a matter of priority, adapt to its European environment and in so doing create a unique combination of the Disney tradition and the expectations of its European customers.

It was easy to lower charges. The number of attractions could easily be increased. More attention was paid to the provision of European-style food. The ban on the consumption of alcohol in Disney theme parks was lifted in order to allow the French and others to consume wine in the park restaurants. In advertising there was much less reference to the USA. The celebration of public holidays was orientated towards Europe and not the USA. Off-season charges were introduced. There was more emphasis on attracting groups or tours since they turned out to represent a larger proportion of the visitors in Europe. There was less emphasis on the traditional American way of individual family visits.

Disney had to accommodate an employment regime hostile to low wages and long hours of work. Employees had trouble with the 'Disney Look' and the shortage of accommodation in the local area. The mass lay-offs in the early period encouraged a high turnover of staff.

By the early 2000s Disneyland Paris was at last beginning to deliver. Disney turned its attention to establishing a theme park in Hong Kong, which it hoped would repeat the success of Japan. Somewhat later in 2002 they also reached an agreement in principle to establish a further park in Shanghai.

Internalization

Intellectual property rights

The mode of entry tends to reflect a need for the enterprise to protect those assets which are the major source of profit. The increasing emphasis on created assets has underpinned a focus on the intellectual property rights held by an enterprise, such as patents, trademarks, copyrights, and even organizational know-how of a more specific kind, and the need of the enterprise to protect these rights. The loss of its intellectual property is a serious threat to an enterprise. Ownership is meaningless if the rights cannot be defended. This is not an easy task. Such protection appears to require a strong legal system and enforceable contractual obligations. The existence of separate legal systems, poor enforcement of property rights and the weakness of international law make this protection deficient.

Only those countries which have a significant accumulation of intellectual property rights to exploit have an interest in protecting those rights. As a consequence, they tend to push this need strongly. Others, since they possess very few intellectual property rights, have an interest in the abuse of others' property rights and regularly do so. At the very least they ignore the flouting of these rights by their citizens, whatever the existing law may appear to show. They are willing to pass laws to protect the rights but are either often unable or unwilling to enforce those laws. This is a reality which has to be confronted when deciding on a mode of entry.

There are various strategies for avoiding such abuse. One may be to choose to license or franchise, seeking relatively low royalties or licence fees, in order to render abuse unprofitable but guarantee at least some revenue. This implies accepting the situation. If there is great difficulty in preventing pirating of copyright, this may be the only realistic strategy.

If the legal system or the nature of the intellectual property is not a sufficient protection and if a company is unwilling to grant licences at very low returns, what alternative method of protection is there for the enterprise? Where the intellectual property is not so easily copied, the most common protective mechanism is a strategy of internalization.

Taking transactions out of the market

Internalization describes a situation in which transactions are taken out of the market and placed within an enterprise – they are internalized. This is increasingly the case at both domestic and international levels. As shown in Chapter 11, it is extremely difficult to write contracts which spell out in detail all the contingencies which relate to the use of intellectual property rights, and even more difficult to persuade courts to enforce the contracts if they are worth enforcing. It is easy for others to backward (reverse) engineer and copy with enough variation to satisfy a court that the product or process is different. Dependence on market transactions is often a high-risk strategy.

Certain kinds of market relations clearly expose the nature of the intellectual property and thereby make that property publicly available. For example, any system of licensing immediately opens the enterprise to the possible entry of a competitor or the release of knowledge previously a source of competitive advantage. Even some forms of investment may be vulnerable to abuse, for example engagement in joint ventures in which the partner is given access to previously guarded knowledge. There is a clear asymmetry in the degree of exposure of property rights to abuse in the different entry modes. Exporting or licensing create a major vulnerability which direct investment does not. However, joint ventures are also vulnerable.

Another problem relates to asymmetrical investment, that is, to the vulnerability to opportunism created by committing many more resources to a series of transactions than a partner. This is a particular danger for an enterprise from a developed economy with a partner from a developing one. This may expose the enterprise to opportunistic behaviour exploiting that situation. It may even invite such opportunism if the contrast is striking. Who gets the most out of a partnership of any kind? It is difficult to prevent a partner exploiting intellectual property rights, even copying technology.

In order to try to avoid these problems, at least the worst of them, and still operate with a system of market-based contracts, the enterprise may be forced to incur a level of transaction costs which is relatively high. These costs would include efforts to:

- find suitable partners who will not exploit the situation
- write contracts which include all possible contingencies
- ensure enforcement, through periodic resort to the courts, government bodies or third parties.

The resulting costs may be much higher than incurred if the transactions are internalized in some way, that is, they occur within the enterprise, between its subsidiaries. There is still a danger of opportunistic behaviour as staff with valuable knowledge are tempted to leave and set up independently, but this is much less likely to occur. There may be good reasons for preferring FDI which internalizes the international transactions within the enterprise, making it much easier to maintain secrecy on the exact nature of the intellectual property and avoid the high transaction costs of using the market. Internalization is a method of protecting all the sources of competitive advantage which reside in created assets. When created assets are more important than locational assets, it creates a strong predisposition to favour the mode of entry involving direct investment. This partly explains the rising relative importance of direct investment as a mode of entry.

The nature of a world (global) enterprise

Strategy in Action SingTel and its Asia Pacific role

Lee Hsien Yang, the present CEO and son of Lee Kuan Yew, has been steadily making SingTel the region's first truly pan-Asian telecom company. Until 2000 the Singapore government, through its holding company Temasek, owned 80% of SingTel. Today that ownership is down to 67.5%, and the government's intention is to take it down further.

In April 1997 Mobile One (M1), backed internationally by Cable & Wireless of the UK and its subsidiary Hong Kong Telecoms, was allowed to enter the domestic mobile phone market. Prices went down by as much as 50–70%, the quality and range of ser-

vices improved significantly and the rate of mobile penetration rose from only 14% to 41%. In just two years, M1 won 32% of the mobile phone market. In 1998 two further licences for mobile phone services were issued. In April 2000 Star Hub, supported internationally by British Telecom and Nippon Telecom and Telegraph, was allowed to enter the fixed-line market. It aimed to be 'the first info-communications company in Asia Pacific to offer total convergence of fixed and mobile communications on a simple, integrated platform'. All licence winners were consortia of companies comprising at least one government-linked corporation, but usually also an international company.

This internal competition compelled SingTel to take an international role in order to retain its own competitiveness, despite facing the specific challenges of:

- How to deal with an interventionist government
- How to remain competitive within a small domestic market with powerful international players
- How to enter and take advantage of the global market, notably the rapidly growing Asian market
- What partners, if any, to take.

There are marked differences between Singapore and other Asian countries (Table 15.7).

Singapore's domestic telecommunications environment is closer to that of a developed economy than most of Asia, in which there were a number of important trends:

1. A strong emphasis on telecommunications infrastructure development by most governments
2. A strong growth of fixed-line and mobile telecommunications networks
3. Acceleration of deregulation and privatization
4. Increased competition from Western telecommunications companies
5. A typical concession/licensing period of 25 years within the build, operate, transfer model (BOT)
6. A strong demand for debt and equity capital to finance expansion
7. Industry rationalization through mergers and acquisitions
8. Upgrading of telecommunications technology, with a significant pricing impact.

The CEO of British Telecom has been quoted as predicting that Asia, which now has only 22% of the world telco market, will within 10 years account for 60%. Recently China has been adding each year as many new telephone lines as are already available in the whole of Switzerland. In Singapore there are already over 50 fixed lines per 100 people, over 40 mobiles and nearly 40 pagers, the latter two well above the average levels for developed economies. SingTel might have an important role to play in infrastructure-poor Asian countries, aspiring to be 'a total service provider with a range that covers the entire spectrum of the telecom business'.

At first SingTel invested in Thailand, Vietnam and Sri Lanka. As its ambitions rose, it quickly shifted its attention, trying to compete in the developed economies of England and Western Europe, and investing in cable television and mobile communications. This proved unprofitable. SingTel failed to achieve its general target of a 15–20% share of total sales accounted for by foreign ventures. Within five years it had disposed of most of these early ventures.

The usual mode of entry is an alliance with a local player, simultaneously buying a minority equity interest. SingTel refocused on the Asia Pacific region, investing:

- S$47.1 million in PT Bukaka Singapore Telecom International in Indonesia, which operates fixed-line telephone services
- S$339 million in 23.6% of Globe Telecom, the number two telecom operator in the Philippines, providing mobile phone, international and fixed-line services (March 1993)
- S$930 million in 12.2% of Belgacom, Belgium's leading telecom player (the only AA rated European telco left) (December 1995)
- S$869.7 million in 21.53% of Advanced Info Services, the number one mobile telephone operator in Thailand (January 1999)
- S$615 million in 24.3% of New Century Infocomm, a fixed-line operator in Taiwan (March 2000)
- S$1.15 billion in 31.5% of the Bharti Group of India's Bharti Tele-ventures (August 2000)
- S$55.6 million in the switched and lease-back services of AAPT and in September 2001, S$15 billion in the purchase of Optus, the second fixed-line and mobile communications provider in Australia, from Cable & Wireless, at fifty times Optus's earnings.

Table 15.7   A comparison of Singapore and Asia

Asia	Singapore
Extremely low tele-density	High tele-density
Low quality and availability of fixed-line services	High quality and availability
High concentration of residential users	Same
Less demand for specialized features	High demand
High vulnerability to credit risk	Low vulnerability
High regulated tariffs	Falling tariffs

It holds 35% of Telkomsel in Indonesia. In 1999 SingTel began an equity joint venture with KDD, Japan's largest international telecommunications operator, to integrate their respective services. It holds a 60% stake in CZC AsiaPac, a company building one of the first private submarine cable systems.

SingTel is carrying a heavy load of debt, some S$9.3 billion (US$5.2 billion), allegedly the result of the ill-timed and overly generous purchase of Optus. Company profits have been declining and the share price falling. SingTel has accumulated some US$30 billion of assets over 1996–2001. It is conservative in its accounting practices, which means that its profit position is rather better than it appears, relative to other telcos. The company has expanded from 1.5 million mobile customers in Singapore in 1997 to 25 million in Asia in 2002. Its national revenues are now 5.8% of its total revenues, 54% of which are already from mobiles and data transfer. Market penetration in SingTel's markets is low – 23% in Thailand, 16% in the Philippines, 5% in Indonesia and 1% in India. The companies in which it has invested, market leaders with the potential to grow quickly from US$2 billion to US$5–6 billion companies, are moving quickly. Bharti has moved from 300,000 mobile customers in August 2000 to 2 million in 2002.

In a global world it is reasonable to expect to find many global enterprises. These would be enterprises which could easily enter the economies and markets of different countries. International entry would be as easy or as difficult as domestic entry today. This is not the case; genuinely global enterprises are rare. There are good reasons why this is true, not least because the world is not global in the sense indicated in Chapter 3.

The world is far from this state, but reference to such a world helps the observer to understand the nature of a global enterprise. A global enterprise is one which would act as if such a world were its venue, severing its links with any particular country, whether the country of origin or the country of greatest activity. In the process the enterprise would shed any home country bias. This is much easier to achieve if the domestic market in the country of origin is small. On the other hand, a large domestic market encourages home country bias; the larger the home market, the greater tends to be the bias.

First, it is necessary to define a global enterprise, as the terminology at present is confusing. Management theorists (Bartlett and Ghoshal, 1989) have defined multidomestic, global and transnational enterprises in a rather special way, making difficult the use of clear and consistent labels. Commonly there is a distinction made between a multidomestic strategy, a global strategy and a transnational strategy (see for example Hitt et al., 2001: 331–4). This is based on the growing primacy of the customer, with his or her wants, and hence the nature of a marketing strategy.

In this account the following definitions are made:

- A *multidomestic strategy* is one in which strategic and operating decisions are decentralized to the strategic business unit in each country in order to customize to the domestic markets which are assumed to differ according to the local cultures.
- A *global strategy* is one in which standardized products are offered to all potential customers, across country markets. Here the marketing strategy is dictated by the home headquarters.
- A *transnational strategy* is one which seeks to achieve both global efficiency and local responsiveness, a difficult task, one combining the benefits of product differentiation with the benefits of low costs. The slogan, 'think globally, act locally' is best understood in this context. One way of combining the strengths of the different

strategies is to simultaneously brand at the world and local level, as Nestlé has sought to do (see the Strategy in Action below).

This use of terminology would leave the term world enterprise for what is often called a global enterprise, that is, an enterprise which has completely transcended all national boundaries. There are as yet no such enterprises, largely because the world is far from the global world defined above. Using the terminology employed earlier, it might be better to use the term transnational rather than global enterprise, if we wish to use the terms in a way familiar to management theorists. However, the term global is more commonly used in everyday discourse.

Characteristics of a global enterprise

The following are the main characteristics of a world (global) enterprise:

- It may have its headquarters in one country but this may not be the country of origin but is chosen for reasons of convenience or efficiency. However, inertia may leave the headquarters in the country of origin.
- It may have production or service facilities all over the world but with no particular concentration of facilities in any one country, least of all the country of origin. Both turnover and assets will be distributed widely. The global enterprise will have an elaborate logistical system, involving a complex international value-adding chain and significant intra-enterprise transfers across national boundaries.
- It is likely to have a presence in all the major markets, notably the triad markets and the fastest growing developing economies such as China, Brazil and India, if only to pre-empt the domination of important markets by competitors.
- It will be engaged in generating FDI flows and be in the process of building significant FDI stocks across the world.
- It will generate most of its profits outside the original home economy, the proportion varying with the business conditions in different areas of the world.
- It is likely to use for internal communication, and often for external negotiation and contact, the universal business language of English.
- It will have a cosmopolitan management team recruited solely on the basis of ability to do the job, and not on the basis of country of origin.
- It is likely to have a distinctive corporate culture, one developed to suit its global nature and offset the natural home country bias.
- It will hold a considerable portfolio of intellectual property rights, which is the basis of the significant benefits to be derived from internalization and a rationale for the very existence of such large global enterprises.

A world enterprise is one which makes the world its venue, severing its links with one particular country. In the process it sheds any home country bias.

Absence of global enterprises

Large multinational enterprises do not conform to this picture. The world's largest engineering conglomerates illustrate the point. In 1999 General Electric, a company which has stressed its own international orientation, had located abroad only 44% of its sales, 35% of its assets and just one-third of its profits. In the same year, the figures for a similar type of Japanese company, Hitachi, were 30%, 17%, but rather higher at 69% for profits since the Japanese market was at the time relatively depressed (Whittington, 2001: 27). The GE figures are typical of the largest enterprises. The title of an article by Y. S. Hu in the *California Management Review* (1992) summarizes the position well; such enterprises are not so much global enterprises as *national firms with international operations*.

Those who support the risk-managing role of diversification are surprised that there is such a bias, particularly in investment. Others feel no surprise at all. In the words of Richard Whittington (2001: 90): 'the great puzzle remains about FDI: why do it at all? Rather than go to all the trouble, risk and expense of setting up and managing manufacturing operations in a strange country, why not export?'

Home country bias

The strong benefits of internalization suggest why multinational companies engage in foreign direct investment. However, offsetting the influence of internalization is the existence of a powerful home country bias. The reason why genuinely global enterprises are rare is linked to the notion of home country bias, which was discussed in Chapter 3 and referred to above. A global enterprise by definition frees itself from such a bias.

The concept of country risk is useful in explaining the lack of a global orientation. It embraces a whole range of factors which deter foreign involvement and encourage a home country bias. These are factors which must be taken into account in any global strategy.

A sense of losing control is implicit in political risk to which an enterprise is exposed when it engages in foreign investment, unless the country concerned has political and economic systems and a culture and social system similar to that of the country of origin. Regional organizations such as the European Union can only arise and remain integrated with basic similarities in these areas, a fact which explains the hesitation to admit Turkey. In their absence the differences predominate. Ignorance or lack of information is one factor which is highly relevant to a home country bias. It is expensive to gain the required information in order to dissipate such ignorance.

Transaction costs rise with the 'distance' between any two countries. They might have their origin in geographical distance or cultural distance. It is always helpful to have a home government ready to back you up in negotiations and bargaining. There is a nervousness which is fully justified if, for example, the legal system does not protect intellectual property rights or foreign governments are apt to favour their own, as is usually the case.

The bias may be reducing but not in a steady manner. There are major cycles. The occurrence of major risk-generating events, such as the terrorist attacks of September 11, 2001 in New York or October 12, 2002 in Bali, tends to increase the bias, if only in the short term. It may temporarily interrupt a tendency to reduced bias which appears so powerful that it obscures the natural biases which have prevailed throughout history.

The strength of home country bias explains why global enterprises are rare. At the root of home country bias is the 'systemic' nature of strategy itself, the fact that strategy differs from one culture and political/economic system to another. Enterprises become expert is making strategy for a particular kind of economic system.

Despite the growing homogeneity of culture in the world, there are still pronounced differences. The very meaning of strategy differs from one society to another. It is extremely difficult to operate effectively in different cultural and political contexts, to change the strategic approach accordingly and with the subtlety required. Such an approach makes heavy demands on the management effectiveness of the enterprise.

An international approach today requires an accommodation to local difference. This is what is often called a transnational approach. A combination of increased stress on product differentiation and market customization makes this desirable. The willingness to pursue such a strategy may quickly disappear if the environment becomes a threatening one and the task perceived as too difficult.

The absence of world enterprises reflects the differentiation of markets in different regions of the world and the growing emphasis on satisfying consumer needs in those local markets. Unless the forces of globalization homogenize the world, there will continue to be very different patterns of demand in different regions. The example of Nestlé described below illustrates one way of reconciling the opposing demands.

Despite the constraints on the emergence of genuinely world enterprises, multinational enterprises do carry out a role of promoting interactions between different countries at the global level. They possess assets which are mobile and can be moved from country to country. These enterprises are beginning to engage in genuinely supranational transactions. They are important agents of increased globalization.

Strategy in Action   Nestlé – a global enterprise?

Nestlé was founded in 1866 in Switzerland. Because of the small size of the domestic Swiss market, it is not surprising that Nestlé, from an early date, sought out international markets for its products. In this and other aspects it is typical of the world's largest enterprises. As the world's largest food company today, it runs a global or transnational strategy, with just a touch of the world strategy about it. In other words, it sells in many international markets, adjusting its marketing to the nature of the different markets. The main growth strategy adopted is to undertake the selling of a handful of strategic brands in emerging markets and then to expand from that base.

As a typical multinational company, Nestlé has the dual requirements of local fit and global scale. In the words of the often quoted adage, 'it thinks globally and acts locally'. Nestlé's self-proclaimed policy is at one and the same time 'to adapt as much as possible to local customs and circumstances ... allowing decisions about products, marketing and personnel to be made at the local level' and to achieve by central activity as many efficiencies as possible. It employs locals and promotes and distributes products in a way suitable to local conditions.

The dual requirement demands a sophisticated attitude to brand management. The policy of brand management illustrates the limitations on a transnational approach. In the words of its CEO Peter Brabeck-Lemathe (www.nestlé.com): 'The Nestlé solution to this challenge [that is, to combine economies of scale from global production with meaningfulness for each consumer] was the establishment of a clear hierarchy of very few corporate strategic brands that now cover almost all our products, as well as the parallel usage of regional and local product brands and product denominations.' Brands are managed at these different levels – international, regional and local, thus recognizing the coexistence of both the transnational and the multidomestic. While the company owns something like 8,500 brands, only 750 of them are registered in more than one country, and only 80 are registered in more than 10 countries. It tries to fit ingredients and processing technology to local conditions and use a brand name which resonates locally.

▶

Nestlé, the largest maker of coffee in the world, produces as many as 200 different types of instant coffee, all developed by its four coffee research stations to have a particular blend of flavour, aroma and colour to suit the consumer tastes in different countries, from the lighter blends which are intended for the USA market to the dark expressos for Latin America. On the grocery shelves of the world there are whole range of names for instant coffee, names like Nescafé, Taster's Choice, Ricore and Ricoffy or for roast or ground coffee Nespresso, Bonka, Zoegas and Louminidis.

How far does Nestlé share the characteristics of a genuinely world enterprise?

- Such an enterprise either has no headquarters or one located according to convenience, efficiency or just plain inertia – Nestlé maintains its headquarters in Switzerland
- It sells in all the most important markets in the world and makes its profits in a significantly large number of countries – Nestlé earns 99% of its US$51 billion sales revenue abroad (1998)
- It internalizes a significant proportion of its international transactions – Nestlé sells products in nearly every country of the world
- It has most of its production capacity widely distributed around a number of different countries – Nestlé operates almost 500 factories worldwide in 76 countries
- It engages in significant foreign direct investment and has a complex and highly international value-adding chain – Nestlé holds 95% of its assets abroad
- It has a cosmopolitan management and worker team – Nestlé employs 225,000 people worldwide, of whom only 3% are Swiss

- It formulates and implements a genuinely global strategy, including a global marketing strategy which exploits global brands – Nestlé produces and sells more than 8,500 products or brands worldwide (38% in Europe, 32% in the Americas and 20% in Africa and Asia)
- It has a global culture – Nestlé has 18 different R&D groups operating in 11 different countries throughout the world
- It uses English as it operating language – Nestlé uses English.

Nestlé is highly decentralized in its management structure, giving considerable autonomy to local units for decision making on price, distribution, marketing and human resource management. There is a kind of matrix structure above this local base using seven strategic business units and five geographical zones. The managers who operate at this upper level come from a variety of countries and typically find themselves working in half a dozen countries during their careers.

One recent event highlights the reassertion of home country bias, even for such a 'global' enterprise. Nestlé decided to put US$100 million into the rescue and reorganization of Swissair on the grounds that Swissair often carried its executives in the course of their business (see the press release on Nestlé's website).

Other enterprises which might qualify as genuinely transnational, or even in part world, enterprises include Asea Brown Boveri, Reuters, Bertelsmann and Citibank. It is striking that all of these have been experiencing difficulties in recent times.

Sources: Hill, 2003: 506–8; Thompson and Strickland, 2003: 209; the Nestlé website www.nestlé.com.

Case Study   Entry into the Chinese automobile industry

Entry into the WTO

China's entry into the World Trade Organization, finally achieved in 2001 after long negotiations with key global players, offers great opportunities to foreign business in the further opening up of China, provided of course the various parts of the agreement are adhered to. The strength of the intent to realize the agreements has yet to be tested.

The impact of the opening up of China will differ significantly from sector to sector. The impact of the entry

on a particular industry can be negative or positive. The automobile industry is one in which the potential impact could be either way. Table 15.8 sets out the main features of the changes as they relate to the vehicle industry.

Tariffs have kept the level of automobile prices high, at least by international standards, and therefore allowed a high level of profits. These profits are now steadily being eroded by competition, lower tariffs and increasing costs. The context in which the present strategies are effective is changing dramatically.

Table 15.8 **Before and after entry into the WTO**

	Before	After
Tariffs	22% in the 1980s, 80–100% in the 1990s	25% by 2006
Input quotas	30,000 vehicles a year allowed for foreign carmakers	Quota to be decreased 20% a year and phased out in 2006
Local content	40% in first year of production, increasing to 60% and 80% in the second and third years	No local content rules to apply
Foreign participation in sales and distribution	Limited to wholesaling through joint ventures and prohibited from consolidating sales organization of importers, joint ventures	Will be allowed to own vehicle wholesale, retail organizations: integrated sales organization permitted by 2006
Auto financing for Chinese customers	Foreign, non-bank financial organizations prohibited from providing finance	Foreign, non-bank financing permitted in selected cities prior to gradual national rollout

In 2002 for the first time bank finance was made available for car purchase at an interest rate of 5.3%. This still accounted for only 20% of all passenger car sales, compared with 75% in the USA. Foreigners are not allowed to make such loans.

There is a transitional period during which the economy will be steadily opened up for competition and much freer entry allowed for global producers. The strategy of foreign companies should be designed to suit the conditions at the end of the transition.

The automobile industry in China

So far global automobile manufacturers have conformed to the general pattern of entry into China by means of joint ventures, with one exception. They have sought out good local partners and with their help established assembly plants in China, sourcing components within China where possible but also importing where this has proved absolutely necessary. The situation in 2000 is set out in Table 15.9. Ford established a 50/50 joint venture with Chang'an Automobile Group in 2001 and began production of a model based on the Fiesta in 2002.

The history of entry goes back to the early period of reform. As long ago as 1984, the first joint venture in China occurred between American Motor Corporation (AMC), which later became Chrysler, and later still ChryslerDaimler, and the Beijing Automotive Works (BAW). The agreement was to build a local version of the Jeep, which was well suited to local road conditions. China was the world's biggest potential market of 4WD vehicles because of its rugged landscape, rural-based population and heavy emphasis on agriculture. The brand name, Jeep, was well established in China. The arrangement was that a 40% share of domestic produc-

tion qualified the project as local manufacture and entitled the enterprise to privileged treatment in importing components and exporting foreign exchange.

The initial investment was to amount to $152 million, at that time the largest manufacturing agreement between a foreign corporation and a Chinese enterprise. Initially AMC put in $8 million in cash and $8 million in technology, which entitled it to an ownership stake of 31.35%. BAW put in the equivalent of $35 million in cash and assets, entitling it to the remaining 68.85% ownership stake. AMC intended to reinvest its share of the profits to take its equity stake to 49%. There were to be seven Chinese members on the board of directors and four Americans. For three years the president and CEO were to be Americans and after that the incumbency would alternate.

The aims of the two partners differed, a not unusual situation. The Chinese wished to assimilate best-practice technology in order to create at the global level a leading automobile manufacturer. The Americans wished to use China as a platform for exporting to a rapidly growing region where the demand for automobiles was rapidly rising. Since the Chinese did not view the initial agreement in the same way as the Americans, the real negotiations began only after the initial agreement. There was disagreement over what was to be produced. The Americans wanted to produce the Jeep Cherokee for the civilian market, the Chinese wanted a version for the military market. The actual outcome was a switch to kit assembly rather than the making of cars.

Initial difficulties over foreign exchange led to the temporary closure of the production facility in 1985. A confidential agreement with the Chinese government papered over the cracks. Unknown to AMC, the Chinese government held the agreement up as a 'model joint

Table 15.9 **Joint ventures**

Joint venture	Local partner	Foreign partner	Year	Market share in 2000 (%)
Shanghai-Volkswagen	Shanghai Automobile Industry Corporation SAIC	Volkswagen	1985	35.6
FAW-VW	First Auto Works FAW	Volkswagen	1985	17.8
TAIC	Tianjin Automobile Industry Corporation TAIC	Daihatsu/Toyota	1987	14.9
Dongfen-Citroen	Dongfeng Motor	Citroen	1992	8.9
Chang'an Suzuki	Chang'an Automobile	Suzuki	1993	8.9
Shanghai GM	SAIC	GM	1998	5.0
Guangzhou Honda	Guangzhou Auto Group	Honda	1998	4.9
Beijing Jeep	Beijing Automobile Industry Group	DaimlerChrysler	1984	1.0

97.0

Chinese firms accounted for the other 3%
FAW 2.0%, others 1%

venture'. The arrangement continued after Chrysler acquired AMC in 1987. For Chrysler its share of the income from the Beijing Jeep Company (BJC) was one-tenth of 1% of its total worldwide sales, hardly a major part of its activity.

The Beijing Jeep sold well in the 1980s, but the factory, which had a productive capacity of 80,000, only ever turned out 10,000 units. Sales have declined to only a few hundred vehicles each month. The company has been making losses and losing market share. It had become used to preferential treatment on tariffs and foreign exchange and finds the recent competitive environment difficult to deal with. The loss of position is not surprising. Private purchase is rising in significance, with a more demanding customer. With the improvement of the road system, there is also an increased demand for compacts and subcompacts. BJC's plant is old, its models outdated and its workforce bloated. It needs to update both technology and models. The introduction of the Grand Cherokee would help. Not unexpectedly the joint partners want to get permission to drop the Jeep and move into production of a compact passenger car.

On the figures currently quoted, Volkswagen still dominates automobile production in China and has done so from the beginning. Since it entered China with the Santana in 1985, it has accounted for over half of passenger cars produced. It has established a dominant position in the market, but one which is under increasing pressure. It has a brand name second to none and is probably making a return on investment in the region of 20%. After Germany, China is VW's next largest market. In 2000 Volkswagen held 54.5% of the market for locally produced cars, but by 2002 this had slipped to the lower 40s. It was the major supplier to the taxi market, most taxis being either Santanas or Jettas. However, its Santana model, on which its dominance has been based, is losing its appeal. VW has added the Polo and the Jetta in an effort to be more competitive. However, the positive side is that the sales of the Group's cars have been rising rapidly, by 19% in 2001, which is still much lower than the growth rate of the total market of 39%, and by a phenomenal 50% in 2002, still lower than the market growth of 60%.

Volkswagen now produces six brands in China, across the whole spectrum of the Chinese market for vehicles, except in the high-growth sub-Rmb100,000 segment, a gap which it plans to fill in 2003. Volkswagen's bigger difficulty is making its partnerships work as effectively as it would like. It needs to cut its parts procurement costs by at least 30% and try to get the same suppliers to serve both partners. It also sees a need to raise its local content, probably from 40% to somewhere between 75 and 80%.

VW had some difficulties. It has had trouble with its partner, the Shanghai Automobile Industry Corporation (SAIC), since it discovered that Chery, an Anhui-based and Anhui-government majority-owned firm, in which SAIC has a 20% stake and which produces a rival model, has been illegally using original Volkswagen parts. This particular problem of conflicting interest has been resolved.

A similar type of problem has arisen for General Motors. SAIC Chery has produced a new car, the QQ model, which has a clear resemblance to a GM model, the Chevrolet Spark, made by one of GM's Chinese joint ventures.

Volkswagen's two Chinese partners, SAIC and FAW, see each other as rivals and are unlikely to work together in assisting Volkswagen.

To defend its position in China, VW is introducing four new models in 2003. It is investing €3 billion over the next five years, in new facilities and in upgrading existing plant. It aims to broaden and deepen its participation in sales, marketing and the building of dealership networks and retail outlets, with a stronger emphasis on brand building. It is hoping to enter the field of financing car purchase. It has been systematically training Chinese staff in Germany. In all of this it faces fierce competition.

The competitors

GM is the second largest foreign player, currently accounting for about 9% of all sales. In 1998 General Motors entered the Chinese market, setting up the Shanghai Automobile Manufacturing Company in Shanghai and investing $1.5 billion. The plant had a capacity of 100,000 units. The main model is the Buick. It is a 50/50 joint venture with SAIC. The aim was to produce 40% of the value of the vehicle with Chinese labour and parts in the first year, 60% in the second and 80% in the third.

Honda is the third largest seller, accounting for about 5.5% of all sales. It has created the first foreign full-service dealership chain. Honda is the first to build a plant designed for exporting. This plant in Guangzhou will be complete by 2004, and will export 50,000 vehicles to Europe and Asia. The government allowed Honda to take a 65% stake in the plant, above the usual 50%.

Different strategies are creeping in. The main alternative to the existing system is to license a Chinese firm to produce a vehicle on your behalf.

Toyota, a late entrant compared with the players discussed above, experimented with this strategy in its initial entry into China. It built up a relationship with Tianjin Xiali, a subsiduary of TAIC. In 2000 it licensed Tianjin Xiali to produce a car under the Chinese firm's marque, a car which was based on the Toyota Platz/Vitz compact (known as the Toyota Echo in the USA). Toyota derived its revenue from the licence. Toyota oversaw production and built up Tianjin's ability to meet Toyota's exacting standards. The takeover of Tianjin Xiali by FAW changed the strategy. The next move was a joint venture between FAW and Toyota to build a completely new model, to be sold under the Toyota brand name. Toyota has only 5% of the Chinese market which it has mainly serviced by imports. However, it has invested $1.3 billion since 1998 and aims to double its market share by 2010. Its plant in Tianjin has a capacity of only 100,000, but Toyota is planning a second much larger plant in 2005. The Vios Sedan has a backlog of orders of 16,000 and is a smash hit at the low price of $13,300.

Toyota is trying to introduce the Toyota Way into China, just as it did in the USA. It is building a workforce which is young, at an average of 21, and deliberately choosing to rely heavily on manual assembly.

Nissan already has a licensing agreement with an affiliate of Dongfeng Fengshen Automobile Company to produce the Bluebird. It considers China so important that it has a dedicated division, on a par with the divisions relating to Japan and the USA. The linchpin of the company's strategy is to set up a joint venture with Donfeng Automobile Company in Wuhan, with car production beginning in July 2003. It is the first domestic–foreign joint venture to have a full vehicle production line. The Bluebird, Sunny and Teana luxury cars will carry the Nissan badge, but the commercial vehicles will bear the Donfeng brand. The aim is ambitious – by 2006, 220,000 passenger vehicles and 330,000 commercial vehicles, at first from existing plants. The initial delay was caused by a number of different factors: Nissan's worry concerning Dongfeng's level of existing debt, which is nearly US$4 billion, a desire to have full management control over the joint venture and the wish to have maximum scope to prune the excessive labour force of Donfeng, currently 120,000. Nissan was in competition with France's Peugeot Citroen to be Donfeng's partner.

BMW has been working on a variant of the original Toyota strategy. It has developed a relationship with Brilliance China Automotive. Brilliance hired the Italian design firm Italdesign and its owner Giorgetto Giugiorno to design the Zhong Hua passenger car. BMW assisted Brilliance to build an assembly plant in Shenyang and trained the staff and workers. Provided the project goes well, BMW intends to use the company to build its 3-series and 5-series models for the East Asian market.

Volvo, a Ford subsidiary, has a 50/50 US$70 million agreement with China National Heavy Truck Corporation to set up a manufacturing plant, initially producing 2,000 but moving to 10,000 by 2010, assembling from imported components at first but then moving to source from China. It already imports 1,000 cars into China each year.

The automobile manufacturers are not the only companies entering China. By the end of 2000 every one of the top ten automotive components suppliers had set up shop in China, many were already exporting components to Europe and North America.

For various reasons China is a good place to produce motorcars and many of the components needed in vehicle manufacture. Some of these reasons originate on the demand side. In the developed economies, demand for motorcars is relatively stagnant. In the future most of the increased demand will come from developing countries like Brazil and China, where demand may be growing at around the 10% annual rate. On some accounts, in the next few years China will account for something like 15% of the global demand.

There are also good reasons on the supply side to locate in China. The technologies of manufacture are well known. China has a cheap labour force which is flexible and easy to train. The educational level of the workforce is rising rapidly. In a number of sectors it is obvious what can be done (see the case study on Haier in Part V). The sheer scale of possible output and the degree of specialization would allow costs to be kept down. The experience curve in China is likely to be very steep.

A strategy for entry

It is helpful to consider one aspect of the industry before analysing the different strategies. It is useful to look at where the profits might lie. A comparative breakdown of the global industry and the Chinese industry is illuminating (Table 15.10).

Unsurprisingly, the most profitable part of the global industry, service, is massively underrepresented in China. By contrast, assembly is overrepresented. There is a lack of development in a whole range of activities, such as retail financing, leasing, servicing, repairs, spare parts and retailing itself. For example, at present only 10% of auto sales are financed by credit from the industry.

The other issue relates to the lack of brand names in China. There is a problem of reputation and quality which needs to be solved before the Chinese industry can begin to compete.

The development of any strategy for China must take account of other strategic players, including the Chinese central government and other levels of government. A process of consolidation has been occurring in the highly fragmented Chinese industry, in which there are as many as 120, for the most part small and unprof-

itable, manufacturers with considerable surplus capacity. Since 1999, if not earlier, the Chinese government has encouraged this process of consolidation. The government's goal has been to merge the top 13 producers, who accounted for 92% of output in 1998, into three large conglomerates, grouped around the Changchun FAW, the SAIC and Wuhan's Donfeng Motor Company. However, it is difficult for central government to push through this process of consolidation since provincial and local governments continue to view automobile manufacture as an important source of tax revenue and employment. It is therefore hard to close any facility.

A sign of the times has been the merger between the TAIC and the FAW in 2002, the first big consolidation since the entry of China into the WTO, creating FAW Xiali. TAIC is to sell just over 50% of its listed Tianjin Xiali and its entire 75% holding of Tianjin Huali Auto, a mini-vehicle manufacturer, to FAW, which is China's largest motor group. FAW already employs 160,000 people. One commentator was provoked to say, 'In many ways, First Automobile Group is a barometer in China's future' (Cheng, 2002: 19).

Some have said that FAW is the first state-owned enterprise to make a consistent and significant profit. In 2002 it made a profit of US$253 million on sales of US$5.85 billion. In 2001 it made $337 million on $7.5 billion. This was after the enterprise made losses for most of the 1980s and early 1990s. It claims to have an attitude of 'customer first' rather than 'production first'. However, its link with Volkswagen is what has carried it through. It produces 100,000 Jettas and 30,000 Audis in the joint venture.

FAW has more than 50 subsidiaries, which are run independently. Two of them are already listed on the stock market, First Autoworks Shiquan Autoparts Co. – a component producer – and First Autoworks Passenger Vehicle Co., which manufactures China's only home-grown passenger sedan, The Red Flag. It is not a good advertisement for the company since only 17,000 were manufactured last year and the enterprise is loss making. However, the company has a plan to produce a family car which will sell for only Rmb100,000 (US$12,000). If it is of a good quality, it will have a large potential market.

The more serious problem is the overmanning of the company. On one estimate 70% of the workforce of 160,000 could be laid off in the future. Whereas Toyota produces on average 24 vehicles a day, GM 22, Ford 19 and

Table 15.10 **Sales and profits in different activities in the automobile industry (%)**

100% =	Global automakers, 2000		Chinese automakers, 2000	
	Sales	Profits	Sales	Profits
Service	33	57	12	14
Retail	7	5	8	14
Original equipment manufacturers	21	17	43	46
Suppliers	39	21	37	26

Source: Gao, 2002.

the best of the Chinese competitors, SAIC, a measly 5.7, FAW produces only 2.6.

Somehow the enterprise has to shift from a low salary, high benefits combination typical of any state-owned enterprise to a high salary, low benefits combination, a difficult task. With the range of benefits still being offered – schools, hospitals, sporting and social facilities and pensions – there is no way the enterprise can compete with the large multinationals.

The occasion for FAW's merger with TAIC is the competition coming from Geely, a private company, which is selling two compacts, the Merrie and the Haoqing at prices undercutting the Xiali by more than Rmb10,000. The Xiali has been losing market share. Tianjin Auto has been forced to cut its price and is losing more than Rmb80 million on the vehicle. There is a need to streamline the supply chain.

Such mergers can create enormous problems for the foreign joint enterprise partners. In this case the partners are Volkswagen and Toyota. The joint enterprises are competing in the same market segment.

The competitive situation in China is intensifying, with the 17 locally produced models of 2000 up to 30 in 2002, and new cars from Toyota and Ford about to hit the market. The high flyers of Shanghai GM, the producers of the Chery, were hitting three-figure growth in the first six months of 2002.

With the expansion planned by all the main players, it could be that China's productive capacity will triple during the next four years. Is this a bubble which will create surplus capacity? How much of the production will be exported?

The advantages and disadvantages of different modes of entry

There are a number of possible strategies for exploiting the opportunities in China's market for automobiles, and the capacity of China to become a platform for the manufacture and export of automobiles. The former might or might not include the latter, that is, developing an automobile manufacturing capacity in China. The possible advantages and disadvantages of each strategy are indicated below.

Exporting finished vehicles direct to China

At present only 6% of total car sales are accounted for by imports. It seems unlikely that the figure will ever rise above 10%. Not only does the Chinese government disapprove of imports in general, it wishes to encourage local content.

In Asia imported cars tend to be expensive niche products, such as Jaguars, Mercedes or Lexus, sold at high prices and with high taxes. There is likely to be great competition in this area. The Chinese government would certainly not favour an approach which allowed for a broader range of imports.

On the other hand, mid-2002 saw the first shipment of 252 Chinese-built cars to the USA by TAIC, at this stage in order to test the vehicles against the exacting safety standards applied in the USA. These consisted of the Xiali.

• *Advantages*
1. This would involve less risk since it would involve a smaller commitment of resources than the other modes of entry
2. Entry could be gradual as the market is tested and the brand names established.

• *Disadvantages*
1. It does not fit in with the Chinese government's intention of building a competitive car industry
2. There is likely to be a lot of competition from local producers, including foreign companies manufacturing in China. This is true even at the luxury end of the market
3. The distribution and financial infrastructures for supporting such sales are weak and difficult for foreign companies to establish without being present in China
4. It may not be very profitable.

Exporting key components to be put together in China by an assembly plant which could be foreign-owned, locally owned or a joint venture

This is a difficult strategy to sustain since it also runs counter to the wish of the Chinese government to maximize local content, unless it involves a partner in a joint enterprise. In theory local content rules will disappear, in practice there may be much pressure to maximize the local content.

• *Advantages*
1. Assembling vehicles in China takes some advantage of lower costs
2. Through a partner, such assembly might allow access to the distribution networks
3. This mode can take advantage of an established brand name.

• *Disadvantages*
1. There may be some loss of quality control if a local manufacturer is involved
2. It is a kind of half-way strategy, unlikely to be sustainable over the medium or long term
3. It almost certainly requires a partner.

An asset-light strategy equivalent to licensing

This strategy would mean that the global partner would provide the design of the product together with its brand name. It would be responsible for the design and development of any new vehicle. The Chinese partner would contract to build the automobile, sourcing components locally, rather as the Finnish company Valmet has already done for Porsche.

• *Advantages*
1. This mode of entry would allow the entrants to take full advantage of the low costs of Chinese manufacturing and the steady build-up of component supply
2. It would allow capital to be saved by the global partner and concentrated on those areas in which the foreign entrant has the most decisive advantage – for example, research and development, design and marketing.

• *Disadvantages*
1. The foreign brands may suffer a loss of reputation if quality controls are poor
2. There may be a danger of establishing potential competitors and eventually losing control of all value-adding activities
3. There may be disputes over the sharing of profits.

Building the whole facility in China independently of any Chinese partners

This is by far the riskiest mode, involving the greatest commitment of resources.

• *Advantages*
1. The foreign company would control most aspects of production and maintain quality
2. The company could train its own managers and workers
3. The company could apply best-practice technology.

• *Disadvantages*
1. The company may not have access to either the key supplier or distribution networks
2. The company may have a disadvantage in poorer access to the government and be vulnerable to action taken by the government to favour Chinese manufacturers or foreign manufacturers with Chinese partners.

Continuing the present system

• *Advantages*
1. With all its strengths and weaknesses, the system is already known
2. The system may be more flexible in allowing the most efficient mode to be adopted, depending on the circumstances of both product and market.

• *Disadvantages*
1. It is very expensive and not very profitable. GM has already invested US$1.5 billion in its Shanghai plant, VW US$1.7 billion in its two facilities. The returns have not yet been commensurate with the level of investment
2. The environment has changed and is changing very rapidly.

The main problems in China for foreign players are twofold. The first involves the local industry. There is a lack of local brand names, a poor design of all vehicles and a generally poor quality control which results in inefficient production methods and overmanning. Local players are too small to take advantage of economies of scale. It is difficult to set up quickly the necessary supply chains in China.

The second issues relates to the role of the government. Any foreign player must take into account the fact that the Chinese government is bound to be a major player, although now constrained by the need to appear to be playing according to the WTO rules. Any mode of entry must satisfy the strategic aims of the Chinese government.

Case Study Questions

1. What are the arguments relevant to the automobile industry in favour of creating joint ventures and the arguments against?
2. Who are the main strategic players in the Chinese automobile market? What is likely to be the influence of their strategies on the mode of entry into the Chinese market?
3. What is the impact of entry into the WTO likely to be for the Chinese automobile industry?
4. What is the present place and likely future place of China in the world automobile market?
5. What are likely to be the main factors relevant to a scenario-building exercise for the Chinese automobile industry? Note in particular the forces of change, the pre-determined elements and the critical uncertainties.

Reading

Cheng, A. T., 'Reform or die', *Asia Inc.*, July 2002: 19.

Dawson, C., 'For Nissan, A game of who'll blink first', *Business Week*, September 9, 2002: 26.

Dawson, C., 'Roaring into China', *Business Week*, April 7, 2003: 72–3.

Dwyer, M., 'Car market not all that it seems', *The Australian Financial Review*, June 18, 2002: 15.

Gao, P., 'A tune-up for China's auto industry', *The McKinsey Quarterly*, 2002 (1): 144–55.

Jopson, B. and George, N., 'Nissan and Volvo in China joint ventures', *Financial Times*, June 10, 2003: 40.

Kynge, J., 'Expanding Chinese carmakers agree merger', *Financial Times*, June 15/16, 2002: 1.

Leggett, K. and Zaun, T., 'Foreign auto makers are racing to get piece of business in China', *The Asian Wall Street Journal*, December 13–15, 2002: A1.

McCathie, A., 'Auto makers lead the German charge to Beijing', *The Australian Financial Review*, October 22, 2002: 14.

McGregor, R., 'VW loses Chinese lead but is still in the race', *Financial Times*, August 20, 2002: 21.

McGregor, R., 'Chery defends using features of rival cars', *Financial Times*, June 19, 2003: 31.

Murphy, D., 'Old Volkswagen chases new China', *Far Eastern Economic Review*, March 6, 2003, (27): 27–9.

Roberts, D., 'Motor nation', *Business Week*, June 17, 2002: 20–1.

Young, M. N. and Tan, J., 'Beijing Jeep at a cross-roads – facing the challenge of China's entry into the WTO', *Asia Case Research Journal*, 2001, 5(1): 1–26.

Key strategic lessons

• Participation in global business requires different participation strategies. The modes of entry differ markedly from enterprise to enterprise and product to product. The process of entry is a dynamic one in which most enterprises prefer to enter in a cautious manner. There may be a sequence of entry modes which allow entry and continuous operation to be characterized over the medium to long term by both higher return and lower risk.

• The distinctive modes of entry into international business include exporting, licensing or franchising, foreign direct investment, joint ventures, acquisitions or mergers and greenfield projects. These modes are principally distinguished by the degree of resource commitment and their levels of return and risk. The special management project mode is intermediate between exporting and licensing, sharing characteristics of each.

• Decisions on the mode of entry are made at periodic intervals, but there may be a logical sequence of modes, which runs from exporting through licensing to investment. Entry may follow a risk-averse path.

• Circumstances determining the appropriate mode of entry include commitment of resources, level of

return, level of and attitude to risk, need and ability to diversify, level of transaction costs under different modes and the degree of home country bias.

• Decisions on the mode of entry must take account of changing determinants, which are analysed in theories which emphasize the role of mobile, created assets, particularly enterprise-based theories, and reflect the demand-side rather than supply-side elements.

• Internalization is a powerful argument in favour of the direct investment mode of entry and within this mode inclines choice away from joint ventures to other forms of direct investment. Reasons for this include the need to defend the intellectual property rights of mobile, created assets and the higher transaction costs for other modes of entry.

• The world is not a global world since most of the features which define such a world are not satisfied and there are no genuinely global enterprises. The main reason for this is the universal existence of home country bias, which is reinforced by negative events and which often offsets the influence of internalization. Any strategy must take this into account and be designed to cater for a home country bias and the cultural differences associated with it.

Applying the lessons

1 Define the following terms: mode of entry, participation strategy, licensing, franchising, portfolio investment, foreign direct investment, joint venture, greenfield development, created assets, location-specific assets and internalization.

2 How do ethical issues influence the choice of mode

of entry? Consider an example of entry in which ethical issues were important. How important were such ethical issues in the making of a choice?

3 'If it were not for market imperfections, the obvious mode of entry would be through exports.' In what sense is this true? List the market imperfections

which cause this to be true. How do such imperfections cause the desired mode of entry to differ from industry to industry? Choose at least two different industries to illustrate your argument.

4 How does the operation of a global value chain affect the strategy of a multinational enterprise? Illustrate from the experience of one company.

5 Choose an industry with which you are familiar. List as many mobile, created assets as you can. Repeat the exercise for location-specific assets. Which are more important? Explain why the mix might differ from one industry to another?

6 What have been the advantages and disadvantages of the use of joint ventures as a mode of entry into the Chinese market? Are these typical of the situation of joint ventures elsewhere in the world?

Strategic project

1 In what sense could there be said to be global or world enterprises?

2 List the ten largest enterprises in the world, defined in a consistent manner.

3 Take each of the characteristics of a world enterprise and choose an operational threshold which will satisfy each.

4 Consider how far each of the top ten has the characteristics of a global enterprise. Indicate with a plus or minus whether the enterprise has those characteristics.

Exploring further

This chapter links up closely with the chapter on globalization (Chapter 3), the chapter on the nature of resources or assets, particularly the growing importance of intangible assets (Chapter 7), the section relating to acquisitions and mergers in the chapter on optimum size (Chapter 11) and the chapter on risk management (Chapter 14). There are many themes in common with all these chapters. The biographical reviews of these chapters therefore contain much reading also relevant to this chapter.

There is a rich literature specific to the choice of the mode of entry. All texts on the international business environment deal directly with the issue. A relevant chapter or section can serve as an introduction to the topic. For example, Part III in Bradley, 1995: 227–448, or Chapter 11 in Grant, 2002: 273–302, both serve as good introductions. A longer and deeper treatment is Root, 1980. A shorter introduction to the topic is Hill et al., 1990: 117–28, or Kim and Huang, 1992: 29–53.

Underlying the theory of choice of mode is a theory of foreign direct investment. On this Dunning is the best authority. See Dunning, 1998, or his student Narula, 1996.

The complexity of the issues which determine choice of entry mode are best handled in Grant, 2002. The impact of country risk on the mode of entry is important and considered in: Meldrum, 2000: 33–40, or Howell and Chaddick, 1994: 70–92. Also interesting is Rugman and Hodgetts, 1995, particularly Chapter 13.

Internalization and the notion of transaction costs have been the focus of considerable attention. A good introduction is Hill and Kim, 1988: 93–104. Further discussion of the issues can be found in Anderson and Gatignon, 1986: 1–26 and Madhok, 1997: 39–61.

Specific modes of entry are dealt with in Contractor, 1982: 73–83, and Kogut, 1988: 319–32.

Part IV

Bringing it all Together

16 Formulating strategy

17 Implementing strategy

18 Monitoring strategic performance

Part IV addresses the nature of the most important activities in the making of good strategy – formulation, implementation and monitoring. The preceding sections have built a strong case for the argument that formulation, implementation and monitoring are parts of a single process rather than separate activities, discrete in their timing. Only in a theoretical sense can they be considered separate activities, in practice they must be pursued jointly. However, they are considered separately in this section in order to make it easier to explore the different issues which each activity raises. It will become obvious from the treatment that the chapters should be read together.

This section analyses the main features of strategy making and the main challenges involved in the process of formulating, implementing and monitoring a strategy. It defines what can be done, identifying the key factors in developing successful strategies and showing how they might be incorporated into the strategic approach of the enterprise.

The issues dealt with include:

- the exercise of creativity to create competitive advantage

- the selection of the appropriate kind of strategic activity to apply this creativity

- the reconciling of different stakeholder goals and the goals of different groups in the enterprise hierarchy and attempts to realize those goals through strategic action

- the need to integrate the actions of all external players and the different functional areas within the enterprise.

The greatest dangers in strategy making are horizontal or vertical fracturing, amounting to

Task	Parts	Chapters				

Task	Parts	Chapters
Starting right	**Part I** **Introducing Strategic Management**	**WHY?** Prologue **WHO?** 1 Introducing strategy and strategy making **WHAT?** 2 Thinking and acting strategically **HOW?** 3 Adopting a global perspective **WHEN?** 4 Reading an uncertain future
Acquiring conceptual tools for the job	**Part II** **Strategic Environments**	General — 5 Identifying opportunity and risk **ENVIRONMENTS** Internal 7 Analysing resources, capabilities and core competencies Immediate — 6 Reading the competitive environment
	and Competitive Advantage	**GENERIC STRATEGIES** 9 Reducing costs 8 Creating and maintaining competitive advantage 10 Differentiating the product
Resolving particular strategic problems	**Part III** **Strategic Dilemmas**	**FIVE DILEMMAS** 11 Determining the size of an enterprise 12 Integrating the strategists 13 When to compete and when to cooperate 14 Managing risk 15 Participating in the global economy
The strategy emerges	**Part IV** **Bringing it all Together**	16 Formulating strategy 17 Implementing strategy → **CONTINUOUS ITERATION** ← 18 Monitoring strategic performance
Analysing strategy making	**Part V** **Strategic Analysis and Audit**	Case studies Epilogue

a failure to achieve the communication or cooperation critical to this integration. This is a failure in the process of iteration which is central to good strategy making, that is, the reciprocal interchange of information between the many different strategists. The nature of the process of strategic iteration is a particular focus of interest.

This section takes a close look at the problems of monitoring the success of a strategy. It sees monitoring as a continuous process which checks the efficiency of implementation but also allows for adjustment, or reformulation, of the existing strategy. The process of benchmarking, and monitoring the achievement of those benchmarks, is usually seen as directed at achieving operational effectiveness and not at the making of good strategy. The argument advanced here is that monitoring must be built into the process of strategy making itself.

The section advocates a realistic approach in which the organization adjusts to its particular environments as they change, and is flexible and innovative, with the ability to adapt to any unexpected change in the external environments. The enterprise manages change in order to maintain competitive advantage and control risk. The section proposes that the sequence of formulation, implementation, and monitoring could easily be reversed and explains why. So the sequence of chapters could easily be reversed, a reversal which would yield a new insight into the nature of strategy making. It is open to the reader to read the chapters in reverse order.

- Chapter 16 considers the way in which strategy formulation should and does occur, including the nature and possible sequencing of steps in the process. Two common models are discussed, in which the starting point is very different, either market position or resource endowment. It argues strongly against such sequencing and in favour of the emergent nature of strategy.

- Chapter 17 considers the challenge, or challenges, of implementation. It does this mainly in the context of the five Cs – command, control, communication, coordination and conflict – and the impact of fracturing in these areas. It also discusses the role of leadership in strategy making. The pros and cons of having a separate division or unit responsible for strategy making are weighed.

- Chapter 18 considers the monitoring of strategic outcomes, seeing it as integral to the whole process of strategy making. It discusses the question, how is it possible to judge whether a strategy is genuinely successful? It returns to the issue of profit as a performance indicator and a motivator and puts the achievement of a satisfactory level of profit into the broader context of the interests of all stakeholder groups.

The case studies in this section are different in their nature from those elsewhere in the book. They are extended case studies which try to take a broad view of the process of strategy making, illustrating many of the concepts and problems introduced at various stages in the book. They consider both successful and unsuccessful strategy making. In Chapter 16 the case studies consider the enterprises General Electric and Nokia, which have been successful in formulating strategy and are well known for their excellent strategy making. In Chapter 17 the case studies consider companies which are perhaps not as innovative in strategy formulation, but are excellent implementers, South African Breweries and Toyota. In Chapter 18 the case studies consider how to monitor and adjust a strategy in a changing environment. Sony and Imclone illustrate the ethical problems which arise in strategy making and the challenges of a change in strategic direction associated with deteriorating performance. These case studies are put together in such a way as to provide the opportunity for a full strategic audit.

16 Formulating strategy

Strategic management requires explicit attention to both the internal and the external, to production and demand, to resources and products. (PRIEM AND BUTLER, 2001: 35)

Learning objectives

After reading this chapter you will be able to:

- understand how the strategy-making process typically evolves within an organization
- identify different steps in the formulation of a strategy
- understand the implications of different methods of sequencing those steps
- know how to encourage, and avoid discouraging, strategic thinking
- define an emergent strategy and identify its component parts
- understand the role of strategic planning in strategy making

Key strategic challenge

How do I ensure the formulation of a successful strategy?

Strategic dangers

That the strategy adopted becomes a rigid plan which restricts what the organization tries to do and that the strategy-making process itself becomes an excessively bureaucratic process which diverts significant resources away from strategic thinking and develops a negative attitude to unanticipated change.

Case Study Scenario   The supreme strategist – General Electric

GE was founded in 1892 to exploit the patents held by Thomas Edison relating to electricity generation, light bulbs and electric motors. It has a long history which covers the whole period in which the concept of strategy has been developed. In the course of the twentieth century GE grew to be the largest company in the world, having by April 2002 the largest capitalization of all companies, at US$396 billion. It has been one of the most diversified companies in the world, retaining its broad portfolio during a period when diversity became unfashionable, producing goods as diverse as financial services, electric turbines and medical equipment. Its sheer size and degree of business success warrants special attention. Both are the result of a deliberate application of strategy.

GE is a classic conglomerate. Over the years it has managed to sustain its growth and profits through a strategy of timely acquisition and divestment. It is equally ruthless at both. It has been quick to spot changes in the environment in which it operates and which justify either acquisition or divestment. It is a living testament to the potential of the portfolio approach for producing a good strategy, if pursued ruthlessly.

GE has been a significant focus of interest for those interested in management theory and strategy making. Its history is almost the history of strategy. Over the years it has pioneered a raft of management and strategic techniques, notably the establishment of the strategic business unit and the use in strategy making of the technique of portfolio management. It

has emphasized the role of marketing and the final consumer. There is probably more written about GE than about any other company.

GE has been characterized by a succession of strong leaders who have imposed their imprint on the company. Because of this GE's strategy has looked more like the model of classical strategy making than that of most other enterprises. It is interesting to consider how far these leaders have built on previous work and rebuilt both organizational design and strategy, taking account of the changing context of the company. Each leader has been leader for a significant period of time; Jack Welch, the last one to retire, being at the helm for almost 20 years. Such a long tenure has helped greatly in bringing consistency to the process and content of strategy making.

Considerable thought went into choosing the successor for each retiring CEO. It was understood to be part of the process of strategy making. Very often the incomer had played an important role in developing strategy under his predecessor, and the newcomer was chosen because their personality and abilities matched the needs of the strategy being pursued. There was significant continuity in the building of a capacity to make good strategy.

Table 16.1 The CEOs of GE

Coffin	1915–21
Swope/Young	1922–39
Wilson	1940–49
Cordiner	1950–63
Borch	1964–72
Jones	1973–80
Welch	1981–2000
Imelt	2000–

Case Study Scenario   Nokia – where did it come from?

'Whatever can go mobile, will go mobile.'
Pekka Ala-Pietila, Nokia's president

In 1990 there were less than 10 million wireless subscribers worldwide; by 2000 over 550 million. In 2003 there were 1.2 billion users, far more than the number using personal computers. The mobile phone was one of the growth products of the 1990s. Nokia was a company which almost became synonymous with the mobile phone. Nokia's reputation has won the world's 11th most valuable of all brand names. For a period it was Europe's highest valued stock market company.

In 1998 Nokia passed Motorola to become the world's

leading maker of mobile phones, currently having 38% of the market, more than the combined share of the next four competitors. In 2003 Nokia has global sales of $30 billion and profits more than $5 billion, despite the recession. In 1992 it was nearly bankrupt. Today it makes the vast majority of the profits generated in the mobile phone industry. Typically Nokia has had operating profit margins of 20%, compared with Motorola's average of just 6%.

In the early 1990s Nokia was a conglomerate with disparate activities, including tire manufacture, paper production, consumer electronics as well as telecommunication equipment. It was unlikely that such a company could outcompete Motorola in producing and selling the mobile phone. The history, geography and political economy of Finland and its Scandinavian neighbours provides some explanation for the success of a regional company. Nokia did many things right. It is interesting to trace the changing strategic stance adopted by the company.

Nokia is part of the new economy, a leader in the development of digital wireless technology. The mobile phone was a product which took off in a surprising way. It answered real needs for small businesses and highly mobile managers, but it also satisfied the utility of sociability, offering improved security and promoting the ability of young people to overcome shyness and interact socially. Nokia emerged during a period in which the mobile phone became fully established in developed economies. Finland leads the way in this revolution, perhaps only headed by South Korea in certain

areas of innovation such as the introduction of broadband. In Finland the mobile phone is already used as a flexible instrument for a multitude of different functions – browsing the web, executing e-commerce transactions, controlling household heating and lighting systems, or purchasing coke from a wireless-enabled vending machine.

Three firms dominate the global market for wireless equipment of various kinds, including the base station equipment and digital switches – two are Scandinavian, Nokia and Ericsson, and one American, Motorola. Nokia is the best performer of the three. How was such a position achieved so quickly by a company with its base in Finland, a country of just five million people, known best for the hardness of its people, its lakes and frozen north, in one of the remotest parts of Europe? Does it reflect the existence of a good strategy?

So far the book has moved steadily in the direction of indicating how a strategy should be formulated. It has described the constraints which limit what can be done in strategy making and has introduced the basic concepts needed to understand what strategy is trying to do. It has also described the recurrent dilemmas which must be confronted in the process of strategy making. It is time to review how the procedure of strategy making should be organized. What is necessary for the formulation of a good strategy?

How to learn good strategy making, the 'core' core competency

Strategy in Action Honda and the revival of a stagnant market

Before the 1960s the motorcycle industry was in the doldrums with a stable but weak market. The room for increased sales seemed slight. The spread of the motorcar had undermined the market for motorcycles, except for a small group of enthusiasts. The image of the motorcyclist was a poor one, associated with such groups as the 'Hell's Angels' or 'Satan's Slaves'. The stereotype of the motorcyclist, reinforced by the leather-jacketed Marlon Brando in the film, *The Wild Ones*, was a leather-jacketed, teenage troublemaker. At that time the industry was dominated by American and European producers, such as Harley-Davidson, BSA, Norton Triumph and Moto-Guzzi. Harley-Davidson was still the leader in the USA market (see the Strategy in Action on Harley-Davidson in Chapter 10).

This was all about to change, but the way in which it changed is rather controversial. There are significant strategic implications. Some issues are uncontroversial and uncontested, but others not. There is no doubt that Japanese producers, led by Honda, reached a position in which they outperformed Western producers in terms of both cost and quality. Large automated facilities equipped with highly mechanized machining and assembly lines allowed them to pursue lean production, and achieve cycle time reduction and zero product defects. Advanced production techniques, such as high-pressure diecasting and hot and cold forging and sintering, reduced processing costs and metal wastage. The close relationship with suppliers was important and helped keep down costs. Honda and the other pro-

▶

ducers continuously innovated, adding new features such as electric starters, four-cylinder engines, disk brakes and five-speed transmissions. They repeatedly upgraded their bikes, introducing annual model changes. By the mid-1970s there was no doubt which company in the world offered the lowest cost and the highest quality bike.

Controversy enters with discussion of the role of strategy in this success. The conventional story on strategy runs as follows. During the 1950s Honda had developed huge production volumes in small motor-cycles in the Japanese domestic market, runs which allowed them to achieve volume-related reductions in production costs. On the basis of supplying the large domestic market, Honda had become potentially competitive internationally, although in 1960 it still exported only 4% of its production. By 1959 it was already the largest motorcycle producer in the world. Honda then used a cost leadership strategy to enter, expand and dominate the American and world markets for motorcycles.

In 1959 Honda established an American subsidiary – the American Honda Motor Company. In the early 1960s it decisively entered the American market on the basis of productive facilities built ahead of sales, with the aim of seeking maximum market share. In order to do this it adopted a strategy of selling small, lightweight bikes to members of the public not previously interested in motorbikes. It deliberately sought to extend the market and counter the poor image by a campaign directed at young families, using the slogan, 'You meet the nicest people on a Honda'. The campaign was extremely successful. Within five years Honda dominated the market.

The real story is rather different. Honda backed into success with the relatively cheap lightweight bike, the 50 cc Supercub, both in Japan and the USA, but reluctantly, since they, in particular Sochiro Honda who was interested in motorcycle racing, preferred to be successful with the larger bikes. Takeo Fujisawa, his partner, was the one who opted for designing the smaller bike, largely because he thought it would appeal to the women who controlled the purse strings in Japanese households. The success in selling the smaller bike surprised even him; it was not the result of a deliberate strategy.

Far from having foreseen and planned success, Honda had not built production facilities in Japan ahead of demand; they had trouble keeping up with the unexpected surge in demand. Nor did Honda deliberately redefine the American market. It thought the market was for large bikes and did not wish to ruin its image by offering and pushing strongly the small bike. Honda was forced, by serious initial technical problems with its larger bikes which arose because of the longer trips and faster movement in American conditions, to run with the smaller one. The slogan came by chance at the right time, initially by a circuitous route from an advertising student, not as a result of any deliberate strategy initiated by Honda. The slogan arrived at the right time but even then was rejected by the most senior staff.

It is a salutary lesson to note the difference in interpretation. Pascale (1996: 80–91) has called the process of tidying up real history as the Honda effect. Other Japanese companies, such as Toyota, had similar initial failures. With hindsight, it is easy to read a long-sighted and systematic strategy into a series of glorious improvisations which in the end prove more successful than anyone expected. It is obviously beneficial to be able to recognize opportunity, even when it is staring you in the face; many companies fail to do so, including some Japanese companies. Honda was in a strong position to exploit the opportunities and had senior mangers able to recognize those opportunities.

Strategy making is simultaneously a learning process and a learned skill. If done well, it promotes learning in every significant area of organizational activity. Where strategy is regarded as important, it assists the staff of the organization to confront positively a series of changing problems, both external and internal.

The phases in learning strategy making

Not all organizations are good at strategy making. Some organizations are better at learning this skill than others. They are better at making strategy and consequently have better strategies. In some cases the learning is implicit, as is the strategy itself, although it suffuses everything that is done by the company; in this case it is not explicitly called strategy or recognized as such. In other organizations strategy making is a self-conscious and deliberate process. There is often much agonizing over how to do it.

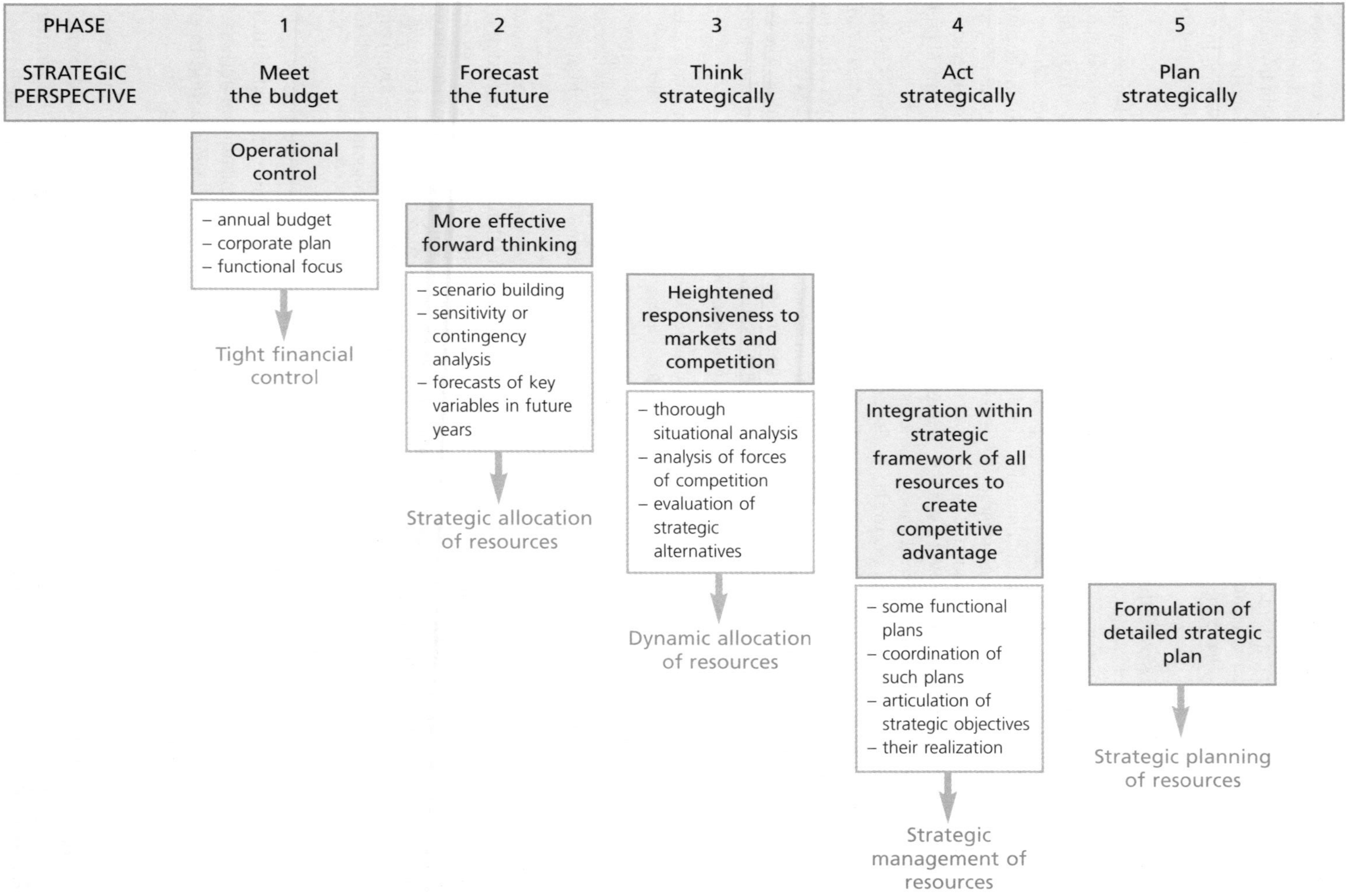

PHASE	1	2	3	4	5
STRATEGIC PERSPECTIVE	Meet the budget	Forecast the future	Think strategically	Act strategically	Plan strategically

Operational control

- annual budget
- corporate plan
- functional focus

Tight financial control

More effective forward thinking

- scenario building
- sensitivity or contingency analysis
- forecasts of key variables in future years

Strategic allocation of resources

Heightened responsiveness to markets and competition

- thorough situational analysis
- analysis of forces of competition
- evaluation of strategic alternatives

Dynamic allocation of resources

Integration within strategic framework of all resources to create competitive advantage

- some functional plans
- coordination of such plans
- articulation of strategic objectives
- their realization

Strategic management of resources

Formulation of detailed strategic plan

Strategic planning of resources

Figure 16.1 Five phases in the evolution of strategy making

It is unusual, probably impossible, for an organization to move quickly from having no strategy-making capacity at all to having a fully developed strategic plan. Since no organization can exist without some strategy, the starting point is usually an incoherent process and an implicit strategy resulting from it. Most organizations tend to move gradually in small steps, unless there is some crisis which moves them forward more rapidly. The case study of GE illustrates neatly the process of learning involved in strategy making and the development of this competency. Sometimes the organization moves too far, the process becomes overly rigid and strategy becomes subject to all the problems described in the next chapter.

There is a simple but graphic way to picture the historical evolution of learning phases in the process of strategy making (Figure 16.1). There are five phases distinguished. This sequence can be regarded as a notional historical unfolding of strategy making for an 'ideal' company. No real company conforms exactly to such an evolutionary path.

Phase 1

All organizations have a corporate plan which covers the coming financial year and have mechanisms for exerting budgetary control in line with the corporate plan. In this first phase the emphasis is very much on key functional areas, notably, but not only, on finance. The aim is to secure the operational control necessary to realize the corporate plan.

Phase 2

Phase 2 sees a more serious attempt to look beyond the next financial year and anticipate events or changes of trend which will have an impact on the organization in the future. Such forecasting is a requirement for any effective project evaluation when the projects involve investment in facilities which have a life well beyond one year.

Phase 3

Phases 2 and 3 could be interchanged since there is nothing to prevent an organization developing its strategy making in either way. Phase 3 draws out the implications of the strategic thinking which has begun in Phase 2, in order to take account of the present and future behaviour of other players. It concentrates attention on how the markets will develop in the future.

Phase 4

Phase 4 is characterized by the beginning of an integration of all facets of strategy making and the achievement of a fit between the evolving opportunities and risks in the external environment and the changing resource position in the enterprise. The framework of a strategy sets the parameters for functional strategies or plans. It also sets the framework within which annual corporate plans are prepared and implemented.

Phase 5

Often the process stops at phase 4. In certain conditions phase 4 can result in genuine strategic planning, which is identified as phase 5. This is unusual and can only take place in exceptional circumstances. In the normal case it is difficult to move beyond phase 4, which corresponds to what has been called strategic management in this book.

By entering into phase 4, the organization is starting to remake its environment. This last phase puts the emphasis on the ability of the enterprise to make the future, that is, not to take the environment as a given. As a consequence, the last two phases can be described as creating the future.

It is difficult to know how long it takes for an enterprise to develop a capacity for strategy making which is effective and relevant to the situation of that organization. It is not an easy thing to do. It requires time for staff to learn and significant resources to support the effort. It is a process whose unfolding is difficult to predict with precision. Sometimes the competency is developed well, but at other times badly. Sometimes the competency is allowed to deteriorate after reaching a respectable level of effectiveness. The ability to make a good strategy is like any core competence – valuable, rare and difficult to imitate. It is highly specific to a particular time and industry. It needs to be continuously renewed. It is a competency which is critical to every organization.

This approach stresses how the capacity of strategy making is developed over real time by any organization. The next section considers the theoretical and empirical breakdown of the process of strategy making into different steps, which in this analysis exist in notional, rather than real, time. The question is, are there steps which must be placed in a particular sequence?

Steps in strategy making

At different points in the course of the book, potentially separate and distinct steps in the process of strategy making have been identified, which correspond to different types of strategic activity, somewhat akin to a value-adding chain. These activities are in principle sufficiently different to have the potential to define independent steps. The first question focuses on the identification of these separate activities and the possible steps in strategy making which might be distinguished.

From the literature on strategy making, it is possible to identify 11 potentially discrete activities in strategy making. They are potentially discrete in that they are often treated as such by commentators. In practice they may be carried out together. These activities and the steps associated with them are often considered independently of each other. It is appropriate later to analyse whether they are genuinely discrete or independent steps. For the moment it is assumed that they are. Most of these steps have been discussed at some length in previous chapters of this book. Some have not. For example, formulation, implementation and monitoring are discussed in this section of the book.

The analysis starts by simply listing the different steps.

The 11 steps

The first two steps are part of an information strategy.

1. Studying, analysing or, in the terminology used in this book, *reading the general environment*, in particular reading that environment for any opportunities or threats relevant to the enterprise.
    This ability has been discussed in two separate chapters: the activity of reading in Chapter 4 and the nature of the general environment which is being read in Chapter 5. In the analysis, reading was broken down into four separate activities, or substeps, but for the purpose of this analysis of steps, it is enough to aggregate the reading into just two steps: scanning and monitoring.

2. *Reading the competitive or industrial environment.*

   The industrial and/or competitive environment is more immediate to the enterprise than the general environment. It is critical to read what other players might do, particularly those who are in some sense competitors or complementors for the enterprise. It is necessary to anticipate how the competitive state of the market might develop in the future. This issue has been dealt with in Chapter 6.

3. *Forecasting*, or more exactly, *scenario building*, notably in the area relevant to the enterprise.

   It is impossible to avoid making some forecast of the future, although this issue is much neglected in many of the textbooks on strategy. This comprises the other two activities in reading the environment, forecasting and assessing. The forecasting is often implicit rather than explicit, but should not be. This has been treated at length in Chapter 4.

4. Locating an attractive industry or part of an industry, and its associated market or market segment (*positioning*), that is, one which, because of its favourable conditions, including competitive conditions, offers opportunities of an above-normal return.

   This has been discussed under the heading 'Forces of competition' in Chapter 6. The discussion assumed that for different industries there are differing levels of barriers to entry, and therefore different returns which persist in the industry or sector.

5. Identifying the positive aspects of the firm's internal environment, that is, *evaluating the organization's resources* and making an audit of all these resources.

   The inventory of resources held by an organization includes a wide spectrum of assets, both tangible and intangible, natural and created. The evaluation of the full range of resources has been discussed in Chapter 8.

6. *Determining the enterprise's capabilities*, given its resources and the different ways in which they can be integrated, and comparing these with those of competitors, particularly as they constitute the enterprise's potential strengths and weaknesses relative to those competitors.

   Resources are put together in combination as capabilities, which are specific to the organization but which change over time, sometimes in an organized way. Again this has been discussed in Chapter 8.

7. *Considering core competencies* as a source of distinctive competitive advantage, in the light of all the possible strategies.

   Capabilities become competencies within the framework of a possible strategy. This analysis is closely linked with the need to develop a strategy which emphasizes a particular source of competitive advantage. Again this has been discussed in Chapter 8.

   It is appropriate, because of the importance of the organization's resource position, to divide all three steps in the 'reading' of the organization's internal environment and treat them as separate activities.

8. *Formulating an appropriate strategy.*
   This is the focus of this chapter.

9. *Acquiring any missing resources*, capabilities or competencies needed to implement the strategy.
   This might or might not be possible. This possibility has to be assessed. This step was discussed in Chapter 8.

10. *Implementing the strategy.*
    This is the subject of Chapter 17.

11. *Monitoring the strategy.*
    This is the subject of Chapter 18.

These steps are not placed in any particular order. Different commentators attach a differing importance to each step and put them in different sequences. In any particular analysis where particular steps, and the activities associated with them, seem unimportant, they can be, and are often, conflated with other steps. There is considerable disagreement in the literature on the number and definition of the steps, let alone on their sequencing.

A sequence of steps?

The next stage is to place the steps in an appropriate sequence, integrating steps where and if necessary.

The first issue to address is the starting step. This question amounts to asking what is given when the process of strategy making begins. Since the process is a continuous one, never reaching completion and never really having a start, the notion of a starting point is a purely theoretical one. It is simply a means of initiating a strategic discussion.

There are two possible, but significantly different, starting points, which yield different sequences, obviously related to two different models of strategy making. Both approaches have their strengths and weaknesses.

What are the factors which determine an appropriate sequence of steps? The answer to this question lies in particular circumstances, notably the differing nature of particular industries or sectors of the economy.

Two alternative models

It is helpful to call the two models the positioning and the resource models, but in many texts they are called the industrial organization model and the resource-based model. The sequencing of steps and activities is markedly different in these two models.

In the industrial organization model the starting point is the external environment of the enterprise. Decisions about where to position an enterprise are regarded as more important than the capacity to implement such a positioning. The potential performance of the organization reflects its ability to position itself well or, in more graphic language, to find a suitable peak or mountain range in the business landscape.

In the second model, the starting point is the resource position of the enterprise. Here decisions about internal organization are regarded as more important. The resources of the organization determine what it can do and what its performance is likely to be. The key issue is not what the enterprise should do but what it can do.

Which particular sequence of steps to adopt in the process of strategy making reflects a judgement about which is more important, the external or the internal environment.

The analysis below examines each of the models in turn.

The positioning model

The sequence of steps is:

1. Read the environment (steps 1, 2 and 3)
2. Locate an attractive industry (step 4)
3. Identify an appropriate strategy to achieve competitive advantage (step 8)
4. Develop or acquire the appropriate resources (a conflation of steps 5, 6, 7 and 9)
5. Implement the strategy, using the firm's resources (step 10).

The resource model

The sequence of steps is:

1. Identify the enterprise's resources (step 5)
2. Determine the enterprise's capabilities (step 6)
3. Determine the enterprise's core competencies and the nature of its competitive advantage (step 7)
4. Locate an appropriate and attractive industry (step 4)
5. Select an appropriate strategy (step 8)
6. Implement the strategy (step 10).

Differences between the models

There are three significant differences in the sequencing of the two models:

1. The starting point in the positioning model is the existence of external opportunity; in the resources model, it is the internal resources of the enterprise. This difference might be expressed differently, using the metaphor of the business landscape – how is the choice made of what peak to locate the enterprise upon? It is assumed that in the first case there is sufficient difference in external opportunity to make positioning significant. The peaks are of significantly different height. In the second the difference is in resources. The issue becomes the ability of the mountaineering teams to climb the different peaks. The first assumes that the enterprise is capable of scaling any peak, the second that some are beyond the capacity of the enterprise and therefore out of reach.
2. Because resources are not a problem in the first model, by assumption being capable of acquisition through the market, the three steps involving resources,

capabilities and competencies are integrated into one. The climbing team can easily acquire the necessary climbing gear, the appropriate skills and whatever transportation is needed. These steps are considered much less difficult to accomplish in the first than in the second model.

3. The resource model does not have, as a separate step, the acquisition of resources. It is impossible to acquire resources it does not already have. It does not require such a careful reading of the external environment as in the other strategy, since what the enterprise can do is largely determined by its existing resource position. In other words, it needs to consider only maps which indicate peaks in its immediate vicinity. There is much less scope for positioning than assumed in the first model. Some peaks are too distant, some too difficult to climb.

The two models are based on very different assumptions about the nature of the world in which the organization or enterprise operates. It is possible that the real world conforms at different times and in different places to each set of assumptions. Alternatively, they may both describe a different aspect of the same world, and both therefore be relevant to strategy making. There may be some choice of peak, but not a completely free choice.

Assumptions of positioning model

This model is the world that the economist typically assumes. First, it is assumed that markets are competitive enough to impose one highly specific but broad objective on the enterprise, notably that which accords with the interests of the owners or shareholders, that is, the maximization of profit. You have to go for the highest peak. Even if managers do not deliberately maximize profit, competition, either in the commodity or capital markets, forces them to do so. Decision makers within the enterprise react in a rational manner to the incentive structure provided by opportunity and the constraints set by resource availability.

Second, all resources held by enterprises within a particular industry are assumed to be similar, that is, homogeneous. The resource positions of different enterprises within the same industry do not lead to different strategies. This assumption places the emphasis squarely on tangible rather than intangible resources, largely excluding or ignoring the role of the latter, which must by their nature be heterogeneous. Here all resources are appropriable and highly mobile; they can be easily acquired or transferred. Any differences arising from the initial resource endowments can be quickly ironed out.

Third, any variation of return results chiefly from differences in competitive conditions between markets and the differing levels of the barriers to entry into the different markets or industries. It therefore assumes that product markets are heterogeneous, that is, characterized by different and changing conditions of competition. The exact positioning of an enterprise largely determines performance in such a world.

The principal axiom of this model is that inter-industry differences in rates of return are more significant than intra-industry differences in returns in determining the performance of an enterprise. This follows on from the other assumptions above. This anticipation of unequal inter-industry returns can be empirically tested. Studies of the real world have thrown considerable doubt on the axiom.

If the real world yields empirical data at odds with the axiom, then it follows that the theoretical assumptions from which it is derived do not hold. They do not describe adequately conditions in real markets. Most data is organized on a national basis, which restricts what can be said. It is perhaps surprising that the variability in return explained inter-industrially is much less than that explained intra-industrially. For the USA over the period 1978–96, the statistics show the following (Ghemawat, 1999: 19–20, 49–50). Only 10–20% of the observed variation in business profitability is accounted for by the industry in which the business operates. Stable within-industry effects account for a much larger share, as much as 30–45%. This predisposes an observer to think that the internal environment of an enterprise is more important than its external environment in explaining where the enterprise locates itself, that the inter-enterprise boundaries are far stronger than the inter-industry boundaries. However, the inter-industry differences are still significant. The most profitable industries such as toiletries/cosmetics and pharmaceuticals yield an average rate of profit greater than 15%, the least profitable, such as steel, a loss greater than 10% and the airlines greater than 5%.

Assumptions of resource model

The second model assumes a rather different world. First, that satisficing is acceptable, that is, profit maximization is impossible, given the constraints on enterprises and that they have different resource endowments.

Second, the unique resources and capabilities of an enterprise define its nature and determine, through the strategic competencies and the enterprise's competitive advantage, its performance. In other words, resources are by their nature dissimilar or heterogeneous. Over time the enterprise develops and integrates these resources in a way which stresses unique capabilities. Each enterprise has a unique history in which it has developed such capabilities and translated them into distinctive competencies. The stress is on intangible resources which differ from enterprise to enterprise.

Third, the resources are relatively immobile. They cannot be transferred without a significant cost. It is difficult to comprehend the nature of such resources, let alone acquire them.

The competencies of an enterprise determine its profitability. Enterprises are endowed with different resources which themselves become the basis for different rates of return. They are the basis for strategy making which seeks, by reshuffling the resources and redefining the capabilities as distinctive competencies, to maintain these higher returns. On the other hand, there are no significant differences between industries in the average rates of return. Product markets are assumed to be homogeneous, notably in their competitive conditions. There are no significant differences between them in the forces of competition, particularly in the ease or difficulty of entry.

Which model?

Towards which model do the circumstances of the world incline – the positioning model or the resources model? Fashion in theory, and therefore in the nature of strategy making, tends to swing dramatically from one model to the other, and back.

A world which has a growing and significant inventory of intangible assets certainly appears to better fit the second model. However, the conditions surrounding an enterprise vary and can justify either model. There are sectors of the economy which better fit the first model, sometimes only briefly. The new economy, for ever changing from period to period, whatever activities it consists of, may for a short time offer a higher return, because of some element of first-mover advantage and a delay in entry of imitators, but this is doubtful.

The fusion of two models

The answer to the apparent contradiction is simple; both models describe different aspects of the same world. Either model is incomplete without the other. Both make rather restrictive assumptions about the nature of the world, assumptions which are unrealistic and need to be relaxed as a basis for identifying a valid basis for strategy making. What an enterprise should do is different from what it can do and what an enterprise can do is limited by its resource position. It is always advisable to consider the width of the gap between aspiration and actuality in determining a desired process of strategy making.

A fusion of the two approaches has two major implications for strategy making. The first is that many of the steps above are not discrete. They must occur simultaneously and as part of the same strategic process. It is impossible to divide steps which must be undertaken simultaneously, for example:

- How is it possible to list and evaluate resources unless it is known in which markets these resources can provide value?
- How is it possible to scan and monitor external environments unless it is known what kind of information is likely to be relevant to the enterprise, given its resources and therefore its potential capabilities or competencies?

Resources and position are inextricably linked. An enterprise should only attempt peaks which represent a reasonable challenge.

The second implication is that even where certain steps can be regarded as discrete, there is no clear-cut sequence, rather an overlapping range of steps and activities. Good strategy making is more a matter of the degree of emphasis given to different activities at different times than a delineation of a clear-cut sequence.

Considering the choice of activities and the associated sequence of steps is only a preliminary step necessary to strategy making. There are two further issues which must be confronted. These issues partly reflect the nature of the strategic situations faced by specific enterprises.

The first concerns the strategic coherence achieved in carrying out these steps. How is it possible to integrate all the different strategic activities discussed above, so that they gel with each other?

The second issue concerns the effectiveness with which the steps are carried out, which influences the quality of the resulting strategy. It is possible to develop any number of feasible strategies, which are coherent, but which is the best strategy? At some point the focus must be on finding the best.

Strategic thinking – making room for creativity

After the arguments which have been developed in the last 15 chapters, it is fruitful to return to the distinction made in Chapter 2 between strategic thinking, strategic management and strategic planning.

The focus was placed on two main aspects of strategy making, the creative aspect and the more humdrum administrative aspect. It was further argued that strategic thinking is a precondition for the achievement of competitive advantage of any kind, but that creativity can only be converted into competitive advantage with the help of a significant managerial and administrative input. The present section considers in detail the role of creativity in strategy making. The next two sections then return to strategic management and strategic planning. The aim of the three sections is to explore the role of each strategic activity as it is best realized in the process of strategy making.

A number of key questions need to be confronted:

• How far can any organization harness the creativity of its strategists?
• How far can the formulation of any strategy take account of the need for creativity?
• How far can a strategy be formulated which first encourages creativity and then incorporates its results into strategy?

Creativity is important for the long-term survival of any organization. It is critically important for any organization to encourage such creativity. This is far from easy, as by its nature creativity cannot be 'planned'.

First it is important to be absolutely clear about what must be encouraged. It is possible to define creativity as the ability of any member of an organization to do something new, which is potentially promotive of the goals of that organization, *without being directly shown or taught how to do this.*

The emphasis is on the autonomy of the creative individual. The results of creativity are either improvements, that is, minor modifications in the current operation of the organization, or innovations, that is, the introduction of completely new activities or new ways of doing things.

As has been shown, innovations have an important strategic dimension, but the aggregation of minor modifications can also have an impressive impact. It is good strategy to encourage such improvements.

Types of creativity

It is useful to give a typology of creativity which helps the reader to understand what is being talking about. The matrix in Figure 16.2 makes two distinctions. Firstly, it distinguishes between the different drivers of, or motivators for, engagement in creative activity. Do these creativity drivers come from outside the individual, as a consequence of some demand from the outside world, expressed as an instruction or an inducement, or are they to be found within the creator? These have been described as either extrinsic or intrinsic motivation.

Secondly, what is the nature of the problem to be solved? Is the problem already formulated? If it is, it can be described as a closed problem. Or is it an open problem, one in which the creator is required to find, invent or discover the problem before trying to find a solution?

It is worth considering briefly each of these different types of creativity.

A. *Responsive creativity* seeks a solution to a specified problem. The motivation for reaching a solution is based on a material reward. This is the type of creative

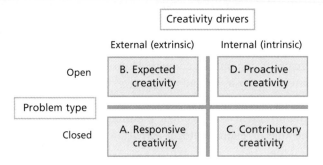

Source: Unsworth, 2001.

Figure 16.2   **A matrix of creativity**

behaviour most often considered and studied. It is the type in which the individual has least control over the nature of the activity. An important mechanism for encouraging this kind of creativity is through focus groups or think-tanks, whose membership is specifically organized to help to solve a particular problem.

Strategies often specify only broad targets without spelling out in detail how to achieve these targets. The strategic framework requires a multitude of specific solutions to the problems thrown up by the detailed strategy as it emerges. Much of the search for solutions to the associated problems requires responsive creativity.

B. *Expected creativity* lacks the focus of a defined problem but is induced by an outside authority. In this case the problems are not specified but a particular context does expect, even require, the exercise of creativity.

In the management context, the activity of quality circles or the practices of total quality management (TQM) would qualify as examples of expected creativity. Any activity carried out by members of a quality circle is relevant. An organization might build in such activity as an integral feature of the strategy-making process, on the assumption that creativity would generate a significant productivity improvement, whose approximate rate can be anticipated. The exact way in which a productivity increase can be achieved is not known in advance. Learning by doing or movement down the experience curve can result from such creative activity.

C. *Contributory creativity* involves the solution of defined problems but with motivation coming from inside rather than outside the individual.

The implication here is that the desire for creativity comes to all of us spontaneously. Job rotation might encourage the application of this kind of creativity to fresh areas. Employees might volunteer to engage in problem solving in areas not strictly relevant to their functional expertise, on the assumption that they bring a fresh mind and consequently new ideas.

D. *Proactive creativity* is the purest kind of creativity, with undefined problems but a motivation which comes from inside the creator. This creativity is in no way forced upon the individual. It is considered by many of those engaged in researching the nature of creativity to be the most fruitful kind of creativity, both in terms of the number of creative ideas or acts generated and the potential impact of those ideas or acts.

In the business world, any suggestions system, particularly if there is no outside incentive offered or instruction given on the area of application, would be an expression of this kind of creativity.

All these different types of creativity should flourish within an organization which is seeking an explicit, strategy-making competence. They may be linked with and reinforce each other. The situation is rather more complex than often presented, and reflects the particular circumstances of the organization. The differences between the types of creativity may not always be as clear-cut as the matrix suggests; they can overlap.

The paradox is that the context of strategy making implies that the driver is external, yet there is a consensus that creativity is best promoted by internal drivers. Moreover, extrinsic motivation, that is, the motivation which rests on pecuniary or material reward, has often been shown to be inferior to intrinsic motivation, that is, the pleasure derived from solving a problem is a better motivator than an external reward. It is often pointed out that extrinsic motivation actually reduces intrinsic motivation. There is plenty of evidence showing that suggestions systems offering no reward do very much better at stimulating creativity than those which offer a reward, in many cases reaching a 100% coverage. It is probably better to reward a team for a good outcome than the individual for a particular contribution. Individuals often show amazing tenacity in trying to solve particular problems, at considerable personal cost or discomfort. The attempt often spills over to fill their spare or recreation time.

Creativity is not just a matter of having creative people. Every person has the capacity to be creative to some, if only a small, degree. It is this universal ability which must be tapped to get the most out of the staff of an organization. The fact that some company suggestions systems have achieved 100% participation shows the extent to which it is genuinely universal. The key is how an organization can release creativity, particularly proactive creativity since this offers the greatest potential.

Focus on Humour
The incompatibility of extrinsic and intrinsic motivation

An old man was greatly disturbed by the newly started practice of the local children playing football on a derelict plot next door to his home. He had grown used to peace and quiet. The play was noisy and prevented his afternoon nap. He knew that he could not use any personal authority or physical presence to prevent the youths from playing, but he found the noise very intrusive and wanted it to stop. He devised an interesting but effective strategy to stop the playing, one which neatly illustrates human nature and its typical motivation.

One day he went out to the youths and thanked them very much for the pleasure that they had given him as he watched their skilful playing. He said that he wanted to show his thanks by giving them a cash reward. He gave them enough for each to

▶

Focus on
Humour
cont'd

receive two dollars. They looked surprised but accepted the money. He repeated the gift for the rest of that week.

The games continued, perhaps initially with even more frequency and enthusiasm. The next week, when the boys reappeared, he repeated the act of rewarding the boys but reduced the amount to one dollar, explaining that he was an old man living on a pension and could not always afford always to be so generous. The boys were no longer surprised but were not so obviously enthusiastic about the gift.

The playing continued. The next week the old man reduced the reward by half, this time provoking almost no response on the part of the boys, rather a stony silence.

Finally, in the fourth week, when the boys started playing, he went to them and said that he had run out of money and could give them nothing to reward them for playing. Their response was unanimous: 'If you think that we are going to play for you for nothing, you are sadly mistaken.' They departed and played their game elsewhere.

Intrinsic motivation, the love of playing, had been converted into extrinsic motivation, the response to a material reward, which was then withdrawn.

How to release creativity

Creativity cannot be planned; it is by its nature unexpected. The policy advice on encouraging creativity is often about what not to do, as much as about what to do. The tacit assumption is that the removal of potential obstacles to creative activity frees the innate desire to be creative. However, creativity must be relevant to the strategic framework. In order to achieve a maximum release of creativity, there are some very simple rules to follow. Hambrick and Frederickson (2001) have shown how an organization can do this through six elements which are described in turn.

Alignment

Alignment is closely linked with the problem of integration, as discussed in Chapter 12. It provides the purpose for which integration is desired. The aim is to harmonize the interests and actions of all staff and stakeholder groups around the key goals of the organization. There needs to be a strong alignment in order to stimulate and channel appropriately the creativity of staff so that they innovate in ways which help achieve the strategic targets. In other words, all staff should be aware of, and therefore headed in, the right direction. Unfortunately alignment is intangible and hard to define with precision. Fortunately complete alignment is not what is needed since it does not allow for gains from unexpected activity outside the parameters of the current strategy.

Strong alignment requires everyone to be clear about the organization's objectives, that is, to be thoroughly conversant with the basis of its strategy – where the organization is going. They need to be committed to initiatives which will promote the achievement of these objectives. Achieving this involves a great deal of communication. The staff will then be ready to move the organization in the desired direction.

Many organizations are misaligned in some way. For various reasons, staff may have no clear notion of what the key targets are, or are actually motivated to act in a way which is contradictory to the strategic intent of their organization. The most frequent tendency is to align an organization towards operating effectiveness rather than strategic creativity. This appears to reduce operating costs, but only in the short term. This orientation involves looking backwards, accepting the organization as it is and concentrating on its existing operational efficiency and not its future development.

Self-initiated activity

Left to themselves, human beings will, without any prompting, initiate creative activity, most effectively in areas with which they are familiar and in which they have an interest. However, they can often see what can be done to improve and innovate in areas new to them. This means that they tend to self-select for the job at hand, provided they are not prevented from doing so by some obstacle, such as a lack of time, excessive supervision or a poor corporate culture. The goal is to avoid the suppression of creativity. The role of the organization is to release what is already there and not in any way obstruct the natural desire to be creative. Any suggestions system can provide the opportunity to do this.

A good suggestions system must have a number of characteristics which encourage creativity and avoid discouraging it. The primary requirement is that someone in a position of authority must respond positively to the ideas advanced by employees. To do this there must be a system which reaches everyone, is easy to use, has strong and prompt follow-through by senior staff, documents suggestions carefully and is transparent and based on intrinsic motivation.

Unofficial activity

Every unexpected creative act begins with a period of unofficial activity, sometimes an activity which takes place in a matter of minutes, sometimes over a much longer period, even years. The benefits of unofficial activity are striking. The unofficial world provides a safe haven for activity which appears to be strange or repellent to many in the organization, and therefore in their view something which should be rejected. Very often the illicitness of the activity stimulates a much bigger input of time and effort, way beyond what would be the case in the official world. Such activity often ignores all the boundaries which limit and constrain creative activity in the official world. Such activity better prepares decision makers to choose between different options. Unofficial activity opens the way for the consideration of a larger number of ideas than would be opened in the official world.

The role of the organization is to make room for this unofficial activity in every way that it can, and certainly not to discourage it. Those working in this unofficial way must be given some space to develop their ideas, even allowed facilities and resources in an informal setting, even if this is done by turning a blind eye. The importance of this is best illustrated by what has happened in Nokia, where a significant number of breakthroughs have been achieved outside the official domain.

Serendipity

Creativity involves serendipity, happy chance discovery. There are two aspects of serendipity, on the one hand the frequency of occurrence of a fortunate accident and on the other the ability on the part of someone, who is in a position to do something about it, to recognize the good fortune in the accident. Fortunate accidents happen all the time in the course of working activities; a good strategy actually stimulates and provokes their occurrence. It encourages staff to recognize the good fortune.

The good fortune depends on the observer of the accident having the potential to analyse and act beyond the strict requirements of the immediate operating needs of the job. In the words of Robinson and Stern (1997: 192): 'If companies have no redundancy or randomness at all, they are optimized for their present environment and so are limited to only what they can anticipate and plan.' In this case they are unlikely to take advantage of serendipity. This is another argument for having a degree of organizational slack in any organization, sufficient to allow observers to exercise their sagacity and recognize a positive, chance discovery, turning it into a happy discovery. The observers require intelligence and experience to recognize the opportunity.

Diverse stimuli

Not all stimuli provoke creative activity. There is no doubt that a wider variety of stimuli helps in this. It is more important for a manager to have a wide range of acquaintances than a small circle of close friends. The former are much more likely than the latter to offer something new, something outside the everyday experience of the manager. Stimuli take various forms and their power differs from person to person. All are sensitive to different stimuli. Stimuli can redirect those stimulated in a completely new direction, or simply give them a fresh insight into what they are already doing.

The organization can deliberately seek to provide stimuli. By rotating the staff through different departments or even different locations, it can increase their exposure to new stimuli. It can encourage outside contacts of a kind which are likely to generate such stimuli, encouraging attendance at classes, courses or conferences. It can encourage staff to build on the stimuli they are already experiencing outside the organization.

Within-company communication

A company's creative potential increases greatly, perhaps exponentially, with its size. The full potential may not be realized. This relationship may help to explain the relentless tendency for enterprises to get bigger and bigger. The larger the company, the more likely that the components which make for creative action are already present, but the less likely that they will come together without help. It is critical for the staff member to understand what the company does and its expertise and capabilities. It should be an organizational priority to encourage staff to respond easily and quickly to requests for help or information. The key to releasing the creative potential of any organization is to promote a high level of within-company communication. Large Japanese companies are particularly good at doing this and most creative activity in Japan seems to occur in large organizations, which does not wholly correspond with the Western experience.

How might a company achieve this within-company communication? It cannot be organized centrally; this contradicts the spontaneity required by creativity. Innovation centres might help, but they often hinder more than help by exposing the organization to the temptation to manage ideas. The key is to try to allow self-organization to occur. The company can help by providing an opportunity for staff to meet outside the immediate work area.

There should be numerous conduits for feedback from those being creative. Creative ideas should feed straight into the strategy-making process. The creativity acts as a critical input into that process. The innovations which result are the stuff of strategy formulation. Since they happen all the time, they cause a continuous revision of strategic targets and objectives, and also the resources needed to achieve those objectives. Creativity means both an improvement in operational efficiency and the consequent freeing up of resources, and the continuous adjustment of strategy to take account of unexpected outcomes and newly revealed opportunities.

All strategists – and everyone as a potential strategic thinker is a strategist – are involved in creative thinking and creative action. Good strategy creates space for this creativity while at the same time providing the level of management appropriate to the circumstances of the industry.

New venture entrepreneurship

The key issue is how a company can maintain the impetus of creative entrepreneurship beyond the period when an entrepreneurial leader usually provides it from above. It is possible to make some generalizations about how this might happen. The impetus has to come from below, in a process of autonomous strategic development, encouraged in the way described above. Any new ventures within a company have to compete for resources, even if there is a specialist, separate division within the company responsible for such activity.

The story can be told in terms of three levels of the enterprise – senior management, middle managers in the new venture area and creative front-line workers. All have important roles to play.

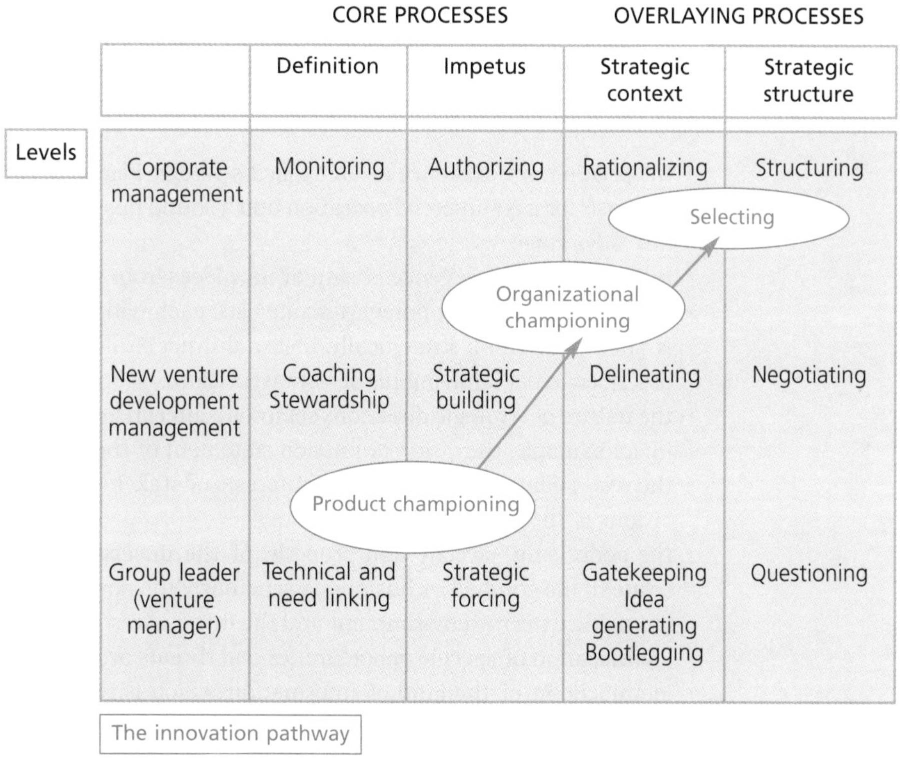

| | CORE PROCESSES | | OVERLAYING PROCESSES | |
Levels	Definition	Impetus	Strategic context	Strategic structure
Corporate management	Monitoring	Authorizing	Rationalizing	Structuring
			Selecting	
		Organizational championing		
New venture development management	Coaching Stewardship	Strategic building	Delineating	Negotiating
	Product championing			
Group leader (venture manager)	Technical and need linking	Strategic forcing	Gatekeeping Idea generating Bootlegging	Questioning

The innovation pathway

Source: Burgelman (1983).

Figure 16.3 **Burgelman's process model of internal corporate venturing (ICV) or intrapreneurship**

It is also told in terms of four processes. Two of these – the so-called core processes – are central to the new venture initiative as it is initially conceived, developed and promoted:

- the cognitive process of *defining* what the initiative means in technological and marketing terms
- the sociopolitical process of imparting impetus to the initiative, during which it is championed by middle managers, especially venture managers.

The other two – the overlaying processes – comprise the way in which senior managers become involved in incorporating the initiative into a strategy:

- the administrative and institutional mechanisms which set up or determine the structural context in which the initiative can be pursued
- the way in which the initiative leads to a revision or redetermination of the strategic context.

Intra-preneurship

Successful encouragement of such acts of intrapreneurship leads to an emergent strategy which is continuously being renewed and a reinterpretation of the past to accommodate the new initiative.

In the business management area, strategic thinking involves a range of features which are critical to good strategy making, particularly the articulation of the vision and the strategic objectives associated with it and their continuing updating to accommodate autonomous strategic developments:

- the preliminary existence of an explicit strategic idea(s) or initiative which can be the basis for a commercial operation and a sound business model based on competitive advantage
- the continuing emergence of similar new ideas from within an existing company
- the existence of many potential strategists, each with his or her own domain, that is, those who think strategically, have a distinct strategic orientation and could be described as each having his or her own vision
- the nature of strategic directions set for an enterprise and how they are articulated in, for example, the vision or mission statement of the organization
- the reconciliation of the different interests of stakeholder groups and the different visions of the strategists
- the addressing, directly and properly, of the uncertainties of the future as they relate to the conduct of business, particularly the potential interactions between a changing external environment and the internal resources of the organization
- identification of specific opportunities and threats or risks outside the enterprise
- identification of the kind of information which is required for realization of the strategic vision and the process by which this information might be acquired
- use of the creative imagination to devise innovative ways of dealing with problems arising from the realization of the strategic vision
- determination of the capacity of the enterprise to engage successfully in strategic

management and an understanding of the limitations on the effectiveness with which strategic management and strategic planning can be used

- the recognition of the limitations of strategic thinking, that business performance depends upon appropriate motivation and efficient management as well as creative strategic thinking.

The nature of strategic management

An emergent strategy

It is impossible to deal with formulation and implementation of strategy as different and distinct stages in strategy making. Since there is a massive overlap between the two, they should occur simultaneously. This fusion is a defining characteristic of an emergent strategy, which is one which emerges as the result of the implementation of a strategy already formulated and its reformulation.

There is a real need to depart from the classical notion that strategy making is a rational, linear and sequential process and that the strategy is formulated and handed down by the grand strategist and then implemented by the managers. It is easy to present the process of formulating a strategy as a clear-cut activity conducted over a defined period of time which precedes and does not overlap implementation, or as a process which yields a choice between a number of well-defined plans, readily available and detailed in their articulation. Strategy making is simply another example of optimizing choice. Specialist strategists assist the leader in implementing the strategy which he or she formulates. In such an account each stage is well defined and independent of the others.

A number of problems with the classical interpretation as a description of what happens in the process of strategy making have been identified. The procedure is to systematically analyse these problems and redefine the process of strategy formulation and implementation to accommodate them.

1. *The need to encourage creativity*

This has already been discussed at length.

2. *The problem of imperfect information, ignorance and uncertainty*

Imperfect information takes two forms. The first is ignorance of what might happen in the future. The faster the change, the less is known about the future. Strategy cannot anticipate every change or cover every possible contingency. Since strategy making takes time, circumstances change, even during the period of time needed for formulation of a strategy. Since change offers as much opportunity as risk, it is not even desirable to ignore the benefits of unanticipated change. The key is to take advantage of any opportunity and suppress any threat.

The second is the need for disaggregation. The formulation of a plan in a large hierarchical organization cannot be completed in a detail which would fully accommodate the requirements at every level of the organization. Strategists at the top have to rely on strategists at the bottom to fill out the strategy as it relates to their domain, that is, to disaggregate in an appropriate way a strategy which by its nature must consist in aggregate targets. The strategists at the top cannot possibly have a complete grasp of all the detail necessary to fully flesh out any plan. Those at the bottom need the discretion to deal with unexpected events or information.

There is always an element of serendipity in the identification of information. It is to some degree a random process. It is certainly a process of learning or discovery, occurring in an unpredictable way in the course of the formulation and implementation of any strategy.

3. *The indeterminateness inherent in strategic risk*

This requires the enterprise to be ready to respond to unanticipated strategic responses by other players – competitors, complementors or even governments. There is no way of knowing fully what competitors or complementors will do in response to any given strategy. This depends on the nature of the situation and the behaviour of the strategic players. The same indeterminateness applies to governments. Nobody can be certain who will be in power and what they might do. This is another source of strategic risk. Any strategy has to be capable of adaptation to meet the reactions of other strategic players and cope with the resulting strategic risk.

An enterprise must go further and, from its reading of others' behaviour, decide whether it is appropriate in a defined strategic situation to cooperate or compete. It also has to decide upon the risk management strategy which is appropriate in a multitude of different situations.

4. *The problem of solving the agency dilemma*

This involves guiding agents away from activity inconsistent with the directions of the strategy adopted, and motivating and empowering agents to behave in a way consistent with that strategy.

This is a problem of identifying the divergent interests of all stakeholders, devising a way of involving them in strategy making and harmonizing the differing objectives within the strategy-making process. It involves dealing with the 'political' issues, negotiating with groups or individuals.

The alignment of all groups and individuals must be achieved without blocking their creative activity. There is a need to reconcile the unpredictability of such activity with the directional framework of a strategy in which the different groups are all similarly aligned.

5. *The necessity of remaking in some way the external and/or the internal environment in order to maintain competitive advantage*

Genuine strategy is about changing things, not just accepting the environment as a given. The strategist must decide what is a given and what can be changed. A strategy must be built on a realistic view of how the enterprise can remake either its external or internal environment and what resources are needed to do this.

6. *The temporary nature of any competitive advantage, or monopoly profit, created by the enterprise*

Central to any successful strategy is the ability to create and maintain competitive advantage. Maintaining competitive advantage requires a sensitivity to market changes and a willingness to embrace any innovation which reduces costs or raises the quality of the product, or generally offers good or better value to the consumer.

This requires a continuous process of innovation. There is no possibility of resting on one's laurels.

The context, reflecting these problems, prevents strategy conforming to the classical view. Emergent strategy summarizes the nature of strategy making as it must occur most of the time. It is never complete. By its nature, any successful strategy must always be open-ended, that is, flexible enough to be adjusted to take advantage of opportunities which arise and head off threats which emerge. In this sense, strategy is more process than content, more perspective than plan – a way of setting targets, identifying resources needed for implementing the strategy rather than a finished, comprehensive and highly detailed set of proposals.

Interactions

Strategy making is also an interactive process in which different strategists steadily reveal what they know, sometimes without realizing its significance, and what they are learning. They can contribute continuously to the making of strategy. A multitude of decisions are made every day which influence the performance of an enterprise and the realization of its strategy. All these decisions are based on a mass of information that cannot possibly be known by one strategist alone. It is important that these decisions are made within a coherent framework and are in some sense consistent with each other: that is one of the main functions of strategy.

Any decisions must be made at an appropriate location in the organization. It is easy to overcentralize or overdecentralize – getting the balance right is difficult. Strategy making includes discovering the appropriate location of decision making and institutionalizing it. The pursuit of competitive advantage requires all to be alert to opportunities and be in a position to exploit those opportunities when they present themselves. Strategy is at its best when it is an active process of revealing the full potential of the organization and its resources.

Learning and discovery

Strategy becomes part of a process of discovery. Discovery is made necessary by the elements indicated above – the imperfection of the information available, the indeterminateness of outcome in the strategic situations likely to occur and the universality of the agency dilemma and the associated opportunism. Since change is relentless, any detailed strategic plan would become obsolete even before it begins to be implemented. Nor could any plan spell out in detail possible strategic reactions to all the contingencies which might occur. Knowledge is highly specific to particular sectors of the economy and highly specific to particular times and circumstances. It is impossible to deal in advance with every eventuality. Strategy is about the emergence of new possibilities, some the result of the release of creativity within the enterprise.

The capacity to make good strategy could be regarded as one of the most important intangible resources available to an enterprise. It is a skill which can be developed, and one which can be easily lost. It may include the emergence of strategists whose main function is to develop strategy, that is, staff who are specialist, 'professional' strategists but, much more importantly, it includes the inculcation in all staff of a strategic perspective – in this sense, all staff are strategists, or should be; they are a vital part of the process of strategy making, whether formulation or implementation. They can all engage in strategic thinking, if only to link an activity which results in improvement and innovation with the objectives contained within a strategic framework. This perspective is best made explicit, rather than left implicit. The adoption of such a perspective is critical to continuing business viability. Given this situation, most discussions of strategy making are oversimplifications of a complex and difficult process. Carried too far, they can be more damaging than helpful.

What is it which emerges or is learned or discovered in the process of strategy making? The answer is new opportunities and new threats, and new ways of making the best of both. In the course of strategy making, an enterprise discovers what it should be doing in order to remain viable. It discovers what it is capable of doing, which may be very different from what it initially thought.

Putting together an integrated strategy

Strategy is not about following a well-defined, sequential process. Rather, it is a process of achieving 'a robust, reinforced consistency among the elements of strategy itself' (Hambrick and Fredrickson, 2001: 50). It means juggling with all these elements simultaneously. What exactly are these elements? They have already been discussed, but the following summarizes the previous discussion:

1. *The arenas or peaks* (or whatever metaphor is helpful)
This is where the enterprise will *position* itself, where it will be most active and where any focus will be on the associated activities. It considers:

• the enterprise's range of business units, with their products and services
• the market segments to which the products and services are sold
• the geographic areas in which the customers in those market segments reside
• the core technologies employed to produce the products and services
• the activities in the value chain on which the enterprise concentrates.

In all these the enterprise needs to be as specific as possible. These issues concerning positioning were all raised in the section on environments in Chapter 6 in which positioning was seen as a key perspective.

2. *The competitive advantage differentiators* – choosing a generic strategy
The choice of a generic strategy raises the following questions:

• How will the enterprise win over its competitors?
• What is the nature of the competitive advantage which is at the heart of its strategy?
• Is it the cost or price level?
• Is it the image or branding of the company and its products?
• Which product attributes or consumer utilities are involved – style or reliability, luxury or prestige, safety or healthiness?
• Can utilities be delivered to the consumer in combination?
• What value does the company offer to consumers?

These issues were dealt with in Chapters 8, 9 and 10.

3. *The vehicles or modes of participation*

How exactly will the enterprise get to where it desires to be? There are various methods which have been discussed already:

- Organic or internal development (see the IKEA case study in Chapter 2)
- A strategic alliance, such as a joint venture (see the Strategy in Action on Renault and Nissan in Chapter 13)
- Licensing (see the case study on Hutchison in Chapter 8)
- Mergers or acquisitions, linked sometimes to demergers, a vehicle in which GE excels (see also the BHP case study in Chapter 11).

All these methods have been discussed in earlier chapters, notably Chapters 11, 13 and 15.

4. *Staging or pacing*

Staging involves:

- How the enterprise will get from its starting point to the target point
- The speed of movement and the exact sequence of moves which are best suited to a successful completion.

The speed of expansion will be driven by a range of different factors including:

- resource availability
- the urgency of movement
- the credibility of the enterprise in trying to do what it is doing
- the early successes achieved which might make possible an acceleration.

If there are key initiatives to be attempted, in what order should they be undertaken? This issue is largely unexplored in the management literature and is so far unexplored in this book. It will be dealt with in Chapter 17.

5. *Economic logic and corporate social performance*

The economic logic of any strategy concerns outcomes as defined by performance indicators. Corporate social performance reflects the need to satisfy stakeholders other than the owners.

From an economic perspective, a successful strategy should produce a desired outcome, which might be an increase in sales, an increase in market share or, more likely, an increase in profit, or possibly all of these. This often comes down to an examination of the bottom line, how performance is to be measured and how profit is to be gained to meet the financial targets.

What are the main factors needed to generate this profit? It asks whether the logic should be purely profit driven or whether there should be a triple or even a quadruple bottom line. How far should all stakeholders be considered in analysing outcomes? From a social perspective, it is desirable to have happy stakeholders. Chapter 18 on

Strategy in Action IKEA and innovative combination

In the case study in Chapter 2, the emphasis was on the creativity of IKEA in combining different elements in an innovative mix, called the IKEA way. For the past 25 years, IKEA has had a strategy which is highly coherent and integrates all five elements, in a way which sees them reinforce each other. The success of IKEA can be interpreted in terms of these elements. This is a creative application of strategic thinking, which culminates in making a successful strategy, producing good profit outcomes, relatively high market shares and happy stakeholders.

These elements fit together well in the IKEA way. For example, the young, white-collar customers, who are the target market segment and like the sense of style, find a low price, a fun, non-threatening shopping experience and instant fulfilment very much to their liking. The last two characteristics are difficult to deliver in anything other than a wholly owned store, which allows IKEA to exercise the level of control required to deliver them.

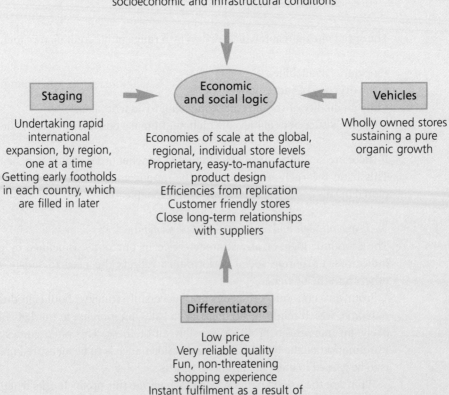

Arenas

Selling inexpensive, contemporary, stylish furniture and furnishings to young, white-collar customers, produced by suppliers using best-practice technology.
Worldwide market reach to countries with similar socioeconomic and infrastructural conditions

Staging

Undertaking rapid international expansion, by region, one at a time
Getting early footholds in each country, which are filled in later

Economic and social logic

Economies of scale at the global, regional, individual store levels
Proprietary, easy-to-manufacture product design
Efficiencies from replication
Customer friendly stores
Close long-term relationships with suppliers

Vehicles

Wholly owned stores sustaining a pure organic growth

Differentiators

Low price
Very reliable quality
Fun, non-threatening shopping experience
Instant fulfilment as a result of immediate availability

Figure 16.4 IKEA's creative combination

monitoring shows how different stakeholders are important at different stages in the life cycle of an organization.

All the different elements stress intentionality, a propensity to look forward and make things happen. They all require careful preparation and the investment of significant resources. All must be aligned with each other so that they are mutually reinforcing. The five elements represent the central hubs for designing an integrated strategic activity system. This is really what constitutes strategy formulation. Underpinning this integrated system are supporting activities – framing functional policies, putting in place the appropriate organizational arrangements, devising operating programmes and instituting various processes, including those for controlling and monitoring strategy. These latter are better seen as parts of strategy implementation. The IKEA Strategy in Action provides a neat illustration of the importance of these five strategic elements and how they can be put together in a strategy.

Developing the best strategy

It might be that a whole series of strategies could satisfy the basic requirement of a fit between these different elements. A good strategist is not interested in just any strategy which happens to be internally consistent. It is a matter of discovering which of all strategies is the best available, or rather will turn out to be best in terms of desired outcomes in different environments. It is not possible to know all the strategies possible at any one time – this is only possible with hindsight. Which has the potential to be the best depends on satisfying a number of key evaluation criteria.

A strategy does not consist of targets and resource allocations written on tablets of stone. Strategy could be likened to a process of developing what is called a rolling plan, that is, one which is continuously being adjusted to fit a changing environment. It sets directions rather than detailed plans. There are clear directions for future movement set in the strategy, with allowance made for the unexpected. Strategy consists in an unrelenting quest to maintain competitive advantage in an ever-changing world and adopt whatever procedure assists in achieving this. A good strategy accommodates the unexpected and the unanticipated.

Since it is not possible to anticipate all the changes in the environment, uncertainty is the normal state of the strategist. If scenario building reveals different possible futures, then it is advisable to have optional strategies ready for these different futures. There might be a best strategy for each future scenario. The common denominator in all these best strategies establishes what could be called the core strategy. On the other hand, differences create what are called contingent strategies, only to be implemented if the nature of the environment so requires. If the scenario actually realized is appropriate to another contingent strategy, then this strategy might have to be taken up.

Most important, the different best strategies define:

- what resources are definitely needed
- what might be needed
- what can with confidence be disposed of
- other assets which might be acquired.

A strategic alliance or an R&D project might establish the equivalent of an option to purchase such a resource, an option which need not be exercised, although creating and maintaining the option generates some cost. The main aim is to retain flexibility. The key evaluation criteria are:

- Does the strategy position the enterprise on one of the peaks of the business landscape, or at least in the highest mountain range with a good route to an accessible peak? Does it place the enterprise to take advantage of any new peak which might appear?
- Does the strategy make full use of the enterprise's resources, capabilities and core competencies, including the competency to make good strategy?
- Are the differentiators at the heart of a generic strategy which creates competitive advantage sustainable over the period envisaged in the strategy?
- Is the strategy achievable with the resources that are already available, those on which there is an option to acquire or those which can be readily and economically acquired? Or is the enterprise likely to be struggling to support the strategy?
- Is it possible to implement the strategy? Is there any reason for believing it is not possible?

Elements of strategic management

Strategic management involves a combination of the following:

- undertaking a scenario-building exercise which outlines possible futures
- formulating core and contingent strategies
- articulating the vision of the enterprise and disaggregating this as objectives and targets in a clear and detailed way
- communicating these detailed objectives to managers
- giving all the functional areas their appropriate place in the realization of enterprise objectives
- integrating different functional areas of management in the achievement of enterprise objectives
- linking specific functional plans with the achievement of enterprise objectives
- considering how to get access to any resources required which are not already available within the enterprise
- considering the role of the business or corporate plan in strategic management
- considering what is meant by a strategic plan and how far the elements of strategic management can be embodied in such a plan.

Strategic planning

It has already been made clear that a strategy is not the same as a plan. In the course of the book, it has frequently been shown how difficult it is to plan thoroughly in the context of ignorance and uncertainty, and rapid change in the environments in which strategy making occurs. The faster the rate of change, the more difficult it is to make the final step to strategic planning, the move to phase 5 discussed in the first section of this chapter.

Planning is probably the most used and misused word in the lexicon of management studies. It is possible to take either a strict or a loose definition of planning:

- A strict definition would insist on the existence of a comprehensive detailed plan covering all functional areas, for several years into the future, usually at least three
- A loose definition would accept a business model, the annual corporate plan or even the general framework of a set of broad long-term objectives as sufficient to show the existence of planning

Of course, there are many possible definitions between these two extremes. It is rare to be able to achieve planning in the stricter sense. Much more typical is planning in the looser sense, sometimes supplemented by more rigorous planning in certain limited functional areas.

It is fruitful to explore the issue at greater length. For the moment, the looser definition is accepted in order to distinguish between four different degrees, even types, of planning. These are:

1. *Minimal planning* – an annual business or corporate plan within the framework of broad long-term aims and an apparently viable business model
2. *Focused planning* – the specification of key targets, often in narrow functional areas, with some detailed analysis of how to achieve them, but little outside the area(s) of focus
3. *Comprehensive planning without all the detail* – specific and coherent aggregate targets but no detailed disaggregation of what is needed in order to achieve these targets
4. A *fully comprehensive plan* which spells out in detail, at all levels of the organization, both targets and the resources needed to achieve those targets.

There is a further type of planning which is flexible, in the sense that it allows for adaptation to unexpected changes in the environment. This can be called *flexible planning*, and the plan, one subject to continuous adjustment, is called a rolling plan. Each of the four types of planning can incorporate some degree of flexibility.

Unhappily, number one is all too common, largely because organizations do not appreciate the importance of strategy making and most of their time are fully absorbed in operational problems. Crisis management is a common condition for many organizations. In this they tend to be reactive rather than proactive. The time and effort of staff is never available for a consistent practice of strategy making. It may be that the enterprise wishes to avoid the commitment of the necessary resources.

The fourth type of planning is only possible with an organization in stable conditions within a mature industry in which there is almost no competition and little change of any kind. The circumstances which make it possible are unusual and so it is rare to find this type of planning actually being practised.

There are four main determinants to the kind of planning which will be used:

1. The rate of change in the industry, on the supply side, particularly the rate of technical change, and on the demand side, the rate of change in tastes or consumer fashions, and the degree to which it is possible to anticipate the changes which are occurring.
2. The point in the industry or product cycle at which a particular product or industry is located – infancy, adolescence, adulthood or old age. Is this sector part of the new or old economy? Has the particular product or service already been 'commoditized'?
3. The competitive conditions in the industry. Is there easy entry and fierce competition? Is there a natural monopoly, or the usual oligopoly or duopoly?
4. The condition of the organization itself. Is it in its infancy? Is it dynamic and profitable, or stable and making a satisfactory profit? Or is it in crisis for some reason, facing a turnaround situation?

Where the rate of change is rapid, the industry is in its infancy, competitive conditions are extreme and the enterprise is dynamic and profitable, the minimal model may apply. These are the conditions under which the evolutionary approach to strategy making is most appropriate. There may be little room for real strategy making, and often no perceived need.

However, for start-ups, whatever the other conditions, it is advisable to move as close to the fourth type as possible – there should be a blueprint for success, which consists in a detailed plan of what should be done. However, start-up companies usually lack the resources to do this. A serious crisis and the need for a turnaround (as illustrated in the Samsung Strategies in Action in Chapter 8) will also prompt the application of comprehensive planning.

In both these conditions, the classical approach is more accurate as a description of what does, or rather what should, occur. Often a fully comprehensive plan does not appear because of the urgency of timing and the absence of the necessary resources. However, an individual strategy maker emerges – the founder or the saviour – to rescue the enterprise through an imposed strategy. The strategy is often in the head of the strategists and develops as the situation unfolds. The return to normality after the crisis means a return to a mixture of types two and three planning.

For the most part, under conditions which are not extreme – moderate change, adulthood of the industry, oligopoly, relative stability and satisfactory profitability – the processual approach best indicates the nature and constraints on planning. In these circumstances, either types two or three planning are the likely location of strategy making, with a touch of adaptation added to the aggregation. This is what has been called emergent strategy, already discussed at the beginning of the previous section.

Finally, it is helpful to comment on systemic differences in the nature of the approach to strategy making and on changes in the nature of the strategy making. For example, there has been a radical change in Japan, reflecting the difficult transition which that economy has been experiencing. Even within particular economies, the approach can shift dramatically, with an emphasis on entrepreneurship or transformation in whole sectors of the economy.

The author of the book has tended to use and prefers to use planning in the fourth sense. Often students find this a restricting usage but it does help to avoid confusion. Much of the criticism of planning is a criticism of planning restricted to this narrow conception, not what this book calls strategic thinking or strategic management. It is better to use planning in the stricter rather than the looser usage.

Elements of strategic planning

Strategic planning therefore involves:

- the fixing of definite time horizons for the achievement of strategic intent, for example a three- or five-year plan
- the establishment of a strategic planning department, or the appointment of particular personnel, professional strategists designated to formulate, oversee the implementation of and monitor and adjust plans
- the identification of appropriate information streams which will allow the preparation of a plan and the later monitoring of planned target achievement
- the establishment of conduits for the communication of the plan to various parts of the enterprise and the generation of continuous feedback from within the enterprise on plan formulation and implementation
- the drawing up of detailed and coherent plans in all the main functional areas of management, for example finance, operations, marketing, human resource management, research and development, all consistent with the broad objectives set and the resources available
- detailed allocations to the various units of the resources needed to fulfil the plans
- the preparation of mechanisms for the adjustment of a plan to take account of the changing external environment.

Case Study 1:   The supreme strategist – General Electric

The early history of GE and strategic planning

Prior to 1947 GE's strategy making consisted of nothing more than an annual plan and a system of capital budgeting to solve the enterprise's internal problems. In that year Charles Wilson, the CEO, asked Ralph Cordiner to analyse the enterprise's growth problems. His conclusion was that the enterprise was overcentralized and that somehow all managers should be encouraged to develop and use the attributes of entrepreneurs. In 1950 he became the CEO. During his incumbency GE developed the foundations of its strategy-making concept, which was based on the twin notions of managers as entrepreneurs and the customers as the prime movers of all strategy.

The main element in strategy making was to be the marketing concept, the notion that all strategy should have market opportunity as its justification. How was this to be achieved? Borch, Cordiner's successor, asked the McKinsey consulting firm how to do this in the light of two principal difficulties, the tendency to overbureaucratization of GE and the problem of integrating all the separate divisions of the enterprise.

McKinsey made two major innovations:

1. A matrix organization, in which strategic teams were superimposed over the line or functional organization, headed by a director of corporate planning and beneath him at the group level a group vice-president. These teams were to be called strategic business units (SBUs). There were as many as 43 of them to go alongside the 10 groups, the 50 divisions and the 170 departments. A business unit was

Industry attractiveness

		High	Medium	Low
Business strengths	High	Invest/grow	Invest/grow	Select/earn
	Medium	Invest/grow	Select/earn	Harvest/divest
	Low	Select/earn	Harvest/divest	Harvest/divest

Figure 16.5 **GE's multidimensional portfolio assessment**

defined by the boundaries of a market having sets of interrelated customers. It was to have a corporate sub-mission, and its own resources, competitive strategies and budgets.

2. The portfolio management of the resources of GE. Each of the SBUs would apply for financial support on a competitive basis. A corporate planning committee would prioritize projects put up by the SBUs. The approach is best summarized in the classic diagram shown in Figure 16.5.

In order to succeed, the portfolio approach required the SBU to make its own 'sub-mission', in which it made its own set of financial objectives, conducted its own in-depth studies of the markets, implemented its own competitive strategies and cost–benefit studies, developed its own corporate resources and established its own intermediate and final goals. The SBU was to be judged, not by short-term profitability but by its role in achieving the targets of the strategic plan.

When Jones replaced Borch in 1972, there were still problems in two main areas: first, the ability of the centre to assert control over the divisions and business units, and second the need to make the strategy-making process itself more effective. Jones moved forward the reorganization of the business activities of the company at a higher global level. He identified six separate broad areas: energy; communication, information and sensing; energy application – productivity; materials and sources; transportation and propulsion; and a pervasive services area, including finance, distribution and construction, as the world markets for GE. He sought the basis for the assertion of control by the centre through the appointment of two or three vice-chairmen supervising the vice-presidents who headed these areas. Market assessments were based on these groupings, although strategic business units could be as large as a division or as small as a department or product line. The vice-chairmen were made responsible for plans and financial results as well as operational

control. They required of the vice-presidents a regular reassessment of their strategic plans from an international perspective. The management layers reviewing the strategic business units and their plans were reduced from 43 to 6.

What was still lacking was a significant reduction in the level of bureaucratization in the strategy-making process. The problems associated with the nature of demanding presentations and the way in which the substance of the strategy was developed still had to be confronted.

The Jack Welch years

Jack Welch had a background in chemical engineering, having completed a PhD at the University of Illinois. He joined GE Plastics in 1960 and worked his way up through the various management levels of the company, never leaving the company. He was not the front runner for the position of CEO of GE until the very last moment. His rise within the company was rapid but it was still a surprise when he attained the position of CEO. His predecessor Reginald Jones argued that he was looking for someone to innovate, to take the company to a new level of achievement by changing things.

Welch himself saw his goal as developing a perception of GE 'as a unique, high-spirited, entrepreneurial enterprise ... a company known around the world for its unmatched level of excellence'. It would be a company which would be 'the most profitable, highly diversified company on earth, with world-quality leadership in every one of its product lines' (quoted in Grant 1999: 346). Note the emphasis on entrepreneurship, global perspective and leadership. Welch saw the leader as a visionary, a communicator and a supreme organizer.

Welch sought to turn GE into a performance-driven enterprise rather than clearly articulating a detailed strategic plan. In order to achieve this goal, every aspect of GE's management had to be challenged. The guiding rules were simple; be number one or number two in the business area or be part of the three priority areas of GE business, which meant developing a technical advantage which could be translated into competitive advantage – or bow out. Disengagement did not mean a management failure, it simply meant

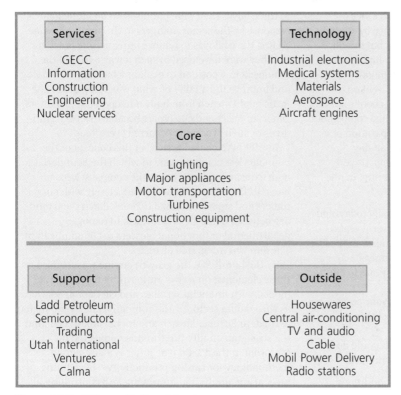

Services

GECC
Information
Construction
Engineering
Nuclear services

Technology

Industrial electronics
Medical systems
Materials
Aerospace
Aircraft engines

Core

Lighting
Major appliances
Motor transportation
Turbines
Construction equipment

Support

Ladd Petroleum
Semiconductors
Trading
Utah International
Ventures
Calma

Outside

Housewares
Central air-conditioning
TV and audio
Cable
Mobil Power Delivery
Radio stations

Figure 16.6 **GE's portfolio of businesses**

that a bad situation was tying up resources and needed to be changed.

The three priority areas comprised 15 business units, covering the core activities, the high-tech businesses and the service businesses (Figure 16.6).

Some of these businesses were shed and some reorganization occurred. By the end of his first decade as CEO, there were 14 business units. As Table 16.2 illustrates, Welch largely succeeded in his aim on performance. At this stage, GE's financial services and communications units were too fragmented to be ranked.

Welch put the emphasis on stretch goals, which were to be clear and concise, easily translated into one or two stretch targets, and benchmarked against the main competitors to show that they were feasible.

Among the objectives was a significant internationalization of the company, the achievement of a share of as much as 25% of total sales in Mexico, India and China. This was premised on the existence in these countries of an infrastructure capable of sustaining a 20–25% return on investment. Initially this was seen as much more likely in India than China.

Welch reorganized the management structure in 1985, removing whole layers of middle management. The aim was to make GE's structure more flexible and

responsive to changing circumstances. Instead of the head of a business unit reporting to the CEO through both group and sector layers, these layers were removed and in future the report was to be direct to the CEO. The office of the CEO was expanded and a corporate executive council set up. Welch believed that the company management structure could be reduced to four levels, and that those running business units could be empowered by this rationalization. He believed that the average span of control could be extended from 6–7 to 10–15 subordinates. As a result, there were large reductions in employment. Between 1980 and 1990, GE's number of employees fell from 402,000 to 298,000, which helped to give Jack Welch the nickname of 'Neutron Jack'. Any growth in employment tended to occur overseas. At the same time, union membership declined dramatically, from 70% to half that by the end of the 1980s.

Welch retained the annual planning cycle but replaced the staff-led, document-driven process by a much less formal and more personal approach. What happened is perhaps best summarized by

Table 16.2 **The position of GE's strategic business units after ten years of Jack Welch**

| SBU | Market standing | |
	in the USA	in the world
Aircraft engines	1st	1st
Broadcasting (NBC)	1st	N/A
Circuit breakers	Tied for first	Tied for first
Defence electronics	2nd	2nd
Electric motors	1st	1st
Engineering plastics	1st	1st
Factory automation	2nd	3rd
Industrial and power systems	1st	1st
Lighting	1st	2nd
Locomotives	1st	Tied for first
Major home appliances	1st	Tied for second
Medical diagnostic imaging	1st	1st

Source: Thompson and Strickland, 1999: 255.

comments made by Bossidy, one of Welch's vice-chairmen in 1988. He startled his audience by stating that GE no longer did strategic planning, but qualified this by saying that, whereas the company had deserted strategic planning, it certainly had not abandoned strategic thinking or strategic management. He went on to indicate that strategic thinking is thinking about markets, customers and the nature of competition and competitors.

Strategy making now involved the preparation of a 'slim' playbook and it was debated at a half-day meeting. The playbook addressed the competitive dynamics of each business unit by answering, in one page, five key questions:

1. What are your market dynamics globally today, and where are they going over the next several years?
2. What actions have your competitors taken in the last three years to upset those global dynamics?
3. What have you done in the last three years to affect these dynamics?
4. What are the most dangerous things your competitor could do in the next three days to upset those dynamics?
5. What are the most effective things you could do to bring your desired impact on those dynamics?

This came down to considering market conditions, technology, competition, profitability and competitive strategies.

Supporting this process was fairly tight budgeting and the establishment of continuously stretched targets, which were directed to improving performance. Budgets could be adjusted if it was shown by the leader of a business unit that conditions had changed significantly but budgets were taken seriously. Net earnings were to grow at 1.5–2 times the growth rate of GDP. In the end good performance showed itself in good earnings.

Staff needed the right incentive to perform, and not to be deterred from trying by punishment for failure. There was an enormous extension of the stock option system and a concentration on and increase in bonuses. Managers were given space to show what they could do. However, they had to deliver, meeting commitments and embracing both the GE role for them of market-oriented and fast-moving entrepreneurs and the company's vision of the future.

Welch believed that it was necessary to embrace change and see the world as it is, not as you hope it will be. The stress should be on 'speed, simplicity and self-confidence'. In order to encourage open and direct communication, in 1989 Welch initiated the Workout, forums in which mangers could speak their minds on the management processes and practices in their areas. These were attended by 50–100 managers and took two to three days. They were premised on an immediate response by the senior mangers in the area concerned. At first the goal was to remove bureaucratic practices, but they were developed in such a way as to put the managers in a position to explain what they were doing and improve the quality of what was being done. The focus might switch from budget to operational matters. Often suppliers and customers became involved. Hundreds of such Workouts occurred every year.

By 1990 Welch had arrived at this concept of the boundaryless company, one in which the boundaries both external and internal to the company were blurred. The company had to work closely with customers and suppliers. It had to break down the boundary between domestic and foreign, to remove departmental or functional barriers to communication. The aim was integrated diversity.

By the late 1990s the growth engine was focused on three elements: on a two- rather than a three-circle model, with financial services and GE Capital Services as the leading sector of the company; global expansion abroad, to Europe, Mexico and increasingly Asia; and the six sigma quality programme, pioneered by Motorola in the 1980s. The latter is a disciplined methodology for raising productivity – by defining, measuring, analysing, improving and controlling all the processes involved in the ultimate delivery of the product or service to the customer. It replaced Workout as the main driver of improvement and rising productivity.

The role of leadership

It is obvious from any account of the history of GE how important its leaders have been. They have certainly imposed their imprint on the company. A leader like Welch, who ran the company for almost 20 years, was bound to have a powerful influence on the company. It is almost unprecedented for any CEO to survive for so long and continue to deliver in terms of company performance.

All the CEOs have always been carefully selected, largely by their predecessors, and closely involved in strategy making for the future. The tendency has been to select the strategy first and then choose the CEO best able to realize that strategy. For example, Welch was chosen because he had demonstrated an ability to match GE's core technology to worldwide market opportunities. He certainly saw his job as internationalizing the company.

The new CEO Jeff Immelt faces a series of problems which are discussed below. They will inevitably change the strategy of the company.

Strategy today

'GE is increasingly like a large shark: it must keep moving, and keep eating, or perish.'

Hill et al., 2002: 26

GE has maintained a very healthy share valuation by providing double-digit growth in net earnings each year for many years. It has done this by a process of strategic acquisitions. The problem is that the bigger GE becomes, the harder it is to continue to do this. In 2001, the European Commission turned down the GE $43 billion bid for Honeywell. However, the failure of gross revenue to continue to grow at anything like the previous pace has led to a reconsideration of the company. The P/E ratio has dropped from a peak of 45 to about 16, which means GE is being priced more like a finance company than a manufacturing company.

How has GE maintained its growth in earnings? The critics argue that it has done so by sleight of hand, leaning on its shareholders and acquisitions.

There are four main criticisms of GE. Over the years there have been *far too many acquisitions*, running at about 100 a year, and the growth in earnings has been sustained by acquisitions rather than innovation and organic growth, that is, internal productivity rise. This is a common argument laid against acquirers who stand accused of using the acquisitions to hide fluctuations in revenue. It is certainly much easier to hide such fluctuations when you are frequently consolidating acquired enterprises into your accounts. Warner (2002: 72) estimates that acquisitions have accounted for about 40% of GE's growth over the period 1985–2000, a high but not enormously high proportion.

There are two main dangers, first, that the profits made are one-off speculative gains, and second, that the profits are deliberately smoothed out to show an even growth, in line with the targets already set, in a double process of massaging the key analysts to influence expectations and the interpretation of outcomes in order to keep the share price up. This is accompanied by a criticism of the process of smoothing of profits over time which have made it appear that profits have grown steadily rather than fluctuated with the economy. There is not much doubt that the company has been adept at both, showing itself as highly competent at meeting targets and achieving stable growth. Over the past ten years there have been only two quarters in which GE has failed to meet its earnings targets.

The accusations seem unfair if only because GE has been just as ready to shed businesses as to acquire them. It has been the greatest of downscopers. At the moment it stands ready to divest three of its most unprofitable, but sometimes defining, businesses – appliances (for

example refrigerators and micro-ovens), lighting and Employers Re, the second largest reinsurer in the USA. In this context the simultaneous occurrence of both acquisition and divestiture have meant that the company regularly restructures itself. It is actively seeking more service contracts, able to make more money by following up with maintenance and add-on services on its sales of aircraft engines or electricity turbines than by the initial sale. It is increasing its R&D expenditures, opening two new research centres in China and Germany.

It is possible but unlikely that the company has been concealing a slowing of growth, or today, even the appearance of losses. Certainly some methods have been used which can conceal more than they reveal. The issue of asset-backed securities, a failure to properly account for reinsurance losses and the use of stop-loss contracts spring to mind.

The company relies too much on short-term debt, at a level way in excess of its bank lines (three or four times), making the company vulnerable to sudden interest rate changes. At one time the level of short-term commercial paper was $117 billion compared with only $33 billion of backup bank loans. Traditionally short-term debt has been 50% of GE Capital's total borrowings. The loans are a cheap form of finance particularly for GE Capital and particularly when interest rates are low. Recently, in order to keep the markets happy, the backup lines have been increased to $57 billion and something like $37 billion of commercial paper replaced with longer term bonds

The level of leverage is excessive, something like 14–16 to 1 which compares badly with the more usual range of 6–12 to 1 for finance companies.

There is not enough accounting disclosure and it is unclear how different business units are doing and how acquisitions have affected the company. Much of this criticism has arisen because of the crash of Enron and the difficulties of Tyco.

Because of these criticisms and the recession, the share price of GE has taken a beating. It has moved down from $60 in August 2000 to $33 on April 24, 2002, implying a fall of $268 billion in the value of the company. The divisional results, as given in Table 16.3, reveal some of the problems.

Altogether in 2001 GE Capital had revenues of US$58.4 billion, down 11.8%, and profits of US$5.6 billion, up 7.6%, which shows its importance in the overall picture.

The figures clearly show the impact of September 11 and the recession. They also show, in the figures on power systems, a dangerous bunching in demand for gas turbines which reflected a temporary shortfall in electricity generating capacity around the world. In this 'turbine

Table 16.3 **GE divisional results**

	Revenues 2001	($ bill) 2002	%	change	Profits 2001	($ bill) 2002	%	change
Aircraft engines	11.4	11.1	5.5	–2	2.6	2.1	2.6	–4
Appliances	5.8	6.1	–1.7	5	0.4	0.5	–6.0	11
Industrial products and systems	9.1	9.8	0.1	7	1.0	1.0	–14.3	–3
Materials	7.1	7.7	–11.2	8	1.4	1.1	–20.8	–21
NBC	5.8	7.1	–14.7	24	1.4	1.7	–10.9	18
Power systems	20.2	22.9	35.6	13	4.9	6.3	84.5	29
Technical products and services	9.0	9.3	13.8	3	1.6	1.6	14.7	–4
Commercial finance	13.9	16.0	N/A	16	2.7	3.2	N/A	17
Consumer finance	9.5	10.3	N/A	8	1.7	1.9	N/A	13
Insurance	23.9	23.3	N/A	–2	1.3	–0.5	N/A	N/A

bubble', occurring over the period 1998–2001, there was a four times increase in demand for gas turbines. GE has 60% of this market and an average profit margin of 24%, well above that of competitors. This demand is now falling way, with a halving between 2001 and 2002, and although an increasing share of the power systems' revenue comes from services, such as maintenance (as much as 40%), the fall is bound to make it difficult to maintain both revenue and profit growth.

The figures also show the increasing reliance on GE Capital, a much more long-term trend, although there were some problems in the area of insurance.

The role of GE Capital

It might be said that GE Capital is a money-making subsidiary which is financing a true conglomerate.

From an early date GE has had a presence in the finance industry. That presence has tended to grow over time, to become a major one. GE Capital is a large financing company involved mainly in consumer and commercial lending, car leasing, mortgage insurance and equipment financing, It has always been very profitable. GE therefore consists of two sets of businesses, GE Industrial which has no debt and generates plenty of cash and GE Capital, a financial operation, which has largely grown by acquisition and is not highly regarded by bank analysts, which must borrow in the rather capricious wholesale market (capricious at least relative to the retail market). Much of the growth has come in the financial area. Without GE Capital the growth rate of GE Industrial would have been rather lacklustre, at just under 6%.

Probably the biggest failure in GE's history occurred in the financial area and was a result of the failure to

recognize the difference between the way a manufacturing company and a financial company are run, in other words to recognize the difference in the required core competencies.

In 1986 GE Capital decided to acquire the securities firm Kidder, Peabody & Co. in order to produce, in combination with GE Capital, a 'force in the world's marketplace second to none'. However, the new CEO Michael Carpenter had no securities experience. Moreover, he did not get on well with the head of GE Capital Gary Wendt. Even in the area of mortgage securities in which GE Capital had a significant role, there was no cooperation and no realization of the synergies intended. Carpenter answered directly to Welch and Kidder, Peabody & Co. behaved independently of GE Capital.

Kidder's strategy proved risky. Carpenter decided to aim for a dominant position in the fixed-income market, notably the mortgage securities market. This required the firm to build up a large body of inventory which reflected the large number of underwritings undertaken. Carpenter assumed that the company could hedge much of the risk and that its traders would make significant profit in trading the securities. The implied financial backing of GE encouraged him to do this. Unfortunately, a rise of interest rates in 1994 caused the failure of this policy. Increasingly large losses were chalked up. Kidder lacked the tight management controls of GE. It had the freewheeling trading culture which was typical of Wall Street.

The immediate cause of the fiasco which revealed the vulnerability of even GE was the huge fictitious trading profits in government securities notched up by a Kidder trader, Joseph Fitch. This forced GE to report a US$350 million pretax loss in early 1994. The GE report, commissioned by a former head of enforcement at the SEEC, concluded that Kidder suffered from 'lax oversight' and 'poor judgement'. Virtually all the Kidder executives, including Carpenter, had to leave and were replaced by GE executives.

This debacle scarcely affected the growth of GE Capital. It shrugged off the difficulty as a local setback. GE Capital continued to grow rapidly. In terms of its asset size, GE Capital is now the fourth largest financier in the USA, just behind the Bank of America. GE Capital operates a broad portfolio of activities throughout the world, including a mixture of consumer and commercial finance, insurance and leasing businesses.

The most distinctive feature of GE Capital is its triple A credit rating, a privilege shared by only eight other American companies, and no financial companies. GE Capital has this privilege because its diversified, industrial parent guarantees its debts. In the words of one commentator, GE is 'the owner of the fanciest and most valuable corporate reputation of all' (*The Economist*, 2002: 57). This reputation rests largely on the superb management of its industrial businesses, from aircraft engines to light bulbs.

However, in the words of Bill Gross of PIMCO, one the most prominent buyers of the $100 billion worth of commercial paper issued by GE: 'GE is at bottom a financial company, open to the same set of risks as any other financial firm.' GE simply disguises these risks rather better than most. Not only does GE Capital currently generate 40% of GE's earnings, its ability to borrow on a triple A rating also markedly reduces the company's cost of capital, nearly all the debt being lodged in GE Capital. Every year since 1992, GE has been a net borrower of money. This helps to finance its acquisitions, whatever they are.

With a lower AA rating, the cost of its current debt would be as high as US$100–200 million more each year: if GE Capital was a separate stand-alone entity, even more, as much as US$400. This is because, if GE Capital had to stand alone, it would almost certainly be rated lower. The comparison with Citigroup, which appears on most indicators to be a better performer, shows the likely size of such a rerating.

Should the situation of GE Capital deteriorate, there are a series of triggers which would cost GE dearly in terms of cash or increased collateral. For example, earnings must not fall below 110 % of fixed costs (interest

Table 16.4 **Comparison with Citigroup, April 8, 2002**

	GE Capital	Citigroup
Total Assets	US$426 billion	US$1.05 trillion
Total outstanding debt	US$240 billion	US$399 billion
Return on assets	1.36%	1.43%
Debt to capital ratio	87.96%	81.87%
Long-term debt rating (Standard & Poor's)	AAA	AA

costs plus a portion of rental expenses) – they are presently at 170%, or the debt-to-equity ratio fall below 8 to 1. It is currently at 7.3 to 1, at which point the crossing triggers obligatory cash flows. Special-purpose entities (SPEs) off the balance sheet also share the high GE Capital rating. They carry US$43 billion in securitized loans, including credit card debt, commercial mortgages and equipment financing. Should the rating fall to AA- because of a series of defaults, they will trigger a need to substitute almost $15 billion in alternative credit. None of this constitutes an immediate liquidity problem but it does create a vulnerability if circumstances change and a target for critics.

Case Study Questions

1. In what areas of strategy making has GE been a pioneer?
2. What do we learn from the experience of GE about the role of the leader in strategy making?
3. What is the relationship between structure and strategy in the history of GE?
4. Which of the various schools of strategy best describes what has been experienced at GE?
5. How would you, as a strategist, deal with the problems which are now confronting GE?

Reading

Brady, D. Scherreik and Timmons, H., 'How does GE grow?', *Business Week*, April 8, 2002: 70–2.

Economist, The, 'The Jack and Jeff show loses its lustre', May 4, 2002: 57–9.

Hill, A., Marsh, P. and Roberts, D., 'GE must hone predatory instincts to ensure survival', *Financial Times*, June 21, 2002: 26.

March, P., 'GE and Siemens chase turbine market', *Financial Times*, June 3, 2003: 27.

Sherman, S.P., 'Inside the mind of Jack Welch', *Fortune*, March 27, 1989: 339–50.

Thompson, A.A. and Strickland, A.J., *Strategic Management: concepts and cases*, 11th edn (Irwin McGraw Hill, Boston, 1999: 255).

Vaghefi, M.R. and Huellmantel, A.B., *Strategic Management for the XXIst Century* (St. Lucie Press, London: 1999), particularly Chapter 2 'Strategic leadership and General Electric'.

Warner, M., 'Can GE light up the market again?', *Fortune*, November 11, 2002: 68–75.

Welch, J. *Jack, What I've learned leading a great company and great people* (Headline, London: 2001).

This case study is also relevant to Chapters 2 and 14.

Case Study 2   Nokia – where did it come from?

Early history

Nokia had it origins in a lumber mill built on the banks of the Nokia River in 1965. In 1967 the Finish Cable Works merged with the Finish Rubber Works and the Nokia Forest Products Company. In the early 1970s the strategic goals of the company were threefold – internationalization, an increased market share of high-tech products and the maintenance of the competitiveness of the original businesses. In the mid-1970s the company even dabbled in the new area of computers. It had not yet learned to focus, mainly because it was not obvious on what it should focus.

The Nordic nations had good reason to be the first region in the world to create a mobile telephone network. A harsh climate and a sparse population made a fixed-line system expensive to build. While it might cost about $800 per subscriber to bring fixed-line communication to remote communities in the north, the wireless cost per subscriber was significantly less, at $500. The demand for such a communication method was strong since the conditions made its use in an emergency literally a matter of life or death. In 1994, 12% of people in Scandinavia owned wireless phones at a time when in the next most important major market, the USA, the level was at less than 6%. By mid-2000 the respective levels in Finland and the USA were 70% and 30%, Finland having maintained its lead.

Another advantage for Finland was the lack of a national telephone monopoly, an unusual situation. Telephone services were provided by about 50 autonomous local telephone companies, whose elected boards set prices by referendum, which guaranteed low prices. The low prices in turn ensured that there would a ruthless and continuing drive to keep down costs. The boards were free to buy from the cheapest source, rather than, as elsewhere, forced to purchase from an expensive monopoly supplier or from its own in-house manufacturer, the telephone monopoly itself, again likely to be expensive. Nokia operated in a fiercely competitive environment.

Nokia had the right background to take advantage of the favourable situation. The new company produced mainly power transmission cables and phone lines. Its introduction to the world of communications was through radio telephones. In the 1970s the army wanted a new type of portable radio telephone and opened the contract to competitive tender. It split the contract, giving orders to three different companies – Salora, Televa and Nokia. The managers of Nokia, realizing that it was difficult to go it alone, began to cooperate with Salora. By 1980 the two companies had formed a 50/50 joint venture, Mobira.

The connection with Salora created what fortunately turned out to be a temporary diversion down a cul-de-sac. Salora produced televisions but was in trouble. This led to Nokia's first major foray into the international scene, focused on televisions. Nokia acquired all of Mobira, and in the process 18% of Salora, and later went on to acquire Televa as well. In 1984 it became more ambitious and acquired the Swedish television producer Luxor. By this stage it had 36% of the Finnish television market and over 20% of the Swedish. To manage its television business in 1989, Nokia established a separate consumer electronics division. Within the Nordic countries, its share in television sales rose to 35%, and about 45% in Finland. It proceeded to move to full ownership of Salora.

Nokia's ambitions were on the rise. The decision to enter the major European markets came in 1986. By that time, in a highly fragmented market, Nokia was already number three in Europe, but still with only 5% of the overall market. To be on a par with the large European players, Philips and Thompson, or its Japanese and South Korean competitors, Nokia needed to sell at least two million sets.

The acquisition of the French company Oceanic in 1987 and in the next year of Standard Electric Lorenz, which gave it markets in Germany and Southern Europe, moved its sales from one to almost two and a half million. Simultaneously, Nokia acquired the personal computer and information systems of the Ericsson Group which became Nokia Data. Nokia was now the ninth largest manufacturer of colour televisions in the world, accounting for 15% of the European market. The culminating act of this story was to come later in 1992 with the acquisition of its only competitor in Finland, Finlux.

The problem with the strategic focus on televisions was that the television business was not profitable and in any event Nokia was losing market share. The television was in the process of commoditization. Profit margins were non-existent or thin. Nokia had further difficulty melding the different cultures in its factories and achieving a consistent branding of product. Televisions proved to be a poor choice for focus.

By the early 1990s Nokia seemed headed into serious trouble, poorly led and not far from bankruptcy. In 1992 the basic goods produced by Nokia were still the same as those produced two decades earlier. The company had changed little in its product mix.

With hindsight, the early 1990s were a transitional period for Nokia, in which the television business was wound down and the telecommunications business wound up. At that time a decision was made to give priority to telecommunications and mobile phones, a decision which proved to be the right one. Only in 1996 was there a total withdrawal from the consumer electronics business, and its main product, the colour TV set. The process of withdrawal began much earlier, with the closure of plants in France in 1990 and Sweden in 1992.

First strategic remake

The seeds of the first remake were sown as early as the 1970s and 80s. The so-called Nordic cellular system was developed during the 1970s by the national telecommunication companies of the Nordic countries, on the basis of original research done by Bell Laboratories. The system began operating in 1981. The system had a unique feature, international roaming. It rapidly became the world's most heavily used system. On its back Ericsson established a lead in supplying cellular network equipment. Nokia made one of the first phones for the system. Table 16.5 shows the extent and the speed of the remake, when it occurred.

The 1972 situation was largely that of 1992. A decade ago Nokia decided to shed its heritage as an enterprise which produced everything from toilet paper to rubber boots and stake its future on wireless communication. This turned out to be an opportune decision. The timing was exactly right. Deciding to focus on the right industry was not enough. The strategic remake was well executed.

Jorma Ollila, the man most closely associated with Nokia's rise and the first remake, was Nokia's account officer at Citibank. In 1985 he moved to Nokia as vice-president of international operations and after a year, at the tender age of 35, he became the chief financial officer.

The company went through a major crisis between 1988 and 1991, not just because of its product mix, but also the suicide of the first CEO of the company, Kairams. The crisis was compounded by the collapse of the Soviet Union, Finland's closest neighbour and major trading partner. The company was having problems mass producing and selling mobile phones. In February 1990 Ollila was put in charge of the mobile phone business. His success in turning the business round meant that in 1993 he became CEO.

As CEO Ollila had to sort out a number of problems. In order to raise the cash needed to buy out disgruntled Finnish shareholders and finance the development of the company, non-core businesses were sold, private placements were made in 1993 and a listing was made

Table 16.5 **Shares of different activities in turnover (%)**

	1972	1995
Paper	19.9	0
Tyres fabric	24.5	0
Electronics	8.0	
Telecom		27 ⎫
Mobile phones		43 ⎬ 99
Consumer electronics		29 ⎭
Cable fabric	47.6	0
Other	0	1

on the New York Stock Exchange. As a result most company stock came to be held by Americans.

Ollila had a strong belief that the mobile phone would become a mainstream consumer product. He decided to create a phone for all digital systems, but rode the GSM wave to success. This became the European standard and Ollila had made the right technological choice. The phone was engineered down to a size which was potentially attractive to owners. The smooth, rounded form became a Nokia hallmark. A software-based menu was developed and a big screen put in. At the end of 1993, the 2100 series was introduced and became Nokia's 'break-away' product. The initial goal was to sell 400,000 but in the event it has sold 20 million (Table 16.6).

Nokia has had half a dozen models that sold as much as 50 times the company's own internal projections. In 1991 Nokia made an operating loss, by 1995 it made $1 billion, and by 1999 it made almost $4 billion.

Another correct decision was to give the company a strong brand name. It succeeded, since in 1991 a decision was made to call the company Nokia. A holistic approach was taken to marketing the company and its products. Marketing was seen as comprising every aspect of design, production and distribution. Advertising only began when all the other aspects were properly in place.

Table 16.6 **The winning products**

Phone model	Year released	Unit sales (in millions)
101	1992	12
2100	1994	20
5100	1998	100 +
3200	1999	45 (Europe only)
8200	1999	35
3300	2000	70 +

Source: Kaihla, p. 66.

As we see below, in considering Nokia's technical creativity, the aim of the leaders of the company was to allow individual groups to be creative. Nokia became known as one of the least hierarchical of the large companies. Success in Nokia was very much a team effort. A largely hands-off management encouraged creativity, entrepreneurship and personal responsibility, as all the best companies are wont to do. There had to be an overarching financial discipline, with an ambitious target of 25% growth per annum set for the revenue of the business, but this simply set the framework for the expression of creativity.

Key people were put in as CFO, as senior vice-president operations, logistics and sourcing, and as chief designer. The Nokia way, as it become known, embraced an emphasis on brainstorming and a clear strategic vision. There was a regular and rapid transmission of information and ideas in both directions, up and down the company. Nokia chose its strategic allies well, usually other creative upstarts such as Orange in Britain or E-plus in Germany.

The emergence of a technically dynamic enterprise

Arguably the R&D division of Nokia is the best product-driven R&D organization in the world. It has been headed by Yrjo Nuevo since he came to Nokia in 1993 at the time of the first remake of the company. Nuevo has an international reputation for his research in digital signal processing. He is a legend in Finland, attaining the rank of professor. More than 100 of his former students worked at Nokia. Nuevo has used his worldwide academic connections to recruit the best researchers. He believes he knows how to unleash the combined energy of thousands of engineers without being swamped by a wave of anarchy.

There are five basic principles to the process:

1. A company should not locate all its R&D in one single place, especially if that place is near the smothering influence of the headquarters of the company. The best policy is to disperse the facilities all round the globe. Nokia's R&D is located at 69 sites, from Boston to Bangalore. While the framework of dispersion existed before Nuevo arrived at the company, he drastically accelerated the number of separate sites.
2. A company should keep the teams of researchers small, not larger than 50 if possible. This will help it to give the individual engineers and their managers significant power and autonomy to drive particular projects or ideas. Nokia did just this.
3. A company should flatten its hierarchy and try to keep the senior managers as close as possible to the engineers and researchers. Hierarchy tends to dissipate energy. In Nokia there are at most only three layers of decision making between the president of the company and the most junior engineer.
4. A company should encourage its engineers to generate original, even crazy, new ideas outside their official work assignments by celebrating their secret tinkering and side projects. Having identified significant breakthroughs, it should get the associated innovation into production with rocket speed. The history of Nokia shows this happening all the time.
5. A company should welcome mistakes. If there are no mistakes, then nobody is doing the kind of thing which generates the great successes. In their impact, the successes will outweigh the failures.

In Nokia there was a rejection of the traditional approach to R&D, which saw it ideally as centralized, hierarchical and no-nonsense, like the German firm Siemens with its huge R&D complex in Munich. In the words of Paul Kaihla (2002): 'Nokia's 18,000 engineers, designers, and sociologists are scattered across the globe and form a kind of federation of rule-breaking, risk-taking hackers.' Nuevo likened the Nokia R&D organization to a jazz band with a leader but plenty of improvisation. When Nuevo began his work at Nokia, Ericsson outspent Nokia in the R&D area by five to one. Within three or four years, the division had tripled in size, now it is eight times the size. Nokia spends about US$3 billion on research and the figure is still rising, at a rate of 16% in 2002 despite the high-tech crash and recession.

The record of Nokia is comparable to Sony's, albeit within a narrower area but also within a shorter period of time. The roles of Ibuka and Nuevo are similar and the five principles seem to be shared and applied equally by the two companies. Nokia achieved a number of technical firsts:

1996 Aulis Perttula was responsible for the first user-changeable mobile phone cover.

1997 Christian Lindholm, an apprentice engineer, discovered Navikey, one of the great design innovations in mobile phone history, now a popular feature on 10 million Nokia phones.

1997 A team at the British R&D site made the first GSM phone with a 3-volt battery. This helped to triple talk time and boost standby time from 20 to 100 hours. This is now an industry standard.

1997 A joint retreat of Nokia and Texas Instruments, known as the Finnish forest meeting, produced the first single-chip phone. This reduced the phone weight by one-third. Within a year, it was the industry standard.

1998 Erkki Kuisma, tinkering at home with equipment more suited to his skiing, produced the first successful antenna internal to the phone.

1999 Stephen Williams, a low-level applications designer, came up with the predictive text PC software, which made text messaging much easier and also quickly became an industry standard.

2000 Lone Sorensen, a young product manager at Nokia's Copenhagen R&D site, created the first chat room for text messaging.

2002 Erik Anderson, vice-president, introduced a user-changeable cover with a built-in electrical circuit.

Of course there were failures when a project went off the rails, as with the 5510 MP3 phone, which was too bulky and expensive and had to be taken off the market.

Second remake

'We foresaw that being too big was a real danger. We had to break up the company in a meaningful way to retain the entrepreneurial thrust we had in the 1990s.'

Jorma Ollila, CEO of Nokia (quoted in Reinhardt, 2002)

Today the time is ripe for a second strategic remake. Nokia's performance is still good, but it is better to be proactive than reactive and anticipate the need for change. Overall profit was up about 6% in 2002 to US$3.7 billion on sales of US$29.7. However, there are telltale signs of a future problem. Profit margins have fallen from 25% to about 18%. The market share of Nokia for handsets peaked at about 37–38% and is down to about 34%. The share price has been falling significantly over the last two years, by something like 70%.

The success of Nokia has been dangerously dependent on one product, the mobile phone, a product which is at a critical stage in its history.

The market for mobile phones in the developed countries is reaching saturation point. This is part of a steady process of commoditization of the basic building blocks of all electronic products including mobile phones. Once esoteric components are now available off the shelf from multiple suppliers. It is even possible to buy ready-to-assemble kits from Motorola, Texas Instruments or the French company, Wavecom. The price trend is clearly downward, although masked by the prevalence of discounting and cross-subsidy. Over the last five years, the average retail price of a handset has fallen from US$275 to US$155.

Despite the speed of technological change, it is difficult to persuade those with mobile phones to replace them with a new generation of phones until that new generation has additional attributes highly desired by the potential purchasers, offering them value which

exceeds the cost of replacement. Such phones are only slowly establishing themselves in new and growing market segments. The third generation (3G) wireless services are catching on much more slowly than originally thought, which is one reason why the industry is in a financial crisis, having built ahead of demand.

Partly because of this general tendency and partly because of the recession in key markets, there has been a dramatic slowdown in sales of wireless phones and the equipment which supports their use. In 2000 there was a 54% increase in sales revenue, but in 2002 the increase was only 5%.

Competition is becoming fierce. The main competitors are South Korean, notably Samsung, and Chinese, notably TCL. Microsoft has been pursuing an active policy of getting a stripped-down version of Windows, the Windows SmartPhone software, into as many mobile phones as possible.

Nokia appears to be losing its technological edge. It is being outpaced in new areas. It is being outsold in colour screen phones by the T68 of Sony Ericsson Mobile Communications Incorporated, a new joint venture of two of Nokia's main competitors. It is trailing Motorola with phones using GPRS, an enhanced version of the dominant European standard GSM. It has less than 10% of the market share in CDMA phones, a market segment dominated by Samsung. Moreover, the vast majority of the camera phones, which take snaps digitally and transmit them wirelessly, come from Japanese producers, such as NEC. One estimate predicts that as much as 50% of the mobile phone market in Japan will be accounted for by phones which include cameras.

For these reasons, Nokia has been conducting a whole series of meetings, which have considered all the strategic options open to the company preliminary to remaking the existing strategy.

Strategic implications

The leaders of Nokia see a need to have the company move faster and be more flexible than it has been in recent years, in short to continue to be entrepreneurial. The market is becoming more competitive and growing more slowly.

Continuing success is premised on the ability of the company to read what consumers want. They may want very different things. In 2002 Nokia introduced 34 new phones but far fewer in 2003. In the developed economies, consumers want more and more attributes, and smaller and smaller size, increasing the convenience of use. In the end convergence will come and Nokia must be ready and well positioned to take advantage of this. It aims to renew the whole industry within the next two years by embracing strong technology but being transparent about the technology developed, believing that by making such knowledge freely available it gains more than it loses. In other words, the expansion of the market will offset any loss of return from loss of technological exclusivity.

Nokia accepts the need to differentiate the product with fancy hardware but most of all fancy software, particularly in the developed countries. Nokia is spending about 60% of its US$2.7 billion R&D budget on software development, up from 30% just five years ago. It takes seriously the need to counter the push by Microsoft into the mobile phone market.

Nokia believes there is still room for expansion of the conventional market, notably in developing countries, although unit sales of handsets grew only 6% in 2002, well down on the heady 40%+ during the 1990s. It hopes to play an important role in increasing the number of mobile phone users in the world, from one billion to 1.5 billion in 2005.

The core of the new strategy is expressed in the new organizational structure which Nokia has put in place. As early as the mid-1990s Nokia began to segment its product lines by 'styles' – basic, classic and fashion. The new structure goes further in distinguishing organizational units by different customer groups. The units are designed to service niche markets. The aim is to produce nimble, market-focused teams, nine of them. Already the groups are producing the products which will drive future growth.

1. *Time-division multiple access group (TDMA)*
   Nokia has 50% of this declining market and clearly does not want to give away market share, although TDMA is an outmoded digital phone standard. There is still a market in some parts of the world, such as Latin America.

2. *Code-division multiple access group (CDMA)*
   Nokia has only 9% of this market. This is the technology sweeping Asia; it is at the heart of most 3G mobile systems.

3. *Mobile phone unit*
   This comprises the high-end GSM phones and their successors, which could generate at least half the profits of Nokia in the future. There is still significant improvement in this area, as the standard Nokia phone shows (Table 16.7).

4. *Mobile entry products unit*
   This unit is responsible for the cheap phones which will be purchased in developing countries like China, India and Russia. The unit will work closely with local operatives to deliver the level of service desired and the low price appropriate to such markets. The 2100s sell for only about US$100.

5. *Imaging unit*
   This unit has launched the much anticipated 7650 camera phone, featuring a colour screen, snazzy graphical software and a tucked-away keyboard. It has also released a cheaper version, the 3650, and a business version, the 6220. The 6600 has a big colour screen and an inbuilt video recorder.

6. *Entertainment and media unit*
   The first priority of this unit is to market the 5510, a hybrid messaging phone and music player that has not yet caught on. An alternative is the 3300 which is a combined phone, FM radio and MP3 player, or the 3100 which is aimed at younger users, with its ability to light up in the dark and a camera shaped like a tear drop.

7. *Business applications unit*
   The aim of this unit is to pitch everything, from smart phones to personal organizers, at corporate customers. The 9210/9290 Communicator leads in this area.

8. *Mobile enhancement unit*
   This unit will sell the range of Nokia accessories, from cordless headsets to Sat Wat-themed phone faceplates.

9. *Mobile services unit*
   This unit will run Club Nokia, which is an online service, a clearing house for technical support information, downloadable ring tones and Java applications. This club is popular with customers and helps to cement brand loyalty.

Each unit is to have its own R&D and marketing. They will be able to draw on a shared central research laboratory and operations and logistics group. They are working closely on screens which can be controlled by

Table 16.7 **Specifications of the standard handset**

Model	Nokia 6150	Nokia 6100
Released	1998	2002
Weight	141g	78g
Volume	130cc	60cc
Standby time	290 hours	320 hours
Talk time	320 mins	360 mins
Electronic components	about 430	345
Functionality	GSM 900/ 1800, infrared	GPRS 900/1800/ 1900, infrared, colour screen, WAP, picture messaging, Java, polyphonic ring tones, hands-free speaker

Source: Durman, 2003.

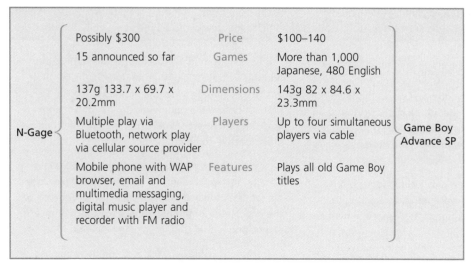

Figure 16.7 **Handset games consoles**

touch. The difficulty is to counter the negative consequences of the tendency to separate the development of different products and the resulting empire building. Such units could easily lose the synergies of being within the one organization. There is a clear overlap between some of them, for example the CDMA unit and the imaging unit.

The future

The remake may be only temporary. There may be much trial and error in finding a new strategy which is successful. In an industry in which technical change is rapid, it is difficult to make a definitive organizational design. Rather it must adjust to different applications and different technologies. Nokia has been slow to position itself for 3G, but has finally mastered the difficulties of adapting its 3G handset, the 6650, so that it links with the existing GSM or 2G networks.

However, the creativity of Nokia is best exemplified by the N-Gage, a mobile phone that doubles as a wireless game console and competes with Nintendo's Game Boy.

Case Study Questions

1. Distinguish the three strategies which have been developed by Nokia in its short history.
2. In each case, what were the reasons for the adoption of the particular strategy and the two changes of strategy?
3. What accounts for the stunning success of the second strategy adopted by Nokia? How far is it to be explained by the technical virtuosity of Nokia?
4. How has Nokia managed to encourage creativity while at the same time maintaining the financial and governance controls needed to keep the company efficient?
5. What do you think is a desirable strategy for Nokia today?

Reading

Durman, P., 'Nokia bets on a mobile world', *Sunday Times*, June 22, 2003, Business 11.

Fitzpatrick, M., 'Sony's flexible approach pays dividends in lab', *Financial Times*, June 25, 2003: 13.

Fox, J., 'Nokia's Secret Code', *Fortune*, May 1, 2000: 78–86.

Kaihla, P., 'Nokia's hit factory', *Business 2.0*, August 2002: 66–70.

Lindell, M. and Melin, L., 'Nokia: the consumer electronics business', in Johnson, G. and Scholes, K. *Exploring Corporate Strategy: text and cases*, 4th edn (Prentice Hall, London, 1997: 731–51).

Reinhardt, A., 'Nokia's next act', *Business Week*, July 1, 2002: 24–8.

This case study is also relevant to Chapters 2 and 12.

Key strategic lessons

• Enterprises have to learn how to make strategy, not an easy thing to do. As with other strategic activities, they learn best by doing. Much of this learning in strategy making may initially be implicit rather than explicit. The unfolding of any specific strategy is itself a learning or discovery process. The strategy evolves with the learning.

• This learning process may include some, but not all of these phases: financial control, forecasting the future, strategic thinking, strategic management and strategic planning.

• The process of strategy making can be separated into component steps including reading the general and competitive environments, forecasting, positioning, evaluating resources, determining capabilities, identifying core competencies, formulation, implementation and monitoring. Some of these steps might be conflated or further split. The steps do not fall naturally into a defined sequence.

• The industrial organization model takes the external environment as the starting point for strategy making, while the resource-based model starts from the internal environment or resource position of the enterprise. Both models are based on real-world behaviour which highlights different elements whose importance may differ from sector to sector but are always present and therefore always relevant to strategy making.

• It is impossible to plan for creativity; the most that can be done is to make space for strategic thinking and the activity following from that creativity. Different types of creativity can be defined according to motivation and the degree of 'closure' of the problems, including responsive, expected, contributory and proactive creativity.

• Creativity requires good alignment of creative activity with other elements of strategy making, room for self-initiated and unofficial activity, recognition of the importance of serendipity, the existence of diverse stimuli and within-company communication.

• Intrapreneurship, which builds creativity into the behaviour of an enterprise as part of an emergent strategy, requires particular kinds of communication and cooperation, particularly product and organizational championing.

• Strategic management should integrate the various elements, notably positioning, the source of competitive advantage, modes of participation, staging or pacing, the role of economic indicators such as profit and the issue of corporate social responsibility.

• Strategic planning can be defined as minimal, focused or comprehensive planning (with or without detailed planning). All plans should be rolling plans, that is, flexible plans capable of adjustment to suit changing environmental circumstances. The role of planning diminishes with the speed of change, the youthfulness of an industry and the degree of competition.

Applying the lessons

1 Define the following terms: responsive creativity, proactive creativity, serendipity, staging, rolling plan, strategic phase, learning, discovery, emergent strategy and core strategy.

2 What are the resources needed in order for an organization to be able to develop the core competency of good strategy making?

3 How might you define a discrete stage in strategy making? How useful is it to make such a separation and think in terms of discrete stages?

4 Under what circumstances would the resource-based approach be a better starting point for strategy making than positioning? Under what circumstances would the positioning approach be a better starting point?

5 What is it that 'emerges' in strategy making?

6 Consider the organization for which you are currently working or one with which you are familiar. Assess how well that organization is encouraging a creative approach to the formulation and implementation of strategy.

Strategic project

1 Select an enterprise which has successfully pursued a good strategy for a number of years. The enterprise can be in any sector of the economy and any size.

2 Do a detailed strategic audit on the enterprise.

3 Indicate the main characteristics which would distinguish a classical from an emergent strategy.

4 Consider in turn each of the following questions. How far does the strategy conform to the classical view of strategy? How far is the strategy emergent? How far has strategic success reflected either type of strategy making?

Exploring further

Much of the reading on strategic thinking in Chapter 2 is applicable here. However, a good start in analysing strategy making is to read Hambrick and Fredrickson, 2001: 48–59. Another short and apposite paper is Porter, 1996: 61–78.

Often the division of strategy making into different stages is indicated by the chapter divisions of textbooks. The two models taking the different starting points of external and internal environments are clearly set out at the beginning of Hitt et al., 2001: 21–6.

An excellent review of how to improve creativity is Robinson and Stern, 1997. Also of interest in arguing in the same way is Unsworth, 2001: 289–97. For the argument that it is much easier to kill creativity than promote it see Amabile, 1998: 77–87.

The general problems of strategy formulation and the nature of a strategy are addressed in Hofer and Schendel, 1978 and Burgelman, 2000. The latter views are found at lesser length in Burgelman and Grove, 1996: 8–28. In the past, Burgelman has written widely about his research on how to encourage entrepreneurship, work which supplements the material above: see Burgelman, 1983: 1349–64 or 1985: 39–54.

The view that strategy integrates all management activities is found in Hart, 1992: 327–51. The emphasis on strategy making as a continuous process is made in Makrides, 1999: 55–63. A discussion of what constitutes an emergent strategy is discussed in Mintzberg and Waters, 1985: 257–72.

17 Implementing strategy

Learning objectives

After reading this chapter you will be able to:

- understand why a strategy fails
- understand what is meant by the interactive nature of strategy making
- appreciate the danger of the vertical or horizontal fracturing of an organization as a threat to good strategy making
- understand the way in which an organization interacts with the world outside that organization
- evaluate different paths and different pacing in the achievement of strategic objectives
- assess the arguments for and against the existence of a separate strategy division

Key strategic challenge

How do I ensure the successful implementation of a strategy?

Strategic dangers

That, in the process of strategy making, different stakeholder groups and different managers, in other words different strategists, pursue their own interests and objectives in an incoherent manner with frequent fractures in the control, coordination and communication systems which support the implementation of the strategy of the organization.

Case Study Scenario 1   South African Breweries – a different global strategy

'We regard ourselves as a driving force in the consolidation of a highly fragmented industry.'

Graham Mackay, CEO of South African Breweries (quoted in Capell, 2002: 31)

In the words of Benson-Armer et al. (1999: 111), the beer industry is 'surprisingly local', 'a collection of tiny players'. So far it has not shared in the dramatic process of consolidation which is sweeping through most consumer product industries. The top four brewers in the world still account for just 20% of the world market. The largest brewer Anheuser-Busch sells as much as 85% of its output on its domestic market. However, most domestic markets are already oligopolies, with two to three players accounting for more than 80% of sales. There are a few exceptions; Germany and China are two, but even in these countries, concentration occurs at the city or provincial level. Local players tend to dominate the local distribution networks. Often special licences are needed to sell on domestic markets.

All this may be about to change. Beer is slowly going global in a number of interesting ways.

At the international level, both consumers and companies have an increasing access to each other. Heineken beer is sold in 170 countries, Corona and Carlsberg in 140. Over the last five years South African Breweries (SAB) has used capital raised through the American depository receipt market to fund its expansion into 11 different countries.

Consumer choice is converging across countries, in both flavour – lager preferred over ales – and packaging – cans preferred over bottles. Within the market for beer, there are segments growing at a different pace. Light beers have established a strong market segment as drink-driving laws spread and a greater concern with health becomes important.

The other rapid rise is in the premium beer segment. This is the segment in which competition is most intense at the international level since premium beers carry prices sufficiently high to offset the cost of transport. There are numerous different brands and temporary fashions which rapidly come and go.

Although price differences are quite marked from country to country, and region to region, there is a movement towards convergence of international price.

The scale of production is steadily becoming more important, highly relevant for a strategy of price leadership. Production must be a certain size to reap economies of scale. There is some specialization occurring, although at present this is relatively unusual. Guinness is the obvious case, with its concentration on stout.

In most of the developed world, the beer industry is displaying little growth, in some cases an actual contraction of demand. This is because of a number of factors including competition from other beverages such as soft drinks, ready-made drinks and wine. There are other countries in which the demand for beer is rising rapidly alongside income levels:

- India, although the size of the market is not yet comparable to the giant markets, such as that of the USA
- China which combines large size of market with a rapid growth of that market. It is the second largest market in the world, after the USA, and is growing at an annual rate of about 5%.

A handful of large brewers may soon dominate the world market. The main players are Anheuser-Busch, Heineken and Carlsberg, and perhaps the lesser known brewers Interbrew of Belgium and South African Breweries. There are three strategies that the various brewers could follow:

1. Integrate on a global scale
2. Specialize, as has Guinness
3. 'Dress up for sale', often by becoming a contract brewer, leaving the product development and marketing to the leaders.

It is expensive to export beer directly; transport costs are a high ratio of the final price. As a consequence, there are three main modes of entry: licensing and joint ventures which usually involve strategic alliances with domestic brewers, and foreign direct investment, usually by acquisition, but sometimes by the building of greenfield breweries.

Case Study Scenario 2   Toyota – still a Japanese company?

'Toyota is the benchmark of the automotive industry, worldwide.'   *Vaghefi and Coleman, 1999: 394*

After establishing a position of dominance worldwide after World War II, the American automobile industry became complacent; temporarily at least it lost its capacity to innovate. Productivity in American automobile assembly stagnated during a long period from the 1950s right through to the mid-1980s. Stagnation continued even longer among the enterprises which were component suppliers to the American automobile industry, in this case until as late as 1990.

In the meantime Japanese producers were improving productivity dramatically, particularly during the 1970s. Competition between the main automobile manufacturers in Japan was fierce and encouraged innovativeness. A series of events during the 1970s highlighted the serious gap in the ability of the two sets of car producers to meet consumer needs at prices which were competitive. The oil crisis of the 1970s highlighted a productivity lead which was by that stage already dramatic. The decisive lead of the Japanese manufacturers, particularly in small and medium-sized vehicles, became obvious. They went on to extend their expertise to large cars and the luxury segment of the market. Toyota led the way and has since continued to lead the way.

Toyota was founded in the 1930s as an offshoot of a textiles firm. From the beginning it devoted significant resources to research and development. In the period after World War II when, in a defeated nation, it could not protect itself from the competition of imports from the USA, it concentrated on the production of small vehicles rather than the large and medium-sized vehicles in which the American manufacturers had a clear competitive advantage. This was not an unusual strategy in Japan (see the Strategy in Action on Harley-Davidson in Chapter 10 and the role of Honda which later adopted a similar strategy for motorcycles).

What was the nature of the strategy which has allowed Toyota to create and maintain a significant competitive advantage and become a brand name synonymous with both high quality and low price?

The key to Toyota's success is the way in which Toyota designs and manufactures its vehicles. The approach has all the hallmarks of an emergent strategy. It involves a combination of central control and local empowerment. It is described as cost leadership. However, this is an oversimplification of Toyota's strategy. Toyota combines both product differentiation and cost leadership. In the words of Spear and Bowen (1999: 106): 'Toyota's ideal state shares many features of the popular notion of mass customization – the ability to create virtually infinite variations of a product as efficiently as possible and at the lowest possible cost.'

The interesting question is how far the Toyota method can be exported. Toyota has shown by its productive presence in the USA that this can be done.

Chapter 12 analysed the dilemma of integrating principal and agent in the making of strategy. It introduced many of the issues discussed in greater depth in this chapter.

There are two main reasons why any strategy is difficult to implement. Firstly, the existence of different departments or divisions within an organization and different stakeholder groups associated with that organization. There is a tendency for each to favour his or her own. Carried to excess, this tendency can be described as empire building. It can lead to a horizontal fracturing, both within the organization and between the organization and outside stakeholders

Secondly, the nature of a hierarchical organization, in which there exists different levels of decision making and strategy making. An excess of bureaucracy can slow and prevent the transfer of appropriate information or instruction. Here the danger is of a vertical fracturing. This fracturing may extend outside the organization to different levels of strategy making at the industry, community, regional or country levels, where these are relevant.

Common weaknesses in strategy implementation

There are a number of problems of approach in strategy making. If formulation cannot be distinguished from implementation, the problems which confront formulation confront implementation. The key to an emergent strategy is the process of learning. Any effective process of strategy making must encourage this process of learning. Anything which discourages it will lead to poor formulation and implementation. The six approaches discussed below discourage the process of learning, but in different ways.

Tokenism

There is a danger of tokenism, which can be defined as the wish to have a strategy because any respectable organization must have a strategy, not because it has any intention to implement it. The strategy is put together quickly, with inadequate preparation, a minimum of effort and little investment of resources. It is then shelved with no attempt to implement or monitor. The original strategy may be poorly formulated, since it is not intended for realization. No self-respecting manager would dream of implementing such a strategy.

Tokenism occurs for a variety of reasons. It often occurs when an organization, already in straitened circumstances, does not wish to commit the resources needed to build a real strategy. It might occur when key individuals for various reasons feel threatened by the existence of such a strategy. They might see the appearance of such a strategy as reducing their discretionary responsibility in key decision-making areas, leading to a loss of status for them, or as restricting their room for manoeuvre. The strategy may also be the vehicle for the advancement of a rival or rival group. Tokenism is a common approach to strategy making.

Bureaucratization

A contrasting danger is to be carried away by the promise of strategy and take strategy making to the opposite extreme, in the belief that it can answer all problems. Strategy making encourages a tendency to excessive bureaucracy – too many reports, too many meetings, too many statistics, far too much detail altogether. In this approach, making strategy may even become a substitute for action, with an assumption that more means better. Following the procedures crowds out real strategic thinking. There may be a team of strategists employed full time in making the strategy, with a significant investment of time and effort by all staff. As the case study in Chapter 16 shows, at times GE has found its strategic process becoming overbureaucratized. In this it is not unusual.

It is hard to hold strategy making poised in a healthy state halfway between tokenism and overbureaucratization. There is always the danger of a movement to one of these extremes.

Strategy as risk control

The next dangers follow from a series of misreadings of what strategy is really about. Strategy making is seen by some to have as its main goal, a negative one, the discouragement of risk taking rather than a positive one, the creation and maintenance of competitive advantage. In this view, strategy is about heading off potential threats. It is possible to interpret risk control as the central activity in strategy making, assuming that the ultimate goal is the avoidance of all risk.

This approach has the undesirable outcome of denying the enterprise many opportunities for a good return, since it is inevitably the case that high returns and high risk go together, just as low returns and low risk do. It would discourage, for example, a deliberate policy of 'disruptive innovation', that is, the introduction of new products and new processes, which helps to maintain a decisive and continuing competitive advantage.

Strategy as short-term profit maximization

Paradoxically, strategy can be used to encourage an obsession with short-term profit, or short-term opportunity at the expense of long-term market share or long-term growth. The short-term opportunities are more obvious and more easily exploited than the medium and long-term opportunities. They may be taken at the cost of the loss of longer term opportunities. The goal of the strategist becomes the achievement of every small or incremental increase in profit that can be recognized and exploited, while neglecting the larger opportunities which can arise in the longer term but are much more uncertain and probably invisible to many decision makers.

This short-termism partly reflects deliberate action, because the external environment is taken as a given and a narrow view of enterprise objectives is taken, and partly it is the market activity which forces this view on the enterprise. This is particularly characteristic of the way in which strategy has been used in the USA and the short-termism of an obsessively market-oriented and bottom-line approach.

Strategy as reproduction of the past

Strategy making can encourage a concentration on the present through the mirror of the past rather than on the present through the mirror of the future, which is seen simply as an extrapolation of the past. The focus is on the existing strengths and weaknesses of the enterprise and existing rather than future markets. This approach puts the emphasis on what is already known rather than what, it is assumed, cannot be known. The implicit assumption is that the future will simply reproduce the past. Strategy is heavily constrained by the parameters of existing circumstances.

Focusing on future markets requires entering a little known world, deliberately anticipating scenarios which accommodate significant future changes in taste and technology and taking action to influence the emergence of these new markets.

Strategy as a vehicle for uncontrolled ambition

One final trap is to assume that everything is possible, that strategy is concerned with breaking free of all the constraints of the past and completely remaking the environments of the organization. Strategy becomes a vehicle for uninhibited ambition. The strategists allow themselves to become carried away by their own exuberance. Nothing is impossible.

The dangers of such an approach are twofold:

1. The creation of a straitjacket from which it is difficult to escape
2. A tendency to self-deception which might be expressed in deliberate distortion, and even rewriting, of performance indicators. The strategists cannot believe that they are failing.

The five Cs and strategy implementation

The first requirement of good strategy is to avoid the biases described in the first section. The next requirement in the implementation of a successful strategy is to focus attention on the five Cs as the basic requirements needed to keep the separate units in any organization working together to achieve the objectives of a strategy. Further analysis of the five Cs focuses attention on the key issues.

Coordination

Coordination must occur at every step in a strategy-making process, certainly in formulation and implementation, between different stakeholders, between different cooperating enterprises and organizational levels, and between different internal units within the enterprise itself. Coordination involves a two-way interaction between any two strategists, whoever they are. Coordination involves the harmonization of objectives as they are disaggregated and the accommodation of the demand for resources to the existing supply.

Communi-cation

Working together requires a minimum transmission of information, which then becomes valuable knowledge if it influences the content of a strategy. Coordination can only occur on the basis of the proper communication of information concerning objectives and opportunities, risks and threats, capabilities and outcomes. Such communication occurs both up and down the organization, and also in and out of the same organization. Like cooperation, it is a two-way process and involves repeated interaction.

The information communicated must be accurate. There should be clear incentives not to suppress information and not to distort it in a deliberate way. Instead, there should be every incentive to communicate appropriate information. Of course the key issue is the selection of information which can become knowledge in the appropriate hands in the context of a strategy.

Command

Command is passed downward, reflecting the hierarchy of authority which characterizes every organization. It should be rarely given and only when absolutely necessary, in a crisis or to resolve a particular conflict. It is held in reserve for when it is needed. Everyone should be aware of the possibility of command but it does not have to be used. There are some occasions when decisive action is necessary, but most of the time staff should be aware of what they need to do without being prompted. Often command is associated with attempts to ensure coordination. Commands are most frequently issued to change objectives or reduce the demand for specific resources.

Control

Control is often exercised indirectly and discretely, through incentive structures and the internalization of a corporate culture. There are direct control systems in certain areas such as finance. It is better that all become committed to following the broad directions of the strategy without explicit instruction. The outlines of a strategy provide the guidelines for any assertion of control. In a really successful strategy, the guidelines are internalized and do not require endless repetition. Each decision maker has his or her own domain or area of control, all well understood, and abstains from intervention in other domains unless invited or if there is a crisis.

Conflict/consensus

Honest disagreement is inevitable in any organization. It is a vital aspect of any creative activity, since creative thinking means thinking outside the normal boundaries. If a new idea is to change behaviour, it needs to be argued out in the forum of the enterprise where there will inevitably be those who cannot agree. Any proposal for change almost always invites conflict of some kind, hostility from those opposed to a new way of thinking or to change as such. Any action resulting from creative thinking follows a process of persuading others to agree and support the action. Any resulting disagreement is not necessarily damaging to the organization. It may assist the participants to understand better their role and potential contribution in the overall strategy.

Conflict often does represent a legitimate clash of viewpoints and a release of energy. The energies released should be harnessed to the achievement of the objectives of the strategy. However, conflict must be contained within reasonable bounds and not allowed to spiral out of control.

Coordination can break down. Communication can be insufficient. Command can be excessive or non-existent when needed, and control overly visible or invisible because absent. Conflict can get out of control and result in widespread antagonism which prevents effective cooperation or communication. The failures are usually symptoms of a degree of self-interested behaviour which has reached a level which is dysfunctional for the enterprise. The need for leadership becomes more obvious in such circumstances. Good leadership can stop any of these failures, but good leadership is not enough.

Usually a strategy implies significant change of some kind, otherwise the strategy is superfluous. Change threatens the status quo. If there are already conflicts and contradictions in a static organization, dynamizing the organization only compounds these difficulties. All organizations develop an inherent inertia, particularly when they have achieved previous successes. Nobody wants to change the tried and tested ways. Change also stimulates active resistance from those with a vested interest in the retention of the status quo. This explains the different degrees of opposition to strategy, particularly where the purpose of strategy is change of some kind. This opposition takes a number of different forms.

'Success breeds failure'

It is necessary to dwell for the moment on the effects of inertia. Olson (1982) has developed a macrolevel model in which protracted stability and success in a national economy stimulates an increasing proliferation of successful rent-seeking coalitions. These coalitions often achieve their objectives because the benefits of their actions are concentrated but the losses, expressed in the reduced efficiency of allocation of resources, are spread so thinly across a large number of people that no one has an incentive to resist with any commitment, even if they notice the damage done. Only a crisis of some kind, such as war or depression, creates the opportunity for a cleansing of the economic system of the rent-seeking coalitions. This picture illustrates well the general problem of inertia for any organization and the way in which success itself creates the conditions for failure. The argument has general validity.

A similar kind of tendency applies at the microlevel, within the enterprise. Over time, an attachment to the status quo develops a realization that change is risky, at least for those who occupy positions of authority. The successful seek to protect what they already have and form informal networks working to this end. There is an increase in the number of those who exploit the commons within the enterprise, trading off the success of predecessors. The successful have time to play the politics of the organization with sustained effort and increasing effectiveness. Empire building is rife, with different divisions pressing their own interests and resisting any change of role and diminution of importance. As in the macroeconomy, there can be a proliferation of different forms of rent-seeking behaviour which in the short run has only an incremental effect on other members of the organization, but over the longer term eventually has a dramatic effect in reducing efficiency.

This is a normal tendency. To extend the successful existence of an enterprise it must be deliberately countered. A comfortable life is a sure prescription for failure. A sufficient measure of discomfort is a stimulus to the kind of action which validates the changes necessary to keep the enterprise competitive. Intermittent but controlled discomfort is one way of countering the forces of inertia.

In a crisis wholesale change must occur. However, the main obstacle ceases to be mere inertia and becomes open opposition. One of the main difficulties in strategy making is organizational, sometimes even organized, resistance. However the organization is designed, there are likely to be relations of conflict between the different divisions, departments or units. Conflict is often a continuing process, that is, a dynamic series of conflict episodes, each of which leaves an aftermath which is an antecedent to its successor, another episode of conflict. No organization ever develops in a pattern of steady and stable growth.

Even enterprises which have the best of intentions can become involved in conflict. Starbucks has an excellent reputation and intentions, yet it has had its share of conflict and hostility.

Strategy in Action Starbucks and being a good citizen

Starbucks has made a great deal of its role as a good global citizen. It has frequently repeated its six guiding principles, which are:

1. Provide a great work environment and treat each other with respect and dignity
2. Embrace diversity as an essential component of the way we do business
3. Apply the highest standards of excellence to the purchasing, roasting and fresh delivery of our coffee
4. Enthusiastically develop satisfied customers all the time
5. Contribute positively to our community and our environment
6. Recognize that profitability is essential to our future success.

While not embracing the triple bottom line, in stating such principles, Starbucks has represented itself as both environmentally and socially responsible.

Despite this statement of principles, Starbucks has managed to get itself into some difficulty with employees. In April 2002 it agreed to a settlement of $18 million to compensate thousands of present and former managers and assistant managers in California stores, who were forced to spend long hours performing menial tasks not in their job description and not compensated at penalty overtime rates. Californian law requires employers to pay a penalty rate, at time-and-a-half base remuneration rates, after eight hours of work in any day, even for managers and supervisors, provided they spend at least 50% of their time performing tasks that are not related to managing (report from the *Los Angeles Times*, reproduced in the *Sunday Age*, April 21, 2002: 16).

Starbucks has proclaimed its environmental friendliness and its unwillingness to exploit the current surplus of coffee in the world which has led to a chronically low price. There have been various attempts to raise the price of coffee and ensure that producers are paid above their costs. There have been various suggestions for 'ethical taxes' to assist the farming communities. Some organizations have voluntarily bound themselves to a fair trade code, which aims to ensure that small farmers receive a fair share of the price paid for their crops. The typical pledge is to buy at least 5% of their purchase in a fair trade. In March 2002, Howard Schultz, founder of Starbucks,

▶

urged coffee executives 'to share the blanket' of prosperity with the growers. Despite this, Starbucks will not certify 5% of its coffee as 'fair trade' as other specialty coffee companies have agreed to do.

THE STRATEGY

The main strategy of Starbucks is to establish a reputation for high-quality coffee, in effect to brand the company so that it can set a premium price, one which offers the company a profit margin way above that normally made in such an industry.

There are various ways in which it seeks to do this. It does it by emphasizing the quality of the product. It roasts the beans itself and after much experimentation created a taste which is unique, or claimed to be unique. It also uses technology, in this case the one-way valve bags to retain the freshness of the beans for the maximum possible period of time. It has developed a mystique about coffee. Another method of emphasizing quality is stressing excellence in everything the company does or sells.

The focus is not just on the product, the coffee. It is also on the nature of the coffee shops themselves and the enthusiasm and good attitude of staff. Any other products which Starbucks uses or sells, such as coffee-making machines, grinders, coffee filters, storage containers or just coffee mugs, must come up to the same high standards as the coffee.

There are three main areas to be considered in discussing the strategy adopted: the treatment of employees, principally the influence of this on their motivation; the choice of location for the stores, since this is vital to the whole coffee-drinking package; and the image presented by the Starbucks name, both domestically and internationally, and the management of that image.

All staff from CEO to baristas (barpeople) are, in theory, regarded as partners, not employees. Even part-time staff receive stock options, so-called 'bean stock'. Starbucks baristas are paid slightly higher wages than is the norm in the food service industry. They are given health insurance, disability and life insurance, and a free pound of coffee each week. The baristas who serve the coffee are usually college or university students. They are carefully selected and receive a significant amount of training, a minimum of 24 hours, ensuring that they can answer any question asked about coffee which may be put to them. Even executive staff have to work in a store for

two weeks to gain customer experience. Starbucks has aimed to have a very flat organizational structure, partly in order to ensure close contact between management at headquarters and the operational staff actually selling the coffee. It is unclear how Starbucks can maintain the initial culture of the staff, the high level of motivation and enthusiasm which marked the early years.

Since venue is critical, the policy on location is an important part of strategy. Starbucks is happy to establish stores in close vicinity with each other, provided the location is good. One joke popular among staff stressed the close vicinity, by inventing a headline, 'Starbucks establishes new store in rest room of existing store'. Starbucks has a team of property managers and others working to find the best sites for retail outlets. It needs to find such outlets at a rate of at least one a day in North America alone. The initial target was the main street of every major North American city, now it is the main street of all regional centres. Starbucks has turned to using espresso carts or kiosks, called Doppio espresso carts. It is in the process of branding the humble cart. An eight-foot by eight-foot cube unfolds into a large stand with a clear Starbucks identity which can be used for street corners, train stations and shopping malls.

What is the population needed to support a coffee shop? This sets the threshold population size. In Seattle there is a store for every 9,400 people, the highest density anywhere. A more realistic target is said to be 55,000 in the USA and 56,000 in Canada (the Coffee Specialty Association of America believes it could be half this figure, although almost half these would be coffee carts rather than stores). This would in theory mean that North America could support almost 5,000 specialty coffee retail outlets. In 1997 Starbucks had just over 1,000 stores, or just over 20% of the maximum possible number. In the large urban markets, it had already reached almost one-third of the potential maximum. Rapid growth since then has moved the number much closer to the notional maximum. Today Starbucks has 4,247 shops, not far off a possible saturation point, although there are still eight states where there are none and Starbucks may not accept the rather conservative views of the various authorities, seeing Seattle as an indication of the potential.

Essential to Starbucks is an integrated and efficient supply chain, whether it is supplying the retail store units, the specialty sales and wholesale channels, the mail order business, which is also important, or the grocery channel. The main growth vehicle is clearly the retail outlet, but the other channels help to boost the demand and establish the reputation.

Starbucks only entered international markets when it had already established itself firmly in the USA. It therefore moved abroad from a position of strength. Its strategy was to seek good partners abroad. It chose to make its international entry in the Asia Pacific area, because of the enormous size of the market and its potential for growth. A higher population base is needed in many Asian countries in order to support one store but the population of Asia is so large that the number of stores could easily outnumber those in the USA within a short period of time. It chose to start in Japan in 1997.

As Starbucks has moved to a point at which the North American market is saturated, overseas expansion has become critical to sustaining rapid growth. In 2002 a further 1,177 stores were opened, bringing the total to 6,000. In three years the aim is to have 10,000 stores worldwide. Starbucks is clearly expanding in dramatic style internationally and at the breakneck pace at which it had already opened up the American market. The eventual goal is very ambitious, 20,000 stores worldwide. It has considerable room for further expansion. The problem is that the nature of the competition in other countries differs from that in the USA.

The model adopted in Japan, in which the foreign expansion began, was very much the same as that used in North America, with one exceptional feature which related to the organizational structure. Starbucks set up a joint venture with a local retail partner, Sazaby Inc, which Starbucks then licensed to use the Starbucks model. Elsewhere in Asia, such as Thailand and South Korea, it initially issued a licence to a local operator, but later converted the local operator into either a partner in a joint venture or a wholly owned subsidiary. With licensing and the use of partners, there is always the problem of maintaining the quality of coffee product and store, and maintaining the brand image. The bigger the organization, the bigger the problem.

| **Degrees of conflict** | There are five levels of intensity of conflict which can be clearly isolated. They represent steps in the build-up and release of situations of conflict. Such conflict has to be managed in some way. These levels are: |

1. *A condition of latent conflict*
Here conflict simmers below the surface. The source of conflict might be the differing interests of various staff and stakeholder groups, bitter individual career and political rivalries and the consequences of resource shortages. Factions may push a particular line on a strategic issue. The conflict may appear to be over issues which do not reveal the real differences or the animosity below the surface. For various reasons, this latent conflict does not become overt. It can continue in a latent form for a long period of time.

2. *A condition of perceived conflict*
A perception emerges on the part of many staff that conflict exists and is significant. This may be encouraged by those for whom the existence of conflict is useful. The perception may be inaccurate, at least initially, since perception inevitably becomes reality if it persists. Perceived conflict may exist alongside and reflect latent conflict, or the two may be completely separate. Perceived issues may differ from the real ones below the surface, or there may be no latent conflict of the kind indicated above.

3. *A condition of felt conflict*
Latent conflict becomes overt conflict. This may be because of a rise in the conflict level or because latent and perceived conflict merge. It is to the advantage of some to

express and make public the conflict. Once triggered by some public expression of dissatisfaction, a significant number of individuals feel a level of tension and anxiety that causes them to begin to express their discontent, perhaps to organize an expression of this conflict. Conflict is often personalized as some kind of threat to individuals or groups and their interests.

4. *A condition of manifest conflict*

Perception becomes action, which generates a conflict situation. Conflict is not just expressed in the feelings of individuals, it is translated into behaviour. Individuals take action to pre-empt and frustrate the attainment of others' aims. This action may not be consistent with the achievement of the objectives of the strategy. This depends on who initiated the action and why.

5. *Conflict aftermath*

There may be two possible outcomes. One is a resolution of sorts, which is by its nature temporary since another conflict is not far away. Most resolutions create the conditions for further conflicts. The other is the suppression of manifest conflict and its return to a condition of latency, for example by the removal of key individual players from the situation in which the conflict has arisen.

From a strategic perspective conflict is not always dysfunctional. The emergence of conflict alerts an organization to the need to cope with a rapidly changing and discontinuous environment. Where change is occurring, conflict is almost universal. Conflict pinpoints the location of stresses arising from that change and therefore draws attention to the sources of change. In conditions of discontinuous change, conflict is more or less inevitable but the organization must manage that conflict, so that it does not completely undermine the stability of the enterprise. It must channel the energy released by this conflict in such a way as to drive strategic change in the desired direction, but it must also manage it in such a way as to prevent a breakdown of the organization.

Conflict is only dysfunctional for strategy if it affects the ability of the enterprise to formulate or implement strategy. In the worst case, it may inhibit the productive or marketing effectiveness of the enterprise or even its adaptability to change. In the best case, it assists in sustaining a momentum for change.

Typical conflict situations

What are the typical situations in which inter-functional conflicts arise? There are many but the discussion below is limited to two common ones in order to illustrate just how significant they can be in strategy making. This discussion focuses on conflicts which are strategic rather than personal. The latter may add a further dimension to strategic conflicts.

The first example involves a potential conflict between the marketing and operations units. Unless the product is homogeneous, customer satisfaction increasingly requires customization of the product or service to meet individual needs. In an extreme case, a product might be customized on an individual basis to suit each and every set of wants. This might mean that every unit of output is individually produced.

There is a cost to customization. Customization requires adjustment of the production line in order to vary specific attributes. The production line needs to be halted regularly to allow adjustment to meet the requirements of different specifications. This increases production costs since economies of scale require long production runs which are only made possible by a homogeneous product. How long these runs have to be to derive maximum benefit depends on the nature of the technology and the optimum size of plant. In this situation the homogeneous product may have specifications which are appropriate to production, but not to sales. This would reduce the costs of production but at the risk of a failure to satisfy the customer.

The answer to the problem might be to devise a plant of an optimum size which fits the likely emergence of separate market niches, or it might be to tool up to allow flexibility and train workers to operate with a minimum loss of time in making a transition from one product variant to another. The conflict must be dealt with at the strategic level, although it will manifest itself frequently at the operational level and in the day-to-day implementation of a strategy.

The second example involves a potential conflict between both the operations or logistics and marketing units and the finance unit. The timely meeting of customer wants requires the existence of a sufficient size and range of inventory to match the inevitable variations in level of demand for particular product variants. There needs to be a stock of the full range of product types available to meet the inevitable fluctuations in demand for particular product variants. The greater the inventory held, the more likely it is that the enterprise is able to meet the customer wants immediately or with minimum delay.

Inventory represents an investment in working capital which can be quite large and has a cost, the return which could otherwise be made on this investment. In theory, the funds locked up in inventory could be invested elsewhere; there is a clear opportunity cost. Any self-respecting finance division would wish to reduce this loss to a minimum. The larger the inventory, the greater the cost. Again there is a contradictory interest.

One answer to the problem is just-in-time (JIT), which involves linking production directly with sales. This is a matter of quick communication of sales information and incentives structured to support the necessary information flow. These features allow production to be adjusted quickly to meet any changes in sales. The link between the nature of the conflict and the strategic nature of any solution is again readily apparent.

These two examples illustrate how a divergence of interests is inherent in any specialized structure and how a strategy might be adopted to limit the costs of such divergences by integrating the relevant units within the framework of an agreed strategy. There are all sorts of trade-offs and compromises which must be agreed by the parties. Once more formulation is so closely associated with implementation that it is impossible to distinguish the two.

The existence of separate functional areas is a major source of pressure on the implementation of any strategy. A functional division may be the general organizing principle of the enterprise or it may occur within the framework of overarching business or regional units. It is a much easier task to integrate the plans of separate business units than it is to integrate the plans of separate functional units. The two examples of conflict described above relate to functional divisions.

It is useful to return to the original dichotomy, that between integration and specialization. For any organization of a size which requires a formal structure, there is bound to be a contradiction between the needs of integration and those of diversity and specialization. Inherent in the structure of any organization are conflicts of interest between its different units with different specialist interests and objectives. These may lead to fracturing at the horizontal level. However the organization is put together, there are bound to be such conflicts of interest. These conflicts typically reveal themselves as emerging operational problems but they really involve strategic decisions or a failure to set appropriate strategic directions. They hinder implementation of strategy if they are combined with personal clashes.

One answer to the problem already discussed, and an increasingly popular one, is a matrix organization which links a product or regional principle with a functional one. In theory this prevents the isolation of functional units and the horizontal fracturing which is the precondition for the type of conflict already discussed.

No strategy can be effectively implemented if there is serious fracturing, whether vertical or horizontal. Such fracturing obstructs the process of good strategy making by interfering with the process of iteration which is at the heart of strategy implementation.

The interactive or iterative nature of strategy making

In one attempt at description, great strategists have been characterized as 'iterative, loop thinkers' (Hambrick and Fredrickson, 2001: 50). Since strategy making is by its nature iterative, with many feedback loops of various kinds, both positive and negative, this is not surprising. There are a number of different senses in which the notion of iteration can be understood. It helps in understanding the problems of formulation and implementation to consider the nature of such iteration. Efficient iteration is vital to good strategy making.

The processes of iteration

Strategy making involves a number of different processes of iteration. All organizations are hierarchical and inevitably the targets or objectives set at the topmost level of the enterprise are more aggregative than they are at the bottom level. The larger the organization, the greater the degree of aggregation. There is more detail at the lower levels, with most at the bottom level. Only those at this level can draw out the specifics of what is needed.

The *core iteration occurs within the enterprise itself*, without which there could be no strategy. The core iteration is between the different levels of an organization as information and instruction are passed between these different levels and the strategic directions are clarified. The communication of new objectives elicits new information. The new information leads to a redefinition of objectives. This is a continuous process. A process of iteration involves procedures whereby objectives are continually reassessed and revised in the light of new and more detailed information.

It is a complex interaction in which commands and communications are transmitted from level to level within an organization, or between units at the same level within that organization. The interaction is reciprocal, both up and down, and side to side, and there are further responses to that interaction which result in further interactions.

This process of iteration is by its nature part of a discovery or learning process and a process of transmitting what has been learned, since aggregate communications or commands are broken down into more detailed instructions or pieces of information. Communications in the reverse direction are aggregated. The aggregation itself creates new information. In this process of iteration all learn something they did not previously know, in this case about the organization and what it is capable of doing.

In conditions of stability, the iteration would fade to insignificance after a few rounds. In conditions of change, the iteration never dies away. The linking of the inside iteration with those iterations linking the organization with the outside confronts the organization with a changing environment.

There are a number of different kinds of iteration. Two external iterations are linked to the core internal iteration.

There is *general iteration between the external and internal environments*. This translates into a process whereby the objectives and targets of the enterprise, reflecting the opportunities thrown up by the external environment, are progressively reconciled with the enterprise's resources. A process of mutual adjustment, which amounts to an iteration when placed in real time, occurs. Since the environment is continuously changing and generating new information, the process of iteration is always being recharged by new inputs from outside. The same argument holds for risk management. An identification of a threat in the external environment is followed by an iterative process of clarification, action and reaction. This happens at every level of the enterprise.

A third iteration is that between the different layers of strategy making at national, community, industry or enterprise levels. Usually this is simpler, in that there are many less layers and in theory there is less distortion and less selection. It may also be much quicker. However, it is equally important. In this case the iteration may be between different strategies as they emerge and it may involve both complementors and cooperators.

The information from these iterations is fed into the core iteration discussed above.

The problems of iteration

There are a number of problems associated with these iterations:

- Iteration takes time, exactly how much depending on the number of different layers in the organizational hierarchy and on the nature of the conduits of communication and command. A significant delay in response ensures that the information available is always out of date.
- Somewhere the iteration may become blocked. There may be a fracturing of the conduits for communication, sometimes deliberate, sometimes inadvertent.

Boundaries

In this book, it has often been argued that the boundary between an enterprise and the external environment is not as clear-cut as might be expected. In many interpretations of strategy making the enterprise is the main, and for some the only, strategy maker in the domestic and global economy. This explains why strategy is often considered and discussed as corporate strategy alone, ignoring the possible existence of strategy at the different levels of an economy.

There is an almost universal propensity of human beings to create boundaries, classify within boundaries and organize within such boundaries. They divide the public world from the private, government from the realm of private business, country from country, industry from industry, enterprise from enterprise and department from department. Such boundaries are necessary in order to make manageable the demands of organization and the understanding of who does what. They are also a vital part of a world which is considered competitive rather than cooperative; they constitute the units which compete with each other.

Some argue that it is dangerous for an enterprise to act in any way other than as an independent entity with fixed boundaries ruthlessly pursuing its own self-interest. On this account the enterprise should ignore the interests of other stakeholders and other strategy makers in the world outside, except insofar as the interests and actions of these groups impinge directly on the profit level of the enterprise. This is as true at the global level as at the domestic level.

However, strategy is made at many different levels of an economy. There are industry issues which may require an industry strategy. An industry association may articulate these interests in a strategy of some kind. There may also be community strategies, even government strategies at the national level which are important to an enterprise. Government policies may be framed with such strategies in mind. The enterprise must anticipate what these policies might be and how they might change. It might wish to influence the nature of these strategies and policies. No government, local, regional or national, takes an entirely neutral attitude to the pattern of economic activity which occurs within its jurisdiction. There may be much less industry policy and deliberate planning than used to be the case but the change made its presence implicit rather than explicit.

At the global level there may be a desire to market or brand a particular country or the industry of a particular country, publicizing tangible and intangible characteristics which favour the particular industry or country. A strategy designed to achieve this can establish a reputation for quality which will benefit all the enterprises within that industry and/or that country. It is a matter of who should organize that strategy and how it should be done. An enterprise can actively encourage and support the emergence of such strategies or it can passively acquiesce in them. A failure to articulate such a strategy will hamper the development of the industry concerned.

All organizations or organizational units are intermeshed in dense networks of relationships with units outside. These relationships take many different forms – political, economic and social. Such different networks of relationships overlap but do not share common boundaries. Although any organizational boundaries acquire a life of their own, they cannot prevent either the penetration of the external environment by the unit or the penetration of the unit by other units from the outside environment.

Theories are built around the contradictions and conflicts arising from the existence of separate units. These theories reinforce the boundaries so that they acquire a significant impermeability. The setting of boundaries creates the possibility of stimulating loyalties to the entities within those boundaries. Performance can benefit from that kind of loyalty. Strategy is seen as independently set by particular organizations, whereas a good strategy clearly benefits from taking account of the strategy of other organizations. Boundaries create separate interests which diverge from each other and enormous coordination and communication problems if the organizations need to work together.

Crossing the boundaries

A critical part of strategy is to understand the need to cross those boundaries and carefully devise the best way of doing so. This may mean positioning the enterprise in different industries, particularly outside the home country. There are a number of other reasons for crossing the boundaries:

- Coordinating the organization or enterprise strategy with strategies outside the enterprise, at whatever level, where this clearly brings benefits to the organization
- Discovering assets, resources or competencies outside the enterprise to which the organization might desire access
- Forming strategic alliances and cooperating with outside organizations, including complementors, competitors and governments.

The resource issue indicates how the assumption of a watertight boundary between an enterprise and its environment is invalid. There are many good reasons to argue that the boundary is extremely porous but this is the most powerful argument for relaxing the assumption. Enterprises can gain access to outside resources; they are not limited by their own resources. One key capability may be the ability to access outside resources. If an enterprise is to remake itself and in some way remake the environment in which it operates, it needs to access these outside resources.

Strategies which ignore the need to cross boundaries are likely to be ineffective. There are examples where the boundaries almost disappear as a consequence of the coincidence of separate motivations. For example, there are many examples of dense networks or clusters of small enterprises working together and with government, but working as if they were a single unit. This usually happens in an environment of successful repeated interaction. It requires trust and a reputation for consistent and fair dealing.

Staging

Staging is concerned with the way in which strategy moves an enterprise from its current position to its target position. It is also concerned with timing. There are two particular aspects of staging which must be considered:

1. There may be alternative routes which are available for moving between the two points. Choosing one path rather than another might be a question of saving time or ensuring arrival at the planned destination in a healthy state.
2. There may be a choice of the speed at which movement occurs on those routes. The speed of movement is not completely under the control of the strategists.

Strategy in Action Lessons from the online broking experience – how to stage?

What are the difficulties of an effective response by the incumbents in an industry when a threat from a new substitute emerges, such as online broking? The main difficulty is the gap between the core competencies already possessed and those required in the new situation. Both newcomers and incumbents wish to exploit the new technology and the new service.

It is useful to describe the typical features of the developing situation:

1. Initially, partly because it is relatively small, the new activity is not very profitable, certainly not as profitable as the traditional activity. It is a low profit margin business.
2. There may be many players offering the new activity, with prices falling in a competitive market, and significant advertising costs as players seek to increase their market share, making themselves known to potential customers.
3. There may be a clear underserving of the needs of traditional customers by the new activity. Certain competencies may be stressed above others, for example the provision of an effective website with a broad range of information, as against the building up of reputation and close customer relationship.
4. A traditional company may cannibalize its own existing operations by developing the new activity, for example Merrill Lynch's 15,000 financial consultants and 700 branches. There may also be considerable resistance within the company to the new activities. Both of these may inhibit entry into the new activity.
5. An incumbent company may lack the expertise to enter the new activity.
6. For a long period it may be unclear exactly which business model will win out for the new activity.
7. All the traditional weaknesses of sloth, arrogance, myopia, bureaucracy and politics may apply. Organizational slack can work two ways, either preventing a quick response or allowing room for a flexible response.
8. The appearance of electronic communication networks (ECNs) may eventually allow traders to bypass brokers completely, since these networks can match orders automatically.

There are a range of possible strategic responses, differing by destination, route to that destination and speed of movement over that route.

For the new entrant, there are two main strategic possibilities:

1. Practice what is called 'judo economics' (see the Strategy in Action on the no-frills airline Southwest in Chapter 9): enter in a small way, carving out a market segment specific to the new technology, provided it is a strategy which initially has little effect on the incumbent and provides no incentive for it to respond decisively. During this early period, the company develops all the competencies required for successful application of the new techniques. Then, as in judo, when the time is ripe, it uses speed and timing to throw the larger incumbent.
2. Enter all market segments simultaneously, trying to win as much of the overall market as possible, in so doing catching the incumbent off-guard. Use any price advantage to win market share. At the same time develop all the core competencies as quickly as possible.

For the incumbent, six strategic options are available:

1. Embrace the new technology and exploit it, alongside existing traditional activities. This is called *straddling*. Go even further and recombine elements from the traditional and the new, producing an effective and competitive hybrid. In any event develop the new competencies as soon as possible.
2. Switch completely to the new activity as soon as possible, developing competencies at the same time. Fight fire with fire.
3. Do not respond at all, at least in the short term. Play to existing strengths or competencies, and try to reinforce the market segments already dominated without changing strategy.
4. Adopt an aggressive position, playing to the strengths and competencies already possessed but trying to outcompete the newcomers. Change the strategy to one in which you resist the newcomers, either through price or promotional competition.
5. Adopt a middle position, slowly aligning the competencies with the changing market and

▶

trying to retain flexibility until it is clear which business model is the best for application of the new technology. Also adjust according to how large are the different market segments.

6. Accept that you cannot compete and *harvest* what you can from the market in which you operate, and then retire gracefully.

A good strategy will fit what is likely to happen in the future. It is sensible to engage in scenario building to consider the future of the whole finance sector. These wider changes are likely to determine the future of broking. Electronic broking may be the catalyst for the use of the Internet for a wide variety of financial services. Electronic brokerages might develop into one-stop financial services enterprises, acting as financial services gateways, where customers can have access to everything from tax advice to ordinary banking, retirement planning to portfolio management for the investment of surplus income.

This development can happen either as brokers expand into other activities or when brokers are acquired by companies which have their main focus in these other areas. There may be synergies in the combination of the back offices for all these activities.

Some strategies are examples of different routes taken to the same destination, or others the choice of different destinations. In other cases the strategy has the same route and the same destination, but a different speed of movement.

Alternative routes

Most strategies involve movement towards simultaneous achievement of a number of key targets. The targets may be achieved at different dates. There may be a necessary sequence in target arrival dates. These targets can be prioritized in two ways, first in importance and second in sequencing. The latter is relevant here. It may be that the achievement of one target is a necessary precondition for the achievement of another. It is often better to phase the undertaking of the tasks associated with the different targets.

This can be illustrated with the help of two examples. The first relates to a strategy which envisages both geographic expansion into new countries and therefore new markets, and product expansion, that is, an extension of the range of products or product variants produced and sold. The company could be Amazon.com or IKEA. Which should come first? It is difficult to sustain both initiatives at the same time, so it is sensible to prioritize. In the example, product breadth is likely to be developed first, before entry into a new market occurs. The desired situation might look like Figure 17.1.

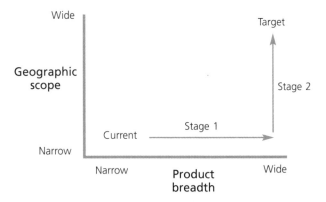

Figure 17.1 **Different strategic routes 1**

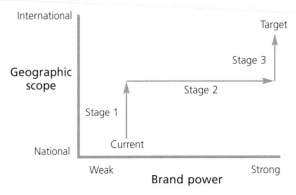

Figure 17.2 **Different strategic routes 2**

Alternatively, there may be a strategy which aims to develop simultaneously the brand power of existing products and the geographic scope of sales of the same products (Figure 17.2). It could be a company such as Nestlé or any number of wine producers seeking to develop a brand name and expand from a position of dominating the domestic market to one of opening up a broader market, including a significant international role.

There is no reason, other than the demands of simplicity, to limit the targets to two. Since strategies are complex, the variations are much greater than often thought. The movement towards a number of such targets should be represented on a flow chart.

Alternative speeds

Another important aspect of strategy implementation is pacing. This is equivalent to asking over what period should an enterprise implement a strategy. Enterprises can move either too slowly or too quickly:

- The former might mean that competitors leave them behind. After all, a miss is as good as a mile.
- The latter might mean that the enterprise is trying too much in the time available and moving in lurches as successive bottlenecks are created and released. It may be a case of less haste, more speed.

There is usually some preferred pace of movement.

The pace chosen must be appropriate to what is being done. Pacing has everything to do with performance measurement. Many performance measures are time-related, setting the pace in the sense of how much is to be produced or sold in a particular period of time. Such measures might be set according to best practice elsewhere or according to previous performance of the departments or individuals. Pacing is concerned with the normal rhythms of production and sales, rhythms which often involve a significant unevenness during the year.

The pace might also reflect various transitions which are critical to an organization, for example turnarounds or product replacements. It is harder to benchmark the pace in such cases. There may be serious time constraints on how quickly these transitions can and should be completed.

Event pacing

The biggest problem is not so much the speed of movement as the lack of control over that speed. The desirable speed may differ from industry to industry. For most enterprises, particularly in fast-changing industries, it may seem perfectly natural to adopt a strategic stance of reaction to outside events. In this situation, the speed is imposed on the enterprise by the changing environment. Such a reactive stance tends to be an opportunistic one. The enterprise tries its best to imitate and exploit whatever opportunities it sees appearing. This stance has been described as event pacing (Eisenhardt and Brown, 1998: 60). It does not reflect the degree of strategic control most organization would aspire to. This is usually not a preferred state of affairs.

Time pacing

Any enterprise wants to be in control, even if the industry is a fast-changing one. By contrast, a better stance is time pacing. Such a pacing is defined as involving regular, rhythmic and proactive movement. It requires focus, efficiency and confidence on the part of staff in order to maintain the chosen speed. With this consistency of speed, a considerable forward momentum can be built up, a momentum determined by the organization itself. Staff internalize the need for, even the rate of, change. This enables managers to manage the speed and rhythm with which the enterprise changes, even during key transitions.

There are simple targets which can be set and which help in controlling the pace. The target may be to generate during a given time period a certain proportion of sales from new products, say 30–40% of the total, or the target may be to introduce a certain number of new products each year. There may be a decision to initiate the design of the next new product before the one about to be introduced is put onto the market. The aim is to choreograph carefully any such phased movement. It is like the pipeline described in the case study on the pharmaceutical industry in Chapter 18. There are a series of unfolding development experiences which are repeated, but require appropriate pacing. They must be linked to each other.

The same might apply to other processes of expansion, for example entry into new markets or making new acquisitions. Folding in new acquisitions into the existing enterprise might be done in the same way as introducing a new product.

The critical dimension of time pacing is setting the right rhythms for strategic change and synchronizing those rhythms, both with changes in the market and what is made possible by the organization's internal capabilities. Sometimes the rhythms are purely external, set by:

- the seasons, where production or sales vary seasonally
- the requirements of product development
- swings in customer spending, reflecting perhaps the introduction of new models, even a retailer's shelf-planning cycle
- the actions of suppliers or complementors and their own rhythms.

Almost any strategic initiative, whatever its nature, can be broken into smaller parts, which can then be paced in a similar way. These parts can be called modules. The introduction of different modules has a timetable. Modularizing new product development helps to establish a clear timetable of events and an even pace of expansion.

Leadership and the role of the centre: a specialized strategy division

It is necessary to look briefly at the specifics of leadership in the area of strategy implementation.

There is a common belief that a leader needs to distance him or herself from operational matters in order to concentrate on strategic issues – to focus on the big picture. Such a classical conception sees the leader as the strategy maker, who hands down the vision for others to implement. The board of directors has some responsibility in this area, but usually acting in concert with the CEO.

Insofar as strategy is seen as one person's vision, leadership could be understood as overseeing the implementation of that strategy. Coherence is allegedly only achieved if one person has the ultimate responsibility for strategy, provided that person tries to involve all the others in the task of strategy making. The ability of the leader to achieve cooperation and control within the framework of the strategy is important. The skills required may be negotiation or communication skills or simply the ability to inspire others with the power of the vision. Different models of strategy conceive leadership in different ways, putting the emphasis on different elements of that leadership, for example on positioning or transformative ability, entrepreneurship, cognitive or rhetorical skills. Each of these conceptions requires different skills and different experience. The leader is the person who takes the initiative in strategy making, particularly where change is occurring.

Where strategy is clearly emergent, a different kind of leader is needed, one capable of guiding an enterprise through the real world, overseeing the complex operations of the enterprise and linking those operations with its long-term goals. Here, the role of the leader is to provide the rationale, interpreting the real world and the response of the organization to unanticipated and unexpected change. In the process, the leader becomes the champion of a particular strategy.

Diversified companies or conglomerates always need central guidance. Without it the individual business units would go off in different directions, even competing against each other for scarce resources. The same is of course true at the level of the business unit, and is repeated endlessly down to the bottom layer. Everyone needs a leader, mainly to interpret and guide.

There is a dictum – centralize strategy, decentralize operations – which is often repeated. It seeks to place operations close to the customer, but define an important strategic role for the centre. It has a measure of truth since the centre acts as an information node, a facilitator of many necessary information transfers.

The centre is far more than this. It is:

- The articulator of the enteprise's mission, setting the objectives in a clear way and ensuring that the company is moving in the right direction. The CEO, often operating with the board, is the person most responsible for ensuring that the strategic directions are right.
- The controller, direct or indirect, if necessary disciplining the various parts of the enterprise to keep them performing as anticipated and within the limits of the strategic objectives.

- The banker, using the internal financial market to allocate corporate funds, doing this at a lower cost than outside finance could manage and providing better monitoring of financial controls, again within the parameters of the strategy adopted.
- The coordinator, particularly in a diversified company where there is a need for joint asset utilization.
- The protector of the intangible assets of the company, the brands and the knowhow which can so easily be dissipated.

At the centre, the CEO provides the nudge, or even the push, to guide the whole enterprise in the direction desired. The CEO reads the subtle changes of direction felt desirable and the abrupt changes which suddenly prove necessary to avoid disaster. A leader needs a good team behind him or her, and choosing that team is an indispensable aspect of that leadership. The emphasis put on leadership may reflect current fads and failures, but the role of the leader in strategy making cannot be ignored.

A separate strategy unit

The importance of strategy, and leadership in making strategy, might be indicated by the establishment of a separate division solely responsible for strategy making. Its very existence may be a signal that the enterprise considers strategy important. This can be done in a number of ways:

- To superimpose in a matrix form a strategy structure on the line management of the company, whatever principle is used in its organization. There may be a structure of strategic business units defined independently of the normal organizational structure, with its own layers of responsibility right up to a deputy chairperson or president.
- To establish a separate functional division alongside, and of equal status with, the other functional units such as operations, finance or marketing. The strategy division might be more like a research department, providing data which is needed for strategy making.
- To be directly answerable to the CEO, particularly where there are separate business units organized on a product or other basis, whose activities need to be harmonized. It may be part of his office.

The division may be under the control of the key senior management officers who give it instruction on what is to be done, or it may be given a free rein to act independently in identifying opportunities or threats. Its function may be to generate strategic thinking and encourage others to generate strategic thinking. For example, it might be the body responsible for scenario building, an activity which is seen as involving all the staff of the enterprise.

Whatever the exact means of incorporating strategy making into the activities of the organization, the purpose of having such a division is to create a certain distance between the long-term view and operational problems. In this way strategic management can be separated from operations management. While there must be a positive interaction between the operational and the strategic, some distance is generally deemed to be good for both sides, but not too much distance. One danger is that the division then remains aloof from the normal operations of the enterprise and becomes irrelevant.

The main aim of a strategic division should be to put the strategists in a position to make an objective overview, free of the demands and noise of everyday activity, but not wholly so, since familiarity with the everyday may be the source of invaluable insights about the changing context. Nevertheless, the division might be lean and mean, designed simply to give the organization the strategic direction it needs.

The need for such a division is likely to be pressing in the unusual case where strategic planning is being undertaken. The formulation of detailed strategic plans and their harmonization may require a concerted and systematic effort which needs to be institutionalized. The regular monitoring of a plan may require permanent staff.

There are various advantages and disadvantages in having such a division:

Advantages
- Its existence signals to all employees the importance of the activity.
- It allows the separation of strategy from other functional interests. A body of specialist skills and knowledge in strategy making, a professionalism, can be built up and built upon.
- There are strategists with the time to consider the broad view and look further ahead than most functional units are able, given the immediate demands of operations.

Disadvantages
- There are the dangers in an extreme detachment of thinkers from doers; it is only in doing that the strategist discovers opportunities and threats. To abstain from doing is to deprive oneself of access to information. Isolation compounds the problem of inadequate data. Involvement in everyday operations may be a highly desirable aspect of any manager's job.
- A second danger is that its very existence encourages an excess of bureaucratization which some already think is inherent in strategy making – presentations which are too long, reports which are made too frequently and at excessive length, and meetings which demand far too much time.
- Strategic thinking may be discouraged by the very existence of such a division. The assumption may be made that strategy is carried out by someone else. Since it is already covered, there is no need for such thinking elsewhere in the organization.

Role of a strategy unit

If such a strategy division exists, there are three possibilities in terms of its role:

1. It could be an extended form of tokenism, a separate division highlighting that you are doing the right thing but without real significance.
2. It may exist as a think-tank, gathering information. At the same time, it may or may not have a role in promoting strategic thinking throughout the organization.
3. It could be the executive arm of the leader or the central strategy-making team. It may have as its task the implementation of the strategy formulated by the leader and handed down.

The argument has been put that strategy is best made by everyone in a process which is integrated into all the core activities of the organization.

Case Study 1   South African Breweries – a different global strategy

History and position of SAB

It is unusual for a company to have gained the position that SAB has without attracting attention. SAB still has a low profile, although it has become one of the driving forces for the consolidation of a highly fragmented industry. It currently raises half its estimated annual revenues of approximately $4 billion from its foreign holdings. Its interests span mainly Africa, Latin America and Eastern Europe, but increasingly Asian countries such as India and China. It is on the verge of entering the markets of North America and Europe.

SAB, founded in Johannesburg as long ago as 1895, at present controls 98% of the South African beer market; it is the dominant producer, almost the only producer in that country. When SAB was establishing itself as dominant within the South African market, it acquired licensing rights to produce locally and distribute and market international brands such as Heineken and Guinness. During the apartheid years, it had limited scope to enter foreign markets and was forced to concentrate its attention on the domestic market. SAB survived the transition from a white to a black regime well. It has acquired a good reputation for developing black entrepreneurs.

After the end of apartheid, it quietly but quickly moved to extend its market abroad. It established a position of dominance in sub-Saharan Africa, now producing two-thirds of all beer in the continent of Africa. It moved into other, fast-growing markets, principally those of the formerly Communist states of Eastern Europe, Latin America and key parts of Asia. In China, SAB is now the second largest brewer. Its main seller Castle is acquiring a brand name which is still not up with the premium brands but is gaining wider recognition.

SAB is a large company by any standards. In all it now has 108 breweries in 24 countries, employing 31,000 people. In the year ended March 31, 2001, SAB had net earnings of US$359 million on a total revenue of US$4.18 billion. This made SAB the third largest brewer in the world, even before the acquisition of Miller, a surprising position for a company which ten years ago had an almost non-existent global role and almost no profile. It is also surprising for a brewer which up to 2002 had no significant operations in any developed country in the world. The real turning point came in 1999 when Mackay become its CEO and SAB moved its headquarters to London. The object of this move was to raise its international profile and increase its ability to raise funds. Today it is certainly a major global player in the beer industry.

Competition

The world beer industry is extremely fragmented. There are hundreds of regional breweries, many of them family-owned. Almost everywhere, there is a strong attachment to local brews, even in developed economies. One of the key issues in entering a new market is access to the local distribution system, hotels, public houses, supermarkets and off-licences. This is not always easy to achieve, which partly explains a tenacious home country bias.

There are two processes which are currently at work, the internationalization of the industry, with some players taking a very active role in entering foreign markets, especially those which offer size or growth, and a process of consolidation, both within national markets and across international boundaries.

SAB Miller has to compete with the small local breweries and the large international players.

The strategy of expansion

Circumstances as well as inclination have forced a strategy on SAB which has led it to move from the domestic market into the markets of undeveloped and developing counties. SAB has embraced this strategy and has used it to escape from the constraints imposed by the South African context. SAB aspires to global leadership in the industry.

The background of SAB was eminently suitable for such an early strategy of expansion into the African market, and then into the markets of other developing countries outside Africa. These countries, with the exception of the Czech Republic, are generally small but fast-growing markets.

SAB is poised to make a significant entrance into the developed markets of the world. The acquisition of Miller marks its entrance into the North America market. This acquisition is clearly part of a strategy of establishing a global position in the industry. Graham Mackay, the chief executive of the company, has emphasized this: 'We'll look to fill in our positions around the world and also look at larger transactions with broader geographical spread as they come available' (quoted in Carpenter, 2002: 5).

SAB's normal mode of entry into foreign markets is primarily through the acquisition of existing breweries, that is, through foreign direct investment rather than export or licensing. The present case study concentrates on three examples of such entry. The first two are examples of the global strategy of consolidating its presence in the emerging markets of developing countries. It considers how SAB has already entered the small but rapidly growing Indian market and how it has chosen to enter the large and rapidly growing Chinese market. The third example indicates a change of strategy; how it proposes to make its first entrance into a large mature market, the USA.

India

The Indian beer market, while still a relatively small one by world standards, is growing quickly, at least 10% per annum, more like 15% per annum over the last five years, and it has an enormous potential for future growth, given the rapid economic growth of India and its large population. At the moment, per head consumption is only about half a litre, well below the champion consumers, Germany and the Czech Republic at 125–140 litres and 100 litres for the USA and UK. However, consumption in these markets is not growing. By contrast, in developing markets such as China, it is already at 20 litres per head and the Philippines 35. As a result, while Germany has about 1,200 breweries and China a similar number, there are only 54 breweries in the whole of India. There is clearly a long way to go for India, but it is a good market to be in.

There are three main producers in India who supply 75% of the market. The biggest player, occupying a dominant position, is United Breweries (UB). Its position has been under threat, from domestic and international competition. Its main competitor, Shaw Wallace, has been catching up in recent years. In 1992 United Breweries sold 15 million cases of beer (a case holds a dozen 65ml bottles) and Shaw Wallace only 4. By 1999 United Breweries was selling 22 million to Shaw Wallace's 15. Shaw Wallace had achieved this by meeting India's increasing preference for strong beer. Fosters had also entered the market.

UB responded in two ways to this competition. Using spare capacity at UB, it created Millennium Alcobev (MABL), as a vehicle attacking the strong beer market, spinning off new brands through a new distribution system. It acquired 51% of Inertia Industries and transferred all the MABL assets into a new company called Inertia-Millennium Industries.

Second, UB is looking for a strategic alliance with a global brewery. It is offering 26% of its equity to such a player, clearly with a view to forging a strategic alliance. Of course such an equity holding could be a prelude to a full merger. A number of breweries are interested. The principal ones are SAB, Carlsberg and Heineken.

SAB intends to be an important player in the bur-geoning Indian market. In the words of its current CEO in India, Richard Rushton: 'Our focus is on desirable capacity footprint and building a powerful brand portfolio in India. The beer industry fragmentation provides consolidation opportunities' (Mohan, 2002: 89). SAB began its Indian operations in October 2000, with the acquisition of Narang Breweries in Gonda, Uttar Pradesh; in an 18-month period, 2001 and the first half of 2002, it acquired Mysore Breweries, outbidding Millennium, Pals Distilleries and Rochees Breweries. Mysore is a relatively small but fast-growing player which has two breweries and sells in the fastest growing part of the Indian market.

SAB intends to merge all these firms with the main company, SAB India, which is a subsidiary of SAB Plc, London. SAB proposes to use this holding company to contain existing production facilities and make further investments in India. It is currently talking with breweries in Goa and Madhya Pradesh to expand operations and is looking to acquire further breweries in India. Already SAB has access to the key beer markets in India – Maharashtra, Delhi, Karnataka, Andhra Pradesh, Uttar Pradesh, Rajasthan and Goa.

Through Mysore, SAB has acquired two important brands, Knockout and Bengal Tiger, brands it intends to revamp and commit significant investment in expanding their markets. SAB has already launched its Castle brand in Delhi and Mumbai.

It plans to invest US$53 million in the Indian beer sector and acquire ten breweries. There are particular difficulties in investing in India, notably a difficult excise tax which is imposed on beer as if it were a spirit and a legacy of licensing policies which used to regulate most industries.

China

The most interesting market is the Chinese one which is about to overtake the American as the largest in the world. The Chinese thirst for beer has risen dramatically, expanding tenfold between 1982 and 1999. In 1990 China accounted for 6% of the world market, by 1999 it was 14%.

The Chinese market is much more fragmented than the American in which Anheuser-Busch accounts for as much as 48% of the beer sold. The largest brewery in China, Tsingtao Brewery, accounts for only 11% of the market and has little international recognition. Until 1996, it accounted for only 2% of the market. Since then there has been a consolidation of the industry but it remains largely locally focused, with something like 500 breweries in the hinterland of China, away from the coast. Since 1995, Tsingtao has acquired 43 breweries, several of which are state-of-the-art operations sold by foreign brewers at bargain prices. The main rivals of Tsingtao, the Beijing Yanjing Beer Group and the China Resources Breweries hold only 15% of the market between them. The local industry has been consolidating but there is a long way to go.

The beer market was only opened to foreign entry in the mid-1990s, but potential players flooded in. Competition from local suppliers was much more intense than expected and the consumer was apparently happy to put up with beers which were of inconsistent quality, higher air content, inferior ingredients, shoddy labels and packaging and even the occasional exploding bottle. In the 1990s China was awash with beer. Competition brought prices down to low levels, sometimes to a third of what foreign companies wanted to charge and less than the price of mineral water. Foreign companies made heavy losses as they confronted the additional problems of finding good wholesalers, retaining brand loyalty from distributors and restaurants and collecting accounts. By the end of the 1990s, Bass Brewers, Fosters and Miller Brewing had had their fingers burned and were withdrawing. Fosters lost US$70 million over five years, wrote off US$100 million on its brewing assets in China in 1998 and sold two of its three breweries.

However, the foreign brewers are returning. Anheuser-Busch has allied with Tsingtao, recently moving its stake up from 4% to 27%. Interbrew acquired 80% of the Nanjing Brewery in 1997 and, in 2002, 24% of the Zhujiang Brewing Group, China's third largest brewer, and a 70% stake in the KK Group (Ningbao-based). SAB's entry into the Chinese market has taken the form of a joint venture. It owns 49% of China Resources Breweries, which is intending to invest US$100 million dollars in the acquisition of other breweries over the next three years (announced in April 2002).

Entry into the Chinese beer market, as with other industries, has typically taken the form of joint ventures. It has not been very successful, with Fosters and Carlsberg notching up large losses and retreating into niche markets in the major cities. These players underestimated the degree of competition in this market, particularly for products which were relatively pricey. There was little brand recognition and local beers could outcompete the expensive foreign intruders. The foreign companies also underestimated the difficulty of cutting cost in local breweries and changing labour regimes. On all these counts, SAB may prove to be much more resilient, despite using the same mode of entry.

The USA

A much more critical step is entry into the American market, a step which many have attempted to make and failed. The specific entry mode into the American market is through the acquisition from Philip Morris of Miller Brewing Company, a brewer almost as large as SAB but one which has a chequered history and is not known for its dynamism. The acquisition made SAB the second largest brewer in the world, behind only Anheuser-Busch. The price tag was US$5.6 billion in stock (US$3.6 billion) and assumed debt (US$2 billion), a commitment well beyond anything previously attempted, including the US$2 billion spent over the last two years in acquiring brewers in emerging markets and certainly dwarfing the Indian investment. The Milwaukee brewer is still number two in the USA, with over $4 billion annual sales, slightly more than SAB.

For a company which aspires to be an international player, the South African connection has proved a major handicap. The fall in the value of the rand has caused the company's earnings to decline over the last two years. At present 47% of SAB's reserves are in rands. This makes it difficult for SAB to play an international role since the rand fell some 80% in value against the American dollar over the twelve years before 2002. The acquisition of Miller will generate a flow of cash in a hard currency and allow diversification of SAB's reserves. It will cut the proportion of the company's earnings received in rands from half to about a third. It will help the company to issue a large tranche of new shares in order to raise additional money for fresh expansion.

The aim of the acquisition is to add to the company's earnings and profits, rather than to reduce costs. Since there is little overlap between the two companies, no cost savings are anticipated in the first year and only US$50 million over three years. Miller is regarded as one of the more efficient American brewers, but has been losing out to Anheuser-Busch. Philip Morris retains a 36% stake in the new company, which is called SAB Miller and listed on the London Stock Exchange. Philip Morris has promised not to sell any shares before June 2005. It has almost a quarter of the voting rights and holds three of the 11 non-executive positions on the new board.

The main problem is to lift demand for Miller's main brands, Miller Lite and Miller Genuine Draft. Philip Morris has made a significant additional investment in marketing since 1999 in order to turn around a fall in demand and restore growth. Whatever the outcome, the acquisition will give SAB the number two distribution system in the USA, a platform for selling its own premium brands such as the Czech beer Pilsner Urquell.

When the deal was announced in 2002, there was a 10% rise in the value of the London-listed shares.

Case Study Questions

1. Consider each of the different modes of entry into a foreign market and show how a beer company wishing to expand might evaluate each of them.
2. What are the main determinants of the mode of entry by beer producers into the various parts of the global market? Consider the best mode of entry into each of the following markets – China, the USA and India. In particular, what are the likely differences in entering developing and developed markets?
3. What are the advantages and disadvantages of South Africa as the home country of a global beer company? How can the disadvantages be played down?
4. What are the advantages and disadvantages of a beer company diversifying into other forms of beverage production and sale?
5. How successfully is SAB implementing its strategy for growth?

Reading

Banzai, S., 'Cheers to combat', *Business India*, September 17–30, 2001: 60–2.

Benson-Armer, R., Leibowitz, J. and Ramachandran, D., 'Global beer: what's on tap?', *The McKinsey Quarterly*, 1999, (1):111–21.

Capell, K., 'This brewer has an unquenchable thirst', *Business Week*, June 10, 2002: 31.

Carpenter, C., 'SA brewer swallows Miller for $10b', *Business Age*, May 31, 2002: 5.

Koppisch, J., Khermosch, G. and Capell, K., 'It's Miller time in Johannesburg', *Business Week*, April 22, 2002: 30.

Lee, C. S., 'China beer battle; Tsingtao's long march' *Fortune*, May 27, 2002: 25–6.

Mohan, D., 'Frothing up', *Business India*, April 29–May 12, 2002: 89.

Sito, P., 'Belgium brewer buys into mainland's KK Corp', *South China Morning Post*, November 2, 2002, Business 1.

Tanzer, A., 'An Asian dream becomes a beer baron's nightmare', *Business Review Weekly*, February 1, 1999.

Viljoen, J. and Dann, S., *Strategic Management* (Longman, Frenchs Forest NSW: 2000), Illustration Capsule 9.6, Foreign beers not China's cup of tea: 354–6.

Wonacott, P., 'Foreign brewers try new route to Beijing', *The Financial Review*, August 2, 2002: 64.

This case study is also relevant to Chapters 14 and 15.

Case Study 2   Toyota – still a Japanese company?

'Toyota is the benchmark of the automotive industry, worldwide.'

Vaghefi and Coleman, 1999: 394

The Toyota brand name, which ranked 20th globally in 1999, is behind only Sony among Japanese companies and only Ford and Mercedes for automobile producers. What was the nature of the strategy which has allowed Toyota to create and maintain a significant competitive advantage and become a brand name synonymous with high quality and low price?

The strategy

Most commentators assume that for any organization there is a trade-off between efficiency and flexibility. The traditional argument is that specialized formal structures of bureaucracy increase efficiency but at the cost of introducing a hierarchy of decision-making levels. This imposes all the negative effects of bureaucratization, including delays in decision making, a web of excessive rules and regulations suffocating the individual, an overemphasis on formalism, a retreat behind the organization and the suppression of initiative. Size and structure can raise productivity but can also reduce the ability to adapt. Toyota has shown that this supposed trade-off is not inevitable. The systems described below show exactly how Toyota has managed to achieve this, although it is difficult to fully understand the system since it is so highly specific. This is why it is so difficult to replicate, not a result simply of cultural difference, as some suppose.

The Toyota system focuses on the particular and the concrete. It requires the specification of all logistical links, both within the company and with its partners outside, as direct customer/supplier relationships. It focuses on a desire for production which is defect-free, with a batch size of one, on a product which can be delivered exactly and immediately to the appointed destination on the terms specified, without any waste and in a work environment that is safe, physically, emotionally and professionally.

There is a paradox at the heart of what needs to be explained. In the words of two researchers on Toyota, 'activities, connections, and production flows in a

Toyota factory are rigidly scripted, yet at the same time Toyota's operations are enormously flexible and adaptable' (Spear and Bowen, 1999: 97). In their view, 'the rigid specification is the very thing that makes the flexibility and creativity possible'. In what sense is this true?

There are four main mechanisms for making possible an organizational system which combines efficiency with flexibility. Toyota effectively uses all four mechanisms:

1. Developing a meta-routine or meta-routines, that is, a series of mechanisms for making the non-routine in some sense routine, but not so routine that it completely removes the desired flexibility. The aim is to build change and innovation into the routine of the organization, to institutionalize change so that the enterprise becomes efficient and flexibile. This can only be done in an organization which encourages the learning process.

     In the case of Toyota, there are clear meta-routines for the changeover process when new models are introduced. So effective are the meta-routines that Toyota can change its models more frequently and more quickly than American producers.

2. Enrichment, the addition of more demanding non-routine tasks to the routine production tasks of any worker. The worker is empowered to discover the rules of the work by confronting and solving problems. The role of supervisors is to draw out problems and solutions by a process of iterative Socratic questioning. Any worker can be sensitized to identify possible improvements while they carry out their routine operational tasks. This challenging of the worker enriches, in the sense that it makes the work more interesting and rewarding. The same mechanism of enrichment can be applied to any work done by the suppliers.

3. Switching, that is, the commitment of specific time to the consideration of non-routine and routine tasks. There may be a clear sequence of tasks within a programme which builds in the non-routine as a natural part of a worker's activity. Switching recognizes that the tasks are separate and to be undertaken at different times but this may occur so frequently and unconsciously that the boundaries are fuzzy. It may occur without any premeditated timing. However, the mechanism stresses that this should be made easy for any worker to achieve. Quality circles might assist in this switching.

4. Partitioning, which further recognizes that there might be subunits specialist in non-routine tasks which operate parallel to or side by side with those which concentrate on routine tasks. A pilot team, consisting of the production team leaders, which looks at the ramifications of a model change might qualify here.

In what context can these four mechanisms contribute to a rich combination of efficiency and flexibility? Clearly, training is required to properly motivate and prepare the workers for operating these mechanisms effectively. Trust is also necessary between participants, trust in the consistency of others to act as they promise, to be capable of fulfilling what they promise and share the pursuit of the same goals.

It is surprising to characterize Toyota as an enabling bureaucracy, in which there is a high level of standardization. There are clearly defined standard skills, standard work processes, although these are more flexible than they appear at first sight, and well-understood design standards. These interact to produce continuous, overlapping product cycles. On the other hand, there are strongly integrative social processes at work within the organization. These involve the deliberate encouragement of mutual respect, the resulting mutual adjustment in the interests of achieving consensus, the putting in place of close supervision or mentoring, and an emphasis on an integrative leadership from the product heads. Once again these interact positively. Toyota managers achieve a cross-functional coordination while still building functional expertise. The right leadership is critical.

Lean production

The lean production system played a central role in Toyota's rise in the 1970s and 80s, although the term was first applied by the International Motor Vehicle programme at MIT. The key to lean production is to treat purchasing, product development and production as a

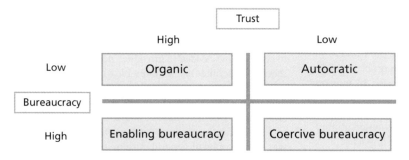

Figure 17.3 **A typology of organizations**

single system. It is necessary to treat each of these elements in turn, starting with production itself, going on to purchasing and concluding with product development. By aiming to optimize the whole system in one go, Toyota achieved a simultaneous and marked improvement of quality and cost levels, a continuous stream of innovation and a significant degree of flexibility in the face of environmental change.

The origins of lean production go back to the 1930s and the beginning of the Toyota Motor Company, when Kiichiro Toyoda, the founder, emphasized the concept of 'just-in-time'. In the 1940s, a Toyota production supervisor wedded elements of Taylorism and the Ford system with this concern with inventories. He sought to standardize work but at the same time allow workers to become multiskilled. During the occupation years (1945–51), American influence brought in the training within industries system developed during the war in the USA. This had a direct influence on Toyota through supervisors trained in the new system. It is ironic that American influence is one source of lean production.

It is overly dramatic to say that the stopwatch and the clipboard were put in the hands of the worker, not the manager, but there is a strong element of truth in this statement. Toyota did not simply imitate, over a lengthy period of time it developed a system which could not be easily imitated. Toyota went on improving the hybrid system and extended it to other Japanese companies.

Lean production is a coherent system in which the independent elements link together to create an impact on innovation, quality and cost which is much greater than the sum of the individual influences. The whole Toyota system must be seen as a coherent, interacting whole. The individual elements are:

1. Design for easy manufacture
Engineers worked intensively on the assembly floor to determine how product design could be modified, not only to improve the quality of the end product, but to make production less costly and faster. Exactly the same principle could be applied to components supplied to the company. Engineers could work in both areas to ensure compatibility and maximize the impact of learning.

2. Total quality control
There was significant empowerment of the workers, which involved giving them training in problem solving, encouraging them to make suggestions for the improvement of the production process, and listening to their suggestions. Teams of workers, problem-solving (quality) circles, are responsible for production quality and minimizing waste. To minimize the impact of breakdown, workers were always allowed to halt the production line to remedy production problems. They

were encouraged to solve a problem which caused defects rather than simply having inspectors remove defective parts.

3. Continuous improvement (kaizen)
All workers engage in continuous improvement, if only to make their lives easier. The phenomenon of a small team learning to operate a work station with fewer workers than planned in order to allow one or more to sleep, have a smoke or simply to relax is common. The trick is to get the workers to share their secrets with the company. In the Toyota system, teams of 4–6, with a designated team leader, identified the optimal procedure for each job without the participation of methods engineers. This involved encouraging a belief that there could be a continuous learning process from which all would gain and sensitizing workers to the possibilities for realizing actual improvement. This required and made possible the taking of swift action, even before problems became known to senior managers or became serious and disruptive. Problems would be fixed where they occurred.

4. Just-in-time (JIT) manufacturing
The core feature of JIT is producing to demand rather than to stock or inventory. The mechanism for achieving this was the *kanban* or 'supermarket system'. In this the downstream production station receives just the right number of components needed, and the upstream production station producing the component produces just enough to replenish what was taken. In an ideal world, there would no inventory at all, but this situation is unattainable, for example there needs to be a safety stock to deal with the less than perfect reliability of processes, and a buffer stock to deal with the volatility of customer demand. The point is to match exactly the countermeasure, in this case the inventory held, to the problem and keep enough inventory at the relevant place, but no more than this. Keeping inventory to a minimum requires that production is kept to the target level, so that all can be confident that the position is a stable one.

5. Flexible manufacturing
The aim of this was to tailor products to specific market segments, that is, to customize as much as possible, and to cut the time needed to introduce new products. This required machines easily adaptable to design changes, work standardization and multitasking, and a shop-floor design that enables the process layout to be easily changed. Toyota tried to eliminate facilities designed exclusively for the production of specific models. There was a philosophy of general purpose plants that could be quickly retooled to produce different models. This would allow production lot sizes to be small, promoting

both wide product lines to accommodate consumer demand and rapid model changes to accommodate changes in that demand.

6. *Rapid cycle time*

The aim was to accelerate the life cycle of a product, to take action now which avoided going down cul-de-sacs late in the process of product development. This was achieved by using parallel rather than sequential development processes, multiskilled engineers, rapid production of prototypes and more prototypes than is the norm, and involving the suppliers of various components as actively as possible in the process of design from an early stage.

7. *Close supplier relationships*

The keys to long-term successful partnerships are joint development of products and strengthened loyalty. Toyota prefers to concentrate on a small number of first-tier, long-term relationships, rather than a larger number of short-term relationships. Information exchanges from early in the development process of a product, incentive structures to improve quality and efficiency, and personnel rotation of staff between Toyota and the suppliers are all part of the establishment of this long-term relationship. This issue is discussed at length below.

All this is made possible by the combination of a consensus approach, in which much decision making originates at the bottom of the company rather than the top, and an individual loyalty to the company. Managers in this system are less functionally specialized, more participatory in productive operations than the norm and act more as mediators for those below them in the hierarchy of communication and coordination. There is absolute discipline, without which there could be massive disruption.

The same approach was applied when Toyota decided to enter the luxury car market with the Lexus brand.

The supplier network

Toyota fashioned its lean production system around a close network of supplier firms. It is a good example of a vertical complementary strategic alliance. There are a number of industries which lend themselves to such alliances because the supplier networks produce a large proportion of the value of the product. Airplane production is one area already encountered in which this is true (see the case study on Airbus Industrie in Chapter 4). It is less true of the wine industry, where suppliers are less important.

In the automobile industry, as much as 70% of the value of output is accounted for by suppliers, so that the relationship with these suppliers is fundamental to success. The dependence is less in the USA. One of the explanations for the success of the leading Japanese automobile producers, such as Toyota and Honda, is that they have developed bilateral and multilateral knowledge-sharing routines with their suppliers, which result in a continuous process of inter-organizational or network-level learning from which all gain and which gives them an advantage over American and European automobile manufacturers.

Several implementation issues are raised by the construction of such a vertical network:

- Long-term relationships of the strategic centre firm with a limited number of suppliers, focusing on the long-term productivity of the whole network, not just the individual enterprises. This approach is to be contrasted with one which involves continually renegotiating short-term contracts and changing suppliers in order to reduce the price paid for components.
- A strong interest on the part of the strategic centre firm in modernizing or updating the suppliers by giving them appropriate technical and financial assistance. The centre firm has to take the initiative in putting together the network and providing a suitable incentive for the suppliers to participate.
- The development of strong ties of trust and transparency on the part of all members of the network, and the strengthening of both multilateral and reciprocal relationships between all the suppliers and the strategic centre firm.

Once again, the distinction between explicit information, that is, information which is easily codifiable, and tacit knowledge, or know-how, that is, information which is difficult to codify and transfer without face-to-face contact, is critical. The Toyota network with its suppliers is designed to facilitate the sharing of not just codifiable but also, and more importantly, tacit know-how. The problems of network creation are twofold: firstly, how to encourage members of such a network to openly share valuable knowledge when they know that that knowledge can become a public good or a 'commons', subject to the free-rider problem; and secondly, how to set up efficient conduits within the network for carrying such knowledge.

Clearly, Toyota became the core or nodal firm in such a network. It was the initiator of gain for others and itself the main recipient of much gain. It sought to encourage the suppliers to identify strongly with the network. The initial lure was a significant subsidy by Toyota, consisting of both knowledge and resources to which the suppliers would not otherwise have had access. Continued membership of the network meant acceptance by the suppliers of the rules or norms of behaviour of the network. There were sanctions for non-compliance, including exclusion from the network and further orders. Strong ties developed within the network which led to internalization of the rules and the protection of the tacit know-how. The assumption was encouraged that the knowledge was not proprietary, but belonged to the network itself. The price of entry into the network was the willingness to open up your own operations for inspection and make available valuable knowledge to the rest of the network. As Dyer and Noeboken (2000) have put it: 'The price of entry into the network is a limited ability to protect proprietary production knowledge. In this sense intellectual property rights reside at the network, rather than the firm, level.'

There are four network-level processes which were important in the transfer of knowledge:

1. The establishment of supplier associations

In Japan there are three regional supplier organizations. Typically these have general meetings which occur every other month. They have linked to them topic committees, for example a quality committee. These associations and their committees select an annual theme which is considered important and relevant at the time. The committees organize training schemes and plant tours. There is an annual quality conference.

2. Toyota establishes consulting teams

Toyota's operations management consulting division trains the consultants who learn how to problem solve and then go on to teach that ability to others. The operations management consulting group within the division has responsibility within Toyota for the acquisition, storage and diffusion of valuable production knowledge. The group spins off consulting teams which go out to the suppliers. The consulting teams provide free advice to the suppliers.

3. Toyota establishes learning teams

These are small groups which have a voluntary membership, consisting of any member of the network who wishes to be represented. The exchange of information is reciprocal. The groups engage in learning which is context-specific and relates to particular plants or facilities which are regularly visited.

4. Toyota encourages inter-firm employee transfers

Each year something like 120–130 individuals were transferred from Toyota to the suppliers where they stayed for significant periods of time. This process built up, and continues to build up, a stock of human capital consisting of individuals with specific knowledge of the links between suppliers and the hub company (see Figure 17.4). The network was not created overnight. The process took time and was carefully prepared:

- *Phase 1: Developing weak ties*
  During this stage there is a sharing of explicit knowledge, achieved through the formal supplier associations and their committee systems.

- *Phase 2: Developing strong ties with Toyota*
  During this stage Toyota, through its consultants, deliberately activated an indebtedness on the part of its suppliers. The aim was to create reciprocal obligations which would modify behaviour. The process of transfer of implicit know-how or knowledge begins at this stage.

- *Phase 3: Developing strong ties among suppliers*
  During this stage there was a move to multilateral links. The small learning teams constituted 'subnetworks'. The process of transferring tacit knowledge among the suppliers really began. Knowledge flowed in both directions. Structural holes in the broad network rapidly disappeared as the density of such teams increased. As the word went out that the process was beneficial, the initiative spread.

In the evolution of the knowledge-sharing network, the network therefore moved from an initiation phase to a mature phase. During the initiation phase, there is one huge network with the core firm as a hub. The relationships of the suppliers with the core firm are bilateral ones

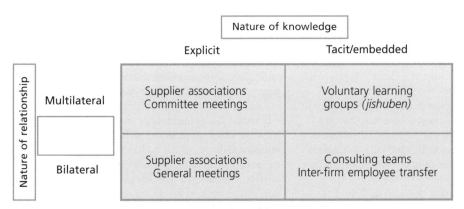

Figure 17.4 **Toyota's network-level knowledge-sharing processes**

and the ties among most members weak or non-existent. There are numerous structural holes. The network is good at transferring explicit knowledge but that is about all. Membership by the suppliers demonstrates a commitment to the core firm because the suppliers see a gain from membership, both in maintaining orders from the core firm and in learning how to improve their own productivity. The core firm deliberately avoided appearing too mercenary in its approach, that is, trying in an obvious way to extract a benefit from the supplier in a reduced price of a component, a reduction directly linked to a specific productivity gain made by that supplier.

During the mature phase the nature of the network has changed and is very different. There is still a large network framework, but one in which there are multiple 'nested networks' fleshing out that skeleton. The relationships have become multilateral. There are strong 'embedded' ties both between the suppliers in the nested networks and between them and the core firm. By 'embedded' is meant incorporated within the highly specific interactions between members. There are few remaining holes, all are linked. The knowledge transferred now is both explicit and implicit; indeed the emphasis has shifted to the latter. As a consequence, the members are learning faster than those competitors who do not share the same relationship with suppliers, with the result that the benefits of participation far outweigh any possible advantages to be derived from isolation. The flows of know-how are reciprocal. The ties established are ones of trust, likely to last for the long term.

The product development system

Toyota is not only effective in its operations, it also innovates well in its products and processes. How is this possible? There is a second paradox. Toyota manages to consider a broader range of designs than any other producer and delay a decision as late as possible, yet has the fastest vehicle development cycle of all. How does it manage to do this?

In the traditional point-based serial engineering system, the development of a new vehicle goes in a well-defined sequence from styling to marketing, body, chassis and manufacture. There are often feedback loops but usually from the downstream functions occurring late in the process, when they might have drastic effects in making necessary a major reworking of the design. On occasion, the whole process has to be aborted, a very expensive outcome. In such a system, there is a natural tendency to have a limited exploration of solutions around a starting point such as the original dominant design. What happens if the starting point is wrong, as may become obvious late in the process?

Toyota has used a system which has been called a point-based concurrent engineering system, which is characterized by much earlier feedback. In this system, the initial styling, or design, is opened to a simultaneous analysis and critique by all those concerned with marketing, body, chassis and manufacturing. In this first phase, the design space is mapped and mapped over a much greater area. This defines the feasible regions, at the same time exploring possible trade-offs by designing multiple alternatives, and communicating to the relevant people sets of possibilities instead of one design. There is really no one original design, but a number of such designs.

In the second phase, there is a search for an intersection of feasible sets, that is, what is feasible from both a design and an operational or manufacturing perspective. Remember that this is being done for all the major components. The key is to keep all the solutions compatible with a range of possible outcomes. In this search, certain minimum constraints are imposed and a conceptual robustness aspired to. In other words, there is considerable play in the systems. This phase is called the integration by intersection phase.

In the next phase, the sets of feasible solutions are gradually narrowed down but in the process become increasingly detailed. All working on the project must stay with the sets, once they are defined. Feasibility is fully established before there is any commitment. The whole process is controlled by managing uncertainty at key process gates.

One Toyota engineer, when asked what makes a good car, replied 'lots of conflict', which of course is likely to occur when so many people from so many disparate backgrounds are involved from the beginning in the process of product development. This is acceptable provided that conflict becomes mutual adjustment.

NUMMI

'NUMMI could ... enjoy the benefits of both discipline and creativity.'

Adler et al., 1999: 61

'No problem is problem.'

Uchikawa, second in charge at NUMMI
(quoted in Ingrassia and White, 1994: 51)

One obvious question to ask is whether the Toyota system is transferable. As Toyota began to build up its productive capacity abroad, notably in the USA, this became a live issue. Toyota has tried to extend the system it developed in Japan to the USA and clearly succeeded.

The beginning of direct activity in the USA by Toyota was a surprising alliance between GM, for so long the dominant American producer, and Japan's version of GM, Toyota. On second consideration, the alliance was not so surprising. GM wanted access to the secret, the method by which Toyota organized a production and product development system which made it so competitive (Ingrassia and White, 1994: 35). On the other hand, Toyota, to achieve entry into the American market by manufacture there, needed a supplier network and a distribution system. An alliance between two such industry leaders is significant.

In 1983, General Motors and Toyota entered an alliance that resulted in the creation of the New United Motor Manufacturing Incorporated (NUMMI), jointly owned by the two parents and with equal representation by each on the board of directors. NUMMI is an excellent case study illustrating how the Japanese strategy achieved a sustained competitive advantage over the big three American automobile manufacturers. Today General Motors and Toyota together account for 25% of global automobile production.

Each partner contributed the equivalent of $100 million, Toyota fully in cash, GM $20 million in cash and the rest in kind, a GM plant at Fremont in California which had been closed between 1982 and 1984 because of labour problems, low productivity and quality, and high rates of absenteeism. The Fremont facility was to be the production facility of the new company.

The goals of the two companies were obvious. GM wanted to learn about the Toyota production system, and in the short term fill a massive gap in its product range with a world-class small car. Toyota wanted to make a successful entry into a new market, the largest in the world, in which it wanted to establish a long-term presence. In order to do this it had to deal with two groups new to it – American suppliers and the United Auto Workers Union representing its workers.

Toyota was to manage the Fremont facility, providing the president, the CEO and the senior officers. The GM participation was limited to at most 16 executives serving three-year terms at Fremont. The initial product was to be a compact car, the Chevy Nova, already made and sold in Japan, selling in the USA for about $7,500. Components were to be sourced from the USA and Japan and the facility was mainly to assemble them.

Toyota tried as far as possible to replicate its production system and familiarize GM with that system. NUMMI has the same bureaucratic organizational structure as in Japan, with the same formalization and standardization, and as many as six levels in the hierarchy. It aimed at the same level of worker participation and commitment. However, this had to be modified to take account of different worker attitudes, more suspicious and potentially adversarial. Toyota persuaded the workers that they had total job security and total involvement in decision making in return for total commitment to the job and the company.

The company managed to turn around labour relations so effectively that on a whole series of indicators the plant became extremely successful. Absenteeism fell from about 20–25% to 2.3–4%. Productivity soared to twice that of the old plant and well above any other GM facility in the USA (something like 40% above), comparable with the sister plants in Japan. The turnaround was clearly a result of a change in worker attitudes and motivation.

Production was extended to three vehicles – the Toyota Corolla sedan and the Geo Prizm (1993) and the Toyota Tacoma pickup truck (1995) – which are marketed separately by the two partners. Collaboration has been extended to other areas, such as the development of alternatives to the internal combustion engine, a high-risk project requiring major investment. For example, in April 1999, the two partners signed a five-year partnership to develop and possibly jointly produce advanced technology vehicles, including those powered by fuel cells.

The acid test came when Toyota operated its own greenfield production facilities in the USA, which it began at Georgetown, Kentucky. This was followed by the extension of the whole Toyota system to the USA. As early as 1989, on the model of the Japanese supplier associations, it set up the Bluegrass Automobile Manufacturers' Association. In 1992 it set up the Supplier Support Centre, again on the model of the consulting group in Japan. In 1994 a plant development activity core group was established in the USA to act as a focus for learning and learning groups. In the USA Toyota has not as yet moved to the next phase, inter-firm transfers of staff. The impact of what has already been done is striking. There has been dramatically improved productivity among suppliers and much reduced levels of inventory.

It does appear that in certain circumstances and with careful preparation the essence of the system can be transferred. Toyota has shown this in the USA. Other enterprises have not achieved the same results. It is clearly both time-consuming and expensive for other companies to imitate the Toyota network. Toyota derives a competitive advantage in the automobile industry from having constructed a network whose efficiency and effectiveness other automobile manufacturers cannot emulate without an enormous effort. Probably the greatest obstacle to the establishment of such networks by others in the USA is the 'adversarial' posture encouraged by the emphasis on a competitive market which is seen as excluding the possibility of cooperation and certainly makes it unlikely that mutual trust will develop. This is true of both manager/worker and company/supplier relationships.

Another question is whether the Toyota system makes

unnecessary its membership in one of the e-commerce alliances involving the exchange of automobile components. Toyota has shown a marked reluctance to be a member of either the GM-based or Ford-based group. This business-to-business commerce assumes a readiness to change component sources according to price and use the combined bargaining strength or clout of the purchasers to lower price. Neither of these practices is consistent with the Toyota system.

To what kind of industry is this network structure relevant? As we have already seen, component suppliers should be important. It is most relevant to the transfer of existing knowledge within a mature industry. It does not appear capable of generating new knowledge in a fast-developing, technologically dynamic industry. This situation is considered below, that is, the capacity of the system to generate innovation.

Weaknesses of the Toyota system

Toyota makes mistakes. Its success is not the result of a consistently applied strategy. The first entry into the USA market in 1958 was a woeful failure. The Toyota Crown shipped to California was totally unsuitable for the American market at that time, greatly underpowered and inadequate for American conditions of high temperatures in summer and long distance routes. The foray ended ignominiously in 1960. The difference is that Toyota worked hard to learn from its failure. GM made poor use of the NUMMI joint venture, learning little from it.

Can Toyota generate a fundamental technological discontinuity, rather than a predetermined development of a mature product using proven technology. The case study on the hybrid electric vehicle (Chapter 5) certainly suggests that it can.

Toyota has shared some of the negative characteristics of the old Japanese model. It has been obsessed with market share, often pursued at the expense of profit. In 1996 when Toyota's market share in Japan fell below 40% for the first time in 15 years, the company entered crisis mode.

Toyota has shared the predisposition to diversify into areas distant from the core business, in Toyota's case into housing, helicopters, banking, software and telecommunications. In the 1990s it was aiming to generate 10% of its revenues outside the automobile industry.

Toyota now accounts for something like 11% of the American market. It is moving to open a new production facility in Mexico, its fifth in North America, which will help it reach its target of two million vehicles sold on that market by 2004. It still outcompetes the American producers in productivity levels and therefore costs. Little seems to have changed.

Case Study Questions

1. How far has Toyota conformed to the old-style Japanese strategic model and how far has it always pioneered a new model?
2. How far has Toyota succeeded in combining its policies on production, purchasing and new product development into a coherent strategy to achieve a sustained competitive advantage?
3. How far has Toyota succeeded in transferring its business model and strategy overseas?
4. Why is it so difficult to imitate the Toyota strategy and business model?
5. How far has it been and is it now necessary for Toyota to change its business model and strategy?

Reading

Adler, P. S, Goldoftas, B. and Levine, D. I., 'Flexibility versus efficiency? A case study of model changeover in the Toyota production system', *Organisational Science*, January–February 1999, **10**(1): 43–68.

Cusamano, M., *The Japanese Automobile Industry* (Harvard University Press, Cambridge, MA, 1989).

Dyer, J. H. and Noeboken, K., 'Creating and managing a high-performance knowledge-sharing network: the Toyota case', *Strategic Management Journal*, March 2000, **21**(3): 345–67 (special issue on strategic networks).

Ingrassia, P. and White, J. B., *Comeback: the Fall and Rise of the American Automobile Industry* (Simon & Schuster, New York, 1994), particularly Chapter 2, The NUMMI commandos.

Porter, M., Takeuchi, H. and Sakakibara, M., *Can Japan Compete?* (Macmillan – now Palgrave Macmillan, Basingstoke: 2000), particularly Chapter 3.

Sobek II, D. K., Liher, J. K. and Ward A. C., 'Another look at how Toyota integrates product development', *Harvard Business Review*, July–August 1998: 36–49.

Sobek II, D. K., Ward, A. C. and Liher, J. K., 'Toyota's principles of set-based concurrent engineering', *Sloan Management Review*, winter 1999, **40**(2): 67–83.

Spear, S. and Bowen, H. K., 'Decoding the DNA of the Toyota Production System', *Harvard Business Review*, September–October 1999: 97–106.

Vaghefi, M. R. and Coleman, J., Case 9. Toyota Motor Corporation, in Vaghefi, M. R. and Huellmantel, A.B., *Strategic Management for the XXIst Century* (St Lucie Press, Boca Raton, FL, 1999), 375–95.

Womack, J. P., Jones, D. T. and Roos, D., *The Machine that Changed the World* (Macmillan – now Palgrave Macmillan, New York, 1990).

This case study is also relevant to Chapters 9 and 15.

Key strategic lessons

- In the process of implementation, much is learned about what a strategy is trying to achieve and what an organization can actually do. In that process the strategy is continuously reformulated or 'emergent'. The processes involved in strategy making are complex; the faster the rate of change, the more complex they will be.

- There are serious pitfalls in strategy making. Particular weaknesses of the strategic approach which can make efficient implementation very difficult include tokenism, bureaucratization, overemphasis on risk minimization, desire for short-term profit, seeing the future as the past and having inflated ambitions.

- The biggest challenge is a fracturing of the lines of communication, coordination or control, a fracturing which can be either vertical or horizontal.

- The states of conflict within an organization are latent, perceived, felt and manifest. There is a repetitive cycle of conflict which can act as an obstacle to strategy implementation or promote it. Examples of conflict between different horizontal units in the enterprise include that between marketing and operations over the degree of customization and between operations/marketing and finance over the level of inventory held.

- The three main 'iterations' within strategy making are between the different vertical levels within the enterprise and the linked horizontal units outside, between sources of outside influence such as stakeholders and the enterprise, and between different levels of decision and strategy making outside the enterprise, including the national or industrial, and the enterprise.

- Emphasis on corporate strategy puts too much stress on rigid boundaries between the enterprise and the outside world. There are good reasons why such boundaries are porous including the need to consider external strategies, the need to access external resources and the proliferation of strategic alliances and their importance in implementing a strategy. There is real meaning in talking about a 'boundaryless' organization.

- Where there are multiple strategic targets, these can be achieved in differing sequences. Choice of an appropriate route is a key strategic decision.

- Pace of movement can either be too fast or too slow and it is better for the enterprise to determine the pace – time pacing, rather than to have it imposed – event pacing.

- As the powerhouse of strategy, a strategy division can play a number of leadership roles including being the source of objectives, the controller, banker, coordinator or protector of assets. Alternatively it can also act as a 'token', a think-tank or the executive arm of the leader.

Applying the lessons

1 Define the following terms: tokenism, vertical fracturing, horizontal fracturing, rent seeking, iteration, time pacing, event pacing and lean production.
2 Under what conditions would the classical approach to strategy be regarded as an accurate account of the strategy-making process and in particular the implementation of a strategy?
3 Consider one enterprise which has put in place a specialized division or unit responsible for strategy making. What are the advantages and disadvantages which have flowed from this decision? What place might this division occupy in the overall organizational design of the company?
4 What are the boundaries which exist between different units within an organization and between an organization and the outside world? What effect do these boundaries have on the process of strategy making?
5 Select five well-known CEOs. How far was their reputation built upon the formulation and implemen-

Applying the lessons cont'd

tation of a successful strategic plan and/or the application of creative strategic thinking?

6 Consider an example of conflict which has become uncontrolled and had a negative effect on strategy making. How far could this have been avoided? How far could the conflict have had positive rather than negative results?

7 Give at least one example of bad strategy making with which you are familiar. What was the cause of the problem?

Strategic project

One framework for examining the implementation of a strategy and judging whether all the different factors are fully aligned with each other is the 7-S model, developed by McKinsey & Company. Choose either an enterprise with which you are involved or an enterprise in one of the extended case studies in Part V of this book. Complete the following list of current actions and recommendations.

1 *Superordinate goals* (guiding concepts, a set of values and aspirations, often unwritten, that may go beyond formally stated objectives. They are succinct, abstract and mean a lot to insiders)

Current actions: ....

Recommendations: ....

2 *Strategy* (the actions to be taken to adjust to changing environments and provide value to customers and maintain competitive advantage)

Current actions: ....

Recommendations: ....

3 *Structure* (the specialized units within the enterprise and their coordination)

Current actions: ....

Recommendations: ....

4 *Systems* (the formal and informal sets of procedures which make the enterprise work)

Current actions: ....

Recommendations: ....

5 *Style* (this reflects the culture as it is symbolically displayed in behaviour)

Current action: ....

Recommendations: ....

6 *Staff* (both hard issues such as incentive schemes and soft issues such as motivation and attitude)

Current actions: ....

Recommendations: ....

7 *Skills* (part of the strengths possessed by the enterprise and their relationship with core competencies)

Current actions: ....

Recommendations: ....

Exploring further

Implementation can be dealt with in a number of ways. In the main textbooks it is either the focus of a whole section as in Hill and Jones, 2003: part four or an individual chapter as in Viljoen and Dann, 2003: Chapter 12. Sometimes it is called strategy execution. All sorts of issues are often raised under this heading, for example organizational design, control systems, managing change, corporate culture and risk management. Many of these have been discussed in separate chapters. There is no uniformity of approach.

A highly intelligent piece of work which raises all the issues above is Davis and Devinney, 1997. More action-oriented is Brodwin and Bourgeois, 1984: 176–90 or Zagotta and Robinson, 2002: 30–4.

There are a number of papers dealing with the pitfalls: Oliver and Garber, 1983: 49–51; Beer and Eisenstat, 2000: 29–40; and Huff et al., 1992 (special issue): 55–75.

Conflict is analysed in Litterer, 1966: 178–86; Kochan, 1972: 359–70; and Pondy, 1967: 296–320. Taking a different perspective is Floyd and Wooldridge, 1992: 27–39. A rather broader treatment is Heracleous, 2000: 75–86.

Iteration is not a term often used in the literature on strategy. It was once discussed more in the literature on planning.

The issue of pacing is raised in Hambrick and Fredrickson, 2001 – see the last chapter for the full reference; and is discussed at greater length in Eisenhardt and Brown, 1998: 59–69.

There are many treatments of leadership. A general one is Pfeffer, 1992. On the one hand there are those who argue for an active role, rather like the classical one – Hambrick, 1989 (special issue): 5–15. Or perhaps an active role adopted under special circumstances: Tichy and Ulrich, 1984: 59–68. Whittington, 2001 has an excellent chapter, Chapter 3. There is the view that the job of the leader is to provide the vision: Westley and Mintzberg, 1989 (special issue): 17–32, or a particular kind of intelligence, Goleman, 1998: 92–105. Some prefer the unobtrusive kind with indirect control: Mintzberg, 1998: 14–148. For a view that strategy is not management: Wrapp, 1967: 91–9.

18 Monitoring strategic performance

Learning objectives

After reading this chapter you will be able to:

- know how to monitor strategy performance
- know how to measure strategy performance
- read financial indicators
- evaluate corporate social performance
- see formulation, implementation and monitoring as continuous processes

Key strategic challenge

How do I check that my strategy is being successfully formulated and implemented?

Strategic dangers

That there is no follow-up in the implementation of a strategy, no attempt to evaluate the degree to which a strategy is being successfully realized, and that consequently there is no continuing adjustment of the strategy to take account of unanticipated changes in technology and taste.

Case Study Scenario 1   Sony – the disruptive innovator

Since 1990 Japan has been going through a crisis. The old model of economic success no longer works; a new model is needed. According to Porter et al. (2000), the current problems have arisen because the old model stressed operational effectiveness at the cost of a genuinely strategic approach and most Japanese enterprises had, and still have, no strategy.

There are systemic differences in the understanding of what constitutes a strategy. The Japanese are suspicious of a monolithic strategy or even a strategic concept systematically applied in the style of the classical model. Following such a method is seen as a weakness:

- It is easy for competitors to read what a competitor is likely to do next. By contrast, in its early history it was impossible to anticipate what an enterprise like Sony would do.
- Any formulaic approach weakens what the Japanese call peripheral vision, the ability to respond to unexpected changes outside the main field of vision of the enterprise. The exploitation of peripheral vision is a process well illustrated by Sony in its first 30 years of life.

The Western strategic approach is seen as oversimplifying reality and imposing an excessively purposive rationality on rather chaotic chains of events. A forced coherence is read into strategic situations. In the words of Richard Pascale (quoted in Mintzberg and Quinn, 1996): 'How an organization deals with miscalculations, mistakes, and serendipitous *events outside its field of vision is often crucial to success over time.*' Is it a distortion to read a clear and deliberately imposed strategy into the past success of Japanese companies?

There is a general crisis in Japan, which can be seen in the fall in its economic growth rate from an average 10% in the 1970s, to 4% in the 1980s and about 1% in the 1990s. The domestic economy is no longer growing. Many Japanese enterprises have become loss making or barely profitable. Whereas the best American enterprises realistically aspire in good times to a return on equity of 20–25%, the best Japanese enterprises are achieving 2–5%. Sony illustrates this experience.

The old model Japanese enterprise, backed by an unequalled level of operational effectiveness, aimed to establish maximum market share, often at the cost of profitability. If increased market share was attained without the momentum of genuine and continuing innovation, other enterprises successfully imitated. Any competitive advantage is transitory if it consists of competencies which can be easily imitated. When foreign enterprises caught up with the methods of improving operational effectiveness, previously successful companies suddenly became uncompetitive and unprofitable.

Initially Sony was not as badly affected by the crisis as other enterprises. The export-oriented have weathered the storm better than the domestic-oriented. However, with its main markets in recession, Sony's growth rate has now slowed and profitability is low. It is in the midst, not just of a transition from the old Japanese model to a new one, but from one strategy based on disruptive innovation in electronic hardware to one which links the electronic hardware with creative software. How successfully has it gone through this transition? What should it do?

Case Study Scenario 2   A blockbuster drug – Imclone and insider trading

During the past 40 years there has been a continuing revolution in man's knowledge of biochemistry. The revolution began, back in the 1960s, with Crick and Watson's discovery of the structure of DNA which recently resulted in the mapping of the human genome, achieved partly by the commercial biotechnology company Celera, which ambitiously mapped the whole human genome. Much less ambitiously Incyte sought to map the 3% of the human genome that involves protein-making genes implicated in disease.

A commercial revolution will follow the intellectual revolution. Researchers are now pinpointing biochemi-

cal structures and designing drugs that target those structures. The biotechnical revolution is beginning to spawn a host of small biotechnology firms which seek to exploit specific breakthroughs in biological knowledge. There are a host of applications which will be the source of commercial opportunity.

One interesting question relates to the development and sale of the resulting new drugs. There are three possibilities:

1. To develop one's own drugs. At any given moment, a large company seeks a pipeline of drugs at different stages in their development. A typical pharma-

ceutical company will plough back something approaching 20% of its revenues into research and development.

2. To acquire drugs already developed by purchasing another company, either a small company which has successfully developed a drug to a key stage in its development or a larger company with a good list of drugs, filling the gaps in the company's portfolio.

3. To form a strategic alliance between a larger company, with all its resources including marketing and distribution facilities, and a much smaller biochemistry research firm. The latter are growing in number and importance.

The latter options allow a small company to specialize in what it does best and take the risk of choosing a winner, reaping a reward when successful, not by selling the drug but through takeover by, or licensing of a drug to, a large company. Another strategy is to operate as a rapid follower, producing similar products to those just patented, but sufficiently different not to fall foul of the law, thereby avoiding significant costs.

This case study focuses on one drug, formerly called IMC-C225, rechristened Erbitux, and one company ImClone which sought to develop the drug as a blockbuster. A drug is considered a blockbuster when it generates at least US$1 billion a year in sales. The company ImClone has risen to prominence on the back of this new drug.

The drug is the leader in a group of proposed new drugs using a revolutionary new technique, which targets and blocks the epidermal growth factor receptor, a protein stuck on the surface of many cancer cells which signals cancer cells to grow and spread. The drug does not cure cancer, but rather turns the cancer into a chronic, treatable disease by preventing the tumours from metastasizing, that is, spreading. How does ImClone illustrate the difficulties of the strategies open to pharmaceutical companies?

Just as it is impossible to distinguish formulation and implementation, it is also impossible to distinguish monitoring from either of these strategic activities. As will become clear, monitoring is a continuous process, one linked closely with both the other activities. It is necessary to evaluate strategy making as well as specific strategies. In the end, strategy must be judged by its results. How is this judgement to be made?

Monitoring

Monitoring is the act of reviewing the appropriateness of a strategy and overseeing the way in which it is implemented. There is no doubt that it is necessary to evaluate both the effectiveness of the general strategy and the efficiency with which the specific targets of a strategy are being implemented.

Effectiveness refers to the general appropriateness for the organization of:

- the arenas chosen or peaks scaled
- the competitive differentiators which are part of the generic strategy
- the vehicles for strategy achievement
- the staging and pacing of any strategy.

It concentrates on the big issues of choice of product or market, and therefore on the appropriate positioning of the enterprise and the attainment of an appropriate resource endowment. *Efficiency* refers to the way in which the resources are used in the achievement of the specific targets of the strategy.

From the very beginning, it is necessary to build monitoring of effectiveness and efficiency into the system of strategy making, from the attainment of a general agreement on strategic intent and the setting of the original objectives to the setting up of appropriate systems of governance and control.

Integration of monitoring into strategy making

Figure 18.1 takes a holistic approach and shows how monitoring can be integrated into the process of strategy making, as it has been described and developed in this book. These should be presented as a circle because the last area is linked in a continuous process of adjustment to the first, as shown in Figure 18.2.

STRATEGIC ACTIVITIES

Strategic intent	Analyse all stakeholder needs and expectations and prioritize them Formulate the mission and the strategic objectives

Identify performance measures

Strategic environments	Analyse the external environment for opportunities and threats Appraise strategy of other players and appraise their past, present and likely future performance Identify own core competencies

Generic strategies	Choose competitive differentiators Choose a pricing policy Consider how to encourage learning and innovation

Strategic situations	Make strategic choices in key arenas: 1. products, services 2. size of organization 3. markets 4. structure 5. functional or value-adding activities

Strategic formulation	Choose a preferred strategy

Develop appropriate control systems

Strategic implementation	Acquire skills and resources Develop organizational structure Manage the culture Manage risk

Strategic monitoring	

Measure strategic performance

Evaluate performance in terms of the strategy

Take any corrective action, including modifying the strategy

Figure 18.1 **Monitoring strategy**

Figure 18.2 The relationship of strategic activities

Those activities which are directly relevant to monitoring are shown in blue text in Figure 18.1. Others are indirectly relevant. From the very beginning strategy making must be made operational, that is, capable of evaluation in terms of performance outcomes. At all stages in the formulation and implementation of a strategy, this imperative must be borne in mind. The following are required as necessary parts of monitoring:

- Key performance indicators must be selected
- Control systems must be put in place to promote the achievement of targets
- Performance must be continuously appraised, in the context of the strategy as a whole, not just from a narrow perspective
- The strategy must be adjusted where necessary. A key aspect of success is the degree to which new ways of meeting the broader aims are thrown up by the strategy process itself.

Having established how monitoring is universal and continuous in the same way as are formulation and implementation, it is necessary to look at the process of strategy making as a whole. It is useful again to return to the original distinction. What are the desired results or outcomes of the different strategic activities – thinking strategically, managing strategically and planning strategically – which make up the whole of strategy making?

At the simplest level, it is appropriate to ask what is the return on the investment in strategy making. The investment might vary significantly according to the level of strategy making undertaken. At one extreme, thinking strategically may involve almost no investment, rather an attempt to build into the corporate culture a strategic perspective and sufficient scope for creative action by every staff member. To achieve this perspective requires purposeful action, and such action absorbs resources, if only in setting up focus groups or running a suggestions scheme.

The strategic canvas

One way of encouraging such a perspective is illustrated by the notion of a strategic canvas, which sees strategy as nothing more than strategic thinking and uses a very simple mechanism for monitoring the strategic performance of the enterprise. All that is needed for a good strategic profile is:

- a focus, either on a particular attribute or a set of attributes of the products or services provided by the enterprise, which stand out as special
- a source of differentiation in these attributes from those of competitor products or services
- a compelling tag line, which summarizes and creates a graphic image of both focus and differentiation. The procedure allows the staff to check whether the enterprise has achieved such a strong strategic profile.

The first two can be represented on a simple diagram. Figure 18.3 uses a hotel as an example.

The staff of the enterprise are regularly involved in articulating the strategic profile of the business. The process of doing this acts as a stimulus to undertaking strategic thinking. It encourage two useful orientations on the part of staff, a customer focus and a consciousness of the position of the enterprise relative to its competitors.

There are four stages, all or some of which could be part of this process:

1. The staff of whatever level are invited to portray visually their view of the existing strategic profile of the business in the way indicated in Figure 18.3.
2. If this does not produce either a distinctive focus or a differentiation from the main competitors, staff are shown that this is the case and asked to explore with customers and complementors how both might be achieved and what they think the strategic profile should become.
3. The different profiles which emerge from the staff are compared and a desirable profile chosen from the alternatives.
4. The desirable profile is communicated to the rest of the company.

This involves a number of meetings but some significant research. This can be part of a series of different strategic activities. It could be supplemented by an exercise in scenario building which would check consistency with the changing external environment.

Audit of strategic performance can be much more systematic. The return on the investment in strategic activity is the improvement in performance which results

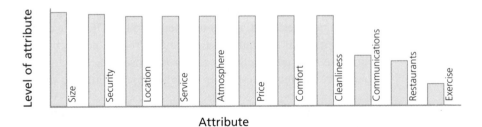

Figure 18.3 **The canvas of a hotel**

from the existence of strategy, in practice difficult to estimate with any accuracy. Part of the activity of a strategy division would be to monitor the results of the strategic plan and its own activity. It might be possible to conduct a strategic audit independently of the strategy division.

Between these two extremes, the one designed simply to evaluate the success of strategic thinking in the creation of a strategic profile, the other to measure the return from the formulation of a strategic plan, is a disparate range of activities which are not fully strategic but involve strategic management of some kind. The level of investment is unclear and difficult to estimate. It is difficult to say whether an activity is strategic or not. As a consequence the return is also difficult to estimate.

Disentangling the results of any strategic activity is an extremely difficult task. All sorts of change, both external and internal to the organization, are occurring continuously. A favourable set of results may simply be a reflection of a benign environment and be nothing to do with the strategy adopted. There may be the unexpected appearance of favourable demand conditions or a change in exchange rates which boosts profitability above what might otherwise have been expected.

Monitoring and learning

The interpretation of strategy as emergent has strong implications for the nature of monitoring. Monitoring is not a discrete activity which occurs at the end of the strategic planning period. It is emergent, and as such it never ceases. It is a process whereby strategists review the appropriateness of a strategy to changing circumstances and incorporate within it any improvements and mechanisms for improvement which are newly discovered. The process is performed on the run. Quick judgements have to be made. Monitoring generates learning, which in turn results in greater efficiency and greater effectiveness in strategy making.

In the sense described here, monitoring is a vital part of the process of generating the information flows on which the making of strategy is based. Monitoring could be regarded as the main information-generating process. This flow of information is critical to strategy making. Consequently, the division between Chapters 16, 17 and 18 is an artificial one which distorts a realistic view of what is strategy making.

Measuring

What is being monitored is highly complex. First, how can monitoring deal with such complexity? It makes the task much easier if what is monitored is reduced to quantifiable indicators. It is much easier to compare what is measurable, whether the comparison is with past performance or the performance of competitors. This is not always possible. The second question is how to make indicators quantitative.

The balanced scorecard

One method of monitoring which is suited to a complex project is to construct a balanced scorecard. The balanced scorecard is a systematic application of monitoring based on the assumption that the processes of formulation, implementation and monitoring of a strategy are both integrated and continuous.

The balanced scorecard is a comprehensive framework which translates an organization's vision and strategy into a coherent set of strategic initiatives and performance measures. It could be described with accuracy as a complete strategic management system. It is not intended to measure compliance with a pre-established plan or put in controls over current operational performance, rather to 'articulate the strategy of the business, to communicate the strategy of the business, and to help align individual, organizational, and cross-departmental initiatives to achieve a common goal' (Kaplan and Norton, 1996a: 56). The scorecard is used as 'a communication, information, and learning system, not as a traditional control system' (56).

The gist of such a method is identifying the key issues which are at the core of a successful strategy. The balance reflects consideration of all the major elements of performance, not just a few. The scorecard is designed to measure accurately and highlight what the strategy is about. Nominating specific measures draws attention to those areas. The measures must come from the business unit's unique strategy.

There are usually four key areas in the standard balanced scorecard. It is possible, and sometimes desirable, to customize the method according to the needs of any specific industry. In the standard models, these are the following areas:

1. *Financial performance*, often reduced to a single measure, usually the level of profit or its growth over time. It should ask the question, is the financial performance of the organization capable of keeping happy its owners, the shareholders?
2. The *performance of the organization in satisfying its customers.* How satisfied are they by the enterprise's performance? How far is it possible to measure that satisfaction? It is possible to discover the level of consumer satisfaction through surveys or the experience of those staff members who deal directly with the customers. Any precision may be spurious insofar as the non-quantifiable is quantified. Quantifying can oversimplify and distort.
3. The *performance of critical processes in the internal value chain*, including innovation. How efficiently are these processes being carried out?
4. *Performance in learning*, and therefore in innovating. Is the organization changing with the times and growing in a way which is acceptable?

These are not the only areas of concern. The choice of area might differ from industrial sector to sector. An example of customization by sector might be for an academic organization such as a university, the replacement of finance with academic management and customers with stakeholders in general, including both the local community, with which the university interacts in many ways, and government which might provide a significant amount of finance.

There are two other areas which should be added, particularly if the analysis is to embrace strategy for all organizations, not just commercial enterprises or corporations. These are:

5. *Performance viewed from the perspective of stakeholder groups* other than the owners, managers or customers, such as suppliers, strategic allies or the local community. Have the expectations of all these stakeholder groups been met? Overall this raises the issue of corporate social responsibility and how the enterprise performs in this area.

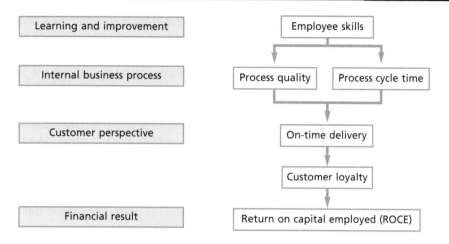

Figure 18.4   **Performance improvement chain**

6. The *performance of people and the development of human capital.* One of the main assets for any enterprise is the human capital embodied in the staff who work for it. What values are people capable of adding for customers with the aid of the skills and experience that they possess and are in the process of further developing?

The first four areas can be written up as four logical but interlinked steps in the process of strategy making. They have the potential to describe entire chains of cause and effect relationships from creating the basic infrastructure of knowledge and skills, through the improvement of critical processes, including innovation, to the satisfaction of customers and a resulting good financial performance. Figure 18.4 gives an example of one chain.

A whole series of such chains could be analysed, some more important than others. It is in this sense that 'a properly constructed balanced scoreboard should tell the story of the business unit's strategy' (Simons, 2000: 201).

There are four steps in the procedure for establishing a balanced scorecard:

1. *Develop goals and measures for critical financial performance*
These are discussed in detail in the next section.

2. *Develop goals and measures for critical customer performance*
This can be tackled in two ways: (i) an evaluation of customer loyalty, considering customer satisfaction, customer retention, customer acquisition, customer profitability and an estimate of market or account shares; (ii) an evaluation of the unique value proposition offered by the enterprise, which consists of the following:

product/service attributes	customer utilities and relationships	image and reputation
uniqueness functionality quality price time	convenience trust requirements	brand equity

3. *Develop goals and measures for critical internal process performance*

Innovation process	Operations process	After-sales service process
	quality	warranty
	cycle times	treatment of defects and returns
	traditional cost	administration of payment
	accounting: activity/process based	

4. *Develop goals and measures of critical learning and growth performance variables*
This relates to people, systems, organization and procedures.

A scoreboard for each of these areas can be put together. It should include:

- the *critical success factors* – that is, those factors that are critical to strong performance in the designated area
- the *measures* – the quantitative indicators which reflect the way in which performance will be measured. These are so-called *lagging indicators* which measure previous operational performance
- the *targets* – the level of achievement envisaged in the strategy and to be attained in the time horizon
- the *initiatives* – the special actions required in order to meet the targets. These are *leading indicators* which are the drivers of future performance.

The balanced scorecard is best described as a strategy measurement system. Its use has a number of advantages:

- Precision in performance evaluation. Managers know exactly what is expected of them.
- An all-round view. Managers must take a balanced view of the performance of the enterprise.
- Generation of important strategic information. Managers can make better informed decisions on strategy making.
- A single integrated report, one which is concise and to the point.

Benchmarking

So far performance has been considered mostly, although not wholly, from a macro-perspective. At the microlevel there must be a focus on performance indicators. One vital aspect of strategy and the achievement of competitive advantage is to benchmark every activity against best-practice international standards. In its many forms, benchmarking is very common. It analyses a concern with quality, which has had many manifestations, including total quality management and quality circles. Quality also requires attention to detail.

The best-known standards adopted by organizations are the ISO standards developed as an international benchmark for quality and adopted by 90 countries around the world. Adherence to the system and acceptance for ISO accreditation gives a guarantee of quality and is good for the reputation of the accredited organization. In some cases it is critical to winning a contract. Clearly, it assumes a stable set of standards, which might not be true of the new economy industries.

Key performance indicators

The key to day-to-day control and evaluation of a strategy is the identification of key performance indicators (KPIs). Successful performance management, which should be a continuous process, requires the specification of such indicators and their continuous monitoring. Key performance indicators are detailed measures established for every major strategic objective and for all the core processes of an organization. They must relate to outcomes and the drivers of those outcomes, that is, the key inputs or processes needed.

There are two steps in this logical progression:

1. What are the outcomes desired?
2. What are the key drivers which influence these outcomes?

The KPIs may relate not just to quality, but to quantity – cost, revenue or the time activity rate. They may relate to efficiency, often shown by a ratio such as cost per item produced, or the extent to which an outcome or result is achieved, such as consumer satisfaction. The key performance indicators are the basic ingredients of a balanced scorecard, but it should be possible to isolate for day-to-day use key monitoring indicators.

There are a number of dangers:

• there are too many KPIs, diffusing any focus
• the measures are poorly constructed or poorly chosen
• the emphasis is on inputs rather than outputs
• no action is taken on the basis of the actual movement of the KPIs and their relationship to the targeted movements.

Day-to-day operational decisions must be considered in the light of the unfolding strategy. The strategy must be adjusted if day-to-day operations suggest that this is desirable. Regular monitoring is a vital part of this iterative process of application and adjustment.

The qualitative

There is a tendency to assume that what is quantifiable is by its nature a good measure of performance. Invariably this is not true. The difficulties of interpreting rates of growth and what they mean and rates of profit and what they mean have been much discussed. None of these concepts is unambiguous. Faster growth or higher profit is often assumed to be better, but this is not true either. Good performance is a more subtle concept, involving as many qualitative as quantitative measures and reflecting the specificity of an industry or economic sector. Timing is a key issue.

The process of strategy making, as summarized in this section, may be enough on its own to improve performance, but detailed measurement of results is impossible and undesirable. Strategy needs to be so integrated into the whole activity of the enterprise that the overall performance of that enterprise is the only possible measure of effectiveness. How is it possible to tell what are the results of strategic thinking if it is conducted by a multitude of different employees? It would be impossible to pinpoint every cause and every effect and, even if possible, costly to carry out such an exercise.

Focus on Theory
ISO 9000

ISO 9000: a set of universal standards which apply to every aspect of design, development, production, installation and servicing, and final inspection and testing. Because not all enterprises involve the full range of activities, ISO has given birth to different standards:

ISO 9001: the superset of the contractual models for quality systems. It covers all aspects except inspection and testing.

ISO 9002: the model for quality systems which include production but not design.

ISO 9003: the model for contractual systems for final inspection and testing, but does not include either production or design.

Source: http://www.bawtech.com.au.

There are two kinds of aim in any strategy. The first is the creation and maintenance of competitive advantage. This will be reflected in performance indicators such as aggregate profits and earnings growth. This may also include indicators such as market sales. The general wellbeing of the enterprise will show the degree of success of the strategy. This may be as far as can be gone in judging whether a strategy is successful.

The second is the existence of a well-defined strategic intent and a series of targets linked to the objectives implicit in that intent. These can be specific, that is, relate to the efficiency in carrying out particular functions. They must be linked to the overall strategy and its objectives. There must be a process of benchmarking to check how far strategy is successful at the functional level. In the process of disaggregation and the creation of any subplans, benchmarks will be specified and evaluated in a comparative context, and their achievement regularly reviewed. As highlighted in the Focus on Humour below, one indicator is not enough.

Focus on Humour
Monitoring performance

Q: I'm surprised to see you operating the plane with only one instrument. What does it measure?

A: Airspeed, I'm really working on airspeed this flight.

Q: That's good. Airspeed certainly seems important. But what about altitude? Wouldn't an altimeter be helpful?

A: I worked on altitude for the last few flights and I've gotten pretty good at altitude. Now I have to concentrate on airspeed.

Q: But I notice you don't even have a fuel gauge. Wouldn't that be useful?

A: Fuel is important, but I can't concentrate on doing too many things well at the same time. So this flight I want all my attention focused on airspeed. Once I get to be excellent at airspeed, as well as altitude, I intend to concentrate on fuel consumption on the next set of flights.

The role of financial controls

This chapter has placed a discussion of financial indicators after the general discussions on monitoring and measurement. Financial performance and financial controls are important parts of a strategy, but an excessive concern with financial indicators can have undesirable outcomes.

The first might be a single-minded obsession with short-term profit and its growth at the cost of longer term profit. The obsession with short-term profits and their growth can lead not just to the distortion of accounting results or a selective choice of performance indicators, but even to the deliberate falsification of both. A reasonable level of profit is a critical outcome, but it is an outcome, not a strategic driver or a prime motivating factor; it follows from good strategy rather than precedes it.

The second could be excessive attention on one stakeholder group, the owners, that is, the shareholders, at the expense of all other stakeholder groups. It may not only reflect a neglect of those groups, but may even encourage such a neglect.

In the end, financial performance is easily the most measurable element in strategic performance. It is the element which produces the most immediate and potentially the most negative feedback if the measures indicate a poor performance. It is impossible and undesirable to ignore profit. However, as a performance indicator, it must be used judiciously. The following analysis provides an appropriate context in which to use profit as a performance indicator.

Financial indicators

There are five kinds of financial indicator, most of them ratios of some kind. Each concentrates on a different area of performance. The combinations in which they are used is critical to good strategy making and particularly monitoring.

By themselves these ratios are not helpful. There needs to be a comparative context:

- past performance of the enterprise
- performance of other enterprises in the industry
- target levels, defined in a way which takes account of what might be considered, on objective grounds, a good performance.

It must always be asked, what is a high figure and what is a low one?

Profitability

The first kind of financial indicator considers the *overall profitability of the enterprise or any business unit within the enterprise*. There are five measures, which are shown in Table 18.1.

Profit is sometimes called net income or net earnings. The key issue is what deductions are made from profits, income or earnings, if any. At one extreme, none are made, that is, the earnings are considered before any deductions are made, before interest is charged, before taxes are paid, and even before an allowance is made for depreciation or amortization (EBITDA). There may also be a liberal interpretation of what constitutes an expense.

Table 18.1 **Profitability ratios**

Ratio	Definition	What it does
1. Gross profit margin	(Total sales − costs)/ total sales	Indicates the total margin available to cover any deductions per unit of sales
2. Net profit margin	Profit after deductions/ total sales	Indicates net profit per unit of sales
3. Growth of profits	Profit this year/ profit last year	Indicates the rate of growth of profits, however defined
4. Return on total assets	Profit after deductions/ total assets	Indicates the return on total investment or assets
5. Breakeven ratio	Fixed costs/contribution margin per unit (selling price per unit − variable costs per unit)	Indicates how many units of product must be sold to cover total costs and make a profit

Distortions of the indicators

Below are three examples which show the way in which earnings may be exaggerated, examples which are relevant to the accounting practices pursued by various enterprises. The first involves the income or revenue side, the others the cost side.

1. It is possible to bring forward incomes already contracted for but which will be received in the future. This has the effect of increasing current profit but reducing future profit.
2. The first cost item involves development costs. If there are certain future income streams with which these can be directly linked, then it is legitimate to regard them as capital expenditures which should be depreciated over time. If this link cannot be established, the cost is a current operating one and should be fully incorporated in cost now.

   In our first measure, deeming something a development or capital cost excludes it completely from the expense side. The rise in the significance of intangible assets, created in a number of different ways but with the incurring of expenses, makes this a difficult issue. There is real ambiguity in defining the nature of the cost. It is possible to take a very liberal interpretation of what is a capital expense.
3. The second cost issue concerns the depreciation of goodwill and the related intangible assets which go onto the balance sheet after a large acquisition. Acquisition is usually at a price which includes a premium which covers this goodwill. Traditionally, the goodwill is written down or amortized over a number of years. There has been a tendency to argue more recently that goodwill can stay on the balance sheet without being amortized, provided that the goodwill is unimpaired and remains intact, which is shown by the level of the share price. This is important for enterprises which are acquiring other companies at a rapid rate. A sudden decline in share prices below the level at the time of the acquisition can lead to a need to write down goodwill in one hit, often with a catastrophic impact on profits.

Earnings are clearly an elastic concept which can be made to appear what they are not. The most popular earnings benchmark has been EBITDA.

At the other extreme, all deductions are made and there is a netting out of all costs. This produces a net figure for earnings which excludes not only taxes and interest but capital charges as well, although amortization is sometimes excluded. It might be better to call this the 'free cash flow'. This is what is really available to pay down debt, finance acquisitions and buy back stock or increase dividend payments to shareholders. Some argue that this is the best indicator of the health of an enterprise.

Some companies are conservative in their treatment of revenue and costs, for example SingTel (see the Strategy in Action in Chapter 15), for whom profits are clearly understated compared with other similar companies. Others are more liberal in their interpretation.

The exact level of the targets set in this area is worth considering. The desired growth in net earnings is often put as high as 15%. This can become the main driving force in any strategy.

Liquidity

The second kind of financial indicator considers the *liquidity position of the enterprise*, that is, what position it is in to meet any immediate demands on its cash income or cope with extreme but temporary fluctuations in the level of that income. It is possible for a business to be fundamentally profitable and yet be unable to meet its short-term obligations. There are three main ratios here, as shown in Table 18.2.

Table 18.2 **Liquidity ratios**

Ratio	Definition	What it does
1. Current ratio	Current assets/ current liabilities	Indicates extent to which the claims of short-term creditors are covered by short-term assets, which can be quickly made liquid
2. Quick ratio ('acid-test' ratio)	(Current assets – inventory)/ current liabilities	Indicates ability of the firm to pay off short-term obligations without running down its inventory
3. Inventory to net working capital	Inventory/(current assets – current liabilities)	Indicates the extent to which the firm's working capital is tied up in inventory

These indicators are critical to any evaluation of whether the enterprise is immediately solvent or not and whether the enterprise is headed for trouble. Once more the problem is to define the obligations appropriately, taking into account any off-balance sheet obligations to which the enterprise is liable and which may add to current short-term liabilities.

Debt levels

The third area of consideration is the *debt position* of the enterprise, or more exactly the *degree of leverage* of the enterprise. Since debt, in contrast with equity, has to be serviced, it lays the enterprise open to additional risk. There are five ratios, as shown in Table 18.3.

Table 18.3 **Debt ratios**

Ratio	Definition	What it does
1. Debt-to-assets ratio	Total debt/ total assets	Indicates the degree to which the firm has used borrowed funds to finance its operations
2. Debt-to-equity ratio	Total debt/ total equity	Indicates the relative share of funds provided by creditors and equity holders
3. Long-term debt-to-equity ratio	Long-term debt/ total equity	Indicates the long-term ratio of debt and equity
4. Times interest earned (or covered ratio)	Profits before deductions/ total interest charge	Indicates the ease with which a company can service its debt
5. Fixed charge coverage	Profits before deductions plus lease obligations/total interest charge plus lease obligations	A more inclusive measure of 4

There are notions of target or optimum debt levels which may differ from industry to industry. A debt-to-asset ratio of more than 50% is often thought to indicate a possible problem. The direction and rate of change of the ratio is also relevant. If it is rising rapidly, this may indicate a deteriorating position.

The costs of any investment funds differ according to whether they are internally generated, raised through an equity issue or borrowing of some kind. As the cost of these funds rises, so does the risk.

Activity rates

The next area introduces the *time element* and comprises what can be called time activity ratios. The five ratios are shown in Table 18.4. The target for the first, the inventory turnover, is often seen as infinity; this is the ultimate goal of JIT, to require no inventory at all. The lower the turnover rate, the greater the cost of holding inventory. The next two indicate the amount of work the capital used by the firm is

Table 18.4 **Time activity ratios**

Ratio	Definition	What it does
1. Inventory turnover	Sales/inventory of finished goods	Indicates how many times the firm turns over inventory each year
2. Fixed assets turnover	Sales/fixed assets	Indicates the ability of fixed capital (assets) to generate sales
3. Total assets turnover	Sales /total assets	Indicates the ability of all capital (assets) to generate sales
4. Accounts receivable turnover	Annual credit sales/ accounts receivable	Indicates how many times the receivables are collected in a year
5. Average collection period	Accounts receivable/ average daily sales	Indicates how long the firm waits to collect payment after sales

doing; they are a measure of the efficiency with which assets are used. The last two consider the amount of credit that is being extended by an enterprise to its customers. The longer the credit is given, the more working capital is tied up. All three types of measure are measures of the work done by the different types of capital. They are most useful when compared with the levels in other firms or the industry as a whole.

Return to shareholders

The final area relates to the *return to the shareholder of the enterprise*. Perhaps unsurprisingly, there are more ratios in this area than any other, as shown in Table 18.5.

An unhappy shareholder is likely to sell. This will put a downward pressure on share prices. A shareholder is interested in the dividends paid out at any time and the notional capital gain over time. A serious fall in either may jeopardize the ability of existing management to stay in office. An increase in the share price keeps the shareholders happy by giving them a capital gain while making it easier and cheaper for the enterprise to raise capital.

There is a natural tendency to simplify the evaluation by reducing the indicators to a small number or just one. This is a mistake. As the balanced scorecard approach has shown, strategy making requires the use of a number of measures, financial or otherwise.

Table 18.5 Shareholder return ratios

Ratio	Definition	What it does
1. Return on equity	Profits after deductions/ total equity	Indicates the net rate of return on the share investment
2. Return on common equity	As above but with dividends on preferred stock subtracted and the value of preferred stock subtracted	As above, with the omission of preferred stock
3. Earnings per share	Total profits after deductions and dividends on preferred stock/number of common shares	Indicates earnings made per share and available either as distributed income or for reinvestment
4. Dividend yield on equity	Annual dividends per share/ current market price per share	Indicates actual rate of return to shareholders, at least that received in the form of dividends
5. Price/earnings ratio	Current market price per share/ earnings after deductions per share	Indicates the view of shareholders about the potentialof future income streams to grow and their riskiness
6. Dividend/payout ratio	Annual dividends per share/ earnings after deductions per share	Indicates the willingness of an enterprise to distribute profit

Strategy in Action Andersen, accounting and the problems of monitoring

A major problem has been created for accounting firms like Andersen by the tendency to overemphasize the growth of net income, usually defined as EBITDA, and to reward managers by granting stock options, the value of which reflects that income performance. There is enormous pressure on managers to deliver a rising level of earnings per share, in the process maximizing share value, usually with targeted rates of 10–15%.

Such targets are unrealistic. Just as a mature developed economy cannot grow consistently above a maximum rate of about 4%, there is also a limit on what is possible for a mature diversified company to sustain for a period of more than one or two years. The situation for a developing country and a start-up company is rather different; they can grow at much higher rates for a long period of time. Consequently, all sorts of devices have been used by mature companies to conceal their real costs and inflate revenues.

The first issue involves stock options which have become popular among the companies operating in the new economy, including many of the start-ups in Silicon Valley. The main issue is that the stock options are not *expensed*, that is, they are not included in the costs of operation. This has made it possible to switch remuneration costs out of expenditures in a way which affects the level of net earnings. The profit performance of the companies which use stock options has looked much better than it really is. Very often the stock options have been matched by purchase of an enterprise's own shares with the help of retained profits.

There is no law or regulation which says a company should expense stock options and, until recently, no tendency to do so; a norm which companies have chosen to embrace. Quite the reverse, to expense stock options is not only difficult to do, since it is a complex issue for which there are no standards, but during the stock market boom, it would have severely disadvantaged any company since it would have reduced apparent earnings levels.

When the context changed in 2002, it paid some enterprises such as Amazon.com to innovate and introduce expensing. In the different environment, this practice had a beneficial effect on the share price,

persuading other companies to follow suit. The practice is fast becoming the norm.

There are also five main ways of exaggerating earnings:

1. To accelerate earnings, in the extreme case to bring forward earnings which will occur in the future so that they appear to be earned today; they may be the result of a signed contract but do not arise in the current accounting period. This is what Xerox did between 1997 and 2001, boosting and overstating its profits by US$1.4 billion.
2. To take expenses, notably those associated with debt, off the balance sheet by devising special-purpose entities, which in reality are not independent of the main company, but are to all intents and purposes invisible, certainly from an accounting point of view. This is what Enron did.
3. To convert operating expenses into capital expenses which are depreciated over a number of years. This is not difficult since many of the assets of companies today are intangible. It is often unclear what is a current and what is a capital expense. This is what WorldCom has done over an 18-month period, converting a loss into a significant profit.
4. To inflate profits and even out the growth of earnings through the acquisition of other companies. This is much easier to do if either the acquirer or the acquired operate in the financial sector.
5. To inflate earnings with the increase in the value of assets held by the companies' pension fund. One view maintains that this is what GE has been doing, but this is unclear.

To keep managers honest, and transparently so, there are various auditing systems. Any organization should have an internal audit committee, which should make a judgement as to whether the accounts meet the standards required. A further check is provided by an external audit, traditionally provided for most large companies by one of the big five accounting firms. The two committees should be independent of each other. In practice. the quality of auditing has left much to be desired.

The downfall of Enron took down the accounting firm Andersen, one of the big five, which as Enron's auditor should have been in a position to reveal the concealment of debt and inflation of earnings, but did not; worse, the accounting firm tried to conceal its knowledge by shredding documents, a clear breach of the law.

One big issue, which has arisen with respect to the accounting firms, relates to the dual activity of auditing and providing advice both to the companies concerned and investors purchasing the shares of the companies. There is a major conflict of interest. The accounting firms have been generating large streams of income from consulting services provided to the very firms which they have been auditing. The number of negative audits has diminished greatly. The so-called Chinese walls which should have divided the two sides are of puny construction. Investment banks looking for consulting work with the large companies have the same problem, since they are also in the business of giving advice to potential purchasers of shares on the value of companies to which they have also been giving advice or providing services.

Satisfying all the stakeholders

In recent years the main concern of the management of any enterprise has been on satisfying one group above all others, the owners or shareholders. From this perspective the aim has appeared to be quite simple. Any strategy should maximize shareholder value. It does this by maximizing what is called market value added (MVA), that is, the amount of wealth that a company has created for investors. It is the difference between what investors originally supplied as equity capital, that is, the money that they put up to acquire and continue to hold the shares, and the market value of that equity today. The first figure should be a net figure. The effect of the size of the enterprise can be taken out by relating this to the total capital of the company. This is a better measure of the effectiveness of the company in adding wealth.

Market and economic value added

The increase in market value added or wealth partly reflects the performance of the enterprise each year in adding value to the equity, although it also includes a component which reflects expected future earnings, that is, the ability of the enterprise to add value in the future. In some years, when the market value declines, there may be a loss of value. On average, the overall economic value added (EVA) for all companies might be expected to net out at zero, since even good companies generate a negative EVA about every four years because of a capital-intensive phase in the capital and growth cycle. In any given year, there is an EVA for each company, which is the difference between the after-tax operating profit earned and the opportunity cost of the capital employed at a similar level of risk.

MVA includes future growth value, which is the total amount of growth in EVA which investors have anticipated and built into share prices. It is arrived at by deducting total capital and current EVA from the total market value of the company. It is possible to relate this growth component to market value, to discover what share of current market value is accounted for by buoyant expectations of growth or what pessimistic expectation is built into the valuation. The relationship between MVA and EVA is therefore not a simple one, since it can be said to depend on the payout or dividend policy of the company and the P/E ratio, which may change according to shareholder expectations of future earnings or simply shareholder confidence. If the expectations are good and confidence is high, the P/E ratio can rise and the rise in MVA might exceed the cumulative value of the annual EVAs, and vice versa if the expectations are poor and confidence is low.

Strategy in Action   General Motors and its value added

The big three American car companies have found themselves outcompeted by the Japanese car manufacturers. This is a classic case of success breeding failure. The success of the American car manufacturers before the 1970s blinded them to the potential improvements in performance displayed by the Japanese. The performance of General Motors (GM) during the 1970s was by any standards poor. The company found itself unable to turn around the situation, even when it became obvious that there was a major problem. During the 1980s and 90s it continued to deliver a poor value added to its shareholders. There was considerable, and probably growing, organizational slack within the company, more than was necessary to allow a flexible response to unexpected external events.

Jensen (1993) has pioneered an attempt to work out the return on the R&D and capital expenditure of GM. This work was further developed and extended by Ghemawat (1999). Superficially, according to the financial indicators, the situation for GM appeared to be sound, with a significant rise in market capitalization and continuing profit making right up to 1990. The market value of the equity of the company rose from US$13 billion in 1980 to over US$26 billion at the end of 1990 (it continued to rise to US$69 billion in 1995, before falling back to US$42 billion in 1997).

The real problem lay in the amount of money being poured into the company over this period compared with the return. From 1980 to 1990 R&D expenditures were US$42.7 billion and gross capital expenditures US$87.5 billion. Much of this was accounted for by depreciation and amortization, in other words a straight replacement of productive capacity, as much as US$63 billion, which leaves a net expenditure of US$24.5 billion. The net injection of funds by shareholders was therefore US$67.2 billion. This went on rising in the early 1990s, as investors supplied the company with a massive US$87 billion of capital between 1980 and 1995 and an even more impressive US$167 billion between 1980 and 1997.

The MVA was clearly negative and growing more negative over time. On Jensen's preferred definition,

it was as high as minus US$115.2 billion from 1980 to 1991. The loss of value from 1980 to 1997 is well over US$100 billion, even if it is conservatively assumed that, in the absence of the investment expenditures, the market value of the equity would have been zero rather than what it was at the beginning of the period. If the timing of the investment is considered, the negative figure rises to well over $200 billion, that is, if value is added to the capital expenditure at an interest rate of 10%. Putting the picture a little differently, for every dollar invested in 1995 there was only 79 cents left and less than 50 cents, possibly as little as 33 cents, in 1997. GM was consuming itself.

Ross Perot (maverick millionaire, one time US presidential candidate) put it even more graphically when he pointed out that, in the mid-1980s, GM could have bought Toyota and Honda with the money it spent on itself, which would have turned out to be a much better investment – on market value in 1985 together they would have cost only US$21.5 billion.

By way of a simple contrast, over the period 1980–90, AT&T had a US$2.1 billion gain, to which you can add the US$125 billion of value in the seven divested Baby Bells, which did not exist in 1980. This is possibly a powerful argument in favour of divestment rather than automatic expansion, although there has been a significant loss of value in recent years.

GE, another divestor, had a gain of US$29.9 billion and Wal-Mart an even greater gain at US$38.2 billion. Between 1990 and 1995 Coca-Cola, which also had a MVA of US$69 billion in 1995, the same as GM, had received only $8 billion from its stockholders. Its MVA was therefore a strongly positive $61 billion. By these standards GM was a poor relative performer. The money invested in it would have been better spent elsewhere, for example returned to the shareholders for them to invest as they saw fit, perhaps in Coca-Cola or Wal-Mart.

Sources: Brigham and Houston, 1998: 45–7; Ghemawat, 1999: 101–3; Jensen, 1993, **48**(3): 831–80.

Total value added and the stakeholders

It is intriguing to ask why shareholders are regarded as owners and accorded such an important role when they could be regarded simply as only one of the groups providing finance, although on different terms to other groups of financiers. This point seems even more telling when the nature of what is owned is considered, intangible assets such as intellectual property and human capital rather than physical assets such as buildings, plant and equipment. In what sense are the shareholders any more owners of such assets than the employees of the enterprise?

In theory, if stakeholder groups other than owners were being taken into account, the concept should be the total value added, but defined so that all the costs should enter the calculation as opportunity costs rather than actual costs. In an imaginary world where perfect competition rules the market, this is how it would work. All stakeholder groups would have a call on the wealth created.

However, it is always open to an enterprise to pay more than the opportunity cost to any group – to share any good fortune by:

- paying workers or managers more than is strictly necessary in a perfectly competitive market or retaining them beyond a time when the level of company activity justifies this
- maintaining the price of supplies above what suppliers might ask in a fully competitive market in order to give them the resources to invest in innovation
- reducing the price or raising the quality of a product for customers, above what the market might demand
- rewarding other groups, such as community groups, in various ways, by contributions to local activities of various kinds and safeguarding, even improving, the quality of the natural environment.

Such procedures would recognize the claim that these stakeholder groups have on the total value added. Nearly all enterprises consciously carry out at least one or two of these acts.

As has been seen in Chapter 1, there are a number of different stakeholder groups who need to be satisfied in order to prevent damage to the performance of the enterprise over the longer term. The key issue is to keep them happy without making strategy inflexible and secure a long-term relationship without losing too much room for manoeuvre. That is one reason why stakeholders are paid more than their opportunity costs.

There has been a tendency to concentrate all the attention on just two stakeholder groups, owners and managers, and ensuring that the latter act as if they were the former. This explains the concentration of attention on shareholder value and a particular definition and model of corporate governance. It also explains the spreading habit of the issue of share options to senior managers. In some cases this has led to a tendency to neglect other stakeholder groups – workers, suppliers, strategic allies, the local community, customers, trade associations and even government. It might be said that many enterprises have lost a sense of corporate social responsibility.

In the developed market economies, there are two concepts which have tended to dominate discussion concerning management over the last ten years: that of good share value, already discussed, and that of governance, or rather what constitutes proper governance, which is discussed now.

Governance and strategy

To most commentators, governance means the attempt to give the board of directors real independence, in other words to ensure that the board is responsive to owners, not senior managers. There are two ways in which this can be achieved:

1. With an independent chairperson, not the CEO, and a majority of independent members on the board, voted on by the shareholders and possessing the required skills needed to make board supervision real. The board can be given an interest in the company's performance by requiring them to take an equity stake in the company.
2. With controls which are objective in nature and application, particularly financial controls. For example, the internal audit committees should have independent membership, including the chairperson, and proper reporting procedures. It is no good having board members who are independent if they are not receiving appropriate information and are therefore ignorant of what is happening within the company. In that situation they would be unable to properly police the managers.

The principal concern has been to ensure that the managers of an enterprise act in the interests of the owners, and not their own. This is achieved by the increasingly prevalent issue of stock options to managers at various levels of the enterprise, especially the topmost level. These options are the right to buy stock at a specially low strike price relative to market prices. The aim is to give managers an interest in maximizing the value of the enterprise's shares, since it will only pay to exercise the option if the price of the share is above the exercise price. The higher the price, the greater the potential profit from sale of the shares. In some cases such options are limited to the CEO and one or two others, including the chief financial officer; in others the options are spread right through the enterprise in an attempt to find a general solution to the principal/agent problem.

It is interesting that the stock options are not normally counted as expenses, although this is changing. Such an issue therefore converts an employment payment from an expense into something else, which is similar to profit and apparently irrelevant to the determination of net earnings.

Satisfying other stakeholders

This ignores the issue of keeping happy other stakeholder groups. How is it possible to keep such stakeholder groups happy? This is done by being aware of and sensitive to their differing interests and involving all the stakeholders in the process of strategy making. It is necessary to ensure that information on strategy formulation and implementation is conveyed to the stakeholders at the appropriate time. Each stakeholder group is likely to respond positively to the empowerment implicit in being consulted and informed about what is being done, and encouraged to respond with an appropriate but positive input.

For example, there is ample evidence to show that better performance results from a good relationship with suppliers. Numerous companies show the wisdom of this, such as Benetton, IKEA and Toyota whose practices are described, respectively, in

Chapters 13, 2 and 17. Sometimes the relationship involves cross-holdings of shares. It usually involves the swapping of staff. Suppliers must know exactly what is expected of them and how they fit into the strategic picture. They must be part of the learning process and feel that they are contributing to the achievement of strategic targets. Any change of direction or adjustment of strategy by the core enterprise must be communicated, particularly if it affects the supplier.

This kind of relationship is only worth nurturing if the relationship is intended to be a long-term one. This is exactly the opposite of a situation in which the relationship is regarded as an arm's length market one, which can end abruptly at any time and involves minimum interaction. The latter is more likely to be an adversarial situation in which there is a minimal exchange of information and no real cooperation.

A long-term close relationship probably involves limiting the number of suppliers and certainly not throwing contracts open to tender every year. The aim is to build up a relationship of trust, notably with those suppliers who are likely to be partners for the long term. A long-term relationship develops the relationship as a non-zero-sum game, not one in which the players are competing for a fixed value added. By increasing the value added to the final product, both can gain, provided there is an agreement on how that gain is to be shared.

Strategic allies, other than suppliers, must also be kept well informed of what the strategy means for them. There may be confidential information, but this is limited. Since some allies are potential competitors, this is a sensitive matter. Many successful companies take the view that it is better to err on the side of releasing too much information rather than too little. Nokia is a company which has tended to behave in this way, even regarding valuable technological knowledge.

Again, it is necessary to keep customers happy. The degree of customer satisfaction with the package of products and services provided is deliberately built into the balanced scorecard approach. It is critical to understand what customers want and whether they are getting what they want. It is also critical to identify any change over time in their wants. Ruthlessly extracting as much as possible out of the customer is not a sensible way to encourage repeat purchase, even when the seller temporarily has the upper hand. Nor does it encourage the dissemination of information by word of mouth, which is the best advertising a company can have.

The local community, that is, local relative to a specific facility, is able to inflict significant damage on any company if it wishes. It is important to take a positive attitude to the role of the company in the local community, which may mean using some of the company earnings to promote the wellbeing of local people. It is good public relations. An apt illustration of this is the way in which oil companies interact with the people of the areas in which they operate, such as the Niger Delta in Nigeria where there is a continuing problem (see Chapter 14). There are many ways in which the community can be kept on side. It is not simply a matter of avoiding conflict. It is important to be a stable employer who treats well any staff laid off in a crisis, giving them advice and smoothing their transition to another employer.

It is good for the company to keep the local community and its representatives well informed on strategy and its implementation. One potential source of concern is the environment and the sustainability of company operations from an environmental perspective. Any company must be attentive to any possible damage to the local environment. It makes little difference whether the company is operating in the oil industry or a winter resort. The organization should pay proper attention to issues such as energy conservation, possible air, water or soil pollution, the minimization of waste and the desirability of recycling.

Government and government agencies may have a particular interest in the behaviour of the organization. The interest may be a general one, in employment generation and tax raising. It is also often necessary for companies to seek approval at different levels of government for certain proposed actions. It is also necessary to avoid falling foul of existing regulations, or in some circumstances to persuade an authority to change the regulations. This requires keeping open lines of communication with government and its representatives, through the nurturing of contacts or even systematic lobbying. There is often a tacit agreement or social compact with government at whatever level that each side – enterprise and government – contributes what the other wants, for example jobs and taxes for government approvals.

The multiple bottom line

As the triple bottom line shows, it is not easy to weigh all these relationships in the balance. The triple bottom line might be a quadruple or even a quintuple bottom line, if it takes account of all stakeholder groups. The term corporate social responsibility has become fashionable. It does summarize the need to take account of all the wider stakeholder groups and their interests. The aim is not just to avoid the obvious and dramatic disasters, such as the Bhopal explosion or the *Exxon Valdez* oil spill, it is to keep all the relationships positive.

The relationships are not static; they are dynamic. They change in two principal ways: first, according to the stage at which the organization is located in its life cycle, and second, according to the prevailing norms of social behaviour.

During the different stages of an organizational life cycle, the managers of an enterprises can adopt one of four strategies towards different stakeholder groups:

1. A *proactive strategy* which anticipates responsibility by taking action to meet the requirement of each stakeholder group
2. An *accommodating strategy* which accepts responsibility but is less active in meeting the requirement than a proactive strategy
3. A *defensive strategy*, in which they admit responsibility by simply meeting the minimum legal requirements
4. A *reactive strategy* which involves denying responsibility, either fighting against addressing a stakeholder's wishes or completely withdrawing and ignoring the stakeholder.

Which strategy is adopted towards particular stakeholder groups depends on the general reference point of the managers, whether they have an expectation of profit or loss, and the prioritization of resources offered by different stakeholder groups during the enterprise's various life-cycle stages. Different stakeholder groups have control over critical resources which vary in importance during the different stages.

Typically there is an expectation of loss during the first and last stages of the life cycle, start-up and decline, and an expectation of profit during the middle two stages, growth and maturity. This can lead to the adoption of:

- a *risk-taking strategy* in the first situation which inclines the strategy towards the reactive end of the scale and a failure to meet the interests of a number of stakeholder groups
- a *risk-averse strategy* in the second which inclines strategy towards the proactive end and an attempt to meet the interests of nearly all groups.

The choice of riskiness of strategy is likely to be influenced by the level of the commitment of resources. The greater the commitment, the more proactive the strategy.

Table 18.6 indicates a typical progression in strategy during the different stages of the life cycle. It does not claim to describe the situation for all groups, rather to indicate a general tendency, and could be written as a longitudinal representation of the real experience of a particular enterprise.

Table 18.6 **A typical strategy towards stakeholder groups**

Life-cycle stage	Type of strategy			
	Proactive	Accommodating	Defensive	Reactive
Infancy (start-up)	Shareholders Creditors Customers	Suppliers Employees	Government Community	Trade association Environment
Adolescence (growth)	Creditors Employees Suppliers Trade association	Shareholders Government Community Environment Customers		
Adulthood (maturity)	Employees Suppliers Trade association Shareholders Government Community Environment Customers	Creditors		
Old age (decline/ transition)	Shareholders Creditors Customers	Employees Suppliers	Government Community	Trade association Environment

Source: Based on Jawahar and McLaughlin, 2001.

Corporate social responsibility

During the periods when the organization is at its best in terms of performance, the typical strategy is to work actively to promote the interests of all stakeholder groups or at worst to accommodate them. When it is at its worst in terms of performance, it is forced to retreat, concentrating on those groups providing critical resources.

What is the return on good behaviour? Corporate social responsibility does not

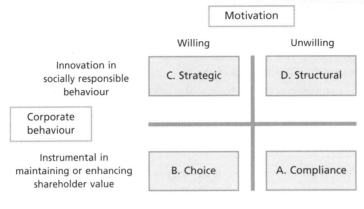

Source: Martin, 2002: 69–75.

Figure 18.5 **The virtuous behaviour matrix**

necessarily produce profits, although it can, but it is often the kind of behaviour which enhances the long-term position of a company, including its reputation. Martin (2002) has indicated the problem neatly through the use of a virtue matrix (Figure 18.5).

As with all matrices, there are two criteria for distinguishing behaviour:

1. The motivation for acting responsibly is sometimes *instrumental* – there is a return for doing so, and sometimes *intrinsic* – it is done because it is deemed appropriate and praiseworthy conduct.
2. The behaviour is sometimes accepted as what, given the norms of the time, *should be done*, and sometimes it is *innovatory*. The two forms of behaviour in the upper half of the matrix can be shifted to the lower half by government action or a change of social norms.

It is possible to distinguish four different types of socially responsible behaviour.

The first two positions lie within what can be described as the civil foundation of any society. The level of the boundary varies from society. On the whole, the civil foundation in prosperous, advanced societies is deep and robust. In poor, less developed societies it is shallow and fragile. A company does not necessarily receive any credit for this kind of behaviour, but will certainly experience a loss for failing to act according to law or convention. A company can receive only social credit for operating at the frontier where it is seen as a pioneer.

A. *Compliance* – with the laws and regulations which already exist in any country, put there in the first place to enforce what is commonly regarded as socially responsible behaviour. It is potentially costly to break the law, both because of the fines incurred and the bad reputation earned. It pays to comply with the law, whatever it is, recognizing that it varies over time and from country to country.
B. *Choice* – whether or not to realize the virtues expressed in the unwritten and

unformalized norms and customs of a society. Again, failing to follow these norms results in lost reputation and the alienation of key stakeholder groups. Often the norms and customs of today are the laws and regulations of tomorrow.

C. *Strategic* – innovating in social behaviour in a way which is potentially imitated by others. In whatever it is doing, the company is setting an example for others to follow. It might be the example on training given in Chapter 13. In many cases this example might be rapidly imitated, so that it becomes the norm, which most organizations are likely to choose to observe. It becomes part of the profit delivery mechanism of any company.

D. *Structural* – innovating in a way which is obviously not part of the profit delivery mechanism and unlikely to be imitated. It might offer the prospect of enormous social benefit, but no, or very little, private gain. The example of a prisoner's dilemma relating to the pollution of the atmosphere, given in Chapter 13, falls into this type. Only collective or government action of some kind can convert such behaviour into compliance behaviour. Otherwise a company engaging in this kind of activity is simply imposing a cost on itself and in the process helping to make itself uncompetitive vis-à-vis those enterprises which do not do the same.

As income rises in particular economies, there is usually a movement of the different types of behaviour from the frontier to the civil foundation, but this is by no means certain. A recession or depression, onerous conditions like war, threatening events like terrorist attacks or simply a change of fashion or policy may reverse the movement. From a social perspective, at any given time there is always an undersupply of socially responsible behaviour in any country. In a global context it is also unclear what might happen when companies engage in international transactions:

- an 'averaging up' of the world, as companies from countries with a higher civil foundation apply their higher standards
- an 'averaging down', as they adjust their behaviour to the lower standards of the countries in which they are operating.

Either could predominate, but today it is dangerous to offend the norms of the most advanced with poor behaviour in the less advanced. There is little forgiveness for the Union Carbides of this world.

Any commercial enterprise needs to generate a value added large enough to allow all stakeholder groups to be kept happy, but not a profit so large as to necessitate the kind of action which undermines positive stakeholder relationships. The acquisition of a reputation for straight and transparent dealing is more important than agonizing over what is the exact level of profit to be targeted or who exactly is to share the value added. Stakeholder groups need to be kept properly informed. They need to learn to trust any representative of the company and what they tell them. How this might be achieved was discussed in general terms in Chapter 1.

It is important to run an audit check on socially responsible performance as part of the monitoring of strategy implementation. Under the pressure of events, implementation is sometimes carried out in a way which allows standards to slip in the name of the bottom line and offends key stakeholder groups. Such behaviour, if allowed to continue, often results in a drift away from socially responsible standards and a disastrous loss of reputation when it is exposed. The response to the immediate pressure to produce short-term profit needs to be monitored.

Strategy only works if those who must be implementors of that strategy are convinced of its value. As in many other areas of social and economic activity, confidence and trust are key parts of any success. Delivering what you say you will deliver, and always believing that you will, is an essential basis for trust and the confidence which goes with it. At the very least it is necessary to explain fully what has gone wrong, in the rare event that you are unable to deliver. There are always mishaps, or an accidental divergence from a strategy, which have to be dealt with. Strategy will be treated cynically if it is obvious that the strategists are only going through the motions, with no real commitment to keep the staff and others informed. All staff need to feel empowered, knowing that they can cause a filling out of, or an adjustment in, the strategy if they make a positive suggestion.

Few companies can claim the independent confidence felt by middle mangers in Intel who, by their day-to-day actions and reactions to Japanese competition, decided, in a fundamental strategic reorientation, to switch the company from the DRAM (memory chips) business to the microprocessor business and had their decision confirmed by top management.

Promoting strategy to stakeholders

In order to win support, strategy making may involve the never-ending selling of strategic thinking to all the stakeholders of an enterprise, including the employees. This is done firstly by regular contact and involvement in the strategy-making process, whether using the strategic canvas method, building scenarios or involving staff in focus groups. All these methods, with the maximum participation of all staff, promote involvement, particularly if they are integrated with strategy making itself. All staff can be involved to some degree in continuously reviewing the current profile of the organization and looking at its future.

Second, it is achieved by making clear the standing of any strategy at any given time. Strategy is best made transparent and best sold on the basis of its results – that strategy delivers outcomes which benefit both the enterprise and all its stakeholders, outcomes with which these groups are very happy. These outcomes must be built into the strategy. For that reason there must be communication conduits which are clearly defined, beyond simply distributing the annual report.

Insofar as strategic thinking is a creative perspective on business, it is essential to ensure that as many stakeholders and employees as possible share this perspective. All become strategists within their own spheres. There is a learning process involved which can be promoted by appropriate strategic action.

The Enron collapse is an illustration of the consequences of behaviour which is not transparent and certainly did not keep the stakeholders informed.

One of the largest crashes of a company in recent times has been that of the American company Enron. In the good times, Enron epitomized what was considered good – a willingness to embrace innovation, and in the bad times, what was considered bad – socially irresponsible behaviour.

Enron is not the only company to collapse in a spectacular manner, since its demise has been accompanied by a whole series of shocks to the reputation of the American accounting system. The Enron collapse was as remarkable for its rapidity and the lateness of the change of attitude of analysts towards the company, as for the size of the fall which rocked many other parts of the economy. It was a watershed and marked the real end of the dynamic 1990s, an end which has already been flagged by the dot-com crash and the telecommunications crisis, events which simply reflected the overshooting so characteristic of market systems.

From every perspective Enron and its CEO, Ken Lay, were held up as models worthy of emulation, the very model of a modern 'virtual' enterprise. It was considered a model of how innovation should be built into the strategy of a modern enterprise. Within a short period of time Enron became very large indeed, one of the largest companies in the USA, positioned in the top ten, a $30-plus billion energy broker.

Enron had taken advantage of the wave of privatizations among energy and other utilities throughout the world to transform itself, within ten years, into a global service powerhouse in energy, water and other infrastructure industries. The share price of Enron rose at an extremely rapid rate, for example 50% in 1999 alone, quadruple the rate of the S&P Natural Gas Index. On the basis of this performance, *Business Week* named Ken Lay as one of the top 25 managers of the year. Enron itself was consistently voted the Most Innovative Large Company in the United States in *Fortune* magazine's Most Admired Companies survey. Some analysts went as far as to argue that Enron's 'audacious executives (now) think they can funda-

mentally alter the way the Internet works'. It was seen as a company which was able to continually reinvent itself with new products and by entering new markets.

In the words of Eisenhardt and Sull, 'Enron began its remarkable transformation by embracing uncertainty' (2001: 114). It was very much a child of the new economy. It moved from transmitting gas interstate to trading in commodities of every variety and even to risk management trading. It was not always easy to understand exactly what Enron was doing. It traded in an enormous variety of different things – fibreoptic bandwidth, pollution-emission credits and weather derivatives offering an insurance against damaging weather. From 1996 it began to handle outsourced energy management on a massive scale, developing sales as high as US$15 billion.

Enron allegedly adopted some very simple strategic rules which superficially seemed to be sensible and safeguard it against any major failure:

- All trades should be balanced with an offsetting trade to minimize unhedged risk
- There should a daily report on the profit and loss situation of any trade
- The customers should be screened. In the energy management business there were boundary rules which could be applied to the screening of customers. Any such customer must have engaged in outsourcing before, not have energy as its core business, have had previous contact with Enron and must be represented initially by the CFO or CEO of the company, or someone with broad responsibility and ability to implement the recommended policy.

It appears unlikely that these simple rules were actually applied in a consistent way. The undoing of Enron was that it had spun off a number of off-balance sheet entities which carried much of Enron's debt and allowed it to present its performance as very much better than it really was.

Choosing the nature of strategy

Much of this book is based on a description of what actually happens when an enterprise tries to 'plan'. Accurate description is always a preliminary to appropriate prescription. There are severe constraints on what is possible in the area of strategy making. It is pointless to advocate what is impossible. This book takes the position that it is unproductive to prescribe a strategy-making method which runs counter to the nature of the enterprise and the world in which the enterprise operates. Imposing models which are oversimplifications of the process undermines the potentially helpful role of strategy, just as centralized physical planning systems have undermined the credibility of all planning at the national level.

Strategic management used to be called business planning which encapsulates the classical view of strategy. This narrowed the conception of strategic management unnecessarily. The change in title is illuminating. Strategy is a much broader concept than planning. Planning is not always the appropriate type of strategic management to adopt. In certain situations, planning may be relevant, but generally this is not the case. Quite rightly there is an extensive literature pointing out the deficiencies, taking a narrow definition of planning. In most circumstances, detailed strategic planning is not feasible, even if it were desirable.

Finding appropriate strategies

Good strategy making plays a critical role in any successful company. Pretending that it does not is just as dangerous as imposing a distorted version of strategic planning on the organization. Part of good strategy making is to decide an appropriate role for strategy itself. This is one of the most important strategic questions. Theory and practice must be combined in order to attain the kind of strategy making which helps the enterprise to remain viable as a business unit. There is a discovery process in finding what is appropriate. What is appropriate may change over time. Strategy making is a core competency required by all successful companies. There is much room for strategic thinking in developing this core competency and making particular strategies.

Strategy making is first of all a matter of 'philosophy', a reflection of the way the world is seen by the strategists. How are people motivated? How do organizations function? There are many questions which reveal what we have called a person's meta-theory, his or her view of how the world is. This is by no means a simple issue, and is worthy of careful consideration since the meta-theory determines whether the enterprise finds a strategy which works. It is what this book is about. It has repeatedly brought the relevant meta-theories to the surface. Good strategy making requires a degree of perceptiveness on the part of would-be strategists and a degree of flexibility in what they do to fit a strategy to the world in which they are operating.

It is important to do this since it stops the enterprise adopting approaches which are counterproductive, approaches which inadvertently block change and undermine competitive advantage. Later it is a matter of the choice of techniques for making good strategy, techniques which are consistent with the nature of the world. As such, strategy making is as much art or craft as science. What works is worth repeating and developing, but it must be adjusted to fit a changing environment.

Strategy is always in the process of emerging (see Chapter 16). This has important implications for monitoring and what it means. Strategy making is a continuous process: it can never cease. Monitoring is also part of this continuous process which can never cease. There are no sequential steps which follow one after another in a defined order and which close the activity when completed. There is no beginning and no end. Strategy is like the real world and its behavioural patterns, a messy business; it cannot be neatly defined. Monitoring this process and its outcomes is difficult and itself messy. The practice usually bears no relationship to the classical description of strategy, which is a distorting oversimplification.

Reversing the accepted sequence of steps

There is even a sense in which implementation precedes formulation and monitoring precedes implementation. In conditions of rapid change, the overlapping increases so much that operations pre-empt the development of the strategy. Monitoring and implementation actually allow formulation to occur because they involve a discovery process, a discovery of the unexpected. In 'doing' you can discover what you are capable of doing. The doing reveals previously unknown possibilities. Strategy is as much about discovering what you can do as realizing what you plan to do.

If change is rapid enough, this discovery process is speeded up. It becomes impossible to formulate and implement a plan fast enough to accommodate the changing environment. Formulation, implementation and monitoring are fused into one simultaneous process. Yet the process must be controlled. It cannot be allowed to spiral out of control. Enterprises cannot behave reactively without eventually suffering disastrous results.

Strategy is about being proactive. Those engaged in current operations and other functional areas now must be kept informed about possibilities for the future and how, through its strategy, the enterprise is trying to remake the external environment to its own liking. There must be some framework in which the organization is operating. Strategy provides this framework. It is systematic monitoring of performance which paradoxically allows a strategist to be proactive.

To produce a detailed plan in such circumstances is to defeat the aim of strategy, whose very existence is premised on the uncertainty that change brings and the benefits which are contained within that change. To deny oneself such benefits is not part of good strategy. Strategy gives shape to the actions of the enterprise as it seeks to realize its objectives, the specific details of which are being redefined at frequent intervals. Such adjustment can result eventually in a major rewrite of the strategy.

Strategy making as a continuous process

As we have seen strategy is continuous in two main senses. It is the result of learning in a context of rapid change in the external environment. It is rather more than the result of an unpredictable process; strategy itself promotes and channels such learning. Learning is a selective process. What is learned must be incorporated into the strategy and become the basis for a further process of discovery. However, what is not yet known cannot be incorporated in any conventional sense into a strategic plan. Knowledge creation cannot be managed in a simple manner. Structure, strategy and culture can all be treated in a way which encourages such a learning process.

Strategy must accept the universality of change and the temporary nature of the present. Strategy guides the learning process and tries to discover the direction in which to move, but this also involves discovering possible destinations and sorting out which is the appropriate one for an organization at a particular moment of time.

This is all part of what is conventionally understood as monitoring. It may involve deciding the choice of destination as late as possible in the strategy-making process.

It is the result of the exercise of a particular kind of leadership by key strategy makers who, through their vision, integrate the disparate efforts of a large number of dependent strategists and stakeholders. The leader or leaders read patterns into the unfolding events and assist in giving direction to the learning process – that is their job. The more uncertain the future, the more important this leadership role.

Continuous monitoring

Leaders must continuously and carefully monitor what is happening, understanding how far they can control events and how far that control is desirable. Detailed formulation and implementation arise from a process of negotiation and bargaining which is never quite completed. Communication of information and coordination of agents continues all the time. Different interests need to be reconciled. Different stakeholders need to be involved in a continuing process of decision making. Monitoring feeds back the information needed to do all these things effectively.

Leadership stresses that strategy is not limited by existing conditions. It aims to remake the environments facing the enterprise to the advantage of that enterprise, even if only to a minor degree. It is always discovering new ways of doing this. Other strategic players are doing the same for their own enterprises and in the process changing the environment for the enterprise. A creative company like Sony has done this over a protracted period of time and in a dramatic way.

Monitoring takes a conventional form in stable circumstances, the regular checking of key performance indicators and the occasional drawing up of a balanced scorecard. Often, however, strategic planning becomes a constraint on the achievement and retention of competitive advantage. This is particularly true of industries which are competitive and subject to rapid change. Monitoring becomes a matter of examining the degree to which the enterprise is responding positively to the opportunities and threats thrown up by the changing environment.

The Soviet Union became hopelessly uncompetitive as a consequence of the comprehensiveness of its planning in a world in which change was rapid on both the supply and demand sides. A simple monitoring of its position showed a serious incapacity to innovate and keep up with changes in taste and technology which were occurring in the outside world. The lessons are clear to all – highly centralized and detailed physical planning which ignores change is not good for either enterprise or economic system. Classical strategy making shares many of these faults.

On the other hand, it is always true that strategic thinking is advantageous, promoting a dynamic and innovating orientation in strategy making. It pays to encourage all to engage in strategic thinking. The extent to which this is actually happening needs monitoring. What mix of thinking and planning goes to establish the desired strategic management is again a reflection of conditions specific to any organization.

Who are the monitors? Since formulation, implementation and monitoring are fused, the monitors are the strategists, who might be everyone, but in some narrow cases might be specialists. All can monitor their own performance and with appropriate information can monitor the performance of the unit or organization in which they work or have an interest.

Focus on Humour

Simplicity has a price. Why are so many business books written in a style appropriate for 10-year-olds?

Who Moved my Cheese? by Spencer Johnson MD, tells a story of mice in a maze. For the past three years it has been the bestselling business book. Ten million people have read it, the publishers claim, and so has my computer.

I used the computer to analyse extracts to assess the reading age the material requires. The program considers the vocabulary and sentence structure. *Who Moved my Cheese?* is less than 100 pages long, set in large print and copiously illustrated. The program judges it suitable for those who have completed five or six years of education. That is about the same as Britain's tabloid newspaper the *Sun*, and rather lower than the requirements of the Harry Potter books.

Yet there is one genre of business writing that blows the computer off the scale. When the program detects unfamiliar jargon, it believes it is in specialist territory that requires an advanced degree or professional qualifications. And that is how it reacts to the convoluted prose and inventive phraseology of management consultants. Computers can look for vocabulary, sentence structure and grammatical consistency. They cannot decide whether what is written has any meaning.

Source: Financial Times, May 7, 2002: 8.

(The current book aims to fall between the two!)

Case Study 1 The disruptive innovator, Sony

'Don't be afraid to make a mistake, but don't make the same mistake twice. If you think it is good for the company, do it. ... Sony motivates executives not with special compensation systems but by giving them joy in achievement, challenge, pride, and a sense of recognition.'

Akio Morita

'Sony's primary mission is to produce something new, unique, and innovative for the enhancement of people's lives.'

Dr Kihara

'Sony can be the No. 1 company in the broadband network society. That will be a much bigger role than Sony has ever had ... We have to take advantage of everything that technology and the new economy provide.'

Noboyuki Idei

History and positioning of Sony

Japan has slipped from being a star global performer to being a struggling developed economy. Japan is a prime case of what can be called 'premature maturity' (a term first used by Nicholas Kaldor, a Cambridge economist, to describe the British economy), that is, a society unable to come to terms with its own high level of economic development. This may be a temporary phenomenon and by 2010 the pendulum may have swung once more. The transition from an old type business model to a new type model encapsulates these changes. It is easy to exaggerate the contrast but it does exist.

The most revealing sign of the failure of old type companies was a decline in their share price and a significant reduction in market capitalization. Many companies fell into this hole, including Nissan for a long period during the 1990s, Matsushita, still in the same hole, Mitsubishi, Hitachi and possibly not so surprisingly Nippon Steel and the retailer Daiei.

By contrast new style companies retained a high price and a high capitalization. These were not necessarily new companies. Some old companies stand out for their ability to make successful strategies. Toyota and Honda are good examples. The video games makers, Nintendo and Sega (see Chapter 6), have also kept themselves ahead of the field, although the latter is now having some trouble. Softbank and SECOM are new and successful players. Nissan has transformed itself to become a turnaround model for others (see Chapter 16). Sony also held its own until recently, but is now seeing a decline in its share price, a 15% fall in the last quarter of the year to March 31, 2003, double the fall of the electrical machinery index on the Tokyo stock market.

The key changes in Japan are interesting. Emphasis has shifted from the supply side, away from scale economies, which followed from mass production in a large domestic market supplemented by export markets, and the scope economies which accompanied diversific-ation – the old companies were nothing if not diversi-fied. There was intense competition in producing a range of homogeneous products at the lowest price. In the new model the emphasis has switched to the con-sumer and the demand side, with successful compet-ition requiring more and more differentiated products.

The speed of response has become essential. Research and development are necessary to keep an enterprise ahead and keep up a drive for high quality and low cost. Enterprises quickly need to develop and access new resources and integrate old resources in new ways. The network economy, sometimes first appearing under the old economy, began to emerge as important (see the Toyota production system – Chapter 17). Successful new industries were often in areas where clusters of related enterprises were the normal condition. Strategic alliances proliferated, eventually resulting in mergers where this was advantageous.

The successful were able to build on their success, partly through increasing returns. In the past, growth was often associated with smaller profits as companies strove to win a greater market share. Now the larger scale was often associated with increasing returns to the successful. The key success factors among the successful were a creative vision at the top which transformed the company from the old to the new style, reinforced by the synchronization and coevolution of different parts of the organization and the ability of enterprises and their staff to self-organize at the grassroots, particularly in networks of interacting enterprises. The main con-straints on the ability of enterprises to achieve success in the new style were:

- market turbulence and slow growth
- difficulty in integrating the different parts of the organization in implementing the strategy
- difficulty in reaching agreement on the identific-ation of what constituted their area of competitive advantage.

Up to the 1980s the business model used by Sony was both highly successful and different from the norm in Japan. Between 1950 and 1980 Sony had initiated as many as 12 such disruptions, a truly impressive number (see the Strategy in Action on Sony in Chapter 2). By doing this Sony achieved two things:

- It created from nothing a succession of huge new growth markets
- It toppled from their positions of leadership competi-tors who had been the leaders in electronic hardware.

The last of these successful disruptions was the Walkman, launched in 1979. The nature of technical

advance changed. From 1980 to the present Sony has been engaged in sustaining innovations, that is, innov-ations which build on the platform of what has already been done. Neither technology nor markets are new. Sony's PlayStation and the Vaio computer notebook are good, successful products, but they are targeted at well-established markets rather than completely new ones, and do not use technology which is radically new.

Following the logic of the distinction made on the nature of innovation, the obvious question to ask is, how did the company's ability to develop sustaining innovation squeeze out its ability to continue generating disruptive ones? The answer lies mainly in the passing of the old guard and the maturing of the company. The role of Morita and his small group of immediate associ-ates was critical. They made every product launch decision themselves. They did this largely on the basis of intuition but an intuition grounded on what became well-practised procedures for shaping and launching such innovations.

There was no market analysis or research done since there was no existing market. In key respects Sony was unlike the older conglomerates in Japan. It carefully avoided involvement with either government or banks. It did not operate within a *keiretsu*-like organization. Staff were appointed on the basis of talent and then given a free hand. Organization was in teams or cells which operated independently of control from above. Development teams were responsible for specific pro-jects. Staff were moved around, potential executives exposed to the production line and/or marketing. The decisions to innovate were freed from the constraints which in established companies lead to the rejection of most innovations made outside the core activities of the company. There was, and still is, active encouragement of intrapreneurship.

In the early 1980s Morita withdrew from an active role in Sony. With his departure a change of balance occurred and the ability to generate disruptive innov-ation was steadily lost. Other external changes, broadly summarized by the term commoditization applied to the areas of electronic hardware, tended to reinforce this transition. New competitors emerged. The transition was, by necessity, accompanied by a beefing up of the marketing side of the company, with the result that only sustaining innovations tended to pass muster.

Entering the world of entertainment

'Software also makes hardware meaningful: hardware does not exist without software. They must be developed mutually.'

Noria Ohga, former CEO, Sony

In the late 1980s and 90s Sony attempted to go through a revolutionary transition, which would change the nature of the company, in which it sought to convert itself from an electronics manufacturer into a comprehensive entertainment business. It pioneered in putting together these two areas, the electronic hardware and the creative software.

This transition involved Sony in a series of acquisitions in the entertainment area. In 1988 Sony Corporation acquired CBS Records for about US$2 billion. This followed a long relationship between the two companies which involved the distribution of CBS records in Japan, a relationship in which the two companies enjoyed an equal role. A second major acquisition was that of Columbia Pictures Entertainment for US$3.4 billion. What was being acquired was not just the capacity to make new films or new music, but a large pool of past productions. Sony was again trying to be a pioneer, this time in combining the medium – the communications hardware, and the message – the entertainment product.

Why did the company do this? There were two incidents which are said to have been important in persuading the senior managers of Sony that they had to change their strategy:

1. The victory of VHS over Beta, which was made certain by the build-up of software compatible with VHS and not Beta. Since nobody wished to carry double inventories of motion picture software, there came a point at which purchase of VHS was inevitable: the software pool had passed a threshold level. Although technically Beta was superior, Sony lost in its attempt to promote it.
2. The introduction of the CD which was only just made possible by the willingness of two record companies to prerecord music for the discs, PolyGram and the joint CBS/Sony venture. Other companies were hostile and nearly prevented this Sony innovation.

There were two underlying factors which were also important and reinforced the impact of the situations above. With the digitalization of electronic hardware, it became hard for one company to establish a clear technological lead over the others and gain and maintain a continuing competitive advantage based on that technology. Yet the demand for entertainment was growing quickly, and particularly quickly outside the USA. The entertainment software was characterized by a clear product differentiation based on talent. The talent for film and music making lay largely in America. It became clear that while the electronic hardware was a facilitator of new businesses, but no longer a large profit generator, the software had become a significant profit generator for such businesses.

These factors became obvious, not only to Sony, but to other players. Matsushita bought MCA, owner of Universal Studios, in 1990, for $6.1 billion. Vivendi bought Universal Studios. Later Viacom, a telecom group, merged with Paramount. Time, Inc., a magazine publisher, merged with Warner Brothers. News Corporation acquired Twentieth Century Fox. A similar process was repeated with the main music companies and radio and television. Whether any of the new information-entertainment (infotainment) conglomerates could make money in the process of construction was at the time unclear. Sony had set the precedent.

Two principles of organization governed the expanded Sony:

1. The 'loose organization' principle. There was very little in the way of formal structure. Talented individuals determined how business was organized.
2. The main company in the USA, SUSA, operated as a US company with a Japanese parent, rather than as a branch or a subsidiary of the main company, a most unJapanese practice. Americans came to dominate the key positions. To some degree Sony learned from its past successes and its initial mistakes.

The entertainment business is unusual in the nature of its economics. The costs are fixed and incurred upfront. For films they are large, less so for television, but still significant. Revenue is only generated on distribution of the product. For all media a small part of the product generates most of the income. It is extremely difficult to predict taste, that is, which films or products will be a hit. These features mean that capital and talent are the key to success. Sony had the former and was seeking to acquire the latter.

The new strategy

Electronic hardware and entertainment software are very different in their strategic implications. For the former it is possible to envisage a timetable of development which runs quite a way into the future, although it is placed in the context of discovery-led planning. For the latter, the entertainment side, this is not possible since tastes are fickle and changing; talent is by its nature unpredictable. It is impossible to control creativity in the same way that you can control finance or follow through all the implications of a new technical paradigm. Moreover, strategy for Sony is complicated by the fact that there must be communication between the two, and any effective strategy must take account of this. Sony has shown itself a pioneer in anticipating the growing importance of the hardware/software link, but the critical issue is whether it can successfully implement the link. This is something which requires a considerable period of time and a significant learning process.

Sony's original core competency was the ability to miniaturize its products, that is, a technical expertise, which has never been lost or neglected. As we have seen this expertise was applied to radios, televisions, transistors, camcorders and the Walkman. Sony has established its name both by its technical brilliance, but even more by its application of that knowledge to products which have strong consumer appeal. It has sought to sell its products on the quality of their attributes. For example, its digital camera, the Mavica, is deliberately designed to be easy to use. Its laptop computer, the Vaio, introduced in 1996, has very attractive styling. Sony was always particularly good at identifying new opportunities that are a product of the rapidly changing technologies – it still is. Its brand name is another vital resource, recently being valued as high as eighteenth in a global assessment. Managing the use of the brand name is one of the key strategic issues for the company.

Sony has used its technical expertise and its name to extend its coverage into the area of content and entertainment. Sony pioneered a strategy of becoming 'a comprehensive entertainment business'. It shares the goal of many companies which sought to take advantage of convergence between computing, telecommunications and entertainment, such as AOL Time Warner, Vivendi, Viacom or News Corp. It made the decision to enter a strategically difficult area. It deliberately acquired both film and television production facilities and television channels, not only in the USA but also most notably in the larger Latin American and Asian countries. In 1999 it produced as much as 4,000 hours of foreign-language programmes compared with 1,700 hours of English-language programmes.

Sony made early mistakes in this strategy. Its initial global strategy did not work, so that it quickly moved away from a global strategy to a multidomestic strategy. It controls 24 TV channels which operate in 62 countries. It is constrained by law from doing this in the US. It displays a considerable cultural sensitivity in the way it now operates.

Sony has not hesitated to enter new areas. It does this with decisiveness. Superficially some of these entries appear to lack a link with the overall strategy, but this is more an indication of the width and depth of Sony's ambition. The margins on Sony's core electronic business have been shaved to a razor-thin 1%. There is even a price war on the games consoles. Sony does need a new strategy and a new business model. Its CEO Nobuyuki Idei does not want Sony to become simply a supplier of electronic components. The future may lie with subscription services for the provision of content of various kinds, on which the price can be increased over time. The strategy is to promote convergence and develop the business model to reap the rewards from the use of software.

Sony is unusual in trying to do everything simultaneously. Perhaps more than any other company, Sony stands at the centre of digital convergence and stands to gain most from its achievement. Today Sony seeks to dominate the television industry, not just the hardware side, but the software side too. It does this through a gorilla rather than a guerrilla strategy. In a guerrilla strategy, the strategist identifies and commandeers a key technology, which all other industry participants must incorporate into their production in order to survive. Microsoft and Intel have adopted this strategy. By contrast, the gorilla strategy requires the envelopment of the whole sprawling industry in a massive grasp. This involves everything from hardware to content. This is the strategy adopted by Sony. It is a risky strategy in that it requires a considerable commitment of resources.

Can Sony succeed under Idei? He has certainly refashioned the company. Sony is being converted into something which looks more like a holding company, one which might in the future spin off some of the product areas. Idei reorganized Sony into five main operating units:

- he retained Sony broadband entertainment, which oversees the creative film, television and music activities
- a home network company, which is responsible for the audio and video hardware used in the home entertainment network and also in ensuring the robustness of compatibility between the various bits of hardware
- a personal IT network company, which deals with the personal computer and wireless side, including camcorders and cameras
- a communications systems solution network company, which is responsible for the technology of the film and television areas
- a core technology and network company, which oversees a wide range of components, such as batteries, magnetic tapes, semiconductors, disc drives, optical and flat-panel displays, and memory sticks.

The company now looks much more like a Western company. The board has been reduced from 40 to 10 members and streamlined to be an effective governance mechanism. It has a heavyweight membership which includes Carlos Ghosn. Japanese employment habits, such as lifetime employment and promotion by seniority, have been dropped. Sony has become much more willing to enter into alliances, since it realizes it cannot succeed without them. Before the late 1990s it was extremely reluctant to engage in partnerships of any kind. There is one major exception. Together with Philips, it co-developed the audio CD, a successful partnership since it still receives 5 cents for every CD sold.

Returning to basics

'Sony is going through a transitional period which makes it a dangerous but exciting place.'

Howard Stringer

There is a strong suggestion in the literature that from the 1980s onwards Sony lost focus as it ceased to be the consumer electronics pioneer and tried to forge a different strategy. The retirement of the founder was partly responsible, but Sony was also caught off guard by the rise of the Internet and the appearance of new competitors. The important electronics unit, responsible for 64% of total sales in the year ending March 31, 2002, fell behind in core areas such as mobile phones and Internet music players. For a period the company, distracted by the attempt to change strategic direction, regularly reorganized itself, frequently changed management personnel and varied the pace at which it introduced new products. The consumer electronics industry is fiercely competitive. There are many low-cost copycats snapping at the heels of Sony. In the 2001/2002 financial year, electronics made a loss for Sony.

Sony has never completely lost it dynamism. In 1995 Sony entered the video game market with PlayStation 1. It is an understatement to say that it offered a good quality console at a low price. PlayStation 2 is not so much a games machine as a super set top box, which could easily upstage the PC as the centre of the digital convergence, so often talked about, and whose arrival has been so often heralded. PS 1 had a DVD drive. PS 2 was designed from the ground up to be a broadband device. Sony developed a cost leadership strategy in order to break into this market. This turned out to be successful and profitable. PlayStation 2 came out in late 2000 ahead of its competitors. Today more than one in five households in the US has a PlayStation. Worldwide Sony has sold 50 million PlayStation 2 consoles over the last three years, compared with the 10 million sales of Microsoft's XBOX. Although games account for only 12% of sales, they account for 53% of profits. However, Sony became dangerously dependent for its profits and growth on PlayStation 2. Now that the console is placed in so many households and it is likely that demand will ease, the key transition is for Sony to generate growth and profit from the games.

Sony is following up by creating a large number of games to play on the console. It is an example of the positive interaction between the hardware and the software. PlayStation 2 is linked with games designed for the console, but also with the first online games. With EverQuest, the online computer game, Sony just provides the playground and the players do the work. Sony provides 47 staffers to continually add items and quests to the game, and 128 'games masters' who function as customer service representatives, providing answers to questions whatever their global source (see the case study on video game wars in Chapter 6).

Recently, with the problems of the new communication/entertainment giants, the company looks to have returned to basics, switching the emphasis back to the hardware, but stressing interconnectivity in its gadgets rather than independence of stand-alone devices. After all it is the only company to produce three digital devices – the PC, the TV and the video game machine – which can be, and are now being, wired into networks, in an example of technical convergence. The new devices, such as the tiny digital music player, the flat-panel TV controlled by mobile phone, the flat wireless device for surfing the Web (called the Sony Airboard) and even humanoid robots that can walk, talk, sing and dance, are designed to share music, video and other data, over a wireless home network or through memory chips that slot into the products. Sony calls the network of personal devices its 'ubiquitous value network' and Guth (2002: 60) describes it as 'a kind of electronic Lego system for grown-ups'. The plan is still to wed the hardware with software, but the emphasis has been subtly shifted. This is still a goal which is largely unrealized and is not generating either profits or growth.

Sony has certainly returned to a display of glorious creativity, as revealed by the 'Sony Dream World' exposition at Yokohama in September 2002, the first of its kind. Revealed were a 'Vaio Content Egg', a plastic pod that will be able to miraculously serve up movies, music and games to Sony gadgets around the house and, even more impressively, gadgets which are designed to anticipate their owner's wants, a 'sensing computer', a hand-held device which learns its owner's habits, and the CoCoon, which stores TV programmes appealing to the owner and linked to a broadband Internet connection. This is really a return to basics, but in a different context. The key issue is how far it can turn this creativity into saleable products.

However, in early 2003 Sony suddenly imparted what come to be known as the 'Sony shock' to the Japanese capital market. In the three months to March 31, the company made a net loss of US$927, most of which was accounted for by electronic operations, a figure well above the expectations of most analysts. It further forecast a drop in profits for the year of 50%. Sony had dramatically cut its inventory as sales fell, ensuring an even bigger fall in production. This downturn came at the end of a steady fall in its profitability which had been going on since 1997, now down to a low 2.5% for the year up to March 31, 2003. The target is to restore the profit rate to 10%. To achieve this Sony is incurring significant restructuring costs and investing in production and research, notably in the areas of chips and networks. It has unveiled a three-year, US$10 billion streamlining and investment plan. Sony is attempting to create competitive productions bases in China and centralize its retail channels, particularly in the USA. By contrast Samsung, one of its main rivals in the area of electronic hardware, continues to turn in profits, with a profit ratio of about 15% in recent years, and now has a market capitalization greater than Sony's. Sony faces falling demand for its products and sliding global prices.

Case Study Questions

1. In what ways has Sony differed in its strategy making from the way in which strategy was usually developed in the old model in Japan?
2. How did Sony manage to sustain a continuing competitive advantage in the area of consumer electronic technology?
3. What prompted Sony's change of strategy which began in the late 1980s? What implications did this change have for the nature and structure of the company?
4. What are the differences between the industries based on electronic hardware and entertainment software in terms of the mix of strategic thinking, management and planning?
5. Has Sony in its present strategy found the appropriate balance between hardware and software?

Reading

Christensen, C. M., Johnson, M. W. and Rigby, D. K., 'Foundations for growth: how to identify and build disruptive new businesses', *Sloan Management Review*, 2002, **43**(3): 23–31.

Economist, The, 'The complete home entertainer', March 1, 2003: 62–4.

Guth, R., 'Inventive Sony gets back into gizmos', *The Australian Financial Review*, September 18, 2002: 60.

Ishibashi, K., 'Sony reports surprisingly weak profit, bearish outlook', *Dow Jones Newswire*, April 24, 2003.

Keighley, G., 'The sorcerer of Sony', *Business 2.0,* August 2002: 49–53.

Klamann, E., 'Sony stuns with weak profits', *Forbes* update, April 24, 2003.

Pesek, W., 'Where Sony goes, Japan may follow', *International Herald Tribune*, April 2003.

Porter, M., Takeuchi, H. and Sakakibara, M., *Can Japan Compete?* (Macmillan – now Palgrave Macmillan, Basingstoke: 2000).

Quinn, J. B., 'Vignette Three; Sony Corporation', in *Intelligent Enterprise* (The Free Press, New York: 1992: 283–92).

Schlender, B., 'Sony plays to win', *Fortune*, May 1, 2000: 55–63.

Relevant website

www.sony.com

This case study is also relevant to Chapters 7 and 8.

Case Study 2   A blockbuster drug – ImClone and insider trading

Drug development

The path for the development of any drug is a long and expensive one, fraught with the risk of failure. Table 18.7 indicates the difficult nature of the path in the USA for all drugs.

The failure rate in the later stages of development and therefore the risk-adjusted cost is likely to rise, at least for a period, because of the nature of the genomic revolution and the relatively immature technology being used to test new compounds. Because of the rapid pace of discovery, the average number of academic papers in the public literature per target has decreased from 100 in 1990 to 8 in 1999. In the words of Edmunds et al. (2001: 17): 'Most pharmaceutical companies are therefore pushing drugs through the R&D pipeline without fully understanding the physiological consequences of the interaction with their intended targets.'

In the development of a blockbuster drug there are at least four core competencies which are necessary for the eventual successful development of a new drug:

1. The ability to do the research which identifies a target or compound as potentially the basis for a new drug.

   In the case of ImClone the epidermal growth factor has become the focus of work being done simultaneously by a number of companies. For example, the Canadian biotech company YM has two of its drugs originating in Cuba, one of which is a therapeutic vaccine that stimulates the immune system into rejecting a protein called the epidermal growth factor.

Table 18.7 **The regulatory path**

	Preclinical	Phase I	Phase II	Phase III	Submission for drug approval	Phase IV
Typical no. of patents	NA	20–80	100–300	1,000–3,000	NA	Varies
Timing (years)	1.6	1.5	1.5	2.5	1.5	5.0
Cost per compound $ million	5.9	7.3	18.9	43.3	1.0	12.5
Attrition rate: no. of compounds tested for each drug approved	10	5	3.5	1.5	1.0	1.0
Total cost per drug $ million	59	30.5	66.2	65	1.0	12.5

The total cost comes to $240 million

There is even a difference between basic research and applied research. The former is usually done in a university since the return from such research is so uncertain and so long in coming. Applied research is a different matter. It is therefore not unusual for biotech companies to be located close to universities or research facilities.

2. The ability to see the commercial possibilities of such research and raise the money to finance it and guide the early stages of development. This is really the core competence of a venture capitalist. There are venture capitalists who specialize in this area.
3. The ability to organize and oversee the necessary clinical trials, interacting positively with the authorities responsible for approval. This is becoming a longer and longer process, absorbing an increasing amount of financial and human resources. Often this requires the services of a large pharmaceutical company.
4. The ability to market and distribute the new drug. This requires either a large sales force or contacts with health management and pharmaceutical benefit organizations. No biotech company has this kind of large infrastructure.

There is no reason why all four competencies should be possessed by one enterprise, although some of the heavy-weight pharmaceutical companies do possess all four. It is possible for the four each to be possessed by different specialist companies. For example, the basic research may be done within a university and the applied research by a biotech company often associated with the university, which specializes in bringing new drugs to the beginning of the trial process. Such a firm may even work on contract in order to reduce the extreme risk which confronts the developer of any drug, as the account below shows.

The history of a drug

The example used in this section is that of a cancer drug IMC-C225. It took 20 years to move this drug from an idea in the mind of its creator, John Mendelsohn, to a point at which its commercial development was about to begin. During this period there was a constant search for the financial resources needed to develop the drug. In 1992 ImClone Systems of New York, a biotech start-up company looking for a project with potential, took up C225 and proceeded to pour $100 million into its development.

The company appeared to be well rewarded since in February 2001 the FDA granted C225 fast-track approval. As a consequence, by the summer of 2001, ImClone, which had never made a cent of profit, was capitalized at US$3 billion. This reflects the fact that the drug could easily reach blockbuster status, at least US$1 billion in annual sales. The cost of treatment per patient could be as high as US$10,000–15,000.

Oncology is a notoriously difficult area to work in. Cancer treatment is just one of a large number of important areas of drug development. Cancer is in reality something like 400 separate diseases. Drugs are usually specialized in targeting a particular disease. C225 was initially targeted at colon cancer. Currently there are over 400 cancer drugs in the process of development, compared with 126 a decade ago.

C225 was conceived and developed by John Mendelsohn of the M. D. Anderson Cancer Centre in Houston. John Mendelsohn had no wish to set up his own business and develop the drug himself, a not unusual position for a researcher. Originally the University of California, San Diego owned the licence to the patent on C225, but it did nothing to develop the drug. In 1990 Hybritech, San Diego's first 'biotech start-up' company, licensed the drug. In 1992 the large pharmaceutical company Eli Lilly bought the start-up company, but C225 did not fit in with its plans for drug development. As a consequence, ImClone took over the licence.

ImClone, set up by two brothers Sam and Harlan Waksal as a vehicle for biotech development, had raised an initial $4 million in venture capital, a drop in the ocean in terms of drug development. The company raised more money by making an initial public offer in 1991. It was a company looking for a product. The brothers decided that C225 was the project that they were seeking.

They made a second significant decision, not to take the usual route for small biotech start-ups, to license their drugs to or partner with a much larger company which could underwrite the substantial development costs of the drug. This massively increases the potential return, if they were successful, but also increases the risk, if they were not. As a consequence, they came very near to bankruptcy early on in the process of development in 1994. The decision reflected their confidence in the drug and reluctance to give away the marketing rights and most of the profits. As an example of the usual practice, Amgen followed the usual route and sold most of the rights to its anaemia drug to Johnson & Johnson: in 2000 the sales of the drug came to US$2.7 billion.

In 1995, at the famous American Society of Clinical Oncology (ASCO) annual meeting, data was presented on the Phase I clinical trials which showed a tumour contraction for the two patients treated with the drug. This was the key turning point. The drug appeared to have a potential which was being realized. In 1998 one case dramatized the potential of the drug more than any other. Shannon Kellman, with an advanced colon cancer, saw an 80% shrinkage after treatment, which allowed the surgical removal of what remained of the cancer: she is still alive. Clinical tests on a greater scale in 1999 and 2000 resulted in further significant success. At the 2001 ASCO meeting, the drug came of age. Approval was given to build a greenfield plant to manufacture the drug, with further plans for a plant with three times the capacity. Pharmaceutical companies began to copy the drug.

At this stage the most likely outcome of the story seemed to be that a large pharmaceutical company with the resources to fully market and promote the drug would acquire ImClone.

Choosing and evaluating a portfolio of drug projects

The key question is, 'How do you make good decisions in a high-risk, technically complex business when the information you need to make those decisions comes largely from the project champions who are competing against one another for resources?' (Sharpe and Keelin, 1998: 45).

The following describes the process of deciding on a portfolio of drugs as developed by Smithkline Beecham. This is conducted at a given moment of time and applied to the existing pipeline of drugs. It raises a lot of strategic issues.

A number of other options were previously considered and tried by the company:

1. A directive top-down approach. The major problem of this approach is the lack of knowledge on the part of those at the top. They are not in a position to make the choice required.
2. (a) Long intensive interrogation sessions of project leaders followed by a decision on a show of hands by the same leaders.
   (b) A more sophisticated points scoring system based on the multiple attributes of a project – commercial potential, technical risk and investment requirements.
   (c) Various quantitative approaches – projections of peak year sales or five-year net present value.

These three variants have a number of common and specific problems:

- a lack of transparency
- the result often depends on the advocacy skills of project leaders
- a lack of a standard approach between the projects
- a spurious degree of accuracy implied by such quantitative approaches.

The decision-making process actually adopted by Smithkline Beecham has three stages.

Phase 1: Generating alternatives

The emphasis at this stage was on developing meaningful alternatives in a fully articulated form. It is critical to avoid premature evaluation which tends to kill creativity. The project teams were instructed to present four alternatives:

1. the present one
2. a 'buy-up' option (more expenditure)
3. a 'buy-down' option (less expenditure)
4. a minimal plan (the project dropped but as much value retained as possible).

Most drugs can be delivered in different ways and directed at different diseases. For example, a cancer drug, such as C225, could be delivered either intravenously or orally and used for different tumour types. The various combinations on product and market should be costed out. The cost tends to rise with the number of delivery mechanisms or target diseases but the return also rises. There may be all sorts of different attributes to be considered – timing of dosage, the nature and timing of clinical trials, and the phasing in of different markets for the drug.

A brainstorming session was likely to give a much better picture of where value was created by a new drug and a fuller picture which considered and took into account previously unconsidered options. The session could create benefits outside the area under consideration for later procedures.

A project review board consisting of managers from key functional areas and key product groups then examined every facet of the alternatives proposed. The alternatives were revised on the basis of their suggestions and presented once again, this time to even more senior mangers, those who would make any final investment decisions. The aim of the exercise was to ensure that every option was considered in detail.

Phase 2: Valuing alternatives

The company chose to use decision analysis for each alternative and, with the help of technical specialists, develop decision trees, making sure that all major uncertainties or risks attached to these alternatives were built into the analysis. There were a number of common requirements for all alternatives – the analysis must use the same type of information, always taken from reliable sources, clearly documented and subjected to intense peer review and comparison with external assessments where possible. Finally, the impact of each variable or attribute had to be identified, so that it was possible to discover the key value drivers. A neutral group carried out the evaluation which was then presented to a peer review for clarification, followed by another review by senior managers. At this stage any linkage effects across projects were also to be considered.

Phase 3: Creating a portfolio and allocating resources

The object was to create the highest value portfolio. The choice was made by a neutral analytic team, not the project managers. The exercise was highly complex, involving four variants for each of 20 different projects. The portfolio needed to be examined on a number of important strategic dimensions – stability under different scenarios, balance across therapeutic areas and stages in the development pipeline and feasibility of success, given Smithkline's technical and commercial resources.

The result of the portfolio choice in this case was a significant departure from the status quo, with only four projects maintaining their existing funding. Six were to be cut back and ten to receive increased funding. The increase in value of the portfolio was 30%, without any new investment, achieved simply by a reallocation of existing resources. More significantly the exercise was relevant to the investment strategy. The marginal return on additional investment had tripled from 5:1 to 15:1. This was seen as justifying an increase in development spending of as much as 50%. Clearly the company had been underinvesting in research and development.

The new process was introduced gradually, being pilot tested twice. The main advantages of the system were to introduce transparency and a reliance on objective data where possible. Everyone in the key areas was involved and therefore empowered by the process. The gains made were obvious.

The exercise can be massively broadened to include all possibilities. There are alternatives to developing drugs yourself. An enterprise can license a drug developed by another enterprise, usually one which does not have the resources to develop and sell the drug itself, possibly one which specializes in the early stages of drug development. There is the choice of the stage in drug development at which the licensee company becomes involved. There has been a dramatic increase in the number of strategic alliances, often between much larger pharmaceutical and small biotechnology companies, made to gain access to expertise in the new techniques of combinatorial chemistry and mass-throughput screening. The pharmaceutical companies offer the resource of their large libraries of chemical compounds built up over many years of research. The result has been an enormous increase in the productivity of the libraries and the number of 'hits', that is, the identification of possible compounds which could be the base for a new drug.

Some pharmaceutical companies take the approach of strategic alliance and licensing. Eli Lilly formed an alliance with Sphinx Pharmaceutical, one of the early biotechnology ventures that focused on combinatorial chemistry and high-throughput screening. The 1991 alliance was translated into an acquisition in 1994. A good example of reliance on licensing is Bristol-Myers Squibb, which specializes in cancer drugs and derives 95% of its oncology revenues from in-licensed products. All its oncology products in late-stage development are licensed. Licensing is becoming more popular, with the number of competitors for any given licence rising. As a result the price charged by licensors is going up, as is the proportion of income of pharmaceutical companies accounted for by licensing – 14 of the 55 semi-blockbuster drugs (those with sales over $500 million) marketed in 1998 by the 10 largest pharmaceutical companies were licensed from external sources, most often after the proof-of-concept stage.

One enterprise can buy another enterprise and its drug portfolio, hopefully one which could fill the gaps in its own pipeline of drugs. This is a more expensive proposition. It also poses all sorts of integration hazards, especially on the side of R&D. There may be different degrees of risk tolerance, different scientific 'tastes' reflected in different portfolio choices, and different approaches to governance and decision making. It is hard to centralize R&D, particularly when the company might have 100 programmes and 2,000 scientists. In this area it is better to try to replicate the role of the small but highly entrepreneurial biotechnology company. Purchase might be postponed to later phases of development, but the price clearly rises the closer the drug is to approval. It is necessary to centralize development, since there may be as many as 500 clinical trials happening at a given time.

Such strategies of licensing and purchase make more complicated the kind of exercise described above.

The exercise has to be a process repeated at frequent intervals. There are particular crisis points when a change of policy must occur. In theory, properly carried out, the approach would avoid most such crises but not all. A good example of such a moment for revaluation would be the ending of patent protection for a major drug. On August 3, 2001 the patent on Prozac expired. This drug had 40 million users. It accounted for one-quarter of Eli Lilly's US$10 billion plus sales and one-third of its US$3 billion profit. What should it do?

The response of the new CEO, Sidney Tawel, was to pump up the level of R&D expenditure to more than US$2.2 billion. In the year 2000 alone, 700 scientists were added to the team, resulting in a full complement of 6,900. The aim was to develop drugs generating a minimum of $500 million in annual sales. Over a period of eight years Eli Lilly was aiming to roll out 15 potential mega-sellers, five already launched over the last five years, 10 over the next three. The CEO took the position that organic growth was much superior to acquisition. He preferred to go it alone and spurned acquisitions. These were regarded as an obstacle to research efforts since they led to an emphasis on cost cutting and culture clashes between the merged entities. He believed that there was no correlation between the size of the research effort and the success in innovation.

The players

Super heavyweights
(ethical drug revenue of over $20 billion)
Pfizer   (merged with Warner-Lambert in 2000, absorbed Pharmacia in 2002)
GlaxoSmithKline

Heavyweights ($10–20 billion)

Merck	AstraZeneca	Bristol-Myers Squibb
Novartis	Aventis	Johnson & Johnson

Middleweights ($7–10 billion)

American Home Products	Roche
Eli Lilly	Abbott Laboratories
Bayer	Schering-Plough

There are some clear advantages to size, but also disadvantages. The biggest companies tend to be the ones which back the most promising products, enter key markets most expeditiously and deploy large sales forces to launch and market products most effectively. Doing these things makes you a giant, as much as being a giant allows you to do these things. The strategy of most companies is to strive to become the next giant in the industry, so that it has the edge in launching new blockbuster drugs, can increase the number of bets a company can place on new technologies, can complete clinical trials as quickly as possible and can increase its desirability as a licensing partner.

For shareholders there seems little long-term relationship between size and the return they receive. The development of blockbuster drugs and a strong presence in the American market seem far more important than size. In the past mergers have often been motivated by a fear of weak earnings.

In the future size is likely to grow in significance. An average drug company is likely to spend something like 25% of its R&D budget on new discoveries. A conservative firm might spend $100 million a year, a more aggressive firm as much as $300 million. This implies a total R&D ratio to sales of between one-third and three-quarters, according to the size of the company. This puts enormous pressure on the smaller firms if they wish to gain access to winning drugs. The industry is receiving more regulatory scrutiny than ever, with more clinical trials required on many more patients. The large companies can speed up the process of moving through the trials to approval in a way in which the smaller companies cannot.

Further choices

ImClone chose not to go down the path of purchase. An alternative was that ImClone would sign an agreement with a large pharmaceutical company to distribute the drug. ImClone did the latter. It entered into an alliance with Bristol-Myers Squibb for the development and promotion of Erbitux (which is what IMC-225 is now called) in the USA, Canada and Japan. This alliance allowed ImClone to leverage Bristol-Myers Squibb's highly respected oncology sales force, providing a lever to expedite Erbitux's inclusion in formularies and distribution by wholesalers. The aim was to accelerate the sales of Erbitux while freeing resources to allow ImClone to develop other promising oncology drugs. The agreement was potentially worth as much as $2 billion to ImClone. There was a further agreement with Merck which applied to the area outside North America, particularly Europe. Under these agreements, ImClone stands to receive large sums of money, as well as an equity investment.

The problem is that both agreements are subject to the drug receiving the relevant FDA (Food and Drugs Administration) approvals. The clinical tests late in 2001 proved to be ambiguous in their results. There was a 123-patient trial against head and neck cancer, funded by the National Cancer Institute. It found that Erbitux, combined with chemotherapy, shrank the tumour in 23% of the patients, compared with only 9% for chemotherapy alone. However, the increase in life expectancy was only a little better, 1.19 months as against 0.96. The FDA tended to attach more importance to the latter than the former. The FDA interpreted this a negative result and responded to the application with 'refuse to file'. It did not refuse the drug approval, but rather refused to consider the application on the ground that the data were incomplete and the trial flawed as a real test. By contrast ASCO scientists took a much more positive line in interpreting the results. One problem is that there is no magic bullet, no cure, only a treatment which offers improvement.

The stock market interpreted the outcome badly, dropping the share price dramatically, as much as 80%, from a peak of $75 in 2001 to $7.10 in 2002, and forcing the resignation of Sam Waksal as CEO, although his replacement is his brother.

The situation has been made even more complicated by allegations of insider trading at the company. The FDA's decision in December 2001 not even to review the evidence on ImClone's cancer drug was a nasty surprise for most investors. They saw much of their share value disappear in a short period of time. Was the decision also a surprise for the senior executives of the company?

There is an allegation that members of the family and friends sold off millions of dollars worth of stock in the weeks leading up to the announcement. Two days before the public announcement on December 28, 2001, Sam Waksal is said to have tried twice and failed to sell shares, on which, as it turns out, there was a con-straint. Without doubt other family members sold $100 million worth of stock. Martha Stewart (TV personality and lifestyle adviser), a family friend, sold her stock the day before the announcement. There is a shareholders lawsuit against ImClone on the grounds of a failure to warn. In this situation issues of transparency in the FDA process of approval and equal access to information for managers and shareholders have become serious. On June 12 Sam Waksal was arrested on insider trading charges.

All of this has serious consequences for Bristol-Myers Squibb, which has based all its projections of revenue and profit on the success of Erbitux, and also for share prices in the areas of pharmaceutical companies and biotechnology companies.

The competition

There has been a race to exploit the new cell growth target. Being first to get approval and arrive on the market is an enormous advantage in the quest for the next blockbuster drug. Because of the delay caused by the FDA rejection ImClone has fallen behind AstraZeneca. AstraZeneca's application for Iressa was accepted by the FDA on the same day that ImClone's was rejected. This guaranteed Iressa a review within six months. Iressa had the pole position. However, AstraZeneca was at that time not ready to present the results of late-stage trials, which may cause some concern about the strength of its data. Both companies presented the results of mid-stage trials, ImClone's conducted on its behalf by Merck.

ImClone's strategy

ImClone's strategy is unusual. In its own words, its 'goal is to become a fully-integrated biopharmaceutical company that has the capability and resources to take its novel pipeline compounds and develop them from the research and development stage through to manufacture, marketing and sales.' It has research, clinical, development and manufacturing departments, and a regulatory affairs and quality assurance group. However, it has showed itself

Table 18.8 **The race for a cancer treatment**

Company	AstraZeneca	ImClone
Drug	Iressa (pill)	Erbitux (intravenous injection)
Target	Growth signals inside the cancer cell	Growth-signal receptor on surface of cancer cell
Disease	Lung cancer. Also being tested against breast, colon, gastric and prostate cancer	Colon cancer. Also being tested against head and neck, pancreatic and breast cancer
Status	FDA application filed in December 2001: drug approved in May 2003	FDA application rejected in December 2001; refiled by year end

willing to use the marketing and sales platform of a large partner pharmaceutical company, in the case of Erbitux, Bristol-Meyers Squibb. It is trying to develop the first three competencies on the back of just one drug.

It is difficult for a small biotechnology company, growing quickly on the strength of one or two potentially blockbusting drugs, to survive a major setback. ImClone is dangerously exposed to just one product, Erbitux. Its early work was on immunology-based diagnostics and on infectious disease vaccines. It has one vaccine at Phase III trials (BEC2 or Mitumomab) and another drug at Phase I (IMC-1C11). Neither appears to have the blockbuster potential of Erbitux. The company is still making a significant loss.

Any further setback to the development of Erbitux could prove terminal, since it could deny financial resources to the company. The irony is that the fate of Waksal and ImClone have diverged widely since December 2001. Waksal pleaded guilty to insider trading, was sentenced to seven years in prison and ordered to pay US$4.3 million in fines and restitution. Data finally was released which showed that Erbitux really does shrink tumours in patients. The share price of ImClone, which peaked at $75 in late 2001 but reached a low of $7 after the scandal became public in 2002, is now back at $36.30. Erbitux may still turn out to be a blockbuster.

Case Study Questions

1. What resources or capabilities has Imclone and what has been the potential to make these strategic, in other words to translate them into core competencies?

2. What has been the strategy of Imclone? How far has ImClone the core competencies which would justify the strategy it has chosen?

3. Assess the relative risks and returns which are associated with the strategy adopted by ImClone on the development of the drug Erbitux.

4. What strategy should ImClone adopt in order to rescue itself from its present troubles?

5. How important is the FDA, the US regulatory agency, in shaping strategy in the pharmaceutical industry?

Reading

Agarwal, S., Desai, S., Holcomb, M. M. and Oberoi, A., 'Unlocking the value in the Big Pharma', *The McKinsey Quarterly*, 2001, (2): 65–73.

Arndt, M., 'Life after Prozac', *Business Week*, July 23, 2001: 53–4.

Arnst, C., 'The birth of a cancer drug', *Business Week*, July 30, 2001: 47–53.

Arnst, C., 'Fighting cancer ... and each other', *Business Week*, May 27, 2002: 39.

Arnst, C., 'Patience, biotech investors, patience', *Business Week*, June 10, 2002: 44.

Barrett, A. and Arndt, M., 'No quick cure', *Business Week*, May 6, 2002: 36–9.

Clifford, L., 'Tyrannosaurus Rex', *Fortune*, October 30, 2000: 94–101.

Dyer, G., 'YM Bio springs a Cuban surprise', *Financial Times*, June 14, 2002: 25.

Economist, The, 'The value of trust', June 8, 2002: 61–3, Special Report on Wall Street.

Economist, The, 'Mercky prospects', July 13, 2002: 51–2.

Edmunds, R. C., Ma, P. C. and Tanis, C. P., 'Splicing a cost squeeze into the genomic revolution', *The McKinsey Quarterly*, 2001, (2): 15–19.

Griffith, V., 'ImClone founder Waksal jailed and fined for fraud', *Financial Times*, June 11, 2003: 21.

Herper, M., 'ImClone CEO leaves, problems remain', Forbes' home page.

Hitt, M. A., Ireland, R. D. and Hoskisson, R. E., *Strategic Management and Globalisation*, 2nd edn, 1997: 307–24.

Sharpe, P. and Keelin, T., 'How Smithkline Beecham make better resource-allocation decisions', *Harvard Business Review*, **76**(2): 45–53, March/April 1998.

Thomke, S. and Kuemmerle, W., 'Asset accumulation, interdependence and technological change: evidence from pharmaceutical drug discovery', *Strategic Management Journal*, 2002, **23**: 619–35.

Relevant website

www.imclone.com

Key strategic lessons

- Strategy making should be a fully integrated process, with formulation, implementation and monitoring overlapping to a significant degree. These strategic activities are part of a single process in which each emphasizes a different aspect of strategy making. They often occur simultaneously and are performed by the same people.

- Monitoring is a continuous process that should be

Key strategic lessons cont'd

built into every part of the strategy-making process and generates new information which is part of a learning process.

• The general performance of the enterprise reflects how well its strategy is formulated and implemented. Monitoring consists of the selection of key performance indicators, the establishment of appropriate control systems and the appraisal of overall performance in terms of aggregate results and specific targets and should result in the continuous adjustment of the existing strategy to take account of the changing environment.

• The quality of monitoring depends on the measurement of performance and can be complex because of multiple targets. The balanced scorecard is a good method of addressing that complexity and consists of the clear specification of strategic goals, measures of goal achievement and initiatives to attain those goals.

• The standard balanced scorecard includes financial performance indicators, measures of customer satisfaction, operational benchmarks for key value-adding activities and rates of learning and innovation, but can be adapted to the circumstances of particular industries.

• Key performance indicators are used as suitable benchmarks through which it is possible to trace the degree of success in achieving strategy targets. These benchmarks can be general, as in the internationally accepted ISO standards or specific to the organization and its strategy, when they are described as key performance indicators.

• There is often excessive focus on short-term profit indicators and owners as the only stakeholder group to be given attention. Any indicator needs a comparative context, whether historical or competitive, and there are grave dangers in the manipulation of financial indicators by managers in order to deceive others or themselves.

• There are five groups of indicators, those relating to overall profitability of the enterprise, its liquidity and debt position, time activity ratios relating to the efficient use of assets and the return to shareholders.

• In each period of time an enterprise creates economic value which cumulatively makes up the market value added of the enterprise. This value added is available to be distributed amongst its various stakeholder groups.

• Corporate social responsibility involves keeping all the stakeholders happy, in a way which might amount to a quadruple or quintuple bottom line.

• The governance of an organization should reflect the existence of all stakeholder groups, for whom involvement equals empowerment and to whom there must be appropriate communication conduits from the strategists of the enterprise. Different stakeholder groups are likely to be treated differently, according to their importance at different points in the life cycle of the enterprise

• Monitoring should be indicative of the emergent nature of strategy, flexible, with continuous adjustment of existing strategy, proactive and 'leadership-driven' at key critical times.

Applying the lessons

1 Define the following terms: monitoring, measuring, benchmarking, a strategic canvas, a balanced scorecard, a strategic management system, lagging indicators, leading indicators, key performance indicators, leverage or gearing, market value added and corporate social responsibility.

2 What would a complete balanced scorecard look like? Apply the balanced scorecard approach to any enterprise which is the subject of a case study in this book and indicate what a balanced score card evaluation would look like.

3 Using Table 18.6, choose an organization of which

you have good knowledge and indicate where on the diagram each of its stakeholder groups is to be found.

4 Consider the three scenarios set out below and choose what you think is a suitable response.

a. You are a university lecturer responsible for an important subject in a masters course which all students must pass. You have been receiving gifts, which have been rising in value, from students enrolled in the course who come from countries in which gift giving is a normal part of social interaction. You suspect that the gift giving is rather more than just gift giving, but you do not wish to upset the group of students. What should you do?

• Accept the gift and continue to teach and assess the subject as normally
• Accept the gift and ask that the work of the student be double marked
• Refuse the gift, explaining to the student that the gift would compromise your independence
• Ask the head of the department to issue a ruling that staff are not to accept gifts from students.

b. You are a senior manager of a large enterprise and frequently have to entertain visiting customers. You tend to use the same restaurant and are well known there. You have visited the restaurant for private dinners and noticed a tendency for the bill to omit certain items and undercharge for others. The manager of the restaurant has discovered that you intend to have a large party to celebrate your son's 18th birthday. He has offered you a price which appears to be well below cost. What do you do?

• Refuse the offer but continue using the restaurant
• Point out the problem to the manager and ask for a new quote which better reflects the cost
• Refuse the offer and quietly move your entertaining elsewhere
• Resolve in future not to mix your private life with your working life.

c. You are friendly with a director of a biotechnology company. Inadvertently you learn from him that there is to be announcement in two days that the company has failed to receive approval for a key drug. You are close to retirement and have your own superannuation fund, a significant part of which is invested in the stock of this company. He is unaware of this. You have already been considering selling. What do you do?

• Go ahead and sell on the basis that this is probably what you would have done
• Put the decision of whether to buy or sell to someone who is unaware of the dilemma and act on their advice
• Retain the stock and hope for the best
• Retain the stock and talk to the director, warning him of the dangers of divulging confidential information and appearing to implicate others in insider trading.

5 Select key performance indicators which are specific to five different industries and show why these indicators differ.

6 Choose an organization and show how the performance indicators relevant to different stakeholder groups might themselves differ.

Strategic project

Take your own organization, select a well-known organization or choose the university in which you are pursuing your studies or, if you have the time, consider each of these organizations in turn.

Apply the strategic canvas method to show:

1 What attributes the organization presently focuses on.

2 How it is differentiated from its main competitor.

Do both of these visually. Consider whether the organization is successfully competing on the basis of a significant competitive advantage.

Invent a tag which summarizes the competitive advantage and could be used in a marketing campaign.

Exploring further

Not many textbooks include a chapter reserved for monitoring or even for a treatment on how to assess strategic performance. Yet strategy making is pointless without monitoring. An exception is Viljoen and Dann, 2000, particularly Chapter 14. A general assessment of the effectiveness of strategy is Moncrieff, 1999: 273–6. Most texts include sections on control systems, which are based on the premise that performance is being monitored.

Two interesting pieces on how the question can be approached are Miller and Cardinal, 1994: 1649–65 and Rogers et al., 1999: 567–77.

There is a considerable literature on the practice of benchmarking. See Watson, 1993, or Camp, 1989. Short and directly relevant to strategy is Bresada, 1992: 30–8. Another interesting comment is Pryor, 1989: 28–32.

The classic text on the balanced scorecard method is Kaplan and Norton, 1996a, or the shorter versions, 1992: 71–9; 1993: 134–47; and 1996b: 75–85. A comment on this approach is Olson and Slater, 2002: 11–16. One conclusion of comments on the balanced scorecard is that it is only as effective as the key success factors or indicators included.

All texts deal with the financial indicators used as part of the financial control system. The same table is present in just about every textbook.

Ethical problems are always important in strategy, but have become more obviously important in recent times. A thorough treatment is Badaracco, 1997. Attempts to conceptualize the problem of corporate social responsibility are to be found in Martin, 2002: 69–75, or Driscoll and Hoffman, 1999: 179–89. An excellent treatment of the relationship between strategy towards different stakeholder groups and stages in the life cycle of an organization is to be found in Jawahar and McLaughlin, 2001: 397–414.

For a position strongly against the notion of corporate social responsibility to the triple bottom line, see Friedman, 1970, or at greater length, Friedman, 1971. Friedman's arguments need to be controverted in order to justify the kind of analysis in this book.

Part V

Strategic Analysis and Audit

Riding the Internet wave: Amazon.com

Finance, a venue for perfect competition: the Deutsche Bank

Haier: pioneering the Chinese export brand

The Hewlett Packard/Compaq merger

Lloyd's of London and 'long-tailed' risk

The Mt Buller winter resort and global warming

Euro Disney and a tale of three cultures

The strategic alliance between Renault and Nissan

Samsung Electronics: a dramatic turnaround

Going global: Singapore Telecommunications (SingTel)

Starbucks: the third place

Sir Richard Branson and many wise virgins

Vivendi Universal: divesting to survive

Wal-Mart: the cost-reducing machine

Forecasting the price of oil

Epilogue: reviewing the nature of strategy

Task	Parts	Chapters
Starting right	**Part I** Introducing Strategic Management	**WHY?** Prologue **WHO?** 1 Introducing strategy and strategy making **WHAT?** 2 Thinking and acting strategically **HOW?** 3 Adopting a global perspective **WHEN?** 4 Reading an uncertain future
Acquiring conceptual tools for the job	**Part II** Strategic Environments and Competitive Advantage	5 Identifying opportunity and risk General 6 Reading the competitive environment Immediate **ENVIRONMENTS** Internal 7 Analysing resources, capabilities and core competencies **GENERIC STRATEGIES** 9 Reducing costs 8 Creating and maintaining competitive advantage 10 Differentiating the product
Resolving particular strategic problems	**Part III** Strategic Dilemmas	**FIVE DILEMMAS** 11 Determining the size of an enterprise 12 Integrating the strategists 13 When to compete and when to cooperate 14 Managing risk 15 Participating in the global economy
The strategy emerges	**Part IV** Bringing it all Together	16 Formulating strategy 17 Implementing strategy → **CONTINUOUS ITERATION** ← 18 Monitoring strategic performance
Analysing strategy making	**Part V** Strategic Analysis and Audit	Case studies Epilogue

In Part V there are 15 long case studies of roughly equal length. They are an integral part of the book, written to reinforce the message of the main text. It is necessary to read at least some of the case studies in order to get a feel for the way in which strategy should be evaluated and therefore how it should be made. They should not be ignored as a disposable add-on.

The aim of each of these case studies is to develop analytical ability in the area of strategy and enable the student to make a full strategic audit of the company. The information provided is intentionally selective and by no means comprehensive. Much work is left for the student to undertake. In order to encourage a systematic approach, the cases have appropriate questions asked throughout the text. The case study is rounded off by a project.

A summary of the different topics which these case studies support and their industry sectors and geographical regions is provided in the Prologue. Additional long case studies are also available on the website accompanying this text.

The Epilogue reviews the nature of strategy making and revisits one last time the definition of strategy.

Riding the Internet wave: Amazon.com

Everything, everywhere ...

Amazon.com slogan

I've been using a computer for eight or ten years now and I still really pay for only three things on the Internet: the Wall Street Journal, *online bridge, and books from Amazon.com. That they are one of only three companies online that have gotten money out of my pocket tells me they are doing something right.*

WARREN BUFFET

Background

Two topics are favourites for analysis – the e-commerce revolution and the development of Amazon.com. The latter has had more case studies written about it than almost any other company. However, despite all the analysis, both topics have many puzzling aspects and unanswered questions.

There has been a lot of talk about the potential for e-commerce at the retail level and its capacity to revolutionize the nature of business and the way it is conducted. In developed economies the spread of the PC was dramatic. There has also been a rapid uptake of the Internet and spread of email as a form of communication. Websites are just about compulsory for all businesses which aspire to operate in the marketplace. There are three main functions of such websites:

- advertising
- providing information
- providing a mechanism for selling.

Most websites are there to promote or advertise the enterprise. In a number of cases, in order to achieve this they have become a major source of information about the product or service on offer.

Has the speed of uptake of e-commerce been much slower than originally envisaged? If so, why is this?

E-commerce at the wholesale or B2B level is catching on fast. Many of the preconditions for e-commerce at the retail level also exist, yet there has been little real success, outside a few areas, such as pornography, gambling, share broking and airline booking. The number of successful companies is limited – eBay has developed a successful model for the conduct of online auctions. The

dot-com collapse has shown the brittleness of the dream for most others, some of whom were dreamers with ideas that could never succeed or who lacked an ability to make the idea work, some of whom were opportunists jumping on the bandwagon and making a profit from the gullible. Only those with something of real value to the consumer and a well-run enterprise have survived the crash. This area illustrates the tendency to exaggerate the forces of change, for markets to overshoot and most strategists to fail to understand the steady momentum and systematic nature of the application of new technical knowledge. There are opportunities but they require systematic application, patience and, most of all, modest claims.

Why should the development of B2B be so much faster than B2C?

At the forefront of the dream has been Amazon.com, which has revolutionized the selling of books, but without actually making a profit until recently.

Amazon has spent many years incurring large costs without making a profit. How can a company survive so long without making a profit?

Amazon.com raises a whole series of questions which have strategic implications and require an analytical treatment. The first relates to its use of the Internet and B2C selling methods. How successful is this likely to be? What are the future rewards likely to be which will justify the large costs and the long delay in profit making? Just how far ahead should a company and its financiers look?

In most respects Amazon.com is a great success. It had a total revenue of over US$3 billion in 2001 and an annual revenue of $4 billion by mid-2003. These revenues are still growing by more than 20% a year. The total number of active customers has risen steadily: 14.1 million in 1999, 19.8 in 2000, 24.7 in 2001 and 27.3 million in 2002. Its customer base is very large indeed. It nearly doubled its international sales in 2002, but this arm of its business is still losing money.

Why might the growth of sales be more important than the growth of profits? Is the obsession with sales growth and customer numbers a trap?

Up until 2002, Amazon.com losses had been truly prodigious, US$1.4 billion in 2002 alone, and a debt crisis always a possibility. In December 2001, for the first time it reported an honest-to-GAAP quarterly profit of US$5 million, but one which reflected favourable exchange rate movements. Successive quarters of small but real operating profit and positive cash flow from operations have followed. Perhaps Amazon has really turned the corner. It is certainly generating significant cash, about $135 million in 2002, rising to an estimated $300 million in 2003. It has started to pay off a significant amount of its debt. Operating profit is expected to be $200 million in 2003. This has made a debt crisis much less likely to occur. On some accounts the upside for profit is very high, with a doubling in revenues and a profit of $800 million expected by the year 2007.

Under what conditions might there be a debt crisis? Just how large would you anticipate the profit to be in the future? What are the main factors which will determine the level of profit?

Jeff Bezos, the dynamic CEO of Amazon.com, has developed the Amazon website in a way which creates an interactivity which has changed the selling of books for good. He has also sought to use the brand name, extending sales into areas beyond books to videos, CDs, toys, electrical goods, tools and kitchen utensils. In theory the same methods could be applied to a whole host of other retail products.

How far can the online purchase of books change the usual mode of distribution in the industry? How far is the model transferable to other products?

The history of Amazon.com

Jeff Bezos was a computer science and electrical engineering graduate who, at the age of 28, became the youngest vice-president in the history of D. E. Shaw, a Wall Street-based investment bank. Prior to that, he had turned down job offers from Bell Labs and Intel in order to take up a position at a start-up company run by two Columbia University professors which built a new telecommunications network for Wall Street firms, and then went on to sell software to pension fund clients for Bankers Trust. He stayed five years working for the D. E. Shaw hedge fund.

How was his background linked to the success of Amazon.com?

He read a prediction about the incredible rise in the Internet and the implications in terms of selling in a new way. After careful research into 20 possible products for sale on the Internet, he chose books as the best candidate for immediate sale for two reasons. First, the largest physical bookstore in the world held only 175,000 books, as compared with the 1.5 million English-language books actually in print and the 3 million books in all languages worldwide, and second, there was no dominant player in the industry. After all, there were 4,200 publishers in the USA alone. The two largest booksellers in the USA, Barnes & Noble and Borders, accounted for only 12% of total sales.

Why are books a good candidate for e-commerce?

When Bezos launched his new venture in Seattle, in July 1995, the venue was carefully thought out. It had a large pool of software engineers and was less than 400 miles from Roseburg, Oregon, the home of the largest book distribution warehouse in the country. The former was very helpful, but the latter turned out to be irrelevant.

Given the 'virtual' nature of the new bookshop, does the venue matter? If so, why?

The original business model saw no need for retail outlets or warehouses. Significant costs could be saved by avoiding investment in such facilities. Within a year, sales were at a level comparable to a large Barnes & Noble superstore. However, the business model had to be amended. Warehouses were needed and had to be added to the facilities of the company. There were three main reasons for this:

- to ensure a good experience for the customer
- to be able to access books at a good price
- to gain as much control over costs as possible.

Amazon had found that it had to build its own warehouses to ensure it could meet its delivery targets. The rapid pick-up in sales meant that the company had to move warehouse several times in its first year of operation. The decision to build Amazon's own warehouses was an expensive one, since each of the six currently used cost about $50 million to construct and are also expensive to run. An issue of $2 billion worth of bonds helped to finance the extension of the business model.

Is part of the reason for the success of Bezos linked to a flexibility of approach? How far was the decision to use its own warehouses a concession to the limitations of the 'virtual' model? How has Amazon managed to finance its own development?

The industry

The traditional structure of the industry is illustrated in Figure C.1. The place of each of the main players is described below.

Publishers
- Publishers sell books on a consignment basis, that is, they bear all the risk and the retailers none. They tend to print far more copies than they can sell, so that about 25% of all books distributed to wholesalers are returned and remaindered or pulped. There are therefore hidden costs in the system which could be avoided.

Why should the publishers bear all the risk?

- The profit comes from only about 10% of book titles. Some 90% of publishers are barely making money. Although there is some consolidation in the industry, with the 20 largest publishers accounting for 60% of retail sales, the industry is still a highly fragmented one.

How far is the problem a matter of anticipating tastes and forecasting creative success?

The finance of the production and sale of a book are relevant. Table C.1 shows the profit margin for a typical book. The profit margin is low and therefore any reduction in costs can have a significant impact.

Wholesalers
- Effective wholesaling depends on speed which itself reflects the range of stocks. Electronic ordering has made rapid response and dispatch much more feasible. Profit margins are even lower than for publishers, at 1.5%. This is by no means a high-margin industry. One indication of Amazon's efficiency is that in the fourth quarter of the 2002/03 year, its operating profit margin was 5%, which approaches even Wal-Mart's margin of 6%.

Why are the profit margins in retailing so low?

- The wholesale side is more concentrated, with Ingram Book Co accounting for as much as 50% of the

Table C.1 **Profit margin for a 'typical book'**

Book list price		US$19.95	
Revenue to publisher (paid by wholesaler or bookstore)	10.37		48% discount off suggested price
Manufacturing price		2.0	Printing, binding, jacket design, composition, typesetting, paper, ink
Publisher overhead		3.0	Marketing, fulfillment
Returns and allowances		3.0	
Author's royalties		2.0	
Total publishing costs		**10.0**	
Publisher's operating profit	0.37		A margin of 3.7%

sales. However, only about 30% of all book sales go through wholesalers. There is also a growing tendency for retailers to deal directly with publishers and bypass wholesalers.

Are wholesalers the most vulnerable players in the industry and therefore the profit margins so low because of the existence of alternative mechanisms for sale?

Retailers
- In 1994, 35–40% of book sales were accounted for by bookstore chains, independents and general retailers, but during the 1990s the relative proportions within this group changed dramatically. The superstores, notably Barnes & Noble and Borders, have expanded and the independents have closed.

Why should the chains be winning in the competition with independents?

Institutions and libraries
- These provide a stable and important share of demand, particularly for books with a limited market. Textbooks for schools and universities offer the highest profit margins of all sales. The market is a relatively stable one, although the degree of competition can be intense.

Why might it be true that this market segment is the one most easily predictable?

Mail order and book clubs
- Mail order sales are declining but book club sales are increasing.

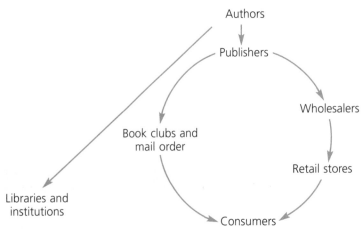

Figure C.1 **The existing structure of the industry**

Competition

There are alternative pathways for the sale of books:

- The superstores are tending to exclude wholesalers, by going straight to the publishers
- Virtual bookstores offer the possibility of the retail layer disappearing
- Electronic book publishing and online distribution by computer-literate authors threatens even the publishers and the virtual bookstores.

How far is it possible for various levels in the chain of sales to be bypassed? What are the attributes of the different pathways for the final purchaser?

Amazon.com claims that it provides four of the most desired attributes of book buying:

- low price
- convenience of purchase
- a wide selection
- rapid and reliable service, although service may be significantly slower than for a normal retail outlet.

Are there other attributes which are important?

- Amazon also provides fun and a wealth of information relating to the specific books and the general area of interest. It supplements the basic information on price and publication with reviews of the book and comments from other readers. It even provides a list of books which those who read the relevant book have also bought.
- What it does not provide is the feel of the book and the opportunity to browse and skim a book.
- It also denies the purchaser the glories of serendipity.

Are these attributes important to a significant number of purchasers?

Amazon.com has a potential cost advantage over other distributors in that it turns over the inventory much faster than a normal bookstore. Its inventory currently turns over every 18 days, which is equivalent to 20 times each year. Virtually every other retailer is below 15. The six warehouses run by Amazon are completely computerized and highly efficient. Their efficiency is now as good as the processing of orders. They have tripled their volume of throughput since 1999.

How far is Amazon's model dependant upon a cost leadership strategy?

Amazon has succeeded in reducing its costs significantly in a number of different areas:

- Since 2000, the cost of operating the warehouses has come down from 20% to less than 10% of revenue.

- Amazon has also managed to reduce its capital expenditure to 1 cent in the dollar from 10 cents in 1999. It does not have to carry all the cost of property, often in prime locations, which book retailers have to carry.
- Marketing was also down from 12.5% in 1999 to 4% in 2002. The brand name is reaching the point at which it sells itself.

Are there other areas of cost saving which are important? How far should cost leadership be accompanied by price leadership?

Using the brand

The book trade as a whole is not expanding very fast – it is old economy. There is a limit to which the Amazon brand name can be used to sell books. Even today in the USA only 7% of book sales occur online. There is a limit to the number of people who prefer to purchase online rather than immediately, with the opportunity to browse lost. Even an extension of the market abroad must reach a market saturation point quite quickly.

What is likely to be the income or the price elasticity of demand for books?

However, most people are familiar with the name of Amazon. The company can use its brand name to sell other products. This is very helpful since it will allow a reduction in costs. Amazon has a high proportion of fixed costs, such as expenditure on:

- innovation
- the technology for setting up and improving its online systems
- the technology for organizing its customer service operations and customer base
- building its warehouses and distribution service
- marketing over a much larger number of products than it does currently.

Why are fixed costs important? Do the proportions of fixed and variable costs differ from more traditional systems of sale? How can Amazon achieve a reduction in fixed costs per unit of sale?

The mechanisms for reducing such costs are:

- *By selling as many products as possible*
There are obvious areas for Amazon to expand into, such as CDs, DVDs or videos. Other areas were not so obvious, such as consumer electronics, tools and kitchen utensils, and sales in these areas by Amazon are still losing money. However, the general principles are the same.

What sorts of product are suitable for sale by Amazon?

● *By expanding its customer base as much as possible*
This can be done partly by selling a wider range of products, but mainly by extending the market abroad. There is not necessarily an enormous overlap between those buying the different products which Amazon sells but there is enough to give it an immediate entry into new markets. Within the American market it is possible to extend the popularity of e-commerce further, by meeting the common reservations expressed about such sales.

● *By selling in as many countries as possible*
Initially these are developed countries, at least those countries with reliable mail services and an easy facility for making payment. The best markets abroad are currently the UK and Germany. The people of different countries differ in their willingness to embrace the new method of selling. Some are quick to take it up, others are slower. It is difficult to make the international side pay immediately but it will not be long before it is making a profit.

● *By finding as many partners as possible who can sell through Amazon.com, paying a commission to do so*
This is an interesting new idea, started in 2001. Amazon is prepared to sell for other distributors and sell second-hand products, anticipating and benefiting from the success of the eBay model. The rival products are shown on the same website. Since this commission business for the most part does not involve the expense of storage and warehousing, it is almost pure profit and helps to spread the other fixed costs. Nor does it put pressure on for an expansion of warehouse capacity. It also illustrates dramatically the competitive level of Amazon's own prices. Already Amazon is acting as email distributor for Toys 'R' Us and Target, although in the first case it does use its own warehouse facilities. Almost 20% of Amazon's unit volume is now sold through others.

The future strategy

The business model has been adapted several times to meet difficulties which have arisen. In particular the model was adjusted to include warehouses and selling other retailers' products on commission. These adjustments have changed the core competencies of Amazon to some degree, but not substantially. Its chief core competencies are in its customer base and in the resulting ability to service customers. Because of these competencies, more than 70% of Amazon's sales are repeat business.

How far did these adjustments leave the basic model unaffected? How have these adjustments added to the core competencies required of Amazon? What are other adjustments and core competencies which are likely to be necessary in the future?

Over its short life Amazon has established its name as probably the best-known one in e-commerce. It needs to manage that name very carefully.

How should Amazon manage its brand name? What are the problems which confront such management? Are there any threats which, if realized, could reduce the value of the brand name? How, for example, can Amazon guarantee the reliability of delivery?

Bezos has clearly adopted a policy of cost and price leadership. It is what was generally expected of an Internet seller. However, this policy had to be reversed during the years of greatest crisis. Recently there has been a resumption of this policy. The introduction of free shipping for orders of more than $25 created an additional demand which more than compensated for the lost revenue.

Is this a sensible policy? Will it continue to generate enough sales to justify the policy? What pricing policy should Amazon adopt? Should it drive down the price by an aggressive cutting of costs?

For Amazon, partners of various kinds are important. For example it has allied itself with Linux.

What partnerships should Amazon form, for example in the area of technology or sales? Is it sensible for Amazon to ally itself with Linux?

Amazon has decisively extended its range of products and also moved abroad into foreign markets. This double extension is not without limits.

The product range now includes books, music, online auctions, electronics, toys, video games, camera and photo products, health and beauty aids, software, kitchen and household items, tools and hardware, cars and outdoor living products. In some areas Amazon quickly became the market leader, since the products lent themselves to Internet selling. For example, Amazon launched its online music in June 1998, and within a short period held 40% of the market. Amazon has experimented with the sale of clothing, and through its commission business the products of a range of specialty-item companies engaged in e-commerce. So far Amazon has gone for a broad product offering rather than a narrow focus, but needs to decide carefully what products to sell and in what markets to sell them. Amazon also has to decide what inventory of any particular product to hold. An uncontrolled expansion will inflate inventory enormously. If sales of a product vary greatly over time, the desired size of inventory is difficult to estimate. One way of limiting the inventory is by selling on commission.

How far can it go in the range of products for sale? Does the sales mechanism create a problem for certain products? Is clothing likely to be a good product for it to sell? How much commission selling should it undertake? What countries would represent suitable target markets?

Key strategic issues

There are a number of other key strategic decisions to be made by Amazon and key areas which should be analysed by the reader. For example, what is the role of the leadership of Jeff Bezos in the success of Amazon? How far could Amazon survive without him? Is there a transition to be effected to turn Amazon into a company run by a team of professionals? Does the high rate of turnover of senior staff at Amazon indicate that there is a problem which will have to be dealt with in the near future?

Strategic analysis and audit

Do a full strategic audit on Amazon.com, concentrating on its financial situation, as it is developing towards a normal and above-normal level of profit. What parts of its activities are more profitable than others? What is the strategic justification for loss-making activities?

Reading

Bayers, C., 'The last laugh', *Business 2.0*, September 2002: 86–93.

Biren, B., 'Music on the Internet: Transformation of the Industry by Sony, Amazon.com, MP3.com and Napster', in Thompson, A. A. and Strickland 111, A. J., *Strategic Management: concepts and cases* (McGraw-Hill Irwin, New York: 2003).

Hanson, D., Dowling, P., Hitt, M. A., Ireland, R. D. and Hoskisson, R. E. 'Amazon.com and Barnesandnoble.com: a continuing rivalry', pp. 64–5 in *Strategic Management: competitiveness and globalization*, Pacific edn (Nelson Thomson Learning, Melbourne: 2002).

Hof, R. D., Green, H. and Brady, D., 'Suddenly, Amazon's books look better', *Business Week*, February 21, 2000: 78–84.

Knight, S., Kobrak, H. and Lewis, P., 'Amazon.com' in Czinkota, M. R., Rokainen, I.A. and Moffett, M. H. *International Business*, Update 2003: 619–24.

Kotha, S., 'Amazon.com: expanding beyond books' pp. C120–40, in Hill, C. W. L. and Jones, G. R. *Strategic Management: an integrated approach* (Houghton Mifflin, Boston and New York: 2001).

Spector, R., *Amazon.com: get big fast* (Harper Business, New York: 2000).

Vogelstein, F., 'Mighty Amazon' *Fortune* **147**(10) May 26, 2003: 60.

Wingfield, N., 'Survival strategy: Amazon takes page from Wal-Mart to prosper on web' *Wall Street Journal* (Eastern edn) New York, November 22, 2002: A1.

www.amazon.com

Finance, a venue for perfect competition: the Deutsche Bank

Background

In recent years the banking industry has seen more change than almost any sector of the economy. The information/communications revolution has had a dramatic impact on the finance sector, an impact whose consequences are still unfolding (see the Strategies in Action in Chapter 7 on Charles Schwab and John Doerr). By improving access to information, the revolution has in theory made all the various markets for financial services more integrated and efficient. The efficient operation of a market depends on:

• the speed at which price or product information is communicated
• how much information can be processed and how quickly
• having many buyers and many sellers
• having homogeneous products.

The integration of a global market by good communications has ensured that this is the case. Across the globe there is now a financial market open at every minute of the day. This is all made possible by the new technologies of communication. Financial markets are just about the closest to the perfect market envisaged by the economist.

What is the nature of perfect competition? How close to perfect competition are the various financial markets? In what way does the efficient operation of a market depend on the speed of communications?

The term 'the democratization of finance' summarizes well some aspects of a revolution which has opened access to finance and a range of financial transactions to most people in developed economies. In developed economies these aspects include:

• the generalization to a majority of the population of share ownership and share trading
• the important role of management by financial institutions of investment portfolios
• the capacity to borrow from a wide range of international institutions
• access to all sorts of risk control mechanisms.

The most visible revolution has been the development of online financial activity of various kinds, including retail banking and the broking of financial transactions in shares and bonds.

What kinds of new opportunities does the democratization of finance open up for business enterprises in the finance sector?

Even efficient markets suffer from two problems, those of volatility and malpractice. These problems can intensify rather than diminish with the improvement of communications and information flow.

• Volatility arises because every market is based on confidence, the level of which can change very rapidly. The financial system has become highly sophisticated without losing its propensity for overshooting in both boom and recession. Attitudes are subject to dramatic and cumulative change. Rising asset values can create bubbles as more and more market participants rush to join in, seeking to reap profits before others can pre-empt them and in so doing pushing up further the value of the assets. Some of the bubbles act to prolong a long period of expansion but guarantee a capping off of that expansion. The greater the rise, the further the subsequent fall. Success tends to reinforce the overshooting, in both directions. The classic cases are the property and shares bubbles in Japan during the 1980s and the high-tech bubble in the USA during the 1990s.

During the 1990s the finance sector was part of a protracted boom in the new economy, which overshot badly. Acquisitions and initial public offers generated enormous investment banking business for institutions. There has been some overshooting in the opposite direction. The inherent volatility and instability of the market system is reflected in the behaviour of the financial system, which tends to magnify that volatility.

How does the overshooting affect the process of strategy making in the finance and other sectors, in particular the time perspective?

• Often the two features, volatility and corruption, go together. During expansionary times, the wave of confidence, even overconfidence, obliterates the memory of the reasons for previous setbacks and removes the usual restraints on behaviour. Current practices deteriorate as prudential checks are not properly made and margin borrowing takes on yet another form. The appetite for risk increases. Conflicts of interest proliferate as all seek profit. Almost all upturns and downturns in financial markets, whatever the particular asset bubbles involved, are accompanied by some degree of corruption and malfeasance. The corruption enters during the upturn and is often revealed during the downturn, which compounds the change of mood and helps propel the market downwards.

How should an enterprise deal with the problem of unfair competition created by those engaging in improper behaviour?

One of the core competencies most important to financial institutions is the establishment and maintenance of a good reputation. It is easy to destroy a good reputation, but difficult to build one up. The former can occur overnight, the later takes years.

What is the impact of the communications/information revolution on the level of competition in banking and other industries? What impact do these changes have on the levels of volatility and malfeasance in the industry? How far does integration of global markets lead to an internationlization of banks?

The role of the financial sector

The financial system is at the core of any market economy. It has three main roles:

● To provide the supply of money or, more broadly, the liquidity required to support the elaborate exchange of products and services which takes place in a developed market economy. The banking system does this by creating bank deposits; other financial institutions play a similar role. The creation of money also involves providing credit, that is, retail banking and its equivalents. In an economy in which credit cards proliferate, the role of creating money has changed its nature. It has probably retreated in importance, since the amount of work a given amount of money can do has risen and can vary quite significantly in the short run. In principle there is not a great deal of need for money in the old sense of the word, that is, in the sense of cash or bank deposits. The level of credit card debt has risen greatly. It helps to stimulate private consumption and discourage households savings which are very low in most developed economies.

● To provide intermediation between lenders and borrowers, those who make the initial savings decisions and those who invest in productive assets of various kinds. This is part of the investment banking role. Intermediation can be indirect, involving a whole series of different and highly specialized intermediaries. A prop-

erly functioning financial system is able to facilitate a rapid change in the structure of an economy, shifting resources from the old to the new economy.

Today the investment bank normally plays an important role for those who invest in productive facilities, participating in any new issues on the capital market and placing the paper in the hands of savers or savings institutions. The role of the investment bank has changed greatly from the time when it lent directly to those who invested. The new role is extremely profitable in expansionary times, but not so in bad times.

Specialist venture capital firms play an important role in financing the development of particular sectors seen as high risk, such as computing and biotechnology. Other institutions such as pension funds, insurance companies and mutual funds hold shares and bonds for long periods of time, managing the savings of individuals or institutions.

Two other groups of institutions are important to the financial sector, brokers who organize the buying and selling of paper and investment analysts who give advice to savers on what shares or bonds to buy and sell. Both investment banks and brokers are in the business of giving such financial advice.

● To control risk, using derivatives to hedge risk of various kinds, or rather to bring together those who have different risk profiles. It is often argued that it is the owners of shares who should diversify away risk, unless that risk is systematic, affecting the whole market simultaneously. According to this view it is not within the scope of enterprise strategists to control risk – that is the job of the financial market. However, the risk position of intermediaries is somewhat different from that of investors. The range of products has increased enormously with the development of derivatives, which allow a vast range of players to engage in swaps, future transactions, hedging and many other risk management operations. A new breed of specialist institutions has emerged, the hedge funds, which specialize in this kind of asset.

How has the relative importance of these functions changed? How does the changing nature of such functions influence the strategy-making process? How far is the risk control function made more effective by the availability of new mechanisms?

The problems of Germany

The reunification of Germany in 1989 has highlighted a series of problems which now confront that economy and appear similar to those confronting the Japanese economy, including the threat of deflation. The rate of economic growth in Germany since that date has averaged barely 1% per annum. Unemployment has rarely dipped below 10%. If anything the situation has deteriorated recently, with growth of GDP in 2001 at only 0.6%, the worst rate in the EU.

What problems does slow growth create for the German banks?

Why is this?

• Reunification proved a much bigger problem than expected. At the parity exchange rate adopted on reunification, most of the industry of East Germany was bankrupted and unemployment spiralled. Massive transfer payments to the East have kept public spending at more than half of gross national product.

• On the other hand, the old model which generated rapid recovery and rapid growth from the 1950s onwards no longer works well. For example, labour costs in the West are high and employment regimes overly rigid, both tending to undermine German competitiveness, resulting in a loss in its share of world exports.

• The restrictions imposed on monetary policy in Germany by the rules of the euro system have not allowed an expansionary policy to be pursued. Its ability to lower interest rates or run a budget deficit is heavily circumscribed.

An interesting question to ask is, what will happen to Germany as the EU changes? Germany has acted as a good European and led the way in integrating Europe, both from an intensive and extensive perspective. It has willingly given up its strong currency, the mark, in favour of the euro and subordinated the conservative Bundesbank to a European Central Bank which might choose to play a different role. It is willing to accept a modelling of Europe on its own federal structure. The expansion of the EU eastwards, by the Treaty of Nice (2001) – Estonia, Latvia, Lithuania, Poland, Hungary, the Czech Republic, the Slovak Republic and Slovenia becoming members of the EU in 2004 – will shift the whole centre of economic gravity of the EU towards Germany. This will have enormous implications for Germany and will provide it with great opportunities to restore its trading and investment pre-eminence in central and Eastern Europe.

What opportunities does the expansion of the EU provide for German banks?

Germany has to adjust to its potential role as the leading economy at the core of one of the triad centres and, like Japan, shake off the political legacy of the aftermath of defeat in World War II and the highly successful recovery model which was applied in

the 1950s and 60s and has continued to sustain Germany ever since. This is yet another example of success breeding failure, of circumstances changing but the strategy remaining the same. Germany's old model of economic development in which the investment bank had an important role to play has developed its own difficulties.

What are the weaknesses of the old model? How do these weaknesses relate to the role of the investment bank in contemporary Germany? What role might the big four German banks play in an expanded Europe?

European banking

The European banking industry is still fragmented, nothing like as concentrated as other important industrial sectors, such as the automobile, petroleum, insurance or even the grocery retailing industries. The five largest banks account for a tiny 16% of the overall market. There are as many as 15,000 separate institutions within the European industry and in Germany more than 2,500 banks distributing banking products.

What factors influence the degree of consolidation in the banking industry?

Since 1996, within national economies there has been a considerable quickening in the pace of consolidation, with as many as 60 mergers and acquisitions worth more than US$1 billion each. In Germany this process is constrained by the existence of German savings banks owned and operated by regional governments which are not currently on offer for privatization. There is little room for further domestic consolidation.

How does the organization of the banking sector differ from country to country?

The banking industry is rather like the airline industry in the past, its retention under German ownership seen as an issue of national sovereignty, and therefore the main domestic players protected from foreign ownership. This view has changed. There are an increasing number of factors encouraging consolidation at the international level:

• With increasing integration of the EU, conditions favour international consolidation. Not only is it impossible legally and morally for governments to prevent consolidation, there are many less barriers to this arising from differing currencies and practices. Both the drive for profits and the scope for economies of scale in financial markets encourage this process.

• However, the potential synergies from domestic mergers are typically much larger than those from international mergers, allegedly 10–25% of the market value of the smaller partner as against only 5% internationally.
• Offsetting this is the tendency that once one merger occurs it usually acts as a domino effect to encourage others. Once one large player enters the game, others who aspire to remain competitive have to follow suit.
• The harmonization of government regulations, notably on the Basel standards, assists concentration, as does consolidation among banking infrastructure providers, such as the perfection of the automated clearing house.

Currently many European banks conduct almost every kind of banking business; they are universal banks.

Will this universality continue to be the case? Will there emerge a small group of large banks competing on world markets? Will there be a simultaneous process of divestment and specialization? To what target state is the process of consolidation headed?

There are four possible models for more specialized banks of the new era:

1. Regional retail distributors
Banks offering ordinary commercial banking services required by typical retail customers, but offering them in a concentrated way in a limited number of regions.

2. Pan-European product specialists
Banks specializing in the provision of particular services, such as insurance, leasing, asset management or the provision of consumer credit, but distributing their products throughout Europe.

3. European and global wholesale banks
Banks which assist in the finance of investment in product facilities not just at the European level but throughout the world.

4. Pan-European service providers
Banks which help to provide the necessary infrastructure which enable banks to operate internationally, for example those for payments, settlement or exchange across Europe as a whole.
   The range of activities is shown in Figure C.2.

Are there other ways in which the universal banks could break up into specialist banks?

Investment banking

The main distinction made above is between the retail and wholesale roles of banks. Different countries have had different banking traditions. For example, commercial banks in Britain have not lent long term, the stock market performs that role. In the USA the banking system has been fragmented by states, rather than organized on a national basis.

Why is there a different organization in different countries? Is it simply the result of path dependence?

In Germany there has been a strong tradition of investment or wholesale banking in the old style, referred to as 'development banking'. This does not mean simply underwriting new issues of stock but actually holding for a significant period a sizeable share ownership, in particular helping to see industrial and infrastructure companies through the start-up period or bad times. It also involved having representatives on the board of directors of the company, joint directors who can make a significant and positive entrepreneurial input. One of the main motivations was to use intensively whatever scarce entrepreneurial talent existed. This was a strategy and style which suited rapid economic development in Germany in the catch-up mode of the middle and late nineteenth century and even during the recovery mode of the post-1945 economic world.

Has the need for this entrepreneurial talent disappeared completely?

As the investment bank model changed to one which involved the underwriting of new share and bond issues rather than continuing ownership, German banks simply added this new role to the old. Such underwriting proved immensely profitable, particularly when the stock market was booming. On the basis of this strategy and the out-

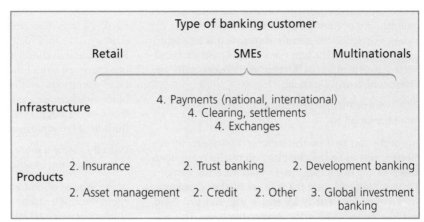

Figure C.2 **The banking value chain**

standing success of the German postwar economic recovery, German banks became masters of European banking, the big four – Deutsche Bank, Dresdner Bank, Commerzbank and HypoVereinsbank – leading the way.

How did the German banks build on their traditional activities?

German banks were not content to limit their activities to the domestic market. They tried to extend the model abroad, led by Deutsche Bank, which sought to turn itself into one of the world's leading banks. However, the attempt to carve out global empires has left German banks exposed.

The high spot of the old strategy came in 2000, when in March Deutsche Bank, Germany's largest bank, announced that it would merge with Dresdner Bank, the third largest, with the goal of creating a European investment and asset management institution which was large enough to reap the economies of scale which would make it competitive with the so-called 'bulge-bracket' of Wall Street, the world giants, such as Citigroup, Goldman Sachs and Merrill Lynch. Neither of the German investment banks had the weight to compete on its own. Such a fusion would create a monster investment bank.

How does international competition affect the German banks?

The retail branch networks were also fragmented and unprofitable; they needed rationalization. The Dresden deal was intended to yield at least €3 billion from savings made in fusing the two retail networks.

Can there be a separation between wholesale and retail banking?

Because profit margins on the wholesale business were much higher than on the retail business, the former was regarded as a better strategic focus for banking activity. Investment banking became the main focus of interest. The acquisition of Bankers Trust and the old Morgan Grenfell had already shown Deutsche's ambitions in this area. The aim was now to integrate Dresdner's investment arm Kleinwort Benson with the investment arm of Deutsche.

Why were profit margins higher on wholesale than on retail banking?

An important part of the strategy, and therefore the merger, was to be the combination of the retail operations of the two banks into Deutsche's retail banking division, Bank 24, and the spin-off of that division as an independent entity in which the merged bank would have less than a 10% ownership stake. This was despite the fact that the new bank would have at least 11 million customers in a number of different countries, although mainly in Germany, and had been pioneering online business, with 20% of all transactions already conducted online. The new bank would shed its retailing operations and act as a global wholesale bank. Out of the two large universal banks would emerge two institutions specialized in retail and wholesale banking.

Was this ever a feasible strategy? Why was it adopted?

The merger failed because of managerial disagreements, and the inability to win the support of their own specialist staffs for the merger. Dresdner staff accused Deutsche of wishing to sell all or part of Kleinwort Benson. The main Deutsche investment staff threatened to walk out if the merger went ahead because they feared dilution of their investment role. There was a danger that the investment bank units would disintegrate. By April 5, 2000 the merger was dead and it was called off. This proved to be a false dawn.

How far does a main core competence of an investment bank rest in the abilities of its staff?

Strategy making in a crisis

Within six months Deutsche's strategy had completely changed, partly by choice and partly by necessity. Previously the investment bank tail had wagged the bank. This ceased to be the case. The high-tech crash and the recession of the early 2000s provided a good reason for rethinking such a strategy. Investment banking looked a different proposition in a recession. The revenue stream generated in the boom diminished significantly. Internal difficulties provided the ultimate persuasion to take a different path.

Why was strategy not framed to take account of possible bad times?

Bank 24 was now to become the heart of a new strategy, one in which Deutsche would build a pan-European retail channel. It decided to reintegrate under one management all the services offered, including the retail operations, and rebrand Deutsche Bank 24, and other divisions, as a unified Deutsche Bank. In spite of this new strategy, Deutsche Bank still generates two-thirds of its revenue from investment banking.

Does this seem a more realistic strategy in the changing business environment?

In the process of doing this Deutsche is retargeting the client base. Deutsche had identified a rich market segment of some 60 million well-educated and prosperous 30–40-year-olds within the EU who are switching their money from deposit accounts to equities and investment funds as part of good savings management and in preparation for retirement. In that sense retail banking was now seen as intimately linked with wholesale banking; the two could not be disentangled. Retail banking would help Deutsche to feed these savers into its wholesale banking business. Such affluent private clients, combined with prominent business clients, would provide a highly profitable core business, not only in Germany but in the southern members of the EU – Italy, Spain and Portugal – and Germany's neighbours, Poland, Belgium and the Netherlands, where Deutsche has most of its foreign branches. Access to savers would be helped by the introduction of the euro. All customers would receive comprehensive financial and advisory services through a single bank account.

What does this mean for the process of specialization of banking activities?

The aim is to offer customers the full range of possible banking services, through a combination of branch offices, the telephone and the Internet, but mainly the Internet. As part of this strategy, Bank 24 will promote the online broking of Maxblue and extend its customer base. Such a strategy requires major expenditures to promote and implement. Information technology is not cheap. Despite the high level of expenditure required, after initially trying to find a partner for its retail operations, the bank has opted to go it alone.

What is the impact of online banking on the traditional banks? How quickly is it likely to grow?

There are a number of problems with the new approach. One is the retention of the universal banking model. Another is the conflict of interest created by the dual role – both advising on savings decisions to buy shares and bonds and underwriting new issues for various companies. The new model leaves most of these problems unresolved.

How has this conflict of interest manifested itself in recent times?

Deutsche intends to close 470 of its private and business client branches, more than one-third of its network of 1,240 outlets in Germany. To offset these closures Deutsche will set up 300 self-service banking terminals and 120 mobile consulting units. Most of the branches outside Germany will be retained.

What is the role of the bank branch in the new context?

Less than ten years ago, in terms of market capitalization, the Frankfurt-based Deutsche Bank was, outside Japan, the biggest bank in the world. Given the setbacks received by the Japanese banks during the 1990s, it

might now be the leader, but, since its share price fall, it is not even in the top 20 in terms of market capitalization. This is despite the fact that in the value of its assets it is second only to Citigroup. The assets have been poorly managed and have generated a low level of profit. It is now a bank vulnerable to acquisition, rather than one looking for acquisitions. The threat is only too real. Dresdner Bank was taken over by the giant insurance company Allianz in 2001. Citigroup itself has shown some interest in buying Deutsche.

What does Deutsche Bank need to do in order to avoid being taken over?

There is a general crisis for German banking. All the German banks are confronted by sky-high costs, the consequences of reckless past lending practices, mounting bad debts and the poor outcomes of ill-conceived forays outside their core areas. In European banks, costs are typically 60% of income, but the figure is as high as 80% in Germany. There is scarcely any profit being made. The German banks have inherited a set of attitudes and practices from the past which now have to change. They are changing, but painfully slowly. Deutsche Bank is a good example of both the crisis and the change.

Why are costs so high in German banking?

There are a number of reasons for the banking malaise which are outside the control of Deutsche:

● The bank receives unfair competition from the state-controlled banks, which offer guarantees on deposits and have close links to municipal and state governments. They have an unfair advantage in competing for funds. This weakens the retail banking of the big four. This special status is to be phased out by 2005.
● The recession has badly affected the German economy, with a rising tide of bankruptcies and the consequent bad debts, some very large, such as the collapses of the construction company, Philipp Holzmann, the media conglomerate, the Kerch Group, the aircraft manufacturer, Fairchild Donier, and the engineering group, Babcock Borsig.
● Germany, as elsewhere, is being opened up to competition from outside banks. Their home patch is no longer their sole preserve.
● Deutsche Bank also has an exposure to the major collapses which have occurred in the USA. It has set aside more than €1 billion to cover losses on loans to WorldCom, Enron and other bankrupt companies. It committed the most to a US$2.65 billion credit line that WorldCom used in May 2002. Its aim in accepting such exposure was to win more lucrative advisory and underwriting business.

How far is the banking crisis a result of external and internal factors?

The year 2002 was the critical year for restructuring the big four banks and making a new strategy to suit the times. There is a general crisis in which all the banks are aiming to cut costs, closing hundreds of branches and laying off thousands of staff. The earnings crisis is indicated by the figures in Table C.2.

Table C.2 **Performance of Germany's big publicly traded banks**

Bank	Core capital ratio	Net income (millions)
Deutsche Bank	9.6%	$426.5
Commerzbank	7.3%	–$320.1
HVB Group	5.6%	–$921.7

DB is less exposed to the German market, with only about 60% of its revenue coming from domestic business. Any increase in profit is coming from cost reduction rather than revenue increase. However, the figures for Deutsche Bank also hide a fourth quarter loss and a further loss of $245 for the first quarter of 2003, one caused by a large write-off of losses in the bank's assets.

To solve Deutsche's difficulties, specifically to reverse the 30% drop in its share price during 2002, it announced a buy-back of 62 million shares or 10% of the bank by September 2003, up to a value of €4 billion (US$4.39 billion). The aim of this buy-back was to improve investor returns and boost the market value of its shares, thereby avoiding becoming prey to a company wishing to take it over. The buy-back was to be funded by the sale of some holdings in the bank's large industrial portfolio worth as much as €15 billion and by a €2 billion cost-cutting campaign, including job cuts of 10% of the workforce.

Why should any company buy back its own shares?

Although Deutsche is planning to cut its private equity holdings, it is happy to retain third-party funds. It intends to accelerate the sales of its industrial holdings, DaimlerChrysler, Munich Re and Allianz, which are at present very substantial. It also intends to divest its money-losing subsidiaries, Banque Worms of France and Deutsche Bank Brown Inc., a USA money manager and investment bank. It has also already divested such low return businesses as global custody and passive asset management. It has also sold large chunks of its Global Securities Services business and its US leasing unit.

Why should Deutsche Bank sell its equity holdings?

The profit position is behaving in a volatile way. Immediately after the decision to reform, the situation deteriorated. In the first quarter of 2002, pretax profits were down by 70% but profits in the second quarter were boosted by a series of disposals, especially the sale of shares in the German reinsurer Munich Re. As indicated above, it then improved before deteriorating again. Some believe that the bank will have to close half its branches and reduce its labour force by 30% rather than by 10%. The banks have even begun to consider the possibility of shifting research functions to countries with low-paid, high-skill graduates.

Do the changes go far enough? Is it necessary to stop bailing out failing companies and reduce its loans to SMEs, turning its attention to the provision of services for which it can charge? Should it concentrate on its core business? Will the whole industry have to consolidate?

The problems of recession caused the new CEO Ackermann to propose to Chancellor Schroeder that, in the event of one of the big banks failing, a banking entity should be created which could take over the bad debts of the big four. In the long run his plan for DB is to boost its market value to put it among the world's top 10 financial institutions, to which it used to belong. This is not going to be easy.

Key strategic issues

Deutsche Bank is a classic case of success creating failure. In what sense has the old business model of the German banks been superseded by a new one, one which has a much more international bias?

This big question raises a number of other questions. How has a. the economic success of Germany before the 1990s, b. the expansion of the EU, c. the communications/information revolution and d. the recent recession in Germany influenced the strategy of Deutsche Bank? How should these events have influenced the strategy? What changes in the external environment have made the universal banking model difficult to sustain?

Strategic analysis and audit

Carry out a full strategic audit on Deutsche Bank. How does its position compare with that of the other large German banks? Has it made the right decision in developing its international activities? Does this insulate the bank, at least partially, from the negative impact of conditions in Germany?

Reading

Economist, The, 'German Banking', April 8, 2000.

Financial Times, 'DB24 reprived to target Europe's forty somethings', November 17, 2000: 33.

Financial Times, 'Germany: Finance', Special Report, June 10, 2003.

Hill, C. W. L., 'Deutsche Bank's pan-European Retail Banking Strategy', in Hill, C. W. L. *International Business,* McGraw-Hill Irwin, New York: 2003: 288–9.

McCathie, A., 'Worst may be over for Europe's banks', *The Australian Financial Review,* July 31, 2003: 21.

Souder, E., 'Deutsche Bank swung to a loss in period on asset write-downs', *Wall Street Journal* (Eastern edn) New York, May 1, 2003: B7.

Walker, M., 'Deutsche Bank plans to make its retail unit a stock outlet', *Wall Street Journal,* October 23, 2000.

Walker, M., 'German banker calls for plans for "worst case"', *Wall Street Journal* (Eastern edn) New York, March 17, 2003: c1.

www.db.com

Haier: pioneering the Chinese export brand

We work in a mixed economy. You have to have three eyes: one for the market, one on the workers, and one on policy.

ZHANG RIUMIN, CEO of Haier

We have a broad product line with a wide price range. We need lower price models for price-only stores that sell commodity goods. We need higher price models for stores that will display our products and have salespeople on the floor. We promote Haier as a global brand – not Chinese or American, but global.

I saw opportunity in the Haier brand. The appliance market is old and has a lot of hang ups like product recalls. Here was a new brand of good products with no baggage and the chance to develop its own Image. I believed in the Haier Brand.

MIKE JEMAL, president of Haier America

Given China's vast geography, disparate market, and multiplicity of national and local authorities, Haier has dealt with many of the problems of globalization without leaving home.

MARSHALL MEYER, Wharton School of Business

We have a dream. China should have world-known brands of her own ... letting the people of China hold their heads high in the world.

Poster at Haier's headquarters

Background

China is the focus for many cost leadership strategies. The potential for exporting from China is enormous, as the rapid growth in exports since 1978 has shown. This potential is largely based on the vast supply of cheap but often skilled labour in China. It is frequently argued that China can become the manufacturing base for the rest of the world. However, it is difficult for an enterprise to make a strategy solely on this basis; any competitive advantage based solely on cost can only be temporary.

Haier is an interesting case to explore the degree to which any enterprise can pursue a pure generic cost leadership strategy. How far is this possible? Under what circumstances is it likely to be feasible?

There are few Chinese companies with an international profile for their products, or international exposure of any kind. If they do, it is usually to export and sell under a variety of brands either relatively unknown or belonging to some other company. Within China, for example, there is growth in the profile of the computer manufacturer Legend, the mobile phone producer China Keijian and the television maker TCL, but as yet these names mean little outside China. Keijian is sponsoring Everton football club in the English premier league, to the tune of $3.2 million over two years. The Keijian name is on every Everton shirt, but the company is not yet selling its mobile phones in Britain. The TCL Corporation is selling its TVs in Europe but under the Schneider name, the name of a bankrupt producer which it purchased. These tentative steps are indicative of a shyness to attempt a serious branding.

Why are the Chinese companies so reluctant to use their own names for selling abroad? What do they need to have done in order to make this possible?

There are good reasons why most Chinese enterprises lack an international orientation:

• Even today the economy is only half-open. Before the initiation of reform in 1978 it was an almost fully closed economy. The opening has occurred in a steady manner without any dramatic move, culminating in membership of the WTO (see the case study on entry into the Chinese automobile industry in Chapter 15). The size, and rate of growth, of the domestic market means that Chinese companies can grow to a reasonable size without having to export.
• It is also revealing that at the time of writing *Fortune*'s first China 100 list contains no privately owned company. There is still a strong legacy from the period of centralized physical planning. Most enterprises are either state-owned or in collective ownership of some kind. This usually means that in some way their domestic market is protected.

The Qingdao Haier Company is an exception to the first, but not to the second. It is not a private company, still being in collective ownership and rated only 57th in the China 100. In terms of size it is still a comparatively small player in China.

Haier already has a prominent international profile. In that, with the possible exception of the oil companies, it is unique in China. Only Tsingtao beer has anything like the same degree of name recognition. The CEO of Haier, Zhang Riumin, has global ambitions, aspiring to place the company in the Fortune 500. It has quite deliberately cultivated its own brand name. Haier sells its products in as many as 138 countries and has factories in 13 countries. Haier is the world's number two refrigerator maker, after Whirlpool. It is the market leader for small refrigerators in the USA. Its total worldwide sales are $7.5 billion, not dramatic by the standards of most large multinational companies, but impressive by the standards of a country just entering the global economy.

How far is what Marshall Meyer says in one of the opening quotes true? What are the different challenges posed by selling outside China?

Haier is a typical Chinese conglomerate. It produces not just refrigerators, but a wide range of white goods – air-conditioners, freezers, washing machines, colour televisions, water heaters and microwave ovens, even computers and mobile phones. It has also ventured into the area of financial services.

Why are Chinese companies so often conglomerates?

The nature of the industry

White goods are fairly standard products produced by the same methods throughout the world. They are products for which there is a stable market which is not growing quickly, at least in the developed economies. In those economies the demand is largely a replacement demand. As the rate of population increase has declined, the growth of the market has decelerated. An Electrolux planning review several years ago found that the annual growth rate of the market was unlikely to exceed 2–3% in the near future. Today the expectation might be even lower. On the other hand Electrolux saw demand growing at a rate of 20% per annum in developing areas within Asia, Eastern Europe and Latin America. There is also a rapidly growing demand in the fast developing economies of Asia, including China.

What does the relative demand growth rate for white goods in different parts of the world indicate about possible strategies for internationalization?

China offers an excellent base for a producer of white goods, although the market is by no means a homogeneous one, with some barriers to trade between provinces. A domestic producer which reached a significant size might have the resources to start considering entry into foreign markets. Up to now the Chinese market has been difficult for foreign producers to enter, but not impossible, as Electrolux has showed.

Electrolux pioneered in developing a manufacturing facility for refrigerators in China through joint ventures, a facility it then used to export to other Asian countries. Both Siemens and the Samsung Group have entered the market. A plethora of local producers have appeared. All this competition has cut profit margins significantly. To be able to compete with the international giants may require entry by domestic producers into the international market and the establishment of independent names abroad. For automatic washing machines the share of foreign producers, such as LG Electronics, Whirlpool and Siemens, has risen from 23% in 2000 to 42% in 2003, largely on the basis of sales in just four main markets.

How does the opening up of China and the increasingly intense competition in the domestic market influence the nature of strategy for a significant domestic player?

What is the nature of the technology and the product in the white goods area?

- In the developed world white goods are products which have been largely 'commoditized'. The technology is currently well known and certainly not subject to rapid change. The product is largely a standard product with standard technical specifications.
- There are significant economies of scale which tend to lead to a concentration of production within mature markets, but worldwide there is plenty of competition for markets.
- In order to differentiate the product there are relatively few small features which can be adopted, apart from the obvious one of size. It is a real challenge to discover a differentiating feature which allows an enterprise to brand its products.
- A key issue for the purchaser is clearly price, or rather value for money. Competitive advantage comes largely from the ability to undercut competitors, provided the product has a reputation for reliability.

What does the nature of technology and the resulting product tell about a likely strategy?

The rise of Haier

Probably the most striking legend which defines how Haier is different from the ordinary run of Chinese enterprises relates to an action of Haier's CEO Zhang Riumin back in 1985, shortly after he took over the enterprise. Having observed a disgruntled customer return a shoddy refrigerator and then inspect a large number of other fridges before he selected one which satisfied him, Riumin did the same, inspecting 400 in stock and finding 76 in a condition which prevented their sale. He then gathered his management team and in public view reduced the refrigerators to mangled wrecks with the aid of a sledgehammer, a dramatic signal of what he wanted in the future. The sledgehammer now hangs on the wall to remind all of the need for quality. The lesson was obvious; it is no good producing a cheap product which is of low quality.

When Riumin took over the enterprise in 1984 it was in a poor state, making large losses and incurring significant debt. The workforce was unmotivated and demoralized. It was not untypical of large state-owned enterprises in China. Although Riumin had worked his way up through the municipal administration in Qingdao and therefore might have been just another administrator without any entrepreneurial or strategic flair, he had familiarized himself with Western management literature and was open to outside influences. This showed itself in two ways when he was put in charge:

- First he purchased German technology from Liebherr-Haushallsgerte, a firm which not only gave Haier its technical base but its name, since Haier is the Chinese phonetic approximation of Liebherr. The German connection ended in 1994 and from then on Haier itself became a generator of new technology rather than a receiver.
- The second foreign influence came from Japan, from Masaaki Imai, the guru of Japanese quality control. From him Riumin took the 5-S self-check system, converting it into a 6-S system. This was vital to restoring staff morale. The five S's comprised the following – discarding the unnecessary, arranging tools in order of use, a clean work site, personal cleanliness and the observing of workshop discipline. Riumin added a sixth, safety. In the Haier Enterprise Culture Centre, Su Fangwen, who joined Haier in 1988, taught discipline and quality control to the staff.

By 1986 Riumin had turned the enterprise round so that it was making a profit. As a result he was given three other white good enterprises which together formed the Qingdao Haier Group in 1991.

As incomes rise in China and a middle class appears and swells in numbers, particularly in those coastal cities having the most rapid economic growth, there is an enormous market for what are, to the people of the developed world, basic household items such as the refrigerator and the washing machine. Already Haier meets a considerable proportion of the demand for these products. It is by far the dominant supplier of not just these products, but also air-conditioners and freezers. Its extraordinary rate of growth has been fuelled mainly by the growth of the domestic market. However, it is becoming harder to sustain both growth and profitability in the Chinese market because of the intense competition. One problem is that competition in China is driving down prices, in the case of washing machines by 10–15% per annum.

Going global

Haier began by establishing its leading position in the domestic market. It currently holds 29% of the Chinese market for refrigerators and 26% of the market for washing machines. In capturing this share of what is a rapidly growing and potentially very large market, it adopted a strategy which differed from the usual Chinese strategy. It emphasized product quality, reflected the results of a study of customer needs and demonstrated the ability to respond quickly by selling products which met those needs, and exerted a relentless pressure to push its brand name. This emphasis on quality is taken for granted on international markets, but not previously in China.

The first international forays were to open factories in Indonesia and the Philippines. However, the most interesting initiative, as for many other enterprises in a variety of industries, is the entry into the American market. At first the mode of entry was by export. In this Haier had surprising success, capturing 50% of the US market for compact refrigerators, that is, refrigerators to suit a student room, office or hotel room. The market for family refrigerators is harder to crack, since there are four manufacturers holding 98% of the market, between which there is already fierce competition. Haier has been making steady inroads even into this market and now claims 25% of that market. Haier has also been innovative in pioneering the sale of new products, such as electric wine cellars, in which it claims a 50% market share. Market shares for chest freezers, at 40%, and air-conditioners, at 18%, are lower but growing. By 2002 overall sales in the USA had reached almost US$500 million, not a startling level, but a good initial base. However, the company claimed to be making a profit and had clearly begun the difficult process of establishing its brand name.

The aim is to increase sales in the USA to $1 billion by 2005. To help achieve this, in 2000 Haier became the first Chinese company to open a major manufacturing facility in the USA – in Camden, South Carolina. While this represented a small investment, $40 million initially, it proclaims Haier's intention to penetrate the family refrigerator market, with an output target from the facility of 200,000 family-sized refrigerators.

Why is it choosing to produce in the USA when so many companies are headed in the opposite direction, producing in China?

There are three main reasons:

- transport costs are high for white goods
- Haier prefers to do its research and manufacture close to the market. Haier also has a design centre in Los Angeles and a trade centre in New York
- the label 'Made in the USA' will help to open this market.

Transferring the Haier culture to the USA, with its emphasis on teamwork, safety and quality, is not easy. Photographs accessible to the workers include one of Riumin wielding his sledgehammer. There has always been an attention to detail to fit the product to the market niche by Haier, an attention which is very un-Chinese. The compact refrigerators for the student market have locks. The Haier mini-fridges with folding computer desks have been selling very well. Door shelves in fridges for the American market are designed to hold gallon jugs. There are see-through vegetable crispers. Haier's chest freezer has an innovative cooling section in addition to the freezing compartment. Most components for Haier's products are locally sourced, although there is some international sourcing, with compressors imported from Brazil. The cost savings come from the location of most research back in China and the import of machinery for the factory from China.

How far is the Haier culture transferable across international frontiers? Can the factories abroad, especially in developed economies, produce at a cost level which is competitive?

Haier has also committed itself to a major advertising campaign to help promote its brand name. It has succeeded in placing its product prominently in well-known department chains such as Wal-Mart, Macy's, Office Depot, Target and Sears.

Competition and entry into the WTO

Haier faces some fierce competition, particularly at the international level. Three of the most potent competitors are Whirlpool, GE and Electrolux, important players in the American market, who have adopted a global role. These companies have enormous resources and a ruthlessness in keeping costs down to the level of their competitors, and below.

With the opening of China this competition will penetrate the domestic economy. Entry into the WTO means that foreign manufacturers can enter the Chinese market, either through exports or foreign direct investment (FDI) of various kinds and local production, taking advantage of low costs.

One interesting project shows the possible role of China in the world market. China entered the WTO with Taiwan and Haier is leading the way in promoting the link between the two. The link is already a strong one, with Taiwan investing heavily in China. Taiwanese investment is worth over the $100 billion mark and comprises over 40,000 factories and businesses of various kinds.

This investment is part of the enormous flow of FDI into China, which has underpinned an enormous growth in exports of all sorts, including white goods. There is no doubt that in many industries China will become a platform for exports to other countries, including Asian ones. The overall export ratio of China, using current exchange rates, is as high as 20%, although on the purchasing power parity exchange rate this exaggerates the level. However, this has been achieved from a base close to zero in 1978.

There are two motives for the Taiwanese involvement in China – access to a massive and growing domestic market, and use of efficient and cheap labour, as a platform for exports from China. In doing this the Taiwanese are worried about a possible overdependence on China and a hollowing out of its own industry, as its companies move their manufacturing facilities onto the mainland.

Haier illustrates how this is happening. In April 2002 an agreement started by which the Taiwanese company Sampo will produce Haier products in its three factories in Taiwan. The Haier refrigerators will sell at $300–400 less than similar Sampo products. In return Haier will distribute Sampo appliances in China. Sampo already has four factories in China producing mostly for export. It is also looking to sell in the rapidly growing Chinese market.

Haier has entered into other strategic alliances, notably with Japan's Sanyo to sell washing machines, dishwashers and refrigerators, with Korea's LG to make digital TVs and with the Hong Kong-based CCT Telecom to manufacture electronics and mobile phones. The aim of all these alliances is to promote exports.

The present and future strategy

There are four arms to the present strategy of internationalization:

- the achievement of markets in China, the USA and the rest of the world which are roughly equal in size.
- an export strategy that consists of entering and developing the difficult markets before easy ones or markets in developing countries – this explains the early entry into the American market.

- a product-focused international market entry strategy, which includes the introduction of innovative products and an attempt to enter the high end of the white goods markets. It has an excellent reputation for speed in turning out new products.
- an attempt to brand itself internationally through an ambitious promotional campaign.

Haier has global ambitions. In November 2002 it named Grey Global Group to develop a national marketing communications platform in mainland China, the first step on the way to international branding. Haier is looking outside for the freedom to develop beyond China as a global player. It already holds 29.9% of a Hong Kong-listed mobile phone company, Haier-CCT Holdings Ltd. It intends to raise this to 40% and fold its Shanghai-listed Qingdao Haier company, with its home appliance business, into this company, thereby further raising its international profile and making the Hong Kong company its flagship for operations in the international capital markets. It needs Chinese government permission to do this. At some point in the future it also intends to list in the USA.

How far is Haier constrained in its strategic objectives by its status as a 'government' enterprise? How might it escape from these constraints?

It may be that Haier is currently overstretching itself, both in product range and geographically, although it is obvious that it is doing this in order to move into areas with higher profit margins than those for white goods. It is highly conscious of the advantages of diversification.

The range of products is wide, typical of a Chinese conglomerate. They include all the main white goods, but also areas in the new economy such as computers and mobile phones, as well as financial services. Computers, TVs and mobile phones may only offer a temporary increase in profit margins, whereas financial services, including insurance and securities, offer a better prospect of a continuing profitability. Haier has laid out large sums to buy into both local and foreign securities and banking companies. For example it bought into the Wuhan-based Changjiang Securities, which is forming China's second joint venture investment bank with France's Paribas. It also signed a $24 million, 50/50 joint venture with New York Life International to begin selling a range of insurance policies in China.

Some critics have observed that it would be wise to choose a focused cost leadership strategy, in other words to concentrate on white goods rather than venturing into IT and finance. How far is this a legitimate criticism?

Not only has the company recently come under criticism, it has also seen pressure on its profits, for example a 45% reduction in net profits in the first half results for 2002, largely because of reduced returns on sales of air-conditioners. This is a sector with thin and decreasing profit margins.

The share price of Haier has also fallen. There is concern that the situation on profit levels and debt is rather opaque and a reference to a culture of secrecy. The main criticism has been directed at Haier's investment in air-conditioners and mobile phones, at its purchase of a refrigerator factory in Modena, Italy, seen as both high cost and less than best practice, and the sheer audaciousness of its overseas ambitions. The response from Haier was not encouraging; it has resorted to issuing a lawsuit against a critic, rather than adjusting its strategy. Haier, surprised by the negative backlash from the media, reached a settlement with Chen Yicong.

Why has there been an increasing trend in China for companies to take media critics to court for alleged defamation? What implications does this have for the type of strategy adopted by Haier? Do such lawsuits threaten the free flow of information vital to good business and good strategy making?

Haier is a pioneer, marking out a new path for other Chinese companies. It has had to decide what to produce and where to sell. It is faced with a wide range of choice in these areas, at least until it has committed resources to the relevant area. It has had to choose a participation strategy appropriate to the different products. In a sense Haier has been swimming against the current. It is in the same position as Japanese and Korean companies which had to move from a national reputation for cheapness and low quality, reflecting their initial relative labour abundance, to a national reputation for innovation and high quality. In achieving this it must balance cost against quality, only allowing cost increases if an adequate price premium justifies them.

How can it manage this balance? Haier is attempting to gain the same brand recognition as Sony or Samsung. How can it achieve this? Is it likely to achieve this?

Key strategic issues

Chinese companies have weaknesses which are often commented upon. How can Haier avoid these traditional weaknesses, in particular overreliance on a single leader, opaque financial dealings, excessive social obligations, a tendency to overdiversify, particularly in an environment which continues to encourage the suppression of criticism, at every level of society? How can it raise the financial resources required for its ambitious international strategy?

Strategic analysis and audit

Carry out a full strategic audit on Haier. Is it doing as well financially as it proclaims? Is it possible to draw firm conclusions on this? How far is Haier improving its profit margins by improving its brand name?

Reading

Biers, D., 'A taste of China in Camden', *Far Eastern Review*, **164**(12) March 29, 2001: 54.

Dolven, B., 'Hubble, bubble, toil and trouble', *Far Eastern Review*, February 20, 2003 **166**(7): 30–3.

Economist, The, 'China and the chaebol', **345**(8048) December 20, 1997 – January 2, 1998: 97–8.

Far Eastern Economic Review, Business Digest, **166**(10) March 13, 2003: 26.

Far Eastern Review, 'A draw between Haier and its critic – China briefing: intelligence', **165**(34) August 2002: 24–5.

Khermoush, G., 'Breaking into the name game', *Business Week*, March 31, 2003.

Lawrence, S. V., 'Gagged by big business', *Far Eastern Review*, **165**(30) August 1, 2002: 24.

Liu, H. and Li, K., 'Strategic implications of emerging Chinese multinationals: the Haier case study', *European Management Journal*, **20**(6) December 2002: 699.

Madden, N., 'Chinese marketer Haier taps Grey', *Advertising Age*, **73**(48) December 2, 2002: 22.

Madden, N., 'China's power brands eye global expansion', *Advertising Age*, **74**(2) January 13, 2003: 12–3.

McGregor, R., 'Analyst apologises for critical Haier report', *Financial Times*, August 20, 2002: 21.

Paul, A., 'China's Haier Power', *Fortune*, February 15, 1999: 55–8.

Roberts, D., Arndt, M. and Zammert, A., 'Haier's tough trip from China', *Business Week*, Online, April 1, 2002.

Sprague, J., 'Haier reaches higher', *Fortune*, **146**(4) 2002: 43–6.

Sprague, J., 'China's manufacturing beachhead', *Fortune*, **146**(8) October 28, 2002: 192B.

www.haier.com/english/
www.haieramerica.com

The Hewlett-Packard/Compaq merger

Michael Dell looms over the PC landscape like a giant, casting a shadow over all his unfortunate competitors.

Fortune, June 21, 2002: 55

HP's breadth and depth of offering is quite deep: It includes services; it includes virtual storage, virtual processing, server provisioning, management software and virtual application environments that will allow workloads to move from machine to machine as needed. It's a very comprehensive offering. But it's hard for me to tell what are products that will be delivered immediately and what are products that will be delivered over time. We'll have to watch and see.

DAN KUZNETSKY, Vice-president of systems software at IDC

The question is: is Hewlett-Packard trying to emulate IBM?' H-P gives 'high-tech, low-cost' solutions, IBM 'high-tech, high-cost', and Dell 'low-tech, low-cost'.

VEVERKA, 2003

The motives for a merger

This case study is concerned with the issue of size and the identity of merging partners (see for comparison the case study on BHP Billiton and the Strategy in Action module on AOL Time Warner, both in Chapter 11). It considers the computer industry and the current stage in its development.

Why do particular enterprises merge or acquire another enterprise? What are the factors which influence them to do so?

There are a host of different possible motives for an acquisition:

- The main one is that it is the quickest way to get bigger. The reasons for getting bigger may themselves be many, including simply using productively surplus profit or cash flow. Most companies take growing bigger as a mark of success.
- It may even be a matter of eating or being eaten, a race to avoid being absorbed by another enterprise. It is a race down the experience curve. An acquisition may therefore be defensive, the need to grow big enough to avoid being taken over by someone more adept at getting bigger.
- It may be also a matter of diversifying or moving into a new area while it is still possible.
- It may be that the industry has matured and offers much lower profit margins, so the acquisition is motivated by the need to gain and protect market share.
- It may be a significant change in the external environment. This might involve sweeping technical change, the communications revolution, or a dramatic change in market segmentation, or even a significant change in government regulation, removal of the restrictions on the cross-ownership of different media or foreign ownership.

In the case of the Hewlett-Packard/Compaq merger, what are likely to be the main motivators?

The usual arguments advanced to explain the justification for any merger or acquisition are twofold. Either there is the putting together of complementary assets which make the sum of the whole greater than the individual parts. It might be linking control over a medium of communication with control over something to communicate, as in so many of the mergers of the 1990s (see the long case study and the Strategy in Action in Chapter 8 on Vivendi).

What assets could be described as complementary in this case?

Or there may be a possible exploitation of significant synergies, common procurement or the sharing of fixed costs of various kinds.

Are these arguments contradictory and therefore mutually exclusive? In this case, which is likely to have more validity?

It is difficult to understand why so many enterprises are keen to acquire or merge, given that studies show that a majority of acquisitions are in some sense a failure, notably for the acquiring enterprise. In particular the experiences of the sectors under analysis have not been happy ones for mergers. There needs to be strong arguments to justify a merger.

One interesting issue is the timing of acquisitions or mergers. Acquisitions tend to peak on a rising stock market. Most acquisitions are concentrated in the periods of upturn. The reason for this is simple. High, and rising, share prices both protect against takeover and provide the means for the acquirer to achieve the takeover of others. If the market particularly favours a sector, it provides that sector with the potential to undertake such takeovers. The movement of share prices therefore often explains the timing of mergers.

Is this merger an exception to this situation, a merger on a falling market? If so, why is this?

Mergers on a rising market may be premature, running ahead of the realization of genuine synergies which are promised by a change in the environment. The use of shares as an acquisition currency which is ever-more valuable is one good reason why this timing might be appropriate. As P/E ratios rise it becomes easier for companies to use either their own shares to purchase or their own share value to raise money. The high valuation put on any company in the new economy, particularly in the communications sector, promoted acquisitions by companies in this area. The general acquisition frenzy which reached a peak in 2000 with the expenditure of $1.8 trillion shows the truth of this. However, this is offset to a significant degree by the increasing prices of the acquired.

Where in the cycle did the Hewlett-Packard/Compaq merger occur?

The cycle is now in reverse, with an enormous drop in acquisition activity. On the whole the process is not completely symmetrical, in that demergers never completely reverse the previous mergers.

Industry background

Even before the recession it was obvious that the market for computers was becoming a mature one. The recession knocked the bottom out of a market which was already growing at a slowing rate and which had become fiercely competitive. Demand fell dramatically, partly because the market in developed economies appeared saturated and partly because users could easily postpone replacement in the absence of any major change in technology which added significant new attributes to a computer. With the fall in demand the computer manufacturers have been under immense pressure to cut their costs. Under competition from Dell they had already been losing market share.

Where in the transaction cycle is the computer industry? How far has the computer been commoditized?

The main motive for the merger is to establish a company with the size to be a dominant market player, one capable of competing on equal terms with Dell. The other motive is to cut costs through various synergies in order to push up the level of profit margins.

What is the role of Dell in this? How far is the iron law of oligopoly reasserting itself in this industry?

In 2001, for the first time since the product was launched, PC sales fell. The era of rapid growth had at last come to an end. The industry had come of age, with a high level of saturation in the markets of the developed economies. Moreover, the product, its components and the services associated with it had been separated and commoditized. There were clear industry standards. Specialist suppliers provided the products, components and services. In particular the computer manufacturers competed to produce what had become a fairly standard product. This also applied increasingly to servers and printers, although Hewlett-Packard had managed better in these markets to defend its market share.

A sign of the times was that IBM, the Big Blue, had largely withdrawn from producing computers to concentrate on computer services. Others were trying to follow suit. Computers are likely to be a slow-growth business with increasingly tight profit margins. The industry is also subject to competition from a host of new devices with attributes superior to the humble PC. The industry was, and still is, ripe for consolidation.

Why are services a potential area for larger profit margins and more rapid growth?

The shadow of Dell

In this sector of the economy one supplier has become increasingly dominant. Dell revolutionized the PC industry though its direct sales model. It divided the business market from the ordinary retail market, carving out a separate market segment in the former. Dell made its machines to order and delivered them direct to the customer. It customized according to the requirements of individual enterprises and individuals within those enterprises. There was to be no middleman, so reducing costs significantly. Thus direct sale gave Dell a tremendous advantage in both the speed of delivery and the cost of the computer to the final customer. As it expanded its market share Dell also used its increased bargaining strength. The company has been likened to Wal-Mart, in that it extracts more and more from its component suppliers.

What is the generic strategy adopted by Dell? Is it a pure price leadership strategy, a pure product differentiation strategy, or a combined strategy? How far has Dell focused successfully in the strategy adopted?

From 1995 to 2001, Dell grew at a compound rate of 42% per annum, well above the rate of growth of even Wal-Mart. The share of the market accounted for by Dell reached a tad under the quarter mark in 2001 and on industry expectations is headed as high as 40%. By contrast the next two suppliers, Compaq and Hewlett-Packard, accounted for 13.3% and 9.7% respectively. Less than ten years ago, in 1994, Compaq was at 13.6% and HP 2.4%, but Dell at only 4.2%. HP has been losing ground, Compaq just maintaining its position. By contrast Dell was rapidly translating itself into a Microsoft or an Intel, in dominating this particular market. It was exceeding the combined performance of the other two. The business model adopted was clearly successful.

What are the strategic implications of such a relative performance?

The background of Hewlett-Packard and Compaq

Hewlett-Packard originated as the world's largest manufacturer of test and measurement equipment. During the early 1960s it diversified, moving into the area of medical equipment. It also began to produce computers and peripherals in the mid-1960s. The company put a great emphasis on innovation. It has always remained technically dynamic, often spinning off employees who 'seeded' numerous small start-ups in Silicon Valley.

How far was HP typical of a company which had not exploited its core competencies and found itself in sectors which were not 'new economy'?

By the late 1990s the leaders of the company were concerned at a slowing rate of growth and an inability to take advantage of the Internet revolution. Its older businesses were growing slowly. An internal review by the CEO Lewis Platt decided that the company was too big and too diversified: it lacked a clear corporate focus. The non-computer areas were to be spun off. Platt resigned in favour of Carly Fiorina who previously had run the global services division of Lucent. As both an outsider and an expert in the computer area she was clearly the new broom seen as necessary in the new environment. She was the architect of the merger with Compaq, having to resist the opposition of the old Hewlett interest in pushing it through. Later she had to defeat an effort from Michael Capellas, former CEO of Compaq and ally, but now president, to accelerate reform even faster.

What is the role of leadership in the recent history of HP?

Compaq found itself in an even worse plight than Hewlett-Packard in the late 1990s as it rapidly began to lose market share and make losses. Compaq had achieved number one position in overall PC sales in the mid-1990s. An attempt to compete with Dell through direct sales fell foul of its distributors. Compaq wished to extend into the area of services and to achieve this bought the Digital Equipment Corporation for the large sum of US$8.4 billion in 1998. It had great difficulty absorbing the company and began to lose customers in the services area. It too had lost focus. In 1999 the CEO Eckhard took the blame for the deterioration in performance and was replaced by Michael Capellas who, just two or more years later, was to strongly support the merger with HP.

Why was Compaq failing despite being in the right areas of the new economy?

Both companies therefore had a history of acquisition and merger and problems arising from such acquisitions. Both had reacted to relentless competitive pressure by trying to grow bigger and strengthen their position in the most rapidly growing areas of the computer industry.

What was the legacy of the previous negative experience of acquisition and merger?

The process of integration

Although there was agreement on the merger between the senior management in both companies, one group on the HP board associated with the founding Hewlett family was bitterly opposed and took their opposition into the courts. This took up significant time of the main protagonists and generated considerable animosity.

How far is the merger an illustration of the need for harmony to make such mergers work?

The process of acquisition and merger absorbs resources. Due diligence exercises, which are critical to a successful outcome, take time and money. It is said that staff from Hewlett-Packard and Compaq devoted more than one million hours of their time to planning this merger, before it occurred or was even approved. This is a prodigious investment and like any investment needs justification. In the short run the process may actually push up costs before any savings are realized.

Is there a tendency to underestimate the cost of implementing a merger? Is it also true that the more preparation there is, the more successful the merger is likely to be?

The expenditure of time is not surprising. It is a major problem to fuse two large organizations which operate throughout the world and which may have entirely different cultures, structures and strategic philosophies. The same process has to be repeated in each country in which they operate, and in very different contexts, which might be more hostile to the very concept of a merger. This involves a significant rationalization of products, markets and staff, a process which differs according to the nature of the enterprises in each country.

How far is there a separate process for each country in which each of the companies operates?

In scoring a merger, there are four main areas relevant to the balancing of arguments for and against:

● *Financial performance*. Most mergers or acquisitions are judged in the short term by the impact of the merger on share values, thereby reflecting market perceptions of the merger, and the overall capitalization of the two companies combined. Initially nearly all acquisitions involve the payment of a premium on market value for the enterprise acquired. The acquiring enterprise very often sees a fall in price. The key time is perhaps one year into the merger and whether the price is down at that time. Perhaps even more relevant is the combined price relative to the individual prices before the merger.

After one year, and perhaps even more so after two or three, the impact of the merger on key success indicators such as profit or the rate of growth of net revenue are clearer. Market value usually reflects profit levels and growth. The financial indicators of profit earnings growth or market capitalization should eventually reflect other factors.

How is it possible to use these indicators while so many other factors affect performance?

● *Impact of the merger on the range of products or services produced and sold*. Many mergers may be designed to diversify either the output or the markets of the company involved. What each company has may be complementary to what the other has. In this case nothing needs to be given up, or is given up, by either company as a result of the merger.

When the merger involves similar companies producing overlapping or competitive products and services, the issue is how far the product range can be rationalized, or who should give up what. What happens when one gives up a product or service? Are at least some of the customers lost? There is often a tendency to an initial loss of customers.

What are the factors which will prevent a rational shedding of products and services?

● *Potential synergies*. In what way can the merger allow a cutting of costs, through the reaping of economies of scale or scope, in other words, the avoidance of duplication. There may also be all sorts of possibilities for cost

saving in merging the procurement of the two enterprises. Their joint buying power may increase their bargaining power and give them the opportunity to drive down the prices of components. Fixed costs may also be spread much wider, whether the costs relate to R&D, the system of distribution or promotion.

● Significant *differences of culture* between the two organizations – are these a plus or a minus?

Are managerial styles compatible? If not, are they appropriate to the functional areas that will be dominated by the partner? Will staff who are a valuable resource leave because of possible conflict? Will the conflict be harmful or can it be channelled into creative flow?

The situation with respect to the Hewlett-Packard/ Compaq merger is:

1. The loss in the second quarter of 2002 was US$163 million, compared with a loss of US$187 million the previous year, a marginal improvement. By the fourth quarter there was a turnaround to a net income of US$309 compared with a loss of US$505 a year earlier. It appears that the new company is being turned around successfully, but that the resulting growth is still unbalanced.

What has been the history of the share price of the company?

The performance and contribution of the four divisions differs markedly.

The loss from the *enterprise systems* group making high-end servers, storage machines and enterprise software rose from $233 million in the second quarter of 2002 to US$574 million in the fourth, compared with a profit of $1 million in the second quarter of 2001. This reflects a serious loss of revenue by this area since the merger. The size of the loss diminished in late 2002 and early 2003 but it is now the only loss-making division.

Is an acquisition a possible way of turning around this division?

The *personal systems* group (PCs, notebooks, hand-held devices and workstations) also has problems. It has seen a serious reduction in revenues and is also significantly loss making. It is in these areas that there was a serious reduction in jobs. However, it has turned around and is now profitable, if only marginally.

The new HP still depends on printers and other services for its major profits. The *printer* division is an area almost unaffected by the merger. There is an enormous expansion in the number of models sold. There are record revenues and a dramatic increase in profit, almost a doubling, so that this division accounts for most of the profit made by the company. Profit margins are up to the high level of 13–15%. Printing generated a $767 profit in 2002 compared with $364 a year earlier. In 2003 the level of profit is still rising.

The *services* division generated a profit of $358 profit in the 2002 quarter compared with $411 a year earlier, and the level is even lower in 2003, due to the high level of competition.

2. In theory the new company has settled on an aggressive adopt-and-grow policy. It has lined up the products of the two companies, adopted the better ones and dropped the worst. The products rejected include most of the HP-branded server computers using processors from Intel, Compaq's Tru64 Unix operating system, HP business PCs and the Jornada hand-held computer from HP. HP is bound to lose more of its products since it produces 62,000 of the two companies' enormous range of 85,000 products. There is much room for more pruning.

The major problem is in the area of PCs. A decision has been made to retain both ranges of PC, on the grounds that dropping one is almost certain to lead to a net loss of sales and revenue slippage, and, even more importantly, add-on sales in printers and digital cameras. Together the two products hold 60% of the retail market. They are different in their market orientation. Compaq's PC is designed for home offices and making a wireless link with the Internet, HP's PC is a home entertainment device and a digital imaging camera for photography enthusiasts. In a contracting market, the failure to make a choice is probably a mistake and certainly does not represent a move to emulate Dell and its successes in selling computers.

Is this sensible as a short-term strategy?

HP is betting on the success of Intel's improved pentium chip in which it is a first mover. One major strength of HP is the raft of technical partnerships it has with good companies. Technically it is still extremely dynamic.

3. It is anticipated that by the year 2004 annual costs will be cut by $3 billion a year, up from the $2.5 billion originally thought. There is an attempt to accelerate the savings. More recently it is claimed that the $3 billion will be saved by the end of 2003. At least one billion can be saved by common procurement alone, because of the increased bargaining power of the very much larger company.

The savings from the payroll were targeted at $1.5 billion, which means shedding 17,900 jobs – with 10,000 by November 2002 and 4,000 on a 50-year-plus generic, early retirement buyout offer. As of April 2003, 16,600 have been laid off, ahead of schedule, and well on the way to the target of 17,900. The problem was morale – $55 million has been committed in retention bonuses to try to stop a brain drain of key staff, notably technical staff. By late 2003 the total labour force will be 140,600, down from 153,500 in May 2000 when the merger occurred.

How far is the cost cutting related to the merger?

4. There is rather a different corporate culture in the two companies. This shows itself in a number of ways:

• HP is rather more laid-back than Compaq. This can affect the nature of the cutbacks and who bears the brunt of them.
• HP is more creativity focused.
• Compaq preferred the direct sales approach, HP a hybrid approach. The retention of both approaches can lead to some channel conflict in marketing the company's products.

The cultural differences are unlikely to be ironed out in less than two years. The continuation of the two brand names has encouraged the survival of the different cultures.

The new strategy

Technology needs to 'yield to the disciplines of business'

CARLY FIORINA, CEO of HP

Hewlett-Packard calls it the Adaptive enterprise, but in reality it's an elaborate strategy that's long on business process re-engineering vision and short on real world experience.

JONES, 2003

A mega-merger will not work simply because the two companies are fused. HP/Compaq must have a strategy which will set its direction for the future and which moves the fused company beyond the production and sale of servers to provide other products and services which the market wants.

Should such a strategy be formulated before merger or after?

A year after the merger the direction was set. In some ways it represented an imitation of the IBM strategy. The new strategy is called the 'adaptive enterprise'. This involves combining hardware, software and services into a utility service to provide computing resources cheaply and efficiently. It is an example of the on-demand model, in which a customer's IT needs are assessed in order to be able to recommend the most economical IT system in terms of effort, cost and risk. It is intended to stress the business agility of the client company, in other words its ability to respond to change. This requires a focus on adaptive technologies. All companies are seen as needing simplified, standardized, modularized and integrated architectures, whether the pressure is competition or new government regulation.

How far should a company imitate the strategy of another successful company?

The centre of the new plan is the Darwin reference architecture services and the existing utility data centre products. The former is used to evaluate the needs of the company, the latter manages the hardware and software that HP/Compaq has available. The role of HP is to provide a total package. Whether this is sensible given the possible role of partners is unclear.

The new HP sees its main competitor as IBM rather than Dell. However, it is under threat from both:

• Typical of the current situation is a contract which HP won for 40,000 PCs from Home Depot. IBM took the much more valuable long-term contract for servers and software designed to help Home Depot to analyse all its logistical and sales data. Customers view HP as a printer and PC company, not a provider of powerful servers and services. HP needs to win more package deals from its corporate customers.

• Dell is also entering a whole series of HP markets, intending to sell printers and ink cartridges from Lexmark under the Dell label. It too is moving into the area of services and advice.

Is HP failing to identify clearly its main competitor?

More in line with what HP is trying to do is the $3 billion agreement with Procter & Gamble by which 2,000 P&G employees, in the areas of managing the company's IT infrastructure, data centre operations, desktop and other services in 48 countries, will become HP employees.

The industry is fiercely competitive. Carly Fiorina has indicated that HP is ready for new acquisitions to build up a weak area such as the enterprise computing area.

Key strategic issues

This case study has explored the issues involved in a merger. It focuses on the obvious questions, why are the two companies candidates for merger and what determines whether a merger or acquisition is a success or not? How does this depend on the conditions in which the two players are operating – the stage in the history of the industry and the degree of competition? How far does it depend on the leadership of Carly Fiorina? How far does it depend upon proper preparation?

Other issues follow. What products and services should be produced by the two companies? What cost synergies are available? How far could the reduction in costs which has occurred have been achieved without the merger?

Fusion only creates an initial departure point. What is the appropriate strategy for the fused entity? What should be the structure of the new company?

More general questions include: How can the success of a merger or acquisition be evaluated? Under what circumstances would a merger provide net benefits large enough to justify that merger? Did the Hewlett-Packard/Compaq merger satisfy these conditions? What are the different strategies on size which have been pursued in the computer industry? What different strategies are likely to be pursued in the future?

An obvious final question is: does a company learn from one merger how to achieve another merger successfully?

Strategic analysis and audit

Carry out a full strategic audit on Hewlett-Packard/ Compaq. Has the merger been a success? Is the present strategy well devised for the new merged company?

Reading

Edwards, C., 'The new HP: how's it doing?', *Business Week*, December 23, 2002: 58–60.

Faletra, R., 'Fiorina's progress so far in HP-Compaq integration does not guarantee success', *CRN 1044* May 5, 2003: 112.

Greenemeier, L. and Babcock, C., 'HP looks to utility computing for growth', *Information Week* **939**, May 12, 2003: 26.

Hill, C. W. and Jones, G. R,. 'Changing the focus at Hewlett-Packard' in Hill, C. W. and Jones, G. R. *Strategic Management: an integrated approach* (5th edn) (New York and Boston, Houghton Mifflin: 2003).

Jones, M., 'HP vision short on experience', *InfoWorld*, **25**(19) May 12, 2003: 16.

Mears, J., 'HP to become more adaptive', *Network World* **20**(19) May 12, 2003: 10.

Tam, P-W., 'Leading the news: HP results signal possible growth', *Wall Street Journal* (Eastern edn) May 21, 2003: A3.

Thibodeau, P., 'HP's 'adaptive' strategy faces challenging market' and 'Step 1: hire a consultant, HP exec says', *Computerworld* **37**(19) May 12, 2003: 4.

Veverka, M., 'Plugged in: HP: hedging on the server curve', *Barron's* **83**(26) June 30, 2003: T3.

www.hewlettpackard.com
www.compaq.com

Lloyd's of London and 'long-tailed' risk

Lloyd's is the most recognized brand in the insurance world. But it is a unique institution that can be confusing to outsiders.

Reactions, 2003

We have to modernise the processes and bring them into the 21st century.

In other cyclical industries you have good years and you have not very good years. It seems in the insurance industry you have good years and then you have unbelievably disastrous years.

Perception, process and price. What do people think about the place? How do we get it to run in the 21st century? And how do we get the cost of doing business here down to a level which people are comfortable with?

LORD LEVINE (quoted for the first two in *Reactions*, 2003 and for the third in Howard, April 2003)

Background

This case study illustrates the need to forecast the future with some accuracy, although the need is to know the probability of various groups of events occurring, not to be able to forecast what will happen in any individual case. The insurance industry is one industry in which it is commercially necessary to have an accurate, if broad, view of future events. However, it is also one in which there is a pronounced cycle of profit and loss, which suggests a failure to forecast accurately.

Are there other industries which rely to the same degree on an ability to forecast the future? What are the differences in the ways in which these forecasts are made?

It is possible to insure against the negative consequences of future events by taking out an insurance policy and paying the associated premiums on this policy. In theory this will include all future events which can have a negative impact on an enterprise. The degree of risk aversion, as well as the probability of occurrence, determines whether an individual or organization actually takes out cover against damage from a particular class of risk-generating events, for example a road accident or a plane crash. The insurer tries to ensure a profit by setting premiums at an appropriate level so they will more than cover the claims made on policies. This requires an accurate forecast of the number and size of claims.

What are the factors which influence firstly the offer of insurance and secondly the wish of those at risk to take up the offer of insurance?

The viability of a commercial insurance industry, or indeed of a particular insurance company, reflects two factors:

- The existence of a large number of potential insurees at risk and willing to cover that risk at a feasible price. If, for example, the premium is high and the risk for certain groups is low, 'adverse selection' may occur, threatening the viability of insurance. In other words, those least likely to claim do not insure. This may push the premiums up to a non-viable level.
- The existence of sufficient information, readily converted into knowledge, for premiums to be accurately calculated. This information consists of past statistics on the frequency of occurrence of potentially negative events, actuarial tables of the probability of negative events. Traditionally the probability of such events occurring could be calculated with some accuracy. This applies to marine, fire, motor and life insurance. In principle the calculations assume that this frequency does not change and also that the cover is for a fixed amount.

What are the basic principles of the law of large numbers which allows the offer of insurance? What do the two features require an insurance company to do in order to be profitable?

The insurance company can then determine an appropriate level of premiums and also reserves adequate to meet any possible bunching of claims. Clearly premiums can be invested to yield a return which is added to reserves and helps to keep those reserves at a level which allows the insurer to cover all claims.

What is likely to be the influence of high interest rates or a stock market boom on the level of premiums determined by insurance companies? Why might the industry be subject to cyclical fluctuations in the levels of profit and premiums?

For much of its history the industry dealt with what it calls 'normal' events but what most people would call abnormal events, events which cause a determinate amount of damage or a fixed loss of income. These include storms, fires, shipwrecks, earthquakes, accidents, illnesses and theft. The law of large numbers meant that the industry had no difficulty dealing with the two factors above. Insurance companies could specialize in different kinds of risk, for example marine or life insurance, medical or more recently automobile insurance.

What might be the definition of a 'normal' event? Has there been any change in the proportion of 'normal' and 'abnormal' events confronting insurance companies?

The same principles were extended and applied to much more expensive items, such as satellites, oil rigs and airliners. With the extension of insurance to a much broader class of valuable assets and therefore to a broader class of potentially damaging events, the risk is more difficult to calculate, partly because it is more difficult to anticipate the frequency of events. Events which occur only rarely and only rarely have an impact on expensive capital items are more difficult to deal with. The size of the cover and therefore possible losses has become much greater, so that both sharing and reinsurance has become much more important.

Is it possible to insure against all risks? If not, is it possible in theory? What are the difficulties in offering insurance against 'abnormal' events?

The risk of the insurance companies, when it becomes large, can be reduced in two ways:

- Horizontally, by a number of companies taking a proportion of and therefore sharing the total risk.
- Vertically, by one company taking all the initial risk but by reinsurance passing on some of that risk and by further retrocession the reinsurers doing the same. One problem that emerges is that with each layer of reinsurance knowledge of the underlying risk becomes more uncertain.

What difficulties are likely to confront those who reinsure?

Insurance has been extended to many new areas, exposing the various players, including insurance companies, to more complex risk. Many of these new areas involve 'long-tailed' risks, that is, risks which only manifest themselves long after the policy has been written. For example, there are diseases with a long gestation period, such as asbestos-related diseases which can take 20, 30 or even 40 years to show themselves. The insurance might also cover an actress's legs, political risk, professional indemnity of various types or exposure to harmful materials or polluting agents. In all these cases it is often difficult to assess the real risk. There is a strong possibility of underestimating the risk and therefore the appropriate levels of premiums.

How is it possible to deal with 'long-tailed' risk? How is it possible to deal with events which are so rare that they have no actuarial background?

In the insurance industry there are institutions which specialize in modelling risk, predicting both frequency and severity of risk-creating events, such as Applied Insurance Research, Eqecut or Risk Management Solutions. This is a highly specialized task. The forecasting has worked quite well for assessing severity, which reflects both the possible size of the shock and the value of the capital at risk. Depending on the nature of the event, it is more difficult to get the frequency right, particularly if it is a rare event. The law of large numbers does not really apply and over a long period of time conditions might change quite dramatically. For events such as terrorist attacks it is very difficult indeed. The insurance cost of the terrorist attacks on September 11, 2001 is something like $35 billion, much of which again has fallen into the lap of Lloyd's. However, Lord Levine, the new chairman of Lloyd's, argues that the problem is an increased risk from natural catastrophes. According to Lloyd's, 12 of the 13 most damaging storms in history have occurred in the past 10 years and mega-catastrophes, which usually occur every 100 years, will start happening every 25 years by 2050.

Is it a feasible and acceptable approach to outsource the actuarial role? Is this not a core competency of an insurance company?

The problem of assessing frequency and severity is compounded if the law courts, in awarding damages, change their policy, both extending the definitions of negligence and malpractice, and awarding much larger sums than was previously the case. The inclination and practice of law courts may differ from country to country. With the increasingly global reach of insurance companies, the pattern of decision making by courts abroad must be considered. All this also has to be allowed for. The amount of knowledge required has become much larger. It could be assumed that a core competency of insurance companies is an actuarial expertise which allows them to make an accurate estimate of probabilities across a broad range of risks and in conditions which might vary significantly. This may involve having ready access to specialist knowledge of particular areas of risk.

How is it possible to deal with the changing litigiousness of the population at large and the greater willingness of courts to grant large damages claims?

Lloyd's

Lloyd's is probably the most famous insurance company in the world and in terms of the size of its total premiums it is the second largest insurer. It is also a market leader in the area of reinsurance, the sixth largest reinsurance group. It claims to be able to undertake any kind of insurance. It has existed for over three hundred years, in which time it claims never to have dishonoured a single insurance claim. It has deliberately erred on the side of generosity in meeting such claims and has therefore acquired an unparalleled reputation for reliability. Lloyd's is a brand name which is unmatched, surviving even the recent crisis of large losses in the early 1990s and a similar situation in the early 2000s.

Is it a sensible approach to be willing to insure anything and err on the side of generosity in meeting claims? Is this not a loss-making prescription?

Lloyd's is in fact a market rather than a single corporation. It is like a franchise, in which the managing agencies writing policies (currently 46 in number) are the franchisees. Each syndicate in the market is like an independent insurance company. Each exploits fully the brand name. On the market all such syndicates both compete for the insurance and cooperate in, for example, providing reinsurance.

How is it possible to avoid the bad behaviour of one or two syndicates destroying the good reputation of the market as a whole?

How did Lloyd's achieve this unparalleled reputation? This required both expertise and the necessary capital. The market needs enough knowledge of the risks to set premiums at appropriate levels and enough capital to deal with any bunching of losses.

What are the core competencies of a successful insurance company?

Before 1969 the individual providers of capital to the syndicates were all British. Moreover, these individuals not only knew each other but knew and were known by the brokers, the underwriters and the agents. It was also true that all the key agents knew their industry very well. They had a known expertise and could be trusted. As a consequence, up to this time most syndicates made very healthy and attractive profits. To become a name, that is, an individual capital provider, was regarded as a highly desired privilege. Under this regime, unlimited liability, to which the names were exposed, was a meaningless vulnerability.

What is the role of information and trust in establishing the reputation of an insurance company? How could Lloyd's have maintained unlimited liability, something which is very unusual for an enterprise of its size and age?

The role of capital provision was in practice dealt with in an unusual way, quite untypical of the modern economy. Each individual providing capital pledged assets or later put up a letter of credit from a bank, backed by shares or bonds. These assets were used as backing for the underwriting of insurance risks. They continued to yield a return for the owner, so that the money worked twice, in giving a return from the investment and from its backing of an insurance. For any agency the aggregate of pledges defined the 'stamp capacity', which fixed the maximum permissible level of premiums, and for individuals their share in profits or losses. Those putting up the capital were individuals, not corporations, and until 1970 a relatively small group of very rich and carefully selected, or 'elected' as the terminology has it, individuals, well under 3,000 in all.

Why was being a name so popular? Is it the case that the double plus of good returns during a boom could become the double negative of large losses during a recession? How could this be avoided?

The underwriters of an agency would consider any insurance proposal made by brokers, and put together a syndicate to back a particular policy or policies. In theory agencies, individuals and syndicates could diversify their portfolio of policies to help reduce risk. One danger was an undiversified portfolio and systematic risk in the policies. Maximizing short-term returns at the cost of massive risk is always a dangerous policy.

What was the role of the underwriters? What makes for a successful underwriter? How could the underwriters reduce the risks to which a syndicate was exposed?

In theory the insuring syndicates were reconstituted at the end of each year, so that individuals could withdraw and be replaced by different individuals. Normally there was immense competition to become a name, so that withdrawals were uncommon. The closing of a syndicate was done always for the year falling three years before to allow most outstanding claims to be settled. This process was called 'reinsurance to close' since a reinsurance premium was paid to cover any outstanding claims. The year was closed if this happened. If it did not, because the outstanding claims were too uncertain, the year remained open. In theory a name could withdraw at this time; in practice few did and when it became desirable for names to withdraw, few could, because the syndicates remained open.

Are there problems associated with the significant time lags in drawing up the accounts? Are there benefits in such a system?

As indicated above, those putting up the money for the syndicates had unlimited liability. Under such a system it was impossible for the syndicates to fail to honour a claim unless the individuals putting up the money (called names, since originally they used to put their names on the back of a policy) all became bankrupt simultaneously, an extremely unlikely event in the pre-1969 environment. Whereas on the stock market for a typical limited liability company there were potentially unlimited returns but limited risk, here the case was the opposite, unlimited risk and limited returns, albeit very generous, since they reflected the permitted total of the premiums.

In the Lloyd's system who bore the risk?

Change and the origins of crisis

A number of critical changes occurred during the 1970s and 80s which culminated in a serious crisis at the end of the 1980s and the early 1990s, from which even today Lloyd's has not fully extricated itself. The changes were:

• The range of events insured expanded enormously. The boast that Lloyd's would insure almost anything became a reality. At the same time competition in the industry became intense, with insurance companies using modern methods with much lower costs.
• The proportion of insurance abroad increased. The industry was going global. For example, for Lloyd's the share of the American market rose to 40%.
• In order to secure an expanded supply of capital, there was a major effort to attract new names. The number of names expanded dramatically to well over 30,000, with the result that entrants were less wealthy. New names were deliberately brought in for fear of losses. The number of syndicates also increased to over 400.
• These names ceased to be limited to residents in Britain, but were increasingly found in North America. They inevitably had less knowledge of what they were doing, trusting in the good name of Lloyd's.
• Reinsurance rose greatly in importance.

How far was the crisis part of a normal cyclical downturn and how far was it a one-off crisis?

The following were the main inputs into the crisis:

• The increase in numbers represented a trading on reputation. The new names were overwhelmed by the reputation of Lloyd's without understanding the full extent of their commitment. It was no longer possible either for the names to know whether the underwriters

had the desired expertise or for the managing agents to know whether the names had the necessary wealth to cover claims in an emergency.
• Expansion into new areas meant a reduction in expertise. There was much greater ignorance and therefore much more risk. Underwriters were much less expert than they had been. This was made more complicated by an element of outright fraud and a failure to recognize and accept the size of the risk.
• In London the so-called reinsurance 'spiral' spun completely out of control, which led to corrupt practices, for some syndicates the disappearance of a majority of premiums into a foreign insurance company doing the reinsurance and therefore the diversion of premiums from names into the pockets of the owners of such companies. This was accompanied by a loss of proper risk assessment, certainly the charging of premiums well below what was reasonable given the real risks. In some cases the spiral of reinsurance was internal and involved the same syndicate in reinsuring different tranches of the risk, which negates the purpose of reinsurance.
• It was said, although this is controversial, that some syndicates, only a few, remained conservative and insiders, aware of the relative riskiness of policies, kept to these syndicates. By contrast new names often landed up in the highest risk syndicates, again only a few.
• There was a delayed reaction to the emerging evidence of greater riskiness. To some degree this was rational since there were enormous delays in processing the claims made, notably in the time taken for the court to make a judgement and finally in the reclaiming of money along the chain of insurers and reinsurers (this alone could take up to 10 years). At a time of high interest rates, above even 15%, and high returns, sometimes much higher, premiums could compound to sums way above the initial value. After all at a 15% rate of return an investment doubles within five years and quadruples in 10. However, the problem was the continuation of practices out of step with the claims already coming in which generated a stream of future claims.

How far was the crisis due to a. corruption, b. a failure to adjust to changing circumstances by Lloyd's, c. a downturn in capital markets and, d. greater riskiness in the external business environment?

The crisis and a changing industry

In 1991 the first loss was reported, for 1988. Unhappily the losses quickly escalated. They began to increase enormously, until they amounted to over $15 billion.

Lloyd's was forced to increase contributions to the central fund which covered the position of those names who either could not or would not meet their obligations. Lloyd's tried to keep the names to their obligations. Names, who found themselves required to find large sums of money to meet losses, began to take legal action against Lloyd's on the grounds that they had been misled and not given adequate information on the basis of which they could make informed decisions, and also on the grounds that Lloyd's had not acted quickly enough to new information on the asbestos claims. For the most part these actions have failed.

The boom in the stock market which began with the end of the recession in the early 1990s and ran right through the 1990s helped Lloyd's cope with the losses which had been incurred. That boom massively increased the return on funds invested to meet future claims. However, the terrorist attacks of September 11, 2001, combined with a recession, pushed Lloyd's back into major loss making. Lloyd's had a £2 billion exposure to the September 11 terrorist attacks. Rating agency Moody's predicts that Lloyd's loss for 2000 and 2001 combined will be £4.5 billion. In 2002 the profit recovered to almost £1.5 billion.

The convergence of three problems is likely to make for a crisis for any insurance company – the incidence of events which create serious claims, poor returns on invested reserves, which can occur when a stock market bubble bursts, combined with low premiums, and organizational problems, which hamper the raising of new capital or limit the capital available to meet claims. Lloyd's has had to confront all these problems.

The attempt to deal with the last has led to a major attempt to reform the Lloyd's system. The preference of successive leaders has been to exclude the names completely and attract new capital from corporate investors without limited liability. The names have resisted this, successfully insofar as they have been allowed to survive. While a significant share of Lloyd's capital comes from corporate sources, the old systems have not disappeared.

The implementation of reform

Lloyd's now has US$40 billion in assets to back its underwriting of insurance, most now coming from corporations and other institutions. It has managed to raise new capital because of its name and its commitment to reform. The limited liability of the names has gone, although the existing names have managed to retain their role, if now a subordinate one, with more than 20% of the capacity of Lloyd's provided by

them. There is an active search by the largest agent Hampden Agencies Ltd for new names, organized in namecos, the limited liability companies specifically designed for Lloyd's names. The lure is still the double revenue, and a potential return on capital of 30%.

What for Lloyd's is a desirable mix of name capital and corporate capital? Would it be better for the company to exclude all names?

Two chairmen of Lloyd's have been faced with the task of reform – Sax Riley who was responsible for putting in the theoretical framework, often against strong opposition, and Lord Levine who was appointed in late 2002 to improve the public image of Lloyd's and implement the reforms. The reconstruction and renewal process of the early 1990s dealt with a turnaround situation and is the basis for the series of reforms now being implemented. The problem of 'long-tailed' risk was dealt with by the establishment of Equitas Ltd as the runoff reinsurer for the pre-1993 liabilities.

How far can a leader impose a strategy on such a diffuse organization as Lloyd's?

Lord Levine is the first chairman to come from outside the industry in more than a century. However, he has considerable experience as a troubleshooter who has played a significant role in turning around a number of troubled enterprises. His job is made rather harder by the structure of Lloyd's. As he says, 'It's very different because if you are chairman of a normal company or even if you are running a government department you can consult people but at the end of the day you can say: "Alright I've heard what you've all had to say, now this is what we are going to do." Here you can't do that because you don't actually control which companies operate in the market' (*Reactions*, 2003).

What kind of leader is required by Lloyd's?

Probably one of the most important functions is to chair the new Franchise Board, established in January 2003, which is responsible for overseeing the underwriting of the syndicates and ensuring that they are implementing their business plans. The decision to model Lloyd's as a franchise led to the appointment of a franchise performance director with a team of assistants with the brief of improving Lloyd's commercial performance. The adherence to the business plans will be monitored by the Franchise Board on a quarterly basis. In the event that the syndicates depart from their plan, their underwriting can be limited and, in extremis, they can be expelled from the market. To ensure profitability, even in a cyclical downturn, there is a need for underwriting discipline.

How far is the Lloyd's strategy simply an amalgam of all the separate syndicate strategies? How far is the job of the chairman simply to coordinate these separate strategies?

A major aim is to even out the nine-year business cycle, which sees high premiums and prices followed by increased capacity and low premiums and loss making. To show that it means business, in the middle of 2003 the Franchise Board ordered 3 of the 71 syndicates to halt underwriting. These 71 syndicates compete for business from the 160 insurance brokers in the market.

What are the main features of the insurance cycle? Why is it a problem?

At the same time Lloyd's has been trying to assess the amount of reinsurance and the strength of the main reinsurers, as part of its own risk control.

A second function is to bring up to date the processes of the market, for example replacing the face-to-face communication and handwritten records with electronic communication and storage in accord with the new information technology. In order to remain competitive in costs, the processes must be modernized which is the aim of an initiative called Project Blue Mountain, the responsibility for the implementation of which is again Levine's. In an increasingly competitive industry, it is necessary to keep costs down.

How important is competition in the insurance industry?

All this action will allow Levine to attain 'the triple p' objective of perception, process and price, which he sees as the main strategic objective of Lloyd's.

Key strategic issues

Lloyd's is an extremely unusual organization, the peculiarities of which compounded the crisis which occurred and have made difficult its reform. It has a strong culture which is difficult to change. How far is the crisis at Lloyd's simply a consequence of strategic drift? Or how far is the change in strategy the result of changes in the environment in which Lloyd's operates? Is it possible for Lloyd's to retain the positive features of the old business model while at the same time modernizing it? How far has Lloyd's managed its brand name cleverly?

Strategic analysis and audit

Carry out a full strategic audit on Lloyd's, taking account of the fact that Lloyd's is really a franchise of many separate businesses. How far are they consistent with each other?

Reading

Hodge, N., 'Lloyd's agency to recruit names', *Business Insurance*, **37**(19) May 12, 2003: 17.

Howard, L., 'Lloyd's chairman outlines challenges', *National Underwriter*, **107**(14) April 7, 2003: 45.

Howard, L., 'Lloyd's assessing re failure risk', *National Underwriter*, **107**(25) June 23, 2003: 5.

Howard, L., 'Would you believe 2010? Lloyd's underwriter', *National Underwriter*, **107**(25) June 23, 2003: 6.

Kemp, S., 'Lloyd's tells syndicates to lift gains', *Business Age*, July 21, 2003: 7.

Luessenhop, E. and Mayer, M., *Risky Business: An Insider's Account of the Disaster at Lloyd's of London* (Scribner, New York: 1995).

Murray, L., 'Get used to higher premiums', *The Australian Financial Review*, July 18, 2003: 72.

Reactions, 'The troubleshooter', London, April 2003: 1.

Veysey, S., 'Lloyd's of London returns to profit', *Business Insurance*, **37**(14) April 7, 2003: 1.

www.lloydsoflondon.co.uk

The Mt Buller winter resort and global warming

It is appropriate to begin by saying something about the resort phenomenon in general and the nature of competitive advantage in such resorts, its creation and even more its maintenance.

Resorts

There are many different kinds of resorts, some privately owned and run by one enterprise, others the amalgam of many enterprises, often quite small. There must be some initial reason for visitors to choose a particular place and to be willing to pay for the privilege. The resort must have some competitive advantage:

• Some resorts are focused on a natural feature such as a beach or a mountain suitable for skiing, or a particular kind of wild life, for example big game
• Others exist independently of natural features and are completely man-made
• There are also seaside or spa resorts which lack the unity of purpose of an isolated resort, and would exist without the attraction, but on a smaller scale
• Some resorts might be organized around a historical event, period or even significant industry which has ceased to have the importance it once had – gold or some kind of mining or agriculture of a particular period in the past
• Some resorts are focused on sporting or recreational rather than working activities
• Some towns offer a casino or casinos; gambling can happen anywhere.

How might a classification of the competitive advantage around which a resort is operated be organized?

Ever since the creation of Disneyland, the putting together of resorts targeted purely for entertainment and without a natural or historical base has gathered pace, often involving the investment of large resources. Such resorts are almost invariably privately run, although they may have significant government assistance, either at the construction or operating stage. In this case the resort becomes free from a specific location; in theory it could be located anywhere. In practice the location reflects where the market is – it must be located so that it is easy and relatively cheap for visitors to gain access.

What are the factors influencing the location of a resort?

It is unclear how far it is possible to stretch the definition of a resort. It depends on what resorts are thought to share in common. This can only be answered if there is an unambiguous definition of what constitutes a resort. It is necessary to attempt this. The definition must have a strategic aspect, that is, the development of the place depends on its nature as a potential resort.

Is it appropriate, for example, to include casinos in this definition or game parks? Is Las Vegas the resort or the gaming houses which constitute its main raison d'être?

Briefly, a resort can be defined as a place of entertainment or recreation which provides a pleasing experience, with the associated services needed to sustain exposure to that experience, and which attracts visitors for significant periods of time. The resort has to provide in some way for the needs of the visitors during this time.

These periods are longer than those required for the performance of a sporting or cultural event, which might only last several hours or several days in some cases.

However, the resort, unlike a festival or major sporting event such as the Olympics or World Cup, must have some continuity of existence, although its main activity may be seasonal.

Can you make a better definition of a resort?

A resort has an identity determined by the nature of the attraction. In some cases the attraction has come to dominate a township which already exists, and is usually but not always separated from the place of residence or work of the local population; visitors resort to it with one aim in view, to be entertained.

How is it possible to define the identity of a resort?

In one significant subgroup of resorts, the resort itself is separated geographically from existing centres of population, perhaps because the population has moved or the nature of the environment has never attracted a large concentration of population. Some resorts may be deliberately established in remote areas, that remoteness being part of the attraction.

Some resorts lend themselves to long stay and therefore include elaborate provision for accommodation of various qualities, hotels for example. Others are frequented mainly by day visitors. If the latter is the case, there is a severe constraint on location, which must be close to existing centres of population so that travel time does not become excessive.

What are the main features of resort identity which have an impact on the making of strategy?

The existence of resorts has been made possible by the increase in discretionary income available to all groups of people in developed economies and growing groups in others. Families or individuals in developed economies are now much better able to find the money required, even if expensive international travel to the resort is required. However, the pricing levels of many package holidays mean they are affordable to increasing numbers of families. There is a regular search for a holiday venue. There is a desire for entertainment for which a resort specifically caters.

What are the factors which influence the way in which recreational wants are satisfied?

The establishment of resorts can become institutionalized. For example, in Japan the passing of the Law for the Comprehensive Resort Areas in 1987 led to every local government drawing up plans to develop resort complexes of various kinds. Often the resorts represent a distorted imitation of life in other countries, such as a Dutch village in Nagasaki. Tokyo Disney was part of this phenomenon.

What is the role of construction and local employment in the development of resorts?

Main features of the resort sector

Resorts must usually satisfy the normal requirements for private enterprises to make a profit. There may be some public involvement which creates an interesting relationship between the private and the public. This has significant implications in terms of strategy making.

Is a resort capable of standing on its own feet? Why would a government subsidize the creation of a resort? How does the public sector pay for its contribution, or does it too require that a project pays its way?

Some defining features of a resort are now discussed.

● *Most resorts require considerable infrastructure*
Typically this is the same as for normal everyday life: transport systems with the outside world and within the resort, including roads, and sometimes rail or air facili-

ties; utilities – energy, water, communications, rubbish disposal; police; sometimes educational and medical services; plus the usual retail outlets selling food and other daily necessities; even hotels and motels. These are required in addition to equipment or facilities necessary for the recreational activity, such as rides or other attractions in a Disney theme park. The infrastructure required for this may also be significant, for example ski lifts or exhibits.

These facilities imply a considerable investment of resources. A resort cannot be built incrementally. There may be economies of scale or scope which, from its inception, make highly desirable a minimum threshold size for the resort. The infrastructure must be paid for and maintained. For example, Disney began to build theme parks alongside existing parks to take advantage of existing infrastructure.

There are important implications arising from the need for infrastructure. How is the finance raised? Over what period is the investment recouped?

● *Most resorts involve networks of cooperating enterprises*
These enterprises may vary enormously in size. Some may be involved in providing inputs of various kinds, others may be directly operating part of the resort, a few may even be involved in assisting in the marketing of the resort or providing its services. Some of the cooperating organizations may be government organizations. In some cases there may be a large number of enterprises. In the case of Disney there was a steady widening of the scope of activity of the Disney company itself in order to capture the returns which were accruing to others, such as those providing attractions or accommodation, evening entertainment or food. Disney seeks to capture as much of the visitors' expenditures as possible.

In what ways does the existence of interacting organizations complicate strategy making?

● *Resorts require coordination of a sophisticated kind*
Where the resort has one owner, the enterprise concerned has the coordinating role. Where there are many different enterprises involved, it is often the case that one organization has the role of coordination. The stress on cooperation may make necessary a higher level of strategy. The strategic coordination may be provided by a leading enterprise, an industry association of some kind or a government body. Or it may be provided by a combination of all these. Often some level of government is involved in strategy making for the resort. These may be organizations deliberately put in place for the purpose or local government organizations which are already there.

What determines which organization is the strategic leader?

Since the resort may have a significant impact on the local region and local communities, generating both jobs and income, there may be a strong government interest in stimulating resort development. Government may feel it worthwhile to encourage resort development by providing infrastructure or services at a low price. This is particularly true of townships already in decline as old industries decay. They may be in the process of actively seeking out new attractions. The exact nature of government involvement is a critical issue.

What is the role of government as a stakeholder in such resorts?

In terms of organizational structure there is a range of possibilities. At one end is a highly decentralized structure of private enterprises, all operating in a market context. At the other end is extreme centralization, with a government body running a number of different resorts, or in some cases one single owner. The nature of strategy making reflects these differences in structure.

What influences the degree of centralization?

It is important that all the cooperating enterprises have a clear idea about the likely future development of the resort, its pace and nature. Plans for investment must be consistent with each other. There must not be any serious bottlenecks arising from the lack of a critical service or input. Without a coordinator, this is difficult to achieve.

Why is coordination so important to both the formulation and implementation of a strategy?

● *The arrival of visitors is uneven*
Some resorts are by their nature seasonal. This may simply result from the timing of public holidays or when workers traditionally take their recreation leave, or it may reflect the regular rhythm of weekdays and weekends. The seasonality of operation is pronounced if the resort relies on particular weather conditions, for example plenty of snow or sunshine. It may mean avoiding some seasons such as the rainy or cyclone season. This means that most visitors come during a particular period of the year, and that the numbers are greatest in a good season, defined by the amount of sun or snow.

What factors influence the pattern of flow of visitors?

During the off-season or a bad season facilities are under-utilized. This creates a problem for the employment of most staff who as a result must be part time. Employment patterns must be flexible. The problem can be solved by the availability of a range of different seasonal activities which maintain year-round employment. There is a definite interest in evening out visits to a resort.

What difficulties does an unevenness of flow create for the operation and development of a resort?

● *Often the product(s) or service(s) has a range of linked attributes*
Attending a resort may involve a main experience, such as skiing, surfing or gambling, and a range of other experiences ranging from good eating and drinking to sporting activities. The range is extended further if it is a family affair, seeking to satisfy the tastes of children as well as adults. The attraction may be particular climatic conditions or simply a good view. It may involve a deliberate attempt to entertain or it might be a purely passive form of enjoyment. Generally it is a complex experience, which makes more difficult the marketing of the product(s).

Choose a particular resort and indicate the attributes which attach to the experience provided by that resort.

● *Marketing is a major activity, partly because of the nature of the product and partly because the leisure sector is a fiercely competitive sector of the economy in which there are many competing resorts*
Branding of place is a key part of the marketing of resorts. This is well shown by the importance of the Disney name in attracting large numbers of visitors to its theme parks, even to the first park, visitors who were already familiar with the main Disney characters from films, comics or cartoons. There are different levels of marketing which may involve branding the country, the region, the resort itself and finally the enterprise and the product it provides.

What is the advantage of branding to a resort?

Customers may be repeat customers or one-off day visitors. The key aim may be to achieve repeat visits by converting one-off visitors into repeat visitors. Promotion may involve ensuring that the customer is happy with the whole experience. However, variety itself may be part of the recreational experience, which puts the emphasis on attracting one-off visitors. One-off visitors may be common. It is harder and more expensive to attract such visitors.

Under what conditions are one-off visitors or repeat visitors likely to be more important?

● *In some cases environmental or cultural issues are important*
Sheer numbers can lead to damage to the environment

which is the attraction in the first place. Solitude itself may be part of the experience. For example, too many visitors to the game parks of Africa can deter the animals which attract the visitors, or the alpine flora and fauna can be badly affected by the construction of alpine villages. There may well be a balance between the desire to attract large numbers of visitors and the damage inflicted by such a high level of visitation. As a result there may be a deliberate attempt to make the resort more exclusive, more expensive and open to fewer people.

Who are the main stakeholder groups concerned with environmental damage? How might they be involved in the strategy-making process?

Alternatively the nature of the experience at a resort may be perceived as damaging to the culture of the host community. In practice it may or may not be – perception is the key. There may be key local groups who suffer negative consequences from the existence of the resort.

Who are the main stakeholder groups concerned with cultural damage? How might they be involved in the strategy-making process?

In these case studies, two resorts are considered, the Mt Buller winter resort and Euro Disney; they raise different strategic problems, particularly for the creation and maintenance of competitive advantage. Disney has sought to apply the same model in different places. The Buller resort raises the issues of seasonality and global warming. By way of contrast it is also helpful to compare the strategic issues raised by events such as Formula One motor racing (see the Strategy in Action module in Chapter 10).

What are the different strategic issues raised by these case studies?

Mt Buller is the premier winter resort in Victoria, Australia. It is one of six resorts, three of which are large. Mt Buller competes for customers with these other resorts as well as with winter resorts in New South Wales and abroad. It has the advantage of being only a three-hour drive from Melbourne, which has well over 3.5 million potential visitors within easy travel time.

Particular problems of a winter resort

• *Dependence on weather conditions*
The skiing season is defined by the presence of adequate snow. Too little snow prevents skiing and other snow sports or activities. The fall of snow at the beginning of the season and its publicizing is particularly important in setting the tone for the season. Snow making itself,

while of increasing importance, can only occur if the temperature is low enough and therefore cannot fully substitute for natural falls. Where the snow season is short and dependent for its length on advantageous weather conditions, there may be bad years when there is little possibility of skiing. A bad season is an inevitable event whose frequency needs to be estimated.

How long is a typical snow season? What is the variability of that season's length? Is it changing?

Fluctuations in the length of the season affect the level of revenues and costs in any one year, not only for resort management but for all businesses in a resort. It is hard to break even with bad conditions and even harder to finance investment in improvements.

How sensitive is an organization's revenue to variations in the length of a season?

The possibility of global warming compounds the problem. Any strategic plan needs to take account of bad seasons and any change over the years in the incidence of bad seasons. Reading the environment includes tracking the degree and effects of global warming. The problem is larger for resorts which are marginal, in the sense that their seasons are already short and variable, generally because of their low altitude.

• *Problem of seasonal visitation*
A short winter season, less than four months for example, leaves the infrastructure of a resort under-utilized for the other eight months. The short season is itself a major deterrent to the provision of the full range of facilities required by a permanent alpine village. A lack of out-of-season activities worsens the problem.

What is the range of activities available in a winter resort? How many occur outside the snow season?

The kinds of activities that might be pursued are wide:

• They include walking, climbing, mountain bike riding, horse trekking and other sporting activities of a more organized nature, even golf, some requiring specific equipment
• The existence of good sporting facilities allows the provision of training facilities for sporting teams
• Educational pursuits, including teaching and research, might be appropriate
• Where there are good hotel and restaurant facilities and good lecture and seminar rooms, conferences and colloquia can be attracted to the resort.

• *Problem of providing a full infrastructure*
Most facilities demand either a minimum size of permanent population or a regular flow of visitors all year round. There is a threshold level of demand below

which any facility is not viable, which varies from facility to facility. This is true even of supermarkets, restaurants or cinemas. It is definitely true of police, fire or medical facilities. The more remote the resort, the truer this is, since day visitors cannot provide the required demand and permanent residents must.

What is the threshold size for a viable resort?

● *Resident/visitor mix*
It may be difficult to build up a significant permanent local population which would justify keeping facilities open out of season without those facilities being there in the first place. The existence of facilities creates a permanent working population. Therefore there is a vicious circle – poor facilities, few permanent residents. The closing of facilities out of season compounds the problem of increasing the permanent population. The domination of a resort by temporary visitors, particularly day visitors, and part-time workers, or workers who live somewhere else, influences the whole nature of the resort.

When is it likely that a resort closes in the off-season?

● *Problem of high operating costs*
There are a number of reasons why the unit costs of supplying services may be higher in a resort than outside:

● If the resort is remote and hard to access, perhaps even impossible at certain times, transport costs for all supplies may become a significant element in the final price of goods and services
● The resort may not be large enough to reap significant economies of scale for basic services
● A short season means that any fixed costs must be covered by a smaller number of sales
● There may be a lack of competition in the provision of some goods and services which keeps prices up within the resort
● Wage costs may be higher because it is necessary to attract staff to a remote place, living costs are higher, including accommodation, or simply because most staff are employed on a part-time basis.

The higher the costs, the higher the price of services and the greater the deterrent to purchase them. Skiing is already an expensive sport in terms of equipment and clothing. A high cost of using the resort further limits the possible market. It is by its nature the sport of either the rich or the deeply committed.

How is it possible to limit the costs of using a winter resort in order to expand the market?

There may be a vicious circle of increasing costs since high operating costs cut use and reduce the effect of any economies of scale in using the infrastructure. Alternatively, it may be possible to generate a virtuous circle of decreasing cost, if an impetus can be given to expansion which brings down the costs.

What are the dynamics of the cost situation – good or bad?

● *Avoiding accidents and disasters*
The areas concerned may be subject to geodisturbances, such as landslides and avalanches. This is a priority area of concern, as the disaster at the Australian ski resort of Thredbo in 1997 showed. The activities may be potentially dangerous since they are pursued in extreme weather conditions, which can change very quickly. A reputation for low safety could badly damage a resort. In the past court decisions have been costly for some resorts where negligence has been proved. This adds to the cost of operating the resort, directly through the level of insurance premiums and indirectly through the cost of measures to control risk.

What are the type of risks which confront a winter resort? What methods are available to control this risk?

● *Avoiding environmental damage*
Alpine ecologies are fragile, but their very existence is part of their attractiveness which needs to be protected. It is easy for resorts to damage these ecologies, for example by clearing natural vegetation for buildings and roads. The problems of water supply, sewerage and rubbish disposal are significant ones.

What needs to be done in order to protect the environment?

● *Maintaining a good relationship with key stakeholder groups*
The strategy-making body must set its objectives with a sensitivity to the objectives of stakeholder groups and then operate the resort in a way which keeps these stakeholders happy.

Who are the main stakeholder groups?

External
● Central government and its ministries
● Local government
● Local and regional communities
● Community groups such as conservationists
● Businesses on route to and from the resort, particularly in local towns serving the area
● Suppliers of inputs to the resort, for example a train or bus company
● Other resorts, competing or cooperating, and their strategy-making bodies.

Internal
- Owners of enterprises operating at the resort who are leaseholders,
  - ski lift and ski school operators
  - hotel operators
  - university or school operators
  - restaurant, cafe and shop owners
- Managers and employees of the resort and the enterprises located there, permanent and part-time
- Customers using the resort, some of whom are also leaseholders
  - owners of apartments on the mountain
  - institutions and individuals with an interest in ski lodges
  - sportspeople who train on the mountain
  - day visitors.

How is it possible for all these groups to have an input into the strategy-making process?

The Mt Buller resort

Since 1998 the Mt Buller resort has been run by its own management board, which is appointed by the Ministry of the Environment and Conservation of the Victoria state government. There are six resorts in Victoria, three of which are large – Mt Buller, Mt Hotham and Falls Creek, and three small, subsidized by the larger ones. The six boards are in theory supervised by the Alpine Resorts Coordinating Council.

What alternative organizational structures are available?

Each board serves for three years. The board members are selected to comprise a range of skills – financial, legal, marketing, environmental and strategy making. Thus it was intended by the minister to be a skills-based board, although there is a pronounced tendency for it to become interest-based. It includes those with pecuniary interests in the resort and outsiders with no such interests. However, it is difficult for the latter to devote the time needed to attend meetings and familiarize themselves with the everyday routines of the resort.

What is the difference between a skills-based board and an interests-based board? How do the alternative structures influence strategy making?

The board acts like a cross between a local government and a utility manager:

- It manages land use, overseeing the leasing and renting of the resort land which is all crown land
- It provides most of the infrastructure and services needed at the resort, such as roads, water supply, sewerage and rubbish disposal

- It supervises the day-to-day operation of the resort but also seeks to develop the resort.

However, it is constrained in the way in which it carries out its responsibilities by the law and government policy.

Are these appropriate activities given the strategic objectives of the board?

The board has an obligation to prepare an annual business plan, setting out the aims for the coming year, and an annual report on the outcome of the previous year. It must do this in the context of longer term objectives, but there is currently no strategic plan. The board has adopted a triple bottom line approach to assessing its goals and its performance in achieving these. It recognizes the existence of a number of aims. It must break even financially but also act in a way which both conserves the environment and satisfies the social interests of its stakeholders.

How should the board accommodate the process of strategy making? How does the use of the triple bottom line influence the strategy-making process?

The board has an extensive system of committees which operate in the main areas of activity, making use of the expertise of individual members of the board. The main committees meet on a regular basis every month, reporting and making recommendations to the board. In 2002, for the first time, the board set up a planning committee.

The strategic context

The main aim of the board is to develop a prosperous and thriving resort.

How might this be done? How can broad aims be translated into specific objectives? This prompts a number of questions which are more easily raised than answered.

- *Can the resort be economically viable at any level of activity?* This is a question which is relevant to every enterprise on the mountain as well as to the board itself. In the absence of a continuing government subsidy, every enterprise which wishes to survive must be viable. Anything done on the mountain should be done in such a way as to contribute to the viability of the resort, whether from the perspective of the board itself or the main stakeholders who have invested in the resort.

Is this possible?

- *The board has to make a further strategic choice, whether to go beyond the goal of immediate economic viability and do more: should it run its budget in such a way as to improve the resort, investing an appropriate part of its revenue back in the resort? Should it also do this in such a way as to encourage private enterprises and individuals who wish to invest in the resort to do so?*

This clearly implies a higher level of charges or the earmarking of certain revenues to this purpose. It also implies structuring charges to favour those likely to develop the resort.

There are three kinds of beds on the mountain, socalled 'hot beds', mainly, but not only, in hotels and two 'cold beds', those in lodges and apartments. The relative proportion of these can be influenced by board decisions and is therefore a matter for strategic choice. There are pluses and minuses for development of the numbers in each group. The proportions of each affect the general nature of the resort.

A resort full of apartments which are only occupied for short periods of the year may be undesirable. The board might prefer to support lodges which make possible low-cost but regular skiing. On the other hand, they might prefer hot beds which increase the permanent population on the mountain, for example the staff of a hotel, its restaurant and other services.

What kind of resort does the board want?

• *What are the activities outside the normal snow sports which can generate revenue streams for the main players, including the board, and which will guarantee viability? How can their growth be encouraged?*

A resort should have a range of activities capable of sustaining the facilities and infrastructure required by a significant permanent population, in particular activities concentrated in the non-winter season.

The main presence on the mountain is a campus of La Trobe University, which concentrates its activity in the off-season, partly in order to have access to cheap accommodation for its students. La Trobe has the same problems as other stakeholders in the high cost involved in providing education services on the mountain.

What are these and how can the board stimulate their introduction and expansion?

• *What is the size of a permanent population needed to support the infrastructure required and the facilities needed, in the role of supplying necessary labour inputs and helping to provide a significant demand for their use?*

There is no work on this issue and therefore no real guidance on what might be a target population.

• *How can such a population be encouraged to live on the mountain at a reasonable cost of living and therefore with a reasonable standard of living?*

The resort must be run and developed in a way which satisfies the socioeconomic aspirations of the main stakeholders: customers who visit the resort for short periods, workers who might live there permanently, the local community living close to the mountain and the government which owns the land.

How might this be achieved?

• *What is likely to be the impact on the environment of developing an alpine resort village?*

The activities in the resort could be carried out without significant damage to the resort's environment. For example, the quality of water in the natural creeks and rivers can be left unaffected by the resort activities. As far as possible, water should be recycled and used in snow making to limit the total demand.

What is the cost of doing all this and how is the money to be raised?

• *What are the implications of different pricing strategies on the choice and level of different activities and the relative size of different visitor groups?*

There are a range of different methods of charging for services and access to the ski slopes. Pricing can be used to favour certain kinds of customers.

How can the board deliberately use price to influence activities and customer use?

Sources of revenue and costs

Without subsidy the board must organize its budget in such a way as to break even, averaging out good and bad years, assuming that this is actually possible given the demand conditions for its services. It has no choice but to try to do so. The government does no more than offer a loan facility which allows the board to effect this evening-out process at a moderate interest cost. Beyond this the board can try to improve, charging in a way which raises the necessary funds. The board can cover deficits by selling off assets, such as the gas facility.

What impact does the financial situation of the board have upon the strategy adopted?

There are some basic principles in charging for service and raising revenue:

• The structure of charges should be consistent with strategic policy objectives. Generally this will mean user pays unless there is good reason to depart from this principle in order to pursue an agreed strategic objective.

• The pattern of revenues raised and costs incurred by the board must be perceived as treating all stakeholders equitably. If there is a departure from user pays, it must be publicly explained and justified.

- The system of charges must be transparent: it is then clear who pays how much for what.
- The system should be as simple as possible.
- The board is not aiming to make a profit for its own sake. It will seek to minimize the costs for users unless there is a good reason for not doing so, that is, the pricing system is being used either to deter certain activities or to encourage others.

In what way do these principles compel the board to be clear about the strategy it is pursuing?

The main sources of revenue for the board are threefold:

1. combined charges for entry and transport within the resort
2. payment of site rent specified by leases of varying duration
3. payment of service charges.

In the short term the latter two are relatively stable sources of revenue, whereas the first depends on how good the snow season is. In the medium to long term, the proportions of revenue raised by the different charges reflect the pricing policy adopted by the board which in its turn should reflect the elasticities of the demand curves, that is, what the customer groups are prepared to pay and how much of the service they will consume at those prices. There is also a capital impost levied on the number of beds, which in theory, because of its nature, should go to capital improvement of the resort.

How can charges be used to achieve strategic objectives?

It is also open to the board to charge different groups of resort users in a way which promotes the kinds of activities the board is seeking. For example, it could give discounts on service charges for summer activity.

What activities or what group might the board seek to discriminate in favour of in order to promote different strategies?

Costs can also be divided into three parts:

1. the administrative costs of running the resort and providing the services
2. the costs of facilitating visitor entry and transportation during the season
3. the costs of improving and developing the resort.

The first is stable, the second varies quite significantly with the number of visitors, the third is highly variable depending on the quality of the season. In a bad year there are no resources to invest back into the resort.

In what ways do costs reflect the nature of the strategy implemented?

The problem is that, at the current level of charging, in an average year it is difficult to break even and in a bad year it is impossible. Without a surplus it is impossible to develop the resort. If the frequency of bad years is increasing, as some believe, then the resort is unlikely to be viable. Increasing the charges simply deters residence on the mountain and visitors. It is unlikely that the elasticities of demand allow much of an increase in charges.

This case study is based on the experience of the author as a board member. It should be read in conjunction with the following case on Euro Disney.

www.mtbuller.com.au

Key strategic issues

How does the strategic situation of Mt Buller show the need for an explicit strategy? How does it show that strategy must be developed with the participation of the main stakeholders and that it must be adjusted to take account of changing environmental circumstances? The first critical issue is what objectives to adopt. What is involved in the development of a winter resort? Does it require the existence of a permanent alpine village, with a significant population, a wide range of activities throughout the year and a developed infrastructure? How should the funds for such development be raised?

Strategic analysis and audit

Carry out a full strategic audit on Mt Buller. How far is a winter resort, located at a relatively low altitude, economically viable, given its short winter season and the impact of global warming?

Euro Disney and a tale of three cultures

When we first launched there was the belief that it was enough to be Disney. Now we realize that our guests need to be welcomed on the basis of their own culture and travel habits.

Whether you open in a downturn, an upturn or in the middle of the cycle, it doesn't make much difference for a product like this.

JAY RASULO, CEO, Euro Disney

Background

This case study should be read in conjunction with the previous one on the Mt Buller winter resort which starts with a background piece on resorts in general.

Everything that Disney did appeared to be marked by success. The CEO Michael Eisner could not put a foot wrong. It was said that everything he touched turned to gold. This applied as much to resorts as to the other areas of commercial interest to Disney, developed earlier. Disney had successfully opened up theme parks in the USA, in California and Florida. It had also extended the model to Tokyo with great success. Could the model be applied throughout the world? The moment had come to enter the European market. Disney was confident of success. The projections of attendance and profits confidently anticipated that the new theme park near Paris would break even within a year and would repeat the success of the other theme parks.

How far is it likely that a common business model relating to resorts can be applied to different countries?

Disney

Disney's first theme park, Disneyland, established at Anaheim, Los Angeles, in 1955, was an offshoot of Disney's incredibly successful film enterprises. It allowed those who had enjoyed the whole range of Disney characters, from Mickey Mouse to Goofy, to reacquaint themselves with their old favourites. This was a successful initiative since the theme parks came to generate a majority of Disney's income. The park was very much in the Disney mould of family entertainment, wholesome but fantastic. It took full advantage of the Disney brand name.

What are the main features of the Disney brand name?

Disney made a significant mistake in Disneyland at Anaheim. The company owned only the land on which the theme park and its car park were located. Consequently it had no control over the sprawl of hotels and motels which were built around it and diminished its image, undermining both the wholesomeness and the fantasy element. Nor were the profits made from the attendance fees comparable with those made from the businesses in the vicinity.

What are the dangers to the value of the brand name in Disney establishing theme parks?

As a response to this, when the plans were laid for Disney World in Florida, which eventually opened in 1971, they included the purchase of a huge tract of undeveloped land outside Orlando, 28,000 acres in all, enough to hold a multitude of hotels and amusement parks. Disney attempted to coordinate its activities and vertically integrate in order to capture the profit made by others. The aim was to cater for all the visitors' needs, including accommodation, entertainment during the evenings and food.

What exactly should be included in the resort?

To a significant degree Disney was successful in its general aim, but not fully. Despite the fact that the company built three hotels with over 2,000 rooms, hotel chains, such as Hyatt and Hilton, still located themselves just outside the Disney-owned area.

Michael Eisner, who became CEO in 1984, used three strategies to further increase the revenue from Disney World:

• to increase the price. He discovered that the price elasticity of demand was low. The entrance price was raised 45% in just two years, with a resulting 59% growth in revenue, the price increase generating as much as 94% of the total earnings growth.

What are the factors influencing the price strategy when a new resort is opened?

• to add attractions and rides to the existing park, and then to add theme parks or gates. For example, the Disney-MGM Park opened in 1989. The existing infrastructure could serve a much wider set of facilities.

Why was it important to locate new theme parks, such as those related to the world of film, close to the existing parks?

- to try to capture more of the money spent by visitors on shopping and night-time entertainment by building facilities such as night clubs and restaurants on site and running the food concessions in the park itself. Disney also entered the hotel business, although usually with partners who helped to finance the hotels.

How far should Disney go in doing this itself or using partners?

The next step was to open a theme park abroad. Disney chose Tokyo as the venue, which turned out to be a shrewd choice. The Japanese were benefiting from a rise in both leisure and income. The park took five years to plan but became profitable very quickly. Targets for visitors were exceeded and came up to American standards. In 2002, 25 million people visited Tokyo Disneyland, about one-fifth of Japan's population. Whereas elsewhere visitors have tended to be tourists, in Japan they are locals. Something like 95% are 'repeaters', mainly from the metropolitan Tokyo area. Visitors spent more than had been anticipated, including admission fees, something like ¥9,600 per person or more than $90.

Why are there different patterns of visitation?

Initially there were some difficulties in transferring the business model and a need for some adjustments:

- The weather made it necessary to put most activities indoors and to cover walkways
- There was also a need for translators.

Overall the park has been a resounding success, more so than other Disney theme parks. This was by no means assured as the rather checkered history of other theme parks in Japan has shown. More or less the same business model had been applied by Disney with success. The next obvious move was into Europe.

Why might the application of the same successful business model appear surprising?

A difficult start-up

Disney had the initial advantage of different European countries competing for the new theme park. After a brief flirtation with England, the competition reduced to two main players, France and Spain. Disney enlisted the support of the French government by stressing the beneficial results in increased tourism and employment but kept as a background threat the possibility of the Spanish city of Barcelona as an interesting and realistic alternative.

What determines the choice of country location? What advantage is there is keeping the choice competitive until the last moment?

The French government stepped in to make an offer Disney could not refuse:

- It offered to purchase 51% of the shares and organize their sale on the market.
- It dangled attractive tax breaks.
- It offered a generous amount of land at a very low price. The French government sold to Disney 4,800 acres in a prime location only 30 km from Paris, at a price equivalent to 1971 agricultural prices.
- It contributed the necessary infrastructure, extending roads, subways and railway lines to the site in Marne la Vallée. It extended the metro to the park and built a station on the high-speed train route opposite the park entrance. It became much easier for visitors to access the park.

What benefits might the French government derive from the park?

The location also appealed to Disney. Apart from the proximity of Paris, the main tourist city in Europe, the park would be central for a large number of visitors from a number of West European countries. The Disney management appeared to have done everything right in the lead-up to the opening of the theme park on April 12, 1992.

Why did Disney choose Paris for the venue?

They had also managed to negotiate partnerships with high-flying allies, like American Express, Coca-Cola, Esso, IBM, Kodak, Mattel, Nestlé, Philips and Renault, to build or finance many of the attractions and state-of-the-art systems in return for favourable sales and/or promotion opportunities within the resort.

Disney succeeded in completing Phase 1 of the detailed plan the day before the opening, including the theme park, six hotels with a total of 5,200 rooms, a convention centre, a golf course and 32 nightclubs, bars and restaurants. The construction had taken five years and been a mammoth organizational effort. By 1992 something approaching $3 billion had been invested in the project. This was by any standards a major commitment of resources.

Disney also had in mind the start of construction of Phase 2, a film studio and a second theme park, by the end of 1993, and at one stage even a third park for the beginning of the new century.

How far ahead is it sensible to look in planning a resort? What are the variables which it is necessary to predict?

Yet, after an initially good start, attendance rates were disappointing, well below expected levels. More threatening, the park failed to reach its financial targets. By October 1993, the park had lost Fr1.5 million. The reaction was to retrench. By then the workforce had been reduced to 11,000 from a peak of 19,000. The start of Phase 2 had already been postponed by one year. These difficulties continued to dog the project.

What are the reasons for the difficulties? After all attendance at Euro Disney in 1993 was not that bad, approaching one million per month, which made the resort Europe's most popular paid tourist destination. What was wrong?

Could Disney maintain that competitive advantage in what proved to be a rather more different environment than envisaged? Was this a typical case of success breeding failure? Did Disney believe that it had a winning formula, a tried and tested strategy, which had delivered competitive advantage and was expected to continue to do so?

On the basis of the successful model, Disney made a whole series of wrong assumptions:

• The pricing strategy was wrong. The early strategy in the USA had been to price at a low level and then raise the initial price level. In the early years satisfied customers who had, they believed, received value for money 'talked up' the parks. By contrast the price for Euro Disney started high and the park was consequently 'talked down' by those who did not think that they had received value for money. What happened to Club Med illustrated what talking up can achieve in terms of a good reputation, even in France. Admission prices at Euro Disney were about 30% higher than at Disney World. Food prices were as much as twice as high. The hotels were $200–300 a night, well above the rates available near the other theme parks.

• Disney was also ignorant of the vacation habits of Europeans. The typical holiday in Europe is 4–6 weeks as against 1–2 weeks in the USA, but the total expenditure on the holiday was about the same, which meant that there was less money spent per day. Disney had also anticipated that guests would on average stay four nights at their three hotels. It turned out to be two, partly because of the high costs of hotel accommodation and partly because there were initially only 15 rides in the park, as compared with 45 at the inception of Disney World.

• Eating and drinking habits were also different. Disney had planned for all-day grazing at the park, as happened in the USA and Japan. However, European eating habits were very different. Visitors looked for a dinner at noon, putting unsustainable pressure on the eating facilities.

They were also used to eating bread and cheese and drinking wine, distinctly un-Disney tastes compared with the usual fare of burgers, fries and coke.

• Purchases of merchandise at the souvenir shops was also at a lower level than anticipated, not surprising since the money was going on the basics of entrance fee, accommodation and food. Many fewer high-margin items such as T-shirts and hats were bought.

The result was a level of expenditure per visitor well below what had been expected.

• The external environment took a turn for the worse. Certainly the times were not auspicious, with recession in Europe and the associated high interest rates. Devaluation of a number of neighbouring countries' exchange rates pushed up the relative value of the franc to levels which implied prices for foreign visitors well above what had been anticipated. This reinforced the feeling that the entrance fee and hotel prices were excessively high.

What is the relative importance of policy mistakes, changes in the external environment and difficulties of cultural difference?

The main problem could be summarized in a graphic phrase applied to the theme park, a 'cultural Chernobyl'. There was a considerable backlash against the American nature of the park. The press was dominated by a storm of criticism. They argued that it was too American and, as a prime example of American cultural imperialism, certainly unlikely to be accepted happily by the French and probably not by other Europeans either. Critics argued that the project was doomed to failure and that the French government should never have supported it.

How far was this reaction peculiarly French and how far is it likely to be more common?

Disney seemed to recognize the validity of at least some part of this argument since within months of the opening they replaced the American chairman of Euro Disney, Robert Fitzpatrick, by a Disney insider of French origin, Philippe Bourguignon. The replacement was seen as a move from American-style to European-style management.

How far can the Disney experience be adapted to remove its excessively American elements?

Robert Fitzpatrick had already prefaced the 1992 annual report: 'that looking at the future, Euro Disney had two primary objectives: to achieve profitability as quickly as possible, and to better integrate Euro Disney into its European environment while reinforcing our greatest asset – our Disney heritage'. The view of the new CEO was that Disney should, as a matter of priority, adapt to its European environment and in so doing create a unique combination of the Disney tradition and the expectations of its

European customers. The emphasis had clearly changed under the pressure of events. However, in his public statements, Bourguignon asserted that he believed there was no crisis, rather the unfolding of natural stages in the development of the park. In his words, 'Euro Disney developed a core strategy and culture of Disney, and then had to work to Europeanize its theme park' (Hitt et al., 1997: 305).

Why did the same difficulties not arise with the Japanese project?

A changing strategy

Some of the changes implemented were simple:

- It was easy to lower charges, but the horse had already bolted. It is much more difficult to offset negative impressions already created than to create positive ones from the beginning.
- The number of attractions could easily be increased.
- Some of the changes were part of the process of Europeanization. More attention was paid to the provision of European-style food. The ban on the consumption of alcohol in Disney theme parks was lifted in order to allow the French and others to consume wine in the park restaurants. In advertising, there was much less reference to the USA. The celebration of public holidays was oriented towards Europe and not the USA.

Other changes represented a change of approach for Disney. Labour relations had proved to be a particular problem. Disney had to accommodate a different employment regime which was hostile to low wages and long hours of work. Employees had had trouble with the so-called 'Disney look' and with the shortage of accommodation in the local area. The mass lay-offs in the early period did not help staff morale. As a result there was a high turnover of staff. Disney moved decisively towards a French system of employment relations.

Off-season charges were introduced. There was more emphasis on attracting groups or tours since they turned out to represent a larger proportion of the visitors in Europe. There was less emphasis on the traditional American way of individual family visits.

Does this constitute a change of business model? Was this kind of change enough?

Another focus of criticism were the financial arrangements put in place by Disney, which were complex, but amounted to a large amount of debt supported by very little equity. This situation was highly risky for all other players in the event of the project failing to deliver the target rate of return. Fortunately for Disney in theory it protected the company from the full effects of failure but rewarded it handsomely for success, but only if it could keep its partners to the letter of the agreements. Euro Disney was a subsidiary in which the Walt Disney Corporation held only a 49% stake, having paid just Fr10 for its shares, whereas the other 51% were sold at Fr72 a share. While the shares did open at Fr165, they quickly fell back to Fr68, much to the chagrin of the investors.

The parent company also contracted to manage the park for hefty management fees. Royalty payments were also considerable. On the assumption that the planned targets were met, 57% of Euro Disney's operating profit would go to the parent company. In the event of losses, Euro Disney would still have to pay the management fees and royalties, if it could. It could not and in the event Disney could not collect such payments.

What was the nature of Euro Disney's risk control strategy?

Losses amounted to $36 million in 1992 and more than $900 million in 1993. Attendance was down 15% in 1993 compared with 1992. The share price continued to slide throughout 1992 and 1993.

Eventually a rescue package was put together in 1994 which raised more money and provided much needed liquidity. It had the goal of halving Euro Disney debt, in practice significantly reducing, but not quite halving, it. The creditor banks were persuaded to accept the waiving of a significant interest debt and to postpone repayment of the principal. Disney retained a controlling interest but saw its share of the project decline to 39%, a sign that it did not think that the theme park was going to be a major generator of profits. Euro Disney was renamed Disneyland Paris.

How did Disney limit damage to itself while keeping the resort going?

Disney also agreed to waive management fees and royalties for five years and only to reintroduce them gently at half the previous level for a further five years. Losses in 1994 still amounted to well over US$300 million. In 1995 there was only a very small profit despite the temporary but significant reduction of costs. The key success indicators, particularly attendance levels, continued to deteriorate.

Why did the key success indicators continue to deteriorate?

Disney Studios Park

In March 2002 Euro Disney, still 39.1% owned by the California-based Walt Disney Company, opened a new theme park Disney Studios Park alongside Disneyland Paris. This time every effort was made to cater for local sensibilities.

By the early 2000s Disneyland Paris was beginning to deliver. Disney now turned its attention to establishing a theme park in Hong Kong, which hopefully would repeat the success of Japan. Disney was very clever in minimizing its commitment of resources and maximizing the investment of the Hong Kong government. Somewhat later in 2002 they also reached an agreement in principle to establish a further park in Shanghai. The organizers in Hong Kong were upset and fearful that this park would compete with the Hong Kong park.

Key strategic issues

The establishment of any resort creates a host of strategic dilemmas. Most resorts have a complex organization and a multitude of stakeholders who have to be consulted and kept happy in the formulation and implementation of any strategy. Relevant questions relate to location, the bundle of services and experiences provided, risk control in the project, sensitivity to cultural difference, the choice of partners, the role of government, particularly in infrastructure development, and the pricing and promotion strategies. The Disney parks highlight the problem of transferring a business model from one country to another.

There are other questions to be asked: How important are the theme parks to Disney? Are they simply there to take advantage of and further develop the brand name, or are they an important source of revenue? Expenditure on resorts is notoriously sensitive to the state of the economy; How does Disney protect itself against the impact of the associated fluctuations in demand?

Strategic analysis and audit

Carry out a full strategic audit on Euro Disney. Is it likely to have turned around its financial position in a permanent way? What is the explanation of the much greater degree of difficulty in making the park work than was experienced by other Disney theme parks?

Reading

Brasor, P., 'Bogus' theme parks becoming the last resort', *The Japan Times*, March 16, 2003: 12.

Hitt, M. A., Ireland, R. D. and Hoskinsson, R. E., *Strategic Management: Competitiveness and Globalization*, 2nd edn (South-Western Publishing, Cincinatti: 1997).

Koranteng, J., 'Euro Disney is preparing to unwrap $600 million Walt Disney Studios Park', *Amusement Business*, **113**(50) December 17, 2001: 12.

Koranteng, J., 'Disney embarks on European marketing push', *Amusement Business*, **114**(11) March 18, 2002: 1.

McDonald, H., 'Hong Kong billions fund Mickey Mouse economy', *The Business Age*, January 11, 2003: 3.

Milhomme, A. J., The Euro Disney Case: early debacle, in Wright, P., Kroll, M. K., and Parnell, J. *Strategic Management Cases* (Prentice Hall, Upper Saddle River, NJ: 1998).

O'Brien, T., 'Walt Disney studios makes Paris debut', *Amusement Business*, **114**(12) March 15, 2002: 3.

Prada, P. and Orwall, B., 'A certain 'je ne sais quoi' at Disney's new park', *Wall Street Journal* (Eastern edn) March 12, 2002: B1.

Wall Street Journal, Leisure Brief – Euro Disney, (Eastern edn) January 23, 2003: D5.

www.disney.com

The strategic alliance between Renault and Nissan

Carlos Ghosn – a Brazilian-born Lebanese with a history of fixing French companies.

(White, 2003)

Background

This industry is one of the most important in the modern economy. Its origins go back to the period before World War I. It has also always been a focus for rapid and significant organizational and technical change. It is one in which many novel management techniques have received their first application. Indeed strategy was first systematically tried out in this industry. The importance of and fierce competitiveness in the industry have ensured that this was the case.

Why is strategy so important for the car industry?

As might be expected, the industry is strongly represented in the triad, with well-developed automobile industries in the USA, various European countries, principally Germany, and Japan. Competition between the three centres has been fierce. In this there have been three phases since World War II:

- At first, during the 1940s, 50s and 60s, American enterprises, notably Ford and General Motors, were dominant.
- The oil price hikes of the 1970s threw the spotlight on the increasing competitiveness of the Japanese, led by Toyota, particularly in the areas of smaller and cheaper vehicles. Toyota and Honda have continued to lead the way in efficient production.
- By the end of the 1980s the American industry was in crisis. It reacted by imitating the methods which had made the Japanese enterprises successful, such as just-in-time, quality circles and outsourcing. In turn, by the mid-1990s, some Japanese enterprises were in trouble, notably Nissan and some of the smaller companies. European producers also reacted by raising their game, leading the way in the premium markets and then using their reputation to extend the branding to other markets. Today the market capitalization of Toyota exceeds the combined value of Ford and General Motors, but an increasing proportion of its output is outside Japan.

Why did the Americans lose their lead in the automobile industry?

The industry has also seen much cooperation alongside the competition. The number of large producers in these countries has tended to decline over the years. The industry has seen many mergers and acquisitions, which can be interpreted as a process of consolidation. There has also been a quest for partnership or strategic alliances, which sometimes are a preliminary to a merger. For example, in the recent past Daimler has acquired Chrysler, General Motors has allied with Honda and Ford purchased Volvo. It is significant that each of these links is across the boundaries of the triad. To be a global player an automobile producer needs a presence in each of the three main markets. There is a strong tendency to oligopoly at the global level.

What are the reasons for the many strategic alliances in the car industry?

One prediction is that there will be only six major players in the near future, two in each of the major markets. To be a main player probably requires at least five million in vehicle production. Currently only Ford and GM sell more than five million vehicles a year. The likely survivors of competition for the prized global positions are often quoted as Ford and GM in the USA, DaimlerChrysler and Volkswagen in Europe and Toyota and Honda in Japan, but this is by no means certain and depends upon the successful formulation and implementation of strategy and the reading of competitors' strategy. The case study concentrates the attempt by Renault-Nissan to be one of these survivors.

Why is it forecast that only six major manufacturers will survive?

There are successful small players who must be taken into account. A rapidly growing industry has recently emerged in South Korea. Its main players, Hyundai, Daiwoo and Kia, are adopting an aggressive and ambitious strategy for entering and gaining a significant market share in the main world markets, particularly the USA. They too have relied on a measure of significant cooperation.

As countries develop economically, is it possible for new car industries to emerge?

Lesser government players also carefully nurture home production, even if sometimes provided by a foreign multinational. Like airlines, automobile producers are regarded as flag carriers. Despite the small size and fragmentation of the industry in China, there is no doubt that the Chinese government attaches great importance to having a thriving automobile industry (see the case study on entry into the Chinese automobile industry in Chapter 15). Car producers see China as a large and rapidly growing prospective market. The same holds for India and even smaller players such as Malaysia.

Why is there so much interest in China?

Because of the strong tendency to a home country bias and the intense competition, there is excess capacity in the industry at the global level. As a consequence all the main players are looking for new markets to develop and old markets in which to increase their market share.

What impact does global surplus capacity have on the industry?

Main features of the industry

● The development and production of a new motorcar takes a long period of time and demands a high level of investment. It is also the product of a group of different specialists – engineers, marketing specialists, financial experts. A mistake in judging the market can bankrupt the enterprise which makes it. Yet successful enterprises must continually update and renew the products they offer. One Japanese achievement is to greatly reduce the time needed to develop a new model.
● There are thousands of components which go into the manufacture of a motorcar, necessitating the establishment of dense networks of supplier enterprises who need to deliver on time and at a quality which is acceptable. Today the value-adding chains are international. The industry has become global in its dimensions. Cost minimization at the global level is a major challenge and a major task, particularly in a world of floating exchange rates.
● The environment in which motorcars are developed and sold can change rapidly and dramatically, whether the focus is on significant changes in the price of oil, the introduction of new environmental requirements or simply the progress of technology and switches in taste.
● Second to the house or flat, the motorcar is the biggest purchase made by individual households, often requiring some financial assistance. This finance is often provided by an enterprise linked in some way to the car producer or

dealer. A strong dealership network to stock and sell the vehicles is important. Often there are exclusive arrangements which give a particular dealer some locational monopoly. It is difficult to establish such distributor chains.
● The industry has excess capacity worldwide, even outside recession years. It is an industry in which there is significant home country bias which assists in producing the excess capacity. Governments have actively sought to protect existing enterprises and, where there are none, to create new enterprises. Despite this, from a global perspective it is a competitive industry, one in which informal protective devices such as export quotas have been adopted to moderate the impact of competition.
● The competitive advantage rapidly changes from country to country, and from large producer to large producer. Price is important but there is also considerable product differentiation, particularly in the premium area.
● In recent years there have been many attempts to cooperate, usually involving enterprises in the different centres of the triad, some temporary, some designed for the longer term.

How do each of these feature influence the content of a strategy and the strategy-making process?

Competition and cooperation

Why should automobile producers cooperate as well as compete or instead of competing?

The main reason is that cooperation has become part of the strategy to improve competitive strength. There are a whole host of particular reasons:

● The enormous cost of developing a new motorcar. The financial requirements create enormous risk for those who commit the resources.
● The benefits of promoting R&D in new technologies with a long development period, particularly those which are environmentally friendly, saving energy and reducing carbon emissions or generally reducing the level of pollution.
● Gaining access to new markets and the distribution systems in those markets, particularly the already large markets of the triad and the rapidly growing markets of some developing countries.
● Negotiating with governments over new regulations or tax systems, or incentives to set up in a particular country.
● Making use of new methods of organization pioneered by competitors, such as e-commerce.
● The existence of excess capacity which is not likely to go away and disadvantages those who lose competitive advantage.

• The need to set an industry standard for a product, a product attribute or the technology used.

Can you find examples of each of these different kinds of cooperation?

A common form of cooperation in the automobile industry is the complementary strategic alliance, usually based on differential access to markets or differential strength in different niches for vehicles. The Renault-Nissan alliance is an example of a complementary alliance.

What form might a complementary alliance take in the automobile industry?

Background to the Renault-Nissan partnership

Renault has been one of the smaller global producers, France's largest, but a relatively efficient one. It has significant government ownership. On the other hand, by the end of the 1990s Nissan had entered a period of financial distress, having failed to make a profit for the previous eight years and having accumulated over $16 billion of debt. It was producing dull cars and trying to imitate Toyota. Nissan stood apart from its better performing domestic rivals, Toyota and Honda. Neither Nissan nor Renault was expected to be among the six major world players that were anticipated to dominate the automobile industry in the future. However, together they could become the fourth largest producer in the world.

The origin of the strategic alliance was a Renault reaction to a decision by Toyota to build a new small car manufacturing plant in France. Competition was reaching into the core market of Renault. Renault reacted positively and strongly. In early 1998 it announced plans to expand its output by half a million units in the period running up to 2002, and simultaneously to reduce its overall costs of production by a significant amount.

One way for Renault to achieve its objective was to form an alliance with Nissan which had significant excess capacity. Annually Nissan could produce a million more vehicles than it actually sold. In 1999 this alliance took place. The first task was to turn Nissan round.

How do manufacturers deal with a situation in which there is surplus capacity in the world? What are the best ways of entering the main markets?

The turnaround has been very successful. Nissan has gone from losing US$5.7 billion in 1999 to earning a record net income of US$2.98 billion in fiscal 2001 and US$4.24 in fiscal 2002 and is likely to go on showing an improvement. It is more profitable than GM or Ford, and about to overtake Honda as the second most profitable car company in Japan. The debt has been removed.

The alliance

The alliance has three stages in the evolution of the cooperation between the two partners. A strategic alliance can be a prelude to a merger, willingly acquiesced in by the partners as a result of previously successful cooperation.

The first stage is now complete. This was a strategic alliance which involved as a priority the turnaround and transformation of Nissan. The initial core act of the alliance was the transfer of $5.4 billion of the debt to Renault in return for a 36.6% equity stake in the Japanese company. However, written into the 1999 agreement was the retention of operating autonomy by both partners, despite the equity stake. Clearly Renault saw significant advantage in the alliance for itself, even at this stage.

Why was operating autonomy retained when the Renault stake would normally be regarded as a controlling interest?

Building on the initial agreement, during stage two of the alliance, there has been a strengthening of cross-shareholdings. Renault has raised its stake in Nissan from 36.65 to 44.4%. Nissan is taking a 15% stake in Renault without voting rights. As a consequence of these cross-holdings, an improvement in the performance of either automatically profits the other.

What is the strategic implication of cross-holdings of this type?

It can be assumed that in a third stage a complete merger might take place.

From the beginning the companies were genuinely complementary:

• There were powerful geographical synergies. Nissan was strong in North America whereas Nissan was weak.
• Renault was expert in innovative design, Nissan in engineering.

A proposed link between Renault and Volvo had fallen through, as had a proposal for DaimlerChrysler to take over Nissan. The alliance was not therefore a random event. The particular areas of focus in exploiting the synergy were in manufacturing operations, purchasing and marketing.

In an unprecedented move, a Brazil-based high flyer, Carlos Ghosn, nicknamed later, perhaps unfairly, 'Le cost killer', was appointed as the new president and CEO of Nissan. He saw his mission to make the changes necessary to make Nissan profitable once more but to do this while retaining and safeguarding the existing identity of Nissan. He was also to reinforce and broaden the alliance.

How important was it that an outsider came in to oversee the turnaround?

In its first stage, the aims and objectives of the alliance were:

- To formulate a revival plan for Nissan
- To update Nissan's products and make them competitive
- To introduce systems in Nissan which rewarded good performance
- To cut Nissan's costs to a competitive level so that it could go into the black and further increase profit
- To reduce Nissan's debt
- To break down barriers between the different parts of the alliance
- To identify and exploit the complementary strengths and synergies of the two partners
- To identify a broad strategic direction for the alliance.

How far did such a plan set the direction for the future?

The process

One of the main problems of the alliance was that it was between two companies with different cultures and philosophies and, more to the point, different expectations on the part of the managers and workers. Ghosn believed that it was imperative to develop trust and to be transparent in what was done.

How might two very different cultures be reconciled?

To achieve success required the dropping of some time-honoured Japanese practices. For example, despite the high level of debt, the company was not without assets. It held significant non-core assets, financial and property investments, particularly in *keiretsu* partners. This amounted to at least $4 billion, resources which could be used productively to assist core activities by financing new investments and reducing debt. This investment was disposed of and the resources released for use in the revival plan.

More directly threatening to the gaining of willing cooperation from staff was the need to change the system of employment, in particular to ditch the seniority rule and revamp the compensation system, putting the emphasis on performance. This was done. In the event it even proved possible to introduce stock options.

Ghosn went about this dramatic change by creating two sets of teams, a set of cross-functional teams (CFTs)

within Nissan itself, and another set of cross-company teams (CCTs) between Nissan and Renault. The first were important to the formulation and implementation of the revival plan, the second to continuing successful cooperation between the two companies. Initially the emphasis was on the first set of teams.

Why were these teams so important?

The aim of the CFTs was twofold, to encourage managers to think differently from the way they had thought in the past and to help sell the message that change was necessary. There were initially nine such groups, each with ten members from middle management. A vice-president sponsored each team and specialist pilots were there to guide their efforts. Each team could create subteams where it was thought desirable. The areas covered were business development, purchasing, manufacturing and logistics, research and development, sales and marketing, general and administration, finance and costs, phase-out of products and parts complexity, and organization. Each team had three months for the review. About 500 people worked in the CFTs and the subteams, a sizeable part of the management of the enterprise. At the top was a nine-member executive committee responsible for processing the recommendations and producing the revival plan itself.

What was likely to be the long-term influence of having so many managers working in the teams?

The CFTs remained in existence after the completion of the plan review and have a continuing role.

Alongside the CFTs are the CCTs, the cross-company teams responsible for making the alliance work. There were eleven of these. Their role increased in importance as the partnership deepened.

Which of the teams were initially more important? Was this relative ranking likely to change over time? If so, why?

The results

The Nissan revival plan

The Nissan revival plan was made public in October, 1999. It included cutbacks and closures as well as major new investment commitments. It also included a plan to reduce purchasing costs by 20% and cut the number of suppliers by 50%.

Some analysts predicted that it would take Renault 8–10 years to produce a return on its investment in Nissan. This was unduly pessimistic. By 2001 Nissan was in the black, a major success. A failure to have achieved a speedy turnaround would have sounded the death knell for Renault.

Why was the turnaround so quickly achieved?

The combined automobile sales reached the magical 5 million level in 2001, after being very close in 2000, when the alliance was among the top five world producers. The partners were almost equal in size: Nissan sold 2.6 million, and Renault 2.4 million. Together they accounted for 9.2% of the total world market. The regional breakdown is interesting – 2.4 million in the EU, 0.8 million in North America, 0.75 million in Japan – that is almost 4 million, or 80%, in the triad. The increasing importance of other areas is shown by the 1.0 million sales, 20% of the total.

How likely is it now that Renault-Nissan will be one of the six survivors?

Areas of cooperation

Platforms and power-trains
These are the two most important parts of the car. Common platforms will account for more than half the two enterprises' production by 2005. There is also an increasing exchange of engines.

Joint purchasing organization
In April 2001 the first joint company, equally owned, was created in this area – the Renault-Nissan Purchasing Organization. This will handle 70% of both groups' purchases, a combined invoice amounting to $50 billion.

Industrial and commercial cooperation
The aim is for each enterprise to help the other where they are weak, Renault using Nissan to return to the Mexican market and also to get back into Australia, Japan and Indonesia, and Renault assisting Nissan in Brazil and Europe.

Joint distribution in Europe
With a dealership hub strategy, a joint distribution organization is being set up in Europe.

Joint IS/IT
A common system was set up in September 2001, for which the Renault-Nissan IS/IT Office (RNIO) is responsible.

One example of cooperation and the first components jointly used is a powerful 3.5-litre, V6 engine which has been developed by Nissan and is being used by Renault in its attempt to break into the lower end of the Euro-

pean premium market, currently dominated by German companies Mercedes and Audi.

How many of these areas of cooperation are irreversible without significant costs?

There are several notable examples of Ghosn's success in reviving Nissan's product mix. The most dramatic achievement was the daring production of the Titan in Mississippi, USA, a pickup fully competitive with the models of the big three American companies. The product range includes the Nissan 350Z sports car and the Infiniti G35 luxury sedan and coupé.

A second stage

The alliance has been so effective that it has entered a second stage in which the cooperative arrangements are being institutionalized. To oversee the making of a common strategy, the new plan of October 30, 2001 proposed the creation of a new, equally owned management company, Renault-Nissan BV, which will represent a strategic command centre for the alliance, in charge of coordinating all its operations worldwide. The CCTs, the driving force of the alliance since 1999, will now report to Renault-Nissan BV. The new Renault-Nissan Purchasing Organization will also report to R-N BV.

The initial steps in this stage were completed by mid-2002. There is a new strategy – 'Nissan 180' – to increase worldwide sales by one million vehicles a year by the end of fiscal 2004 while achieving an 8% operating profit margin and zero net debt.

Does this represent a fusion of the strategy-making process?

However, success in this merger may not be enough. The joint enterprise is still not large enough to compete with the really large players. Renault is still seeking other acquisitions. Logically, from the perspective of market proximity, the alliance should look for another partner in the USA.

Who might such a partner be?

The future

As the alliance is developing there is every chance that Renault and Nissan will merge their manufacturing processes and production methods in the near future. Is it likely that others will follow in merging their activities?

Key strategic issues

The most interesting strategic question relates to the way in which a strategic alliance can become a merger. Does this require a meeting of equals, or is it necessary for one to take the lead? How likely is such a merger to occur? In what areas is the cooperation becoming irreversible? Is it using a common technology or common components, power sources or platforms? Or is it in common procurement systems? In which markets is each taking the lead? What products are they selling? In the case of Renault and Nissan, is it likely that they will look for new partners?

Strategic analysis and audit

Carry out a full strategic audit, assuming that Renault and Nissan constitute a single unit. From a financial perspective, which is the stronger of the partners? Who is the dominant partner in making strategy?

Reading

Ghosn, C., 'Saving the business without losing the company', *Harvard Business Review*, January 2002: 37–45.

Jusko, J., 'How Ghosn's driving Nissan', *Industry Week*, **252**(4) April 2003: 15.

McElroy J., 'No more mergers, please', *Ward's Auto world* **38**(11), November 2002: 21.

Magee, D., *Turnaround* (Harper Business, New York: 2003).

Naughton, K., 'Comeback, by design', *Newsweek*, **141**(16) April 21, 2003: 50.

Sawyer, C. A., 'Nissan's product-led transformation', *Automotive Design and Production* **115**(3) March 2003: 38.

Siciliano, J. and Gopinath, C., *Strategize! experiential exercises in strategic management* (South-Western, Cincinatti: 2002), Strategy Session 10.

Tierney, C., 'Now Renault is driving upmarket', *Business Week*, March 19, 2001.

White, J. B., 'From the brink of disaster' A review of Magee, 2003, *Wall Street Journal* (Eastern edn) January 31, 2003: W8.

Zau, T., 'Nissan's profit jumped by a third in fiscal year', *Wall Street Journal* (Eastern edn), April 23, 2003: A2.

www.renault.com
www.nissanmotors.com
www.toyota.com
www.honda.com
www.gm.com
www.ford.com
www.daimlerchrysler.com
www.citroen.com
www.kia.com
www.hyundai.com

Samsung Electronics: a dramatic turnaround

Samsung Electronics has become a global company living in accord with global standards.

JEFFREY D. JONES, President of the American Chamber of Commerce in Korea

We are living a nomadic life. We move on if other companies catch up.

HWANG CHANG GYU, President of Samsung's memory division (quoted in *Business Week*, 2003)

Background

The economic structure of South Korea was, and still is, similar in many ways to that of Japan. There was some deliberate imitation of the Japanese model. After all between 1910 and 1945 Korea was a colony of Japan. Japanese influence was, and still is, strong, despite the legacy of hostility from World War II. The *zaibatsu* or *keiretsu* organization of the Japanese economy was closely paralleled by the *chaebol* system of South Korea. In alliance with the *chaebol*, government institutions engaged in a significant degree of guidance planning. The conglomerates were largely responsible for South Korea's impressive rate of growth between the 1960s and 1997.

Reform of the *chaebol* system was considered necessary as a result of the 1997 crisis. What is it that has made reform necessary? What changes of environment have turned a plus into a minus?

Samsung was one of the leading *chaebol*. It was an enormous group, comprising 25 different companies and producing a wide range of products, catering mainly for the domestic market. In the area of electronics Samsung was, in the pre-1997 world, by reputation a low-end maker of refrigerators and VCRs and similar products. It was an imitator rather than an initiator. In this it also followed Japan and its pattern of development. Backward engineering allegedly allowed this copying. The competitiveness of products was based on low cost, which reflected the existence of cheap labour. The name of South Korea and its *chaebol* had almost no brand value, certainly not at the international level. The strategy was very much one of cost or price leadership.

Is the transition from a cost leadership strategy to a product differentiation strategy a natural part of economic development?

The South Korean economy was badly affected by the Asian economic crisis of 1997. The South Korean currency, the won, experienced a dramatic decline in value, as capital was withdrawn. However, its speed of descent in 1998 was more than matched by the speed of ascent in 2000. Recovery was speedy and dramatic.

The four leading *chaebol* were all put under enormous pressure by the crisis. Daewoo, the weakest of them, nearly went bankrupt. Samsung responded extremely well, much better than the other two large *chaebol*, Hyundai and Lucky Goldstar. It developed a turnaround strategy which has left it much better placed in the world economy than previously, although it still carries a legacy of the old Korea Inc., notably in its top-down hierarchy and the rigid control by Chairman Lee Kun Hee and his family, although they own only a small fraction of the shares of the company. There still exists a complex web of affiliate holdings. The present case study is focused on Samsung Electronics rather than the whole *chaebol*. It leaves unanalysed the role of the *chaebol* and the perceived need for structural reform.

Why have the *chaebol* responded so differently to the turnaround situation created by the 1997 crisis? The obvious strategic questions to ask are: how far did the *chaebol* suit a strategy which characterized rapid economic development in its early stages? How far have circumstances made the old structure out of date? Should the *chaebol* change both strategy and structure to suit the new times?

Samsung has reinvented itself as a breathtakingly innovative competitor seeking to 'snatch Sony's crown' (Larkin, 2002: 36). It has set out to establish a reputation for quality and innovative ability. In doing this it has sought to differentiate its products. The generic strategy adopted now stresses product differentiation as much as cost leadership. It has also focused on certain key markets, principally the largest and most demanding of all markets, the highly developed American market, and also on the fastest growing market, the Chinese market. It has emerged as a top three player in a host of product areas and as a top five receiver of patents on a worldwide basis.

Is Sony a good role model for Samsung to emulate?

Changing the strategy

In the depths of the 1997/8 crisis Samsung was losing millions of dollars every month. It emerged from the crisis with a mountain of debt. In 1997 debt reached an unsustainable $10.8 billion. Yet by 1999 the company was once more profitable. In 2000 the position improved further, with a net income of over US$5 billion. Since then it has flourished, with the level of profit sustained during recession and the debt level having fallen to just $1.4 billion.

How was such a dramatic turnaround achieved in such a short time?

Until 1997 Samsung, as other *chaebol*, was hierarchical in structure and deferential in the corporate culture inculcated in its staff. In 1997 Yun Jong Yong became the CEO. He had the advantage of speaking fluent Japanese and significant Japanese work experience. There was a pronounced change of leadership and leadership style. He turned the group into what amounted to Korea's first great global company.

How far is one person responsible for the choice of strategy and the successful implementation of that strategy?

Initially Yun Jong Yong dispensed the traditional painful medicine, a 30% cut in costs in five months. Overall the company shed 30,000 of its 70,000 workforce. It also shed a number of non-core units. However, the turnaround required rather more than this, nothing short of a profound change of attitude, in particular an increased stress on performance, achieved through an emphasis on creativity and open-mindedness. Yun's greatest achievement was to change the corporate culture, although yielding nothing in the exercise of decisive leadership.

How far is it possible for one man to change the culture of a company? How is it possible to reconcile the exercise of leadership with a culture which empowers staff to innovate?

The company has thoroughly internationalized itself. The group began to hire American-educated staff or those with significant experience in the USA. Three non-South Koreans become members of the board of directors. Two of the three possible heirs to Yun Jong Yong could speak English. Foreigners owned 60% of the shares of the group, including significant ownership by companies such as Apple. The company now generates 70% of its revenues outside South Korea, manufacturing in 14 different countries, including China and Mexico.

Why is internationalization so important to a company like Samsung?

In 1999 Eric Kim, a very experienced marketing director, who also had significant early experience in Japan and later in the USA, was attracted to the company. He set out his main strategic objective immediately: 'Samsung is going to be the first Korean company to create a truly global brand' (Solomon, 2002: A1). This became the driving force of Samsung's strategy.

Is a stress on marketing a critical part of the turnaround strategy?

The new strategy

The strategy which was adopted in the recovery is distinctive, partly because it differs significantly from that of its main competitors (see the Sony case study in Chapter 18). The strategy has been focused on five main aspects:

- *Hardware*, rather than software, despite the general belief that profit margins are wider and lead times longer in the latter. The company believes it is much better off buying the software rather than the hardware from outside. In this emphasis, Samsung is different from its main competitor Sony. The strategy does lay it open to a problem of getting the software needed.
- *Vertical integration*, producing rather than buying the chips and display screens required for its consumer electronics. This has meant that it has invested vast sums in investment in new productive facilities and has had to maintain a wider range of competencies than other companies operating in its markets. For example, over the last five years Samsung has put over $19 billion into new chip facilities, which are getting more expensive and more competitive.
- A so-called '*nomadic*' strategy. On the hardware side prices are falling relentlessly and the life cycle of products is short. However, something like 90% of the cost of most digital devices are accounted for by the chips and displays. Getting the cheapest but best-practice inputs is important. Samsung believes it can outcompete others through a nomadic strategic, that is, a strategy wherein it moves on when the area becomes overpopulated. A stress on technical advance allows it to do this. A stream of improvements and innovations will support such a strategy.
- *Product differentiation*, aiming to increase prices and profit margins by going upmarket, selling high-quality

products and gaining a reputation for doing this. It has not only put an emphasis on new technology but also on design. It needs a strategy of successful disruptive innovation, a stream of new and exciting products. CEO Yun has decreed that Samsung will sell only high-end goods, so it is investing an enormous amount in research in order to place it at the cutting edge of best practice.

This applies not only to final consumer products, but to the necessary inputs. By going upmarket Samsung is able to ride the recession better than its competitors. For example, in 2002 Samsung sold more memory chips than Micron Technology, Hynix Semiconductor and Infineon Technologies combined, each of which made a loss. Samsung's memory-chip business produced as much as US$2 billion in profit. Samsung has succeeded by avoiding the mass market and going for niches that command higher prices and larger profit margins. Something like 70% of profits comes from specialty products: graphics chips for game consoles, high-density memory modules for powerful servers and flash memory chips for hand-held computers, mobile phones and camcorders. Whereas Samsung gets two-thirds of its memory business from DRAM, its competitors get as much as 90%. Diversity has helped Samsung in difficult times. By 2006 it is hoping to get half of its memory business from flash chips, sales of which have been growing rapidly.

There was a deliberate attempt to upgrade the general image of Samsung, particularly in the USA. In this Sony was used as the benchmark model. In the words of Idei, Sony's CEO, Samsung 'found Sony a model or a benchmark of their brand image'. Sony sees Samsung rather as a supplier, from whom it can purchase semiconductors or display units, rather than as a threat or a competitor. This view seems to be a mistaken one, and represents a basic misunderstanding of what Samsung is trying to do.

- A 'digital-convergence strategy', which again is similar to the goal of Sony and other operators in the area of electronic products. It appears that Samsung may win the race.

How coherent is this strategy? How risky is this strategy? What are the sources of incoherence or risk?

Realizing the strategy

The first step in the rebranding of Samsung Electronics was to reduce the 55 advertising agencies working for Samsung to just one. Samsung signed a $400 million contract with a Madison Avenue firm, Foote, Cone & Belding Worldwide, whose task was to create a global brand image for Samsung Electronics. An expensive

marketing campaign was undertaken, the cost of which in 2002 was $450 million. The aim was to take Samsung upmarket, rebrand it as a maker of stylish best-practice products. Samsung pulled out of the cheap distribution outlets, such as Wal-Mart and Target, and moved upmarket to chains such as Best Buy and Circuit City.

Why is it important to have just one company controlling all the aspects of brand creation?

At the same time there was a move to effect a partnership with American technology, or the main purveyors of American technology. At the beginning of 1997 Samsung had almost no presence in mobile phones outside South Korea, but later that year Samsung won an order for 1.8 million handsets worth $600 million from Sprint PCS Group, an order which most might have expected to go to Nokia or Ericsson. The service was based on the CDMA standard in which Samsung had an early lead due to a strategic alliance with Qualcomm Inc. Not only did Samsung complete the order but it did it in 18 months, half the contracted time. Its silver, clamshell-shaped model the SCH-3500 was an instant hit and Samsung became world leader in CDMA technology. As a consequence the partnership with Sprint has grown, involving the new 3G Sprint wireless system. Samsung now has a reputation for high-end mobile handsets. It is growing in importance as a supplier in this industry.

This example showed a happy knack of making the right partnerships. How far can Samsung's success be explained by its strategic alliances? Are such alliances more a matter of good timing in finding a helping hand rather than one of a continuing partnership? How important are they likely to be in the future?

Three years ago Samsung had no significant retail presence in the USA. It has changed that by forging new partnerships, like those with Best Buy, Radio Shack and Circuit City. In these stores there are often lavish displays highlighting Samsung's products. In 2001 it sold $500 million worth of products, and targeted sales of $1 billion for 2002. The best sellers are its DVD/VCR players and the mobile phone, which also serves as a PDA. Since 1999 Samsung's total sales in the USA have doubled to $2.8 billion. Mobile phones have more than doubled the revenue generated, to over $1 billion, DVD players quadrupled to $129 million.

Why is it important to establish a position in the American market?

The company has succeeded in upgrading the brand name of Samsung very well. Samsung, for example, became a regular and reliable supplier to the main computer companies in the USA, supplying digital components to Dell and forming a $US16 billion R&D partnership with that company, supplying set-top boxes to AOL Time Warner, digital products to Microsoft and components to both the giants, IBM and Hewlett-Packard/Compaq. These links have helped Samsung stay at the frontier of best-practice technology.

The key to success has been design. Samsung sought to rank alongside Sony and Motorola as premier brands, not to outcompete them by undercutting them through price. Its technology and design have been excellent. Over the past few years only Apple has won as many design awards as Samsung. Even with the TVs and the DVDs it has deliberately moved upmarket. As early as 1996, but accelerated by the crisis of 1997, it has aimed to differentiate its products on the basis of design. There are 300 talented designers in Seoul and four design bureaux in the USA, Europe and Japan. The emphasis has been on style, best practice, simplicity and a quick response to market changes.

Why is design so important to a company like Samsung?

Samsung Electronics is the most dynamic part of Samsung. While it generates only a quarter of total revenue, it accounts for three-quarters of net income. In 2001 net profit was W2.95 trillion, on a total revenue of W32.4 trillion. In US dollars the profit is 2.41 billion, an impressive figure by any standards. The capitalization of Samsung is now, at US$48 billion, just below that of Sony at US$52 billion, poised to overtake it.

Table C.3 **Sales in 2001**

	%
Telecommunications (mainly mobile phones)	27.9
Digital media (mainly TVs and PCs)	29.1
Semiconductors	27.4
Home appliances (refrigerators, microwave ovens etc)	9.6
Other	6.0
Total US$26.64 billion	

Table C.4 **The sales and profit situation in 2002**

Telecommunications	Digital media
Sales: $10.4 billion	Sales: $8.2 billion
Profits: $2.5 billion	Profits: $32 million
Semiconductors	Digital appliances
Sales: $10.7 billion	Sales: $3.1 billion
Profits: $3.2 billion	Profits: $11 million

Would Samsung Electronics be better off on its own, without the other parts of the *chaebol*?

In the restructuring of the late 1990s three strategic business units were created within Samsung Electronics – digital media, telecommunications and semiconductors (memory chips), to go alongside the domestic or digital appliances which were the traditional area of sales, but one which had a poor profit potential, if the standard products with low profit margins were considered. The biggest advance was in the first business unit, which now stands alongside handsets and semiconductors for sales, but not yet for profits. Tables C.3 and C.4 show the relative proportions of sales and profits.

Is this product structure a suitable one for Samsung?

The home market of South Korea gives Samsung an advantage in a number of the product areas in which it operates. It is a good test market for new products. Fifty-six per cent of South Koreans have mobile phones. Typically they upgrade their phones about every eight months. This creates a market for the most up-to-date products. More than 70% are already broadband subscribers, way above comparable figures in developed countries. Samsung has also participated in an early 3G project which allows users to download and view up to 30 minutes of video and watch live TV.

Is it important to have a sophisticated and technology-sensitive domestic market? If so, in what ways?

One result was a combined mobile phone and hand-held computer, the NEXIO (Next Generation Internet Office), which was in direct competition with Nokia's Communicator. It has produced a sophisticated refrigerator with a screen on the door and potential connections with other devices. It has also perfected new digital and plasma TVs. It continues to produce less expensive and more conventional products, such as the i330 or i500 Smart phones, in partnership with Sprint.

Samsung in China

During the mid-1990s many South Korean companies entered China. Samsung was one of them, incurring, like the others, huge losses. The crisis of 1997 led to a change of policy, even in China. Every individual factory was now required to break even. Attention was concentrated on the ten main cities. Within a short period the situation changed dramatically. Overall sales grew by more than five times between 1998 and 2001. The goal was to push them up even further, from US$1.8 billion in 2001 to US$7 billion by 2005. In 1998 Samsung was still making a loss in China, but by 2001 this had been turned into a profit of more than $200 million, and an increase of 160% in 2002. China has enormous potential for a company such as Samsung.

Why was it so important for Samsung to be in China? Why have so many companies failed initially to make a profit in China?

China neatly illustrates the attempt by Samsung to stress quality rather than quantity. Even in China the strategy was a differentiation strategy, based on the attempt to establish a reputation for high quality. Many of the sales in China were still of the conventional electrical products, such as home appliances like washing machines or refrigerators. Often these were produced in China by joint ventures involving a Chinese partner. Yet Samsung still wanted to go upmarket. It believed that there was a growing middle class in China with rapidly increasing purchasing power and extremely willing to buy higher quality products. The market was becoming segmented and Samsung was happy to encourage this process of segmentation.

What is the best mode of entry into China by Samsung? Does the likely size of the market for high-quality white goods justify the Samsung strategy?

There are two examples which show this strategy at work:

• The first involved a plant producing washing machines in Suzhou which in 1998 had lost over US$2 million. Instead of reacting to competition by reducing prices or trying to slash costs, in 2000 Samsung began to produce a stylish but rather pricey alternative model. Within a short time the plant was profitable and annual sales rose from 32,000 to 170,000, showing that Samsung's reading of the market was quite correct.
• The second involved the mobile phone. Samsung sold models in China which were not cheap by Chinese standards: the A-288 of which it managed to sell 300,000, the N-628 and even the NEXIO, whose starting price was as high as US$800. Every few months Samsung introduced a new model. By this strategy it managed to capture 8% of the mobile phone market. One of the secrets of success was a good distribution system, which was made possible by the high profit margins.

Today

Samsung is aiming to put in place a range of global brands which impress by their advanced technology and design. In 2003 the Global Digital Tour, an extravagant exhibition of Samsung's products in the USA, has four stops, the first at the Guggenheim Museum in New York. It is the American market which is the key to increasing the brand value. On one valuation it has more than doubled since 1999, to US$8.3 billion. Samsung is rapidly acquiring a brand name based on the quality of its products.

How does having a valuable brand name help a company like Samsung? What mechanisms are there for using this brand name? How quickly can a brand name be won?

Today Samsung is the world's largest producer of memory chips and flat-panel monitors, number two in DVD players, number three in mobile phones, well behind Nokia but catching up on Ericsson. It is most definitely by reputation a high-end maker of mobile phone handsets, DVD and MP3 players, and digital television sets. It has emerged as a leader in the linking of wireless technologies with gadgets ranging from PDAs to refrigerators. From virtually nowhere a decade ago Samsung has moved into a prominent position in a whole range of areas in the new economy. This reflects success in using the technical advances made by Samsung and applying them to its own products.

Table C.5 Products in which Samsung now holds number one spot in the world

Market share (%)		Other players
DRAM (dynamic RAM)	32	Micron 19%, Hynix 13%, Infineon 12%
SRAM (static RAM)	27	
Flash memory	14	Intel 27%
CDMA mobile handsets	26	
All mobile phones	10	Nokia 36%, Motorola 15%
TFT-LCDs	18	LG Philips 17%, AU Optronics 12%, Sharp 9%
Computer monitors	22	
Big-screen TVs	32	Sony 25%, Mitsubishi 25%, Hitachi 11%
VCRs	17	
DVD players	11	Toshiba 15%, Sony 14%
MP3 players	13	Sonicblue 18%, Apple 17%
Microwave ovens	25	LG 22%, Galanz 19%

Table C.5 shows how Samsung is well placed in a number of advanced areas – from semiconductor chips to screens for TVs and computers, from microwave ovens, mobile handsets to MP3 or DVD players.

Samsung is definitely prepared to take a bet on the pattern of future demand. It is assuming that there is a large potential demand for thin-screened television and computer screens. It believes such televisions may be the next 'must-have' appliance. Samsung is already number one in the ultra-thin screens used in most high-tech computers and televisions. It intends to reinforce this lead and has announced a W20 trillion (US$16.75 billion) programme through to 2010 to build a flat-panel, liquid-crystal display production complex in Asan north of Seoul, which by 2005 will have monthly capacity of two million units. By that stage it is highly likely that the cost and the price of production of such display screens will have fallen under the twin influences of significant economies of scale and increased competition. Samsung wishes to derive first-mover advantage from being ahead of the field, using best-practice technology which it has developed itself. It has another such plant under consideration if demand warrants its construction.

Key strategic issues

In many ways Samsung is trying to repeat the success of Sony in generating a whole range of disruptive innovations in the period up to the 1980s. It is trying to retain the emphasis on hardware and technology. Can this be done in the changed conditions of the current business context? Can it be done at the new level of technology? Is Samsung trying to do too much in vertically integrating and producing itself many of the basic inputs in the digital world of communication, despite the high cost of R&D and investment in manufacturing? Is the strategy of going upmarket likely to stave off the impact of commoditization?

Strategic analysis and audit

Carry out a full strategic audit on Samsung Electronics. In particular compare the financial performance of Samsung with that of Sony and relate this to the difference in strategies adopted. How has this financial performance changed recently?

Reading

Edwards, C., Moon, I. and Engardio, P., 'The Samsung way', *Business Week*, June 16, 2003: 56.

Hwang Chang Gyu, President, Memory Division, Samsung Electronics, South Korea, *Business Week*, no. 3836, June 9, 2003: 48.

Larkin, J., 'Samsung tries to snatch Sony's crown', *Far Eastern Economic Review*, December 10, 2001: 36–43.

Marketing Magazine, 'Samsung's fairy tale', **108**(23) June 16, 2003: 22.

Moon, I., 'The secrets of Samsung's success', *Business Week*, no. 3816, January 20, 2003: 70.

Wall Street Journal (Eastern edn), 'Business brief: Samsung Electronics Company', June 12, 2003: 1.

Ward, A., 'Samsung invests $17bn in flat screens', *Financial Times*, June 12, 2003: 29.

Ward, A., Nakamoto, M. and Hille, K., 'Gambling on flat screen revolution', *Financial Times*, June 14/15, 2003: 14.

www.samsung.com

Going global: Singapore Telecommunications (SingTel)

Background

Until recently, throughout the world, telecommunication companies, or telcos for short, have been government-owned. Because of the high cost of the fixed-line networks required for telephony, there was a tendency to monopoly, which was one of the main reasons for government ownership. However, the possibility of renting or leasing use of the fixed networks was never really considered until quite recently. In practice the organization responsible for the service was given a monopoly, usually by government regulation. Since it was regarded as wasteful to duplicate these networks, and probably potentially unprofitable, the alternative to a government monopoly was a private monopoly. The present overcapacity is perhaps a hint at the wisdom of the previous approach.

What were the reasons for government ownership and monopoly? What has changed to end the dominant role of government and the existence of a monopoly? Has privatization been a success in this area? How is success to be measured? How is the role of the government likely to change in the future?

The existence of this huge indivisible investment created a barrier to entry which was more or less insurmountable. Even today it is difficult to enter the industry unless the new entrant has large resources or limits itself to hiring capacity from existing network operators and retailing it. Unfortunately unless the regulators limit the level of both price and profit, network owners can charge prohibitively high prices. For example, to use the 'last mile' network in Singapore costs something like five or six times the charges levied in New York.

What are the monopoly elements which are inherent in the industry? What kind of regulation does government introduce to avoid the exploitation of these monopoly elements? How likely is it that government will maintain such regulation?

The process of privatization, which has spread throughout the world, has released many of these organizations from government tutelage but simultaneously exposed them for the first time to competition. They have become either partially or fully privately owned. The former is usually a step towards the latter. SingTel is at present almost one-third privatized. The intention of the Singapore government is to increase that share. Most telcos have been corporatized and are expected to behave like a private company. This change has significant strategic implications, since it means a clear change in the goals of the enterprise, with an increasing emphasis on the bottom line, profit, rather than social aims such as providing communications to remote areas.

How far does privatization mean not only the introduction of the profit motive as a main objective but the break-up of the old utilities into different components?

Changes in technology have tended to break down any monopoly. Today there are numerous rival systems. There are satellite and other wireless systems, fibre-optic as well as copper wire networks. Increasingly there are wireless systems of various kinds. It would be difficult to maintain a monopoly situation in such a world. The transmission of voice messages is beginning to take second place to data transmission on a scale previously not envisaged.

What are the factors making for increased competition in the area of telecommunications? How much competition is there likely to be in this sector in the future? How is technical change likely to affect the level of competition? How would an analysis based on Porter's forces of competition look?

Given the close connection between telcos and the governments of the countries in which they have operated, the broad strategic aim of government is highly relevant to the strategy adopted by telcos, even after privatization. This is particularly true when the government has a history of taking an interventionist stance in promoting the development of the economy, in the way the Singapore government has.

What is the likelihood of such an interventionist stance continuing? What is likely to be the nature of government regulation in the future? Is it possible to forecast the nature of that regulation in any specific country?

The Singapore government has run a development state, where one of its primary roles is seen as promoting economic development. One of the prerequisites of economic development is a good infrastructure, including a good communications infrastructure. When SingTel was fully under government control, the aim was to establish this infrastructure. In this it was very successful, prompting Heracleous and Singh to write: 'In some respects, Singapore has almost the most advanced information technology hardware infrastructure in the world' (2000: 50).

How important is the infrastructure in the operation of a telco?

The problems of the telcos

Even in normal times the challenges faced by telcos are immense. These are compounded by the overexpansion which resulted from the communications bubble and the following world recession. There are a number of problems facing the telcos in general, and some facing SingTel in particular. The most significant general challenges are:

- how to meet the increased level of competition, both domestically and internationally. In all countries there are now rival providers of telecommunication services and some of these have serious international pretensions.
- how to meet the requirements of a changing regulatory environment and accommodate the evolving role of government. This is a dynamic process since technology itself is changing and causing government regulations to adjust.
- how to absorb the changing technology of communications, which constitutes a continuing revolution. Despite the long life of much of their infrastructure, telcos have to keep up with rapid technical change. For example, how will they cope with the pressure of broadband Internet telephony, which may be almost costless if associated with massive movements of data?
- how to cope with the much-increased internationalization of the industry. Which companies see themselves as international players? In what areas do they see themselves competing?
- how to cope with the wave of mergers, acquisitions and alliances in the industry, beginning in the mid-1990s, creating larger, more global and better endowed companies. This process has only just started.
- how to cope with the massive overcapacity in the industry, notably in broadband, and the downward pressure on prices exerted by this overcapacity. This overcapacity may be temporary but nobody knows just how temporary.

Why did the industry end up with such overcapacity? How quickly will the level of demand catch up with the oversupply?

Telecommunications is a sector of the economy in which there is considerable scope for strategic choice.

Any strategy must deal with the issues raised above. It is a sector in which scenario building on all these issues is useful – on competition, government regulation, technology, internationalization, consolidation and the fit between demand and supply. The large investments involved in the sector create considerable risks for the main players.

Can you construct scenarios for the future of each of the key areas relevant to strategy making?

SingTel and its history

There are a number of key dates in the development of SingTel. As late as 1972 SingTel became the monopoly government-owned postal and telecommunication services provider in Singapore. In 1986 the plan to privatize SingTel was announced, a plan not yet fully realized.

In April 1997 Mobile One (M1) was allowed to enter the domestic mobile phone market. M1 was backed internationally by Cable & Wireless of the UK, and its subsidiary Hong Kong Telecoms, and two local companies SPH and Keppel Corporation. The impact of this entry was beneficial. Prices went down by as much as 50–70%, the quality and range of services improved significantly and the rate of mobile penetration rose from only 14% to 41%. In just two years M1 won 32% of the mobile phone market. In 1998 two further licences for mobile phone services were issued, and one for fixed-line telecommunication services to start operation in April 2000. All licence winners were consortia of companies which comprised at least one government-linked corporation. International companies were often part of the consortia.

What has been the impact of privatization in Singapore? How far does privatization compel SingTel to move into international transactions?

In April 2000 Star Hub was allowed to enter the fixed-line market. Again the backing for the new company was strong. Star Hub was supported internationally by British Telecom and Nippon Telecom & Telegraph, and locally by Singapore Technologies Telemedia and Singapore Power. Star Hub had an ambitious strategy. In its own words, it aimed to be 'the first info-communications company in Asia-Pacific to offer total convergence of fixed and mobile communications on a simple, integrated platform. This means your home, office and mobile phones can all be linked, so you can be reached anywhere with just one number.'

In this context, what is convergence?

Domestic competition more or less compelled SingTel to take an international role in order to retain its own competitiveness. In Asia a race developed between rival telecommunication companies to become the largest pan-regional operator.

Are there first-mover advantages in putting together a regional network? Are there factors encouraging the iron law of oligopoly?

The challenges specific to SingTel include:

- how to deal with the interventionist Singapore government. Right up to 2000 the Singapore government, through its holding company Temasek, owned 80% of SingTel. Today that ownership is down to 67.5%, still a majority stake, and the government's intention is to take it down further. The free trade agreement with the USA compels them to do so. Even with zero ownership the government's wishes cannot be ignored. SingTel also intends at the right time to divest Singapore Post.
- how to remain competitive within such a small domestic market with powerful international players.
- how to enter and take advantage of the global market, notably the rapidly growing Asian market. Which countries should SingTel enter? Some countries have a low level of country risk, implying political and economic stability. However, other countries, while riskier, have greater potential for growth.
- how to select any partners. Just who are likely partners and who are likely strategic allies?

Is there really such considerable scope for strategic choice? Or is it the case that there is very little choice?

A comparison between other parts of Asia and Singapore

There are some very marked differences between Singapore and the other countries in Asia which determine the way in which SingTel might interact with them and therefore should be noted.

Do geographic and cultural affinities to Asian countries give SingTel an advantage in developing a pan-Asian role?

Generally Singapore differs from most parts of Asia in its recent rapid growth and current high level of GDP. It has all the trappings of a rich developed economy. Singapore's domestic telecommunications environment is more similar to that of a developed economy than those of most of the rest of Asia. In Singapore there are

Table C.6 Characteristics of the two markets

Asia	Singapore
Extremely low tele-density	High tele-density
Low quality and availability of fixed-line services	High quality and availability
High concentration of residential users	Same
Less demand for specialized features	High demand
High vulnerability to credit risk	Low vulnerability
High regulated tariffs	Falling tariffs

over 50 fixed lines per 100 people, over 40 mobiles and nearly 40 pagers, the latter two figures well above the average levels even for developed economies. This translates into significant differences in the characteristics of telecommunications between Singapore and large, but infrastructure-poor, countries such as India and China and suggests that SingTel might have an important role to play in these countries.

Are there particular reasons why telecommunications in Singapore are so well developed? Will this help SingTel in the future?

Singapore is a potentially competitive player mainly because of its strong infrastructural support, developed market for telecommunications, access to investment funds and openness to competition. However, nearly all Asian countries share participation in certain key trends:

- A strong emphasis on telecommunications infrastructure development by nearly all governments in the area
- A strong growth of fixed-line and mobile telecommunications networks throughout the region
- Acceleration of deregulation and privatization of government institutions
- Increased competition resulting from the early entry of Western telecommunications companies
- A typical concession/licensing period of 25 years within the build, operate, transfer model (BOT)
- A strong demand for significant amounts of debt and equity capital to finance expansion
- Industry rationalization through mergers and acquisitions
- Upgrading of telecommunications technology, with a significant pricing impact.

Do these factors make it likely that SingTel, operating in a fast-growing industry, will itself grow quickly?

The scale of the expansion in some countries is enormous. Recently, for example, China has been adding as many new telephone lines each year as are already available in the whole of Switzerland. The CEO of British Telecom has been quoted as predicting that Asia, which now has only 22% of the world telco market, would account for 60% within 10 years.

Which Asian countries would be the most advantageous to move into?

The strategy

SingTel aspires to be 'a total service provider with a range that covers the entire spectrum of the telecom business'. It therefore has little option but to go global. It has adopted an aggressive strategy to move out of its home market – but selectively. The key issues are which markets to enter, when and how to enter those markets, and also which technology to develop and when and how to apply it.

How important are staging and pacing to SingTel? How complex are the issues involved in entry into different markets?

At first SingTel invested in Asia, specifically in Thailand, Vietnam and Sri Lanka. However, its ambitions rose and it quickly shifted its main focus of attention. SingTel tried to compete in the developed economies of Europe, particularly in England and Western Europe, investing in cable television and mobile communications. This proved premature and unprofitable. SingTel also failed to achieve its general target of a 15–20% share of its total sales accounted for by foreign ventures. Within five years it had changed strategy and disposed of most of these early ventures. The entry into these markets appeared to be an expensive mistake.

Why was the movement into Europe a failure?

SingTel then refocused on the Asia Pacific region. Its main investment was in Australia, at first on a minor scale, S$55.6 million in the switched and lease-back services of AAPT and then later, in September 2001, on a much more dramatic scale, in Optus, the second fixed-line and mobile communications provider in Australia.

The purchase of Optus was greeted with a negative initial reaction. The price was the main issue. The purchase was from Cable & Wireless and cost SingTel an enormous S$15 billion. There has been much debate about whether the price, at fifty times Optus's earnings level, was too high. At first it appeared so, but later outcomes may prove SingTel to have been right. Most of the other investments were much smaller but highly strategic in their focus.

Was the purchase of Optus good strategy? Was it implemented at too high a price?

Some investments were relatively small, such as the S$47.1 million in PT Bukaka Singapore Telecom International in Indonesia, which operates fixed-line telephone services. However, others were larger, although not quite at the Optus level:

• As early as March 1993 it bought 23.6% of Globe Telecom, the number two telecom operator in the Philippines, providing mobile phone, international and fixed-line services, for S$339 million.
• In December 1995 it bought 12.2% of Belgacom, Belgium's leading telecom player (the only AA rated European telco left), for S$930 million: although recently SingTel has been reconsidering the commitment and there is a hint of eventual disinvestment.
• In January 1999 it bought 21.53% of Advanced Info Services, the number one mobile telephone operator in Thailand, for S$869.7 million.
• In March 2000 it bought 24.3% of New Century Infocomm, a fixed-line operator in Taiwan, for S$615 million.
• In August 2000 it bought 31.5% of the Bharti Group of India's Bharti Tele-ventures for S$1.15 billion.
• It also holds 35% of Telkomsel in Indonesia. In 1999 SingTel began an equity joint venture with KDD, Japan's largest international telecommunications operator, to integrate their respective services. It also holds a 60% stake in CZC AsiaPac, a company which is building one of the first private submarine cable systems.

Is the gradual strategy using partners in Asian countries a good strategy? Does the strategy for developed and developing countries differ significantly?

Not all these investments have been an immediate success. Share prices of telcos are down and judged in this way the purchases do not appear well made. However, they are long-term rather than short-term investments. SingTel also had a number of failures in its attempt to purchase, notably the Hong Kong arm of Cable & Wireless and Time dot.com, the telecommunications arm of the Renong Group in Malaysia. This is a highly competitive industry, one in which a commitment to purchase a stake in a country may sometimes be beyond even the largest players.

As can be seen from the above, the usual mode of entry in most cases is by an alliance with a local player, simultaneously buying a minority equity interest. The venues are carefully chosen for their potential – India, Thailand, Taiwan, the Philippines and Indonesia. However, there are one or two example of purchasing a whole company, notably Optus in the developed Australian market, which now generates more than half of SingTel's gross income.

What are the advantages of entering through a minority equity holding in a partner enterprise?

Future strategy

At present SingTel appears to be carrying a heavy load of debt, some S$9.3 billion (US$5.2 billion), some say the result of the ill-timed and overly generous purchase of Optus. Certainly for a period company profits were declining and the share price also falling. In reality SingTel is a very strong company.

SingTel has turned around Optus, which started to make a profit a year earlier than forecast. The main effort has been directed at reducing costs, for example improving procurement and debt collection. It has helped Optus to restructure an unprofitable pay-television business, enabling it to resell content instead of buying all its own programming. It has cut capital expenditures by as much as 37%.

How has SingTel managed to improve the performance of Optus?

In total SingTel has accumulated some US$30 billion of assets over the period 1996–2001. It is very conservative in its accounting practices, which means that its profit position is rather better than it appears relative to other telcos.

Lee Hsien Yang, the CEO and son of Lee Kuan Yew (prime minister of Singapore until 1990), has been steadily putting in place the building blocks to make SingTel the region's first truly pan-Asian telecom company. He is well on his way to achieving this. The company has already expanded from 1.5 million mobile phone customers in Singapore in 1997 to 25 million in Asia in 2002. Its national revenues are now only 5.8% of its total revenues. Of these revenues 54% are already from mobiles and data transfer rather than from fixed-line telephony.

Is the SingTel strategy changing the company in a desirable way?

Market penetration in the markets of SingTel's partners is still low – 23% in Thailand, 16% in the Philippines, 5% in Indonesia and a measly 1% in India. However, the companies in which it has invested are moving quickly. Bharti in India has moved from 300,000 mobile phone customers in August 2000 to 2 million in 2002. All the previous acquisitions are market leaders, with the potential to grow quickly from US$2 billion companies to $5–6 billion companies. They will clearly at some stage outgrow the home Singapore and its Optus base.

Key strategic issues

It is inappropriate to make a judgement on SingTel's strategy in a recession. It may appear that it has overpaid for its portfolio of assets. How should such assets be priced? Any strategy must be evaluated as a long-term strategy. Much of SingTel's strategy reflects its location in a small but highly developed base. As a response to the opening of its own limited market to outside competition, SingTel has had no choice but to internationalize. How should it have done this? What mode of entry is open to telcos? Is entry through a partner the right strategy? Is the combination of markets entered appropriate? What other markets should it enter in the future? How should it reinforce its role in these markets?

Some questions are those addressed by all companies: Should SingTel try to offer the whole range of services? What kind of pricing policy should it adopt?

Strategic analysis and audit

Carry out full strategic audit of SingTel. In doing this you should pay particular attention to the financial performance of Optus and other international investments and the prospects for the future.

Reading

Bedell, D., 'SingTel/Optus gets investor pans but analyst raves', *Corporate Finance* (198), May 2001: 3.

Buckman, R., 'SingTel's overseas moves pay off; Singapore firm's success contrasts with problems of other state companies', *Wall Street Journal* (Eastern edn) July 8, 2003: B5.

Day, P., 'In Asia, dispute erupts over cable access', *Wall Street Journal* (Eastern edn) May 22, 2003: B3.

Heracleous, L. and Singh, K., 'Singapore Telecom: strategic challenges in a turbulent environment', *Asia Case Research Journal*, (4) 2000: 49–77.

Luh, S. S., Borsuk, R., Webb, S. and Witcher, S. K., 'SingTel chief aims to mesh two cultures', *Wall Street Journal* (Eastern edn) April 23, 2001: B4B.

Saywell, T., 'Slow and steady at SingTel', *Far Eastern Economic Review*, October 4, 2001: 76–8.

Saywell, T., 'Nobody has done well', *Far Eastern Economic Review*, **165**(40) October 10, 2002: 48.

Saywell, T., 'Stoking SingTel's regional ambitions', *Far Eastern Economic Review*, December 10, 2002: 467.

Witcher, S. K., 'SingTel seals deal on stake in C&W unit – Singapore firm will expand Asian reach', *Wall Street Journal* (Eastern edn) March 26, 2001: A15.

www.singtel.com
www.optus.com.au

Starbucks: the third place

You get more than the finest coffee when you visit Starbucks. You get great people, first-rate music, a comfortable and upbeat meeting place, and sound advice on brewing excellent coffee at home. At home, you're part of a family. At work you're part of a company. And somewhere in between there's a place where you can sit back and be yourself. That's what a Starbucks store is to many of its customers – a kind of 'third place' where they can escape, reflect, read, chat or listen.

HOWARD SCHULTZ (quoted in Hitt et al., 2001: C-576)

Our main advertising media is the store itself.

LIN, vice-president of Starbuck's joint venture partner in China (quoted in Fowler, 2003)

Yet cup by cup, Starbucks is caffeinating the world, its green-and-white emblem beckoning to consumers on three continents. In 1999, Starbucks Corp. had 281 stores abroad. Today, it has about 1,200 – and it's still in the early stages of a plan to colonize the globe.

(Holmes et al., 2003a)

Background

The coffee shop or coffee house is not a new phenomenon. Lloyd's of London had its origins in one such coffee house. The founder of Starbucks, Howard Schultz, found his inspiration in the expresso bar so popular in Italy. Coffee shops had always been community gathering places, which is what Starbucks has intended its own stores to become.

How far does a strategy build competitive advantage on ideas used successfully by others, often used in a new combination with other ideas, some new, some old?

Schultz began his career with Starbucks Coffee Company in 1982, when it was a retailer of whole bean coffees. He visited Italy in 1983 and was inspired by the large number of expresso bars in Milan. He was unable to persuade his board of directors to embrace the idea of establishing the coffee bar as a vehicle to sell the coffee which it was selling directly. So he started his own company Il Giornale, and after two years of great success, he returned to purchase the Starbucks assets and, more importantly, the name, which he used for all the stores.

In building a strategy on a new idea, how often is there considerable resistance from the interests of those already in the sector? Is it true that good strategy comes from a clear objective whose realization is consistently and persistently pursued?

Coffee consumption in the USA appears to have fallen quite significantly from a peak in the 1960s and 70s and only began to recover in the 1990s. The Americans are not among the highest coffee consumers in the world, Scandinavians consuming as much as twice the American level. So the success of Starbucks depended on reversing the trend and lifting the level of coffee consumption.

How often is success built on a strategy which in some way remakes the environment? In broad terms how has Starbucks done this?

The industry

Fast food

The modern world is one of supermarkets or hypermarkets, which seem to get bigger and bigger, and fast-food chains, such as McDonald's, which cater for the need to avoid the time-consuming activity of preparing meals. Speed, convenience and low cost are the features of the new world of shopping and eating, largely an American invention. Scale is the key to low cost, as Wal-Mart has shown. Starbucks has managed to apply the methods of mass production and mass sales to an industry which sells something which can be regarded as more of a luxury or aspirational good, and with a surprising degree of success. It has also done this by sticking to its core business.

What does Starbucks have in common with a supermarket? How far could Starbucks be described as pursuing a price leadership strategy?

It is interesting to compare the success of Starbucks with that of IKEA. There are some illuminating parallels, for example the mix of generic strategies, the package of product attributes, the importance of size for product procurement and logistics.

What are the parallels with the IKEA way? Are there significant differences?

Coffee

Coffee is reputedly the second most traded commodity after oil. There are two categories of coffee, specialty and basic coffee. Whether such a distinction is real is something to be considered. The latter is the typical coffee bought in the supermarket and also used in instant coffee. Specialty coffee has recently been experiencing a rapid rate of growth, largely at the expense of the latter. The distinction goes right back to the grower and what is grown.

How far are there real differences in the input and therefore the final product, if seen simply as coffee?

The commercial bean is usually the Robusta variety, the specialty bean the Arabica. The latter are seen as high-quality beans which command a price premium. These beans move from the grower to the specialty coffee seller through as many as five separate steps and five different intermediaries. The farmer passes the coffee to the collector, who moves it to the miller and from there it goes to the exporter, the importer and finally to the coffee speciality seller. There has been a dramatic increase in the proportion of specialty beans moving through this chain. During the 1980s the Arabica accounted for less than 10% of all coffee beans sold. By the end of the century it had just about reached equality with the humble Robusta bean.

How far are Starbucks and its imitators responsible for the changing demand for the different coffee beans?

Key success factors

Why is specialty coffee the basis for the success achieved by Starbucks? There are a number of factors which have been important:

- There has been a switch in demand towards real coffee, and away from instant coffee, largely associated with the notion of real coffee as the superior product. There is also a tendency to replace low-quality coffee with higher quality coffees. This is partly a reflection of rising incomes and more informed consumers. Consumers have more discretionary income and the income elasticity of demand for specialty coffee rises with income. Consumers also know much more about coffee, which has developed something of the mystique of wine. It is now as socially valuable to know something about good coffee, as it is about good wine.
- The attempt to adopt a healthier lifestyle, particularly strong in the USA, and the campaign against drink driving, everywhere in the advanced world, has pushed consumers towards the consumption of non-alcoholic beverages. Coffee is an attractive alternative.
- After an initial emphasis on home entertainment, with videos and pay television, there is a return to regular 'going out' in developed countries, as shown by the revived popularity of cinema going. The coffee bar is a place where people 'going out' can easily meet and talk. It has also long been a locus of business activity for independent consultants, creative people and teleworkers, but is also becoming a job search centre for the professional unemployed.
- Specialty coffee is an affordable luxury or aspirational good. Drinking Starbucks coffee conjures up the image of relaxed affluence (Fowler, 2003). It is part of what has been called a 'democratization of luxury'. The neologisms 'masstige' or 'boutiqeing' have been coined to capture the combination of both mass market and prestige which attaches to the products which qualify as aspirational. Middle-market consumers selectively trade up to higher levels of quality, taste and aspiration. This involves the creation of the perception of luxury in goods and services that are hardly luxurious. Starbucks is in good company with the 'super housewife' Martha Stewart or designer pet food.

How far does competitive success often follow from a recognition of changes in behaviour and taste, which are often parts of broader changes, such as a greater concern for health? Can you give other examples of this? What generational differences exist which might reduce demand for Starbucks coffee? How far is coffee a candidate for budget cuts in conditions of slower economic growth?

Competitive forces

Barriers to entry

There are very few barriers to entry into this industry. It is relatively easy for a small player to set up a coffee shop. Little in terms of financial resources is needed to set up one retail outlet. It is also possible to enter as a small player without an intention to grow bigger. It can be done with little delay after the initial intention is articulated.

There is nothing in the technology of coffee production which could establish significant difficulty in entering the industry, nothing that could not be quickly mastered. There are insignificant economies of scale or scope, although the relationship with suppliers reflects the size of orders.

It is also unlikely that current players could respond to entry with a set of major deterrent actions. However, in theory this could be done by a large chain simply dropping its price.

The one entry problem is location. There are finite good locations in the centre of any city or town, but usually enough to ensure a new entrant can find an attractive venue, although at a cost which is likely to be higher the better the site. Unlike IKEA and the furniture industry, a significant attribute of the product is the centrality of the place at which it is delivered; a central location is important, a location easily accessible by potential customers, such as shoppers or businesspeople during the day and those attending entertainment events in cinemas, theatres or concert halls during the evening. With the advent of the espresso cart, the importance of location is retained but access to suitable locations made much easier.

The saturation of good locations by Starbucks is a deterrent, the company being prepared to cannibalize existing stores, with an initial loss of as much as 30% of sales, on the assumption that the additional stores will expand total demand to compensate. Starbucks has a reputation for predatory rental behaviour, paying over the odds in rent for a good location. It might even rent or lease and keep a venue empty.

Although Starbucks spends as little as $30 million on advertising, or 1% of its revenues, its brand name is an increasing factor in deterring entry, established by word of mouth and repeated visits.

Existence of substitutes

In its broadest sense a substitute is anything offering the same experience. The sale of specialty coffee in grocery stores and its consumption at home is a substitute. In its narrow sense tea, juice, soft drinks, alcohol and other flavoured coffee and non-coffee-related drinks are possible substitutes. Starbucks provides some of these.

The Starbucks coffee experience is a package of attributes. The overall experience comprises the ambience of the venue, including decor and musical background, the nature of the clientele, predictability of the product, convenience and ease of payment and even the availability of Internet facilities. Starbucks innovates to cut transaction costs and speed up service, introducing automatic espresso machines in some stores and prepaid Starbucks cards. In its 60 Denver stores it is possible to prepay on the phone or the Starbucks Express website and have the coffee waiting on arrival at the store.

Starbucks claims the largest Wi-Fi network in the world, a high-speed wireless Internet service to about 1,200 stores in North America and Europe, developed together with Mobile International and Hewlett-Packard. The coffee house works as an office where you can check your emails and download multimedia presentations. Starbucks provides an initial 24 hours of free wireless broadband, backed up by a variety of monthly subscription plans. The aim is to fill the stores in the period between the breakfast and lunch rushes and win the support of the generation just entering the workforce.

What exactly does the customer want? There may be distinct market segments. This has long been recognized by those who sell alcohol, who have adjusted the nature of the bar according to the tastes of the clientele and adjusted the price of the drinks. A premium is paid for the right ambience and company.

Bargaining power of suppliers

Because Starbucks purchases high-quality coffee, suppliers give priority to Starbucks and work closely with the company to ensure prompt delivery and good quality.

Since 1989 the price of coffee has plummeted, peaking at US$3.15 per pound, but now at an average price as low as US$45 cents. The grower receives far less, since the intermediaries take their cut. The first International Coffee Agreement was negotiated in 1962, a complicated set of quotas for more than 60 coffee-growing countries, designed to keep prices reasonably stable. This it managed to do for 25 years, despite endless renegotiation. In 1989 the USA withdrew its support; the agreement was suspended and the price began to fall. Before 1989 the price had hovered around the US$1.20 mark. Supply ran ahead of demand, with new producing areas such as Vietnam becoming significant. During the 1990s world production rose by 21%, demand by 10%.

The typical coffee producer is small, although the purchase by cooperatives or middlemen, including exporters, increases somewhat the market power of suppliers. The cooperatives do not have the market clout of Starbucks, which could easily apply considerable pressure on producers, hardly necessary, given the level of coffee prices in world markets. To access a wide variety of coffees and hedge the risks to local supply, Starbucks buys 50% of its beans from Latin America, 35% from the Pacific rim and 15% from East Africa. Increasingly Starbucks blends the coffees. With a global reach and access to modern procurement techniques, Starbucks makes purchases to minimize cost.

Starbucks has never considered integrating vertically back into the growing of coffee beans. However, because Starbucks purchases more high-quality coffee than anyone else in the world, exporters are keen to sell to the company. Because of this suppliers give priority to Starbucks and are willing to work closely with the company to ensure prompt delivery and good quality. Starbucks takes samples at every stage to ensure that the quality is maintained.

The planned massive expansion in retail outlets and therefore in demand for quality coffee beans make Starbucks' task of finding suitable supply more difficult. Potentially it may increase the market power of the supplier of good coffee, shifting the balance back to the growers.

Bargaining power of purchasers

The typical customer of Starbucks is someone who visits one of their retail outlets. However, Starbucks also has agreements with retailers, wholesalers, restaurants and other service providers to carry Starbucks coffee. Starbucks deliberately seeks out leaders in the various fields, those with an excellent reputation who would enhance Starbucks' own reputation. This includes an airline, United Airlines, supermarket chains Nordstrom and PriceCostco using a special brand name Meridian, a bookstore Barnes & Noble, and a supplier of business services ARAMARK. Starbucks has also worked with well-known companies to develop new products, with Pepsi with whom Starbucks has developed the frappuccino, a milk-based cold coffee beverage in a bottle, with Red Hook Breweries supplying an ingredient for a stout, and with Dreyers' Ice Cream with whom Starbucks has developed its own ice cream which it distributes through Dreyers' grocery channels. These companies have much more resources than the usual Starbucks customer and can negotiate from a stronger position.

Intensity of competition

In developed economies there is a 'retailing war' between coffee chains, and between the local retail outlets of such chains and individual coffee shops. Starbucks is the largest player. In the USA there is no nationwide competitor. McDonald's McCafe outlets are expanding rapidly, but they have a downmarket image. The strategy of McDonald's has changed, from simply capturing the passing trade through low price, to making the outlet a 'destination'. Back in 1997 in North America when it was beginning to take off, there were 3,485 competitors, mostly one-store establishments with no plans to expand. Starbucks' main competitor in the specialty coffee area was Second Cup, a Canadian company, a franchiser, traditionally

mall-based but increasingly using stand-alone locations like Starbucks.

The forces of competition are strong in this industry, so that it is remarkable that Starbucks has established itself as such a dominant player. The notion of an aspirational product largely explains this (see the Strategy in Action on the democratization of luxury in Chapter 10).

What about the role of complementors? How are future changes likely to change the forces of competition?

Being a good citizen

Starbucks has made a great deal of its role as a good global citizen. It has frequently repeated its six guiding principles, which are:

1. Provide a great work environment and treat each other with respect and dignity
2. Embrace diversity as an essential component of the way we do business
3. Apply the highest standards of excellence to the purchasing, roasting and fresh delivery of our coffee
4. Develop enthusiastically satisfied customers all of the time
5. Contribute positively to our community and our environment
6. Recognize that profitability is essential to our future success.

While not embracing the triple bottom line in stating such principles, Starbucks has represented itself as both environmentally and socially responsible.

Despite this statement of principles Starbucks has managed to get itself into some difficulty with employees. It has recently agreed to a settlement of $18 million to compensate thousands of present and former managers and assistant managers in California stores, who were forced to spend long hours performing menial tasks not in their job description, and unremunerated at penalty overtime rates. Californian law requires employers to pay time-and-a-half after eight hours of work in a day, even for mangers or supervisors, provided they spend at least 50% of their time performing tasks that are not related to managing (report from the *Los Angeles Times* reproduced in the *Sunday Age*, April 21, 2002: 16).

Starbucks has also proclaimed its environmental friendliness and its unwillingness to exploit the current chronic surplus of coffee in the world which has led to the low price. There have been various attempts to raise the price of coffee and ensure that producers are paid above their costs. There have been various suggestions for 'ethical taxes' to assist the farming communities. Some organizations have voluntarily bound themselves to a fair trade code, which aims to ensure that small farmers receive a fair share of the price paid for their crops. The typical pledge is to buy at least 5% of their purchase in a fair trade. In March 2002 Howard Schultz urged coffee executives 'to share the blanket' of prosperity with the growers. Starbucks does have a good reputation for its treatment of suppliers. Despite this Starbucks will not certify 5% of its coffee as 'fair trade' as other speciality coffee companies have agreed to do.

Do these two examples show the danger of proclaiming your own virture?

The strategy

Starbucks' main strategy is to establish a reputation for high-quality coffee, in effect to brand the company so that it can set a premium price, one which offers the company a profit margin way above that normally made in such an industry.

How much of a price premium can Starbucks charge for its coffee?

There are various ways in which it seeks to create a price premium:

- It has developed a mystique about coffee in general.
- It emphasizes the quality of the product. It roasts the beans itself and after much experimentation created a taste which is unique, or claimed to be unique.
- It uses technology, in this case one-way valve bags, to retain the freshness of the beans for the maximum possible period of time.

What other ways are there for creating a price premium?

Another method of emphasizing quality is stressing excellence in everything the company does or sells. The focus is not just on the product, the coffee, but on:

- the nature of the coffee shops themselves
- the enthusiasm and good attitude of staff
- the quality of other products which Starbucks uses or sells, such as coffee-making machines, grinders, filters, storage containers and mugs.

What other activities or features are important in establishing a reputation for quality?

There are three main areas to be considered in discussing the strategy adopted:

- *the treatment of employees – principally the influence of this on their motivation*

All staff from CEO to baristas are, in theory, regarded as partners, not employees. Even the part-time staff receive stock options, so-called 'bean stock'. Starbucks baristas are paid slightly higher wages than is the norm in the food service industry. They are given health insurance, disability and life insurance and a free pound of coffee each week. The baristas who serve the coffee are usually college or university students. They are carefully selected and receive a significant amount of training, a minimum of 24 hours, ensuring that they can answer any question asked about coffee which may be put to them. Even the executive staff have to work in a store for two weeks to gain real customer experience. Starbucks has aimed to have a flat organizational structure, partly to ensure close contact between management at headquarters and operational staff. However, it is unclear how Starbucks can maintain the initial culture of the staff, the high level of motivation and enthusiasm which marked the early years.

How far is it true in a business such as Starbucks that the reputation of the company rests on the behaviour of its staff? How is it possible to maintain the motivation of staff beyond the initial period of operation of a business?

- *the choice of location for the stores, since this is vital to the whole coffee-drinking package*

Since venue is critical the policy on location is an important part of strategy. Starbucks is happy to establish stores in close vicinity with each other, provided the location is good. One joke popular among staff stressed the close vicinity, by inventing a headline, 'Starbucks establishes new store in rest room of existing store'. Starbucks has a team of property managers and others working to find the best sites for retail outlets. It needs to find such outlets at a rate of at least one a day in North America alone. The initial target was the main street of every major North American city, now it is the main street of all regional centres. Starbucks has also turned to using espresso carts or kiosks, called Doppio espresso carts. It is in the process of branding the humble cart. An eight-foot by eight-foot cube unfolds into a large stand with a clear Starbucks identity which can be used for street corners, train stations and shopping malls.

Daniels (2003) says that: 'The strategy is simple: Blanket an area completely, even if the stores cannibalize one another's business.' Starbucks has only 7% of the USA coffee-drinking market and less than 1% of the world market. What is the population needed to support a coffee shop? This sets the threshold population size. In Seattle there is a store for every 9,400 people, the highest density anywhere. A more realistic target is 55,000 in the USA and 56,000 in Canada (the Coffee Specialty Association of America believes it could be half this figure, although almost half these would be coffee carts rather than stores.). In theory this would mean that North America could support almost 5,000 specialty coffee retail outlets. In 1997 Starbucks had just over 1,000 stores, or just over 20% of the maximum possible number. In the large urban markets it had already reached almost one-third of the potential maximum. Rapid growth since then has moved the number much closer to the notional maximum. By 2002 Starbucks already had 4,247, not far off a possible saturation point, although there are still eight states where there are none and Starbucks may not accept the rather conservative views of the various authorities, seeing Seattle as an indication of the full potential.

What is saturation point in North America? What factors determine the size of the catchment area required by a Starbucks store? What are the locational factors which influence this catchment size?

As Starbucks has moved to a point at which the North American market is saturated, overseas expansion has become critical to sustaining rapid growth. In 2002 the plan was to open a further 400 stores, an expansion of 35%. The aim was the same in 2003, and by 2004 the objective is to have 10,000 stores worldwide. Since Starbucks is nearly debt-free and generates $300 million in free cash flow annually, it has every opportunity to do this. Starbucks is clearly expanding in dramatic style internationally and at the breakneck pace at which it had already opened up the American market. The eventual goal is very ambitious, 20,000 stores worldwide. It obviously has considerable room for further expansion.

Can the business model be transferred abroad easily?

• *the image presented by the Starbucks' name, both domestically and internationally, and the management of that image*
The image in North America has been very much an aspirational one, but this is more difficult to establish abroad.

What might Starbucks have to do to create an aspirational image in countries which already have a tradition of coffee drinkers or an alternative tradition of tea drinking?

Starbucks only entered international markets when it had already established itself firmly in the USA. It therefore moved abroad from a position of strength. However, it is by no means clear that the overseas expansion has been a success. At present Starbucks' 1,532 overseas stores, which account for 23% of its stores yet only 9% of its sales, are losing money. In the 30 countries in which it operates it has faced a host of problems. To many in Europe Starbucks' coffee appears to be an overpriced imitation of the real thing. Both in Europe and Asia it faces a multitude of competitors.

What are the kinds of difficulties which are likely to confront the use of Starbucks' business model abroad?

It chose to make its international entry in the Asia Pacific area, because of the enormous size of the market and its potential for growth. A higher population base is needed in many Asian countries in order to support one store but the population of Asia is so large that the number of stores could easily outnumber those in the USA within a short period of time. It chose to start in Japan in 1997. It has over 450 stores there but the Japanese chain is losing money, which has caused Starbucks to experiment with selling alcohol.

Why did Starbucks choose Japan for its first foreign venture? Why is it having difficulties in Japan? Is the real test for Starbucks its entry into Italy?

Starbucks' strategy has been to seek good partners abroad. The model adopted in Japan, in which the foreign expansion began, was much the same as that used in North America, with this one exceptional feature. Starbucks set up a joint venture with a local retail partner, Sazaby Inc, which Starbucks then licensed to use the Starbucks' model. Elsewhere in Asia, such as Thailand and South Korea, it initially issued a licence to a local operator, but later converted the local operator into either a partner in a joint venture or a wholly owned subsidiary. With licensing and the use of partners there is always the twofold problem of maintaining the quality of coffee product, stores and brand image, and controlling costs, notably property and labour costs. The bigger the organization, the bigger these problems are likely to be.

Is the joint venture the appropriate mode of entry for Starbucks?

Key strategic issues

The key strategic issues confronting Starbucks in its breakneck pace of expansion relate to reaching saturation point in the North American market and the transferability of the business model abroad. Are the attributes of the product different abroad? This raises a number of questions. Location is a difficult problem in countries in which change is occurring rapidly – how does Starbucks deal with this issue? Is it sensible to change the nature of the coffee house by selling alcohol? In making the transfer abroad, the mode of entry is an important strategic dilemma for Starbucks. With the use of the joint venture mechanism, what criteria are appropriate for the choice of partner? Is Starbucks, like MacDonald's, soon likely to reach a turnaround situation?

Strategic analysis and audit

Carry out a full strategic audit on Starbucks. How do the financial results differ for the operations in the USA from those abroad? Why are the foreign operations still loss making?

Reading

Daniels, C., 'Mr. Coffee', *Fortune* **147**(7) April 14, 2003: 139.

Economist, The, 'United States: Make mine a latte; the labour market', **367**(8328) June 14, 2003: 48.

Fowler, G. A., 'Starbuck's road to China', *Wall Street Journal* (Eastern edn) July 14, 2003: B1.

Greene, T., 'Starbucks gets win-win from Wi-Fi', *Network World* **20**(28) July 14: 1.

Hitt, M. A., Ireland, R. D. and Hoskisson, R. E. *Strategic Management: competitiveness and globalization,* 4th edn (South-Western Publishing, Cincinatti: 2001).

Holmes, S., Bennett, D., Carlisle, K. and Dawson, C., 'Planet Starbucks: to keep up the growth, it must go global quickly', *Business Week* (3798) September 9, 2003a: 100.

Holmes, S., Kunii, I. M., Ewing, J. and Capell, K., 'For Starbucks, there is no place like home', *Business Week* (3836) June 9, 2003b: 48.

Mason, T., 'Indian Tea board to fight coffee bars', *Marketing,* June 12, 2003: 5.

Webb, R., 'Melbourne awash with coffee chains', *The Sunday Age,* April 21, 2002: 16.

www.starbucks.com

Sir Richard Branson and many wise virgins

The Virgin name was inspired by the nubile young women who passed through Sir Richard's west London squat in the 1960s, by the entrepreneur's lack of business experience, and by a religious experience he had at a funeral, depending on which story he feels like telling.

(The Economist, 2002: 22)

If we have an aim in life, it's to create the most respected brand in the world.

BRANSON (quoted in *Business Age*, July 2003)

He is a serial entrepreneur. Some of his ventures will succeed and probably more than half of them won't, but that's the nature of the animal.

PHILIP KENDALL, head of public company corporate finance at PricewaterhouseCoopers in London (quoted in *Business Age*, July 2003)

Background

Successful leadership, particularly when it is based on charisma of some kind, can lead to the favourable branding of the person. Often the name of the person lives on with the company. The name, whether it is Gucci or Lloyd's, then sells the products or services. There are particular moments in the history of an enterprise which lend themselves to the emergence of a leader. The foundation of a new enterprise or the turnaround of an existing enterprise already in trouble are such moments. Even Lloyd's and Gucci have had their times of trouble in which questions have been raised about the enterprise and its name. What has been striking has been the tenacity of many brand names, which have managed to survive these times.

How far is the development of a brand name associated with a person? What happens to the brand name once that person departs?

However, while there is obviously a relationship between the reputation of the leader and business success, in some cases the relationship seems a tenuous one. The degree of success does not seem to justify the branding. The company may never quite achieve the success it promises; however, it keeps going. The reputation of some leaders survives failure; they display an uncanny ability to bounce back, to persuade others to back them. There is an aura about them which attracts support.

What causes the leader to lose the charisma or aura? What does the case of Messier and Vivendi in Chapter 8 tell us about this?

This case study considers the history of a person who has had mixed business success and still excites considerable interest and support, Sir Richard Branson, the creator of the Virgin brand. Over a period of 35 years Branson has created a stable of companies which today have a gross turnover of at least £4 billion, not enormous by the standards of the largest multinational companies, but impressive and still growing. Sir Richard describes his business as the reverse of a faceless corporation or conglomerate, what he calls a 'branded venture capital' organization. Virgin looks at business sectors around the world which are 'fat, lazy or oligopolistic and do not serve the customers well' and applies the Virgin brand to that sector.

How far has the Virgin brand become independent of Branson, with an appeal of its own? Are there other examples of branded venture capital organizations which spring to mind?

The key question to ask is why Richard Branson's Virgin group of companies should command so much respect. They operate in very competitive industries, by no means limited to the new economy, and they do so often with what is to many a questionable management competency. Many of the enterprises appear to be scarcely profitable or even loss making. Nor is this situation new.

How is it that such companies have a status above their measured performance? How important are factors other than profit in establishing the reputation of a strategist-manager, particularly when he or she is a founder of a new enterprise?

Branson's character and history

What is it about Richard Branson which attracts attention and wins respect? He has obvious good looks and charm, and is prepared to behave with a flamboyance which lends itself to media presentation. His behaviour is in conventional terms most unBritish but much admired.

Most of all he is seen as a counterculture figure, someone who is prepared to cock a snook at the stuffy gentility of old Britain and to be representative of the entrepreneurship and glamour of new Britain, the Britain of the Beatles, Tony Blair and Princess Diana. His appeal transcends class, despite his upper-class background. Some of the reasons for this appeal are obvious:

• He tends to see no division between public and private life. His style is to involve in his business dealings all those who come into contact with him, family friends or neighbours. He has often operated his businesses from home rather than an office.
• He totally immerses himself in a new project, initiates it and then passes it over to good management and financial people who are given a stake in the enterprise and given room to make the enterprise succeed. Success then depends on his ability to choose good lieutenants.
• He puts his staff first, followed by the customers and only then by the shareholders. This is unusual in the current fashion for giving priority to the shareholders and often ignoring the other stakeholder groups, except where they can impact dramatically on profit.
• He looks much more to long-term rather than short-term profit. He is able to do this because his enterprises as private companies do not have to spell out the immediate profit situation.
• He prefers organic growth to acquisitions which have been rare.
• He accepts the challenge of entering markets where there are long-established incumbents who have become conservative. He enjoys confronting them, as he did famously with British Airways and Coca-Cola. He is popular for his emphasis on fair play.

How far are these characteristics specific to Branson, his time and place, and inimitable? Are there examples of others who have behaved in a similar way?

The structure of the Virgin companies reflects the nature of Branson himself. It is an unusual structure, a vast sprawling alliance of about 270 companies held together mainly by the trade name and Branson's role as shareholder, chairman and public relations supremo. The empire is organized into layers of holding companies, in which Branson's stakes are held by family trusts based in tax havens like the Virgin Islands. The Virgin group has been likened to a Japanese *keiretsu* or a franchising operation – in reality it is somewhere between the two. The companies are nominally independent of each other but linked by the small group of executives and advisers who guide strategy, plan new business development and exercise overall financial control. There is no real headquarters and almost no middle management. Close personal ties and a strong

culture made up for the lack of a formal structure. The aim is to empower the managers of the companies and ensure that they act in an entrepreneurial way.

How far can this structure survive the disappearance of the founder? How far has it solved the principal/ agent problem?

The structure and performance of Virgin companies

There are currently two characteristics which mark out the stable of Virgin companies as different from most of the enterprises discussed in the case studies in this book.

• The first is that all the enterprises are private companies. In 1986 Branson flirted briefly with the notion of a public company. He floated his music and entertainment empire. The timing was very unfortunate since in 1987 the stock market crashed and the economy went into recession, leaving Virgin shares at almost half their initial offer price. In 1988 at the cost of about £100 million Branson reprivatized the company, buying back the shares at their float price.

There is a web of trusts which act as holding companies for the enterprises. Because they are private companies Branson argues that they do not have to be obsessed with profits and therefore also avoid the short-term obsessions of the stock market. He maintains that they are much more concerned with cash flows and capital value. The downside is that nobody knows the profit position of the various companies.

What are the disadvantages of the private company and the advantages of the public company as a vehicle for any enterprise? Are there differences for enterprises of a different size at a different point in their life?

• The second characteristic is that Branson almost always operates with a partner, often very good partners who supply much needed managerial expertise and credibility in the relevant areas. Singapore Airlines owns 49% of Virgin Atlantic. Patrick has recently acquired half of Virgin Blue in Australia. Stagecoach holds 49% of Virgin Rail, T-Mobile 50% of Virgin Mobile (UK) and AMP half of Virgin Money. Branson prefers to retain control but to be allied with competent and strong partners. The downside is that Branson does not always see eye to eye with his partners.

What are the problems in selecting a partner? Is Branson's personality likely to make conflict with partners inevitable?

The strategy

The Virgin brand name is undoubtedly the most valuable asset which the Virgin group of enterprises possesses. It is said to be more of an image than a brand. It is an asset closely associated with the name of Richard Branson, reflecting his sense of fun, his humour, his style and his irreverence. The nature of the brand as it relates to the products and services is difficult to define exactly but is a highly individual one. It includes value for money but also a certain modern style and status. The brand is used to set up a new business, in almost any area of the economy, and then to raise capital by selling off part of the enterprise. The initial expansion is the key to maximizing early value. Much depends on Branson himself who is an articulate but flamboyant speaker. He is a master of publicity.

Branson finds it easy to get press coverage and is much quoted and much talked about. Below is a sample of his sayings and comments about him.

The biggest risk any of us can take is to invest money in a business that we don't know. Very few of the businesses that Virgin has set up have been in completely new fields.

Branson does not expand Virgin Blue to Hobart (as he did recently). Rather, he 'allows grandmums and granddads to come and see their grandkids on the mainland'. He does not push Virgin Mobile into the US (as he did recently), he 'helps ordinary Americans get a better deal on phones, and makes it fun along the way'.

I have not depended on others to do surveys or market research, or to develop grand strategies. I have taken the view that the risk to the company is best reduced by my own involvement in the nitty-gritty of the new business.

'Greed is fun – that's true' says Branson.

I think he sees his business as having a definite social value, rather than just a way to make money. Brown, M., Richard Branson: The Inside Story.

Reduce the scale of ... risk through joint ventures ... (and) have a way out of a high risk venture.

Branson's headmaster: You will either go to prison or become a millionaire.

As businesses grow, watch out for management losing touch with the basics – normally the customer.

Rowan Gormley, CEO of Virgin Wines: A big part of why he's successful is because he's instinctive. Rather than analysing things backwards and forwards, he simply asks, 'Would I like it as a customer?'

My goal is to set enormous, some say unachievable, challenges and rise above them.

Brown: You can go to any Virgin event or get on any Virgin plane, and everybody seems to feel that they know him personally.

[Our] 'keep it small' rule enables ... more than usual numbers of managers the challenge and excitement of running their own businesses.

he is the little guy

Pursue a 'buy, don't make' strategy.

Source: Adapted from Mintzberg et al., 1998: 130; and Elder, 2002.

How far does Branson act on intuition and gut feeling and base his success on his personal relations with staff and key strategic players?

The extension of the brand may carry its own dangers. It is a brand name which has been applied to a wide range of products and services, including airlines, railroads, cosmetics, financial services, music, mobile phones, retailing and soft drinks. Other brand names have been used in this way, including Harley-Davidson and Gucci, but never quite as widely. How far the brand name can be used in an international context is unclear since Branson is so quintessentially British. It does seem to work in North America and Australia, but not so well elsewhere.

What are the limits of the branding, in terms of the range of products and services and geographically? Is it possible for individuals to brand themselves universally? What are the sources of such a branding success? What does the success of Bill Gates, Jeff Bezos and Jack Welch tell us about this process?

The broader the portfolio of business units within the Virgin stable, the greater the potential need for financial resources to cover losses and meet the need of future expansion. However, a diverse portfolio can hide a multitude of sins. In recent years Branson has regularly raised money to finance expansion and is likely to continue to do so. It is never clear in any individual case whether he is raising money to cover losses or finance expansion.

How does the Virgin stable avoid the problem of needing a multitude of core competencies to operate in so many fields? How independent is the management and operation of the individual businesses?

In 1999 he sold 49% of Virgin Atlantic Airways to Singapore Airlines for £600 million. This could be interpreted in two ways, either as a shrewd choice of partner for future development, or as reflecting a need for cash to cover losses incurred by existing companies. Since then he has raised a further £700 million by selling stakes in a number of companies including Virgin Blue, Virgin Radio, Virgin Cinema and Virgin Active, a chain of health clubs. The partners were all well chosen.

How important are the inputs of the partners? Do they supply the missing core competencies?

There is a further plan to float as many as eight of the companies, beginning with Virgin Blue in 2003, but stretching over a period of eight years. This will raise at least £2 billion, which will become available either to cover losses or finance new projects; which of these is true depends on the authority consulted. It supplements the £1.3 billion pounds already raised over the last three years. The obvious question to ask is, is the money to be raised by these public offers for future extension of Branson's interests or is he in desperate need of cash?

Is there an obvious closure to this process of expansion?

There are some obvious areas of planned expansion:

• The airline business is probably the one ripe for expansion. Virgin hopes to build a domestic airline in the USA since Branson believes that the development of Southwest still leaves plenty of room for further expansion of no-frills services. He also wishes to extend his network of airlines and their route coverage, perhaps moving from the no-frills focus to a more hybrid airline, linking up the Virgin Atlantic routes with the Virgin Blue routes. Virgin Blue already has 30% of the domestic Australian market where it was assisted by the demise of Ansett (see the case study on Qantas in Chapter 3).
• Virgin is also making a bid to expand dramatically its mobile business. In 2002 Branson put up US$160 million of his own money into the start-up of Virgin Mobile USA in Australia and its retailing in Japan.

How far can the expansion of successful individual businesses be taken without the business model changing and Branson's role itself changing?

Branson has shown a marked reluctance to close down or completely dispose of any company he has created, whatever its profitability or lack of it. In the past there have been only two complete divestitures, Virgin Records to EMI and Virgin Radio to the Scottish Media Group.

Branson has a reputation for making predictions on sales or profit levels which are seldom attained. For example, he predicted a 60% rise in sales in 2003 and a turnaround in profitability of almost £1 billion, converting the Virgin stable from significant losses to significant profits. By his account Virgin will in 2003 produce nearly US$9 billion of sales round the world and profits of around US$500 million, with barely any public debt, despite huge continuing investment in new growth. He has always been much more optimistic than the markets have justified but this is part of his image.

What is the significance of revenue or profit forecasts? How can a failure to meet the forecasts upset a strategy?

The flamboyant gesture is a Branson trade mark, part of his image. There are numerous examples but the following give a flavour of the type of behaviour engaged in:

• To publicize the start-up of Virgin Mobile USA, Branson appeared in a body suit with the Broadway cast of *The Full Monty* on a giant mobile phone dangling above Times Square in New York
• The route from London to Australia, the so-called Kangaroo route, by 2002, the timing of which was always regarded as impossible
• The one pound bid for each Concorde, later raised to one million pounds, intended to keep the plane in the air, is bound to be refused by British Airways since it flew Concorde to enhance its own image and would not wish to give this enhancement away, least of all to a competitor.

What do such gestures achieve? How should they be employed in seeking to achieve strategic objectives?

Key strategic issues

The case of Branson and Virgin raises a whole series of questions about the role of leadership in strategy making. How far is the strategy the implicit strategy of Branson and what would happen if he left the Virgin companies without his guidance? He is faced with a whole series of questions. What product areas to move into? What foreign market to open up? What business areas to exit? What portfolio of businesses to operate? How to raise investment funds for expansion? What partners to work with and on what basis? What input to allow the partners into the strategy-making process?

Strategic analysis and audit

Carry out a full strategic audit on the Virgin group of companies. Since they are not public companies, it is impossible to get a full financial evaluation so the nature of the audit will be different from the norm.

Reading

Baker-Said, S., 'Sir Richard wants respect for a logo that gets around', *Business Age*, July 25, 2003: 2.

Branson, R., 'Reflections of a risk-taker', *McKinsey Quarterly*, Summer 1986: 13–18.

Branson, R., *Losing my virginity: the autobiography* (Random House, London: 1998).

Branson, R., 'Sir Richard rejects negativity, says Virgin's record speaks for itself', *Business Age*, June 10, 2002: 14.

Brown, M., *Richard Branson: the inside story* (Joseph, London: 1988).

Elder, J., 'The Virgin Knight', *The Age*, Sunday Life, November 24, 2002: 26–31.

Kapner, S., 'Questions arise as Virgin flirts with the public once more', *Business Age*, May 27, 2002: 3.

Rochfort, S., 'Virgin addresses Kangaroo route', *Business Age*, July 25, 2003: 2.

Steiner, R., 'Branson bids 5m pounds for Concorde', *Sunday Times*, June 22, 2003 Business 3.2.

www.virgin.com

Vivendi Universal: divesting to survive

Jean-Marie Messier you have shown truly exceptional leadership and vision in taking the helm of the prestigious but somewhat stodgy company, Generale des Eaux, a major actor in water services and construction activities, and changing it almost overnight – well, five years – into the service group of the 21st century. You have shown along the way a clear will to become a major actor of globalization and seize the opportunities it offers, instead of concentrating on the threats that it can bring. On a more personal note you are the prototype of a new breed of executives that dispels the traditional clichés about France. You have championed a new type of corporate governance, more in line with international and, yes, American standards, and more attuned to the expectations of investors worldwide. In you and with you, Jean-Marie Messier, the chamber recognizes today the new French economy that has enjoyed a tremendously good coverage in the American press, an economy of entrepreneurs (reminding us all that this is a French word), of business creation, of internet start-ups that are the avant-garde of 'la France qui gagne'.

The French ambassador to the United States, Francois Bujon de l'Estaing in making Messier the Franco-American chamber of commerce person of the year (quoted in the *Guardian*, June 24, 2003)

In the end he pursued his vision of a converged media company with a breathtaking financial recklessness.

(*The Economist*, June 2003)

Background

Sony set the pattern, the putting together of both hardware and software in the area of communications/information/entertainment. It also set the precedent of entry into areas in which the acquiring company had no, or very little, expertise, and the takeover of a Hollywood studio, the invasion of the home turf of America. After the acquisition it had to learn how to run a film studio and a television channel. A number of competing giants later emerged at the international level, including News Corporation, Disney, AOL Time Warner, Bertelsmann and Viacom, who all imitated this model of fusion, some more dramatically than others. Some of these fusions were achieved very quickly, but none more quickly than that of the French company Vivendi.

In what ways did Vivendi differ from the other giant conglomerates?

Unfortunately for Vivendi the acquisition of the entertainment empire occurred late in the stock market boom which had been fired by the communications/information/entertainment revolution. The deal whereby Vivendi acquired Seagram and with it the Universal film and music business was concluded on June 9, 2000. Even later in 2001 Vivendi acquired, for more than US$10 billion, the cable TV business in the USA of Barry Diller. Most of the other new giants for various reasons overreached themselves and had to confront turnaround situations (see the Focus on Theory on McDonald's in Chapter 1). This is true of AOL Time Warner, Disney and Bertelsmann, but Vivendi found itself in the most difficult situation of all.

What are the most common reasons for the development of a turnaround situation? What are likely to be the short- and long-term responses to such a situation? How did a turnaround situation show itself for the other companies pursuing a similar strategy to Vivendi?

The history of Vivendi

Vivendi, a 149-year-old French water and sewerage utility, was converted during the late 1990s and early 2000s through takeovers into a communication/entertainment giant to rival, in size and spread of assets, even the new AOL Time Warner. The total value of the takeovers amounted to US$77 billion in value. The initiator was its CEO Jean-Marie Messier, a 45-year-old former investment banker. At its brief peak it controlled a vast array of businesses and assets (see Table C.7 below), from an international water business, through transport interests to environmental services as well as media and telecommunication interests. It possessed a valuable art collection and a fleet of aeroplanes, including an Airbus A319.

Does it matter what the platform is for the build-up of a media/entertainment company? Does it matter that the original company has no core competency in the area? How is it possible for a company to acquire these competencies?

Messier's strategy was an ambitious one. As the quotation above shows Messier cleverly played on the need to modernize the French business community and also the degree of competition between the French and the Americans. In 2000 he bought Seagram, the owner of Universal Music Group, one of the big five music companies, and Universal Studios, a major Hollywood studio; Canal Plus, Europe's biggest pay-TV business; US publisher Houghton Mifflin; and in 2001 the broadcasting interests of Barry Diller's USA Interactive. Vivendi rode the stock market boom, using shares to put together the giant conglomerate in a remarkably short period of time. On the basis of the increase in stock prices it could use its own shares to purchase other companies. This gave enormous leverage to its cash flows and allowed it to do more than might be expected.

How far is this typical of the construction of such companies, the significant role of one man, in this case not the founder or the saviour, but the formulator and implementer of the strategy?

Initially the markets reacted well. At its peak the value of the company reached €154 billion, but, when Messier resigned under pressure on July 1, 2002, the decline in the share price, which had followed Moody's cut in the company's creditworthiness rating to below investment level, had reduced its value to one-tenth of that high, about €15 billion.

Why is the behaviour of the share price important in the implementation of such a strategy?

The company had reached a crisis point because:

- it lost the confidence of the capital market. It could no longer raise money on the market, limited by its low share price. The low share price undermined confidence in the existing management and the strategy pursued.

How far was this inevitable in the circumstances of the time?

- its strategy of delivering movies and music via mobile devices did not work; it is unlikely to be successful for a number of years.

How far was this a mistake which was common to all the new giants?

- all the key players lost confidence in the ability of the CEO Messier to realize the strategy he was pursuing.

What were the weaknesses of Messier? Were they the same features which in a rising market had made him successful?

- the build-up of the company left it with a high level of debt which has to be serviced, as much as €17 billion worth. Its bankers showed themselves unwilling to roll over the existing debt. The liquidity position of Vivendi became critical, with €5.6 billion of debt to be refinanced by March 2003.

Was this a matter of poor timing, excessive ambition or a failure to massage the bankers properly?

For a time Messier survived with the assistance of the French directors, but the refusal of the main bankers to grant a new standby credit line at the end of June 2002 and the final loss of confidence by the French directors, who joined the Americans in seeking a replacement of the CEO, spelled the end for Messier. He saw his end as the result of a 'man hunt à la francaise', organized by French corporate capital, principally *Le Monde* and the chairman of AXA, Bebear, panicked by the high-tech and dot-com crash. Others saw him as 'the victim of his own reckless vanity and overweening self-belief' (*The Economist*, June 2003). On his resignation he urged the new management not to break up the business which he had created. In his final letter to Vivendi's 380,000 employees he argued that the vision of a transatlantic media and entertainment giant to rival the Americans was a sound one.

Why did the French directors cease to support him?

In the circumstances the new management had little choice. The company is likely to be unbundled at an even faster rate than it was constructed. Fortunately many of the businesses are performing reasonably well in operational terms.

How far was the problem one in which the purchases were made at prices appropriate to a rising and buoyant market, but not to the conditions which ruled in 2002?

The turnaround situation

In a turnaround situation of this kind there are a number of stages in recovery, which confront the short-, medium- and long-term problems of the company:

- The need to keep short-term creditors happy in order to generate sufficient liquidity to prevent the company becoming bankrupt.
- The need to divest assets in an ordered way in order to meet the requirements of the creditors and, more important, achieve an acceptable equity/debt ratio.
- The need to devise a strategy which takes account of the new environment and the need to contract the asset base. Such a strategy should have as its principal focus the establishment of a clear identity and a choice of core activities. The medium-term divestment should be guided by this strategy.

How far is it possible to control the process of turnaround? How far is it possible to move beyond the short-term response?

As a distressed seller the company needed to divest about US$20 billion of assets in order to achieve its medium-term objectives. For a significant period of time a fire sale threatened. The main aim of the new management has been to establish some control over the process. The implications of such a weak position are clear. Although the company managed to persuade the bankers to extend a loan sufficient to see it through its short-term debt problems, the loan was extended on the condition of action to meet the medium-term needs.

How much time did Vivendi have? How might the short- and medium-term strategies be devised to cope with the unhelpful business environment and support a strong long-term strategy?

In the short term the scope for choice of strategy was limited. Quickly a French publishing unit and a Norwegian pay-TV unit were sold off, at rock bottom prices. News Corp. was originally prepared to pay €1.5 billion for Telepiu, but because of Vivendi's parlous position it managed to drop the price to only €1 billion.

What is the relative bargaining strength of the transactors in such a situation?

Jean-Rene Fourtou, the new CEO and semi-retired former vice-chairman of Aventis, the European pharmaceutical company, has to deal with the immediate crisis but in a way which retains as much value for the company as possible and a set of assets which have some strategic coherence. He admits to having no experience or expertise in running a business like Vivendi Universal. In order to do this he has to devise a new strategy. This may involve all three time perspectives. The short-term and medium-term strategies involve selling off non-core assets in order to allow Vivendi to reduce the level of debt and service and roll over remaining debts.

This raises the question, what is a non-core asset? How is such an asset to be defined? What are the factors which determine the core assets for a company in the condition of Vivendi?

What, on most criteria, might be defined as non-core assets may not be the assets for which there is any kind of a market in a recession. This may make inevitable a sale of assets which might be regarded as core assets. The key strategic issue is for the company to give itself some space in which to manoeuvre. A successful short-term strategy would provide more scope for the formulation and implementation a new long-term strategy. A long-term strategy might even involve the sale or demerging of Vivendi Universal Entertainment and Universal Music Group.

How is it possible for Vivendi to gain the space required? What are the immediate strategic objectives in gaining such space?

The strategy

It has been difficult to read the strategic intentions of Fourtou, which may be a good strategic ploy to gain the required time and space. He clearly saw part of this job as maximizing the price of any assets sold. This meant avoiding a fire sale but also massaging the potential bidders in any auction in order to keep as many players as possible in play.

The first goal, successfully accomplished, was to persuade Vivendi's banks to extend a lifeline to allow time to arrange a sale. A $1 billion short-term loan achieved this. Fourtou even managed to raise the funds to prevent Vodafone's bid for BT's stake in France's Cegetal in order to maintain control in the cable television company.

In return for the extension of the short-term loans, Fourtou promised to raise US$16 billion by the end of 2004 by disposing of significant assets; but which assets?

Table C.7 is just one reading of the situation in terms of the early intentions on what to sell.

What alternative strategies could be pursued, given the assets held?

What is for sale reflects partly what can be sold or rather for what there is some kind of a market. Prices reflect the current state of the market and the urgency of the sale. A turnaround strategy involves difficult decisions, which should be made in some kind of strategic framework.

What should Vivendi sell?

The auction

Early in 2003 Vivendi made a decisive move and announced its plan to auction its international entertainment business, including the film studio, the theme park business and the cable TV channels. It was also willing to sell its music business. The sale of such a set of assets is unprecedented. Unhappily the ownership of Universal Music has changed hands four times in a decade. Vivendi had the wish and the expectation of shedding at least US$7 billion of debt.

Table C.7 **Status of principal assets (August 2002)**

Assets	Comment	Estimated value €billions
For sale		
Houghton Mifflin	US publisher	1.5–2.0
Canal Plus International	Non-French pay TV (includes Telepiu)	2.0
Canal Plus (after proposed purchase and IPO)	51% of French pay-TV operator	2.0
Canal Plus Technologies	Decoder manufacturer	0.25–0.35
Express-Expansion	French press	?
Vizzavi	50% of internal portal	up to 0.15
Paris St Germain	Football club	0
Undecided		
DuPont	16.4 million shares	0.7
Maroc Telecom	35% stake	1.3–1.5
Universal Pictures	Hollywood studio	2.2–4.0
USA Networks/SciFi Channel	Cable channels	4.0–5.0
Universal Music	Global music group	6.3–8.5
Recreation	Theme parks	1.8–2.5
Echostar	10% stake	1.2
Not for sale		
Cegetel	44% of telecoms subsidiary	5.0–6.5
Vivendi Environnement	40.6% stake in water utility	3.5
Canal Plus	49% of French pay-TV operator	2.0
Vivendi Universal Publishing	Rump European business	3.0

Source: Johnson and Burt, 2002: 20.

The sale was not a simple one. Vivendi set out a list of 32 questions which bidders had to answer. The sale was complex because it had all sorts of tax implications for the main players. For this reason two of the early bids were for a partial purchase which would have left Vivendi with a significant ownership stake.

There were originally six bidders, the identity of which was surprising for its absentees, such as News Corp., AOL Time Warner and Disney, companies otherwise occupied or with their own turnaround problems. After the first round of bids six bidders were reduced to five, with either Metro-Goldwyn Meyer or Liberty Media as favourites. The former raised its bid to US$11.5 billion but threatened to withdraw if it did not get more detailed financial information. Vivendi, believing that it was in a strong position, refused to provide it. There are obvious synergies for MGM putting together the film studios. Liberty turned its attention elsewhere, spending US$7.9 billion on the shopping channel QVC. The others have a varying degree of interest. NBC with the backing of its owner GE clearly has the resources but it was initially unclear that it had an interest in running a film studio. Viacom only wanted the cable television channels. Edgar Bronfman,

the former boss of Seagram, was probably only interested in pushing up the value of his shares, and lacked the ability to raise the capital required to purchase. The deal in which he sold Seagram to Vivendi, including the entertainment assets, was for shares which, with the 71% fall in value since that date, have cut his holding from $6.5 billion to just one billion. Another shareholder (6.9%) is Barry Diller, who, it was rumoured, might partner with either Liberty or Viacom to buy.

The bids made turned out to be too low to persuade Vivendi to take any of them seriously. The highest, allegedly the only, cash bidder was MGM. MGM raised its initial bid to US$11.5 billion for Vivendi Universal Entertainment, but Vivendi executives indicated that they expected around US$14 billion, a value well beyond what MGM regarded as reasonable, or at least that is what the representatives of MGM said. It may have been a ploy to get the assets cheaper if the auction process failed, since MGM is the only film studio without other major links. Vivendi protracted the sale, but the expected bidding war did not materialize.

In response to the failure to raise the price anticipated, Vivendi had a number of options. It could:

● offer the assets separately rather than continue to insist on their sale together. This might be helpful in that most of the bidders were interested in only some of the assets. It cast the focus on the particular cost synergies which might make an acquisition desirable.
● float its entertainment assets.

Unfortunately the net revenue position of Vivendi is deteriorating. However, the debt position has been improved, by a combined process of closures and sales, from €35.1 to €13.6 billion over the year to July 2002 and was still further improved when eventually a deal was struck with GE, worth $5.5 billion, of which $1.7 billion was a shedding of further debt, but meant that Vivendi retained Universal Music and 20% of the equity in the television studios and channels transferred.

Was Vivendi overvaluing the assets in the current climate? Why were the bidders behaving so conservatively? What is likely to be the strategy of purchasers, in linking the assets acquired with other assets already held and the way in which the purchase is organized?

Key strategic issues

Vivendi is a symbol of the 'hype' of the stock market boom which accompanied the communications revolution. It is in the most difficult situation of all the communication/information/entertainment giants. Why is this? In what ways did the strategy of Vivendi and its implementation differ from that of the other communication/ information/entertainment giants which had preceded it?

Is it the case that the content of the Messier strategy was correct but the timing was completely wrong? Is this partly the result of being a follower rather than an initiator, particularly in the light of the collapse of confidence which came with the recession?

There are other questions which arise from the turnaround situation. How can a company like Vivendi decide what is a core business activity? Why should a company with so many business units earning an operating profit, and so much potential interest by other players in the communication/information/entertainment market in purchasing such assets, find itself in a turnaround situation?

Strategic analysis and audit

Carry out a full strategic audit on Vivendi. What are the current values of assets held by Vivendi, particularly those which are on the market? How many of these assets need to be sold to produce a viable enterprise, both from the perspective of profitability and a viable long-term strategy?

Reading

Cullen, L. T., 'A fallen mogul stirs', *Time* **161**(22) June 2, 2003: 52.

Economist, The, 'Himself: Jean-Marie Messier', **367**(8328) June 14, 2003: 103.

Economist, The, 'That's entertainment: Vivendi', **368**(8333) July 19, 2003: 59.

Guardian, the, three extracts published: 'A fairytale beginning for Vivendi' June 24, 2003, 'The night the music died' June 25, 2003, and 'The day the undertaker called' June 26, 2003.

Johnson, J. and Orange, M., *The man who tried to buy the world: Jean-Marie Messier and Vivendi Universal* (Viking, London: 2003).

Larsen, P., 'MGM halts $11.5 billion Vivendi bid', *Financial Times,* July 29, 2003.

Larsen, P., Johnson, J. and Burt, T., 'A Hollywood studio, a music major, TV assets, theme parks: Messier's legacy is up for grabs', *Financial Times,* June 23, 2003: 17.

Milner, M., 'Viva Vivendi', *Guardian,* February 17, 2003.

Orwall, B., 'Vivendi saga rolls on as MGM pulls out', *Financial Times,* July 31, 2003.

Timms, D., 'Vivendi's entertainment revenues fall 23%', *Guardian,* July 31, 2003.

www.vivendi.com

Wal-Mart: the cost-reducing machine

For a lot of years, we avoided mistakes by studying those larger than we were – Sears, Penney, Kmart. Today we don't have anyone to study ... When we were smaller, we were the underdog, the challenger. When you're number one, you are a target. You are no longer the hero.

GLASS, former CEO of Wal-Mart

Wal-Mart's secret was to focus its IT investments on applications that directly enhanced its core value proposition of low prices.

(Johnson, 2002: 42)

Background

One of the major changes which has marked modern business has been the application of methods of mass production and mass selling, and the consequent reduction in cost which this has made possible. This has happened in the area of retailing through discount department stores which sell just about everything and through the supermarket or hypermarket, ever-increasing in size, which sell mainly, but not only, foodstuffs. The former paved the way for the latter.

For what kind of product is discount retailing suitable? Is there any limit on the size of a retail outlet? If so, what is the nature of this limit?

The discount department chain has been the instrument for a dramatic decrease in price for a wide range of products, including clothing, electrical goods, furniture and cosmetics. The supermarket has been the mechanism for a dramatic reduction of the price of foodstuffs and other merchandise products. Part of this decrease in price is accounted for by a decrease in profit margins, offset by the much greater scale of sales. Competition has forced the profit margins down as low as 1–2%.

How is it possible for a retailer making only a 1–2% profit margin to be successful? Can profit margins be reduced any further without the 'iron law of oligopoly' reasserting itself?

The sheer volume of sales has allowed the supermarket to outcompete local stores, in terms of price and the range of items on offer, which is enormous. The corner shop has been disappearing, despite its compensating offer of personal service and knowledge of the consumer and his or her tastes. The attributes of the new supermarkets have been valued more highly. One of the most important attributes is price.

What are the different attributes offered by the supermarket and the corner shop? Is it possible for the single store to compete with the chains by emphasizing different attributes? If so, how can they manage to do this?

In its turn the supermarket has been increasingly replaced by the hypermarket, a largely French innovation. Modern methods of communication and information processing have supported an enormous expansion of logistical capability and therefore made possible a significant increase in the size of retail outlets. The historical experience seems to show no limit on the scale of such retail outlets. The methods of the supermarket have in turn been copied in the sale of many other types of product.

The attrition rate of discounters has always been high. They tend either to fail or are taken over. From this process, as it has unfolded in the USA, Wal-Mart has emerged as America's and the world's largest retailer. Perhaps to describe Wal-Mart as a discounter is to misdescribe it – that issue will be dealt with later. Of the top ten competitors faced by Wal-Mart in the USA in 1962, not one has survived. There has been a tendency to consolidation within the discount retail sector. Whereas in 1986 the top five discounters had accounted for 62% of industry sales, in 1993 they accounted for 71%. In 1993 Wal-Mart had larger sales than the next four discounters combined. The second player Kmart has recently gone bankrupt.

Is there space for more than a few retail outlets of the Wal-Mart type? What is the likely outcome of oligopoly? From what quarter does Wal-Mart face its main competition?

Since the 1960s when the Waltons first entered discount retailing, there has been a rapid growth in total sales, initially at a rate of 25% per annum, more recently around the 10% mark, perhaps slowing markedly today. Wal-Mart recognized that the domestic market was reaching saturation point, although as late as 2001 it continued to open new stores. To counter the slowing growth of the domestic market, in 1991 Wal-Mart began to internationalize, transferring its successful

Table C.8 **Retailers go global – number of new countries entered**

	1981–85	1986–90	1991–95	1996–2001
Ahold	1	1	3	20
Carrefour	1	2	5	14
Kingfisher	0	0	3	12
Metro	2	3	1	9
Tesco	1	−1	2	6
Wal-Mart	0	0	4	5
H&M	0	1	2	5

Source: McKinsey Quarterly, 2002: 3.

business model to new markets. By 2001, 1,000 of its 4,000 stores were foreign.

What is a saturation level in retailing? How far can a similar growth experience be replicated in countries abroad?

The opening up of new markets by deregulation, the saturation of domestic markets and the improvement in the technology of both communications and logistics has encouraged a movement of many retailers onto the international stage. As yet this process is in its infancy. In 2000 the market share of the world's 50 largest retailers was only 20%. The 10 largest had on average entered only 10 countries.

From Table C.8 it is obvious that internationalization is a new phenomenon. However, now no major player can afford not to be in the game. Wal-Mart has been comparatively slow in joining this trend and has concentrated most of its efforts into neighbouring countries such as Mexico and Canada. The other, more recent, area of expansion is in Hong Kong as a possible springboard into China.

Are there advantages in being the first mover in internationalizing a retail chain?

The model which underpins this strategy of internationalization differs from retailer to retailer. There are three main models:

- For retailers like Benetton and Starbucks, the model is *replication*. A simple format and business system are reproduced wherever the company goes. This provides significant economies of scale and enormous clout in purchasing from suppliers who themselves are often major international players, such as Unilever, Procter & Gamble and Kellogg's.

This is very much the model adopted by Wal-Mart. Internationally Wal-Mart sought to reproduce the model which had served it so well domestically.

- For Ahold and Kingfisher the model is one of *performance manager*. In this model the company acquires a portfolio of existing retail businesses and develops them as distinct entities with their own brands and product profile. Management is decentralized. The problem with this model is twofold, finding cheap acquisitions and managing an enterprise of increasing size and complexity.
- For Carrefour and Tesco the model is that of the *reinvestor*. The company has one or more store concepts or business models such as the hypermarket concept of Carrefour, which are then adapted to suit each local market. There are standard back-end processes and systems which help to achieve economies of scale and economize on costs, at least in these limited areas. This model lies between the first two.

What determines which of these models is adopted? Is it the nature of the environment or the enterprise?

However, there are threats to such leviathans, whether they are global or not:

- There are real discounters at large who undercut even these retailers (see the Strategy in Action module on Aldi in Chapter 9).
- Specialist stores are also undercutting the department chains at the domestic level.
- Another threat comes at the global level, from e-commerce on the model of Amazon.com, discussed in Chapter 5.

Which of these constitutes the greatest threat? Why?

The nature and history of Wal-Mart

When in 1995 Wal-Mart, with it origins and headquarters in Bentonville, Arkansas, finally won its five-year battle with local leaders to open its first store in Bennington, Vermont, it had a store in every state of the union. This was in fact Wal-Mart's 2,158th store. By the end of 1997 it had two more stores in Vermont. The typical Wal-Mart store occupies an area of 200,000 square feet and is built close to a major highway. In Vermont Wal-Mart showed itself ready to compromise with only a 50,000 sq. ft area located downtown.

The history of Wal-Mart is rather briefer than often thought. Sam Walton opened his first Ben Franklin franchise in Newport, Arkansas in 1945 but failed to persuade Franklin to go into discounting. The first discount department store was opened by Wal-Mart in November 1962. The Ben Franklin stores were gradually phased out, disappearing finally in 1976. The company was incorporated in 1969 and went public in 1972 with only 18 Wal-Mart and 15 Ben Franklin stores. The US$3.3 million raised in the public float went to help meet the cost of a warehouse, which at the time cost more than $5 million.

After that, geographic growth, which began in the south and mid-west, began to accelerate. The pattern of advance never jumped ahead, it was systematic. Steadily it covered the whole country.

What were the alternative strategies on geographical expansion? What are the advantages and disadvantages of these strategies? Why did Wal-Mart choose the strategy which it did?

The initial store format was the traditional Wal-Mart store that sold a wide range of basic consumer merchandise, from household products to clothes and electronics. Two new concepts were introduced in 1987, which brought in groceries as an addition to the basic merchandising mix:

• These were the hypermarket, the 200,000 sq. ft plus store which sells everything, including food, and the super-centre which is a scaled-down version of the hypermarket, combining supermarket and discount store. The super-centre usually covered about 120,000–130,000 sq. ft. The hypermarket idea was borrowed from France. It covered an enormous area, over 220,000 sq. ft, carried as many as 20,000–30,000 items and, when well run, has gross margins as high as 13–14%. After giving it a try Wal-Mart opted for the super-centre, now the fastest growing part of Wal-Mart, mostly replacing existing Wal-Mart stores. In 1995 there were just 68 super-centres, by 2000 over 800. The super-centre became the main engine of Wal-Mart's growth.

Why did Wal-Mart not opt for the hypermarket?

• Wal-Mart also moved into the no-frills warehouse business which mainly served other businesses. Called Sam's Club, these are deep discount stores that carry a limited range of low-priced merchandise and food. This is real discounting.

Are the market segments for the super-centre and Sam's Club distinct?

The unique strategy of Wal-Mart

When Wal-Mart established its first supermarket in 1962 it was not a new concept. Discount retailing was already known. Whereas most discounters eventually failed, Wal-Mart did not. Wal-Mart's success did not come from discounting as such, but rather the way in which it was pursued.

The Wal-Mart business model had a number of unique features which allowed it to achieve unprecedentedly low levels of cost, while providing value to the customer. It built the leanest supply chain in the industry:

• Wal-Mart pioneered the development of the hub-and-spoke distribution system, in which a central distribution warehouse served a cluster of stores (IKEA has also used this system). The speed at which Wal-Mart could replenish stock in its stores was accelerated. Inventories held could be smaller, thereby reducing costs, and sales per square foot of store space much greater. This system was introduced for the conventional stores but applied to all the new stores as they were introduced. To supply the super-centres with food Wal-Mart acquired the McLane chain of warehouses and further developed these. Wal-Mart expanded the number of warehouses rapidly.
• Wal-Mart combined its network of warehouses with an early use of computer-based information systems which tracked in-store sales and transmitted the information to suppliers. This also assisted in pricing policy and the better management of inventories. Suppliers were encouraged in various ways to keep down their own costs, which became easier to achieve the bigger Wal-Mart became and the more important as a buyer.

How important is it in retailing to keep inventories down? How can this be achieved? Is just-in-time as relevant to retailing as to manufacturing?

Simultaneously, Wal-Mart reconfigured its stores, with three aims:

1. to strip away all inessentials from the store. The physical amenities of the typical department store, such as carpeting or chandeliers, were discarded.
2. to configure the store in such a way that it could handle the flow-through of large numbers of shoppers. This applied to the whole store, from parking spaces to shopping aisles and checkout points.
3. to put fewer salespeople on the floor and rely on customers to serve themselves.

Which is more important, reducing costs or increasing the range of products on offer? What are the attributes of the shopping experience which are desired by customers? Do they differ according to the type of retail outlet?

These three features had obvious cost advantages. Wal-Mart did this in just the same way as Kmart had done, but it went further, putting its stamp on the supermarket. It combined cost minimization with a more subtle strategy. There were three parts to the strategy which marked Wal-Mart out as different and its strategy as unique:

• In the words of Walton himself, the key strategy of Wal-Mart 'was to put good-sized stores into little one-horse towns which everybody else was ignoring'. The towns targeted had populations of 5,000–25,000, like Rogers, Arkansas where the first supermarket was located. Much of America lived in such areas. Walton believed that, given the opportunity, people would shop locally, provided there was no significant price disadvantage in so doing.

In the major cities competition was intense. By putting a supermarket of some size into a relatively small place Wal-Mart pre-empted entry by competitors. In the mid-1980s about one-third of Wal-Mart stores were located where there was no competition. Entry into this market would be suicidal for the new entrant as well as the existing player since it would lead to a split of customers and probably a price war. Expansion eventually moved Wal-Mart into areas where there was competition, but it was still true that Wal-Mart had an advantage. In 1993, 55% of Wal-Mart stores faced direct competition from Kmart and 23% from Target, whereas 82% of Kmart stores faced competition from Wal-Mart and 85% of Target stores. The strategy gave Wal-Mart a continuing advantage.

What are the conditions for the success of this strategy? In what other areas can it be pursued?

• Wal-Mart also took account of the customer's concern with quality. From the start it promised national brands at everyday low prices, rather than the usual private or own label goods, second-tier brands or price promotions. Its prices were consistently lower than those of its competitors for the same products.

How far did Wal-Mart qualify as a pure cost leadership strategy?

• Rather as Richard Branson and Howard Schultz did later, Wal-Mart used the charismatic personality of Sam Walton to sell itself. The nature of Walton's leadership was critical. Sam Walton was ruthless in his single-mindedness, obsessed with keeping costs down but zany in his behaviour and the way he promoted the stores. He sought to empower his associates but to keep an eye on them, to use every element of technological superiority he could and build loyalty among associates and staff, customers and suppliers. As a result the culture of Wal-Mart was dynamic and egalitarian. Staff were empowered to take responsibility, provided they were committed to excellence of performance and motivated to perform by stock incentive schemes. This raised productivity and kept down costs.

What problems did Wal-Mart face with the passing of the foundation leadership?

Wal-Mart also unashamedly copied the good ideas of its competitors, for example taking the concept of Sam's Club from the Price Club of Sol Price.

Wal-Mart as cost leader

Allegedly the rate of growth of retail productivity in the USA, as measured by value added per hour, jumped from 2% between 1987 and 1995 to 6.3% between 1995 and 1999, which appears to explain as much as one-quarter of the economy-wide acceleration in productivity occurring at that time. The acceleration has attracted much attention, often being accounted for by the communications and information revolution. Although general merchandising accounts for only 15% of retail sales in the USA, the sector is heavily concentrated in five enterprises – Wal-Mart, Kmart, Target, Costco and Sears – accounting for 60% of the total sales.

Has there really been an acceleration in productivity? How would the communications and information revolution affect the level of productivity in retailing?

More than half the productivity acceleration in retailing of general merchandise is explained by what has happened to Wal-Mart alone. Certainly Wal-Mart has been the market leader. In 1987 it had 9% of the market share, in 1995 27%. At the earlier date, in terms of real sales per employee, Wal-Mart was 40% more productive than its competitors, at the latter date 48%.

There is some suspicion about the statistics on the size of the productivity acceleration and its implications. It has been argued that the tendency of consumers to favour higher quality items has automatically pushed up productivity, without any real increase. Whatever the true value of the productivity increase, Wal-Mart led a real improvement in the retail sector.

There were five areas of advantage and innovation undertaken by Wal-Mart which underpinned this surge in productivity improvement:

• the extremely large-scale, 'big-box' format of the super-centre stores, with the detailed attention to layout and throughput, which further raised the efficiency with which each customer was served and increased sales per square foot well over what any other store could achieve
• the concept of 'everyday low prices' for products which have brand names, which allowed a consistent underselling of competitors
• the system of electronic data interchange (EDI) with suppliers, which closely linked demand and supply and minimized the inventory which needed to be carried
• the location of an expanded number of stores around the warehouses and central distribution centres
• the application of IT.

Wal-Mart was:

- among the first retailers to use computers to track inventory (1969)
- one of the first to adopt bar coding (1980), starting regular use of electronic scanning of uniform product codes at the point of sale in 1983 and installing the system in all its stores by 1988, two years ahead of Kmart
- among the first to introduce EDI (1985), which enables most vendors, including the large ones like Proctor & Gamble, General Electric and Wrangler, to receive orders and interact directly with Wal-Mart electronically, allowing Wal-Mart itself to reduce inventory
- one of the first to put in wireless scanning guns (the late 1980s).

Wal-Mart has a well-deserved reputation for its use of IT. It has the largest private satellite system to control distribution. The first installation of the satellite system was made in 1983. The use of this system allows a much better link up between the stores, distribution centres and the head office at Bentonville, Arkansas. It also makes possible the daily collection and analysis of sales data. Managers could tell immediately how fast stock was moving and thus avoid, on the one hand, overstocking and the need for deep discounting and, on the other, empty shelves and disappointed customers. Between 1987 and 1993 Wal-Mart spent over US$700 million on its satellite communications network, computers and related equipment. Each year it spends in excess of $500 million on IT. Today it employs over 1,200 staff in this area alone.

How far are these advantages simply the result of faster movement down the experience curve and the resulting economies of scale or the result of genuine innovations?

However, at least half of Wal-Mart's productivity edge came from traditional areas of improvement, such as inbound logistics, cross-training of employees, better training of cashiers and continuous monitoring of the level of utilization in its stores. Distribution is usually through the distribution centres, rather than direct from suppliers. However, a 'cross-docking' scheme allows merchandise often to move straight through the distribution centres.

How far is Wal-Mart simply better at doing the conventional things?

Over the period 1995–99 Wal-Mart's competitors began to catch up. From 1994 they began to copy the Wal-Mart system with its innovations.

Wal-Mart's productivity rose by 22%, that of its competitors at a faster rate of 28%.

However, Wal-Mart has outcompeted and outlasted

Table C.9 **Real sales per employee ($1000s)**

	1995	1999
Wal-Mart	148	181
Kmart	109	133
Sears	87	118

Kmart which has filed for bankruptcy. This is not surprising since Wal-Mart, with about the same number of stores, sells about three times the value of products. Per square foot of area the sales by Wal-Mart are about twice those of Kmart. Wal-Mart has been investing about four times the capital each year in expansion and innovation. There is clearly a neat virtuous circle in which Wal-Mart spends more and therefore makes more, makes more and therefore can spend more.

Is it true that the first-mover advantages of Wal-Mart make imitation irrelevant to its competitive advantage? How far is there a virtuous circle for any successful business which reinvests a significant proportion of its profits?

It is interesting and significant to note that Wal-Mart has the largest and most complex commercial database of all enterprises. It has recently doubled the size of its central data warehouse, so that it now can hold 200 terabytes of information (a terabyte equals 1,000 gigabytes or one million megabytes). As recently ago as 1996 the capacity was raised from 3.5 to 7 terabytes. One forecast is that Wal-Mart will be the first commercial enterprise to have a petabyte capacity (one petabyte equals 1,000 terabytes).

Why is the capacity to store and process information important to Wal-Mart?

The new warehouse could store all the books and research data in the Library of Congress twenty-five times. The attainment of this storage capacity has been made possible by the dramatic reduction of costs. It now costs just 15 cents for the hardware and the software to store one megabyte of information. A decade ago it cost $15. Within five years the cost will be down to one cent.

The facility is a real strategic asset. It enables Wal-Mart to analyse the large quantities of data available to it, in the process interpreting and predicting consumer buying patterns and the demand for particular consumer products on a day-to-day basis. This helps Wal-Mart meet demand with the minimum of stocks. The main information going into this database relates to transactions within the Wal-Mart stores. Every point-of-sale transaction is reported, stored and analysed. Through the retail link system this information is made available to Wal-Mart's suppliers. Some information going in may be personal and is likely to be the subject of debate on grounds of privacy.

How important is information to a retailer? Why is it important? What ethical issues are raised by the collection of information?

International expansion

Can Wal-Mart export the model to other countries? Entry into Mexico by Wal-Mart has shown that it can, although other experiences have not been as favourable.

Mexico was chosen because of the establishment of NAFTA which removed obstacles to entry. Wal-Mart chose not to establish franchisees because it believed that franchisees could not operate its model, or a greenfield enterprise because it did not know enough about the local culture and business practices to be confident of success. It therefore formed a joint venture with one of the largest Mexican retailers, Cifra, eventually, when it had the necessary experience and confidence, turning its partner into a majority-owned enterprise.

What are the advantages and disadvantages of a joint venture as a mode of entry into a foreign market for a retailer? What alternatives are there?

Initially there were serious difficulties, which defeated other entrants from the USA, such as Kmart and Sears, some of these general to the economy as a whole, others specific to Wal-Mart. The general included:

• the peso devaluation of 40% in 1994 and the ensuing recession
• the poor infrastructure.

The specific included:

• The initial lack of distribution centres prevented the recreation of the important logistics system in the USA. However, it was simply a matter of time and scale before they were introduced.
• It took Wal-Mart a decade to introduce its electronic supply management system into Mexico, partly because of the resistance of suppliers and partly because of confusion in the minds of its own employees, as well as the problem of the local infrastructure.

Wal-Mart now has 10 super-efficient distribution centres. The distribution centre in Mexico City became Wal-Mart's most efficient centre anywhere because of the low labour costs in Mexico. Wal-Mart surmounted the teething problems and did so remarkable quickly.

How far are these difficulties likely to occur everywhere and how far were they specific to Mexico? Does export of the model become more difficult the greater the physical or cultural distance from the USA?

Mexico is now the brightest star in the company's international division, with more than 500 stores generating over US$9 billion in sales and $458 in profit. Wal-Mart (Walmex) now captures half of all Mexican supermarket sales nationwide, just a decade after entering the country. The Mexican companies are losing ground, with their sales and profits falling. Without foreign partners they find it difficult to achieve the costs to match Wal-Mart's 'everyday low' prices (Table C.10).

Not surprisingly Wal-Mart has a $600 million budget set aside for the establishment of a further 63 stores by mid-2003.

Wal-Mart has also entered Germany and Britain through acquisitions, in the latter acquiring Asda, a nationwide discount food chain. The model adopted is that of the replicator, but on occasion it can come unstuck, as it did in Indonesia. Local tastes turned out to be the problem. In 1996 Wal-Mart established a number of efficient, clean superstores only to find that the customers preferred Matahari, which is a chain of shabbier local stores, more akin to the traditional local markets in which the customers loved to haggle and regularly buy fresh produce. In 1998 Wal-Mart left Indonesia. There is nevertheless much scope for extension of a replicator model since today only 15% of Wal-Mart's total sales are abroad.

Table C.10 **Mexico's retail landscape (2001)**

	Walmex	Commercial Mexicana	Gigante	Soriana
Net sales ($bill)	9.67	3.61	3.25	3.03
Net profit ($mill)	458.00	82.90	68.70	160.30
No. of stores	579	225	445	115

Key strategic issues

Given the differences in culture and tastes from country to country, can the replicator model work in all countries? If not, where can it work and why? Is it likely that Wal-Mart may have to change its international strategy, when, for example, it moves into Asian countries? If it wishes to continue growing, does it have a choice about internationalizing? Where should it expand? Should it enter foreign markets, gently learning how to adapt its business model and therefore spreading its expansion broadly, or should it concentrate on one or two markets in order to achieve size and first-mover advantages?

Strategic analysis and audit

Do a full strategic audit on the performance of Wal-Mart in both its domestic and foreign activities. Show from its key financial ratios how it is outcompeting other retail chains, either domestically or internationally.

Reading

Foley, S. and Mahmood, T., 'Wal-Mart Stores, Inc.' in Ghemawal, P. *Strategy and the Business Landscape: text and cases* (Addison-Wesley, Reading, MA: 1999).

Hill, C. W. L., 'The global grocer', in Hill, C. W. L. *International Business* (McGraw-Hill, Irwin, Boston: 2003: 3–4).

Hill, C. W. L.,'Wal-Mart's Mexican Adventure' in Hill, C. W. L. *International Business* (McGraw-Hill, Irwin, Boston: 2003: 515–19).

Johnson, B. C., 'Retail: the Wal-Mart effect', *McKinsey Quarterly*, (1) 2002: 40–3.

London, S., 'Customer information is the new commodity', *Financial Times*, June 15/16, 2002: 12.

McKinsey Quarterly, 'Travel tips for retailers', (3) 2002: 127–33.

Pettet, J., 'Wal-Mart yesterday and today', *Discount Merchandiser*, December 1995: 66–7.

Shah, A. and Phipps, T., 'Wal-Mart Stores, Inc. – 1998' in David, F. R. *Strategic Management: concepts, cases* (Prentice Hall, Upper Saddle River, NJ: 1999: 24–38).

Smith, G., 'War of the mega-stores', *Business Week*, September 16, 2002: 64–5.

www.walmart.com

Forecasting the price of oil

This case study is rather different from the others in form and aim. It is intended to illustrate how scenario building occurs. It supplements the text in the last section of Chapter 4.

Background

The price of oil has an influence on a myriad of economic decisions, both by oil producers and oil users, and not least by governments interested in the state of the global political economy:

• Oil companies have to make decisions about whether to open up new oilfields or expand old fields, whether to expand or upgrade refining capacity, and whether to construct new oil tankers to transport the oil
• There may also be decisions on where to locate oil or gas pipelines, running from oilfields to the ports or consumption areas
• Those who design and build aeroplanes, motorcars and industrial motors using fuel oil are also influenced by the price of oil, as are a multitude of other decisions which involve oil as an input
• It might be possible to accelerate the development of the hydrogen cell in order to phase out the internal combustion engine.

Because of its enormous economic importance the price of oil has widespread political significance. Control over sources of supply and the supply routes between the producing and consuming countries are critical political issues. The largest countries, in terms of population and GDP, are increasingly dependent on oil imports to meet their energy needs.

From the end of World War II until the 1970s, in a buoyant world economy growing at historically unprecedented rates, the demand for oil rose at a consistently rapid rate of about 6% per annum. Despite this high rate the real price of oil fell and had fallen ever since oil became an important commodity in the world economy back in the 1880s. Yet, because the costs of production and delivery were very low, the price was adequate for high rates of return by the oil companies. Any mistake which resulted in supply temporarily getting ahead of demand was quickly rectified by later increases in demand. Falling real prices encouraged consumption in a wide range of possible uses, from

powering machinery, generating electricity, heating houses and providing the fuel for transport.

The downward trend in price came to a grinding halt in the 1970s:

• The first oil price hike in 1973 – the result of political events – caught most decision makers unprepared and slow to react (van der Heijden, 1996: 4). Price suddenly rose by a factor of four times.
• The further hike in 1979 of about three times reinforced the impact of the first rise.

The economic system was slow to respond to such a price rise. Refining capacity went on increasing for another seven years, although demand had ceased to grow. Tanker capacity went on increasing for four more years. Decision makers behaved as if the hikes would be reversed, and as if the growth of oil demand would resume at its old rate. Such strategic failures are very expensive. Slow reactions imposed massive costs on the industry.

The impact of the price hike was extensive and striking:

• At the macrolevel it initiated a break in trend and momentum, slowing growth, increasing unemployment and accelerating the general rise in prices. The price hikes of 1973 and 1979 together constituted a shock which helped to move the world economy away from rapid growth and high employment to a condition of 'stagflation', the combination of rising prices and rising unemployment.
• At the microlevel it diverted oil from wasteful use in simply powering industrial motors and heating homes to its use as a feedstock in the petrochemical industry and for transport.
• As an extra it threw the American automobile industry into a crisis which is still with us today.

Ever since the 1970s the level of the price of oil has become a major factor in the world economy. There has been no real trend. Since 1979 the price of oil has fluctuated, quite dramatically at times, around what had become the 1979 level. If anything the price has tended to fall in real terms, which is due to substitution of other fuels and greater energy efficiency and better oil-extraction technologies, largely stimulated by the hikes of the 1970s. It has become quite reasonable for expectations of future movements of price to differ quite markedly from the trend suggested by extrapolations of past behaviour. Simply extrapolating past trends no longer works well in forecasting the future. There has been, and still is, a strong measure of uncertainty concerning even the direction of movement.

The level of uncertainty is such that in ten years the price of a barrel of oil might range anywhere from $10 to $30. At the time of writing, it is at the higher end, partly because the American invasion of Iraq built a five-dollar 'war premium' into the price.

The aim of the present exercise is to suggest a way to change the level of uncertainty about the price level, reducing the range of possible future scenarios which are worth considering, in other words to move from complete uncertainty through a range of possible outcomes to a limited number of discrete possibilities.

It is useful to skip ahead for a moment. It might be possible to simplify the problem by considering just three scenarios. These represent three feasible futures:

- The first involves an outcome with a relatively low price of $10 per barrel
- The second assumes a medium price of $20 which is close to the level before the Iraq War of 2003
- The third has a price at the high end of $30.

The analysis below develops these scenarios and considers the different probabilities.

Price determination

Clearly the price of any product or service reflects both supply and demand and their interaction. The movement of price over time reflects shifts in demand and/or supply conditions over time. The starting point for any discussion must therefore be the state of both.

How is it possible to conceptualize demand and supply conditions?

Focus on Theory The demand curve	This is the construct of the economist. A demand curve is drawn for a given moment of time. It represents the level of demand for a particular product at different price levels, assuming that it is known. A comparison of different points on the curve does not represent change over time. Change over time is shown by a comparison with a new curve.

A demand curve can be drawn for a whole market or an individual; the former consists of an aggregation of all the latter.

A well-behaved demand curve is one which shows consistently higher levels of demand at lower and lower prices. In other words it is consistently downward sloping. The relationship between a change to price and a change in quantity demanded is referred to as the price elasticity of demand (% change in quantity demanded divided by the % change in price). Demand is said to be elastic if the ratio is greater than one, inelastic if less than one. Elasticity is sometimes represented as the slope of the demand curve. The steeper the slope of a demand curve, the more inelastic is demand.

The price of a product is determined by the intersection of a demand and supply curve for that product. These curves represent the situation at a given moment of time. These curves trace out the quantity of the product demanded or supplied at different price levels. It is assumed that well-behaved curves fall in the case of the demand curve and rise in the case of the supply curve, so that there is always an equilibrium price which equates demand and supply. The stability of the equilibrium price, that is, the ability of the market to return to that level, depends on the exact slope of the curves. However, such a comment is to introduce dynamics into

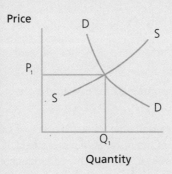

Figure C.3 **The demand curve**

Focus on Theory
                  cont'd

what is a static analysis. Strictly speaking there is no time in such analysis.

Change over time would be represented by shifts in the curves. For example, the situation for oil might be as follows. As world demand increases with world output, the demand curve shifts upwards. The rate of shift is likely to reflect the rate of substitution of other sources of energy for oil. As new sources of supply are found, this tends to push outwards the supply curve, but it can be countered by using up existing reserves.

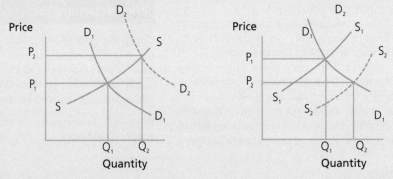

Figure C.4 **Movement in demand and supply over time**

In an extreme case the demand curve may move upwards and outwards and the supply curve downwards, increasing the equilibrium price of oil. If OPEC totally dominated supply, it could either fix the price and supply as much oil as is demanded at that price or it could fix the quantity and allow demand to fix the price. In the first case the supply curve is horizontal at the given price, that is, infinitely elastic with respect to price. In the second case the supply curve is vertical at the given quantity, that is, has zero elasticity with respect to price. The former better represents the behaviour of OPEC. If the non-OPEC producers are willing to sell at a lower price than OPEC, the supply curve will be well behaved up to the point at which the OPEC price cuts in. It is possible that OPEC policy may change from one position to the other in an unpredictable way.

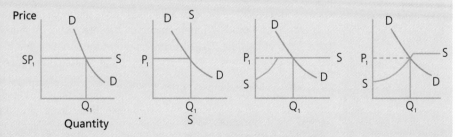

Figure C.5 **Price determination under different conditions**

In the case of oil, supply at any given time reflects the size of existing reserves, with annual output often about 10% of the reserves of a given field. It takes significant time to develop new fields, and even to bring back into production fields which have been closed for some reason, as by the impact of the strike in Venezuela in 2003 or war in Iraq.

Focus on Theory
cont'd

Fields are explored and developed over fairly lengthy periods of time. Some parts of the world have been closely explored and are using up their initial reserves, such as the second largest producer in the world, the USA. The USA is also the largest consumer of oil in the world, burning up about a quarter of the total annual oil consumption. Imports are rising as a proportion of America's total consumption, now accounting for half. Japan is also a major importer and China is fast becoming one. The rapidly growing Asia Pacific area is energy deficient and increasingly dependent on Middle East oil to meet its needs.

On the other hand Saudi Arabia has by far the largest reserves and is the only supplier which has the capacity to act as the balancing supplier in the short term.

It is possible from the reserve position to have a good idea of the short-term production potential. It is also easy to underestimate the likely size of reserves in the medium-term future. The underestimates in the past have been dramatic. Ever since the 1880s there have appeared to be reserves for just a further 30 years of consumption. In practice the reserves have gone on increasing. While the oil companies controlled production it was probably true that in any given period the size of reserves directly determined production levels. There was no real incentive for this to cease to be true. This is no longer necessarily the case.

Table C.11 Crude oil reserves and production in 2001

	Reserves in billions of barrels	Production in millions of barrels per day
Saudi Arabia	261.8	8.8
Iraq	112.5	2.4
UAE	97.8	2.4
Kuwait	96.5	2.1
Iran	89.7	3.7
Venezuela	77.7	3.4
Russia	48.6	7.1
USA	30.4	7.7
Libya	29.5	1.4
Mexico	26.9	3.6

Source: The Economist, 2002: 22.

OPEC and non-OPEC production

Oil was an inviting target for those who wished to increase government revenue. The concentration of oil reserves in certain countries, mostly otherwise poor, assisted in the motivation and achievement of government control. Such governments had every incentive to assert control of the oilfields and tap them as a source of revenue. When governments began to control supply, the possibility emerged of slowing the exploitation of reserves with no loss of immediate revenue, indeed with an increase because of the price inelasticity of demand. Why should governments expand output in such a way as to push down price and reduce their own actual and potential income?

Since there are a limited number of producers, certain producers, mainly located in the Middle East and in particular the Persian Gulf area, account for a large share of the reserves, output and exports. Saudi Arabia is the swing producer (the price setter). It has enormous reserves of oil that can be extracted at low cost, something like a quarter of the world's proven reserves (four of its neighbours each account for about a further 10%). Even today the equivalent of a barrel of oil can be lifted out of the ground in the Persian Gulf for barely a dollar.

If the oil market were a completely free one, with many suppliers acting independently of each other, it would concentrate production on Saudi Arabia and its neighbours since their cost of production is only 1–2 dollars per barrel compared with costs in other producers which are many times that, levels of cost which would with a lower world price make them uneconomic suppliers. Saudi Arabia, as the swing producer, can decide to maintain oil revenue at the $60 billion it currently earns, either by producing 6 million barrels per day at a price of about $30 a barrel or by producing 10 million barrels a day at a price of around $17. In theory it has it in its power to vary output by this amount. The motives for doing either are as much political as economic.

By reaching an agreement to control, or rather limit, output levels, the main producers are able to move price up to a point on the demand curve at which revenue is at a maximum. A cartel of producers or exporters can thus maintain prices at a higher level than would be the case in a competitive market. Such a cartel was formed in 1961, called the Organization of Petroleum Exporting Countries (OPEC), consisting of 11 main oil producers, notably, but not only, those in the Middle East who determine supply. Price is determined by a combination of political and economic factors. Political factors have had an important role to play, and at key moments in recent decades often a critical role. OPEC producers account for about 80% of world reserves, but only 40% of world exports. However, the cartel is not monolithic. It has its own tensions between members. It also makes mistakes, that is, does things which undermine its own intentions. For example, in 1997 it released an increased supply of oil onto a weakening economy and oil prices collapsed to around $10 a barrel.

Given these factors, the focus shifts to two issues. First, can the OPEC cartel hold together? Second, is it a sufficiently homogeneous group to maintain its cohesiveness?

It is clearly in the interest of any one producer to break any agreement on output and sales and to sell as much as possible at the higher price, provided the others continue to act as a cartel. If enough producers follow suit, the price will be forced down and the cartel will break up. Consequently all will lose. Any maverick or free rider can threaten the integrity of the group.

What keeps the group together, apart from self-interest, and what factors break the group up? Is self-interest enough? Is it relevant that many of the producers are geographically and culturally close?

A second important question to ask is, what is the level of production outside the cartel? Does the cartel account for a sufficiently large proportion of output to really control the market, or are outsiders willing to go along with the cartel, limiting their own output in an acceptable manner?

Ironically, higher prices have encouraged higher cost non-OPEC producers who may produce at the margin of profitability but in normal times cause supply to tend to outstrip demand. On the whole these producers have met specific requests from OPEC to limit output with a positive response. The location of world reserves and their relationship to output levels are relevant here, as is the near exhaustion of fields outside OPEC countries. Further exploration is becoming increasingly expensive. It is likely that in the future the potential for non-OPEC production will decline. At any given time Saudi Arabia and its neighbours could expand output and make the marginal oilfields very uneconomic.

Much of the literature points out that the price level is largely determined by the cartel of producers, OPEC, and discusses oil price fixing in this light. Is this an appropriate approach to the issue of price fixing?

The case study below shows how to use scenario building as a technique for forecasting future oil prices.

Case study   Scenario building

Chapter 4 outlined the different stages in the construction of a number of scenarios and these are repeated here.

Step 1

The first step in scenario building is to define the scope of the topic.

What is the nature of the interest in the issue?

● The interest might be a broad one, that of a government considering the implications of oil import dependence at different price levels, particularly if the regions which are the sources of oil are unstable.
● The interest might be that of an oil company wishing to open up a new oilfield, asking the question whether it should or should not do so. The decision might hinge upon the level of the price of oil.

● The decision maker might be an automobile producer planning a new car. The type of car with its power source, its planned size and engine capacity might depend on the price of oil (see the case study on the HEV in Chapter 5).

These are the kinds of decisions which will provide the appropriate focus and motivate an interest in the topic.

Step 2

The second stage involves the identification of stakeholders and the success indicators relevant to them. The main stakeholders are the governments, the owners of the enterprises who produce and use oil or produce or sell products complementary to oil or oil using products, and those who manage or work in such enterprises.

- For the governments of oil-producing countries revenue from excise taxes or directly from oil sales is the main success indicator. It depends upon price and quantity sold.
- For the government of an oil-importing country the aim might be to keep the cost of such imports at a manageable level.
- For an oil company or an automobile producer profit is the main performance indicator. In the first case the price has a direct impact on profitability, in the second an indirect impact, since the demand for automobiles and their use when purchased will reflect to some degree the running costs of cars, including the cost of the petrol consumed.

What are the interests of the main players? What motivates them?

Step 3

The third stage is to identify three groups of key factors – possible driving forces, predetermined elements and critical uncertainties.

What are these elements?

1. *Driving forces*
- Environmental concerns requiring the reduction in the consumption of carbon fuels and encouraging energy efficiency and the development of alternative sources of energy
- Muslim fundamentalism and the nature of international conflict in a post-Cold War world, particularly as it relates to issues relevant to countries in the area of the Persian Gulf, including Israel, and members of OPEC
- The energy position of both developed and rapidly growing economies, as for example the rising dependence of some major oil consumers – USA, Japan, China and India – on imports from the Middle East
- Probably the chief driving force in the oil industry is, as we have seen, the behaviour of OPEC. The overall supply and demand conditions create the environment in which OPEC seeks to set the price. In normal circumstances OPEC seeks to fix the price at between $18 and $24 per barrel. Demand may reflect government regulations to limit energy consumption and carbon emissions.

2. *Predetermined elements*
- The size of existing oil reserves and the level and rate of growth of potential production in the near future
- The relationship of energy consumption to economic development as determined by the nature of known technology

- National and cultural divisions in the world
- The organization of the industry which has changed significantly over the history of that industry. The key players in the industry today are the owner producers, the governments of the countries in which the main oil reserves are to be found
- The conditions of supply and demand which are relatively stable over time. Most oil production in any period comes from existing fields. Reserves are well known. Equally, in the short term, demand is relatively fixed, except that the level of activity in the world economy determines the overall level of demand, which fluctuates with the business cycle.

3. *Critical uncertainties*
- The possibility of an oil shock of various kinds. This might take the form of a war which closes significant facilities or the overthrow of moderate political regimes in oil-producing countries
- The exact rate of growth of the world economy over the medium to long term, with the implied level of world activity in ten years time
- The strength of environmental pressure to reduce carbon fuel use and the level of investment in new technology which determines the economics of alternative energy sources – how much the governments of importing countries deliberately try to limit consumption
- The external political environment of OPEC countries
- The nature of political regimes in OPEC countries such as Saudi Arabia and Iraq – how far OPEC remains united and reacts in a concerted way to changes in that environment – how much of world production OPEC controls
- The state of the Israeli/Palestinian conflict
- The productive potential and attitude of non-OPEC oil-producing countries – how non-OPEC countries behave in response to OPEC initiatives.

It is clear that in this area there are more uncertainties than certainties. Is it possible to reduce further the uncertainties? The listing is general and needs to be made more specific. How can this be done?

Step 4

The next stage is to analyse those critical uncertainties whose unfolding can be regarded as the key to different outcomes.

What determines the behaviour of OPEC? What are the influences beyond the narrowly economic?

The political situation in the world and in particular in the Middle East is a major factor in this, as the price hikes of the 1970s showed so well. The state of the Israeli/Palestinian confrontation, the role of Iraq and its stance vis-à-vis the outside world, Islamic fundamentalism and its popularity, the nature of the regimes in Iran and other oil-producing countries are all key issues.

How homogeneous is OPEC? Equally, how far can OPEC persuade non-OPEC countries to go along with it? Specifically, what are the policies of countries like Russia, the former Soviet republics, Norway and Mexico, possibly important sources of new reserves and significant reserves of gas which is competitive with oil.

Step 5

The next stage, a preliminary outline of the scenarios, might take three possible outcomes from the unfolding of the element(s) of critical uncertainty.

1. At one extreme it might assume a resolution of the Israel/Palestine problem and the prevalence of moderate Arab governments in charge of the oil-exporting countries, including Iraq, with a decline in the influence of extreme views.
2. At the other extreme there is the continuation of major conflict, and the domination of fundamentalist governments prepared to use their oil muscle to reduce output and push up the price of oil as a political weapon.
3. In between these two extremes there is the continuation of the present uncertainty with unresolved conflicts and a mixture of moderate and fundamentalist regimes. This regime may be an uneasy one, punctuated by intermittent crises. In this case there are occasional events which threaten to destabilize the situation, events which can rapidly get out of control.

What outcome in the areas of critical uncertainty defines each scenario?

Step 6

The next stage is to consider these different scenarios in the light of the likely price outcomes and their plausibility. It is possible to label the scenarios to give them some focus:

1. 'peace reigns'
2. 'clash of cultures'
3. 'continuing instability'.

The 'peace reigns' scenario may mean that the intervention in the market determination of price is mild and that the price simply fluctuates within the desired range according to market conditions. If there is significant growth in the developed economies, the price may be relatively high, at around $24; if these economies are in recession, the price may be at the lower end, at about $18. Even in this scenario, if OPEC loses its control over price as new producers enter the market or as members become free riders maximizing their own advantage by increasing production and hoping that the price stays up, prices could drop to $10 per barrel, particularly if the world economy is in recession.

The 'clash of cultures' scenario could mean that production will be badly and significantly affected by damage to wells, deliberate curtailment of production or embargoes and sanctions from outside. Depending on who was affected and by how much, and how far producers outside the area could compensate for lost production, the price may rise to $30 and above, in some cases well above, even to a level of $50.

The 'continuing instability' scenario is the most difficult to interpret. Within this scenario there might be a whole range of possible prices, all the way from $10 to $30, possibly all these prices at different times. It depends on the exact mix of economic conditions, the strength of OPEC, the share of oil production accounted for by OPEC and the nature of the political environment at the time.

What is the range of possibilities in each of these scenarios?

Step 7

The next stage involves developing a narrative of how in each case the political situation will develop and how OPEC will respond to this situation. This needs to be done at different levels. It requires a consideration both at the global political and economic level and at the level of the oil producers themselves. This is a major task. For example it requires an analysis of the stability of key regimes like Saudi Arabia and Iraq.

Can you construct a narrative for each of these scenarios?

Stage 8

At this stage it is necessary to draw out the implications of the scenarios for the decisions.

Are the outcomes sufficiently different to make a difference to any decisions to be made, whether by governments or private enterprises? Are there ways of making a strategic decision more compatible with all scenarios?

Step 9

The final step is monitoring the actual outcome. This stage involves identification and recognition of key indicators, or signposts, which can be monitored. The signs may be weak and require close attention. Oil prices move continuously from day to day but may not be the best means of tracing the unfolding of the actual scenario. Political events in combination with economic trends may be more helpful. There may be a combination of signposts, such as the rate of growth of world output, the proportion of world reserves within OPEC countries compared with the proportion of output accounted for by OPEC and the level of income per head in the oil-producing countries.

Key strategic issues

The reader should flesh out each of these stages. This is best done as a project which repeats the stages above. The following case study questions help in asking the relevant questions. The starting point might be one of the following.

Imagine that you control an enterprise with significant reserves of oil shale or tar sands. You wish to develop those reserves. Which of the scenarios will allow you to do so?

Imagine that you are a major car producer planning the development of a new motorcar? How will the future price of oil influence your decision?

An answer to these questions requires an answer to the following questions.

In the future what factors will influence the demand for energy in general and the demand for oil in particular? In the future what factors will influence the supply of energy in general and the supply of oil in particular?

After constructing the scenarios you should be able to give a better answer to the question: What is likely to be the price of oil in 12 months, 5 years, 10 years and 25 years?

Strategic analysis and audit

Since the situation on oil pricing is so volatile, repeat the exercise of scenario building imagining that you are undertaking the same exercise without the benefit of hindsight in 1970, 1980, 2000 and 2010. Repeat the same stages of scenario building.

Reading

Adelman, M. A., *The Genie out of the Bottle: world oil since 1970*, (MIT Press, Cambridge, MA and London, 1995).

Bartlett, D. L., 'The U.S. is running out of energy', *Time* **162**(3) July 21, 2003: 36.

Economist, The, 'Don't mention the "o" word', September 14, 2002: 22–4.

Kassler, P., 'Scenarios for world energy: barricades or new frontiers?', *Long Range Planning*, **28**(6): 38–47.

Salameh, M. G., 'Quest for Middle East oil: the US versus the Asia-Pacific regions', *Energy Policy*, **31**(11): 1085.

Epilogue: reviewing the nature of strategy

The book started by indicating the difficulty of defining in a precise way what strategy is. It also referred to a number of different and possibly contradictory approaches and the existence of analytical treatments and definitions from as many as fourteen different schools which have analysed the nature of strategy, all differing and some apparently mutually exclusive. It also asserted that the whole book could be seen as an extended definition of strategy. All these statements are true. They bear testimony in different ways to the significance of strategy but also to the need to take great care in handling the concept. They justify the length of the book.

To attempt a simple definition of strategy is to reduce a subtle concept to the strait-jacket of a rigid interpretation. In any area of management it is important to emphasize what is possible, not what should be prescribed. To prescribe the impossible – not an unusual occurrence – is to subvert the positive role of strategy as an instrument of management. What is possible in strategy making is defined by the particular circumstances of an enterprise, circumstances which differ markedly from enterprise to enterprise and industry to industry. Finding an appropriate definition is part of the process of learning how far it is possible to generalize about strategy in such different circumstances. It is possible to generalize, even if it is impossible to produce a set of simple principles on how to make strategy. As in all theory, the core of the problem is to reconcile the need to generalize with the uniqueness of the experience.

The present book has taken as its starting point what is possible:

- It analyses strategy as the central foundation of any attempt to guide the enterprise into an uncertain future and as a practical means of enhancing the performance of that organization in that uncertain future. No organization is successful without a good strategy, even if it is often implicit.
- It has shown how, by taking a strategic approach, it is possible to resolve recurrent dilemmas.
- It takes a plural motivation of stakeholders as the norm but accepts the usual primacy of the 'single' bottom line over the 'triple' or 'quadruple' bottom line. Corporate social responsibility is easily incorporated into the analysis once the nature of any organization as a coalition of interests is accepted. This requires a move away from a monopoly concern with the one stakeholder group, the share-owners.
- It prefers to emphasize an emergent view of strategy rather than one which stresses clear objectives and a clear but simple choice between ready-made strategies designed to achieve those objectives. Strategy requires learning and discovery about what an organization can do and how it can do it.

- There are some exceptional circumstances which would justify a deliberative or classical approach.
- Most importantly, the book takes a realistic view of the role of planning, defining it in a narrow manner as the preparation and implementation of a comprehensive and detailed set of plans, and pointing out its rarity.

There is an enormous amount of evidence on the effectiveness of strategy making under different conditions and at different levels. Since every set of circumstances in which an enterprise finds itself is unique, every strategy is also unique. The paths by which strategy making unfolds are dependent on these unique but changing circumstances. It is necessary to recognize the universality of contingency. Circumstances are never exactly the same, nor events ever repeated in all their detail. The process of strategy making is always particular to an organization and a particular time, every good strategy tailored to that organization's needs and to the circumstances at that moment of time.

The fourteen different schools have considered different aspects of a complex concept. All have some validity, but no single one exhausts the full meaning of the concept. Some may be a good description of what happens in certain circumstances and at certain times. Others may simply pick out a narrow aspect of the activity of strategy making. In some way all have been dealt with in this book, although at varying lengths. It is barely possible to draw together all these definitions in one compound definition. This is attempted in a loose way in the next few paragraphs.

The distinction between strategic thinking and strategic planning is reflected and highlighted in the two schools of thought which stress the entrepreneurial and planning aspects of strategy. There is a dramatic contrast between strategy as an intent to create something dramatically new, that is, a vision of a new future, and strategy as a detailed but coherent linking, through a defined strategic purpose, of existing resources and environments. In the latter sense strategy sees the strategist to some degree locked in by the constraints of the past and even by the constraints of reason itself. There is a striking contrast between the two pictures, strategy as remaking yourself and even your environment, and strategy as making the most of what you already have and the environment which already exists and is developing.

There are two different ways in which these views can be interpreted, either as prescriptions of what strategy should be, or simply descriptions of what strategy can be in different circumstances. Such views characterize enterprises operating in different circumstances but both can be interpreted as comprising a deliberative element, strategy as making possible both the remaking of the future context of the enterprise and making the most of what already exists. This deliberative action focuses on the creation and maintenance of competitive advantage.

One of the schools, the episodic, or configurative, and perhaps even a variant of this, the transformative or revolutionary school, emphasizes the dominance of unexpected contingency and the need for a comprehensiveness of reaction, the need to transform the whole organization to keep ahead of rapid or discontinuous change. Other schools prefer to take that context as fixed and strategy as only marginally pliable. This is best summarized in the use of the term 'logical incrementalism'. The design school considers how to achieve a fit between the external and internal environments, the positioning school emphasizing one particular element of the external context. These latter schools tend to take the environments as largely given, at least from the perspective of strategy made at a given moment in time.

There are a number of obvious constraints on what any strategy can do:

- Cognitive, a matter of the way in which strategy is thought about or conceived. This is also true of the way in which it is discussed or talked about. Again the rationality school adopts a particular cognitive approach, which reflects the dominating metatheory in both economics and management studies. The learning school introduces another constraint, the limitations of information and information processing and the role of strategy as stimulating, and always reflecting, an ongoing learning process.
- Environmental, political and cultural contexts, all part of a broader external context but identifiably separate parts of that context. These contexts shape the way in which strategy is, or can be, made. They place severe limitations on the nature of such strategy. These schools tell us much about how decision making in strategy actually occurs and warn us to apply a reality check to any prescription about what strategy should be or should do. Decision makers are social animals. They have interests other than the economic welfare of the enterprise. They are also political animals. They wield power for its own sake, they negotiate and bargain with others, they compromise.

These constraints tempt the strategist into adopting simple rules, and there are occasions when this is a valid approach. However, strategy must take into account every activity which occurs within an enterprise. To engage in strategy making is to participate in an integrative process which pulls together all these different activities, not simply as current operations but also as activities capable of future development, in a way which helps to realize a set of integrated individual and group objectives. Strategy is also complex, in that it is relevant at different levels of decision making, some of which are broader than corporate strategy making, such as the industry or community levels. Even a good corporate strategist must take account of these different levels. Good strategy must always take into consideration other strategy makers, including both competitors and cooperators (complementors); they are part of the environment.

It is useful to ask the corollary question, who or what is a strategist? A strategist is a person who makes strategy. Since strategy making is a complex process, a strategist is likely to have to embrace this complexity.

On one interpretation everyone is a strategist; it is clearly beneficial to the enterprise that every employee engages in strategic thinking. However, turning the focus onto strategic management or strategic planning can change the definition of a strategist, reducing the number of potential strategists, in an extreme and unlikely case to just one. Both of these extreme answers to the question – all or just one – are untenable. All may act at some time as strategists, within a narrow domain, some may spend a significant amount of their time dedicated to strategy making, one may have a large responsibility for making strategy.

There are certain characteristics of a good strategist which become more evident the more senior the manager and the greater the size of his or her domain. These include:

- the desire to identify and describe alternative directions for the future development of the enterprise and to take new approaches, all consistent with likely scenarios of the future which are relevant to the organization
- an entrepreneurial vision embracing action which creates competitive advantage and articulates at least part, if not the whole, of the strategic intent and tries to realize it
- a willingness to consider the long-term interests of all stakeholders, not just shareholders
- an ability to provide the kind of leadership which empowers all employees to act freely without hindrance within their own domains but coherently within the framework of a generally accepted strategy
- the drive to build an organization designed and structured in a way that fits the vision and which makes full use of the existing corporate identity and corporate culture
- the ability to integrate strategy with corporate identity and corporate culture
- the ability to ride luck, that is, to recognize and take unexpected opportunities and avoid unexpected threats.

The senior strategists must be clear on objectives, embracing as a core aim the creation of value for customers; aware of the significance of changes in the environment, but able to ignore passing fads and fashions; and willing, if necessary, to take quick decisions regardless of resistance or threats.

In the end strategy is judged by its results. If it produces positive results, it will survive as something useful. If it does not produce results, it will be discarded. In reality the absence of an explicit strategy does not mean there is no strategy. It simply means that strategy making for some reason is implicit. A good reality check is not a prescription for treating strategy simply as another management tool which can be easily discarded, and ignoring the theory which argues for the universality of strategy making. It is always easier to get a positive outcome if the justification of what is being done is understood. If it works, why does it work? If it does not work, why not? All can benefit from answers to these questions. This book has sought to show what strategy is and the various ways in which it might assist in the development of an organization.

Glossary

Acquisition The process of acquiring by purchase other enterprises, assets or business units.

Advantages of agglomeration The benefits that come from having as many economic activities as possible occurring in close proximity.

Adverse selection The tendency of those at low risk not to insure against that risk.

Agent The person who acts to complete a particular strategic task under delegation from a principal.

Alliance capitalism The type of capitalism based on a proliferation of strategic alliances which is said to prevail today.

Allocentric strategy A strategy which takes account of the actions of other strategic players.

Anti-monopoly legislation Laws intended to prevent the creation of monopoly elements in a market.

Aspirational good One whose consumption provides status or the feeling of consuming a luxury good.

Assessing The evaluation of the relevance for strategy making of information about any future change. The fourth step in reading the general environment.

Asset specificity A situation in which there is a close link between the nature of certain assets and a particular activity and/or enterprise.

Asset stripping The act of breaking up and selling the assets of a business unit which has been acquired.

Asymmetrical information A situation in which strategic players have differing access to information.

Asymmetrical investment A situation when the partners to a transaction make different commitments of resources in order to try to achieve a successful conclusion.

Attribute A particular characteristic of any product or service which might create a demand for that product or service.

Backward (reverse) engineering Gaining an understanding of a product or technique by taking the product to pieces in a systematic manner.

Backward-sloping demand curve A curve which slopes the opposite way to that which is normal, that is, which shows higher demand associated with a higher price for at least some part of the curve.

Balancing The ability to keep all the resources used in a blend in appropriate proportions and in good condition.

Balanced portfolio of products One which includes products at different points in their life cycles.

Balanced scorecard A complex method of monitoring the performance of a strategy.

Benchmarking The practice of establishing performance indicators which enable strategists to measure the performance of an organization relative to best practice.

Best strategy The strategy which performs best on the relevant performance indicators.

Bilateral monopoly A situation where both parties to a transaction have a monopoly.

Bilateral relations The political and economic links between two countries.

Blending The combining of resources to maximum effect in achieving competitive advantage.

Boundary The border of an organization, enterprise or department or any other unit relevant to strategy making.

Bounded rationality The constraint put on the application of reason to the solution of problems by the existence of

limited information or a limited capacity to process that information.

Branding The process by which a person, product or region becomes known by its name alone because there are certain desirable qualities attached to that name.

Bubble An excessive price increase for a particular type of asset such as property or shares over a short period of time.

Business landscape A simplified expression of the opportunities and threats facing an enterprise, with performance represented by height above sea level and risk by the rapidity of change in gradient. In making strategy the enterprise moves through the landscape with the aim of gaining greater height but avoiding the precipices.

Business plan A plan, usually covering a short period such as a year, which sets out the targets for achievement, particularly the financial targets.

Capability An ability to carry out a potentially value-adding activity made possible by a particular combination, or blending, of the resources available to an organization.

Cause An event(s) or circumstance(s), or their combination, from which follow further events or circumstances.

Chaebol The Korean equivalent of a *keiretsu*.

Characteristic A distinguishing feature which helps to define the meaning of or identify a concept or object.

Chief learning officer The organization official put in charge of the process of knowledge acquisition by all the staff of that organization.

Civil foundation The laws, conventions and customs relating to behaviour with respect to the environment and society in general.

Civil society The mix of societies, clubs, associations or voluntary groups of various kinds which exists between government and commercial organizations.

Classical approach A deliberate, explicit and rational process with an emphasis on the strategist formulating and passing down the strategy for managers to implement.

Closed problem A problem which is articulated in an explicit way and requires a particular solution.

Cluster A network in which enterprises are located in close proximity to each other.

Codification The detailed articulation of the main features of some process or procedure, for example the codification of the strategic intent.

Coevolution The tendency of different parts of a whole system to develop in a way which makes them compatible with each other.

Command The issue of instruction.

Commitment The dedication of assets or resources to a particular task or activity.

Commoditization The process by which any product, including manufactured goods, can become a 'commodity'.

Commodity A homogeneous product, formerly one produced in mining or agriculture, but the term is now extended to the manufacturing sector.

Commons Any asset which is available for less than its real cost.

Communication The transfer of information to an appropriate point in an organization, without distortion.

Competencies Capabilities which assist an organization to implement its strategy.

Competition policy A policy of deliberately fostering increased competition.

Competition reducing alliance A cooperative venture intended to reduce the forces of competition in a market.

Competition response alliance A cooperative venture intended to assist in meeting new competition.

Competition risk The risk which arises from the uncertainty created by the exis-

tence of competitors with their own strategies.

Competitive advantage A perceived association with a commodity or service of a tangible or intangible attribute or condition of supply, which makes that product or service more attractive to consumers than the goods or services of competitors.

Competitive environment The immediate competitive context in which an organization or enterprise operates.

Competitive strength matrix A growth share matrix with more dimensions on the growth and share scales.

Complementary alliance A cooperative venture to which the partners bring assets which are different but potentially combine well.

Complementor An individual or organization which provides a product or service which promotes either a reduction in costs or an increase in value of a product. The opposite of a competitor.

Conflict Disagreement which persists beyond an immediate confrontation and is significant enough to influence behaviour.

Consensus Agreement on the main points of a strategy.

Consequence The result of a circumstance or an event, or a combination of such circumstances or events.

Contingency testing The testing of a strategy for its robustness in the event of the occurrence of an event which has a potentially negative impact.

Contingent strategy That part of a strategy which is not likely to be part of any alternative strategy.

Contrarian A person who deliberately takes the opposite view to that adopted by the general market, notably with respect to future movements in that market.

Control Direct or indirect guidance of other players within an organization to behave in a certain way.

Convergent problem A problem which, according to a generally accepted criterion, has either only one, or rather only one obviously best, solution.

Conversion A synonym for implementation.

Coopetition A strategy which combines both cooperation and competition.

Coordination The harmonizing of the actions of separate departments or individuals.

Core activities Those activities which assist significantly in the production and sale of the main products or services of an organization.

Core (distinctive) competency A competency which is made necessary by the strategy of an organization and is central to the making of that strategy.

Core resources Those resources necessary to support the core activities of an organization.

Core strategy That part of a strategy which is likely to be part of any other feasible strategy.

Corporate culture The set of attitudes, values and behavioural patterns which characterize a particular enterprise.

Corporate plan Usually a synonym for a business plan.

Corporate social responsibility The notion that there is an obligation to take account of the interests of all the stakeholders of an organization.

Cost drivers The factors which determine the level of the costs of production or distribution.

Cost leadership A generic strategy which aims to produce and sell a commodity or service at a cost lower that that of competitors.

Country risk The risk which arises for business transactions from the existence of separate countries with their own sovereignties and currencies.

Created assets Assets which are the product of human creativity.

Creating the future Remaking the environment of an enterprise by strategic activity.

Creative destruction The simultaneous process of destruction of the old by the creation of the new.

Creativity The ability to develop a new idea or to innovate.

Creativity driver Any motivation which causes an individual to be creative.

Critical uncertainties Areas of uncertainty concerning variables of change critical to a particular problem.

Crony capitalism A form of market economy in which the impersonal links of the market are superceded by personal links based on the relationships of those in government with business-people.

Cultural cluster A group of countries sharing the same culture.

Culture The set of attitudes, values and patterns of behaviour which characterize a particular society and the artefacts which are deemed typical in some way of that society.

Definition The drawing out of the technical and marketing implications of a new venture initiative.

Deflation The general tendency for prices to fall.

Demand curve A curve which represents for a given moment in time the relationship between the level of demand for a product or service and the price which a purchaser is willing to pay for it.

Demand-based explanation An explanation which focuses on consumption or the consumer.

Demerger The opposite of a merger. It represents the separation of business units which previously existed within one conglomerate.

Despotic power The ability of a political leader to satisfy a personal whim, but not necessarily to implement policy.

Development state A government which actively promotes the process of economic development.

Differential pricing The varying of price according to the demands of individual consumers.

Discovery-driven planning A form of planning which makes space for as yet unknown discoveries and innovations.

Disruptive innovation An innovation which marks a decisive break with either the technology or the pattern of demand which has prevailed before in an area of the economy.

Divergent problem A problem which has more than one solution, the choice of which reflects divergent criteria.

Diversification A technique for spreading risk by holding a range of assets or engaging in a range of activities; assets or activities which are subject to independent risk elements.

Diversifying strategic alliance A cooperative venture intended to widen the range of products or services produced.

Divestment The sale or spinning off of business units not regarded as strategically necessary to the enterprise.

Dominant strategy One which is clearly preferred by all players.

Downscoping The divestment of activities or business units not regarded as part of the core activities of the business.

Driving forces The main independent variables which influence the rate and direction of change in an area of the economy.

Duopoly The existence of two sellers in a market or industry. A *duopolist* is an enterprise which sells in such a market.

Eclectic theory A theory which is complex since it borrows and combines elements from other existing theories.

E-commerce Economic transactions organized through the Internet.

Economic value added (EVA) The value added to the initial raw material inputs in the process of preparing a product for final consumption.

Economism The tendency to interpret all human motivation in terms of economics.

Economy of learning A saving in costs which results from the process of discovery or learning experienced in the operation of a business facility.

Economy of scale A saving in costs which arises when an enterprise increases the level of its production.

Economy of scope A saving in costs which arises from the synergies when an enterprise produces more than one product or service.

Efficient price A price whose determination takes into account all the information which is currently available.

Egocentric strategy A strategy which fails to take into account the strategy of other players.

Elaboration The translation of objectives into strategic actions designed to achieve those objectives.

Elasticity of substitution The degree to which one product is substituted for another when their relative prices are changed.

Embedded process An activity whose organization is specific to the organization, but whose exact nature is unclear.

Emergent strategy A strategy which is always in the process of being articulated – it emerges through a process of learning.

Empowerment The granting to all staff of an organization of as much scope for decision making as is feasible within the framework of a strategy.

Enrichment Empowerment.

Entrepreneurship The ability to innovate and create a viable new enterprise.

Environment The context, surroundings or conditions of an organization or enterprise.

Environment segments The various parts of the environment as conventionally classified, e.g. political or economic.

Equidistance The notion that the communications and transport revolutions have removed the significance of location, leaving every place equally distant from every other.

Equilibrium price A price which equates demand and supply of a product or service.

Equity The value of ownership in an enterprise net of any debts – the value of the shares.

Equity strategic alliance A cooperative venture which involves equity ownership by one or both partners.

Ethnocentric Oriented towards a national or local perspective.

Event pacing The setting of a speed of strategy implementation which is determined by outside events.

Evolutionary approach A process by which a dominant strategy is the result of a process of competition in which those strategies failing to perform well are culled.

Evolutionary stable strategy A strategy which persists in being chosen as best.

Experience curve The curve which describes the relationship between the level of output and the level of unit costs. It assumes the relationship is an inverse one, in which learning from increased activity levels progressively reduces the level of unit costs.

Explicit strategy An explicit strategy is one whose main outline is spelt out.

External environment The external environment is the context, outside the boundary of an organization, in which that organization has to operate.

Extreme events Events which cause large fluctuations in the behaviour of important performance indicators.

Extrinsic motivation Motivation based on a pecuniary reward.

Feasible strategy A strategy which can be implemented.

First-mover advantage The advantage reaped by the first to innovate in a particular area.

Fixed costs The costs which are incurred irrespective of the level of output.

Floating exchange rate The relative price of two currencies left free to be determined by the movement of supply and demand. A *dirty float* is when there is some intervention by a government authority to smooth out the abrupt movements which can occur in an uncontrolled market.

Focusing A pronounced orientation towards one strategy, policy or activity rather than others.

Focused cost leadership Occurs when an enterprise concentrates on getting

the costs of a particular product or activity below those of competitors.

Focused product differentiation Occurs when an enterprise concentrates on marketing or branding of a certain product or products from the whole range it produces and/or sells.

Forcing mechanism A device which compels an organization to carry out a certain activity at a particular time.

Forecasting The process of making predictions relevant to strategy. The third step in reading the general environment.

Foreign direct investment (FDI) An active form of investment in productive facilities in a country other than one's own.

Foresight The ability to read well, and influence significantly, the future.

Formal structure The design framework of an organization which indicates the links between different specialized units.

Formulation The activity of articulating a strategy.

Founder enterprise An enterprise still run by its founder.

Franchising A form of licensing in which the franchisee pays to use the name and all or some part of the business model of the franchisor.

Free rider Someone who exploits the existence of public goods or the commons.

Function A discrete area of management activity, such as finance or marketing.

Game theory An approach to conceptualizing business problems which sets them up as games with defined rules.

Gearing The ratio of debt to equity.

General environment The overall context of an organization, including all the various environment segments.

Generic strategy A group of broad strategies which have significant characteristics in common.

Geocentric Oriented towards a global perspective.

Global enterprise An enterprise which has very significant international activities.

Globalization The process of movement towards a global world.

Gorilla strategy A strategy in which the enterprise seeks to dominate every part of the value-adding chain of production and sales.

Governance The way in which management control of an organization is exercised by key stakeholder groups, notably but not only the shareholders: it is often used to refer in particular to the way in which the owners control the managers of an enterprise.

Graduated entry A systematic movement from small and less risky modes of entry into international markets to decisive and much more risky modes.

Greenfield project A project which starts from scratch.

Group thinking The tendency for the views of any group of people to converge.

Growth share matrix A matrix which relates the growth potential of a market to an enterprise's existing market share and therefore competitiveness.

Guerrilla strategy A strategy in which the enterprise positions itself to dominate a key point in the value-adding chain of production and sales.

Guidance planning A form of national planning in which the government guides private strategists in the direction it desires by providing information and using persuasion.

Hardware The physical equipment in an area.

Hedging A means of gaining cover against particular kinds of risk, such as transfer or economic risk.

Home country bias The tendency to favour one's own country in consumption, savings, investment or employment decisions.

Honda effect The tendency with hindsight to read a clear and deliberate strategy into a set of opportunistic actions.

Horizontal alliance A cooperative venture which involves potential competitors.

Horizontal fracturing A failure to maintain links between departments at the same level within an organization.

Horizontal integration The combining into one enterprise of business units or companies operating at the same point in the value-adding chain or the same markets.

Hybrid A mix of at least two different types.

Hybrid organization An organization based upon at least two different design principles.

Hyper-competition A heightened and intensive competition which is often associated with globalization.

Hypothesis The statement or assertion which is to be tested in any piece of research.

Ideal type A pure form of structure or principle which rarely exists in practice.

Imitation The tendency to copy what is perceived as existing best practice.

Imperfect information Information which is less than perfect, that is, less than full, or inadequate for the purpose required.

Impetus The successful championing of a new venture initiative.

Implementation The activity of putting into effect a strategy.

Implicit strategy A strategy whose main outline is left unsaid and unwritten but tacitly expresses the intent of the strategist.

Income elasticity of demand The responsiveness of the demand for a product to a rise in income. As a ratio it is the proportional increase in demand over the proportional increase in income.

Incrementalism A tendency to engage in marginal or gradual change.

Indeterminateness The lack of a unique and predictable price or output level in a market.

Industrial organization (positioning) model A set of procedures for strategy making which start with the positioning of an enterprise with respect to product, value-adding activities or markets.

Industry risk This is the risk characteristic of a particular industry.

Inflation The general tendency for prices to rise.

Inflection point A point at which an enterprise needs to change its business model and/or strategy.

Informal structure The unofficial way in which an organization functions and the patterns of interaction which this involves.

Information strategy The strategy for discovering information necessary in making a strategy.

Infrastructural power The ability of a government to use its administrative penetration of a society and economy to implement its policies.

Innovation The introduction of a significant new element into business activity, whether a new process, a product or even a new method of organization.

Intellectual property rights Ownership rights in ideas with a commercial relevance.

Interactive process A process of mutual influence and of action, response and reaction by interacting players.

Intermediate products Products intermediate between raw materials and the final product, sometimes called components.

Internal environment Anything which is internal to an organization, that is, within its boundary, including resources, structures and culture.

Internalization The process by which economic transactions are taken out of the market and organized as transactions within the boundaries of an enterprise.

Internationalization The increased interaction between national units, most often in international business transactions, taking the form of exports or foreign direct investment.

Intrapreneurship The deliberate encouragement of entrepreneurship within an existing organization.

Intrinsic motivation Motivation which is based on pride in doing something well, without material reward.

Iron law of oligopoly The tendency for any market to be dominated by a few sellers.

Iteration The process by which information is passed backwards and forwards between players in the making of a strategy.

Joint production economies Either economies of scale or economies of scope.

Joint venture A cooperative enterprise, which may involve the creation of a separate enterprise, jointly owned.

Just-in-time The practice of minimizing inventory by delivering inputs as and when they are required.

Keiretsu Large conglomerate enterprises which have dominated the Japanese economy since 1945, the successors of the *zaibatsu*.

Key performance indicators Specific measures of performance which are critical to the implementation of a strategy.

Lateral thinking This is a mode of thinking which is creative or intuitive rather then rational.

Law of large numbers The tendency of a variable to converge to an anticipated value as more cases are considered.

Law of one price The process by which riskless exchange or arbitrage equalizes the price of homogeneous products or services.

Lean production The practice of minimizing the costs of production by continuous improvement (*kaizen*).

Leverage (1) The ability to make the most of a resource available to the organization and to use that resource to improve performance to the maximum degree. (2) The ability to incur increased debt.

Licensing The use of another's name, product or process in return for a payment.

Liquidity trap The inability of the monetary authorities to reduce the rate of interest below zero.

Logical incrementalism The tendency to make marginal change which follows from and is compatible with the existing organizational strategy and structure.

Long-tailed risk An event whose negative consequences become evident long after the original event.

Luxury good A good the price of which excludes consumption by all but a few wealthy consumers.

Macro-invention An invention with the capacity to change radically the technology in key areas of an economy.

Managing change The process of accurately reading the nature of change in the environment and responding appropriately to that change.

Market The use of price to allocate resources, dispose of products and distribute income between independent transactors. Or such a mechanism as it operates in a particular part of the economy.

Market failure An inability for a market to function in the normal way.

Market imperfection Anything which prevents a market from functioning with maximum efficiency.

Market structure The rules of market activity, the number of players operating in the market and the nature of the interaction between these players.

Market value added (MVA) The net addition to the market value of an enterprise over a given period of time net of all fresh injections of money from any source.

Matrix A matrix represents combinations of two characteristics, often expressed by a simple diagram with vertical and horizontal axes.

Matrix design structure A design which embodies two different principles, for example product and regional principles.

Merger The voluntary fusion of two or more enterprises.

Meta-routine A flexible timetable under which there is space allowed for activities which by their nature cannot be timetabled exactly, for example innovation.

Metatheory The underlying theory which establishes the assumptions on the basis of which strategists, or those commenting on or writing about strategy, think.

Micro-invention An invention which assists in realizing a macro-invention or continues the general process of innovation in an incremental way.

Mission statement A statement of how an organization sees itself and where it hopes to go in the future.

Mode of entry The way in which an enterprise participates in international business and enters an international market.

Model A well-formulated theoretical framework or system.

Monitoring (1) The process of following an interesting development as it develops over time and the drawing out of its implications. The second step in reading the general environment. (2) Alternatively it is the activity of checking on the implementation of a strategy.

Monopolistic competition A situation in which there are a number of sellers in a particular market who compete by differentiating their products.

Monopoly The existence of a single seller in a market or industry.

Monopsony The existence of a single buyer in a market or industry.

Moral hazard The tendency of those who are given automatic cover against risk to engage in riskier behaviour than they would otherwise do.

Multidomestic strategy A strategy, particularly a marketing strategy, which is tailored to suit the conditions of different countries.

Multilateral institutions The international institutions which set the rules of international behaviour, for example the World Trade Organization and the International Monetary Fund.

Negative reference group A group by which a person identifies undesirable characteristics.

Network A web of strategic alliances which persists over a significant period of time.

New economy That part of the economy which is being established as a result of significant innovation and the application of new technology.

No-frills model Reduction of the attributes of a product or service to the minimum possible number.

Non-equity strategic alliance A cooperative venture in which there is no cross-ownership.

Normal profit Either the minimum rate of profit which would ensure the continuing presence of an enterprise in a particular market or the opportunity cost of using the capital invested in the enterprise, that is, what could be earned in the next best alternative use.

Old economy The set of industries which have reached maturity or adulthood.

Oligopoly The existence of only a few sellers in a market or industry.

Open problem A problem which is not articulated explicitly and requires definition, and therefore has a multitude of possible solutions.

Opportunistic behaviour Behaviour which exploits the possibility of short-term gain at the expense of long-term advantage.

Opportunity An opportunity is a possibility for advancing the aims of an organization, notably by making a profit or improving performance in another way.

Opportunity cost The value of any benefit lost by making a particular choice rather than the next best.

Optimization The process of finding the optimum solution to a problem, usually involving the achievement of a maximum or minimum value of a variable.

Option A future possibility for action kept open, usually at some cost.

Organic growth Growth which results from activities having their origin and location within the enterprise.

Organizational slack The failure of an organization to work with the full efficiency which is possible, with a resulting surplus of resources above what is strictly necessary.

Output gap The degree to which aggregate supply tends to run ahead of demand in an economic system.

Outsource To purchase an input from outside the enterprise rather than to make it.

Paradigm The unique set of attitudes, beliefs and behavioural patterns which characterize any organization.

Paradigm shift A major change in the unique set of attitudes, beliefs and behavioural patterns which characterize any organization.

Participation strategy The strategy for entering an international market.

Partitioning The development of separate specialized units or activities.

Path dependency The tendency for the present state of any organizational unit to reflect its unique history or experience. Sometimes referred to as *hysteresis*.

Perception device A mechanism for improving the ability to read and understand a situation.

Perfect competition The existence of so many sellers and buyers in a market or an industry that no single one can influence the level of price.

Peripheral vision The ability to recognize strategic information which is to be found outside the main focus of attention.

Person culture A corporate culture which stresses the role of the individual.

Pillar industry A sector of the economy which is of critical importance to that economy.

Point-based concurrent engineering system A system in which different activities, design, manufacturing and engineering, are conducted at the same time.

Point-based serial engineering system A system in which the different activities are conducted in a defined sequence.

Political clout The ability to influence government agencies in their decision making.

Political risk That which arises as a consequence of political uncertainties

and which can involve the imposition of a cost or reduction of revenue from an investment abroad.

Polycentric approach One which recognizes the existence of many different cultures and therefore markets.

Portfolio A group of assets or products.

Portfolio investment A passive form of investment in paper assets such as shares or bonds.

Positioning The location, whether deliberate or not, of an organization with respect to product, industry, activity or market segment.

Power culture A corporate culture which stresses the role of the person or persons in power.

Practical reason This is the application of the principles of reason to action rather than thought.

Predetermined elements Those features of a strategic environment which are unchanging.

Predict Anticipate a future event or series of events.

Present value This is the value today of a stream of net benefits which will accrue in the future.

Price elasticity of demand The responsiveness of demand for a product to a change in price. As a ratio it is the proportional change in demand for the product over the change in price.

Price leadership Price leadership is a generic strategy in which an enterprise uses price to outcompete its competitors.

Pricing strategy The deliberate use of price as part of a business strategy.

Primary activities Those activities which are central elements in a value-adding chain.

Principal The person responsible for initiating or organizing a particular strategic act.

Prisoner's dilemma The dilemma common in situations in which there is a lack of communication and/or trust between players which leads each of them to seek to maximize their advantage at the cost of a loss to all.

Procedural rationality The application of reason to the process of deliberation relevant to a particular problem.

Processual approach An approach to strategy making which stresses the constraints on the process itself.

Product bundle A set of attributes associated with a particular product.

Product differentiation A generic strategy in which an enterprise persuades its customers that its product or service is superior to that of its competitors.

Production function The formula by which economists interpret the conversion of inputs into outputs in the act of production.

Public good A good to which the exclusion principle cannot be fully applied, that is, one which is available at less than full cost.

Pure reason The system of reasoning which uses the criteria of logic to draw inferences from initial axioms.

Quasi-integration A limited degree of integration of the value-adding chain in which there is not full ownership of the units in the chain.

Rationality This is the belief in the consistent and systematic application of reason to the solution of problems.

Reading the general environment The process of identifying information in the external environment of an organization.

Reader The person who does the reading.

Reference group A group by which a person measures him or herself.

Regionalism The tendency for countries which are in close proximity to integrate economically and politically.

Reinsurance Where the insurer obtains partial or complete insurance coverage from another insurer for a risk on which a policy has already been issued.

Rent seeking Behaviour which seeks to redistribute existing income in one's own favour rather than to create new income by innovation.

Resource Anything which directly or indirectly adds ultimate value to a final product or service.

Resource audit A review and listing of all the resources to which an organization has access.

Resource-based model A system of procedures for making strategy which takes as its starting point the resources to which the enterprise has access.

Revenue management policy This involves charging different prices according to the intensity of customer demand for the product.

Risk The calculable probability of a harmful event or outcome occurring.

Risk appetite The degree to which individuals are willing to bear risk.

Risk assessment The process of assessing and measuring the level of risk in different areas of the economic system.

Risk aversion A distaste for engaging in risky activities.

Risk avoidance The deliberate avoidance of any activities which seem to be risky.

Risk control The attempt to reduce the level of uncertainty confronting an enterprise by avoiding, managing or mitigating risk, and limiting the possible impact of any threat or shock which occurs.

Risk management The process of protecting an organization against the various threats in its environment by redistributing the risk to others, by a commercial transaction or a strategic alliance.

Risk mitigation The attempt to reduce the level of risk confronting an organization.

Risk premium The additional return required of a project or activity which justifies exposure to additional risk.

Risk-generating events Events which can potentially cause a large negative fluctuation in a performance indicator.

Role culture A corporate culture which stresses the importance of specialized positions.

Rolling (flexible) plan A plan which is adjusted according to changing circumstances.

Satisficing The strategy of aiming to produce outcomes which satisfy all stakeholder groups, rather than aiming at a single maximizing outcome for a performance indicator such as profit, which satisfies the owners alone.

Scanning The process of quickly casting an eye over a mass of information relating to the future. The first step in reading the general environment.

Scenario A possible path of future development with respect to an area or performance indicator.

Scenario building The process of constructing scenarios.

Scenario planning The process of making strategy on the basis of scenario building.

Search costs The costs of searching for partners in any market transaction.

Self-organization The capacity of any disorganized system to develop systematic and persistent patterns of organization.

Sensitivity analysis The testing of the sensitivity of a strategy to a change in the value of a variable.

Serendipity The recognition of a chance discovery as potentially useful.

Shock An unexpected event with a significant negative impact on economic performance.

Signal An indication by one strategic player to others of what action is intended, an indication which may be correct or not.

Signal effectiveness The effectiveness with which any signal is given.

Signal reaction The way in which a player reacts to a signal.

Small numbers contracting A situation where there are few potential partners to a desired transaction.

Social web The complex network of human interactions which occur within an organization.

Software Whatever makes hardware operate to the benefit of a consumer, for example the instructions of a computer program, or comprises the content of what is being communicated, for example music, film or data.

Staging The choice of a pathway by which to implement a set of strategy objectives.

Stakeholder Any individual or group with a significant interest in the performance of an organization.

Stock option An option to buy a share at a fixed price and usually at a fixed time.

Strategic action A series of acts informed by a strategic intent.

Strategic activities Conceptually separate activities relevant to the making of a strategy, such as formulation, implementation, monitoring, thinking, management or planning.

Strategic alliance A systematic act of cooperation between separate organizations.

Strategic audit A systematic evaluation of the success of a strategy, notably the appropriateness to environments and the effectiveness of implementation.

Strategic business unit The units responsible for making strategy in a particular product area.

Strategic canvas A visual method by which an organization can show its relative success in achieving different attributes for a product or service.

Strategic centre enterprise An enterprise which is at the centre of a network of strategic alliances.

Strategic coherence The alignment of all the elements of strategy making in a way which makes them consistent with each other.

Strategic context The aspects of a strategy relevant to a particular activity.

Strategic danger Any negative influence of a failure to properly formulate, implement or monitor a strategy on the economic performance of the organization.

Strategic dilemma A potentially recurrent situation in which there are strategic decisions to be made.

Strategic domain The area of decision making relevant to the particular employee.

Strategic drift The growing gap between the strategy being implemented and a strategy appropriate to the changed environment.

Strategic empowerment The giving of power to individuals or groups to make strategic decisions in their 'domain' area.

Strategic inertia A failure to adjust strategy to suit changing circumstances.

Strategic intent An expression of the aims and objectives of a strategy.

Strategic management The carrying out of various management functions in order to further the achievement of the strategic intent.

Strategic management system A means for ensuring the coherence of different functional areas of an organization in strategic management.

Strategic orientation The underlying view of the nature of strategy making held by the strategists.

Strategic planning The spelling out in detail of comprehensive written plans.

Strategic player Any individual or organization whose behaviour is likely to influence the outcome of a strategy.

Strategic risk A combination of country and competition risk.

Strategic situation A situation in which the decisions made should be informed by a strategic orientation.

Strategic thinking The combined use of creativity and rationality in the development of an innovatory strategic framework.

Structural context The formal context of an activity.

Structure The formal framework of an organization.

Substantive rationality The application of reason in the achievement of given goals when any action is subject to constraints.

Super-additivity A condition in which combination of two units results in

profits greater than the aggregated separate profits of the two units.

Super-brand status A brand which has a particularly high power to attract purchase on a continuing basis.

Supply-based explanation An explanation which focuses on the production or cost side.

Supply curve A curve which represents the relationship between the level of output and the level of costs at a given moment of time.

Support activities Those activities which assist in the successful operation of the primary activities but are outside the value-adding chain.

Supranationalization The ability of business transactions to become genuinely global, moving beyond national influence.

Sustaining innovation An innovation which represents a change which is within the existing technical or market parameters.

Swing producer The producer who can change price by varying its supply to the market.

Switching The act of moving from one activity, supplier or consumption good to another.

Switching costs The costs incurred, whether financial or psychological, in changing from the use or consumption of one product to that of another or from one source of supply to another.

Synergistic alliance A cooperative venture intended to lead to a significant reduction in costs by the partners.

System This is a complex set of interacting elements which have some overall coherence, such as an engineering system.

Systemic approach A perspective which stresses the influence of cultural difference on the nature of strategy.

Taper integration The retention of alternative sources of supply by an integrated enterprise.

Task culture A corporate culture which stresses the importance of the particular job or project.

Technique The process by which certain inputs are converted into outputs and the way in which such a process is organized.

Technology A set of techniques which belong to the same system.

The five Cs Command, control, coordination, communication and conflict (consensus).

The triad The three centres, or poles, responsible for most economic activity in the world – North America, the European Union and Japan.

Threat Any event which could damage the profitability or viability of an organization.

Three pillars The three elements of lifetime employment, promotion by seniority and enterprise unions which are alleged to have constituted the essence of the Japanese employment relations system.

Time activity rate A measure of some quantitative indicator over a conventional period of time.

Time horizon The time period which is relevant to strategy making.

Time pacing The setting of a speed of strategy implementation according to the requirements of the strategy itself and the enterprise implementing that strategy.

'Tit-for-tat' strategy A strategy in which a player repeats the play of the other player.

Tokenism The tendency to do something for the sake of form but not to do it with real intent to achieve its basic purpose.

Total factor productivity A measure of the efficiency with which all factors of production are used.

Total value added The difference between the opportunity cost of all inputs and the prices consumers are willing to pay for the final product.

Transaction costs The costs associated with a particular transaction, usually defined to include search, negotiation and enforcement costs.

Transaction cycle The pattern of stages through which a typical product passes during its lifetime.

Transaction economies Reductions in transaction costs.

Transfer risk That which arises as a consequence of uncertainties concerning the value of a currency and which can involve a reduction in the income arising from an international transaction.

Transformation situation A set of circumstances which make necessary a radical change in the organization, whether of structure or strategy or both.

Triple bottom line Performance as measured by profit, plus some measure(s) of environmental impact and some measure(s) of social impact.

Turnaround A situation in which the performance of an organization has deteriorated so badly that it makes necessary a transformation.

Turnkey project One in which an organization carries out all the activities from design to operational testing before turning the project over to another enterprise to operate. Sometimes called BOOT (build, own, operate, transfer) and, in some economies, such as China, BOT (build, operate, transfer).

Uncertainty A state of ignorance of what might happen in the future.

Uncertainty reducing alliance A cooperative venture intended to reduce risk.

Uniqueness drivers The factors which differentiate one product or service from another.

Utility A set of perceived wants related to a feature such as luxury or youth which is a powerful source of value to the consumer of a product.

Valuation ratio The relationship between the market and the book values of an enterprise.

Variable costs The costs whose level changes with the level of output.

Variance A measure of the variability of a performance indicator.

Vertical alliance A cooperative venture which involves enterprises operating at different points on the value-adding chain.

Vertical fracturing A failure to maintain links between the different levels of decision making within an organization.

Vertical integration The combining into a single enterprise of activities at different points in the value-adding chain.

Vertical thinking The application of rationality, or sustained reason, in the solution of a problem.

Virtue matrix A representation of the degree of corporate responsibility set out in a matrix.

Vision The core of a strategic intent which envisages a significant remaking of both external and internal environments as an aim of the organization.

Wicked problem A problem of some complexity with divergent solutions requiring creative lateral thought for a solution.

Winner-takes-all politics The mechanism by which the winners, those in power, systematically ensure that the distribution of any rewards favours them and disfavours the losers.

World enterprise An enterprise which has broken its connections with a particular country and has become truly global.

Zero-sum game A game or transaction in which if one wins the other loses, rather than a non-zero-sum game in which both can win.

Bibliography

Aaker, D.A. *Building Strong Brands* (The Free Press, New York: 1996).

Aaker, D.A., 'Managing assets and skills: the key to sustainable competitive advantage', *California Management Review*, **31**(2) 1998: 91–100.

Aaker, D.A. *Developing Business Strategies*, 6th edn (Chichester, New York: 2001).

Aaker, D.A. and Jacobson, R., 'The risk of marketing: the role of systematic, uncontrollable, and controllable unsystematic, and downside risk' in Bettis, R.A. and Thomas, H. (eds) *Risk, Strategy and Management* (JAI Press, London: 1990): 137–60.

Aaker, D.A. and Joachimsthaler, E. *Brand Leadership* (The Free Press, New York: 2000).

Abernathy, W.J. and Wayne, K.,'Limits of the learning curve', *Harvard Business Review*, Sept–Oct 1974: 109–19.

Ackoff, R.L., 'Beyond prediction and preparation', *Journal of Management Studies*, **20** Jan 1983: 59–69.

Aggrawala, R., 'Technology and globalization as mutual reinforcers in business: reorienting strategic thinking for the new millennium', *Management International Review*, **39**(2) 1999: 83–104.

Alchian, A. and Demsetz, H., 'Production, information costs, and economic organization' *American Economic Review*, **62** Dec 1972: 177–95.

Amabile, T.M., 'How to kill creativity', *Harvard Business Review*, Sept–Oct 1998: 77–87.

Anderson, E. and Gatignon, H., 'Modes of foreign entry: a transaction cost analysis and proposition', *Journal of Business Studies*, **17** 1986: 1–26.

Anderson, K. and Norman, D. *Global Wine Production, Consumption and Trade, 1961–2001: a statistical compendium* (Centre for International Economic Studies, Adelaide: 2003).

Ansoff, H.I. *Corporate Strategy* (McGraw-Hill, New York: 1965).

Anslinger, P.L. and Copeland, T.E., 'Growth through acquisition: a fresh look' *Harvard Business Review*, Jan–Feb 1996: 126–35.

Argenti, J. *Corporate Collapse: causes and symptoms* (McGraw-Hill, New York: 1976).

Axelrod, R. *The Evolution of Cooperation* (Basic Books, New York: 1984).

Axelrod, R., 'A survey of globalisation', *The Economist*, September 29, 2001.

Ayres, F.L. and Logue, D.E., 'Risk management in the shadow of Enron', *Journal of Business Strategy*, **23**(4) 2002: 36–50.

Badaracco, J.L. *Defining Moments: when managers must choose between right and wrong* (Harvard Business School, Boston, MA: 1997).

Barney, J., Wright, M., and Ketchen, D.J. Jr, 'The resource-based view of the firm: ten years after 1991', *Journal of Management*, **27**(6) 2001: 625–41.

Barney, J.B., 'Firm resources and sustained competitive advantage', *Journal of Management*, **17** 1991: 99–120.

Barney, J.B., 'Looking inside for competitive advantage' *Academy of Management Executive*, **9**(4) Nov 1995: 49–61.

Barney, J.B., 'Is the resource-based view a useful perspective for strategic management research? Yes', *Academy of Management Review*, **26**(1) 2001: 22–66.

Bartlett, C.A. and Ghoshal, S. *The Transnational Solution: managing across borders* (Harvard Business School Press, Boston, MA: 1989).

Bartlett, C. and Ghoshal, S. (eds) *Trans-national Management* (Irwin, Homewood, IL: 1992).

Baumol, W.J., 'Entrepreneurship in economic theory', *American Economic Review*, **58** May 1968: 64–71.

Beer, M. and Eisenstat, R.A., 'The silent killers of strategy implementation and learning', *Sloan Management Review*, **41**(4) 2000: 29–40.

Bernstein, P.L. *Against the Gods; the remarkable story of risk* (John Wiley, New York: 1998).

Bettinger, C., 'Use corporate culture to trigger high performance', *Journal of Business Strategy*, **10**(2) 1989: 38–41.

Biggadike, H.R., 'The risky business of diversification', *Harvard Business Review*, **57** May–June 1979: 103–11.

Bingelli, U. and Pompeo, L., 'Hyped hopes for Europe's low-cost airlines', *McKinsey Quarterly*, (4) 2002: 86.

Bower, J.L. and Hout, T.M., 'Fast-cycle capability for competitive power', *Harvard Business Review*, **66**(6) 1988: 110–18.

Bowman, C. and Faulkner, D. *Competitive and Cooperative Strategy* (Irwin, Burr Ridge, IL: 1996).

Bradley, F. *International Marketing Strategy*, 2nd edn (Prentice Hall, London: 1995).

Brandenburger, A.N. and Nalebuff, B.J., 'The right game: use game theory to shape strategy', *Harvard Business Review*, July–Aug 1995: 57–71.

Brandenburger, A.N. and Nalebuff, B.J. *Coopetition* (Doubleday, New York: 1996).

Branigan, T. and Vidal, J., 'Naked power play from the mamas', *The Age*, July 27, 2002: 22 (*Financial Times* Special Report: Nigeria, June 10, 2003).

Branson, R., 'Reflections of a risk-taker', *McKinsey Quarterly*, summer 1986: 13–18.

Bresada, A., 'Strategic benchmarking', *Financial World*, September 29, 1992: 30–8.

Brigham, E.F. and Houston, J.F. *Fundamentals of Financial Management* (The Dryden Press, Fort Worth et al.,1998), MVA and EVA: 45–7.

Brodwin, D.R. and Bourgeois, L.J., 'Five steps to strategic action', *California Management Review*, **26**(3) 1984: 176–90.

Brush, T.H., 'Predicted changes in operational synergy and post acquisition performance of acquitted businesses', *Strategic Management Journal*, **17** 1996: 1–24.

Bryan, D. and Rafferty, M. *The Global Economy in Australia: global integration and national economic policy* (Allen & Unwin, St Leonards, NSW: 1999).

Burgelman, R.A., 'Corporate entrepreneurship and strategic management: insights from a process study', *Management Science*, **29** 1983: 1349–64.

Burgelman, R.A., 'Managing the new venture division: research findings and implications for strategic management', *Strategic Management Journal*, **6** 1985: 39–54.

Burgelman, R.A. *Strategy is Destiny* (The Free Press, New York: 2000).

Burgelman, R.A. and Grove, A.S., 'Strategic dissonance', *California Management Review*, winter 1996: 8–28.

Business Week, 'The stateless corporation', 14 May, 1991: 98–104.

Buzzell, R.D., Bradley, T.G. and Sultan, R.G.M., 'Market share: a key to profitability', *Harvard Business Review*, Jan–Feb 1975: 97–111.

Calverley, J. *Country Risk Analysis* (Butterworth, London: 1985).

Camp, R.C. *Benchmarking: the search for industry best practices that lead to superior performance* (ASQC Quality Press, Milwaukee: 1989).

Camuffo, A., Romano, P. and Vinelli, A., 'Back to the future: Benetton transforms its global reach', *MIT Sloan Management Review*, **43**(1) 2001: 50.

Catoni, L., Larssen, N.F., Naylor, J. and Zocchi, A., 'Travel tips for retailers', *McKinsey Quarterly*, **3** 2002: 126.

Caulkin, S., 'Who's in charge here? Nobody', *The Japan Times*, May 19, 2003: 13.

Chandler, A.D. Jr *Strategy and Structure: chapters in the history of industrial enterprise* (MIT Press, Cambridge, MA: 1962).

Chandler, A.D. Jr *The Visible Hand – the managerial revolution in American business* (Belknap Press, Cambridge, MA: 1977).

Chandler, A.D. Jr *Scale and Scope: the dynamics of industrial capitalism* (Belknap Press, Cambridge, MA: 1990).

Cheng, A.T., 'Reform or die', *Asia-Inc.*, July 2002: 19.

Chessell, J., 'Greed', *The Age*, April 3, 2002.

Christensen, C.M., *The Innovator's Dilemma* (Harvard Business School Press, Boston: 1997).

Christensen, C.M., 'Glass half full', *Global Cosmetic Industry*, **171**(2) Feb 2003: 40, 45.

Christensen, C.M. and Bower, J., 'Customer power, strategic investment and the failure of leading firms', *Strategic Management Journal*, March 1996: 197–218.

Christensen, C.M., Johnson, M.W. and Rigby, D.K., 'Foundations for growth: how to identify and build disruptive new businesses', *Sloan Management Review*, **43**(3) 2002: 23–31.

Clement, R.W., 'Culture, leadership, and power: the keys to organizational change', *Business Horizons*, **37**(1) 1994: 33–9.

Coakley, J., Kulasi, F. and Smith, R., 'Current account solvency and the Feldstein-Horioka Puzzle', *The Economic Journal*, **106** May 1996: 620–7.

Coase, R., 'The nature of the firm', *Economica*, **4** 1937: 386–405.

Coleman, J., 'Social capital in the creation of human capital', *American Journal of Sociology*, **94** (Supplement) 1988: 95–120.

Collis, D.J. and Montgomery, C.A., 'Competing on resources: strategy in the 1990s', *Harvard Business Review*, July–Aug 1995: 118–28.

Coltman, T., Devinney, T.M., Lutukefu, A.S. and Midgley, D.F., 'Keeping E-business in perspective', *Communications of the ACM*, **45**(8) 2002: 69–73.

Commons, J.R. *Institutional Economics* (Macmillan, New York: 1934).

Contractor, F.J., 'The role of licensing in international strategy', *Columbia Journal of World Business*, winter 1982: 73–83.

Cooper, R. and Kaplan, R.S., 'Measuring costs right: make the right decision', *Harvard Business Review*, **66**(5) 1988: 96–103.

Coplin, W.D. and O'Leary, M.K. *The Handbook of Country and Political Risk Analysis* (Political Risk Service, New York, 1994).

Costa, P.R., Harned, D.S. and Lundquist, J.T., 'Rethinking the aviation industry', *McKinsey Quarterly*, 2002: 89–100.

Courtney, H., Kirkland, J. and Viguerie, P., 'Strategy under uncertainty', *Harvard Business Review*, **75** Nov–Dec 1997: 66–79.

Coyne, K.P. and Dye, R., 'The competitive dynamics of

network-based businesses', *Harvard Business Review*, **76**(10) 1998: 99–109.

Cravens, D.W. *Strategic Marketing* (McGraw-Hill Irwin, Boston: 1997).

Daniels, J.D., Radebaugh, L.H. and Sullivan, D.P., 'Risk management and asset protection', in J.D. Daniels *Globalization and Business* (Prentice Hall, Upper Saddle River, NJ: 2001).

Das, T.K. and Bing-Sheng Teng, 'Managing risks in strategic alliances', *Business Horizons*, **31**(1) 1988: 34–41.

D'Aveni, R.A. *Hypercompetition: the dynamics of strategic manoeuvring* (The Free Press, New York: 1994).

Davis, J.G. and Devinney, T.M. *The Essence of Corporate Strategy: theory for modern decision making* (Allen & Unwin, St Leonards, NSW: 1997).

Davis, S.M. and Lawrence, P.R., 'Problems of matrix organizations', *Harvard Business Review*, **56**(3) 1978: 131–42.

de Bono, E. *Lateral Thinking: a textbook of creativity* (Penguin Books, London: 1970).

de Bono, E. *Lateral thinking for management: a handbook* (Penguin, Harmondsworth: 1971).

de Bono, E. *Serious Creativity: using the power of lateral thinking to create new ideas* (Harper Business, New York: 1992).

de Bono, E. *Six Thinking Hats* (Little, Brown, Boston: 1999).

de Geus, A.P., 'Planning as learning', *Harvard Business Review*, March–April 1988: 70–4.

de Souza, G., 'New service businesses must manage quality', *Journal of Business Strategy*, **10**(3) 1989: 21–5.

de Wit, R. and Meyer, R. *Strategy – Process, Content, Context: an international perspective*, 2nd edn (International Thomson Business Press, London: 1998).

Dixit, A. and Nalebuff, B., 'Anticipating your rival's response', in A. Dixit and B. Nalebuff *Thinking Strategically* (W.W. Norton, New York: 1991).

Dow, K. *Beyond Values at Risk: the new science of risk management* (John Wiley, London: 1998).

Dower, J.D. *Embracing Defeat: Japan in the wake of World War II* (W.W. Norton/The New Press, New York: 1999).

Doz, Y.L. and Hamel, G. *Alliance Advantage: the art of creating value through partnering* (Harvard Business School Press, Boston: 1998).

Drejer, A. *Strategic Management and Core Competencies: theory and application* (Quorum Books, Westport, CT, 2002).

Driscoll, D.-M. and Hoffman, W.M., 'Gaining the ethical edge: procedure for delivering values-driven

management', *Long Range Planning*, **32**(2) 1999: 179–89.

Dumaine, B., 'Asia's wealth creation confronts a new reality', *Fortune*, December 8, 1997: 42–52.

Duncan, R., 'What is the right organizational structure?', *Organizational Dynamics*, winter 1979: 59–80.

Dunning, J., 'Governments and macro-organisation of economic activity: a historical and spatial perspective', in J.H. Dunning (ed.) *Governments, Globalisation and International Business* (Oxford University Press, Oxford: 1997a): 31–73.

Dunning, J. *Alliance Capitalism and Global Business* (Routledge, London: 1997b).

Dunning, J. *Globalization, Trade and Foreign Direct Investment* (Elsevier, Oxford: 1998).

Durack, T., 'Topless performer', The Sunday Review, *Sunday Times*, September 1, 2002: 35.

Economist, The, 'The Jack and Jeff show loses its lustre', May 4, 2002: 57.

Economist, The, 'Cheers mate! A smart beermat may help to stop drug-facilitated rape', June 1, 2002: 97.

Economist, The, 'Dynastic progression', **364** July 13, 2002: 52.

Egan, C. *Creating Organisational Advantage* (Butterworth-Heinemann, Oxford: 1995).

Eisenhardt, K.M. and Brown, S.L., 'Time pacing: competing in markets that won't stand still', *Harvard Business Review*, March–April 1998: 59–69.

Eisenhardt, K.M. and Sull, D.N., 'Strategy as simple rules', *Harvard Business Review*, **79**(1) 2001:107–16.

Elder, J., 'The Virgin Knight', *The Age*, Sunday Life, November 24, 2002: 26–31.

Elenkov, D.S., 'Strategic uncertainty and environmental scanning: the case for institutional influences on scanning behavior', *Strategic Management Journal*, **18** 1997: 287–302.

Ellman, M. *Socialist Planning*, 2nd edn (Cambridge University Press, Cambridge: 1989).

Fahey, J., 'Love into money', *Forbes*, **169**(1) 2002: 30.

Fama, E.F., 'Agency problems and the theory of the firm', *Journal of Political Economy*, **88** 1980: 375–90.

Feldstein, M. and Horioka, C., 'Domestic saving and international capital flows', *The Economic Journal*, **90** June 1980: 314–29.

Fischer, D.H. *The Great Wave: price revolutions and the rhythm of history* (OUP, New York: 1996).

Fisher, M.L., 'What is the right supply chain for your product?', *Harvard Business Review*, **76**(3) 1997: 139–47.

Fitzgerald, B., 'Miners see red over Africa's black devolution', *The Age*, July 30, 2002.

Fitzmaurice, E., '$300 bread a bit rich', *The Herald Sun*, September 8, 2002.

Floyd, S.W. and Wooldridge, B., 'Managing strategic consensus: the foundation of effective implementation', *Academy of Management Executive*, **6**(4) 1992: 27–39.

Foreign Affairs, 'The clash of civilisations', **72**(3) 1993: 22–8.

Forster, J. and Browne, M. *Principles of Strategic Management* (Macmillan, Melbourne: 1996).

Franzen, J. *The Corrections* (Fourth Estate, 2001), quoted by Andrew Cornell in 'Cult of Luxury: the new opiate of the masses', *Weekend Australian Financial Review*, April 27–28, 2002: 47.

Friedman, M., 'The social responsibility of business is to increase profit', *The New York Times Magazine*, September 13, 1970.

Friedman, M. *Capitalism and Freedom* (Chicago University Press, Chicago: 1971).

Friedman, T. *The Lexus and the Olive Tree* (HarperCollins, New York: 1999).

Fukuyama, F. *The End of History and the Last Man* (Avon Books, New York: 1992).

Fukuyama, F. *Trust: The social virtues and the creation of prosperity* (Hamish Hamilton, London: 1995).

Galbraith, J.R. *Designing Organizations* (Jossey-Bass, San Francisco: 1995).

Garvin, D., 'What does product quality really mean?', *Sloan Management Review*, **26** 1984: 25 –44.

Geller, D. *The Brian Epstein Story* (Faber & Faber, London: 2000).

Ghemawat, P., 'Building strategy on the experience curve', *Harvard Business Review*, March–April 1985: 143–9.

Ghemawat, P. *Commitment: the dynamic of strategy* (The Free Press, New York: 1991).

Ghemawat, P. *Games Businesses Play: cases and models* (MIT Press, Cambridge, MA: 1997).

Ghemawat, P. *Strategy and the Business Landscape: text and cases* (Addison-Wesley, Reading, MA: 1999).

Ghoshal, S. 'Global strategy: an organizing framework', *Strategic Management Journal*, **21** 2000: 51–80.

Giddens, A. *Runaway World: The Reith Lectures revisited (1999)*, to be found at www.globalisationguide.org.

Goleman, D., 'What makes a leader?', *Harvard Business Review*, Nov–Dec 1998: 92–105.

Goll, I. and Rasheed, A.M.A., 'Rational decision-making and firm performance: the moderating role of environment', *Strategic Management Journal*, **18** 1997: 583–91.

Goold, M. and Luchs, K., 'Why diversify? Four decades of management thinking', *Academy of Management Executive*, **7**(3) 1993: 7–25.

Grant, R.M. *Contemporary Strategy Analysis: concepts, techniques, applications* (Blackwell, Oxford: 1991).

Grant, R.M. *Contemporary Strategy Analysis: concepts, techniques, applications*, 4th edn (Blackwell, Oxford: 2002).

Hall, W.K., 'Survival strategies in a hostile environment', *Harvard Business Review*, Sept–Oct 1980: 78–81.

Hambrick, D.C., 'High profit strategies in mature capital goods industries: a contingency approach', *Academy of Management Journal*, **26** 1983: 687–707.

Hambrick, D.C., 'Putting top managers back into the picture' *Strategic Management Journal*, **10** (special issue) 1989: 5–15.

Hambrick, D.C. and Fredrickson, J.W., 'Are you sure you have a strategy?' *Academy of Management Executive*, November 2001: 48–59.

Hamel, G., 'Strategy as a revolution', *Harvard Business Review*, **74**(4) 1996: 69–82.

Hamel, G., 'Bringing Silicon Valley inside', *Harvard Business Review*, **7**(5) 1999: 70–84.

Hamel, G. and Prahalad, C.K., 'Strategic intent', *Harvard Business Review*, May–June 1989.

Hamel, G. and Prahalad, C.K. *Competing for the Future* (The Free Press, New York: 1994).

Hampden, C. and Trompenaars, A. *The Seven Cultures of Capitalism: values systems for creating wealth in the United States, Japan, Germany, France, Britain, Sweden and the Netherlands* (Currency Doubleday, New York: 1993).

Handy, C.B. *Understanding Organizations*, 4th edn (Penguin, London: 1983).

Hanlon, P. *Global Airlines: Competition in a trans-national industry*, 2nd edn (Butterworth Heinemann, Oxford: 1999).

Hannan, M., 'Corporate growth through internal spinouts', *Harvard Business Review*, **47**(6) 1969: 55–66.

Hannen, M. and Way, N., 'Run the risk', *Business Review Weekly*, July 25–31, 2002: 51.

Harrigan, K.R., 'A framework for looking at vertical integration', *Journal of Business Strategy*, **3**(3) 1983: 3–7.

Harrigan, K.R., 'Formulating vertical integration strategies', *Academy of Management Review*, **9** 1984: 638–52.

Harrigan, K.R., 'Vertical integration and corporate strategy', *Academy of Management Journal*, **28** 1985a: 397–425.

Harrigan, K.R. *Strategic Flexibility* (Lexington Books, Lexington, MA: 1985b).

Hart, S.L., 'An integrative framework of strategy making processes' *Academy of Management Review*, **17** 1992: 327–51.

Haspeslagh, P. and Jemison, D. *Managing Acquisitions* (The Free Press, New York: 1991).

Hegert, M. and Morris, D., 'Accounting data for value chain analysis', *Strategic Management Journal*, **10** 1989: 175–88.

Held, D., McGrew, A., Goldblatt, D. and Perraton, J. *Global Transformations: politics, economics and culture* (Polity Press, Cambridge: 1999).

Henderson, B.D. *Henderson on Corporate Strategy* (Abt Books, Cambridge, MA: 1979).

Henderson, B.D. *The Logic of Business Strategy* (Ballinger Publishing, Cambridge, MA: 1984).

Henderson, J.C., 'Plugging into strategic partnerships; the critical is connection', *Sloan Management Review*, **31**(3) 1990: 7–18.

Heracleous, L., 'The role of strategy implementation in organization development' *Organization Development Journal*, **18**(3) 2000: 75–86.

Herzberg, F., 'One more time: how do you motivate employees?', *Harvard Business Review*, **65**(4) 1987: 109–20.

Hextall, B., 'S. African plan could claim BHP assts', *Australian Financial Review*, October 11, 2002: 58.

Hill, A., Marsh, P. and Roberts, D., 'GE must hone predatory instincts to ensure survival', *Financial Times*, June 21, 2002: 26.

Hill, C.W.L. *International Business: competing in the global marketplace* (McGraw-Hill Irwin, Boston: 2003).

Hill, C.W.L. and Deeds, D., 'The importance of industry structure to the determination of industry profitability: a neo-Austrian approach', *Journal of Management Studies*, **33** 1996: 429–51.

Hill, C.W.L. and Jones, G.R. *Strategic Management: an integrated approach* (Houghton Mifflin, Boston, 2001).

Hill, C.W.L. and Jones, G.R. *Strategic Management*, 5th edn (Houghton Mifflin, Boston: 2003).

Hill. C.W.L. and Jones, T.M., 'Stakeholder-agency theory', *Journal of Management Studies*, **29** 1992: 131–54.

Hill, C.W.L. and Kim, W.C., 'Searching for a dynamic theory of the multinational enterprise: a transaction cost model' *Strategic Management Journal* **9** (Special issue on Strategy Context) 1988: 93–104.

Hill, C.W.L., Huang, P. and Kim, W.C., 'An eclectic theory of the choice of intended entry mode', *Strategic Management Journal*, **11** 1990: 117–28.

Hill, C.W.L., Heeley, M. and Sakson, J., 'Strategies for profiting from innovation', in L.R. Gomez-Mejia *Advances in Global High Technology Management* (JAI Press, Greenwich, CT: 1993), **III**: 79–95.

Hilmetz, S.D. and Bridge, R.S., 'Gauging the returns on investments in competitive intelligence: a three-step analysis for executive decision makers', *Competitive Intelligence Review*, **10**(1) 1999: 4–11

Hirschhorn, L. and Gilmore, T., 'The new boundaries of the "boundary-less" company', *Harvard Business Review*, May–June 1992: 108–15.

Hirst, P. and Thompson, G. *Globalization in Question: The international economy and the possibilities of governance*, revised 2nd edn (Polity Press, Cambridge: 2001).

Hitt, M.A., Dacin, T., Tyler B. and Park, D., 'Understanding the difference in Korean and U.S. executive strategic orientations', *Strategic Management Journal*, (**18**) 1996: 159–67.

Hitt, M.A., Ireland, R.D. and Hoskisson, R.E. *Strategic Management: competitiveness and globalization*, 2nd edn (South-Western Publishing, Cincinnati: 1997).

Hitt, M.A., Ireland, R.D. and Hoskisson, R.E. *Strategic Management: competitiveness and globalization*, 4th edn (South-Western Publishing, Cincinatti: 2001).

Hofer, C.W. and Schendel, D. *Strategy Formulation: analytical concepts* (West Publishing, St Paul, MN: 1978).

Hoffman, R.C., 'Strategies for turnarounds: what do we know about them?', *Journal of General Management*, **14** 1984: 46–66.

Hofstede, G. *Cultures and Organizations* (McGraw-Hill, London: 1991).

Hogarth, R.M. and Makridakis, S., 'Forecasting and planning: an evaluation', *Management Science*, **27**(2) 1981: 115–38.

Holloway, N., 'Branding machine', *Business Review Weekly*, August 1–7, 2002: 82–4.

Howell, D. and Chaddick, B., 'Models of political risk for foreign investment and trade', *Columbia Journal of World Business*, **29**(3) 1994: 70–92.

Hu, Y-S., 'Global or stateless corporations are national firms with international operations', *California Management Review*, **34**(2) 1992: 107–26.

Huff, J.O., Huff, A.S. and Thomas, H., 'Strategic renewal and the interaction of cumulative stress and inertia', *Strategic Management Journal*, **13** 1992 (Special issue): 55–75.

Humble, J., Jackson, D. and Thomson, A., 'The strategic power of corporate values', *Long Range Planning*, **27**(6) 1994: 28–42.

Huntingdon, S. *The Clash of Civilizations and the Remaking of the World Order* (Simon & Schuster, New York: 1996).

Jacobson, R., 'The Austrian school of strategy', *Academy of Management Review*, **17** 1992: 782–807.

James, C., 'No more weekends at Bernie's', *Sport Age*, May 15, 2002: 8.

Jawahar, I.M. and McLaughlin, G.L., 'Towards a descriptive stakeholder theory: an organizational life cycle approach', *Academy of Management Review*, **26**(3) 2001: 397–414.

Jeannet, J.-P. and Hennessey, H.D., *Global Marketing Strategies*, 4th edn (Houghton Mifflin, Boston: 1998).

Jensen, M.C., 'The modern industrial revolution, exit,

and the failure of internal control systems', *Journal of Finance*, July 1993, **48**(3): 831–80.

Johnson, B.C., 'Retail: the Wal-Mart effect', *The McKinsey Quarterly*, (1) 2002: 40–3.

Johnson, G. and Scholes, K. *Explaining Corporate Strategy* (Prentice Hall, New York: 1993).

Johnson, J. and Burt, T., 'Vivendi needs firesale to service debt', *Financial Times*, August 21, 2002: 20.

Jones, R. and Hill, C.W.L., 'A transaction cost analysis of strategy-structure choice', *Strategic Management Journal*, **9** 1988: 159–72.

Jones, R. and Hill, C.W.L. 'National institutional structures, transaction cost economizing, and competitive advantage', *Organizational Science*, **6** 1995: 119–31.

Kamprad, I. and Torekull, B. *Leading by Design: the IKEA Story* (HarperCollins: 2000).

Kaplan, R.S. and Norton, D.P., 'The balanced scorecard – measures that drive performance', *Harvard Business Review*, Jan–Feb 1992: 71–9.

Kaplan, R.S. and Norton, D.P., 'Putting the balanced scorecard to work', *Harvard Business Review*, Sept–Oct 1993: 134–47.

Kaplan, R.S. and Norton, D.P. *The Balanced Scorecard* (Harvard Business School, Boston: 1996a).

Kaplan, R.S. and Norton, D.P., 'Using the balanced scorecard as a strategic management system', *Harvard Business Review*, Jan–Feb 1996b: 75–85.

Katzenbach, J.R. and Santamaria, J.A., 'Firming up the front line', *Harvard Business Review*, **77**(3) 1999: 107–17.

Kenwood, A.G. and Lougheed, A.L. *The Growth of the International Economy 1820–2000*, 4th edn (Routledge, London: 1999).

Kerr, S., 'On the folly of rewarding A while hoping for B', *Academy of Management Executive*, **9**(1) 1995: 7–14.

Kiechel, W., 'The decline of the experience curve', *Fortune*, October 5, 1981.

Kim, W.C. and Huang, P., 'Global strategy and multinationals' entry mode', *Journal of International Business*, Jan–March 1992: 29–53.

Kim, W.C. and Mauborgne, R., 'Value innovation: the strategic logic of high growth', *Harvard Business Review*, Jan–Feb 1997: 102–15.

Kindleberger, C.P. *The World in Depression, 1929–1939* (Penguin, Harmondsworth: 1987).

King, E., 'Still in the bag?', *The Age*, July 31, 2002, The Culture: 4.

Kochan, T.A., 'Conflict: towards conceptual clarity', *Administrative Science Quarterly*, **13** 1972: 359–70.

Koestler, A. *The Act of Creation* (Arkana, London: 1989).

Kogut, B., 'Joint ventures: theoretical and empirical perspectives', *Strategic Management Journal*, **9** 1988: 319–32.

Kohn, A., 'Why incentive plans cannot work', *Harvard Business Review*, **71**(5) 1993: 54–63.

Kotler, P. *Marketing Management*, 9th edn (Prentice Hall, Englewood Cliffs, NJ: 1996).

Kotter, J.P. and Heskett, J.L. *Corporate Culture and Performance* (The Free Press, New York: 1992).

Krayenbuehl, T.E. *Country Risk Assessment and Monitoring* (Woodhead-Faulkner, Cambridge: 1985).

Kulkani, S., 'Purchasing: a supply-side strategy', *Journal of Business Strategy*, **17**(5) 1996: 17–20.

Larkin, J., 'Samsung tries to snatch Sony's crown', *Far Eastern Economic Review*, December 10, 2001: 36–43.

Latham, F. and Slajkovic, A.D., 'Reinforce for performance: the need to go beyond pay and even rewards', *Academy of Management Executive*, **13**(2) 1999: 49–57.

Lauenstein, M.C., 'Diversification: the hidden explanation of success', *Sloan Management Review*, Fall 1985: 49–55.

Learned, E.P., Christensen C.R., Andrews, K.R. and Guth, W.D. *Business Policy: text and cases* (Irwin, Homewood, IL: 1965).

Legge, J. and Hindle, K. *Entrepreneurship: how innovation creates the future* (Macmillan Education Australia, South Melbourne: 1997).

Levi, M.D. *International Finance: the markets and financial management of multinational business*, 3rd edn (McGraw-Hill, New York: 1996).

Levitt, T., 'The globalisation of markets', *Harvard Business Review*, May–June 1983: 92–102.

Liberman, M. and Montgomery, D., 'First-mover advantages', *Strategic Management Journal*, **9** (special issue) summer 1988: 41–58.

Liedtka, J.M., 'Linking strategic thinking with strategic planning', *Strategy and Leadership*, **26**(4) 1998a: 30–5.

Liedtka, J.M., 'Strategic thinking: can it be taught?', *Long Range Planning*, **31**(1) 1998b: 120–9.

Linneman, R.E. and Klein, H.E., 'Using scenarios in strategic decision making', *Business Horizons*, **2**(1) 1985: 64–74.

Litterer, J.A., 'Conflict in organization: a re-examination', *Academy of Management Journal*, **9** 1966: 178–86.

Loehle, C. *Thinking Strategically: power tools for personal and professional advancements* (Cambridge University Press, Cambridge: 1996).

Lubatkin, M. and Chatterjee, S., 'Extending modern portfolio theory into the domain of corporate diversification: does it apply?', *Academy of Management Journal*, **37**(1) 1994: 109–36.

Luce, R.D. and Raifa, H. *Games and Decisions* (Wiley & Sons, New York: 1957).

Lyons, B. and Varoukis, Y., 'Games theory, oligopoly and bargaining', in Hey, J. (ed.) *Current Issues in Microeconomics* (Macmillan, London: 1989).

McColl-Kennedy, J.R. and Kiel, G.C. *Marketing: a strategic approach* (Thomas Nelson, Melbourne: 2000).

McGahan, A. and Porter, M., 'How much does industry matter, really?', *Strategic Management Journal*, 1987: 15–30.

Mack, T., 'It's time to take risks', *Forbes*, October 6, 1986: 125–33.

McKinsey Quarterly 2002 (special edition: Risk and Resilience): 89–100.

Mackintosh, J., 'Carmakers reap benefit of taking no currency chances', *Financial Times*, June 3, 2003: 27.

Macmillan, I.C. and Jones, P.E., 'Designing organisations to compete', *Journal of Business Strategy*, **5** spring 1984: 12–16.

Macmillan, I.C. and Jones, P.E. *Strategy Formulation: power and politics* (West Publishing, St Paul, MN: 1986).

Madhok, A., 'Cost, value and foreign market entry: the transaction and the firm', *Strategic Management Journal*, **18** 1997: 39–61.

Madura, J. *Financial Markets and Institutions* (South-Western Publishing, Cincinatti: 2001).

Mahoney, D., Trigg, M., Griffin, R. and Pustay, M. *International Business: a managerial perspective* (Prentice Hall, Sydney: 2001).

Makridakis, S. *Forecasting, Planning and Strategy for the 21st Century* (The Free Press, New York: 1990).

Makrides, C.C., 'A dynamic view of strategy', *Sloan Management Review*, **40**(3) 1999: 55–63.

March, J.G. and Simon, H.A. *Organizations* (Wiley, New York: 1958).

Marks, M.L. and Mirvis, P.H., 'Rebuilding after the merger: dealing with survivor sickness', *Organisational Dynamics*, autumn 1992: 18–33.

Martin, R.L., 'The virtue matrix: calculating the return on corporate responsibility', *Harvard Business Review*, March 2002: 69–75.

Maslow, A. *Motivation and Personality* (Harper & Row, New York: 1954).

Mauri, A.J. and Michaels, M.P., 'Firms and industry effects within strategic management: an empirical examination', *Strategic Management Journal*, **19** 1998: 211–19.

Meldrum, D.H., 'Country risk and foreign direct investment', *Business Economics*, **1** Jan 2000: 33–40.

Meyer, A.D., 'What is strategy's distinctive competence?', *Journal of Management*, **17** 1991: 821–33.

Miller, A. and Dess, G.G., 'Assessing Porter's (1980) model in terms of its generalizability, accuracy and simplicity', *Journal of Management Studies*, **30** 1993: 553–85.

Miller, C.C. and Cardinal, L.B., 'Strategic planning and firm performance: a synthesis of more than two decades of research', *Academy of Management Journal*, **37** 1994: 1649–65.

Miller, D., 'Configurations of strategy and structure: towards a synthesis', *Strategic Management Journal*, **7** 1986: 233–49.

Miller, D. and Shamsie, J., 'The resource-based view of the firm in two environments: the Hollywood film studios from 1936 to 1965', *Academy of Management Journal*, **39**(3) 1996: 519–43.

Miller, K.D., 'A framework for integrated risk management in international business', *Journal of International Business Studies*, **23**(2) 1992: 311–31.

Mintzberg, H., 'Strategy-making in three modes', *California Management Review*, **16**(2) 1973: 44, 53.

Mintzberg, H., 'Organizational design: fashion or fit', *Harvard Business Review*, **59**(1) 1981: 103–16.

Mintzberg, H. *The Rise and Fall of Strategic Planning* (Prentice-Hall International, Hemel Hempstead: 1994).

Mintzberg, H., 'Musings on management', *Harvard Business Review*, July–Aug 1996: 5–11.

Mintzberg, H., 'Covert leadership', *Harvard Business Review*, Nov–Dec 1998: 140–47.

Mintzberg, H. and Lampel, J., 'Reflecting on the strategy process', *Sloan Management Review*, spring 1999: 21–30.

Mintzberg, H. and Quinn, J.B. (eds) *The Strategy Process; concepts, contexts, cases*, 3rd edn (Prentice Hall, Upper Saddle River, NJ: 1996).

Mintzberg, H. and Waters, J.A., 'Of strategies, deliberate and emergent', *Strategic Management Journal*, **6** 1985: 257–72.

Mintzberg, H., Ahlstrand, B. and Lampel, J. *Strategy Safari: a guided tour through the wilds of strategic management* (The Free Press, New York: 1998).

Mische, M.A. *Strategic Renewal: becoming a performance organization* (Prentice Hall, Upper Saddle River, NJ: 2001).

Mittelman, J.H. *The Globalisation Syndrome: transformation and resistance* (Princeton University Press, Princeton, NJ: 2000).

Mokyr, J. *The Lever of Riches: technological creativity and economic progress* (Oxford University Press, New York: 1990).

Moncrieff, J., 'Is strategy making a difference?', *Long Range Planning*, **32**(2) 1999: 273–6.

Nagle, T.T. *The Strategy and Tactics of Pricing: a guide to profitable decision making* (Prentice Hall, Englewood Cliffs, NJ: 1987).

Narula, R. *Multinational Investment and Economic Structure: globalization and competitiveness* (Routledge, London: 1996).

Nelson, C.A. *International Business: a manager's guide to strategy in the age of globalisation* (International Thomson Business Press, London: 1999).

Nolan, P. *China's Rise, Russia's Fall: politics, economics and planning in the transition from Stalinism* (Macmillan – now Palgrave Macmillan, Basingstoke: 1995).

North, D.C. *Structure and Change in Economic History* (Norton, New York: 1981).

North, D.C. *Institutions, Institutional Change, and Economic Performance* (Cambridge University Press, Cambridge: 1990).

O'Brien, K., 'Frugal brooders who spark a chain reaction', *Australian Financial Review*, September 27, 2002a: 72–3.

O'Brien, K., 'Aldi enters succession phase', *The Age*, September 26, 2002b, Business: 8.

O'Reilly, C., 'Corporations, culture and commitment: motivation and social control in organizations', *California Management Review*, 31(4) 1989: 9–25.

Ohmae, K. *The Borderless World: power and strategy in the interlinked economy* (Harper Perennial, London: 1991).

Ohmae, K. *The End of the Nation State: the rise of regional economies* (HarperCollins, London: 1995a).

Ohmae, K., 'Managing in a borderless world', in K. Ohmae (ed.) *The Evolving Global Economy: making sense of the new world order* (A Harvard Business Review Book: 1995b): 269–85.

Oldfield, S., 'Blacks-first policy sparks fears for BHP's future in South Africa', *Australian Financial Review*, July 30, 2002.

Oliver, A.R. and Garber, J.R., 'Implementing strategic planning: ten sure-fire ways to do it wrong', *Business Horizons*, 16(2) 1983: 49–51.

Olson, E.M. and Slater, S.F., 'The balanced scorecard, competitive strategy and performance', *Business Horizons*, May–June 2002: 11–16.

Olson, M. *The Rise and Decline of Nations* (Yale University Press, London: 1982).

Orr, D., 'Biotech wizard', *Forbes*, June 24, 2002: 6–19.

Pascale, R.T., 'The Honda effect', *California Management Review*, 38(4) 1996: 80–91.

Penrose, E.T. *The Theory of the Growth of the Firm* (Basil Blackwell, Oxford: 1959).

Perraton, J., 'The global economy – myths and realities', *Cambridge Journal of Economics*, 25(5) 2001: 669–84.

Peteraf, M.A., 'The cornerstone of competitive advantage: a resource-based view' *Strategic Management Journal*, March 1993: 179–91.

Peters, T., 'Rethinking scale', *California Management Review*, 35(1) 1993: 7–29.

Pfeffer, J. *Managing with Power* (Harvard Business School Press, Boston: 1992).

Pinchot, G. *Intrapreneuring* (Harper & Row, New York: 1985).

Pine, B.J. *Mass Customization: the new frontier in business competition* (Harvard Business School Press, Boston: 1993).

Pollock, T.H. and Gorman, P., 'Global strategic analysis: frameworks and approaches', *Academy of Management Executive* (1) February 1999: 70–82.

Pondy, L.R., 'Organizational conflict: concepts and models', *Administrative Science Quarterly*, 2 1967: 296–320.

Porter, M. *Competitive Advantage: techniques for analysing industries and companies* (The Free Press, New York: 1980).

Porter, M. *Competitive Advantage: creating and sustaining superior performance* (The Free Press, New York: 1985).

Porter, M. *On Competition* (Harvard Business Review Press, Cambridge, MA: 1998a).

Porter, M., 'Clusters and the new economics of competition', *Harvard Business Review*, 6(6) 1998b: 77–90.

Porter, M., 'Towards a dynamic theory of strategy', *Strategic Management Journal*, 12 (special issue) winter 1991: 95–118.

Porter, M., 'What is strategy?', *Harvard Business Review*, 74(6) 1996: 61–78.

Porter, M., 'Strategy and the Internet', *Harvard Business Review*, 79(3) 2001: 63–78.

Porter, M., Takeuchi, H. and Sakakibara, M. *Can Japan Compete?* (Macmillan – now Palgrave Macmillan, Basingstoke: 2000).

Powell, W., 'Japan v. Botswana', *Fortune*, June 13, 2002.

Prahalad, C.K. and Doz, Y.L. *The Multinational Mission: balancing local demands and global vision* (The Free Press, New York: 1987).

Prahalad, C.K. and Hamel, G., 'The core competencies of the corporation', *Harvard Business Review*, 70(3) 1990: 79–93.

Priem, R. and Butler, J.E., 'Is the resource-based "view" a useful perspective for strategic management research?', *Academy of Management Review*, 26(1) 2001a: 22–40.

Priem, R. and Butler J.E., 'Tautology in the resource-based view and the implication of externally determined resource value: further comments.' *Academy of Management Review*, 26(1) 2001b: 40–66.

Pryor, L.S., 'Benchmarking: a self-improvement strategy', *Journal of Business Strategy*, 10(6) 1989: 28–32.

Quick, J.C., 'Crafting an organisational culture: Herb's hand at Southwest Airlines', *Organisational Dynamics*, autumn 1992: 45–56.

Quinn, J.B. *Intelligent Enterprise* (The Free Press, New York: 1993).

Raynor, M.E., 'Quality as a strategic weapon', *Journal of Business Strategy*, **13**(5) 1992: 3–9.

Reeb, D.M., Kwok, C.C.Y. and Baek, H.Y., 'Systematic risk of the multinational corporation', *Journal of International Business Studies*, **29** 1998: 263–79.

Reed, S.R. *Making Common Sense of Japan* (University of Pittsburgh Press, Pittsburgh: 1993).

Reinhardt, A., 'Nokia's next act', *Business Week*, July 1, 2002: 25.

Rennie, P., 'BHP risks floating into indifference', *Business Review Weekly*, **24**(18) 2002: 38.

Reuters, 'Schumacher may face charges of betting fraud after tainted race.', *Sport Age*, May 17, 2002: 5.

Ringland, G. *Scenario Planning: managing for the future* (John Wiley & Sons, New York: 1997).

Robinson, A.G. and Stern, S. *Corporate Creativity: how innovation and improvement actually happen* (Business and Professional Publishing, Warriewood, NSW: 1997).

Robinson, D., 'Keys to successful strategy execution', *Journal of Business Strategy*, **23**(1) 2002: 30–4.

Robock, S.H., 'Political risk: identification and assessment', *Columbia Journal of World Business*, July/Aug 1971: 6–20.

Rodrik, D. *Has globalization gone too far?* (Institute of International Economics, Washington, DC: 1997).

Rogers, P.R., Miller, A. and Judge, W.Q., 'Using information processing theory to understand planning/performance relationships in the context of strategy', *Strategic Management Journal*, **20** 1999: 567–77.

Ronen, S. and Shenkar, O., 'Clustering countries on attitudinal dimensions: a review and synthesis', *Academy of Management Review*, **10**(3) 1985: 449–55.

Root, F.R. *Entry Strategies for Intended Markets* (D.C. Heath, Lexington, MA: 1980).

Rosen, S., Simon, J., Vincent, J.R., MacLeod, W., Fox, M. and Thea, D.M., 'AIDS is your business', *Harvard Business Review*, February 2003: 80–7.

Rugman, A.B. and Hodgetts, R.M., *International business: A strategic management approach* (McGraw-Hill, New York: 1995).

Rumelt, R., 'How much does industry matter?', *Strategic Management Journal*, March 1991: 167–86.

Rumelt, R., 'The evaluation of business strategy', in Mintzberg, H. and Quinn, J.B. (eds) *The Strategy Process; concepts, contexts, cases*, 3rd edn (Prentice Hall, Upper Saddle River, NJ: 1996).

Sachs, J., 'Sachs on globalisation: a new map of the world', *The Economist*, June 24, 2000.

Sanchez, R., 'Strategic flexibility in product competition', *Strategic Management Journal*, **16** (summer special issue) 1995: 105–40.

Saunders, A. *Financial Institutions in a Modern Perspective* (Irwin/McGraw-Hill, Boston: 2000).

Scheiber, H.N., 'Regulation, property rights and definition of "the market": law and the American economy', *Journal of Economic History*, **41** 1981: 103–11.

Schelling, T. *The Strategy of Conflict* (Harvard University Press, Cambridge, MA: 1960).

Schendel, D., Patton, G.R. and Riggs, J., 'Corporate turnaround strategies: a study of profit decline and recovery', *Journal of General Management*, **2** 1976: 1–22.

Schlender, B., 'All you need is love, $50 billion, and killer software code-named Leghorn', *Fortune*, July 8, 2002: 38-47.

Schmalensee, R., 'Do markets differ much?', *American Economic Review*, June 1985: 341–51.

Schmalensee, R., 'Inter-industry studies of structure and performance', in Schmalensee, R. and Willig, R.D. *Handbook of Industrial Organization, 1.* (North Holland, Amsterdam: 1989).

Schoeffler, S. *Nine Basic Findings on Business Strategy* (The Strategic Planning Institute, Cambridge, MA: 1980).

Schoeffler, S., Buzzell, R.D. and Heany, D.F., 'Impact of strategic planning on profit performance', *Harvard Business Review*, March–April 1974: 137–45.

Schoemaker, P.J.H., 'Multiple scenario developments: its conceptual and behavioural foundation', *Strategic Management Journal*, **14** 1993: 193–213.

Scholz, C., 'Corporate culture and strategy – the problem of strategic fit', *Long Range Planning*, **20** August 1987: 78–87.

Schumpeter, J.A. *The Theory of Economic Development* (Oxford University Press, London: 1934).

Schumpeter, J.A., 'The creative response in economic history', *Journal of Economic History*, November 1947: 149–59.

Schumpeter, J.A. *Capitalism, Socialism and Democracy* (Harper & Row, New York: 1950).

Schwartz, H. and Davis, S.H., 'Matching corporate culture and business strategy', *Organizational Dynamics*, summer 1981: 30–48.

Schwartz, P. *The Art of the Long View: planning for the future in an uncertain world* (Doubleday, New York: 1996).

Semler, R. *Maverick: the success story behind the world's most unusual workplace* (Warner Books, New York: 1993).

Semler, R. *The Seven-day Weekend: finding the work/life balance* (Century, London: 2003).

Senge, P.M. *The Fifth Discipline: the art and practice of the learning organization* (Doubleday, New York: 1990).

Serwer, A., 'Dell does domination', *Fortune*, June 21, 2002: 55.

Seth, A. and Thomas, H., 'Theories of the firm: implications for strategy research', *Journal of Management Studies*, **31**(2) 1994: 165–91.

Shank, J.K. and Govindarajan, V., 'Strategic cost analysis of technological investments', *Sloan Management Review*, Fall 1992: 39–51.

Shank, J.K. and Govindarajan, V. *Strategic Cost Management* (The Free Press, New York: 1993).

Siafter, S. *Corporate Recovery: successful turnaround strategies and their implementation* (Penguin Books, Harmondsworth: 1984).

Simon, H.A., 'A behavioural model of rational choice', *Quarterly Journal of Economics*, **6**(4) 1955: 99–111.

Simon, H.A., 'From substantive to procedural rationality', in Latsis, S.J. *Method and Appraisal in Economics* (Cambridge University Press, Cambridge: 1976).

Simons, R., 'Control in the age of empowerment', *Harvard Business Review*, **73** March–April 1995: 80–8.

Simons, R. *Performance Measurement and Control Systems for Implementing Strategy: text and cases* (Prentice Hall, Upper Saddle River, NJ: 2000).

Singer, A.E. *Strategy as Rationality: redirecting strategic thought and action* (Avebury, Aldershot: 1996).

Slater, S.F. and Olson, E.M., 'A fresh look at industry and market analysis', *Business Horizons*, **45**(1) 2002: 15–22.

Smith, K.G., Grim, C.M. and Gannon, M.J. *Dynamics of Competitive Strategy* (Sage, London: 1992).

Solomon, J., 'Seoul survivors', *Wall Street Journal* (Eastern Edition), June 13, 2002: A1.

Stachey, J. and White, D., 'When and when not to vertically integrate', *Sloan Management Review*, spring 1993: 71–93.

Stalk, G., Evans, P. and Schulman, L.E., 'Competing on capabilities: the new rules of corporate strategy', *Harvard Business Review*, **70**(2) 1992: 57–69.

Stuart, T.E., 'Network positions and propensities to collaborate: and investigation of strategic alliance formation in a high-technology industry', *Administrative Science Quarterly*, **43** 1999: 668-698.

Sun-Tzu, *The Art of War* (Oxford University Press, New York: 1971).

Sykes, T., 'Rupert Murdoch's game plan: filling in the gaps', *Weekend Australian*, Financial Review, October 12–13, 2002: 10.

Thomas, H., Pollock, T. and Gorman, P., 'Global strategic analysis: frameworks and approaches', *Academy of Management Executive*, (1) Feb 1999: 70–82.

Thompson A.A. and Strickland, A.J., 'Matrix Organization in a Diversified Global Company: The Case of Asea Brown Boveri', in Thompson, A.A. and Strickland, A.J. *Strategic Management; concepts and cases* (Irwin/McGraw-Hill, Boston: 1999).

Thompson, A.A. and Strickland, A.J. *Strategic Management; concepts and cases*, 11th edn (Irwin/McGraw Hill, Boston: 1999).

Thompson, A.A. and Strickland, A.J. *Strategic Management; concepts and cases*, 13th edn (Irwin/McGraw Hill, Boston: 2003).

Thurow, L. *Head to Head: the coming economic battle among Japan, Europe, and America* (William Morrow, New York: 1992).

Tichy, N.M. and Ulrich, D.O., 'The leadership challenge: a call for the transformational leader', *Sloan Management Review*, Fall 1984: 59–68.

Trompenaars, A., 'National cultures in four dimensions', *International Studies of Management and Organization*, spring/summer 1983: particularly pp. 54–5.

Trompenaars, A. *Riding the Waves of Culture* (Economist Books, London: 1998).

Tushman, M.L. and O'Reilly, C.A., 'The ambidextrous organization: managing evolutionary and revolutionary change', *California Management Review*, **38** 1996: 8–30.

Uhlen, S. and Lubatkin, M., 'ABB in China, 1998', in Hitt M.A., Ireland, R.D. and Hoskisson, R.E. *Strategic Management: competitiveness and globalisation* (Nelson, Cincinatti: 2000).

Unsworth, K., 'Unpacking creativity', *Academy of Management Review*, **26**(2) 2001: 289–97.

Vaghefi, M.R. and Huellmantel, A.B. *Strategic Management for the XXIst Century* (St Lucie Press, London: 1999).

van der Heijden, K. *Scenarios: the art of strategic conversation* (John Wiley & Sons, New York: 1996).

Venkatesan, R., 'Strategic outsourcing: to make or not to make', *Harvard Business Review*, **70**(6) 1992: 98–107.

Viljoen, J. and Dann, S. *Strategic Management; planning and implementing successful corporate strategies* (Longman, Frenchs Forest, NSW: 2000).

von Clausewitz, C. *On War*, trans. J. Howard and P. Paret (Princeton University Press, Princeton, NJ: 1984).

Wack, P., 'Scenarios, uncharted waters ahead', *Harvard Business Review*, Sept–Oct 1985a: 73–90.

Wack, P., 'Scenarios, shooting the rapids', *Harvard Business Review*, Nov–Dec 1985b: 131–42.

Wack, P., 'According to plan', *The Economist*, July 22, 1989: 60–3.

Watkins, M.D. and Bazerman, M.H., 'Predictable surprises: the disasters you should have seen coming', *Harvard Business Review*, March 2003: 72–85.

Watson, G.H. *Strategic Benchmarking: how to rate your company's performance against the world's best* (John Wiley, New York: 1993).

Wernerfelt, B., 'A resource-based view of the firm', *Strategic Management Journal*, **5** 1984: 171–80.

Wernerfelt, B., 'The resource-based view of the firm: ten years after', *Strategic Management Journal*, **16** 1995: 171–4.

Westley, F. and Mintzberg, H., 'Visionary leadership and strategic management', *Strategic Management Journal*, **10** (special issue) 1989: 17–32.

Wheatley, M.J. *Leadership and the new science: learning about organization from an orderly universe* 2nd edn (Berrett-Koehler, San Francisco: 2000).

White, C.M., 'The proper concerns of economic history', *Scandinavia Economic History Review*, **XL**(2) 1992: 47–50.

Whittington, R. *What is Strategy and Does it Matter?* 2nd edn (Routledge, London: 2001).

Williams, J.R., 'How sustainable is your competitive advantage?', *California Management Review*, **34** spring 1992: 29–51.

Williams, J.R. *Renewable Advantage: crafting strategy through economic time* (The Free Press, New York: 1999a).

Williams, J.R., 'Economic time', *Across the Board*, Sept 1999b: 11.

Williamson, O.E. *Markets and Hierarchies* (The Free Press, New York: 1975).

Williamson, O.E. *The Economic Institutions of Capitalism: firms, markets, relational contracting* (The Free Press, New York: 1985).

World Bank, *The East Asian Miracle: economic growth and public policy* (Oxford University Press, New York: 1993).

Wrapp, E., 'Good managers don't make policy decisions', *Harvard Business Review*, Sept–Oct 1967: 91–9.

Yasai-Ardekani, M. and Nystrom, P.C., 'Designs for environmental scanning systems: test for contingency theory', *Management Science*, **42** 1996: 187–204.

Zagotta, R. and Robinson, D., 'Keys to successful strategy execution', *Journal of Business Strategy*, **23**(1) 2002: 30–4.

Zahra, S.A. and O'Neill, H.M., 'Charting the landscape of global competition', *Academy of Management Executive*, **12**(4) 1998: 36–42.

Name index

A

Aaker, D. A. 265, 374, 529
Ackermann 714
Ackoff, R. L. 155
Adler 645
Aggrawala, R. 155
Al-Bukhary, Syed Mokthat 183
Ala-Pietila, Pekka 569
Alchian, A. 494
Amabile, T. M. 613
Ambani, Anil 430
Ambani, Dhirubai 429–30
Ambani, Mukesh 430–1
Anderson, E. 563
Anderson, Erik 609
Andrews, Kenneth R. 10
Anslinger, P. L. 415
Ansoff, H. I. 10, 42
Argenti, J. 301
Armani, Georgio 452, 453
Arnault 452
Axelrod, R. 494

B

Badaracco, J. L. 697
Barney, J. 265
Barrichello, Rubens 352–3
Bartlett, C. A. 112
Baumol, W. J. 42
Bazerman, M. H. 131, 155
Beatles, the 48, 774
Bebear 779
Beckham, David 234, 258, 259, 261
Benetton, Carlo 461
Benetton, Gilberto 461
Benetton, Guiliana 461
Benetton, Luciano 461
Benson-Armer 615

Bernstein, P. L. 529
Best, George 261
Bettinger, C. 455
Bezos, Jeff 173–5, 257, 703
Biggadike, H. R. 415
Bing-Sheng Teng 529
Blair, Tony 774
Borch 599
Bossidy 602
Bourguignon, Philippe 321, 546, 547, 745
Bouw, Pieter 106
Bowen 616, 641
Bower, J. L. 77, 301
Bowman, C. 277
Brabeck-Lemathe, Peter 554
Bradley, F. 563
Brandenburger, A. N. 31, 42, 231, 469, 494
Brando, Marlon 570
Branigan, T. 527
Branson, Sir Richard 325, 359–60, 362, 773–7, 786
Bresada, A. 697
Bridge, R. S. 155
Brigham, E. F. 670
Bronfman, Edgar 781
Brown, M. 362
Brown, S. L. 633
Browne, M. 116, 494
Brush, T. H. 415
Bryan, D. 82
Buffett, Warren 129, 702
Bullmer, Steve 421–2, 428–9
Burgelman, R. A. 587, 613
Butler, J. E. 265, 568
Buzzell, R. D. 42

C

Calverley, J. 529
Camp, R. C. 697

Camuffo, A. 466, 461
Capell, K. 615
Capellas, Michael 400, 724
Cardinal, L. B. 697
Carpenter, Michael 604
Caulkin, S. 426
Chaddick, B. 563
Chandler, Alfred 5, 9, 14, 431, 455
Chaney, Michael 517
Charlton, Bobby 259
Chatterjee, S. 529
Cheng, A. T. 559
Chessell, J. 315
Christensen, C. M. 51, 301
Clement, R. W. 455
Coakley, J. 112
Coase, Richard 415
Coleman, J. 494, 615, 640
Collis, D. J. 265
Coltman, T. 291
Commons, J. R. 494
Contractor, F. J. 563
Cook, Scott 257
Cooper, R. 337
Copeland, T. E. 415
Coplin, W. D. 529
Cordiner, Ralph 599
Cornell 342
Costa, P. R. 316
Cotsakos, Christos 249
Courtney, H. 155
Coyne, K. P. 494
Cravens, D. W. 374
Crick 652

D

D'Aveni, R. A. 231
Daniels, J. D. 529, 770
Dann, S. 697
Das, T. K. 529
David, Elizabeth 46, 48
Davidson, Willie 353

Davis, S. M. 455, 456
de Bono, E. 77
de Geus, A. P. 155
de Korte, Donald 526
de Sole, Domenico 418, 451–2
de Souza, G. 374
de Wit, R. 5, 6, 43, 53
de l'Estaing, Francois Bujon 778
d'Estaing, Giscard 322
Deeds 232
Dell, Michael 722
Demsetz, H. 494
Dess, G. G. 374
Devinney, T. M. 456
Devlin, Stuart 370
Diller, Barry 286, 778, 779, 781
Dior, Christian 452, 453
Dixit, A. 494
Doerr, John 256–7, 708
Dosé, André 106
Dow, K. 529
Dower, John W. 45
Doz, Y. L. 112, 494
Drejer, A. 9, 42
Driscoll, D. M. 697
Dumaine, B. 423
Duncan, R. 455
Dunning, John 487, 494, 563
Durack, T. 343
Durman 610
Dye, R. 494

E

Ecclestone, Bernie 348, 353
Eckhard 400, 724
Edmunds 688
Egan, C. 13, 42
Eisenhardt, K. M. 42, 633, 679

Eisner, Michael 395, 545, 743
Elder, J. 363, 775
Elenkov, D. S. 155
Ellman, Michael 77
Epstein, B. 48–9
Evans, Sir Christopher 254
Evert, Chris 371

F

Fahey, J. 353
Fama, E. F. 455
Feldstein, M. 112
Ferguson, Alex 262
Ferrari, Enzo 345–6
Figo 258
Fiorina, Carly 400, 724, 726, 727
Fischer, D. H. 139
Fisher, M. L. 337
Fitch, Joseph 604
Fitzpatrick, Robert 547, 745
Ford, Tom 418, 451–2
Forden 417
Forster, J. 116, 494
Fourtou, Jean-Rene 286, 780
Fowler 767
Franzen, J. 342
Fredrickson, J. W. 592, 613, 626
Friedman, M. 697
Friedman, Thomas 86, 112
Fukuyama, Francis 93, 494

G

Galbraith, J. R. 441
Gao, P. 559
Garvin, D. 374
Gates, Bill 421–2, 428–9, 524
Gatignon, H. 563
Geller, D. 49
Ghemawat, P. 8, 11, 23, 42, 163, 231, 301, 337, 494, 670
Ghoshal, S. 112, 551
Ghosn, Carlos 463, 481, 686, 748, 750

Giddens, Anthony 78, 111
Gilbertson, Martin 408
Gilmore, T. 112
Glass 323, 783
Goll, I. 155
Goodyear, Chip 379
Goold, M. 529
Gormley, Rowan 362, 775
Govindarajan, V. 337
Grant, R. M. 265, 337, 563, 600
Gross, David 353
Gross, W. H. 605
Grove, A. S. 613
Gucci, Aldo 417, 450
Gucci, Guccio 450
Gucci, Maurizio 417, 450–1
Gucci, Rodolfo 417, 450
Guth, W. D. 687

H

Hall, W. K. 374
Hambrick, D. C. 337, 584, 592, 613, 626
Hamel, Gary 34, 42, 125, 155, 265, 301, 494
Hampden, C. 16, 42
Handy, Charles 445
Hanlon, P. 79
Hannan, M. 415
Hannen, M. 517, 521
Harrigan, K. R. 415
Hart, S. L. 613
Haspeslagh, P. 415
Hegert, M. 337
Held, D. 111
Heller 234
Henderson, Bruce 42, 337
Henderson, J. C. 415
Hennessey, H. D. 374
Herzberg, F. 455
Heskett, J. L. 455
Hewett 267
Hill, C. W. L. 232, 301
Hill, Charles 42, 198, 415, 555, 563
Hilmetz, S. D. 155
Hindle, Kevin 77

Hirschhorn, L. 112
Hirst, P. 111
Hitt, M. A. 42, 546, 551, 613, 746, 766
Hocq, Robert 341
Hodgetts, R. M. 563
Hofer, C. W. 613
Hoffman, R. C. 301, 697
Hofstede, G. 22, 42, 171, 198
Hogarth, R. M. 155
Holmes 766
Holmes A'Court, Robert 408
Horioka, C. 112
Hoskisson, R. E. 75, 413, 694, 772
Houston, J. F. 670
Hout, T. M. 77
Howell, D. 563
Hu, Y. S. 553
Huang, P. 563
Huellmantel, A. B. 25, 42
Humble, J. 42
Huntingdon, Samuel 87, 112, 170
Hwang Chang Gyu 754

I

Ibuku, Masuru 50–1, 626
Idei, Noboyuki 683, 686
Imai, Masaaki 310, 718
Immelt, Jeff 602
Ingrassia, P. 31, 645
Ireland, R. D. 75, 413, 694

J

Jacobson, R. 232, 529
James, Clive 352
Jawahar, I. M. 675, 697
Jeannet, J. -P. 374
Jemal, Mike 243, 716
Jemison, D. 415
Jensen, M. C. 670
Jin, Kim Taek 229
Joachimstaler 374

Johnson, B. 52
Johnson, Gerry 35, 42
Johnson, Spencer 683
Jones, Jeffrey, D. 281, 754
Jones, T. M. 42, 415, 455

K

Kaihla, Paul 607, 608
Kairams 607
Kaldor, Nicholas 683
Kamprad, Ingvar 44
Kaplan, R. S. 337, 658, 697
Katzenbach, J. R. 455
Keating, Paul 408
Kendall, Philip 773
Kenwood, A. G. 112
Kenyon, Peter 262
Kerr, S. 455
Keynes, John Maynard 140
Kidman, Nicole 452
Kiechel, W. 337
Kiel, G. C. 374
Kihara 683
Kikimatsu, Ogawa 45–6
Kim, Eric 282, 755
Kim, W. C. 301, 563
Kindleberger, C. P. 96
Kirch, Leo 348
Kirdar, Nemir 450
Klein, H. E. 529
Koestler, Arthur 77
Kogut, B. 563
Kohn, A. 455
Kotler, P. 374
Kotter, J. P. 455
Kozlowski, l. Dennis 353
Krayenbuehl 529
Kruger 267
Kuisma, Erkki 609
Kulkani, S. 337
Kuznetsky, Dan 722

L

Lampel, Joseph 4, 20, 42
Larkin, J. 282, 754
Latham, F. 455
Lauenstein, M. C. 415

Lawrence, P. R. 455
Lay, Ken 679
Learned, E. P. 10, 42
Lee Hsien Yang 549, 764
Lee Kuan Yew 549, 764
Lee Kun Hee 754
Legge, J. 77
Levi, M. D. 112
Levine, Lord 729, 730, 733–4
Levitt, T. 112
Lewis 339
Li Ka-Shing 267
Liberman, M. 301
Liedtka, J. M. 46–7, 77
Lin 766
Lindholm, Christian 608
Linneman, R. E. 529
Liu, Alex 423
Loehle, Craig 43, 77
Logue, D. E. 519
Lorie, Roland 371
Lougheed, A. L. 112
Lubatkin, M. 438, 529
Luce, R. D. 468, 494
Luchs, K. 529
Luger, S. 31
Lyons, B. 494

M
Mack, T. 155
Mackay, Graham 637
Macmillan, I. C. 42, 455
Madhok, A. 563
Maharta 303, 332, 335
Mahathir, Mohammed 183
Mahoney, D. 112, 171, 198
Maiden 379
Makinwa, Bunmi 496
Makridakis, S. 113, 155
Makrides, C. C. 613
March, J. G. 42
Mark, Rebecca 504
Marks, M. L. 415
Marsh, P. 457, 489
Martin, R. L. 676, 697
Maslow, A. 340–1
Mauborgne, R. 301

Mauri, A. J. 231
McCallum 409, 411
McColl-Kennedy, J. R. 374
McCormack, Mark 234
McGahan 231
McGahan, A. 231
McLaughlin, G. L. 675, 697
Meldrum, D. H. 563
Mendelsohn, John 689
Messier, Jean-Marie 286, 778–9
Meyer, A. D. 5, 6, 43, 53, 265
Meyer, Marshall 716
Michaels, M. P. 231
Miller, D. 265, 337, 374, 697
Miller, Kent 529
Mintzberg, Henry 4, 20, 42, 57, 164, 363, 455, 613, 652, 775
Mirvis, P. H. 415
Mische, M. A. 101, 112
Mittelman, J. H. 78, 84, 111
Mohan 638
Mokyr, Joel 198
Moncrieff, J. 697
Montgomery, D. 265, 301
Morita, Akio 50, 683–5
Morris, D. 337
Mundie, Craig 429
Murdoch, Rupert 259, 537, 538
Murthy, Naraya 332

N
Nagle, T. T. 374
Nalebuff, B. 31, 42, 231, 469
Narula, R. 563
Nelson, C. A. 112
Nolan, Peter 77
Norton, D. P. 658, 697
Nuevo, Yrjo 608
Nystrom, P. C. 155

O
O'Brien, K. 332
O'Leary, Michael 316

O'Neill, H. M. 198
O'Reilly, C. A. 301, 455
Ohga, Noria 684
Ohmae, K. 43, 46, 101, 111, 112
Ollila, Jorma 609
Olson, E. M. 697
Onassis, Jackie 344
Oppenheimer, Sir Ernest 339, 371
Orr, D. 255

P
Paltrow, Gwyneth 453
Panke, Helmut 346
Pascale, R. T. 23, 571, 652
Pele 261
Penrose, Edith 415
Perraton, J. 111
Perrin 199
Perttula, Aulis 608
Peteraf, M. A. 265
Peters, Tom 415
Phumaphi, Joy 496
Pinault, Francois 452
Pinchot, G. 77
Pine, B. J. 374
Platt, Lewis 400, 724
Poetl, Wolfgang 352
Porter, Michael 11, 42, 163, 204–6, 231, 265, 301, 337, 374, 480, 494, 613, 652
Posh Spice 259
Prahalad, C. K. 112, 125, 155, 265
Prescott, John 408
Price, Sol 325, 786
Priem, R. 265, 568
Princess Diana 774
Pryor, L. S. 697

Q
Quick, J. C. 455
Quinn, J. B. 42, 51, 155, 301, 455

R
Rafferty, M. 82
Raifa, H. 468, 494
Rao 303
Rasheed, A. M. A. 155
Rasulo, Jay 743

Raynor, M. E. 374
Reagan, Ronald 353
Reeb, D. M. 529
Reed, S. R. 494
Rennie, P. 379
Ringland, G. 155
Robinson, A. G. 613
Robock, S. H. 232
Rodrik, D. 78
Rogers, P. R. 697
Ronaldo 258
Ronen, S. 88, 112, 198
Root, F. R. 563
Rosen, S. 495, 524, 525
Rugman, A. B. 563
Rumelt, R. 42, 231
Rushton, Richard 638
Russell, Kevin 267

S
Sachs, J. 112
Sanchez, R. 374
Santamaria, J. A. 455
Scheiber, H. N. 131
Schelling, T. 494
Schendel, D. 301, 613
Schlender, B. 429
Schmalensee, R. 231
Schoeffler, Sidney 42
Schoemaker, P. J. H. 138, 155
Scholes, K. 35, 42
Scholz, C. 455
Schroeder, Helmut 714
Schultz, Howard 621, 766, 770, 786
Schumacher, Michael 352–3
Schumpeter, J. A. 42, 77, 232
Schwartz, Peter 136, 138, 155, 455
Sculley, John 386
Semler, Ricardo 425–6
Senge, P. M. 155
Seth, A. 265
Shamsie, J. 265
Shank, J. K. 337
Sharpe, P. 690
Shaw 457, 489
Shenkar, O. 88, 112, 198
Siafter, S. 301

Simon, Herbert 42, 116, 155
Simon, J. 371
Simons, R. 455, 659
Singer, A. E. 20, 42
Singh 303
Slajkovic, A. D. 455
Slater, S. F. 231, 697
Sloan, Alfred 9
Smedly, J. 228
Smith, Adam 8, 14, 468
Smith, K. G. 231
Solomon, J. 282, 755
Sorensen, Lone 609
Souter, John 491
Spear 616, 641
Stachey, J. 415
Stalk, G. 265
Stern, S. 613
Stewart, Martha 693
Stonecipher, Harry 149
Strickland, A. J. 438, 555

Stringer, Howard 687
Stuart, T. E. 494
Su Fangwen 310
Suharto 219
Sull, D. N. 42, 679
Sun-Tzu 77

T

Tawel, Sidney 692
Thomas, H. 198, 265
Thompson, A. A. 111, 438, 555
Thompson, J. Walter 369
Thurow, L. 112
Toyoda, Kiichiro 642
Trigano 321
Trompenaars, A. 16, 22, 42, 198
Tushman, M. L. 301

U

Uchikawa 645
Uhlen, S. 438
Unsworth, K. 613

V

Vaghefi, M. R. 25, 42, 615, 640
Van der Heijden, K. 113, 137, 155, 790
Varoukis, Y. 494
Venkatesan, R. 415
Veverka 722
Vidal, J. 527
Viljoen, J. 697
von Clausewitz, Carl 8, 77

W

Wack, P. 155,
Waksal, Harlan 689
Waksal, Sam 689
Walton, Sam 323–5
Warner 603
Watanabe 161
Waters, J. A. 613
Watkins, M. D. 131, 155
Watson, G. H. 652, 697

Way, N. 411, 517, 521
Wayne, K. 337
Welch, Jack 405, 412, 569, 600–2
Wernerfelt, B. 265
Wheatley, M. J. 24
White C. M. 177
White, D. 415, 748
White, J. B. 31, 645
Whittington, Richard 13, 14, 21, 42, 553
Williams, J. R. 77
Williams, Stephen 609
Williamson, O. E. 415
Wilson, Charles 599

Y/Z

Yasai-Ardekani, M. 155
Yun Jong Yong 282, 755
Zahra, S. A. 198
Zhang Riumin 243–4, 309–10, 716–18
Zidane 258, 261

Organization index

3DO 200, 225
@Home 257

A

A. G. Edwards 249
AAPT 550, 763
AC Milan 260
Accenture 334, 335,
 361
Acerdia 411
ACI 488
Activision 227
Advanced Info Services
 550, 763
Africa Comprehensive
 HIV-AIDS
 Partnerships
 (ACHAP) 524
African Development
 Bank 97
Age, The 52, 777
Ahold 535, 784
Air France 106, 316
Air Lib 104
Air New Zealand 79,
 105, 107, 108, 109
Airbus Industrie
 114–15, 147–53, 204,
 643
Aldi 329, 331, 332,
 351, 784
Allianz 100, 713, 714
Alpine Resorts
 Coordinating Council
 740
Altria Group 360
Amazon.com 111, 173,
 174, 257, 392, 535,
 631, 668, 784
America Online 257
American Depository
 Receipt Market 615
American Express 303,
 334, 514, 744
American Motor
 Corporation 556

American Society of
 Clinical Oncology
 690
Ameritrade 250, 251
AMF Corporation 353
Amnesty 95
AMP 360, 774
Andean Community
 97
Andersen Consulting
 361
Andersons 74
Anglo American 410,
 521, 526
Anglo American
 Platinum 525
Anglo Gold 525, 526
Anheuser-Busch 615,
 638, 639
Ansell 361
Ansett 104, 105, 107,
 108, 473, 776
AOL Time Warner 283,
 286, 394, 395, 722,
 757, 778
Apple 282, 283, 344,
 386, 755, 757
Applied Insurance
 Research 507, 730
ARAMARK 206, 769
Arbed 411
Arcelor 411
Argyle 339, 370, 371,
 372, 373
Armani, Georgio 452–3
Arrows 347
Arsenal 259, 260, 261
Asda 788
Asea Brown Boveri
 437–8, 555
Ashton 370
Asia-Pacific Economic
 Cooperation (APEC)
 97
Asian Development
 Bank 97

Association of South-
 East Asian Nations
 (ASEAN) 97
AstraZeneca 692, 693
AT Kearney 423
AT&T 404, 670
Atari 200, 225
Atlantic Excellence
 Alliance 104
Aurias 372
Australian Airlines
 108
Australian Competition
 and Consumer
 Commission 107
*Australian Financial
 Review, The* 153, 196,
 230, 413, 561, 562,
 688, 715, 734
Australian and New
 Zealand Closer
 Economic Relations
 Trade Agreement 97
Australian Wine and
 Brandy Corporation
 491
Australian Wine Export
 Corporation 490
Austrian 104, 106
Aventis 692
AVIVA 361

B

B. Vijaykumar and
 Company 372
Babcock Borsig 713
Baby Bells 404, 670
Bang & Olufsen 344
Bank 24 223, 712, 713
Bank of America 605
Bank of International
 Settlements 95
Bank of Scotland 262
Bankers Trust 222,
 703, 712
Banksia Wines 492

Banque Worms 714
Barnes & Noble 173,
 206, 703, 704, 769
Barron 250, 728
Bass Brewers 639
Bayern Munich 259
BBC 260
Bechtel 437
Beijing Automotive
 Works (BAW) 556
Beijing Yanjing Beer
 Group 639
Belgacom 333, 550,
 763
Bell Laboratories 607
Ben Bridge 372
Ben Franklin 323, 324,
 784
Benetton 461, 462,
 465–7, 535, 672, 784
Beringer Blass 41, 491
Bertelsmann 394, 395,
 555, 778
Best Buy 282, 756
Bharat Petroleum 431
Bharti Group 550, 764
BHP Billiton 361, 370,
 372, 370, 379,
 408–12, 413, 434,
 517, 522, 722
BHP Steel 410–13
BMW 28, 346, 509,
 558
BMW Williams 347
Boeing 28, 114, 115,
 148, 149, 150, 151,
 153, 437
Boeing Capital 149,
 153
Borders 173, 703, 704
Boston Consulting 11,
 42, 351, 392, 393
Botswana Institute of
 Development Analysis
 526
Bottleshop.com.au 293

Brick, The 74
Bridgestone 153
Bristol-Myers Squibb 693
British Aerospace 114
British Airways (BA) 105, 107, 108, 109, 303, 317, 359, 435, 438, 774, 776
British Dutch Corus 411
British Petroleum 101, 361
British Steel 408
British Telecom 511, 549, 550, 762, 763, 780
Broken Hill Proprietary (BHP) 15, 28, 372, 379, 405, 408, 409, 410, 411, 412, 413, 432
Brokerage America 250
BSA 570
BSkyB 259, 260, 261, 262, 263
Bundesbank 216, 710

C

Cable & Wireless 549, 550, 761, 763
Cadbury Schweppes 434
California Management Review 32, 553
Cambridge University 254
Canadian Eastern Life Assurance 432
Canal Plus 286, 287, 779, 781
Cap Gemini 335
Caribbean Community 97
Carlsberg 615, 638, 639
Carlton Communications 234
Carrefour 535, 784
Cartier 199, 341, 343, 451
Caterpillar 325, 326

Cathay Pacific 107, 108, 109
Cato Institute 522
CBS Records 685
CCT Telecom 719
Celera 652
Central American Common Market 98
Central Selling Organisation 339
Cerent 257
CGU 361
Chanel 346, 452
Changjiang Securities 720
Charles Schwab 240–1, 251, 255, 708
Chevron Texaco 100, 527
China Keijian 243, 716
China National Heavy Truck Corporation 558
China Resources Breweries 639
Chrysler (*see also* DaimlerChrysler) 30, 31, 542, 556, 557
Cifra 536, 788
Circuit City 282, 756
Cisco 257
Citibank 437, 555, 607
Citigroup 100, 222, 223, 334, 605, 712, 713
Cititrade 251
Citroen 557, 558
Club Med 313, 320, 321, 322, 745
Coca-Cola 72, 89, 262, 349, 359, 361, 514, 670, 744, 774
Coffee Specialty Association of America, 771
Columbia Pictures Entertainment 685
Commerzbank 712, 714
Companhia Siderurgia Nacional 411
Compaq 256, 400, 401, 402, 724, 726, 727, 757

Compass 107
Concours Group 334
Consignia 361
Consolidated Foods 361
Constellation 491, 492
Cooperative Automotive Research for Advanced Technology 193
Corona 615
Costco 330, 786
CRA 370
Credit Suisse First Boston 451
Crossair 105, 106
CSC 334
CSFB Durel 250
CZC AsiaPac 551, 763

D

D. A. Davidson 249
D. E. Shaw 173, 703
Daewoo 754
Daiei 683
Daihatsu 194, 557
Daimaru 540
DaimlerChrysler (*see also* Chrysler) 100, 114, 194, 195, 347, 463, 509, 714, 748, 750
Dain Rauscher 249
Datang 298
Datek 251
David Jones 74
Davnet 361
De Beers 339, 340, 357, 369–74, 525, 526
Debswana 525
Dell 196, 257, 283, 291, 293, 294, 363, 400, 402, 722–4, 726, 727, 756
Delta 104, 527, 673
Department of Energy 193
Desmo Owners Club 354
Deutsche Bank 216, 222, 223, 255, 699, 708, 709, 711, 712, 713, 714, 715, 716
Deutsche Bank Brown Inc. 714

Diamond 370, 371, 372
Digital Equipment Corporation 400, 724
DirecTV 538, 539
Disney 89, 321, 394, 514, 545, 546, 547, 738, 742, 743, 744, 745, 746, 747, 778, 781
Disney-MGM Park 545, 743
Disney Studios Park 746, 747
Disneyland 514, 545, 546, 547, 735, 743, 744, 746, 747
Disney World 545, 546, 547, 743, 745
DoCoMo 267, 298
Donfeng Motor 559
Dow Chemical 437
Dresdner Bank 222, 712, 713
Dreyers 206, 769
Ducati 353, 354, 355
DVT Holdings 361

E

E*Trade 240, 241, 249, 250, 251
Eastman Kodak 436
easyJet 105, 106, 316
eBay 292, 702, 706
EchoStar 287, 538, 539, 781
Economic Community of Central African States 97
Economic Community of West African States 97
Economist, The 53, 112, 335, 362, 430, 605, 773, 778, 779, 793
EDS 334, 335
Eidos 228
Elders 361
Electrolux 244, 310, 717, 719
Electronic Arts 227, 229

Eli Lilly 689, 691, 692
Email 412
Emirates 109, 149, 153
Enron 100, 504, 603,
   668, 678, 679, 713
Eqecut 507, 730
Equitas Ltd 733
Ericsson 143, 267,
   282, 284, 298, 570,
   606, 607, 608, 609,
   756, 758
Esso 514, 744
Euro Disney (Paris)
   321, 514, 546, 547,
   699, 738, 742, 743–7
Euro-money 501
European Aeronautical
   Defence and Space
   Company 114
European Bank for
   Reconstruction and
   Development 97
European Central Bank
   97, 216, 710
European Champions
   League 263
European Commission
   of Transportation
   106
European Free Trade
   Association 97, 178
European Union 87,
   95, 97, 98, 553
Exxon Mobil 100

F
Fairchild Donier 713
Federal
   Communications
   Commission 538
Federal Drugs
   Administration (FDA)
   202, 689, 693, 694
Ferrari 345, 347, 352,
   417
Feyenoord 258
Fidelity 250, 251
Financial Times 153,
   299, 335, 373, 526,
   527, 561, 562, 605,
   611, 683, 694, 715,
   721, 759, 782, 789
Finlux 606

Finnair 106, 107
First Auto Works (FAW)
   557, 558, 559, 560
Foote, Cone & Belding
   282, 756
Forbes 196, 256, 260,
   263, 688, 694
Ford 30, 100, 193, 194,
   257, 347, 418, 434,
   451, 452, 556, 558,
   559, 560, 640, 642,
   647, 748, 750
Fortune 679, 722
Free Trade.com 250
Freedom 74
FreeMarkets 257

G
Gallo 491, 492
Gates and Merck
   Foundation 524,
   526
GE Capital 303, 602–5
GE Plastics 600
Gembel Group 372
Gemstar 538
General Atlantic 257
General Electric (GE)
   100, 334, 405, 437,
   552, 569, 599–605,
   670, 781
General Motors (GM)
   30, 106, 161, 194,
   406, 538, 542, 646,
   748
Glasgow Rangers 258,
   260
Globe Telecom 550, 763
Goldman Sachs 222,
   250, 450, 712
Gomez Advisers 250
Granada 234, 261, 262
Greenpeace 95, 96
Grey Global Group 720
Guanazhou Auto 557
Guardian, the 778
Gucci 344, 345, 346,
   417, 418, 430, 450–3,
   773, 775
Guggenheim Museum
   758
Guinness 361, 615,
   637

Gulf Cooperation
   Council 97

H
Haier 243, 309–11,
   699, 716, 717, 718,
   719, 720, 721
Haier-CCT Holdings
   720
Haier Enterprise Culture
   Centre 718
Handspring 257
Harley-Davidson 70,
   570, 616, 775
Harley Owners Group
   (HOG) 353
Harrods 343
Harvard AIDS Institute
   524
Harvard Business Review
   526
Harvard Business
   School 9, 256, 425
Harvard University
   386
HCL 334
Heineken 615, 637, 638
Hennes & Mauritz
   (H&M) 467
Hermes 343, 344, 345
Hewlett-Packard 699,
   722–8
Hilton 545, 743
Hindustan Petroleum
   431
Hitachi 125, 553, 683,
   758
Home Depot 402, 727
Honda 194, 195, 354,
   542, 616, 670, 683,
   750
Hong Kong Telecoms
   549, 761
Houghton Mifflin 286,
   779
Huaxia Bank 432
Hughes Electrics 538
Hutchison Whampoa
   267, 299
Hyatt 545
Hybritech 689
Hynix Semiconductor
   756

HypoVereinsbank 712
Hyundai 748, 754

I
IBM 100, 123, 124,
   212, 283, 294, 327,
   334, 335, 388, 402,
   404, 514, 722, 723,
   744, 757
IDOMO 74
IKEA 44–45, 52, 70–4,
   75, 225, 324, 538,
   594, 631, 672, 766,
   768, 785
Il Giornale 766
Imclone 567, 652, 694
Impulse 107
Infineon 125, 756,
   758
Infosys 303–4, 332–5
ING Group 100
Ingram Book Company
   174, 704
Institutional Investor
   232, 501
Intel 125, 212, 226,
   229, 257, 294, 726
Interbrew 615, 639
International
   Management Group
   234
International Monetary
   Fund 95
International
   Telecommunications
   Union 296
Intuit 256, 257
Investcorp 450–1
Itochu 100
ITV Digital 234, 259

J
J. P. Morgan 450
Jaguar Racing 347
Jet Blue 316
John F. Welch
   Technology Centre
   304
Johnson & Johnson
   264, 272, 690, 692
Jordan Honda 347
Juniper Networks 257
Juventus 235, 260

K

KDD 551, 763
Keijian 716
Kellogg's 535, 784
Keppel Corporation
    761
Kerch Media 234
Kingfisher 535, 784
KK Group 639
Kleiner, Perkins,
    Caulfield & Byers
    256, 257
Kleinwort Benson 223,
    712
Kmart 324, 325, 330,
    331, 536, 783, 786,
    787
Komatsu 325, 326
Korea Inc. 282, 754
Kraft 360
KTF 267

L

La Trobe University
    741
Ladbroke 262
Le Monde 779
Legend 243, 716
LG Philips 284, 758
Liberty Media 781
Library of Congress
    331, 787
Lidl 331
Liebherr-Haushallsgerte
    309, 718
Linux 706
Lion-Nathan 492
Lloyd's 731
Lochheed 114, 150
Louis Vuitton Moet
    Hennessy (LMVH)
    344, 345, 346, 351,
    352, 371, 452, 491
London Stock Exchange
    639
Los Angeles Times 621,
    769
LOT 104
Lotus 256, 257
LTU 104, 105
Lucas Arts 229
Lucent 298, 400, 724
Lucky Goldstar 754

Lufthansa 104, 106,
    316

M

M. D. Anderson Cancer
    Centre 689
McDonnell-Douglas
    114, 149, 150, 153
Macintosh 327
McKinsey 11, 42, 196,
    392, 561, 599, 640,
    649, 694, 777, 784,
    789
McLane 324, 785
McLaren Mercedes 347
Macromedia 256
McWilliams 492
Maersk-Sealand 183
Manchester United
    234–5, 258–63
Marks & Spencer 341
Massachusetts Institute
    of Technology (MIT)
    641
Matahari 536
Matsushita 683, 685
Mattel 514, 744
MCA 685
Mercedes 345, 640
Merck 525, 693
Mercosur 97
Merlin Biosciences 254
Merrill Lynch 222,
    241, 250, 251, 630,
    712
Metro 784
Metro-Goldwyn Meyer
    (MGM) 781
Meyers 74
Micron Technology
    756
Microsoft 99, 200, 213,
    226, 227, 228, 229,
    283, 294, 388,
    421–2, 426, 428–9,
    609, 610, 757
Mildara-Blass 491
Miller 637
Minardi 347
Ministry of the
    Environment and
    Conservation of
    Australia 740

Mitsubishi 100, 683
Mitsui 100
Mobile International
    205,
Mobile One 549, 761
Mobilkom 267
Mobira 606
Moody 286, 501, 502,
    733, 779
Morgan Grenfell 222,
    712
Morgan Stanley 250,
    450
Moto-Guzzi 570
Motorola 267, 283,
    569, 570
Mt Buller Winter Resort
    280, 281, 699,
    735–42
MU Finance 262
Munich Re 714
MUTV 262

N

Nanjing Brewery 639
Narang Breweries 638
National Renewable
    Energy Laboratory
    193
NBC 781
NCSoft 229
NEC 125, 267, 609
Nestlé 106, 514,
    554–5, 632, 744
Netscape Navigator
    256
Netto 331
New Century Infocomm
    550, 764
New United Motor
    Manufacturing
    Incorporated
    (NUMMI) 645–7
New York Life
    International 720
New York Stock
    Exchange 354, 450,
    607
New York Yankees
    260, 262
News Corporation 395,
    537–9, 685, 778
Nike 90, 259

Nintendo 200, 225,
    226, 227, 228, 229,
    683
Nippon Steel 683
Nippon Telegraph and
    Telephone (NTT)
    100, 267
Nissan 41, 463, 464,
    482–3, 484, 542,
    593, 748–53
Nokia 267, 298, 567,
    569, 757
Nordstrom 206, 333,
    769
Nortel 267
North American Free
    Trade Agreement 98
North Atlantic Treaty
    Organization 98
Norton Triumph 570

O

O_2 267, 268
Oceanic 606
Office Depot 310, 719
OneSteel 411, 412
Oneworld 104, 107,
    109
Open University
    274–5
Optus 267, 550, 551,
    763, 764, 765
Orange 267
Organization for
    Economic
    Cooperation and
    Development (OECD)
    411
Organization of
    Petroleum Exporting
    Countries (OPEC)
    98, 141–2, 144, 147,
    793–4
Orlando-Wyndham
    491
Oxfam 96, 95

P

Pacific Dunlop 361
Paine Webster 250
Pan Am 79
Paramount 685
Paribas 720

Partnership for a New Generation of Vehicles 193
Patrick 109
Penney 323, 783
Penny Market 331
PepsiCo 206
Petaluma 492
Pfizer 434, 692
Philip Morris 360, 639
Philipp Holzmann 713
Philips Electronics 200
Pinault-Printemps-Redoute 452
Porsche 345
Port of Tanjung Pelepan (PTP) 182–3
Prada 344, 452, 453
Price Club 325, 786
PriceCostco 206, 769
PricewaterhouseCoopers 521, 773
Procter & Gamble 535, 784
Prudential Securities 250
PT Bukaka Singapore Telecom International 550, 763

Q
Qantas 41, 80, 103–9, 151, 473–4
Qualcomm 298, 534, 756
Qualifying Alliance 104
QVC 781

R
Radio Shack 282, 756
RAI 260
Rare 228
Real Madrid 258, 259, 260, 261, 263
Red Cross 95, 235
Red Hook Breweries 206, 769
Reebok 229, 333
Reliance 332, 430–1
Renault 41, 347, 462–3, 481–2, 484, 514, 593, 744

Renault-Nissan BV 482, 752
Renong Group 763
Reuters 352, 555
Ricard Pernod 491
Rio Algom 408
Rio Tinto 370, 408, 410, 522
Risk Management Solutions 507, 730
Robert Mondavi 492
Rolex 371
Rosemount Estates 491
Royal Mail 361
Ryanair 105, 106, 316

S
Sabena 104, 105, 109
Salora 606
Sampo 719
Samsung 125, 244, 281, 282, 283, 598, 609, 754–9
Sanyo 719
Sara Lee Corporation 361
Sauber Petronas 347
Sauder 74
Sax Riley 733
Sazaby Inc. 623, 771
Seagram 286, 778, 781
Sears 310, 323, 536, 719, 783, 786, 787
SECOM 683
Second Cup 206, 769
Sega 200, 226, 227
Semco 425–6
Semiconductor Industry Association 125
Shanghai Automotive Industry Group (SAIC) 557, 558, 559, 560
Shanghai Municipality 101
Sharpe 284
Shaw Wallace 638
Shell, Royal Dutch 41, 100, 126, 136, 155, 437, 430
Shougang 432
Siemens 244, 267, 298, 347, 717

Singapore Airlines 104, 109, 360, 775
Singapore Power 761
Singapore Technologies Telemedia 761
Singapore Telecommunications (SingTel) 760–5
Sky Italia 538
SLEC 348
Smart Money 250
SmithKline Beecham 690, 694
Smorgon 412
Softbank 683
Software Engineering Institute 334
Sony 50–1, 200, 226, 228, 282, 284, 394, 611, 652, 683–8, 754, 755, 756
Sony Ericsson Mobile Communications 609
South African Airways 104
South African Breweries 567, 615, 637
Southcorp 41, 491, 492
Southwest 315–16, 630, 776
SPH 761
Sphinx Pharmaceutical 691
Sprint PCS 756
Squibb 452
SSD 52
Standard Electric Lorenz 606
Standard & Poor 299, 404, 501, 502, 605
Star Alliance 109
Starbucks 205–6, 343, 344, 535, 621–3, 766–72, 784
Stream 260, 538
Sun Microsystems 257
Suzuki 557
Swatch 371
Swiss International Airlines 105, 106, 109

Swissair 41, 79, 103–9
Swisscom 105

T
T-Mobile 267, 774
TAP Air Portugal 104
Target 310, 330, 706, 719, 756, 786
TCL 243, 609, 716
TD Waterhouse 250, 251
Telepiu 260, 286, 538, 780
Televa 606
Telkomsel 551, 763
Telstra 267, 408
Temasek 762
Terra Lycos 262
Tesco 535, 784
Texas Instruments 298, 437, 608, 609
Texas Pacific Group 354
Thompson 606
Tiffany 450
Tokyo Disneyland 546, 744
Toshiba 125, 758
Total Finn Elf 100
Toyota 100, 161, 194–6, 318, 347, 462, 542, 557–9, 560, 567, 571, 615, 640–7, 670, 672, 748, 750
Transparency International 172
Tribeca 361
Tsingtao Brewery 638
TWA 79
Twentieth Century Fox 685
Tyco 353, 603

U
UNAIDS 496, 524
Unilever 535, 784
United Airlines 206, 769
United Auto Workers Union 542, 646
United Breweries 638
United Nations (UN) 95, 96

Universal   260, 286,
   394, 699, 778, 779,
   780, 781, 782
Universal Entertainment
   287, 780, 781
Universal Music Group
   286, 287, 779, 780,
   781
Universal Studios   286,
   685, 779
USA Interactive   286

V
Vendome Luxury Group
   451
Verant Interactive   229
Versace   453
Viacom   394, 395, 685,
   686, 778, 781
Virgin   105, 777
Virgin Active   360, 776
Virgin Atlantic   109,
   360, 774, 775, 776

Virgin Blue   107, 108,
   360, 473–4, 774,
   775, 776
Virgin Cinema   360,
   776
Virgin Mobile   360,
   774, 775, 776
Virgin Money   774
Virgin Radio   360, 776
Virgin Rail   774
Virgin Records   776
Virgin Wines   362,
   775
Vivendi   229, 260,
   286–7, 394, 685,
   686, 778–82
Vodafone   259, 263,
   267
Volare   104
Volkswagen   509,
   557–8, 560, 562,
   748
Volvo   463, 558, 750

W
W. J. Deutsch   490, 491
Wal-Mart   100, 294,
   310, 324–5, 330–2,
   344, 351, 670, 719,
   723, 756, 783–9
Wall Street Journal   702
Warner Brothers   685
Warsteiner   347
Washington Redskins
   260
Waterford   344
Wavecom   609
Wedgwood   344
Wellcome Trust Sanger
   Institute   254
Wells Trade   251
Whirlpool   244, 310,
   717, 719
Wine online   293
Wine Planet   293
Winepros   293
Wipro   334, 335

World Bank   77, 95, 96,
   181
World Cup   234–5
World Trade
   Organization (WTO)
   95, 96, 99, 181, 184,
   202, 310, 518, 519,
   531, 555, 556, 559,
   561, 562, 716, 719
WorldCom   668, 713
Wrangler   330, 787

X/Y/Z
Xerox   668
Yankee Entertainment
   Sports   262
YM   688
Yves St Laurent (YSL)
   344, 345, 452, 453
Zara   467
Zurich Financial
   Services   262

Subject index

A

A380 113–5, 148–53
Accounting
  problems of 663–4, 668–9, 679
Acquisitions 395–402
  difficulties of 397
  international 537
  motivations for 396
  timing of 402
Activities
  core 258
  down-stream 251
  primary 251–4, 367
  support 251–4, 367
  up-stream 251
  in value-chain 319
Activity rates 666–7
Administration 67–9
Advantage see competitive
  advantage
  first mover 149–50, 297–8
Adverse selection 505–6
Agent(s) 419–21, 424–6, 590
  effect of organizational structure
    on 427–8
  motivating 428
Africa
  risk environment of 496–7
AIDS 133, 412, 496–7, 522–6
  cost of 525
  incidence of 523
  its spread 523
  treatment of 524–5
  virus types 523
Aircraft manufacturing
  demand for 148
  nature of 147–8
Airline(s) 79–80
Airline industry 79–80
Alignment 584–5
Alliances see strategic alliances
Anti-monopoly legislation
Arenas 592, 594
Argentina
  financial crisis in 179–81
Asbestos-related diseases 730

B

Asia 189
Asian economic crisis 133, 282,
  511–12, 754
Asian economic miracle 176, 303
Aspirational goods 342–4
  demand for 351–2
Assessing 124, 575
Asset specificity 390
Asymmetries
  of information 210, 420, 442
  of investment 210
Assets
  country-specific 542–3
  enterprise-specific 543–4
Australian Rules Football 262
Australian wine industry 487–92
Automobile industry 748–9
  in China 531–3, 555–61, 749
  competition and cooperation in
    749–50
  new technology in 161, 193–6
  political economy of 30–1
  role of Toyota 615–16, 640–7
  in the USA 541–2
  value chain 318–20
Aviation industry see airline
  industry

Back-office services 303, 334
Bags
  icon 344–5
Balanced score card 657–60
Balancing 242
Bank(s)
  structure of 255–6
Banking
  in Europe 216–17, 710–11
  investment banking
    222–3, 711–72
Bargaining power 206, 210, 308,
  319
  for Starbucks 768–9
Barriers to entry 205, 207–9,
  767–8
Barriers to exit 406

Basel standards 711
Beer see brewing industry
  consumption per head 638
Beijing Jeep 556–7
Benchmarking 567, 660–1
Bhopal 674
Bilateral organizations 98–9
Bilateral relations 98–9
Bioengineering revolution 191–2
Biotech companies 27
Birth rates see demography
Blending 242
Boeing 737 151, 153, 316
Boeing 747 114, 150–1, 153
Book distribution 173–5
BOOT (build own operate transfer)
  534, 550
Botswana 339, 371, 496
  AIDS in 522–6
  problems of 502–3
Boundary(ies) 7, 235, 375, 627–9
  crossing 629
  and strategy 629
Bounded rationality 115–16
Brand(s) 234–5, 349, 359–63
  creating 370–4
    for Amazon.com 705–6
    for beers 637–40
    for Harley-Davidson 353–5
    for Lloyd's 731
    in sport 258–63
    for Virgin and Branson
      359–60, 773
    for wine 491
  and names 360–1
Brewing industry 637–40
  in China 638–9
  in India 638
  South African 637–40
  in USA 639
Bribe Payers Index 172
Broking
  business models for 249–51
  online 240–1, 630–1
Budget 572–3
Bureaucratization 617

Business landscape 162–4
Business plan 57–9
Business success
    its temporary nature 168–9

C
Capabilities 239–42, 340, 575–80
Capacity utilization 308
Capitalism
    alliance 486–7
Chaebol 281–3, 754
China
    brewing industry in 638–9
    economic reform 518–19,
        716–17
    entry in the automobile industry
        531–2, 555–61
Choice matrices 392–3
Cluster(s) 403, 480, 540
    cultural 87–8
Codification 57
Coffee 205–6, 767
Cognitive map 22,
Command 439–40, 619
Commoditisation 215, 326, 717
Commodity 326
Commons, the 464–6
Communication(s) 440, 619
    speed and cost of 85
    within company 587
Communications industry 385–7,
    394–5
Communications revolution
    188–9, 291–2
Competencies 243–58, 340
    core 243–6, 575
        'core' 258, 570–4
        determinants of 247
        new 271
        number of 258
    distinctive 244–6
Competition 270
    and competitive advantage 290
    degree of 205
    intensity of 210–11
    for Starbucks 206, 769
Competitive advantage 63–4,
    269–75, 539–42, 575, 590
    differentiators of 592 594
    strategies for gaining 275,
        289–90
Competitive environment 162,
    199–232, 575

Competitive forces *see* forces of
    competition
Complementing 32–4
Complementor(s)
    economic 32,
    existence of 211
    political 33,
    role of 204
Complexity 162
Computer industry 388, 723–4
Concorde 151
Conflict 440, 619–620
    aftermath of 624
    degrees of 623–4
    felt 623
    latent 623
    manifest 624
    perceived 624
    situations 624–6
Consensus 440, 619
Consumer society 349
Consumer utilities 357
Contact lenses
    cosmetic 272
Contingency testing 132, 572,
    573
Control 440, 619
    systems 35,
Convergence 93–4
    cultural 88–9
    economic 93–4
    organizational 761–2
    political 93–5
    technical 756
Convergent problem 6,
Conversion 57
Coordination (*see also* cooperation)
    619, 629
Cooperation 308, 439, 567
    government imposed 480–1
    methods of 477–80
    spontaneous 477
    in the wine industry 478–80
Corporate culture 34–5
Corporate plan (*see also* business
    plan) 57
Corporate social responsibility 29,
    593, 675–7, 769–70
Corruption 172–3
Cost(s) 304
    fixed 208, 305
    sunk 245
    variable 305

Cost drivers 305–9, 319
Cost leadership 278, 304–5,
    317–18, 330–2
    focused 278
    fragility of 329
    limits of 325
    minimization 317–22
    prerequisites 304
    for Wal-Mart 786
Country risk 219–21
Creativity 6, 594
    how to release 584–7
    types of 581–4
Crimson Skies 227
Critical success factors 660
Critical uncertainties 138, 141–2,
    518–19
Culture 170–3
    corporate 441–3, 498
    differences in 171
    homogenization of 87–9
    organizational 445–8
        person 446–8
        power 445
        role 445–6
        task 446
Customers 340
Customization 624–5

D
Dabhol project 504
Debt 665–6
Decision making
    rational 117
Decision tree
    on entry into a new market
        474
    on mode of entry 532
Deflation 139–40
Demand curve 146–7, 791–3,
    304
    backward sloping 488
Demerger(s) 379
    of BHP Steel 408–11
Democratization 89–90, 769
    of luxury 353–7
Demography 172–3, 176–7
    fall in fertility rates 186–7
Design school model xxiii, 10
Differentiation 207–8, 278–9,
    353–7
    definition of 355
    demand side of 364–5

sources of 355–7
strategy 363–9
supply side of 366
Diseases 133
Diseconomies of scale 382
Diseconomies of scope 382
Divergent problem 6
Diversification 391, 410
and risk 516–17
Divestment 406–407, 569, 778–82
strategy of 407
Doppio espresso carts 622, 770
Downscoping 405–6
Downsizing 404–7
Driving forces 518–19

E
E-commerce 173–5, 240–1,
291–2, 386, 702–3
Earnings before interest, taxes,
depreciation and amortisation
(EBITDA) 665
Economic development,
its limited spread 187–8
Economic growth 176–7
causes of 177
Economic theory 116, 139–40,
149–50, 181
Economic value added (EVA) 275,
669–71
Economies of scale 208, 306,
382, 389, 395
Economies of scope 208, 306,
382, 389, 395
Effectiveness 653
Efficiency 653
Ekati diamond mine 409
Elaboration 57
Electronic data interchange (EDI)
330, 786–7
Embedded processes 245, 246
Enrichment 641
Enterprise
identity of 235–7
size of 380–415
advantages of size 381–2
bias in favour of size 385
disadvantages of size 382–3
414
reducing 385
optimum size of 380–7
Entertainment industry 385–6,
394–5, 684–8

Entrepreneurship 17, 66–9, 587
Environment(s)
competitive see competitive
environment
conservation of natural 190–1
external 162, 590–1
general 120–4, 162–7, 201
immediate, industrial or
competitive 162, 575
internal 162, 590–1
remaking 288–9
segments of 169–85
economic 176–81
political 182–5
social (cultural) 170–3
technical 173–6
Epidermal growth factor receptor
653
Erbitux 653, 689, 692–3
Ethics 19
EverQuest 229, 687
Exchange rates
floating 180
pegged 179–80
Experience curve 559
Exporting 533–4
Extrapolation of past
strategy as 618
Exxon Valdes 674

F
Failure
causes of 286
Family
extended 192
nuclear 192
Family firms 422–4
in Asia 423
Fashions (fads) 24–5
Feedback effects 212–13
Fertility rates see demography
Fidelio 292
Financial control(s) 57
role of 663–5
Financial crisis 476
Financial indicators 665–71
Financial sector 708–9
Finland
wireless communication in
569–70, 606–11
First-mover advantage 149–50,
297–8
Five Cs 439–40, 618–26

Focusing 281–3, 402–3
Forces of change 138, 141
Forces of competition 204–13, 575
dynamic 211
for Starbucks 767
Forecasting 124, 129–31, 572–3,
575, 790–7
reasons for failure of 131–2
Foreign direct investment (FDI)
534–539
Formula One 346–8, 738
Founder enterprises 420–1
Four Ps of marketing 350–1
Franchising 534
Free riding 464–6
Fuel cell technology 191–2,
195–6

G
Game Boy Advance 229, 611
Game theory 467–71
elements of 469–71
win–win game 479
GAMECUBE 226
Generic strategies 279–81
Germany
banking in 216
problems of 709–10
Global enterprise 190, 544–55
absence of 552–4
characteristics of 552
Nestlé as an example 554–5
Global strategy 551
Global warming
impact on winter resort 280–1
Global world 80, 93–4
Globalization
accelerated 84
benefits and losses from 81
bridging 84
definition of 80
elements of 83–90
incipient 84
opportunities and risks 102–3
viewpoints on 82
Globalization drivers 102
Golden straitjacket 86
Governance
and strategy 672–4
Government
imposing cooperation 480–1
role of policy 183–5, 760–2
as stakeholder 27, 30

Grand Theft Auto: Vice City   201
Grand Theft Auto 3   227
Greenfield project(s)   537
Growth/Share Matrix   11, 392–3
Gulf War   80, 105, 133

H

Halo   228
Hardware   200–1, 225–6, 685–6,
   755
Hassidic Jews,
   and diamonds   371
Hedging   509–10
Hierarchy   419
   of needs   340–2
HIV *see* AIDS
Home country bias   79, 90–3, 555
   in holding foreign equities   91
   reasons for   91–2
   removal of   92–3
Horizontal fracturing   565–7, 616
Horizontal integration   391
Hybrid electric vehicle (HEV)   161,
   193–6, 794
   advantages and disadvantages
   193
Hydrogen cell   191–2, 195–6
   advantages and disadvantages
   195

I

Identity   36,
Immigration   186
Imperfect competition   213–15
Incentive(s)
   systems   443–5
Indeterminateness   216–18, 590
India
   advantages over China   303
   beer industry in   638
   country risk   219–20
Indonesia
   in the Asian Economic Crisis
   219–20
   Japanese investment in   219
Industries
   age of   63–4
   how to classify   62–3
   infancy of   218
Information
   costs of   120
   imperfect or limited   115–20,
   589–90
   perfect   118, 120

Information industry   387, 394–5
Information strategy   122, 119–20
Innovation   212, 268, 284–9
   disruptive   285–6
   pathway   587
   policy of Nokia   608–9
   role of   285
   strategy   287–9
Input prices   318
Insurance   505–7, 729–30
Integration   387–95, 404
   benefits of   387–90
   of strategy   592–3
Intellectual property rights   547–8
Intermediation   709
Internal combustion engine
   improvements in   195–6
Internal environment,
   reading   576
International Coffee Agreement
   206
Internationalization   7–8, 83,
   547–9
   of retailing   535–6
   of services   191–2
Internet   173–4, 228, 273–5, 293,
   303
Intrapreneurship   66–7, 285, 588,
   612
Invention(s)
   macro-   175, 191
   micro-   175
Iraq War   105, 133
Ireland
   growth of   178–9
ISO 9000   662
IT enabled services (ITES)   303, 335
Iteration   566, 626–8
   core   626
   general   627

J

Jacob's Creek   491
Jains
   and diamonds   372
Japan
   economic crisis in   652
   fall in fertility rates   186
   old and new model   683–4
   risk rating of   502
Joint production economies   389
Joint venture   483, 536–7
Just-in-time   625, 642

K

Kaizen (continuous improvement)
   642
Keiretsu   281, 774
Key (critical) success factors   660
Key performance indicator(s)   661
Knowledge
   explicit   245
   sharing by Toyota   644
   tacit   244
Korea, South
   as market for electronic goods
   282
   structure of the economy
   281–2

L

Lateral thinking   5,
Law for the Comprehensive Resort
   Areas (Japan)   736
Leadership   38–9, 634–6, 773–7
   charismatic   39
   institutional   39
   team   39
   traditional   38–9
Lean production   641
Learning   18, 241–2, 591–2, 657
   economies   307
Leveraging
   debt   665–6
   resources   239, 241
Licence Raj   303
Licensing   534
Lineage   229
Lion King, The   395
Liquidity   665
Location   308
Luxury products   343–6, 371

M

Macroeconomic stability   139–40
Malaysia
   role of government in growth of
   182–3
Management control system(s) *see*
   strategic control system(s)
Managing change   167–9, 285–6
Managing risk   495–529
   universality of   497
Market(s)
   competitive conditions in   62–3
   cycle of competitive advantage
   in   63–4

evolution of 215
failure 389–90
how to classify 62–4
imperfections 291
instability of 211, 212
integration of world markets
83–4
segment(s) 358–9, 363–4
structures 213–15, 289–91
and cooperation 460
Market Value Added (MVA)
669–70
Marketing 346
Matrix structure 437
MBA 273–5
Measuring performance 657–8,
660–1
Merger(s) 379, 395–402
between BHP and Billiton
408–10
between Hewlett-Packard and
Compaq 400–2, 722–8
Meta-routine(s) 641
Metaphor
use of 163–4
Metatheories 20–5
Mexico
retailing structure 536
Wal-Mart in 788
Mission statement 55
Mode of entry 532–42, 593, 719
of automobile companies into
China 531–2, 555–61
advantages and disadvantages
of different modes 539–42
and competitive advantage
539–42
determinants of 540
Model(s)
hybrid 579–80
positioning 163, 576, 577
assumptions of 578
resource-based or resources
235–6, 263, 576, 577
assumptions of 579
Monitoring 123, 441–3, 575
Monopolistic competition 213–15
Monopoly 62, 213–15
Moral hazard 510–11
Mortality rates see demography
Motivation
extrinsic 443, 583–4
intrinsic 443, 583–4

Multi-divisional structure 432–3
Multi-domestic strategy 551
Multilateral organizations 95–6
Multilateral relations 95
Multinational enterprise (MNE)
99–101, 190

N
N-Gage 229, 611
Names, the 507–9, 731–4
Nation state
number of 86
National sovereignty
loss of 86–7
Navikey 608
Needs 340–6
Negotiation to reduce risk 515
Network(s) 403, 485
Network economics 221
Nigeria 673
the Niger Delta 'mamas' 527
No-frills airline 288, 315–17

O
Oil prices 138–144, 790–7
Oligopoly 213–15, 224, 290, 381
the iron law of 382–3
Opportunism 222, 390, 473,
475
Opportunity(ies) 184, 292
Opportunity cost 398
Optimization 116–17
Option 596
Organization(s)
know-how
systems 35
typology of 641
Organizational design 431–9
customer group 436
federal 431
functional 435
hybrid 438–9
inverted 431
matrix 437–8, 555, 635
product 433–4
regional 434
spider's web 431
'starburst' 431
Organizational slack
reducing 309
Output gap 139
Outsourcing 405
Ownership 308

P
Pacing 593, 632–3
event 633
time 633
Paradigm 35–6, 55
Participation strategy see mode of
entry
Partitioning 641
Partner selection 485
Path dependency 217–18
Patterns of change 167–8
Pay television 538–9
Perception device 137
Perfect competition 213–15
Performance areas 658–9
Pharmaceutical industry 688–94
stakeholders 27,
PIMS (profit impact of marketing
strategies) 11
Planning 596–9
comprehensive 597
determinants of the nature of
597
discovery-driven 285
feasible 596–7
flexible 597
focused 597
minimal 597
Planning period 128–9
Play Station (1, 2 and 3) 200,
225, 226, 227, 228, 229, 394,
687–8
Pokemon 228
Political risk 221
Pop Idol 395
Portfolio
approach to risk 516–17
of business units 392–3
of drugs 689–94
of products and services 384
Portfolio management 273, 413,
600–1
Positioning 163–4, 270, 575
Power
orientation 171
sources of 39–40
structures 36
Predetermined elements 127, 128,
138, 141, 518–19
Prediction see forecasting
Price determination 147, 791–3
Price/earnings ratio 402
Price efficient 118

Price leadership 472
Price strategy 311–17, 471–3
  differential 313–17
  predatory 473
Pricing stance 312
  aggressive 311–12
  tame 311–12
Principal 419–20, 424–5, 454–5
  principal/agent behaviour
    424–5
  principal/agent relationship
    419–20
Prisoner's dilemma 468–71
  universality of 471–7
Problems
  tame 50
  wicked 50, 53
Product attributes 340, 365–6,
  656–7
  intangible 358
Product design 308
Product development,
  at Toyota 645
Product differentiation see
  differentiation
Professional liability 130–1
Profit
  above normal 57–8
  distortion of 664–5
  maximization of 29
    strategy as 618
  measurement of 664–5
  monopoly 590
Public liability 130–1

R
Rational economic man 117–18
Rationality 5–6, 19
  bounded 115–16
  criteria 116
  procedural 116
  substantive 116
Reading
  the environment 120–4, 574–5
    political problems of 121
  the environment as economic
    169
  the future 120–4
Reason
  practical 116
  pure 116
Reform
  gradual 518–20

Regional organizations 96–8
Regionalism 98
Reinsurance 506–7, 732
Reproduction rates 186
Reputation 246, 352
Resorts 545–7, 735–42, 743–7
  problems of a winter resort
    738–40
Resource(s)
  acquiring 399, 575, 629
  balancing 242
  blending 242
  control over 39
  conserving 242
  core 236
  defining 235–6
  evaluating 575
  extracting 242
  intangible 237–9
  leveraging 241–2
  recycling 242
  tangible 237–9
Resource audit 239
Responses see strategic responses
Restructuring 439
Retailing 535–6, 704, 783–4
  and IT 786–7
Risk(s) 220, 221, 391, 460,
  495–529
  competitive 224, 520
  country 133, 224, 520
  economic
    enterprise 134–5
  global 133
  government guarantee against
    510–11
  industry 133–4
  insolvency 135
  liquidity 135
  long-tailed 130, 507–9, 729–34
  market 134
  maturity 134–5
  off-the-balance sheet 135
  operational 135
  political 135, 221, 521–2
  price 134
  strategic 150–1, 221–4, 520–1,
    521
  technical 135
  transfer 136, 221
Risk appetite 497–9
Risk assessment 500
Risk aversion 497

Risk avoidance 497, 503–4,
  511–12
Risk control 132–6, 497, 709
  strategy as 617–18
Risk environment 132–6, 497,
  499
Risk evaluation see risk assessment
Risk-generating events 499
Risk management 134–6, 497,
  500
  as part of strategy 520–1
  principles of 521–2
  strategy of 500, 505–12,
    513–15
Risk manager(s) 500–3
Risk matrix 133–4
Risk mitigation 497, 512, 514–15
Risk premium 513
Risk rating 501–3
Risk response 503–18
Risk sharing 510
Rituals 35
Routine(s) 35, 126
Rule(s) 459, 470

S
Sabre 292
Sanctions 442–3
Santana 557
SARS 105, 526
Saudi Arabia 795, 796
  oil reserves 793
Scanning 122–3, 574
Scenario(s)
  goal 136
  learning 241
  macro 137
  naming of 143
  reasons for 145
Scenario building 126, 136–45,
  517–19, 572, 575
  components of 138
  for the price of oil 138, 794–7
  role in strategy making 145
  steps in 138–44
Scenario planning 520
Self-organization 477–8
Sensitivity analysis 132, 572
Serendipity 585–6
Services 295–6
  internationalization of 191
Shareholder(s)
  returns to 666–9

Shock(s)
  therapy 519
Silicon Valley 400, 668
Sims, the 229
Singapore,
  role of government in growth of
    182–3, 549–50, 760–1
Six Sigma quality programme
  602, 718
Small numbers contracting 389
Social responsibility see corporate
  social responsibility
Social web 33–40
Software 200–1, 225–6, 303, 685
Sonic cruiser 150–1
South Africa
  beer industry 637–40
  political risk in 521
Specialization 253
Sports industry 234–5
Staging 593, 594, 629–33
  alternative routes 631–3
Stakeholders 20–33, 671–2,
  673–4, 682
  definition 26
  mapping of
    economic stakeholders 31,
    political stakeholders 32,
  strategy towards 677–8
  who they are? 26–8
Star Hub 761
Star Wars Galaxies 229
STEP (sometimes called PEST)
  169
Strategic action(s) 5, 43–77,
  203–4
Strategic activities 61, 654–5
Strategic aims 28
Strategic alliance(s) 403, 481–7,
  629
  complementary 483
  equity 483
  horizontal 483–4
  international 485–7
  managing 484–5
  non-equity 483
  between Renault and Nissan
    462–4, 750–1
  and risk sharing 510
  types of 483–4
  vertical complementary 483
Strategic allies 27
Strategic analysis 699–801

Strategic approaches 13–16
  classical 13
  evolutionary 14
  processual 14–15,
  systemic 15–16,
    American 22
    Anglo-Saxon 16
    Japanese 16
Strategic audit 567, 699–801
Strategic business unit (SBU)
  599–600
Strategic canvas 655–7
Strategic choice 592–6, 680
  evaluation criteria of 596
Strategic constraints 800
Strategic control see monitoring
Strategic design 10
Strategic dilemmas 379
Strategic drift 36–8
Strategic elements 5–6
Strategic inertia 36
Strategic intent 5, 654
Strategic leadership 634–5
Strategy making
  learning 570–3
  levels of 7
  steps in 574–80
Strategic management 128, 572,
  589–99
  definition 56–7
Strategic mission 634
Strategic objectives 54–5
Strategic performance 6–7
Strategic perspectives 14, 572–3
Strategic planning 9–12, 128–9,
  572
  definition 59–61
  when appropriate 64–5
Strategic players 201–4, 458–61
  global 95–101
Strategic responses 203–4
Strategic schools 16–20, 799–800
Strategic situations 654
Strategic stance 34–5
Strategic steps 574–80
  reversing the sequencing 681–3
  sequencing 576–80
Strategic thinking 5–6, 45–61,
  127–9, 572–3, 581–9
  contexts of 49–53
  definition 45–7
  explicit 46–7
  implicit 46–7

Strategist(s)
  who are they? 7–8, 26–7, 800–1
Strategy(ies)
  in a crisis 712–14
  definition of 5
  emergent 589–91
  formulation of 10, 566,
    568–613, 570, 580, 654
  generic 277–80, 365–70, 654
  gorilla 686
  guerrilla 686
  history of concept 8–13
  hybrid 279
  impact of globalization on
    101–2
  implementation of 10, 566,
    580, 614–50, 654
    weaknesses of 616–18
  learning of 568–70
  making 7
    context of 33–4
    evolution of 572
  meanings of 13–21
    as adaptation 19
    as cognitive psychology 18,
      33
    as design 17
    as entrepreneurship 17
    as ethics 19
    as learning process 18
    as organizational culture 18,
      33–40
    as planning 17
    as political process 18, 33–41
    as positioning 17
    as rationality 19
    as rhetoric 19
    as simple rules 19
    as transformation 18
  monitoring of 566, 580,
    651–98
  nature of 798–800
  nomadic 755
  origins of concept 8–9
  promoting 678–9
  resource based view 12
  stages in development of
    concept 9–13
Strategy division 634–6
  role of 636
  separate 635–6
    advantages and disadvantages
      of 635–6

Structure(s) 418–49
  formal 418
  informal 441
  principles of 418–20, 432–3
Substitutes 204–5, 209–10
  for Starbucks 205, 768
Supervision 426
Supplier(s)
  for Toyota 642–7
Supply curve 146–7, 314, 791–3
Sustainability 29
Switching 641
SWOT 10, 17

T

Take-over,
  danger of 449–53
Teams
  cross-company 463–4, 482,
    751
  cross-functional 463–4, 751
Technical change
  waves of 173–6
Technique(s) 307
  choice of 322–3
Technology 322–5
  accelerated diffusion of new 85
Telecommunications 760–1
  in Asia 762–3
Terrorist attacks 80, 220, 322,
  473, 553, 733
Threat(s) 184, 185
Three pillar system 443–5
Time horizon 127–8, 511
Time orientation 171
Tokenism 617
Tomb Raider 228
Total quality management (TQM)
  641–7

Toy Story 395
Training,
  provision of 474–6
Trans-national strategy 551
Trans-national world 93
Transaction costs 549, 553
Transaction cycle 327–9
Transformation 18, 236–7
Transition
  from planned to market
    economy in India 303
Treaty of Nice 216
Triad, the 99, 188, 189–90, 544,
  748
Triple bottom line 674–5
Trust 246, 641
Turnaround(s) 36–8, 284–5
  of Nissan 751–2
  of Vivendi 779
Turnkey projects 534

U/V

Uncertainty 169, 211–12,
  589–90
  levels of 119
  orientation 171
Uniqueness drivers 366–8
Value 275
  creation of 276
  strategic implications of 276–9
Value added
  economic 276
    definition 275
Value analysis 275–7
Value chain 251–7
  in banking 216–17, 711
  use for cost leadership 318–22
Vertical fracturing 565, 567,
  616, 626

Vertical integration 253,
  388–91
  benefits and costs of 390
  and competition 388
  types of 390–1
Vertical thinking 5
Videogame(s)
  consoles 200–1, 225–7
  industry 224–30
    driving forces in 224–5
    features of 225
Virtue matrix 676
Vision 55–6

W

Wants 340–6
  creation of new 348
White goods industry 717
Wi-Fi 205, 768
Windows 213, 421–2, 429, 609
Wine industry 457–8
  in Australia 293, 457–8,
    487–92
    industry associations 489
  in California 480
Wireless technology 267–8, 282,
  296–9, 394–5, 541, 606
World Cup (football) 258, 735
WWF Raw 228

X/Y/Z

XBOX 225, 226, 227, 228, 687
Yellow Tail 490
Zero-sum game 458